CD-12043, 120044

118679

KT-556-500

CISCO SYSTEMS

Cisco Networking Academy Program

HP IT Essentials I: PC Hardware and Software Companion Guide

Second Edition

Cisco Systems, Inc.

Cisco Networking Academy Program

Cisco Press

800 East 96th Street

Indianapolis, Indiana 46240 USA

www.ciscopress.com

Cisco Networking Academy Program

HP IT Essentials I: PC Hardware and Software Companion Guide

Second Edition

Cisco Systems, Inc.

Cisco Networking Academy Program

Copyright © 2005 Cisco Systems, Inc.

Published by:
Cisco Press
800 East 96th Street

Indianapolis, Indiana 46240 USA

Printed in the United States of America 3 4 5 6 7 8 9 0

Library of Congress Cataloging-in-Publication Number: 2003114382

ISBN: 1-58713-136-6

Third Printing December 2005

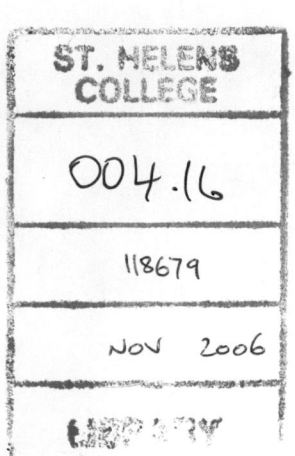

Trademark Acknowledgments

All terms mentioned in this book that are known to be trademarks or service marks have been appropriately capitalized. Cisco Press or Cisco Systems, Inc., cannot attest to the accuracy of this information. Use of a term in this book should not be regarded as affecting the validity of any trademark or service mark.

Warning and Disclaimer

This book is designed to provide information about PC Hardware and Software from the Cisco Networking Academy Program HP IT Essentials PC Hardware and Software course. Every effort has been made to make this book as complete and as accurate as possible, but no warranty or fitness is implied.

The information is provided on an "as is" basis. The author, Cisco Press, and Cisco Systems, Inc., shall have neither liability nor responsibility to any person or entity with respect to any loss or damages arising from the information contained in this book or from the use of the discs or programs that may accompany it.

The opinions expressed in this book belong to the author and are not necessarily those of Cisco Systems, Inc.

This book is part of the Cisco Networking Academy® Program series from Cisco Press. The products in this series support and complement the Cisco Networking Academy Program curriculum. If you are using this book outside the Networking Academy program, then you are not preparing with a Cisco trained and authorized Networking Academy provider.

For information on the Cisco Networking Academy Program or to locate a Networking Academy, please visit www.cisco.com/edu.

Corporate and Government Sales

Cisco Press offers excellent discounts on this book when ordered in quantity for bulk purchases or special sales.

For more information please contact:
U.S. Corporate and Government Sales   1-800-382-3419 corpsales@pearsontechgroup.com

For sales outside the U.S. please contact:
International Sales international@pearsoned.com

Feedback Information

At Cisco Press, our goal is to create in-depth technical books of the highest quality and value. Each book is crafted with care and precision, undergoing rigorous development that involves the unique expertise of members from the professional technical community.

Readers' feedback is a natural continuation of this process. If you have any comments regarding how we could improve the quality of this book or otherwise alter it to better suit your needs, you can contact us through e-mail at networkingacademy@ciscopress.com. Please make sure to include the book title and ISBN in your message.

We greatly appreciate your assistance.

Publisher	John Wait
Editor-in-Chief	John Kane
Executive Editor	Mary Beth Ray
Cisco Representative	Anthony Wolfenden
Cisco Press Program Manager	Jeff Brady
Production Manager	Patrick Kanouse
Development Editor	Deborah Doorley
Senior Editor	Sheri Cain
Project Editor	San Dee Phillips
Copy Editor	John Edwards
Technical Editors	Shawn McReynolds, Allan Reid
Editorial Assistant	Tammi Barnett
Designer	Louisa Adair
Composition	Octal Publishing, Inc.
Indexer	Tim Wright

CISCO SYSTEMS

Corporate Headquarters
Cisco Systems, Inc.
170 West Tasman Drive
San Jose, CA 95134-1706
USA
www.cisco.com
Tel: 408 526-4000
    800 553-NETS (6387)
Fax: 408 526-4100

European Headquarters
Cisco Systems International BV
Haarlerbergpark
Haarlerbergweg 13-19
1101 CH Amsterdam
The Netherlands
www-europe.cisco.com
Tel: 31 0 20 357 1000
Fax: 31 0 20 357 1100

Americas Headquarters
Cisco Systems, Inc.
170 West Tasman Drive
San Jose, CA 95134-1706
USA
www.cisco.com
Tel: 408 526-7660
Fax: 408 527-0883

Asia Pacific Headquarters
Cisco Systems, Inc.
Capital Tower
168 Robinson Road
#22-01 to #29-01
Singapore 068912
www.cisco.com
Tel: +65 6317 7777
Fax: +65 6317 7799

Cisco Systems has more than 200 offices in the following countries and regions. Addresses, phone numbers, and fax numbers are listed on the
Cisco.com Web site at www.cisco.com/go/offices.

Argentina • Australia • Austria • Belgium • Brazil • Bulgaria • Canada • Chile • China PRC • Colombia • Costa Rica • Croatia • Czech Republic
Denmark • Dubai, UAE • Finland • France • Germany • Greece • Hong Kong SAR • Hungary • India • Indonesia • Ireland • Israel • Italy
Japan • Korea • Luxembourg • Malaysia • Mexico • The Netherlands • New Zealand • Norway • Peru • Philippines • Poland • Portugal
Puerto Rico • Romania • Russia • Saudi Arabia • Scotland • Singapore • Slovakia • Slovenia • South Africa • Spain • Sweden
Switzerland • Taiwan • Thailand • Turkey • Ukraine • United Kingdom • United States • Venezuela • Vietnam • Zimbabwe

About the Technical Editors

Shawn McReynolds, CCAI, CCNP, MCSA, A+, is an assistant professor at Southwest Virginia Community College, where he teaches Cisco Certified Network Professional and Cisco Sponsored Curriculum courses full-time. He is also a partner in a regional information technology consulting venture specializing in PC hardware and application training. Each summer, Shawn works with gifted programs for middle and high school students, instructing in multimedia creation and digital video. Shawn resides in Tazewell, Virginia, with his wife, Stephanie.

Allan Reid is a professor and coordinator for the networking, computer hardware, and operating system programs in the School of Business at Centennial College in Toronto, Ontario, Canada. He has designed, developed, and instructed numerous courses and programs for computer and networking technology and has more than 25 years of experience developing innovative solutions for business, academic, and technical environments.

Overview

Table of Contents

Cisco Systems Networking Icon Legend

Cisco Systems uses a standardized set of icons to represent devices in network topology illustrations. The following icon legend shows the most commonly used icons that you might encounter throughout this book.

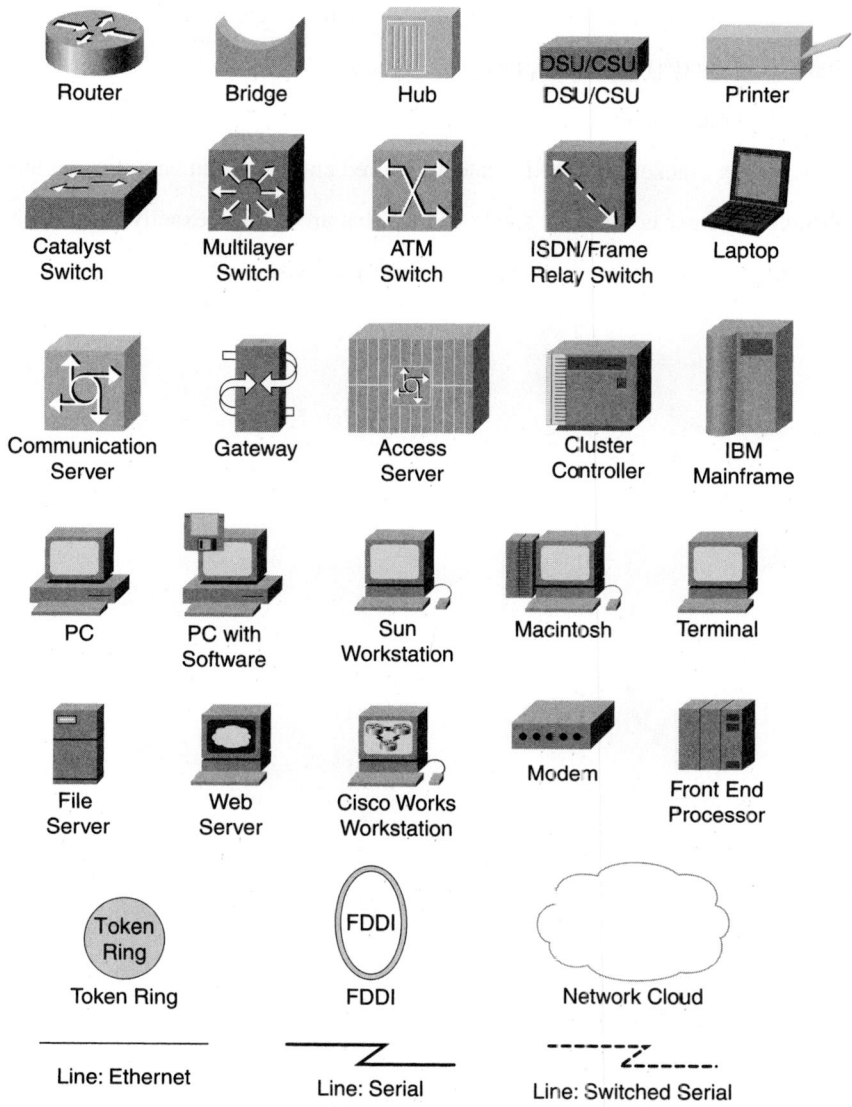

Command Syntax Conventions

The conventions used to present command syntax in this book are the same conventions used in the Cisco IOS Software Command Reference. The Command Reference describes these conventions as follows:

- Vertical bars (|) separate alternative, mutually exclusive elements.

- Square brackets ([ ]) indicate optional elements.

- Braces ({ }) indicate a required choice.

- Braces within brackets ([{ }]) indicate a required choice within an optional element.

- **Boldface** indicates commands and keywords that are entered exactly as shown.

- *Italic* indicates arguments for which you supply values.

Foreword

Throughout the world, the Internet has brought tremendous new opportunities for individuals and their employers. Companies and other organizations are seeing dramatic increases in productivity by investing in robust networking capabilities. Some studies have shown measurable productivity improvements in entire economies. The promise of enhanced efficiency, profitability, and standard of living is real and growing.

Such productivity gains aren't achieved by simply purchasing networking equipment. Skilled professionals are needed to plan, design, install, deploy, configure, operate, maintain, and troubleshoot today's networks. Network managers must assure that they have planned for network security and for continued operation. They need to design for the required performance level in their organization. They must implement new capabilities as the demands of their organization, and its reliance on the network, expands.

To meet the many educational needs of the internetworking community, Cisco Systems established the Cisco Networking Academy Program. The Networking Academy is a comprehensive learning program that provides students with the Internet technology skills essential in a global economy. The Networking Academy integrates face-to-face teaching, web-based content, online assessment, student performance tracking, hands-on labs, instructor training and support, and preparation for industry-standard certifications.

The Networking Academy continually raises the bar on blended learning and educational processes. The Internet-based assessment and instructor support systems are some of the most extensive and validated ever developed, including a 24/7 customer service system for Networking Academy instructors. Through community feedback and electronic assessment, the Networking Academy adapts the curriculum to improve outcomes and student achievement. The Cisco Global Learning Network infrastructure designed for the Networking Academy delivers a rich, interactive, and personalized curriculum to students worldwide. The Internet has the power to change the way people work, live, play, and learn, and the Cisco Networking Academy Program is in the forefront of this transformation.

This Cisco Press title is one of a series of best-selling companion titles for the Cisco Networking Academy Program. Designed by Cisco Worldwide Education and Cisco Press, these books provide integrated support for the online learning content that is made available to Academies all over the world. These Cisco Press books are the only authorized books for the Networking Academy by Cisco Systems, and provide print and CD-ROM materials that ensure the greatest possible learning experience for Networking Academy students.

I hope you are successful as you embark on your learning path with Cisco Systems and the Internet. I also hope that you will choose to continue your learning after you complete the Networking Academy curriculum. In addition to its Cisco Networking Academy Program titles, Cisco Press also publishes an extensive list of networking technology and certification publications that provide a wide range of resources. Cisco Systems has also established a network of professional training companies—the Cisco Learning Partners—who provide a full range of Cisco training courses. They offer training in many formats, including e-learning, self-paced, and instructor-led classes. Their instructors are Cisco certified, and Cisco creates their materials. When you are ready, please visit the Learning & Events area on Cisco.com to learn about all the educational support that Cisco and its partners have to offer.

Thank you for choosing this book and the Cisco Networking Academy Program.

Kevin Warner
Senior Director, Marketing
Worldwide Education
Cisco Systems, Inc.

Introduction

Cisco Networking Academy Program HP IT Essentials I: PC Hardware and Software Companion Guide, Second Edition, supplements the online course and its corresponding classroom and laboratory instruction. This book parallels the online course to provide support for the information and skills you need to pursue a career in information technology as a PC technician or a network administrator. In addition to a course certificate, students can take the CompTIA A+ certification exam. The objectives for this certification were updated in November 2003 for both exams; one focuses on hardware and the other is on operating systems.

This *Companion Guide* starts with the basics of technology and progresses through the assembly of a computer system. Features and functions of computer components are introduced, and then the process of preparing and installing the components is detailed in a step-by-step manner.

After the computer system is up and running, this book explains operating systems, which include the Disk Operating System (DOS). After learning the basics of DOS, students are introduced to the Windows 9x operating systems, including the file system, file management, Control Panel, and system tools. Windows NT/2000 is also discussed, and the differences between the installation of each operating system are presented. The new chapter on Windows XP explains the features and the different editions of XP, including Home, Professional, and Media.

The topic of hardware fundamentals for servers is also covered. It discusses RAID for the network server, including the different types and configuration issues. The fundamentals of networks are then introduced, which cover understanding the types of networks, adding a network interface card, and understanding the physical components of a network. Printers and their operation and maintenance are also discussed.

Information on preventive maintenance and troubleshooting for hardware, software, and the network server is detailed, as is information covering careers available to IT professionals.

Hands-on experience, along with the review questions and worksheets, provides the foundation for students who will be taking the CompTIA A+ certification exam and continuing their studies in HP IT Essentials II: Network Operating Systems. The CD-ROM included with this book further reinforces important topics, such as the floppy drive, the CD-ROM drive, the sound card, and other interactive elements.

The Goal of This Book

The goal of this book is to lay a foundation for the basic information required to build a computer and troubleshoot problems that occur. It is designed to prepare students to pass the CompTIA A+ certification exams and, when studied in conjunction with the IT Essentials II: Network Operating Systems course and its related titles, the CompTIA Server+ certification exam.

The Audience for This Book

This book is intended for students who want to pursue a career in information technology or who want to have knowledge about how a computer works, how to assemble a computer, and how to troubleshoot hardware and software issues. Students who will be seeking their A+ certification will find this book particularly useful.

This Book's Features

The features in this book facilitate an understanding of computer systems and troubleshooting system problems. The highlights of each chapter are as follows:

- **Objectives**—Each chapter starts with a list of objectives that should be mastered by the end of the chapter. The objectives provide a reference of the concepts covered in the chapter.

- **Figures, examples, tables, and scenarios**—This book contains figures, examples, and tables that help explain theories, concepts, commands, and setup sequences, as well as help you visualize the content covered in the chapter. In addition, specific scenarios provide real-world situations that detail problems and solutions.

- **Chapter summaries**—At the end of each chapter is a summary of the concepts covered in the chapter. The summary provides a synopsis of the chapter and serves as a study aid.

- **Key terms**—Each chapter includes a list of defined key terms that are covered in the chapter. These terms serve as a study aid. In addition, the key terms reinforce the concepts introduced in the chapter and help you understand the chapter material before you move on to new concepts. You can find the key terms highlighted in blue throughout the chapter, where they are used in practice.

- **"Check Your Understanding" review questions**—Review questions are presented at the end of each chapter to serve as an assessment. In addition, the questions reinforce the concepts introduced in the chapter and help test your understanding before moving on to subsequent chapters.

- **Lab Companion references**—Throughout this book are references to worksheet and lab activities found in *Cisco Networking Academy Program HP IT Essentials I: PC Hardware and Software Lab Companion*. These labs allow you to make a connection between theory and practice. References to the labs are marked with the following icon:

 Worksheet   Lab Activity

- **CD Activity references**—Throughout the book are references to e-Labs, PhotoZooms, and Videos found on the book's accompanying CD-ROM. These activities are designed to supplement the material found within the book to solidify your understanding of hardware components and networking concepts. References to these activities are marked with the following icon:

 e-Lab Activity   PhotoZoom   Video

How This Book Is Organized

This book is divided into 14 chapters, two appendixes, and a glossary of key terms. These sections are described as follows:

- **Chapter 1, "Information Technology Basics"**—Different computer systems, programs, and computer types are discussed in this chapter. The Windows Desktop environment is identified, and relevant computer terminology is defined. Number systems that relate to the computer industry are covered in order to perform binary, decimal, and hexadecimal conversions. The safety requirements are emphasized, as are the tools used to assemble a computer.

- **Chapter 2, "How Computers Work"**—This chapter details the features and functions of computer components in preparation for the assembly process. This includes the case, power supply, motherboard, expansion slots, memory, I/O ports, SCSI disk types, and system resources. Detailed information is provided on the floppy drive, hard drive, and CD-ROM drive. In addition, the components of portable computers are discussed.

- **Chapter 3, "Assembling a Computer"**—The first step in the assembly process is gathering the components and completing the computer inventory. Preparing and installing the components are detailed in a step-by-step process. In the final steps, you review the checklist, assemble the case, and boot the system for the first time.

- **Chapter 4, "Operating System Fundamentals"**—The operating system and terminology important to the technician are explained in this chapter. The emphasis is on the Disk Operating System (DOS). You learn the basics of DOS, the commands used, and the file structure. Additionally, memory management is detailed, along with the tools that are used to adjust and optimize memory.

- **Chapter 5, "Windows 9x Operating Systems"**—This chapter provides an in-depth discussion of Windows 9x, although the focus is on Windows 98. This includes the file system, file management, the Control Panel, and system tools. It is important to understand the requirements for installing Windows 98 in order to install the operating system and troubleshoot errors that might occur.

- **Chapter 6, "Windows NT/2000 Operating Systems"**—This chapter compares the file systems and discusses the differences between the installation of Windows 98 and Windows 2000. Topics include the Windows 2000 boot system and administrative tools.

- **Chapter 7, "Windows XP Operating System"**—The focus of this chapter is the Windows XP operating system. The differences between the Home Edition, Professional Edition, and Media Edition are discussed. Topics include the features of Windows XP and new enhancements.

- **Chapter 8, "Multimedia Capabilities"**—Multimedia is an important part of a computer system. This chapter covers the basic hardware required, including video cards, sound cards, CD-ROM drives, and DVD drives.

- **Chapter 9, "Advanced Hardware Fundamentals for Servers"**—The focus of this chapter is RAID for the network server. You learn about the different types of RAID along with configuration issues. In addition, adding hardware to the server and upgrading server components are covered in detail.

- **Chapter 10, "Networking Fundamentals"**—In this chapter, you are introduced to the fundamentals of a network, including understanding the types of networks, adding a network interface card, and understanding the physical components of a network. Of importance is the OSI model, TCP/IP, and network protocols. You learn about LAN architectures and the media needed to connect to the Internet.

- **Chapter 11, "Printers and Sharing"**—Printers are extremely important in a network environment. This chapter discusses the different types of printers, how they work, and the maintenance required to ensure optimal performance. In addition, you learn about print sharing and management, and how to solve printer problems.

- **Chapter 12, "Preventive Maintenance"**—A computer system and a network are kept in good working order with preventive maintenance. You learn about electrostatic discharge (ESD) and how to create an ESD-free environment. Maintaining computer components, including the keyboard, monitor, and mouse, is covered along with information on cleaning and disposing.

- **Chapter 13, "Troubleshooting PC Hardware"**—This chapter details the troubleshooting cycle and the steps to take when there is a computer problem. These steps help the technician determine and fix problems relating to the hardware box and peripheral devices.

- **Chapter 14, "Troubleshooting Software"**—Problems that are attributed to software can be complicated. In this chapter, you use system tools to troubleshoot Windows-specific problems relating to the operating system and registry, and programs that are running on the computer.

- **Appendix A, "The Information Technology Professional"**—The careers available to an IT professional is the focus of this appendix. Career paths are detailed, including related fields, degree fields, and fields where certification is necessary.

- **Appendix B, "Answers to the Check Your Understanding Questions"**—This appendix lists the answers to the Check Your Understanding review questions that are included at the end of each chapter.

- **Glossary of Key Terms**—This glossary provides you with a complete list of the key terms defined in each chapter.

CompTIA-Authorized Quality Curriculum

The contents of this training material were created for the CompTIA A+ Certification exam covering CompTIA certification exam objectives updated as of November 26, 2003.

How to Become CompTIA Certified

This training material can help you prepare for and pass a related CompTIA certification exam or exams. In order to achieve CompTIA certification, you must register for and pass a CompTIA certification exam or exams.

In order to become CompTIA certified, you must

1. Select a certification exam provider. For more information, please visit www.comptia.org/certification/general_information/test_locations.asp.

2. Register for and schedule a time to take the CompTIA certification exam(s) at a convenient location.

3. Read and sign the Candidate Agreement, which will be presented at the time of the exam(s). The text of the Candidate Agreement can be found at www.comptia.org/certification/general_information/candidate_agreement.asp.

4. Take and pass the CompTIA certification exam(s).

For more information about CompTIA's certifications, such as industry acceptance, benefits, or program news, visit www.comptia.org/certification/default.asp.

CompTIA is a nonprofit information technology (IT) trade association. CompTIA's certifications are designed by subject-matter experts from across the IT industry. Each CompTIA certification is vendor-neutral, covers multiple technologies, and requires demonstration of skills and knowledge widely sought after by the IT industry.

To contact CompTIA with any questions or comments, please call + 1 630 268 1818 or send an e-mail to questions@comptia.org.

About the CD-ROM

A CD-ROM complements this book. This CD-ROM contains three test engines consisting of A+ and Server+ questions, interactive e-Lab Activities, high-resolution PhotoZooms, and instructional video vignettes. These materials review and reinforce the content covered in this book. This CD-ROM also includes supplemental material on the Windows XP operating system and a certification map that aligns chapters to A+ certification exam objectives. Additionally, this CD-ROM provides the following:

- An easy-to-use graphical user interface

- Accurate and concise feedback

- Frequent interaction with content

- Support for guided and exploratory navigation

- Learner direction and support

- Flexibility to learners at different levels of expertise

Upon completion of this chapter, you will be able to perform the following tasks:

- Describe the different computer systems, programs, and computer types
- Identify and navigate the Windows Desktop environment
- Use the features of Microsoft Windows, including creating shortcuts and adjusting display properties
- Define relevant computer terminology that is used in digital math
- Perform number conversions, including decimal, binary, and hexadecimal
- Understand the safety procedures that are promoted throughout this course
- Identify and use the tools in the PC technician's tool kit

Chapter 1

Information Technology Basics

This chapter discusses the basics of Information Technology as they relate to the computer technician. It covers different computer types and software applications. A brief overview of the Internet is also included. You identify the basic features of the Windows operating system and the elements of the Windows Desktop.

Additionally, you learn some vocabulary that is important to the technician. You also examine the methods that are used in number conversions, including binary to decimal, decimal to binary, and so on. An explanation of analog and digital is included, as is an introduction to algorithms.

Safety is the first priority when working with computers. This chapter details safety procedures that pertain to the labs that are used throughout this course and in the workplace.

Getting Started in IT

This section provides an introduction to computers and software along with a short history of the Internet. The following topics are covered:

- Computer systems and programs
- Computer types
- Connecting computer systems
- The birth of the Internet
- The cost of technology

Computer Systems and Programs

A *computer system* is shown in Figure 1-1. A computer system consists of hardware and software components. Hardware is the physical equipment such as the case, floppy disk drives, keyboards, monitors, cables, speakers, and printers. The term *software* describes the programs that operate the computer system. Computer software, also called *programs*, instructs the computer on how to operate. These operations can include identifying, accessing, and processing information. Essentially, a program is a sequence of instructions that describe how data is processed. Programs vary widely, depending on the type of information that is to be accessed or generated. For example, instructions for balancing a checkbook are different from instructions for simulating a virtual reality world on the Internet.

Figure 1-1 Computer System

HP Deskjet 630 Printer

HP Pavillion bg922 PC

The two types of software are applications and operating systems.

Application software accepts input from the user and then manipulates this input to achieve a result. This result is known as the output. Applications are programs that are designed to perform a specific function for the user or for another application program. Examples of applications include word processors, database programs, spreadsheets, web browsers, web development tools, and graphic design tools. Computer applications are detailed later in this chapter.

An *operating system (OS)* is a program that manages all the other programs in a computer. The OS also provides the operating environment for applications that access resources on the computer. Operating systems perform basic tasks like recognizing input from the keyboard or mouse, sending output to the video screen or printer, keeping track of files on the drives, and controlling peripherals such as printers and modems. The Disk Operating System (DOS), Windows 98, Windows 2000, Windows NT, Linux, Mac OS X, DEC VMS, and IBM OS/400 are examples of operating systems.

Operating systems are platform specific, meaning that they are designed for specific types of computers. For example, the Windows operating system is designed for an IBM-compatible personal computer (PC). The Mac OS only works with Macintosh computers. PC and Macintosh are called platforms. A platform is the computer system on which different programs can be used.

Firmware is a program that is embedded in a silicon chip rather than stored on a floppy disk. Any change to either the hardware or software can cause firmware to become outdated. This can lead to device failure, system failure, or data loss. When this happens to older firmware, the only solution is to replace it. Modern firmware is flashable, meaning that the contents can be upgraded, or flashed. This subject is covered in more depth in a later chapter.

Computer Types

Two types of computers are detailed in this section. The first is the mainframe, which has provided computing power for major corporations for more than 40 years. The second is the personal computer, which has arguably had more impact on people and business than any other device in history.

Mainframes

Mainframes are powerful machines that allow companies to automate manual tasks, shorten marketing time for new products, use financial models that enhance profitability, and so on. The mainframe model consists of centralized computers that are usually housed in secure, climate-controlled computer rooms. End users interface with the computers through dumb terminals. These terminals are low-cost devices that usually consist of a monitor, a keyboard, and a port to communicate with the mainframe. Initially, terminals were hard wired directly to communication ports on the mainframe, and the communications were asynchronous. A mainframe computer is shown in Figure 1-2.

NOTE

Asynchronous means "without respect to time." In terms of data transmission, asynchronous means that no clock or timing source is needed to keep both the sender and the receiver synchronized. Without the benefit of a clock, the sender must signal the start and stop of each character so that the receiver knows when to expect data.

Figure 1-2 Mainframe Computer

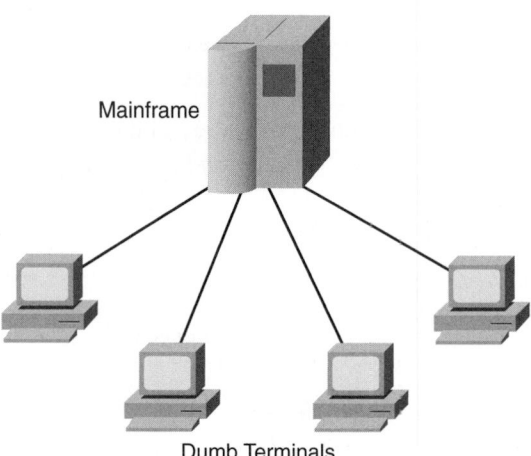

Mainframe

Dumb Terminals

A mainframe environment consists of a single computer or group of computers that can be centrally managed and maintained. This configuration has the additional advantage of being more secure for two reasons. First, the computer is stored in a secure room. Second, the ability of the end user to introduce viruses into the system is decreased. Virus protection and eradication cost companies hundreds of millions of U.S. dollars annually.

At its peak in the late 1970s and early 1980s, the mainframe and minicomputer market was dominated by IBM and Digital Equipment Corporation (DEC). However, the high-powered mainframes came with high price tags. The cost of entry into the mainframe market was typically several hundred thousand to several million U.S. dollars. The minicomputer was a smaller and less expensive line of mainframes. The minicomputer began to bring similar capabilities at a lower price, but the minicomputer configurations often cost more than US $10,000.

Mainframes continue to be prominent in corporate computing. It is estimated that 24 million dumb terminals are currently in use worldwide. In addition, 15 million PCs are currently deployed to function primarily as mainframe terminal emulators. These dumb terminals are American Standard Code for Information Interchange (ASCII) character–based devices. These terminals are often referred to as green screens because many of them display green characters.

The term *mainframe* used to refer to the cabinet that housed the CPU. Today, the term refers to a large computer system. Table 1-1 lists the advantages and disadvantages of mainframes.

Table 1-1 Advantages and Disadvantages of Mainframes

Advantages	Disadvantages
Scalability, the ability to add more users as the need arises	Character-based applications
Centralized management	Lack of vendor operating system standards and interoperability in multivendor environments
Centralized backup	Expensive, with a high cost for setup, maintenance, and initial equipment
Low-cost desktop devices (dumb terminals)	Potential single point of failure (non-fault-tolerant configurations)
High level of security	Timesharing systems, which indicate a potential for a bottleneck

PCs

A *personal computer (PC)* is a stand-alone device. This means that it is independent of all other computers, as shown in Figure 1-3. With the advent of the PC, the *graphical user interface (GUI)* gained wide introduction to users.

Figure 1-3 Personal Computer

A GUI, pronounced *goo-ee,* uses a graphics display to represent procedures and programs that can be executed by the computer. An example is the Windows Desktop, as shown in Figure 1-4. These programs routinely use small pictures, called icons, to represent different programs. The advantage of using a GUI is that the user does not have to remember complicated commands to execute a program. The GUIs first appeared in Xerox and Apple computers. Along with the GUI, thousands of Windows-based applications were also introduced.

As PC technology has improved, the power of the PC has risen to the point that it can perform enterprise-level functions. Enterprise-level functions refer to the professional tasks required by businesses, e-business, schools, government agencies, etc.

The advantages and disadvantages of PC computing are listed in Table 1-2.

Figure 1-4 Typical GUI

Table 1-2 Advantages and Disadvantages of PC Computing

Advantages	Disadvantages
Standardized hardware	Desktop computers cost, on average, five times as much as dumb terminals, according to some industry estimates
Standardized, highly interoperable operating systems (interoperable refers to the compatibility of the software)	No centralized backup
Graphical user interface	No centralized management
Low-cost devices (when compared to mainframes), low cost of entry	Security risks can be greater (physical access, data access, and virus security)
Distributed computing	High management and maintenance costs, although they are generally cheaper to maintain than mainframes
User flexibility	
High-productivity applications	

Connecting Computer Systems

The PC as a stand-alone device can be adequate for use as a home computer. However, businesses, government offices, and schools need to exchange information and share equipment and resources. This exchanging and sharing is known as networking. Networking was developed as a method to connect individual computers. The individual computers in a network are referred to as workstations, as illustrated in Figure 1-5.

Figure 1-5 Stand-Alone Computer Workstations

A *network* is a group of computers that are connected to share resources, as illustrated in Figure 1-6. Computers that are used by students, teachers, and administrators in a school are all connected through networks. This saves the expense of having to buy peripheral equipment for each computer. For example, the printer in the school computer lab is shared with all the students. A network also allows users to share files. If work is being done on a group project, a file can be saved to a central computer called a server. This file can then be accessed from any other computer in the school.

Figure 1-6 Connecting Computer Systems

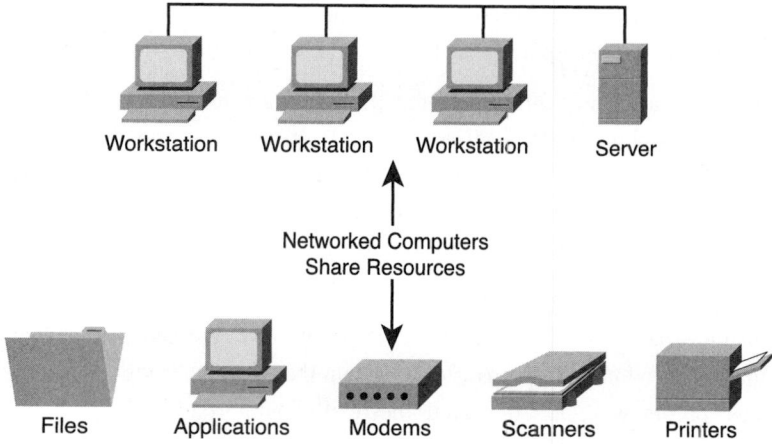

Networks are not limited to a building or school campus. Networks can encompass an entire school district or all the offices in a company. A school, for example, is connected to a main district office, as are all the other schools in a district. The Internet is the ultimate network, because it connects millions of smaller networks.

Most connections are made by wiring the devices together. However, wireless connections are becoming more prominent. Cable can carry voice, data, or both. Homes can have modems that plug into telephone jacks. The telephone line carries voice signals when the telephone is plugged into the phone jack. However, the phone line carries data signals, which are encoded to appear as if they are voice signals, when the modem is connected. Other, faster connections to the Internet are available. These connections include digital subscriber line (DSL), cable, and T1, T3, or E1 lines. In some parts of the world, Integrated Services Digital Network (ISDN) is used as well. Most of these technologies are used by businesses because their cost is often prohibitive for home users. Some of the high-speed services are only available in a limited area. However, improvements in communication devices and an ever-increasing demand for high-speed links mean that many home users should have access to these Internet connections in the next few years.

Birth of the Internet

As the Cold War between the West and the former Soviet Union intensified in the 1960s, the U.S. Department of Defense (DoD) recognized the need to establish communications links between major U.S. military installations. The primary motivation was to maintain communications if a nuclear war resulted in the mass destruction and breakdown of traditional communications channels. Major universities, such as the University of California and the Massachusetts Institute of Technology (MIT), were also involved in networking projects.

The DoD funded research sites throughout the United States. In 1968, the Advanced Research Projects Agency (ARPA) contracted with Bolt, Beranek, and Newman, Inc. (BBN) to build a network. This network was based on packet-switching technology, which was developed for better transmission of computer data.

The Growth Begins in the 1970s

When the Advanced Research Projects Agency Network (ARPANET) project began, no one anticipated that the network would grow to the extent that it did. Throughout the 1970s, more nodes, or access points, were added, both domestically and abroad.

More Is Better in the 1980s

In 1983, the ARPANET was split. The Military Network (MILNET), which was integrated with the Defense Data Network (DDN), took 68 of the 113 existing nodes. The DDN had been created in 1982.

The *Domain Name System (DNS)* was introduced in 1984. This system provided a way to map friendly host names to IP addresses. It was much more efficient and convenient than previous methods. These methods are discussed in Chapter 9, "Advanced Hardware Fundamentals for Servers." In 1984, more than 1000 host computers were on the network.

During the last half of the 1980s, networking increased considerably. For example, the National Science Foundation (NSF) created supercomputer centers in the United States at Princeton, the University of California, the University of Illinois, and Cornell University. The Internet Engineering Task Force (IETF) was also created during this time. By 1987, there were 10,000 hosts on the network. By 1989, that number increased to over 100,000.

The Net Becomes Big Business in the 1990s

The phenomenal growth rate of the 1980s was nothing compared to what came in the 1990s. ARPANET evolved into the Internet, with the U.S. government getting involved in pushing the development of the so-called information superhighway. The National Science Foundation Network (NSFNET) backbone was upgraded to T3 speed (that is, 44.736 Mbps), and in 1991, the backbone sent more than 1 trillion bytes per month. The Internet Society (ISOC) was formed, and in 1992, more than 1 million hosts existed on the Internet.

The 1990s saw the explosion of commerce on the Internet. As more college students, faculty, home users, and companies of all sizes became connected, the business world recognized the opportunity to reach a large and expanding affluent market. By 1995, online advertising became prominent, online banking had arrived, and even a pizza could be ordered over the Internet.

The last five years of the 20th century ushered in new major developments on an almost daily basis. Streaming audio and video, "push" technologies, and Java and ActiveX scripting took advantage of higher-performance connectivity that was available at lower prices. Domain names became big business, and particularly desirable names have sold for upward of US $1 million. Currently, millions of sites exist on the Word Wide Web, and millions of host computers participate in this great linking. Table 1-3 shows a timeline of significant events in PC networking history. The graph in Figure 1-7 shows the growth of the Internet.

Figure 1-7 Exponential Growth of the Internet

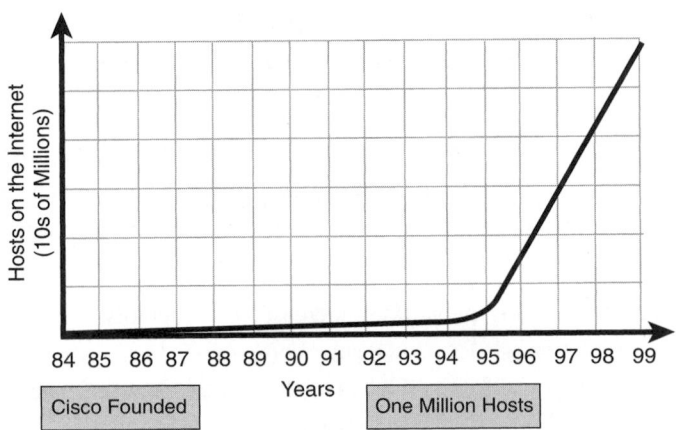

Table 1-3 Internet Timeline

Year	Event
1957	ARPA created by the DoD.
1969	ARPANET connects the first four universities in the United States.
1970	ALOHANET developed by University of Hawaii.
1973	ARPANET goes international, with connections to University College in London, England, and the Royal Radar Establishment in Norway.
1974	BBN opens Telnet, the first commercial version of the ARPANET.
1982	The term *Internet* is used for the first time.
1983	Transmission Control Protocol/Internet Protocol (TCP/IP) becomes the universal language of the Internet. ARPANET is split into ARPANET and MILNET.
1984	The number of Internet hosts exceeds 1000. DNS is introduced.
1986	NSFNET is created, with a backbone speed of 56 Kbps.
1987	The number of Internet hosts exceeds 10,000.
1988	Computer Emergency Response Team (CERT) is formed by DARPA.
1989	The number of Internet hosts exceeds 100,000.
1990	ARPANET becomes the Internet.

Table 1-3 Internet Timeline (Continued)

Year	Event
1991	The World Wide Web (WWW) is born.
1992	Internet Society (ISOC) is chartered. Number of Internet hosts breaks 1 million.
1993	Mosaic, the first graphics-based web browser, becomes available.
1996	The number of Internet hosts exceeds 10 million. The Internet covers the globe.
1997	The American Registry for Internet Numbers (ARIN) is established. Internet 2 comes online.
1999	Internet 2 backbone network deploys IPv6.
2001	The number of Internet host exceeds 110 million.

The tremendous growth in the computer industry means exciting job possibilities. According to projections from the U.S. Bureau of Labor Statistics, eight of the ten fastest-growing occupations will be computer related. This means that the number of jobs for IT technicians and computer-support personnel will almost double by 2010.

The Cost of Technology

As computer and networking technologies have advanced over the past few decades, the cost of the increasingly sophisticated technology has fallen dramatically. Those falling prices are at least partially responsible for the rising popularity of connectivity solutions in the business world and in personal lives.

In the 1970s and 1980s, the PC shown in Figure 1-8 was considered state of the art and cost several thousand U.S. dollars. Online services existed, but they were expensive. Only big businesses and the wealthy could afford them at the cost of US $25 or more per hour of access. PC veterans can still remember the announcement of the Prodigy bargain rates of only US $9.95 an hour for online access. The available speeds were 1200 or 2400 baud (bits per second), which would be considered unusable by the current user.

Today, a user can buy a computer system in the United States for less than US $1000 that is capable of doing much more than a system purchased just five years ago. Such a machine can also operate better and faster than the mainframe version of 20 years ago, which cost US $500,000. Internet access at speeds equivalent to T1 is available through DSL or cable modem service for US $30–40 per month, and prices are continually decreasing. Basic Internet access at 56 kbps can be obtained for much less—even free—if the user can tolerate on-screen advertising.

Figure 1-8 Legacy PC

Windows Desktop Environment

The Windows Desktop environment allows users to work more efficiently and provides the ability to customize features. This section includes the following topics:

- Starting, shutting down, and restarting Microsoft Windows
- Using Windows Explorer
- Navigating the Desktop
- Working with icons
- Recognizing an application window
- Resizing a Desktop window
- Switching between windows

Starting, Shutting Down, and Restarting Microsoft Windows

The basic functions of a computer include turning the computer on, restarting the computer, and shutting down the system. Because most computers have both the power button and reset button on the front of the machine, it is important to know how to differentiate between them.

Turning on the PC

To turn on a PC, you must activate an external switch or a pair of switches. The rear switch, if included, provides the physical connection between the house power from the wall outlet and the computer power supply. This switch must be on prior to turning on the front switch. However, most PCs only have a single switch in the front that is activated to provide power.

In most cases, the monitor also has a power switch. This switch is usually in the front or lower-right portion of the display case. Switches can be push-type or rocker switches. They are manufactured to withstand thousands of cycles and typically outlast the PC itself.

Starting up a computer is also referred to as booting the system. A *cold boot* is performed when the PC is turned on using the power button. At the end of this process, the Windows operating system Desktop is displayed.

Shutting Down a Computer

To shut down the computer, click the **Start** button on the lower-left corner of the Windows Taskbar and select **Shut Down**, as shown in Figure 1-9. Alternatively, press **Ctrl-Alt-Delete** and click the Shut Down button.

Do not switch the computer off until a message displays indicating that it is safe to do so. Important data that is stored in memory while the system is operating needs to be written to the hard disk before switching off the computer. Newer computers automatically shut off power when the shutdown process is complete.

Figure 1-9 Shutting Down a Computer

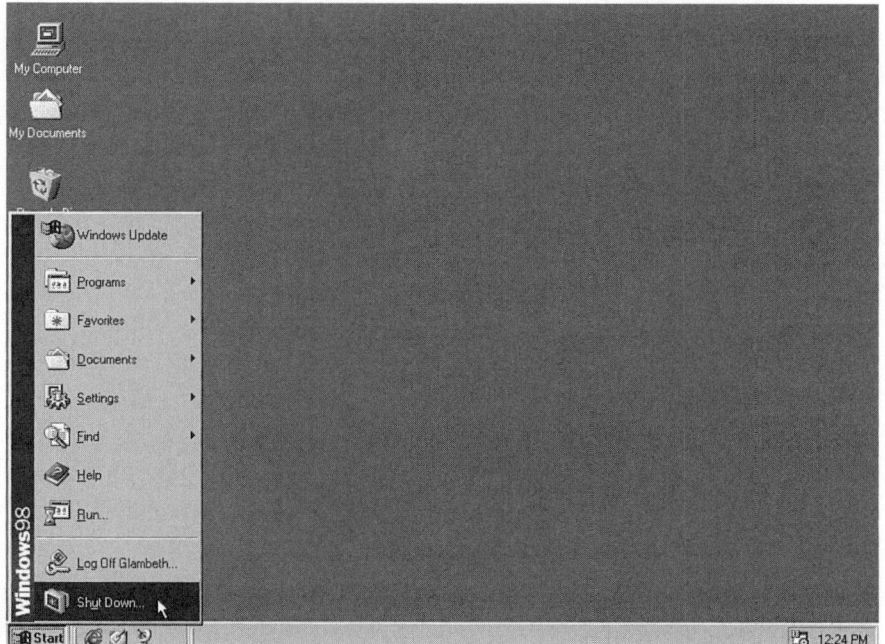

NOTE

It is extremely important not to shut down the computer with the power switch. Most operating systems, such as Macintosh OS X and Microsoft Windows, have a specific method for turning the system off. In Windows, choose **Shut Down** from the Start menu. On a Macintosh, choose **Shut Down** from the Special menu.

Restarting the PC

Restarting a PC that has already been powered up is referred to as a *warm boot*. This can be achieved by pressing the reset button on the front panel of the computer. Alternatively, in Windows 98, press **Ctrl-Alt-Delete** and choose **Restart** from the menu that displays. The options that display with the **Ctrl-Alt-Delete** command will vary depending on the version of Windows installed on the system. The concepts of warm boot and cold boot are discussed more thoroughly in Chapter 2, "How Computers Work."

Using Windows Explorer

The Windows Explorer file manager provides the ability to create, copy, move, and delete files and folders. As shown in Figure 1-10, Explorer displays the hierarchy of folders that are stored on the hard disk or other storage device in the left pane. When a user clicks a folder in the left Explorer pane, its contents are displayed in the right pane. Two or more instances of Explorer can be launched to drag and drop files and folders between them.

Figure 1-10 Windows Explorer in Windows 2000

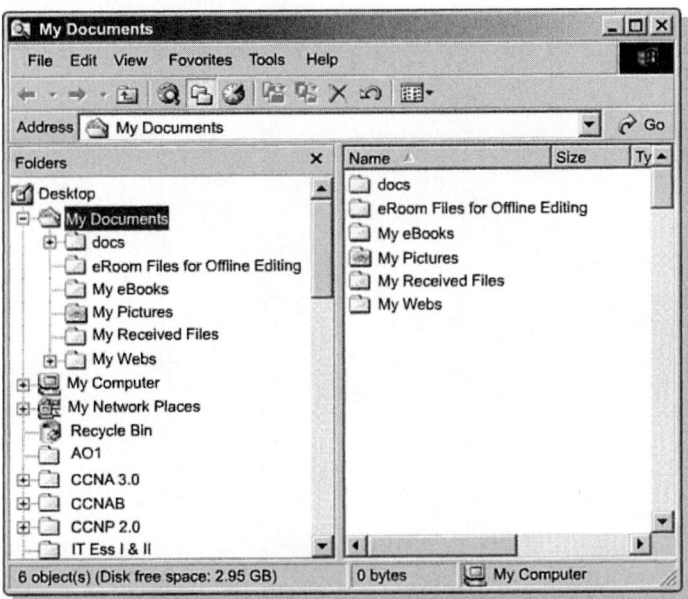

TIP

Know the different ways to open Windows Explorer.

You can access Explorer in Windows 95, 98, and Me (Millennium Edition) by choosing **Start**, **Programs**, **Windows Explorer** from the Windows Desktop, as shown in Figure 1-11. In Windows 2000, choose **Start**, **Programs**, **Accessories**, **Windows Explorer**, as shown in Figure 1-12. Another way to open Windows Explorer in Windows 9x, Me, 2000, and XP is to right-click the Start button and select **Explore**.

Figure 1-11 Accessing Windows Explorer in Windows 98

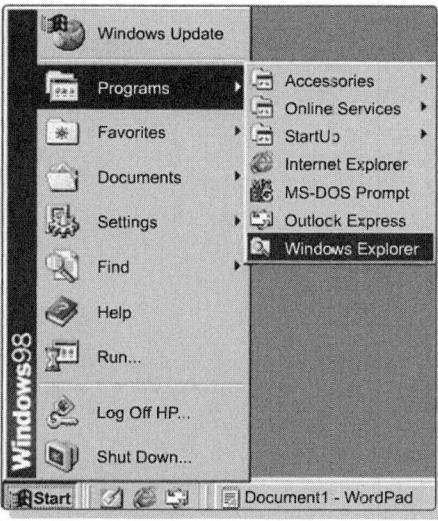

Figure 1-12 Accessing Windows Explorer in Windows 2000

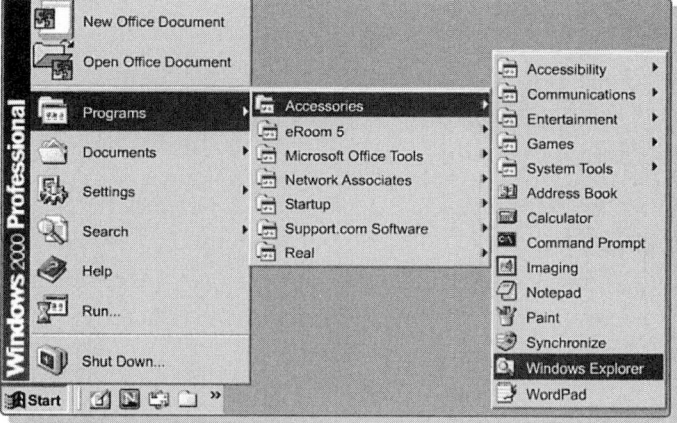

Navigating the Desktop

The main display screen in Windows is known as the ***Desktop***. The Windows Desktop has remained consistent for most versions, including Windows 95, 98, 98 SE (Second Edition), Me, NT, 2000, and XP. Figure 1-13 shows the Desktop in Windows 98. However, some variations can be seen in older versions of Windows 95 or in a special type of installation, such as that on a laptop or network, when certain features are disabled.

Figure 1-13 Windows Desktop

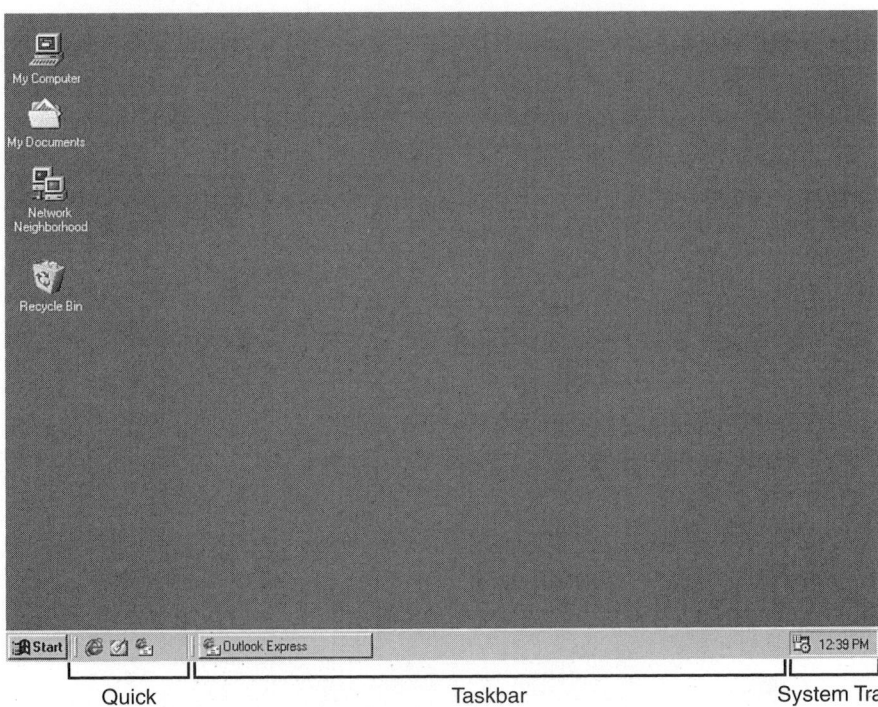

An *icon* is an image that represents an application or a capability. Typically, an icon is selectable as a shortcut to a program or file on the Desktop. An icon can also be nonselectable, as in a company logo on a web page.

TIP

Practice navigating the Desktop with both the mouse and keyboard.

Some of the icons on the Desktop, such as My Computer, Network Neighborhood, My Network Places, Recycle Bin, and My Documents, are shortcuts to those directories. Directories are discussed in Chapter 4, "Operating System Fundamentals." Other icons that can be on the Desktop, such as Microsoft Word, Microsoft Excel, or Adobe Photoshop, are shortcuts to those applications.

Clicking the *My Computer icon* gives access to all the installed drives, which are computer storage components.

The *My Documents icon* is a shortcut to personal or frequently accessed files. The Network Neighborhood icon allows you to see neighboring computers in a networked environment. The Recycle Bin is discussed in the section "Basic Features of Windows," later in this chapter.

The Taskbar is located at the bottom of the Desktop. The Taskbar contains the Start button, quick launch buttons, and the System Tray. The Start button displays the Start menu. This menu allows access to almost every program and function on the PC. The Start menus for Windows 98 and Windows 2000 are shown in Figure 1-14.

Figure 1-14 Windows Start Menus

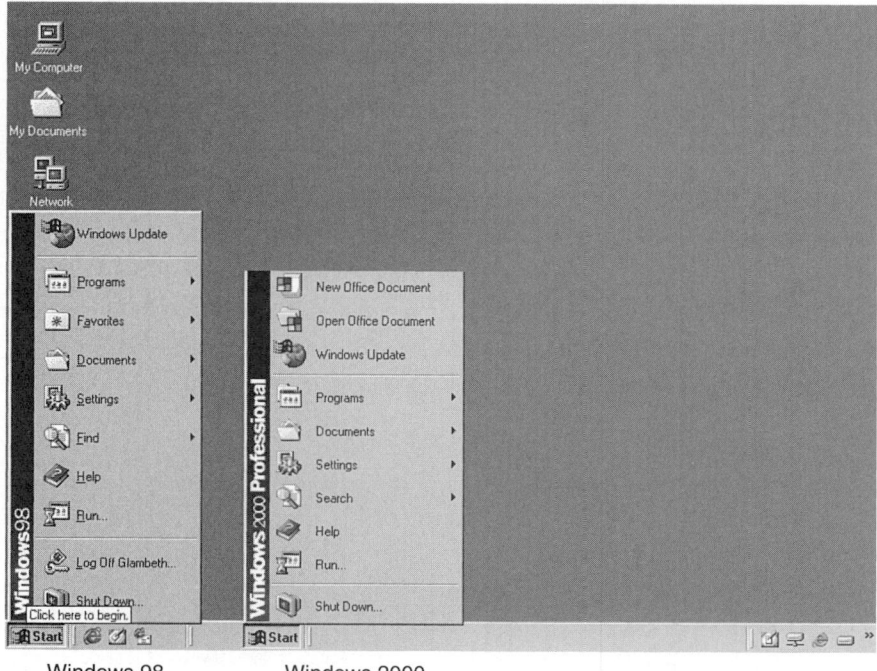

Windows 98   Windows 2000

The quick launch buttons are located on the Taskbar next to the Start button. These buttons allow immediate access to the Desktop from any application, as well as access to e-mail and the Internet. Quick launch buttons are similar to Desktop icons because these buttons are shortcuts to applications. The buttons are particularly useful when several applications or documents are open and you need a quick way to open another application.

Working with Icons

This section explains how to select and move Desktop icons. You also learn how to recognize basic Desktop icons such as the hard disk, directory tree, directories or folders and files, and the Recycle Bin. Finally, this section explains how to create a Desktop shortcut icon or a Desktop menu alias.

Creating Shortcuts (Icons)

To create a shortcut (icon), navigate to a program or file in Windows Explorer. Right-click the program or file, and select **Create Shortcut**. The shortcut icon appears as the last item in the menu that appears. This icon can be moved using cut and paste or drag and drop. An icon can also be created directly on the Desktop. Right-click the Desktop, and select **New**, **New Short-cut**, or **Create Shortcut**. Enter the path for the program or file, and the shortcut displays on the Desktop.

Moving Icons

To move the created icon or another Desktop icon to another position on the Desktop, click and hold and then drag the icon to the desired location, as shown in Figure 1-15. The icon becomes semitransparent while being dragged. To restore the icon to full intensity, click outside of it. If the icon does not move, disable the Auto Arrange function on the Desktop. To do this, right-click an empty space on the Desktop and deselect the Auto Arrange option, as shown in Figure 1-16. Shortcut icons can be created for frequently used programs such as web browsers, word processors, spreadsheets, and instant messengers.

Figure 1-15 Moving an Icon

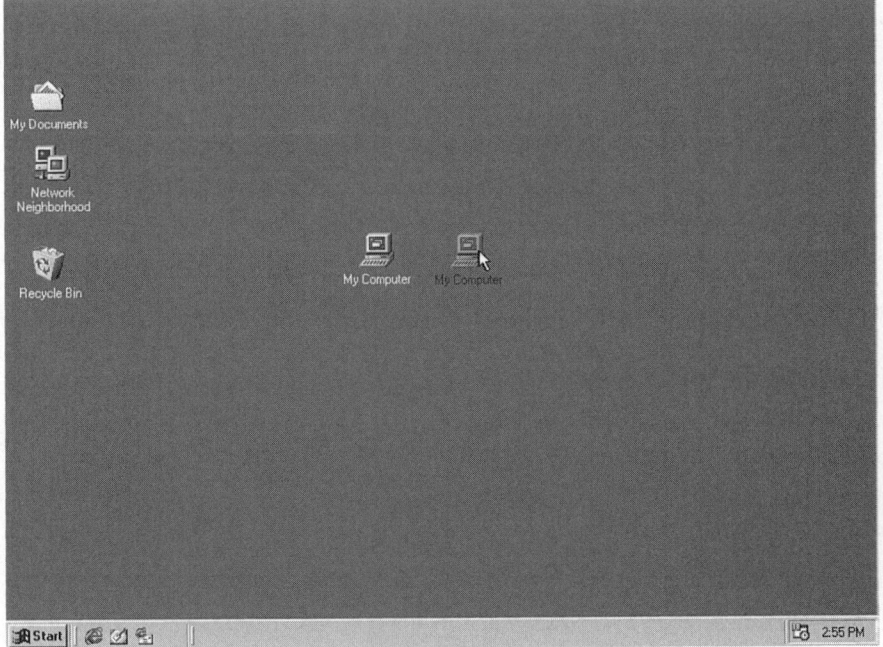

Selecting Multiple Icons

To simultaneously select and move several icons, press and hold down **Ctrl** and click all the icons that are to be moved. Then drag the group of icons to the new location and release the mouse button, as shown in Figure 1-17. Deselect the icons by clicking an empty part of the Desktop.

Figure 1-16 Arranging Icons

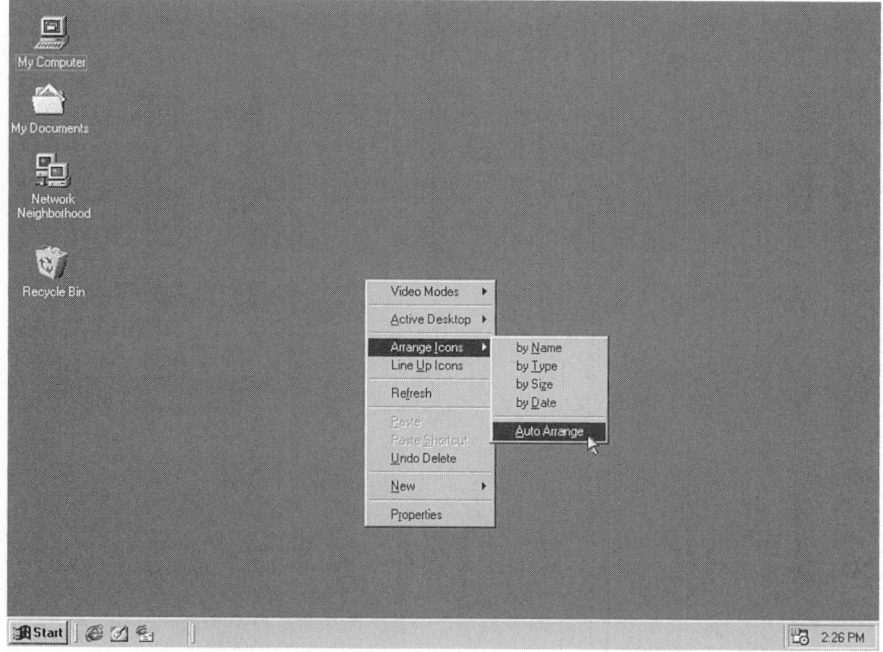

Figure 1-17 Moving Multiple Icons

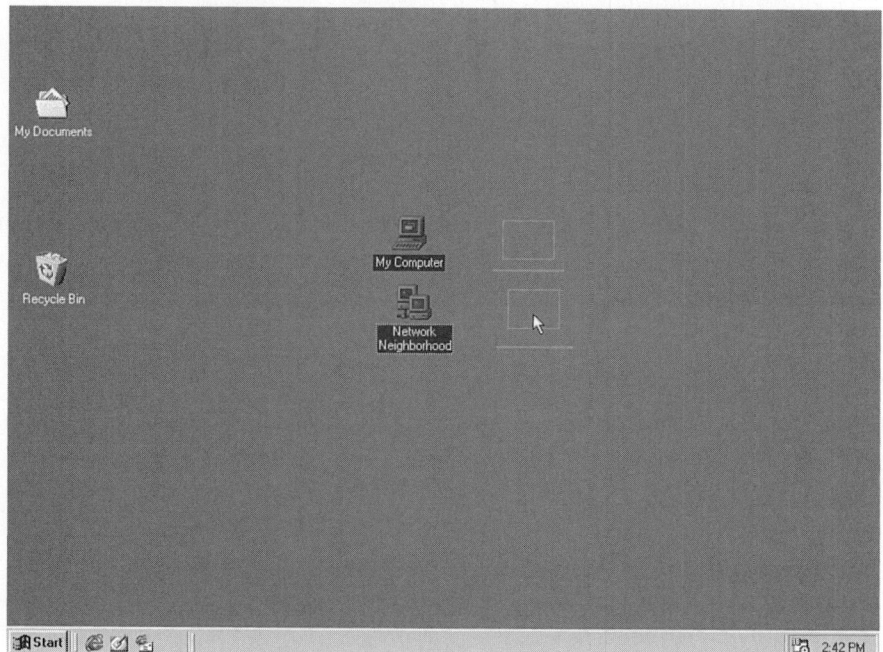

Renaming Icons

You can rename an icon in two ways. The first way is to simply click the name under the icon, as shown in Figure 1-18. Then type in a new name, as shown in Figure 1-19. Click an empty part of the Desktop or press **Enter** to complete the action. The second way is to right-click the icon and select **Rename**.

Figure 1-18 Highlighting the Icon Name

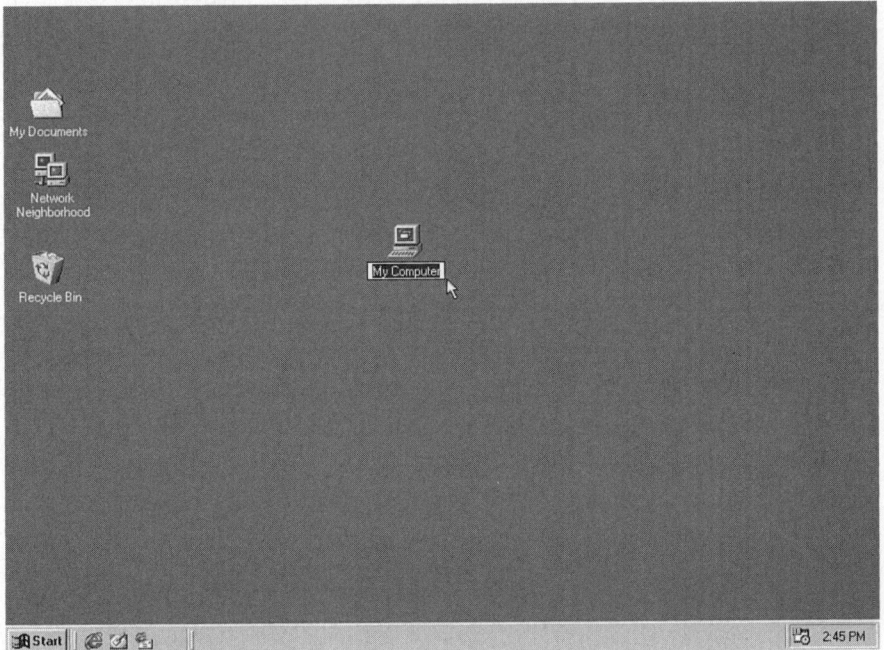

It is easier to navigate and work with the Desktop by using icons. Because icons are simply shortcuts that point to programs and files, they can be copied, moved, and even deleted without affecting the program or file.

Recognizing an Application Window

Application windows typically have a title bar, toolbar, menu bar, status bar, and scroll bar. In this section, WordPad is used to demonstrate the features that are common to most Windows applications, as shown in Figure 1-20. WordPad—or Notepad on some Windows computers—is a simple word processing program that can be accessed by choosing **Start**, **Programs**, **Accessories**, **WordPad**.

Figure 1-19 Changing the Icon Name

Figure 1-20 WordPad Application Window

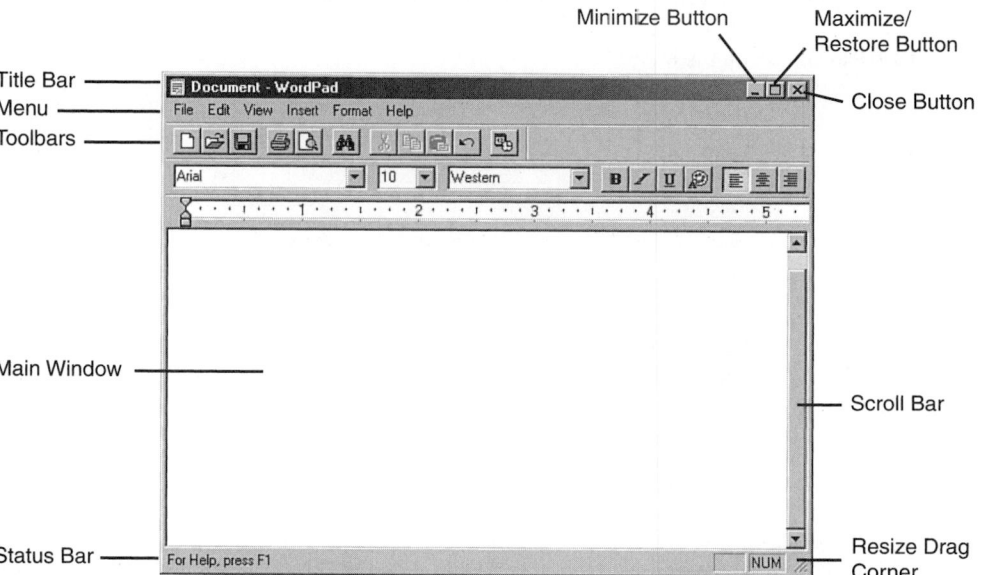

The functions of the toolbar are easy to understand and are described in Table 1-4.

Table 1-4 Toolbar Descriptions

Toolbar	Description
Title bar	Displays the name of the document and application. In Figure 1-20, it is Document – WordPad. Also located in the title bar are the Minimize, Maximize, and Exit buttons that are discussed later in this chapter.
Menu bar	Contains menus for manipulating the document, such as creating new documents, copying text, inserting images, and so on. To see the menu for each item, click a button. A drop-down menu displays.
Status bar	Located at the bottom of the window, the status bar shows information such as page number, whether the file is being saved, how to access the Help feature, and so on.
Scroll bar	Windows can have scroll bars that appear on the right side of the window, the bottom of the window, or both. These scroll bars appear when the document is too large to be viewed in the window. Clicking the arrows on either end of the scroll bar moves the images or text through the window. Clicking and dragging the scroll bar moves image or text even more quickly through a window.

Figure 1-21 shows an example of a file option on the menu bar.

Figure 1-21 File Option on the Menu Bar

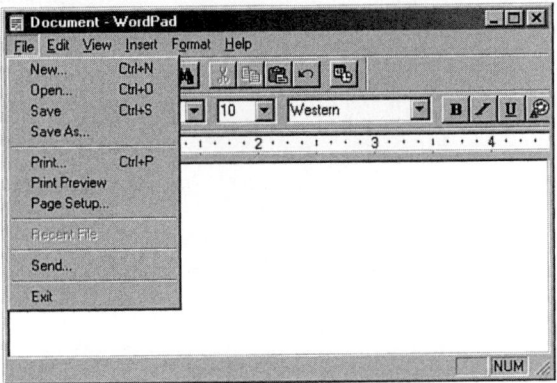

You might want to move a window to another location on the screen, particularly if more than one window is open on the screen. Click and hold the title bar, and then drag the window to the desired position, as shown in Figure 1-22. The window dynamically follows the cursor around, similar to moving a piece of paper on a real desktop.

Figure 1-22 Moving an Application Window

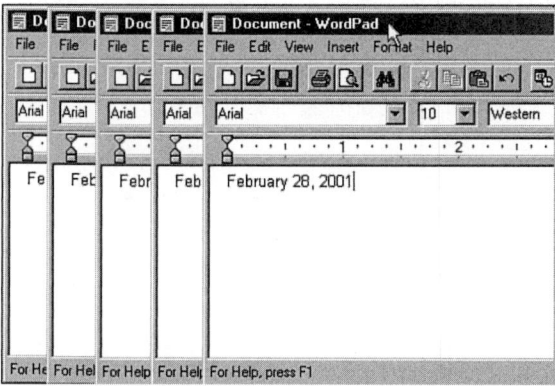

Most Windows applications have similar-looking menus and functions. Differences depend on the type of application.

Resizing a Desktop Window

Windows that display applications, such as WordPad, can have sizes ranging from full-screen to very small. To resize a window, move the cursor to any corner or side of the application window. A double-headed arrow appears, as shown in Figure 1-23. Click and drag the window edge to change the window size.

Figure 1-23 Double-Headed Arrows

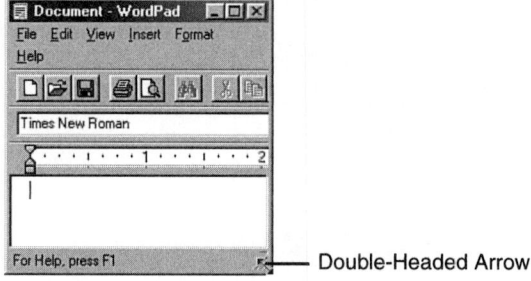

Double-Headed Arrow

Many types of arrows, pointers, cursors, and other items allow you to navigate around in Windows, as shown in Figure 1-24. To modify the mouse pointer, choose **My Computer**, **Control Panel**, **Mouse**, **Pointer**.

Figure 1-24 Arrows, Pointers, and Cursors

Switching Between Windows

When more than one window is open, you can switch between windows by pressing **Alt-Tab**. As shown in Figure 1-25, a window appears that indicates which applications are open. While holding down **Alt**, keep pressing **Tab** to find the desired window.

Figure 1-25 Switching Between Windows

Document windows can also be selected by clicking the desired document on the Desktop Taskbar, which displays at the bottom of the screen.

   Video   Getting to Know Windows

In this video, you explore the basic features of Windows.

Basic Features of Windows

You have several options for viewing the Desktop and accessing system information in Windows. This section includes the following topics:

- Viewing the basic system information of a computer
- Setting the clock and date

- Minimizing, maximizing, and exiting
- Adjusting the screen display
- Working with Desktop settings
- Adjusting audio volume
- Using the Start menu options
- Understanding the Recycle Bin

Viewing the Basic System Information of a Computer

This section discusses how to find system information in Windows 2000. It also shows how to view information such as the type of operating system, the type of processor, and the type and amount of random-access memory (RAM) that is installed. This information is valuable to the PC technician for troubleshooting and for updating the system or applications.

To view information about the system in Windows 2000, click the **Start** button and choose **Programs**, **Accessories**, **System Tools**, **System Information**, as shown in Figure 1-26.

Figure 1-26 Nested Menu Display

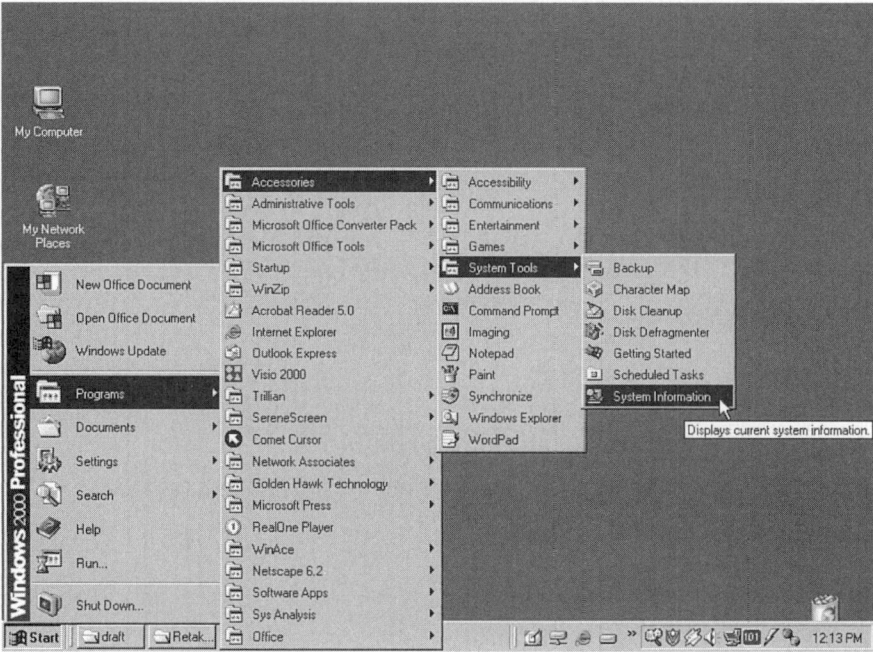

A window opens that shows the OS name and version, the system manufacturer and model, the processor type and manufacturer, the BIOS version, and the amount of memory. Figure 1-27

shows this window. This information can be saved as a text file by selecting **Action**, **Save As Text File**, as shown in Figure 1-28. You can specify the location where the file is to be saved, as shown in Figure 1-29. Figure 1-30 shows the *System Info.txt* file in the My Documents directory.

Figure 1-27 System Information

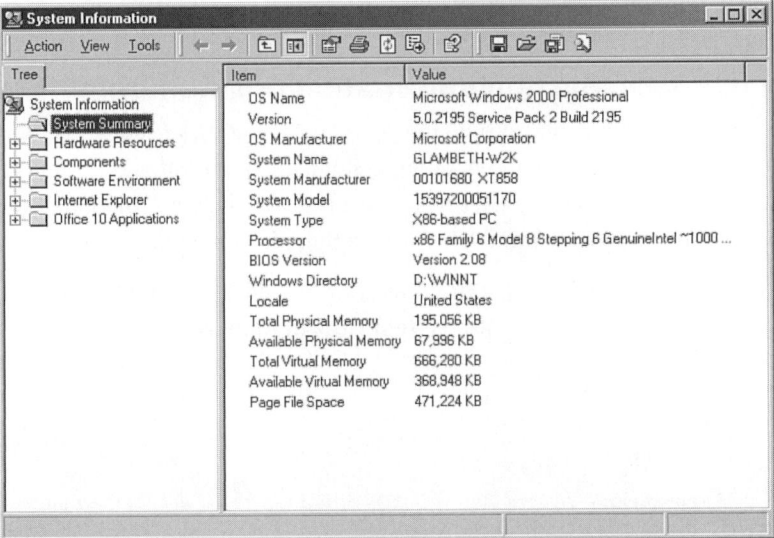

Figure 1-28 Saving the System Information

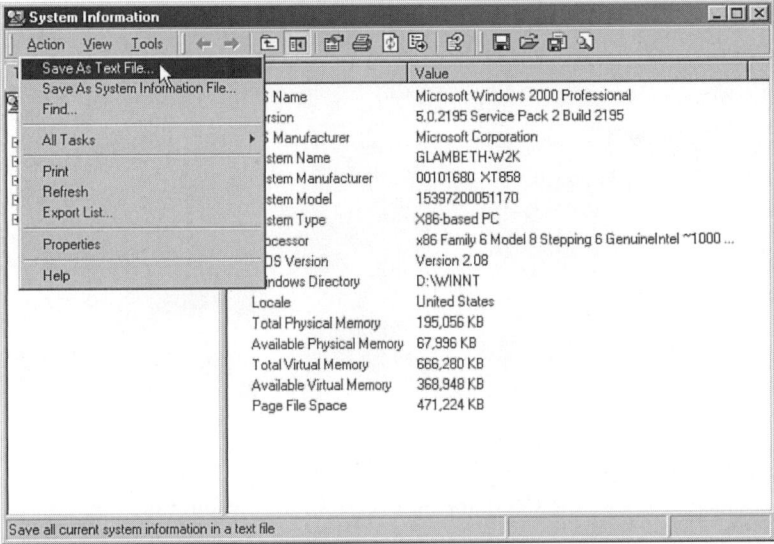

Figure 1-29 Saving the System Information as a Text File

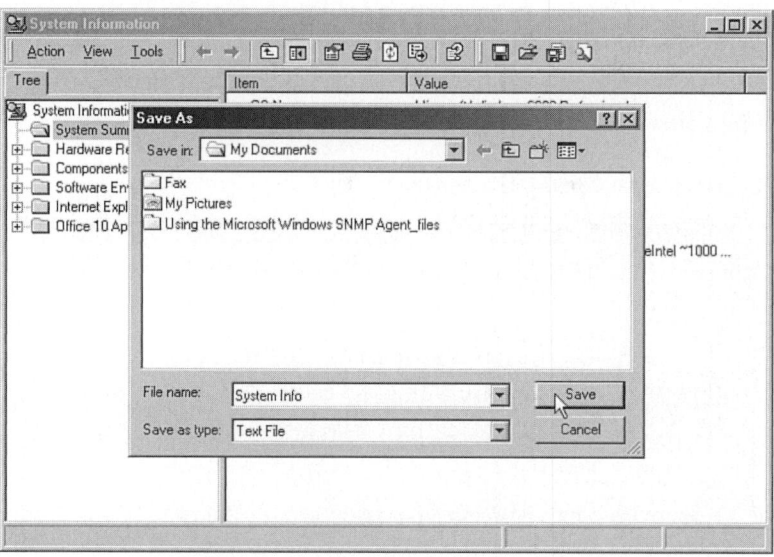

Figure 1-30 Verifying That the System Information Is Saved

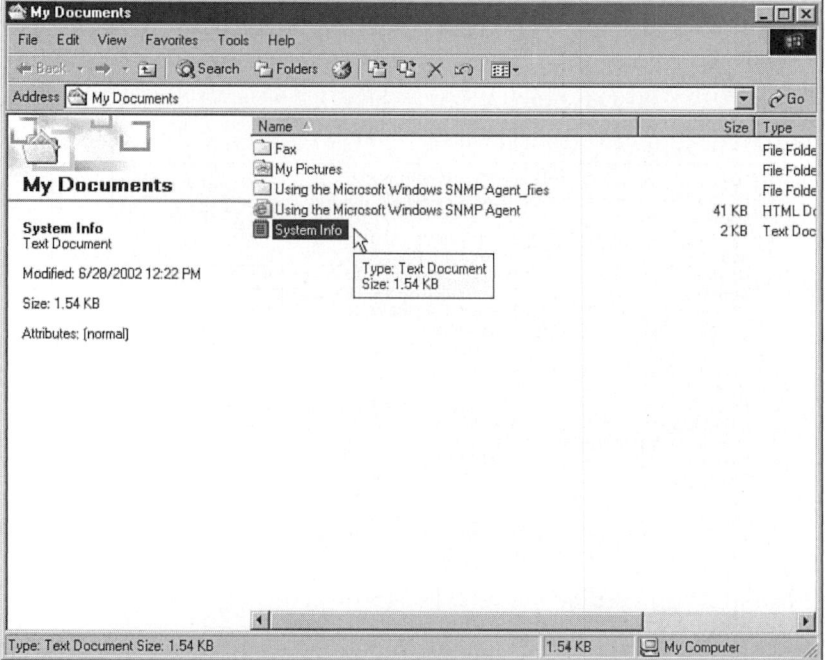

You can open the *System Info.txt* file in Notepad by double-clicking the filename. If the file is too large, Windows prompts you to open it in WordPad instead. The contents of the file are similar to what is shown in Figure 1-31. The text can then be copied and pasted into a word processing program, such as Microsoft Word, or a spreadsheet program, like Microsoft Excel, so that the information is easier to read, as shown in Figure 1-32.

Figure 1-31 System Info.txt Displayed in Notepad

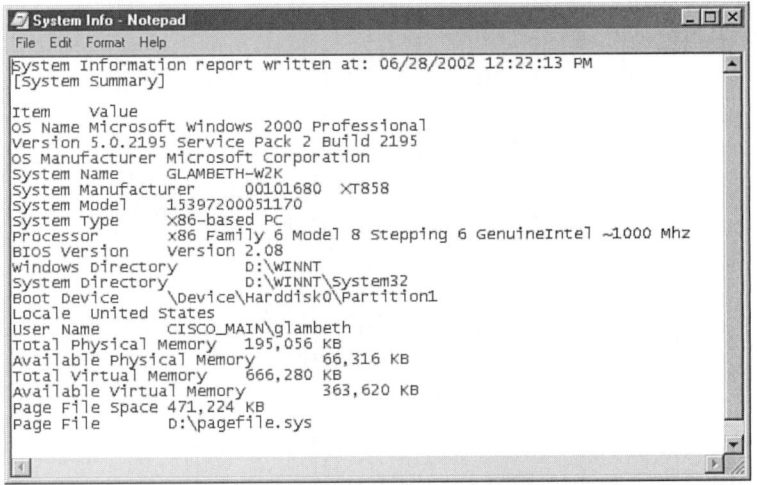

Figure 1-32 System Information Reformatted in Microsoft Word

System Information report written at: 06/28/2002 12:22:13 PM
[System Summary]

Item	Value
OS Name	Microsoft Windows 2000 Professional
Version	5.0.2195 Service Pack 2 Build 2195
OS Manufacturer	Microsoft Corporation
System Name	GLAMBETH-W2K
System Manufacturer	00101680 XT858
System Model	15397200051170
System Type	X86-based PC
Processor	x86 Family 6 Model 8 Stepping 6 GenuineIntel ~1000 Mhz
BIOS Version	Version 2.08
Windows Directory	D:\WINNT
System Directory	D:\WINNT\System32
Boot Device	\Device\Harddisk0\Partition1
Locale	United States
User Name	CISCO_MAIN\glambeth
Total Physical Memory	195,056 KB
Available Physical Memory	66,316 KB
Total Virtual Memory	666,280 KB
Available Virtual Memory	363,620 KB
Page File Space	471,224 KB
Page File	D:\pagefile.sys

Setting the Clock and Date

The next few sections show you how to use the Microsoft Windows graphical user interface (GUI) to adjust or make changes to the Desktop. You can change the date and time, the volume settings for the speakers, and other Desktop display options such as the background, screen settings, screen saver, and so on.

To adjust the date and time, double-click the clock on the Taskbar. A pop-up window similar to Figure 1-33 displays. Click the down arrow next to month to select the current month, as shown in Figure 1-34. Change the year in the same manner, if necessary. To adjust the date, click the desired numerical day of the month. Set the clock by entering the new time in the field and selecting AM or PM.

Figure 1-33 System Clock, Where You Can Set the Time, Date, and Time Zone

Figure 1-34 Adjusting the Month Using a Drop-Down Menu

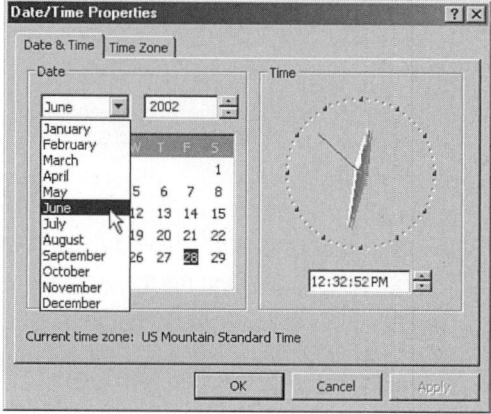

Click the Time Zone tab. Figure 1-35 shows the Date/Time Properties window. Click the down arrow, and choose the appropriate time zone, as shown in Figure 1-36. The clock is automatically adjusted for daylight-saving time changes annually.

Figure 1-35 Choosing the Time Zone

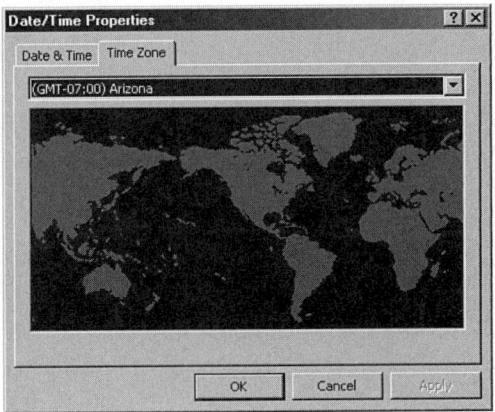

Figure 1-36 Adjusting the Time Zone Using a Drop-Down Menu

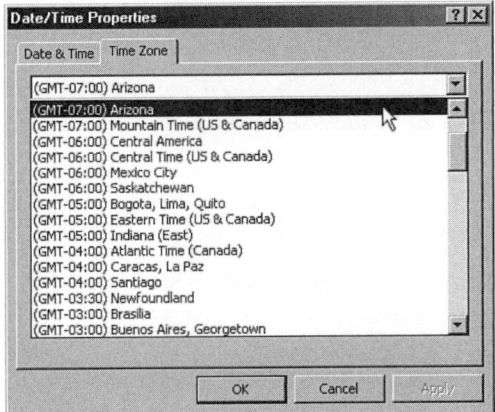

In Windows 98, the display window that is used to adjust the date and time properties is different from that in Windows 2000. In Windows 98, the Time Zone drop-down menu is located in the Date & Time tab. To select the time zone, click the Time Zone down arrow. This opens a drop-down menu, from which you can select a time zone.

Minimizing, Maximizing, and Exiting

Most Windows applications have three small icons in the upper-right corner of the screen that minimize the screen, maximize/restore the screen, or close the application. Figure 1-37 shows these icons.

Figure 1-37 Minimize, Maximize/Restore, and Exit Buttons

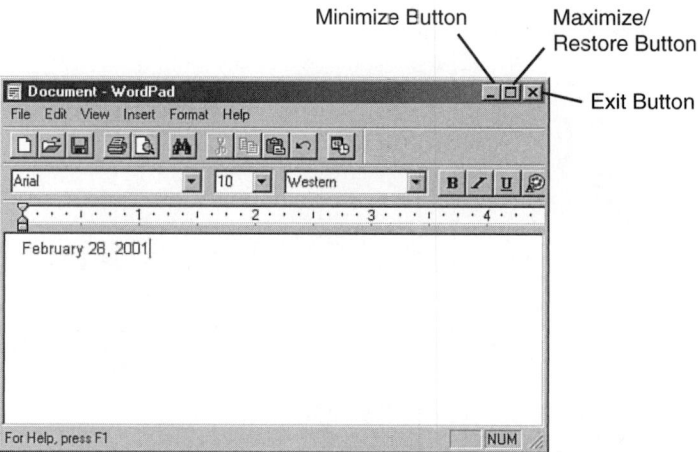

By clicking the Minimize button (the left button), the application is placed on the Taskbar. The application is still open and can be accessed by clicking it on the Taskbar.

The middle button, which is the Maximize or Restore button, changes depending on whether the window being viewed is opened partially or fully. Click this button to make the application screen smaller or larger. The Close button (the right button) is marked with an *X* and closes the application.

TIP

The fastest way to minimize all windows quickly is to click the Show Desktop icon next to the Start button. Clicking the icon again restores all windows.

Adjusting the Screen Display

The screen resolution setting depends on the requirements of the user, the application being used, and the version of Windows that is installed. Young children, older adults, and those with vision difficulties might prefer larger text and images. In addition, older video cards might not support more detailed colors or speed of display as demanded by the most advanced computer games, computer graphics, design software, or video-editing tools.

To adjust the screen display, first minimize all windows that are open. Right-click an empty space on the Desktop and choose **Properties** to open the Display Properties window, as shown in Figure 1-38. Alternatively, choose **Start**, **Settings**, **Control Panel**, **Display**.

Figure 1-38 Opening the Display Properties Window

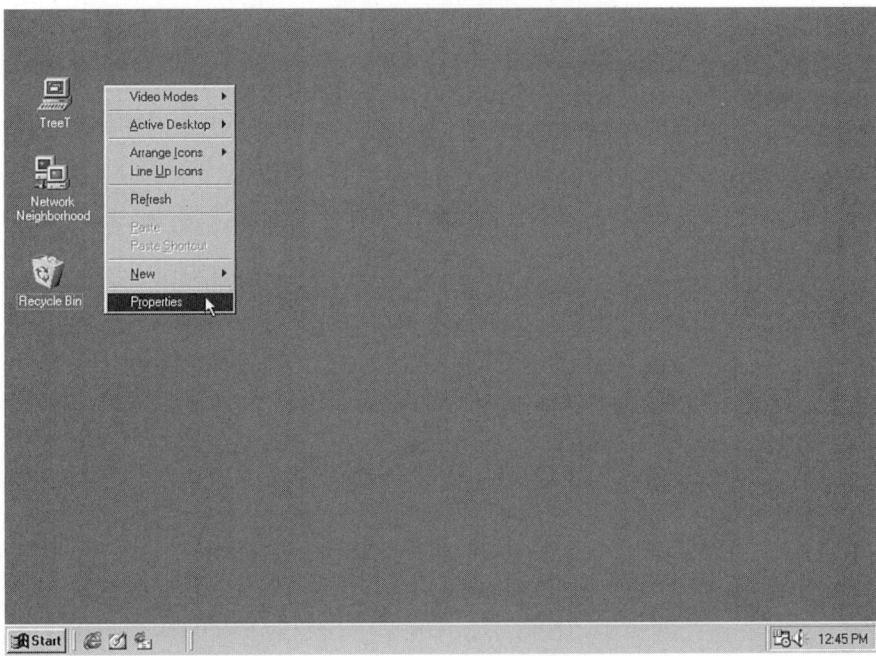

The following list details the tabs that are found in the Display Properties window:

- The Background tab, as shown in Figure 1-39, allows you to choose what is displayed as background for the Desktop. The Windows default background is a blue screen.

Figure 1-39 Display Properties: Background

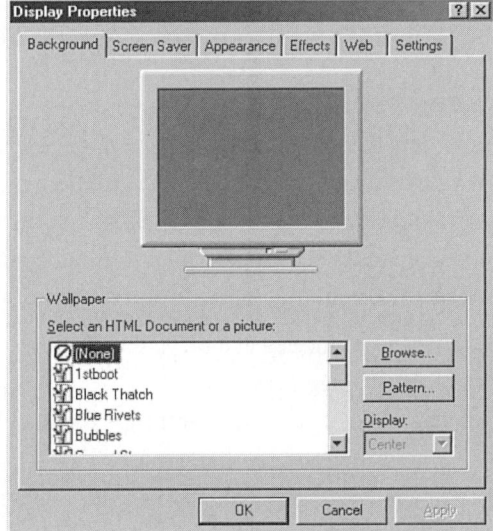

- The Screen Saver tab, as shown in Figure 1-40, permits you to select a screen saver and to indicate when the screen saver should activate on the Desktop. The screen saver can also be set up to require a password. Energy-saving features of the monitor are also applied on this tab.

Figure 1-40 Display Properties: Screen Saver

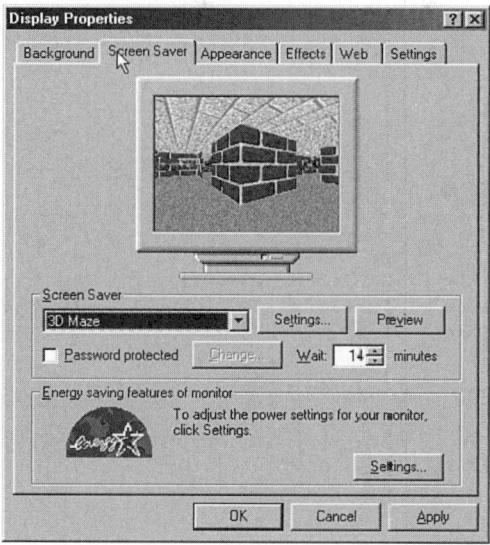

- The Appearance tab, as shown in Figure 1-41, allows you to choose the size and color of text and backgrounds for applications.

Figure 1-41 Display Properties: Appearance

■ The Effects tab, as shown in Figure 1-42, allows you to choose visual effects such as fade, large icons, and the ability to show contents while dragging windows.

Figure 1-42 Display Properties: Effects

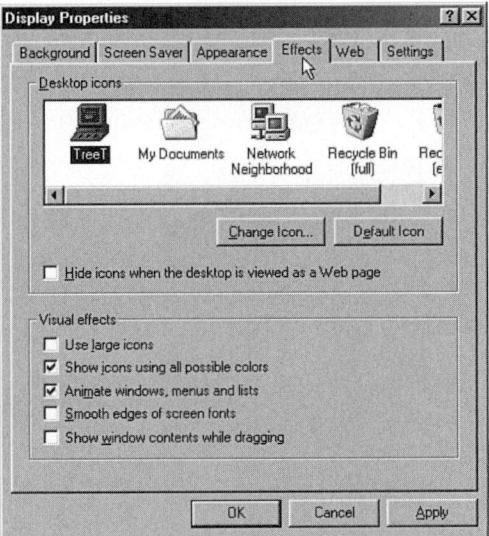

■ The Web tab, as shown in Figure 1-43, allows you to decide whether to show web content on the active Desktop. This tab is not available in Windows 95.

Figure 1-43 Display Properties: Web

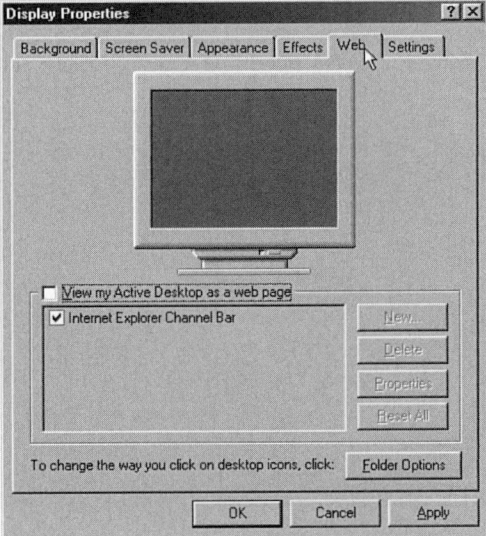

■ The Settings tab, as shown in Figure 1-44, allows you to adjust the screen area display and colors.

Figure 1-44 Display Properties: Settings

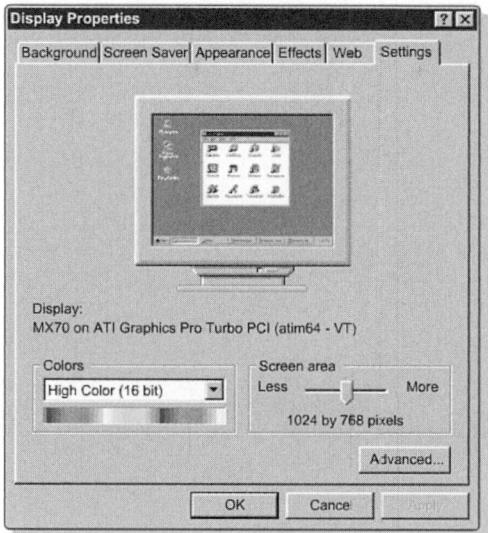

Setting the screen display properties allows you to customize your screen to your preferences.

Working with Desktop Settings

To adjust the Desktop settings, open the Display Properties window, as described in the previous section. On the Settings tab, adjust the number of colors and the number of pixels that are to be displayed, as shown in Figure 1-45. Pixels are the tiny dots that make up the light on the screen and determine the intensity of a screen image. For example, lower values tend to display cartoon-like color images, which are grainy with few details. Higher values display more realistic color images, which approach a true color (16.7 million colors) and have superb detail. Once the color or number of pixels has been selected, click the Apply button. The message in Figure 1-46 appears. Click the OK button. The message in Figure 1-47 appears. Click the Yes button to reconfigure the Desktop. The screen display might become blank, or the Desktop screen could jump around. Don't worry. Windows is adjusting the Desktop to match your new settings.

NOTE

When first installing a video card, Windows defaults to the lowest settings of 640×480 resolution and possibly eight colors. When a video card driver is installed with driver software that is supplied by the manufacturer, more colors and resolutions can be displayed. This topic is discussed in more detail in the "Display Components" section in Chapter 2.

Figure 1-45 Changing the Color Settings

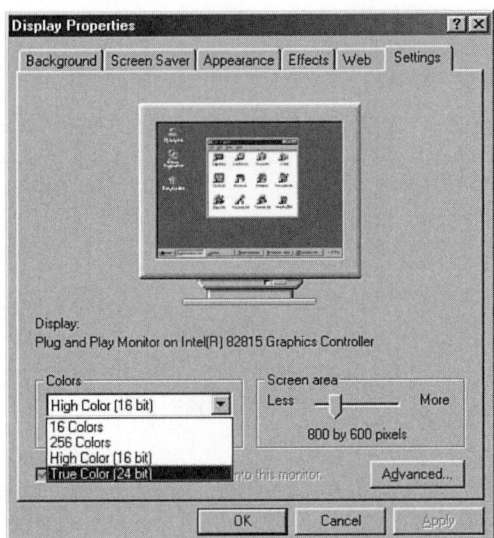

Figure 1-46 Confirm the New Settings

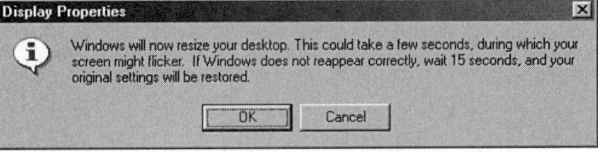

Figure 1-47 Accept or Reject the New Settings

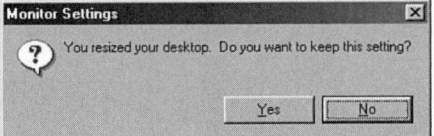

Adjusting Audio Volume

To access the volume control, click the speaker icon on the Taskbar. Audio properties can also be accessed from the Sounds and Multimedia icon in the Control Panel. Slide the bars up and down to adjust the volume level and other audio settings. The volume control screen includes a mute option that allows you to turn off the sound, as shown in Figure 1-48.

Figure 1-48 Adjusting Volume Controls

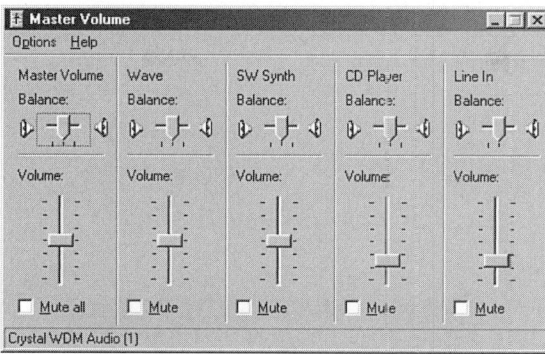

Using the Start Menu Options

The Start button is located on the Windows Taskbar in the lower-left corner of the Desktop. Imbedded in the Start button are several useful Windows features. Clicking the Start button, as shown in Figure 1-49, allows you to easily access these options.

Figure 1-49 Start Menu Options

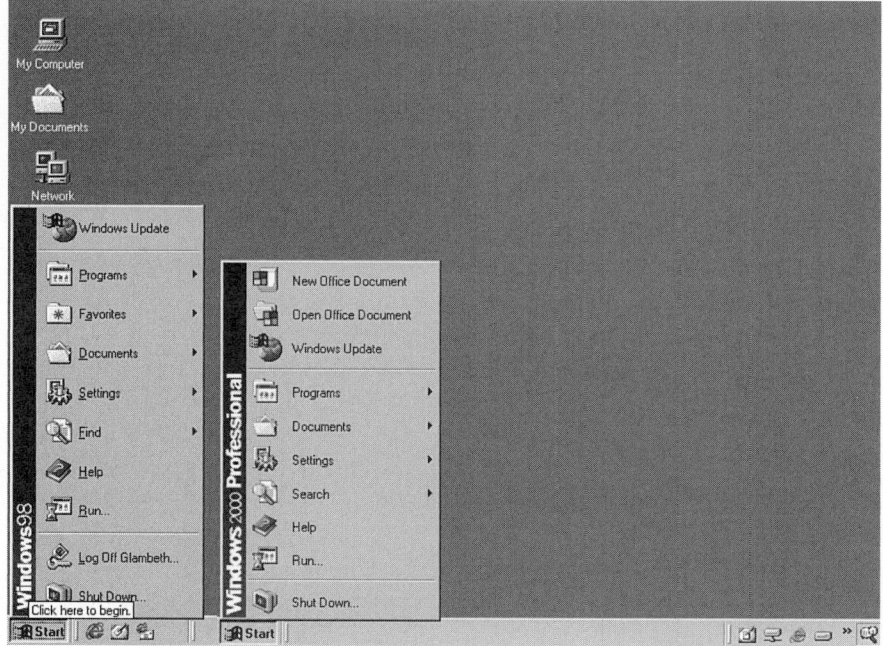

Windows 98   Windows 2000

Run

The Run feature is another method of starting a program. This feature can be used instead of clicking the program shortcut icon on the Desktop or in the list of programs within the Programs directory. This directory is discussed more thoroughly in Chapter 4. Access the Run feature by choosing **Start**, **Run**. A command-line entry space appears, as shown in Figure 1-50. You can now enter the program name and any necessary parameters as you would in a DOS prompt window.

Figure 1-50 Run Dialog Box

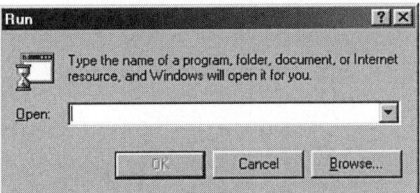

Help

The *Help* feature provides tips and instructions on how to use Windows. The Help feature includes an index and search function, as shown in Figure 1-51.

Figure 1-51 Windows Help

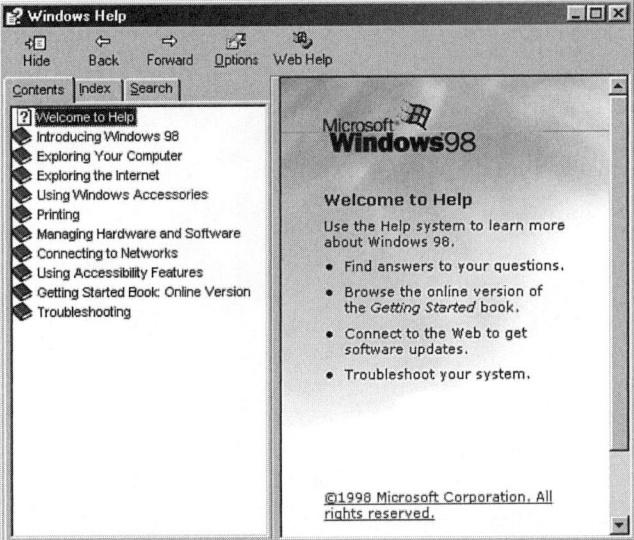

The Help feature for Windows is easy to use, and learning to navigate it allows you to find useful information quickly. The following steps show you how to search for help in formatting a floppy disk:

Step 1   Select **Start**, **Help**.

Step 2   Click the Index tab, and type the keyword phrase **formatting disks**.

Step 3   Click the Display button, as shown in Figure 1-52.

Figure 1-52 Index Tab on the Help Screen

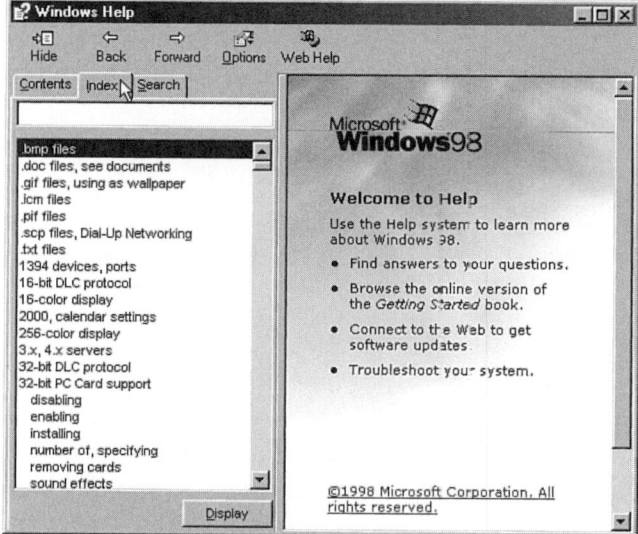

As shown in Figure 1-53, the right side of the screen displays instructions on how to format a disk.

Find/Search

In Windows 95, 98, and NT, the Find feature allows you to locate files, folders, and network connections to other computers and peripherals. In Windows 2000 and XP, Find has been renamed Search.

Documents

The Documents menu shows a list of the most recent documents that have been accessed or created. This menu can also be used as a shortcut method for returning to these documents. These documents are linked to the applications that created them. The application launches when the document is opened.

Figure 1-53 How to Format a Disk

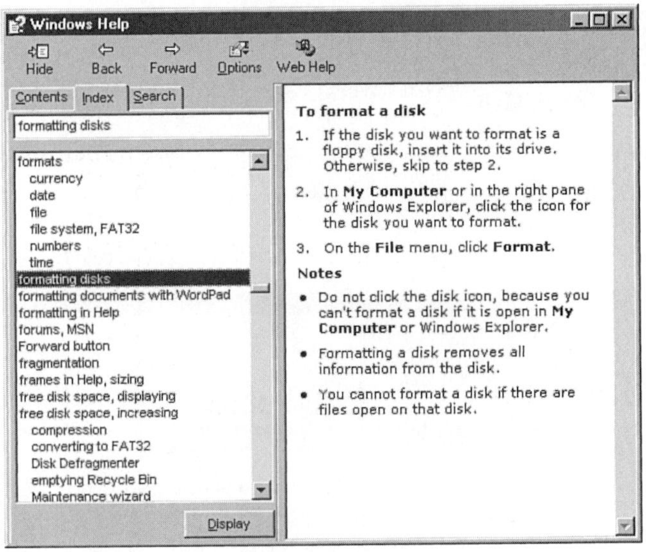

Programs

The Programs menu lists all the programs that are installed on the computer. To start a program, choose **Start**, **Programs**, locate the program to be started, and select it. You can create shortcut icons on the Desktop for programs that are used regularly.

Understanding the Recycle Bin

The *Recycle Bin* stores files, folders, graphics, and web pages from the hard disk that have been deleted. These items can be undeleted, or restored, to their original location. Items remain in the Recycle Bin until they are permanently deleted from the computer. When the Recycle Bin becomes full, Windows 2000 automatically removes enough files to accommodate the most recently deleted files and folders. Figure 1-54 shows the Recycle Bin in Windows 98 and Windows 2000 with deleted files and folders.

Lab 1.3.8   Getting to Know Windows

In this lab, you navigate the Windows Desktop, use Windows Help features, resize windows, and learn the proper way to shut down the system.

Worksheet 1.3.8   Windows Navigation and Settings

This worksheet tests your knowledge of navigating in Windows and Desktop settings.

Figure 1-54 Recycle Bin for Windows 98 and Windows 2000

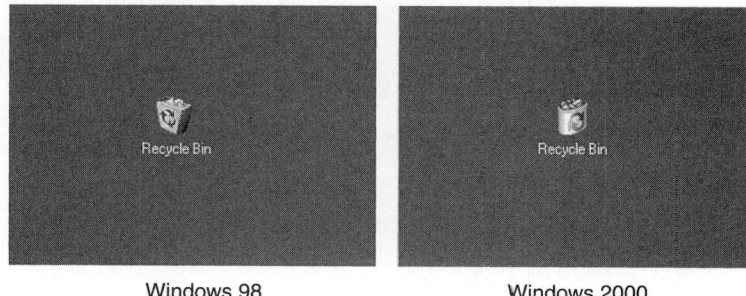

Windows 98   Windows 2000

Overview of Software Applications

Troubleshooting software problems starts with an understanding of how the most popular software applications work. This section includes the following topics:

- Word processors
- Spreadsheets
- Databases
- Graphics applications
- Presentation applications
- Web browsers and e-mail

Word Processors

As discussed earlier in this chapter, software applications are the programs that allow you to complete tasks. These tasks include writing a report, keeping track of clients, drawing a company logo, displaying web pages, and writing e-mails.

A *word processor* is an application that creates, edits, stores, and prints documents. Figure 1-55 shows Microsoft Word 2000 as an example of a word processor. All word processors can insert or delete text, define margins, and copy, cut, and paste. These features, called text editors, are only supported by word processors. Most word processors support additional features that enable the manipulation and formation of documents in sophisticated ways. Examples include file management, macros, spell checkers, headers and footers, merge capabilities, advanced layout features, multiple windows, and preview modes. The most prominent word processors are Microsoft Word, Corel WordPerfect, and Lotus Notes.

Figure 1-55 Microsoft Word 2000

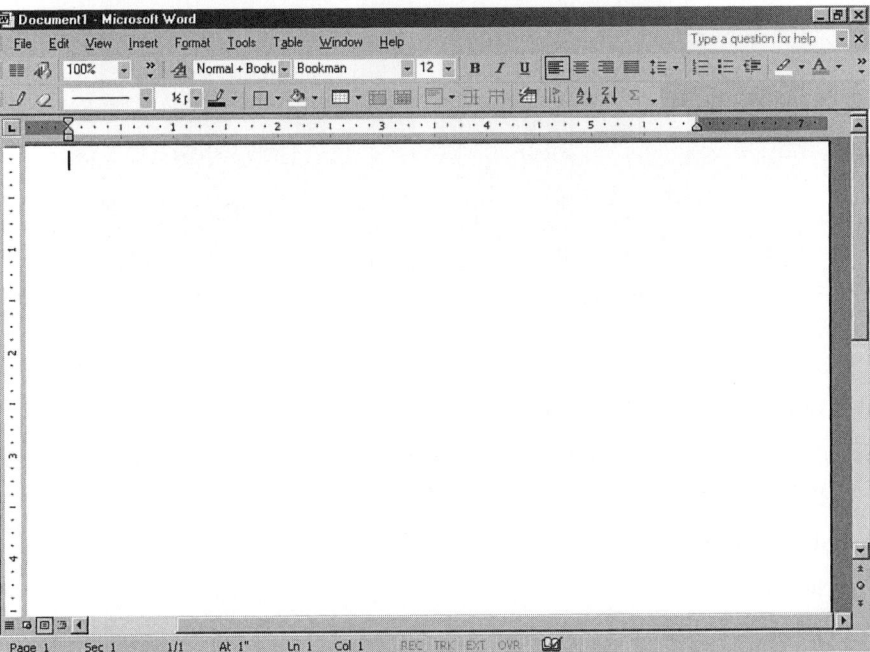

Spreadsheets

In a *spreadsheet*, numerical data is stored in cells that are arranged on a grid. A cell is identified by its position in the grid according to the column and row that it occupies, such as A3. The data in a cell could be a number, text, or calculation. Consider that cell A3 contains the value 10 and the adjacent cell, B3, contains the calculation =A3*2.54 (that is, the value in cell A3 multiplied by 2.54). The cell B3 would display the value 25.4. In other words, a value in inches in cell A3 is converted to centimeters in cell B3, because 2.54 is the conversion factor.

Spreadsheets calculate a range of numerical values and carry out large and complex calculations. Many spreadsheets can plot data in the form of graphs, bar charts, and pie charts. Microsoft Excel, as shown in Figure 1-56, and Lotus 1-2-3 are both examples of spreadsheet applications.

Databases

A *database* is an organized collection of data that can be easily accessed, indexed, searched, managed, and updated. Microsoft Access, Oracle Database, and FileMaker by FileMaker, Inc. are examples of database applications. Microsoft Access is shown in Figure 1-57. PC databases are divided into two categories: flat-file and relational.

Figure 1-56 Microsoft Excel 2000

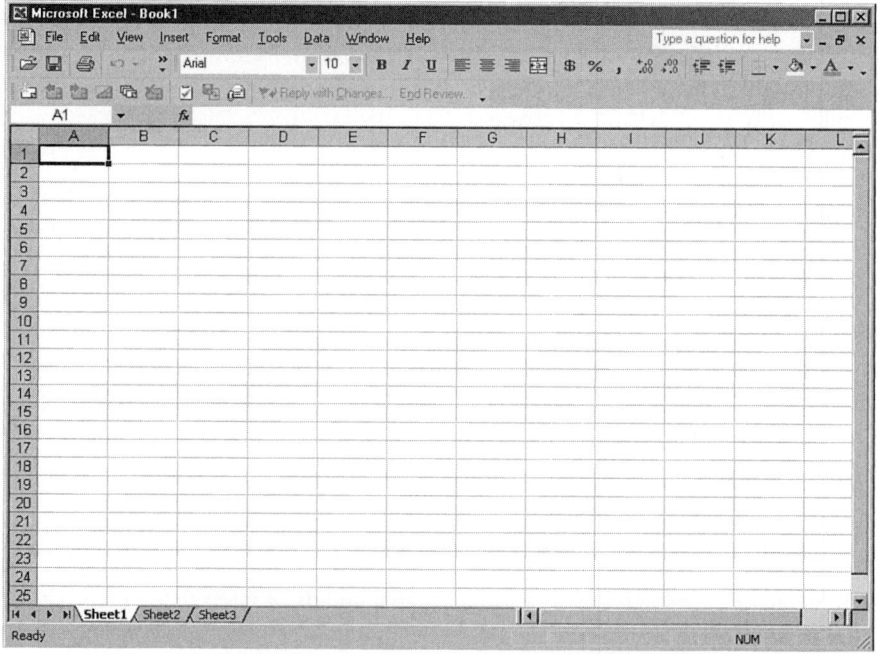

Figure 1-57 Microsoft Access 2000

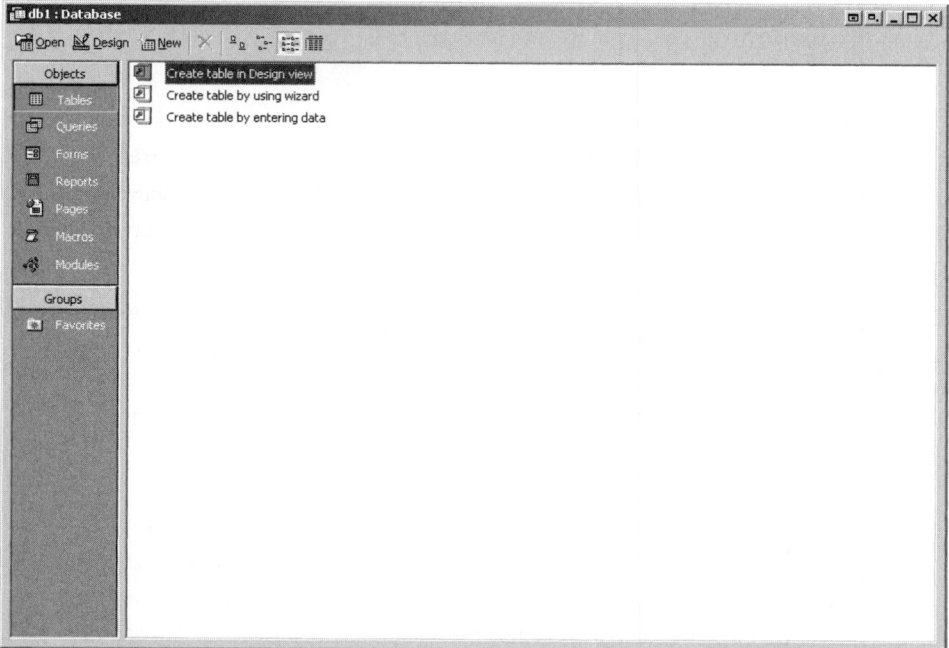

Flat-File Database

A *flat-file database* stores information in a single table. Each column, called a field, contains a particular piece of information such as first name, last name, address, or telephone number. Each row, called a record, contains information for a particular database item. An ordinary telephone directory might be stored in this format.

Relational Database

A *relational database* is a collection of flat-file databases, or tables, that are linked through some particular relationship. For example, a bank would use a relational database to store information about its clients. Individual tables would contain the names and addresses of clients, detailed information about each bank account, the amount in each account, passwords, and so on. A unique identifier, called a key, forms the relationship between each record in the different tables and links the information in these tables. For example, when money is withdrawn from an ATM, the details of the bank card and the password number are verified in a security table. Next, the account balance table is accessed to ensure that sufficient funds are available. Finally, the transaction is stored in an account transaction table.

Relational databases are the best way to store large amounts of interrelated data. These databases can manage multiple relationships with a minimum duplication of data; this is the primary advantage over flat-file databases. For example, each bank account has many transactions stored in conjunction with that account, known as a one-to-many relationship. A single flat-file database would be overwhelmingly large and inefficient for the task. Flat-file databases are two dimensional, whereas relational databases have three or more dimensions.

Graphics Applications

Graphics applications create or modify graphical images. The two types of graphical images are (a) object- or vector-based images and (b) bitmaps or raster images. To understand the difference, imagine creating a letter *T,* as shown in Figure 1-58. A bitmap would represent the *T* as if it were drawn on graph paper, with the corresponding squares shaded in. A vector-based graphic would describe the *T* with geometrical elements, such as two rectangular shapes of the same size, one standing up and the other resting on top at its middle. The vector-based graphic can be enlarged or shrunk to any size. However, the bitmap shows the individual squares if the image is enlarged. Bitmaps often require much more file space than vector graphics.

Figure 1-58 Vector-Based Versus Bitmap Image

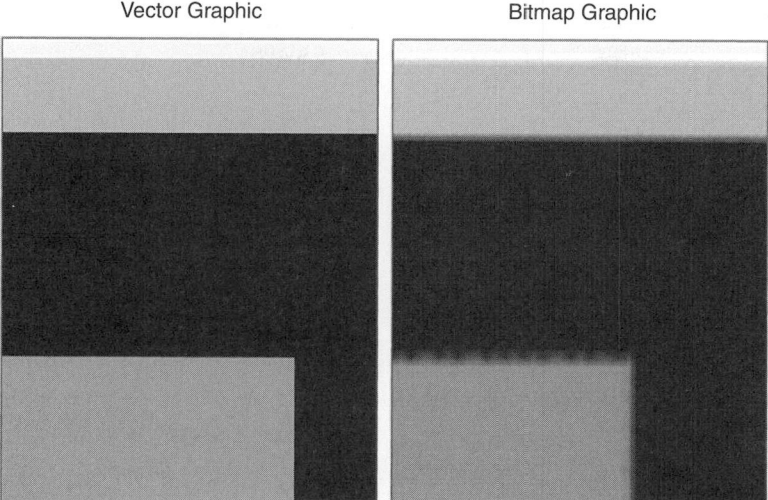

Several types of graphics programs exist; they can be listed in the following main categories:

- **Image editing**—The process of creating bitmaps or raster images. The industry-standard image-editing software is Adobe Photoshop, as shown in Figure 1-59. Its vast tool set allows you to manipulate and create raster or bitmap images.

- **Illustration**—The process of creating object- or vector-based images. The most prominent illustration software is Adobe Illustrator. It has a tool set that is similar to Photoshop's. This tool set creates vector-based images as opposed to raster images. Figure 1-60 shows an example of this program.

- **Animation**—The process of creating sequential images that give the impression of continuous movement when played in a series. You can accomplish this process in many ways. The most prominent types of animation are frame-by-frame animation and keyframe animation. Frame-by-frame animation involves the creation of each frame. Keyframe animation allows the animator to define two key points and uses the computer to calculate the "in between" frames. This process is commonly known as *tweening*.

- **3D graphics**—The process of using a simulated, three-dimensional environment to create geometric objects, which can be textured, painted, and animated. The geometry of 3D graphics can have real-world scale and depth to assist in creating floor plans, model cars, or even movie special effects.

Other graphics applications are used in multimedia, audio, and games.

Figure 1-59 Adobe Photoshop

Figure 1-60 Adobe Illustrator

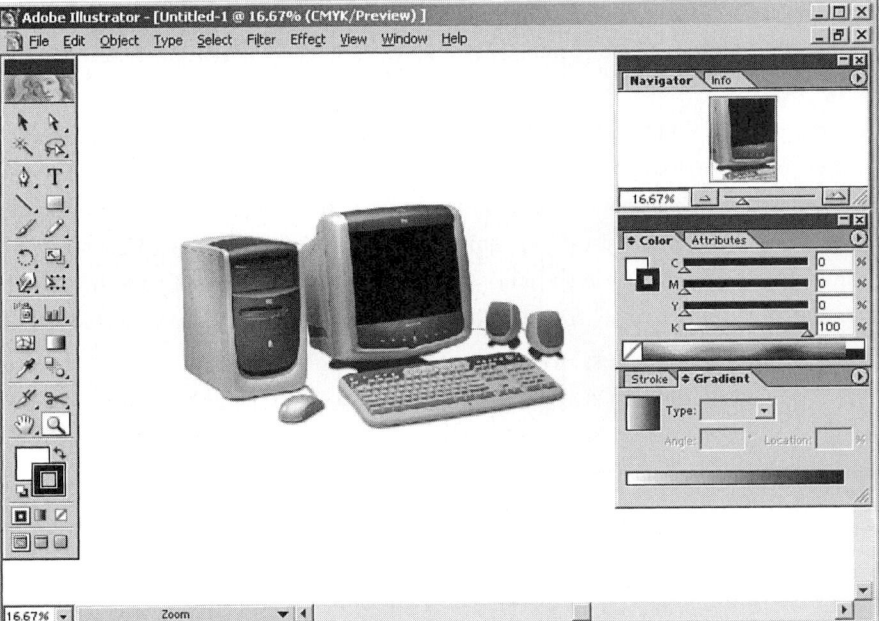

Computer-Aided Design

Another type of application worth mentioning is ***computer-aided design (CAD)***. CAD software requires high-speed workstations or desktop computers. CAD is available for generic design or specialized uses such as architectural, electrical, and mechanical.

More complex forms of CAD are solid modeling and parametric modeling, which allow objects to be created with real-world characteristics. For example, objects that are created in solid modeling can be sectioned, or sliced down the middle, to reveal their internal structure.

Presentation Applications

Presentation applications, also known as business graphics, permit the organization, design, and delivery of presentations in the form of slide shows and reports. Bar charts, pie charts, graphics, and other types of images can be created based on data that is imported from spreadsheet applications. Figure 1-61 shows Microsoft PowerPoint, which is a prominent presentation application.

Figure 1-61 Microsoft PowerPoint 2000

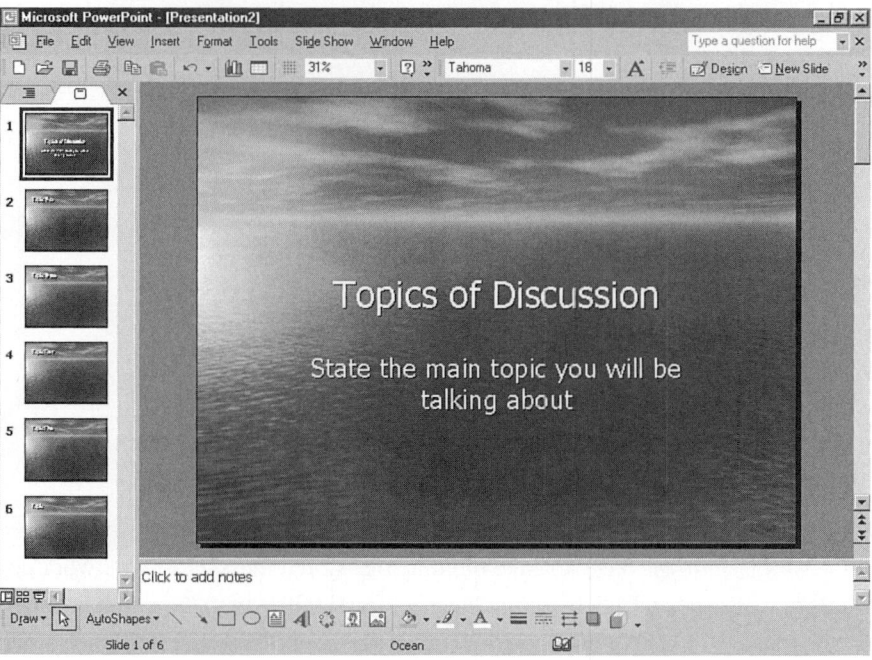

Web Browsers and E-Mail

NOTE

A plug-in is an auxiliary program that works with a major software package to enhance its capability. An example of a plug-in is a filter that adds special effects in an imaging program such as Photoshop. Plug-ins are added to web browsers to enable them to support new types of content, including audio, video, and so on. Although the term plug-in is widely used for software, it can also refer to a module for hardware.

A *web browser* is an application that locates and displays pages from the World Wide Web (WWW). The two most common browsers are Netscape Navigator, shown in Figure 1-62, and Microsoft Internet Explorer, shown in Figure 1-63. These are graphical browsers, which means that they can display graphics as well as text. In addition, most modern browsers can present multimedia information, including sound and video, although they require plug-ins for some formats.

Figure 1-62 Netscape Navigator

E-Mail

Electronic mail (e-mail) is the exchange of computer-stored messages by network communication. Both Netscape and Microsoft include an e-mail utility with their web browsers. Figure 1-64 shows the Netscape e-mail utility. Internet service providers (ISPs) offer e-mail as a service to their customers, Free e-mail is also available from a variety of websites, including HotMail at msn.com and Yahoo! mail at yahoo.com. Free e-mail accounts require the user to sign up, and they limit the amount of space for e-mail storage. Multiple e-mail accounts for individuals are common. Each account can have a separate purpose, such as surfing, friends and family, and business.

Figure 1-63 Microsoft Internet Explorer

Figure 1-64 Netscape Navigator E-Mail Client

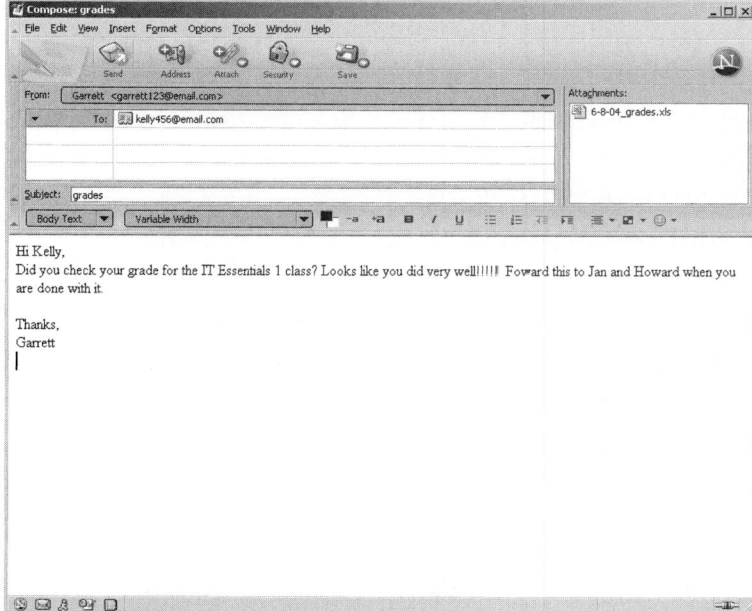

Math for a Digital Age

NOTE

A common error is confusing KB with kb and MB with Mb. An uppercase *B* indicates bytes, whereas a lowercase *b* indicates bits. Remember to do the proper calculations when comparing transmission speeds that are measured in KB with those measured in kb. For example, modem software usually shows the connection speed in kilobits per second, such as 56 kbps. However, prominent browsers display file-download speeds in kilobytes per second. Therefore, the download speed with a 56-kbps connection would be a maximum of 7 KBps.

The IT technician needs a thorough understanding of the terminology used along with the ability to work with number systems and perform conversions. This section includes the following topics:

- Measurement-related terminology
- Analog and digital systems
- Boolean logic gates
- Decimal and binary number systems
- Decimal-to-binary conversion
- BASE16 (hexadecimal) number system
- Binary-to-hexadecimal conversion
- Hexadecimal-to-binary conversion
- Converting to any base
- Introduction to algorithms

Measurement-Related Terminology

When working in the computer industry, it is important to understand the terms that are used. Whether reading the specifications about a computer system or talking with another computer technician, you should be familiar with the terminology. The technician needs to know the following terminology:

- *Bit*— The smallest unit of data in a computer. A bit can take the value of either 1 or 0. A bit is the binary format in which data is processed by computers.
- *Byte*—A unit of measure that describes the size of a data file, the amount of space on a disk or other storage medium, or the amount of data that is being sent over a network. One byte consists of 8 bits of data.
- *Nibble*—Half a byte, or 4 bits.
- *Kilobyte (KB)*—1024, or approximately 1000, bytes.
- *Kilobytes per second (KBps)*—A measurement of the amount of data that is transferred over a connection such as a network connection. A data transfer rate of 1 KBps is approximately a rate of 1000 bytes per second.
- *Kilobit (kb)*—1024, or approximately 1000, bits.

- *Kilobits per second (kbps)*—A measurement of the amount of data that is transferred over a connection such as a network connection. A data transfer rate of 1 kbps is approximately a rate of 1000 bits per second.

- *Megabyte (MB)*—1,048,576 bytes (approximately 1 million bytes).

- *Megabytes per second (MBps)*—A common measurement of the amount of data that is transferred over a connection such as a network connection. A data transfer rate of 1 MBps is approximately a rate of 1 million bytes or 1000 kilobytes per second.

- *Megabits per second (Mbps)*—A common measurement of the amount of data that is transferred over a connection such as a network connection. A data transfer rate of 1 Mbps is approximately a rate of 1 million bits or 1000 kilobits per second.

- *Megabit*—1,048,576 bits (approximately 1 million bits).

In practice, the download speed of a dial-up connection cannot reach 56 kbps because of other factors that consume bandwidth at the same time as the download. The technician needs to know the following terminology:

- *Hertz (Hz)*— A unit of frequency measurement. It is the rate of change in the state, or cycle, in a sound wave, alternating current, or other cyclical waveform. Hertz is synonymous with cycles per second, and it describes the speed of a computer microprocessor.

- *Megahertz (MHz)*—One million cycles per second. This is a common measurement of the speed of a processing chip.

- *Gigahertz (GHz)*—One billion cycles per second. This is a common measurement of the speed of a processing chip.

Analog and Digital Systems

The variables that characterize an analog system can have an infinite number of values. For example, the hands on the face of an analog clock can show an infinite number of times of the day. Figure 1-65 shows a diagram of an analog signal. Analog signals can have any voltage. The voltage is continuous and, as time progresses, resembles waves. The variables that characterize digital systems only occupy a fixed number of discrete values. In binary arithmetic, such as that used in computers, only two values are allowed: 0 and 1. Computers and cable modems are examples of digital devices. Figure 1-66 shows a diagram of a digital signal. This signal does not have continuous pulses, and the voltage can jump between levels. In addition, a digital signal can only have one or two voltage levels.

NOTE

PC processors are becoming faster all the time. The microprocessors used on PCs in the 1980s typically ran at less than 10 MHz, and the original IBM PC featured a 4.77-MHz processor. In early 2000, PC processors approached the speed of 1 GHz, and in 2004, speeds approached 3 GHz.

Figure 1-65 Analog Signals

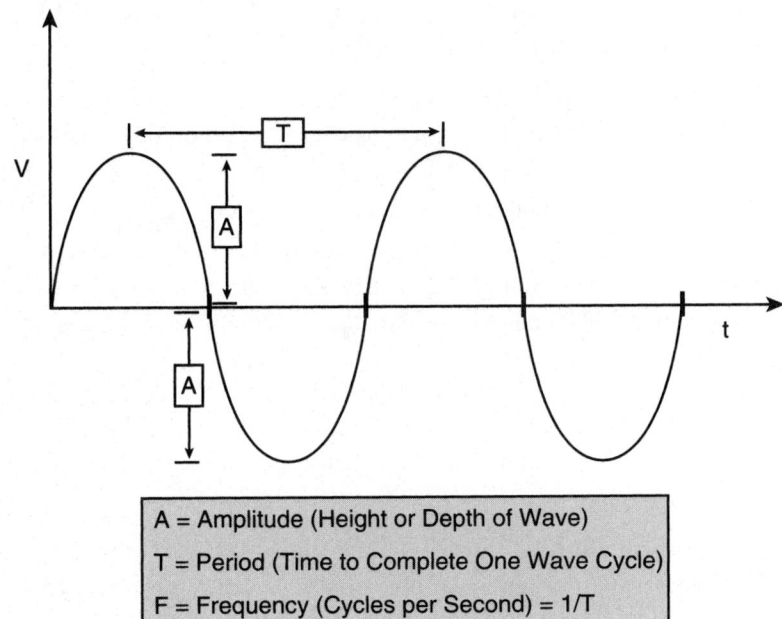

A = Amplitude (Height or Depth of Wave)

T = Period (Time to Complete One Wave Cycle)

F = Frequency (Cycles per Second) = 1/T

Figure 1-66 Digital Signals

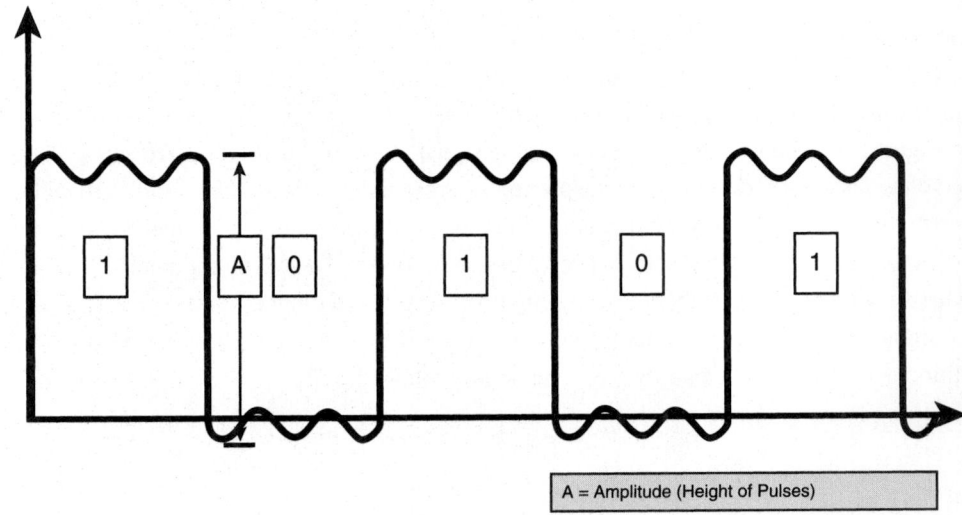

A = Amplitude (Height of Pulses)

Boolean Logic Gates

Computers are built from various types of electronic circuits. These circuits depend on AND, OR, NOT, and NOR *logic gates*. These gates are characterized by how they respond to input signals. Figures 1-67, 1-68, and 1-69 show logic gates with two inputs. The *x* and *Y* represent inputs, and the *f* represents output. Think of 0 as representing off and 1 as representing on.

Figure 1-67 Boolean Logic Gates: AND and OR

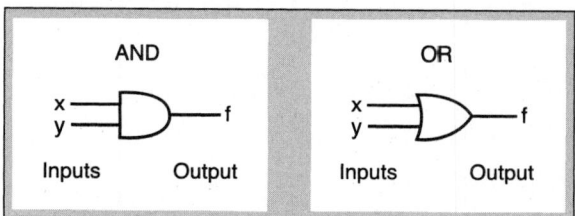

Figure 1-68 Boolean Logic Gate: NOR

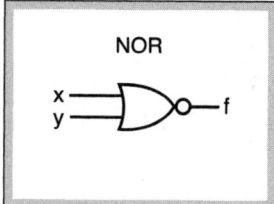

Figure 1-69 Boolean Logic Gate: NOT

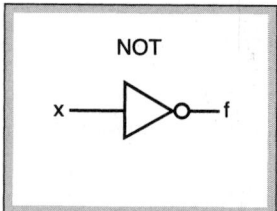

Figure 1-70 Boolean Logic Gate: Truth Tables

OR	AND	NOR	NOT
0 OR 0 is 0.	0 AND 0 is 0.	0 NOR 0 is 1.	NOT 0 is 1.
0 OR 1 is 1.	0 AND 1 is 0.	0 NOR 1 is 0.	NOT 1 is 0.
1 OR 0 is 1.	1 AND 0 is 0.	1 NOR 0 is 0.	
1 OR 1 is 1.	1 AND 1 is 1.	1 NOR 1 is 0.	

Only three primary functions for logic gates exist. They are AND, OR, and NOT; each is described as follows:

- **AND gate**—If either input is off, the output is off.
- **OR gate**—If either input is on, the output is on.
- **NOT gate**—If the input is on, the output is off and vice versa.

The NOR gate is a combination of the OR and NOT gates and should not be presented as a primary gate. A NOR gate acts as follows: If either input is on, the output is off.

The truth tables shown in Figure 1-70 represent these statements in a compact form. Other logic gate combinations or extensions such as XOR, NAND, and so on are beyond the scope of this course.

 Lab Activity 1.5.3   Boolean Operations

In this lab, you are introduced to the AND, OR, NOR, and NOT Boolean operations. You also learn how to calculate the output of combinations of Boolean operations based on input.

Decimal and Binary Number Systems

The decimal, or BASE10, number system is used every day for doing math such as counting change, measuring units, telling time, and so on. The decimal number system uses ten digits: 0, 1, 2, 3, 4, 5, 6, 7, 8, and 9.

The binary, or BASE2, number system uses two digits to express all numerical quantities. The only digits used in the binary number system are 0 and 1. An example of a binary number is 10011101010010100101.

It is important to remember the role of the digit 0. Every number system uses the digit 0. However, whenever the digit 0 appears on the left side of a string of digits, it can be removed without changing the string value. For example, in BASE10, 02947 equals 2947. In BASE2, 0001001101 equals 1001101. Sometimes, 0s are included on the left side of a number to serve as placeholders.

When working with binary numbers, another important concept is the powers of numbers. The numbers 2^0 and 2^3 are examples of numbers represented by powers. These examples are spoken as "two to the zero power" and "two to the third power." The power is the number of times that a value must be multiplied by itself. For example, $2^0 = 1$, $2^1 = 2$, $2^2 = 2 \times 2 = 4$, $2^3 = 2 \times 2 \times 2 = 8$. Using powers is commonly confused with doing simple multiplication. For example, 2^4 is not equal to $2 \times 4 = 8$. However, 2^4 is equal to $2 \times 2 \times 2 \times 2 = 16$.

In BASE10, powers of ten are used. For example, 23,605 in BASE10 means the following:

$$(2 \times 10{,}000) + (3 \times 1000) + (6 \times 100) + (0 \times 10) + (5 \times 1).$$

A decimal number can be expressed in terms of powers of 10, such as 10^0, 10^1, 10^2, and so on. However, the actual value of a decimal number should be expressed in the expanded form of the powers, such as 1, 10, 100, and so on. Use tables to help keep your numbers organized. Table 1-5 shows the BASE10 number 23,605 as it relates to the powers of 10.

Table 1-5 The Decimal Number System

Power of 10 representation	10^4	10^3	10^2	10^1	10^0
Decimal representation	10,000	1000	100	10	1
BASE10 representation	2	3	6	0	5

Binary

The same method is used with binary numbers and powers of 2. Consider the binary number 10010001. Table 1-6 can be used to convert the binary number 10010001 into decimal notation as follows:

$$10010001 = (1 \times 128) + (0 \times 64) + (0 \times 32) + (1 \times 16) + (0 \times 8) + (0 \times 4) + (0 \times 2) + (1 \times 1) =$$
$$128 + 16 + 1 = 145$$

NOTE

Note that $10^0 = 1$, $10^1 = 10$, $10^2 = 100$, $10^3 = 1000$, and $10^4 = 10{,}000$.

CAUTION

Although $0 \times 10 = 0$, do not leave this portion out of the previous equation. If it is omitted, the BASE10 places all shift to the right and result in the number 2365 instead of 23,605. A 0 within a number should never be ignored. However, the value of a number is not affected by adding 0s to the beginning of the number or by ignoring 0s that are at the beginning of the number. For example, 23,605 can also be expressed as 0023605.

Table 1-6 The Binary Number System

Power of 2 representation	2^7	2^6	2^5	2^4	2^3	2^2	2^1	2^0
Decimal representation	128	64	32	16	8	4	2	1
BASE10 representation	1	0	0	1	0	0	0	1

The table method is an efficient way to convert binary numbers to decimal, and it is important for the IT technician to understand how the process works. However, scientific calculators are available that are fast, accurate, and easy to use.

Decimal-to-Binary Conversion

More than one method exists to convert binary numbers. One method is explored in this section. However, you should feel free to use another method if it is easier for you.

To convert a decimal number to binary notation, first find the largest power of 2 that "fits" into the decimal number. Use Table 1-7 to convert the decimal number 35 into binary notation.

Table 1-7 Converting the Decimal Number 35 to Binary Form

Power of 2 Representation	2^6	2^5	2^4	2^3	2^2	2^1	2^0
Decimal Representation	64	32	16	8	4	2	1
BASE10 Representation	0	1	0	0	0	1	1

The following steps help to clarify the conversion process:

- 2^6, or 64, is larger than 35. Place a 0 in that column.
- 2^5, or 32, is smaller than 35. Place a 1 in that column. Calculate how much is left over by subtracting 32 from 35. The result is 3.
- 2^4, or 16, is larger than 3. Place a 0 in that column.
- 2^3, or 8, is larger than 3. Place a 0 in that column.
- 2^2, or 4, is larger than 3. Place a 0 in that column.
- 2^1, or 2, is smaller than 3. Place a 1 in that column. Subtract 2 from 3. The result is 1.
- 2^0, or 1, is equal to 1. Place a 1 in that column.

The binary equivalent of the decimal number 35 is 0100011. Ignoring the first 0, the binary number can be written as 100011.

This method works for any decimal number. Consider the decimal number 1 million. The largest power of 2 that fits into the decimal number 1,000,000 is 2^{19}, or 524,288, because 2^{20}, or 1,048,576, is larger than 1,000,000. According to the procedure that was used for the previous conversion, the decimal number 1 million is converted to the binary number 11110100001001000000.

This technique can rapidly become cumbersome when dealing with very large numbers. A simpler technique is shown later in the section, "Converting to Any Base."

e-Lab Activity   Decimal-to-Binary Conversion

In this interactive lab, you follow the steps that are presented on the enclosed CD-ROM to perform a decimal-to-binary conversion.

e-Lab Activity   Binary-to-Decimal Conversion

In this interactive lab, you follow the steps presented on the enclosed CD-ROM to perform a binary-to-decimal conversion.

BASE16 (Hexadecimal) Number System

The BASE16, or hexadecimal, number system is used frequently when working with computers because it can represent binary numbers in a more readable form. The computer performs computations in binary form. However, in some instances, a computer binary output is expressed in hexadecimal form to make it easier to read. One way for computers and software to express hexadecimal output is by placing 0x in front of the hexadecimal number. Whenever 0x is used, the number that follows is a hexadecimal number. For example, 0x1234 means 1234 in BASE16. This would typically be found in a router configuration register.

BASE16 uses 16 characters to express numerical quantities. These characters are 0, 1, 2, 3, 4, 5, 6, 7, 8, 9, A, B, C, D, E, and F. An A represents the decimal number 10, B represents 11, C represents 12, D represents 13, E represents 14, and F represents 15. Examples of hexadecimal numbers are 2A5F, 99901, FFFFFFFF, and EBACD3. The hexadecimal number B23CF is equal to 730,063 in decimal format, as shown in Table 1-8.

Table 1-8 Hexadecimal Number System

Power of 16 Representation	16^5	16^4	16^3	16^2	16^1	16^0
Decimal Representation	1,048,576	65,536	4096	256	16	1
BASE16 Representation	0	B	2	3	C	F

The traditional conversion between decimal and hexadecimal is outside the scope of this course. However, some shortcuts for conversion to any base, including decimal and hexadecimal, are discussed in this chapter.

Binary-to-Hexadecimal Conversion

Binary-to-hexadecimal conversion is uncomplicated for the most part. First, observe that 1111 in binary form is F in hexadecimal form, as shown in Table 1-9. Also, 11111111 in binary form is FF in hexadecimal form. One useful fact when working with these two number systems is that one hexadecimal character requires 4 bits, or 4 binary digits, to be represented in binary.

To convert a binary number to hexadecimal, first divide the number into groups of 4 bits at a time, starting from the right. Then convert each group of 4 bits into hexadecimal form. This method produces a hexadecimal equivalent to the original binary number, as shown in Table 1-9.

Table 1-9 Binary-to-Hexadecimal Conversion

Binary	Hexadecimal
0000	0
0001	1
0010	2
0011	3
0100	4
0101	5
0110	6
0111	7
1000	8
1001	9
1010	A
1011	B
1100	C
1101	D
1110	E
1111	F

For example, consider the binary number 1111101110011000010000. Breaking this number into groups of 4 bits produces 1111 0111 0011 0001 0000. This binary number is equivalent to F7310 in hexadecimal, which is a much easier number to read.

As another example, the binary number 111101 is grouped as 11 1101. Because the first group does not contain 4 bits, it must be "padded" with 0s to produce 0011 1101. Therefore, the hexadecimal equivalent is 3D.

 e-Lab Activity   Binary-to-Hexadecimal Conversion

In this interactive lab, you follow the steps that are presented on the enclosed CD-ROM to perform a binary-to-hexadecimal conversion.

Hexadecimal-to-Binary Conversion

Use the reverse of the method described in the previous section to convert numbers from hexadecimal to binary form. Convert each hexadecimal digit to binary form, and then string together the solution. However, be careful to pad each binary representation with 0s to fill four binary places for each hexadecimal digit. For example, consider the hexadecimal number FE27. F is 1111, E is 1110, 2 is 10 (or 0010), and 7 is 0111. Therefore, the binary conversion of FE27 is 1111 1110 0010 0111, or 1111111000100111, as shown in Table 1-10.

Table 1-10 Hexadecimal-to-Binary Conversion

Hexadecimal	Binary
0	0000
1	0001
2	0010
3	0011
4	0100
5	0101
6	0110
7	0111
8	1000
9	1001

continues

Table 1-10 Hexadecimal-to-Binary Conversion (Continued)

Hexadecimal	Binary
A	1010
B	1011
C	1100
D	1101
E	1110
F	1111

Converting to Any Base

Most people already know how to do many number conversions. For example, consider converting inches to yards. First, divide the number of inches by 12 to determine the number of feet. The remainder is the number of inches left. Next, divide the number of feet by 3 to determine the number of yards. The remainder is the number of feet left. These same techniques are used for converting numbers to other bases.

Consider that decimal is the normal base and octal, BASE8, is the foreign base. To convert from decimal to octal base, divide by 8 successively and record the remainders, starting from the least significant remainder.

Convert the number 1234 in decimal and to octal form as follows:

1234 / 8 = 154 R 2

154 / 8 = 19 R 2

19 / 8 = 2 R 3

2 / 8 = 0 R 2

The remainders, in the order of least to most significant, provide the result of 2322 in octal form.

To convert back to decimal form, multiply a running total by 8 and add each digit successively, beginning with the most significant number, as follows:

$2 \times 8 = 16$

$16 + 3 = 19$

$19 \times 8 = 152$

$$152 + 2 = 154$$

$$154 \times 8 = 1232$$

$$1232 + 2 = 1234$$

The same results in the reverse conversions can be achieved by using numerical powers, as follows:

$$(2 \times 8^3) + (3 \times 8^2) + (2 \times 8^1) + (2 \times 8^0) = 1024 + 192 + 16 + 2 = 1234$$

NOTE

Any number raised to the power of 0 is 1.

Using Numerical Powers to Convert

You can use similar techniques to convert to and from any base, simply by dividing or multiplying by the foreign base.

However, binary form is unique because odd and even determine 1s and 0s without recording the remainders. You can determine the binary equivalent of 1234 in decimal form simply by dividing the number by 2 successively. If the result is even, the bit associated with it is 0. If the result is odd, the binary digit associated with it is 1. The following is an example of this process:

1234 is even. Record a 0 in the least significant position, 0.

$1234/2 = 617$ is odd. Record a 1 in the next most significant position, 10.

$617/2 = 308$ is even, 010.

$308/2 = 154$ is even, 0010.

$154/2 = 77$ is odd, 10010.

$77/2 = 38$ is even, 010010.

$38/2 = 19$ is odd, 1010010.

$19/2 = 9$ is odd, 11010010.

$9/2 = 4$ is even, 011010010.

$4/2 = 2$ is even, 0011010010.

$2/2 = 1$ is odd, 10011010010.

With practice, the running dividend can be mastered and the binary form can be written quickly.

Note that just as a hexadecimal digit is a group of four bits, an octal is a group of three digits. Group the previous number into groups of three, starting at the right, as follows:

010,011,010,010 = 2322 octal

For hexadecimal form, group the binary number by 4 bits starting from the right, as follows:

0100,1101,0010 = 4D2 hexadecimal, or 0x4D2

This is a quick and easy method that you can use to convert to any base.

Lab Activity 1.5.9   Converting Numbers Overview

In this lab, you identify the places in binary and decimal numbers as they relate to the powers of 10 and the powers of 2. You manually convert binary and decimal numbers and describe the difference between them.

Worksheet 1.5.9   Number Systems Exercises

Practice number conversions, and increase your understanding of decimal, binary, and hexadecimal forms.

Introduction to Algorithms

An *algorithm* is a systematic description or method of how to carry out a series of steps to complete a certain task. Computers use algorithms in practically every function that they perform. Essentially, a software program is many algorithms pieced together into a huge set of code. Learning computer programming means learning how to create and implement algorithms. Many algorithms are prepackaged for use in programs. This keeps programmers from having to start from scratch every time that a program is written. The concept, especially with object-oriented programming, is to use existing code to build more sophisticated programs or code. Three particular examples of algorithms are described in the following sections.

Euclidean Algorithm

The Euclidean algorithm allows you to do long division when dividing two numbers.

Dijkstra Algorithm

The Dijkstra algorithm is used by networking devices on the Internet. This algorithm finds the shortest path between a specific networking device and all other devices in its routing domain. This algorithm uses bandwidth to measure the shortest path.

Encryption Algorithm

Encryption algorithms prevent hackers from viewing data as it passes through the Internet. For example, an encryption algorithm is used by 3DES (pronounced triple dez). 3DES is an encryption standard that secures connections between networking devices and hosts. Further details about 3DES are outside the scope of this course.

Algorithms are step-by-step procedures that perform a specific task. Computers use algorithms to accelerate and simplify procedures. Most algorithms used by computers are fairly complex and require some background in computer science to understand.

More information can be found at the Dictionary of Algorithms and Data Structures. Visit http://www.nist.gov/dads/.

Laboratory Safety and Tools

Using the right tools in the right way is important for the safety of the IT technician and for the equipment. This section includes the following topics:

- Basic lab safety principles
- Workspace practices that help reduce ESD potential
- Tools of the trade
- Workspace cleaning supplies
- Workplace testing equipment
- Lab safety agreement

Basic Lab Safety Principles

In the following modules, you assemble a computer. Observe the following guidelines to help create a safe, efficient work environment, as shown in Figure 1-71:

- The workspace should be large enough to accommodate the system unit, the technician's tools, the testing equipment, and the electrostatic discharge (ESD)–prevention equipment. Near the workbench, power outlets should be available to accommodate the system unit power and the power needs of other electrical devices.
- The optimal level of humidity in the workspace should be 30–70 percent to reduce the likelihood of ESD. The temperature of the workspace should also be controlled to a maximum of 75°F.
- The workbench should be a nonconductive surface that is flat and cleanable.
- The workspace should be distant from areas of heavy electrical equipment or concentrations of electronics. For example, a workspace should not be near a building's heating, ventilation, and air conditioning (HVAC) or phone system controls.
- The workspace should be cleaned of dust. Dust can contaminate the workspace, causing premature damage to computer components. The work area should have a filtered air system to reduce dust and contaminants.
- Lighting should be adequate to see small details. Two different illumination forms are preferred, such as an adjustable lamp with a shade and fluorescent lighting.

- Temperatures should be maintained so that they are consistent with the specifications of the components. Extreme variations of temperature can affect computer components.
- AC electrical current should be properly grounded. Figure 1-72 shows the components of an outlet. Power outlets should be tested with an outlet tester for proper grounding.

Figure 1-71 Typical Workbench

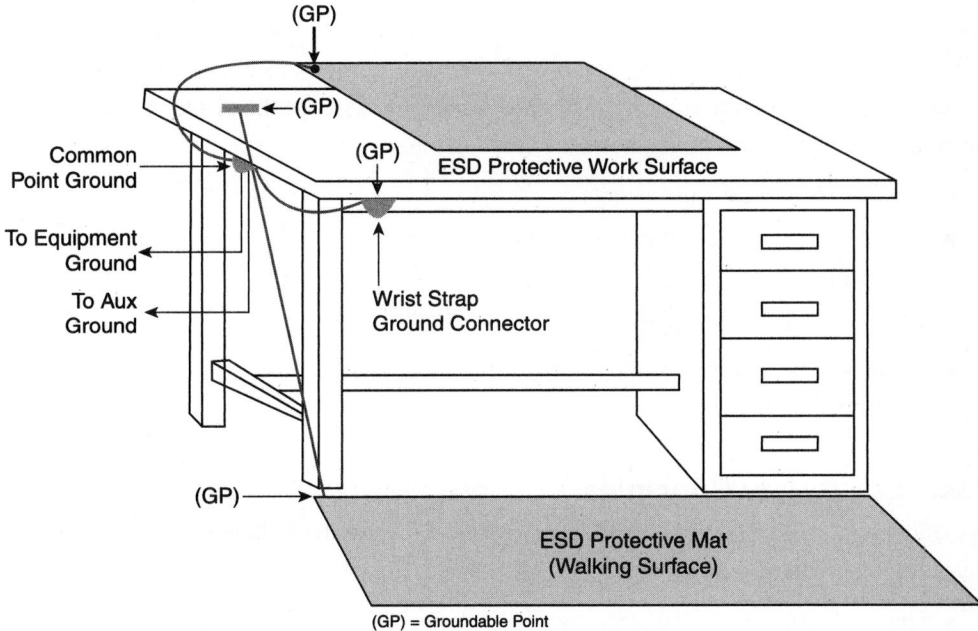

Figure 1-72 AC Outlet

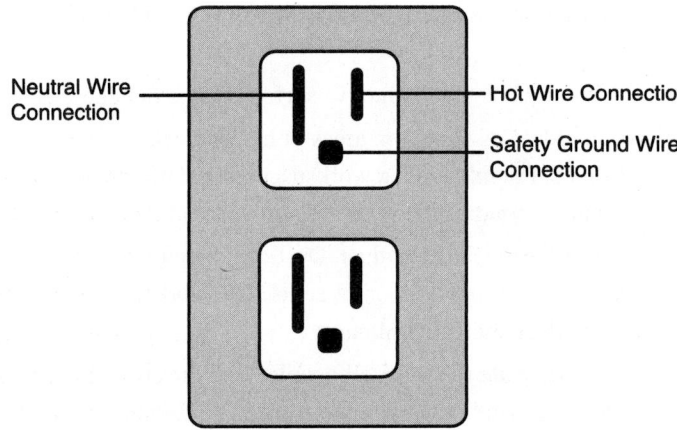

Workspace Practices That Help Reduce ESD Potential

The workspace should be situated away from carpeted areas, because carpets can cause the buildup of electrostatic charges. If distance from carpeting is not possible, the carpeted surface could be covered with a plastic antistatic mat, such as those commonly used under desk chairs. The use of ESD-protection tools such as a wrist strap and a mat, which are commonly sold in kits, can largely eliminate this type of danger.

When working with components, lay the mat on the workspace next to or under the system case. Clip the mat to the case to provide a grounded surface on which parts can be placed as they are removed from the system. Always handle all components by their edges. Avoid touching pins, chips, or anything else made of metal. This practice reduces the chance of producing a damaging electrostatic discharge. Reducing the potential for ESD reduces the likelihood of damage to delicate circuits or components.

Avoid touching the computer screen while it is turned on. Even brief touches to an active screen can put an electrostatic charge in your hand; this can discharge through the keyboard.

Using a Wrist Strap

A *wrist strap*, as shown in Figure 1-73, is a device that is attached to the technician's wrist. This device is then clipped to the metal system chassis on which work is being performed. The wrist strap prevents ESD damage by channeling static electricity from the person's body to the ground.

Figure 1-73 Wrist Strap

After the wrist strap is attached, wait 15 seconds before touching sensitive electronic components with your bare hands. This pause allows the wrist strap to neutralize the static electricity that already exists on the technician's body. ESD potential can also be reduced by not wearing clothing made of silk, polyester, or wool. These fabrics tend to build static charges.

A wrist strap can only offer protection from ESD voltages that are carried on the body. ESD charges on clothing can still cause damage. Therefore, avoid making contact between electronic components and clothing. If you still experience static shocks in the workspace while

TIP

Electrostatic discharge (ESD) is the discharge of static electricity from one conductor to another conductor of a different potential. Know when and how damage from ESD occurs.

working near a computer, try using a fabric softener or an antistatic spray on your clothing. Be certain to spray clothing and *not* the computer. A wrist-grounding strap does not discharge electrostatic charges that have built up on hair. Take precautions to ensure that hair does not rub across any components.

When a Wrist Strap Should Not Be Used for Grounding

There are some exceptions to wearing a wrist strap to provide a safe ground. A wrist strap is never worn when working on a monitor or when working on a computer power supply. Monitors and power supplies are considered replaceable components. Only highly skilled professionals should attempt to open and repair these units.

Components inside a monitor can hold a charge for a long time, even after the unit has been unplugged from its power source. The amount of voltage that a monitor can contain, even when turned off and unplugged, is enough to kill someone. Wearing a wrist strap helps heighten the risk of contacting the monitor's dangerous electric current. The cathode ray tube (CRT) in the monitor is charged to 20,000 volts or more. This charge can last for weeks after the monitor is turned off.

Storage of Equipment

Electronic components or circuit boards should be stored in shielded antistatic bags, which are easily recognized by a shielding characteristic. These bags usually have a silver color and a shiny, transparent appearance. Shielded antistatic bags are important, because they protect components from static electricity. Shielded antistatic bags need to be in good condition, without crinkles or holes. Even tiny openings from crinkles can limit the ability of the bag to provide protection from electrostatic discharges.

When original packaging is not available, circuit boards and peripherals should be transported in a shielded antistatic bag. However, never put a shielded antistatic bag inside a PC. In addition, never plug in a motherboard while it is sitting on top of an antistatic bag. Remember that antistatic bags are partially conductive. A motherboard could easily be shorted out while starting up if several hundred pins from its components are touching the conductive bag.

If computer components are stored in plastic bins, the bins should be made of a conductive plastic. A nonconductive plastic bin can build an electrostatic charge. Make a habit of touching the bins to equalize the bin charge to your body before reaching for the components in the bin. Also, remember to touch the hands of another individual before passing a component to that individual.

Tools of the Trade

Most tools that are used in the assembly process are small hand tools. They are available individually, or they can be included as part of PC tool kits that can be purchased at computer stores. If a technician is working on laptop computers, his or her tool kit should include a small Torx screwdriver. This tool does not come in all PC tool kits. Figure 1-74 shows a typical tool set that is used by a technician.

Figure 1-74 Technician's Toolset

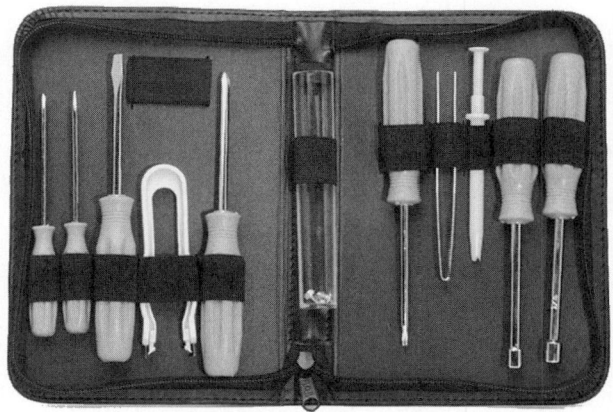

The correct tools can save time and help the technician avoid causing damage to the equipment. Tool kits range widely in size, quality, and price. PC technicians typically have the following tools:

- ESD wrist strap
- Flat-head screwdriver, large and small
- Phillips screwdriver, large and small
- Tweezers or part retriever
- Long-nosed pliers
- Wire cutters
- Chip extractor
- Hex wrench set
- Torx screwdriver
- Nut driver, large and small
- Three-claw component holder
- Digital multimeter

- Wrap plugs
- Small mirror
- Small dust brush
- Soft, lint-free cloth
- Cable ties
- Scissors
- Small flashlight
- Electrical tape
- Notebook and pencil or pen

The following materials should also be readily available:

- Additional screws
- Expansion card inserts
- Drive faceplates
- Mounting kits
- Extra cables

Organizational Aids

Keeping the tools, parts, and documentation organized allows the IT technician to work more efficiently. The following items are workspace organizational aids:

- An organizer for small parts, such as screws and connectors
- Adhesive or masking tape to make labels that identify parts
- A small notebook to keep track of assembly or troubleshooting steps
- A place to keep quick references and detailed troubleshooting guides
- A clipboard for paperwork

Diagnostic Software for System Repair and Maintenance

Once a computer system has been assembled, you must load the software that allows it to boot. If problems occur when booting a new system, you can use testing software, which is available on floppy disk.

The following software tools are commonly used in PC troubleshooting:

- **Partition Magic**—Advanced drive-partitioning software
- **CheckIt Professional**—Diagnostic software for field service or bench work
- **Spinrite**—Hard drive scanning tool

- **AmiDiag**—PC diagnostic software
- **DiskSuite**—Hard drive defragmenting software
- **SecureCRT**—Feature-filled terminal software
- **VNC**—Remote access software
- **Norton Antivirus**—Prominent virus-protection software

Information on each of these software tools can be found at the respective manufacturer's website. Always determine what a particular software tool can do before purchasing it to ensure that it meets your job requirements.

Workspace Cleaning Supplies

Although a new system does not need to be cleaned during the assembly process, computer systems can gather dust and other residues over time. Dust particles can contain chemical residues that can degrade or short-circuit chips, contact surfaces, and wire contacts. Oil from your fingers can contaminate or corrode a sensitive electrical connection. Even perspiration from your skin contains chemical salts that can corrode electrical connections. A technician should hold all electronic boards by their edges and not where the metal contacts are located.

The component surfaces of a computer need periodic cleaning. A cleaning constitutes more than blowing off or vacuuming out the dust and lint. Commonly used cleaning products include spray contact cleaner, canned air, solvents, swabs, and cleaning pads. Most vendors provide guidelines for the cleaning supplies that should be used with the equipment they produce. Be familiar with these guidelines, and obtain the recommended supplies. Figure 1-75 shows an image of canned air.

Figure 1-75 Canned Air

Spray contact cleaner is a mixture of solvent and lubricant. Contact cleaner can penetrate a small area such as a contact point. The cleaner can usually has a long, thin plastic nozzle inserted into the head that enables the head to precisely discharge the solution.

Spray contact cleaner is useful when removing corroded electrical contacts or when loosening adapter boards that have adhesive residues on the connection points.

Solvents are used with swabs to remove residues that adhere to circuit boards or contacts, especially when boards or contacts cannot be easily reached with regular cleaning pads. Isopropyl alcohol is a reliable and frequently used solvent; it is commonly sold in pharmacies.

Prepackaged cleaning pads are used for open, flat, easily accessible surfaces. These types of swabs and cleaning pads can be obtained at an electronics supply store.

Be especially careful when using cleaning chemicals. Take measures to protect your eyes against volatile solutions. You must also be careful when storing volatile cleaning chemicals, because their vapors can escape from the storage container.

Workplace Testing Equipment

When assembling a computer system, the technician might need to test electrical signals on a motherboard or its components. The technician might also need to test the external power environment. A troublesome power source can cause difficulties for the computer systems that are plugged into it. Figure 1-76 shows a Fluke 110 *multimeter*, which tests high-voltage devices. In addition to the outlet tester and digital multimeter, wrap plugs should be part of the standard equipment kept in the workspace. These plugs are also referred to as loopback plugs or loopback connectors.

Figure 1-76 High-Voltage Tester

CAUTION

Do not confuse isopropyl alcohol with rubbing alcohol. Rubbing alcohol is relatively impure and can contaminate electrical connections. Swabs that resemble typical cotton swabs, but have a foam or chamois cloth on the end, should be used with isopropyl alcohol. Cotton swabs should not be used, because they can shred and leave strands on the components.

Loopback connectors test signaling ports that are located on the back of the computer. The loopback plugs are wired to either loop or send the signals back on themselves. These plugs are used in conjunction with suitable test software to check the integrity of computer ports.

 PhotoZoom   Fluke 110 Multimeter

This interactive PhotoZoom activity, which you can find on the enclosed CD-ROM, explores the basic features of the Fluke 110 Multimeter.

Lab Safety Agreement

The Lab Safety Agreement details the procedures to be followed when working with computers. The classroom instructor will provide a copy of the agreement for you to sign.

Because many classroom lab exercises do not use high voltages, electrical safety might not appear to be important. Do not become complacent about electrical safety. Electricity can injure or cause death. Abide by all electrical safety procedures at all times. General safety issues are discussed further in Chapter 3, "Assembling a Computer."

Before repairing an electronic device, you must know the hazards and safety factors. Use extreme care, and follow these safety procedures at all times:

- ❑ Remove all jewelry.
- ❑ Unplug the power cord before removing or reinstalling any electrical component or circuit board, or when performing maintenance on electrical equipment.
- ❑ Do not touch any exposed circuit with power applied.
- ❑ Only have power applied when taking voltage measurements or waveforms.
- ❑ Insert test probes with one hand only. Do not insert probes with both hands. Keeping one hand behind your back or under the test bench reduces the chance of fatal electrocution. This is referred to as the one-hand rule.
- ❑ Do not leave objects, such as screws, nuts, or washers, loose on the equipment. They can fall into the equipment.
- ❑ Before handling or replacing integrated-circuit (IC) processors, properly ground yourself by touching the outside metal of the equipment and by using an antistatic wrist strap that is connected to the chassis. Make sure that the equipment is grounded prior to removing its case. This reduces ESD damage.
- ❑ Do not troubleshoot electronic equipment without having appropriate documentation, unless instructor approval is given.

- ❏ Never solder a connection with the power on.
- ❏ After soldering, look for possible solder splashes, cold solder joints, or damaged insulation.
- ❏ Always maintain a clean and safe work area.
- ❏ Take your time.
- ❏ Be certain about what you are going to do. If you are unsure about a procedure, ask for help.
- ❏ **If in doubt, don't touch it!**
- ❏ Other: The instructor covers fire extinguisher locations, fire evacuation procedures, safety/first aid kit locations, and emergency phone numbers in class.
- ❏ Shoes, shirt, and long pants are required when soldering and working on equipment.

STUDENT ACKNOWLEDGMENT:

- ❏ I have read and understand this document.

_____

Student Signature

_____

Print Name

_____

Date

Worksheet 1.6.6   Lab Safety Checklist

Use this worksheet to test your knowledge about the safety requirements for an IT technician's workspace.

Summary

This chapter discussed the basics of Information Technology. Some of the important concepts to retain from this chapter include the following:

- A computer system consists of hardware and software. Hardware includes physical equipment such as the case, the drives, the monitor, and the mouse. Computer software, or programs, includes the OS and applications that perform specific functions for the user.

- Work with the Desktop to start the system and shut it down properly. Navigate the Desktop to view system information, use shortcut icons, switch between windows, set up the Desktop, and recover deleted files from the Recycle Bin.

- Open programs and documents, use help features, search for files, and open a command line with the Run command on the Start menu.

- Understand computer terminology; know the difference between a byte, kilobyte, and megabyte. Understand how frequency is measured, and know the difference between Hz, MHz, and GHz.

- Use the most effective method of converting number systems, including binary to decimal form and back again, and binary to hexadecimal form and back again. Identify the places in binary and decimal numbers, and know the value of each.

- Safety is the number one concern when working with computer systems. Proper safety procedures must be followed to reduce the risk of ESD that can damage computer components. Proper safety procedures also keep the IT technician safe.

The next chapter introduces you to computer theory. It discusses the various components of a computer and explains how these pieces come together to make a functional system.

Key Terms

algorithm A systematic description or method of how to carry out a series of steps to complete a certain task.

application software Accepts input from the user and then manipulates it to achieve a result. This result is known as the output.

asynchronous Without respect to time. In terms of data transmission, asynchronous means that no clock or timing source is needed to keep both the sender and the receiver synchronized.

bit The smallest unit of data in a computer. A bit can take the value of either 1 or 0. A bit is the binary format in which data is processed by computers.

byte A unit of measure that describes the size of a data file, the amount of space on a disk or other storage medium, or the amount of data being sent over a network. One byte consists of 8 bits of data.

cold boot Performed by turning the PC on using the power button.

computer-aided design (CAD) Used for generic design or specialized uses such as architectural, electrical, and mechanical. More complex forms of CAD are solid modeling and parametric modeling, which allow objects to be created with real-world characteristics.

computer system Consists of hardware and software components. Hardware is the physical equipment such as the case, floppy disk drives, keyboards, monitors, cables, speakers, and printers. The term *software* describes the programs that operate the computer system.

database An organized collection of data that can be easily accessed, managed, indexed, searched, and updated.

Desktop The main display screen in Windows.

Domain Name System (DNS) A system that provides a way to map friendly host names to IP addresses.

electronic mail (e-mail) The exchange of computer-stored messages by network communication.

electrostatic discharge (ESD) The discharge of static electricity from one conductor to another conductor of a different potential.

firmware A program that is embedded in a silicon chip rather than stored on a floppy disk.

flat-file database Stores information in a single table.

gigahertz (GHz) One billion cycles per second. This is a common measurement of the speed of a processing chip.

graphical user interface (GUI)   A graphical display that represents the procedures and programs that can be executed by the computer.

graphics application   Creates or modifies graphical images. The two types of graphical images include object- or vector-based images, and bitmaps or raster images.

Help   Tips and instructions on how to use Windows.

hertz (Hz)   A unit of frequency measurement. It is the rate of change in the state, or cycle, in a sound wave, alternating current, or other cyclical waveform. Hertz is synonymous with cycles per second, and it describes the speed of a computer microprocessor.

icon   An image that represents an application or a capability.

kilobit (kb)   1024, or approximately 1000, bits.

kilobits per second (kbps)   A measurement of the amount of data that is transferred over a connection such as a network connection. A data transfer rate of 1 kbps is a rate of approximately 1000 bits per second.

kilobyte (KB)   1024, or approximately 1000, bytes.

kilobytes per second (KBps)   A measurement of the amount of data that is transferred over a connection such as a network connection. A data transfer rate of 1 KBps is a rate of approximately 1000 bytes per second.

logic gates   Electronic circuits that respond to AND, OR, NOT, and NOR signals.

mainframe   A powerful machine that consists of centralized computers that are usually housed in secure, climate-controlled rooms. End users interface with the computers through dumb terminals.

megabit   1,048,576 bits (approximately 1 million bits).

megabits per second (Mbps)   A common measurement of the amount of data that is transferred over a connection such as a network connection. A data transfer rate of 1 Mbps is a rate of approximately 1 million bits or 1000 kilobits per second.

megabyte (MB)   1,048,576 bytes (or approximately 1 million bytes).

megabytes per second (MBps)   A common measurement of the amount of data that is transferred over a connection such as a network connection. A data transfer rate of 1 MBps is a rate of approximately 1 million bytes or 1000 kilobytes per second.

megahertz (MHz)   One million cycles per second. This is a common measurement of the speed of a processing chip.

multimeter   A device that tests high-voltage devices.

My Computer icon   Provides access to all the installed drives, which are computer storage components.

My Documents icon   A shortcut to personal or frequently accessed files.

network   A group of computers that are connected to share resources.

nibble   Half a byte, or four bits.

operating system (OS)   A program that controls the hardware and manages all the other programs in a computer.

personal computer (PC)   A stand-alone device that is independent of all other computers.

presentation application   Permits the organization, design, and delivery of presentations in the form of slide shows and reports. Also known as business graphics.

program   Instructs the computer on how to operate. Also known as computer software.

Recycle Bin   Stores files, folders, graphics, and web pages that have been deleted from the hard disk.

relational database   A collection of flat-file databases, or tables, that are linked through some relationship.

spreadsheet   Calculates a range of numerical values and carries out large and complex calculations.

tweening   A process used primarily in graphic design that defines two key points in a frame and then uses the computer to calculate the "in between" frames.

warm boot   Restarting a PC that has already been powered up.

web browser   An application that locates and displays pages from the World Wide Web (WWW).

word processor   An application that creates, edits, stores, and prints documents.

wrist strap   A device that is attached to the technician's wrist and then clipped to the metal system chassis to prevent ESD damage by channeling static electricity from the person to the ground.

Check Your Understanding

1. ARPANET was a precursor to the modern Internet. In the 1960s, which U.S. government agency was instrumental in developing ARPANET?

   A. Department of Defense

   B. Department of Commerce

   C. Department of Transportation

   D. Department of Communication

2. Which software application allows the user to collect and organize information so that its contents can be easily accessed, managed, and updated?

   A. Word processing software

   B. Imaging software

   C. Database software

   D. Presentation software

3. What is the hexadecimal equivalent to the binary number 11100110?

   A. 230

   B. E6

   C. 346

   D. A95FCE

4. While working on computer equipment, it is essential to have a safe, efficient work environment. Which of the following is a basic lab safety principle?

   A. To reduce the likelihood of ESD, the workspace should maintain a humidity level of 5–10 percent.

   B. To reduce the likelihood of encountering high voltage, the workbench should not be grounded.

   C. Workbench power outlets should be properly grounded and sufficient in number to accommodate the system power and other electrical needs.

   D. Filtered air should not be used around the work area because of the possibility of ESD.

5. What is the binary conversion of the decimal number 204?

   A. 11011000

   B. 11100110

   C. 10111010

   D. 11001100

6. It is important to wear an ESD wrist strap while working on all computer components except which of the following?

   A. Video monitor

   B. Motherboard

   C. Hard drive

   D. Video card

7. Which of the following would be a primary attribute of a mainframe environment?

   A. Decentralized management

   B. Windows GUI

   C. Dumb terminal use

   D. Standard operating system

8. What is the most accepted safe method to shut down a computer while in the Windows 9*x* environment?

   A. Depress the on/off switch on the computer system case.

   B. Select the **Shut Down** option from the Start menu.

   C. Right-click an empty space on the Desktop, and then select **Shut Down** from the options that appear.

   D. Right-click the Start button, and select **Shut Down** from the options that appear.

9. Which numbering system is based on powers of 2?

   A. Octal

   B. Hexadecimal

   C. Binary

   D. ASCII

10. The CRT in a monitor can be charged to as much as how many volts?

   A. 1000

   B. 5000

   C. 10,000

   D. 20,000

Upon completing this chapter, you will be able to perform the following tasks:

- Define and understand the computer's four basic functions: input, processing, output, and storage

- Understand the actions of the boot sequence, which initializes and tests the system hardware

- Distinguish the features and functions of the hardware components that make the computer work

- Identify the components of portable computers as they relate to their desktop counterparts

- Understand system resources, including IRQs, DMA, and I/O

Chapter 2

How Computers Work

This chapter discusses how computers work. You learn the boot process, which includes initializing and testing the system, loading the operating system (OS), and running the boot sequence that is required to operate the computer.

Computer hardware is explained in detail, and illustrations are included. In addition to the components of the desktop computer, this chapter provides information that relates to laptops and portables.

System resources are shared between computer components and devices. Interrupt requests (IRQs), direct memory access (DMA), and input/output (I/O) addresses enable the CPU to handle multiple requests.

Computer Operations

It is important to understand the four basic operations that are performed by a computer system. These operations facilitate the communication between the user and the computer system.

This section covers the following operations:

- Input
- Processing
- Output
- Storage

Input, Processing, Output, and Storage

The OS is the software that controls functionality and provides lower-level routines for application programs. Most operating systems provide functions to read and write data to files. An operating system translates requests for operations on files into operations that the disk controller can perform. The operating system helps the computer perform the four basic operations of input, processing, output, and storage. Figure 2-1 illustrates these four operations.

Figure 2-1 Input, Processing, Output, and Storage

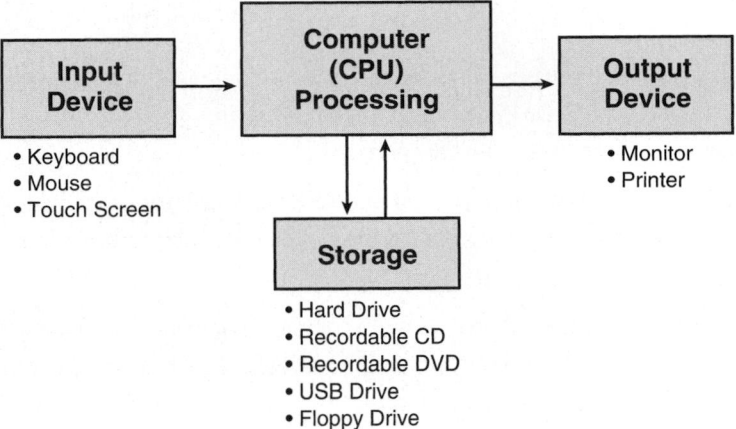

The most common way to input data into a computer is with a keyboard and mouse, as shown in Figure 2-2. Another way to input data is with a touch screen, as shown in Figure 2-3. On full-screen computers, touch screens have on-screen buttons that can be accessed with a finger or a stylus. These applications are custom designed and typically simple to use. Therefore, these applications can be used by anyone. Touch screens are also used on PDAs and tablet computers. Because of the smaller screens that are found on these units, a stylus is required for precise interaction with screen objects. Input devices allow the user to open a web page, send an e-mail file, or access a file from a network server.

Processing, as discussed here, refers to the function of the central processing unit (CPU). When the computer is on, the CPU is always processing data from both internal and external sources. The CPU processes the internal data to boot the system and run the programs that test for functionality when a computer is first turned on. When the user is working with an application—for example, a word processing program—the CPU processes the data that is entered to display on the monitor and processes the data when it is sent to the printer.

Figure 2-2 Input Device

Figure 2-3 Touch Screen

Processing data usually results in output. Examples of output include a word processor file or a spreadsheet. The most common way to output data is to send the data to an output device such as a computer monitor, as shown in Figure 2-4, or to a printer. Most computers have a connection to the Internet. Other ways to output the data include sending the data to the Internet using e-mail or through a web page.

Figure 2-4 Output Device

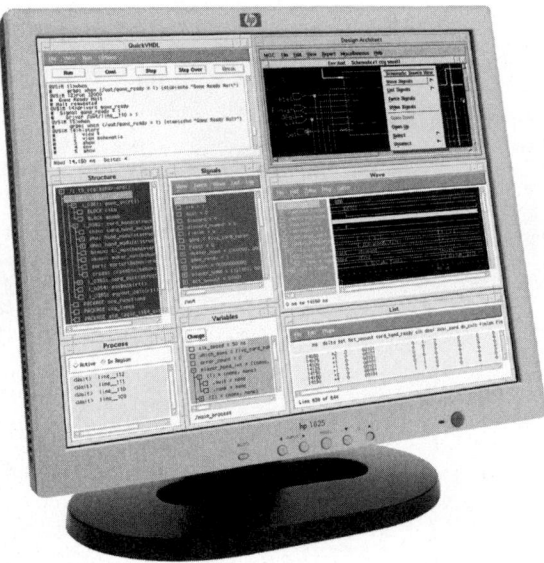

Data storage is probably the most important of the four basic computer functions. Hard drives, recordable/rewritable CD-ROM drives, and floppy disk drives are examples of storage devices. The most common way to store a file is to save it to a hard drive. Hard drives can be compared to large file cabinets. An operating system finds a place on the hard drive, saves the file, and remembers the location of the file.

The Boot Process

The steps of the boot process are automatic and generally do not require user intervention when the computer is turned on. However, it is important to understand these steps when troubleshooting the system. This section includes the following topics:

- Initializing the system hardware
- Loading the operating system
- Running the boot sequence

Initializing the System Hardware

For an operating system to run, it must be loaded into the computer's RAM. When a computer is first turned on, it launches a program called the bootstrap loader on the Basic Input/Output System (BIOS) chip or firmware. The primary functions of the bootstrap loader are to test the computer hardware and to locate and load the operating system files into RAM. Because the ***bootstrap program*** is built into the BIOS chip, the program is also referred to as BIOS control. During the execution of the BIOS firmware routines, the following operations are performed:

1. The power-on self-test (POST) is run.

2. Initialization is completed.

3. The BIOS moves the starting address and mode information into the DMA controller and then loads the Master Boot Record (MBR).

Power-On Self-Test

To test the computer hardware, the bootstrap program runs a program called the power-on self-test (POST). In this test, the computer CPU checks itself first and then checks the computer system timer. The POST checks the RAM by writing data to each RAM chip and then reading that data. Any differences that are found indicate a problem.

If the POST finds errors, it sends a message to the computer monitor. If these errors cannot be displayed on the monitor, the POST sends errors in the form of beeps. If the POST finds no errors, it sends one beep and the screen begins to display OS loading messages.

The POST is an important phase of the bootstrap process. Consult your motherboard manual or visit the website of the motherboard manufacturer to learn more about the BIOS and the audio POST codes. Both the BIOS and the POST process are discussed in greater detail in Chapter 3, "Assembling a Computer."

Loading the Operating System

Next, the bootstrap program needs to locate and copy the OS boot file to the computer RAM. The order in which the bootstrap program searches can be changed in the system BIOS setup. The most common order for the OS search is the floppy drive, and then the hard drive, and finally the CD-ROM drive.

When the bootstrap program finds the OS boot record, the record is copied to the computer RAM. Then the bootstrap program turns over control of the boot process to the boot record. The boot record looks for files on the hard disk that help the hard disk find and locate the rest of the OS. As files are located and loaded into RAM, the boot record is no longer needed. The OS that was stored on the hard disk is now in control of the boot process. Figure 2-5 demonstrates the loading of the bootstrap program.

The last step of the boot process is for the OS to find the hardware configuration files that are specific to the computer. If the computer has a modem or a sound card, the OS finds the configuration files and loads them. Configuration files are also called *hardware drivers*.

Figure 2-5 Bootstrap Loading

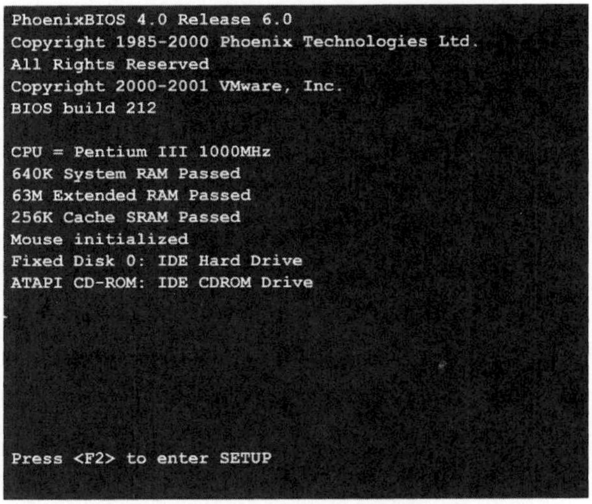

```
PhoenixBIOS 4.0 Release 6.0
Copyright 1985-2000 Phoenix Technologies Ltd.
All Rights Reserved
Copyright 2000-2001 VMware, Inc.
BIOS build 212

CPU = Pentium III 1000MHz
640K System RAM Passed
63M Extended RAM Passed
256K Cache SRAM Passed
Mouse initialized
Fixed Disk 0: IDE Hard Drive
ATAPI CD-ROM: IDE CDROM Drive




Press <F2> to enter SETUP
```

Running the Boot Sequence

The PC boot sequence defines a set of actions and the order in which these actions take place. The boot sequence occurs during a cold boot, when the PC power switch is turned on. When the PC is restarted or reset (referred to as a warm boot), a limited boot sequence is performed.

Perform a warm boot in one of the following ways:

- Choose **Start**, **Shutdown**, **Restart**.
- Press the computer reset button.
- Press **Ctrl-Alt-Delete** twice.

A cold boot begins whenever the PC power switch is turned on. A cold boot involves more events and bootstrap activities than a warm boot. A cold boot causes the BIOS to guide the computer boot sequence through a series of steps that verify the integrity of the system.

The exact steps and the number of events in the boot sequence can vary depending on a number of factors, as follows:

- The version of Windows that is running
- The BIOS manufacturer
- The BIOS version
- The system hardware configuration
- Warm or cold boot

The steps that are listed in Table 2-1 represent a generic cold boot on a PC.

Table 2-1 Generic Cold Boot Sequence

Step		Description
1	Power supply	The power supply initializes. The chipset then waits for the Power Good signal from the power supply.
2	BIOS ROM	The processor looks for the start of the BIOS (Basic Input/Output System) boot program at the end of system memory, where a pointer tells it where to get the BIOS startup program.
3	POST	The BIOS performs the POST. If fatal errors are encountered, the boot process stops.
4	Video	The BIOS looks for the video card BIOS program and executes it to initialize the video card.
5	Other BIOS	The BIOS looks for any other device BIOS, such as a hard disk, and executes it.
6	Startup screen	The BIOS displays the Startup screen.
7	Memory	The BIOS tests other system components and performs a memory count-up test.
8	Hardware	The BIOS tests the system to find the various hardware in the system. Hard drives and memory timings are configured at this time.
9	Plug and Play	The BIOS configures Plug and Play devices.
10	Configuration screen	The BIOS displays a configuration summary of the system.
11	Boot drive	The BIOS searches for a drive to boot from based on the boot sequence.
12	Boot record	The BIOS searches the first boot device in the sequence for either the Master Boot Record (MBR) on a hard drive or the volume boot sector on a floppy disk.
13	Operating system	The BIOS begins to boot the operating system, where boot information code takes over from the BIOS code.
14	Error	If the BIOS does not find a bootable device in the boot sequence, the BIOS displays an error message and halts the system.

Hardware Components

This section covers the components that make up a computer system. The following topics are included:

- Computer cases
- Power supplies
- Cooling systems
- The motherboard
- CPUs
- BIOS ROM
- Expansion slots
- Riser cards
- Bus types

Computer Cases

The computer case and the power supply are two important parts that determine the performance of a system. The type of case and power supply usually determines the type of motherboard used. The power supply is usually included in the computer case.

When building a computer, you must first decide which type of case to use. The case is made up of a metal frame and a cover. The cover is usually constructed of metal or hard plastic. The case is the housing unit for the internal components; it protects against dust and damage. The case usually comes with the power supply that's needed to power the computer and the installed components.

Computer cases are either desktop or tower models, as shown in Figure 2-6 and as described in the following list:

- **Desktop model**—Sits on a desk horizontally. The monitor can be placed on top of the case. This choice can be a space saver.
- **Tower model**—Stands upright in a vertical position that allows easy placement on the floor. Mini-tower, mid-tower, and full tower cases are available.

The choice of a desktop or tower case is a matter of personal preference. However, it is important to consider your workspace before choosing a case.

Figure 2-6 Desktop and Tower Models

Hardware components are installed in the bays of the case. The bays are placeholders for the drives. Devices can be easily interchanged from bay to bay if necessary. Drive bays are 5-1/4 or 3-1/2 inches wide. Some drive bays are left unfilled in a new computer. This allows the machine to be upgraded with a ZIP drive, tape backup drive, or CD-ROM drive.

Table 2-2 summarizes the different parts of a typical computer case. Table 2-3 explains the factors to consider when selecting a case.

Table 2-2 Typical Parts of a Computer Case

Part	Purpose
Frame	The main board and all the objects inside and outside are attached to the frame. The frame is what defines the size and shape of a computer.
Cover panels	These panels attach to the frame to enclose all the parts of the PC. You should not operate the computer without the cover panels in place, because they protect the internal parts, direct airflow to cool the circuits, and contain the radio frequency interference/electromagnetic interference (RFI/EMI) emissions of the power supply unit.

continues

Table 2-2 Typical Parts of a Computer Case (Continued)

Part	Purpose
LEDs and button connectors	These connect the buttons and LEDs on the front of the case to the motherboard.
Speaker and connector	The speaker connects to the motherboard and provides a basic way to diagnose startup problems.
I/O template	This is a metal template on the back of the case that provides access holes to the motherboard's peripheral connectors. On some cases, the template can be replaced to provide the correct access holes, depending on the motherboard connector locations and spacing.
Expansion slots	These are also known as *sockets*. They are receptacles on the computer motherboard that allow additional devices to be added. Video cards, I/O cards, and sound cards are examples of components that can be located in expansion slots.
Case fan and connector	Most modern cases provide a secondary fan at the front of the unit to draw air in to circulate over the circuits and devices in the system. The fan connects to the main board or the power supply to receive power.
5-1/4-inch drive bays	These are the large bays where a 5-1/4-inch-wide device, like the CD-ROM drive, can be installed in the case. A plate usually covers the bay in the front and must be removed before the installation.
3-1/2-inch drive bays	These are the smaller bays where 3-1/2-inch-wide devices, like a floppy disk drive or a hard disk drive, can be mounted. If a hard disk is installed, the metal or plastic cover plate does not need to be removed because the hard disk is not removable.
Vent holes	The design of the case dictates where the appropriate venting holes are placed. The manufacturer locates these holes to ensure the correct airflow within the case.
Power supply mounting area	This area is for mounting the power supply unit, if the case does not have one. Some cases come with a power supply already installed.
Front cover plate	This plate fits on the front of the case, providing a place for the LEDs and buttons and the air intake control, as well as an aesthetically pleasing look.
Feet	The feet on the bottom of the case provide stability on uneven or slick surfaces. Some cases draw air from the bottom of the case, and the feet elevate the case to ensure proper airflow.

Table 2-3 Factors to Consider in Choosing a Computer Case

Factor	Rationale
Model type	There are four main case models. One type is for desktop PCs, and three types are for tower computers. The type of motherboard that you choose determines the type of case that can be used. The size and shape must match exactly.
Size	If a case has more components, it needs more room for airflow to keep the system cool.
Available space	Desktop cases allow space conservation in tight areas because the monitor can be placed on top of the unit, but these cases can be difficult to upgrade.
Number of devices	The more devices that need system power, the larger the power supply must be. This relates to the mounting area of the power supply in the case.
Power supply	Depending on the type of motherboard that you choose, you must match the power rating and connection type to the power supply that you use.
Environmental conditions	If the system will be operated in a dusty area, you should purchase a case that's designed to reduce the amount of dust that enters the system. To trap dust, some cases offer easily replaceable filters for the case fan.
Aesthetics	For some people, the look of the case doesn't matter; for others, it is critical. If you need to have a case that is attractive and aesthetically pleasing, a number of manufacturers consider this when designing a case.
Status display	What is going on inside the case can be important. LED indicators that are mounted on the front of the case can tell you whether the system is receiving power, when the hard drive is being used, and when the computer is in Standby mode.
Vents	All cases have a vent on the power supply, and some cases have another vent on the back to help draw air into or out of the system. Some cases are designed with more vents in case the system needs to dissipate an unusual amount of heat. This situation can occur when many devices are installed close together in the case.
Rigidity	When choosing a case, remember that the internal components are not designed to bend. The case should be sturdy enough to keep all internal components from flexing.

PhotoZoom PC

In this PhotoZoom, you explore the basic PC components.

Power Supplies

A power supply, as shown in Figure 2-7, provides the needed voltage to power the various electronic circuits that make up the PC. The power supply receives the external AC power.

Figure 2-7 External View of a Typical Power Supply

The power supply is contained in a metal box. Within this box, a transformer converts the voltage that is supplied from standard outlets into voltages that the computer components need to operate.

A fan that is installed in the power supply maintains airflow to prevent the computer and its components from overheating. These components must be kept at a consistent operating temperature to ensure the best performance. The fan is built into the power supply, with openings on the back side of the case. Never block or cover the fan inlet port.

Several different types of power supplies are available. Although power supplies vary in size and design, basically, the two form factors are the AT and ATX. Today, the ATX is the most common power supply. The ATX power supply conforms to the standard ATX motherboard and case and uses color-coded wires and industry-standard keyed connectors. AT-type power supplies are no longer used in new systems; they are generally found on computers built prior to the mid-1990s. *Switch mode power supplies (SMPS)* have replaced the linear mode power supplies in most computers. A SMPS uses a high-frequency switch or transistor to maintain the output voltage. Like the linear mode power supply, the SMPS can step-down a supply voltage, but it also provides a step-up function.

The devices that attach to the power supply use +5V, +12V, and +3.3V DC power. Older devices also use –5V and –12V DC power. Examples of older devices are those found in PC/XT and early AT systems. The power supply must support the type of processor that is to be used. Each power supply comes with all these specifications. Table 2-4 describes the components of a typical ATX power supply. Table 2-5 describes the factors to consider when selecting a power supply.

Table 2-4 Components of a Power Supply

Part	Description
Case and cover	Isolate the power supply from the rest of the PC and keep electromagnetic emissions inside the unit.
Power cord	Connects the unit to a receptacle to supply AC power.
Voltage selector switch	Allows the power supply to accept 110/120-volt AC power (in North America) or 220/240-volt AC power (outside North America).
	The following website offers more information: http://kropla.com/electric.htm.
Power switch	Directs power from the AC outlet to the computer.
Power converter	Converts AC to DC power for use within the PC.
Motherboard power connector	Supplies the necessary power to the motherboard.
Disk drive power connectors	Supply the necessary power to the drives, auxiliary fans, and other devices inside the case.
Fan	Circulates air inside the case to keep itself and all the electronics and devices cool.
Fuse	Protects the power supply from damage if a power surge occurs. The fuse will blow if it is subjected to excessive voltage.

Table 2-5 Factors to Consider When Selecting a Power Supply

TIP

Electrical current, or current, is the flow of charges that is created when electrons move. In electrical circuits, current is caused by a flow of free electrons. When voltage is applied and a path for the current exists, electrons move from the negative terminal along the path to the positive terminal. The negative terminal repels the electrons, whereas the positive terminal attracts them.

Factor	Rationale
Wattage	To upgrade the PC with more equipment or faster processors, the power supply must provide enough power to the additional equipment without becoming overloaded.
Form factor	Depending on the type of case and motherboard selected, the power supply must adhere to the same form factor requirements as these items so that it fits inside the case and correctly powers the motherboard and other devices.
CPU type	Different CPUs require different voltages. For example, some AMD chips and motherboards might require more power than some Pentiums.
Expandability	If the power supply only has enough power to supply the current CPU, motherboard, and devices, it might not have enough power to supply an upgrade to the system.
Energy efficiency	Each power supply has an efficiency rating. The higher the rating, the less heat that is generated by the power supply when converting voltage.
Fan type and direction	The power supply must have a high-quality fan. The fan is the primary source of airflow inside the case. Some fans can change direction to allow air to be blown directly on the CPU and to regulate the quality of the air that enters the case.
Signals	Modern power supplies can be regulated by the motherboard. The main board can regulate the speed of the fan, depending on the temperature inside the case. The board can also turn off the fan to save power, and some smart power supplies can turn off the computer in the event of a fan failure, before the components overheat.
Fault tolerance	If you have a PC that needs to be on at all times, consider buying a dual power supply. If one of the units fails, the other one takes over immediately. Some designs enable one power supply to be replaced while the computer remains powered by the second one.
Line conditioning	DC voltages that are supplied to the PC must be kept at normal levels during power spikes or brownouts. One way to achieve this is to install a power supply that has built-in conditioning. These units ensure that the DC voltages supplied to the system remain stable, even when the AC current coming in is not.

Worksheet 2.3.2   Power Supply

In this worksheet, information relating to the power supply is reviewed.

 PhotoZoom   Power Supply and Connectors

Use this interactive PhotoZoom to review the parts of the power supply and the power supply connectors.

Cooling Systems

The power supply fan helps prevent the computer components from overheating by maintaining airflow in the case. Older computer cases could accommodate an additional fan, as shown in Figure 2-8. However, cases are currently designed to accommodate up to six additional fans.

Figure 2-8 Case Fan

Overheating is a critical problem that can cause a computer system to malfunction or fail. A heat sink, made of a material that absorbs the generated heat, can be used to protect against overheating. The heat sink then disperses the heat away from the CPU. Installing a heat sink is covered in Chapter 3.

Other cooling methods are becoming more widely available. Computer cases made of aluminum create a much cooler environment for the installed components. However, aluminum cases are more expensive. Liquid-cooled cases introduce water as a cooling agent. Liquid-cooling units fit most cases that allow the installation of a rear exhaust fan. These units include a pump, a reservoir, the fan and radiator, and the CPU block. The system can be used to keep the components an average of 8–10 degrees cooler than a standard air-cooled system.

The Motherboard

The *motherboard* is the nerve center of the computer system. Dual-processor and single-processor motherboards are available. Figure 2-9 shows a single-processor motherboard. The need for processing power continues to grow. Single-processor boards cannot always meet the demand for power, especially in corporate networking environments. As a result, dual-processor boards are usually installed for an advanced network operating system, such as Windows 2000.

Figure 2-9 Single-Processor Motherboard

The motherboard is also called the *system board* or the main board. Everything else in the system plugs into, is controlled by, or depends on the motherboard to communicate with other devices in the system. The motherboard is the largest of the printed circuit boards, and every system has one. The motherboard generally houses the following components:

- CPU
- Controller circuitry
- Buses

- RAM
- Expansion slots for additional boards
- Ports for external devices
- Complementary Metal Oxide Semiconductor (CMOS) chip
- Other read-only memory (ROM)
- BIOS chips
- Support chips that provide varied functionality

If the computer is a desktop case, the motherboard is generally located at the bottom of the computer case. If the computer is a tower-type case, the motherboard is mounted vertically along one side of the case. All the components that relate to the system unit connect directly to the motherboard. External devices would not be able to communicate with the system unit without the motherboard. External devices include the mouse, the keyboard, and the monitor.

Motherboard Form Factors

Printed circuit boards are constructed from sheets of fiberglass. These boards are covered with sockets and various electronic parts, including different kinds of chips. A chip is made up of a very small circuit board that is etched on a square of silicon. Silicon is a material with the same chemical structure as common sand. Chips vary in size, but many are roughly the size of a postage stamp. A chip is also referred to as a *semiconductor* or *integrated circuit*. The individual wires and hand-soldered connectors that are used in older system boards have been replaced by aluminum or copper traces that are printed on circuit boards. This improvement has significantly reduced the amount of time it takes to build a PC; this, in turn, has reduced the cost for the manufacturer and the consumer. In addition, printed circuit boards with aluminum or copper traces have improved performance and reliability. Figure 2-10 shows an ATX motherboard.

TIP

Understand the difference between motherboard form factors.

Motherboards are usually described by their form factors. Form factors describe the physical dimensions of the motherboard. The two most common form factors currently in use are the Baby AT motherboard and the ATX motherboard. Most new systems come with the ATX motherboard form factor. The ATX motherboard is similar to the Baby AT motherboard, except the ATX unit has the following enhancements:

- The expansion slots are parallel to the short side of the board, allowing more space for other components.
- The CPU and RAM are located next to the power supply. These components consume a lot of power, so they need more cooling by the power supply fan.
- An integrated I/O port and PS/2 mouse connectors are included on the motherboard.
- 3.3-volt operation from an ATX power supply is supported.

Figure 2-10 ATX Motherboard

Table 2-6 provides a general summary of the motherboard form factors in use today.

Table 2-6 Motherboard Form Factors

Form Factor	Dimensions (Inches)	Notes
Baby AT	8.5×10–13	Used by older PCs; becoming outdated
ATX	12×9.6	Most common form factor in use today
Mini-ATX	11.2×8.2	Used in newer, smaller PCs
LPX	9×11–13	Found in older PCs, uses a riser card to save space
Mini-LPX	8–9×10–11	Found in older PCs, uses a riser card to save space
NLX	8–9×10–13.6	Found in newer PCs, setup provides easier access to components

Motherboards are sometimes described according to the type of microprocessor interface, or socket, that they present. Motherboards can be described as Slot 1, Socket 370, and so on. Slot 1 is first-generation ATX board. Single Socket 370 is second-generation ATX. Sockets and slots are discussed in the section "CPUs," later in this chapter.

Motherboard Components

The components that are found on a motherboard can vary, depending on the age of the motherboard and the level of integration. The most common items that are found on a typical modern motherboard are listed in Table 2-7.

Table 2-7 Motherboard Components

Component	Description
Chipset	Set of microcircuits that define how much RAM a motherboard can use, the type of RAM chip, the cache size and speed, the processor types and speeds, and the types of expansion slots that the motherboard can accommodate.
CPU interface	Socket or slot that the CPU connects to on the motherboard.
Expansion slots	Receptacles on the motherboard that accept printed circuit boards. All computers have expansion slots that allow devices to be added.
Dip switches/jumpers	Devices that change various aspects of how the motherboard is configured.
I/O support	Connectors for input and output devices that are controlled by the main board.
Internal buses	Channels for data to move between the devices attached to the system, to the CPU, and to its components.
Power supply socket	Connection for the power supply that provides power to the motherboard.
BIOS chip	Chip that provides the computer with basic instructions to start the computer and check hardware for errors.
Battery	Device that keeps the system time and provides a way for the BIOS to remember certain settings.
RAM sockets	Connectors for inserting memory chips in the computer.

Motherboard Chipset

The motherboard chipset determines the compatibility of the motherboard with several other vital system components. The chipset determines the performance and limitations of the motherboard. This chipset consists of a group of microcircuits that are contained on several integrated chips or combined into one or two Very Large Scale Integration (VLSI) integrated chips. VLSI chips have over 20,000 circuits.

The chipset determines the following items:

- How much RAM a motherboard can use
- The type of RAM chip
- The cache size and speed
- The processor types and speed
- The types of expansion slots that the motherboard can accommodate

Although new microprocessor technologies and speed improvements tend to receive all the attention, chipset innovations are just as important.

A number of chipset manufacturers are shown in Table 2-8. Intel currently produces some of the fastest chipsets.

Table 2-8 PC Motherboard Chipset Manufacturers

Manufacturer	Website
Advanced Micro Devices, Inc.	http://www.amd.com
VIA Technologies	http://www.via.com.tw/en/Products/prodindex.jsp
Intel Corp.	http://developer.intel.com/design/chipsets/index.htm
Ali Corp. (Ali), formerly Acer Laboratories Inc.	http://www.ali.com.tw/eng/product/product_index.htm
Silicon Integrated Systems Corp.	http://www.sis.com/products/index.htm
Opti Inc.	http://www.opti-inc.com/html/products.html

 Lab 2.3.6 Motherboard Identification

In this lab, you learn how to identify, remove, and replace motherboards, and you use the motherboard manuals to identify a number of the system components.

PhotoZoom   Motherboard

Use this interactive PhotoZoom to review the parts of the motherboard.

e-Lab Activity   Motherboard

The components of the motherboard are identified in this e-Lab activity.

CPUs

The computer cannot run without a CPU. The CPU is often referred to as the brains of a computer. On the motherboard, the CPU is contained on a single integrated circuit called the *microprocessor*. The CPU contains two basic components: a *control unit* and an *Arithmetic/ Logic Unit (ALU)*.

The control unit performs the following functions:

- Instructs the computer system on how to follow the program instructions
- Directs the movement of data to and from processor memory
- Temporarily holds data, instructions, and processed information in its ALU
- Directs control signals between the CPU and external devices such as hard disks, main memory, and I/O ports

The ALU performs both arithmetic and logical operations. Arithmetic operations are fundamental math operations like addition, subtraction, multiplication, and division. Logical operations, such as AND, OR, and XOR, make comparisons and decisions. Logical operations determine how a program is executed.

The processor handles most of the operations that are required of the computer by processing instructions, sending signals, checking for connectivity, and ensuring that operations and hardware are functioning properly. The processor acts as a messenger to components such as the RAM, monitor, and disk drives.

The microprocessor is connected to the rest of the computer system through three buses: the data bus, the address bus, and the control bus. The bus types are discussed in detail later in this chapter.

Many different companies produce CPUs. They include Intel, Advanced Micro Devices (AMD), and Cyrix. Intel is credited with making the first modern, silicon-based CPU chip in 1971.

Processor Socket Types

Microprocessor work uses specific terminology, including Socket 7, Socket 423, or Slot 1. Socket X (where X is any number) is a descriptive term for the way that certain processors plug into a computer motherboard. The processor plugs in to make contact with the built-in circuitry or data bus of the motherboard. Manufacturers can have different socket types for their processors. Socket 7, which is mostly outdated, is the best known of the major connection variations that have been designed. Socket 7 was used at some time by each of the three major processor types. Socket types that are followed by a larger number are more current. For example, Socket 370 is more current than Socket 7. Processor technology and speed have improved with each update. Table 2-9 summarizes the information on socket types and indicates the different processor types that use them. More information can be found at http://www.firmware.com/support/bios/pentium.htm.

Table 2-9 CPU Socket Types

Socket Type	AMD	Intel
Socket 1	AM486DX-4, Am5x86	486SX/SX2, DX, DX2, DX4, Overdrive Processor
Socket 2	AM486DX-4, Am5x86	486SX/SX2, DX, DX2, DX4, Pentium Overdrive Processor
Socket 3	AM486DX-4, Am5x86	486SX/SX2, DX, DX2, DX4, Pentium Overdrive Processor
Socket 4	—	Pentium 60–66 MHz, Pentium Overdrive 120–133 MHz
Socket 5	K5	Pentium 75–133 MHz, Pentium Overdrive 125–166 MHz, Pentium Overdrive MMX 125–180 MHz, Pentium MMX 166–200 MHz
Socket 6	—	The last 486-class socket standard that was created by Intel. It is not used in modern motherboards.
Socket 7	K5, K6 166–300 MHz, K6-2 266–550 MHz, K6-3 400–450 MHz	Pentium 75–200 MHz, Pentium Overdrive 125–166 MHz, Pentium Overdrive MMX 125–200 MHz, Pentium MMX 166–233 MHz
Socket 8	—	Pentium Pro 150–200 MHz, Pentium II Overdrive 300–333 MHz

Table 2-9 CPU Socket Types (Continued)

Socket Type	AMD	Intel
Slot 1	—	Celeron, Pentium II 233–450 MHz, Pentium III 450 MHz (and higher).
Slot 2	—	Pentium II Xeon 400–450 MHz, Pentium III Xeon 500 MHz–1 GHz
Slot A	Athlon 500 MHz–1 GHz	—
Socket 370	—	Celeron, Pentium II 233–450 MHz, Pentium III 450 MHz–1.13 GHz
Socket A	Duron 600 MHz*, Athlon 750 MHz*	—
Socket 423	—	Pentium 4 at 1.3 GHz*
Socket 478	—	Pentium 4 at 1.0–2.3 GHz*
Socket 603	—	Xeon at 1.0–1.4 GHz*

*   No top speed to date

Socket-type processors use the ***zero-insertion-force (ZIF) socket***. A ZIF socket allows the easy insertion of the microprocessor. A typical ZIF socket contains a lever that opens and closes to secure the microprocessor in place. In addition, the various sockets have a differing number of pins and pin layout arrangements. Socket 7, for example, has 321 pins. The number of pins generally increases with the socket numbering.

Processor Slots

Slot-type processors were only on the market for a year. Intel moved from the socket configuration to a processor packaged in a cartridge that fits into a slot in the motherboard for its Pentium II processor. Similarly, AMD has progressed from Slot A, similar to Slot 1, to Socket A for its high-end AMD Athlon and Duron processors.

Pentium Processors

The current family of Intel Pentium microprocessors includes the Pentium II, III, IV, and Xeon. The Pentium class is the current standard for processor chips. These processors represent the Intel processor second and third generations. By combining memory cache with microprocessor circuitry, the Pentium supports processor speeds of 1000 MHz (1 GHz) and more. The combined chips cover less than 2 square inches and comprise more than a million transistors.

The Pentium processors offer several improvements over their predecessor, which evolved from the Intel 80486 chip. For example, the Pentium data bus is 64 bits wide and can take in data 64 bits at a time. Compare this to the Intel 486 with 32 bits. The Pentium has multiple caches of storage totaling as much as 2 MB, compared to the 8 KB of the Intel 486.

Improvements in processor speeds allow the components to get data in and out of the chip more quickly. The processor does not become idle waiting for data or instructions. This enables the software to run faster. These components need to handle the flow of information through the processor, interpret instructions so that the processor can execute them, and send the results back to the PC memory. The manufacturer's website, http://www.intel.com, provides more details about the Pentium family of processors.

AMD Processors

The best-performing AMD processors are the Athlon, Athlon XP, Thunderbird, and Duron series. These processors, along with the Intel Pentium IIIs, are currently the most used microprocessors in high-end desktop systems, workstations, and servers. The AMD Athlon processor system bus is designed for scalable multiprocessing. The number of AMD Athlon processors that are possible in a multiprocessor system is determined by chipset implementation. The manufacturer's website, http://www.amd.com, provides more details about the AMD family of processors.

Processor Speed Rating

CPU descriptions such as Pentium 133, Pentium 166, or Pentium 200 are well known. These numbers are specifications that indicate the maximum operating speed at which the CPU can reliably execute instructions. The CPU speed is controlled by an external clock that is located on the motherboard, not the microprocessor. The speed of the processor, determined by the frequency of the clock signal, is typically expressed in megahertz (MHz). The higher the number, the faster the processor. Processor speeds are getting faster all the time. Processors with speeds of 3.0 GHz (3000 MHz) are currently available.

The CPU can run at a much higher speed than the other chips on the motherboard. Therefore, the CPU speed and the frequency of the clock signal are not always at a one-to-one ratio. A variable-frequency synthesizer circuit that is built into the motherboard circuit multiplies the clock signal so that the motherboard can support several speeds of CPUs. The following three factors generally determine how much information can be processed at any given time:

- Size of the internal bus
- Size of the address bus
- Processor speed ratings

BIOS ROM

Read-only memory (ROM) chips are located on the motherboard. ROM chips contain instructions that can be directly accessed by the microprocessor. Unlike RAM, ROM chips retain their contents even when the computer is powered down. The contents cannot be erased or changed by normal means. Data transfer from ROM is slower than from RAM but faster than from any disk. Some examples of ROM chips that can be found on the motherboard include BIOS ROM, *electrically erasable programmable read-only memory (EEPROM)*, *erasable programmable read-only memory (EPROM)*, and Flash ROM.

Basic Input/Output System (BIOS)

The BIOS contains the instructions and data in the ROM chip that control the boot process and the computer hardware. The BIOS is sometimes called *firmware*. The ROM chip that contains the firmware is called the ROM BIOS chip, ROM BIOS, or simply BIOS. This chip is usually marked BIOS on the motherboard. The system BIOS is a critical part of the computer. If the CPU is considered the brains of the computer, the system BIOS is considered the heart of the system. The BIOS determines what hard drive the user has installed, whether a 3-1/2-inch floppy drive exists, what kind of memory is installed, and many other important parts of the system hardware at startup. The responsibility of the BIOS is to serve as a liaison between the computer operating software and the various hardware components that support it. These responsibilities include the following:

- Hosting the setup program for the hardware
- Testing the system during the POST
- Controlling all aspects of the boot process
- Producing audio and video error codes when a problem occurs during the POST
- Providing the computer with basic instructions to control devices in the system
- Locating and executing BIOS codes on expansion cards
- Locating a volume or boot sector from any drive to start the operating system
- Ensuring hardware and system compatibility

The BIOS is easy to locate because it is larger than most other chips. It often has a shiny plastic label that contains the manufacturer's name, the serial number of the chip, and the date that the chip was manufactured. This information is vital when selecting an upgrade for the chip. The unique role that the BIOS plays in the computer functionality is described in Chapter 3.

EPROM, EEPROM, and Flash ROM

ROM is the most common way to store system-level programs that must be available to the PC at all times. The most common example is the system BIOS program. This program is stored in a ROM chip called the system BIOS ROM. Having this program in a permanent ROM chip means that it is available when the power is turned on. Therefore, the PC can use it to boot the system.

EPROM and EEPROM are ROM chips that can be erased and reprogrammed. EPROM is a special type of programmable read-only memory (PROM) that can be erased by shining ultraviolet light through a clear window on the top of the chip. Because the ROM chip holds the instructions that enable a device to function properly, it sometimes must be reprogrammed or replaced when upgraded device instructions are required. Unlike EPROM, EEPROM chips are erased using a higher-than-normal electric voltage instead of with ultraviolet light. When the system BIOS is contained on an EEPROM chip, it can be upgraded by running special instructions.

Flash ROMs are special EEPROM chips that have been developed as a result of advancements in EEPROM technology. Toshiba created the term for the ability of the chip to be erased in a flash, or very quickly. *Flash ROM* holds the BIOS in most new systems. It can be reprogrammed under special software control. Upgrading a BIOS by running special software is known as *flashing*. The BIOS that is implemented on a flash memory chip currently supports Plug and Play devices. These chips retain data when the computer is powered off so that information is permanently stored. Flash memory is less expensive and denser than EEPROM chip technology.

Lab 2.3.8 Identifying ROM and BIOS Chips

In this lab exercise, you learn to locate and identify the ROM chip, BIOS chip, and BIOS manufacturer on a motherboard.

Worksheet 2.3.8 BIOS/ROM

Define BIOS, and know the difference between RAM and ROM.

Expansion Slots

Expansion slots are receptacles on the computer motherboard that accept printed circuit boards. All computers have expansion slots, which allow devices to be added. Devices include video cards, I/O cards, and sound cards.

Several types of expansion slots are found on a motherboard. The number and type of expansion slots in the computer determine the possibilities of future expansion. Figure 2-11 shows the different slot types.

Figure 2-11 Expansion Slot Types

Table 2-10 summarizes the different slots. The most common expansion slots are the ISA, PCI, and AGP slots.

Table 2-10 Expansion Slots

Slot Type	Speed	Data Bits	Use
ISA	8 MHz	8-bit, 16-bit	Modems, 8-bit expansion cards.
MCA	10 MHz	16-bit and 32-bit	This bus is now obsolete.
EISA	8 MHz	32-bit, but able to support 8-bit and 16-bit	Specialty roles; mostly obsolete and being replaced by PCI slots in new systems.
VESA	33 MHz	32-bit	Once used for faster video performance than the ISA bus, this bus has since become obsolete.
PCI	33 MHz	32-bit, 64-bit	Audio and video cards, networking cards, modems, SCSI adapters and more. Not for use with serial or parallel ports.
AGP	66 MHz	32-bit	Video adapter only.

The *Industry Standard Architecture (ISA)* is a 16-bit expansion slot that was developed by IBM. It transfers data with the motherboard at 8 MHz. ISA slots are becoming obsolete and are being replaced by PCI slots in new systems. However, many motherboard manufacturers still include one or two ISA slots for backward compatibility with older expansion cards. In 1987, IBM introduced the 32-bit, Extended ISA (EISA) bus, which accommodates the Pentium chip. EISA became fairly popular in the PC market.

The *Peripheral Component Interconnect (PCI)* is a 32-bit local bus slot that was developed by Intel. PCI also supports a 64-bit local bus slot. Because they communicate with the motherboard at 33 MHz, PCI bus slots offer a significant improvement over ISA or EISA expansion slots. With the PCI bus, each add-on card contains information that the processor uses to automatically configure the card. The PCI bus is one of the three components necessary for Plug and Play compatibility. The main purpose of the PCI bus is to allow direct access to the CPU for devices such as memory and video. PCI expansion slots are the most commonly used type in current motherboards.

The *Accelerated Graphics Port (AGP)* was developed by Intel. AGP is a dedicated high-speed bus that supports the high demands of graphical software. It is also *backward compatible*. This slot, reserved for video adapters, is the standard graphics port in all new systems. On AGP-equipped motherboards, a single AGP slot holds the display adapter, and the PCI slot can be used for another device. Slightly shorter than the white PCI slot, the AGP slot is usually a different color and is located about an inch beyond the PCI slot. AGP 2.0 currently defines an interface that supports 1x and 2x speeds at 3.3V, and 1x, 2x, and 4x speeds at 1.5V signaling. AGP 3.0 is the latest specification that defines the new signaling scheme for 4x and 8x speeds at 0.8V signaling levels. AGP 3.0 delivers over 2.1 GBps of bandwidth to support graphic-intensive applications, including digital photos and video. A summary of the different AGP modes, with the clock rate and transfer rate, is shown in Table 2-11.

Table 2-11 AGP Modes

AGP Mode	Approximate Clock Rate (MHz)	Transfer Rate (MBps)
1x	66	266
2x	133	533
4x	266	1066
8x	533	2133

Lab 2.3.9   Identifying Computer Expansion Slots

In this lab exercise, you learn to identify safety issues, specifications, and components that relate to expansion slots. You should also be able to list the advantages and disadvantages of each expansion slot.

 Worksheet 2.3.9   Expansion Slots

Review the information that you have learned regarding expansion slots.

Riser Cards

A *riser card*, shown in Figure 2-12, is used when a computer is fully loaded. It physically extends a slot so that a chip or card can be plugged in. In low-profile, space-saving cases, cards are plugged into riser cards that reside parallel with the motherboard.

Figure 2-12 Riser Card

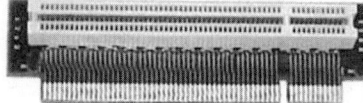

Audio/Modem Riser (AMR)

An *Audio/Modem Riser (AMR)*, shown in Figure 2-13, is a plug-in card for an Intel motherboard. It contains audio or modem circuits. Intel specifies a 46-pin edge connector to provide the digital interface between the card and the motherboard. The AMR contains all the analog functions, or codecs, that are required for audio or modem operation.

Figure 2-13 AMR Slot

The AMR evolved into the *Communications and Networking Riser (CNR)* card, which added LAN and home networking functions. The CNR slot is shown in Figure 2-14. The CNR is a 30-pin interface that accommodates two formats, making various audio/modem and audio/network combinations possible.

Figure 2-14 CNR Slot

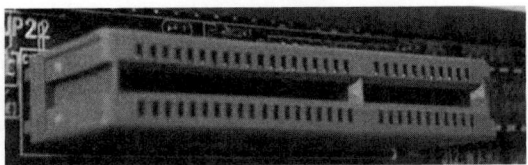

The ***Mobile Daughter Card (MDC)*** is the equivalent of the AMR for laptop computers.

Bus Types

The basic components of the computer are connected by communication paths, called ***buses***. The ***system bus*** is a parallel collection of conductors that carry data and control signals from one component to the other. Recall that the conductors in modern computers are metallic traces on the circuit board.

The three major system bus types can be identified based on the type of information that they carry. These include the address bus, data bus, and control bus.

Address Bus

The ***address bus*** is a unidirectional pathway. *Unidirectional* means that information can only flow one way. The function of the pathway is to carry addresses that are generated by the CPU to the memory and I/O elements of the computer. The number of conductors in the bus determines the size of the address bus. The size of the address bus determines the number of memory locations and I/O elements that the microprocessor can address.

Data Bus

The ***data bus*** is a bidirectional pathway for data flow. *Bidirectional* means that information can flow in two directions. Data can flow along the data bus from the CPU to memory during a write operation, and data can move from the computer memory to the CPU during a read operation. However, should two devices attempt to use the bus at the same time, data errors will occur. Any device that is connected to the data bus must have the capability to temporarily place its output on hold when it is not involved in an operation with the processor. This is also called a *floating state.* The data bus size, measured in bits, represents the computer word size. Generally, the larger the bus size, the faster the computer system. Common data bus sizes are 8 bits or 16 bits for older systems and 32 bits for new systems. Systems with 64-bit data buses are currently being developed.

Control Bus

The *control bus* carries the control and timing signals that are needed to coordinate the activities of the entire computer. Control bus signals are not necessarily related to each other, unlike data and address bus signals. Some are output signals from the CPU, and others are input signals to the CPU from I/O elements of the system. Every microprocessor type generates or responds to a different set of control signals. The most common control signals in use today are as follows:

- System clock (SYSCLK)
- Memory read (MEMR)
- Memory write (MEMW)
- Read/write line (R/W line)
- I/O read (IOR)
- I/O write (IOW)

Memory Components

Computer systems require memory to boot up, process data, and maintain system functions. This includes memory that is saved and memory that is volatile. This section includes the following topics:

- RAM
- SIMMs and DIMMs
- Cache/COASt memory

RAM

Random-access memory (RAM) is the place in a computer where the OS, application programs, and data in current use are kept so that they can be quickly reached by the processor. The *cache* (pronounced *cash*) is a data storage area that provides high-speed access for the system. Because most programs access the same data or instructions repeatedly, memory cache on high-speed static RAM (SRAM) is used. *COASt*, which stands for "cache on a stick," provides cache memory on many Pentium-based systems.

RAM is considered temporary or volatile memory. The contents of RAM are lost when the computer power is turned off. RAM chips on the computer motherboard hold the data and programs that the microprocessor is processing. RAM is memory that stores frequently used data for rapid retrieval by the processor. The amount and type of memory in the system can make a big difference in the system's performance. Some programs have more memory

TIP

Know the definition of volatile memory.

requirements than others. Older computers running Windows 95 or 98 would have 64 MB RAM installed. Considered to be the minimum required amount of RAM, 64 MB would severely limit the performance of a computer system. Modern computers have at least 128 MB or 256 MB RAM, especially if they are running newer operating systems such as Windows 2000 or other network operating systems.

Two classes of RAM are commonly used today: *static RAM (SRAM)* and *dynamic RAM (DRAM)*.

SRAM is relatively more expensive, but it is fast and holds data when the power is turned off for a brief period of time. This is useful in circumstances such as an unexpected short loss of power. SRAM is used for cache memory. DRAM is inexpensive and somewhat slow. It requires an uninterrupted power supply to maintain the data. DRAM stores data in tiny capacitors that must be refreshed to maintain the data.

RAM can be installed on the motherboard, either as a permanent fixture or in the form of small chips. The chips are referred to as *single in-line memory modules (SIMMs)* or *dual in-line memory modules (DIMMs)*. SIMMs and DIMMs, as shown in Figures 2-15 and 2-16, are removable cards that can be replaced with larger or smaller increments of memory. Although having more memory installed on the computer is a good thing, most system boards have limitations on the amount and type of RAM that can be added or supported. Some systems can require that only SIMMs be used. Other systems can require that SIMMs be installed in matched sets of two or four modules at a time. In addition, some systems use only RAM with parity, whereas others use nonparity RAM. Parity RAM has error-checking capability built into the RAM chip to ensure data integrity. Nonparity RAM has no error-checking capability.

Figure 2-15 72-Pin SIMM

SIMMs and DIMMs

A SIMM plugs into the motherboard with a 72-pin or 30-pin connector. The pins connect to the system bus, creating an electronic path through which memory data can flow to and from other system components. Two 72-pin SIMMs can be installed in a computer that supports 64-bit data flow. With a SIMM board, the pins on opposite sides of the module board are connected to each other, forming a single row of contacts.

Figure 2-16 168-Pin DIMM

A DIMM plugs into the system memory bank using a 168-pin connector. The pins establish a connection with the system bus, creating an electronic path through which data can flow between the memory chip and other system components. A single 168-pin DIMM supports 64-bit data flow for nonparity, and 72-bit data flow for parity. This configuration is now being used in the latest generation of 64-bit systems.

Another DIMM that should be mentioned is the small-outline DIMM (SO DIMM). A SO DIMM can have 72 pins, which can support 32-bit transfers, or 144 pins, which in turn support a full 64-bit transfer. SO DIMMs are used in laptop computers.

Newer or more specialized forms of RAM are frequently brought to market. *Random-access memory digital-to-analog converter (RAMDAC)* is a specialized form of memory that converts digitally encoded images into analog signals for display. The RAMDAC chip is made up of an SRAM component for storing the color map and three digital-to-analog converters (DACs), one each for the red-green-blue (RGB) electron guns. *Video RAM (VRAM)* and *Windows RAM (WRAM)* are currently the best memory types for video. Both VRAM and WRAM are optimized for video cards and are designed to be dual-ported. This means that the chipset processor and RAMDAC chip can access the memory at the same time. Simultaneous access greatly increases video throughput. The newest types of video cards also support the newest system RAM types, such as synchronous DRAM (SDRAM).

Most other types of RAM, such as Extended Data Out (EDO) RAM and Fast Page Mode (FPM) RAM, are too slow for current computing standards. They are no longer used in new computers. Table 2-12 provides a summary of the different types of RAM.

Table 2-12 RAM Types, Usages, and Capabilities

Type	Usage	Capabilities	Notes
SRAM (static RAM)	L1 and L2 cache	Very fast; does not need to be refreshed.	Very large, very expensive.
DRAM (dynamic RAM)	Main memory, expansion cards	Smaller and less expensive than SRAM.	More complicated and slower than SRAM, this memory is considered outdated.
FPM RAM (Fast Page Mode RAM)	Main memory, video memory	Does not need a row and column for each access; does not require special support.	Slowest type of memory in modern PCs. This memory type is also considered outdated.
EDO RAM (Extended Data Out RAM)	Main memory, video memory	One access to the memory can begin before the last one has ended.	Does not work well at 75 MHz and beyond; same cost as FPM RAM.
SDRAM (synchronous DRAM)	Main memory, video memory	Synchronized with the system clock and can read/write in burst mode at speeds of 100 MHz and higher.	Supports internal interleaving, allowing one access to begin halfway through a previous one.
DDR SDRAM (double data rate synchronous DRAM)	Main memory, video memory	Doubles bandwidth by transferring data twice per clock cycle.	More expensive than SDRAM.
DRDRAM (direct Rambus DRAM)	Main memory, video memory	Based on a high-speed 16-bit bus with a clock rate of 400 MHz.	Proprietary to Intel and Rambus.
SLDRAM (synchronous link DRAM)	Main memory, video memory	Uses a 64-bit bus running at 200 MHz clock speed transferring data twice on each cycle.	Open standard.

Lab 2.4.2   Identifying RAM and RAM Sockets

In this lab exercise, you learn to identify the various types of random-access memory (RAM) and RAM sockets.

Worksheet 2.4.2   Identifying RAM and RAM Sockets

Review the information that you learned regarding random-access memory (RAM) and RAM sockets.

Cache/COASt Memory

Cache is a specialized form of computer chip, or firmware, and it is designed to enhance memory performance. Cache memory stores frequently used information and transfers it to the processor much faster than RAM does. Most computers have two separate memory cache levels, as follows:

- L1 cache, located on the CPU
- L2 cache, located between the CPU and DRAM

L1 cache is faster than L2 cache, because L1 cache is located on the CPU and does not have to access the main memory on the motherboard. The L1 cache is the first place that the CPU looks for its data. If data is not found in the L1 cache, the search continues to the L2 cache and then on to main memory.

L1 cache and L2 cache are made up of SRAM chips. However, some systems use COASt modules. COASt modules provide cache memory on many Pentium-based systems. Noted for its reliability and speed, the COASt module uses the pipeline-burst cache. The pipeline-burst cache is significantly faster than SRAM cache. Some systems offer both SRAM sockets and a COASt module socket. The COASt module resembles a SIMM, except the COASt module is taller and has a different connector. A COASt module is shown in Figure 2-17.

Figure 2-17 COASt Module

Display Components

Text, graphics, and other types of output are viewed on a monitor. The interface between the computer and the monitor is the video card. This section includes the following topics:

- Monitors/display devices
- Video cards

Monitors/Display Devices

Computers are usually connected to a display device, also called a *monitor*. A monitor is a display device that works with the installed video card to present output from a computer. The clarity of a CRT monitor is based on several characteristics, which are described in a list later in this section.

A monitor is shown in Figure 2-18. Monitors are available in different types and sizes and with various characteristics. When purchasing a new computer, you might have to purchase the monitor separately.

Figure 2-18 HP Monitor

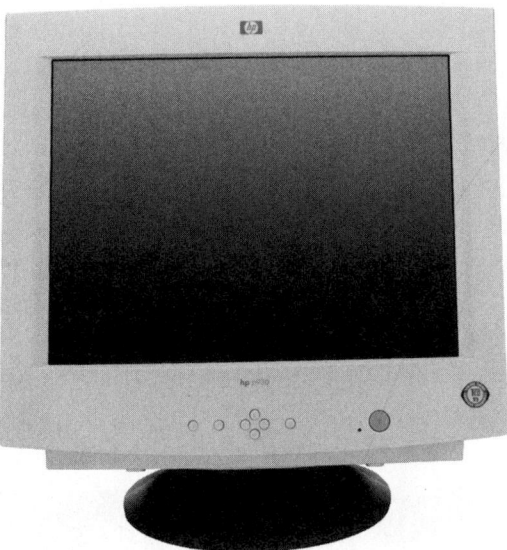

Understanding the characteristics of a good monitor can help you determine which monitor is best suited for a specific system. The following terms relate to monitors:

- **Pixels**—Picture elements. The screen image is made up of pixels, or tiny dots. The pixels are arranged in rows across the screen. Each pixel consists of three colors: red, green, and blue (RGB).

- **Dot pitch**—A measurement of how close each phosphor dot (pixel) is to its adjacent dot on the screen. The finer the dot pitch, the better the image quality. Most modern monitors have a 0.25-mm dot pitch. Some have a 0.22-mm dot pitch, which gives a fine resolution and excellent picture.

- **Refresh rate**—The rate at which the screen image is refreshed. Refresh rates are measured in hertz (Hz), which means times per second. The higher the refresh rate, the more steady the screen image. The screen image should look steady to the naked eye, but in reality, the image flickers every time the electron beam refreshes the phosphor-coated dots. Refresh rate is also called *vertical frequency* or *vertical refresh rate.*

- **Color depth**—The number of different colors, measured in bits, that each pixel can display. The higher the depth, the more colors that can be produced.

- **Video RAM (VRAM)**—The memory size of a video card. The more VRAM the video card has, the more colors the card can display. The video card also sends out the refresh signal, thus controlling the refresh rate.

- **Resolution**—Varies based on the number of pixels. The more pixels in the screen, the better the resolution. Better resolution means a sharper image. The lowest screen resolution on modern PCs is 640×480 pixels, which is called Video Graphics Array (VGA). Super Video Graphics Array (SVGA) and Extended Graphics Array (XGA) resolutions are now available, with up to 1600×1200 pixels, as shown in Table 2-13.

- **Monitor screen sizes**—Measured in inches. The most common sizes are 14-, 15-, 17-, 19-, and 21-inch screens, measured diagonally. The visible screen size is smaller than the measurement size because of the mask that surrounds the screen. Keep this in mind when shopping for a computer monitor.

- **Display colors**—These colors are created by varying the light intensity of the three basic colors. The 24- and 32-bit colors are the usual choice for graphics artists and professional photographers. For most other applications, a 16-bit color is sufficient. The following is a summary of the most common color depths:

  — **256 colors:** 8-bit color

  — **65,536 colors:** 16-bit color, also called 65K or High Color

  — **16 million colors:** 24-bit color, also called True Color

  — **4 billion colors:** 32-bit color, also called True Color

A high-quality monitor and a high-quality video card are required for both a high resolution and a high refresh rate.

Table 2-13 Summary of Monitor Characteristics by Type

Standard	Resolution (Pixels)	Number of Pixels	Screen Size (Inches)	Refresh Rate (Hertz)
VGA	640×480	307,200	14	60–72
SVGA	800×600	480,000	15, 17	75–85
SVGA	1024×768	786,432	17, 19	75–85
XGA	1152×864	995,328	17, 19, 21	75–85
XGA	1280×1024	1,310,720	19, 21	75–85
XGA	1600×1200	1,920,000	21	75–85

PhotoZoom Monitor

This PhotoZoom details the parts of a monitor.

Video Cards

The video card, shown in Figure 2-19, is the interface between the computer and the monitor. The video card tells the monitor which pixels to illuminate, what color the pixels should be, and how intense the color should be. The video card can be an expansion card installed into one of the motherboard expansion slots, or it can be built into the motherboard. The display capabilities of a computer depend on both the video adapter and the monitor. A monochrome monitor, for example, cannot display colors, regardless of how powerful the video adapter is. *Video memory* is a generic term that is used to refer to memory in the computer video system. Video memory is not the same as VRAM.

Figure 2-19 Typical Video Card

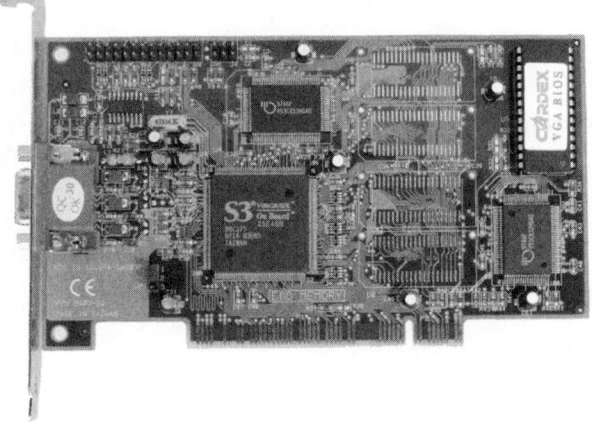

VRAM

Video RAM (VRAM) is a special type of memory that is used on video cards. Most modern video cards contain VRAM, which is a special form of DRAM that has two separate data ports. One port is dedicated to updating the image that is viewed on the computer screen. The other port is used to change the image data that is stored on the video card. The VRAM stores displays so that the computer RAM does not have to. A 64-bit AGP video card with 4 MB RAM should be sufficient for most computers. However, more graphics intensive games might perform better with a video card having 32 MB or more VRAM. Some video cards even include a graphics coprocessor for performing graphics calculations. These adapters are referred to as graphics accelerators. A newer form of VRAM is Windows RAM (WRAM).

Accelerated Graphics Port

The Accelerated Graphics Port (AGP), as discussed earlier, is an expansion slot on the Pentium II motherboard that is available for installing a video card. The AGP is designed exclusively for video cards. An AGP card allows games and 3D applications to store and retrieve more realistic textures in system memory rather than video memory, without incurring performance problems. A significant advantage of the AGP is that the PCI bus is relieved of handling graphics data. Therefore, the PCI slot can concentrate on other demanding duties. The AGP also doubles the PCI bus's transfer speed.

Video adapters are also known as video cards, video boards, and video display boards. At a minimum, a video card should be a PCI adapter with at least 4 MB RAM, depending on the type of graphics that will be run.

PhotoZoom   Video Card

Identify the video card by the markings on the card.

Lab 2.5.2   Video Card Identification

In this lab, you identify the video card by any markings on the card. These markings can include a manufacturer's name or part number. Some cards are identified only by their physical layout.

Worksheet 2.5.2 Video Cards

Review the terms that relate to video cards.

Connector Components

External computer components are connected to the computer with specific cables to specific ports. The type of interface that you use depends on the type of device that you are connecting. This section includes the following topics:

- Serial and parallel ports
- PS/2 (6-pin mini-DIN) ports and 5-pin DIN ports
- Universal serial bus ports and FireWire buses
- IDE, EIDE, Ultra, and SCSI controllers
- SCSI disk types

Serial and Parallel Ports

An I/O port is a pathway into and out of the computer through a connector that is typically on the back of the computer. Newer cases have added ports, usually for USB devices and headphones, on the front of the case. All peripheral devices that connect to the computer use I/O ports. Different types of I/O ports on the computer serve different purposes. This section explores the various types of ports and the types of devices that use them to interface with the computer.

Serial Ports

A *serial port* connects devices that use a serial interface. Devices such as a modem, scanner, and mouse use a serial interface. Generally, a PC can identify up to four serial ports. A typical computer contains only two serial ports, referred to as COM1 and COM2. Serial ports are sometimes called the RS-232 ports, because they use the RS-232C standard as defined by the Electronics Industry Association (EIA). A serial port transmits data bits one after the other (serially) over a single line. Figure 2-20 shows a DB-9 (9-pin) connector that is used on most new computers for the serial ports. Older printers use a larger, 25-pin connector for the serial port interface, as shown in Figure 2-21. The mouse is sometimes used in serial port 1, which is a 9-pin male connector. The modem is typically used in serial port 2, which is also a 9-pin male connector. Both serial ports are located in the back of the computer system.

Figure 2-20 9-Pin Male Serial Connector

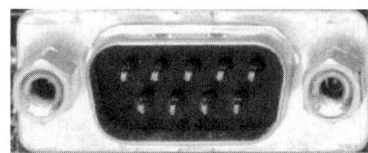

Figure 2-21 25-Pin Male Serial Connector

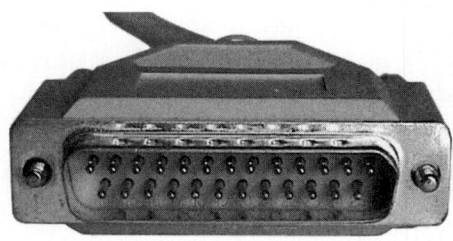

Parallel Ports

A *parallel port* is a socket on the computer that connects newer printers or other peripheral devices such as a portable hard disk, tape backup, scanner, or CD-ROM drive. The parallel port contains eight lines for transmitting an entire byte (8 bits) across the eight data lines simultaneously. The parallel port interface offers 8-bit parallel data transfer and nine I/O control lines at a DB-25 socket, or 25-pin female connector. A DB-25 socket can be found on the back of the computer. Figure 2-22 shows a female DB-25 parallel port. Figure 2-23 shows the Centronics 36-pin female parallel port that is typically found on a printer. Parallel ports can be configured as LPT1, LPT2, or LPT3.

Figure 2-22 DB-25 Female Parallel Port

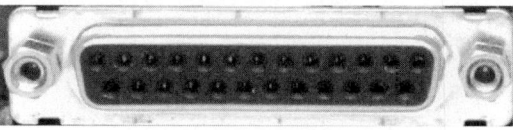

Figure 2-23 Centronics 36-Pin Female Parallel Port

Parallel ports were originally used for printers. However, they are currently used for both data input and output devices. This type of parallel port is called a bidirectional port. A parallel port is often used for the rapid transmission of data over short distances. The newer, enhanced parallel ports can be converted from unidirectional to bidirectional through the CMOS setup screen. In older PCs, the parallel printer interface was located on the back of the video adapter card, on a multiple I/O card, or on a dedicated parallel printer card.

Today, on Pentium system boards, the parallel port is located directly on the back plate of an I/O card or is connected through a ribbon cable to the 25-pin connector on the back of the unit. Avoid using a parallel cable longer than 15 feet when connecting an external device such as a printer to the computer parallel port. A shorter cable reduces the chance for errors and ensures data integrity.

PS/2 (6-Pin Mini-DIN) Ports and 5-Pin DIN Ports

PS/2 keyboard or PS/2 mouse ports connect the PC to its keyboard and mouse. Although both ports look identical, the mouse and keyboard ports are not interchangeable. Both ports are usually color-coded or labeled to avoid confusion, as shown in Figure 2-24. The cable that connects the PS/2 keyboard or mouse uses a PS/2-type connector. The PS/2, or 6-pin mini-DIN, connector has become popular since its introduction by IBM in 1987 with the IBM PS/2 computer. However, the 5-pin DIN XT/AT connector–type ports and serial mice are still common. The 5-pin DIN AT connectors typically connect the AT keyboard directly to the motherboard. One advantage of the PS/2 port is that a mouse can be connected to the computer without using a serial port.

Figure 2-24 PS/2 Keyboard and Mouse Ports

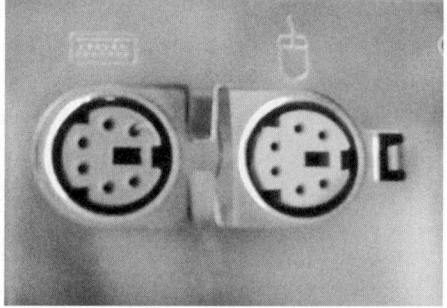

Universal Serial Bus Ports and FireWire Buses

Newer types of interfaces include the universal serial bus (USB) port and the FireWire bus. USB ports are used for low-speed peripherals such as the keyboard, the mouse, a joystick, a scanner, a printer, and telephony devices. FireWire is also known as the IEEE 1394 standard. This high-speed serial bus, developed by Apple and Texas Instruments, is widely used for downloading video from digital camcorders to the computer.

USB Ports

The ***universal serial bus (USB)***, shown in Figure 2-25, is an external port that allows the user to connect up to 127 external PC devices. These peripherals include the following:

- Keyboards
- Mice
- Printers
- Modems
- Scanners
- Digital cameras
- Digital video cameras
- External disk drives

Figure 2-25 USB Port/Connector

USB is an emerging technology. It offers a data transfer rate of up to 12 Mbps. The latest version, USB 2.0, is much faster than version 1.0 and transfers data at a rate of up to 480 Mbps. Seven USB devices can typically be connected directly to the computer using the standard USB 4-pin connector. By using external hubs, each of the seven devices can be connected to the others, creating a daisy chain of up to 127 devices. An external hub is a networking device that is discussed further in a later chapter. USB devices can be hot-plugged. This means that they can be attached while the computer is powered up and running. USB devices are also Plug and Play compatible.

USB 2.0 supports three modes: low-speed (1.5 Mbps), full-speed (12 Mbps), and high-speed (480 Mbps). USB 2.0 is also backward compatible with the USB 1.0 standard.

A USB cable serving a full-speed device has a length limit of 16 feet, 5 inches. The length limit for cables that are used between low-speed USB devices is 9 feet, 10 inches.

USB, introduced in the late 1990s, was not supported by Microsoft Windows 95 and NT 4.0. Support for USB is one reason that Windows 98 or 2000 is a preferred operating system. This port might eventually replace all ports except the VGA port. Most PC USB peripherals can also be used on a Macintosh. However, some devices lack the necessary drivers.

FireWire Port

FireWire is a high-speed, platform-independent communication bus. The FireWire bus interconnects digital devices such as digital video cameras, printers, scanners, digital cameras, and hard drives. FireWire is shown in Figure 2-26. It is also known as IEEE 1394. Developed by Apple, FireWire was designed to allow peripherals to seamlessly plug into a computer. The i.LINK communication bus is a type of FireWire developed by Sony. The benefits of FireWire include the following:

- Compatible, smaller connectors
- Hot-plug connection
- Shared memory
- A single connection
- Backward compatibility
- Speed

Figure 2-26 FireWire 6-Pin Cable and Connector

FireWire can support up to 63 devices using cable lengths up to 14 feet, the length limit for cabling. Like USB peripherals, FireWire devices can be hot-plugged.

FireWire is based on a shared memory model that allows devices to directly access locations in memory. This prevents having to wait for information to flow in a stream. FireWire is much faster than the original version of USB, transferring data at rates up to 400 Mbps.

e-Lab Activity   Identifying Input and Output Devices

Identify by name and usage the I/O ports that are listed in the e-Lab.

IDE, EIDE, Ultra, and SCSI Controllers

IDE, EIDE, Ultra, and SCSI refer to an interface between the computer and hardware such as hard disks, CD-ROM drives, and tape drives. The controller that is used depends on the type of motherboard and hardware that is installed. You should understand the difference between the versions of ATA interfaces.

IDE Controllers

Integrated Drive Electronics (IDE) is a type of hardware interface that connects hard disks, CD-ROM drives, and tape drives to a PC. IDE is popular because it is an economical way to connect peripherals. Currently, hard drives ranging from 20 GB to 120 GB are common; these units cost less than half a cent per megabyte.

The IDE interface is officially known as the AT Attachment (ATA) specification. The ATA Packet Interface (ATAPI) defines the IDE standard for CD-ROM drives and tape drives. ATA-2 (Fast ATA) defined the faster transfer rates that are used in Enhanced IDE. ATA-3 added interface improvements, including the ability to report potential problems.

With IDE, the controller electronics are built into the drive itself, requiring a simple circuit in the PC for connection. IDE drives were attached to earlier PCs using an IDE host adapter card. Currently, two Enhanced IDE (EIDE) sockets are built into the motherboard. Each socket connects to two devices through a 40-pin ribbon cable. Starting with ATA-66 drives, the cable uses 80 wires and 39 pins. It plugs into the same socket with one pin removed.

IDE drives use Programmed Input/Output (PIO) mode for data transfer. This mode uses the registers of the CPU for data transfer. This is in contrast with direct memory access (DMA), which transfers data directly between main memory and the peripheral device.

EIDE Controllers

Enhanced Integrated Drive Electronics (EIDE), also called the ATA-2 disk drive, is an enhanced version of the standard IDE interface. The EIDE interface can handle up to 8.4 GB, more than the 528 MB that the IDE interface can support. The IDE interface can support only two drives. EIDE can support up to four devices using two IDE cables that have 40 pins and a maximum length of 18 inches. In addition, EIDE supports nondisk peripherals that follow the ATAPI protocol. The EIDE interface is often described as an AT Attachment Packet Interface (ATAPI) or a Fast AT Attachment (Fast ATA) interface. ATAPI is the protocol that is used by Enhanced IDE devices such as EIDE CD-ROM drives and EIDE external tape backup drives.

The EIDE/ATA-2 specification, developed in 1994, was subsequently modified to final form in 1995. The EIDE/ATA-2 specification covers the interface signals on the 18-inch, 40-pin cable connector; the drive commands that are issued by the BIOS; the cable specifications; and the drive configuration circuitry. ATA-3 added interface improvements, including the ability to report potential problems.

Each disk drive that is attached to an IDE/ATA, EIDE/ATA-2, or EIDE/ATA-3 disk controller must have a jumper set on the back of the disk drive. The jumper setting specifies the role that one disk performs in relationship to the other disk on the same channel. A single IDE or EIDE disk is usually set to the master role. A second IDE or EIDE disk attached to the same channel must be set to the slave role. The disk hardware on the master disk drive controls both the master and slave disk drives.

An option called **Cable Select (CSEL)** allows the IDE adapter to select which IDE or EIDE disk drive will function as master and which IDE or EIDE disk drive will function as slave. If both IDE and EIDE disk drives are on a single channel and both are set to master, the disk subsystem will not work. The same is true if both are set to slave. The drive must be jumpered for Cable Select, and the IDE cable must support this feature for it to work.

Read your drive documentation carefully, because industry standards do not apply to the jumper settings for IDE or EIDE disk drives.

Beginning with the ATA-4 controllers, either the word "Ultra" or the transfer rate was added to the name in various combinations. For example, at 33 MBps, terms such as Ultra ATA, Ultra DMA, UDMA, ATA-33, DMA-33, Ultra ATA-33, and Ultra DMA-33 have all been used.

Ultra ATA Disk Drives

Ultra ATA disk drives are typically much faster than the older ATA and ATA-2 disk drives. These Ultra disk drives are installed and configured the same way that ATA-2 disk drives are configured: master, slave, or CSEL. However, the faster versions, ATA-66 and ATA-100, require the use of a special ribbon cable to connect the disk drives to the ATA adapter. This special cable contains 80 conductors. However, the cable still uses the same 40-pin connectors that were used by earlier ATA disk drives. Failure to use these special cables for these high-speed disks can result in disk system problems and possible data loss.

Sector translation and continuous technological improvements have allowed hard drives to grow larger in size.

SCSI Controllers

The *Small Computer System Interface (SCSI)* controller was developed in 1979 at Shugart Associates Standard Interface (SASI). Like EIDE peripherals, SCSI (pronounced *scuzzy*) devices have the controlling electronics on each of the drives. However, SCSI is a more advanced interface controller than ATA-2/EIDE. It is ideal for high-end computers, including network servers.

SCSI devices are typically connected in a series, forming a chain that is commonly referred to as a *daisy chain.* The daisy chain is shown in Figure 2-27. The SCSI devices at either end of the daisy chain must be terminated when using an external cable. The other devices do not need to be terminated.

Figure 2-27 Internal and External Daisy Chain

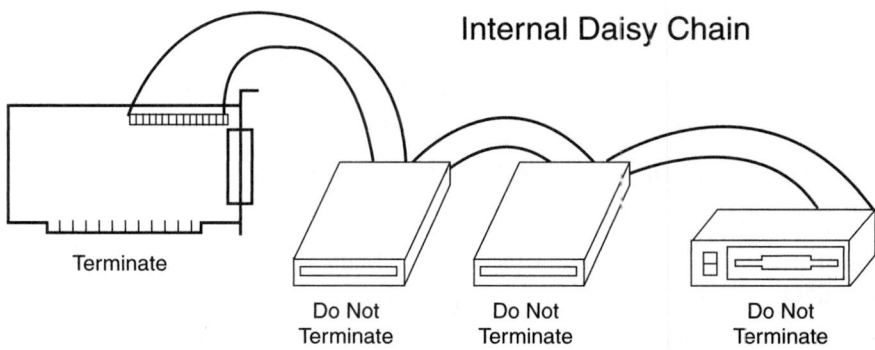

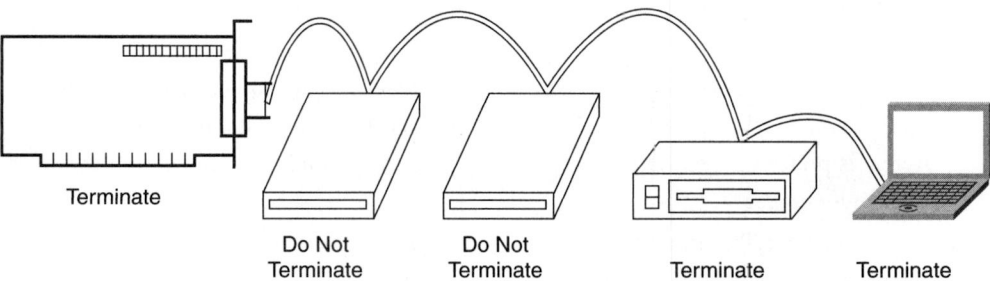

When you are using only an internal cable, the adapter card and the device at the end of the cable need to be terminated. Do not terminate any of the devices in between.

If you are using both an internal and an external cable, the two devices that are located at the end of each cable must be terminated. Do not terminate the rest of the devices, including the adapter or controller card.

Each end of the SCSI bus must be terminated. The SCSI controller is generally on one end of the SCSI bus and usually has onboard termination. The other end of the SCSI cable is terminated either by a resistor on the last disk drive on the chain or by a physical terminator on the end of the SCSI bus.

SCSI ID Numbers

The SCSI bus identifies each device by a SCSI ID number. Most SCSI buses can handle a total of seven devices and one SCSI controller per channel. The channels are numbered from 0 through 7. Some versions of SCSI support a total of 15 devices and 1 SCSI controller per channel. These channels are numbered 0 through 15. Each device on a SCSI channel must have a unique SCSI ID. Devices can include hard drives, CD-ROM drives, tape drives, scanners, and removable drives. Each SCSI device in the chain, including the SCSI controller card, is given a SCSI ID number from 0 to 7. The number 0 is for the primary boot device, or hard drive. The number 7 is for the SCSI controller card.

Each device on a SCSI channel must have a unique SCSI ID. SCSI ID numbers do not have to be sequential. However, no two devices can have the same number.

SCSI ID numbers are generally set by jumpers on the SCSI disk drive. Duplication of the SCSI IDs on a SCSI channel can cause the channel to become inaccessible. If a user wants to be able to boot from a SCSI disk drive, the drive should be given a SCSI ID of 0 or 1.

SCSI Termination

The three types of SCSI termination are as follows:

- **Passive termination**—Controls the resistance at the ends of the SCSI bus by using resistor packs. It is cheap to implement but should be used only for lower-speed SCSI channels with short cables.

NOTE

Impedance is the opposition that an electronic component, circuit, or system offers to alternating or direct electric current. Impedance is calculated based on resistance and reactance.

- **Active termination**—Works to control the impedance at the ends of the SCSI bus by using a voltage regulator, not just the power that is supplied by the interface card. Active is preferred over passive termination, because it can handle much higher speeds and longer cables.

- **Forced Perfect Termination (FPT)**—This is the best method, although it is more complex than the others. FPT can compensate for variations in impedance caused by different cables, devices, and terminators that are used in high-speed SCSI systems. Although the costs to implement FPT are higher, it provides a more reliable system.

SCSI termination can be implemented in several ways. Both ends of the SCSI bus must be terminated, and the SCSI adapter must be on one end of the SCSI bus. Therefore, one termination point is on the SCSI adapter. This is usually done automatically. No additional changes to the SCSI adapter are needed for it to terminate the SCSI bus at that end. On the other end of the SCSI bus, the last disk drive on the SCSI channel must be terminated. This is usually done by a jumper on the disk drive or a special terminator that is inserted on the last connector on the SCSI cable. Low-voltage differential SCSI devices often do not have the capability to terminate the SCSI bus on the device. A special terminator that is inserted in the last connector on the SCSI cable must be used.

SCSI Disk Types

Three major versions of the SCSI standard are currently on the market: SCSI-1, SCSI-2, and SCSI-3. Installation of the three SCSI devices is similar. The differences are mainly in the size of the SCSI connector that connects the SCSI disk drive to the SCSI cable.

Three signaling systems can be used by SCSI devices:

- Single-ended (SE)
- Differential (DIFF), also known as high-voltage differential (HVD)
- Low-voltage differential (LVD)

There is no difference in the connectors that are used among the three different signaling systems. A system of symbols has been devised to identify the different signaling systems that are used by SCSI controllers and drives. Figure 2-28 shows the SCSI symbols.

Figure 2-28 SCSI Symbols

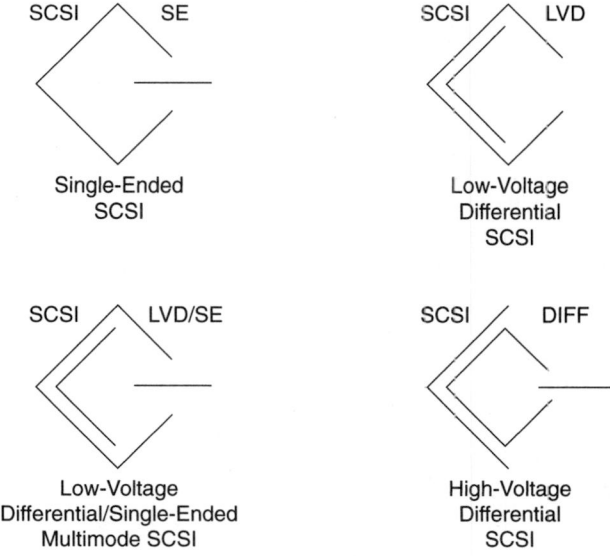

SCSI-1

SCSI-1, originally known just as SCSI, was used by many Apple computers in the early 1980s. By current standards, it was slow. The SCSI bus ran at 5 MHz using an 8-bit data path. This allowed a data transfer rate of 5 MBps. SCSI-1 generally supported a single channel per SCSI controller. The SCSI-1 internal cable was a ribbon cable that was attached to the disk controller by a 50-pin connector. Many early SCSI controllers used a DB-25, 25-pin connector for external SCSI devices. The termination for the SCSI-1 was usually a set of three resistors on the SCSI controller. Two other possible terminations were (a) a set of three resistors on the last SCSI disk drive on the bus or (b) an actual terminator that was attached to the end of the SCSI bus. The maximum cable length of SCSI-1 was 6 meters.

SCSI-2

SCSI-2 uses two different signaling systems. The systems are known as single-ended interface and differential interface. The two signaling systems are incompatible and cannot be mixed on the same SCSI bus. All devices, including the SCSI-2 controller, should use either the single-ended interface, or all should use the differential interface. Because of bus length restrictions, single-ended SCSI-2 cabling is usually found inside a server chassis. The differential interface allows longer cable lengths and is generally found connecting the server to an external SCSI device. SCSI-2 uses the same 50-pin connector on the internal SCSI cable that is used by SCSI-1 devices.

SCSI-2 also has a variant called Wide SCSI-2. Wide SCSI-2 can transfer 16 bits at a time, as opposed to the 8 bits that are used by normal SCSI-1 and normal SCSI-2. This extra bus width requires the use of a 68-pin connector. Wide SCSI-2 allows 16 devices on the SCSI-2 channel. Normal SCSI-2 and SCSI-1 only allow eight devices on the SCSI channel. Normal SCSI-2 is also called Narrow SCSI-2.

Another variant of SCSI-2 is Fast SCSI-2. Fast SCSI-2 doubles the bus speed from 5 MHz to 10 MHz. Fast SCSI-2 requires an active termination technique. Because of the increased speed, the maximum cable length is reduced from 6 meters to 3 meters. A Fast-Wide SCSI-2 implementation is also available. It requires 68-pin cables, active termination, and a short cable length (3 meters maximum). However, the Fast-Wide implementation can transfer data at 20 MBps. Narrow SCSI-2 uses 50-pin connectors on the internal SCSI-2 devices. Wide SCSI-2 uses 68-pin connectors on the internal SCSI-2 devices.

Figure 2-29 shows an example of a 50-, 68-, and 80-pin SCA connector. The Fast SCSI-2 and Fast-Wide SCSI-2 variants require active termination. Regular SCSI-2 and Wide SCSI-2 units can use passive termination, although active termination is preferred.

Figure 2-29 SCSI 50-, 68-, and 80-Pin Connectors

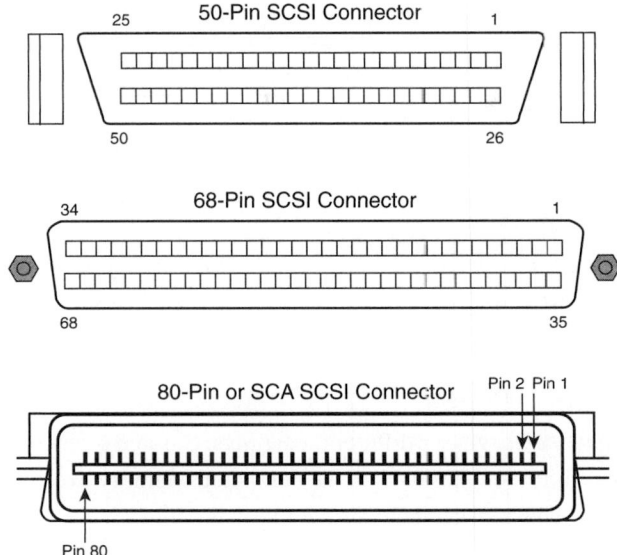

SCSI-3

SCSI-3 is the latest standard of the SCSI family. It combines all the best features of the previous SCSI standards. It uses LVD signaling and supports up to 15 devices on a single cable. The cable can be up to 12 meters long. SCSI-3 supports the following three bus speeds:

- **Ultra**—20 MHz
- **Ultra2**—40 MHz
- **Ultra3**—Double-clocked 40 MHz

Each of the three SCSI-3 bus speeds have both narrow (8-bit) and wide (16-bit) implementations.

Ultra SCSI-3 and Ultra2 SCSI-3 both use 50-pin connectors. The wide variants—Wide Ultra SCSI-3 and Wide Ultra2 SCSI-3—use 68-pin connectors. Ultra3 and Ultra160 SCSI-3 also use 68-pin connectors. All versions of SCSI-3 require active termination. Table 2-14 summarizes the maximum cable lengths for various types of SCSI.

SCSI-1, SCSI-2, and SCSI-3 disk drives can be mixed on the same SCSI channel, but the practice is not recommended. Mixing disk drives from the different SCSI versions can impact performance of the SCSI channel.

Table 2-14 Maximum SCSI Cable Lengths by Type

SCSI Type	Maximum Cable Length (Meters)
Standard	6
Fast	3
Wide Ultra	1.5
Low-voltage differential	12
Differential	25

Storage Components

The terms *storage* and *memory* have different meanings. Storage refers to where data (files, documents, graphics, and so on) is saved on the computer. Memory executes instructions and processes system data. This section includes the following topics:

- Floppy drive
- Hard drive
- CD-ROM drive
- DVD formats and drives
- Backup hardware

Floppy Drive

A *floppy disk drive (FDD)*, as shown in Figure 2-30, magnetically reads information from and writes information to floppy disks. Floppy disks, introduced in 1987, are a form of removable storage media. The 3-1/2-inch floppy disks that are currently in use have a hard plastic exterior shell that protects the thin, flexible disk inside, as shown in Figure 2-31. The main parts of a typical floppy disk include the floppy protective case, the thin magnetic flexible disk, a sliding door, and a sliding door spring.

Figure 2-30 Floppy Disk Drive

Figure 2-31 Typical Floppy Disk

An FDD is mounted inside the system unit and is only removed for repairs or upgrades. The floppy disk can be removed at the end of a computer working session. The main drawback to the floppy disk is that it only holds 1.44 MB of information. This is plenty of space for most text documents, such as MS Word and Excel files. However, for files containing rich graphical content, a floppy disk often has insufficient capacity.

PhotoZoom   Floppy Disk Drive

This PhotoZoom details the internal components of the floppy drive.

Worksheet 2.7.1   Floppy Drive Identification

This worksheet provides a review of the components of the floppy drive.

Hard Drive

This section provides an overview of the components, operations, interfaces, and specifications of the hard drive. The *hard disk drive (HDD)* is the main storage medium of the computer. An HDD, as shown in Figure 2-32, shares many physical and operational characteristics with the floppy disk drive. However, the HDD has the following advantages over an FDD:

- It has a more complex design and provides a greater access speed.
- It has a much larger storage capacity than the floppy drive, which is beneficial for long-term storage.
- It stores programs and files as well as the operating system.

Figure 2-32 Typical Hard Disk Drive

The HDD contains platters that are made from aluminum or glass. These inflexible platters can also be made from aluminum alloys, glass composites, and magnesium alloys. The inflexibility led to the name hard disk drive. The hard drive is typically not removable. This is why IBM often refers to hard disk drives as fixed disk drives. In short, a hard disk drive is a high-volume disk storage device with fixed, high-density, rigid media.

Figure 2-33 shows the following components, which are shared by all hard disk drives:

- Disk platters
- Read/write heads
- Head actuator assembly
- Spindle motor
- Logic/circuit board
- Bezel/faceplate
- Configuration jumpers
- Interface connectors

Disk platters, as shown in Figure 2-34, are the media on which data is stored in the hard disk drive. Hard disk drives typically have two to ten platters, which have the following characteristics:

- They are usually either 2-1/2 inches or 3-1/2 inches in diameter and are typically constructed of aluminum or a glass-ceramic composite material.
- They are coated with a thin-film media that is magnetically sensitive.
- They are double-sided, with the magnetically sensitive media on each side.
- They are stacked, with spaces between them, on a hub that holds them in position, separate from one another.

The hub is also called the spindle. Newer hard drives are manufactured with single platters that can hold up to 30 GB of data.

Figure 2-33 Hard Disk Drive Components

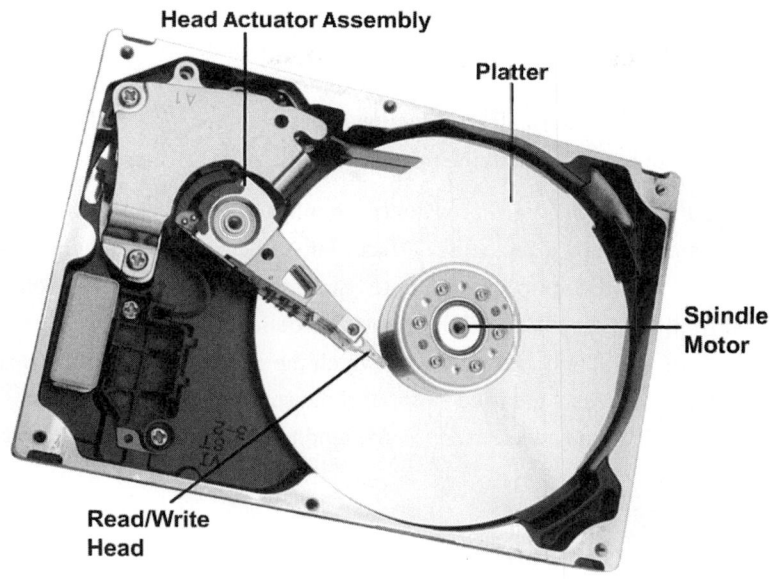

Figure 2-34 Hard Disk Drive Platters

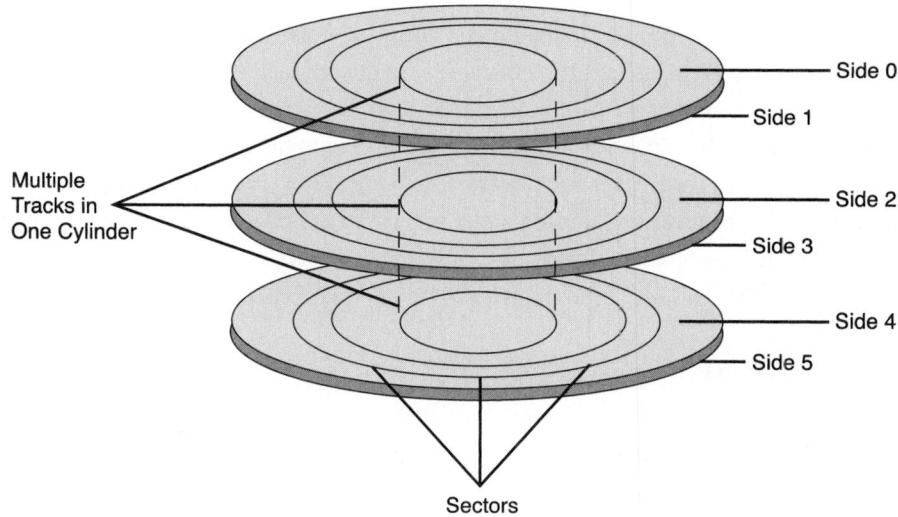

NOTE

Users should never open a hard disk drive to attempt to repair it because the hard disk is contained in an extremely clean environment. The disks are sealed in a protective housing and should never be opened to the atmosphere. Repairs are performed in special facilities called ultra-clean rooms. Even small particles, such as smoke, dust, and hair, have been removed from the air in ultra-clean rooms.

The disk platters require a read/write head for each side. The read/write head accesses the media. These heads are stacked, or ganged, on a carrier called a rack. Because the heads are mounted together, they move in unison across the platters with the rack. The heads are joined to the rack by arms. The arms extend from the head actuator assembly. The head itself is a U- or V-shaped device of electrically conductive material that is wrapped with wires. The wires cause the head to be sensitive to the magnetic media of the platters.

The read/write heads on floppy disk drives directly contact the media surface. Those of hard disk drives float a small distance above the surface. This is because the platters typically spin at speeds of 3600–15,000 revolutions per minute (rpm); most drives operate at either 5400, 7200, or 10,000 rpm. This speed causes air pressure to build between the platters and the read/write head. The central hub, or spindle, on which the platters are mounted is spun by a spindle motor. No belts or gears are used to connect the spindle motor to the hard disk platter spindle. Belts and gears are an added expense and tend to be noisy. They can also cause reliability problems.

How the Hard Drive Functions

The hard disk drive functions in much the same way as a floppy disk drive. The disk platters spin at a high speed while the drive heads access the media to conduct read or write operations. Understanding how the heads read and write the data structures on the platter media is critical to knowing how the drive functions.

The media on the drive platters is a layer of magnetically sensitive material. In general, modern hard disk drives use a film of a cobalt metal alloy that is laid down in several microthin layers. The magnetic particles in this media are randomly aligned when the disk is empty of data. However, as the read/write head writes to an area, the head causes the particles on that track to align in a specific direction. This is done according to the direction of electric current flow in the heads. This local magnetic direction in the media is referred to as a *flux*. The current in the head can be reversed, causing a flux reversal. Flux reversal is the opposite magnetic orientation in the media. As the platter spins, the head lays down a flux pattern along the length of a track. This pattern of flux transitions on the track represents the recorded data.

Evolution of the Hard Drives and Drive Capacity

Personal computers have at least one HDD installed inside the system unit. If more storage capacity is needed, another HDD can usually be added. The capacity of the HDD is a measure of how much information it can store. The capacity of an HDD is normally measured in megabytes or gigabytes. Older hard disks retained about 5 MB and used platters up to 12 inches in diameter. Current hard disks generally use 3-1/2-inch-diameter platters for desktop computers and 2-1/2-inch-diameter platters for notebooks. Modern hard disks can hold several gigabytes of data. A 2 gigabyte (GB) HDD, for example, can store close to 2,147,483,648 characters. With current applications and operating systems, 2 GB can be quickly consumed, leaving little space for data storage purposes.

Some of the older hard disk interfaces used a device-level interface. These hard disks had many problems with compatibility, data integrity, and speed. The original hard disk interface used in the IBM PC/XT was developed by Seagate Technologies. It was referred to as Modified Frequency Modulation (MFM). MFM used a magnetic disk encoding method with the ST-506 interface.

Run Length Limited (RLL) is an encoding scheme that is similar to MFM. RLL has a larger number of sectors than MFM. RLL is an encoding method that is commonly used on magnetic disks. The integrated disk controller within the drive determines which encoding scheme is used. The most common hard disk drive standards are currently IDE, EIDE, and SCSI.

PhotoZoom   Hard Drive

This PhotoZoom details the components of the hard drive.

Worksheet 2.7.2   Hard Drive Identification

This worksheet is a review of the hard drive components.

CD-ROM Drive

This section discusses CD-ROM drives and media. The technology behind the *compact disc (CD)* dates back to the late 1970s. In 1978, Sony and Phillips Corporation introduced the audio compact disc. Today's media and the basic design of the CD-ROM (CD read-only memory) drive remain virtually unchanged. Almost every system unit assembled today includes a CD-ROM drive. The drive consists of a spindle, a laser that flashes onto the uneven surface of the disc, a prism that deflects the laser beam, and a light-sensitive diode that reads the flashing light. Currently, the consumer has many choices of CD drives. They include the CD-ROM, CD-R, CD-RW, and DVD-ROM, as described in Table 2-15.

The *compact disc read-only memory (CD-ROM) drive* is a secondary storage device that reads information that is stored on a compact disc (CD). Whereas floppy and hard disks are magnetic media, the CD-ROM drive reads optical media. The life span of optical media is counted in tens of years, making the CD a useful storage medium.

CD-ROM drives use CDs to install programs, to run applications that install some of the files to the hard drive, and to execute the program by transferring the data from the CD to memory while the program is running.

Table 2-15 CD Drive Types and Their Utilities

Drive Type	Name	What It Can Do
CD-ROM and CD-ROM multiread	Compact disc read-only memory	Reads CD-ROM and CD-R media.
CD-R	Compact disc recordable	Reads CD-ROM and CD-R media. Writes once on special discs named CD-Rs.
CD-RW	Compact disc rewritable	Reads CD-ROM and CD-R media. Writes and rewrites on special discs named CD-RWs.
DVD	Digital versatile disc	Reads all CD formats. Reads DVDs.

The CD used in a computer possesses the same form factor, or physical dimensions, as its music counterpart. The CD is a layered disc with a polycarbonate body, approximately 4.75 inches in diameter. The body is coated with a thin film of aluminum alloy, and the data is laid on the alloy film. A plastic coating protects the disc from scratches.

The major components within a CD-ROM drive are the optical head assembly, head actuator mechanism, spindle motor, loading mechanism, connectors and jumpers, and logic board. Internal CD-ROM drives are housed inside the computer case. External CD-ROM drives are connected to the computer by a cable.

How the CD-ROM Drive Works

The CD is usually produced, or mastered, at a factory. The recording technique for a CD is not magnetic, as it is for the floppy and hard disk media. For a CD, a laser etches the data onto a master disc. The production laser burns pits into the smooth surface of the disc, leaving flat surfaces in between. The patterns of pits and lands represent data. Up to 682 MB of text, audio, video, and graphical data can be written to a disc. Once the master is produced, it is used to make copies. Once the copies have been made, they are then sealed for distribution.

When data is being read, light from the laser is bounced off the pits and the lands that are located on the underside of the disk. The pits reflect less light, so they are read by the CD-ROM drive as 0s. The lands reflect more light, so they are read as 1s. Together these 1s and 0s make up the binary language that is understood by computers.

CD writers are now commonly available for PCs. These units provide a widespread ability to write CDs in a process known as *CD burning.*

One specification for a CD-ROM drive is its speed. The faster the disc spins, the faster the data can be transferred to the computer memory. The CD-ROM drive speed is indicated by a number with an *x* after it. For example, a 12-speed CD-ROM drive is labeled as a 12x drive. The larger the number, the faster the disc can spin, as shown in Table 2-16. Two other important specifications to consider are the access time and the data transfer rate.

Table 2-16 CD-ROM Drive Speed Ratings

CD-ROM Drive Rating	Data Transfer Speed	Rotational Speed (Revolutions/Minute, Outer to Inner Track)
2x	300 KBps	400–1060
4x	600 KBps	800–2120
8x	1.2 MBps	1600–4240
12x	1.8 MBps	2400–6360

CD-ROM drive speed ratings for external drives can vary. Check the manufacturer's documentation for more information.

Other specifications directly or indirectly influence speed, access time, or transfer rate. These specifications are seek time, cache memory, interface type, error correction, access time, and data transfer rate. Table 2-17 describes each of these specifications.

Table 2-17 CD-ROM Drive Transfer Rate Specifications

Specification	Definition/Description
Seek time	The amount of time it takes for the device to locate a piece of data.
Cache memory	Stores commonly accessed data so that the processor does not need to locate and retrieve it from the disc each time the data is needed. The more often cache memory is used, the faster the data can be accessed, because memory is much faster than the drive.
Interface type	CD-ROM drives have different interfaces. For example, a SCSI connection is capable of much faster transfer rates than an IDE interface.

continues

Table 2-17 CD-ROM Drive Transfer Rate Specifications (Continued)

Specification	Definition/Description
Error correction	Uses over 10 percent of the space on the disk to be able to recover from faulty data being transferred. The more the drive must use error correction, the slower it becomes.
Access time	The amount of time it takes for the device to locate a piece of data plus the device's latency period (that is, the time it takes to position the laser over the desired data location). Note that this is different from seek time.
Data transfer rate	The speed of data being transmitted from the CD-ROM drive to the main memory of the computer.

PhotoZoom   CD-ROM Drive

This PhotoZoom shows the components of the CD-ROM drive.

Worksheet 2.7.3   CD-ROM Drive Identification

This worksheet is a review of CD-ROM drive components.

DVD Formats and Drives

The digital versatile disc (DVD) is a type of optical disc that uses the same 4.75-inch-diameter size as a CD. The DVD looks like a CD, but the storage capacity of the DVD is significantly higher. DVDs can be recorded on both sides, and some commercial versions can support two layers per side. This can provide more than 25 times the storage of a CD.

DVD originally stood for digital video disc. As the technology evolved in the computer world, the Video portion was dropped, and the term became simply D-V-D. The DVD Forum (http://www.dvdforum.org) was founded in 1995 for the purpose of exchanging and disseminating ideas and information about the DVD format and its technical capabilities, improvements, and innovations. The DVD Forum started using the term digital versatile disc. Currently, both terms—digital versatile disc and digital video disc—are acceptable.

Two types of media have been developed for DVDs: plus and minus. The DVD Forum supports DVD media with a hyphen, such as DVD-R and DVD-RW. This media is called minus R or minus RW. The DVD +RW Alliance (http://www.dvdrw.com) was created in 1997. The DVD +RW Alliance developed the plus standards. These include DVD+R and DVD+RW.

The plus and minus formats were confusing until recently. In 2002, drives that support both the plus and minus types of media were introduced. Table 2-18 describes the types of DVD media and the sides, layers, and capacity.

Table 2-18 DVD Media

Type	Number of Sides	Number of Layers	Capacity (GB)
Read-Only			
DVD-Video and DVD-ROM	1	1	4.7 (DVD-5)
	1	2	8.5 (DVD-9)
	2	1	9.4 (DVD-10)
	2	2	17.0 (DVD-18)
Rewritable (100,000 Cycles)			
DVD-RAM ver. 1	1	1	2.6
	2	1	5.2
DVD-RAM ver. 2	1	1	4.7
	2	1	9.4
DVD-RAM (80-mm)	1	1	9.4
Re-Recordable (1000 Cycles)			
DVD-RW ver. 2	1	1	4.7
DVD+RW ver. 2	1	1	4.7
DVD+RW	2	1	9.4

An external DVD writer is shown in Figure 2-35. As the price of DVD recordable and rewritable drives decreases, these units will be installed in more computer systems. Currently, DVD players and combo drives are affordable and included in many computers. Combo drives combine a CD recorder with a DVD player or recorder in a single drive.

Figure 2-35 External DVD Writer

How the DVD Drive Works

As with a CD, data is stored on the DVD in the form of indentations and bumps on its reflective surface. The indentations are called *pits,* and the bumps are called *lands.*

When data is being read, light from the laser is bounced off the pits. The pits reflect less light, so they are read by the DVD drive as 0s. The lands reflect more light, so they are read as 1s. Together, these 1s and 0s make up the binary language that is understood by computers.

Speed, Access Time, and Transfer Rate

One specification for a DVD drive is its speed. The faster the disc spins, the faster the data can be transferred to the computer memory. The DVD speed is indicated by a number with an *x* after it. For example, a 12-speed DVD is labeled as 12x media. The larger the number, the faster the disc can spin.

Two other important specifications to consider are the access time and the data transfer rate. Access time refers to how quickly the data can be located and the laser positioned. ***Data transfer rate*** is how fast the computer can transfer the information into memory.

DVD speed ratings for external drives can vary. Check the manufacturer's documentation for more information.

Other specifications that directly or indirectly influence speed, access time, or transfer rate are seek time, cache memory, interface type, and error correction.

Backup Hardware

A tape drive is the most common type of device that is used to back up data on a network server disk drive. Tape devices are known for their long-lasting performance. Their performance is partly due to the tape drive mechanics that some systems include. A variety of tape devices use different tape formats for storing data. Many tape drives can also compress the data before it is stored on the tape. In most cases, the compression ratio is 2:1. This has the effect of doubling the storage capacity of the tape.

Quarter-Inch Cartridge

In 1972, 3M created the Quarter-Inch Cartridge (QIC, pronounced *quick*). QIC is a tape standard. As the name implies, a QIC tape is one-quarter-inch wide. Many versions of the QIC tape drives have been used over the years. Table 2-19 summarizes QIC standards. Early QIC tape drives were attached to the floppy disk controller in the computer. Later versions could be attached to the computer's parallel port. Still later versions used the IDE hard disk drive interface. The QIC standard has limited storage capacity and is used only in entry-level network servers.

Table 2-19 QIC Tape Standards

Standard	Tape Cartridge	Storage Capacity, Native/Compressed	Interface
QIC-40	DC-2000	40 MB/80 MB	Floppy
	DC-2060	60 MB/120 MB	Floppy
QIC-80	MC-2010	125 MB/250 MB	Floppy, parallel
	MC-2120 Extra	400 MB/800 MB	Floppy, parallel
QIC-80XL	MC-2120XL	170 MB/340 MB	Floppy, parallel
QIC-3020XL	MC-3020XL	680 MB/1.36 GB	Floppy, parallel, IDE
	MC-3020 Extra	1.6 GB/3.2 GB	Floppy, parallel, IDE
QIC-3095	MC-3095	4 GB/8 GB	IDE, SCSI-2
QIC-3220	MC-3220	10 GB/20 GB	SCSI-2
QIC-5010	DC-5010	16 GB/32 GB	SCSI-2
QIC-5210	DC-5210	25 GB/50 GB	SCSI-2

Travan Cartridge Tape

The Imation Company, which is a 3M spin-off, introduced the Travan cartridge tape standard in 1994. Table 2-20 summarizes the Travan tape standards. Travan is based on QIC technology. In many cases, it is either read or write compatible with some QIC tape cartridges, or it is read compatible with QIC cartridges. Travan tape drives have a higher storage capacity than the older QIC tape drives. The most recent standard that was implemented on Travan tape drives was hardware compression. This freed the server's processor, allowing it to do other tasks while the tape drive was operating. Travan tape drives have the capacity to back up low-end network servers, but they are relatively slow. Backup speed is about 1 MBps.

Table 2-20 Travan Tape Standards

Standard	Tape Cartridge	Storage Capacity, Native/Compressed	Interface
Travan-1	TR-1	400 MB/800 MB	Floppy, parallel
Travan-2	TR-2	800 MB/1.6 GB	Floppy, parallel
Travan-3	TR-3	1.6 GB/3.2 GB	Floppy, parallel
Travan-4	TR-4	4 GB/8 GB	SCSI-2, EIDE
Travan NS-8	NS-8	4 GB/8 GB	SCSI-2, EIDE
Travan-5	TR-5	10 GB/20 GB	SCSI-2, EIDE
Travan NS-20	NS-20	10 GB/20 GB	SCSI-2, EIDE

8-mm Tape

Exabyte Corporation pioneered tape technology that uses 8-mm tape. This technology uses a tape that is similar to 8-mm videotape and the helical scan system that is used by a VCR. Table 2-21 reviews 8-mm tape technologies. Mammoth 8-mm tape technologies are an improvement over the original 8-mm tape technologies, with higher storage capacities and faster transfer speeds. Table 2-22 reviews Mammoth 8-mm tape technologies.

Table 2-21 8-mm Tape Standards

Technology	Storage Capacity, Native/Compressed (GB)	Transfer Speed (KBps)
8200	2.5/5.0	246
8500	5/10	500

Table 2-22 Mammoth 8-mm Tape Standards

Technology	Storage Capacity, Native/Compressed (GB)	Transfer Speed (MBps)
Mammoth-1	20/40	3
Mammoth-2	60/120	12

Advanced Intelligent Tape

Advanced Intelligent Tape (AIT) technology was originally developed by Sony and introduced in 1996. AIT technology features 8-mm tapes that use the same helical scan recording hardware as a VCR. AIT tapes have memory in the tape cartridge. This is known as Memory In Cassette (MIC). MIC stores the tape log to facilitate locating a file during a restore operation. Table 2-23 summarizes AIT standards. For more information about AIT technology, visit the AIT Forum website at http://www.aittape.com/.

Table 2-23 AIT Standards

Standard	Tape Media	Storage Capacity, Native/Compressed (GB)	Tape Speed (MBps)
AIT-1	SDX-125C	25/50	3
	SDX-135C	35/70	3
AIT-2	SDX-236C	36/72	6
	SDX-250C	50/100	6
AIT-3	SDX-700C	100/260	12
AIT-4	Prototype	200/520	24

Digital Audio Tape

The Digital Audio Tape (DAT) standard uses 4-mm digital audiotapes to store data in the Digital Data Storage (DSS) format. Table 2-24 summarizes the DAT tape.

Table 2-24 DAT Standards

Format	Storage Capacity, Native/Compressed (GB)	Transfer Speed (MBps)	Tape Cartridge
DDS-1	2/4	1	DAT4
DDS-2	4/8	1	DAT8
DDS-3	12/24	2	DAT24
DDS-4	20/40	6	DAT40

Digital Linear Tape

Digital Linear Tape (DLT) technology offers high capacity and relatively high-speed tape backup capabilities. DLTs record information on the tape in a linear format. This is unlike the 8-mm tape technology, which uses helical scan recording techniques. DLT drives support high storage capacity. Depending on the media used, the DLT drives allow up to 220 GB of compressed data as well as a fast transfer speed. However, DLT drives are expensive. Table 2-25 compares DLT formats.

Table 2-25 DLT Standards

Standard	Storage Capacity, Native/Compressed (GB)	Transfer Speed (MBps)
DLT-2000	10/20	1.25
DLT-2000XT	15/30	1.25
DLT-4000	20/40	1.5
DLT-7000	35/70	5
DLT-8000	40/80	6
SDLT 220	110/220	11

Linear Tape-Open

Hewlett-Packard, IBM, and Seagate developed the Linear Tape-Open (LTO) technology. LTO is available in two forms. One form, Ultrium, is designed for high storage capacity. The other, Accelis, is designed for fast access. Table 2-26 reviews the LTO tape formats. For more information about LTO tape technology, visit the LTO website at http://www.lto-technology.com/.

Table 2-26 LTO Standards

Standard	Storage Capacity, Native/Compressed (GB)	Transfer Speed, Native/Compressed (MBps)
Ultrium	100/200	20/40
Ultrium 2	200/400	40/80
Accelis	25/50	20/40

Tape Arrays

Several network server vendors offer an array of tape drives with fault-tolerance characteristics. Most of these technologies use four identical tape drives and implement the tape version of RAID, called Redundant Array of Independent Tapes (RAIT). RAIT can be used to mirror tape drives, or it can be implemented as data striping with parity with at least three tape drives. Therefore, if a tape is damaged or lost, data recovery can still occur.

Tape Autochangers

A tape autochanger, also known as a tape auto loader, allows the tape drive to load a new tape when the current tape gets full while performing a backup. This relieves the operator from having to remove one tape and insert a new tape. This technology is helpful because backups are usually performed during the night. Most tape autochangers support unloading and loading of ten or fewer tapes.

Tape Libraries

A tape library is usually an external system that has multiple tape drives, tens or hundreds of tapes, and an automatic mechanism for locating the tapes. The mechanism can load the tapes into the tape drives and return the tapes to the proper location. Tape libraries are the high ends of backup systems, and they are expensive.

USB Flash Memory

USB flash memory, as seen in Figure 2-36, is a relatively new type of storage device. A USB flash memory device can hold hundreds of times the data of a floppy disk. These devices are available to store 16 MB, 32 MB, 64 MB, 128 MB, 256 MB, 512 MB, and 1 GB of data. The USB 1.1 standard is capable of read speeds of up to 1 MBps and write speeds of up to 900 KBps. The latest standard, USB 2.0, can store up to 2 GB of data. This standard is capable of read speeds of up to 6 MBps and write speeds of up to 4.5 MBps.

Figure 2-36 USB Flash Memory

Network Components

This section focuses on the components of a network. How a network works is discussed in a later chapter. The following topics are covered in this section:

- Modems
- Network interface cards

Modems

A *modem* is a device that converts the digital data used by computers into analog signals, suitable for transmission over a telephone line, and converts the analog signals back to a digital signal at the destination. The word modem is an acronym for modulator/demodulator.

A modem uses a dialup networking connection. A computer that is not connected to a network by some other means, such as a network interface card (NIC), typically has a modem card installed. A modem that is plugged into one of the expansion slots inside a PC is known as an internal modem. Such a modem usually has two types of connectors called registered jack type 11. One jack is for the phone line, whereas the other is used to attach a traditional telephone handset. Registered jack type 11 is more commonly called an RJ-11 jack.

Modems come in the form of expansion cards, also known as modem cards. The modem card handles all the data transmission on the computer serial port with the help of a special chip called the *Universal Asynchronous Receiver/Transmitter (UART)* chip. Almost every modern PC contains a 16550 UART chip, which permits a high-speed connection to the Internet. The number 16550 represents a generational evolution of these chips. The three generations are as follows:

- **8250**—The original chip in XT computers, it has only a 1-byte buffer. A buffer is temporal storage for data as it is sent out bit by bit over a serial line such as a phone line.

- **16450**—Introduced with the AT systems, this chip has a single-byte buffer.
- **16550**—The most popular chip used in Pentium-class computers is currently the 16550A chip. It has a first-in, first-out (FIFO) buffer that effectively eliminates data overrun. Data overrun occurs when a system port runs faster than the CPU can process the data.

The major difference among the different UART chips is the speed at which they can enable data transmission. Notable advanced UART versions include the 16450 and 16550. The 16450 was the 16-bit improvement of the 8250. The 16550 is a high-performance UART with an on-board 16-byte buffer.

Modems and their role in Internet connectivity are discussed in further detail in Chapter 10, "Networking Fundamentals."

Network Interface Cards

A *network interface card (NIC)*, as shown in Figure 2-37, connects a local computer to a group of other computers. NICs connect computers so that they can share data and resources in a networked environment. A NIC is also known as a network adapter. All network interface cards on a local-area network (LAN) are designed to use Ethernet, Token Ring, or another similar protocol to communicate with other machines in the network.

Figure 2-37 Typical NIC

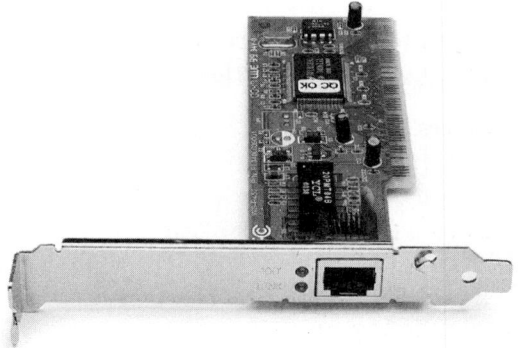

NICs come in the form of a PCI or ISA expansion card installed in one of the computer's expansion slots. The network cable plugs into the computer through the adapter card or NIC. The connection is made with an RJ-45 connector, as shown in Figure 2-38. This connector is very similar to the RJ-11, which was discussed earlier. The RJ-45 has eight wires inside instead of the four wires that are in the RJ-11 phone jack. For two networked computers to communicate, they must be connected at the same speed and use the same Layer 2 technology. Layer 2 technology refers to the TCP/IP networking model. This is discussed in greater detail in Chapter 10.

Figure 2-38 RJ-45 Plug

With the NIC, the RJ-45 jack is used with unshielded twisted-pair (UTP) LAN cabling. Another type of connector, the British Naval Connector (BNC), is provided for coaxial cable connections. Network cabling, or networking media, as well as NICs are discussed in more detail in a later chapter.

System Resources

Computers use both physical and logical system resources. The term *logical system resources* refers to computer activity; these resources are tracked by the operating system. Physical resources allow the computer system to operate. This section includes the following topics:

- What are system resources?
- Interrupt requests
- Direct memory access
- Input/output addresses

What Are System Resources?

In the context of computer configuration, the term *system resources* refers to the mechanisms that interface, communicate, and control individual device adapters along with the serial, parallel, and mouse ports. System resources are shared among the different hardware components of the computer system that need to communicate with the CPU.

The CPU is a complete computation engine that is fabricated on a single chip. It not only controls the functions of the computer, but it also handles requests from many input and output devices. Computers appear to handle multiple requests at the same time. However, the CPU is only capable of handling one request at a time. System resources prevent two or more devices from communicating at the same time. System resources also enable the CPU to identify the hardware device that is making a request.

Interrupt Requests

Modern computers and operating systems are very reliable. The reliability comes from the organization of the internal transactions. Various hardware devices, for example, might want to tell the CPU that information is available for transfer. The devices indicate this by making an *interrupt request (IRQ)*. IRQs cannot generally be shared. A device IRQ causes the operating system to stop momentarily as the device asks the CPU to service the request. IRQs are critical to the proper functioning of the system. You should follow the default device IRQ assignments, as shown in Table 2-27.

TIP

Know the device or port that each IRQ is assigned to.

Table 2-27 Common IRQ Default Assignments

IRQ	Common Device or Port Assignment
0	System timer
1	Keyboard
2	Programmable interrupt controller (cascade IRQs 8–15)
3	COM2 and COM4
4	COM1 and COM3
5	Parallel port 2 (LPT2), sound card, or network card
6	Floppy disk controller
7	Parallel port 1 (LPT1) or sound card (shared)
8	Real-time clock
9	Cascade IRQ2
10	Available
11	Available
12	PS/2 mouse (available if not used)
13	Numerical processing unit (that is, math coprocessor)
14	Primary IDE controller (that is, hard disk controller)
15	Secondary IDE controller

Cascaded IRQs

The concept of cascading IRQs is shown in how the controllers worked with the XT and the AT system board BIOS. The XT BIOS provided eight IRQ lines, 0 through 7. The more advanced AT BIOS provided eight more IRQ lines, 8 through 15. Now, to make AT PCs backward compatible with XT PCs and to "up" the priority of the new IRQ lines, two interrupt controllers are cascaded or redirected. This results in IRQ 8–15 having the same priority as IRQ2. If two IRQs are active at the same time, the one with the higher priority is serviced first. Cascaded IRQs are described in Table 2-28.

Table 2-28 Cascaded IRQs

IRQ	Common Device or Port Assignment		
0	System timer		
1	Keyboard		
2	Programmable interrupt controller Cascaded IRQs 8–15 have the same priority as IRQ 2		
	IRQ	**Common Device or Port Assignment**	
	8	Real-time clock	
	9	Cascade IRQ2	
	10	Available	
	11	Available	
	12	PS/2 mouse (available if not used)	
	13	Numerical processing unit (i.e., math coprocessor)	
	14	Primary IDE controller (i.e., hard disk controller)	
	15	Secondary IDE controller	
3	COM2 and COM4		
4	COM1 and COM3		
5	Parallel port 2 (LPT2), sound card, or network card		
6	Floppy disk controller		
7	Parallel port 1 (LPT1) or sound card (shared)		

Therefore, if IRQ 2 is being used by BIOS instructions, IRQ 9 is also being used. This behavior is described as cascading, redirecting, or vectoring. Note that all three words refer to the same process of pointing to somewhere else. When source information is redirected to a destination, the destination receives cascaded information from the source.

Direct Memory Access

Direct memory access (DMA) channels allow devices to bypass the processor and directly access the computer memory. Therefore, devices with a DMA channel assignment have faster data transfers. DMA channels are typically used by high-speed communication devices to transfer large amounts of data at high speeds. Examples of such devices include sound cards, some network cards, some SCSI cards, some disk drives, and some tape backup drives.

A device signals the intention to use the DMA channel. Then the DMA controller takes control of the data bus and address bus from the microprocessor or CPU. Data and address buses are communication lines that bring information to the computer memory. The CPU is temporarily disconnected from the buses and is put in a floating state. After the transfer is complete, the DMA controller releases the data bus and address bus to the CPU. The CPU can then continue with its normal functions. There is one drawback of DMA use, especially with older systems. The CPU can be put on hold while the DMA device is working, slowing all other functions until the DMA transfer is complete.

As with IRQs, devices that want to make a DMA transfer are assigned a priority level. If a device DMA has a low number, it has higher priority than a device with a higher number. It is important to understand the DMA assignments that are summarized in Table 2-29.

Table 2-29 Common DMA Default Channel Assignments

DMA Channel	Default Device	Channel Can Also Be Used For
0	Dynamic RAM memory refresh	—
1	Sound card (low DMA setting)	Network cards, SCSI adapters, parallel printing ports, and voice modems
2	Floppy disk controller	—

continues

Table 2-29 Common DMA Default Channel Assignments (Continued)

DMA Channel	Default Device	Channel Can Also Be Used For
3	Available	Network cards, SCSI adapters, parallel printing ports, voice modems, and sound cards (low DMA setting)
4	Cascade for DMA 0–3	—
5	Sound card (high DMA setting)	Network cards, SCSI adapters
6	Available	Network cards, sound cards (high DMA setting)
7	Available	Network cards, sound cards (high DMA setting)

Input/Output Addresses

In addition to an IRQ, computer components also need to be assigned an *input/output (I/O)* port number. An I/O port number is a memory address where data is temporarily stored as it moves in and out of the devices. The I/O address is similar to a post office box. As mail comes in, it is temporarily stored in the post office box. If two boxes have the same number, the mail can end up in the wrong box. The same is true for I/O ports. No two devices can have the same I/O address. Table 2-30 shows I/O settings for common input and output devices.

Table 2-30 I/O Address Assignments

I/O Port Address (In Hexadecimal Form)	Typical Device or Port Assignment
000-00F, 081-09F	Direct memory access controller
010-01F, 0A0-0A1	Programmable interrupt controller
040-043	System timer
060-060, 064-064	Keyboard
061-061	PC speaker
070-071	CMOS/Real-time clock
0F0-0FF	Math coprocessor
130-14F	SCSI host adapter

Table 2-30 I/O Address Assignments (Continued)

I/O Port Address (In Hexadecimal Form)	Typical Device or Port Assignment
170-177	Secondary hard disk controller
1F0-1F7	Primary hard disk controller
200-207	Game port joystick
220-22F	Sound card
294-297	PCI bus (data communication line)
278-27F	LPT2 or LPT3
2E8-2EF	COM4 serial port
2F8-2FF	COM2 serial port
376-376	PCI IDE controller
378-37F	LPT1 printer port
3E8-3EF	COM3 serial port
3F2-3F5	Floppy disk controller
3F6-3F6	PCI primary IDE controller
3F8-3EF	COM1 serial port
E000-E01F	USB host controller
E800-E87F	Fast Ethernet adapter
F000-F00F	IDE controllers

Portable Devices

Portable computers have come a long way since the first portable computer was introduced 20 years ago. The focus in this section is notebook and laptop computers, but the issues discussed are common to all portables. This section includes the following topics:

- Notebook computers
- Portable hardware
- PCMCIA cards
- Portable computer displays
- Docking stations

- Upgrading and troubleshooting notebooks
- Infrared devices
- Wireless access points

Notebook Computers

Portable devices incorporate the system unit, input unit, and output unit into a single, light-weight package. Portable devices, unlike the towers or desktops, can be carried around by the user. These devices are also called notebook computers, laptop computers, palmtops, or personal digital assistants (PDAs), depending on their size and function.

Producing portable computers has not been without problems. Early attempts at developing a portable computer produced heavy systems with short operating times between battery recharges. Advancements in technology, particularly in integrated circuits (ICs) and peripheral component designs, now produce a portable that competes with desktop and tower systems in speed, power, and number of features. A typical notebook computer, such as the one depicted in Figure 2-39, has many the following features:

- A video display that is larger than those typically associated with the older PC-AT machines
- A hard drive with a capacity in the tens of gigabytes
- CD-ROM/DVD drives

Figure 2-39 Typical Notebook Computer

Using a notebook computer is different from using a desktop in several ways. The built-in keyboard on a notebook is smaller than the keyboard for a desktop. To keep the computer compact, notebooks do not have a separate mouse but instead use one of the following input devices:

- **Trackball**—A rotating ball that allows the cursor to move on the screen. A trackball is shown in Figure 2-40.

- **Trackpoint**—Moves the cursor when the user pushes the point with a finger. Figure 2-41 shows a trackpoint.

- **Touchpad**—Allows the movement of the cursor by sliding a finger across the pad. It allows the user to scroll and even click to open programs. A touchpad is shown in Figure 2-42.

Figure 2-40 Trackball

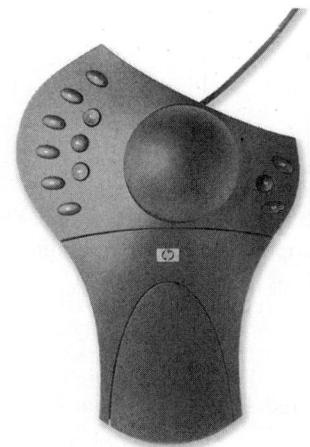

Figure 2-41 Trackpoint

Figure 2-42 Touchpad

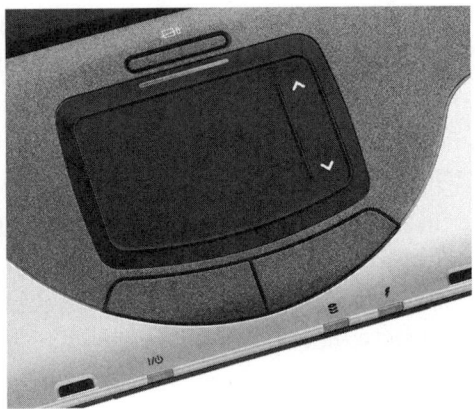

As technology improves, notebook components are using less power and are becoming more rugged. These concepts are explored further in the sections that follow.

Portable Hardware

Portables are built to be lightweight and to fit within a certain size or form factor. This has led to special considerations in developing the hardware components that go into a portable computer. This section explores some of these components.

Power Sources

Notebook computers typically come equipped with an AC-to-DC power adapter. In addition, auto adapters are available so that using the notebook and recharging batteries can be done in a car. These adapters are proprietary, so availability depends on the manufacturer. Notebooks and other portable devices are built to be used anywhere, even where power outlets are not available. To solve this problem, batteries have been incorporated as an integral component of portable systems.

Originally, portables used nickel-cadmium (Ni-Cad) batteries, as shown in Figure 2-43. These batteries were in an external battery pack that would attach to the portable device. When first introduced, Ni-Cad batteries would operate a device for only 30–45 minutes before requiring a recharge. The time to operate increased to 45–75 minutes with certain power-saving features enabled. In addition, it could take nearly a day to recharge these batteries. Better batteries have since been developed to address these limitations.

Figure 2-43 Ni-Cad Battery

More recently, nickel metal-hydride (NiMH) and lithium-ion batteries, as shown in Figure 2-44, have been used in portable devices. These batteries are usually constructed in a plastic holder that can be easily inserted into the portable device. These batteries usually last for just over 2 hours, depending on their size and the power consumption of the device. Also, it only takes 3–5 hours to recharge them.

Figure 2-44 Lithium-Ion Battery

One drawback of portable systems is that no industry standards currently exist for the power supplies. Therefore, a battery in one portable device is usually not compatible with a different portable device.

Power management software is installed on many notebook computers to extend the battery life or to conserve battery power when the charge is low. When a notebook battery's charge gets low, the computer runs slower. The power management software monitors how the notebook is being used. The software can then indicate that the power supply is running low, giving you time to save any work. When this warning is received, plug in the computer AC adapter or power off the unit and recharge the battery.

Hard Drives

As with most components of a portable device, hard drives have been specially developed to be smaller and to use less power to accommodate size and power limitations. The size of hard drives in portable devices varies dramatically. Power is further saved when the hard drives power down after they have not been accessed for a certain amount of time.

Storage Devices/Removable Storage

Current notebooks not only have adequate hard drive storage but also have CD-RW and floppy drives. To make the notebook smaller, some manufacturers provide an external CD-ROM and floppy disk drive. Because notebooks typically have a USB port, these computers can also take advantage of the new USB storage units.

PCMCIA Cards

The *Personal Computer Memory Card International Association (PCMCIA)* card was introduced in 1989. The PCMCIA card is a special expansion card that was primarily designed to accommodate the needs of the portable computer market. These cards can be used to upgrade a notebook by adding memory, a modem, a network connection, or a peripheral device. Recently, the term *PCMCIA* has been used less often and has been replaced by the term *PC card.* The following three types of PCMCIA slots and cards are available, as shown in Figure 2-45:

- **Type I**—3.3-mm-thick cards that are used as memory expansion units
- **Type II**—5-mm-thick cards that are used for any expansion device except hard drives
- **Type III**—10.5-mm-thick cards that are designed to be used solely for hard drives

The newer mini-PCI card is used primarily for notebooks, web pads, Internet appliances, and other mobile data applications. The following types of mini-PCI cards are available:

- **Type I**—Used primarily in full-featured systems, typically desktop replacements.
- **Type II**—Designed for value-priced systems with on-board modular connectors. Type II cards are the simplest to maintain and warranty.
- **Type III**—Designed for thin notebook systems, which are becoming increasingly prevalent in the high-end notebook segment.

Figure 2-45 PCMCIA Card Types

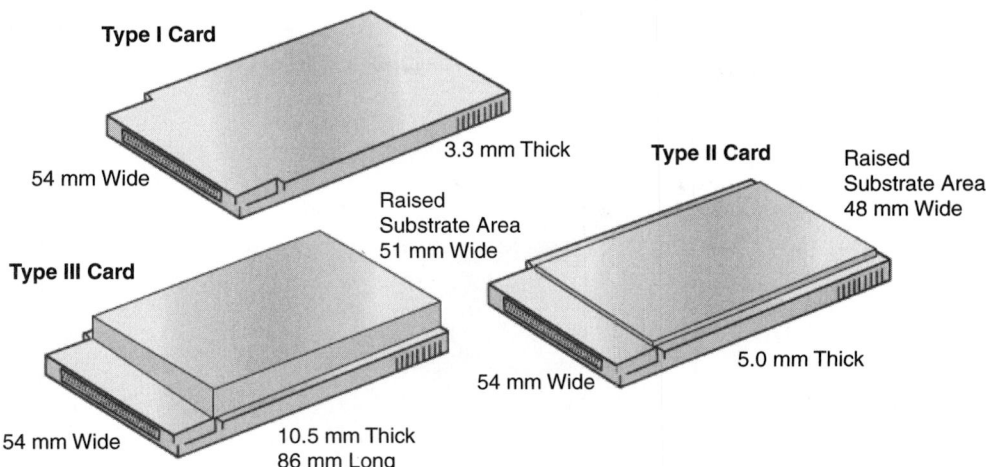

Memory

The standard small-outline dual in-line memory module (SODIMM) is used most often in notebook computers. Some notebooks use the manufacturer's proprietary memory modules. At least 64 MB RAM is recommended to have sufficient memory for the operating system and applications software. Check the user documentation for information on upgrading notebook memory. Some notebooks are equipped with access panels that facilitate plugging in additional memory chips.

Most portable computers do not use a standard type of memory. To upgrade the memory of most notebooks, the owner must visit the manufacturer's website or consult the user manual for more information. Memory types can vary among different products or different versions of the same product. Careful research is required before upgrading the memory in a portable.

Portable Computer Displays

Because of the compact nature and limited power supply of notebook computers and other portables, non-CRT-type displays are used. Two examples of such displays are the liquid crystal display (LCD) and the gas-plasma panel. These two types of display systems are suited to the portability needs of notebook computers for the following reasons:

- They are lighter and more compact than CRT monitors.
- They require less electrical energy to operate.
- They can be operated from batteries.

LCDs are the flat-panel displays that are used with most of the newer portable systems. These displays have the advantage of being thin, flat, and lightweight, and they require little power to operate. In addition, these displays offer better reliability and longer life than CRT units. Figure 2-46 shows an LCD on a PDA.

Figure 2-46 Liquid Crystal Display (LCD)

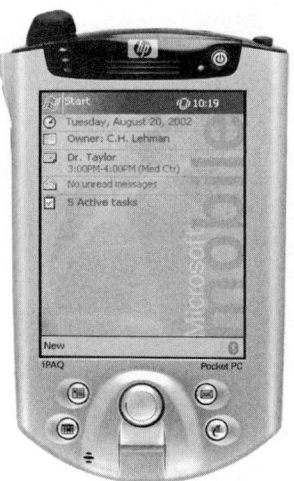

Docking Stations

A docking station, as shown in Figure 2-47, is a device that allows the portable PC to operate with hardware devices that are associated with desktop computers. A docking station is also called a docking port. A notebook is inserted into the docking station. Then the extension bus in the docking station plugs into the expansion connector in the notebook. A docking station usually provides standard PC expansion slots. Therefore, non-notebook peripheral devices, such as network adapters, sound cards, and so on, can be used with the system. When a notebook computer is in a docking station, its normal input/output devices are disabled and the docking station peripherals take over. Input/output devices include the display or monitor, keyboard, and pointing device. This makes it possible for the notebook to use a collection of desktop devices that otherwise would not be available to it. Desktop devices include an AC power source, a CRT monitor, a full-size keyboard, a mouse, a modem, and standard personal computer port connectors.

Figure 2-47 HP Omnibook Docking Station

The notebook and the docking station communicate with each other through a special docking port connector in the rear of the notebook. However, most docking stations are proprietary. This means that they can only be used with the portable that they were designed for. These products are proprietary for the following reasons:

- The connector in the notebook must correctly align with the docking port connection in the docking station.
- The notebook unit must fit correctly within the docking station opening.

Currently, no standards exist for portable systems. Therefore, there is little chance that two different manufacturers would locate the connectors in the same places or design the same case outline.

Port Replicator

A port replicator, as shown in Figure 2-48, is a device that serves a similar purpose to a docking station. The port replicator connects multiple peripherals to a notebook. However, the port replicator does not contain slots for expansion, speakers, or peripherals. The desktop devices are permanently plugged into the port replicator. The port replicator connects to the notebook through a large plug and socket that duplicate all the cable lines for the monitor, printer, keyboard, and mouse.

Figure 2-48 Compaq 1800 Series Port Replicator

Upgrading and Troubleshooting Notebooks

Currently, most notebook computer components can be upgraded to provide more memory, faster processing, increased storage, and faster Internet connections. Figure 2-49 shows a notebook computer. Because notebooks are proprietary, you must verify that the components are upgradeable. The best source for this information is the user documentation or the manufacturer's website.

Figure 2-49 Notebook Computer

Like their desktop counterparts, notebooks need regular maintenance. Using the system tools on a weekly basis can keep the system running smoothly. System tools are covered more thoroughly in Chapter 12, "Preventive Maintenance."

A common problem for notebook computers is overheating. Overheating can cause the system to run slowly and malfunction. When the notebook restarts without notice, this can be a sign that the unit is overheating. Keeping the notebook cooler can be as simple as raising it slightly to allow air to circulate beneath it. Inexpensive devices can also be purchased to achieve this effect. Also, notebook cooler pads can be purchased. These pads feature fans that are powered by the USB port to help keep the notebook cool.

Infrared Devices

An infrared (IR) port allows IR devices to communicate with each other. Figure 2-50 shows the receiving port. IR technology is used for wireless transmissions between computer devices and in remote controls for television and stereo systems. Bidirectional communication is used for all specifications. IR frequencies are higher than those of microwaves but lower than those of visible light. To successfully link two devices (a transmitter and receiver), an unobstructed line of sight is required between the devices. Computer devices, such as PDAs or laptops, are usually placed close to the device for communication. However, an IR printer, for example, can be up to 2.5 feet away from the transmitting computer.

Figure 2-50 Infrared Receiver

Wireless Access Points

Wireless networking technologies allow computers to broadcast their information to one another using radio signals. Computers in a client/server network communicate through a wireless access point. This is the wired controller that receives data from and transmits data to the wireless adapters that are installed on each system. Installing a wireless adapter on a notebook computer allows the user to go anywhere within range of the wireless access point. Wireless devices are shown in Figures 2-51 and 2-52.

Figure 2-51 Linksys Wireless Devices

Figure 2-52 Wireless Adapter

Summary

This chapter discussed the theory and operation of the various components of a computer. Some of the important concepts to retain from this chapter are as follows:

- The OS helps the computer perform four basic operations: input, processing, output, and storage. Entering data with a keyboard is the most common form of input, processing is manipulating data according to the instructions, output is the processed data on a screen or printer, and storage occurs on the hard drive or floppy disk.

- The bootstrap loader is a small program that is stored in the BIOS. The primary functions of the bootstrap loader are to test the computer hardware using the POST and to load the OS into RAM.

- A cold boot is the process of starting a computer from the off position. The cold boot requires the system to go through the boot sequence and POST. A warm boot is restarting the computer.

- You should consider many factors when choosing a computer case. Most modern cases have the power supply installed. The motherboard that is to be used and the components that are to be installed are the major considerations.

- The motherboard, or system board, is the nerve center of the computer. It houses the CPU, the controller circuitry, the bus, the RAM, expansion slots for additional boards, and ports for external devices.

- The computer display, or monitor, is available in various types and sizes and with various characteristics. Important monitor-related terms include pixels (the tiny dots that make up the image), refresh rate (measured in hertz), resolution (the sharpness of the image), and screen size.

- The video card is the interface between the computer and the monitor. This card determines which pixels illuminate, the color of the pixels, and the intensity of the pixels on the monitor. The video card is either installed as an expansion card or is built into the motherboard.

- I/O ports are the connectors on the back of the computer that allow peripheral devices—such as the printer, scanner, and so on—to connect to the computer. You should understand the difference between USB, FireWire, serial, parallel, PS/2, and 5-pin DIN ports.

- The hard drive and other devices use either Enhanced Integrated Drive Electronics (EIDE) or Small Computer System Interface (SCSI) connections.

- The internal hard drive is connected to a disk controller with a cable. The hard drive and other devices can use either EIDE or SCSI connections.

- A floppy disk drive (FDD) magnetically reads information from and writes information to floppy disks, which are a form of removable storage media. A hard disk drive (HDD) shares many physical and operational characteristics with the floppy disk drive but has a more complex design and provides a greater access speed. The HDD has a much larger storage capacity than the floppy disk drive and is therefore used for long-term storage. The HDD stores your programs and files as well as the operating system. Typically, the HDD is an internal drive that cannot be removed from the computer.

- A compact disc (CD) is an optical storage medium. CDs can be played and written to using CD-ROM, CD-RW, and other types of CD drives. Music CDs have all but replaced cassette tapes as the medium of choice for musical recordings.

- A modem is typically an expansion card that connects a computer to the Internet with a dialup network connection. Modems are available in the form of internal expansion cards, also known as modem cards. The modem card handles all the data transmission on the computer's serial port with the help of a special chip called the Universal Asynchronous Receiver/Transmitter (UART) chip. The UART chip controls the flow of information into and out of the serial port.

- Portable computers or notebooks are built to be lightweight and to be within a certain size form factor. Special components include the batteries, hard drives, and memory. The PCMCIA card (more recently called the PC card) is a special expansion card. PC cards include Type I for memory expansion, Type II for devices, and Type III for hard drives.

- System resources are shared among the different hardware components or devices of the computer system that need to communicate with the CPU. The CPU can handle only one communication request at a time. System resources identify the device and prevent two or more devices from communicating at the same time.

- Each device is assigned an interrupt request, or IRQ, that cannot be shared. The IRQ causes a program to stop momentarily as it asks the CPU to handle the request. A cascading IRQ is an IRQ that is redirected or vectored.

- Direct memory access (DMA) channels allow devices to bypass the processor and directly access the computer memory. Devices with a DMA channel have faster data transfers.

- An input/output (I/O) port number is a memory address where data is temporarily stored as it moves into and out of the devices, much like a post office box. An I/O address can be assigned to only one device.

The next chapter discusses how to use the hardware components to assemble a working computer.

Key Terms

Accelerated Graphics Port (AGP)   Dedicated high-speed bus that supports the high demands of graphical software. This slot is reserved for video adapters only.

address bus   A unidirectional pathway that carries addresses that are generated by the CPU to the memory and I/O elements of the computer.

Arithmetic/Logic Unit (ALU)   Performs fundamental math operations and logical operations in order to make comparisons and decisions. How a program is executed is determined by logical operations.

Audio/Modem Riser (AMR)   A plug-in card for an Intel motherboard that contains all the analog functions, or codecs, that are required for audio or modem operation.

backward compatible   Hardware or software systems that can use interfaces and data from earlier versions of the system or with other systems. Also known as backward-compatible or backwards compatible.

Basic Input/Output System (BIOS)   The program stored in a ROM chip in the computer that provides the computer with basic code to control the computer's hardware and to perform diagnostics on it. The BIOS prepares the computer to load the operating system.

bootstrap program   A small program located in the BIOS chip that locates and loads the operating system into RAM.

bus   The media through which data is transferred from one part of a computer to another. The bus can be compared to a highway on which data travels within a computer. See also *address bus*, *control bus*, and *data bus*.

Cable Select (CSEL)   A setting that allows the IDE adapter to select which IDE or EIDE disk drive will function as master and which IDE or EIDE disk drive will function as slave.

cache   A data storage area that provides high-speed access for the system.

central processing unit (CPU)   On the motherboard, it is a chip contained on a single integrated circuit called the microprocessor. The CPU contains two basic components: a control unit and an Arithmetic/Logic Unit (ALU).

COASt   An acronym for "cache on a stick," COASt provides cache memory on many Pentium-based systems.

cold boot   Powering up a computer from the off position.

Communications and Networking Riser (CNR)   A 30-pin interface with LAN and home networking functions. CNR accommodates two formats, making various audio/modem and audio/network combinations possible.

compact disc (CD)   An optical storage medium that can store up to 680 MB of data. CDs can be played and written to using CD-ROM, CD-RW, and other types of CD drives.

compact disc read-only memory (CD-ROM) drive   A storage device that reads information that is stored on a compact disc (CD).

control bus   Carries the control and timing signals that are needed to coordinate the activities of the entire computer. Control bus signals are not necessarily related to each other. Some are output signals from the CPU, and others are input signals to the CPU from I/O elements of the system.

control unit   Instructs the computer system on how to follow the program instructions, directs the movement of data to and from processor memory, and temporarily holds data, instructions, and processed information in its ALU.

data bus   A bidirectional pathway for data flow. Data can flow along this bus from the CPU to memory during a write operation, and data can move from the computer memory to the CPU during a read operation.

data transfer rate   Refers to how fast the computer can transfer information into memory.

direct memory access (DMA)   A method for transferring data from the computer's main memory directly to the device that needs it without requiring the data to pass to and from the CPU. This makes the data transfer faster.

dual in-line memory module (DIMM)   A circuit board with a 64-bit data bus that holds memory chips.

dynamic RAM (DRAM)   A type of RAM that only holds its data if it is continuously accessed by special logic called a refresh circuit.

electrically erasable programmable read-only memory (EEPROM)   A special type of PROM that can be erased by exposure to an electrical charge.

Enhanced Integrated Drive Electronics (EIDE)   An enhanced version of the standard IDE interface that connects hard disks, CD-ROM drives, and tape drives to a PC.

erasable programmable read-only memory (EPROM)   A special type of memory that can be erased by exposure to ultraviolet light.

expansion slot   An opening in a computer where a PC card can be inserted to add capabilities to the computer.

FireWire   A high-speed, platform-independent communication bus. The FireWire interconnects digital devices such as digital video cameras, printers, scanners, digital cameras, and hard drives.

Flash ROM   A special type of memory that can be reprogrammed in blocks of data instead of 1 byte at a time.

floppy disk drive (FDD)   A device that spins a magnetic floppy disk to read data from and write data to it.

hard disk drive (HDD)   The device that stores and retrieves data from hard disks.

Industry Standard Architecture (ISA)   A 16-bit expansion slot that transfers data with the motherboard at 8 MHz.

input   Supplying information to the computer using the keyboard or mouse.

input/output (I/O)   An operation, program, or device that transfers data to or from a computer. Typical I/O devices are printers, hard disks, keyboards, and mice.

Integrated Drive Electronics (IDE)   A type of hardware interface that connects hard disks, CD-ROM drives, and tape drives to a PC.

interrupt request (IRQ)   A request from a device for communication with the CPU.

microprocessor   A chip that contains a CPU.

Mobile Daughter Card (MDC)   Contains audio and/or modem circuits for a laptop computer. It is the equivalent of the AMR for laptop computers.

modem   Short for modulator/demodulator. A device that converts digital and analog signals. At the source, a modem converts digital signals to a form that is suitable for transmission over analog communication facilities. At the destination, the analog signals are returned to their digital form. Modems allow data to be transmitted over voice-grade telephone lines.

monitor   A display device that works with the installed video card to present output from a computer. The clarity of a CRT monitor is based on video bandwidth, dot pitch, refresh rate, and convergence.

motherboard   The main circuit board in a computer. This board connects all the hardware in the computer.

network interface card (NIC)   This card typically is inserted into a PCI or PCMCIA (PC card) slot in a computer and connects to the network medium, which in turn is connected to other computers on the network.

output   Data that is sent to the video screen or printer.

parallel port   A type of bus that transfers multiple streams of data simultaneously.

Peripheral Component Interconnect (PCI)   A 32-bit local bus slot that allows the bus direct access to the CPU for devices such as memory and expansion boards and allows the CPU to automatically configure the device using information that is contained on the device.

Personal Computer Memory Card International Association (PCMCIA)   An organization that developed the standards for small, credit card–sized devices called PC cards. PC cards are designed to add memory and peripheral devices to portable computers.

pixel   An element that is the smallest part of a graphics image. Many pixels placed close together make up the image on the computer monitor.

power-on self-test (POST)   Diagnostic tests that are run by the computer to test the hardware when the computer is powered on.

processing   Manipulating data according to the user's instructions.

random-access memory (RAM)   Computer memory that can be accessed randomly, that is, any byte of memory that can be accessed without touching the preceding bytes.

random-access memory digital-to-analog converter (RAMDAC)   A specialized form of memory that is designed to convert digitally encoded images into analog signals for display. This memory is composed of an SRAM component (for storing the color map) and three digital-to-analog converters (DACs), one for each electron gun.

read-only memory (ROM)   A type of memory, prerecorded on a chip, that can only be read. This type of memory retains its contents when power is not being supplied to the chip.

riser card   Physically extends a slot so that a chip or card can be plugged into it.

serial port   A type of bus that transmits data 1 bit at a time.

single in-line memory module (SIMM)   A circuit board with a 32-bit data bus that holds memory chips.

Small Computer System Interface (SCSI)   A parallel interface standard that supports multiple devices on the same cable and achieves faster data transmission rates than standard buses.

static RAM (SRAM)   A type of RAM that holds its data without being refreshed, for as long as power is supplied to the circuit.

storage   Keeping track of files for later use. Examples of storage devices include floppy disks and hard drives.

switch mode power supplies (SMPS)   Uses a high-frequency switch or transistor to maintain the output voltage.

system board   See *motherboard* .

system bus   A parallel collection of conductors (the metallic traces on the circuit board) that carry data and control signals from one component to the other.

Universal Asynchronous Receiver/Transmitter (UART)   An integrated circuit, attached to the parallel bus of a computer, that is used for serial communications. The UART translates between serial and parallel signals, provides transmission clocking, and buffers data that is sent to or from the computer.

universal serial bus (USB)   An external bus standard that can connect up to 127 USB devices at transfer rates of up to 480 Mbps.

video RAM (VRAM)   This type of memory is used by video adapters and can be accessed by two different devices at the same time.

warm boot   Restarting a computer that is already turned on by pressing **Ctrl-Alt-Delete** twice or by pressing the reset button.

Windows RAM (WRAM)   This special type of VRAM provides even better performance than standard VRAM by supporting two ports for memory exchange.

zero-insertion-force (ZIF) socket   A special type of chip socket that permits the insertion and removal of the chip without tools and by using virtually no force.

Check Your Understanding

The following are review questions for the A+ exam. Answers are found in Appendix B.

1. Which basic operating system function receives data from the keyboard?

   A. Input

   B. Processing

   C. Output

   D. Storage

2. Which I/O port address does the LPT1 printer port commonly use?

   A. 2F8

   B. 3F8

   C. 278

   D. 378

3. In MS-DOS, which of the following actions results in a warm boot?

   A. Replacing the CPU

   B. Pressing **Ctrl-Alt-Delete** twice

   C. Powering on the system

   D. Regaining power after a power outage

4. Which type of motherboard supports 3.3 volts?

   A. AT

   B. Baby AT

   C. LPX

   D. ATX

5. Which computer resource allows hardware devices to communicate with the processor?

   A. DMA channel

   B. I/O channel

   C. IRQ number

   D. Port setting

6. Which process uses special software to upgrade the BIOS (Basic Input/Output System)?

   A. Plug and play

   B. Formatting

   C. Resetting

   D. Flashing

7. What type of RAM (random-access memory) is used for cache memory?

   A. SIMM (single in-line memory module)

   B. DIMM (dual in-line memory module)

   C. SRAM (static random-access memory)

   D. DRAM (dynamic random-access memory)

8. How many universal serial bus (USB) devices can be connected to a USB port?

   A. 256

   B. 127

   C. 64

   D. 128

9. Which type of storage device uses a laser to record information?

   A. Hard disk drive

   B. Floppy disk drive

   C. CD-RW drive

   D. Tape drive

10. Which of the following performs a quick self-diagnostic check of the system hardware early in the boot sequence?

   A. The POST, which is located on the CPU

   B. The POST, which is located in ROM

   C. DOS

   D. HIMEM.SYS

Upon completion of this chapter, you will be able to perform the following tasks:

- Understand ESD and the safety precautions that must be taken prior to the assembly of the computer
- Create an inventory to ensure that the components required to assemble the computer are available
- Prepare the motherboard and its components for installation
- Install and secure the floppy drive, hard drive, and CD-ROM drive in the computer case
- Install and secure the video card in the computer case
- Perform the final steps and boot the system
- Determine the BIOS configuration and CMOS setup, and remedy POST errors

Chapter 3

Assembling a Computer

This chapter discusses how to install computer components and how to assemble a functional computer. Safety precautions are emphasized and reviewed to protect you and expensive computer components. Upon completion of this chapter, you will be able to boot the system and explore the BIOS configuration and CMOS setup. You will also be able to troubleshoot initial boot problems using POST errors.

Overview of the Assembly Process and Safety Issues

The highest priority when working with computers is safety. The procedures detailed can help to protect the technician and the computer components. This section includes the following topics:

- Overview of general safety issues
- ESD precautions
- Process demonstration

Overview of General Safety Issues

Computer assembly helps IT professionals learn about the inner workings of a computer. It also helps create the confidence that is needed to advance in the IT profession. Before beginning an assembly project, it is good to review the following safety procedures:

- Keep the work area free of clutter, and keep it clean.
- Keep food and drinks out of the work area.
- Avoid opening a computer monitor unless you are trained to do so. A monitor can store up to 25,000 volts, a voltage that is potentially lethal.
- Remove all jewelry and watches.
- Make sure that the power is off and that the power plug has been removed.

- Do not look into the laser beam that is found in computer-related equipment such as CD-ROM and DVD drives.
- Make sure that a fire extinguisher and a first aid kit are available.
- Cover sharp edges with tape when working inside the computer case.

Safety is a concern when leaving the computer plugged in while working inside of it.

If the computer is plugged in, an unequal electric potential can exist between a person and the computer case. This potential difference can discharge through the person. In North America and some parts of Asia, 120 volts are present inside the case. This value can be 220 volts or more in Europe and the rest of the world. By moving the machine when it is plugged into the power outlet, the technician might accidentally press the power button. This would create a live machine and a dangerous situation.

If the computer is plugged in and the power supply has a short to the ungrounded power line, the chassis can be energized. This creates a lethal situation, even if the computer is turned off.

To remedy these concerns, the computer should be plugged into a power strip to keep all components at equal potential. The power strip should then be turned off, along with the machine and the power supply on the back of the case. This removes the concern of live power. When the technician connects a wrist strap to the chassis, the ground connector in the power cord protects the equipment from electrostatic discharge (ESD), which is commonly referred to as static electricity.

The technician should also know where the main power or the circuit breakers are located in case of a fire or short.

The importance of protecting the technician and the computer hardware cannot be overemphasized. Consult the student lab safety agreement from Chapter 1, "Information Technology Basics," for more information. Recall that this is a contract that requires the technician to work in accordance with the safety procedures in this document.

Technicians are required to handle computer components, so it is best to take precautions to protect yourself and the computer hardware by following these basic safety procedures:

- Use an antistatic mat and a grounding wrist strap.
- Use antistatic bags to store and move computer components. Do not put more than one component in each bag, because stacking components can cause some of them to break or become loose.
- Do not remove or install components while the computer is on.
- Ground yourself often to prevent static charges from building by touching a piece of bare metal on the chassis or power supply.

- Work on a bare floor, because carpets can build static charges.
- Hold cards by their edges to avoid touching chips or the edge connectors on the expansion cards.
- Do not touch chips or expansion boards with a magnetized screwdriver.
- Turn off the computer before moving it. This protects the hard drive, which is always spinning when the computer is turned on.
- Keep installation/maintenance CDs and floppy disks away from magnetic fields, heat, and cold.
- Do not place a circuit board onto a conductive surface, especially a metal foil. The lithium and nickel cadmium (Ni-Cad) batteries that are used on boards can short out.
- Do not use a pencil or metal-tipped instrument to change dip switches or to touch components. The graphite in the pencil is conductive and could easily cause damage.
- Do not allow anyone who is not properly grounded to touch or handle computer components. This is true even when working with a lab partner. When passing components, always touch hands first to neutralize any charges.

ESD Precautions

ESD is a concern when handling computer components. Static charges can build in the body just by walking across the room. It might not be apparent, but these charges can be enough to damage computer components. A static charge of 2000 volts is enough for a person to notice. You might have been experienced this when walking across a room and touching a doorknob or other metal surface. A static charge of only 200 volts is sufficient to damage a computer component.

ESD is probably the greatest concern when a user unwraps newly purchased computer parts and components in preparing to assemble the computer. Always review the ESD precautions before beginning the assembly process. The following recommendations can help prevent ESD-related damage:

- Keep all computer parts in antistatic bags.
- Keep the humidity at 20–50 percent.
- Use grounded mats on workbenches.
- Use grounded floor mats in work areas.
- Use wrist straps when working on computer parts, except when working on monitors.
- Touch unpainted grounded metal parts of the computer frequently to lower the static energy of the body.

Remember that just because a discharge cannot be felt does not mean that it cannot harm a computer component. Components can sustain minor damage or be destroyed. Minor damage allows the component to function to some degree or can cause intermittent errors. This type of ESD damage is the most difficult to detect, because it only takes a small amount of electricity to damage a component. When computer cases are closed properly, they are designed to provide ESD protection for the components inside. Computer cases channel ESD away from sensitive components. ESD becomes a threat when the case is opened and the components inside are exposed. The same threat applies to the components when they are removed from the antistatic bags in which they are shipped.

The best way to protect against ESD is to use an antistatic mat, a grounding wrist strap, and antistatic bags. The grounding wrist strap, as shown in Figure 3-1, can be connected to the mat. The mat is then grounded to a wall outlet. The wrist strap can also be clipped to the metal frame of the computer case.

Figure 3-1 Wrist Strap

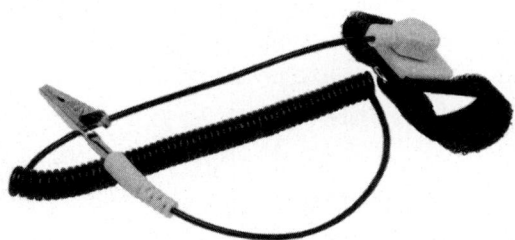

Process Demonstration

The video, "Assembling a Computer," on the accompanying CD demonstrates how a computer is assembled. Note the safety procedures that are followed by the technician as the computer is assembled.

 Video Assembling a Computer

This video shows the step-by-step procedures that are used to install the basic computer components.

Creating a Computer Inventory

Taking several preparations before the assembly process begins can save time. Completing the inventory and the checklist provides important information when the computer is assembled and aids troubleshooting issues in the future. This section includes the following topics:

- Importance of an inventory
- Inventory checklist

Importance of an Inventory

When building a computer, it is important to make a list of all components and the parts purchased. Not all expansion cards or computer parts are clearly labeled with manufacturer information. With these details, the required device drivers or other information can be found and downloaded. The list should include specific warranty information for each part bought. Make sure that the specifics about installation and maintenance requirements are saved so that warranties remain valid. Use a small secure box to hold all the manuals and disks that were used in the assembly of the computer. Label the box with a name that identifies the computer to which it is associated, and store the box in a secure location. If information is needed in the future, all the documentation will be easily available. Table 3-1 shows a sample inventory form.

Table 3-1 Sample Inventory Form

Computer Configuration Worksheet (**One Sheet per Computer**)					
Computer Invoice No.:					
Operating System(s)					
Manufacturer	Version	Service Updates	Network Capable	Security	
Application Software					
Manufacturer	Version	Service Updates	Network Capable	Install Directory	Data Directory

Inventory Checklist

In a lab environment where many students use the same kits, it is not possible to preserve the original packaging and repackage the parts upon dismantling the computer. Documentation for each component should be readily available. In addition, an inventory checklist should be used, such as the one that follows. This ensures that all the components needed to assemble a computer are available.

Sample Inventory Checklist

Computer Identification

Name:

Number:

Computer Case

Manufacturer:

Type (mini, mid, full, desktop):

Number of

3-1/2-inch bays:

5-1/4-inch bays:

Case Fans

Size:

Number of fans:

Motherboard

Manufacturer:

Model:

Bus speed: _____ MHz

Form factor:

  ❏ AT

  ❏ ATX

Chipset manufacturer:

Model:

BIOS manufacturer:

BIOS version:

Does the CPU use a socket or a slot?

Number of CPU sockets/slots:

Number of ISA slots:

Number of PCI slots:

Number of EIDE connectors:

Number of floppy connectors:

Number of serial ports:

Number of parallel ports:

Is there an AGP slot?

Number of USB ports:

Number of other ports or slots:

What kind(s) are they?

CPU
Manufacturer:

Model:

Speed: ___ MHz

Memory
Number of memory slots:

Number of 30-pin SIMMs:

Number of 72-pin SIMMs:

Number of 168-pin DIMMs:

Number of 160-pin RIMMs:

Number of 184-pin RIMMs:

Fastest type of memory supported:

Maximum memory supported:

AGP Slot
Speed:

Hard Drive
Manufacturer:

Model:

Size:

Number of cylinders:

Number of heads:

SPT:

Interface type:

    ❏ IDE

    ❏ SCSI

CD-ROM Drive

Manufacturer:

Model:

Speed:

Interface type:

    ❏ IDE

    ❏ SCSI

Rewritable CD-ROM Drive

Manufacturer:

Model:

Speed:

Interface type:

    ❏ IDE

    ❏ SCSI

DVD Drive

Manufacturer:

Model:

Speed:

Interface type:

    ❏ IDE

    ❏ SCSI

Floppy Disk Drive

Manufacturer:

Monitor

Manufacturer:

Model number:

Size:

Video Card

Manufacturer:

Model:

Memory: ____ MB

Type:

❑ ISA

❑ PCI

❑ On-board

❑ AGP

Sound Card

Manufacturer:

Type:

❑ ISA

❑ PCI

❑ On board

Network Interface Card (NIC)

Manufacturer:

Model:

Mouse

Type:

- ❏ PS/2
- ❏ Serial
- ❏ USB
- ❏ Wireless

Keyboard

Connector:

- ❏ 5-pin DIN
- ❏ 6-pin mini-DIN
- ❏ USB
- ❏ Wireless

Does it match the connector on the motherboard?

Power Supply

Type:

- ❏ AT
- ❏ ATX
- ❏ Other:

Power supply wattage:

Tape Backup

Manufacturer:

Model:

Scanner

Manufacturer:

Model:

Interface:

Speakers

Manufacturer:

Model:

Additional information:

Computer Case and Power Supply

This section focuses on the issues and concerns that affect the purchasing and gathering of parts for assembling a computer. The following topics are discussed:

- Computer cases and system units
- Desktops
- Towers
- Power supplies

Computer Cases and System Units

Whether you are buying a tower or desktop computer, it should conform to the ATX standard and have at least a 250-watt power supply. Make sure that the case that you purchase comes with a tray that allows easy access to the internal components and provides enough room for expansion. Look for spare drive bays, easily removable motherboard mounting plates, and drive racks. Verify the sturdiness of the case, because some of the cheaper ones can be flimsy. The considerations for choosing a computer case are listed in Chapter 2, "How Computers Work."

A *system unit* is typically a metal-and-plastic case that contains the basic parts of the computer system. The three basic system unit styles are desktops, towers, and portables. Each design adapts the system for different environments. These characteristics include mounting methods for the printed circuit boards, ventilation types, total drive capacity, footprint (the amount of desk space that the computer uses), and portability. The desktop and tower design styles are examined in the sections that follow. Portable system units are discussed in Chapter 2.

Desktops

The desktop design, as shown in Figure 3-2, is a familiar case style. Desktop units are designed to sit horizontally on the desktop. The first IBM computers and the original IBM-PC, XT, and AT designs were configured for this case style. Along with the standard and slimline form factors, desktop cases today include mini, micro, and small.

Figure 3-2 Desktop Computer Case

You should consider two important characteristics when choosing a desktop case style for a computer: available desktop space and the form factor.

Available Desktop Space

Available desktop space is important when the computer has to share space with the monitor and other peripherals. If this is the case, a tower case might be a better choice. Desktop cases are generally small and have little room for expansion. Furthermore, not all motherboards fit all desktop models.

Form Factor

The form factor is another characteristic to consider. The form factor describes the general layout of the computer case, the positioning of the slots in the case, and the type of motherboard that the case can accommodate. Cases come in different form factors. The newest form factor, and the one most often encountered, is the ATX. The ATX form factor is designed for better airflow and easier access to the common components.

Towers

Tower cases are usually designed to sit vertically on the floor beneath a desk. To provide more usable workspace on the desktop, some users in the past resorted to standing the desktop cases on their sides under the desk. This prompted computer makers to develop cases that would naturally fit under the desk. In general, tower cases have enough bays to hold floppy drives, CD-ROM drives, tape drives, DVD drives, and anything else that might be installed. The internal design of a tower system resembles that of the desktop unit. Tower cases come in the following three sizes:

- Mini-towers
- Mid-towers
- Full-size towers

Mini-towers and mid-towers, as shown in Figure 3-3, are shorter and less expensive than their full-size counterparts, as shown in Figure 3-4. The major drawback when choosing the smaller towers is that they have little room for internal add-ons or disk drives.

NOTE

External devices can be added to mini- and mid-tower computers if there is insufficient room inside the case for an internal device. Typically, these external devices cost slightly more and use external ports.

Figure 3-3 Mini- and Mid-Towers

Figure 3-4 Full-Size Tower

Many easy-access schemes have been built in to allow quick or convenient access to the inside of the system case. Some towers, for example, use removable trays that allow the motherboard and I/O cards to be plugged in before being slid into the unit. Other tower cases use hinged doors on the side of the case, allowing the system and I/O boards to swing away from the chassis. Either of these features facilitates the process of assembling the computer.

The ventilation characteristics of some tower units tend to be poor because of the I/O cards that are mounted horizontally. When the heat that is generated by the boards rises, it passes the upper boards, which are then subjected to additional heat. Because of this, most tower cases include a secondary case fan to help increase the airflow and dissipate excessive heat.

Power Supplies

TIP

The power supply converts AC current to DC current.

It is important to understand the *power supply* because it provides electrical power for every component inside the system unit. As mentioned in the previous chapter, the computer power supply performs the critical role of converting commercial electrical power received from a 120-volt AC, 60-Hz or 220-volt AC, 50-Hz (outside the United States) outlet into other levels required by the components of the computer. The power supply unit also provides the ground for the system.

In both the desktop- and tower-style cases, the power supply is a shiny metal box that is located at the rear of the system unit. The large bundle of cables provides power to the components of the system unit and its peripheral devices.

The two basic types of power supplies are AT and ATX. AT power supplies are designed to support AT-compatible motherboards. ATX power supplies are designed according to recent ATX design specifications to support the ATX motherboard. Figure 3-5 shows an ATX power supply.

Figure 3-5 ATX Computer Power Supply

Two major distinctions exist between the old AT and the new ATX power supplies. The *AT power supply* has two 6-pin motherboard power connectors, P8/P9, whereas the *ATX power supply* uses a single 20-pin power connector, P1. In the ATX-compatible power supply, the cooling fan pulls air through the case from the front and blows it out the rear of the power supply unit. Conversely, the AT design pulls air in through the rear of the power supply unit and blows it directly on the AT motherboard.

Table 3-2 gives a summary of some important factors to consider when shopping for a power supply. Review Chapter 2 for additional information.

TIP

Know the difference between the AT and ATX power supplies.

Table 3-2 Selecting a Computer Power Supply

Factor	Rationale
Wattage	To upgrade the PC with more equipment or faster processors, the power supply must provide enough power to the equipment without becoming overloaded.
Form factor	Depending on the type of case and motherboard selected, the power supply must adhere to the same form factor requirements to fit inside the case and correctly power the motherboard and other devices.
CPU type	Different CPUs require different voltages. For example, an AMD chip and motherboard require much more power than a Pentium chip and motherboard.
Expandability	If the power supply only has enough power to supply the current CPU, motherboard, and devices, enough power might not be available to upgrade the system.
Energy efficiency	Each power supply has an efficiency rating. The higher the rating, the less heat generated by the power supply when converting voltage.
Fan type and direction	The power supply must have a high-quality fan. The fan is the primary source for airflow inside the case. Some fans can change direction to allow air to be blown directly on the CPU and to regulate the quality of the air entering the case. Some fans can adjust their speed to match the cooling requirements of the system.

continues

Table 3-2 Selecting a Computer Power Supply (Continued)

Factor	Rationale
Signals	Modern power supplies can be controlled by the motherboard. The main board can regulate the speed of the fan depending on the temperature inside the case and can turn off the fan to save power. Some "smart" power supplies can turn off the computer in the event of a fan failure before the components overheat.
Fault tolerance	For a PC that needs to be on at all times, consider a dual power supply. If one of the units fails, the other one immediately takes over. Some designs enable a power supply to be replaced while the computer is still powered on.
Line conditioning	One way to ensure that the DC voltages supplied to the PC are kept at normal levels during spikes or brownouts is to install a power supply that has built-in conditioning. These units ensure that the DC voltages supplied to the system remain stable even when the AC current coming in is not. (These concerns are addressed in Chapter 12, "Preventive Maintenance.")

Levels of DC Voltage from the Power Supply

The power supply produces four different levels of regulated DC voltage for the system components to use. These are +5V, −5V, +12V, and −12V. In ATX power supplies, the +3.3V level is also produced and is used by the second-generation Intel Pentium processors. The IC devices on the motherboard and adapter cards use the +5V level.

Table 3-3 summarizes the use of each DC voltage level that is produced by computer power supplies and indicates the power supply form factors where these are produced. The power supply form factor indicates whether those listed accommodate the voltage.

Table 3-3 DC Voltages Produced by PC Power Supplies

Voltage	Wire Color	Use	Power Supply Form		
			AT	ATX	ATX v12
+12V	Yellow	Disk drive motors, fans, cooling devices, and the system bus slots	*	*	*
−12V	Blue	Some types of serial port circuits and early programmable read-only memory (PROM)	*	*	*

Table 3-3 DC Voltages Produced by PC Power Supplies (Continued)

Voltage	Wire Color	Use	Power Supply Form		
			AT	ATX	ATX v12
+3.3V	Orange	Most newer CPUs, some types of system memory, and AGP video cards		*	*
+5V	Red	Motherboards, Baby AT and earlier CPUs, and many motherboard components	*	*	*
–5V	White	ISA bus cards and early PROMS	*	*	*
0V	Black	Ground—Used to complete circuits with the other voltages	*	*	*

*   DC voltage level is produced by power supply form factor.

You must be able to identify the uses for each voltage level and the corresponding color-coded wire. This allows you to test the wires using a multimeter to determine whether problems exist with the power supply. Note that the computer power supply can produce a voltage only when some component in the machine is running.

The voltage levels are available for use through the expansion slot connectors of the motherboard. Motherboard power connectors provide the motherboard and the individual expansion slots with up to 1 ampere of current each. The power supply delivers power to the motherboard and its expansion slots through the motherboard power connectors. The ATX motherboard connector is a 20-pin, P1, keyed connector. It is keyed so that it cannot be connected incorrectly.

The Pentium 4–type connectors are different from the normal ATX (that is, Pentium II) connectors. This information is typically contained in the motherboard manufacturer's manual or is automatically detected by the on-board BIOS.

 Lab Activity 3.3.4   The Computer Case and Power Supply

Identify the type of computer case to be used, the form factor of the unit, and the voltage selector switch on the power supply.

TIP

The power supply voltage is tested with a multimeter.

WARNING

Never attempt to repair a defective power supply. Capacitors inside a power supply box store electricity and can discharge through the body if touched. The capacitor holds the electricity even if the unit is turned off and disconnected from a power source. Defective power supplies are replaced rather than repaired.

Worksheet 3.3.4   Power Supplies

This worksheet reviews the information that was covered on power supplies, including the voltage supplied to different computer components and the voltage for each color of wire.

Preparing the Motherboard for Installation

Motherboards, also called main boards or system boards, are an integral part of the computer system. The motherboard location map provides the information needed to configure the motherboard and to set the jumpers. It is also used to correctly install the CPU, the heat sink and fan, and for proper placement of RAM in the system. This section includes the following topics:

- Motherboard location map
- Motherboard configuration
- Motherboard jumpers
- Installing the CPU
- Installing the heat sink and fan
- Installing RAM

Motherboard Location Map

A *motherboard location map* shows where the major components and hardware are located on the motherboard. A motherboard map can be found in the documentation that comes with the motherboard. Typically, everything that is listed in the specifications section of the motherboard manual is depicted and labeled on the location map. This map is intended to help orient the board layout so that components can be identified and properly installed according to the instructions. For example, on the location map, you might notice that the processor socket location is labeled "Slot 1–Type CPU."

The location map also provides additional information that is useful during installation and assembly. On the map shown in Figure 3-6, notice that the main memory is subdivided into slots, and the slots are identified and numbered in the sequence DIMM bank 1, DIMM bank 2, and DIMM bank 3. This indicates that when the dual inline memory modules (DIMMs) are installed, they must be installed in the sequence that is indicated on the map. Study the motherboard location map before proceeding with an installation.

Figure 3-6 Motherboard Location Map

NOTE

The tiny 1s next to the jumper of three or more pins indicate the position of pin 1 for that jumper.

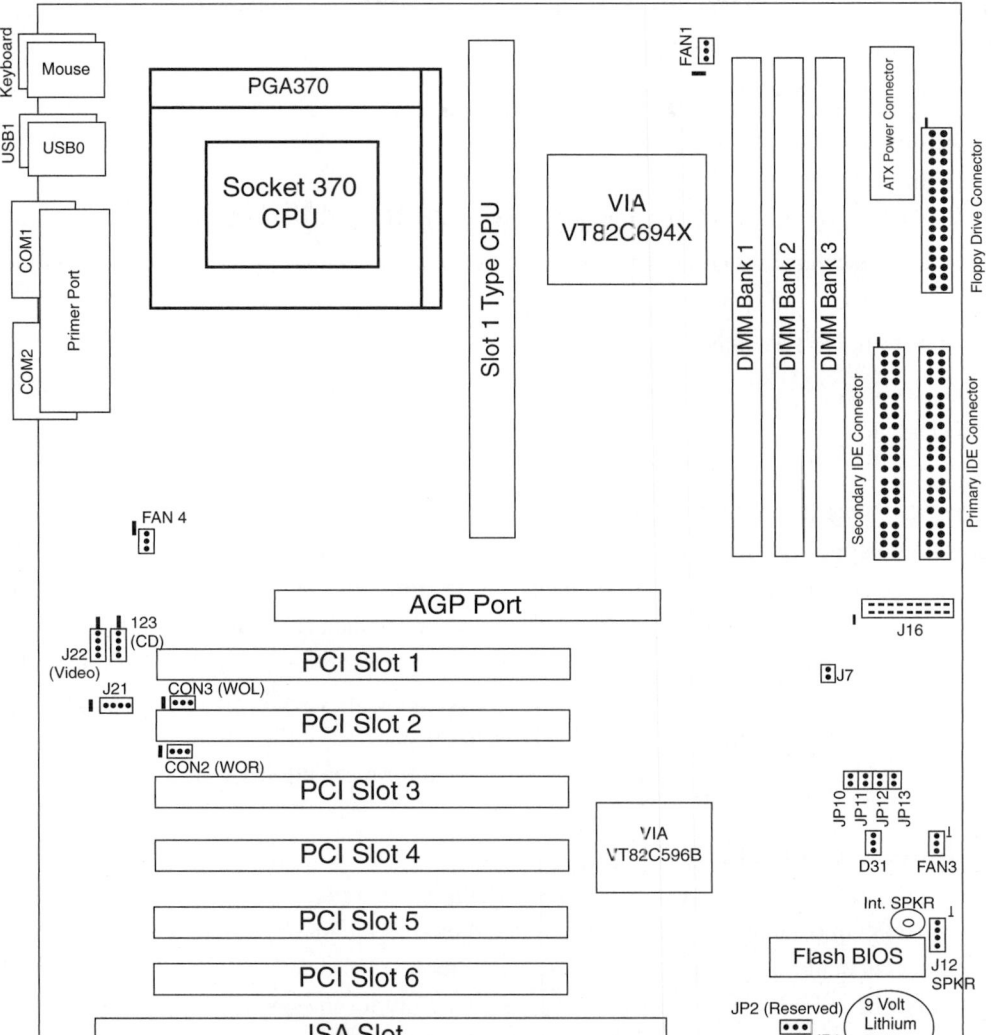

The more you know about a particular motherboard, the easier it is to assemble the rest of the computer. If you are working with a lab partner, you should study the map together.

Motherboard Configuration

The configuration of the motherboard, also known as setting the system hardware, is an important task. Motherboard configuration requires the following:

- Installing the CPU
- Installing the heat sink and fan
- Installing RAM
- Connecting the power supply cables to the motherboard power connectors and connecting miscellaneous connectors to the correct switches and status lights on the case front panel
- Setting the system BIOS

In the sections that follow, information for configuring the connectors, BIOS, and processor is provided.

Configuring the Connectors

Location maps allow the correct configuration of the motherboard for the case controls and monitor lights on the case front panel, which is sometimes called the bezel or faceplate. For the disk controllers, remember that a colored stripe on the data cable indicates pin 1. Most modern connectors are keyed by a missing pin or a blocked connector so that they cannot be connected incorrectly. The colored wires in a power cable are usually positive, and the white or black wires are ground or negative. I/O connectors generally follow industry standard conventions. You should review the motherboard manual for more information.

Configuring the BIOS

The *ROM BIOS* and *Complementary Metal Oxide Semiconductor (CMOS)* (pronounced *see-moss*) chip contain the software that sets and records the master configuration for all components in the system, including those on the motherboard and the logic chip sets. ROM BIOS is where the BIOS is stored, allowing accessibility for the system. The CMOS chip specifically stores the settings that you make with the BIOS configuration program. The BIOS typically has an interface that can be accessed after the initial POST (power-on self test) diagnostics are run. The BIOS sets up other components, such as the type of hard drive, CD-ROM drive, and floppy drives. The BIOS interface can be keyboard driven, or it can be graphical and mouse driven. When drives are replaced, memory is upgraded, or adapter boards are added, the BIOS setup must be updated to reflect the configuration changes and then saved to the CMOS chip. The BIOS is discussed more thoroughly later in this chapter.

Configuring the Processor

The motherboard must be configured for the frequency of the installed processor. Table 3-4 shows the jumper settings for each frequency and the corresponding host bus frequency. These settings differ for each motherboard and processor type. All specifications come from the manufacturer and are found in the manual included with the product. The motherboard manual typically details how the CPU and bus frequencies are related. Make sure that the CPU that is being used supports both the bus speed and CPU clock speed. The fact that the motherboard is capable of all these speeds does not mean that the CPU is capable of running all the variations that can be configured.

Table 3-4 Frequency Configuration Chart

Processor Frequency (MHz)	Jumpers J9C1-C	Jumpers J9C1-D	Host Bus Frequency (MHz)
233	5-6	1-2 and 4-5	66
200	5-6	1-2 and 5-6	66
166	5-6	2-3 and 5-6	66
150	4-5	2-3 and 5-6	60
133	5-6	2-3 and 4-5	66
120	4-5	2-3 and 4-5	60
100	5-6	1-2 and 4-5	66
90	4-5	1-2 and 4-5	60

NOTE

The 233 MHz Pentium processor with MMX technology and the 100 MHz Pentium processor have identical jumper settings. The Intel LT430TX motherboard automatically detects which processor type is installed.

CPU voltage configuration is discussed in the later section, "Installing the CPU." In practice, when you are working on most new systems, motherboard configuration parameters are handled by a Plug and Play BIOS. It is still important to know how to configure these parameters so that you can check the BIOS setup and ensure that everything is configured according to manufacturer specifications.

Motherboard Jumpers

Jumper pins are the electrical contact points. These contact points are set into the computer motherboard and some adapter cards. To set jumper pins, place a jumper (the connector plug) on the pins to complete, or close, the contacts. Closing or opening the contact points establishes logic levels to select functions for the operation of the board. Data generally does not travel through these circuits. Most jumper pins relate to the CPU on newer motherboards. Figure 3-7 shows the motherboard, the jumper location, and an example of the jumper that is used to set the contacts.

Figure 3-7 Motherboard Jumpers

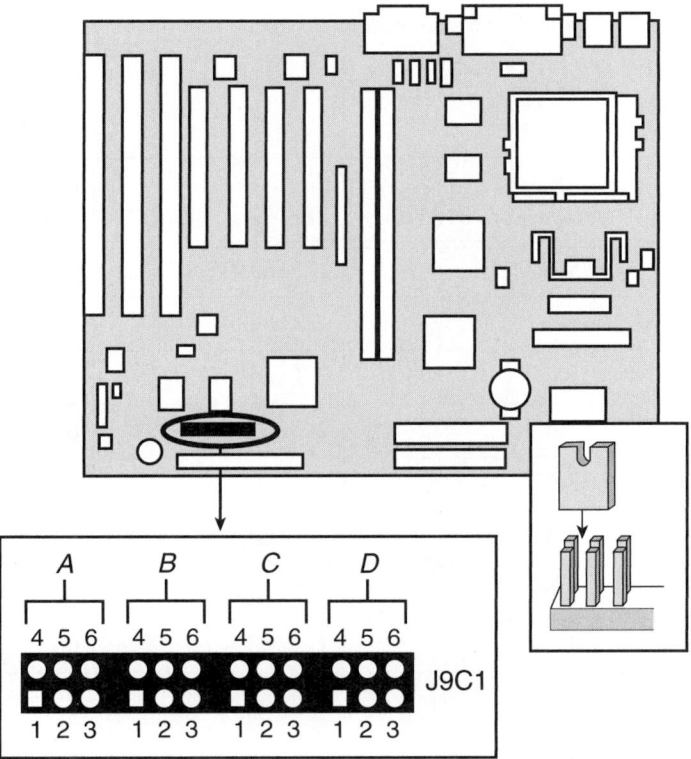

Configuring Motherboard Jumpers

Motherboard jumper pins are configured by using a jumper to bridge a pair of pins that are to be connected on the board. Removing or inserting the jumper on a set of pins enables or clears a given option, as specified in the motherboard manual. For all settings, you should closely follow the instructions that accompany the motherboard manual. Table 3-5 is a sample of how this information is presented in the manual. Remember that the jumper specifications for any board are provided by the manufacturer.

Additional information regarding motherboard jumpers can be found at the motherboard manufacturer's website.

Table 3-5 Motherboard Jumper Connectors

Function	Jumper	Configuration	
Processor voltage	J6M2	1-2	Standard voltage
		2-3	VRE (Voltage Regulator Enhanced) voltage (default)
Password	J9C1-A	1-2	Password enabled (default)
		2-3	Password cleared/disabled
CMOS (NVRAM and ESCD) clear	J9C1-A	4-5	Keep (default)
		5-6	Clear
BIOS setup access	J9C1-B	1-2	Access enabled (default)
		2-3	Access denied
Reserved	J9C1-B	4-5	(Reserved)
		5-6	(Reserved)
Host bus frequency	J9C1-C	Refer to Table 3-4	
Processor frequency	J9C1-D	Refer to Table 3-4	
BIOS recovery	J8A1	1-2	Normal (default)
		2-3	Recovery

Additional Jumpers

Several additional jumper settings might have to be set along with the general motherboard configurations. These settings are summarized as follows:

- **BIOS recovery**—This jumper is for recovering BIOS data from a floppy disk in the event of a catastrophic failure. Leave this jumper set to the default values. Check the technical product specifications for details.

- **Clear CMOS**—This jumper, when provided, resets the CMOS settings to the default values.

- **Password clear**—Use this jumper, if provided, to clear the password if the password is forgotten. The default setting is "password enabled."

- **BIOS setup access**—This jumper enables or disables access to the Setup program. The default setting is "access enabled."

- **Processor voltage**—This jumper, when provided, sets the output of the on-board voltage regulator. The two choices are usually standard voltage and Voltage Regulator Enhanced.

CAUTION

When installing a processor in the motherboard for the first time or upgrading to a new processor, check the processor documentation for the correct voltage setting. Operating the processor at the wrong voltage can cause unreliable performance or damage to the system components.

Any jumper that needs to be removed should be saved along with other spare parts.

Installing the CPU

Microprocessor installation is not a complicated process, but it is important to handle the microprocessor with care.

The two main types of CPU interfaces—the socket type and the slot type—are shown in Figure 3-8. For more information regarding CPU interfaces, see Chapter 2. Socket 7 has been the standard interface, although the most recent systems now use different sockets. Socket 7 is the only interface that is used by at least one generation of Intel Pentium processors—Pentium I—as well as AMD and Cyrix chips. Older-technology processor chips, such as the Intel P24T, P24D, 80486DX4, and 80486DX2/DX/SX-SL; AMD AM486DX4/DX2/DX; and Cyrix CX486DX2/DX/S and 5X86, attach to the motherboard by means of a specially designed socket, commonly called socket 3. These technologies are quite old, so you are unlikely to encounter them.

Figure 3-8 Slot 1 and Socket 7 Processors

Slot-type interfaces use a slot that is similar to an expansion card. Slot 1 is the Single Edge Contact (SEC) interface, which is used only by the Intel Pentium II processor family. SEC is a cartridge that contains the CPU and L2 cache chips. The installation of the CPU differs depending on the processor being used and the interface type.

This course gives instructions on how to install a socket 7 chip. All the newer socket-type interfaces are derived from socket 7; they differ mainly by the number of pins that they have. The latest technologies, such as socket A and socket 370, are installed using the same steps as those for socket 7.

Step-by-Step Installation of the CPU

Almost all socket 7 systems use the *zero-insertion-force (ZIF) socket*. To install a socket 7 or similar chip, follow this general procedure:

Step 1   Turn over the chip and inspect the pins to make sure that none are damaged. All pins should stick straight out of the chip.

Step 2   Locate pin 1 on both the chip and the socket, and position the chip. Notice that the chip is always marked at pin 1. The mark might be slightly different for different chips. On the socket, pin 1 is commonly identified by a notch on one corner or a large 1. In some cases, an arrow on the motherboard points to that particular corner of the socket. As always, consult the motherboard manual for additional guidance. Align pin 1 on the chip with pin 1 on the socket for a correct installation. This is shown in Figure 3-9.

Step 3   After positioning the chip, open the ZIF socket. Shift the lever slightly away from the socket, from its default closed position, and raise it to the open position. Do this with care to avoid breaking the lever. A little resistance on the way up is normal. When fully raised, the top part of the ZIF socket slides over.

Step 4   With the socket open, you can insert the processor. Align pin 1 according to the orientation that was determined in Step 2. Insert the processor chip into the socket so that all the pins slide into the matching holes. With any ZIF socket, the CPU pins should slide easily into the corresponding holes in the socket. Generally, the chip can go in only one way. Avoid forcing the processor into the socket because the pins can be damaged.

Step 5   Check to make sure that no gap exists between the bottom of the CPU chip and the socket. If you see a gap, the processor chip needs to be reinserted.

Step 6   To secure the installed chip, push the lever gently back down to the closed position. A little resistance might be felt, but the lever and ZIF socket should close fairly easily.

Figure 3-9 The Missing Corner Pin on the CPU Chip

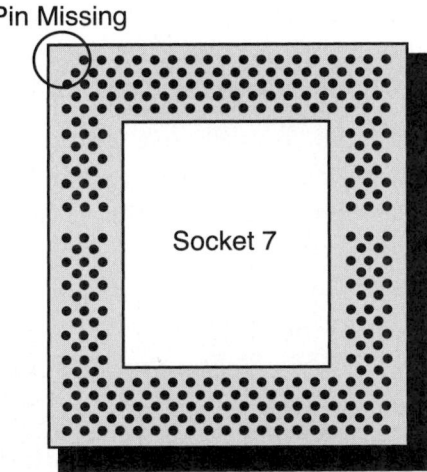

Configuring the CPU Voltage

The correct voltage must be present for the proper performance of the processor. Most CPUs are specific about the amount of voltage that they can handle. Pentium II and most current CPUs adjust automatically to the voltage, so they do not require voltage configuration. While this has been a great development, it has yet to be done to the older CPUs. If the proper voltage is not set, damage to the system could occur. With some hands-on experience, the voltage for any motherboard can be configured.

The information that you need for voltage setting should be contained in the section "Jumper Settings and Connectors" of the processor manual. CPU voltage varies from 1.8V to 3.5V. Dual voltage requirements accompany some CPUs. This means that two separate voltages—a core voltage and an I/O voltage—are required for these CPUs to function, as shown in Table 3-6. The AMD-K6 CPU family, for example, requires dual-voltage power for operation.

Table 3-6 I/O and Core voltages

Operating Voltage (V)	I/O Voltage (V)	Core Voltage (V)
2.2	3.3	2.2
2.9	3.3	2.9
3.2	3.3	3.2

*   Dual voltage requirements for some CPUs such as the AMD-K6 include I/O and core voltages.

Installing the Heat Sink and Fan

Most microprocessors produce a lot of heat, which can cause system problems. One way to dissipate heat from processors is to use a *heat sink* and cooling fan. Proper installation is crucial to the performance of this unit. Although the heat sink can be mounted before installing the processor chip on the motherboard, you risk causing damage to the pins on the chip. Only on Pentium II processors is the fan attached before the CPU installation. Figure 3-10 shows the installation of a heat sink.

Figure 3-10 Installing a Heat Sink

Step-by-Step Installation of the Heat Sink and Fan

Use the following steps when installing a heat sink and fan to socket 7 and other socket-type processors:

Step 1   If the CPU fan did not come with the heat sink already attached to it, use the screws that came with the fan to attach it to the heat sink.

Step 2   Some setups use heat sink compound or thermal grease. Apply the heat sink compound to the surface of the chip. Apply a thin layer—just enough to cover the surface of the chip. The heat sink compound or thermal grease improves contact between the CPU surface and the heat sink, thereby permitting better heat dissipation.

Step 3   Attach the heat sink carefully. Place the heat sink squarely on top of the processor, and press the heat sink down gently. The most recent heat sinks use a set of clips on each side to hold them down. You might need to use slight force to bend the clip in place. If the orientation is not right, the clips will be difficult to bend down into the right position. Sometimes it takes a few attempts to get the right position. In other cases, the heat sink compound is the only attachment between the heat sink and the processor.

Step 4   Make sure that the heat sink maintains a good contact with the processor chip surface. When the heat sink is inserted backward, the chip surface and heat sink usually become staggered. If this happens, remove the heat sink, turn it around, and reattach it.

Step 5   Wipe off the excess heat sink compound or thermal grease that might have oozed out the sides of the contact surfaces.

Step 6   Carefully plug the power cord from the fan to the fan power pins that are provided on the motherboard.

Boxed processors come with the fan and heat sink already attached to them. These units cost more but are more convenient and safer to install. Boxed processors are referred to as original equipment manufacturer (OEM) processors and have a better warranty coverage than processors without the fan and heat sink attached.

Installing RAM

Two types of memory modules are used on most PCs: 168-pin dual inline memory module (DIMM) cards and 72-pin single inline memory module (SIMM) cards, as shown in Figure 3-11. DIMMs and SIMMs share common edge connectors and fit into slots on the motherboard called RAM sockets. RAM sockets used for DIMM cards are often called DIMM sockets, while those used for SIMM cards are called SIMM sockets.

When either card is inserted into the slot, each edge connector makes contact with a corresponding gold trace on the motherboard. Each gold line represents an individual data path. Just as the gold lines leading to the CPU make up the processor bus, these gold lines make up the memory bus. The memory bus data highway transfers data between the RAM and the CPU.

Configuring Memory

The motherboard manual usually shows the permissible combinations of DIMM types that can be installed in the system. New motherboards do not use SIMMs. You might find, for example, that the DIMM sockets on the motherboard map are grouped into three or four banks of one slot each. Using the information that is provided in Figure 3-12, identify DIMM1 and DIMM2. DIMM1 and DIMM2 are Bank 0 and Bank 1. In some cases, motherboards have more than two slots for RAM. These slots would be DIMM3 and DIMM4, and the memory banks would be Bank 2 and Bank 3. Each bank can have any type of synchronous dynamic random-access memory (SDRAM), which is the most commonly used form of RAM.

Figure 3-11 Types of Memory Modules

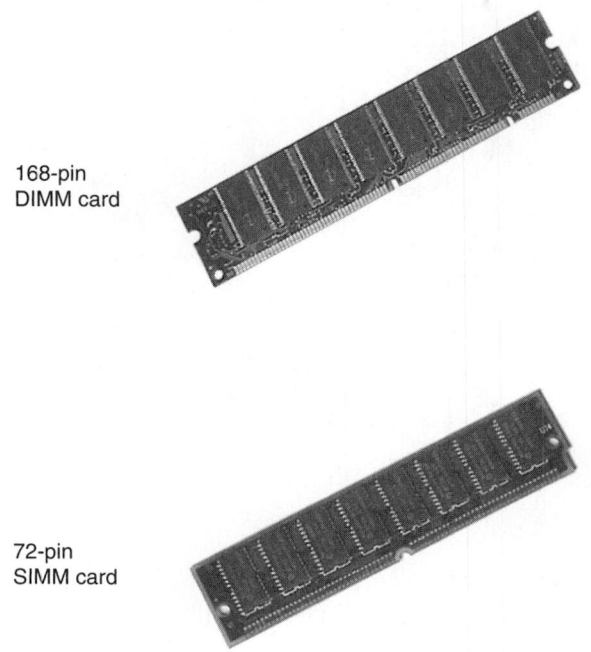

168-pin
DIMM card

72-pin
SIMM card

The memory banks should be filled in the exact combinations shown in the system board manual. For example, the manual might state that the maximum memory size is 512 MB and that the size of each DIMM can be 8 MB, 16 MB, 32 MB, 64 MB, or 128 MB. Any combination of these sizes can be used, depending on memory needs. When DIMM sizes are mixed on the motherboard, you must place the DIMM with the largest memory size in the first bank. The system automatically reads the size of the first DIMM and records it as the largest. If a smaller DIMM were put in the first bank, the system would read it as the largest and might fail to recognize or use the additional memory capacity of the DIMMs that are placed in the subsequent banks.

Banking with SIMM modules is slightly different. Each bank of memory for a SIMM has two sockets. You must fill the first bank before moving on to the next. In addition, each bank must be filled with RAM modules that have the same access time and size.

Figure 3-12 The Memory Banks on a Motherboard

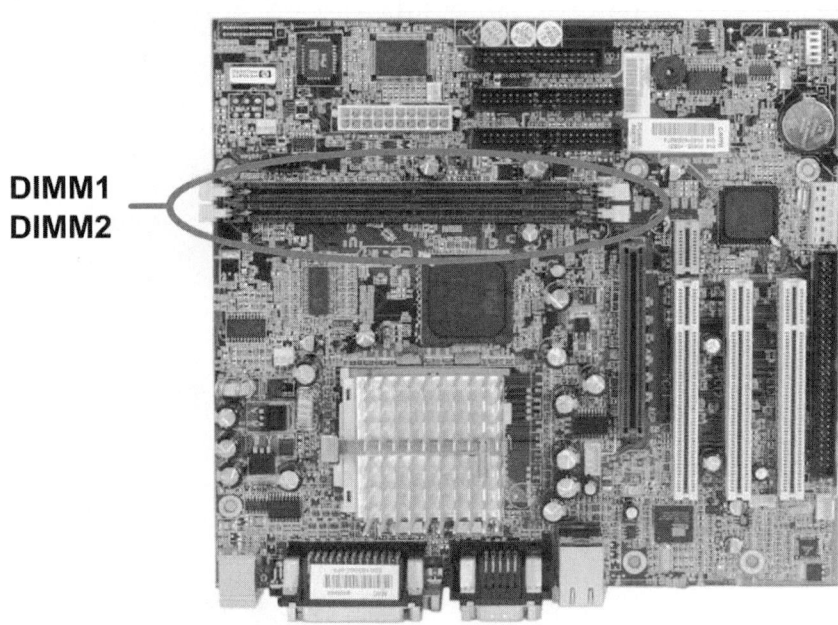

DIMM1
DIMM2

NOTE

When using other types of memory modules such as Rambus inline memory modules (RIMMs), other considerations must be taken into account. Unlike DIMMs and SIMMs, RIMMs modules use only the direct Rambus dynamic random-access memory memory chips (RDRAM). Some systems require RIMMs to be added in identical pairs, and others allow single RIMMs to be installed. Information on specific memory types can be found in the User Guide, the motherboard manual, or at the manufacturer's website.

Instructions for Installing RAM

This procedure describes the installation of DIMMs and SIMMs. The following steps summarize the installation process:

Step 1   Decide on which slots to use, and then orient the SIMM or DIMM chip over it. Both SIMMs and DIMMs are keyed so that they can be installed only one way.

Step 2   Insert the DIMM straight into the slot. The SIMM is inserted at an angle of about 45 degrees.

Step 3   Lock the memory module into place. With a SIMM, rotate it from the angled position to the vertical position. Some resistance is normal, but do not force it. If difficulty is encountered, check to see whether the chip is being installed backward. If this is the case, reverse the chip and reinstall it. When the SIMM is vertical, the small metal or plastic clip should snap in place, securing the SIMM vertically in the memory slot.

With a DIMM, simply close the levers on either side of it. If the levers do not close, the DIMM is usually not fully inserted into the slot or it is installed backward. If the DIMM is inserted properly, the levers should snap into place without further action.

Step 4   Repeat Steps 1 to 3 for the rest of the memory modules. When finished, check your work to be sure that each module is well seated on both ends in the slot.

Installing the Motherboard

Safety procedures and ESD precautions are critical when installing a motherboard. Before touching any part of the motherboard, ground yourself by touching the case of your computer or any other metal object with both hands. This section includes the following topics:

- Installing the motherboard into the case
- Attaching the LEDs, keylock, and speaker
- Connecting the power supply cables to the motherboard

Installing the Motherboard into the Case

Before installing the motherboard, review the section on motherboards in Chapter 2. Be sure to handle the board by the edges. Figure 3-13 shows the installation of a motherboard.

Figure 3-13 Installing a Motherboard

The following steps summarize the motherboard installation process:

Step 1   Locate the holes on the motherboard and the corresponding holes on the case. Hold the board just above the case so that you can see the holes on the case and motherboard for alignment purposes. The expansion card slots give you a good indication of how the board should be oriented.

Step 2   Insert the spacers that came with the motherboard securely into the holes on the case or mounting plate.

Step 3   Install plastic standoffs into the holes on the motherboard that line up with an eyelet—a hole that is long and key shaped—so that you can slide things into the eyelet. Some cases do not have an eyelet and instead use the metal spacer screws to hold the motherboard in place.

Step 4   Carefully slide the board into the case, making sure that it sits on the spacers and that all the spacers line up with an available hole on the motherboard.

Step 5   Inspect the screws to be used. It is a good practice to insert plastic washers on each screw before the screws are installed. This prevents the metallic screws from overlapping and possibly destroying or shorting any part of the circuitry near the holes.

Step 6   Tighten the board to the case, first by hand, and then finish with a screwdriver. The screws only need to be tight enough to prevent the board from moving around in the case.

Step 7   Check your work, and verify the following:

- The back of the motherboard is not touching any part of the case.
- All the slots and connectors line up properly with the holes on the back of the case.
- The board is securely held in place.
- When pressed at any point, the board does not bend.

These are general steps. Some cases have additional features. After becoming familiar with assembling PCs, some of the steps can be combined or bypassed.

Attaching the LEDs, Keylock, and Speaker

Light-emitting diodes (LEDs), or status lights, indicate whether the components inside the computer are on or working. Connecting the LEDs is usually the next step of assembling a computer, after the motherboard is securely installed. LEDs could be installed to indicate power on, turbo mode, and hard drive activity. The following list provides some important tips when connecting LEDs:

- **Turbo mode LED**—Both the turbo mode LED and the turbo switch are now mainly legacy items, and many new computer cases do not include them. If a case has a turbo mode LED, it can be connected by plugging it into the corresponding pins, although this step can be skipped. The turbo mode LED might instead be connected to a different component, such as the SCSI adapter, where it serves as the SCSI drive activity light.

- **Power on LED**—On older systems, the power LED is combined with the keylock switch as one 5-pin plug. Check the labels on the motherboard for a matching connector. To connect the LED, plug the connector into the corresponding plug on the system board. Make sure that the LEDs are connected separately if the system provides a separate power LED and keylock switch.
- **Hard drive activity LED**—This LED comes in either 2-pin or 4-pin plugs. Occasionally, only 2 pins of the 4-pin plug provide the connectivity. Consult your manual for installation procedures.

The keylock and speaker are two other wire leads that are usually connected at the same time as the LEDs. They all make up a group of small connectors and plugs that need the same amount of attention to attach them.

- **Keylock switch**—The keylock switch is common with older systems. It was mainly used to prevent unauthorized individuals from booting the computer and changing the BIOS settings. These switches are rare in newer systems. As previously mentioned, most AT or older systems combine the keylock switch with the power LED in one 5-pin plug. Check the motherboard manual for additional instructions on plugging in the keylock switch.
- **PC speaker**—Most computer cases use a 4-wire plug to connect the PC speaker. Plug the speaker wire into the designated plug, making sure that it plugs into pins 1 and 4.

Additional information about connecting LED devices, the keylock switch, and PC speakers can be found in the User Guide. Because LEDs involve small connectors, one or two connections could be wrong. If the wrong connector is used, the LED will not illuminate when the computer is powered on. Turn off the system and switch the connectors between different plugs until all the LEDs illuminate. LEDs are polarity sensitive, and you might have to reverse the connector if they do not illuminate properly. Figure 3-14 shows an HP Vectra that has hard drive activity and power LEDs as well as a keylock switch.

Connecting the Power Supply Cables to the Motherboard

After successfully installing the motherboard in the computer case, you can attach the appropriate power supply connectors to it. Figure 3-15 shows power supply cables. This process is easy with an ATX because there is only one connector and it is keyed to fit only one way. Take more care with the older AT systems because they contain two separate but physically identical connectors that must be attached in a specific way. This topic is covered in the next section.

Figure 3-14 LEDs on a HP Vectra

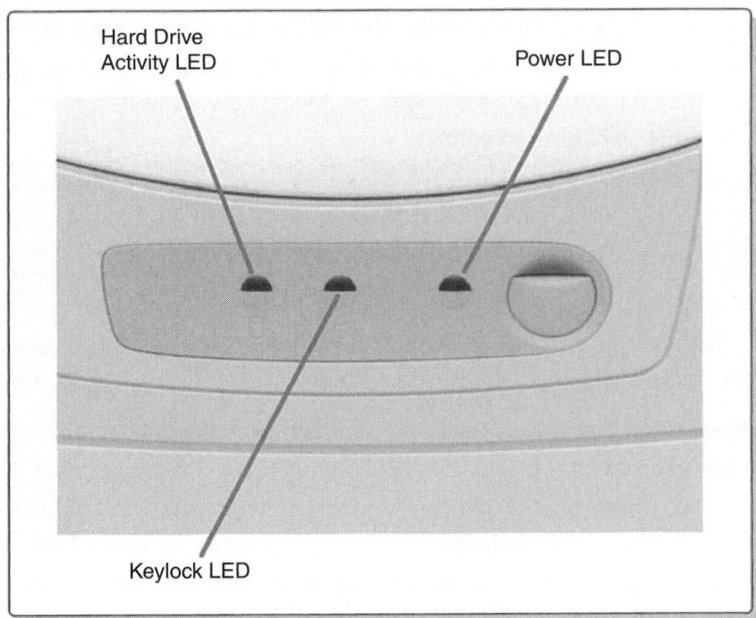

Figure 3-15 Power Supply Cables

Use the following steps to connect the power supply cables to the motherboard:

Step 1   On an AT system, locate the two large wire leads, labeled P8 and P9, that come from the power supply.

Step 2   Locate the large 12-pin power connector on the motherboard. It is usually found directly behind the keyboard connector.

Step 3   Plug the P8 and P9 wire lead connectors into the 12-pin power connector.

On an ATX system, you find one large 20-pin (P1) connector. It is keyed for easy installation.

To allow maneuvering room to work inside the case, do not attach the power connector to the board until all the components that need to go on the motherboard have been installed.

Lab Activity 3.5.3   Motherboard Installation

Use this lab to prepare and install a motherboard.

Installing the Floppy Drive, Hard Drive, CD-ROM Drive, and DVD Drive

The procedures for installing the floppy drive, hard drive, CD-ROM drive, and DVD drive are similar. Continue to follow the safety procedures to prevent ESD damage. This section includes the following topics:

- Attaching the floppy drive to the case
- Attaching the hard drive and CD-ROM drive to the case
- Connecting the floppy drive, hard drive, CD-ROM drive, and DVD drive to the system
- Connecting the power cables to the floppy drive, hard drive, and CD-ROM drive

Attaching the Floppy Drive to the Case

The following step-by-step process for installing a floppy drive is used for a 3-1/2-inch drive. Make sure that the floppy drive cable and power cables are long enough to reach the drive before starting. Verify that the drive is mounted right side up or it will not work. Figure 3-16 shows a 3-1/2-inch floppy disk drive.

Figure 3-16 A 3-1/2-Inch Floppy Disk Drive

Use the following steps to attach the floppy drive to the case:

Step 1   Select which drive bay is to be used for the floppy drive, and remove the faceplate of that bay. Save the faceplate for future use. You typically can choose
between a 3-1/2-inch and a 5-1/4-inch bay. Be sure to choose the correct bay
for the floppy drive that is being installed. You need a special bracket to mount
a 3-1/2-inch drive in a 5-1/4-inch bay. This bracket is usually supplied with the
new floppy drive.

Step 2   Without making any connections, insert the drive into the chosen bay, making
sure that it fits properly.

Step 3   Select the correct-size screws (preferably those that came with the drive). If
using brackets to hold the drive in place, secure them now, or you can use the
screws to attach the drive to the bay. First, tighten the screws by hand, and then
use a screwdriver to secure the screws. Make sure that they are not too tight,
and take care not to cross thread or strip the screws.

Step 4   Attach the power and ribbon cable to the drive. If other drives are to be
installed, you can skip this step. This provides more maneuvering room in the
case, especially if no removable drive bays are available. The drive cable and
power cord can then be connected after all the drives have been installed.

Step 5   Check your work.

Attaching the Hard Drive and CD-ROM Drive to the Case

This section describes how to attach both the hard drive and the CD-ROM drive to the case.

Before proceeding, make sure that the interface cable can reach the drive in its intended location. With IDE/ATA drives, the length of the cable is limited to 18 inches, and less in some
instances. Also, make sure that the power cable can reach the drive from the power supply.
Do not mount the drive upside down or backward. Verify that the label of the drive is up and
that the circuit board is down. The first step is to set the jumpers.

Master/Slave Jumper Settings

The designation of a hard drive or CD-ROM drive as either *master* or *slave* is generally determined by the jumper configuration. The only exception is if the drive is set to "cable select"
and both the system and ribbon cable support cable select. In this case, master and slave are
determined by the position on the data ribbon cable. Depending on how the system controls
the cable, the select line on the ribbon cable determines where the master and slave need to be
attached. Refer to the system manual for more information. The following description applies
only to a situation where both drives are attached to the same IDE channel, where the CD-ROM

drive is set to slave. For better performance, always attach the drives to separate channels. The hard drive should be attached to the primary IDE channel as primary master, and the CD-ROM drive should be attached to the second IDE channel as secondary master.

It is easier to configure these drives before installing them in the computer case because you have more room to set the jumpers. Before setting the jumpers, determine the types and number of drives to install. This section assumes that you have two IDE drives. The jumper settings are often printed on top of the drive itself. If not, consult the manual. In either case, use needle-nosed pliers or tweezers to set the jumpers. Always save spare jumpers for future use by hanging them on one pin.

Hanging the jumper on one pin or parking the jumper means the same as not jumpered—that is, no circuit configuration has been selected. Figure 3-17 illustrates some typical jumper settings on an IDE drive.

Figure 3-17 Jumper Settings on an IDE Drive

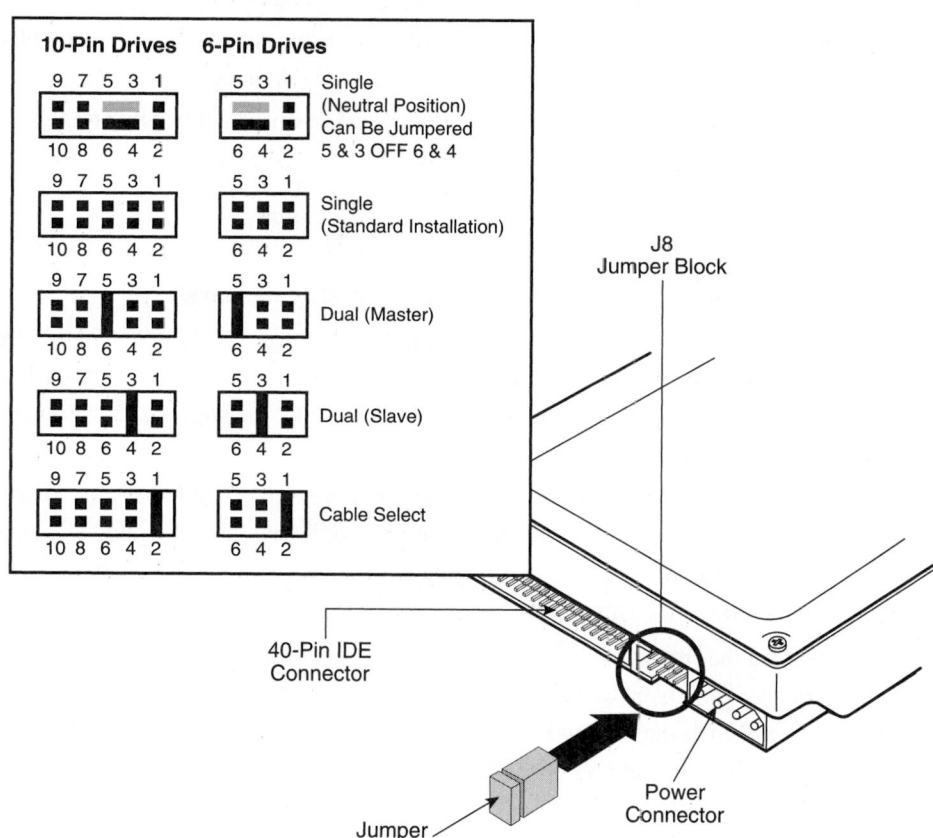

In a basic system that has only one hard drive, set the jumper to master. Some drives have another setting called *single*. This setting essentially tells the drive that it is alone on that IDE channel and works the same as the master. You should use this setting, if available, on a single-hard-drive system. The CD-ROM drive is also easy to configure. However, jumpers can be located in different places on each drive and could be labeled differently. Set the CD-ROM to master if it is the only drive that is connected to the second IDE channel.

Installing the Hard Drive

Technically, the hard drive can be inserted in any free bay in a computer case. However, consider the following points:

- Hard drives, especially the newer 7200-rpm and 10,000-rpm drives, can generate a lot of heat. Therefore, keep these drives as far away from other hardware as possible.
- If you need to install a drive cooler, make sure that you have enough room.
- Install a hard drive away from the power supply. Poorly designed cases might allow room under the power supply to install the hard drive. However, this is not a good place for a hard drive. Power supplies act like magnets and can damage data.
- Try to keep the hard drive near the front of the case. The drive will benefit from the cooling effect of the air that is drawn into the case through the front by the system cooling fans.

With these considerations in mind, follow these general steps to install a hard drive:

Step 1   Set the hard drive jumper to master, as previously explained.

Step 2   Slide the drive into the selected drive rail of the case. The faceplate in this area does not need to be removed. Modern ATX cases usually provide a hard drive bay without a faceplate. If the drive is smaller than the bay, add rails or a mounting bracket to allow the drive to fit.

Step 3   Use the screws that are packaged with the drive or use similar screws. Screws that are too long can damage the circuit board. Screw the drive into place, making sure not to force anything. Tighten the screws by hand first, and then tighten them with a screwdriver.

Step 4   Attach the ribbon cable and the power cord to the hard drive, the same way as with the floppy drive. Connecting the ribbon cable is discussed in the section "Connecting the Floppy Drive, Hard Drive, CD-ROM Drive, and DVD Drive to the System," later in this chapter.

Attaching the CD-ROM Drive and DVD Drive

CD-ROM drive and DVD drive installation is similar to hard drive installation. For the CD-ROM drive, first remove the drive bay cover. Then set the CD-ROM drive jumper to master, because it will be connected to the secondary IDE channel. Now slide the drive into the bay from the front, making sure that the drive is flush with the front panel, and screw it into place. Use the same procedure used for installing a DVD drive.

NOTE

Do not tighten the screws until the cables have been connected to the drive.

In some computer cases, particularly the mini-towers, it can be challenging to work behind the CD-ROM drive because of its length and because it is obstructed by the power supply. Removing the CD-ROM drive can solve this problem. Make sure to reinstall the drive properly when work is complete.

Role of the Drive Rails

As with the hard drive, the installation of the CD-ROM drive and DVD drive depends on the case design or type. Some cases come with drive rails to help install the hardware. Simply screw a drive rail in the correct direction to each side of the CD-ROM drive. Then slide the CD-ROM drive into the computer case from the front, using the rails as a guide, until it snaps into place. Use the same procedure to install a DVD drive. Drive rails make hardware installations relatively easy.

Connecting the Floppy Drive, Hard Drive, CD-ROM Drive, and DVD Drive to the System

The floppy drive, hard drive, CD-ROM drive, and DVD drive communicate with the rest of the system using ribbon cables. This section discusses the types of ribbon cables used as well as how to connect them to the various drives.

Characterizing Ribbon Cables

Ribbon cables connect peripherals, such as floppy drives and hard drives, internally. They are rarely used outside of the system case. Ribbon cables are thin, flat, multiconductor cables that must be connected correctly for the component to work.

Floppy Drive Cable

The floppy drive exchanges data with the motherboard devices, including the microprocessor, through a 34-pin flat ribbon cable. The ribbon cable typically connects from a 34-pin male connector at the rear of the floppy drive to a 34-pin male connector on the motherboard. The cable plugs, drive connector, and floppy controller interface are all keyed for proper alignment. A stripe (usually red) on the edge of the cable identifies pin 1, as shown in Figure 3-18.

Figure 3-18 Pin-1 Ribbon Cable Identification

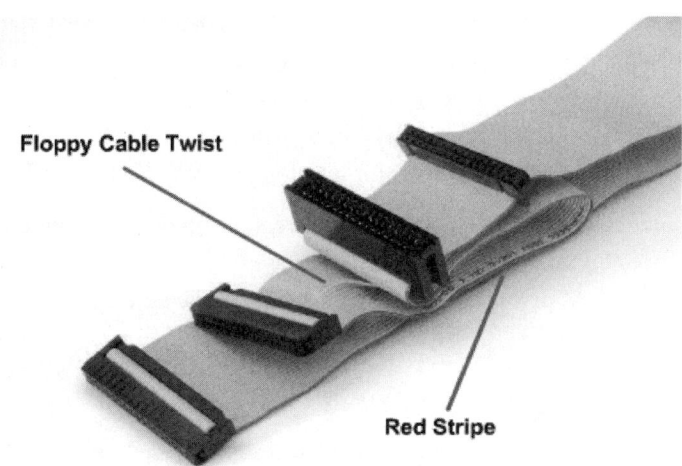

Floppy Cable Twist

Red Stripe

Aligning the red-stripe edge of the ribbon cable with pin 1 of the drive connector or drive controller interface ensures correct alignment.

Current system BIOS versions can support up to two floppy drives on one controller through a daisy-chain cable arrangement. Cable pin-outs 10 through 16 are cross-wired between the middle drive connector and end drive connector. This produces a twist that reverses the Drive Select (DS) configuration of the drive that is plugged into the end connector of the ribbon cable. The twist consists of seven data wires. This feature, called cable select, automatically configures the drive on the middle connector as drive B and the drive on the end connector as drive A. This greatly simplifies installation and configuration of the floppy drives. In this example, only one 3-1/2-inch floppy drive, drive A, is being used.

Hard Drive and CD-ROM Drive Cables
The hard drive, CD-ROM drive, and DVD drive exchange data signals with the controller on the motherboard by means of a flat ribbon cable, just like the floppy drive. The ribbon cable pin-outs and cable width are dependent on the type of interface. In this course, the IDE interface is used. The ribbon cable that is used in this case looks physically similar to the floppy cable previously mentioned, but the ribbon cable is wider, as shown in Figure 3-19. Pin 1 is also identified by a red edge. However, an IDE cable typically has 40 pins and can also have two devices attached to it, like the floppy cable. In this case, though, one device must be set as the master and the other as a slave using jumpers. A second cable is called IDE 2, and it can have a master and a slave. The cable connectors and plugs, just like the floppy cable, are keyed for proper alignment.

Figure 3-19 A Hard Drive Ribbon Cable

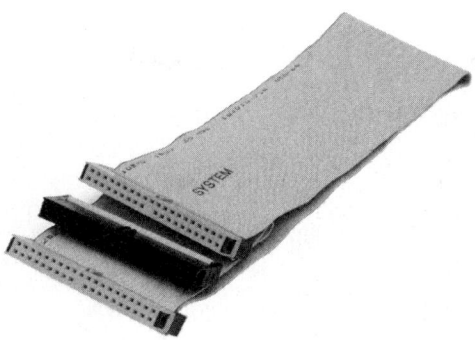

You should now be familiar with ribbon cables and be able to connect these components to the system board.

Instructions for Connecting the Floppy Drive

The following steps detail how to connect the floppy drive to the motherboard:

Step 1   Identify the appropriate ribbon cable that goes with the floppy drive. The cable has a 7-wire twist toward one end and is narrower—with 34 pins—than the 40-pin IDE ribbon cable.

Step 2   Identify pin 1, the red edge of the cable, and align this with pin 1 on the rear of the floppy drive. Gently push on the cable connector until it is fully inserted. In most cases, the connectors are keyed. If any resistance is experienced as the cable is attached, recheck the pin-1 alignment. Because this drive is being installed as drive A, use the connector located just after the twist in the cable.

Step 3   Identify the floppy controller on the system board by consulting the motherboard manual. Attach the connector on the far end of the ribbon cable to the floppy controller on the board. Make sure that pin 1 is properly aligned for the cable and controller interface connectors.

Step 4   Check your work, making sure that no pin is bent or displaced.

If pin 1 has accidentally been reversed, the drive will not work and the drive LED will stay on until the problem is corrected.

Instructions for Connecting the Hard Drive and CD-ROM Drive

The following steps detail how to connect the hard drive and CD-ROM drive to the motherboard:

Step 1 Identify the two 40-pin IDE ribbon cables that go with the hard drive and CD-ROM drive. These are wider than the floppy drive cable and have no twist at one end.

Step 2 Attach one end of one cable connector to the rear of the hard drive connector and one end of the second cable to the rear of the CD-ROM drive. You might have to slide the CD-ROM drive out a few inches to have enough access at the rear. Both cable connectors are keyed. Make sure that pin 1 is properly aligned for the cable and drive connectors. The end of the cable with the longer span is usually connected to the motherboard.

Step 3 Attach the free end of the hard drive cable to IDE controller no. 1, the primary IDE, on the motherboard. Attach the free end of the CD-ROM cable to IDE controller no. 2, the secondary IDE, on the motherboard. Make sure pin 1 on each cable is aligned with pin 1 of the corresponding controller interface. Installing the hard drive and CD-ROM on separate IDE channels can improve performance.

Step 4 Check your work, making sure that all cable connectors are properly seated, that none of the pins are displaced, and that all pin 1s are aligned.

If the hard drive cable is placed backward, you might receive errors that indicate that the hard drive is defective. If this happens, remove the hard drive cable and reinstall it.

NOTE

Pin 1 on both the hard drive and CD-ROM drive is usually located on the side closest to the power connector. Pin 1 might be labeled on the back of the hard drive. Conversely, pin 1 on the motherboard might not be properly labeled, so consult your manual to make this determination. The CD-ROM drive audio cable can remain disconnected until a sound card is installed.

Connecting the Power Cables to the Floppy Drive, Hard Drive, and CD-ROM Drive

Small cable drive connectors from the power supply provide power to the floppy drive, hard drive, CD-ROM drive, and DVD drive. The cable connectors have a female 4-pin plug that connects to a male 4-pin connector at the rear of each drive. The pin-outs or wire scheme is color-coded to identify the proper voltages of the wires.

Power Voltage Requirements

Two different power voltages are required for the proper functioning of these drives. The circuit board and the logic chips that each drive uses are designed to use +5V power. The drive motors use +12V power. For more details, see Table 3-7.

Table 3-7 Power Connector Pin-Outs

Pin No.	Signal	Wire Color
1	+5V	Red
2	Ground	Black
3	Ground	Black
4	+12V	Yellow

Connecting the Drives

All the connectors are keyed and can only be inserted one way. This makes it easier to attach the power cables to the drive. Verify that the proper connector is being attached to the appropriate drive based on the following guidelines:

- **Floppy drive**—Identify the proper connector that goes with the 3-1/2-inch drive. These connectors are usually the smallest plugs that are coming out of the power supply. Push the plugs in gently. Do not rock them back and forth to secure a connection.

- **Hard drive and CD-ROM drive**—Identify the proper power connectors for these drives. The connectors are larger than those for the floppy drive; the labels on these power plugs can be marked P1, P2, P3, and so on. These connectors are harder to push in, so rock them gently back and forth, if needed, until they snap into place.

As always, double-check all your work, making sure that all power plugs are properly inserted and secure.

 Lab Activity 3.6.4   Floppy Drive, Hard Drive, CD-ROM Drive, and DVD Drive Installation

Use this lab to prepare and install the floppy drive, hard drive, CD-ROM drive, and DVD drive.

Video Card Installation

Chapter 2 detailed the video card as the interface between the computer and monitor. To test the newly assembled computer system and complete the configuration, a video card must be installed so that system information can be viewed. Information relating to the different types of video cards and upgrading video cards is provided in Chapter 8, "Multimedia Capabilities." This section covers the step-by-step installation of the video card.

The video card, as shown in Figure 3-20, is the only expansion card that needs to be installed before booting the PC for the first time. This card is critical for displaying vital information that is needed to configure the BIOS during the initial boot process. All the other cards can be installed after the computer is up and running. To learn more about the video adapter, review the section "Display Components" in Chapter 2.

Figure 3-20 Video Card

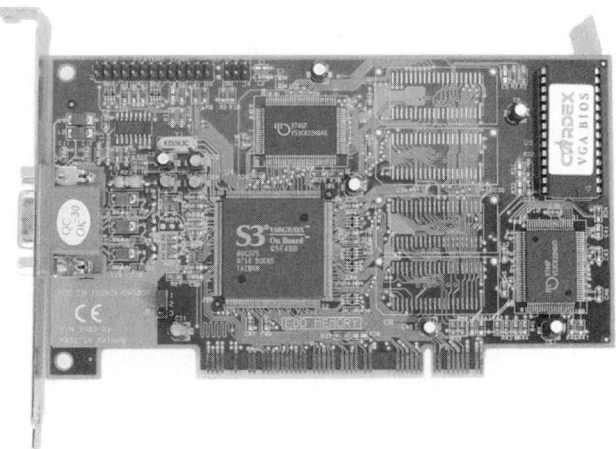

CAUTION

Some motherboards have built-in video. If that is the case, this video must be disabled in the CMOS when installing an external video card. Built-in video that is not disabled causes a system conflict that must be resolved before the new external video card can be recognized.

Installation of the video card is a four-step process, as follows:

Step 1   Locate an expansion slot type that matches the video card. AGP slots are used for newer (ATX) motherboards, whereas ISA and PCI slots are used for older boards.

Step 2   Remove the slot insert that corresponds to the slot that you plan to fill on the motherboard. Some cases have punch-out inserts, whereas other inserts are screwed in.

Step 3   Insert the video card into the slot by aligning the pins and gently applying pressure alternately to the front and back of the board until all the pins are in place. Older ISA cards can be more difficult to insert because of their length. When pushing the card into the slot, try not to bend the motherboard. You can prevent bending the board by placing your hand under the board while seating the video card. Make sure that you are properly grounded to the case.

Step 4   After the card is in place, secure it to the case with a screw. Check your work.

These general steps can also be used to install other expansion cards, such as a modem card or sound card.

If you are installing a Plug and Play video card, the system will detect the new hardware and install the proper driver. If the proper driver is not detected, use the driver that came with the video card. Current drivers can also be downloaded from the video card manufacturer's website.

 Lab Activity 3.7.1   Video Card Installation and System Booting

Install the video card using the steps covered in this section. Then connect the mouse, keyboard, and monitor. The final step is to boot the system.

Final Steps

After all the components are installed in the case, you can complete the PC assembly process. This section addresses the following topics:

- Fitting the case together
- Connecting the keyboard, mouse, monitor, and power cord

Fitting the Case Together

You need to address several items before the case can be fitted together. First, check the cable connectors. Make sure that all the pin 1 indicators on the cables line up with all the pin 1 indicators on the sockets. Next, make sure that all the connections are secure. If a connection does not look correct, push on it gently to seat it. Do not force any connection, because the pins and circuit boards bend and break easily. No connection should be too difficult to attach. After all the cables are secured, make sure that all the screws are properly tightened. These screws should be secure, but not overly tight. Finally, when securing the case, make sure that no cables or wires are sticking out or are caught between the parts of the case.

Postassembly Check List

You should install any extra system components later, after the initial bootup. This ensures that the basic computer is working properly before you add new hardware. Double-check all your work before turning on the power for the first time. The following postassembly checklist should be used before closing the case:

- All expansion cards are fully inserted into appropriate slots.
- The CPU fan is attached to power.
- The 110/220-volt switch is configured properly.

- Drives are properly connected to power.
- Ribbon cables are attached correctly.
- No wires are protruding into the fans.
- CPU voltage settings are correctly configured.
- The power switch is off, and power supply connectors are properly connected to the motherboard.
- All connections are sufficiently tight.
- All pins are properly aligned.

Close the newly assembled computer before testing it to avoid accidental contact with the internal parts while the machine is running.

Connecting the Keyboard, Mouse, Monitor, and Power Cord

The last step before turning on the power is to connect the basic input and output (I/O) devices that the computer needs to start up. These devices can be connected in any order. The following list includes instructions for connecting these devices:

- **Connect the keyboard to the back of the case**—Older model motherboards use a 5-pin connector, but most computers use a 6-pin PS/2 port. Sometimes, the keyboard connector and port are color-coded to distinguish them from the mouse.

- **Connect the mouse to the back of the computer**—If you are connecting a PS/2 mouse, the mouse port is usually adjacent to the keyboard connection. Follow any color codes where applicable. If you are connecting a serial mouse, plug it into the serial port. Some motherboards have numbered ports, and because the mouse is the first serial device in the system, plug it into serial port 1.

- **Connect the monitor**—If the motherboard has video capabilities, the connection point for the monitor is near the mouse and keyboard connections. If the motherboard has a video adapter card, plug the monitor into the connector that is located on that card. Because the connector is large, it normally has two screws to hold it in place. Twist the tops of the screws until the connection is secure.

- **Connect the main power supply**—Plug one end of the AC power cord into the back of the power supply and the other end into the wall socket. If the power supply has a switch, turn it on as well. (This does not usually power up the computer because it is just the power switch for the power supply.)

Start up the computer by depressing the power switch that is located on the front of the case.

Booting the System for the First Time

After the computer is assembled and switched on, the process of configuration begins. Proper configuration is critical for a computer system to function properly. This section addresses the following topics:

- What is the BIOS?
- Entering the BIOS configuration
- Standard CMOS setup screen
- BIOS features and chipset features setup screens
- Power management and Plug and Play screens
- Integrated peripherals and hard disk detection screens
- Password screens and the Load Setup Defaults screen
- BIOS exit options
- Startup sequence

What Is the BIOS?

BIOS stands for *Basic Input/Output System*. The BIOS contains the program code that is required to control all the basic operating components of the computer system. In other words, the BIOS contains the software that is required to test the hardware at bootup, load the operating system, and support the transfer of data among hardware components. In this section and those that follow, the crucial role of the system BIOS is covered.

The final step in the configuration of a new computer is the BIOS setup. Enter the BIOS setup screen during the bootup process by following the screen instructions. Figure 3-21 shows the system entering the BIOS setup after pressing F2. Some computers require you to press a different key to access the BIOS setup. Check the screen as the system boots. For more information, refer to the section, "Entering the BIOS Configuration," later in this chapter.

BIOS setup allows you to customize a computer to function optimally based on its hardware and software profiles. The BIOS code is typically embedded in a ROM chip on the motherboard; this is discussed in Chapter 2. The ROM chip is a read-only chip. This protects the ROM from hard disk, RAM, or power failures that could corrupt the ROM. In addition, this feature ensures that the BIOS code is always available, because it is required for the system to boot. Although the BIOS cannot be changed while loaded in memory, the basic BIOS program can be updated. Newer BIOS ROM chips are of the type called electrically erasable programmable read-only memory (EEPROM), also called flash BIOS. *Flash BIOS* allows you to upgrade the software in the BIOS chip from a floppy disk that is provided by the manufacturer, without replacing the chip. BIOS upgrades are typically used by manufacturers to fix flaws or bugs in the BIOS code and to improve system capabilities.

Figure 3-21 Entering the BIOS Setup

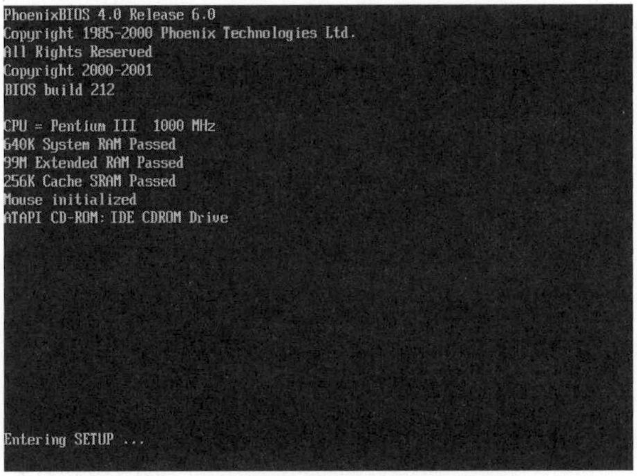

```
PhoenixBIOS 4.0 Release 6.0
Copyright 1985-2000 Phoenix Technologies Ltd.
All Rights Reserved
Copyright 2000-2001
BIOS build 212

CPU = Pentium III  1000 MHz
640K System RAM Passed
99M Extended RAM Passed
256K Cache SRAM Passed
Mouse initialized
ATAPI CD-ROM: IDE CDROM Drive




Entering SETUP ...
```

Evolution of the BIOS

The basic design standard of the system BIOS was originally developed in the early 1980s by the IBM Corporation for use in its XT and AT computer systems. Unfortunately, the IBM BIOS only worked with IBM hardware. Therefore, other manufacturers who built clones of these systems had to guarantee compatibility of the computers with the IBM standard. Cloning was necessary to guarantee that the computer software applications that were developed for IBM systems would run on other systems. By the late 1980s, a few companies had developed compatible BIOSs that other manufacturers could use. The following companies have since come to dominate the BIOS market:

- Phoenix Technologies, Ltd.
- AMI (American Megatrends, Inc.)
- Award Software, Inc.

NOTE

Award Software, Inc. is now a division of Phoenix Technologies, Ltd.

Of the three manufacturers, Phoenix Technologies, Ltd. now concentrates primarily in the specialized laptop computer market, while AMI and Award are the chief suppliers to the modern non-IBM computer market.

BIOS Function

The ***BIOS function*** is simple. It initially runs basic device test programs and then seeks to configure these devices. The system BIOS and the information that is required to configure it are stored on a CMOS chip. The CMOS chip is a battery-powered storage chip that is located on the system board. This chip has rewritable memory, which allows the BIOS upgrade.

Configuration of the BIOS on a computer is called the BIOS setup. It is also called the CMOS setup, named for the chip that stores the BIOS settings. It is especially important to get the BIOS setup right the first time. Because the BIOS scans the system at boot time and compares what it finds against settings in the CMOS, the BIOS must be properly configured to avoid errors. Proper operation of the system depends on the BIOS loading the correct program code for its devices and internal components. Without the correct code and device drivers, the system either does not boot properly or works inconsistently with frequent errors.

If a system crashes, or fails unexpectedly, it can be restarted thanks to the BIOS. Built into the BIOS is a comprehensive self-diagnostic routine called the power-on self test (POST), which checks the internal system circuits at bootup and gives error codes. The POST is discussed more thoroughly in Chapter 2. After the initial circuit checks, the BIOS also checks the internal components against a known list of operating devices that is stored in the CMOS chip. Any problems are indicated using error codes or messages. These error messages can help in diagnosing and repairing the problem. For the BIOS to have meaningful diagnostics and error checking, the internal components and devices of a newly assembled computer need to be configured properly in the CMOS.

 Worksheet 3.9.1   What Is BIOS?

This worksheet reviews the information about the BIOS that was covered in this section.

Entering the BIOS Configuration

When setting up the computer for the first time, you must run the *CMOS Configuration setup utility.* As mentioned in the previous section, the computer checks the CMOS to determine what types of options are installed in the system. The system BIOS allows access to this configuration information through its CMOS configuration setup utility. Simply press the appropriate key, depending on the system, during the bootup sequence to provide access to the BIOS. In general, early in the startup process, the BIOS displays a prompt to tell the user that the CMOS setup utility can be accessed by pressing a special key or key combination. Note that the keys, or key combinations, that access the setup menus can vary among BIOS manufacturers, and sometimes from one BIOS version to another.

Press the proper key or key combinations within a predetermined amount of time to access the setup utility. If the key is not pressed within that time, the BIOS program continues with the bootup process, possibly with undesirable results. Pressing the appropriate key or keys within the allotted time stops the bootup routine and displays the main menu screen of the setup utility.

A sample BIOS setup menu is shown in Figure 3-22. Your menu might be different than that shown in this figure, depending on the BIOS and version in use. The values that are input in the BIOS setup are stored in the system CMOS configuration registers. These registers are examined each time the system is booted up in the future to tell the computer what types of devices are installed.

Figure 3-22 BIOS Main Menu

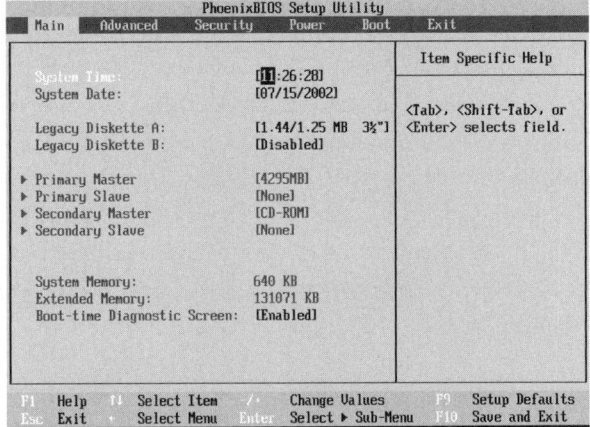

Standard CMOS Setup Screen

The instructions regarding choices in the CMOS setup screen can be found in the corresponding section in the motherboard manual. A typical configuration setup screen is shown in Figure 3-23. Through this screen, you can enter the desired configuration values into the CMOS registers. The cursor on the screen can be moved from item to item using the keyboard cursor control keys. The standard CMOS setup screen includes the basic operating parameters that must be set for the system to work correctly. These CMOS features are typically universal for all PCs.

Several fields are available for entering CMOS configuration data. These fields are described as follows:

- **Date and Time**—These two fields are used for setting the clock that controls the settings in the operating system. The date and time are required for many types of software applications to manage data. The format that you use is very important. For the initial system setup, a default date, such as January 1, 1980, is usually assigned. The time is given in the 24-hour format, similar to military time.

- **Hard Disks**—This section contains fields that identify devices attached to the two IDE controllers that are integrated on the motherboard. IDE controllers can have up to two hard drives, or one hard drive and another IDE device such as a CD-ROM drive. Normally, one device is configured as a master and the other as a slave. Four configuration entries are possible: Primary Master, Primary Slave, Secondary Master, and Secondary Slave. You should usually set the drive type to Auto. This allows the BIOS to autodetect and configure the hard drives so that this information does not have to be entered manually.

- **Drive A and Drive B**—These two sections identify the types of floppy drives that use the available options. In this example, only one drive—a 3-1/2-inch, high-density, 1.44-MB floppy drive—is installed. "None" is shown for drive B, because a second drive is not installed.

- **Video**—This section identifies the video adapter. The choices here are few, and the default EGA/VGA has been the standard for everything since 1990. Whether the video adapter is VGA, SVGA, or anything more advanced, all video adapters since 1990 can support the basic VGA BIOS instructions that are built into the system BIOS.

- **Halt On**—This is the last user-definable field in the standard CMOS screen. The choices here allow a specific system response to errors so that problems can be reported before they corrupt data.

In addition, the informational box in the lower-right corner of the screen shows non-user-definable information about the memory configuration of the system.

Figure 3-23 A Standard CMOS Setup Screen

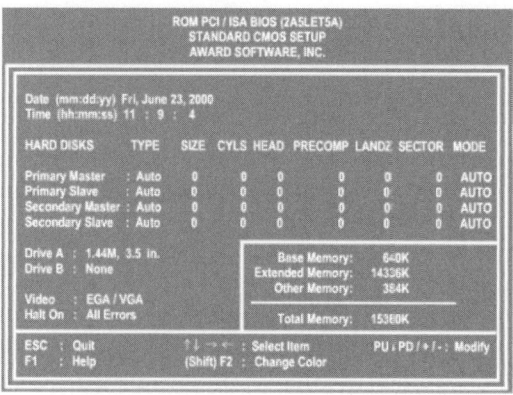

BIOS Features and Chipset Features Setup Screens

The *BIOS Features setup screen*, as shown in Figure 3-24, provides advanced features that control the behavior of the system. This setup screen is where you can fine-tune the system hardware for optimal performance. The disable and enable features for advanced troubleshooting can also be used. Unless there is a good reason to change them, most of the features should be left at their default settings.

Figure 3-24 BIOS Features Setup Screen

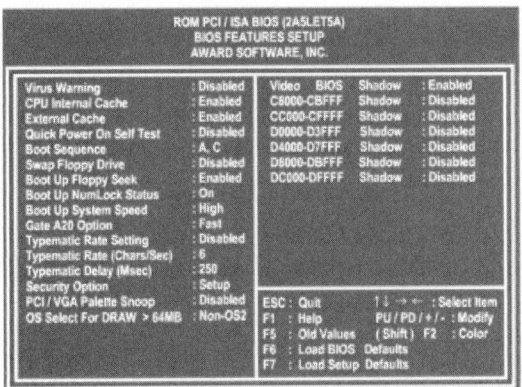

One important setup option on the BIOS Features setup screen allows you to specify the system boot order. For example, on newer systems, it is preferable to boot from the hard drive or CD-ROM drive rather than from the 3-1/2-inch floppy drive, as older systems did. Table 3-8 summarizes the various boot sequence configuration options that are available.

Table 3-8 Boot Sequence Configuration Options

Boot Sequence	Description
A, C	System first searches for a master boot record on the floppy drive, and then the hard drive.
C, A	System first searches for a master boot record on the hard drive, and then the floppy drive.
C, CD-ROM, A	System first searches for a master boot record on the hard drive, and then the CD-ROM drive, and finally the floppy drive.
CD-ROM, C, A	System first searches for a master boot record on the CD-ROM drive, and then the hard drive, and finally the floppy drive.

Chipset Features Setup

Every chipset variation has a specific BIOS designed for it. Therefore, certain functions are specific to the design of system boards that use that chipset. The Chipset Features setup screen, as shown in Figure 3-25, allows you to fine-tune the control parameters for the main system chipset. Recall from Chapter 2 that the chipset controls the memory, system cache, processor, and I/O buses. Because of the potentially disabling nature of these settings, the first feature set choice is Automatic Configuration, with the default set to Enabled. The default should be left at Enabled unless you have a good reason to disable Automatic Configuration. The remaining features are not automatically configured. The setup process for both BIOS and chipset features are covered in future labs.

Figure 3-25 The Chipset Features Setup Screen

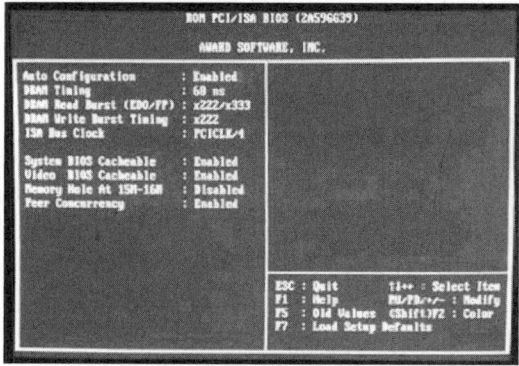

Power Management and Plug and Play Screens

This section discusses power management. As with other setup screens, the instructions in this environment can be found in the corresponding section in the motherboard manual. Use the feature settings found in the *Power Management setup screen*, as shown in Figure 3-26, to control the optional power management for devices on the computer. Power management features can be enabled to allow devices to go into sleep or suspend mode. However, some software applications and operating systems might not deal well with components being powered down, because the software might no longer recognize such devices properly. If this is the case, you should disable the power management feature.

Figure 3-26 Power Management Setup Screen

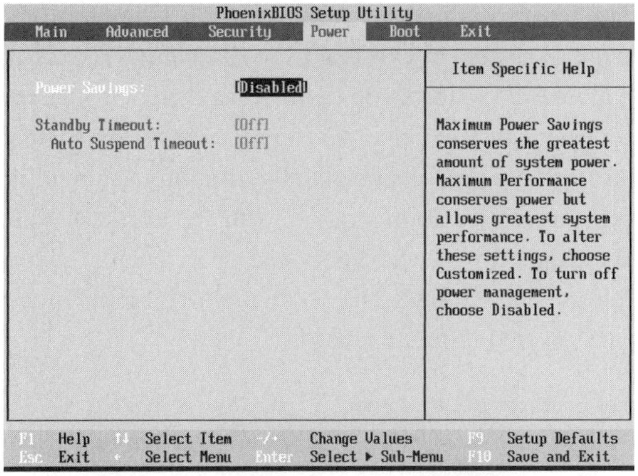

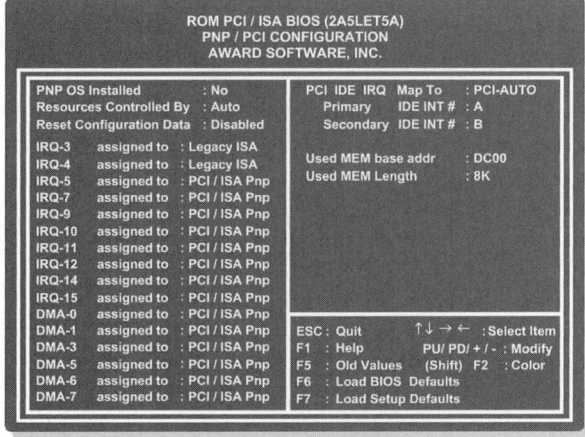

PnP/PCI Configuration Setup

The ***Plug and Play (PnP) configuration screen*** and the ***Peripheral Component Interconnect (PCI) configuration screen*** contain the feature settings that control the system I/O bus and IRQ (interrupts) and DMA (direct memory access) allocation for ISA and PCI PnP devices, as shown in Figure 3-27. For PnP to work, the device or adapter being installed, the BIOS, and the operating system must all support Plug and Play.

Figure 3-27 The PnP/PCI Configuration Screen

The Resources Controlled By setting is set by default to Auto. This allows the BIOS to automatically manage the IRQ and DMA channels on the I/O bus for the PnP devices to avoid conflicts with any legacy, non-PnP, ISA devices. Sometimes IRQs or DMAs must be manually designated for some nonconforming PnP expansion boards or adapter cards. In such cases, such designated resources must be removed from BIOS handling.

In general, the default settings should be used for this section of the BIOS setup when working on newer systems, because any manual configurations require knowledge of the installed bus devices. If any conflicts occur, you can use the Reset Configuration Data feature to clear this portion of the BIOS setup and return it to its defaults upon rebooting the system. Consult the system board manual before making any changes here.

Integrated Peripherals and Hard Disk Detection Screens

This section discusses the features of the BIOS setup that configure the integrated peripheral support on the motherboard. Integrated peripherals typically include devices such as the onboard floppy and hard drive controllers, USB controller, serial ports, parallel ports, and sound card chip. An example of the Integrated Peripherals Configuration screen is shown in Figure 3-28. Setting these features to Auto (the recommended option), when applicable, permits the BIOS to issue the appropriate IDE drive commands to determine what mode the hard drives can support. The USB Controller feature is used to enable or disable the controller chip for the USB ports on the motherboard.

Figure 3-28 Integrated Peripherals Configuration Screen

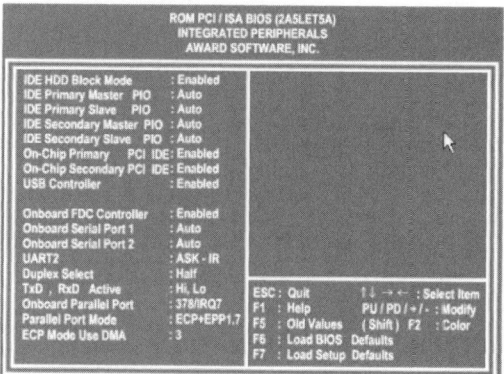

Fixed Disk Detection

From the standard CMOS setup screen discussed earlier, recall the Hard Disks feature, which allowed an Auto setting for automatically detecting the hard drive geometry. At times, this feature does not work with certain IDE hard drives. IDE Auto Configuration is used for such situations. It allows you to manually run the IDE autodetection program and select the auto-detection for each drive on the controller channel. The BIOS then scans and reports drive parameters that can be accepted or rejected. Any drive parameters that are accepted are then entered into the standard CMOS setup.

As usual, the Reset Configuration Data feature is an escape mode for resetting this section to defaults and returning to the last known functional configuration during reboot. Instructions for configuring each feature are included in the motherboard manual.

Password Screens and the Load Setup Defaults Screen

Passwords add security to a network system. The system administrator sets passwords for users and for the supervisor to manage the system. Figure 3-29 shows the two password options that are encountered in the BIOS setup—Set User Password and Set Supervisor Password.

Figure 3-29 PhoenixBIOS Security Options

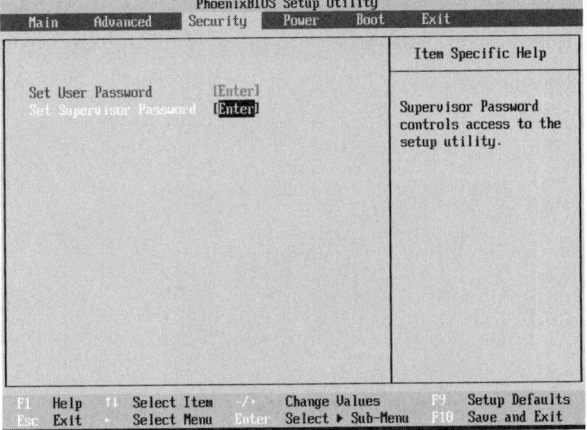

Set User Password

The Set User Password option allows you to insert a BIOS password. The system will not boot unless the proper password is entered. This option also prevents access to the BIOS, eliminating the possibility of other people changing the BIOS setup on the computer. This option is particularly useful when booting up the computer for the first time. You should fol-low the on-screen and password instructions in the motherboard user manual.

Set Supervisor Password

The Set Supervisor Password feature is normally used only in large institutions, where BIOS settings are kept standardized by computer support personnel. Once set, these computer BIOS setups are locked with a master password that is only known to the network administrator or an administrator designee. The instructions for using this option can also be found in the motherboard manual.

If no password is required but this screen is accidentally engaged, complete the following actions to move to the next screen:

1. When prompted for a password, press **Enter** without entering a password.

2. At the second screen labeled Password Disabled, press any key to return to the main setup screen.

Load Setup Defaults Screen

The Load Setup Defaults screen resets the BIOS setup to default settings. This feature does not affect those settings in the standard CMOS setup screen because these settings are the minimums required for the system to function. When configuring the system for the first time, if you encounter problems, use this method to restore the system to its default settings.

Additional information regarding this feature can be found in the motherboard manual.

BIOS Exit Options

In addition to exiting the BIOS, options are provided to save or discard any changes and to continue to work in the utility. Another option on the exit screen is Load System Defaults. System defaults allow the BIOS to return to the manufacturer's original settings.

Two *BIOS exit options* exist: Exit Without Saving Setup and Save and Exit Setup. The Exit Without Saving Setup option allows you to exit the BIOS setup program without saving any changes that you made. The Save and Exit Setup option allows you to exit the BIOS setup program and save your changes to the CMOS chip. Although you can use shortcuts to do this, always use the Save and Exit Setup option to avoid accidental loss of your setup modification entries.

When using the Save and Exit Setup option, the computer will restart according to your new configuration. The startup floppy disk can be inserted to allow the system to boot to a command prompt. The hard drive can now be partitioned in preparation for installing the operating system. Figure 3-30 shows a PhoenixBIOS with the available exit options.

NOTE

Keep a written copy of the BIOS settings with your checklist inventory.

Figure 3-30 PhoenixBIOS Exit Options

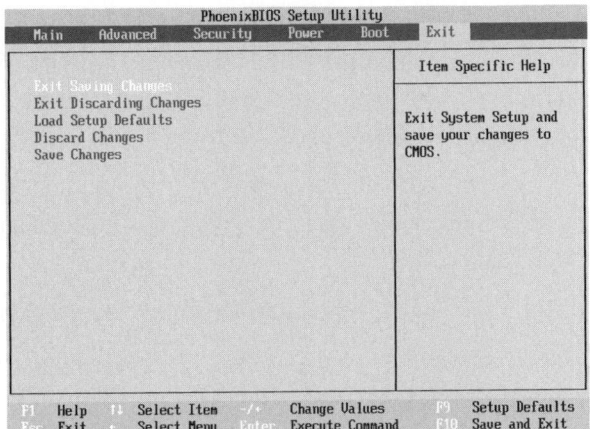

Startup Sequence

Even after careful postassembly inspection, you can still run into problems with the first bootup. If this happens, depending at what stage of the boot sequence it occurs, you might not have an opportunity to access the BIOS menu to configure the BIOS setup. This section describes the critical role of the POST. The POST allows you to troubleshoot many common startup problems.

When a computer starts up, a series of tests are automatically performed to check the primary components in the system, such as the CPU, ROM, memory, and motherboard support circuitry. The routine that carries out this function is referred to as the POST. POST is a hardware diagnostics routine that is built into the system BIOS. The basic function of the POST routine is to make sure that all the hardware the system needs for startup is there and that everything is functioning properly before the boot process begins. The POST routine therefore ensures that the computer is ready to begin the boot sequence. The POST also provides some basic troubleshooting to determine what devices have failed or have problems initializing during this startup hardware check.

POST Errors and Troubleshooting

The POST routine provides error or warning messages whenever it encounters a faulty component. POST error codes take the form of a series of beeps that identify a faulty hardware component. If everything has been installed correctly during the assembly process and the new system is functioning normally, you usually hear one short beep at the completion of the POST. If a problem is detected, a different number of beeps is heard, sometimes in a combination of short and long tones. These are mainly BIOS-dependent codes. They vary according to BIOS manufacturer and even among different BIOS versions.

The beep codes can be used to troubleshoot hardware failures that occur during the POST routine. Although the POST routine is not thorough compared to existing disk-based diagnostics, it is a first line of defense, especially in detecting severe motherboard problems. The POST typically provides three types of output messages: audio codes (beeps), onscreen text messages, and hexadecimal numeric codes that are sent to an I/O port address. The POST generally continues past nonfatal problems, but fatal problems cause the POST to stop the boot process. If problems occur early, before any drivers are loaded for the monitor, the POST can only signal that a problem exists using beeps. Beeps are issued through the computer's system speaker. Conversely, if the POST and the boot sequence can advance to a point where the system can use the system video to display messages, an error message is often displayed on the screen. The message indicates what problems occurred and the probable cause. These are referred to as visual error codes. These error messages are usually in the form of a numeric code, such as 1790-Disk 0 Error.

In many instances, you need to consult the BIOS manual or the manufacturer's website for help in decoding some of the more detailed error codes. Table 3-9 gives a summary of the major groups of visual error codes that are frequently encountered. These codes are some of the major groups of POST hardware diagnostics messages that are commonly used on PC systems. Although most of the major BIOS manufacturers use many of these codes, none of the manufacturers use all the codes. Consult the manufacturer's manual for a specific system BIOS.

Table 3-9 Common POST Hardware Diagnostic Message Groups

Error Code/Range	Possible Problem
1xx	System board or BIOS
16x	CMOS, options or time not set
2xx	Main memory
3xx	Keyboard
5xx	Color monitor
6xx	Floppy drive
17xx	Hard drive
86xx	Mouse

Problems that occur during the POST are usually caused by incorrect hardware configuration or installation. Actual hardware failure is rare. A POST error can indicate that the system must be powered off. Unplug the system from the wall outlet, and carefully double-check the assembled computer to make sure that all the steps in the following list were properly carried out:

- All cables are correctly connected and secured.
- All drivers are properly installed.
- CMOS/BIOS setup configuration settings are correct.
- Motherboard jumper settings are correct, if changed from the original settings.
- No device conflicts exist.
- The expansion boards and disk drives are installed correctly.
- The power supply is set to the proper input voltage of the user's country or region.
- A keyboard, monitor, and mouse are properly attached.
- A bootable hard disk is properly installed.
- The BIOS is the right version and supports the drive installed, and the parameters are entered correctly.
- A bootable floppy disk is in drive A, if necessary.
- All SIMMs or DIMMs are installed correctly.

Summary

This chapter discussed the steps that are required to assemble a computer. Some of the important concepts to retain from this chapter include the following:

- The general safety issues are provided to keep the technician safe and to prevent ESD damage to computer components.
- The inventory checklist provides an accounting of the components that were used in the assembly of a computer.
- The computer case should conform to the ATX standard, with at least a 250-watt power supply. The required wattage depends on the installed components. In addition, make sure that the case has enough space to install the components and upgrades.
- Follow the detailed steps to prepare and install the motherboard. In addition to using spacers to keep the motherboard from touching the case, use caution when handling the motherboard.
- Refer to the motherboard manual for the correct jumper configuration. Jumpers establish logic levels to select functions for the operation of the motherboard. Do not move jumpers with the power on.

- Additional jumpers might have to be set for BIOS recovery to clear the CMOS, to clear the password, or for BIOS setup access.

- The LEDs indicate that the system is getting power. The LEDs for the floppy drive, hard drive, and CD-ROM drive indicate whether the devices have been installed properly.

- The floppy drive, hard drive, and CD-ROM drive are installed similarly. Make sure that the proper ribbon cables are installed and that the devices are mounted right side up.

- The video card is the only expansion card that must be installed before booting the PC for the first time. This card provides the information that is required to configure the BIOS during the initial boot process.

- Before booting the system for the first time, review the final checklist and double-check all your work.

- Entering the BIOS/CMOS setup is required when setting up the computer for the first time. Configuration data must be entered for date, time, hard drive, drive A, drive B, video, and halt on. In addition, advanced features that control the behavior of the system can be fine-tuned for optimal performance.

- The POST is a series of tests that are automatically performed to check the primary components in the system. One short beep is heard at the completion of the POST if everything is installed and functioning correctly. To determine the meaning of other series of beeps that indicate a problem or error, refer to the motherboard manual for documentation.

Disk operating System (DOS) is a collection of programs and commands that control overall computer operations in a disk-based system. The next chapter focuses on the components and functions of DOS.

Key Terms

AT power supply   Uses two 6-pin motherboard power connectors, usually labeled P8/P9.

ATX power supply   Uses a single 20-pin power connector, P1.

Basic Input/Output System (BIOS)   Contains the program code that is required to control all the basic operating components of the computer system.

BIOS exit options   The two options are Exit Without Saving Setup and Save and Exit Setup.

BIOS Features setup screen   Provides advanced features that control the behavior of the system.

BIOS function   Runs basic device test programs and then seeks to configure the appropriate devices.

BIOS setup   Allows you to customize a computer to function optimally based on its hardware and software profiles.

CMOS Configuration setup utility   Used to determine and change if necessary the options that are used in BIOS.

Complementary Metal Oxide Semiconductor (CMOS)   The chip that stores the settings that you make with the BIOS configuration program.

flash BIOS   Allows an upgrade of the software in the BIOS chip from a floppy disk that is provided by the manufacturer, without replacing the chip. The upgrade can also be accomplished by downloading an update from the website for the manufacturer.

heat sink   A device that dissipates heat from electronic components into the surrounding air.

jumper   A pair of prongs that are electrical contact points set into the computer motherboard or an adapter card.

light-emitting diode (LED)   Also called a status light, the LED indicates whether components inside the computer are on or working.

master jumper setting   Designation of primary for an IDE device or hard drive.

motherboard location map   Shows where the major components and hardware are located on the motherboard.

Peripheral Component Interconnect (PCI) configuration screen   Contains the feature settings that control the system I/O bus and IRQ and DMA allocation for ISA and PCI PnP devices.

Plug and Play (PnP) configuration screen   Contains the feature settings that control the system I/O bus and IRQ and DMA allocation for ISA and PCI PnP devices.

Power Management setup screen   Controls the optional power management for devices on the computer.

power supply   Provides electrical power for every component inside the system unit.

ROM BIOS   The chip where the BIOS is stored allowing accessibility for the system.

slave jumper setting   Designation as secondary for a hard drive or CD-ROM drive.

system unit   Typically a metal-and-plastic case that contains the basic parts of the computer system.

zero-insertion-force (ZIF) socket   A special type of chip socket that permits the insertion and removal of the chip without using any tools and by using virtually no force.

Check Your Understanding

1. Which computer component can contain a dangerous amount of voltage?

   A. Motherboard

   B. Monitor

   C. Hard drive

   D. CD-ROM drive

2. What is the purpose of the computer's power supply?

   A. Convert DC (direct current) to AC (alternating current)

   B. Convert AC (alternating current) to DC (direct current)

   C. Eliminate spikes in the electricity

   D. Eliminate brownouts in the electricity

3. What is the result of incorrectly attaching the LED connectors to the motherboard?

   A. The motherboard will short out.

   B. The LED status light will still work.

   C. The LED status light will not work.

   D. The computer will beep constantly when powered on.

4. How are hard drives and CD-ROM drives configured to be master and slave drives?

   A. In the CMOS setup utility

   B. During partitioning

   C. By setting jumpers

   D. During formatting

5. How many volts do disk drive motors require?

   A. 3.3

   B. 5

   C. 12

   D. 120

6. What color is the ground wire for a computer power supply?

   A. Red

   B. Black

   C. Yellow

   D. Blue

7. What is the purpose of a heat sink?

   A. To cool the computer processor

   B. To set the processor voltage

   C. To set the processor speed

   D. To ground the processor

8. Which of the following is a valid statement about the P8 and P9 connectors on a power supply?

   A. They connect to the floppy drive in the computer.

   B. They connect to the motherboard with black wires in the middle.

   C. They connect to the motherboard with black wires on the outside.

   D. They ground the processor.

9. When booting the system, keys/key combinations allow the user to access the CMOS setup screen. They include Delete, Ctrl-Alt-Esc, and F2 depending on the version of BIOS used.

   A. True

   B. False

10. How do you best prevent damaging a computer with static electricity?

    A. Always use a rubber mat as a work surface.

    B. Always touch a ground point on the chassis to discharge static electricity.

    C. Always take off your shoes before working inside a computer.

    D. Always wear an ESD strap when working inside a computer.

11. What type of current can kill you?

    A. AC.

    B. DC.

    C. Voltage kills; current is only a measurement.

    D. AC and DC.

12. The power supply voltage can be checked by measuring the P8 and P9 connections with which of the following devices?

    A. Multiprobe

    B. Cable tester

    C. Multimeter

    D. Battery

13. What is a memory bank?

    A. The cache where memory is stored

    B. The actual slot that memory is inserted into

    C. The collection of all memory

    D. Virtual memory

14. To install a DIMM, you need to do which of the following tasks?

    A. Line up straight over the socket and press in

    B. Tilt 45 degrees and push in

    C. Press down on the lever

    D. Line up all metal pins and slide in

Upon completion of this chapter, you will be able to perform the following tasks:

- Explain the three basic elements that make up the major design components of any operating system
- Understand the components and functions of the operating system
- Modify DOS commands with switches
- Create a DOS boot disk, which is used to boot a computer to the DOS prompt
- Use system memory tools to help simplify the task of placing TSRs into upper memory
- Resolve memory conflicts that can lead to general protection faults

Chapter 4

Operating System Fundamentals

This chapter discusses the basics of the operating system. The operating system is the program that manages computer operations. This chapter describes the components, functions, and important terminology related to an operating system. The chapter focuses on the Disk Operating System (DOS). You learn the basics of DOS, the commands that are used, and the file structure. You also learn about memory management and the tools that adjust and optimize memory.

Operating System

The operating system is what runs the computer system. It is the first program that is loaded when the computer is turned on and is a major consideration in the troubleshooting process. This section includes the following topics:

- Components of an operating system
- Operating system functions
- Operating system types: basic terminology

Components of an Operating System

An *operating system* is a software program that provides an interface between the user and the computer and manages thousands of applications. Most computer systems are sold with an operating system installed. Computers that are designed for individual users are called personal computers (PCs). PC operating systems are designed to control the operations of programs such as web browsers, word processors, and e-mail applications.

TIP

Know the definition of an operating system as it relates to a PC.

The development of processor technology has enabled computers to execute more instructions per second. Advanced operating systems are capable of performing many complex tasks simultaneously. When a computer needs to accommodate concurrent users and multiple jobs, Information Technology (IT) professionals usually rely on faster computers with powerful operating systems.

Computers that are capable of handling concurrent users and multiple jobs are called **network servers** or **servers**, as shown in Figure 4-1. Servers use operating systems called **network operating systems (NOSs)**. A fast computer with an NOS installed can manage operations for a large company or a large Internet site; this involves keeping track of many users and many programs. A server environment is shown in Figure 4-2.

Three basic elements make up the major design components of an operating system. These components are described as modular, because each has a distinct function and can be developed separately. These basic elements are described in the following list:

- *User interface*—The means by which a user interacts with the operating system. The user interface is the part of the operating system that issues commands. The user either types these commands at a command prompt or points and clicks the mouse on a graphical user interface (GUI).

- *Kernel*—The core of the operating system. The kernel usually interacts with the hardware through the system BIOS. The kernel is responsible for loading and operating programs or processes and managing input and output.

- *File-management system*—What the operating system uses to organize and manage files. A file is a collection of data. Virtually all the information that a computer stores is in the form of a file. There are many types of files, including program files, data files, and text files. The way an operating system organizes information into files is called the file system. Most operating systems use a hierarchical file system, which organizes files into directories in a tree structure. The beginning of the directory system is called the root directory.

Figure 4-1 Network Server

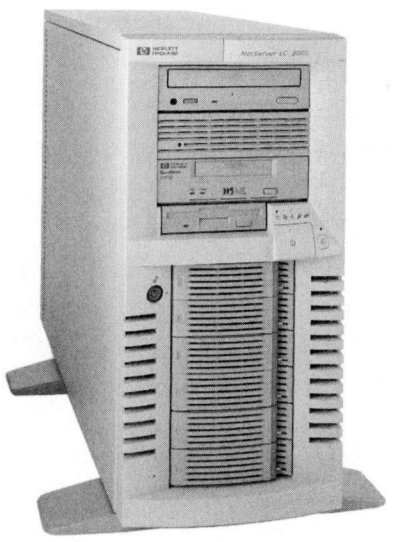

Figure 4-2 Network Server Environment

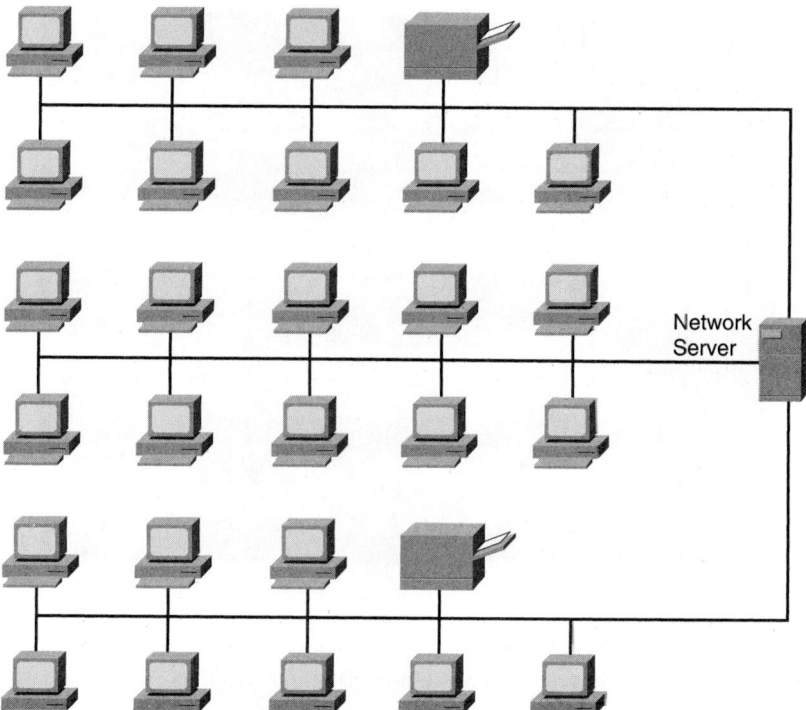

Operating System Functions

Regardless of the size and complexity of the computer and its operating system, all operating systems perform the same basic functions. These functions and their descriptions are included in the following list:

- **File and folder management**—An operating system creates a file structure on the computer hard drive where user data can be stored and retrieved. When a file is saved, the operating system saves it, attaches a name to it, and remembers where it put the file for future use.

- **Application management**—When a user requests a program, the operating system locates the application and loads it into the primary memory, or RAM, of the computer. As more programs are loaded, the operating system must allocate the computer's resources.

- **Support for built-in utility programs**—The operating system uses utility programs for maintenance and repairs. *Utility programs* help identify problems, locate lost files, repair damaged files, and back up data. Figure 4-3 shows the progress of the Disk Defragmenter, which is found by choosing **Start**, **Programs**, **Accessories**, **System Tools**, **Disk Defragmenter**.

Figure 4-3 Defragmenting Drive C

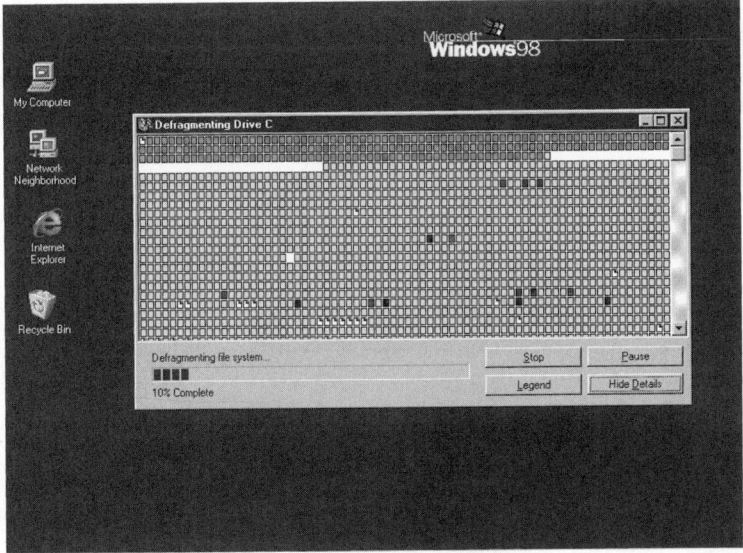

- **Control of the computer hardware**—The operating system resides between the programs and the Basic Input/Output System (BIOS). The BIOS controls the hardware. All programs that need hardware resources must go through the operating system. The

W-7-Req

GHz / 64-bit processor

Memory   2GB minimum

Graphic Card - Direct X 9 graphics
Processor with WDDM driver model
I/O (not absolutely necessary)
        only required for Aero

HDD free disk Space 20 GB

Optical Drive DVD)   (disk space)
        To have Windows XP mode also
                        require 1GB RAM

operating system can either access the hardware through the BIOS or through the device drivers, as shown in Figure 4-4. The Windows 2000 NOS bypasses the system BIOS and controls the hardware directly.

Figure 4-4 Functions of the Operating System

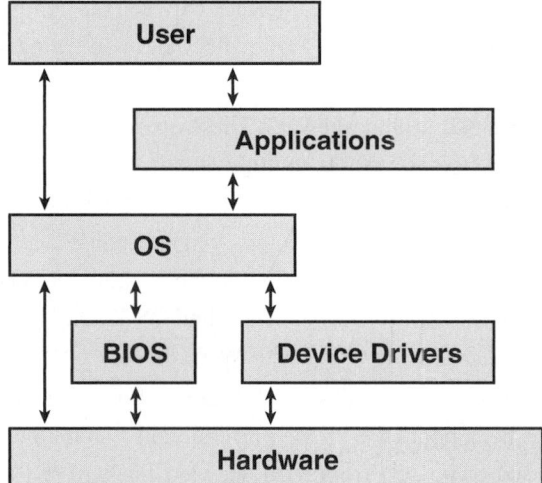

All programs are written for a specific operating system. Programs written for the UNIX operating system do not work on a Windows operating system. The operating system allows programmers to write applications without having to consider hardware access. If the operating system did not transmit information between the application and the hardware, programs would have to be rewritten every time they were installed on a new computer.

Operating System Types: Basic Terminology

To understand the capabilities of an operating system, you should understand some basic terms. The following terms are often used when comparing operating systems:

- ***Multiuser***—Two or more users can work with programs and share peripheral devices such as printers at the same time.
- ***Multitasking***—The computer is capable of operating multiple applications at the same time.
- ***Multiprocessing***—The computer can have two or more central processing units (CPUs) that programs share.
- ***Multithreading***—A program can be broken into smaller parts that can be loaded as needed by the operating system. Multithreading allows individual programs to be multitasked.

Most modern operating systems are multiuser and multitasking and support multithreading.

The following is a list of some of the most popular operating systems:

- **Microsoft Windows 95, 98, and Me**—Windows is one of the most popular operating systems. These operating systems are designed for PCs with Intel-compatible CPUs. Windows-based PCs use a GUI as the interface between the computer and the user. The Desktop for Windows 98 is shown in Figure 4-5. These operating systems are designed for a single user.

- **Microsoft Windows NT, 2000, and XP**—These operating systems are designed to support multiple users and to operate multiple applications simultaneously. Windows NT, 2000, and XP have incorporated many networking features.

- **Macintosh**—The first Macintosh computers, which became available in January 1984, were designed to be user-friendly compared to the existing DOS computers. The latest release of the Macintosh operating system is called OS X. OS X is highly functional and is based on the UNIX core technology. The Apple iMac Desktop is shown in Figure 4-6.

- **UNIX**—Introduced in the late 1960s, UNIX is one of the oldest operating systems. UNIX has always been popular with the professionals that maintain computer networks. UNIX-based computers from IBM, Hewlett-Packard (HP), and Sun Microsystems have helped maintain Internet operations since the beginning of the Internet. Many different versions of UNIX are available today.

- **Linux**—A UNIX-like OS. The Linux kernel was created by Linus Torvalds and was introduced on the Internet in 1991. Many versions, called distributions, of Linux are available. Figure 4-7 shows a KDE Desktop on a Linux system.

Windows, UNIX, and Macintosh operating systems are proprietary operating systems—that is, they must be purchased. Linux is an open source operating system that is available as a free download or at a low cost from developers. Developer editions of Linux cost much less than a Windows OS. As UNIX-based computers have become more powerful and GUIs have become more common, the popularity of Linux has increased.

 Worksheet 4.1.3 Operating System Fundamentals

This worksheet reviews operating system fundamentals by providing true-or-false questions.

Figure 4-5 Windows 98 Desktop

Figure 4-6 iMac Desktop

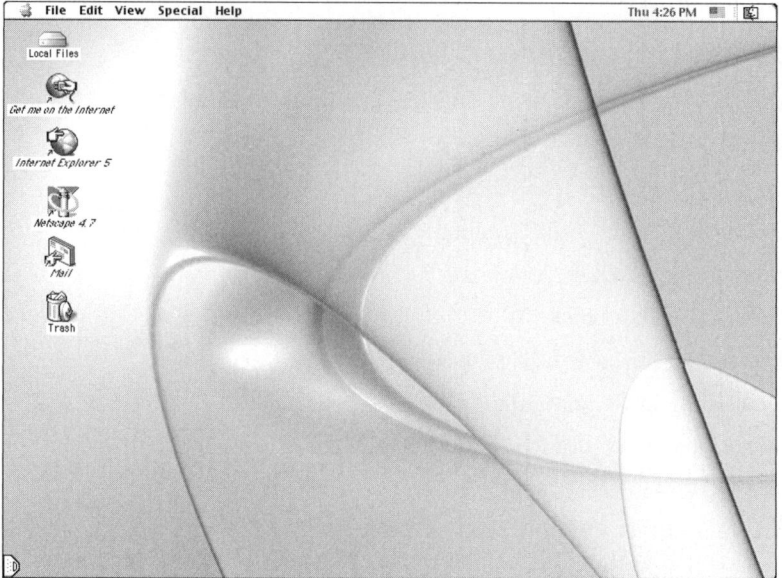

Figure 4-7 KDE Desktop

Disk Operating System (DOS)

The ability to work in and understand the DOS environment is always important for the IT technician. This section includes the following topics:

- What is DOS, and why learn about it?
- Understanding the DOS file structure
- Learning the basic DOS commands
- Creating a DOS boot disk
- Booting the system with a DOS disk
- Understanding DOS configuration files
- Editing system configuration files: SYSEDIT.EXE

What Is DOS, and Why Learn About It?

Microsoft developed the *Disk Operating System (DOS)* in 1981. DOS, which is sometimes called MS-DOS, was designed for the IBM PC. Windows 98 and Windows 2000 both support

DOS commands to reduce compatibility problems with older applications. DOS is a collection of programs and commands that control overall computer operations in a disk-based system. Figure 4-8 shows an example of a DOS prompt. The following three distinct sections make up DOS:

- **Boot files** — Used during the boot process, or system startup
- **File-management files** — Enable a system to manage its data in a system of files and folders
- **Utility files** — Enable the user to manage system resources, troubleshoot the system, and configure the system settings

Figure 4-8 DOS Prompt

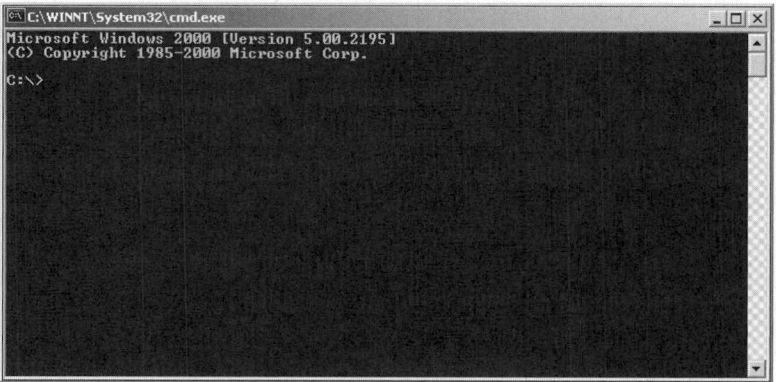

DOS programs usually work in the background and allow the user to input characters from the keyboard, define a file structure for storing records on the disk, and output data to a printer or monitor. DOS is responsible for finding and organizing data and applications on the disk.

The introduction of operating systems with GUIs, such as Microsoft Windows, has made DOS mostly obsolete. However, DOS is still important in many areas, including programming, operating older applications, and installing Windows operating systems, especially on older computers. All generations of Windows support DOS commands for backward compatibility with older applications. You should understand the basics of DOS before proceeding with a Windows operating system installation.

Basic Elements of DOS

DOS is useful as a troubleshooting aid when Windows will not boot. DOS allows the hard drive to be accessed without the GUI and provides the ability to run troubleshooting or diagnostic programs. The following are some of the basic properties of DOS:

- It is a command-line operating system and is not user-friendly. The best way to learn about DOS is to use it.
- It can only run one program at a time. It does not support multitasking.
- It can only run small programs and has memory limitations.
- It is an essential tool for IT professionals and is used extensively for troubleshooting.
- It is able to access only FAT16-based file systems, not the NT File System (NTFS) or the HP File System (HPFS).

To access DOS from Windows 98, choose **Start**, **Run**. A separate window opens that allows commands to be entered. Then type **command** to access the DOS prompt. In Windows 2000 and XP, type **cmd** to access the DOS prompt.

Understanding the DOS File Structure

To understand basic DOS commands, first look at the structure of the hard disk. Programs and data are stored on a disk in the same way that a document would be filed in a file cabinet. Program and data files in DOS are grouped together in directories. Directories are similar to folders in a file cabinet. The files and *directories* are organized for easy retrieval and use. Directories can be kept inside other directories, just like a folder can be placed inside another folder. Nested directories are referred to as *subdirectories*. Directories are called folders in Windows operating systems.

What Is a File?

A *file* is a block of related data that is given a single name and is treated as a single unit. Examples include programs, documents, drawings and other types of illustrations, and sound components. A record is kept of the location of every directory, subdirectory, and file on a disk. This record is stored in a table called the *File Allocation Table (FAT)*. *FAT32*, which was introduced in Windows 95 OSR2, is an improved version of the original FAT (FAT16). FAT32 allows a more efficient use of disk space for storing files.

Files are referred to by filenames. In DOS, filenames can be up to eight characters long, with extensions up to three characters long. The extension, which identifies the file type, is separated from the main portion of the filename by a period (.). An example of a DOS filename is MYNOTES.TXT.

In DOS, all files have *attributes*, which are a set of parameters that describe a file. The nature of a file can be determined by the attributes of a file. The common attributes for DOS files include the following:

- *Hidden*—These files cannot be seen by the user when performing a normal file search in a DOS environment.
- *Read-only*—The user can open and read this type of file but cannot modify the file.
- *Archive*—This is a bundle of other files contained in one file itself. Archives do not compress files; they just tie files and their structure together. Today many archive formats feature built-in compression to save space.
- *System*—The DOS operating system must have these files for a successful bootup.

Hidden files are important files that must be concealed and protected from unauthorized users. A hidden file is not listed in a standard DOS directory listing; the file can only be seen with a specific command. However, a hidden file can still be accessed and modified. To see hidden files, type **DIR /AH** at a command prompt.

Directory Structures and Organization

Hard drives organize the disk into directories and subdirectories. The main directory is called the root directory. All other directories branch out from the *root directory*, similar to the branches of a tree. In MS-DOS, a graphical representation of the directory organization is called a *directory tree*, as shown in Figure 4-9. You should understand how DOS organizes disks when preparing a hard drive for a Windows installation.

Figure 4-9 DOS Directory Tree

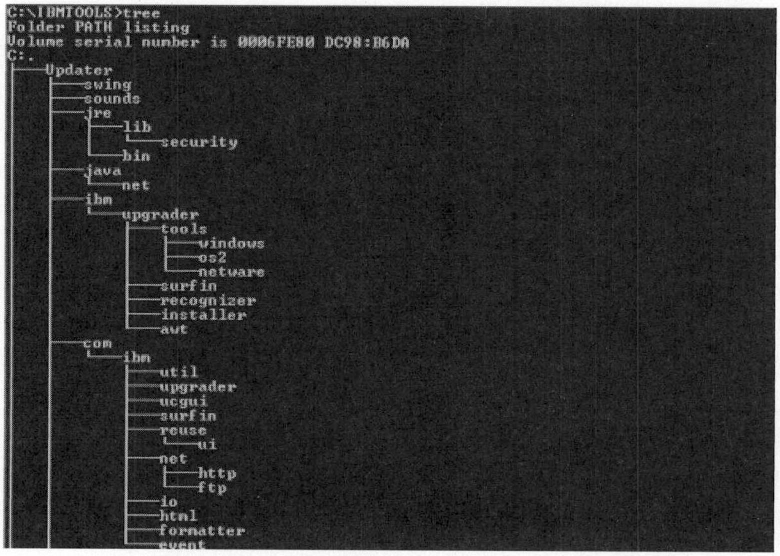

To find a file, you must know the drive, directory, and subdirectory in which the file is located. The first hard drive in most computer systems is the C drive. Each hard drive in the computer can be thought of as a file cabinet, or *root*. The root of the C drive is represented by C:\. Any files or directories within the root are represented by the root followed by the name of the file or directory, such as C:\EXAMPLE. Any directory or file that is located within a directory is represented by the directory name, followed by a backslash (\), followed by the name of the file or subdirectory, such as C:\EXAMPLE\FILE.EXE. In MS-DOS, the format for specifying the path to a file is as follows:

C:*directory* *subdirectory* *subdirectory* *filename*

The components of this representation are as follows:

- C:\ specifies the C drive of the computer.
- The backslash (\) after each item signifies the presence of a directory or subdirectory.
- The first backslash indicates the root directory, which is present on all DOS disks.
- The filename, which is found at the end of the path, is located in the final subdirectory.

Learning the Basic DOS Commands

A *DOS command* is an instruction that DOS executes from the command line. Internal commands, such as DIR and COPY, are built into the COMMAND.COM program and are always available when DOS is operating. Many external commands, such as FORMAT and XCOPY, are individual programs that reside in the DOS directory.

Internal Versus External DOS Commands

DOS contains internal commands, which are built into the operating system, and external commands, which must be executed from a file. Basic commands are generally internal, and more advanced commands are usually external. *External commands* are stored on disk for future use. *Internal commands* are located in the COMMAND.COM program and are loaded into memory during the bootup process. Examples of internal and external commands are discussed later in this chapter.

What Is a Command Line?

The operating system usually provides the user interface. In DOS, the main user interface is the command line. The *command line* is the space that follows the DOS prompt (C:\>). C:\ represents the hard disk drive root directory, and > is known as the prompt. All DOS commands are typed to the right of the prompt and are executed by pressing Enter. All DOS functions can be entered and executed from the command line. For example, you can view all system files on the C drive by typing **DIR *.SYS** at the DOS prompt.

Commonly Used DOS Commands and Switches

DOS commands instruct the disk operating system to perform a specific task. Many DOS commands can be modified by adding switches to the end of the command. *Switches* are options that modify the output of the command. A switch includes a space, a forward slash (/), and a single letter. An example of a command that includes a switch is C:\>DIR /W. The /? switch (help switch) shows you the switch options that are available for each command.

In this example, /W is the switch. The /W switch modifies the DIR command by presenting the screen output in a wide format. The rest of this section focuses on some commonly used DOS commands and switches. The following commands are helpful for various operating system installations:

- *ATTRIB*—Displays, sets, or removes one or more of the four attributes that can be assigned to files and directories. The four attributes are read-only, archive, system, and hidden. The ATTRIB command is an external DOS command. A plus sign (+) or minus sign (–) used in the ATTRIB command sets or clears an attribute. The format of the ATTRIB command is as follows:

  ```
  ATTRIB [+ or -] [variable] [directory\filename] /[switch]
  ```

  The following variables can be used with the ATTRIB command:

  R—Indicates a read-only file

  A—Indicates an archive file

  S—Indicates a system file

  H—Indicates a hidden file

- *DEL*—Deletes named files. The DEL and ERASE commands are synonymous. The switch /P prompts the user for confirmation before deleting each file. The format of the DEL command is as follows:

  ```
  DEL [directory\filename] /[switch]
  ```

- *EDIT*—Allows a user to view, create, or modify a file. The format of the EDIT command is as follows:

  ```
  EDIT [directory\filename] /[switch]
  ```

  The following switches are commonly used with the EDIT command:

  B—Displays monochrome mode.

  H—Displays the maximum number of lines possible for the hardware.

  R—Loads files in read-only mode.

  [*file*]—Specifies initial files to load; wildcards and multiple file specs can be given.

- *FORMAT*—Erases all the information from a floppy disk or a hard drive. This command prepares a hard drive for installation of a Windows OS. A typical FORMAT command is as follows:

  `FORMAT [drive] /[switch]`

  The following switches are commonly used with the FORMAT command:

  > *Q*—Performs a quick format but does not clear the FAT, so file recovery is possible

  > *S*—Copies system files to the formatted disk

  > *U*—Performs an unconditional format, and all previous data, including the FAT, is erased

NOTE

The /S switch must be added when formatting to make a system disk. If this switch is not used, the disk can be reformatted or the DOS SYS command can be used.

- *FDISK*—Allows users to delete and create partitions on the hard disk drive. This command prepares the hard drive before installing a Windows OS. The FDISK command is entered at the command prompt as follows:

  `FDISK /[switch]`

  A commonly used switch is *STATUS*, which displays partition information when used with the FDISK command.

- *SCANDISK*—A DOS program that is designed to detect and repair errors on a hard drive or floppy disk. The SCANDISK command is entered at the command prompt as follows:

  `SCANDISK /[switch]`

  Switches commonly used with the SCANDISK command are as follows:

  > *ALL*—Checks and repairs all local drives at once

  > *AUTOFIX*—Automatically fixes errors and saves lost clusters by default as files in the root directory

  > *CHECKONLY*—Checks the drive for errors but does not make repairs

- *MEM*—Displays a table that shows how memory is currently allocated. The MEM command is entered at the command prompt as follows:

  `MEM /[switch]`

  Switches commonly used with the MEM command are as follows:

  > *C*—Lists the programs that are currently loaded into memory and shows how much conventional and upper memory each program is using

  > *D*—Lists the programs and internal drivers that are currently loaded into memory

  > *F*—Lists the free areas of conventional and upper memory, which are discussed later in this chapter

  > *P*—Pauses after each screen of information

- *COPY*—Copies one or more files from one location to another. This command can also be used to create new files. By using the COPY CON command to copy files from the keyboard console to the screen, files can be created and then saved to disk. The COPY command is entered at the command prompt as follows:

COPY /[*switch*]

Switches that are commonly used with the COPY command are as follows:

Y—Replaces existing files without providing a confirmation prompt.

–Y—Displays a confirmation prompt before copying over existing files.

A—Copies ASCII files and applies to the filename preceding it and to all following filenames.

B—Copies binary files and applies to the filename preceding it and to all following filenames.

V—Checks the copy to make sure that a file was copied correctly. An error message is displayed if the copy cannot be verified.

- *MORE*—Displays output one screen at a time. The MORE command is entered at the command prompt as follows:

MORE | [*filename*]

The CD, MKDIR, RMDIR, and DELTREE commands are slightly different because they do not use switches. A brief description of these commands is as follows:

- *CD*—Changes or displays the current directory on the specified drive.
- *MKDIR* or *MD*—Creates a new directory.
- *RMDIR* or *RD*—Removes an empty directory. Can only be used after all subdirectories and files within the directory have been deleted or moved.
- *DELTREE*—Deletes a directory, including all files and subdirectories that are in the directory.

Table 4-1 summarizes the most commonly used DOS commands.

Table 4-1 Common DOS Commands

Command Name	Type	Function
DIR	Internal	Displays the contents of a directory
CD	Internal	Changes to a specified directory
MD	Internal	Creates a new directory
RD	Internal	Removes a directory

continues

Table 4-1 Common DOS Commands (Continued)

Command Name	Type	Function
DEL	Internal	Deletes a file
REN	Internal	Renames a file
SET	Internal	Displays the contents of the environment variables
MEM	External	Displays memory properties
COPY	Internal	Copies a file
TYPE	Internal	Displays the contents of a text file
FDISK	External	Partitions fixed disks
TIME	Internal	Sets the system time
DATE	Internal	Sets the system date
CHKDSK	External	Displays the status of a disk
DISKCOPY	External	Copies one floppy disk to another
EDIT	External	Opens a file for editing
FORMAT	External	Formats a disk
PRINT	Internal	Prints a text document or displays the contents of the print queue
ATTRIB	External	Changes the attributes of a file

TIP

Be able to perform DOS operations, and know the most common DOS commands.

Wildcards can be included at the command prompt. An asterisk indicates a wildcard. For example, typing **DIR *.*** at the C:\> prompt returns all files in the root directory of the C drive.

Video   Basic DOS Commands

This video shows you the basic DOS commands that are detailed in this chapter.

Lab 4.2.3   Basic DOS Commands

In this lab, you navigate the DOS command line and perform file-management tasks.

Worksheet 4.2.3   DOS Commands

In this worksheet, you match the DOS command to the function that it performs.

Creating a DOS Boot Disk

At some point, you will be unable to boot a computer. To troubleshoot the problem, you need an alternate method of starting the system. A DOS boot disk is an important tool that performs this task. DOS boot disks can also be used to boot up a newly assembled computer to install the operating system.

Video   Creating a DOS Boot Disk

This video shows the step-by-step procedures that are used to create a DOS boot disk.

A DOS boot disk is shown in Figure 4-10. The boot disk is a floppy disk that contains the following necessary system files:

- COMMAND.COM
- IO.SYS
- MSDOS.SYS

Figure 4-10   Contents of a DOS Boot Disk

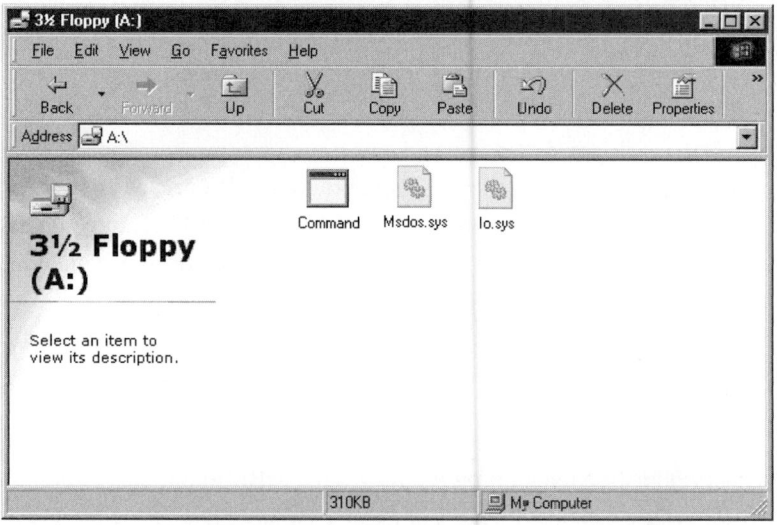

NOTE

The DOS boot disk can also contain a file called DRVSPACE.BIN. This file is only necessary to read a drive that has been compressed. The data on a compressed drive cannot be accessed without this file.

Diagnostic programs should also be included on the boot disk. To create a boot disk, perform the following steps on a computer with DOS installed on the hard disk:

Step 1   Boot the computer.

Step 2   Insert a blank floppy disk in the floppy drive. In this example, the floppy drive is the A drive.

Step 3   Type **FORMAT A: /S** at the command prompt, and press **Enter**.

Step 4   If the disk is already formatted, type **SYS A:** and press **Enter**.

Lab 4.2.4   Creating a DOS Boot Disk

In this lab, you learn about the files used and the commands necessary to create a boot disk.

Booting the System with a DOS Disk

A *DOS boot disk* boots a computer to the DOS prompt. The first section of a DOS disk contains the *boot sector*. The boot sector includes information about how the disk is organized. Sometimes, the boot sector contains a small *Master Boot Record (MBR)* that can access a larger and more powerful bootstrap loader program, which is located in the root directory.

The MBR is usually found at sector 1, head 0, and track 0 of the first logical hard drive or on the boot disk. The MBR is the required boot record on any boot or *system disk*. The MBR can boot up the hardware system to the operating system. A boot disk simplifies the process of preparing a hard drive and installing an operating system.

Booting the System

Insert a boot disk in the floppy disk drive, and power on the computer. The BIOS executes the bootstrap loader program, which is a small BIOS program that initiates and controls a large portion of the bootup process. The bootstrap program moves the MBR into RAM, and then the BIOS begins loading the operating system. If the system performs a standard DOS bootup, the system usually displays the date and time prompts on the monitor, followed by the DOS command-line prompt A:\>. This prompt indicates that DOS is operational and that the floppy drive A is the currently active drive. The following actions take place:

1. The BIOS searches for a Master Boot Record.

2. The primary bootstrap loader program moves the MBR into main memory.

3. The system executes the secondary bootstrap loader program from the MBR.

4. The bootstrap loader program looks at the partition table to find the active partition and then checks the root directory of the active partition for the IO.SYS and MSDOS.SYS files.

5. The secondary bootstrap loader program moves IO.SYS and MSDOS.SYS into main memory.

6. The IO.SYS file executes the MSDOS.SYS file to load file-management functions.

7. The IO.SYS file looks for the CONFIG.SYS file.

8. If CONFIG.SYS is found, the IO.SYS file reconfigures the system in a three-step process: device, install, and shell.

9. The IO.SYS file executes COMMAND.COM.

10. COMMAND.COM looks for the AUTOEXEC.BAT file.

11. If COMMAND.COM finds the AUTOEXEC.BAT file, COMMAND.COM executes the file.

12. If an AUTOEXEC.BAT file does not exist, COMMAND.COM displays the time and date prompts. Finally, the command-line prompt is displayed.

Understanding DOS Configuration Files

Two important configuration files are included in MS-DOS: CONFIG.SYS and AUTOEXEC.BAT. These files, which optimize the system, can be included in the DOS bootup process.

At the beginning of the boot procedure, the BIOS checks the root directory of the boot disk for the CONFIG.SYS file. Then, the BIOS searches for the COMMAND.COM interpreter. Finally, the BIOS looks in the root directory again for the AUTOEXEC.BAT file. The AUTOEXEC.BAT and CONFIG.SYS files can play important roles in optimizing the system memory and in the disk drive usage. The order of file execution during the bootup process, as shown in Figure 4-11, is as follows:

1. IO.SYS

2. MSDOS.SYS

3. CONFIG.SYS

4. COMMAND.COM

5. AUTOEXEC.BAT

TIP

Remember the files that are involved in the DOS bootup process and the order of their execution. In Windows 9*x*, CONFIG.SYS is primarily needed to install real-mode drivers for devices that are not supported by Windows 9*x*'s 32-bit device drivers. Real-mode is discussed later in this chapter.

Figure 4-11 Bootup Process

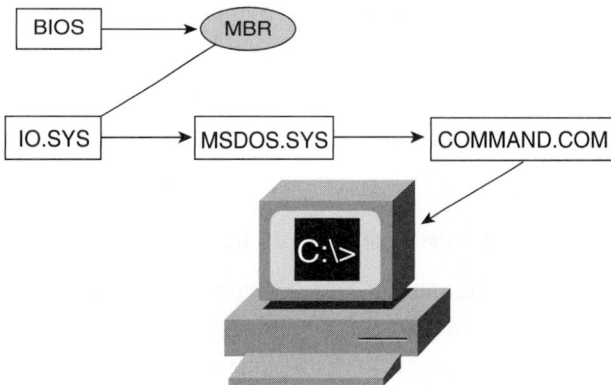

CONFIG.SYS

The ***CONFIG.SYS*** file resides in the root directory; this file loads drivers and changes settings at startup. Installation programs often modify CONFIG.SYS to customize the computer for their own use. Most CONFIG.SYS files in Windows 9*x* are empty, plain-text files that are available for changes that the user wants to make to the system. After switching from DOS to Windows 9*x*, most of the values that were formerly located in this file move to the IO.SYS file. To override the values in IO.SYS, enter the appropriate statements and values in CONFIG.SYS. CONFIG.SYS also runs memory managers.

During the boot process, while the MS-DOS message "Starting DOS" is on the screen, the following special function keys can be used to alter CONFIG.SYS and access AUTOEXEC.BAT:

- ***F5*** (also the left Shift key)—Skips the CONFIG.SYS file, including the AUTOEXEC.BAT file
- ***F8***—Proceeds through the CONFIG.SYS file and AUTOEXEC.BAT file one step at a time, waiting for user confirmation

AUTOEXEC.BAT

The AUTOEXEC.BAT file contains DOS commands that are automatically executed when DOS is loaded into the system. The following commands are normally located in the AUTOEXEC.BAT file:

- ***DATE***—Causes DOS to prompt the user for the date.
- ***TIME***—Causes DOS to prompt the user for the date and time.
- ***PROMPT=PG***—Causes the active drive and directory path to be displayed on the command line.

- *SET TEMP=C:\TEMP*—Sets up an area for temporarily holding data in a directory called TEMP.
- *PATH=C:\;C:\DOS;C:\MOUSE*—Creates a specific set of paths that DOS uses to search for executable .COM, .EXE, and .BAT files. In this example, DOS first searches for executable files in the root directory of drive C, followed by the DOS directory, and finally the MOUSE directory.
- *DOSKEY*—Loads the DOSKEY program into memory. A shortcut tool used when typing in DOS.
- *SMARTDRV.EXE 1024 2048*—Configures the system for a 1-MB disk cache in DOS and a 2-MB cache in Windows.
- *CD*—Causes the DOS default directory to change to the root directory.
- *DIR*—Causes a DOS DIR command to be performed automatically.

Editing System Configuration Files: SYSEDIT.EXE

SYSEDIT is a standard text editor that edits system configuration files such as CONFIG.SYS and AUTOEXEC.BAT. This utility (the file SYSEDIT.EXE) can also be used to edit the Windows initialization files that are generally referred to as INI files. INI files were created when Windows 3.x was added to the DOS structure and have been included in the Windows directory of more recent Windows operating systems for backward compatibility. Common examples are WIN.INI and SYSTEM.INI. CONFIG.SYS and AUTOEXEC.BAT are found at the root directory (C:\). To access these configuration files in Windows 95, choose **Start**, **Run** and type **SYSEDIT** in the command line. Figure 4-12 shows the files in several windows.

Figure 4-12 Accessing Configuration Files in Windows

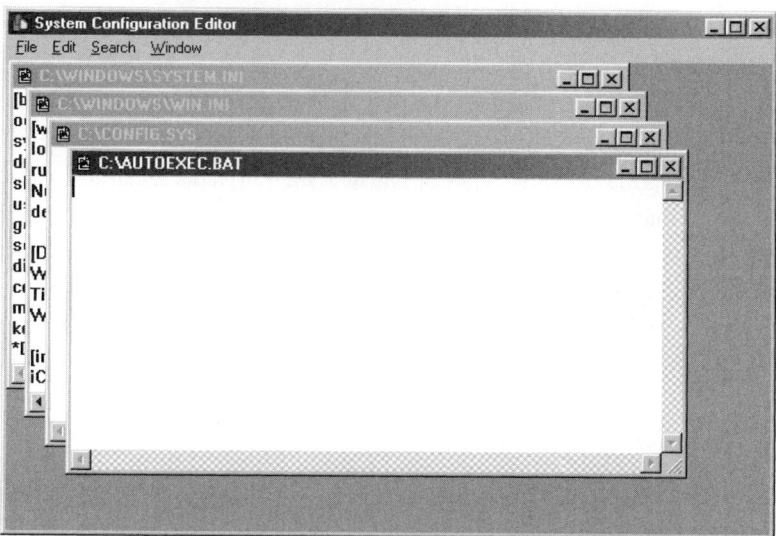

These files can also be accessed for editing in MS-DOS by typing **EDIT CONFIG.SYS** or **EDIT AUTOEXEC.BAT** at the DOS command prompt.

Worksheet 4.2.7   DOS Basics

Review the basics of DOS by answering true or false to the questions provided.

Memory Management

This section provides information on the different types of memory used in a computer system. You can adjust memory, optimize the system, and troubleshoot memory conflicts that can cause system failures. The following topics are included:

- Memory types
- Memory-management tools: adjusting and optimizing system memory
- Other types of memory
- Memory conflicts: General protection faults
- Real- versus protected-mode memory addressing

Memory Types

The operating system that runs the computer uses physical memory and virtual memory. *Physical memory* is called *RAM* and is also referred to as *system memory*. The four categories of system memory in the operating system are conventional, upper, high, and extended memory.

The logical divisions of memory were originally created because MS-DOS and early IBM PC microprocessors had a maximum memory of 1 MB. This 1 MB of memory was split into two pieces. The first 640 KB was for the user and the operating system, and the second (upper) 384 KB was for the BIOS and utilities. Because Windows 9x is built on an MS-DOS foundation, Windows 9x supports different types of physical memory specifications from the original IBM PC and its many descendants. These physical memory specifications are discussed in this section, and virtual memory is discussed in a later section. Figure 4-13 illustrates the allocation of physical memory.

Figure 4-13 Physical Memory Allocation

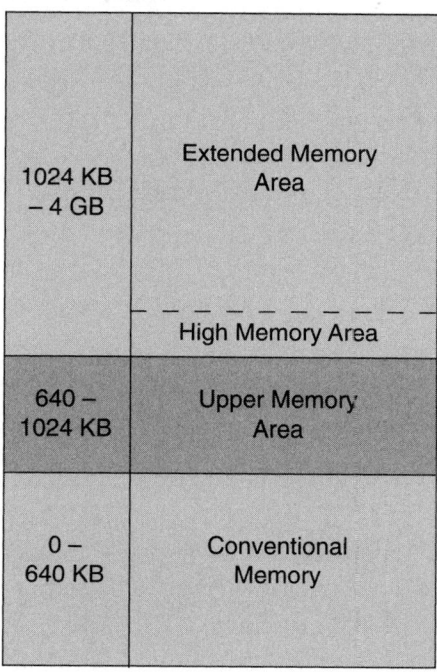

Conventional Memory

Conventional memory includes all memory addresses between 0 and 640 KB. It is also called *base memory*. This is the area where MS-DOS programs normally operate. In older DOS machines, this is the only memory that is available for running the operating system files, application programs, memory-resident routines, and device drivers. Memory-resident routines include terminate-and-stay-resident (TSR) programs such as the mouse and CD-ROM drivers. Figure 4-14 illustrates the allocation of conventional memory.

Figure 4-14 Conventional Memory Allocation

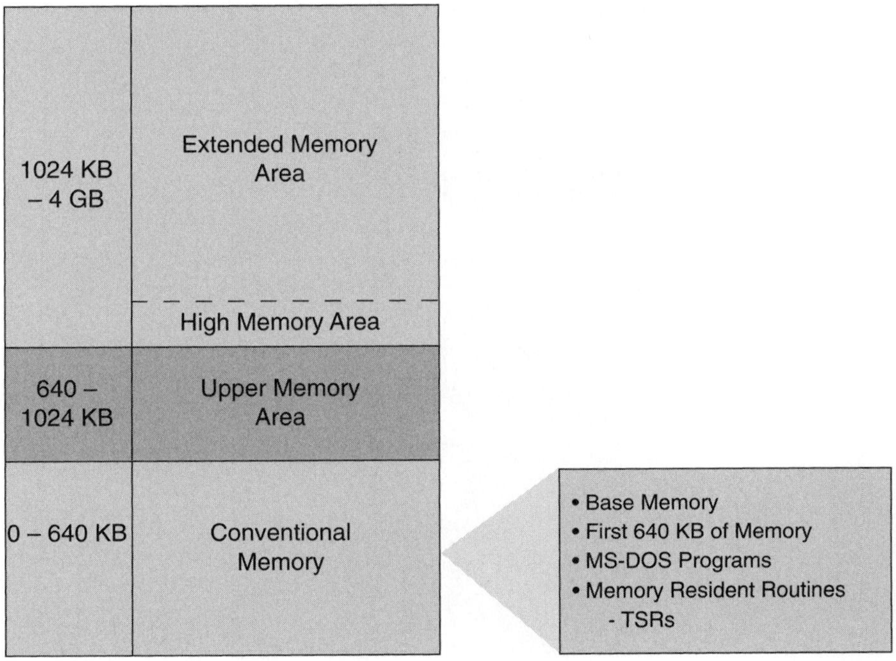

1024 KB – 4 GB	Extended Memory Area
	High Memory Area
640 – 1024 KB	Upper Memory Area
0 – 640 KB	Conventional Memory

- Base Memory
- First 640 KB of Memory
- MS-DOS Programs
- Memory Resident Routines
  - TSRs

Upper Memory/Expanded Memory

Also known as *reserved memory*, upper memory includes memory addresses that fall between 640 KB and 1024 KB (1 MB). Upper memory follows conventional memory, has a size of 384 KB, and is available in the form of *upper memory blocks (UMBs)*. Programs that operate in upper memory include the system BIOS, the Plug and Play BIOS, the video BIOS, and video RAM. Depending on the system, from 96 KB to 160 KB of this memory space is not used by hardware; these addresses are only available if an appropriate memory manager, such as EMM386.EXE, is installed during the startup process. Figure 4-15 illustrates the allocation of upper memory and expanded memory.

Expanded memory is another memory area that is similar to upper memory. *Expanded memory* is also called the *Expanded Memory Specification (EMS)*. This memory that can be accessed in 16-KB pages from a 64-KB page frame. These pages are established in unused UMBs. The primary device driver that allows the use of EMS is EMM386.EXE. This program frees conventional memory by allowing unused portions of the reserved memory area to be used for DOS drivers and memory-resident routines.

Figure 4-15 Upper Memory/Expanded Memory Allocation

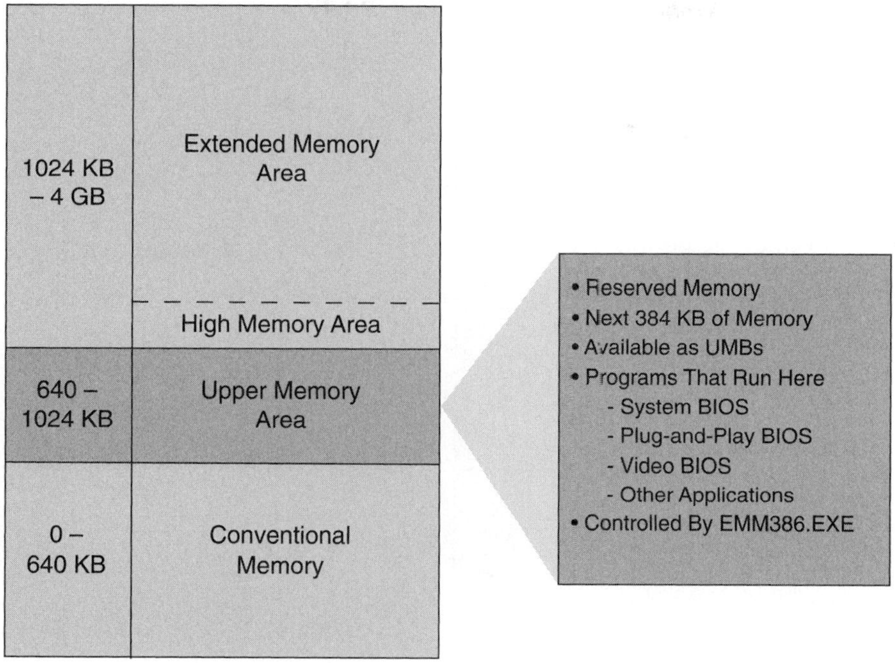

Extended Memory

The 80286 microprocessor and its protected operating mode allow it to access physical memory locations beyond the 1-MB limit of the 8088 and 8086 microprocessors. Memory above this address is generally referred to as *extended memory*. This area of memory is also called the *Extended Memory Specification (XMS)*. XMS is the primary memory area that is used by Windows 9x. A device driver that is loaded by the operating system controls this memory area. Windows 9x loads the XMS driver HIMEM.SYS during startup. HIMEM.SYS makes extended memory available to Windows 9x and other compatible MS-DOS programs. Figure 4-16 illustrates the allocation of extended memory.

High Memory

After the XMS driver is loaded and extended memory becomes available to the operating system, the first 64 KB of extended memory is called the high memory area (HMA). HIMEM.SYS usually activates the DOS=HIGH option, which allows the MS-DOS kernel used by Windows 9x to be copied into the HMA. DOS uses the HMA, which frees conventional memory for use by applications. Figure 4-17 illustrates the allocation of high memory.

Figure 4-16 Extended Memory Allocation

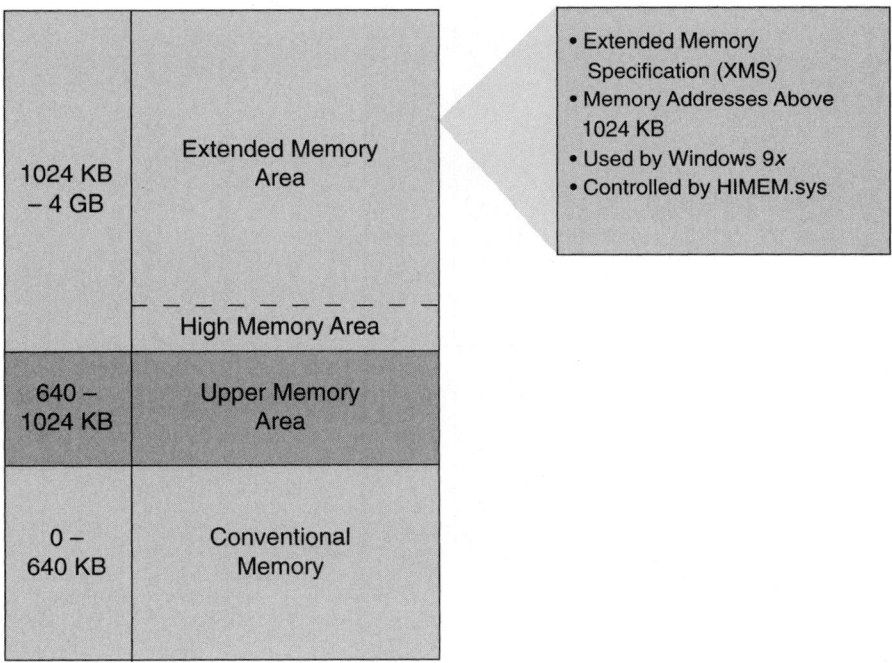

 e-Lab Activity   MS-DOS Memory Layout

In this e-Lab, the logical divisions of memory are identified.

Memory-Management Tools: Adjusting and Optimizing System Memory

Several tools are used to manage and optimize system memory. A description of these tools and a discussion of how they are used are explored in this section.

EMM386.EXE

The *EMM386.EXE* memory manager emulates expanded memory and thus makes upper memory available for use by the operating system. This memory manager can be used as follows:

■ To load MS-DOS TSR utilities into upper memory blocks, include the following line in the CONFIG.SYS file:

```
DEVICE=C:\WINDOWS\EMM386.EXE NOEMS
```

The NOEMS (no Expanded Memory Specification) option tells the OS not to convert extended memory to expanded memory. This is shown in Figure 4-18.

Figure 4-17 High Memory Allocation

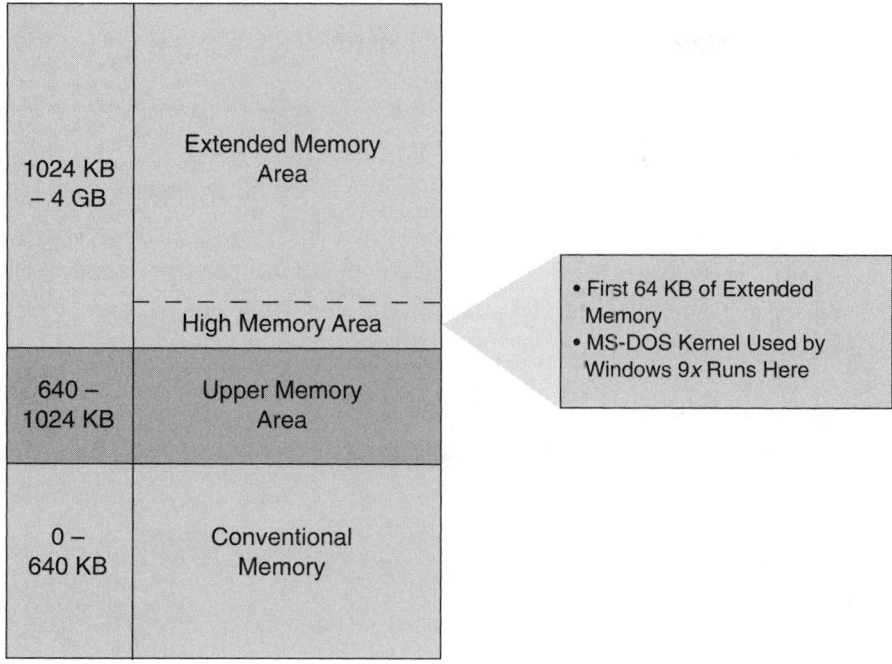

Figure 4-18 Loading MS-DOS TSR Utilities into UMBs

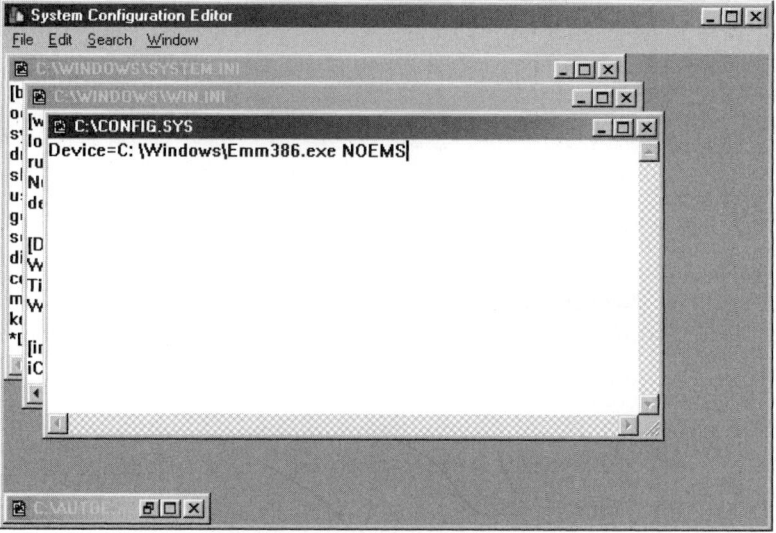

The IO.SYS file adds the following statement to the memory configuration to make UMBs available to MS-DOS TSRs:

```
DOS=UMB
```

- To load MS-DOS applications that need access to EMS memory, include the following statement in the CONFIG.SYS file:

```
DEVICE=C:\WINDOWS\EMM386.EXE RAM
```

This statement, shown in Figure 4-19, converts XMS memory space to a common pool of XMS/EMS memory that is available to both Windows 9*x* and DOS applications. Note that again the DOS=UMB statement is added by IO.SYS to make unused UMBs available to MS-DOS TSRs.

Figure 4-19 Loading an MS-DOS Application with Access to EMS Memory

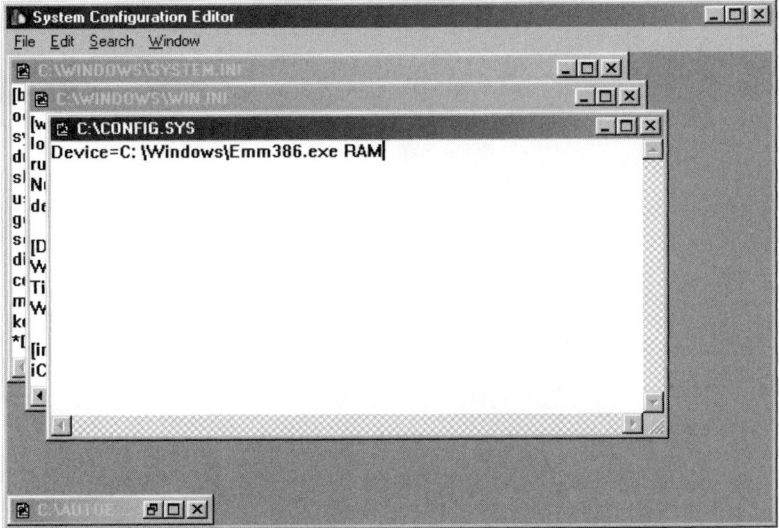

HIMEM.SYS

Load the **HIMEM.SYS** device driver to convert memory starting at 1 MB that is available as XMS or extended memory. This driver is loaded from the CONFIG.SYS file. The syntax for this command is as follows:

```
DEVICE=C:\DOS\HIMEM.SYS
```

DOS=HIGH

The **DOS=HIGH** option, added to the CONFIG.SYS file, tells the operating system to move a portion of itself (such as the MS-DOS kernel) into the high memory area. The DOS=HIGH option is usually combined with DOS=UMB, which tells DOS to create an upper memory block. The command uses the following syntax:

```
DOS=HIGH, UMB
```

DEVICEHIGH/LOADHIGH

The *DEVICEHIGH* option (used in CONFIG.SYS) and the *LOADHIGH* option (used in AUTOEXEC.BAT) both put upper memory blocks to use, once HIMEM.SYS and EMM386.EXE have been loaded. To load a mouse driver into upper memory, for example, use the following syntax:

```
DEVICEHIGH=C:\DOS\MOUSE.SYS
```

Other system memory tools include *MemMaker*, included with DOS 6.0, to help simplify the task of placing TSRs into upper memory. Use this utility to make the needed entries in the CONFIG.SYS and AUTOEXEC.BAT files.

Other Types of Memory

RAM drives and virtual memory are two other important types of memory. Creating a RAM drive and using virtual memory can speed overall performance, but they reduce the amount of physical storage.

Virtual Memory: Swap File or Page File on Disk

Virtual memory is memory that is not what it appears to be. Hard drive space is manipulated to act like RAM. The combination of virtual memory and physical memory gives the illusion of more memory than is actually installed on the system. Virtual memory is the basis of multitasking in Windows 9*x*. Without virtual memory, it would be difficult to use many current versions of software. Windows 3*.x* and 9*x* both implement virtual memory in files called *swap files*. Software called the memory manager or Memory Management Unit (MMU) creates virtual memory by swapping files between RAM and the hard drive, as illustrated in Figure 4-20. This memory-management technique creates more total memory for the system applications to use.

> **NOTE**
>
> Because the hard drive is slower than RAM, an overall reduction in speed occurs with virtual memory operations. In fact, virtual memory is the slowest of any memory type.

Most operating systems since Windows 3*.x* use some form of virtual memory operations. This includes Windows 9*x,* NT, 2000, and XP; UNIX; and Linux. Many older operating systems used a permanent swap file with a PAR extension. Current operating systems generally use temporary swap files with SWP extensions. A permanent swap file is always present and has a constant size. A temporary swap file has a variable size and is created when Windows starts. Control of Windows 95, 98, and Me virtual memory operations is established by choosing **Start**, **Settings**, **Control Panel**, selecting the **System** icon, and clicking the **Performance** tab, as shown in Figure 4-21.

Figure 4-20 Virtual Memory

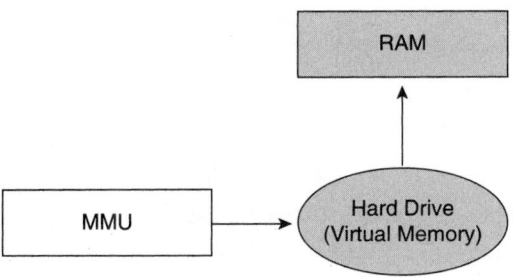

Figure 4-21 System Performance in the Control Panel

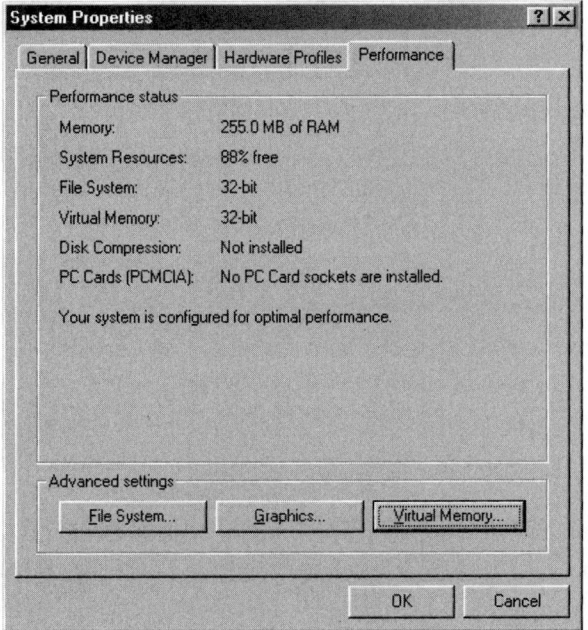

Clicking the Virtual Memory button produces the Virtual Memory options screen. The default setting is "Let Windows manage my virtual memory settings. (Recommended)," as shown in Figure 4-22.

The Windows 95 swap file is called WIN386.SWP. This file is dynamically assigned, and its size is variable. The Windows 2000 swap file or page file is named PAGEFILE.SYS. This file is created when Windows 2000 is installed. Its default size is typically set at 1.5 times the amount of RAM that is installed in the system.

Figure 4-22 Controlling Virtual Memory in Windows

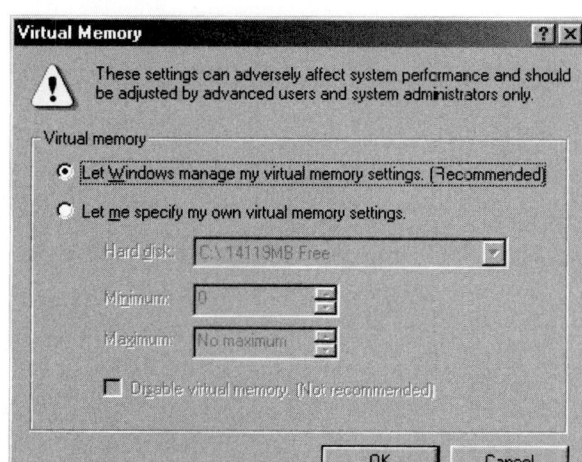

RAM Drives

Setting aside a portion of RAM to emulate a drive creates a *RAM drive*. For example, on a machine that has a hard drive partitioned into drives C and D, a RAM drive of 4 MB (4096 KB) can be created as drive E with the following command:

```
DEVICE=C:\DOS\RAMDRIVE.SYS 4096
```

This command is entered in the CONFIG.SYS file. The RAM drive becomes the next available drive letter and can be any size, up to the amount of RAM that is installed in the computer. Because data that is stored on the RAM drive only exists in RAM, it is cleared during each reboot. As a result, you should not store data files on a RAM drive.

Memory Conflicts: General Protection Faults

Several things can cause a memory conflict. A memory conflict can be caused by two memory managers that are operating at the same time, such as memory managers from a third party and those supplied by MS-DOS. Diagnostic tools, such as the Microsoft Diagnostics (MSD) utility, can diagnose these types of problems.

Memory conflicts can lead to *general protection faults (GPFs)*. Figure 4-23 shows an example of a GPF, which is also known as the "blue screen of death." It indicates that an error has occurred and lists the choices that are available to the user. Your best choice is usually to restart the system.

Figure 4-23 General Protection Fault (GPF)

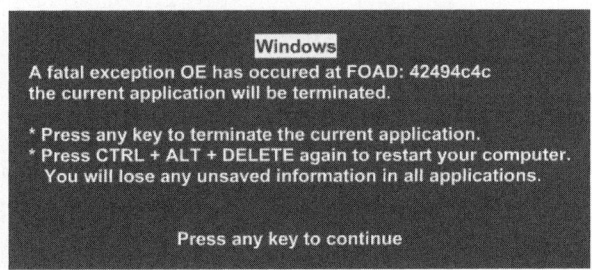

GPFs were introduced in the 16-bit Windows 3.x operating system, which was used for Windows 16 applications. GPFs typically occur when an application attempts to violate the system integrity in one of the following ways:

- Tries to use a memory address or space that is reserved by another application
- Tries to interact with a failing hardware driver
- Tries to gain direct access to the system hardware

Other conflicting situations occur when multiple memory-resident routines, such as TSRs, attempt to access the same upper memory space or address at the same time. A GPF is usually manifested by a nonresponsive system or application. Figure 4-24 shows the error message that is generated when a GPF occurs. Diagnostic utilities can provide a diagnosis of these conflicts. After identifying the conflicting applications, the problem can be resolved by reassigning different memory areas with the various memory-management and optimization tools that were described earlier in this chapter.

Figure 4-24 Sample GPF Error Message

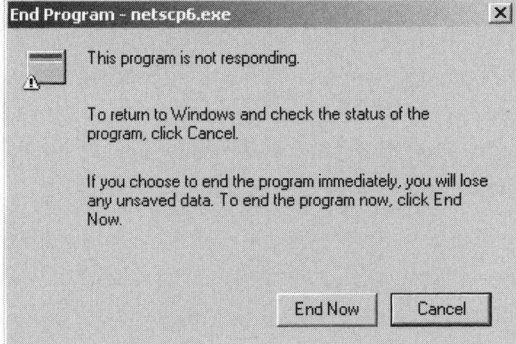

Real- Versus Protected-Mode Memory Addressing

The concept of real- versus protected-mode memory addressing is frequently included in discussions about memory space above upper memory. This includes all memory above 1024 KB.

Real Mode

Real-mode memory addressing means that software such as DOS and its applications can only address 1024 KB (1 MB) of RAM. The microprocessor chip addresses the first 1024 KB of conventional and upper memory by assigning real addresses to real locations in memory. For example, an 80286 system running in real mode acts essentially the same as the 8088/86 system and can run older software with no modifications.

Protected Mode

The counterpart to real mode is *protected-mode memory addressing*. Unlike real mode, *protected mode* allows one program to fail without bringing down the entire system. The theory behind protected mode is that one area of memory has no effect on other programs. When operating in protected mode, a program is limited to its own memory space allocation, but it can access memory above 1 MB. The 80286 processor could address up to 16 MB of memory, but software could use the chip to access even more memory. Before programs that run concurrently are truly safe from each other, the microprocessor and other system chips require an operating system that can provide that protection. Nearly every operating system other than DOS operates in protected mode.

Figure 4-25 Real- Versus Protected-Mode Memory

Protected Mode

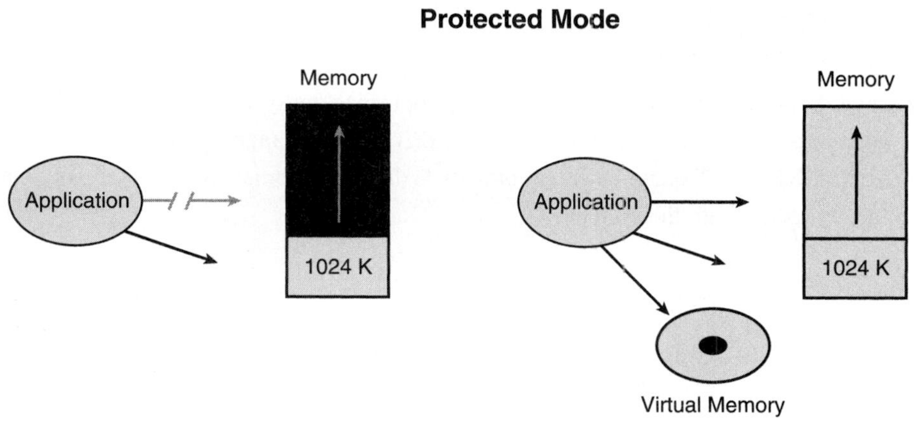

Summary

This chapter discussed the basics of the operating system. Some important concepts to retain from this chapter include the following:

- The three elements that make up the operating system are the user interface or shell, the kernel, and the file-management system.

- The operating system is in charge of operating the computer. The operating system is a software program that controls thousands of operations, provides an interface between the user and the computer, and runs applications.

- Multiuser means that the OS is capable of running programs and sharing devices for two or more users. Multitasking means that the operating system can handle multiple applications. An operating system is multiprocessing if it can support a computer with two or more CPUs. Multithreading is the ability of a program to be broken into smaller parts that can be loaded as needed by the operating system.

- The graphical user interface (GUI) is what makes Windows one of the most popular operating systems. The GUI makes the computer easier to use.

- The Disk Operating System (DOS) is primarily responsible for finding and organizing data and applications on the hard drive. The sections that make up DOS include boot files, file-management files, and utility files.

- DOS is a useful troubleshooting tool when Windows does not boot. Understanding the DOS command line and common commands and switches enables the technician to access the hard drive and run diagnostic programs.

- A boot disk boots the computer to the DOS prompt. The boot disk must include the COMMAND.COM, IO.SYS, and MSDOS.SYS system files. Diagnostic tools can also be added for troubleshooting.

- In DOS, two configuration files are used to optimize the system. CONFIG.SYS resides in the root directory; this file loads drivers and changes settings at startup. AUTOEXEC.BAT contains DOS commands that are automatically carried out when DOS is loaded into the system.

- The two main types of memory are system memory, which is also known as physical memory or RAM, and virtual memory. The four categories of system memory are conventional, upper or expanded, high, and extended. You should understand how system memory is divided into logical types. Virtual memory is memory that is not what it appears to be. The combination of virtual memory and installed physical memory gives the appearance of more memory than is actually on the system.

- Memory conflicts occur when two memory managers that are operating at the same time collide. Memory conflicts can lead to general protection faults (GPFs). A GPF typically occurs when an application attempts to violate the system integrity.

The next chapter goes beyond the DOS operating system to explain the Windows operating system. You learn about the Windows file structure and find out how the file-management system works. A Windows 9x installation is also described.

Key Terms

archive file   This is a bundle of other files contained in one file itself. Archives do not compress files; they just tie files and their structure together. Today many archive formats feature built-in compression to save space.

ATTRIB   Command that displays, sets, or removes one or more attributes.

attribute   A set of parameters that describe a file.

AUTOEXEC.BAT   Configuration file that is used by the operating system. The file contains a batch of DOS commands that are automatically carried out when DOS is loaded into the system.

base memory   See *conventional memory*.

boot file   A file that starts the system.

boot sector   Contains information about how the disk is organized.

C drive   Generally the label for the first hard drive in a computer system.

CD   Command that changes or displays the current directory on the specified drive.

CD   Command in the AUTOEXEC.BAT file that causes the DOS default directory to change to the root directory.

command line   The primary user interface in DOS.

CONFIG.SYS   Configuration file that is used by the operating system. This file loads drivers and changes settings at startup.

conventional memory   Includes all memory addresses from 0 to 640 KB.

COPY   Command that copies one or more files from one location to another.

/A   Switch that is added to the COPY command to copy ASCII files.

/B   Switch that is added to the COPY command to copy binary files.

/V   Switch that is added to the COPY command to verify an action.

/–Y   Switch that is added to the COPY command to display a confirmation prompt before overwriting an existing file.

/Y   Switch that is added to the COPY command to replace an existing file without a confirmation prompt.

DATE   Command in the AUTOEXEC.BAT file that causes DOS to prompt the user for the date.

DEL   Command that removes named files.

DELTREE   Command that removes the directory, including all files and subdirectories.

DEVICEHIGH   Option that puts upper memory blocks into use, once HIMEM.SYS and EMM386.EXE have been loaded.

DIR   Command in the AUTOEXEC.BAT file that causes a DOS DIR command to be performed automatically.

directory   Related program and data files organized and grouped together in the DOS file system.

directory tree   A graphical representation of a disk drive's directory organization.

Disk Operating System (DOS)   A collection of programs and commands that control overall computer operations in a disk-based system. DOS, which is sometimes called MS-DOS, was designed for the IBM PC.

DOS boot disk   Disk that boots a computer to the DOS prompt.

DOS command   An instruction that is executed from a DOS command line.

DOS=HIGH   Option that is added to the CONFIG.SYS file to tell the operating system to move a portion of the OS into the high memory area.

DOSKEY   Command in the AUTOEXEC.BAT file that loads the DOSKEY program into memory.

EDIT   Command that views, modifies, or creates files.

> */B*   Commonly used with the EDIT command, this switch displays monochrome mode.
>
> */H*   Commonly used with the EDIT command, this switch displays the maximum number of lines possible for the hardware.
>
> */R*   Commonly used with the EDIT command, this switch loads files in read-only mode.

EMM386.EXE   Memory manager that emulates expanded memory and makes upper memory available for use by the operating system.

expanded memory   Memory that is closely related to upper memory. It is also called the *Expanded Memory Specification (EMS)*. This memory can be accessed in 16-KB pages from a 64-KB page frame.

extended memory   Memory above 1 MB.

Extended Memory Specification (XMS)   Primary memory area used by Windows 9*x*.

external command   Command that is not part of COMMAND.COM and that must be loaded from secondary storage before being executed.

F5   Pressed during the boot process, this key causes the system to skip the CONFIG.SYS file, including the AUTOEXEC.BAT file.

F8   Pressed during the boot process, this key allows the system to proceed through the CONFIG.SYS file (and the AUTOEXEC.BAT file if needed), waiting for confirmation from the user.

FAT32   Offered first in Windows 98, this is an improved version of the original FAT (FAT16).

FDISK   Command that deletes and creates partitions on the hard drive.

> *\STATUS*   Switch that displays partition information when used with the FDISK command.

file   A block of logically related data that is given a single name and is treated as a single unit.

File Allocation Table (FAT)   A table of records that includes the location of every directory, subdirectory, and file on the hard drive.

file-management file   Enables the system to manage data.

file-management system   Used by the operating system to organize and manage files.

filename   The logical name that is given to a collection of data.

FORMAT   Command that erases all information from a computer disk or hard drive.

> */Q*   This switch, added to the FORMAT command, performs a quick format but does not clear the FAT.

> */S*   This switch, added to the FORMAT command, copies system files.

> */U*   This switch, added to the FORMAT command, performs an unconditional format.

general protection fault (GPF)   A memory conflict.

hidden file   A file that is not listed in a standard DOS directory listing; the file can only be seen with a specific command.

HIMEM.SYS   Device driver that converts memory, starting at 1 MB, to be available as XMS or extended memory.

internal command   A command that is built into the operating system. These commands are part of the command interpreter and are loaded into RAM when the system first boots.

kernel   The core of the operating system that loads and runs programs or processes and manages input and output.

LOADHIGH   See *DEVICEHIGH*.

Macintosh   An operating system, based on the Unix core technology, that is designed to be user-friendly.

Master Boot Record (MBR)   The required boot record on any disk that is created as a boot or system disk.

MD   See *MKDIR*.

MEM   Command that displays a table showing how memory RAM is currently allocated.

> */C*   This switch, when added to the MEM command, lists programs that are currently loaded into memory and shows how much conventional and upper memory each program is using.

> */D*   This switch, when added to the MEM command, lists the programs and internal drivers that are currently loaded into memory.

> */F*   This switch, when added to the MEM command, lists the free areas of conventional and upper memory.

> */P*   This switch, when added to the MEM command, pauses the display at each screen of information.

MemMaker   System memory tool that simplifies the task of placing TSRs into upper memory.

MKDIR   Command that creates a new directory.

MORE   Command that displays output one screen at a time.

multiprocessing   Allows a computer to have two or more CPUs that programs share.

multitasking   The computer's ability to run multiple applications at the same time.

multithreading   The capability of a program to be broken into smaller parts that can be loaded as needed by the operating system.

multiuser   The ability for two or more users to run programs and share resources.

network operating system (NOS)   An operating system that enables the server to track multiple users and programs.

network server   A computer that is capable of handling multiple users and multiple jobs.

operating system   A program that controls thousands of operations, provides an interface between the user and the computer, and runs applications.

PATH=C:\;C:\DOS;C:\MOUSE   Sample command in the AUTOEXEC.BAT file that creates a specific set of paths that DOS uses to search for executable files.

physical memory   Memory that is divided into four categories: conventional, upper/expanded, high, and extended.

PROMPT-PG   Command in the AUTOEXEC.BAT file that causes the active drive and directory path to be displayed on the command line.

protected mode   An area of memory that has no effect on other programs.

protected-mode memory addressing   Allows one program to fail without bringing down the rest of the system.

RAM   See *physical memory*.

RAM drive   A drive that is created by setting aside a portion of RAM to emulate the drive.

RD   See *RMDIR*.

read-only file   A file that can be opened and read but not changed.

real-mode memory addressing   Assigns real addresses to real locations in the first 1024 KB (1 MB) of RAM for DOS applications.

reserved memory   See *upper memory*.

RMDIR   Command that removes a directory or subdirectory.

root   The top level of a directory.

root directory   The file system's main directory.

SCANDISK   DOS program that is designed to detect and repair errors on the hard drive or floppy drive.

   /ALL   This switch, added to the SCANDISK command, checks and repairs all local drives at once.

   /AUTOFIX   This switch, added to the SCANDISK command, fixes errors without further input.

   /CHECKONLY   This switch, added to the SCANDISK command, checks for errors but makes no repairs.

server   See *network server*.

SET TEMP C:\TEMP   Command in the AUTOEXEC.BAT file that sets up an area for temporarily holding data in a directory called TEMP.

SMARTDRV.EXE 1024 2048   Command in the AUTOEXEC.BAT file that configures the system for a 1-MB disk cache in DOS and a 2-MB cache in Windows.

subdirectory   A directory within a directory in DOS.

swap file   Implements virtual memory by swapping files between RAM and the hard disk drive.

switch   An operation that is added to a DOS command to modify the output of that command.

SYSEDIT   Standard text editor that edits system configuration files.

system disk   A disk that is created to boot the computer to the operating system for troubleshooting purposes. It contains the three required system files. Also known as a DOS boot disk.

system file   A file that is required by DOS to boot the system.

system memory   See *physical memory*.

TIME   Command in the AUTOEXEC.BAT file that causes DOS to prompt for the date and the time.

UNIX   An operating system that is used primarily to run and maintain computer networks.

upper memory   Includes memory addresses that fall between 640 KB and 1024 KB.

upper memory block (UMB)   Allocated memory in upper memory.

user interface   The part of the operating system that allows the user to communicate with the computer. User interfaces can be command-line text oriented or the simplified GUI.

utility file   Enables the user to manage system resources, troubleshoot the system, and configure the system settings.

utility program   Program that maintains and repairs the operating system.

virtual memory   Created by manipulating hard disk space to provide more memory than is actually installed.

Check Your Understanding

1. What is the definition of an operating system?

   A. Software that executes other software

   B. An interface between a user and the software

   C. A software program that controls thousands of operations, provides an interface between the user and the computer, and runs applications

   D. Software that is manipulated by hardware

2. Which of the following is not a valid operating system?

   A. DOS

   B. Windows

   C. LAN

   D. UNIX

3. What does DOS stand for?

   A. Disk Operating Sectors

   B. Disk Operating System

   C. Disk Operating Services

   D. Disk Organizing Software

4. What is the maximum length of a DOS filename?

   A. 8 characters with an extension of 3 characters

   B. 12 characters; the extension is optional

   C. 16 characters with an extension of 4 characters

   D. 32 characters with an extension of 3 characters

5. What three files are necessary on a DOS boot disk?

   A. AUTOEXEC.BAT, IO.SYS, COMMAND.COM

   B. IO.SYS, COMMAND.COM, SYSTEM.INI

   C. IO.SYS, MSDOS.SYS, COMMAND.COM

   D. WIN.INI, SYSTEM.INI, COMMAND.COM

6. Where is the statement LOADHIGH used?

   A. CONFIG.SYS

   B. AUTOEXEC.BAT

   C. SYSTEM.INI

   D. MSDOS.SYS

7. When typing in DOS, which program is a good shortcut tool?

   A. MSD

   B. DIR

   C. CLS

   D. DOSKEY

8. Which of the following is an external DOS command?

   A. DIR

   B. HELP

   C. FDISK

   D. CLS

9. Which of the following is an internal DOS command?

   A. GRAPHICS

   B. UNERASE

   C. DISKCOPY

   D. DIR

10. Which of the following commands shows all the system files within a directory?

    A. DIR *.SYS

    B. DIR SYS

    C. DIR SYS /ALL

    D. DIR *.SYS /ALL

11. The .INI file type usually contains what type of information?

    A. Where files that are used by the operating system reside

    B. The names and locations of startup files

    C. User instructions

    D. Parameter information about a program

12. When inserted in the CONFIG.SYS file, what does the DEVICE= statement mean?

    A. It identifies the devices on the computer.

    B. It sets up the driver configuration.

    C. It tells the operating system what drivers are running.

    D. It loads a device driver.

13. What is another name for conventional memory?

    A. Common memory

    B. Base memory

    C. Usable memory

    D. Conventional memory

14. What are the memory addresses from 0 to 640 KB called?

    A. Common memory

    B. Basic memory

    C. Usable memory

    D. Conventional memory

15. What is extended memory?

    A. All memory above 640 KB

    B. Memory between 640 KB and 1024 KB

    C. All memory below 640 KB

    D. All memory above 1024 KB

16. What is the first 64 KB of extended memory called?

    A. XMS

    B. UMB

    C. HMA

    D. Conventional

17. What is virtual memory?

    A. Swapping memory in and out of the high memory area

    B. Simulating RAM by using a file on the hard drive

    C. Paging memory between conventional memory and the HMA

    D. The process of manipulating disk space to create more memory

18. What program is used to find and repair lost clusters?

    A. SCANDISK

    B. DEFRAG

    C. MSD

    D. DOS

19. Which program is used to set up a partition on a hard drive?

    A. PARTITION

    B. FDISK

    C. FORMAT

    D. DISKPART

20. What does TSR stand for?

    A. Terminate-and-stay-resident

    B. Terminate-and-stay-real

    C. Transfer-and-stay-resident

    D. Terminal-and-stay-resident

    E. DOS

    F. IO.SYS

21. Why would a read-only attribute be applied to a file?

    A. So it cannot be changed

    B. So it can only be read by DOS

    C. So changes can be tracked

    D. So the user knows that it is a system file

22. What key/key sequence do you press to step through the startup files when DOS starts?

    A. F5

    B. F6

    C. F8

    D. Shift-F5

Upon completing this chapter, you will be able to perform the following tasks:

- Understand the Windows 9x file structure and file management system
- Manage Windows with the Control Panel
- Use the system tools
- Prepare the hard dive for operating system installation
- Install Windows 9x
- Troubleshoot the installation process

Chapter 5

Windows 9*x* Operating Systems

Windows 9*x* refers to Windows 95, Windows 95 OEM Service Release 2 (OSR2), Windows 98, and Windows Millennium Edition (Me), collectively. In this chapter, you learn about the Windows file structure and file-management system. This chapter provides information on the registry and the system tools that manage the information that is contained in the operating system. Other topics covered include preparing a hard drive, installing an operating system, and troubleshooting the system.

Windows 9*x* File Structure and File-Management System

You need to understand how the Windows file structure and file-management system work. The ability to navigate through and use the features that are discussed is essential to the IT technician. This section includes the following topics:

- Naming files in Windows
- Understanding directories and folders
- Using a text-editing application to create a file (document)
- Copying, moving, and creating shortcuts
- Viewing document details
- Recognizing file types in Windows
- Selecting, copying, and moving files
- Searching for a file, folder, or directory
- Making backup copies of files on a floppy disk
- Using the Recycle Bin

Naming Files in Windows

In addition to being a descriptive name for the file, a filename must conform to the Windows file structure. The terms *directory* and *folder* both describe a place to store information. Prior to the introduction of Windows, files were stored in directories and subdirectories using a tree structure. This structure still exists in the graphical Windows environment, but the terminology has changed from directories to folders. Figure 5-1 shows the folders on drive C. A *subfolder* is simply a folder within a folder. These names are now used somewhat interchangeably. Files, directories, and folders are discussed more thoroughly in a later section.

Figure 5-1 Folders on Drive C

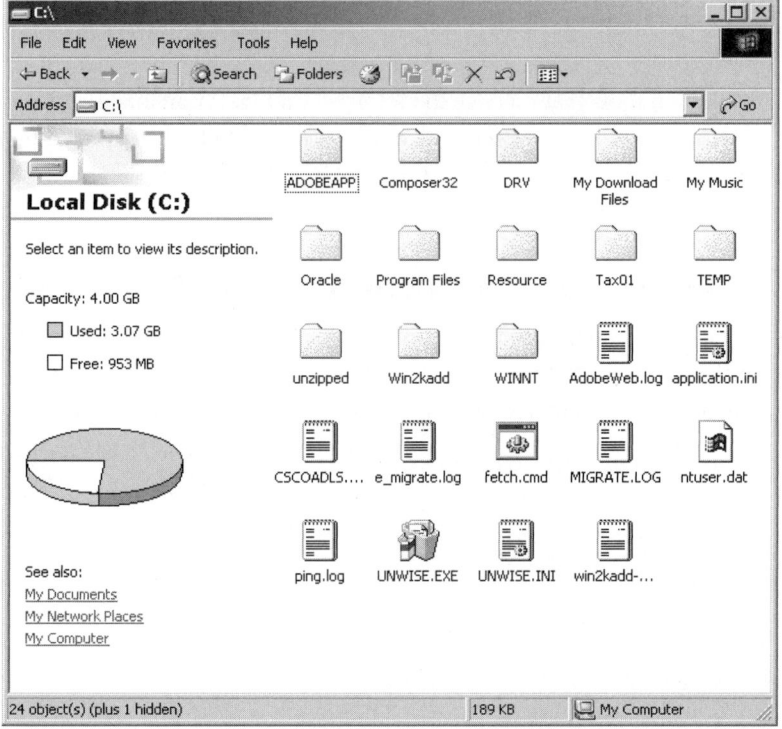

Windows 3.x and DOS filenames are limited to eight characters plus a three-letter suffix, called an *extension*. This format is referred to as an 8.3 convention. Windows 98 and later versions allow extended filenames of up to 255 characters. Folder names use the same rules as filenames.

The following characters should not be used in filenames because they are associated with special functions when executing commands from a command prompt:

```
/ \ : * ? " < > |
```

If these characters are used, a warning prompts the user to rename a file, as shown in Figure 5-2. Valid characters include all other characters and numbers that are available on a standard computer keyboard.

Figure 5-2 Invalid Filename Error Message

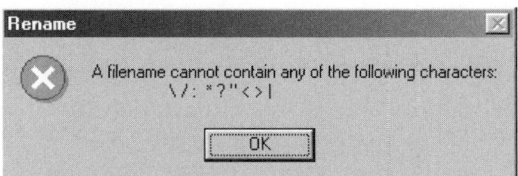

Uppercase characters are treated the same as lowercase characters in Windows. A file named BOB.TXT is the same as a file named bob.txt. However, this is not the case on the Internet, which uses many UNIX servers. UNIX treats filenames more uniquely.

Drive Letters

Drive letters use the 26 letters of the alphabet followed by a colon. The letters A and B are reserved for floppy drives. The letter C refers to the first hard drive, and D typically represents the CD-ROM or DVD-ROM drive.

The ***My Computer*** window, as shown in Figure 5-3, lists all the hard drives, floppy drives, CD-ROM drives, DVD-ROM drives, and network drives that are part of the computer or that can be accessed over a network. Take care when assigning drive letters, because many DOS and Windows programs make references to a specific drive letter.

In Windows 98, in addition to the drive letter, each drive can be assigned a name, called a drive label. The ***drive label*** can be up to 11 characters in length.

Understanding Directories and Folders

You need to understand how files are managed in Windows. This section covers the basic directory structure and file management in Windows.

To understand files, folders, and subfolders, imagine a tree. The trunk of the tree is the main starting place and is like the root folder in Windows. Folders are similar to branches of the tree and connect to the trunk. Minor branches attach to the major branches, just as subfolders are inside and attached to folders. Leaves that are attached to the major and minor branches are like files that are inside and are attached to folders and subfolders. A Windows application called ***Windows Explorer*** represents this concept of a tree and branches in the Windows file-management structure.

Figure 5-3 My Computer Window

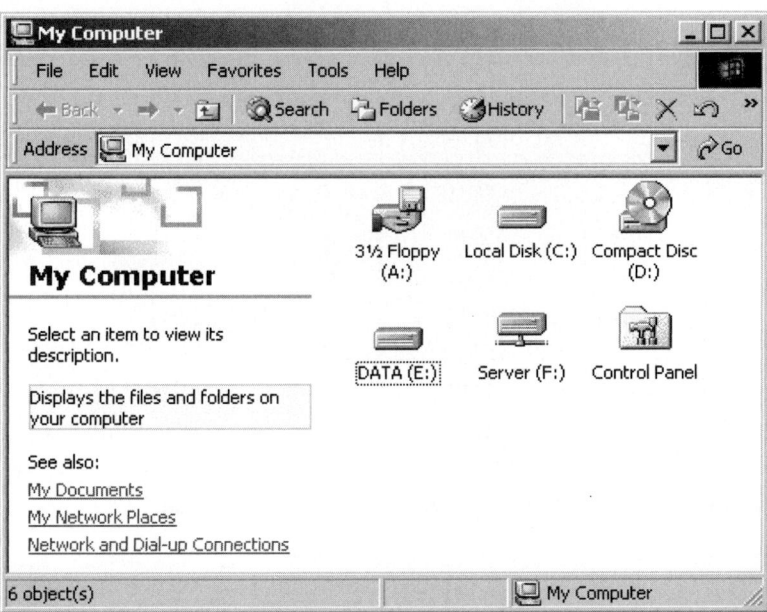

Windows Explorer displays file management as a hierarchical structure of files, folders, and drives on a computer. To open Windows Explorer, choose **Start**, **Programs**, **Windows Explorer**, as shown in Figure 5-4. Alternatively, right-click the **Start** button and choose **Explore** from the pop-up menu that appears. The Windows Explorer window contains the following three main parts:

- The area at the top is known as the title bar.
- The left pane is labeled Folders.
- The right pane displays filenames and possibly file details, such as size and type.

Details Mode

Files can be viewed in different modes by using the View menu on the title bar, as shown in Figure 5-5. The *Details mode* gives the most information about each file. Other modes can simplify viewing by showing only the name of the file, as in the List mode.

Figure 5-4 Windows Explorer

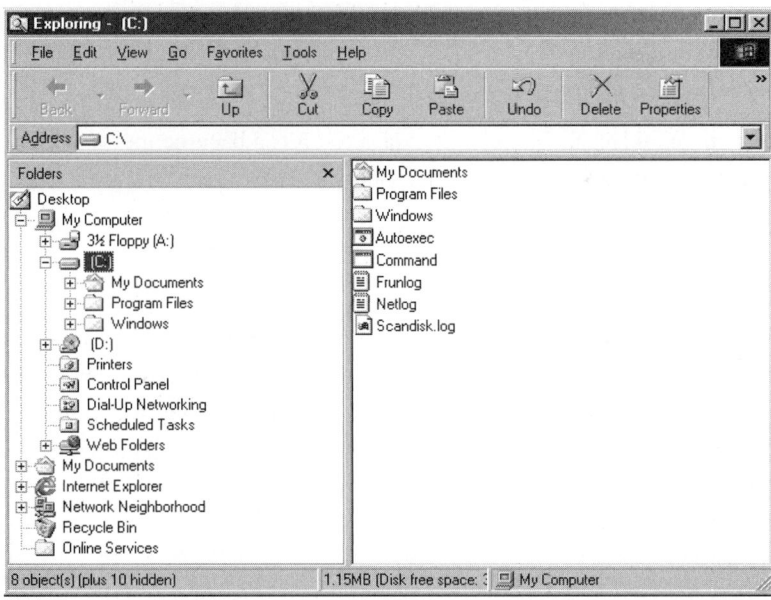

Figure 5-5 View Menu in Windows Explorer

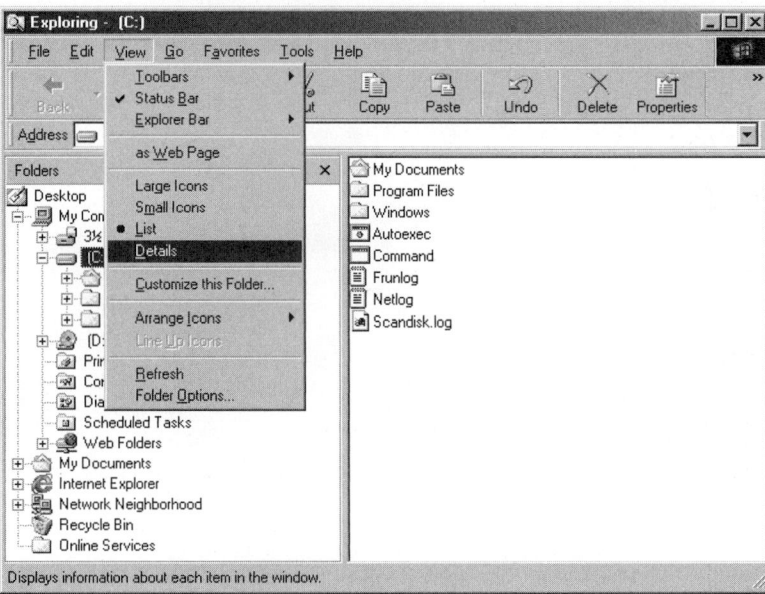

NOTE

The best way to understand the concept of Windows Explorer is to open it and practice viewing folders and files. Click the plus sign to display contents, and click the minus sign to collapse the folders. Also, try the different view options, and notice the information that each provides.

A plus sign (+) appears next to folders that contain subfolders. Click the plus sign to view subfolders. Click a specific folder in the left pane, and the folder contents appear in the right pane. Notice that the plus sign becomes a minus sign (–). Click the minus sign to collapse the subfolders back into the folder.

File management organizes a computer. Just as a room can become messy with many items scattered around, so can files on a computer. Folders store computer files in a logical and neat manner.

Creating a New Folder

To create a folder in Windows Explorer, use the scroll bar that is between the left and right panes to locate the Desktop. The ***Desktop*** is the screen that appears when Windows 98 boots. It allows easy access to files, folders, hardware devices, applications, and possibly the Internet or other computers. Click Desktop in the left pane of Windows Explorer. With the Desktop highlighted, move the cursor over to the right pane. Right-click in a blank area, and choose **New**, **Folder**, as shown in Figure 5-6.

Figure 5-6 Creating a New Folder in Windows

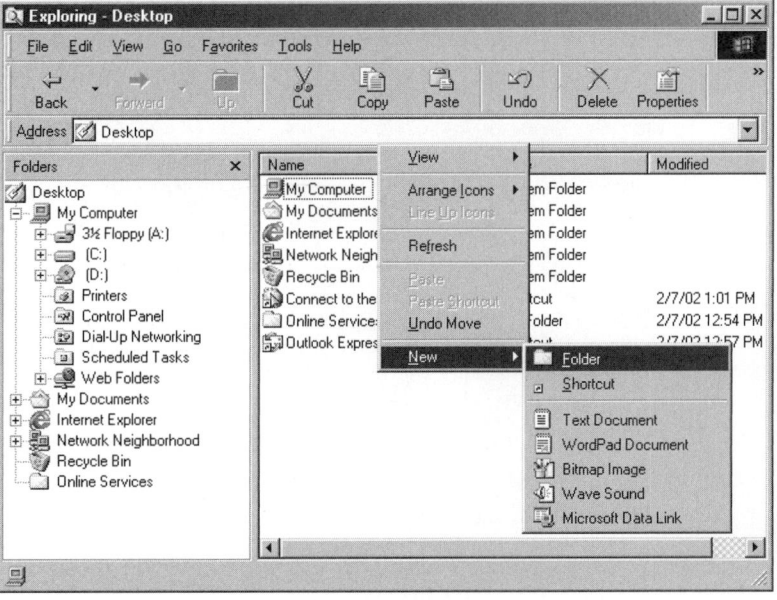

NOTE

Another way to rename a folder is to click the folder name once. Then right-click the name, and select **Rename** from the menu that displays.

When the folder is created, the words "New Folder" are highlighted. The folder can now be renamed. Start typing the new folder name, and the changes appear on the screen. Press **Enter** or click in a blank area of the screen when you are finished typing. Remember that a folder name can be up to 255 characters long and can only contain valid characters. The folder can be renamed later by clicking once on the folder to highlight it and pressing F2. The name highlights. Type the new name. In Figure 5-7, the folder is given the name Projects.

Figure 5-7 Renaming a Folder

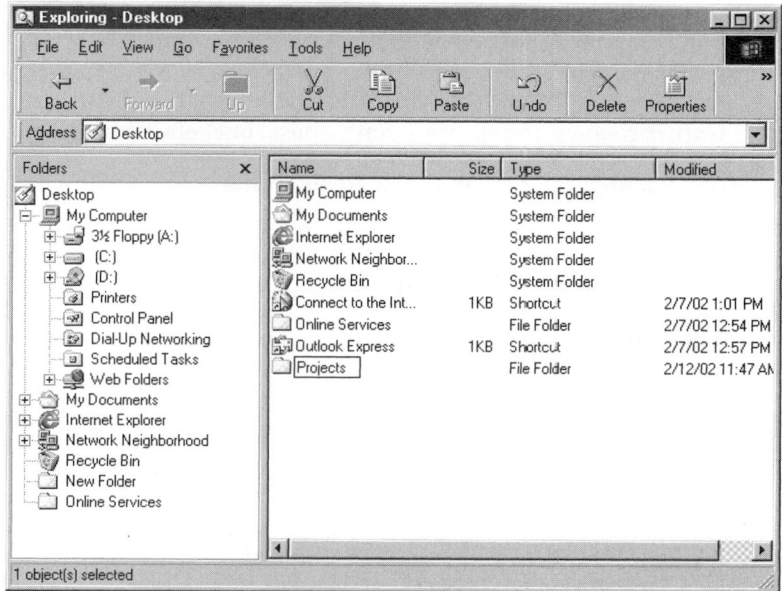

Using a Text-Editing Application to Create a File (Document)

In this section, you create a file using WordPad to demonstrate the process of saving a file and then moving it. To begin, open WordPad and complete the following steps:

Step 1   In WordPad, type the steps to wash a car, as shown in Figure 5-8.

Step 2   Choose **File, Save As**, as shown in Figure 5-9, and enter the filename **Car Wash Steps**, as shown in Figure 5-10.

The document can be saved to the Desktop as a Word for Windows document, which is the default format in Windows 98, or it can be changed to a Rich Text Format (RTF) file.

Step 3   Change the file from a Word for Windows file to an RTF file by choosing **File, Save As**.

The Save As dialog box opens.

Step 4   In the Save as Type text box, choose **Rich Text Format (RTF)**, as shown in Figure 5-11.

NOTE

The filename Car Wash Steps.rtf illustrates that spaces, as well as uppercase and lower-case letters, are valid characters in filenames.

Figure 5-8 Car Wash Steps in WordPad

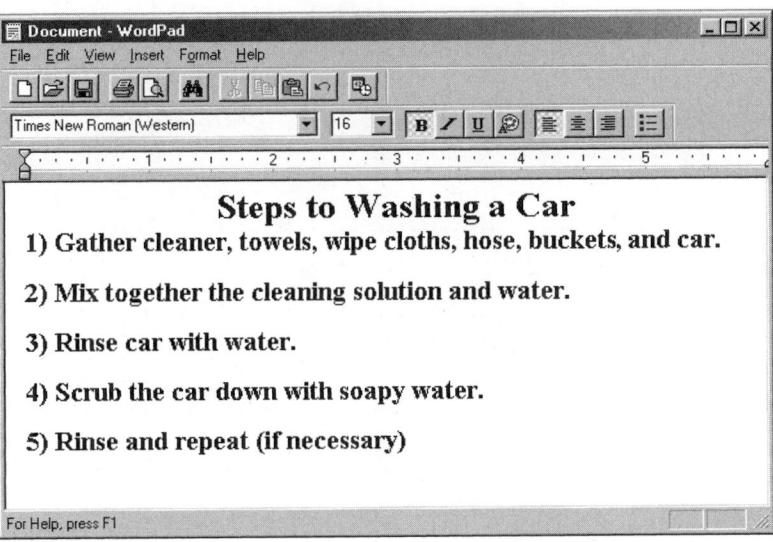

Figure 5-9 Saving the Document

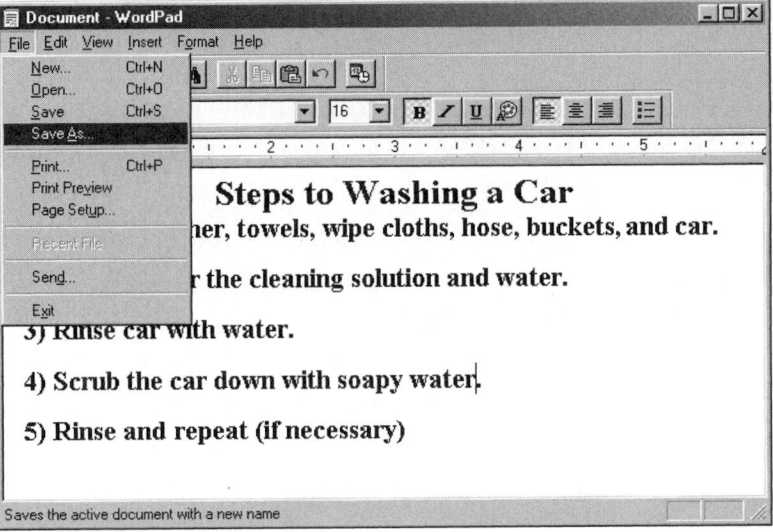

Figure 5-10 Save As Dialog Box

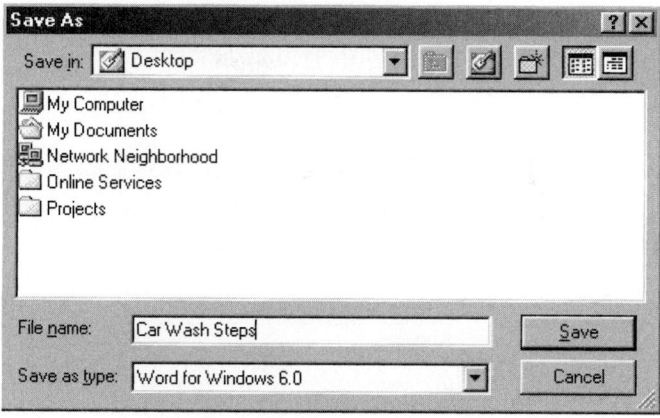

Figure 5-11 Saving the File as a Rich Text Format (RTF) Document

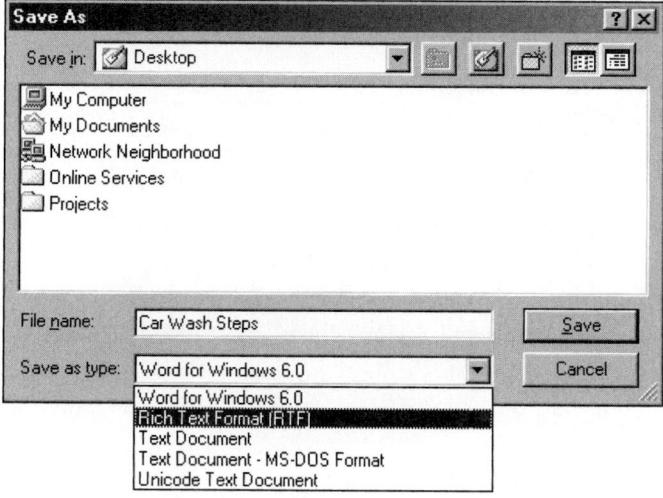

Step 5   Click the **Save** button.

Step 6   Open Windows Explorer, as shown in Figure 5-12. In the left pane, click **Desktop**. The Desktop items are displayed in the right pane.

Figure 5-12 Locating a Document in Windows Explorer

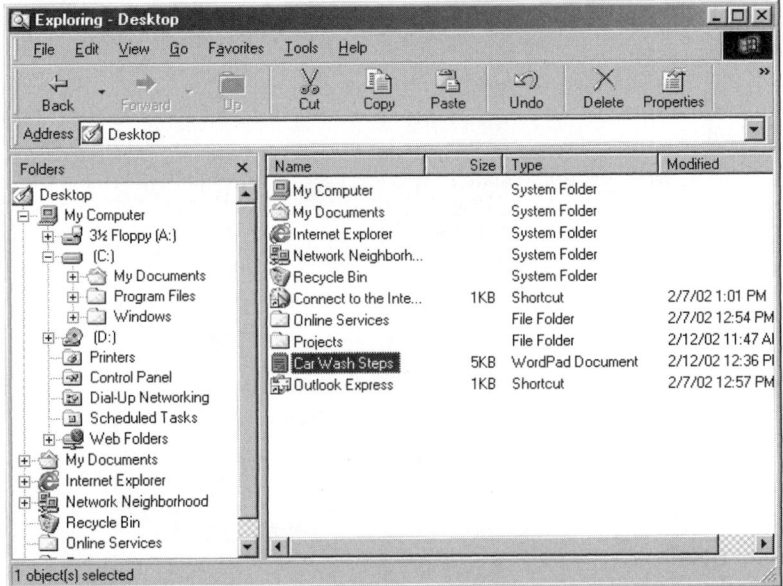

Step 7   To view the full name of the file, move the cursor to the file properties bar, which is between the Name and Size headings, as shown in Figure 5-13. Note that the cursor changes to a double-headed arrow. Double-click between Name and Size. The filename region adjusts automatically to display the full name of every file.

Step 8   Move the Car Wash Steps.doc file to the Projects folder by using one of the following methods:

- On the Desktop, click and hold down the mouse button while dragging the file over to the Projects folder. Release the mouse button. The file becomes semitransparent until it is dropped into the Projects folder, as shown in Figure 5-14.

Figure 5-13 Expanding the Name Column

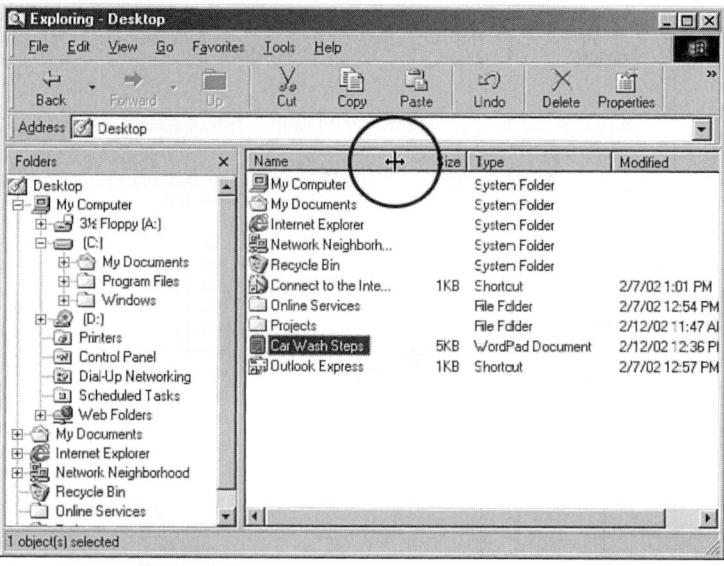

Figure 5-14 Moving a Desktop Item into a Folder

- In Windows Explorer, you can drag the file to the Projects folder, as shown in Figure 5-15.

Figure 5-15 Moving a Windows Explorer File into a Folder

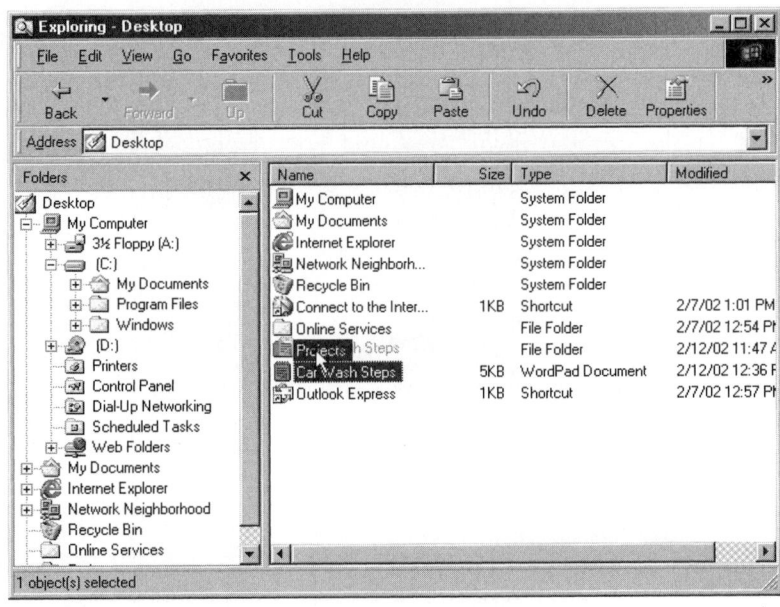

- You can cut and paste the file to the Projects folder. Right-click the file and select **Cut** from the menu that appears. Move the cursor to the Projects folder, right-click the folder, and select **Paste** from the menu that appears. The results are shown in Figure 5-16.

Copying, Moving, and Creating Shortcuts

The ability to copy or cut files and text is made possible by the Clipboard. When a file or text is cut or copied, it is held temporarily on the Clipboard. Each time the cut or copy option is used, the previous Clipboard contents are replaced and are no longer accessible. Right-click a file, as shown in Figure 5-17, and a menu displays with all the options that are available for that file. Selecting the *copy* option leaves the original file in the current location and places a duplicate on the Clipboard. Navigate to the new folder, right-click that folder, and select **Paste** from the menu that appears. The *paste* command copies the file to the indicated folder. Having two files with the same name is permitted as long as the files are not in the same folder.

The *cut* feature is similar to the copy feature, except that cut removes the file from the current location and places it on the Clipboard. The file on the Clipboard can now be pasted to a new location.

Figure 5-16 Verifying the Recently Moved Document

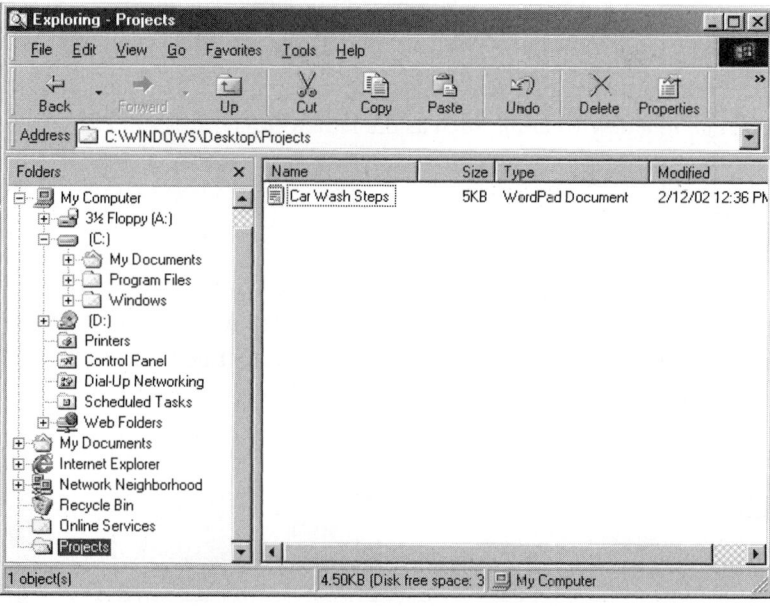

Figure 5-17 Right-Click a File to See the Available Options

Another option, *Create Shortcut*, establishes an additional link to a program, folder, or file. The link can be accessed just as the original file. Right-click a file, for example, and select **Create Shortcut** from the menu that appears. The shortcut is created and displayed in the same location folder as the original file. The shortcut displays as "Shortcut to . . ." The shortcut can be dragged to a new location, such as the Desktop. The shortcut can also be given a new name by using the Rename option that was previously discussed.

Viewing Document Details

File details provide the directory information for a file. The right pane in Windows Explorer provides details of the directory, folders, and files, as shown in Figure 5-18. Details include the creation or last-modified date of a file or folder, the type of item (folder, MS Word document, Excel spreadsheet, and so on), and the file size.

Figure 5-18 Viewing File Attributes

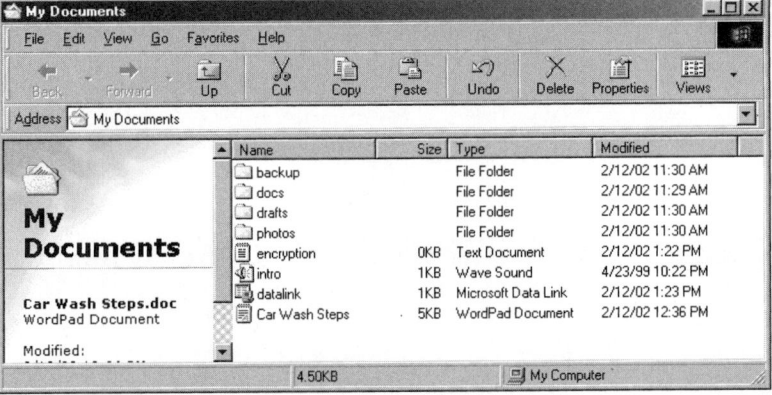

Including the date that the file was last modified in the filename can aid in tracking the latest versions. Adding numbers or the letter *v* to filenames can indicate the different versions. The author's name or organization can also be useful in names, especially if multiple people share the files.

Recognizing File Types in Windows

This section discusses how to recognize the most widely used types of files in a directory/folder. Examples include word processing files, spreadsheet files, database files, presentation files, Rich Text Format (RTF) files, and image files. The main parameter that is used is the *file extension*, as mentioned earlier in this chapter.

The file extensions that are shown in Table 5-1 describe the file format or the type of application that created the file. The asterisk (*) in the first column is a *wildcard* that indicates the filename (for example, myfile), without the extension.

Table 5-1 File Extensions and Their Descriptions

File Extension	Description
*.doc	Microsoft Word or WordPad file
*.xls	Microsoft Excel file
*.dbf, *.dat	Database file
*.txt	ASCII text file with no formatting (bold, underline, and so on)
*.exe, *.com	Executable file (program)
*.sys	Windows driver
*.dll	Windows dynamic link library
*.htm, *.html	Hypertext Markup Language (web page) file
*.ini	Initialization file
*.rtf	Rich Text Format file (a safer form of a Word document that has no macros but retains page formatting)
*.wks, *.wk1	Lotus 1-2-3 spreadsheet file
*.bmp, *.jpeg, *.mpg (or *.mpeg), *.gif, *.tif	Image file
*.ppt	PowerPoint file
*.wav, *.mp3	Audio file
*.log, *.bat	Log file or batch file

Video   Changing File Views in Windows

Changing file views in Windows is demonstrated in this video.

Lab 5.1.6   Changing File Views in Windows (Showing File Extensions)

This lab provides a practice scenario for changing the file view based on the user's needs or preferences in Windows Explorer.

Selecting, Copying, and Moving Files

This section explains how to select a file individually or as part of a group. Copying and pasting files within directories/folders to make a duplicate copy are also explained.

Selecting and Moving Files

To select several files (even discontinuous ones), hold down **Ctrl** while clicking the filenames. The files become highlighted. To deselect a file, continue holding **Ctrl** and click again on the file.

To select a range of files, highlight the first file, hold down **Shift**, and highlight the last file in the range. To deselect any file from within the highlighted range, hold down **Ctrl** and click to deselect it.

To highlight all files, choose **Edit, Select All**. To deselect all the files, click in a blank area or press **Esc**. Once files are highlighted (selected), they can be moved, copied, deleted, or opened.

Copying and Moving Files

To copy a file, right-click the file and select **Copy** from the menu that appears, as shown in Figure 5-19. Click the folder to which the file is to be pasted.

Figure 5-19 Copy Option

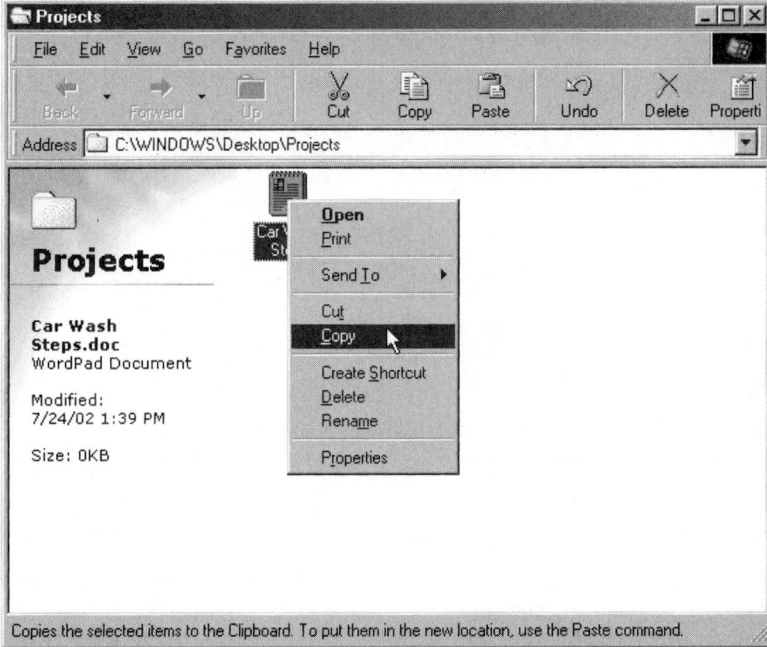

Right-click the destination folder in Explorer's right pane, and choose **Paste** from the menu that appears, as shown in Figure 5-20. A duplicate copy of that file is now available.

Figure 5-20 Paste Option

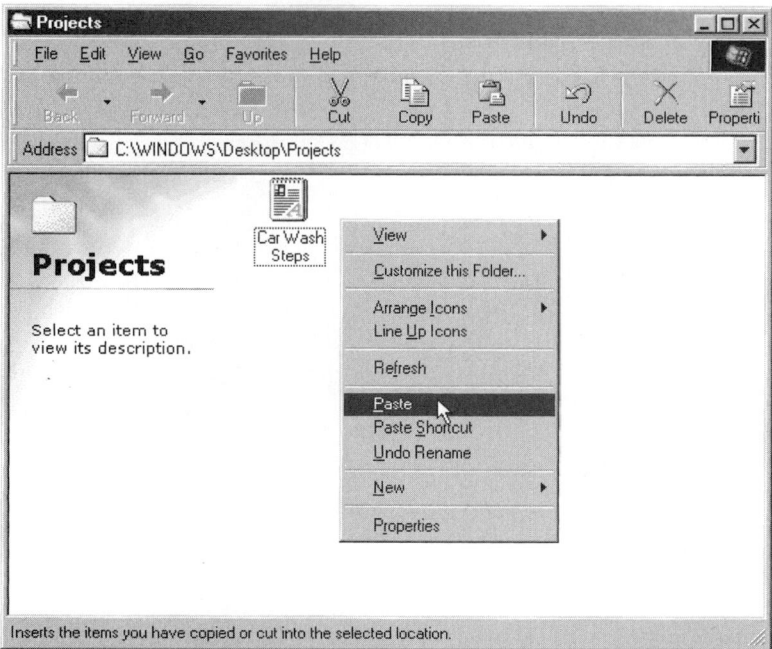

Video   Text Editing and File Management

This video demonstrates how to edit text and manage files.

Lab 5.1.7   Text Editing and File Management

In this lab, you practice text editing and file management by creating a file, saving it, and then moving it to a floppy disk.

Searching for a File, Folder, or Directory

To find a file or folder, choose **Start**, **Find**, as shown in Figure 5-21. Next, choose **Files or Folders**, and type in the name or part of the name of the file, as shown in Figure 5-22. An efficient search uses part of the filename or folder name that is unique. In this example, Wash, Car Wash, or Steps can narrow the search to just a few files. Files or folders that contain the search word are searched for, as shown in Figure 5-23. You can also sort by date modified or by type of file. Double-click the file to open it.

NOTE

A shortcut to the Files or Folders option is to press the **Windows** key, press **F** (for Find), and then press **F** again (for Files and Folders).

Figure 5-21 Find Files and Folders

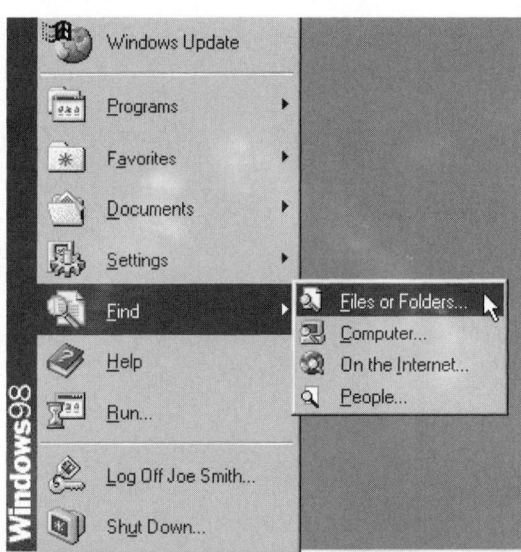

Figure 5-22 Enter a Unique Part of the Filename

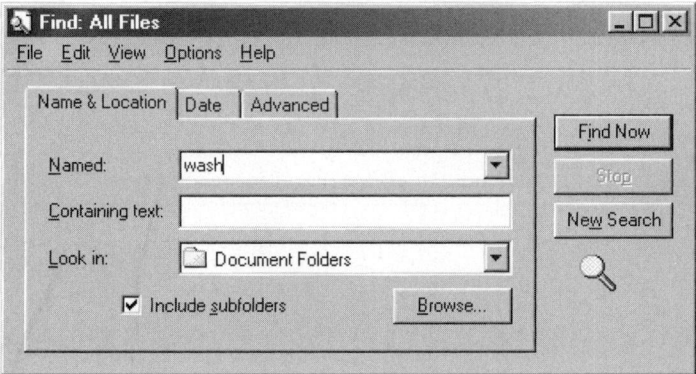

In addition to the text that is being searched for, you must indicate where to search. For example, the system can look in the entire hard drive, on the Desktop, or in specific folders.

Making Backup Copies of Files on a Floppy Disk

To copy a file or folder to a floppy disk, right-click the file and choose **Send To**, **3-1/2 Floppy (A)** from the menu that appears, as shown in Figure 5-24. You can also drag and drop selected files to the drive A icon.

Figure 5-23 Search Results

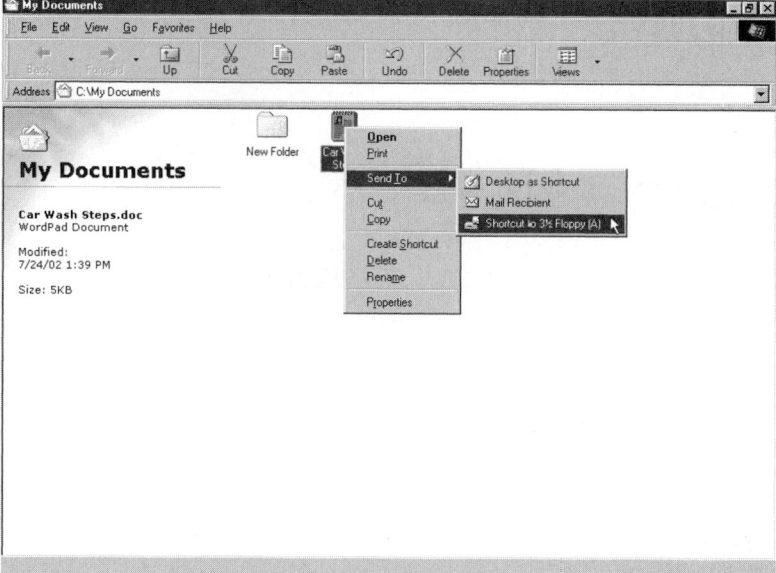

Figure 5-24 Sending (Copying) a File to a Floppy Disk

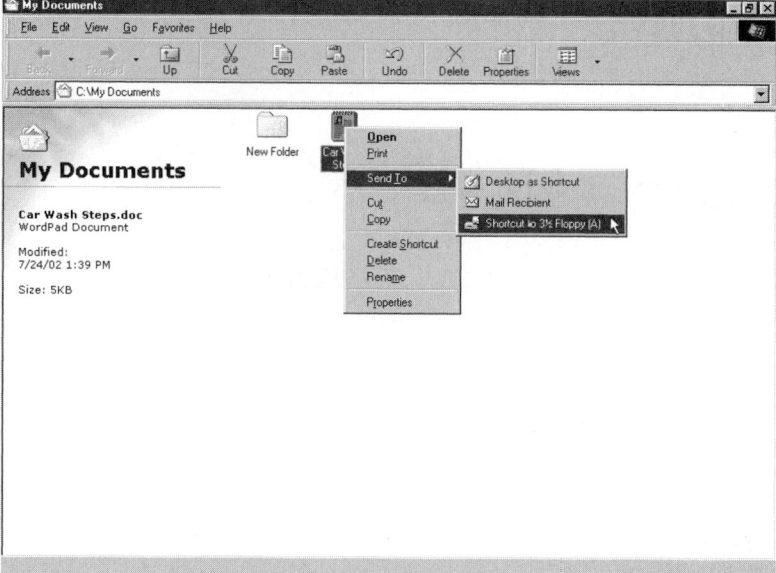

Using the Recycle Bin

The *Recycle Bin* can be used to temporarily hold deleted files or to permanently delete files from the computer. Files remain on the hard drive until the Recycle Bin is emptied. Files can be restored from the Recycle Bin to the original location. In Windows 98, 10 percent of the hard drive space is allotted for the Recycle Bin by default.

Double-clicking the Recycle Bin icon on the Desktop opens a window that shows the files that have been deleted. Right-click a filename and select **Delete** from the shortcut menu that appears, as shown in Figure 5-25, to remove the file from the Recycle Bin. (This permanently deletes the file from the computer.)

Figure 5-25 Permanently Deleting a File

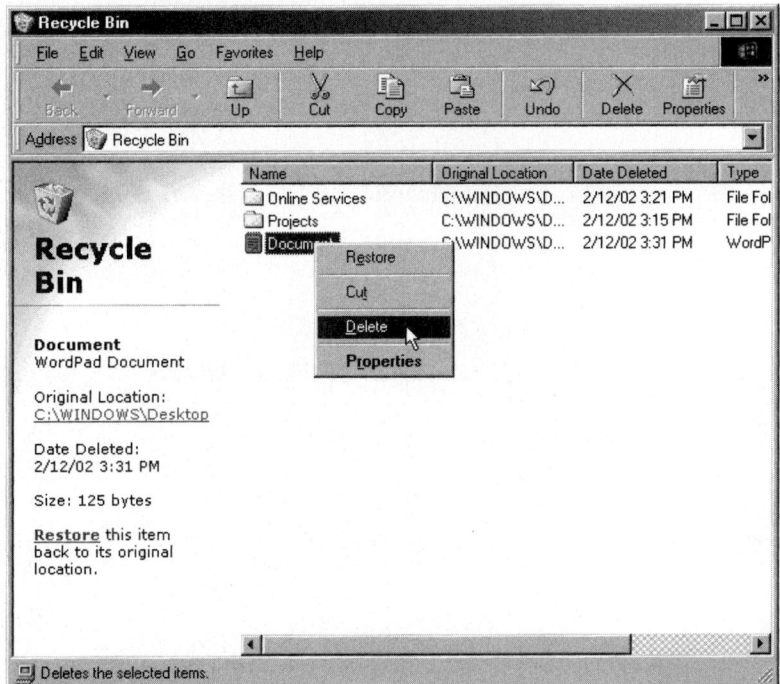

NOTE

The same restore process works for folders. By restoring a file that was previously in a folder, that folder is also automatically restored. An empty folder cannot be restored.

Right-click a filename and select **Restore** from the shortcut menu that appears, as shown in Figure 5-26, to restore the file to its original folder on the hard drive.

Right-click the file and select **Properties** from the menu that appears to view the document's properties. The window that opens displays the original location of the file and other details, as shown in Figure 5-27.

Figure 5-26 Restoring a File

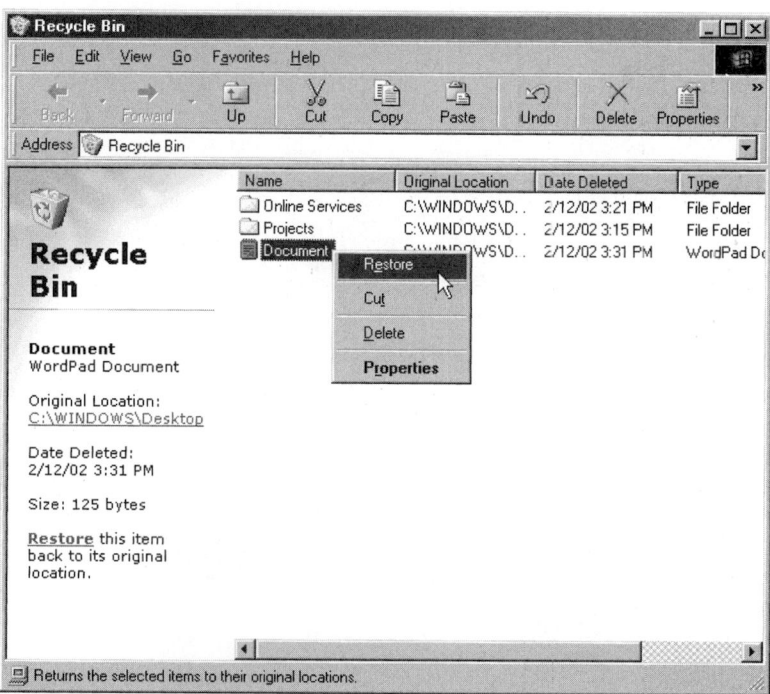

Figure 5-27 Document Properties Window

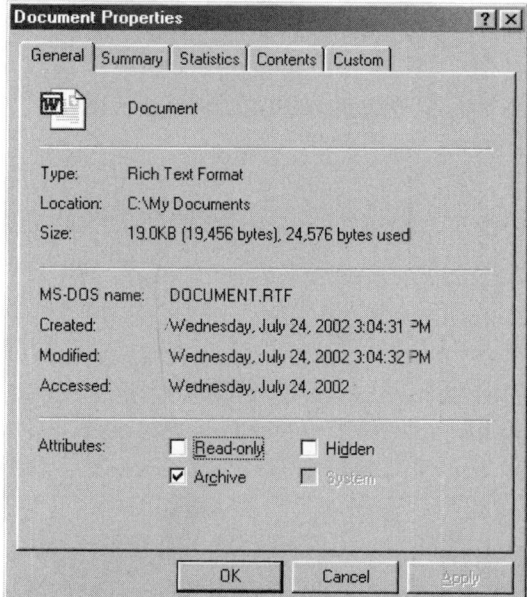

A Recycle Bin that contains at least one file or folder is shown in Figure 5-28. Right-clicking this Recycle Bin opens the menu that is shown in Figure 5-29. Select **Empty Recycle Bin** from the menu that appears to remove all the contents from the Recycle Bin.

Figure 5-28 Recycle Bin

Figure 5-29 Right-Click to Empty the Recycle Bin

Files and folders can be viewed in the Recycle Bin in the same way as in Windows Explorer. In the Recycle Bin, choose **View**, **Details** to verify that the correct file is being removed or restored.

Worksheet 5.1.10   Windows Files and Folders

This worksheet provides a review of the important concepts that are covered in this section.

Windows Management with the Control Panel

The Control Panel is the command center for Windows. It allows computer settings to be changed or adjusted. The view can be changed in the Control Panel. Choose **View** and select **Large Icons**, **Small Icons**, **List**, or **Details**. Some settings rarely need to be accessed, and others are used more frequently. The more widely used features are detailed in this section. The following topics are included:

- Using the System Properties applet
- Using a printer
- Adding and removing programs
- Adding hardware
- Adjusting the display and sounds

Using the System Properties Applet

One of the most useful tools in the Windows Control Panel is the *System Properties* window. This tool can be accessed from the Control Panel by choosing **Start**, **Settings**, **Control Panel**, **System**, as shown in Figure 5-30.

Figure 5-30 Control Panel

The System Properties window includes a series of tabs across the top. The following paragraphs detail each of the tabs.

General

The default tab is the General tab, as shown in Figure 5-31, which lists information that relates to the system. This includes the operating system version, licensing information, and system specifics, such as processor type and amount of memory.

Figure 5-31 General Tab

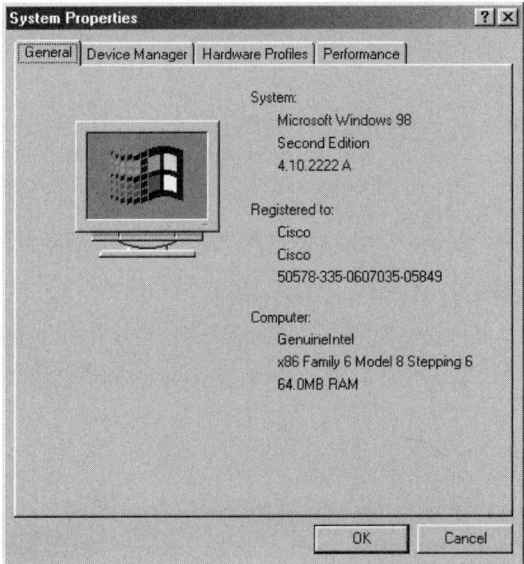

Device Manager

The next tab is the *Device Manager* tab, as shown in Figure 5-32. The Device Manager provides a list of all the hardware within the system and allows the user to view which system resources are being used. It can also be used to update device drivers, disable or enable devices, and change resource settings.

Hardware Profiles

The third tab is the *Hardware Profiles* tab, as shown in Figure 5-33. This tab allow the user to have different hardware configurations for the same operating system. Most users do not need to set up hardware profiles. However, a laptop user can have one profile for the system when it is docked and a different profile when it is not docked.

Figure 5-32 Device Manager Tab

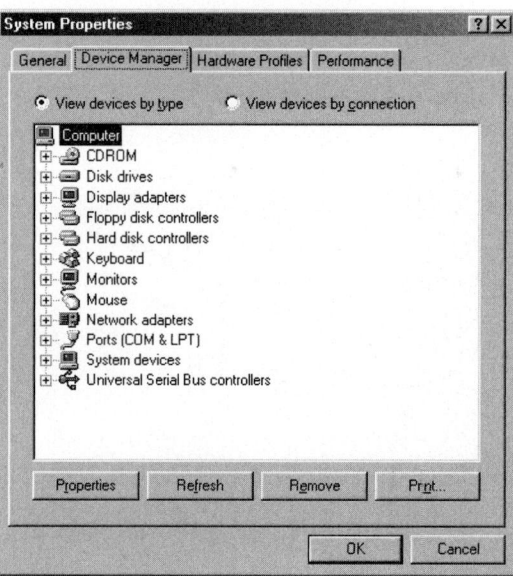

Figure 5-33 Hardware Profiles Tab

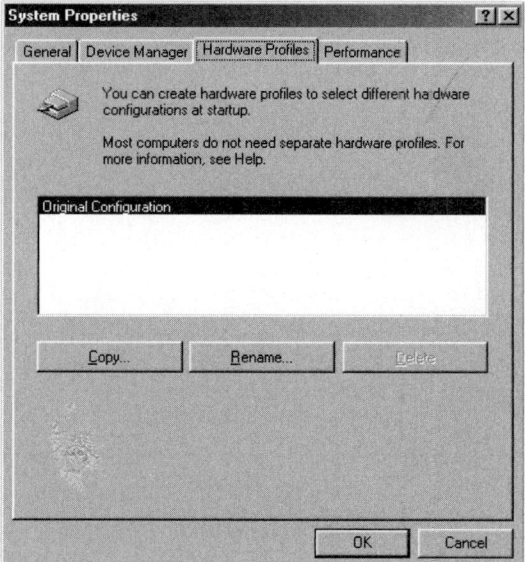

Performance

The fourth tab is the *Performance* tab, as shown in Figure 5-34. This displays information about the performance statistics of the current system and allows access to virtual memory and file system settings.

Figure 5-34 Performance Tab

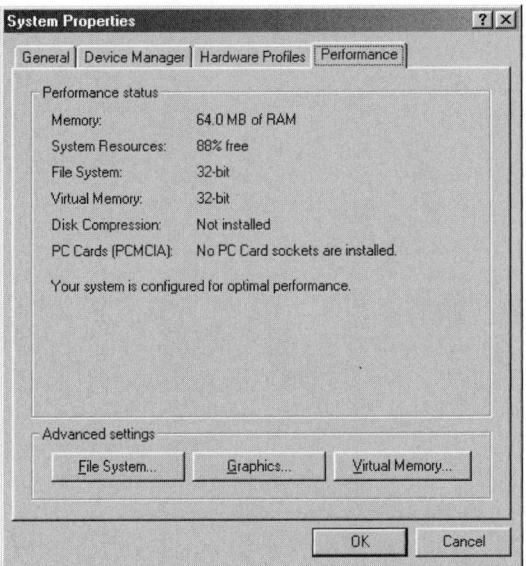

Using a Printer

This section provides information on printing to an already installed printer, changing the default printer, and viewing the progress of a print job.

To print an open document from an installed printer, choose **File**, **Print**, as shown in Figure 5-35.

The Print dialog box displays, as shown in Figure 5-36. The user can select options to print the entire document, print the current page or a range of pages, select the number of copies to be printed, modify the layout of the document, and alter the characteristics of the printer output.

Figure 5-35 Document File Menu

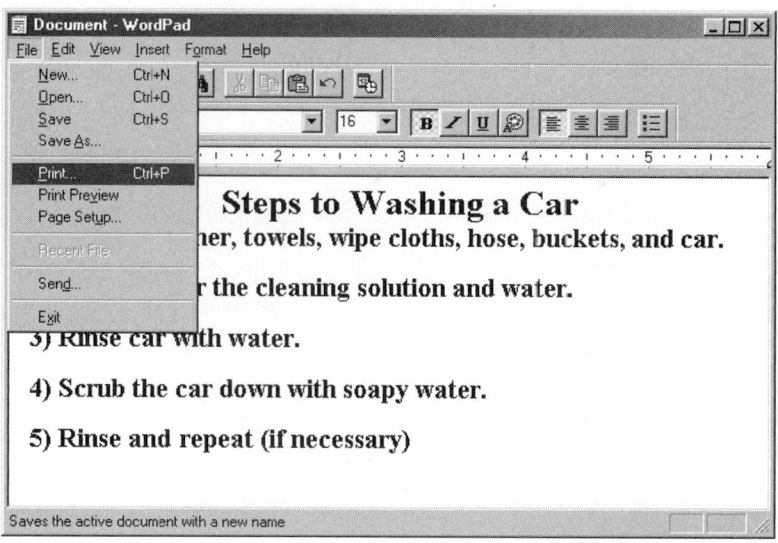

Figure 5-36 Print Dialog Box

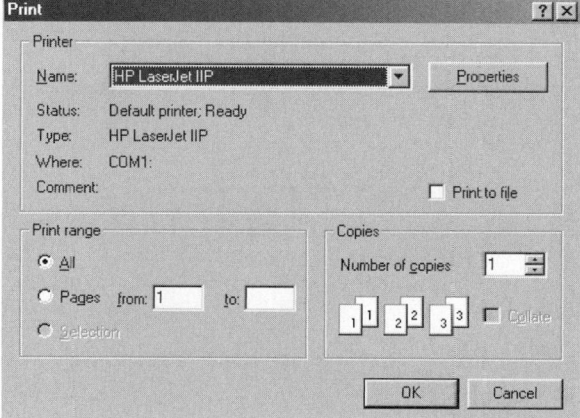

Adding a Printer

The *Add Printer Wizard* is used when a new printer needs to be added. The following steps detail how to add a printer:

Step 1   Choose **Start**, **Settings**, **Printers**, as shown in Figure 5-37.

Figure 5-37 Adding a Printer

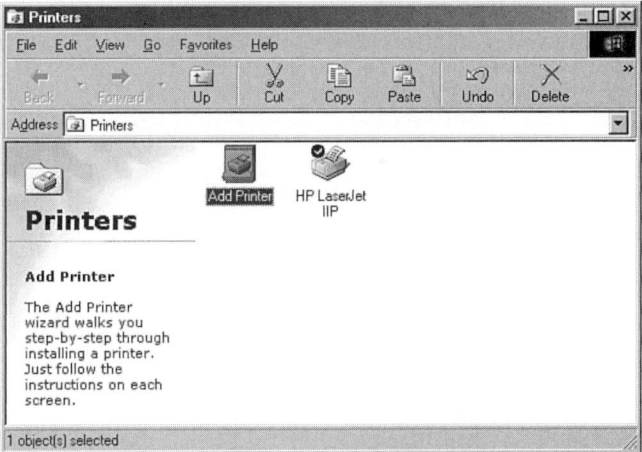

Step 2   Double-click the **Add Printer** icon.

The Add Printer Wizard displays, as shown in Figure 5-38.

Figure 5-38 Add Printer Wizard

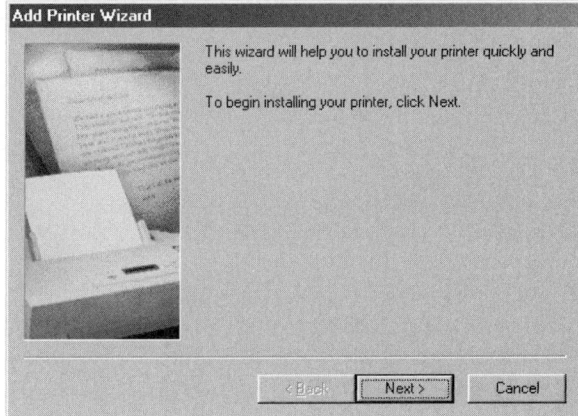

Step 3   Click the **Next** button to start the wizard, and follow the screen commands to add the printer.

The first option is to select a local or a network printer.

Step 4 Select **Local printer** if the printer is directly connected to the computer, as shown in Figure 5-39. Select **Network printer** if the printer is part of a network.

Click the **Next** button.

Figure 5-39 Select Local or Network Printer

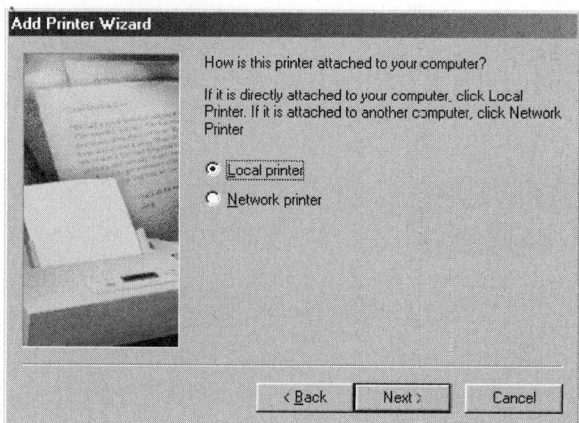

Step 5 Choose the printer manufacturer and model from the list that displays, as shown in Figure 5-40. In this example, the HP LaserJet Series II is selected.

Click the **Next** button.

Figure 5-40 Selecting the Printer Manufacturer and Model

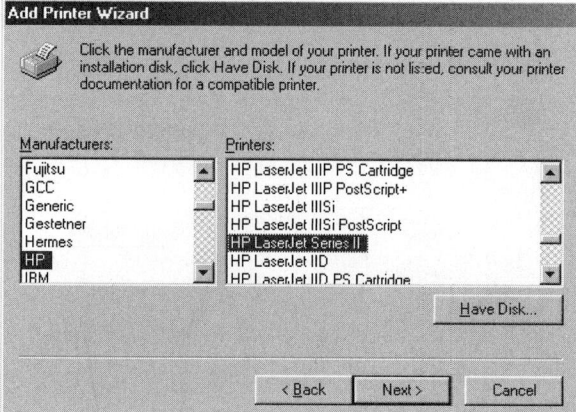

Step 6 Choose to keep the existing printer driver or to replace it. The example in Figure 5-41 shows the recommended option of keeping the current driver.

Click the **Next** button.

Figure 5-41 Keep or Replace the Printer Driver

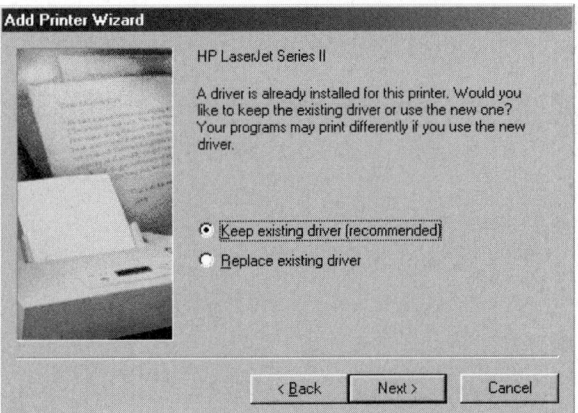

Step 7 Select the printer port from the list of available ports that displays. The LPT1 port is the default port, as shown in Figure 5-42.

Click the **Next** button.

Figure 5-42 Choose the Printer Port

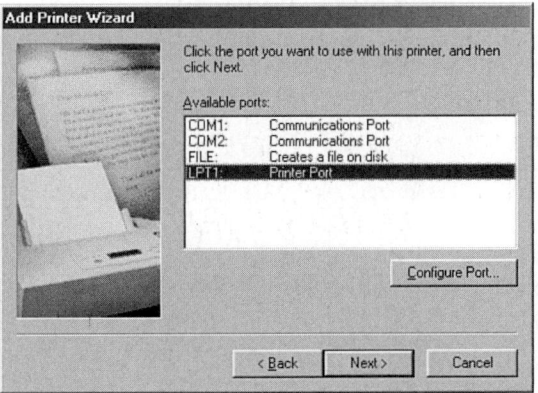

Step 8 Enter a name for the new printer, as shown in Figure 5-43.

The default printer name is its model name. Alternatively, you can change this to Tim's printer or Floor2West, for example. Renaming the printer is useful if, for example, many printers are being used on a network or in an office. You must also indicate whether this is the default printer for Windows-based programs. Click the **Next** button.

NOTE

To share this printer with others on the network, give it a shared name, such as Floor2West or Accounting.

Figure 5-43 Name the Printer

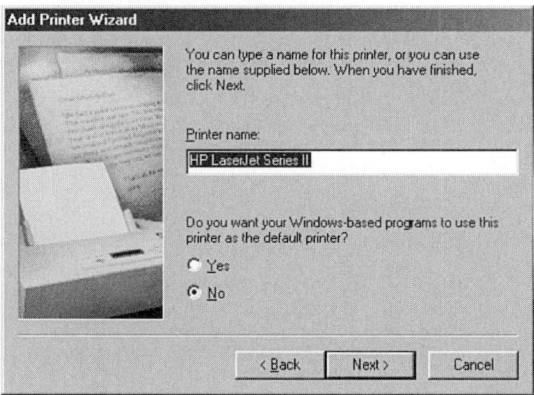

Step 9   Print a test page.

This is recommended because it will demonstrate whether the printer is working properly and that it has the correct drivers installed. Choose **Yes**, as shown in Figure 5-44, and then click the Finish button.

Figure 5-44 Print a Test Page

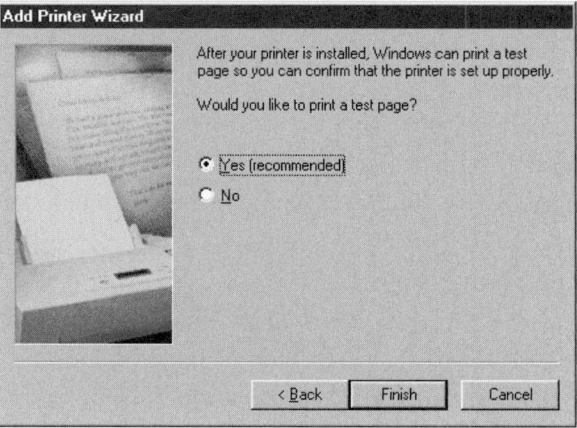

A printer that has been successfully added is displayed as an icon in the Printers window. The example in Figure 5-45 shows that the HP LaserJet Series II printer is now added.

Figure 5-45 Newly Added Printer

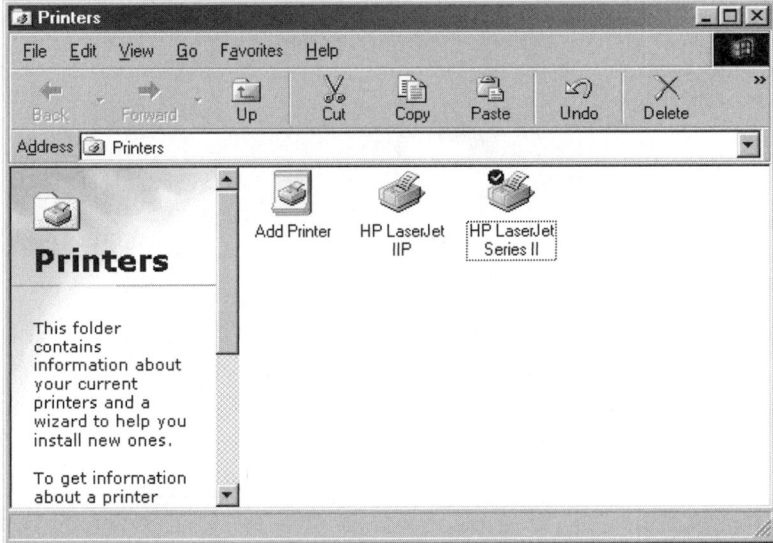

A check mark next to the new printer icon indicates that this printer is the default printer. All print jobs are sent to this printer unless a different printer is chosen in the program that is being used.

Changing the Default Printer

The default printer is the printer that the system automatically prints to. Networks usually have several printers to choose from, and users can select a different printer from an application. However, this choice does not change the default printer. To change the default printer, right-click the icon for the new default printer, as shown in Figure 5-46. Select **Set as Default** from the menu that appears. The check mark now appears on the new default printer.

Viewing a Print Job's Progress

The Desktop Print Manager displays the print job as it starts, is in progress, and finishes. The Print Manager can be accessed by double-clicking the printer icon on the Taskbar. It can also be accessed by choosing **Start**, **Settings**, **Printers**, as shown in Figure 5-47. Double-click the printer that the print job was sent to.

Figure 5-46 Changing the Default Printer

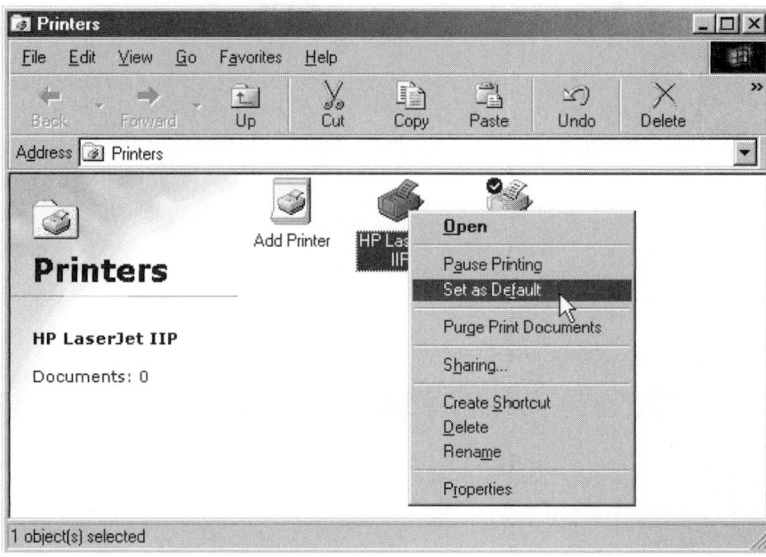

Figure 5-47 Accessing the Print Manager

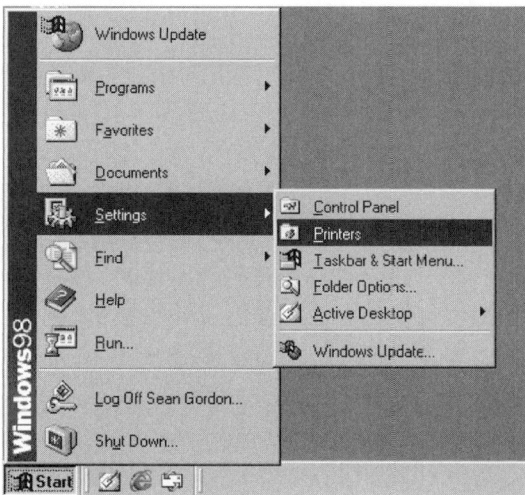

A window opens that displays the current print jobs, as shown in Figure 5-48. Figure 5-49 shows the options that are available in the Printer menu, including Pause Printing, Set as Default Purge Print Documents, and Properties. The Purge Print Documents option is used to empty the printer queue on a local printer. Network printers do not allow documents to be purged because many users are sending jobs to the printer.

NOTE

If a printer malfunctions, the print jobs can be deleted. This is especially important if the printer jams.

Figure 5-48 Accessing the Current Print Jobs

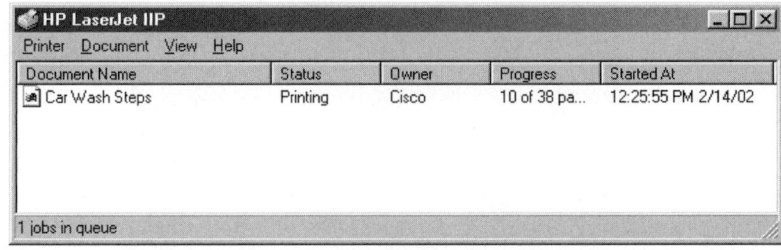

Figure 5-49 Printer Options

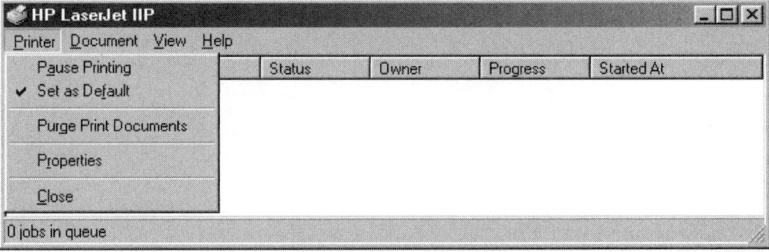

Figure 5-50 shows that the document is experiencing an error in printing. A window appears explaining the nature of the problem, as shown in Figure 5-51.

Figure 5-50 Print Error

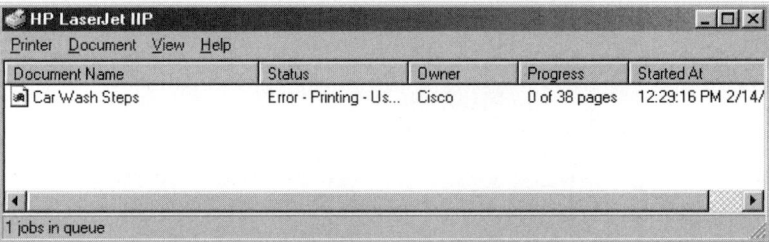

Figure 5-51 Printer Error Message

If the wrong document is being printed or the document is too long, it can be deleted from the printer queue. Highlight the document, and select **Document**, **Cancel Printing**, as shown in Figure 5-52. The print details show that the document is being deleted from the queue, as shown in Figure 5-53. On a network printer, a user can only cancel document printing for documents that he sent.

Figure 5-52 Canceling a Print Job

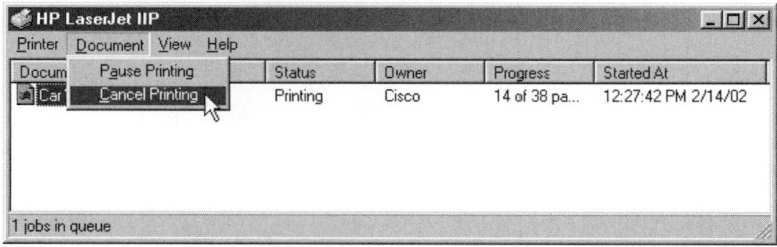

Figure 5-53 Deleting the Document from the Printer Queue

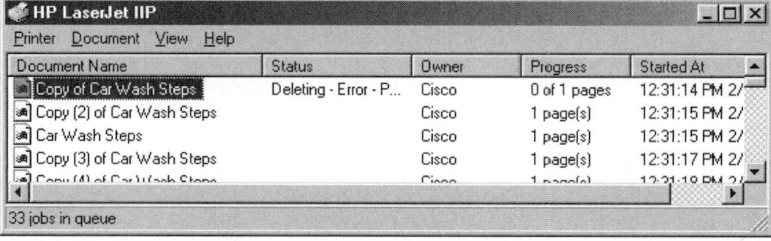

 Worksheet 5.2.2   Managing Printers

This worksheet reviews the steps of adding a printer and accessing printer information.

Adding and Removing Programs

Another important tool in the Control Panel is the *Add/Remove Programs* utility, as shown in Figure 5-54. This utility removes installed programs, installs Windows-specific components that were not installed initially, and creates a Windows startup disk. You should use the Add/Remove programs utility and click the Add/Remove button when uninstalling software. This ensures that the uninstalled application is removed from the system, along with all its associated components.

Figure 5-54 Add/Remove Programs Utility

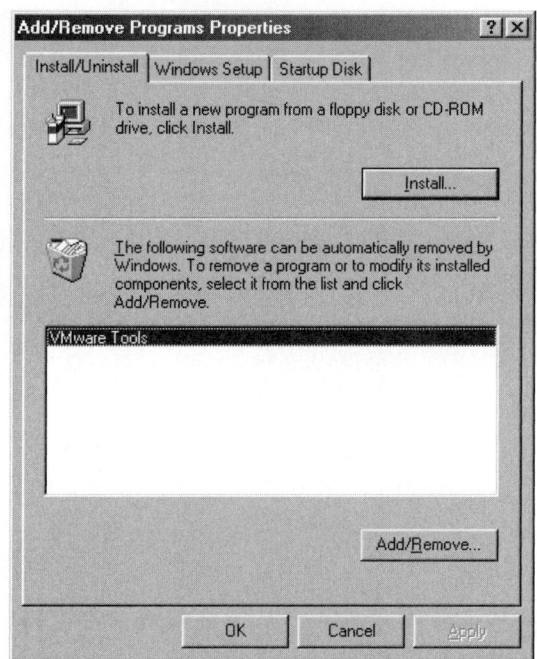

Adding Hardware

The *Add/Remove Hardware* utility in the Control Panel is a tool that automates the addition of a new piece of hardware to the system. The wizard searches the computer for new hardware and installs the appropriate drivers, as shown in Figure 5-55. If the appropriate driver is not found automatically, the wizard allows you to select the type of device from a list and installs the drivers from a specific location.

Adjusting the Display and Sounds

Two tools that are useful when changing the display and sounds that are associated with Windows are the Display utility and the Sounds utility. The *Display utility*, shown in Figure 5-56, can be accessed either by selecting it in the Control Panel or by right-clicking the Desktop and selecting **Properties** from the menu that appears. This allows the user to set a screen saver, change the background color, change the look and feel of Windows, and adjust display resolution settings.

Figure 5-55 Add New Hardware Wizard

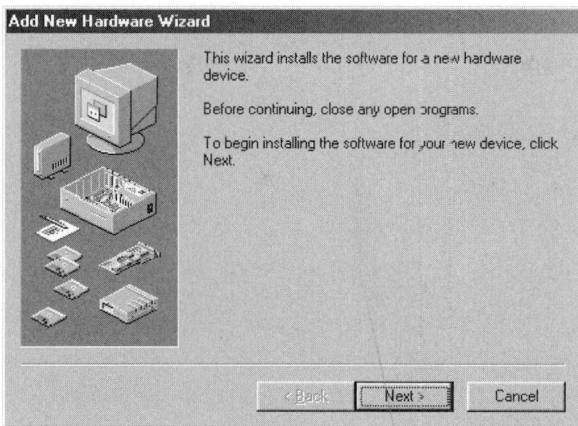

Figure 5-56 Display Utility

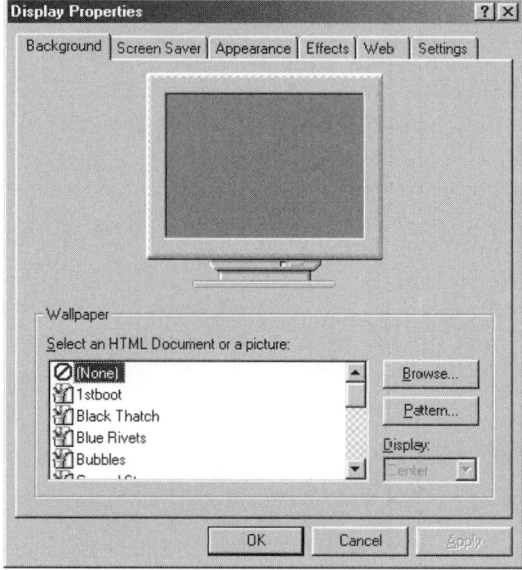

The *Sounds utility*, shown in Figure 5-57, allows the user to choose sounds that are played for different system events, such as when the computer is booted up or shut down. Themes can also be used to coordinate the background, the look and feel of Windows, and the sounds so that they create a uniform environment.

Figure 5-57 Sounds Utility

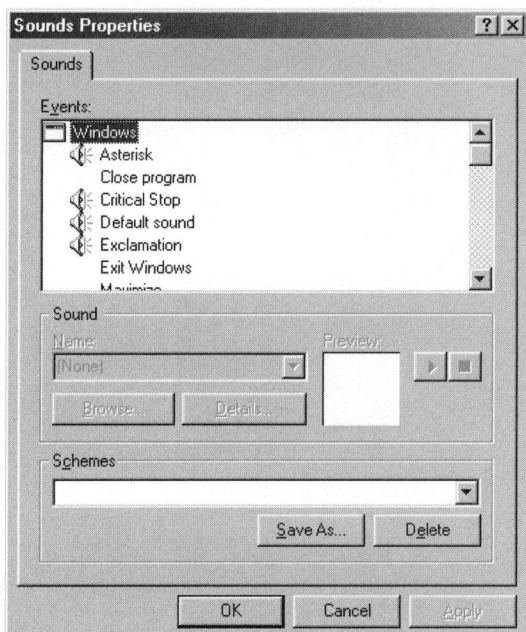

System Tools

This section details information regarding system configuration. The utilities and tools that troubleshoot and optimize are especially important for the IT technician. The following topics are covered:

- Understanding the registry
- Using REGEDIT and SCANREG
- Understanding MSCONFIG, the Startup menu, and safe mode
- Using WSCRIPT.EXE, HWINFO.EXE, and ASD.EXE

Understanding the Registry

The *registry* is a hierarchical database that manages the information that is needed by the Windows operating system. Older versions of Windows stored system and user data in initialization files (INI files), which were usually scattered across multiple directories and could easily be edited by programs or the user. The registry takes all those files and stores them in a separate location.

The Registry is made up of the SYSTEM.DAT and USER.DAT files. The **SYSTEM.DAT** file contains information about the hardware in the system. The **USER.DAT** file contains user-specific information. Windows 98 can still use the SYSTEM.INI and WIN.INI files to run applications that are designed for Windows 3.x. Since the release of Windows 98, the registry consists of two files: SYSTEM.DAT and USER.DAT. POLICY.POL is an optional file if the system policies are configured (see Figure 5-58). The functions of the SYSTEM.DAT and USER.DAT files remain the same as they were prior to Windows 98. The registry is more thoroughly discussed in Chapter 6, "Windows NT/2000/XP Operating Systems."

Figure 5-58 Windows 98 Registry Files

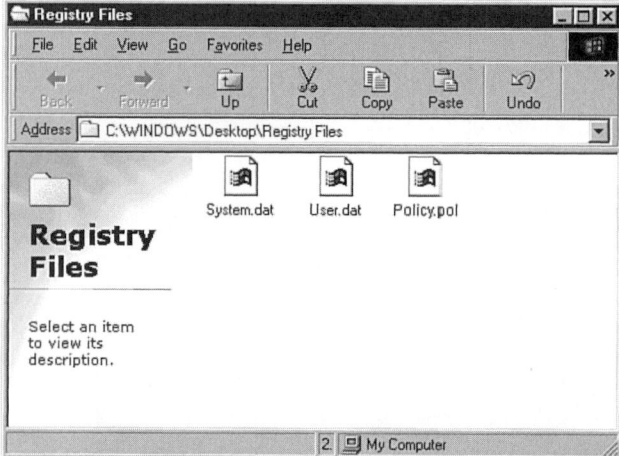

Using REGEDIT and SCANREG

Because the registry is a hierarchical database, it can be viewed by using the **REGEDIT.EXE** utility. The Registry Editor displays the registry in a format that is similar to Windows Explorer, as shown in Figure 5-59. **SCANREG.EXE** was implemented in Windows 98. It backs up or repairs the registry.

Understanding MSCONFIG, the Startup Menu, and Safe Mode

The **MSCONFIG.EXE** file is an excellent tool for Windows 98 and Me users. It is not included in Windows 95. MSCONFIG.EXE, as shown in Figure 5-60, allows the user to control how the system is started. It provides quick access to important Windows configuration and initialization files, including CONFIG.SYS, AUTOEXEC.BAT, SYSTEM.INI, and WIN.INI. It also allows the user to select what programs are loaded automatically when the computer is started.

CAUTION

Required system files are listed in the Startup menu and should not be removed. Only advanced users should edit these files, because the purpose of these files might not be obvious to a new user.

Figure 5-59 Registry Editor

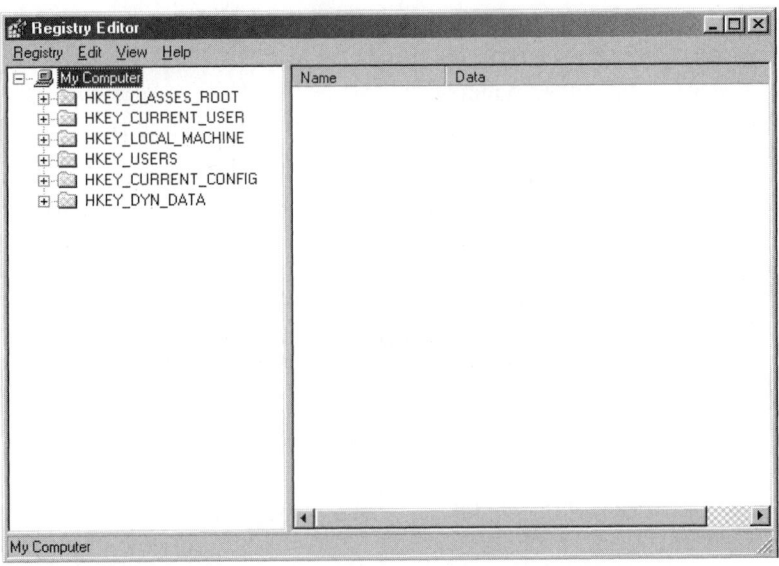

Figure 5-60 System Configuration Utility

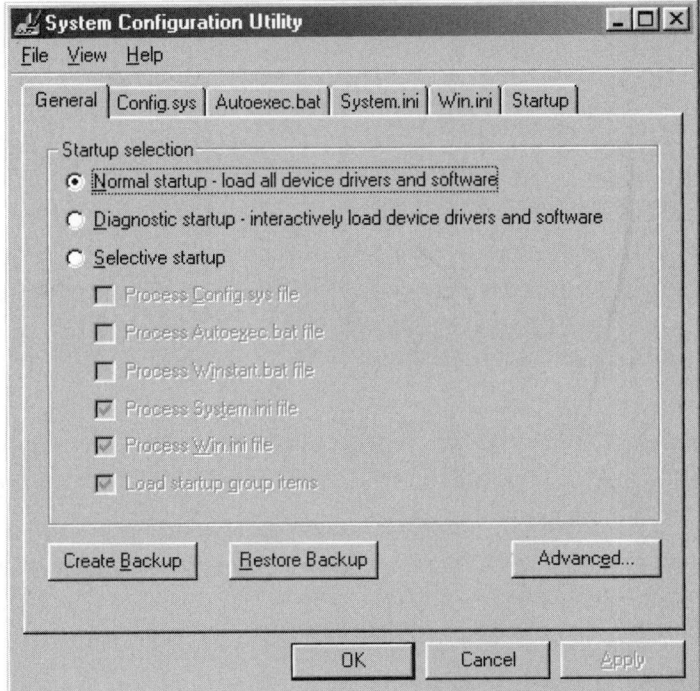

Recall that when the operating system is loaded, it checks the Startup menu in CONFIG.SYS for programs that are listed. These programs are automatically initialized on startup.

This utility can also be used to help troubleshoot problems that occur during the bootup process. Another startup method that can be used in the troubleshooting process is safe mode. Safe mode allows the user to load Windows without specific device drivers or allocated resources. Only the basic user interface and generic drivers are loaded so that the system is operable. For more information, refer to Chapter 14, "Troubleshooting Software."

TIP

Know the difference between safe mode and normal mode.

Using WSCRIPT.EXE, HWINFO.EXE, and ASD.EXE

The *WSCRIPT.EXE* command allows you to configure the properties that are related to the Windows scripting host, as shown in Figure 5-61. The Windows scripting host allows scripts to be easily run within the operating system.

Figure 5-61 Windows Scripting Host

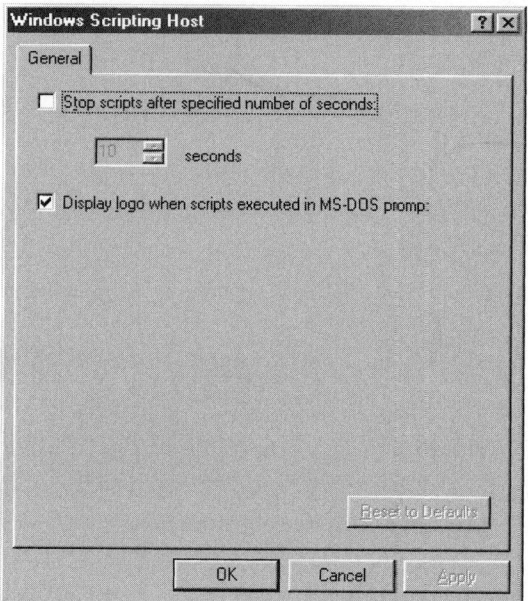

The *HWINFO.EXE* file is a utility that provides detailed information about the computer, as shown in Figure 5-62. If the proper switches are not used, this command does not provide the desired results. The /ui switch is used when running this program to get a detailed list of information about the computer.

Figure 5-62 HWINFO.EXE File

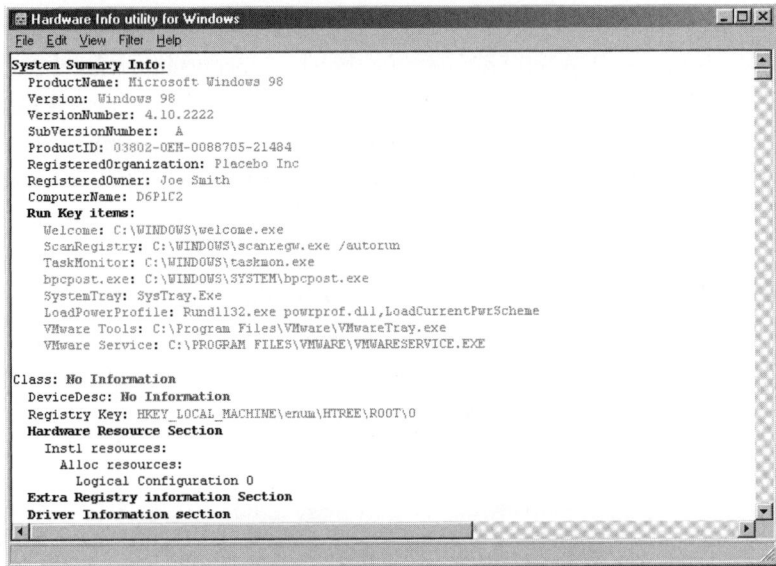

The *ASD.EXE* file skips a driver when the operating system fails during bootup. This troubleshooting utility should be used when a problem exists with a driver that cannot be solved by booting into safe mode.

Preparing a Hard Drive for Operating System Installation

Preparing a hard drive includes the designation of the primary and extended partitions, along with the logical drives. In addition, the drive must be formatted, a process that enables the drive to store data. This section includes the following topics:

- Partitioning a hard drive
- Formatting a hard drive

Partitioning a Hard Drive

When a new hard drive is installed, it is blank. No space is available to store files and folders. To create those spaces, a hard drive must first be divided into logical sections. These sections are called *partitions*. The partitioning process creates spaces of contiguous sectors on the hard drive. Each partition can receive a file system for an operating system. Without a file system, the partition is useless.

Primary and Extended Partitions

Typically with DOS, when the hard drive is divided into more than one partition, the first partition is referred to as the ***primary partition*** and the second is called the ***extended partition***. Logical drives are created on the extended partition and assigned sequential drive letters. Only one partition can be the active partition. DOS is loaded from the active partition by the bootstrap loader during the boot process. Figure 5-63 illustrates a hard drive as it is divided into primary and extended DOS partitions with ***logical drives***.

Figure 5-63 Primary and Extended DOS Partitions

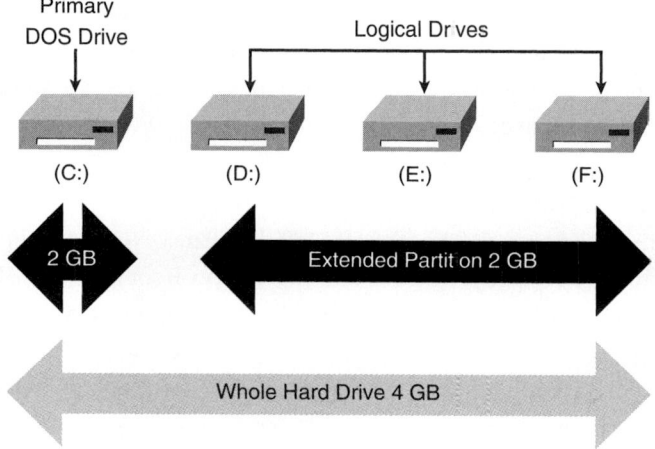

A hard disk can have up to four partitions, as follows, depending on the user's needs:

- Four separate primary partitions
- Three primary partitions and one extended partition
- Two primary partitions and one extended partition
- One primary partition and one extended partition

DOS allows up to four separate partitions on a hard disk. The extended partition uses the free hard disk space and is normally assigned all the available space outside the primary partition(s). DOS can only address a maximum of 2 GB of hard disk space when using FAT16. FAT32 increases the limit to 2 terabytes (TB) of hard disk space. The File Allocation Table (FAT) is discussed later in this chapter.

Logical Drives

When a hard drive is partitioned, the extended partition uses all the free hard disk space that is not included in the primary partition(s). Only one extended partition is permitted per disk.

NOTE

Only the primary partition on a hard drive can be designated as active. DOS, Windows 95, and Windows 98 can only manage one primary partition per hard drive. Windows NT 2000, as well as some third-party disk-management utilities, can manage multiple primary partitions on a hard drive. A primary partition cannot be subdivided into smaller units.

Unlike the primary partition, the extended partition can be subdivided into a maximum of 23 sections, called logical drives. Having multiple logical drives in the extended partition provides the following advantages:

- Logical drives permit rapid retrieval of information.
- Logical drives allow multiple operating systems, such as MS-DOS and Windows 98, to be installed on the same computer. However, both drives must have the same file system.
- Logical drives physically separate information for organizational and security reasons.

By creating a second logical drive on a formatted hard disk, another complete file-tracking structure is created on the hard drive. The operating system views this new structure on the hard drive as a completely new disk. Therefore, a unique drive letter is assigned to the logical drive, as previously mentioned.

FDISK, the Boot Sector, and the Partition Table

FDISK is a partitioning program for MS-DOS, Windows 9*x,* UNIX, and Linux. When partitioning a hard drive, the FDISK program creates the Master Boot Record (MBR) and the FORMAT command creates the disk **boot sector**. Typically, the MBR is the first area on each logical DOS disk or partition. When formatting the hard drive, the information that boots the operating system is recorded in the boot sector. During the partitioning process, FDISK also establishes partition information in the form of a special table called the partition table. The **partition table** is located at the end of the MBR. Critical information found in the partition table includes the following:

- The location and starting point of each logical drive on the disk
- Information on which partition is marked as active
- The location of the MBR

The partition table must be at the beginning of the disk, because this is where the system looks for bootup information.

Formatting a Hard Drive

NOTE

Each sector on a DOS disk holds 512 bytes. Files can occupy several sectors on the hard drive. The maximum file size depends on the file system.

After the drive has been partitioned, it must be prepared to store data. This process is called formatting. **Formatting** a hard drive prepares the tracks for storage. A **track** is a ring of sectors on one side of a hard disk surface platter. The number of tracks per disk is determined by the hard drive manufacturer. These tracks are then broken into pieces of 512 bytes called **sectors**. The tracks of the disk are numbered from the outer edge of the disk inward, beginning with 00. In computers, numbering begins with 0, instead of 1. The combination of two or more sectors is called a cluster. A **cluster** is sometimes called a **block**. The size of each cluster depends on the size of the hard disk and the version of DOS in use.

A cluster is the minimum unit that DOS can use to store a file. Even if a file is only 1 byte long, an entire cluster is still used to store the file. The disk capacity is determined by the number of tracks and sectors and, therefore, by the number of clusters that can be created on the disk surface by formatting it.

In a hard disk drive where several platters are stacked and rotate on a common spindle, all the tracks that have the same number are referred to collectively as a *cylinder*. Figure 5-64 shows a detailed view of a hard drive.

Figure 5-64 Tracks and Sectors on a Hard Disk

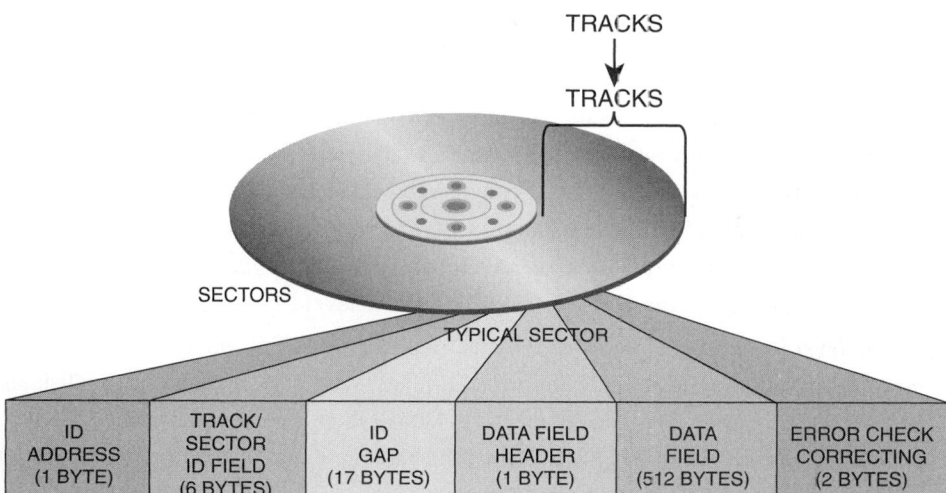

File Allocation Table

During formatting, the *File Allocation Table (FAT)* is created and located on the disk sector 0. The FAT is a reference table that the operating system uses to locate files on the disk. DOS provides additional protection by storing a second identical copy of the original FAT that was created during formatting at another location. The first copy is the normal working copy, and the second FAT is used as a backup in case the contents of the first FAT become corrupted. Under normal circumstances, the contents of either copy of FAT are hidden.

The original FAT that was associated with DOS was called FAT16 (a 16-bit FAT); since then, other versions have been created. VFAT is the version that came with the original version of Windows 95. FAT32 (32-bit) is a more efficient form of FAT that was introduced with Windows 95 OSR2, Windows 98, and Windows Me (collectively called Windows 9*x*). Only DOS and the 16-bit Windows 3.*x* still use FAT16. When written as FAT, with no number associated with it, the version is understood to be FAT16. The FAT is created when a hard drive is formatted for installation of DOS. When a hard drive is formatted for the installation of Windows 9*x*, FAT32 is created as the file system in the disk partition where the Windows 9*x* operating system is to be installed.

A built-in program, such as CVT1.EXE or other third-party utilities such as Partition Magic, can convert FAT16 to FAT32 without destroying the data in the disk partition. However, you cannot convert a FAT32 partition to a FAT16 partition. FAT, FAT32, and other file systems, including NTFS (the NT File System), are discussed more thoroughly in Chapter 6.

Low-Level and High-Level Formatting

You must understand two important concepts about formatting a hard drive. These include low-level formatting and high-level formatting, which are described as follows:

- *Low-level formatting* divides the disk into sectors and cylinders and defines their placement on the disk. Integrated Drive Electronics (IDE) and Small Computer System Interface (SCSI) are system-level drive types and normally receive the low-level format at the factory. Some SCSI devices might still require a low-level format, but you should never perform a low-level format on an IDE hard drive unless the drive has failed. Most drive manufactures provide special utilities for low-level formatting of an IDE drive.

- *High-level formatting* is performed by using the FORMAT command. This procedure creates logical structures on the disk that tell the system what files are on the disk and where these files can be found. When using MS-DOS or a Windows 9*x* boot system that contains the FORMAT.EXE file to format the hard drive, the formatting process creates a blank FAT and root directory structure on the disk. Perform a high-level format when preparing the hard drive for the operating system installation.

When using a Windows 98–bootable disk that contains the FORMAT command to format a hard drive, enter the following syntax at the DOS command prompt:

```
A:\>FORMAT C:
```

In this case, C is the hard disk, A is the floppy boot disk, and A:\> is the command prompt.

Entering a space and the switch /s after the drive letter designation in the command formats the hard drive and transfers the system files, making the drive bootable. The syntax at the DOS command prompt is as follows:

```
A:\>FORMAT C: /s
```

Lab 5.4.2 Hard Drive Preparation Using FDISK and FORMAT

In this lab, you partition the hard drive into two drives. You also install the three system files on the hard drive to make it a bootable drive.

Worksheet 5.4.2   Preparing the Hard Drive

This worksheet is a review of the steps that were covered for partitioning and formatting a hard drive.

Installing Windows 9*x*

You should understand the Windows 9*x* installation process. This section includes the following topics:

- Windows 9*x* versions overview
- Requirements for installing Windows 98
- Steps of a Windows 98 installation
- Windows 98 setup options
- Upgrade installation

Windows 9*x* Versions Overview

Before discussing the installation procedure in detail, you should understand the various Windows 9*x* versions and how they relate to each other. This section gives a basic summary of the Windows evolution. It covers the departure from DOS to the creation of the graphical user interface (GUI)–based Windows operating system.

Windows has been through many revisions. Windows 9*x* refers to all the releases of the Microsoft Windows operating systems from Windows 95 to Windows Millennium Edition (Me). The original version, 3.1, started with a basic GUI. Prior to the release of Windows 3.1, Windows went through several revisions to reach the polished look that can now be seen on many Desktops.

Windows 3.1

Windows 3.1, released in April 1992, was more stable and included scalable TrueType fonts. This version became one of the most popular operating systems from its release date until the mid-1990s. One of the main limitations of this version was that it relied on DOS to run. Therefore, it had all the Windows INI files built into the basic DOS structure to enable startup.

Windows 3.11

By the end of 1993, Microsoft released Windows for Workgroups, version 3.11. This was the first version with integrated networking and workgroup capabilities. Features included e-mail utilities, group task scheduling, file and printer sharing, and calendar management. It offered improved NetWare and Windows NT compatibility and improved stability. Although networking was integrated, it was hard to use. This version still required DOS for its operation.

Windows 95

Windows 95 was released in August 1995, with many more features and benefits than any other previous Windows version. This was the first version of Windows that could be defined as a true operating system; it did not require DOS to be loaded prior to the Windows software installation. This release was also considered to be a more user-friendly version than previous releases, thus mainstreaming PCs to users. Windows 95 also introduced long-filename support, advanced networking features, and Plug and Play capabilities. Some limitations in this version included higher system requirements, a steeper learning curve because of the new look and feel, and inconsistencies with Plug and Play features.

In 1996, Microsoft released Windows 95 OSR2. This version included several bug fixes as well as improvements to various embedded features. It also included the Internet Explorer 3.0 web browser and supported the new and more efficient 32-bit file-management system called FAT32 as well as universal serial bus (USB). This release of Windows had one major limitation. Windows 95 OSR2 was only available to manufacturers and resellers. Therefore, most users could not acquire the improvements unless they purchased a new PC.

Windows 98

Windows 98 was released in June 1998. This version included Internet Explorer 4 and improved support for USB. It supported newer technologies such as Advanced Configuration and Power Interface (ACPI) power management. Despite many improvements, the major limitation with Windows 98 was its lack of stability. However, in May 1999, Microsoft released Windows 98 Second Edition (SE). This version included year 2000 (Y2K) updates, USB support, Internet Explorer, and several other updates. It is the most functional version of Windows to date. Although Windows 98 lacks complete stability, it is still regarded by many technicians as the most stable version of Windows 9x.

Microsoft released the Windows Millennium Edition (Me) in September 2000. This version included enhanced multimedia capabilities and improved Internet support, and it was the last version of Windows to run on the Win9x kernel, a significant component of the operating system that is memory resident and is responsible for process, task, disk, and memory management. Windows Me exhibits poor stability in comparison to Windows 98 Second Edition (SE).

As Microsoft continues to develop and release newer versions of the Windows operating systems, users should anticipate new features and more stability. However, as with any new operating system technology, some limitations and lapses should be expected. Windows 2000 and Windows XP are detailed in Chapters 6 and 7. Figure 5-65 is a time line that summarizes the various releases of the Windows operating systems.

Figure 5-65 Timeline of Windows Operating System Releases

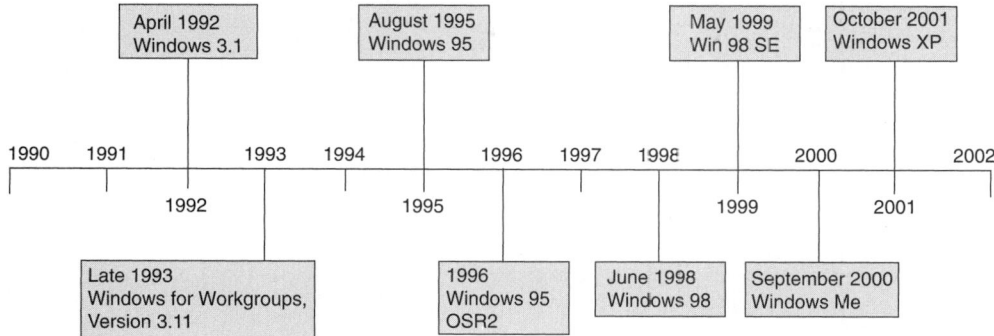

Requirements for Installing Windows 98

The following minimum hardware platform is required to install and run Windows 98:

- An 80486DX/66-MHz or faster processor that operates with at least 16 MB RAM. A minimum of 32 MB RAM or 64 MB RAM is recommended if the system can support it.

- A keyboard, a mouse, and a 16-color VGA monitor or better. An SVGA monitor is recommended.

- An available 255–355 MB of free hard drive space is required to install the full version of Windows 98 on a FAT16 drive. You must have 175–255 MB of free space on a FAT32 drive.

- Approximately 195 MB of free hard disk space is required to upgrade from Windows 95. Free-space requirements can range from 120 MB to 255 MB, depending on the options that are installed.

- A modem might be required to download device driver upgrades from various sources on the Internet. The minimum required is a 14.4-kbps modem. A 28.8-kbps or faster modem is recommended.

- A 3-1/2-inch high-density floppy disk drive and a CD-ROM drive are required.

NOTE

The actual amount of hard disk space that is used depends on the type of installation being performed. Options include New, Upgrade, Custom, Portable, and so on. Regardless of the installation type, a minimum of a 2-GB hard drive is needed for a Windows 98 installation. The information outlined in the previous list is summarized in Table 5-2.

Table 5-2 Requirements for Installing Windows 98

Type of Installation	Processor	Memory (MB)	Free Hard Drive Space (MB)	Floppy Disk Drive	Video Resolution	Modem
Upgrade from Windows 95	486DX 66-MHz or faster processor (Pentium CPU recommended)	16 (24 recommended)	195 (120–295, depending on the options that are installed)	Yes	VGA or higher (16-bit or 24-bit color SVGA recommended)	14.4-kbps required for Internet access (28.8-kbps or faster recommended)
Full installation on a FAT16 drive	486DX 66-MHz or faster processor (Pentium CPU recommended)	16 (24 recommended)	225 (165–355, depending on the options that are installed)	Yes	VGA or higher (16-bit or 24-bit color SVGA recommended)	14.4-bps required for Internet access (28.8-kbps or faster recommended)
Full installation on a FAT32 drive	486DX 66-MHz or faster processor (Pentium CPU recommended)	16 (32 recommended)	175 (140–255, depending on the options that are installed)	Yes	VGA or higher (16-bit or 24-bit color SVGA recommended)	14.4-kbps required for Internet access (28.8-kbps or faster recommended)

Steps of a Windows 98 Installation

This section explains the installation procedure for Windows 98. Most of the steps in the installation are automated through the built-in utility Setup utility. Understanding each stage of the installation or setup process is useful when performing an installation.

Video   Installing Windows 98

The Windows 98 installation process, from preparation to the final steps, is detailed in this video.

The steps of the installation procedure are divided into four phases. Each of these phases is described in the following sections.

Phase 1: Preparing to Run Windows 98 Setup

During this phase, the Setup utility performs the following actions that prepare the ***Windows 98 Setup Wizard*** to guide you through the installation process:

- Creates a SETUPLOG.TXT file in the drive's root directory.
- Identifies the source and destination drive locations for the Windows 98 files that will be installed, as shown in Figure 5-66.

Figure 5-66 Selecting the Directory in Which to Install Windows 98

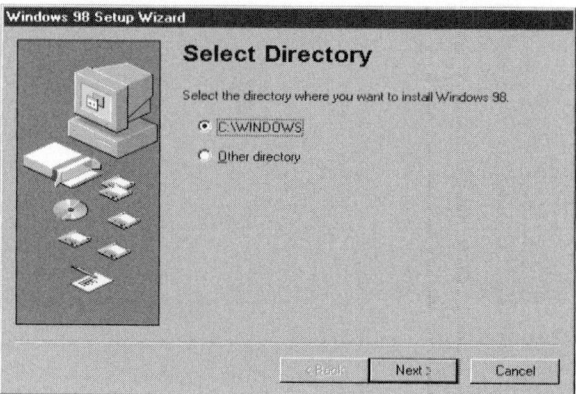

- Copies a minimal Windows 98 setup cabinet file, called MINI.CAB, to a special directory that it creates in the root directory (C:). This directory is called Wininst0.400.
- Extracts the major setup files, known as PRECOPY1.CAB and PRECOPY2.CAB, to the Wininst0.400 directory.

Phase 2: Collecting Computer Information

After the setup files have been successfully copied to the hard drive, the Setup Wizard displays the licensing agreement. Read this agreement, become familiar with the terms and conditions of using the software, accept the agreement, and proceed. The Setup Wizard asks you to enter the product key. This key, which verifies product authenticity, is found on the software Certificate of Authenticity or on the back of the CD case. When the product registration is completed, the Setup utility starts to gather critical information about the system. Some of the actions that are performed by the Setup utility include the following:

- Determines the directory into which the Windows 98 installation files need to be moved.
- Verifies that enough space exists on the selected drive to hold the Windows 98 installation files and the temporary files that are required to complete the procedure.
- Determines the type of installation desired, such as Typical, Portable, Compact, or Custom. Typical is aimed at the general user, while Custom is for more specialized installations. Table 5-3 summarizes the different installation options.
- Sets up company names and usernames. For a personal computer, only the user name is required.
- Determines the Windows 98 components that the user wants the Setup utility to install.
- Sets up computer network identification. A network ID can be entered here, even though the system might not be in a networked environment.
- Determines the Internet location from which the system can receive regional update information. This is important for the system to function with a proper date and a time for the local time zone.

Table 5-3 Windows 98 Setup Options

Option	Result
Typical	This option installs all the components that are usually installed with Windows 98. Most users should select this option.
Portable	This option installs the options that are generally required for portable computers.
Compact	This is the smallest possible installation of Windows 98. For example, you might want to perform a Compact installation if your hard disk has little free space. The Setup Wizard then installs no optional components. To later use an optional component, such as games or WebTV for Windows, you must install it. To install an optional component after the Setup Wizard is completed, use the Add/Remove Programs feature in the Control Panel.

Table 5-3 Windows 98 Setup Options (Continued)

Option	Result
Custom	This option allows you to choose which optional components are installed. If you do not select a Custom installation, the Setup Wizard installs only the optional components that are selected by default. If you know that you are going to need certain Windows components, you might want to select a Custom installation and ensure that those components are included during the setup phase. Pan-European users should choose this option to set up the required regional settings and keyboard layout for their locale.

When the Setup utility has gathered all the installation information, it stops and prompts you to create a startup disk. This step can be skipped by selecting **Cancel**, but you should create a startup disk during this phase. Follow the on-screen instructions to create a startup disk. The Setup utility then begins the installation process for Windows 98. Figure 5-67 shows the Setup Wizard ready to start copying files.

Figure 5-67 Start Copying Windows 98 Files

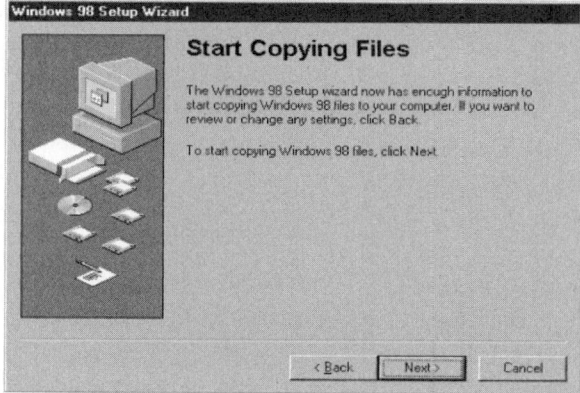

Phase 3: Copying Windows 98 Files and Restarting the Computer

Most of this phase of the Setup utility is automated. It begins by displaying the Start Copying Files window, as shown in the previous figure. Because this phase is automated, no input is required from the user.

After the Setup Wizard has copied the Windows 98 files to their proper locations, it displays a prompt that asks you to restart the system. The system restarts automatically if no user input is detected within 15 seconds.

CAUTION

If the Setup utility is interrupted while copying Windows 98 files to their different locations, the system might not start up properly.

Phase 4: Setting Up Hardware and Finalizing Settings

The system should restart automatically, and the Setup Wizard finalizes the installation process. The wizard uses the information that was provided in Phase 3 to install the following items:

- Contents of the Start menu
- Settings for DOS programs
- The Control Panel
- Application Start functions
- Basic Windows 98 Help functions
- Time zone information
- System configuration information

The Setup utility automatically restarts the computer again after completing these steps. Log on at the prompt (if any logon information was entered). Then the Setup Wizard establishes a system driver database, updates the system settings, establishes personalized system options, and displays the Welcome to Windows 98 window on-screen. The screen displays the message "New Hardware Detected" if Windows detects any new hardware, such as a video card. Windows finds stock hardware drivers and auto-installs the hardware with the proper driver. The Windows 98 Desktop is displayed when the setup process is complete.

Any drivers that were auto-installed by Windows are stock drivers. Drivers typically need to be updated with their most current versions. These drivers are available on the installation CD or on a floppy disk that came with the hardware. The best source of up-to-date drivers is the manufacturer's website. Drivers can usually be downloaded free of charge.

Windows 98 Setup Options

You have the following options for installing Windows 98:

- Install directly from the CD by booting the system from the CD-ROM drive.
- Copy all the installation files to the hard drive and perform the installation from the hard drive.
- Install from DOS.

These options are described in the following sections.

Installing Windows 98 from the CD-ROM Drive

The most common way to install the Windows operating system is from the CD-ROM drive. The autostart feature of the drive should detect the Windows CD and initiate the installation process. The steps that are required to install from the CD are covered in Lab 5.5.5.

Lab 5.5.5   Windows OS Installation

This lab details the steps of installing Windows 98 from a CD.

Installing Windows 98 from the Hard Drive

During a Windows 98 installation, the overall installation process can be sped up by copying the files to the hard drive. Follow these steps to install Windows 98 from the hard drive:

Step 1   Verify that you have at least 200 MB of free disk space in which to store the Windows setup and CAB files. A CAB file (CABinet file) is a Microsoft file format that holds compressed files. A Windows extraction program is run at the DOS command prompt to decompress the files.

Step 2   Create a floppy boot disk that contains the drivers for the CD-ROM drive. Insert the floppy disk in the computer, and power the unit on. When prompted, select the option to boot the system with CD-ROM support, and wait for the computer to boot to the DOS prompt.

Step 3   Create a directory from the DOS prompt called SETUP98 to store the setup files. Type **MD C:\SETUP98**, where C is the drive letter that is assigned to the hard drive.

Step 4   Copy all the files from the SETUP98 directory on the CD-ROM to the corresponding directory on the hard drive. Type the following command:

```
COPY D:\SETUP98\*.* C:\SETUP98
```

This command assumes the usual configuration, where the hard drive is referred to as the C drive and the CD-ROM drive is referred to as the D drive.

Step 5   Revert to the SETUP98 directory on the hard drive to start the installation. Type **CD SETUP98**, press **Enter**, type **SETUP**, and press **Enter**. This starts the Windows 98 setup process.

Copying the setup files to the hard drive and performing the operating system installation provides the following advantages:

- The installation goes much faster. With current-technology drives, regardless of the speed of the CD-ROM drive, the hard drive is always faster.

- When adding new hardware or Windows software, you might be prompted to provide the Windows setup files. Having the files on the hard drive allows you to simply direct the application to the SETUP98 directory. You do not have to retrieve the Windows CD—which might not be conveniently located.

- If you need to perform a complete format frequently, you can create two partitions on the hard drive—one for Windows and a smaller one for the Windows setup files. You can then reformat only one partition and quickly run the Setup Wizard from the smaller partition.

Installing Windows 98 from DOS

If problems occur during the Windows 98 installation process, you might have to run the setup procedure from DOS. Follow these steps to do so:

Step 1   Create a bootable floppy disk with CD-ROM drivers.

Step 2   Insert the bootable disk, and power on the computer. When prompted, select the option to boot with CD-ROM support. Allow the system to boot to the DOS prompt.

Step 3   From the command line, change to the CD-ROM drive by typing **D:** and pressing **Enter**. (In this case, D is the CD-ROM drive letter.)

Step 4   Initiate the setup process as follows: Type **CD WIN98**, press **Enter**, type **SETUP**, and press **Enter**. This starts the Windows setup process.

The Role of ScanDisk in the Installation of Windows 98 in a New Computer

To install Windows 98 on a new or reformatted hard drive, you must boot the system from the Windows CD or run the SETUP.EXE program from the DOS prompt.

When the installation is initiated from the DOS prompt, the Windows 98 Setup program runs a real-mode version of the *ScanDisk utility*, which looks at all the files on the drive. This requires the CD-ROM driver or network driver to be present and loaded. *ScanDisk* performs a complete check of the FAT, directory, and files that are on the drive and creates a ScanDisk log file. If errors are detected, ScanDisk displays an error message. This log can be accessed through the ScanDisk View Log selection. After the ScanDisk inspection has been completed, the Setup program initializes the system and begins copying installation files to the drive.

Upgrade Installation

Windows 95 users can upgrade to Windows 98 to gain its added features and usability. The process of upgrading is easy. To retain settings, such as the background and user files, the Windows 98 Setup program needs to be run from within Windows 95.

Upgrading Windows 95 to Windows 98

Inserting the Windows 98 installation CD in the CD-ROM drive typically initiates the Setup program. However, to start the program manually, navigate to the CD-ROM drive using Windows Explorer and double-click the setup.exe file in the root directory of the installation CD. This should start the Setup program, which guides you through the installation process.

Although the upgrade can go smoothly, you might have problems with upgrading to Windows 98. In this case, back up any required data files, reformat the hard drive, and perform a clean installation of Windows 98.

Upgrading Windows 98 to Windows 2000

The upgrade from Windows 98 to Windows 2000 is simple and straightforward. You can start the upgrade from within Windows 98 in one of the following ways:

- Use the installation CD's autoplay feature (as shown in Figure 5-68).
- Manually run the SETUP.EXE program

Figure 5-68 Upgrading to Windows 2000

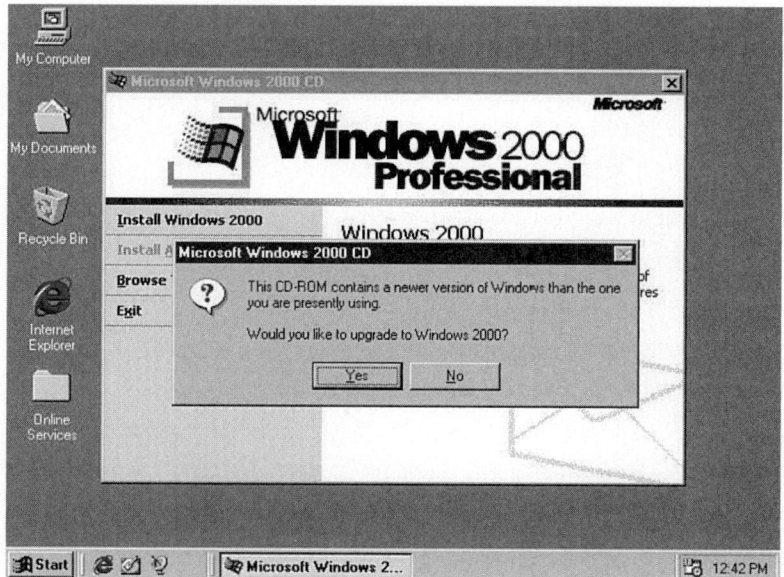

Once the Setup program has begun, follow the on-screen prompts and instructions to install the upgrade. Be aware that a Windows 2000 upgrade can be uninstalled only once on the same system. Detailed information for installing Windows 2000 is provided in Chapter 6.

Troubleshooting the Installation Process

To effectively troubleshoot installation problems, you need to identify and resolve the different types of installation errors. This section includes the following topics:

- Using systematic troubleshooting techniques and finding help
- Understanding Windows 98 setup errors
- Using the System Properties window
- Adding software drivers
- Making a Windows startup disk
- Uninstalling Windows 98

Using Systematic Troubleshooting Techniques and Finding Help

Knowing the various tips and tricks in troubleshooting a Windows installation can make the difference between a good technician and an excellent technician. This section discusses some common problems that occur in the Windows operating system installation and what you can do to fix them. This discussion is limited to problems that are related to the Windows operating system installation. General troubleshooting is discussed more thoroughly in later chapters.

General Troubleshooting Concepts

When troubleshooting any microprocessor-based equipment such as the PC, it is good practice to begin from the outside of the system and move inward. Proceed systematically in the following manner:

- Start the system in a logical order to see what symptoms are produced.
- Isolate the problem as being either software or hardware related.
- Isolate the problem again to a particular section of the hardware or software.
- Determine the appropriate solution, implement it, and verify that the problem is solved.
- Document the problem and solution for future reference.

Most successful troubleshooting results from careful observation combined with deductive reasoning and an organized approach to solving problems.

Unsuccessful First Boot Process

Problems can happen when installing the Windows operating system and restarting the computer. The correct action to take depends on whether the system is a newly assembled computer or a previously functioning machine. This section assumes that the Windows 98 operating system is being installed to complete the computer-assembly process, as discussed in Chapter 3, "Assembling a Computer."

After installing the operating system, if the computer does not successfully boot, a screen does not display, or the keyboard does not respond, first attempt to restart the machine using the reset button. Also try to restart the computer using a Windows 98 startup disk if you have one. If the problem persists, power off the computer and check one or more of the following items:

- Ensure that the CPU cooling fan is running. If it is not, determine that the power cable is plugged into the motherboard, the power cable is plugged into the surge suppressor, and the surge suppressor is turned on.
- Ensure that the power and data cables are properly connected to the hard drive.
- Verify that the monitor cable is connected to the video adapter card.

- Check the boot sequence in the CMOS. The default setup is for drive A to boot first.

- Determine whether the keyboard lights flash during the power-on self test (POST). This flashing indicates that the system passed the POST.

- Watch for the floppy light to come on during the boot process. This is another indication that the system passed the POST.

- Adjust the contrast and brightness controls on the monitor to make sure that the display can be seen.

- Verify that the DIMM(s) are correctly seated in their sockets. If the RAM chip is not correctly seated, a typical symptom would be a blank monitor.

- Check all expansion cards to ensure that they are correctly seated.

- Verify that the CPU is installed properly and correctly seated. If the CPU is not well seated, the monitor can be blank.

- Verify that a power connector is attached to the floppy drive, hard drive, CD-ROM drive, and motherboard.

- Check the keyboard connections.

Using Windows 98 Help Tools, Tips, and Tricks

Some basic setup troubleshooting tools are built into Windows and are available as third-party add-ons. A few such tools are discussed in the sections that follow, and more help is available on the Internet.

Safe Mode/Device Manager

If Windows 98 becomes unavailable, shut off the computer and restart it. Then listen for a beep as the unit restarts.

Press and hold the left Ctrl key. This opens the Windows 98 Startup menu. Choose *Safe mode* from the list of available options. In this mode, Windows loads only the basic devices that it needs to run. Figure 5-69 displays the safe mode dialog box.

You should also check the Device Manager to ensure that no conflicts exist with any devices.

ScanDisk/Defragmenter

ScanDisk, as shown in Figure 5-70, is a powerful tool for troubleshooting Windows 98. ScanDisk searches the hard drive for disconnected file clusters and converts them into a form that can be checked and manipulated. This allows the user to check for lost clusters that can be restored. ScanDisk can also detect cross-linked files and delete them from the hard drive.

Figure 5-69 Safe Mode Dialog Box

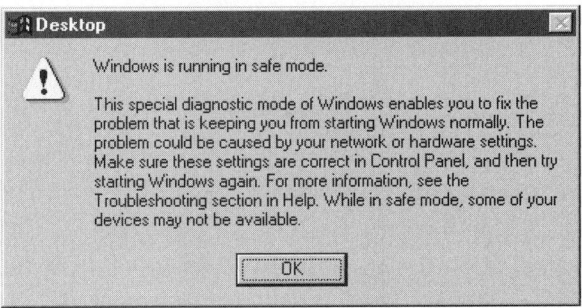

Figure 5-70 Running ScanDisk

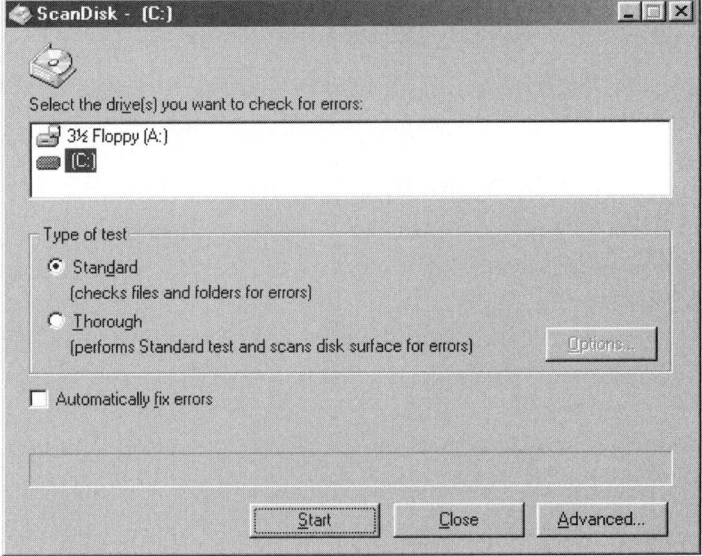

ScanDisk permits you to run two types of tests: Standard and Thorough. Select the **Automatically fix errors** check box to allow ScanDisk to attempt to fix the errors that it finds. The Standard and Thorough options are described as follows:

- **Standard**—Checks the folders and files on the drive for errors
- **Thorough**—Checks the folders and files on the drive for errors and examines the hard drive's physical surface for errors

The *Defragmenter* program rearranges clusters to allow for more efficient hard drive access. It does this by making the files more readable by the system. You should run ScanDisk prior to running the Defragmenter. Figure 5-71 shows the Defragmenter dialog box.

Figure 5-71 Running the Defragmenter

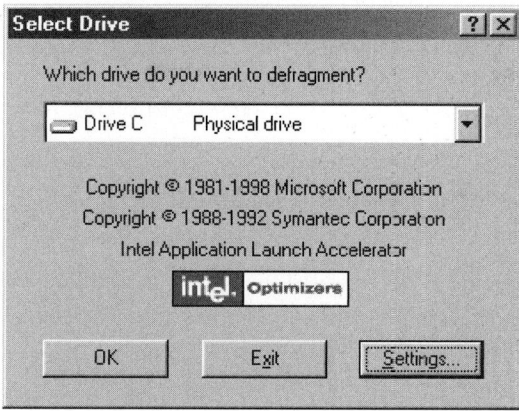

Virus Scan

A **Virus Scan** utility checks all the hard drives for viruses. If a virus is detected, this utility can eliminate them from the hard disk. If the errors persist, check the online help resources for additional help with DOS, Windows, hardware, and software.

FDISK /MBR

The **FDISK /MBR** command, an undocumented MS-DOS command, can be helpful when troubleshooting. The Master Boot Record (MBR) is essentially the hard drive's table of contents. When the computer does not boot, one common problem is that the MBR has been corrupted. Type **FDISK /MBR** at the DOS prompt to rebuild this crucial operating system boot record.

Understanding Windows 98 Setup Errors

Setup errors are probably the most crucial set of problems to deal with. Understanding the error codes that are generated by the operating system can save time when troubleshooting Windows installation problems. In this section, the more frequent setup errors—and the solutions to these errors—are summarized. You might see the following errors when setting up Windows:

- **Not enough disk space**—To correct this problem, delete unnecessary files on the hard drive. If this does not work, reformat the drive and reinstall the operating system.

- **Not enough memory**—This error indicates that the system lacks sufficient conventional memory to continue the installation. Conventional memory is the total memory that is available for copying and moving files. When this problem occurs, install more RAM. A minimum of 32 MB RAM is recommended for a Windows 98 system.

WARNING

Reformatting a hard drive erases all data on the drive.

- **An earlier version of setupx.dll or neti.dll is in use**—This error indicates that other applications are open during the installation. Choose either the option to replace the file and continue, or cancel the setup and close all running applications. If the same error message repeats, attempt to install Windows 98 from DOS. Use the DOS boot disk that you created earlier.

- **CAB file error messages**—These messages indicate that the computer might be infected by a virus, it might not have enough conventional memory, or it might have a hardware problem, especially with the CD-ROM drive. A clean installation of Windows can eliminate problems that are related to a virus or insufficient conventional memory. Another remedy is to attempt to copy the CAB files to the hard drive and run setup from there.

- **Unrecoverable setup error. Setup cannot continue on this system configuration. Click OK to quit setup**—When you see this message, the best course of action is to try installing Windows 98 from DOS. Use the previously created DOS boot disk to boot to the DOS prompt.

- **Setup cannot create files on the startup drive and cannot set up Windows 98. There might be too many files in the root directory of the startup drive, or the startup drive letter could have been remapped (SU0018)**—Remember that the root directory of a drive holds a maximum of 512 files or folders. Either move or delete some files so that the Setup program can continue.

- **Setup cannot write to the Temporary Directory**—This error message indicates that there is insufficient room in the TEMP directory. Delete all files from the C:\WINDOWS\TEMP directory. Note that this is the same directory as the temporary directory that is specified in the AUTOEXEC.BAT file by the line TEMP=.

- **SU0011**—This error indicates that the computer is password protected. Remove the password, which is usually in the BIOS setup, and restart the Windows 98 Setup program.

Only a few of the errors that can occur while installing Windows 98 have been covered. To learn more about setup errors, refer to the SETUP.TXT file that is on the Windows installation disks or CD.

Using the System Properties Window

The System Properties window has four categories of information. This information can be accessed by clicking on each of the tabs, as follows:

- **General**—This tab shows general system information, such as the version of Windows 98 installed, total RAM, type of CPU, percentage of system resources used, and so on. The type of information can vary depending on the computer manufacturer. Figure 5-72 shows general information for a system that is running Windows 98.

Figure 5-72 General Tab

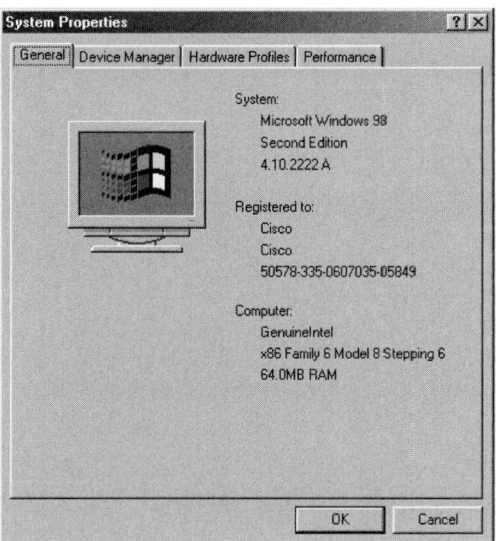

■ **Device Manager**—This tab displays the hardware that is installed and the status of
these devices, as shown in Figure 5-73. Devices can be viewed by type or connection.
The Device Manager provides the options to view the properties of the devices listed,
to refresh the list to ensure that any changes that have been made can be viewed, to
remove a device, and to print.

Figure 5-73 Device Manager Tab

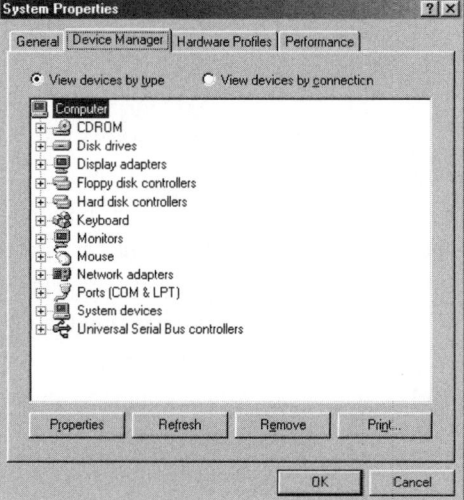

■ **Hardware Profiles**—Most PCs have no need for different hardware profiles. However, a laptop that is used at different locations, such as at home and at work, might need different profiles. The Hardware Profiles tab allows various hardware configuration profiles to be created and then selected when the system boots up, as shown in Figure 5-74.

Figure 5-74 Hardware Profiles Tab

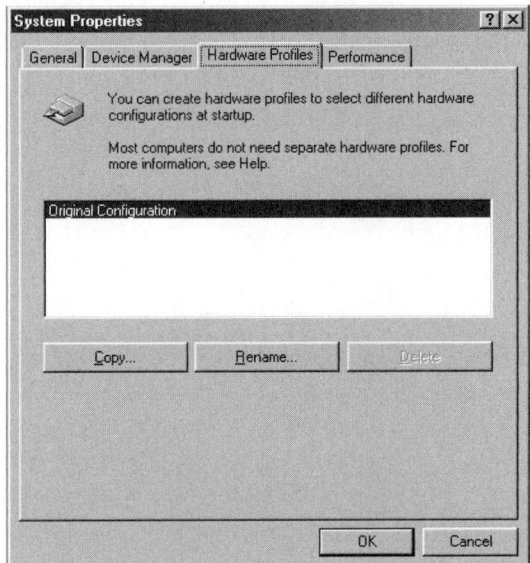

■ **Performance**—This tab shows the detailed performance status and indicates whether the system is configured for optimal performance, as shown in Figure 5-75. Advanced settings can be edited for the file system, graphics, and virtual memory.

Identifying Special Icon Symbols Using the Device Manager

The Device Manager is included with Windows 98 and allows the user to manage, view, and change computer resources. The Device Manager provides a graphical representation of the devices that are configured in the system. This utility identifies installed ports, updates device drivers, and changes I/O settings on the computer. It can also manually isolate hardware and configuration conflicts. The Device Manager allows examination of any problem device to see where the conflict is occurring. Right-click My Computer, select **Properties** from the menu that appears, and then click the Device Manager tab to view the icons in the Device Manager.

Figure 5-75 Performance Tab

From the Device Manager menu, you can determine whether problems exist with installed devices on the system. Within a device, the following types of problems can be identified:

- **An exclamation point inside a yellow circle**—This means that a device is experiencing a direct hardware conflict with another device, as shown in Figure 5-76.

- **A red X appears at the device's icon**—This indicates that the device has been disabled or removed or that Windows is unable to locate the device.

- **Other device appears in place of icon**—This means that Windows cannot recognize the device that is being installed. The drivers have not been installed or were uninstalled, or the device is not working properly and the driver needs to be upgraded.

The Device Manager Properties page provides tabs to access general information, device settings, device driver information, and device resource requirements and usage. The system resources can also be viewed in the Device Manager. If hardware conflicts exist (for example, if two devices are assigned the same IRQ), click the offending device in the list. Make sure that the selected device is the current device in the computer. Also, examine the other conflicting device to make sure that the same device has not been installed twice.

 Lab Activity 5.6.1   Troubleshooting 101

Use the basic troubleshooting skills and a systematic approach to problem solving.

Figure 5-76 Performance Tab

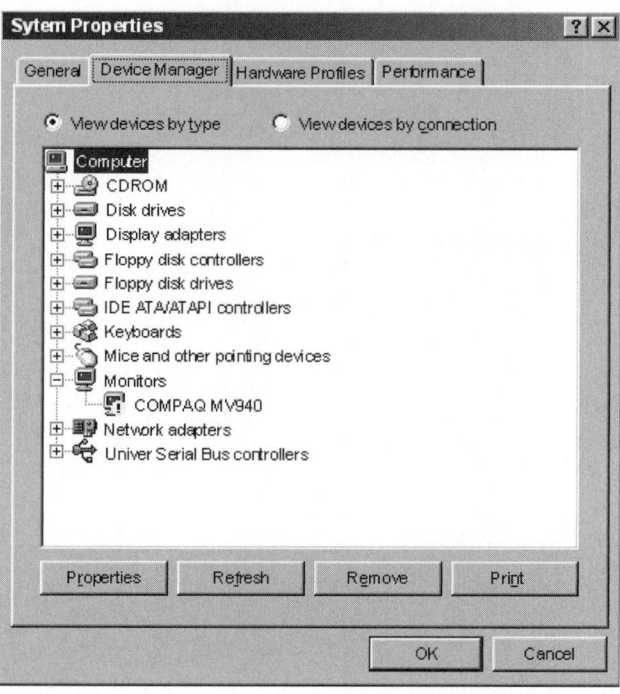

Adding Software Drivers

Device drivers now give PCs the ability to add a wide variety of devices to the system. A *device driver* is software that is designed specially to enable the computer to recognize the hardware or devices that are installed on the system. Such devices include CD-ROM drives, hard drives, and expansion cards. They can also include external devices, such as a mouse or keyboard. Sometimes all the problems that follow the installation of a Windows operating system are linked to the absence of the appropriate device drivers. The device driver not only allows the basic system to recognize the presence of a device, but it also enables the computer to work with the device.

Although the process of installing equipment and their drivers in a PC has become increasingly easy, the technician must still be able to install any drivers that are necessary. A device driver can be installed in two ways. The following sections outline these installations.

Autodetect and Install from Windows 98 Stock Drivers

The new card or device should already be installed in the system before performing this procedure. Use the Windows 98 Driver Installation Wizard to autodetect and install the hardware device, as shown in Figure 5-77. This wizard is a program that is designed specially to show a series of screens that guide the user through hardware setup steps. The first option that is normally available is to use the Autodetect function. Figure 5-78 shows the screen that displays the search for new hardware.

Figure 5-77 Add New Hardware Wizard

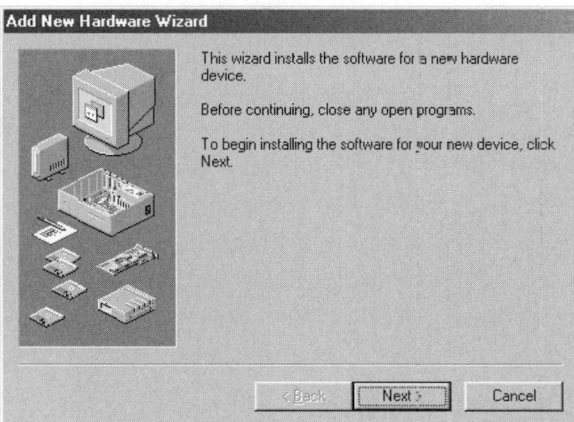

Figure 5-78 Add New Hardware Wizard Automatic Search

After the autodetect option is selected, a hardware detection progress indicator bar appears on-screen. When it completes the search, the wizard indicates what hardware has been found, as shown in Figure 5-79. After the hardware has been found, the wizard searches for the driver software to install and completes the installation process. If the wizard does not detect the hardware, attempt to manually locate the device in the list of supported devices in the wizard.

Figure 5-79 Add New Hardware Wizard: Hardware Found

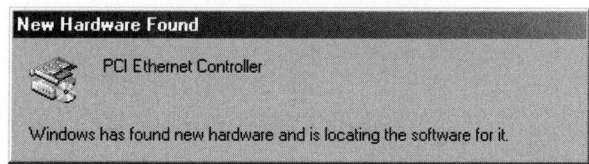

Using the OEM Installation Disk or CD

The original equipment manufacturer (OEM) is the vendor that is responsible for the final packaging of computer hardware and software, including the drivers. The only other option for installing hardware devices is to obtain an OEM disk or CD that has the drivers for the device. Unfortunately, all driver CDs do not have an autostart function. As a result, you can use the following procedures:

- Click the **Have Disk** button and supply the file location to complete the installation process.
- Boot the system to the C:\> prompt. If necessary, type **CD** to change to the directory where the new driver is located. Type **SETUP** at the command line to initiate the driver installation. Follow the on-screen instructions. The readme.txt file contains important information and can be found on the floppy disk or CD.

The main advantage of using the OEM driver disk is that the drivers are likely to be more current. Using the Autodetect feature with Windows 98 stock drivers can lead to device malfunction or poor performance. Stock drivers that are prepackaged with the Windows 98 installation CD can be outdated.

When the driver installation is complete, reboot the system to activate the changes in a Windows 98 system. After every hardware installation, you should update the device drivers to ensure maximum performance.

Lab Activity 5.6.4 Install a Driver

Install the driver for a roller-ball mouse. The same process is used when installing any new device on your system.

Making a Windows Startup Disk

A Windows 98 startup disk is essential if the system crashes, if the system hangs during startup, or if Windows 98 setup fails before completion. The Windows 98 setup is easier with a

Windows 98 startup disk. This section provides an overview of the Windows 98 startup disk and describes how to make one.

A Windows boot disk, or startup disk, is a floppy disk that allows the user to boot the computer without having to access the hard drive. A typical Windows boot disk contains all the necessary files that the operating system needs to start up. The boot disk is a handy tool that no Windows user should be without. The boot disk that is created under Windows 98 includes a generic CD-ROM driver. It also includes both a generic IDE/ATAPI driver and a generic SCSI driver.

The Windows 98 startup disk can be used to boot the system to the command prompt to troubleshoot problems. (The command prompt is not the Windows Desktop.) In addition, if a hard drive fails or if the Master Boot Record is corrupted by a virus, the startup disk can help recover the system. If important operating system files are accidentally deleted or become corrupt, a bootable floppy disk can be of help. If you need to reformat the hard drive or reinstall Windows 98 in the future, you will need the startup (boot) disk.

> **NOTE**
>
> A boot disk that is created under Windows 98 can boot a Windows 95 machine with no conflicts. However, the Windows 98 startup disk provides CD-ROM support that is not available with the Windows 95 startup disk.

Creating a Windows 98 Startup Disk

A Windows 98 startup disk can be created in two ways. The first way is to insert the floppy disk in the computer when prompted during the installation process. Figures 5-80 and 5-81 show the dialog boxes that are displayed while installing Windows 98.

Figure 5-80 Creating a Startup Disk During Windows 98 Installation

Figure 5-81 Insert a Blank Floppy Disk

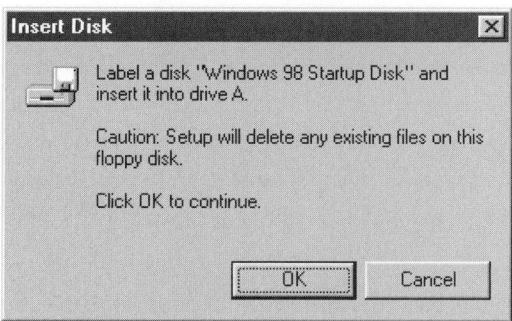

The second way is to create the startup disk after the Windows operating system is already installed and running. The Windows Startup Disk tab is used to create a startup disk. Follow these steps to do so:

Step 1   Choose **Start**, **Settings**, **Control Panel**, as shown in Figure 5-82.

Figure 5-82 Accessing the Control Panel

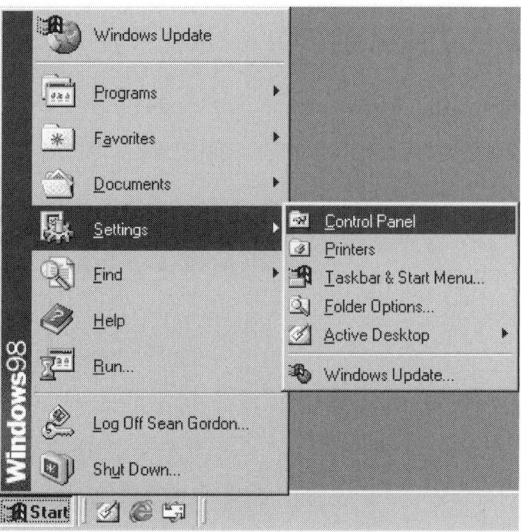

Step 2   In the Control Panel window, double-click the Add/Remove Programs icon.

Step 3   Click the Startup Disk tab, and click the Create Disk button, as shown in Figure 5-83.

Figure 5-83 Creating a Startup Disk

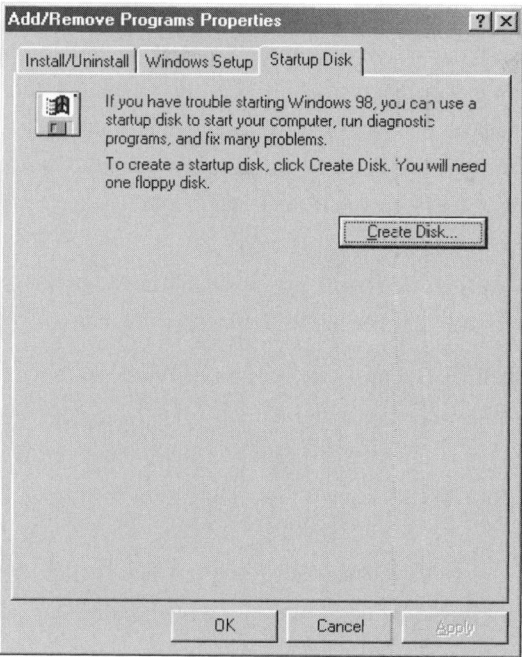

Step 4   When prompted, insert the Windows 98 CD into your CD-ROM drive and place a floppy disk in the floppy drive.

The system notifies you when the startup disk has been created.

In addition to the critical operating system files that copied to the startup disk, three important disk utilities, which are needed for preparing or troubleshooting the hard drive during operating system installations, are also included on the disk. These files are SCANDISK.EXE, FDISK.EXE, and FORMAT.EXE.

Video   Creating a Windows Startup Disk

In this video, you review the steps for creating a startup disk.

Lab Activity 5.6.5   Create a Startup Disk

Create a Windows 9*x* startup disk that can boot the computer for troubleshooting purposes.

Uninstalling Windows 98

Sometimes, it is necessary to remove the Windows operating system from the computer. The uninstall procedure allows the system to return to a previous version of Windows. In some instances, uninstalling Windows 98 is the only solution when an attempted upgrade fails, especially if a system backup was not made before trying to upgrade. Formatting the hard drive deletes all data, because this process removes any previously stored data. Uninstalling Windows is usually referred to as a solution of last resort.

Understanding When Windows 98 Should Be Uninstalled

Windows 98 can be uninstalled under the following circumstances:

- If the user upgraded from a previous version of Windows, such as Windows 95.
- If the Save Uninstall Information option was selected during Windows 98 setup. Note that when this option is selected, the Setup utility creates the WINUNDO.DAT and WINUNDO.INI files, which contain the uninstall information.

Understanding When Windows 98 Cannot Be Installed

Windows 98 *cannot* be uninstalled under the following conditions:

- The previously mentioned conditions are not met.
- The files WINUNDO.DAT and WINUNDO.INI become corrupted or are deleted.
- The hard disk was compressed prior to installing the Windows 98 operating system.
- The hard disk was compressed or converted to FAT32 after installing Windows 98.

Step-by-Step Process for Uninstalling Windows 98

> **CAUTION**
>
> Uninstalling Windows 98 is a drastic course of action and should be your last course of action. Many side effects could occur, such as the malfunctioning of applications that were installed after the installation of Windows 98.

If all the conditions to uninstall the operating system have been met, follow these steps to uninstall Windows 98:

Step 1   Choose **Start**, **Settings**, **Control Panel**.

Step 2   In the Control Panel, double-click the **Add/Remove Programs** icon.

Step 3   In the Add/Remove Programs window, choose **Uninstall Windows 98**, click the **Add/Remove** button, and click the **Yes** button when prompted.

ScanDisk prompts you to check the hard drive for errors.

Step 4   Allow ScanDisk to check the hard drive by clicking the **Yes** button when prompted.

Step 5   When prompted to continue the Uninstall, choose **Yes** and follow the on-screen instructions to uninstall Windows 98.

The requirements and options for uninstalling other versions of Windows can differ, but the steps are similar. Understanding these steps can help the technician troubleshoot problems that occur. Installing Windows 2000 is covered in Chapter 6.

 Worksheet 5.6.6   Troubleshooting Windows Installation

This worksheet is a review of the steps that are used to troubleshoot the Windows installation process.

Summary

This chapter discussed the Windows 9*x* operating systems. Some of the important concepts to retain from this chapter include the following:

- Windows uses a hierarchical structure, or tree view, of files, folders, and drives. DOS allows filenames of up to eight characters in length. Windows allows filenames of up to 255 characters. Illegal characters include the following:

  / \ : * ? " < > |

- Drive letters use the 26 letters of the alphabet. Within Windows Explorer, clicking on the plus sign expands the drives and folders. Files can be moved and copied between drives and folders. Use the Recycle Bin to restore files that have been deleted.

- The Control Panel provides access to the system properties, printers, add/remove hardware, add/remove software, and display options.

- The system registry is a hierarchical database that is an efficient way to manage the operating system. It includes the USER.DAT file, which contains user-specific information, and the SYSTEM.DAT file, which contains hardware-specific or computer-specific settings.

- If preparing the hard drive for the operating system, installation includes partitioning the drive. The partitioning process creates spaces of contiguous sectors on the hard drive. DOS can have up to four partitions on a hard drive.

- The requirements for installing or upgrading Windows are basically the same. A new installation requires more preparation for the hard drive. Do not stop an installation before it has completed.

- Knowing the different tips and tricks can help a technician when troubleshooting is required. Follow the troubleshooting steps, and work from the outside in.

The next chapter details the Windows NT and 2000 operating systems. It covers the differences between these operating systems and the Windows 9*x* operating systems.

Key Terms

Add New Hardware Wizard Installs new hardware on the computer.

Add Printer wizard Installs a new printer on the system.

Add/Remove Programs Installs programs on and removes programs from the computer.

ASD.EXE Skips a driver when the operating system fails during bootup.

block See *cluster*.

boot sector The first area on each logical drive.

Clipboard Temporary storage area that is used with the Cut, Copy, and Paste commands.

cluster A combination of two or more sectors.

copy Makes a duplicate of a document or file and places it on the Clipboard. The document can then be pasted to another location.

Create Shortcut Creates a link to a file or application.

cut Removes a file and saves it to the Clipboard.

cylinder All the tracks on a hard disk with the same number.

defragmenter Rearranges clusters for more efficient hard drive access.

Desktop The area of the screen that Windows boots to.

Details mode The view option that provides the most details of a file.

Device Manager Displays a list of all the hardware that is installed on the system.

directory A place to store data in the Windows file-management system.

Display utility Allows the user to adjust the look of the computer screen.

drive label A name that is assigned to a newly created drive. It can be up to 11 characters in length.

drive letter Distinguishes the logical drives in Windows.

extended partition Second partition on the hard drive.

FDISK A partitioning program.

FDISK /MBR DOS command that helps to rebuild the operating system boot record on the hard drive.

file allocation table (FAT) The reference table that the operating system uses to locate files on the hard disk.

file details Attributes for an individual file that include the size, type, and date modified.

file extension   Describes the file format or the type of application that created a file.

file management   The hierarchical structure of files, folders, and drives in Windows.

folder   A place to store data in the Windows file-management system.

formatting   Preparing a hard drive to store data.

Hardware Profiles   Tab that allows the user to set up different hardware configurations for the same operating system.

high-level formatting   Creates the logical structure on the drive that tells the system what files are on the disk and where they can be found.

HWINFO.EXE   A utility that provides a detailed collection of information about the computer.

logical drive   Section that the partition can be divided into.

low-level formatting   Marks off the disk into sectors and cylinders and defines the placement of the sectors and cylinders on the disk.

MSCONFIG.EXE   Allows the user to control how the system is started.

My Computer   Window that displays the drives on the computer.

partition table   Partition information created by FDISK.

paste   Places a copy of what is on the Clipboard to the indicated location.

Performance   Tab that displays information about the system.

primary partition   First partition on the hard drive.

Recycle Bin   A repository that holds deleted files, folders, and so on.

REGEDIT.EXE   Displays the registry in a hierarchical format.

registry   A hierarchical database for the information that is used by the Windows operating system.

safe mode   An option when booting the system that loads only the basic devices that Windows needs to run. It is used for troubleshooting.

ScanDisk   Performs a complete check of the FAT, directory, and files on the drive and creates a ScanDisk log file.

ScanDisk utility   Prior to installation, this tool looks at all the files on the drive.

SCANREG.EXE   Backs up or repairs the system's registry.

sector   Unit of storage (512 bytes) within a track.

Sounds utility   Allows the user to adjust the system sounds.

subfolder   Folder within a folder in the Windows file system.

SYSTEM.DAT   A file that contains information about the hardware in the system.

System Properties   A tool in the Windows Control Panel that displays information relating to the system.

track   Magnetic area that is created by formatting the hard drive.

USER.DAT   File that contains user-specific information.

Virus Scan   Utility that checks all hard drives for viruses.

Windows 98 Setup wizard   Guides the user through the installation process.

Windows Explorer   A Windows utility that represents the file-management structure.

WSCRIPT.EXE   Allows configuration of the properties that relate to the Windows scripting host.

Check Your Understanding

1. What does Windows Explorer display?

   A. System resources available

   B. Date and time

   C. Hierarchical structure of files, folders, and drives

   D. Progress of the installation process

2. What is the first thing that needs to be done with a new hard drive?

   A. Partitioning

   B. Formatting

   C. ScanDisk

   D. Defragmenting

3. What is the second thing that needs to be done with a new hard drive?

   A. Partitioning

   B. Formatting

   C. ScanDisk

   D. Defragmenting

4. In Windows 98, what utilities are used to set up the hard drive?

   A. ScanDisk and Newdrive

   B. ScanDisk and FDISK

   C. FDISK and FORMAT

   D. ScanDisk and FORMAT

5. What is another name for the active partition?

   A. Bootable partition

   B. Usable partition

   C. First partition

   D. Logical partition

6. The extended partition can be subdivided into a maximum of how many logical drives?

   A. 4

   B. 8

   C. 16

   D. 23

7. What section of the hard drive stores the location of the operating system?

   A. Boot sector

   B. SYSTEM.INI

   C. Boot cylinder

   D. Boot track

8. When upgrading Window 98, what is the earliest DOS version that will allow it?

   A. Version 3.2.

   B. Version 3.

   C. It is not possible to upgrade from DOS; a previous version of Windows must exist in order to upgrade.

   D. It is not necessary to have an operating system installed.

9. What is the first thing you should try if the computer does not boot after installing the operating system?

    A. Restart the computer.

    B. Reinstall the operating system.

    C. Reinstall the hard drive.

    D. Flash the CPU.

10. Is it possible to upgrade a Windows 98 computer to Windows 2000?

    A. Yes

    B. No

    C. Only if you have 64 MB of memory

    D. Only if you have 32 MB of memory

11. What does ScanDisk do?

    A. Removes viruses from the hard drive

    B. Erases temporary files from the hard drive

    C. Erases bad clusters

    D. Marks bad clusters

12. What program is used to edit the registry?

    A. Edit

    B. Registry

    C. SYSEDIT

    D. REGEDIT

13. What should you do if the Windows 98 installation procedure fails?

    A. Remove any hardware listed in the error.txt file.

    B. Restart the computer using safe mode.

    C. Remove any hardware that is listed in the fault.txt file.

    D. Use a clean boot disk to start the computer.

14. What does the IO.SYS file do in Windows 98?

   A. Loads the basic device drivers and sets the basic system headings

   B. Tells the operating system which hardware the user has access to

   C. Controls the video system of the computer

   D. Tells the operating system which software the user has access to

15. In Windows 98, how do you remove or view devices and their properties?

   A. Choose **Start, Settings, Control Panel, System**.

   B. Choose **Start, Settings, Control Panel, System, Device Manager**.

   C. Choose **Start, Settings, System, Devices**.

   D. Choose **Start, Settings, Start, Devices**.

16. In Windows 98, how do you make a startup disk?

   A. Choose **Start, Programs, Startup, Bootdisk**.

   B. Choose **Start, Settings, Control Panel, Add/Remove Programs, Startup Disk tab, Create Disk**.

   C. Choose **Start, Settings, Programs, Add/Remove Programs, Startup Disk tab, Create Disk**.

   D. Double-click My Computer and choose **Add/Remove Programs, Startup Disk tab, Create Disk**.

17. How do you restore a file if you delete it from the Windows 98 Desktop?

   A. Choose **Start, Control Panel, Undelete**.

   B. Choose **Start, Programs, Undelete**.

   C. From the Recycle Bin.

   D. From My Computer.

18. By default, how much space on the hard drive is set aside for the Recycle Bin in Windows 98?

   A. 10%

   B. 20%

   C. 30%

   D. 40%

19. How can you view the version of Windows that is currently installed?

    A. Choose **Start**, **Help**, **About**.

    B. Right-click My Computer and choose **Properties** from the menu that appears.

    C. Right-click My Computer and choose **Version** from the menu that appears.

    D. Choose **Start**, **Help**, **Version**.

20. How do you view the file or folder properties in Windows 98?

    A. Click the icon and select **Properties** from the menu that appears.

    B. Right-click the icon and select **Properties** from the menu that appears.

    C. Drop the icon on the Taskbar.

    D. Choose **Start**, **Properties** and then enter the name of the object.

21. How do you locate an object in Windows 98?

    A. Choose **Start**, **Settings**, **Find**.

    B. Open My Computer and choose **Settings**, **Find**.

    C. Choose **Start**, **Help**, **Find**.

    D. Choose **Start**, **Find**.

22. Which of the following characters cannot be used when naming a DOS file?

    A. ~ (tilde)

    B. > (greater-than sign)

    C. – (dash)

    D. _ (underscore)

23. If a printer is changed in DOS, what must be done?

    A. Change the DOS printer driver.

    B. Change each application's printer driver.

    C. Change the printer in the CMOS.

    D. DOS will find the printer driver automatically.

24. Creating a shortcut in Windows 98 allows the user to do which of the following?

    A. Find shortcuts more easily.

    B. Execute applications more easily.

    C. Have quick access to the Device Manager.

    D. Make use of the Desktop.

25. Windows 98 does not support which of the following types of applications?

    A. DOS programs

    B. UNIX programs

    C. 16-bit Windows programs

    D. 32-bit Windows programs

Upon completing this chapter, you will be able to perform the following tasks:

- Understand the advantages and disadvantages of the different file systems that are used in Windows

- Apply the added security features of Windows 2000, such as setting permissions and encrypting folders and files

- Understand the Windows 2000 boot process and know how it differs from that of Windows 98

- Identify the main components of the Windows 2000 registry and know the purpose of the registry subtrees

- Create an ERD for Windows 2000 and use the Recovery Console

- Install or upgrade from Windows 98 to Windows 2000 and understand whether to use FAT32 or NTFS

Chapter 6

Windows NT/2000 Operating Systems

This chapter explores the differences between the Windows NT, 2000, and XP operating systems and the Windows 9x operating systems. It also discusses the operating system environment, types of file systems, and security issues. You learn the administrative tools that are specific to Windows NT, 2000, and XP. The special requirements for installing or upgrading to the Windows 2000 operating system are also discussed.

Windows 9x Contrasts

DOS and Windows are the most widely used operating systems in the United States and many other parts of the world. For the most part, the file systems used by DOS and Windows are the standard. An IT technician must understand the original FAT file system and know how it evolved into the current NT File System (NTFS).

This section covers the following topics:

- NTFS versus FAT
- Security and permissions
- Windows 2000 boot process
- Plug and Play drivers

NTFS Versus FAT

The Windows NT, 2000, and the recent Windows XP operating systems have some obvious differences from the Windows 9x operating system. However, many differences are unseen. Knowing these differences is important to fully understand the environments in which these operating systems are used. The following factors must be considered when choosing an operating system:

- Whether the operating system will be for the office or the home
- Whether the computer will be part of a network
- Security issues
- The types of programs that will be used on the operating system

All of these factors determine the choice between the Windows 9*x* operating system and the Windows NT, 2000, and XP operating systems. The biggest differences between these operating systems are the Windows NT File System (NTFS) and the File Allocation Table (FAT) file system.

The main purpose of any file system is to store and retrieve data from the computer's hard disk. The file system on the hard drive determines how the data is organized, optimized, and retrieved. Hard drives store information on platters. A file system organizes the data on these platters.

Original FAT File System

Bill Gates invented the original FAT file system in 1976. The main purpose of this file system was for storing programs and data on floppy disks. The FAT file system is a database that keeps track of every file on the hard disk. Intel was the first company to incorporate the FAT file system design. This design was used for an early version of an operating system for the Intel 8086 chip. Bill Gates bought the rights to this operating system, rewrote it, and then created the first version of DOS.

FAT16 File System

The FAT16 file system, in which 16 refers to 16-bit, is used for most hard drives with DOS, Windows 3.1, and the first version of Windows 95. FAT16 has characteristics that distinguish it from the FAT32 file systems. The original FAT directory structure, which came before Windows NT and Windows 95, limits filenames to eight characters with a three-letter extension. For example, the filename COMMAND.COM is a valid filename according to the FAT16 file structure regulations because it is seven characters long and has a three-letter extension. The FAT structure also maintains a set of attributes for each file. These include the following:

- **S**—Indicates a system dataset
- **H**—Indicates that the file is hidden in the directory display
- **A**—Indicates that the file will be archived the next time the disk is backed up
- **R**—Indicates that the file is read-only

A date and time stamp are also placed on the file when it is last changed.

The FAT file system carries out many administrative input and output (I/O) tasks to areas of the partition without using a lot of memory. This ability gives the FAT file system a true advantage. However, a file can become fragmented because of this capability, thereby reducing performance. The FAT file system includes optimization tools to prevent fragmentation from occurring.

FAT File System Utilities

Two important optimization tools that the FAT16 file system uses are the CHKDSK and SCANDISK utilities. These utilities can be used during crashes so that data is not lost. A FAT file system can remove a disk area from the chain of free space without having assigned it to a permanent new dataset.

The CHKDSK utility checks for errors on a disk. Error messages (if problems are found) are displayed, and the utility issues a report. The SCANDISK utility is a disk-analysis and -repair tool that checks a drive for errors. SCANDISK can correct problems that it finds. Both CHKDSK and SCANDISK keep the file system running at an optimal level.

Sectors and Clusters

The underlying difference between the FAT16 file system and the FAT32, or NTFS, file system is the way that it arranges and stores files on the hard disk to maximize space. The size of partitions that the FAT16 file system can use is an important difference as well. The FAT16 file system can only recognize partitions up to 2 GB, or 2048 MB, in size. The FAT32 file system was created to support partitions larger than 2 GB in size, whereas NTFS can handle larger partitions of 2 terabytes (TB) or more in size.

Files are stored in clusters. Under this system, the hard disk is divided into 512-byte pieces called *sectors*. The sectors are grouped into larger pieces called *clusters*. Each cluster can hold only one file. The computer assigns these clusters a specific location to simplify finding them. The size of the clusters is determined by the size of the partitions that are made on the hard disk. Table 6-1 demonstrates the cluster sizes for the FAT16 file system according to the size of the partition.

Table 6-1 FAT16 Partition Cluster Sizes

FAT16 Partition Size (MB)	Cluster Size
0–32	512 bytes
33–64	1 KB
65–128	2 KB

continues

Table 6-1 FAT16 Partition Cluster Sizes (Continued)

FAT16 Partition Size (MB)	Cluster Size
129–256	4 KB
257–511	8 KB
512–1023	16 KB
1024–2047	32 KB
2048–4095	64 KB

FAT32 File System

The FAT32 file system is still based on the original FAT system and works in a similar fashion to remain compatible with existing programs, networks, and device drivers. As the technology of computers and hard drives improved, the FAT16 file system was no longer an efficient means of storing and organizing data on a hard drive that was larger than 2 GB. For example, if a hard drive were larger than 2 GB and only one or two partitions were needed, the FAT16 file system would not work because FAT16 is only capable of dealing with partitions up to 2 GB in size. The FAT32 file system solved this problem. The FAT32 file system is designed to support hard drives up to 2048 GB (2 TB) in size. The FAT32 file system also solves the problem of limited cluster size. Table 6-2 reviews the cluster sizes that are available with the FAT32 file system according to partition size.

Table 6-2 FAT32 Partition Cluster Sizes*

FAT32 Partition Size	Cluster Size
32 MB–8 GB	512 bytes
8–16 GB	1 KB
16–32 GB	2 KB
32 GB	4 KB

   * Windows 2000 works with existing FAT32 volumes of larger sizes (created in other operating systems), but it limits new FAT32 volumes to a maximum size of 32 GB.

The FAT32 file system stores data on the hard disk in a much more efficient manner. The previous FAT16 version wasted useful space because only one file could be stored in a cluster at a time. For example, storing a small file of 1 KB in a 32-KB cluster wastes 31 KB of space. Conversely, the FAT32 file system allows a 4-KB cluster with a 2-GB partition, reducing the amount of wasted space. Table 6-3 shows the utilization of disk space with different cluster sizes. This factor, combined with the ability to recognize partitions larger than 2 GB, made the FAT32 file system an obvious improvement to the DOS file system.

Table 6-3 Utilization of Disk Space

Disk Size	Cluster Size (KB)	Efficiency (%)
260 MB	4	96.6
8 GB	8	92.9
60 GB	16	85.8
2 TB	32	73.8

Added FAT32 Features

The new FAT32 file system has added features and advantages that are important when compared to the FAT16 file system. As processor speeds and hard disk size advanced, FAT16 was not reliable enough for future computer use. FAT32 has many advanced features that still make it a reliable file system today.

In the FAT16 file system, the root directory can be located only at the beginning of the hard disk. This poses problems if this part of the hard disk becomes damaged. If this happens, the entire hard disk can become unusable. With the FAT32 file system, the root directory can be located anywhere on the hard disk. This is useful, because if the section of the hard disk that contains the root directory were to become damaged, the root directory can be moved to another section of the hard disk and the damaged portion can be repaired.

Another benefit of FAT32 is its ability to use both the default and original copies of the FAT. Both FAT16 and FAT32 file systems maintain two copies of the FAT, which are the default and backup copies. However, only FAT32 can use the backup copy as well as the default copy. This means that if the FAT32 file system is being used and a file allocation table becomes corrupted or fails, a backup copy can be used until the default copy is repaired. FAT16 can use only the default copy to run the operating system. This means that if the FAT becomes damaged or fails, the system will crash and become unusable.

These added features of FAT32 make disk space usage more efficient and improve the overall performance of the operating system.

NT File System

The Windows *NT File System (NTFS)* was designed to be capable of managing global and enterprise-level operating systems. NTFS supports all Windows NT and 2000 operating systems. The FAT file system can still be used in the Windows NT, 2000, and Windows XP operating system environments. However, limited access is available to the full features of the operating systems when the FAT file system is used. NTFS4 was first deployed with the Windows NT operating system. At the time of the release of Windows NT, the NTFS4 file system was simply referred to as NTFS. The NTFS has been improved, and many new features have been added with the latest releases of Windows 2000 and Windows XP.

The original version of NTFS that was released with Windows NT is now referred to as NTFS4. The latest version of the NTFS is now referred to as NTFS5. NTFS5 is included with the Windows 2000 release and can control file encryption as well as provide additional security that NTFS4 could not. NTFS5 also includes *disk quotas*, which provide the system administrator with the ability to assign limits to the amount of hard disk space that users are allowed to occupy on the server or workstation.

The main reason for creating the NTFS is that the FAT16 and FAT32 file systems were too limited to provide the advanced features that are necessary for an enterprise-level operating system. The NTFS provides support for added features like file and directory security by using discretionary access control lists (DACLs) and system access control lists (SACLs). Both of these features can perform operations on a file and monitor events that trigger the logging of actions. In addition, NTFS allows the administrator to set local permissions on files and folders to specify which users have access to them. This includes setting the level of access that is permitted. NTFS file and folder permissions apply both to users who are working at the computer where the file is stored and to users who are accessing the file over the network from a shared folder. Share rights for folders can also be set to operate in combination with file and folder permissions with NTFS. FAT only supports share rights. Figure 6-1 demonstrates the attributes that can be set up in the Filename Properties dialog box.

NTFS provides support to more efficiently manage large hard disks and volumes that exceed the FAT16 or FAT32 size limitations. In fact, the NTFS is designed to map disks up to sizes that are expected to be operational for the next 20 years. Table 6-4 shows default cluster sizes for NTFS based on the size of the partition.

Table 6-4 NTFS Partition Cluster Sizes*

NTFS Partition Size	Cluster Size
0–512 MB	512 bytes
513 MB–1 GB	1 KB
1025 MB–2 GB	2 KB
2 GB and greater	4 KB

*   Note: These are defaults. You can choose any of them, depending on your partition needs.

Figure 6-1 Filename Properties—Advanced Attributes

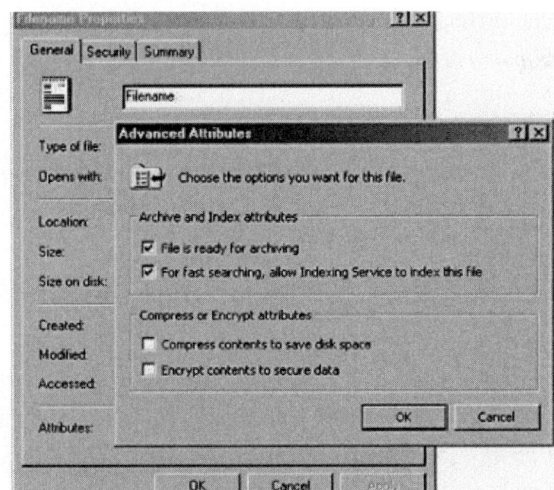

Enables Use of Native Language

An area where the FAT file system fails is the inability to recognize non-English filenames. This is because the FAT file system uses the ASCII 8-bit character set for its file and directory name scheme. NTFS employs the Unicode 16-bit character set for its name scheme, which allows users anywhere in the world to manage files using their native language. Its 16-bit character set has a greater ability to accommodate a native alphabet and a non-English language than an 8-bit character set. This is an important feature for a global and enterprise-level operating system.

The Windows NT, 2000, and XP operating systems were designed to appeal to the corporate and business markets. Features like security and the ability to access large volumes of data are required for large corporations and businesses. NTFS has built-in transactional logging so that every time a modification occurs, NTFS makes a note of it in a special log file. If the system crashes, NTFS can examine this log file and use it to restore the disk to a consistent state with minimal data loss. This feature is called *fault tolerance*. This is another feature that the corporate and business community considers important, because the loss of crucial data due to a computer crash could cost a lot of time and money. FAT has no provision for fault tolerance. The FAT on-disk structures can become corrupted if a system crashes while creating or updating files. This situation can result in the loss of valuable data that is being modified, a general corruption of the drive, and a considerable loss of hard disk data. This risk is clearly unacceptable for the Windows NT, 2000, and XP target market.

High Performance File System

The ***High Performance File System (HPFS)*** is a seldom used and much more obscure type of file system. However, it is worth mentioning, because the OS/2 software that uses this file system is still in use. Microsoft used this file system with its Windows NT 3.51 operating system. However, Microsoft stopped using this file system when it launched the Windows NT 4.0 operating system.

The HPFS directory structure was the same as that of the FAT file system, but it allowed long filenames, up to 254 characters. The FAT16 file system used the 8.3 naming system. Another important aspect of HPFS was its ability to map hard disks up to 8 GB in size instead of 2 GB. Also, HPFS used physical sectors instead of clusters as the unit of management on the hard disk. Overall system performance increased because of this file system, but the file system lacked the necessary tools and security that NTFS would provide.

Table 6-5 summarizes the evolution of the file system, from the introduction of the original FAT16 with DOS to the newer NTFS5, which was introduced with Windows 2000. Other file systems are in use today by other popular operating systems such as Novell NetWare and Linux. However, these are not within the scope of this course.

Table 6-5 File System Evolution*

File System	OS That File System Was Introduced With	Year Introduced	Other OSs That Use the File System
FAT16	DOS	1981	Windows 3.1, 9x, Me, 2000, and XP
HPFS	OS/2	1989	Windows NT 3.51
NTFS4	Windows NT 4.0	1994	Windows 2000 and XP
FAT32	Windows 98	1998	Windows Me, 2000, and XP
NTFS5	Windows 2000	2000	Windows XP

*   Summary timeline and the evolution of file systems from the original FAT16, introduced with DOS, to the newer NTFS5, introduced with Windows 2000.

Security and Permissions

The Windows 9*x* environment lacks the robust security and permissions features of the Windows NT, Windows 2000, and Windows XP environments. If NTFS is used in these environments, these operating systems benefit from enhanced system security features like file encryption. Permissions can also be set on files, directories, or folders.

Permissions

File and directory *permissions* specify which users and groups have access to which files and folders. Permissions also set what can be done with the contents of a file or folder. Assigning permissions is an excellent means of providing security. It is also effective for files or directories that are accessed over a network. However, permissions that are assigned for directories are different from those that are assigned for files. Tables 6-6 and 6-7 describe the different permission types that can be set on folders and files. These features are only available in the Windows NT, Windows 2000, and Windows XP operating systems if NTFS is used in place of the FAT file system.

Table 6-6 Folder Permissions*

Permission	What the Permission Allows the User to Do
Read	See files and subfolders in the folder and view folder ownership, permissions, and attributes.
Write	Create new files and subfolders within the folder, change folder attributes, and view folder ownership and permissions.
List Folder Contents	See the names of files and subfolders in the folder.
Read and Execute	Move through folders to reach other files and folders, even if the user does not have permission for those folders, and perform actions permitted by the Read permission and the List Folder Contents permission.
Modify	Delete the folder, plus perform actions permitted by the Write permission and the Read and Execute permission.
Full Control	Change permissions, take ownership, and delete subfolders and files, plus perform actions permitted by all other NTFS folder permissions.
No Access	Prohibit unauthorized access to files or folders.

* Directory for folder permissions specifies which users and groups can gain access to folders and what they can do with the contents of the folder.

Table 6-7 File Permissions*

Permission	What the Permission Allows the User to Do
Read	Read the file and view file attributes, ownership, and permissions.
Write	Overwrite the file, change file attributes, and view file ownership and permissions.
Read and Execute	Run applications, plus perform the actions permitted by the Read permission.
Modify	Modify and delete the file, plus perform the actions permitted by the Write permission and the Read and Execute permission.
Full Control	Change permissions and take ownership, plus perform the actions permitted by all other NTFS file permissions.

* File permissions specify which users and groups can gain access to files and what the users can do with the contents of the file.

Access Control Lists

Tracking who has the rights to certain files and folders when assigning permissions can be difficult. Permissions management can become difficult for an administrator to handle when dealing with large networks. The *Access Control List (ACL)* is a tool that provides a list of files that a user has access to and the type of access that they have been granted. Every file and folder in an NTFS volume has an ACL. If a user wants to access a resource, the ACL must contain an entry called an *Access Control Entry (ACE)*. This entry allows the requested access. A user cannot access the specified file or folder without this entry.

Encryption

Encryption is another security feature that is included with the Windows 2000 and Windows XP operating systems. Microsoft provides a specific file system for encryption called the *Encryption File System (EFS)*. This allows administrators to encrypt a file or folder so that only the person who encrypted the file can view it. The administrator can also specify which other users can view the file.

The EFS is an integrated service that runs on the operating system. This means that it is easy for an administrator to manage and it is transparent to the file owner. However, other users can be granted access if they are assigned a *public key*. This allows a user to work with the file. Anyone without the public key cannot access the file.

The administrator should encrypt folders, not individual files. Any files that are placed in a folder become encrypted as soon as the folder has encryption enabled. This simplifies management of the encrypted folders. Click the **General** tab in the Properties dialog box for the folder to encrypt it. On the General tab, click the **Advanced** button and then select the **Encrypt contents to secure data** check box.

Compression

Microsoft has a *compression tool* that saves space by compressing files and folders. After compression, a file or folder takes up less space on the Windows 2000 or Windows XP volume. A file can be compressed or uncompressed, which determines the *compression state* of the file. If a compressed file must be accessed, a user can do so without uncompressing it first. The operating system automatically uncompresses it upon opening and then recompresses it when the work is finished. Then the file is closed.

Compressing files and folders creates more disk space. However, NTFS allocates disk space based on the uncompressed file size. When a user tries to copy a compressed file to a volume with enough space for the compressed file but not enough space for the uncompressed file, an error message appears. The message states that there is insufficient disk space to copy the file. This is because NTFS bases the file size on the uncompressed state and not the compressed state.

Compression follows the same recommendation as encryption. Compress the folder first, and then add files to it. Right-click the folder or file in Windows Explorer to set the compression state of a folder or file. Click **Properties** from the menu that appears, and click the **Advanced** button. In the Advanced Attributes dialog box, select the **Compress contents to save disk space** check box. Click the **OK** button, and then click the **Apply** button in the Properties dialog box. Compression is less important today because drives are increasing in size and cost less to buy.

Windows 2000 Boot Process

The Windows 2000 boot process uses more files and steps than the Windows 9x boot process. This is because of added security and logon features. Many of the features that are supported in Windows 98, such as specific device drivers or VxDs, are not supported by the Windows NT and Windows 2000 operating systems. A VxD is a type of device driver that has direct access to the operating system kernel. This allows the driver to interact with system and hardware resources at a very low level, without limiting system resources.

NOTE

A folder or file can be either compressed or encrypted, but not both.

NOTE

This chapter refers to a boot process that is on an Intel-based system. The boot process is different for non-Intel-based systems because the NTLDR is not needed. On these systems, a file called OSLOADER.EXE performs this function. The NTDETECT.COM file is also unnecessary in non-Intel-based systems because this function is performed during the POST. The information that is gathered from the POST is given to NTOSKRNL.EXE through OSLOADER.EXE. Intel-based and non-Intel-based systems boot the same way from this point forward.

Windows 2000 goes through a series of steps as it boots the computer. The details of the boot process are not important if everything works properly. However, understanding how the boot process works is helpful when troubleshooting boot problems. The Windows 2000 boot process occurs in the following five stages:

1. The preboot sequence

2. The boot sequence

3. The kernel load

4. The kernel initialization

5. The logon process

Knowledge of the stages of the boot process and its supporting files helps to effectively troubleshoot problems with the operating system.

Before looking at the details of the boot process, examine the files that are required to complete a successful boot and see where they are located. Table 6-8 reviews the files that are used in the Windows 2000 boot process.

Table 6-8 Windows 2000 Boot Files

Boot File	Location
NTLDR	Root directory of the active partition (C:\)
BOOT.INI	Root directory of the active partition (C:\)
BOOTSECT.DOS (only if dual-booting)	Root directory of the active partition (C:\)
NTDETECT.COM	Root directory of the active partition (C:\)
NTBOOTDD.SYS	Root directory of the active partition (C:\)
NTOSKRNL.EXE	C:\Winnt\System32
HAL.DLL	C:\Winnt\System32
SYSTEM registry key	C:\Winnt\System32\Config
Device drivers	C:\Winnt\System32\Drivers

Step 1: Preboot Sequence

After the computer is powered on, the first step in the boot process is the ***power-on self-test (POST)***. Every computer performs a POST, regardless of its operating system. During the POST, a computer tests its memory and verifies that it has all the necessary hardware, such as a keyboard and mouse. After completing the POST, the computer allows other adapter cards, such as a SCSI card, to run their own POSTs. After a POST routine is complete, the computer locates a boot device and loads the *Master Boot Record (MBR)* into memory. This, in turn, locates the active partition and loads it into memory. The MBR allows programs, such as the Disk Operating System (DOS), to load into RAM. Up to this point, hardware has played an important role, because an operating system cannot load without properly functioning hardware. At this time, the computer loads and initializes the NTLDR file, which is the operating system loader, and begins to load the operating system.

Step 2: Boot Sequence

After the NTLDR loads, the boot sequence gathers information about the hardware and the drivers. NTLDR is the key component of this step. NTLDR uses the NTDETECT.COM, BOOT.INI, and BOOTSECT.DOS files. The BOOTSECT.DOS file is only used if a computer is set to dual-boot. One important function that is provided by NTLDR is the ability to switch a processor into 32-bit flat-memory mode from real mode, or the mode that 8086 and 8088 CPUs run in. Real mode is discussed in Chapter 8, "Multimedia Capabilities." Next, NTLDR starts the file system, which is FAT or NTFS, so that files from the disk can be read. NTLDR reads the BOOT.INI file to enable the on-screen display of the boot menu. The user can select which operating system to load if the computer is set to dual-boot. If an operating system other than Windows 2000 is selected, NTLDR loads the BOOTSECT.DOS file and passes control, which then boots the other operating system. If Windows 2000 is selected or if the computer is not dual-booting, NTLDR runs NTDETECT.COM, which gathers information about the computer hardware. Press **F8** at this time for troubleshooting and advanced startup options. The NTDETECT.COM utility can detect the following hardware components:

- Computer ID
- Bus/adapter type
- Keyboard
- COM ports
- Parallel ports
- Floppy disk drives
- SCSI adapters
- Mouse and other pointing devices
- Floating-point coprocessors
- Video adapters

NTDETECT.COM collects all the hardware information, whereas NTLDR loads NTOSK-RNL.EXE and passes this information.

The NTLDR loads the kernel, NTOSKRNL.EXE. The information that is collected during this process is passed to NTDETECT.COM.

Step 3: Kernel Load

The *kernel load* phase begins with NTOSKRNL.EXE loading with the HAL.DLL file. At this point, NTLDR still plays a role in the boot process. NTLDR reads the SYSTEM registry key into memory and selects the hardware configuration that is stored in the registry. The NTLDR loads the configuration that is needed for the computer to boot. During this point of the boot process, you can select which hardware profile is to be loaded if more than one hardware profile is available. NTLDR loads any device drivers with a start value of 0x0 from the registry. Now all the files are loaded into memory.

Step 4: Kernel Initialization

The kernel load phase is now complete. The kernel now begins to initialize. It recognizes everything that was previously loaded so that the NTLDR can give control to the operating system kernel. The operating system now begins the final stages of loading. The graphical user interface (GUI) displays a status bar that indicates that it is loading. Next, the following four additional steps occur:

1. **The hardware key is created**—Once the kernel completes the initialization process, information that is collected during the hardware-detection phase is used to create the registry key HKEY_LOCAL_MACHINE\HARDWARE. This key contains all the hardware information from the computer motherboard and the interrupts that are used by the hardware devices.

2. **The clone control set is created**—The kernel references the registry subkey HKEY_LOCAL_MACHINE\SYSTEM\Select and then creates a clone, or copy, of the Current Control Set value in the registry. The computer uses this clone to maintain an identical copy of the data that configures the computer. Therefore, this registry value does not reflect changes that are made during the startup process.

3. **Device drivers are loaded and initialized**—During this step, the kernel initializes the low-level device drivers that were added in the kernel load phase of the boot process. Now the kernel must scan the following registry subkey for device drivers with a value of 0x1:

   HKEY_LOCAL_MACHINE\SYSTEM\CurrentControlSet\Services

   This value indicates at which point in the process a driver loads. This is also true for a device driver value in the kernel load phase.

NOTE

The 0x in front of a number indicates that it is a hexadecimal number. See Chapter 1, "Information Technology Basics," for more information.

4. **Services are started**—The final step is starting the Session Manager. The Session Manager starts when the SMSS.EXE file loads. The Session Manager is responsible for loading the programs in its BootExecute Registry entry. The Session Manager also loads the required subsystems, which start the WINLOGON.EXE file. This file starts the Local Security Administration (LSASS.EXE) file, and the Ctrl-Alt-Delete window appears. The Service Controller (SCREG.EXE) checks the registry for services with a start value of 0x2 and then loads them. Services with start values of 0x3 start manually. Services with start values of 0x4 are disabled.

Step 5: Logon

The final step in the bootup process begins with the *logon* screen. A bootup is not successful or complete until a user logs on. Once a user logs on, the clone of the Current Control Set value from Step 4 is copied to the Last Known Good control set value in the registry. This is a safety measure so that a user can reboot the computer if a problem arises. For example, a bad device driver might load so that a user cannot log on. Select the Last Known Good control set during startup to load the last successful boot configuration that was saved without the bad device driver. This allows the user to log on.

Plug and Play Drivers

The ability to add many devices to modern computers has become increasingly easier with the advances made in Plug and Play technology. Figure 6-2 shows Windows searching for new Plug and Play hardware. An administrator must handle resource conflicts that result from the many nonstandard devices. Dealing with these issues can be confusing and time consuming. The Plug and Play specification, which is also called PnP, was developed to resolve this ongoing problem. The goal of *Plug and Play* is to create a computer whose hardware and software work together to automatically configure devices and assign resources. Another aim of this technology is to allow hardware to be changed without large-scale resource assignment tweaking. The goal is to be able to plug in a new device and immediately use it without a complicated setup. The plug-and-play concept was first introduced with the Windows 95 operating system. Plug and Play technology has advanced a great deal with the latest operating system releases. However, Windows NT 4.0 does not support Plug and Play. Only Windows XP, Windows 2000, Windows Me, Windows 98, Windows 95 OSR2, and Windows 95 support this feature.

Figure 6-2 New Hardware Detection

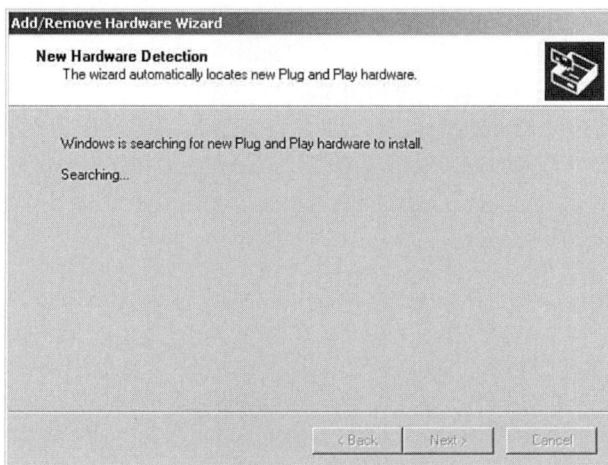

Drivers

Device drivers are programs that tell an operating system how to control specific devices. They act as a communication interface between the operating system and the device so that the two can recognize each other. The Windows 2000 and Windows XP operating systems come with a large driver database already installed. This simplifies the installation of non-standard devices. This preloaded database also simplifies the use of Plug and Play capabilities. For example, if a device or expansion card is attached to the computer and the operating system already has the required driver in its database, the system automatically installs the card without further configuration from the user. Windows 98 also comes with this driver database installed. The latest Microsoft operating system releases contain the most recent drivers and the updated drivers for the new operating systems.

System Tools

The network administrator uses system tools to maintain the network. This includes setting up local users and managing disk storage space. A crucial part of the system is the registry. You should understand the six main components that access the registry and store data. In addition, troubleshooting and recovery tasks require the administrator to use safe mode and to use the Recovery Console to diagnose the operating system. This section includes the following topics:

- Administrative tools
- Windows 2000 registry

- Startup menu and safe mode
- ERD and Recovery Console for Windows 2000

Administrative Tools

The *Administrative Tools* utility is a feature that is unique to the Windows NT, Windows 2000, and Windows XP operating systems. This powerful system tool enables an administrator to control almost everything that is related to the local computer. Logon permissions can be controlled from this utility by creating local user accounts. The Disk Management utility allows an administrator to control and manipulate computer hard drives. A Services tab is available to start or stop any programs that are running on the computer. This feature is helpful when troubleshooting problems with the system. One of the main features of the Windows NT, Windows 2000, and Windows XP environments is security. The Administrative Tools utility includes a Local Security Policy utility that enables an administrator to choose additional security options. These options allow control over user rights and audit policies to control the local environment.

Local Users

A local user does not exist in the Windows 9*x* environment. Anyone who turns on the computer has access to it. You cannot track who uses the computer or who is allowed to use the computer. This might be fine for some users if they are in an environment where limited access is not a problem. The logon process must be very secure because the target market of the Windows NT, Windows 2000, and Windows XP operating systems is the corporate business community. Therefore, local users were created to be the only people who can successfully log on to the computer.

A local user account must first be created on a local computer before a user can log on. This allows the administrator to allow only authorized users to log on. This procedure only works on computers that are not part of a domain. *Local user* accounts allow access to resources only on the computer where they are created. An account is created in a specific security database. It does not replicate the local user account information to any other networked computer.

Disk Management

An administrator must maintain and manage hard drive storage for user Desktops and servers. The administrator must know how to properly manage storage space in the Windows NT, Windows 2000, and Windows XP operating system environments. Proper *disk management* enables administrators to keep hard drives in the best working condition and maximizes them for optimal free space. For example, free space on the hard disk must be partitioned and formatted to store data on that part of the disk. If more than one hard disk is active, each disk must be partitioned and formatted so that it can store data. Setting up a new hard disk or the remaining free space on a hard disk involves tasks that an administrator needs to understand. To access disk management, right-click **My Computer** and select **Manage** from the menu that appears, as shown in Figure 6-3.

Figure 6-3 Accessing Computer Management

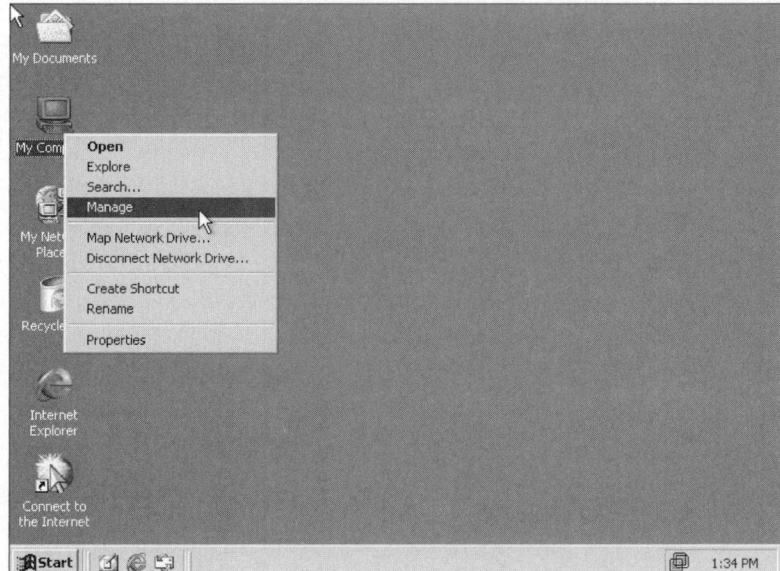

The two types of disks that are available in Windows 2000 and XP are basic disks and dynamic disks. A system with one disk needs to be either basic or dynamic, because both types cannot be used on the same physical hard disk. However, one can be basic and the other can be dynamic if the system has more than one hard disk.

Basic Disks

A *basic disk* is a physical disk that contains primary partitions, extended partitions, or logical drives. Basic disks can also contain the following partitions:

- Spanned volumes, or volume sets
- Mirrored volumes, or mirror sets
- Striped volumes, or stripe sets
- Redundant Array of Inexpensive Disks (RAID)–5 volumes, or stripe sets with parity

RAID is discussed in Chapter 9, "Advanced Hardware Fundamentals for Servers." A basic disk can contain up to four primary partitions, or up to three primary partitions and one extended partition for a maximum of four partitions.

The operating system treats these partitions on a single hard drive as separate drives, depending on how many partitions exist. A basic disk can contain primary partitions, extended partitions, and logical drives. If a second hard disk is added to the system, the computer recognizes it first as a basic disk. Basic disk is the default identity in Windows 2000 and Windows XP. All new disks that are added are considered to be basic disks until they are converted to dynamic disks. *Basic disk storage* is referred to as the industry standard. All versions of Microsoft Windows, MS-DOS, Windows NT, Windows 2000, and Windows XP support basic storage. Figure 6-4 describes a basic disk in Windows 2000 Disk Management.

Figure 6-4 Basic Disk in Computer Management

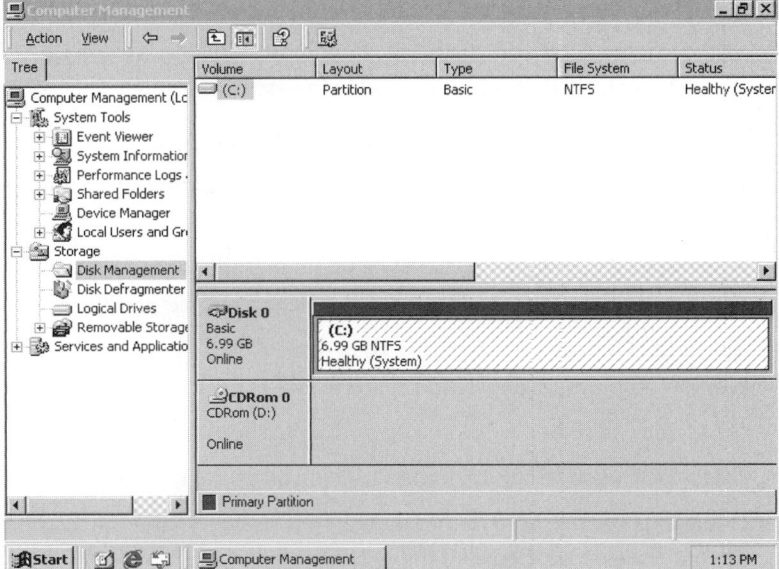

Dynamic Disks

An operating system does not need the Disk Management tool to support basic disks. Basic disk storage was the standard for all the Windows operating systems that existed before Windows NT, Windows 2000, and Windows XP. Basic disk storage is no longer efficient when dealing with the large hard drives that businesses use today.

One of the main reasons to have a disk-management tool is to be able to use multidisk volumes. Multidisk volumes are referred to as hard disk space when using *dynamic disk storage*. This is because the hard drives are not treated as one complete disk divided by partitions, but as multidisk volumes. These multidisk volumes consist of many disks. Drives can span different disks to combine areas of unallocated space more efficiently. Multidisk volumes improve disk performance by allowing more than one hard drive to read and write data. The main difference between basic and dynamic disks is that dynamic disk volumes can be worked on while an operating system is running. This makes dynamic disk management easier than creating partitions. Multidisk volumes allow the use of RAID-5 technology to make volumes fault tolerant. Dynamic disks must be used for any of these multidisk structures in Windows 2000. The Windows 2000 Professional Edition does not support the mirrored and RAID-5 fault-tolerant volumes. Only the Windows 2000 Server Edition supports these types of volumes.

Dynamic Disk Volumes

An administrator can use the Upgrade to Dynamic Disk command to convert a basic disk to a dynamic disk. He or she then decides which type of volume to create. The process of upgrading a basic disk to a dynamic disk involves the following steps:

NOTE

A dynamic disk cannot be returned to a basic disk once an upgrade is complete unless all volumes are deleted from the dynamic disk. All data on a deleted volume will be lost.

Step 1   Open the Computer Management window, as shown in Figure 6-5.

Step 2   Expand the Storage folder, and select **Disk Management**, as shown in Figure 6-6.

Step 3   Right-click the disk that needs to be upgraded. Figure 6-7 shows the options that display. Be sure to right-click the disk and not the partition.

Step 4   Select the **Upgrade to Dynamic Disk** option. The Upgrade to Dynamic Disk window displays, as shown in Figure 6-8.

Step 5   Select the disk that needs to be upgraded, as shown in Figure 6-9.

Step 6   Click the **Upgrade** button. Figure 6-10 displays the next confirmation screen.

Step 7   Click the **OK** button to reboot and complete the dynamic disk upgrade. Figure 6-11 shows the Confirm dialog box.

Step 8   Open the Computer Management window to confirm that the disk was upgraded after the system reboots. Figure 6-12 shows the upgraded disk.

Figure 6-5 The Computer Management Window

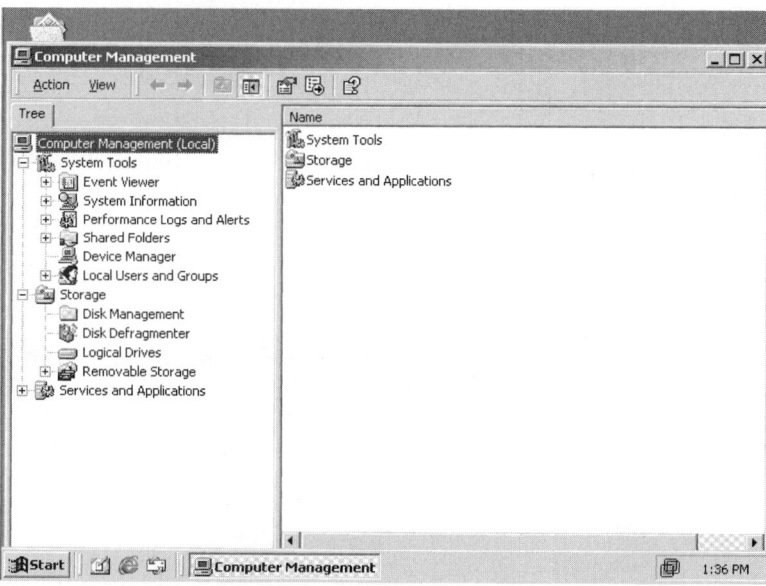

Figure 6-6 Select Disk Management

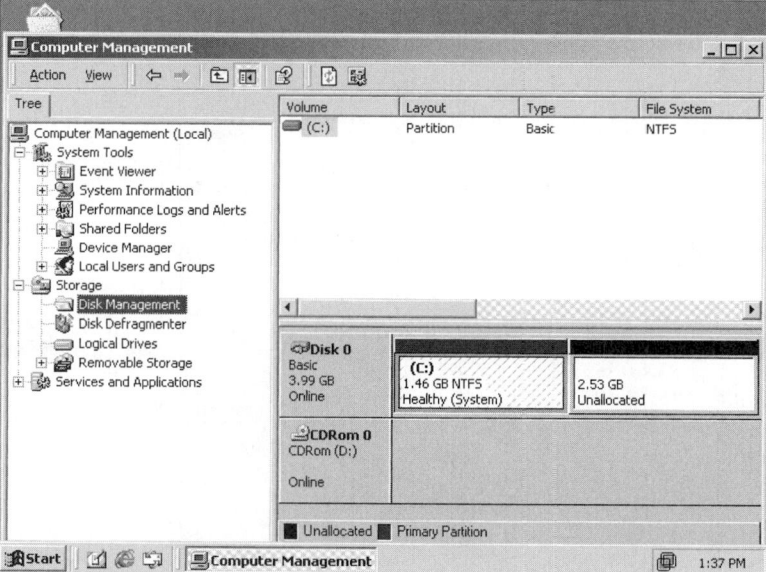

Figure 6-7 Select the Option to Upgrade

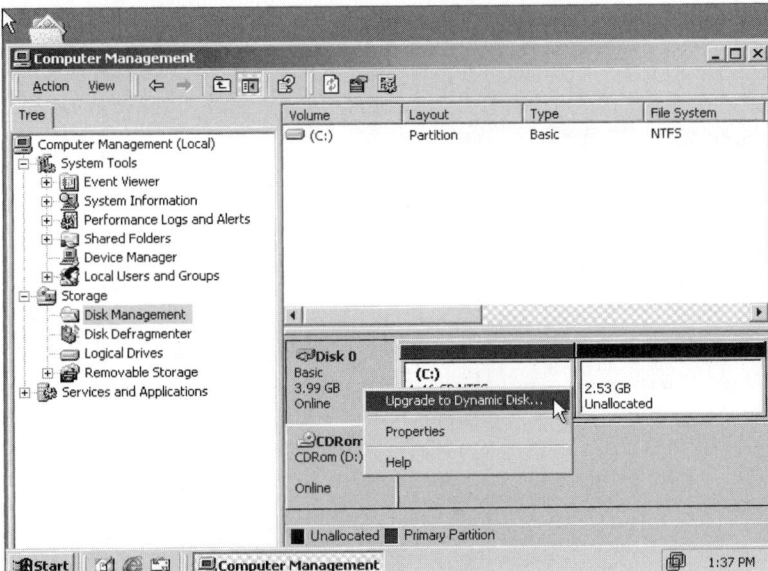

Figure 6-8 Upgrade to Dynamici Dialog Box

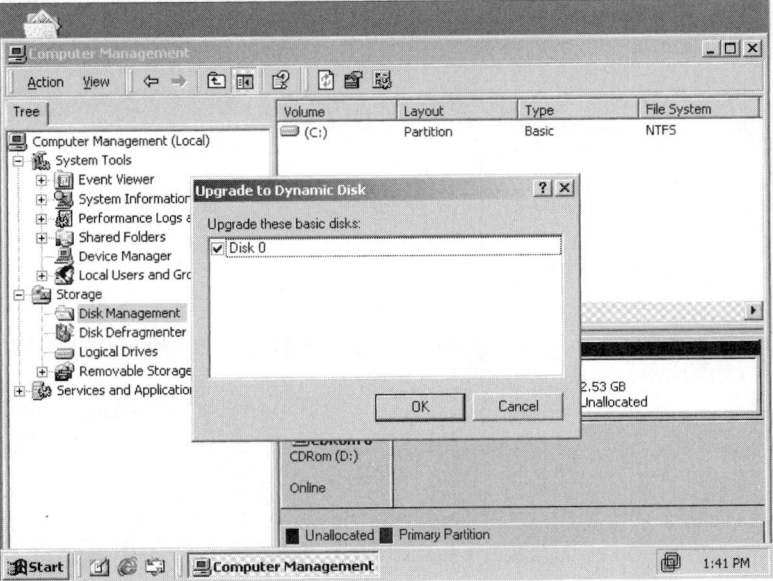

Figure 6-9 Select the Disk to Upgrade

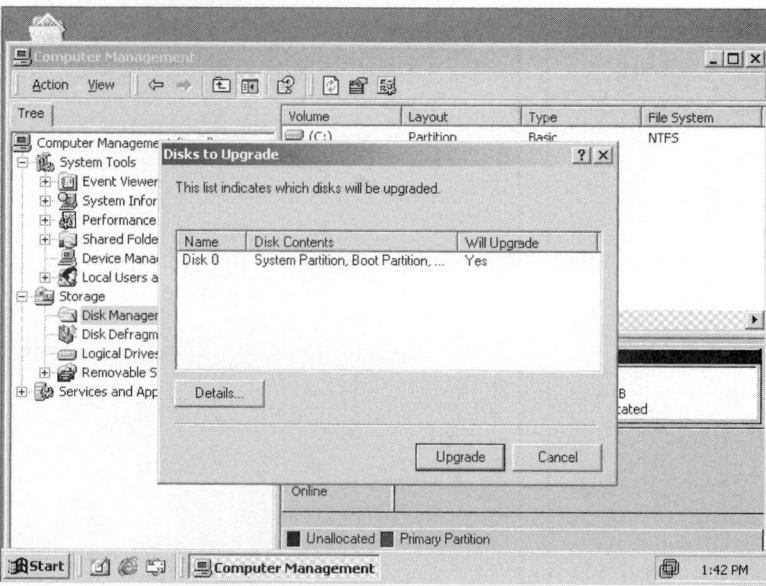

Figure 6-10 Confirm the Upgrade

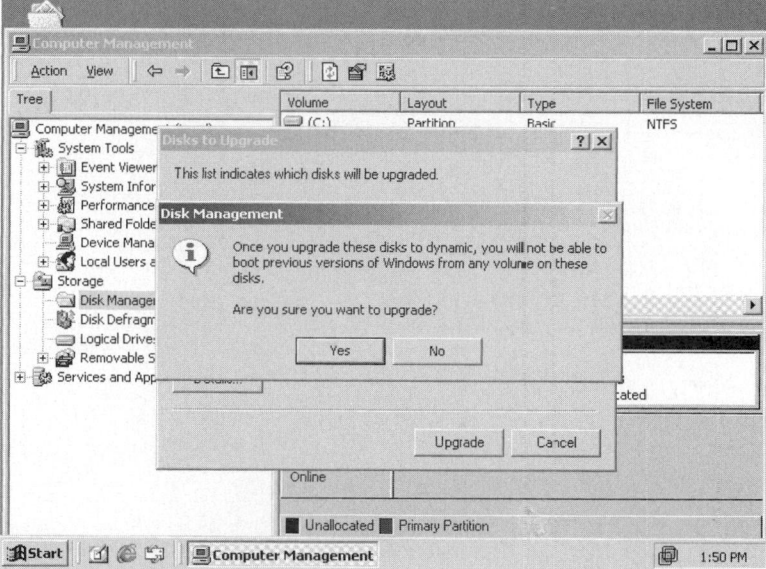

Figure 6-11 Reboot to Complete the Upgrade

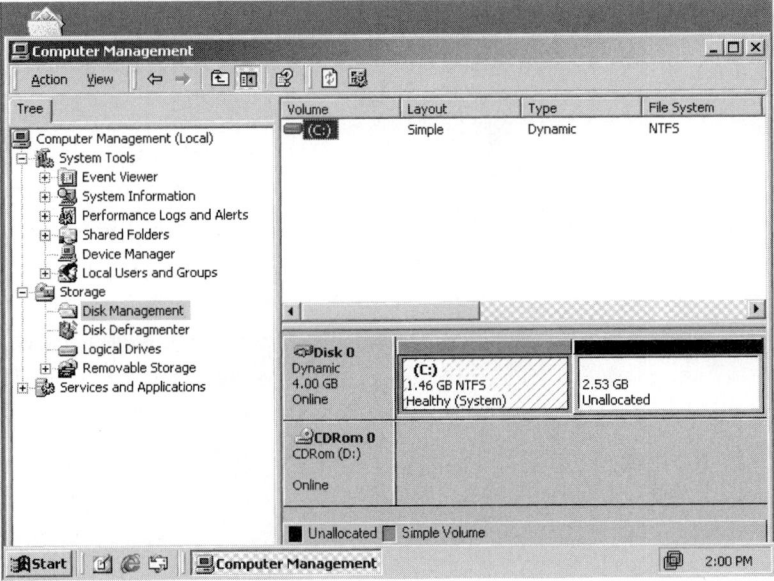

Figure 6-12 Basic Disk Is Converted to a Dynamic Disk

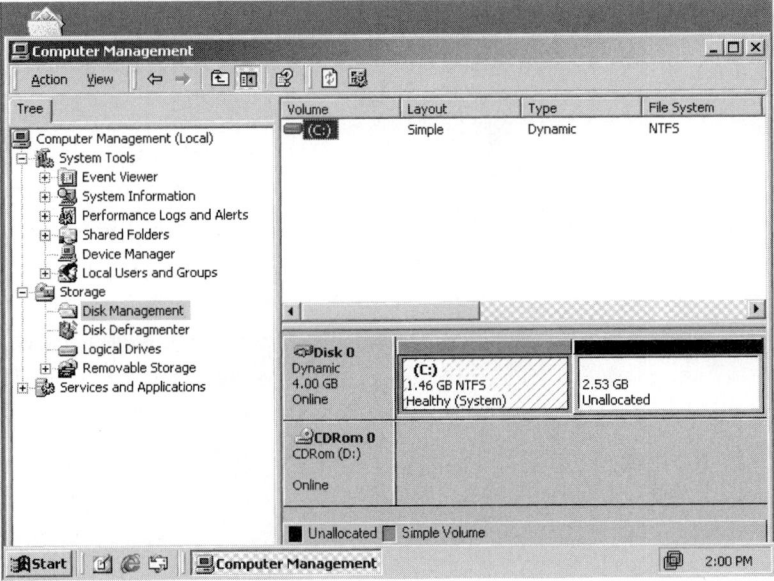

The type of volume that is created depends on the need for storage space. It also depends on how crucial the data is and whether those volumes need to have a backup plan in case they fail.

The three types of volumes that can be created with Windows 2000 Professional are simple, striped, and spanned, as described in the following list:

- *Simple volume*—This volume acts as a basic disk that contains disk space from a complete single disk. It is not fault tolerant.

- *Spanned volume*—This volume includes disk space from multiple disks. Up to 32 disks can be used in a spanned volume. In a spanned volume, the operating system writes data to the first disk until it runs out of space. Then the operating system continues to write data to the proceeding disks for as many disks as are included in the volume. A spanned volume is not fault tolerant. If one disk in a spanned volume fails, the data in the entire volume is lost.

- *Striped volume*—A striped volume, also known as RAID-0, combines areas of free space from up to 32 multiple hard disks into one logical volume. This volume optimizes performance by allowing data to be written to all the disks at the same rate. This volume is also not fault tolerant, so if one disk in the volume fails, all the data is lost.

The types of volumes that can only be created with the Windows 2000 Server operating system are mirrored and RAID-5 volumes, which are described as follows:

- *Mirrored volume*—This volume contains two identical copies of a simple volume that stores the same data on two separate hard drives. Mirrored volumes provide fault tolerance in the event of a hard disk failure. If one disk fails, a new one can replace it. All the data is backed up on the other disk.

- *RAID-5 volume*—A RAID-5 volume consists of three or more parts of one or more drives. It can also consist of three or more entire drives. Users can have up to 32 hard disks. Data is written to all the drives in this volume in equal amounts to improve performance. Each drive contains parity information, which holds copies of the data that is being written to the other two disks. This enables fault tolerance because if one of the drives fails, the remaining two disks can re-create the data automatically without shutting down the server. The data is restored to the new drive when the failed drive is replaced. This is known as *striping with parity*. RAID is discussed in detail in Chapter 9.

The Services section of the Administrative Tools utility is useful for troubleshooting problems with the computer. The Services tab lists all the services that are running on a computer. It allows an administrator to start or stop services that are running. For example, if files are being copied from one computer to another or from a hard drive, and an antivirus program is installed on one system, the Services function can be used to stop the antivirus program temporarily. Files can be copied faster because they do not need to be scanned by the antivirus program. Once the files are copied, the antivirus program should be restarted.

Local Security Policy

The *Local Security Policy* is a function of the Administrative Tools utility that allows the administrator to select additional security options. Almost 40 security options are available to increase the effective security on a computer, as shown in Figure 6-13. One option is to set the number of days before a user is prompted to change his password. Double-click **Prompt user to change password before expiration**. Figure 6-14 depicts the window that displays. The administrator can increase or decrease the number of days before the system prompts a user to change a password. Domain-level policies override local security policies.

Figure 6-13 Local Security Policy

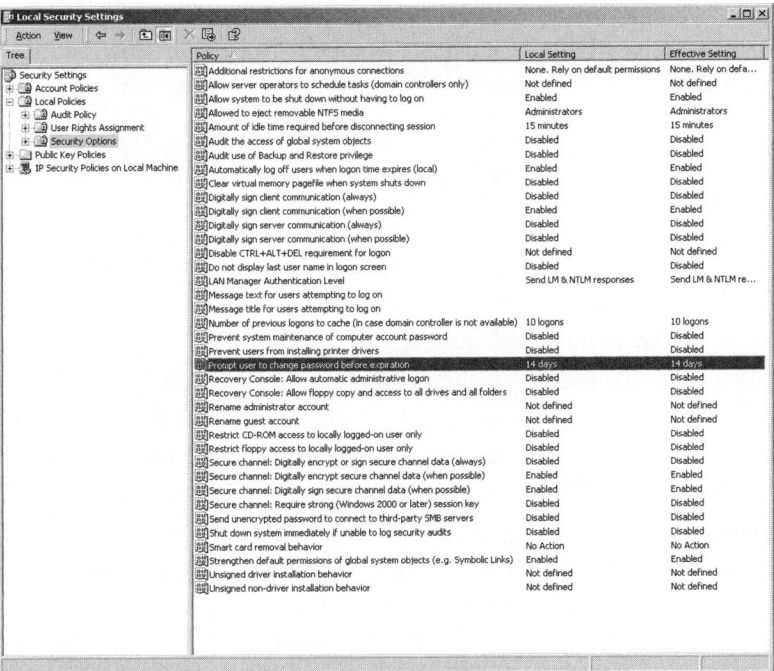

Figure 6-14 Local Security Policy Setting

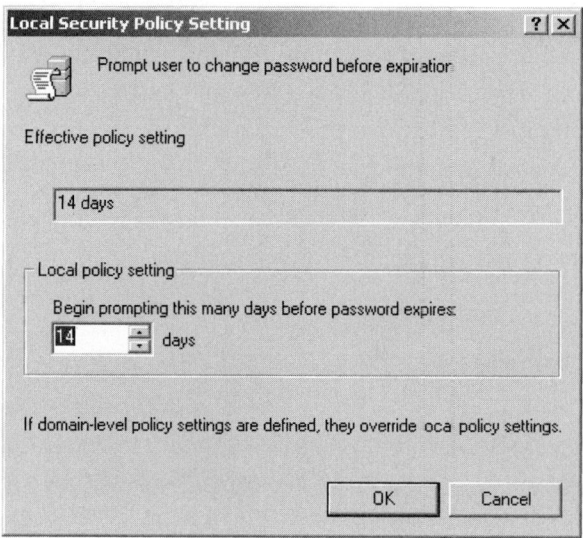

The lab activities for this section require a system that runs Windows 2000 with NTFS to perform the following tasks:

- Assign permissions
- Create user accounts
- Create an Emergency Repair Disk

Lab 6.2.1a   Creating User Accounts in Windows 2000

In this lab, you create users and groups and assign the necessary properties.

Lab 6.2.1b   Assigning Permissions in Windows 2000

In this lab, you create a folder and assign the proper permissions.

Windows 2000 Registry

Microsoft Windows 2000 centrally stores hardware and software settings in a hierarchical database called the registry. The registry for the Windows 2000 and Windows XP operating system replaces many of the .INI, .SYS, and .COM files that are used in earlier versions of Windows. The registry acts as a backbone to the operating system and provides appropriate initialization information to start applications. It loads components such as device drivers and network protocols.

The Registry Editor, as shown in Figure 6-15, accesses the Windows 2000 registry.

Figure 6-15 Windows 2000 Registry Editor

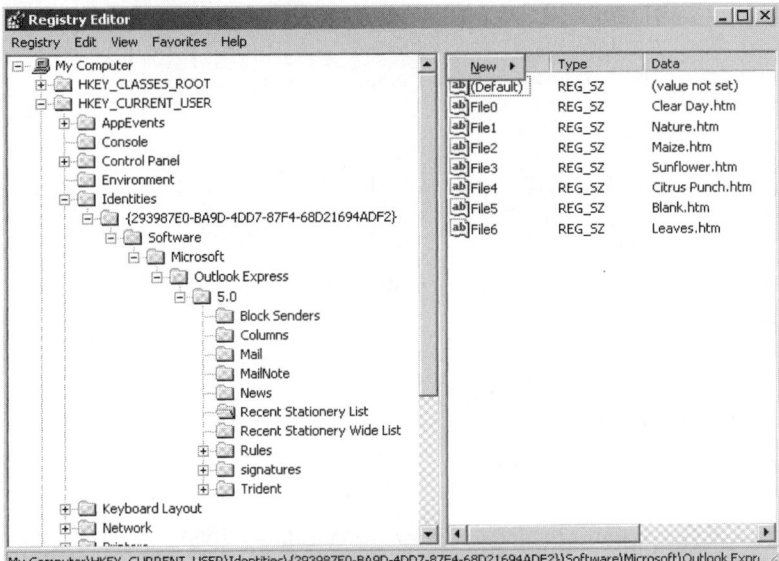

Purpose of the Registry

The purpose of the registry is to maintain a database of configuration settings in Windows 95, Windows 98, Windows NT, and Windows 2000. The main component of the registry is the hardware that is installed on the computer. This includes the CPU, bus type, pointing device or mouse, and keyboard. It also includes device drivers, installed applications, and network adapter card settings. The registry contains a vast amount of data and is critical to how a system operates. The structure of the registry is designed to provide a secure set of records about the components that control the operating system. These components read, update, and modify data that is stored in the registry. Six main components access the registry and store data, as described in the following list:

- *Device drivers* — The registry sets the configuration settings for the system's device drivers. Information is written to the registry when device drivers are updated or referenced.
- *Setup programs* — A setup program adds new configuration data to the registry when new hardware and applications are installed. The setup programs also attempt to scan the registry to verify that components are installed.
- *User profiles* — Windows NT, Windows 2000, and Windows XP create user profiles that maintain all the settings for the users who log on to the computer. These settings are first changed in the registry and then updated in the user profile. The name of the file that holds the user profile information is NTUSER.DAT.
- *Windows NT kernel* — The registry plays an important role during the boot process. The Windows NT kernel, or the NTOSKRNL.EXE file, loads the correct device drivers in the proper order.
- *NTDETECT.COM* — The NTDETECT.COM file and its role in the boot process are explained in the section "Windows 2000 Boot Process," earlier in this chapter. Only Intel-based systems use this file to detect hardware and to store the data that is collected during this process.
- *Hardware profiles* — Windows NT, Windows 2000, and Windows XP can save two or more profiles in which an administrator can control whether a piece of hardware loads. The registry stores these hardware profile configurations.

Registry Subtrees

The registry can be navigated and edited manually by using REGEDT32.EXE. When this command is typed at the command prompt, an interface displays that searches all the values in the Registry Subtrees window. An example of a *registry subtree* is shown in Figure 6-16.

Figure 6-16 Windows Registry Subtree

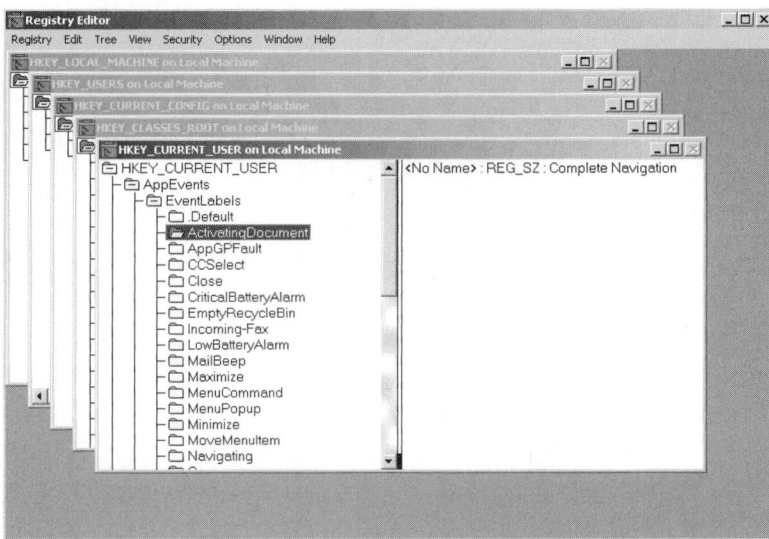

Familiarity with these subtrees and their purposes helps with troubleshooting. A key for every process that is running on a system is found here. The following five subtrees, which contain the subtree keys, display in the Registry Editor window, as follows:

■ *HKEY_USERS*—This subtree contains the system default settings that control individual user profiles and environments, such as the Desktop settings, the Windows environment, and the custom software settings. Figure 6-17 shows an example of the HKEY_USERS screen.

Figure 6-17 HKEY_USERS Screen

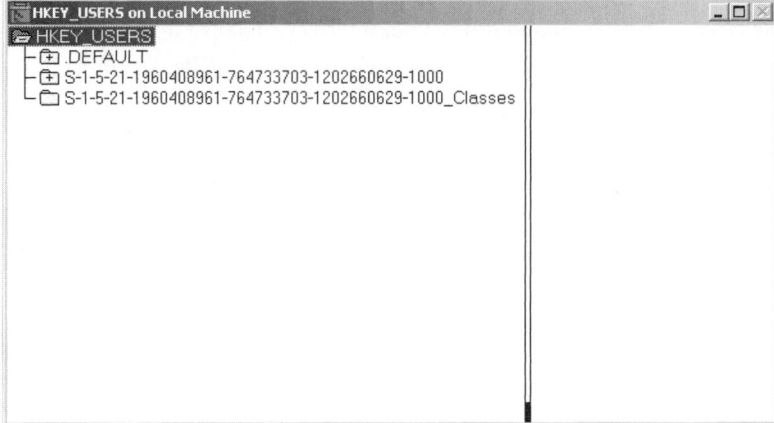

- ***HKEY_CURRENT_CONFIG***—This subtree contains data on the active hardware profile that is selected during the boot process. This information is used to configure settings
  such as which device drivers to load and which display resolution to use. Figure 6-18
  shows an example of the HKEY_CURRENT_CONFIG screen.

Figure 6-18 HKEY_CURRENT_CONFIG Screen

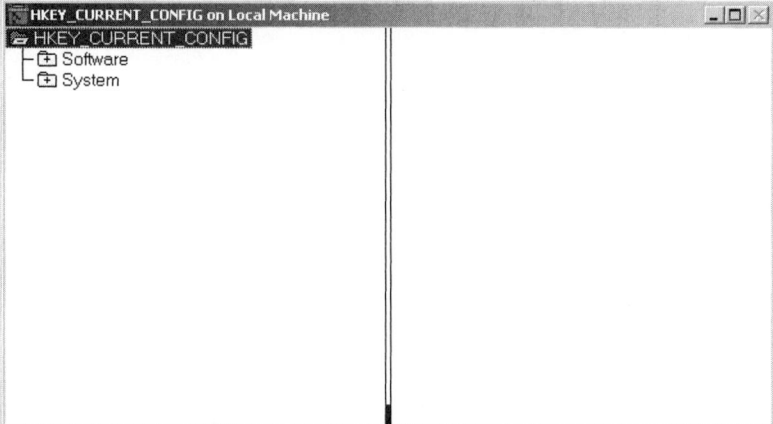

- ***HKEY_CLASSES_ROOT***—This subtree contains the configuration data of all the software that is installed on the computer. Figure 6-19 shows an example of the HKEY_
  CLASSES_ROOT screen.

Figure 6-19 HKEY_CLASSES_ROOT Screen

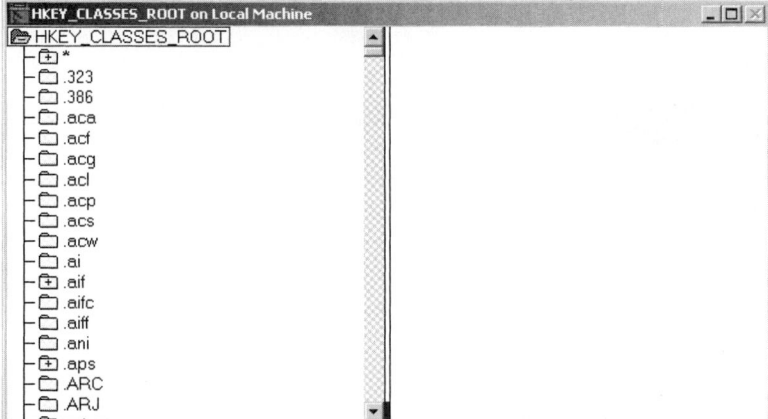

■ *HKEY_CURRENT_USER*—This subtree contains data about the user that is currently logged on to the computer. This key retrieves a copy of each user account that can log on to the computer and stores it in the registry. Figure 6-20 shows an example of the HKEY_CURRENT_USER screen.

Figure 6-20 HKEY_CURRENT_USER Screen

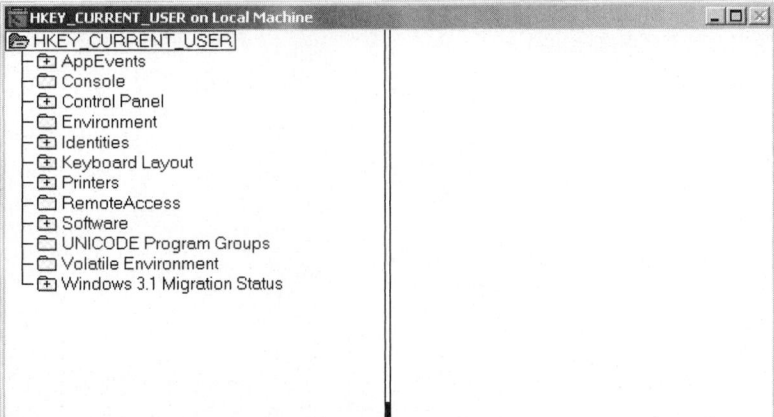

■ *HKEY_LOCAL_MACHINE*—This subtree contains all the configuration data for the local computer, including hardware and operating system data, such as bus type, system memory, device drivers, and startup control data. Applications, device drivers, and the operating system use this data to set the computer configuration. The data in this subtree remains constant regardless of the user. Figure 6-21 shows an example of the HKEY_LOCAL_MACHINE screen.

Figure 6-21 HKEY_LOCAL_MACHINE Screen

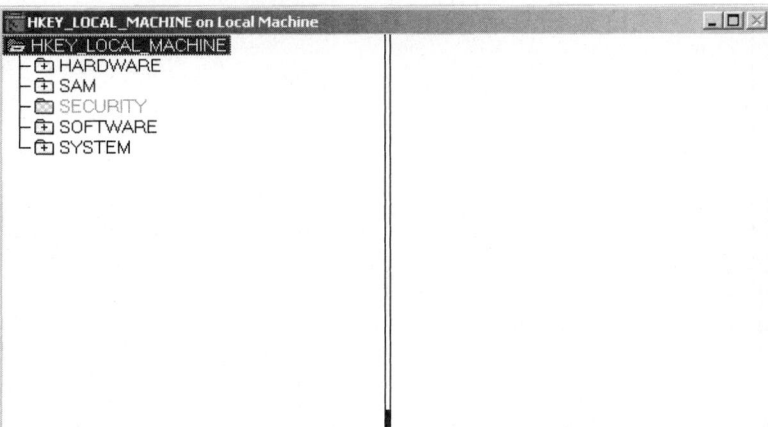

Startup Menu and Safe Mode

The Windows NT, Windows 2000, and Windows XP operating system *Startup menus* are security features that are not found in the Windows 9x operating system environment. The Windows NT, Windows 2000, and Windows XP operating systems must go through a multi-step process to get to the Startup menu.

An advanced startup feature for troubleshooting is safe mode startup. Use this advanced startup option if a computer does not start normally. Enter safe mode by pressing F8 during the operating system selection phase. This displays a screen with advanced options for booting Windows 2000, as shown in Figure 6-22. *Safe mode* loads and uses only basic files and drivers, including the mouse, VGA monitor, keyboard, mass storage, and default system services, and no network connections, which is similar to the Windows 9x safe mode. With Windows 2000, it is easy to recognize the safe mode state because the background becomes black and the words "Safe Mode" appear in each corner of the screen.

Figure 6-22 Windows 98 Startup Menu

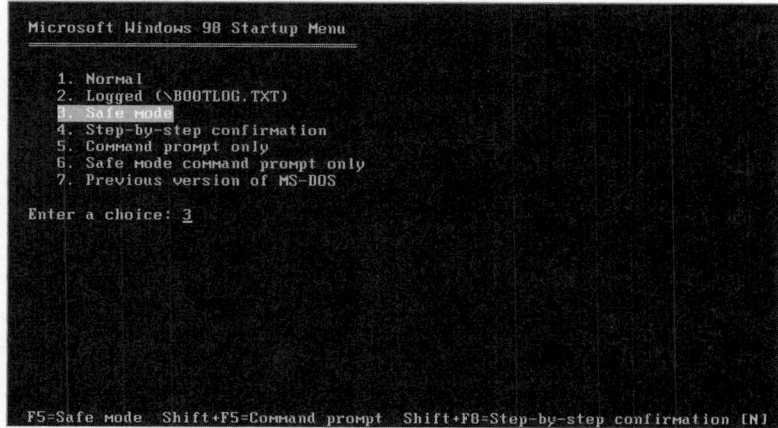

Press **F8** to view a selection of safe mode options. Figure 6-23 reviews the options that are available when using the Safe Mode startup feature. One of these options is Safe Mode with Networking, which is identical to Safe Mode, except that it adds the drivers and services that are required for networking when the computer restarts. Another option is Safe Mode with Command Prompt, which is the same as Safe Mode, except that when the computer restarts, a command prompt displays.

Figure 6-23 Booting into Safe Mode in Windows 2000

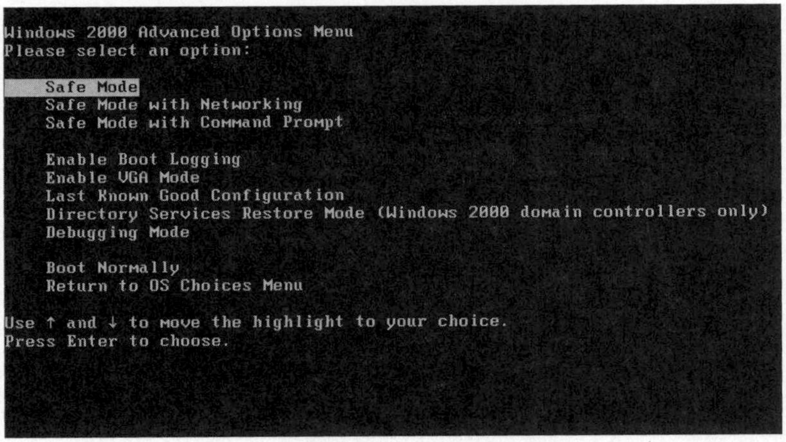

```
Windows 2000 Advanced Options Menu
Please select an option:

   Safe Mode
   Safe Mode with Networking
   Safe Mode with Command Prompt

   Enable Boot Logging
   Enable VGA Mode
   Last Known Good Configuration
   Directory Services Restore Mode (Windows 2000 domain controllers only)
   Debugging Mode

   Boot Normally
   Return to OS Choices Menu

Use ↑ and ↓ to move the highlight to your choice.
Press Enter to choose.
```

The ERD and Recovery Console for Windows 2000

A systems administrator can encounter computers with corrupted operating systems that cannot function or boot up. Sometimes a critical file or program was deleted or changed so that the operating system no longer recognizes it. Therefore, the system no longer works. In Windows 2000, an Emergency Repair Disk (ERD) can be created or the Recovery Console feature can be used. These options repair files or copy new files that have been damaged to avoid reformatting the hard drive and losing valuable data.

Emergency Repair Disk

The *Emergency Repair Disk (ERD)* allows the reinstallation of any service packs that were loaded since the original installation. The ERD also copies files from the CD and overwrites the corrupted files. An ERD can provide a solution if a file system becomes corrupt and cannot start. If a service pack was applied since the original installation, it must be reapplied. This is because the copied files are original installation files taken from the Windows CD.

Creating an ERD

To create an ERD, follow these steps:

Step 1   Choose **Start**, **Programs**, **Accessories**, **System Tools**, **Backup** to run the Backup program. The Windows 2000 Backup and Recovery Tools are displayed in Figure 6-24.

Figure 6-24 Windows 2000 Backup and Recovery Tools

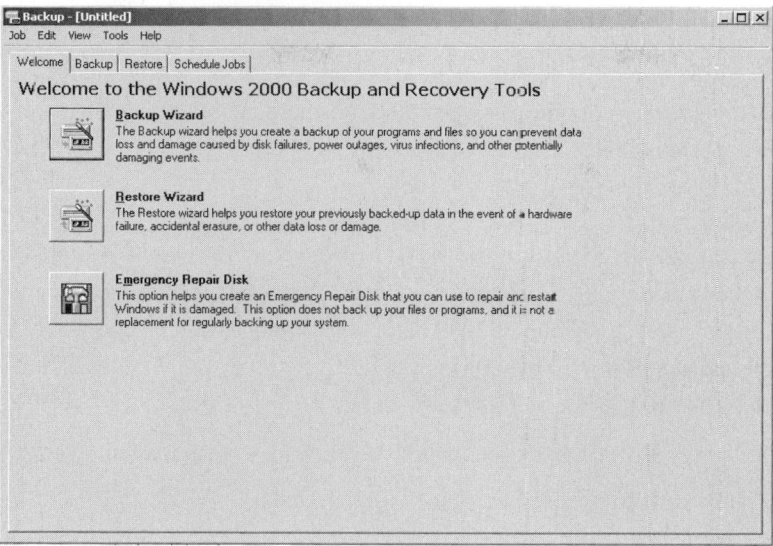

Step 2 Click the **Emergency Repair Disk** button on the Welcome tab. The dialog box that displays is shown in Figure 6-25.

Figure 6-25 Emergency Repair Diskette Dialog Box

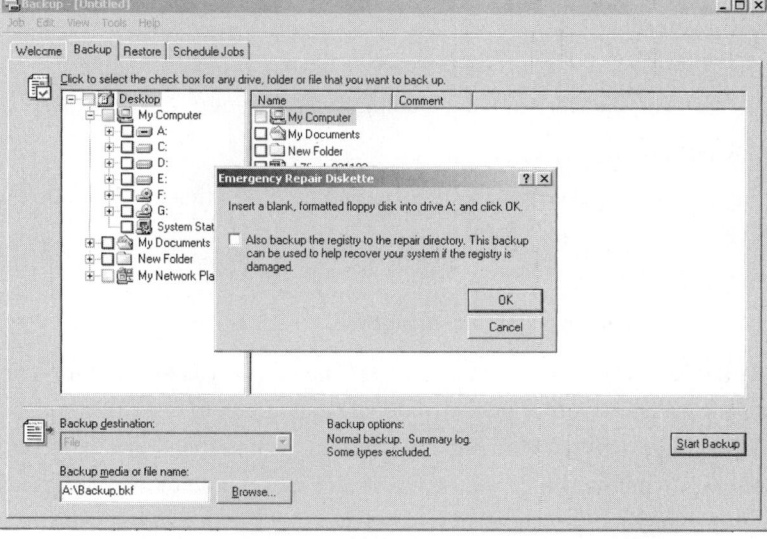

Step 3   Insert a blank, formatted 3-1/2-inch floppy disk in drive A.

Step 4   Select the **Also backup the registry to the repair directory** check box.

Step 5   Click the **OK** button.

Step 6   Remove the floppy disk and label it Emergency Repair Disk, with the current date.

Using an ERD

The emergency disk can be used in two ways. If the system supports a bootable CD-ROM drive, insert the Windows 2000 CD and boot from it. If the system does not support a bootable CD-ROM drive, insert the Windows 2000 Setup disk 1 and restart the computer. A prompt for Setup disk 2 appears, followed by a prompt to insert Setup disk 3. The steps to use an ERD with a CD or a floppy disk are as follows:

Step 1   Press **Enter** when asked whether you want to install Windows 2000.

Step 2   Press **R** to use the Emergency Repair Disk.

Step 3   Press **F** to select the Fast option when presented with the choice of a Fast or Manual option.

Step 4   Press **Enter** to use the Emergency Repair Disk.

Step 5   Insert the Emergency Repair Disk, and press **Enter**.

Step 6   Reboot the operating system after the files are repaired.

Recovery Console

The Windows 2000 *Recovery Console* is a command-line interface that performs a variety of troubleshooting and recovery tasks, including the following:

- Starting and stopping services
- Reading and writing data on a local drive and on drives that are formatted with the NTFS
- Formatting hard disks
- Removing, replacing, or copying corrupt files

You can start the Recovery Console in two ways. The first way is to insert the Windows 2000 CD and wait for the Microsoft Windows 2000 CD dialog box to open. If it opens, close it. If it does not open, choose **Start**, **Run** and type **cmd** in the command line. This brings up a command-prompt window, where the administrator can switch to the drive letter of the CD-ROM drive, change to the I386 folder, and run the WINNT32 command with the CMDCONS switch. After the Recovery Console installs, it is accessible from the Please Select Operating System to Start menu. The second way to access the Recovery Console is to select the option to use the Windows 2000 setup disks.

Lab 6.2.4   Create an ERD in Windows 2000

In this lab, you create and use an ERD. This lab requires a system that is running Windows 2000 with NTFS.

Overview of the Installation Process

Windows 2000 provides additional features that are not found in Windows 9x. Although the installation process simplifies the partitioning and formatting process, it can also change the hardware requirements. Of importance is the use of the Hardware Abstraction Layer and the Client Access License. This section includes the following topics:

- Differences between Windows 2000 and 9x installation
- Hardware requirements
- Windows 2000 features

Differences Between the Windows 2000 and 9x Installation

The differences between the Windows 9x and the Windows 2000 environments exist primarily because the operating systems serve different functions. They are intended for use in different environments, and they come with different installation processes. These differences are because of the added security and file system features that are present in the Windows 2000 operating system. Figure 6-26 shows the Windows 2000 startup screen.

Figure 6-26 Windows 2000 Startup Screen

NOTE

This section refers to the system administrator more often than the technician, because Windows 2000 is more likely to be used in a networked environment. A system administrator manages the network and addresses the problems that occur.

Hardware Requirements

The major difference between the Windows 2000 and the Windows 9x installation process is the hardware requirements for the two operating systems. Windows 2000 is a more robust operating system with many more features than the Windows 9x operating system. Therefore, Windows 2000 requires hardware that is capable of handling the operating system fast enough without crashing.

The Windows 9x operating system requires an 80486DX/66-MHz system with the following requirements:

- A minimum of 16 MB RAM
- A minimum of 120–355 MB of free hard drive space
- A modem (supported but not required)
- A 16-color VGA monitor (minimum)

Windows 9x installation is more thoroughly discussed in Chapter 5, "Windows 9x Operating Systems." The hardware requirements for Windows 2000 are higher than those for Windows 9x. To successfully install Windows 2000, a computer system might require a hardware upgrade.

Partitioning and Formatting

Familiarity with *partitioning and formatting* is important when performing installations. These tasks prepare the hard drive for the operating system installation. When installing one of the Windows 9x operating systems, the hard drive must be partitioned with either the FDISK.EXE utility, as shown in Figure 6-27, or with a third-party utility like Partition Magic. After partitioning, insert the installation CD and install the operating system. Hard drive partitioning for a Windows 9x installation is discussed in Chapter 5.

Figure 6-27 FDISK Options

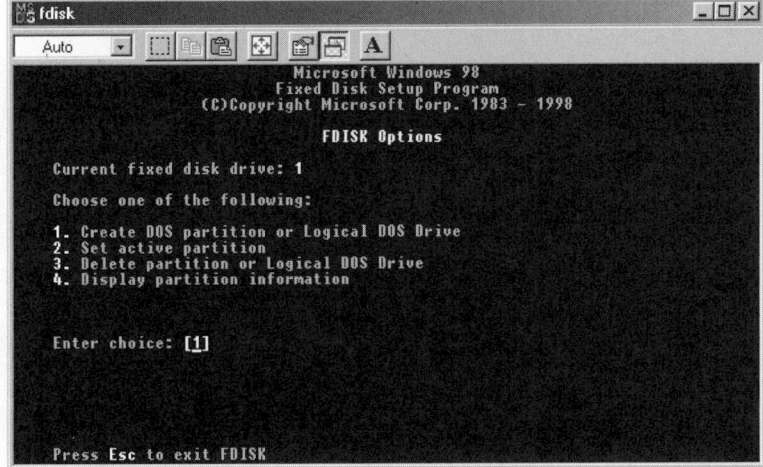

Windows 2000 provides an easy way to prepare a hard drive for the operating system installation. The administrator can use an unformatted, unpartitioned hard drive and begin installing Windows 2000. The setup process prompts the system administrator to select which partition to install the operating system on. If no partitions exist, they can be created by using the Setup program.

You are then prompted to format the partition that has just been created or to reformat the existing one. The file system that is to be used must be selected before formatting can begin. Windows 2000 can format the partition using the FAT file system or the NTFS. If the drive is formatted with a FAT file system, it can be changed to NTFS after installation is complete.

Device Drivers

Device drivers play an important role in all operating systems from Windows 9*x* to Windows 2000. A system cannot run or boot up without the proper device drivers. Windows 2000 has a definite advantage in this area. Different sets of drivers are needed, depending on the system being installed. This is because the internal structures of the two operating systems are so different. For example, a piece of hardware can be installed in a Windows 98 system, and the proper device driver can be loaded and work properly. The same piece of hardware installed in a Windows 2000 system with the same driver will not work. This is why multiple types of drivers exist for one piece of hardware.

The main advantage that Windows 2000 has, when compared to Windows 9*x*, is the ***Hardware Abstraction Layer (HAL)***. The HAL is a library of hardware drivers that function between the operating system and hardware. The HAL enables Windows 2000 to work with different types of processors from different manufacturers. This feature prevents Windows 2000 from interacting with the hardware as it does in Windows 9*x*. The HAL controls all direct access for hardware operations, thereby expanding the hardware compatibility of the system. The HAL is what distinguishes Windows 2000 as a network operating system (NOS), as compared to Windows 9*x*, which is not.

Windows 2000 Features

A few other features are unique to the Windows 2000 installation process. The computer can be added to a domain or workgroup. Only users/administrators with the appropriate rights can add a computer to an existing domain. When a computer is added to a domain, an account is created for the computer in the domain. The Client Access License (CAL) is another important feature of Windows 2000 installations. The CAL gives client computers the right to connect to computers that are running the Windows 2000 Server Edition so that network services, shared folders, and print resources are available.

Installing Windows 2000

The steps for installing Windows 2000 are detailed in this section. Although Windows 2000 provides a setup wizard, it is important for the technician to understand what happens in each step so that he can troubleshoot any errors that occur. The following topics are included:

- Requirements for installing Windows 2000
- Steps of a Windows 2000 installation
- Windows 2000 setup options

Requirements for Installing Windows 2000

Some things must be taken into account before installing Windows 2000. Check to make sure that the hardware is capable of running Windows 2000. Microsoft recommends the following requirements prior to installing the operating system:

- The computer must have at least a Pentium-class processor. Microsoft recommends a 133-MHz or higher processor.
- The system must have at least 64 MB RAM.
- The hard drive or partition where the operating system files are installed must have at least 650 MB of free space.
- The unit must have at least a VGA monitor.
- The system must have a CD-ROM drive.
- A network interface card (NIC) is required if the computer is to connect to a network.

The Microsoft *Hardware Compatibility List (HCL)* is a tool that can be used before installation to verify that your hardware will work with Windows 2000. Microsoft provides drivers for only those devices that are included on this list. The use of hardware that is not listed on the HCL might cause problems during and after installation. The HCL can be viewed by opening the HCL.TXT file in the Support folder on the Windows 2000 Professional CD, as shown in Figure 6-28.

Figure 6-28 HCL in WordPad

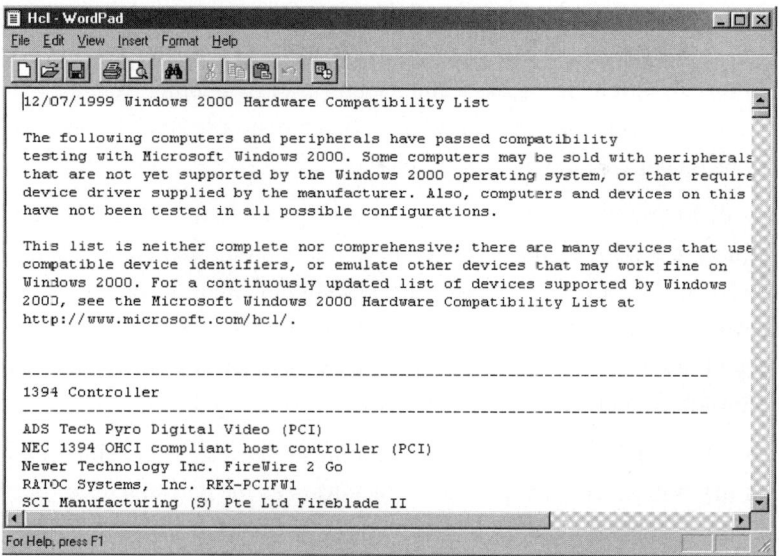

Steps of a Windows 2000 Installation

The Windows 2000 installation process contains four main steps. The installation begins when the Setup program runs. This prepares the hard disk and copies files. The Setup program then runs a wizard that provides informational pages, which are used to complete the rest of the installation. The stages of the Windows 2000 installation process are summarized in the following list:

1. Using the Setup program

2. Using the Setup Wizard

3. Installing Windows networking

4. Completing the Setup program

The Setup Program

The installation process begins by copying the files that run the Setup Wizard, which is the second step, to the hard drive. At this point, the text portion of the setup is seen. The Windows 2000 installation can start by using the Setup boot disks or by booting from the CD. Insert the first disk into the computer and power it on if the Setup boot disks are chosen. Insert the next three disks to begin copying the files.

The Windows 2000 Professional CD is easier to use. After booting from the CD, a minimal version of Windows 2000 is copied into memory; this version starts the Setup program. This is the text-based portion of the Setup program. The administrator must read and accept the licensing agreement. If necessary, a partition can be deleted to reconfigure the hard disk partitions. A new partition can be formatted or an existing partition can be reformatted; Windows 2000 is then installed on one of these partitions.

After deciding which partition to install the operating system on, select either FAT or NTFS as the type of file system. The Setup program then formats the partition according to the selected file system. Once the partition is formatted, the Setup program begins to copy the necessary files to the hard disk and saves the configuration information. Setup then automatically restarts the computer. Next, the Windows 2000 Setup Wizard starts. The Windows 2000 operating system files are installed in the C:\Winnt folder by default. Figures 6-29 through 6-33 demonstrate the steps that the Setup program performs.

Figure 6-29 Welcome to Setup Screen

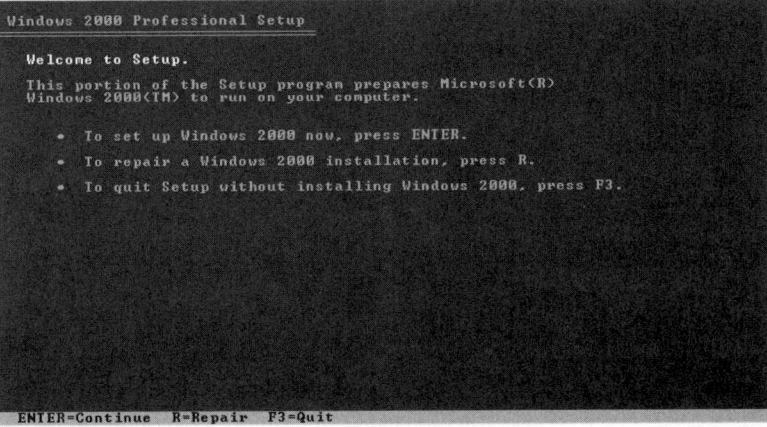

Figure 6-30 Windows 2000 Licensing Agreement

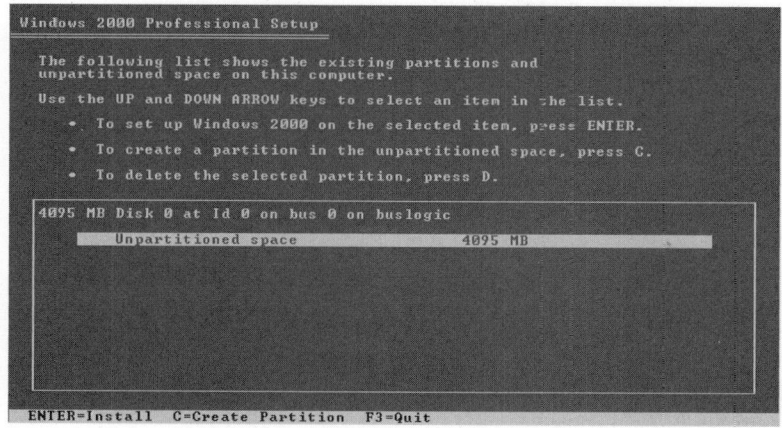

```
Windows 2000 Licensing Agreement

MICROSOFT WINDOWS 2000 PROFESSIONAL

END-USER LICENSE AGREEMENT FOR MICROSOFT
DESKTOP

OPERATING SYSTEMS

IMPORTANT-READ CAREFULLY: This End-User
License Agreement ("EULA") is a legal agreement between
you (either an individual or a single entity) and the
manufacturer ("Manufacturer") of the computer system or computer
system component ("HARDWARE") with which you acquired the
Microsoft software product(s) identified above ("SOFTWARE
PRODUCT" or "SOFTWARE"). If the SOFTWARE
PRODUCT is not accompanied by new HARDWARE, you may not use
or copy the SOFTWARE PRODUCT. The SOFTWARE
PRODUCT includes computer software, the associated media, any
printed materials, and any "online" or electronic documentation.
This EULA is valid and grants the end-user license rights ONLY if
the SOFTWARE PRODUCT is genuine and a genuine Certificate of
Authenticity for the PRODUCT SOFTWARE is provided with the
SOFTWARE PRODUCT. Any software provided along with the
SOFTWARE PRODUCT that is associated with a separate end-user
license agreement is licensed to you under the terms of that
license agreement. You agree to be bound by the terms of this
EULA by installing, copying, downloading, accessing or otherwise
using the SOFTWARE PRODUCT. If you do not agree, Manufacturer

F8=I agree   ESC=I do not agree   PAGE DOWN=Next Page
```

Figure 6-31 Partition Options

```
Windows 2000 Professional Setup

   The following list shows the existing partitions and
   unpartitioned space on this computer.

   Use the UP and DOWN ARROW keys to select an item in the list.

       •  To set up Windows 2000 on the selected item, press ENTER.

       •  To create a partition in the unpartitioned space, press C.

       •  To delete the selected partition, press D.

   4095 MB Disk 0 at Id 0 on bus 0 on buslogic

          Unpartitioned space                  4095 MB

ENTER=Install   C=Create Partition   F3=Quit
```

Figure 6-32 Formatting the Partition

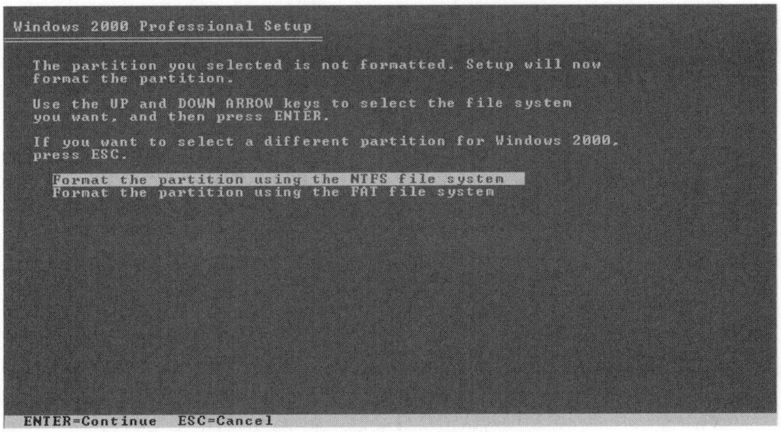

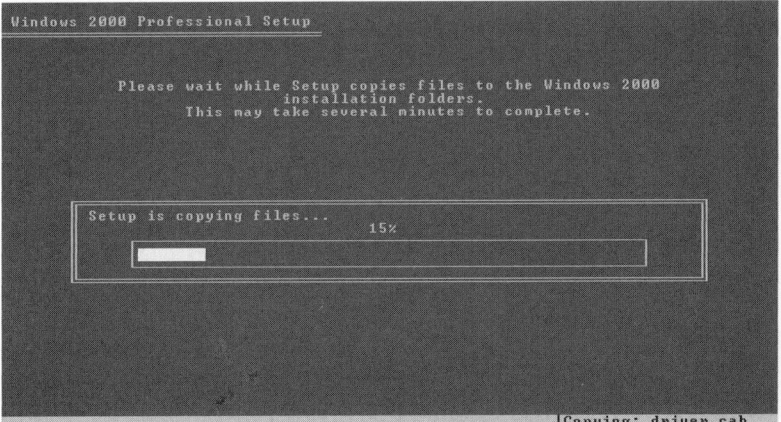

Figure 6-33 Setup Program Copies the Files

The Setup Wizard

The Setup Wizard prompts the administrator through the second stage of the installation process. It gathers information about the administrator, the organization, and the computer. It also installs some security features and configures the system devices. The wizard then prompts the administrator for the following information:

- **Regional settings**—Windows 2000 is designed to be a global operating system. Information that customizes language, locale, and keyboard settings must be entered. Windows 2000 can configure multiple languages and regional settings.

- **Name and organization**—The name of the person who is going to use this computer and the name of the organization to which this copy of Windows 2000 Professional is licensed must be entered.

- **Product key**—Microsoft ships every copy of Windows 2000 with a unique 25-character product key. Most keys are located on the back of the CD case.

- **Computer name**—A unique name identifies each computer on a network. The name must be less than 15 characters long. The Windows 2000 Setup Wizard displays a default name, which can be changed based on the organization name that was entered earlier in the setup process.

- **Password for the administrator account**—Windows 2000 can store different profiles for multiple users of a computer. A built-in administrator account can include privileges to make any changes to a computer. To do so, an administrator must supply the password for this account.

- **Modem-dialing information**—Most networks now use high-speed local-area networks (LANs) and network cards. Therefore, entering this information depends on whether a modem is being used. Most laptops still use modems, so it might be necessary to enter information. First, select the country or region where the computer is located. This is sometimes already completed, based on the selected regional settings. The area or city of the computer's location and the number for obtaining an outside line must be entered. Then select tone dialing or pulse dialing, as dictated by the phone system.

- **Date and time settings**—Specify the correct date, time, and time zone for the computer. Indicate whether Windows 2000 is to automatically adjust the computer's clock settings for daylight-saving time.

Figures 6-34 through 6-38 demonstrate the steps that are involved in the Setup Wizard.

Figure 6-34 Enter Regional Settings

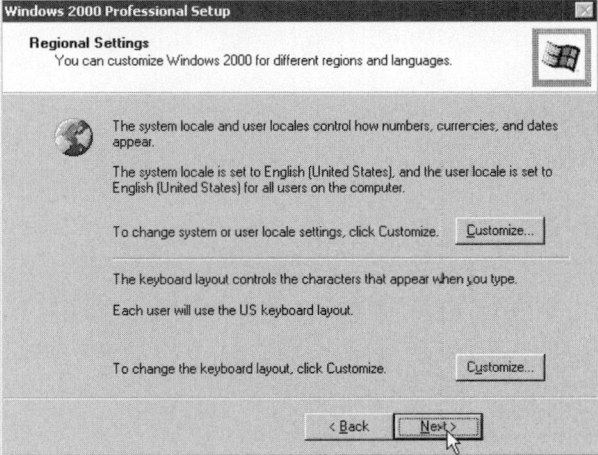

Figure 6-35 Personalize the Software

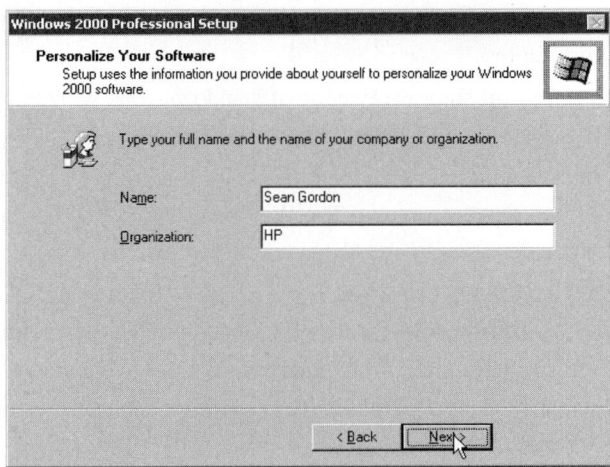

Figure 6-36 Enter the Windows 2000 Product Key

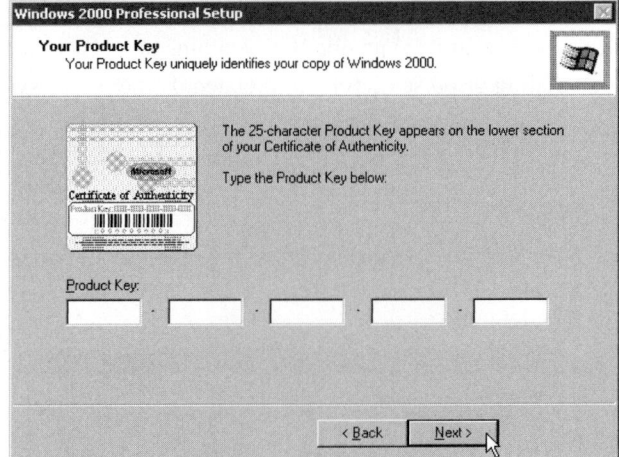

Figure 6-37 Enter the Computer Name and Set the Administrator Password

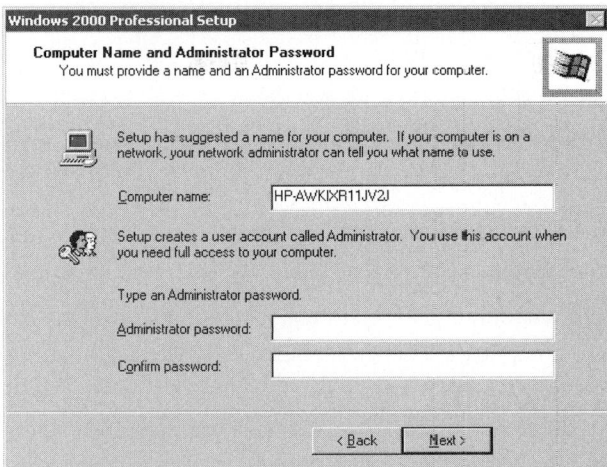

Figure 6-38 Enter Date and Time Settings

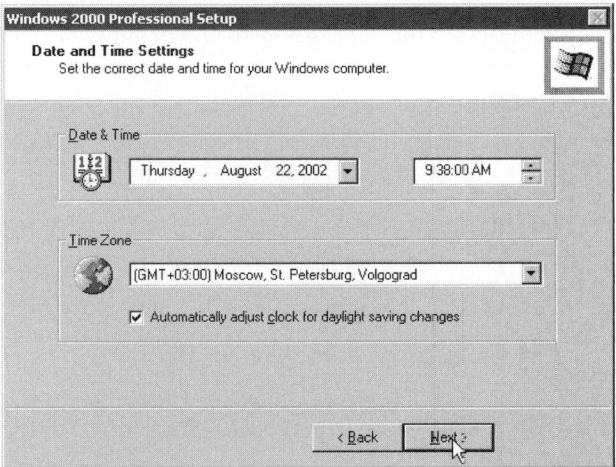

Installing Windows Networking

Windows 2000 is designed to be a network operating system. Installing the network settings is a major step. After gathering information about the computer, the Windows 2000 Setup program automatically installs the network software.

The Windows 2000 Professional Edition installs networking components in the following steps:

Step 1   **Detect network adapter cards**—The operating system must first detect the network cards. If none are installed, this step is skipped.

Step 2   **Install networking components**—Network components are the files that allow a computer to connect to other computers, networks, and the Internet. The Setup program prompts an administrator to choose typical settings or customized settings to configure the networking components. If Typical is chosen, the system installs the default settings. If Custom is chosen, the administrator can enter information that is specific to a company network. For example, Client for Microsoft Networks allows a computer to gain access to network resources. File and Printer Sharing for Microsoft Networks allows other computers to gain access to file and print resources on the computer. TCP/IP is the default networking protocol that allows a computer to communicate over LANs and wide-area networks (WANs). Other clients, services, and network protocols can be installed at this stage if the network requires them. Some examples of these items are NetBIOS Enhanced User Interface (NetBEUI), AppleTalk, and NWLink, or an IPX/SPX NetBIOS–compatible transport.

Step 3   **Join a workgroup or domain**—The administrator decides whether the computer is to be part of a domain or a workgroup. If a computer account is created in the domain for the computer during the installation, the Windows 2000 Setup Wizard prompts the administrator for a name and a password to join the domain.

Step 4   **Install components**—The last step is to install and configure the networking components that have just been selected.

Figures 6-39 through 6-42 demonstrate the steps that are involved in installing these components.

Figure 6-39 Installing Network Components

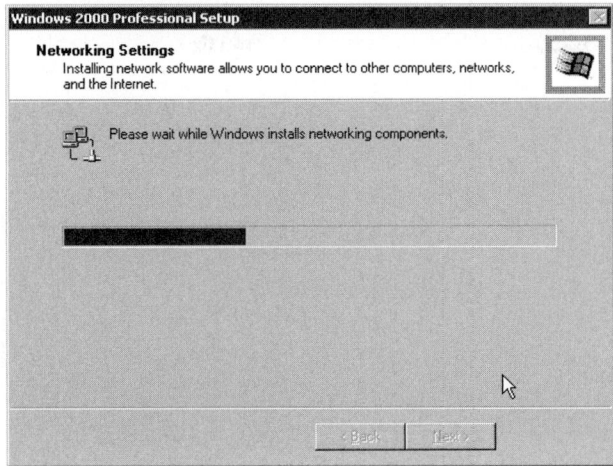

Figure 6-40 Choosing Network Settings

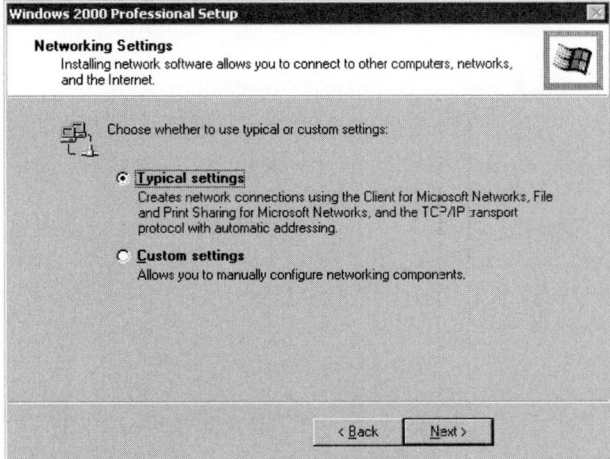

Figure 6-41 Choosing Workgroup or Computer Domain Settings

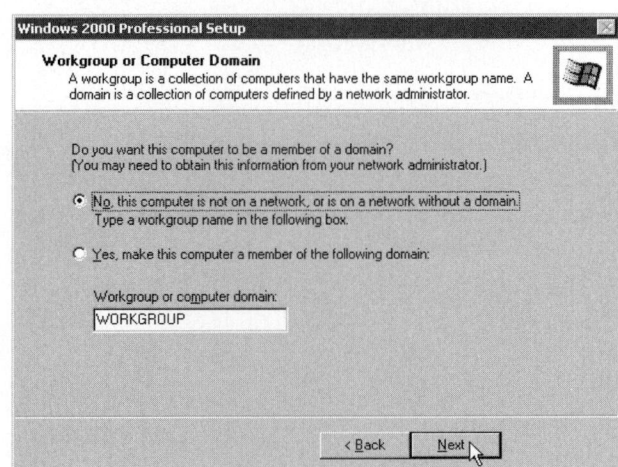

Figure 6-42 Installing Windows 2000 Components

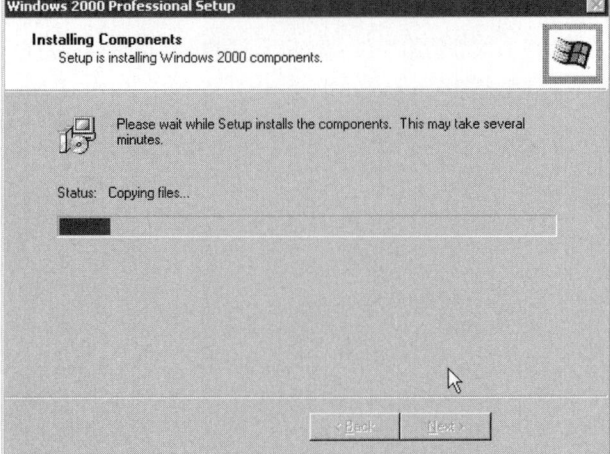

Completing the Setup Program

After the networking components are installed, the Setup Wizard copies additional files to configure the Windows 2000 Professional Edition. The Setup program, shown in Figures 6-43 through 6-47, automatically performs the following four steps:

Step 1   **Installs the Start menu items**—Shortcut items that appear on the Start menu are installed.

Step 2   **Registers components**—Windows 2000 begins to apply the configuration settings that were specified in the Windows 2000 Setup Wizard.

Step 3   **Saves the configuration**—The configuration settings are applied and saved to the hard drive, to be used every time the computer is started.

Step 4   **Removes temporary files**—Many files need to be temporarily copied during the operating system installation. The Setup Wizard automatically deletes these files when the installation procedure is complete. After completion, the computer automatically restarts. An administrator can now log on to finish the installation procedure.

Figure 6-43 Performing Final Tasks—Install Start Menu Items

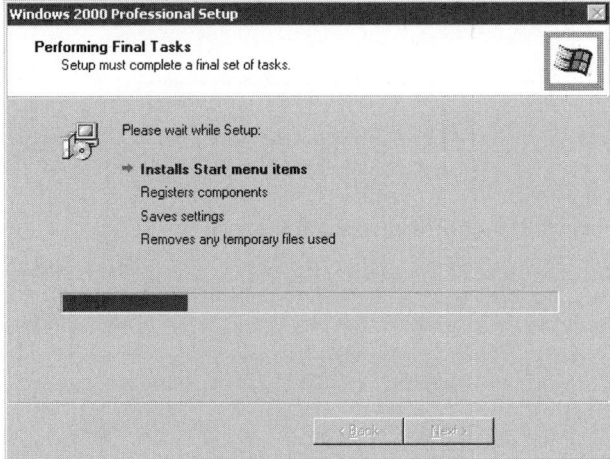

Figure 6-44 Performing Final Tasks—Register Components

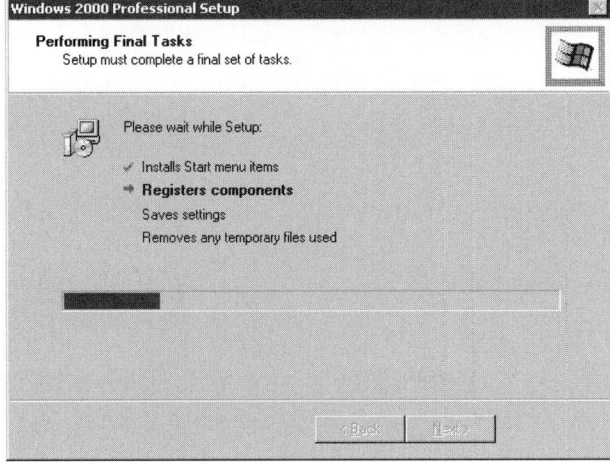

Figure 6-45 Performing Final Tasks—Save Settings

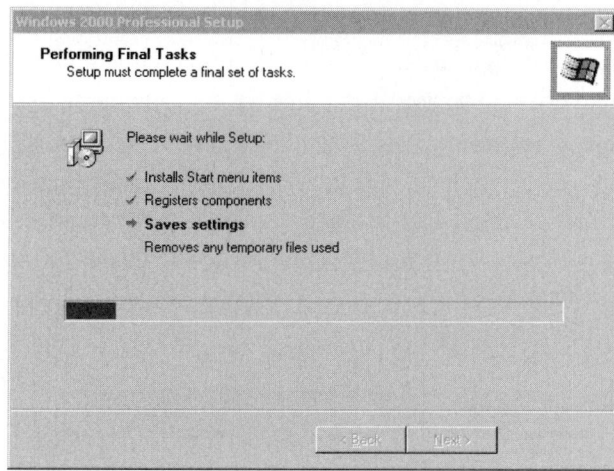

Figure 6-46 Performing Final Tasks—Remove Temporary Files

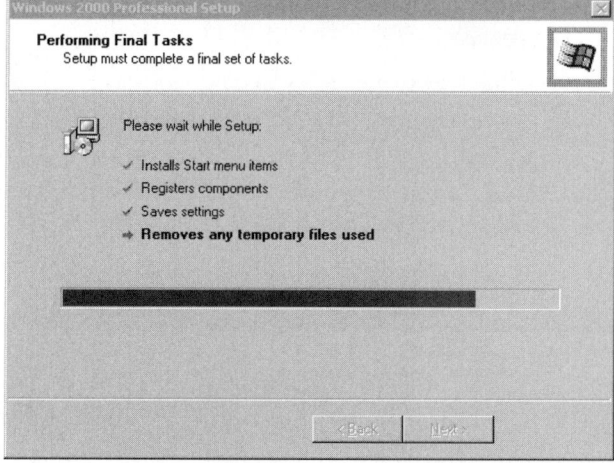

Figure 6-47 Completing the Windows 2000 Installation

Windows 2000 Setup Options

The installation steps for the default, or typical, installation are described in the previous section. Other setup options are available in Windows 2000. The Portable installation installs the options that a portable computer, such as a laptop, might require. The Compact installation can be used when installing Windows 2000 on a computer that has a limited amount of hard drive space. Finally, the Custom installation can be chosen if the device configurations require customization. Select Custom installation if hardware devices or adapter cards that are not Plug and Play–compatible are being used. Table 6-9 summarizes the Windows 2000 setup options.

Table 6-9 Windows 2000 Setup Options

Setup Option	Result
Typical	Installs all the components that are usually installed with Windows 2000. Most users should select this option.
Portable	Installs the options that are generally required for portable computers.

continues

Table 6-9 Windows 2000 Setup Options (Continued)

Setup Option	Result
Compact	This is the smallest possible installation of Windows 2000. For example, you might want to perform a Compact installation if your hard disk has little free space. Setup will not install optional components. If you later want to use an optional component, such as games or WebTV for Windows, you must install it. To install an optional component after the Setup program is completed, choose the Add/Remove Programs icon in the Control Panel.
Custom	Installs the options that you choose. If you do not select a Custom installation, the Setup program installs only the optional components that are selected by default. If you know that you are going to need certain Windows components, you might want to select a Custom installation and ensure that those components are included during the Setup program. Pan-European users should choose this option to select the required regional settings and keyboard layout for their locale.

Lab 6.4.3   Installation Demonstration of Windows 2000

This lab details the process for properly installing Windows 2000.

Special Installations

The IT technician must be aware of special installation instructions that relate to upgrading a Windows 9x or a Windows NT workstation. In addition, there are requirements necessary to prepare a system to dual boot. This section includes the following topics:

- Upgrading from Windows NT Workstation 4 to Windows 2000
- Replacing Windows 9x with Windows 2000
- Dual-booting Windows 9x/Windows NT 4 and Windows 2000

Upgrading from Windows NT Workstation 4 to Windows 2000

Upgrading a computer system from Windows NT 4.0 is faster than performing a clean installation of Windows 2000. It is similar to the upgrade process for computers that are running Windows 9x. Microsoft planned ahead for the circumstances that require a large corporation or business to upgrade their computers. This can involve a few hundred to a few thousand computers. While upgrading, the computers that are waiting to be upgraded—which are still running Windows NT 4.0—can connect and communicate with the Windows 2000 computers.

During the upgrade process, the Windows 2000 Setup utility replaces existing files with the new Windows 2000 files. However, existing applications and settings are saved. Verification of hardware compatibility requirements is necessary to upgrade directly to Windows 2000. The Hardware Compatibility List can help you determine whether a computer meets these requirements.

The upgrade process starts when you complete the following procedure:

Step 1   Insert the Windows 2000 CD in the CD-ROM drive.

Step 2   Choose **Start**, **Run**.

Step 3   Type **D:\i386\winnt32** in the command line, where *D* is the drive letter for the CD-ROM drive.

Step 4   Press **Enter**.

The Welcome to the Windows 2000 Setup Wizard appears.

Step 5   Select **Upgrade to Windows 2000**, which is recommended.

Step 6   Click the **Next** button.

The License Agreement page appears.

Step 7   Read the license agreement, and choose **I accept this agreement**.

Step 8   Click the **Next** button.

The Upgrading to the Windows 2000 NT File System page appears.

Step 9   Choose **Yes, upgrade my drive**.

Step 10 Click the **Next** button.

The Copying Installation Files page appears, and then the Restarting the Computer page appears. The computer now restarts.

After the computer restarts, the upgrade process continues, with no further user intervention.

Replacing Windows 9*x* with Windows 2000

The process for upgrading from Windows 9*x* to Windows 2000 is similar to the process of upgrading Windows NT 4.0 to Windows 2000. The Hardware Compatibility List can be used to ensure that your computer(s) will work with the Windows 2000 operating system.

The Windows 2000 Setup program starts the upgrade to Windows 2000 if the computer passes the hardware compatibility test. The upgrade process for Windows 2000 should start automatically. If it does not, use the following steps :

Step 1   Go to Start > Run. Enter the WINNT32.EXE command.

Step 2   Accept the license agreement.

Step 3 Create a domain-specific computer account if the computer is already a domain member.

Windows 95 and Windows 98 clients do not require a computer account. However, Windows 2000 Professional clients do.

Step 4 Provide upgrade packs for the applications that need them.

These packs update software so that it works with Windows 2000. Upgrade packs are available from the software manufacturer and can be found on the Internet. During the upgrade process, users have the option of visiting the Windows compatibility website to find the latest product updates and compatibility information.

Step 5 Select **Upgrade to NTFS** unless the client computer can dual-boot operating systems, because FAT16 and FAT32 cannot recognize NTFS.

Step 6 Start the Windows 2000 compatibility tool to generate a report.

If the report reveals that a computer is Windows 2000 compatible, continue with the upgrade. If the report shows that the computer is incompatible with Windows 2000, terminate the upgrade process.

Step 7 The upgrade finishes at this point, without further user intervention. Enter the password for the local computer administrator account after the upgrade is complete.

If the computer is Windows 2000 compatible, it becomes an upgraded member of the domain. Figures 6-48 through 6-59 demonstrate the process of upgrading Windows 9*x* to Windows 2000.

Restart the system to complete the installation process. After rebooting, the system proceeds through a typical Windows 2000 installation, as discussed previously.

Figure 6-48 Upgrading from Windows 98 to Windows 2000

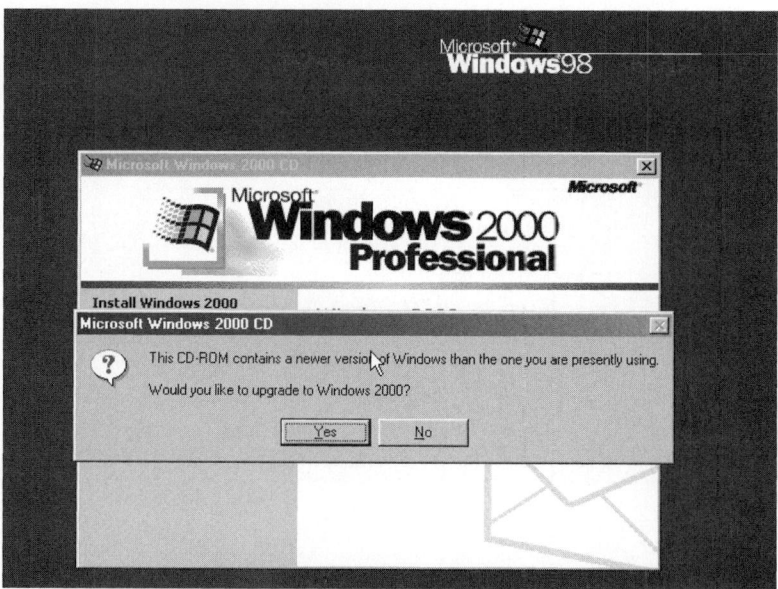

Figure 6-49 Selecting Upgrade Options

Figure 6-50 Windows 2000 License Agreement

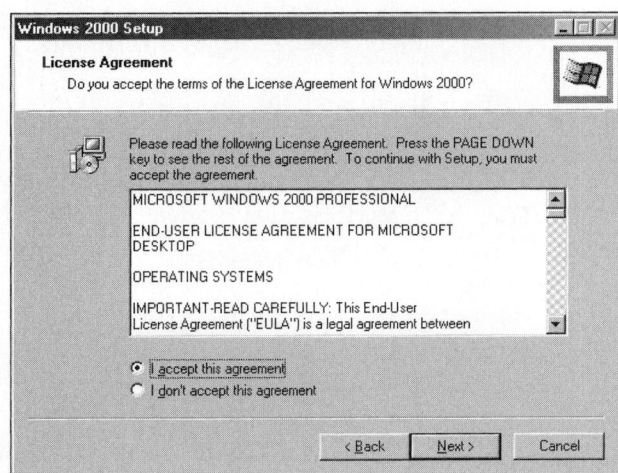

Figure 6-51 Entering the Windows 2000 Product Key

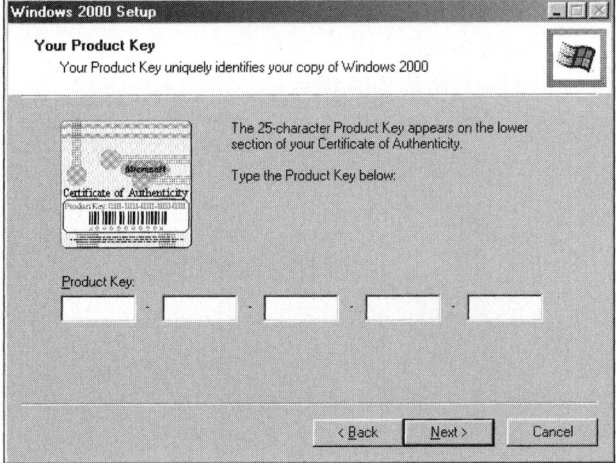

Figure 6-52 Preparing to Upgrade to Windows 2000

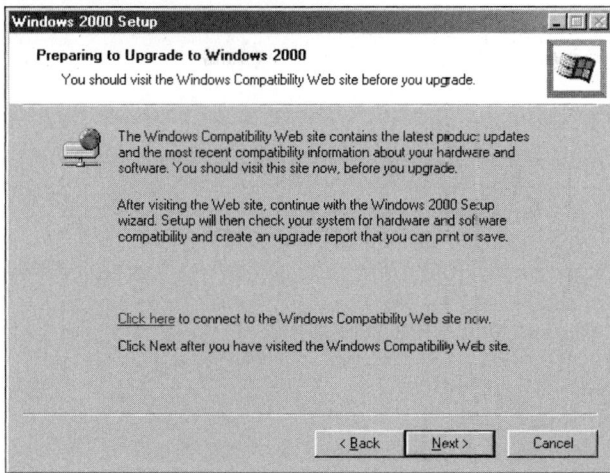

Figure 6-53 Providing Upgrade Packs

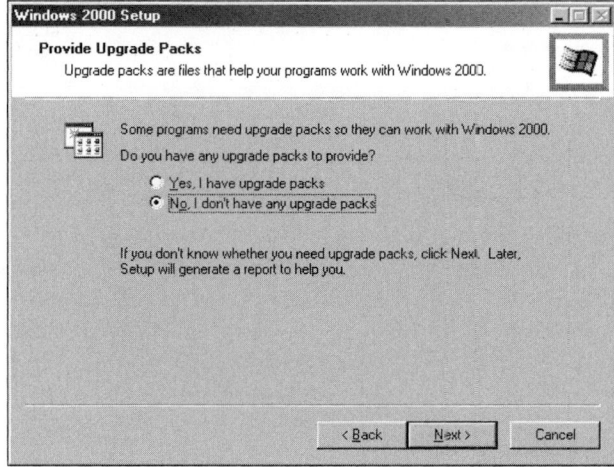

Figure 6-54 Converting an Existing FAT Partition to NTFS

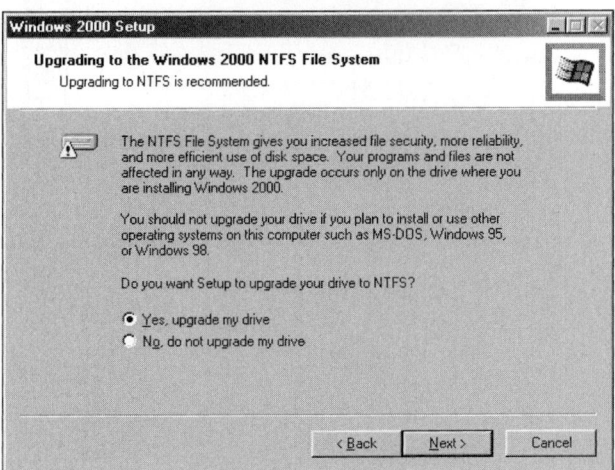

Figure 6-55 Loading Information File

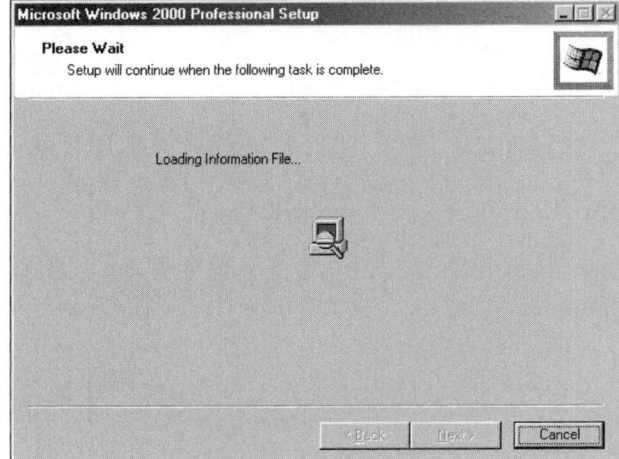

Figure 6-56 Preparing an Upgrade Report

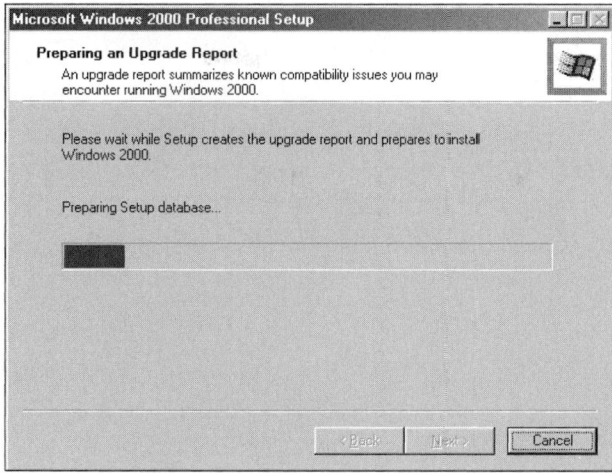

Figure 6-57 Displaying the Upgrade Report

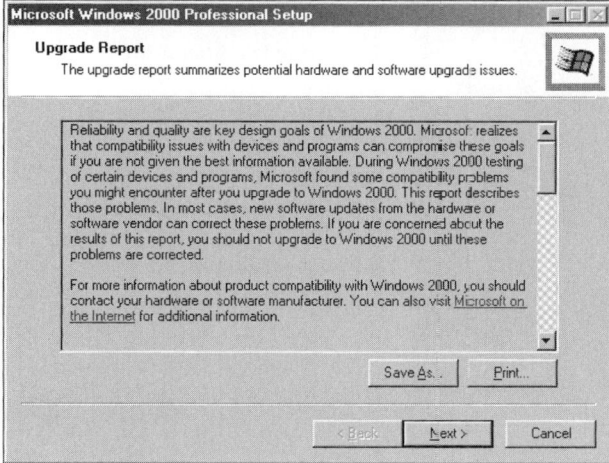

Figure 6-58 Ready to Install Windows 2000

Figure 6-59 Restarting the Computer

Dual-Booting Windows 9x/Windows NT 4 and Windows 2000

Windows 2000 can be set to dual-boot with Windows 98 operating systems. *Dual-boot* is an option for one computer system to have two different operating systems installed and for the user to be able to boot to either operating system. This is done because the Windows 98 and Windows 2000 registries are not compatible. When the computer is started, a menu is displayed with the option to boot to a Windows 98 or a Windows 2000 environment, for example. A clean installation of Windows 98 is recommended before installing Windows 2000. Figure 6-60 shows an example of a dual-boot system. The Microsoft Windows 2000 Professional Setup option starts Windows 2000, and the Microsoft Windows option starts Windows 98.

Figure 6-60 Figure 6-60 Dual-Boot Options

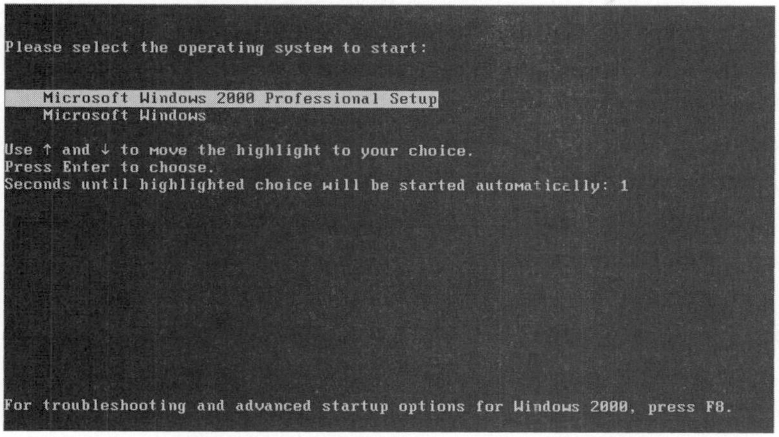

When using a dual-boot system, each application must be installed separately on each operating system's partition.

If two operating systems are incompatible, two separate partitions can be created to separately house each operating system. Logical drives can also be created on which to separately install the two operating systems. However, if the hard drive is NTFS formatted, the Windows 98 operating system cannot read files in the Windows 2000 NTFS partition. Microsoft recommends that if a computer is set to dual-boot with Windows 98 and 2000, both partitions must be formatted with the FAT file system. Windows 2000 can operate with the FAT file system, and the other partition files can be read.

Summary

This chapter discussed the Windows NT, Windows 2000, and Windows XP operating systems. Some important concepts to retain from this chapter include the following:

- The main differences between the Windows NT/2000/XP operating systems and Windows 9x are the added features that provide extra security for the system. The ACL simplifies assigning permissions. Encryption allows administrators to control who has access to folders and files.

- The FAT32 file system solves some problems of the FAT16 system. FAT32 supports hard drives up to 2048 GB in size. In contrast, FAT16 only supports partitions up to 2 GB in size. FAT32 also solves the problem of limited cluster size. FAT32 changes the way that the root directory is located on the hard drive. It has the ability to use both the default and original copy of the File Allocation Table if one becomes corrupt.

- NTFS solves even more of the limitations of FAT16 and FAT32. NTFS is designed as an enterprise-level operating system with directory and file security features. NTFS can more efficiently recognize and address large volumes and hard disks than FAT16 or FAT32.

- The Windows 2000 registry differs from the Windows 98 registry in many ways, including where it is located and how it is backed up. The structure of the Windows 2000 registry is based on subtrees that provide a key for every process that is running on a system. These are useful for maintenance and troubleshooting. The six main components that store data and access the registry are device drivers, setup programs, user profiles, the Windows NT kernel, NTDETECT.COM, and hardware profiles.

- Safe mode is a security feature in Windows NT, Windows 2000, and Windows XP that loads only basic files and drivers. It is a troubleshooting tool that is accessed during the bootup process by pressing F8. Safe Mode with Networking and Safe Mode with Command Prompt options can also be chosen.

- An Emergency Repair Disk (ERD) or the Recovery Console can help fix problems with corrupt operating systems. The ERD copies the original files from the installation CD. The Recovery Console is a command-line interface that helps with recovery tasks and troubleshooting.

- Knowledge of the Setup Wizard and the steps that are required to install or upgrade Windows 2000 in a network environment simplifies troubleshooting. Use the HCL when upgrading to Windows 2000 so that compatibility issues can be addressed before the installation.

The next chapter details the Windows XP operating system. It describes both the Home Edition and the Professional Edition.

Key Terms

Access Control Entry (ACE)   An entry to the ACL.

Access Control List (ACL)   A list managed by the administrator that displays files that a user has access to and the type of access that has been granted.

Administrative Tools   Utility that enables the administrator to control the computer system.

basic disk   A physical disk that contains the primary partition, extended partition, or logical drive.

basic disk storage   Industry standard for all versions of Windows.

compression state   Describes whether a file is compressed or uncompressed.

compression tool   An option to compress a file or folder to make it smaller.

device driver   Program that tells the operating system how to control specific devices.

disk management   The process of optimizing disk space.

disk quotas   Provide the ability to assign limits to the amount of hard disk space that users are allocated.

dual-boot   An option that provides the choice to boot the system to either Windows 2000 or Windows 98, if both are installed.

dynamic disk storage   A method of data storage that uses the hard drive(s) to create multi-disk volumes.

Emergency Repair Disk (ERD)   Disk that restores the operating system.

encryption   A security feature that applies a coding to a file so that only authorized users can view the file.

Encryption File System (EFS)   A Microsoft-specific file system for encryption.

fault tolerance   The ability to restore a disk to a consistent state with minimal data loss.

Hardware Abstraction Layer (HAL)   A library of hardware drivers that communicate between the operating system and the hardware that is installed.

Hardware Compatibility List (HCL)   A tool that verifies that hardware is compatible with the operating system.

hardware profile   Windows NT, Windows 2000, and Windows XP can save two or more profiles in which an administrator can control whether a piece of hardware loads. The registry stores these hardware profile configurations.

High Performance File System (HPFS)   Older file system that was used with Windows NT 3.51.

HKEY_CLASSES_ROOT Contains configuration data of the software that is installed on the computer.

HKEY_CURRENT_CONFIG Contains data on the active hardware profiles that are selected during the boot process.

HKEY_CURRENT_USER Contains data about the user who is currently logged on to the computer.

HKEY_LOCAL_MACHINE Contains configuration data for the local computer.

HKEY_USERS Default settings that control individual user profiles and environments.

kernel load Boot phase that begins with NTOSKRNL.EXE loading with the HAL.DLL file.

Local Security Policy The options that are selected to ensure a secure computer network.

local user An account created that gives a user access to the network.

logon The final step in the bootup process.

Master Boot Record (MBR) Allows programs such as DOS to load into RAM.

mirrored volume Contains two identical copies of a simple volume that stores the same data on two separate hard drives.

NTDETECT.COM Used by Intel-based systems to detect hardware that is installed in a system.

NT File System (NTFS) Designed to manage global and enterprise-level operating systems.

partitioning and formatting Prepare the hard drive for the installation of an operating system.

permissions File and directory permissions that specify which users and groups can gain access to files and folders.

Plug and Play (PnP) Automatically configures devices and assigns resources for new hardware.

power-on self-test (POST) A diagnostic test of memory and hardware when the system is powered up.

public key Provides access to encrypted files.

RAID-5 volume Consists of three or more parts of one or more drives or three or more entire drives.

Recovery Console Command-line interface that is used for troubleshooting purposes.

registry subtree Part of the hierarchical structure of the registry.

safe mode Advanced feature that is used for troubleshooting purposes.

setup program   Adds new configuration data to the registry when new hardware and applications are installed.

simple volume   A basic disk that contains disk space from a complete single disk and is not fault tolerant.

spanned volume   Includes disk space from multiple hard disks (up to 32 disks). It is not fault tolerant.

Startup menu   Unique security feature in the Windows 2000/NT operating systems. A multistep process is used to get to the Startup menu.

striped volume   Also known as RAID-0. Combines areas of free space from multiple hard disks—up to 32—into one logical volume. It is not fault tolerant.

user profile   A specific setting for the user who is logged on to the computer.

Windows NT kernel   Loads the correct device drivers in the proper order.

Check Your Understanding

1. Why is a system attribute applied to a file?

    A. So that it cannot be changed or deleted

    B. So that it can only be read by DOS

    C. So that changes to the file can be tracked

    D. So that the OS knows it is a system file

2. What file system limits filenames to eight characters in length?

    A. FAT32

    B. FAT16

    C. NTFS

    D. HPFS

3. The FAT32 file system is designed to support hard drives up to what size?

    A. 2048 GB

    B. 512 MB

    C. 640 MB

    D. 20 GB

4. Which of the following file systems is capable of managing global and enterprise-level operating systems?

   A. FAT

   B. FAT32

   C. NTFS

   D. HPFS

5. What file system is used by OS/2?

   A. FAT

   B. FAT32

   C. NTFS

   D. HPFS

6. Which of the following is an advanced startup feature that is available for troubleshooting?

   A. Recovery mode

   B. Safe mode

   C. Command mode

   D. Help mode

7. What is the term for the ability to restore a disk to a consistent state with minimal data loss?

   A. Fault tolerance

   B. Disk Recovery System

   C. Disk tolerance

   D. Fault recovery

8. What is the Windows registry?

   A. A database for file storage

   B. A driver that is used when booting up

   C. A database of configuration settings

   D. A database of users

9. What does POST stand for?

   A. Pre-operating system test

   B. Power of system test

   C. Pre-operation self test

   D. Power-on self-test

10. Which of the following describes the Plug and Play feature?

    A. Eliminates the need to manually configure jumpers on the hardware

    B. Allows the user to plug and unplug hardware that is connected to the computer

    C. Loads hardware drivers for system components

    D. Configures BIOS information

11. Which of the following is a tool that provides a list of files that a user has access to?

    A. User Access List

    B. Administrator Access List

    C. Access Control List

    D. Access Control Directory

12. Users can gain access to an encrypted file if they are assigned which of the following?

    A. Public key

    B. Password

    C. De-encryption code

    D. Administrator key

13. The NTLDR uses which of the following files?

    A. NTDETECT.INI, BOOT.INI, BOOTSECT.INI

    B. NTDETECT.COM, BOOT.SYS, BOOTSECT.INI

    C. NTDETECT.SYS, BOOT.SYS, BOOTSECT.SYS

    D. NTDETECT.COM, BOOT.INI, BOOTSECT.DOS

14. Which of the following is a portion of a disk that functions as a physically separate unit of storage?

    A. Partition

    B. Slave drive

    C. Cluster

    D. Sector

15. Which of the following provides a secure set of records about the components that control the OS?

    A. BIOS

    B. Registry

    C. .ini files

    D. System log

16. Which of the following is a library of hardware drivers that operate between the OS and hardware that is installed on the system?

    A. Hardware Abstraction Layer

    B. Hardware Detail Report

    C. Library Detail Report

    D. Library Report Layer

17. Which of the following is a tool, used before installing Windows 2000, that verifies that the hardware will work?

    A. Hardware Compatibility Report

    B. Hardware Comparison List

    C. Hardware Compatibility List

    D. Windows Hardware Report

18. The Windows Compact installation option is used for which of the following?

    A. Computer with a limited amount of hard drive space

    B. Computer with a small tower case

    C. Installations that need to be done quickly

    D. Temporary installations

19. In Windows NT/2000/XP, which of the following allows the administrator to control just about everything that is related to the local computer?

A. Local Tools

B. Administrative Tools

C. User Tools

D. Account Tools

20. What is the term for setting up Windows to boot to Windows 2000 or Windows 98?

A. Double booting

B. Multi-booting

C. Dual-booting

D. Semi-booting

Upon completing this chapter, you will be able to perform the following tasks:

- Understand the different versions of Windows XP
- Determine the hardware requirements for the installation
- Review the installation of Windows XP
- Compare the features of Windows XP to previous versions of Windows
- Evaluate the requirements for upgrading and creating a dual-boot environment

Chapter 7

Windows XP Operating System

Windows XP is designed as an operating system for both the home and office. Microsoft has released four versions of the XP operating system: the Home Edition, the Media Center Edition, the 32-bit Professional Edition that is suitable for a large corporation or business environment, and the 64-bit Professional Edition that was created for businesses with specialized and technical applications. A Windows XP version is also available for the tablet PC; however, this version is not within the scope of this course.

This chapter briefly describes the different Windows versions and lists some features that are new to Windows XP. Windows XP is built on the Windows 2000 code base and provides the same reliability and performance. Windows XP also enhances the new features of the Windows Me operating system, including System Restore, Windows Media Player, and Windows Image Acquisition. Microsoft has designed Windows XP to replace Windows 98, Windows Me, and Windows 2000.

Windows XP Versions

The Windows XP operating system has become the standard that is preloaded on most new computer systems. This section includes the following topics:

- Windows XP Home Edition
- Windows XP Professional Edition
- Windows XP Professional 64-Bit Edition
- Windows XP Media Center Edition

Windows XP Home Edition

Windows XP Home Edition is the least expensive version of Windows XP. The Home Edition is typically marketed to users and customers who use PCs in their homes and small businesses. Figure 7-1 shows a package of Windows XP Home Edition. This edition is intended for inexperienced users who do not need to connect to corporate networks and do not require the extra security options that Windows XP Professional Edition contains. Windows XP Home Edition can be run on most desktops or notebook PCs that meet the minimum system requirements.

Figure 7-1 Windows XP Home Edition

Windows XP Home Edition includes many enhancements and features that are not included in Windows 2000 Professional Edition or in any of the previous Windows 9*x* releases. Some of these features include improved software and hardware compatibility, simplified security such as Simple File Sharing versus Windows 2000 Sharing, a new logon screen, Fast User Switching, enhanced multimedia support, and DirectX 8.1 multimedia libraries for gaming.

Windows XP Professional Edition

The Windows XP Professional Edition operating system includes everything that the Home Edition provides, plus all the networking and security components that are required to join a Windows NT, 2000, or XP domain in a corporate network. Windows XP Professional also includes support for high-performance hardware, such as a dual-processor motherboard. Figure 7-2 shows a package of Windows XP Professional.

Figure 7-2 Windows XP Professional Edition

The *kernel* of the Windows XP Home Edition and Windows XP Professional Edition operating systems are identical. The file and folder management, the web browser, and most of the system-management tools and troubleshooting tools are also the same. The digital media–management applications are similar.

Windows XP Professional contains the following features that are not included in the Windows XP Home Edition:

- **Power user**—The new Remote Desktop feature in Windows XP Professional allows mobile users to access their corporate Desktop remotely. System administrators now have the ability to administer clients on a network remotely. Automated System Recovery (ASR) aids in system recovery from a catastrophic error that might render the system unbootable. Windows XP Professional, like Windows 2000 Professional, supports dynamic disks. The Home Edition supports only the basic disk type. The Home Edition does not include the Internet Information Services (IIS) web server software that is found in the Windows XP Professional Edition.

- **Management**—Windows XP Professional provides added operating system–management features. The Professional Edition can be used to log on to an Active Directory domain. Group Policy for domain users can also be supported. The Professional Edition also includes a change and configuration management tool known as IntelliMirror. IntelliMirror uses policy-based change and configuration management to enable user data, software, and settings to follow the user throughout a distributed computing environment.

NOTE

This chapter refers to the system administrator more often than to the technician because Windows XP Professional, like Windows 2000, is more likely to run in a networked environment. Therefore, the system administrator is the person who attends to most of the problems that occur.

- **Roaming profiles**—With Windows XP Professional, users can log on to any computer on the network and automatically receive their customized settings. The user profile is stored in a shared network folder. When the user logs on to a machine, the information in this folder is copied to the hard disk of the machine that is being used. When the user logs off, the profile information is copied back to a shared network folder.

- **Corporate deployment**—Windows XP Professional is designed for use in corporate networks, and it contains support for multiple languages. XP Professional also provides Sysprep support, which is used to install the operating system on multiple machines in a large or corporate network.

- **Networking features**—Windows XP Professional provides added networking features that are needed when deploying the operating system in a large corporate network. These include Simple Network Management Protocol (SNMP), the user interface for IP Security (IPSec), SAP Agent, Client Service for NetWare, Network Monitor, and simple TCP/IP services.

Windows XP Professional contains additional security features. For example, each user in the Windows XP Home Edition is automatically assigned to the Owners local group. This group is the Windows XP equivalent of the Windows 2000 Administrator account. Anyone who logs on to a Home Edition machine can have full control of the operating system. The Backup Operators, Power Users, or Replicator groups do not exist in the Windows XP Home Edition. However, the Windows XP Home Edition includes a Restricted Users group, which grants limited access to the operating system for selected users.

Windows XP Professional 64-Bit Edition

The Windows XP Professional 64-Bit Edition is the first 64-bit operating system from Microsoft. This operating system is designed to accommodate specialized, technical applications. For example, digital-content creators, including digital artists, 3D animators, gaming developers, and engineers, can view more-complex models and simulations to improve their product. Financial applications also benefit because of the ability to calculate large sets of data in real time.

The Windows XP Professional 64-Bit Edition is also designed to address the most demanding business needs of the Internet-based world, including e-commerce, data mining, online transaction processing, memory-intensive high-end graphics, complex mathematics, and high-performance multimedia applications. Note that 32-bit systems will continue to be the best environment for customers who use only 32-bit applications; these 32-bit systems do not work with data sets larger than 2 GB.

A PC system that is built around an Intel Itanium 64-bit processor must be used in conjunction with the Windows XP Professional 64-Bit Edition. The 64-Bit Edition also takes advantage of increased floating-point performance, which is the raw number of calculations that can be processed in a given period of time using the Intel Itanium platform. Another advantage of the 64-Bit Edition is its memory support; this edition currently supports up to 16 GB RAM. One terabyte—1 trillion bytes (1 TB)—of system cache and a 512-TB page file will also be supported as hardware and memory capabilities increase to 16 TB of virtual memory.

The Windows XP 64-Bit Edition provides a scalable, high-performance platform for a new generation of applications that are based on the Win64 application programming interface (API). When compared to 32-bit systems, the Win64 API architecture provides more efficient processing of extremely large amounts of data. With the 64-Bit Edition, applications can pre-load substantially more data into virtual memory to enable rapid access by the Intel 64-bit processor. Table 7-1 shows a comparison of 64-bit and 32-bit architectures.

Table 7-1 Comparison of 64-Bit and 32-Bit Architectures

Address Space	64-Bit Windows XP	32-Bit Windows XP
Virtual memory	16 TB	4 GB
Paging file	512 TB	16 TB
System cache	1 TB	1 GB

A 64-bit motherboard and chipset are required for the Windows XP Professional 64-Bit Edition. Table 7-2 shows some of the minimum requirements for this edition.

Table 7-2 Requirements for the Windows XP Professional 64-Bit Edition

System Device	Minimum	Recommended
64-bit processor	900-MHz Itanium	1-GHz Itanium
Memory	1 GB	1 GB
Video	VGA	3D graphics

Windows XP Media Center Edition

The Windows XP Media Center Edition is a new Microsoft product that is preinstalled and available only on Media Center PCs. This edition is designed to fulfill the needs of those users who want a powerful digital media center in their home. The Media Center Edition allows users to watch live television, record TV programs, listen to digital music, view slide shows and picture albums, and play DVDs all from one location.

XP Media Center is a packaged hardware and software system, built on the Windows XP Professional Edition platform, that focuses on multimedia. The XP Media Center computer system features hardware that is not typically found on a standard PC. Some of the hardware includes the following:

- An advanced graphics card
- A TV tuner to capture a cable, antenna, or satellite signal and display that signal on the monitor
- A hardware encoder to record the captured TV signal to the computer's hard disk
- Digital audio output that allows the digital audio of the PC to integrate into the existing home entertainment system

A Media Center remote control that communicates with the computer through an infrared sensor is also included. Figure 7-3 shows the Windows XP Media Center Edition.

Figure 7-3 Windows XP Media Center Edition

Overview of the Installation Process

To gain a good understanding of the installation process, this section addresses some of the key differences between Windows XP and previous versions of Windows, as well as some of the requirements and features.

This section includes the following topics:

- Differences between the installation of Windows 2000/9x and Windows XP
- Windows XP hardware requirements
- Windows XP features

Differences Between the Installation of Windows 2000/9x and Windows XP

The Windows family of operating systems has always been user friendly when it comes to installation. Windows XP is no different. Just like Windows 2000 and Windows 9x, Windows XP provides a wizard that takes you step by step through the installation process. Windows XP is more intuitive when it comes to the installation process. The Files and Settings Transfer Wizard allows the user to migrate settings and files from an old computer to a new computer, as shown in Figure 7-4. The user can save settings from any 32-bit version of Windows, including Windows 95.

Figure 7-4 Windows XP Files and Settings Transfer Wizard

The following options enable saved files and settings to be restored on the Windows XP Home Edition or Professional Edition:

- A direct connection between two computers can be made with a serial cable.
- The computers can be connected across a network.
- Files can be compressed and saved to removable media, such as a floppy disk, Zip disk, or CD-RW.
- A removable drive or network drive can be used to transfer data.

Another important feature for Windows XP is the *User State Migration Tool (USMT)*. This tool is similar to the Files and Settings Transfer Wizard. IT administrators who are performing large deployments of Windows XP Professional in a corporate environment use the USMT. The USMT provides the same functionality as the wizard on a large scale for the purpose of migrating multiple users.

Windows XP Hardware Requirements

The hardware requirements for Windows XP depend on the type and number of hardware devices that are to be installed. Windows XP can require more hardware capabilities than previous versions of Windows to support newer hardware devices and to allow the operating system to function efficiently.

Prior to installing Windows XP, ensure that the system hardware is capable of running the XP operating system. The following is a list of requirements that Microsoft recommends:

- A Pentium 233-MHz processor or faster, with 300 MHz recommended
- At least 64-MB RAM, with 128 MB recommended
- A minimum of a 2-GB hard drive with at least 650 MB of free space available (2 GB of free space and a larger drive are recommended)
- A CD-ROM or DVD-ROM drive
- A keyboard
- A mouse or other compatible pointing device
- A video adapter and monitor with Super VGA resolution of 800×600 or higher
- A sound card
- Speakers or headphones

The Hardware Compatibility List (HCL) shown in Figure 7-5 is provided on the Windows website. It allows the user to determine if his or her system will support the Windows XP operating system.

Windows XP Features

Windows XP offers many new features over Windows 2000 and Windows 9x. For reliability, Windows XP was built on the base code of Windows NT and Windows 2000. Code protection keeps kernel data as read-only so that drivers and applications cannot corrupt the data. The device driver verifier and IP security have been enhanced to help protect data that is transmitted across a network.

Figure 7-5 Hardware Compatibility List (HCL)

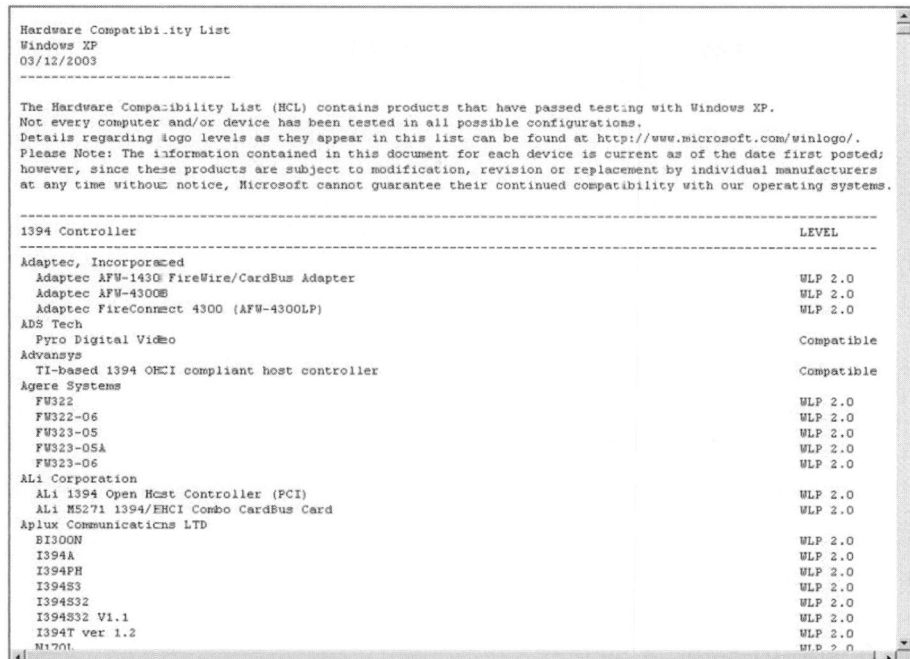

Because Windows is moving toward the .NET environment, Windows XP has been upgraded with smart card capabilities. Windows XP includes support for smart card logons to terminal server sessions that are hosted on a Windows .NET server. Smart cards enhance software-only solutions for client authentication, interactive logon, and secure e-mail.

With each successive version, Windows becomes easier to work with and install. Windows XP removes the clutter from the Taskbar by grouping similar applications together. For example, multiple copies of Internet Explorer are grouped and accessed by clicking the drop-down box, as shown in Figure 7-6.

Figure 7-6 Grouping Applications

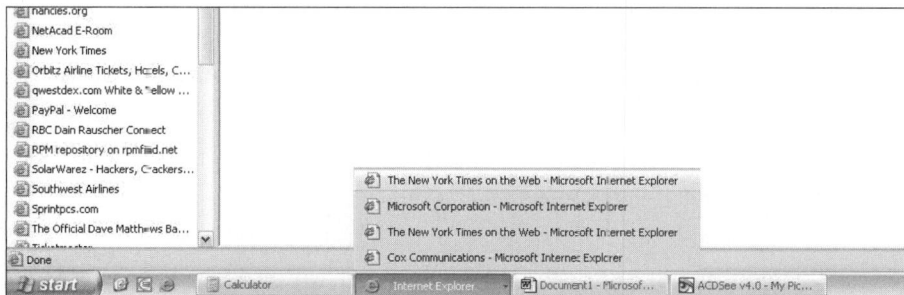

Windows XP allows you to burn CDs from Windows Explorer and to publish files to the web. Another new feature in Windows Explorer is the information that is provided just by scrolling over a file folder. When the user holds the mouse pointer over a folder, an information box displays the size of the folder and the files inside.

For the network administrator, Windows XP has improved the setup routine, provided more security, updated remote access, and developed the *Resultant Set of Policy (RSoP)*. With RSoP, administrators have a powerful and flexible tool to plan, monitor, and troubleshoot Group Policy.

Installing the Windows XP Operating System

A successful installation of Windows XP starts with a review of the basic requirements. Three types of installations can be performed, and the installation process goes through four main steps. Understanding these steps can help the technician should errors occur. This section includes the following topics:

- Requirements for installing Windows XP
- Understanding the steps of a Windows XP installation
- Windows XP setup options

Requirements for Installing Windows XP

The following considerations are important for a Windows XP installation:

NOTE

Some system hardware requires that you use a manufacturer-supplied recovery disk and procedure for installing the operating system. In this case, refer to the manufacturer's documentation for specific instructions.

- Make sure that the computer is ready for Windows XP by checking the system requirements.
- When upgrading, check the Microsoft website to make sure that the version of Windows that you are currently running is eligible for an upgrade. For example, Windows 2000 Professional Edition can upgrade to Windows XP Professional, but you cannot upgrade 2000 Professional Edition to Windows XP Home Edition.
- Use the Compatibility tool or download the Upgrade Advisor to ensure that the system, devices, and software can work with XP. To save time, load updated drivers for any component that is not compatible before performing the installation.
- Review the documentation before starting a new installation. Microsoft provides "Getting Started" guides at its website.
- Run your antivirus software before starting the installation, but be sure to disable this software during the installation process.

Understanding the Steps of a Windows XP Installation

Before setting up Windows XP, first choose one of the following three types of installations:

- **Clean install**—Sets up a fresh copy of Windows XP. This new copy replaces any previous versions of Windows that were installed on the computer.

- **Upgrade of an existing version**—Upgrades Windows 98, Windows 98 Second Edition, or Windows Me to the Windows XP Home or Professional Edition. You can upgrade to Windows XP Professional from Windows NT Workstation 4.0 with Service Pack 6, or you can upgrade Windows 2000 Professional with or without the service packs. You cannot upgrade Windows 3.x or Windows 95 to Windows XP. In these cases, you must perform a clean install.

- **Dual-boot installation**—Allows the user to preserve the currently installed version of Windows. Windows XP needs to be installed on a hard drive partition that is different from the partition on which the current version of Windows resides. When the installation is complete, the user can choose the operating system from which to boot.

The following four main steps are required for the Windows XP installation process:

1. File copy
2. Text mode setup
3. GUI mode setup
4. Windows Welcome

Each of these steps is described in the following sections.

File Copy

This step copies the Windows setup files to a folder on the partition where they can run when the system is restarted. If the system is booted from a CD, the Setup program skips this step and copies files directly from the CD.

Text Mode Setup

During a clean installation, the user selects the partition where the Windows XP system files are to be installed. The partition can be created and formatted in this step.

GUI Mode Setup

Windows Setup uses a graphical wizard to guide the user to input the regional settings, product key, computer name, and administrator password.

Windows Welcome

As the last portion of the setup process, the user has the option to create user accounts and to activate Windows before using it for the first time.

 Lab 7.3.2 Installation Demonstration of Windows XP

This lab is a step-by-step demonstration of a Windows XP Professional installation.

Windows XP Setup Options

Windows XP installation starts with options to set up Windows XP or to repair Windows XP, as shown in Figure 7-7. To run the installation, press **Enter**. To repair an installation, press **R** to open the Recovery Console. The Recovery Console is discussed later in this chapter.

Figure 7-7 Windows XP Setup

```
Windows XP Professional Setup

    Welcome to Setup.

    This portion of the Setup program prepares Microsoft(R)
    Windows(R) XP to run on your computer.

        •  To set up Windows XP now, press ENTER.

        •  To repair a Windows XP installation using
           Recovery Console, press R.

        •  To quit Setup without installing Windows XP, press F3.









    ENTER=Continue   R=Repair   F3=Quit
```

The next option in the setup process is to partition and format the hard drive. This step is not always required. Proceed with the installation if a partition is already available. If a partition needs to be created, set up a smaller partition to speed the installation. In Lab 7.3.2, you should set up a 4-GB partition.

The system then automatically starts copying files after the partitioning and formatting are complete. This allows the installation wizard to provide step-by-step instructions for the rest of the process. Options for language, time/day, and network settings must be entered before the installation can continue. During the installation, Windows XP displays information on new features and shows the time remaining to complete the installation.

If the installation is for a computer on a network, a username and password, provided by the network administrator, is required to connect to the network.

Special Installations

This section discusses upgrading to Windows XP from a previous edition of Windows. In addition, information on setting up a system to dual boot is included. This section includes the following topics:

- Upgrading Windows NT Workstation 4/2000 to Windows XP
- Upgrading Windows 98 to Windows XP
- Dual-booting Windows 9*x,* NT 4, 2000, and Windows XP

Upgrading Windows NT Workstation 4/2000 to Windows XP

Upgrading a computer system in the home or small office is generally error free. On more complex systems, a clean install is recommended. Using an upgrade CD requires that the system have a Windows operating system already installed. Ideally, the Windows XP operating system should be installed clean. A clean installation requires that the drive is reformatted and repartitioned. To upgrade Windows 2000 to Windows XP, boot up the current version of Windows and insert the Windows XP CD. Choose to install Windows XP. The Setup Wizard displays. This wizard is designed to make the installation process easy. On the first page of the Setup Wizard, select **Upgrade** and click the **Next** button. Figure 7-8 shows the first page of the Setup Wizard. The wizard then asks the user for some information, including the product key, to complete the process. The Setup program then replaces the existing Windows files and saves the user settings, programs, and files that had been previously installed on the computer. After several required reboots, the installation is completed.

The process of upgrading a computer system from Windows NT 4.0 to Windows XP is faster than performing a new install of Windows XP. The Windows XP Setup program replaces the existing files with Windows XP files during the upgrade process. However, the XP upgrade does not replace existing applications and settings or saved documents. The administrator should verify that the computers meet the hardware compatibility requirements for upgrading directly to Windows XP. The HCL can be used to determine whether a computer meets the necessary requirements.

Figure 7-8 Beginning an Upgrade to Windows XP

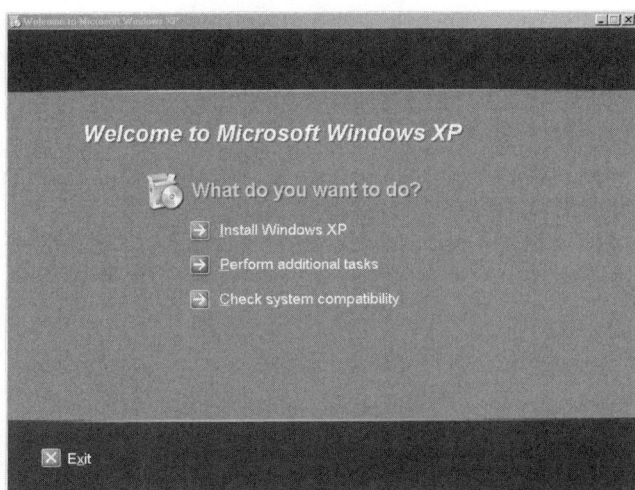

Start the upgrade process by inserting the CD to auto start the program and completing the following steps:

Step 1 Insert the Windows XP CD in the CD-ROM drive. The Welcome to the Windows XP Setup Wizard appears. If Setup does not auto start automatically, choose **Start > Run**. In the Run box, type **D:\i386\winnt32**, where D is the drive letter for the CD-ROM, and then press **Enter**.

Step 2 Select **Upgrade to Windows XP**, which is recommended, and click the **Next** button.

The License Agreement page appears.

Step 3 Read the license agreement, and choose **I accept this agreement**. Click the **Next** button.

The Upgrading to the Windows XP NTFS File System page appears.

Step 4 Choose **Yes, upgrade my drive**, and click the **Next** button.

The Copying Installation Files page appears, and then the Restarting the Computer page appears. Finally, the computer restarts.

After the computer restarts, the upgrade process should continue without requiring any further user intervention.

Upgrading Windows 98 to Windows XP

The process of upgrading Windows 98 to Windows XP is similar to the process of upgrading Windows 98 to Windows 2000. Use the HCL to ensure that the computer being upgraded can accept the Windows XP operating system.

If the computer passes the hardware compatibility test, follow these steps to start the upgrade to Windows XP:

Step 1   Insert the Windows XP CD in the CD-ROM drive.

The Welcome to the Windows XP Setup Wizard appears.

Step 2   Select **Upgrade to Windows XP**, which is recommended, and click the **Next** button.

Step 3   Accept the license agreement.

Step 4   If the computer is already a member of a domain, create a computer account in that domain.

The Windows 98 client does not require a computer account; however, Windows XP Professional clients do.

Step 5   Provide upgrade packs for any applications that might need these packs to work with Windows XP.

Upgrade packs are available from the software manufacturer and can be found on the Internet. Users have the option of checking compatibility at the Microsoft website.

A prompt to upgrade to the NT File System (NTFS) appears.

Step 6   Choose to upgrade to the NTFS unless the client computer will be dual-booted to different operating systems.

This distinction is critical for dual-boot systems, because FAT16 and FAT32 cannot recognize NTFS.

The Windows XP compatibility tool runs and generates a report.

Step 7   If the report shows that the computer is Windows XP compatible, continue with the upgrade. If the report shows that the computer is incompatible with Windows XP, terminate the upgrade process. Remove or upgrade the incompatible devices.

The upgrade should finish without further user intervention. After the upgrade is complete, enter the password for the local computer administrator account.

If the computer is Windows XP compatible, it is now upgraded and is a member of the domain. Figure 7-9 shows the Windows XP upgrade screen.

Figure 7-9 Upgrading Windows 98 to Windows XP

The system needs to be restarted for the installation process to complete. After the system reboots, the computer proceeds through a typical Windows XP installation, as discussed previously.

Dual-Booting Windows 9x, NT 4, 2000, and XP

NOTE

If your system is set up to dual-boot, each application must reside in the partition from which the system is booted. If you need to use the same application with both operating systems, the application must be installed in both partitions.

Windows XP can be set up to dual-boot with another operating system such as Windows 98 or Windows 2000. When the computer system is set up for a dual-boot, a menu offers the user choices of different operating systems during startup. To provide a dual-boot system, perform a clean install of Windows 98 before installing Windows XP. Figure 7-10 shows a startup screen that has options for booting to two different operating systems.

Figure 7-10 Dual-Boot Startup Screen

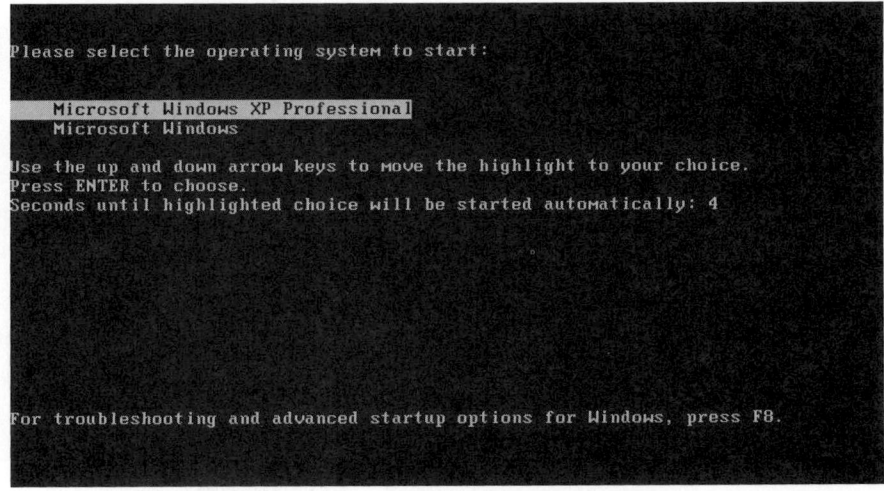

In this example, the Microsoft Windows XP Professional option starts Windows XP Professional and the Microsoft Windows option starts Microsoft Windows 2000.

Alternatively, separate logical drives can be created, and each operating system can be installed on its own logical drive. However, if the hard drive is formatted with NTFS, the Windows 98 operating system cannot read files in the Windows XP NTFS partition. Microsoft recommends that both partitions be formatted with the FAT file system if the computer is set up to dual-boot with Windows 98 or 2000 and XP. Windows XP can operate with the FAT file system, and files in the other partition can be read.

Windows XP and Windows NT/2000/Me/9x Contrasts

The key features that are provided by Windows XP include enhanced security, Internet enhancements, and a new look of the GUI. This section includes the following topics:

- Keeping user files private
- Simple File Sharing versus Windows 2000 Sharing
- Internet enhancements
- System properties
- Graphical user interface

Keeping User Files Private

When a user upgrades from Windows 98 or Windows Me, the Setup program automatically creates a user account with no password. To add a password to the user account, go to **Start > Control Panel > User Accounts**. A dialog box displays, which allows the user to make his or her files and folders private.

NOTE

If the user profile is stored on a FAT32 drive, this option does not display.

NTFS provides the option of making files and folders private so that only the user has access to them. Windows XP allows you to make all or certain selected folders private. For example, the user might want his roommate to have access to the My Documents folder but not to certain files in the folder. The user can create a subfolder in the My Documents folder and make that subfolder private. Any files that the user does not want his roommate to have access to can be placed in the private subfolder. In Windows 2000, this procedure required rights and permissions to be set on files and folders.

Figure 7-11 shows that the file system has been formatted with NTFS. Right-click the local disk drive C. Select **Properties** from the drop-down menu. Look under the **File System** option to determine whether the partition has been formatted with NTFS.

Figure 7-11 Local Disk Properties

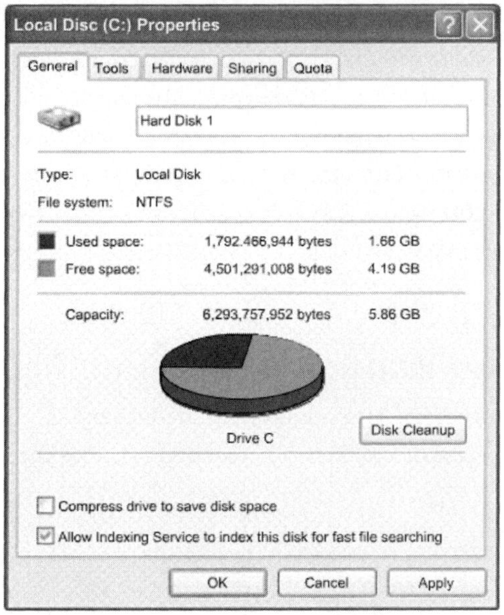

Simple File Sharing Versus Windows 2000 Sharing

File and resource security is another feature of Windows XP. Windows XP uses a system called Simple File Sharing, which provides a stripped-down interface that eases the setup of common security arrangements. Simple File Sharing differs from classic Windows NT and 2000 file sharing in several ways, as shown in Figures 7-12 and 7-13.

In Windows XP, permissions are set for local users and network users at the folder level only. Windows XP cannot apply permissions to individual files. Network users who connect to a computer are authenticated using the guest account of the computer. The guest account provides only those privileges and permissions that apply to the computer that is being accessed or shared. Windows XP also provides an option to switch from the Windows XP interface to the classic Windows 9x or 2000 interface.

In the Windows XP Home Edition, Simple File Sharing is the only option. In Windows XP Professional Edition, both interfaces are available. The user can switch between these interfaces by choosing **Tools**, **Folder options** in Windows Explorer. Click the **View** tab, and select or deselect the **Use Simple File Sharing** check box.

Figure 7-12 Simple File Sharing

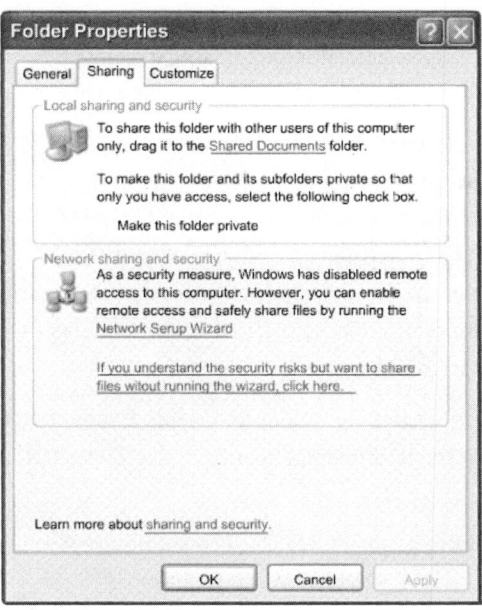

Figure 7-13 Classic File Sharing

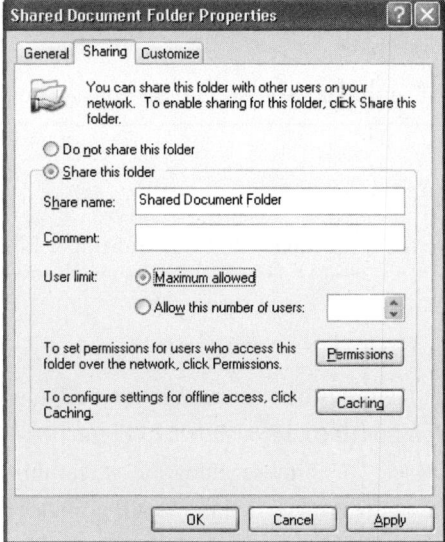

Troubleshooting Folder and File Sharing and Security

To share a folder over the network, right-click the folder and select **Properties** from the drop-down menu to display the Properties dialog box. If the Sharing and Security tabs are missing, determine whether the computer is set up with file and printer sharing for Microsoft networks.

If a user cannot view a shared folder from other computers on the network, determine whether a firewall is prohibiting access to the computers. Check the LAN connection to make sure that the Internet Connection Firewall option is only enabled for the Internet connection. Go to **Control Panel > Network Connections** and right-click on the LAN connection to access the Network Connections Properties dialog box. Make sure that the Internet Connection Firewall check box is selected appropriately. These firewall settings are necessary, but they can cause problems if they are not configured correctly.

To make a folder private, right-click the folder and select **Properties** from the drop-down menu that appears to access the Sharing and Security tabs. These tabs might not be accessible for the following reasons:

- The drive was not formatted using NTFS. The sharing option is not available if the drive is formatted with FAT32.
- The user did not create a folder or have it under his profile to make it private. Users cannot make the profiles of other users private.
- The parent folder or the user profile does not have the **Make This Folder Private** option selected, or all subfolders are already set to private.

Video   Simple File Sharing

A demonstration of setting up Simple File Sharing is provided in this video.

Lab 7.5.2   Using Simple File Sharing to Share Files

In this lab, you use the techniques and tools of Simple File Sharing.

Internet Enhancements

The Internet Enhancements feature is new to the Windows XP environment. Windows XP is shipped with Internet Explorer 6 (IE 6). IE 6, shown in Figure 7-14, is the most recent version of Microsoft's Internet browser. This browser integrates streaming media playback tools into the task pane on the left side of the browser. Windows XP provides a control to protect privacy. This control enables the user to build a custom policy that can block or allow cookies on a site-by-site basis.

Figure 7-14 Internet Explorer 6

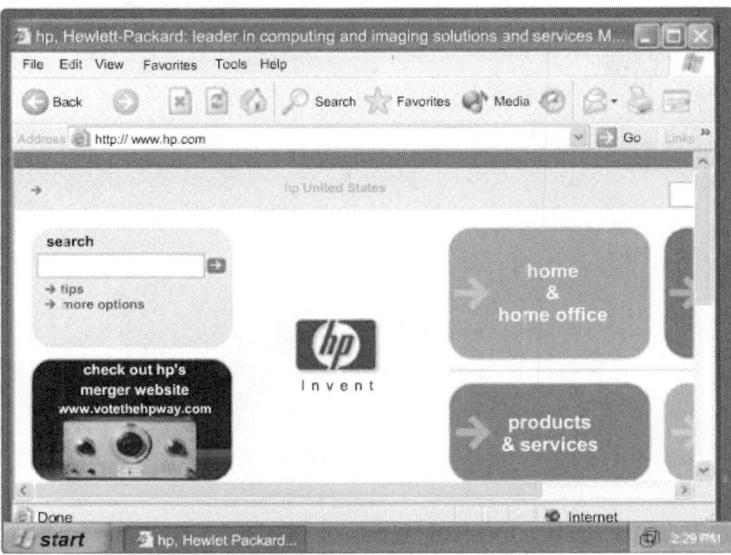

A *cookie* is a small text file that is stored on the PC's hard disk. The cookie allows a website to track the user's personal association to that site. To manage cookies in IE 6, choose **Tools**, **Internet Options** and select the **Privacy** tab. On the Privacy tab, select the desired cookie control with the slider tab on the left. Some websites might not function properly if the Block All Cookies option is selected. To view a nonfunctioning site, choose a lower cookie setting.

Windows XP includes the built-in Internet Connection Firewall (ICF) feature to stop common attacks from the Internet. This feature is significant for users who have high-speed Internet connections, such as cable and DSL connections, that are always active. Chapter 12, "Preventive Maintenance," provides more information on firewalls.

Remote Desktop Connection

The *Remote Desktop Connection* feature uses a Terminal Services technology that allows the user to work on a Windows XP Professional computer from any other computer. For example, a user might have been working on a file at home and forgot to bring it to work the next day. By remotely logging on to the home PC, the user can access the file and can navigate the home computer as if he were sitting in front of it.

To set up Remote Desktop, two computers need to be connected through a local-area network (LAN) or through a dialup or high-speed Internet connection. The computer that the user needs access to is referred to as the *remote computer.* The computer that accesses the remote computer is referred to as the *client computer.* The remote computer must be operating under

Windows XP Professional and have a known public IP address. The client computer needs to be operating under a version of Windows such as Windows 95, 98, Me, 2000, NT, or XP. For the remote connection to work on machines that do not have Windows XP, client software from the Windows XP Professional CD must be installed on the remote computer. Also, to use Remote Desktop, the client machine must have access through a LAN, Virtual Private Network (VPN), or dialup line. Figure 7-15 shows the Remote Desktop Connection interface.

Figure 7-15 Remote Desktop Connection

To run the Remote Desktop Connection, go to **Start** > **All Programs** > **Accessories** > **Communications** > **Remote Desktop Connection**. When using the Remote Desktop, users can encounter problems with the number of colors that are displayed and with audio that does not play properly. The number of colors that is displayed must be set at the lowest value of either computer. The client computer determines screen resolution. If the colors are not being displayed properly, check the group policy of the remote computer. If the value is less than that of the client machine, the group policy prevails. To increase the number of colors on the client machine, open the group policy on the client machine by right-clicking on the **My Computer** icon and selecting **Manage**. Then choose **Computer Configuration**, **Administrative Templates**, **Windows Components**, **Terminal Services**, and double-click **Maximum Color Depth Policy**. Choose **Enable**, and then specify the maximum color depth allowed for remote connections.

NOTE

Options for screen resolutions or audio must be set before making a connection.

During a Remote Desktop Connection, audio is considered a low priority. Audio problems can occur because the firewall is enabled. Check the firewall logs to determine if audio is being blocked. If this is the case, a rule can be entered to allow audio traffic to pass.

A Remote Desktop file (.rdp) is saved in the My Documents\Remote Desktops folder by default. To edit an .rdp file and change the connections settings it contains, right-click the file and select **Edit**. These files contain all the information for a connection to a remote computer, including the Options settings that were configured when the file was saved. You can customize any number of .rdp files, including files for connecting to the same computer with different settings. For example, you can save a file that connects to MyComputer, with the Maximum Color Depth Policy enabled and another file that connects to the same computer with Maximum Color Depth Policy disabled.

A Remote Desktop Connection must be logged off properly to end the session. Use the following steps to log off:

Step 1   In the Remote Desktop Connection window, click **Start**, and then click **Shut Down**. The Shut Down Windows dialog box appears.

Step 2   In the drop-down menu, select **Log Off** *<username>*, and then click **OK**.

Video   Remote Desktop Connection

This video demonstrates how to set up the Remote Desktop Connection.

Lab 7.5.3a   Remote Desktop Connection

In this lab, a Windows XP Remote Desktop Connection is used to establish a connection to another computer.

Lab 7.5.3b   Internet Connection Firewall

Set up a firewall to protect the system from threats from the Internet.

System Properties

The System Properties dialog box is a new feature in Windows XP. The tabs in this dialog box include Automatic Updates, Remote, and System Restore. These new features give the user added reliability and troubleshooting methods.

To access the System Properties dialog box, right-click the **My Computer** icon and select **Properties** from the drop-down menu that appears.

Automatic Updates Tab

Automatic Updates, as shown in Figure 7-16, allows the user to configure when and how the system will check for critical updates.

Figure 7-16 Automatic Update

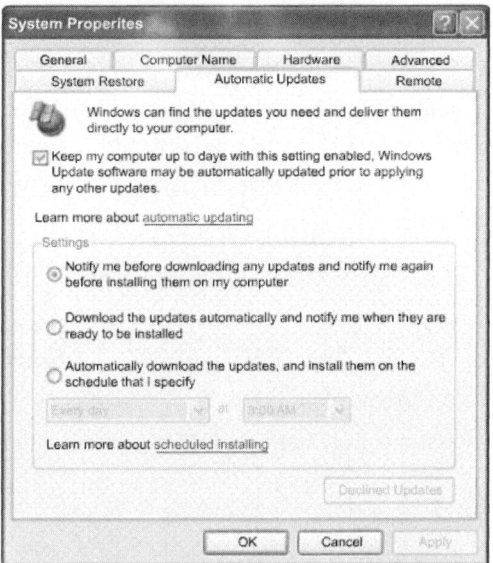

In addition to the option to turn off the Automatic Updates feature, the following three types of notification settings are included:

- **Notify me before downloading any updates and notify me again before installing them on my computer**—This notification prompts the user by displaying an icon in the System Tray. At that time, the user has the option to download or not download the update. If this option is accepted, the Automatic Update feature prompts the user again to install or not to install the update. This setting provides added security for the user. It also lets the user decide when to download an update, because the download considerably slows a dialup Internet connection.

- **Download the updates automatically and notify me when they are ready to be installed**—This option notifies the user when the update is downloaded and available to install. This setting is most useful for a high-speed, always-on Internet connection.

- **Automatically download the updates and install them on the schedule that I specify**—This setting fully automates the updating process.

Remote Tab

The Remote tab contains two new features: Remote Assistance, as shown in Figure 7-17, and Remote Desktop, which was discussed previously. The Windows XP Home Edition includes only the Remote Assistance feature. Both features are included with XP Professional.

Figure 7-17 Remote Tab Showing Remote Assistance

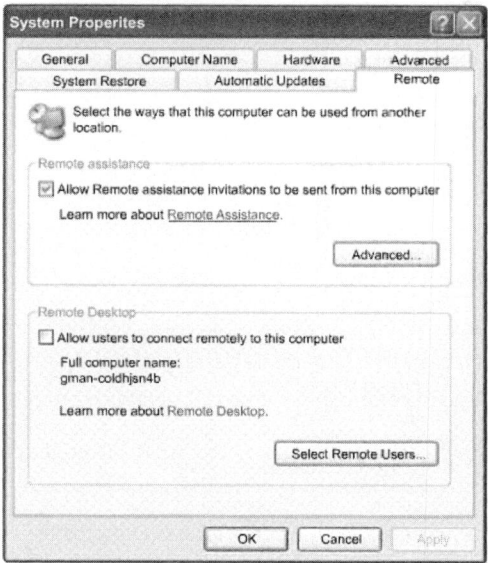

Remote Assistance

Remote Assistance is a convenient troubleshooting tool that allows administrators to connect to a client machine across any distance over the Internet. Remote Assistance can create a secure, reliable connection to ensure that neither computer is compromised. The interface hides the complexity of the process to allow the user to navigate with ease. The Remote Assistance screen is shown in Figure 7-18.

To enable Remote Assistance, two parties must establish a session. These parties are known as the novice and the expert. Both parties must be using Windows XP for this feature to work. Also, both parties must have active Internet connections or be on the same LAN. The connection cannot be established if third-party firewalls are set to block this type of connection. If the Windows XP Internet Connection Firewall is the only firewall in use, Windows XP automatically opens the port when the user requests a Remote Assistance connection.

Figure 7-18 Remote Assistance Screen

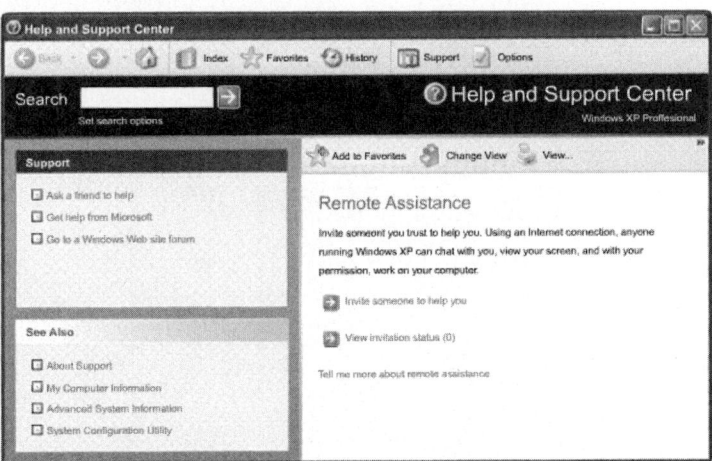

Use the following three steps to establish a Remote Assistance connection:

Step 1   The novice sends an invitation to the expert through Windows Messenger or e-mail.

Step 2   The expert accepts the invitation, which opens a terminal window that displays the Desktop of the novice machine. The terminal window is read-only for the expert.

Step 3   If the novice enables the Allow Expert Interaction option, the expert can manipulate the novice's machine.

The expert can communicate with the novice through text chat or voice chat.

System Restore

The *System Restore* feature is a Windows XP service that runs in the background. This service allows the user to restore the OS to a predefined point in time. The System Restore tab is located in the System Properties dialog box, as shown in Figure 7-19. This feature keeps a log of the continual changes in folders, files, and settings that are crucial to the operating system. These logs are stored in the Filelist.xml file, which is located in the %SystemRoot%\System32\Restore directory.

Figure 7-19 System Restore Tab

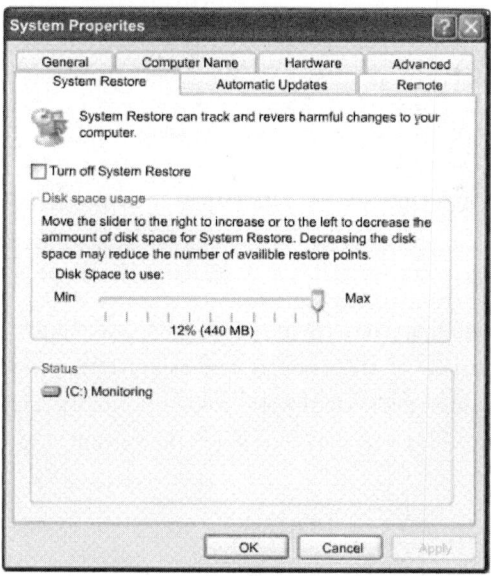

The system files are copied to hidden archives for security at regular intervals. System Restore also takes snapshots of the system state—including user accounts, hardware and software settings, and startup files—at regular intervals. Windows XP creates an initial restore point whenever an install or upgrade takes place. Also, if the computer is left on, restore points are created every 24 hours regardless of user activity. If the computer is turned off and more than 24 hours have passed since the prior restore was completed, the service creates a restore point when the computer is turned on. Windows XP also allows the user to manually create a restore point at any time.

Restore points are automatically created during the following actions:

- An unsigned device driver is installed.
- An application that uses an installer that is compatible with System Restore is installed.
- A Windows update or patch is installed.
- The system is restored to a prior configuration using System Restore.
- A backup set, which was created with the Windows XP backup program, is restored.

System Restore does not monitor the following files or folders:

- Page files
- Any files that are stored in the personal data folders such as My Documents, Favorites, Recycle Bin, History, or Temporary Internet Files
- Images and graphics files
- Microsoft Outlook and Outlook Express e-mail files
- Files that use extensions commonly associated with data files, such as .doc, .xls, .mbd, or .pdf

If a problem is encountered that causes Windows XP not to function properly, the System Restore Wizard can be started in Safe Mode as well as in Normal Mode. The system can then be set back to a point at which the system was working normally. This new service to XP can be helpful when conflicts with drivers arise or when the system stops working for an undetermined reason.

A driver might not work for one of the following reasons:

- A new program could be conflicting with the installed driver.
- A new driver could be installed that causes instability in the system.

When the system suddenly stops working, a restore date prior to the problem can be selected. After the system is restored, it should return to normal operation.

System Restore cannot protect against viruses, worms, or a Trojan horse. When one of these items is detected, the user might not be able to determine how long the virus has been in the system and what files it has infected. System Restore could actually restore the virus, even though the objective was to remove it. Be sure to use and update your antivirus software.

Graphical User Interface

Windows XP has a new graphical user interface (GUI), as shown in Figure 7-20. The Start menu, the Task Manager, and the Taskbar remain. However, the icons for My Computer, Network Places, and My Documents are no longer on the Desktop by default. The Start menu has been given a different appearance, compared to earlier versions of Windows. This menu now includes access to My Computer, Network Places, and so on. This change allows the user to more easily access these directories when other windows are open on the Desktop. The Start menu can be customized to display shortcuts to the most commonly used items. The logon and logoff user icons have been updated as well.

Figure 7-20 Windows XP GUI

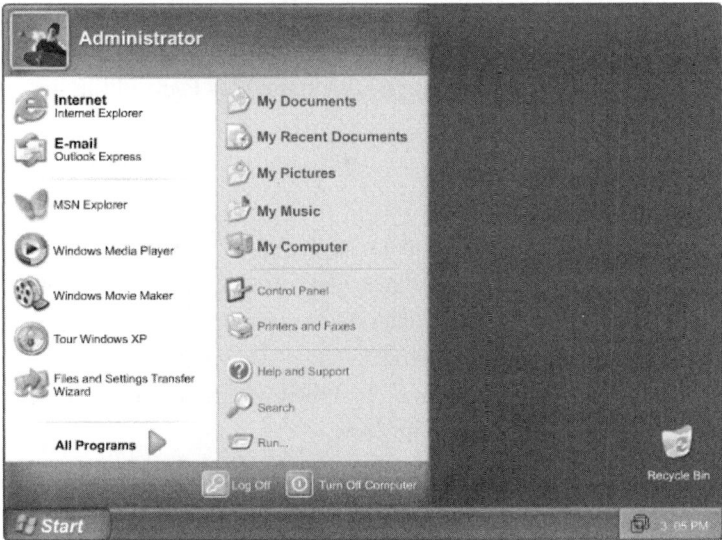

With previous versions of Windows, the Taskbar would become cluttered if multiple windows were opened. Windows XP organizes common items into groups—such as word processing files, spreadsheet files, and so on—on the Taskbar. Clicking an item on the Taskbar opens a pop-up menu that displays the files that are in use for a given application.

Windows XP has new visual styles and themes that can be easily related to specific tasks, as follows:

- **Brighter colors**—Windows XP is capable of displaying color settings of 24-bit and 32-bit True Color because of advances in video card technology. Windows XP uses these enhanced color features to offer brighter and bolder color schemes than those used in previous versions of Windows.

- **Three-dimensional windows and buttons**—The Windows XP GUI appears to have a three-dimensional look, because the windows and buttons have rounded edges and smooth shadows. Buttons, tabs, and windows shift colors as the mouse pointer moves over them.

- **Sharper icons**—Microsoft has redesigned all the icons to make them brighter and stand out more. The properties of these icons can be changed to make them appear about twice as large as they did in previous versions of Windows. Windows XP includes an option to view the large icons in a Tiles View, which adds a few lines of detailed information about the icon.

■ **Integrated themes**—Schemes, fonts, sizes, and sounds can be saved in Windows XP. Theme support is tightly woven into the Windows XP Control Panel Display utility. Changes can be made to window borders and common controls as well as to the Startup menu. Desktop themes were first introduced in the Plus Pack add-in that was supplied with Windows 95.

Putting Pictures on Folder Icons

Folder icons in Windows XP provide a preview of the folder contents in the thumbnail view, as shown in Figure 7-21. For example, a folder icon could display the art from a music CD that has been placed on the hard drive. A folder that contains pictures can display a preview of up to four of those pictures on the folder icon. When a folder contains videos, the folder icon displays the first frame of up to four videos. The Preview option can be accessed from the Customize tab in the Folder Properties dialog box.

Figure 7-21 Pictures on the Folder

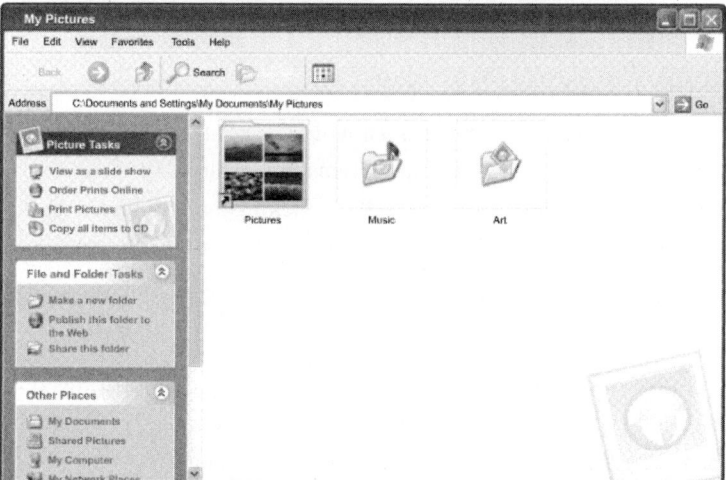

Fast User Switching

On a shared work or home computer, users can quickly switch between accounts without having to log off. This feature was initially designed for home use and is enabled by default with the Windows XP Home Edition. The Fast User Switching feature is also available on the Windows XP Professional Edition if it is installed on a stand-alone or workgroup-connected computer. If the user joins a domain with a computer that uses Windows XP Professional, the user cannot use Fast User Switching.

For example, consider two users who share one computer. The first user is downloading music. The second user can check her e-mail without disrupting the music download of the first user. Both users can share the computer with no logoff time delay.

Windows XP takes advantage of Terminal Services technology and operates each user session as a unique Terminal Services session. This technique enables each user's data to be separated from the other's.

Enhanced Networking Features

Windows XP has incorporated features that are compatible with the latest advances in networking technology. For example, wireless access enhancements follow the IEEE 802.11b standard.

Windows Explorer

Windows Explorer is improved in Windows XP. Windows XP has incorporated a new organized approach with its new appearance, as shown in Figure 7-22. When a folder window is open, the Folder button toggles the left pane between the familiar Folders tree and the new task pane. This pane consists of a set of links that offer quick access to common tasks, related locations, shortcuts, and details. The new Tiles View can be seen easily in the My Computer window.

Figure 7-22 Windows Explorer

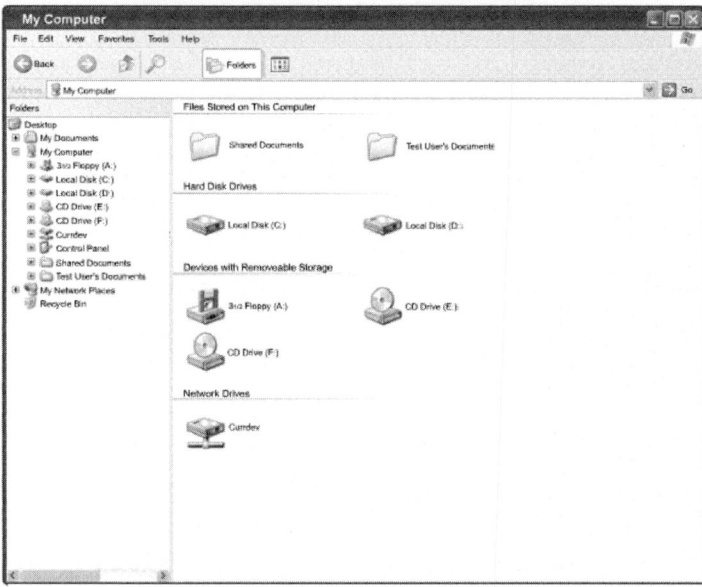

Windows Explorer takes a much more organized approach to browsing folders and files. For example, the folders, hard drives, removable storage devices, and network in My Computer are all grouped into categories.

The user can better organize the files in the My Documents folder by arranging them into various groups. The user can also view documents by type or group files according to the last modification date.

Windows XP uses Webview technology to better manage files and filename space. For example, a selected file or folder can have a list of available options that allow the user to rename, move, copy, e-mail, remove it, or publish it to the web. This functionality is similar to that of Windows 2000. If the user right-clicks a file or folder, Windows XP displays this information directly on the Desktop.

Windows XP makes Taskbar management easier by grouping multiple instances of the same application together. For example, instead of having nine instances of a Microsoft Word file, each arranged horizontally on the Taskbar, Windows XP groups them together onto one Taskbar button. In this scenario, only one Taskbar button appears; this button shows the number of files that are open for the application. Clicking the button shows a vertical list of all filenames. In addition, the files can all be cascaded, tiled, or minimized at the same time.

Video   Using the Windows XP Start Menu and Windows Explorer

This video shows the new look of Windows XP, featuring the Start menu and Windows Explorer.

New Logon Procedure

Windows XP provides a new logon procedure, as shown in Figure 7-23. If a profile is set up on the system, the user can click the icon next to the correct name and type in a password. An administrator cannot log on from this screen.

Windows XP can display a photo or other image beside the names of account holders on the Welcome screen. Although an account administrator can assign pictures for all users, any account holder can choose his or her own picture.

Lab 7.5.5   Using the Windows XP Start Menu and Windows Explorer

This lab explores the Windows XP Start menu and Windows Explorer.

Figure 7-23 Windows XP Logon

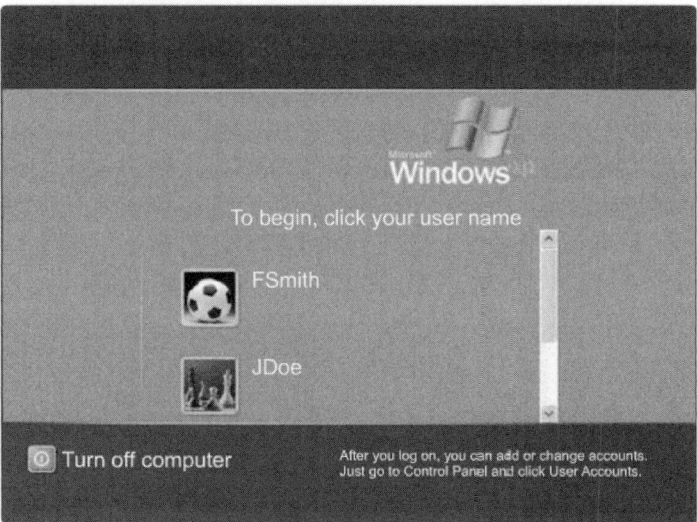

Summary

This chapter discussed the Windows XP operating systems. You should retain the following important concepts from this chapter:

- Windows XP features Simple File Sharing, Internet enhancements, and a new graphical user interface.
- The four different editions of Windows XP that were covered in this chapter are the Home Edition, the Professional Edition, the Professional 64-Bit Edition, and the Media Center Edition.
- Similar to Windows 2000, you must verify that a given computer system will be compatible with the Windows XP OS. Use the Hardware Compatibility List (HCL) before installing Windows XP to verify that the hardware will work with the OS.
- Three types of installations exist: a clean installation, an upgrade, and a dual-boot installation.
- The minimum hardware requirements for Windows XP Professional can vary based on the type of installation that is performed.
- IT administrators who are performing large deployments of Windows XP Professional in a corporate environment use the User State Migration Tool (USMT). The USMT provides the same functionality as the Files and Settings Transfer Wizard on a large scale for migrating multiple users.

- The process of upgrading a computer system from Windows NT 4.0 to Windows XP is faster than performing a clean install of Windows XP. Similar to the upgrade to Windows 2000, the computers that use Windows NT 4.0 or 2000 can connect and communicate with the Windows XP computers.

The next chapter discusses the multimedia capabilities of the PC. You gain an understanding of the basics of multimedia presentations. You also learn how to install the various devices that play and record sound and images.

Key Terms

Automatic Update   Allows the user to configure when and how the Windows Update feature checks for critical updates.

cookie   A small text file that is stored on the PC's hard disk that allows a website to track the user's personal association to that site.

kernel   The main module of the operating system that provides all the essential services that are needed by applications.

Remote Assistance   A troubleshooting tool that allows administrators to connect to a client machine across any distance over the Internet.

Remote Desktop Connection   Allows the user to work on a Windows XP Professional computer from any other computer.

Resultant Set of Policy (RSoP)   A Windows XP tool that plans, monitors, and troubleshoots group policy.

System Restore   A Windows XP service that runs in the background and allows the user to restore the OS to a predefined point in time.

User State Migration Tool (USMT)   Used by IT administrators for migrating multiple users in large deployments of Windows XP Professional in a corporate environment.

Check Your Understanding

1. Which of the following is not included in the Windows XP Home Edition?

   A. Roaming profiles

   B. Fast user switching

   C. Individual user logon

   D. NTFS support

2. Which setting prompts the user after updates have been downloaded and are available to install?

   A. Automatically download the updates and install them on the schedule that I specify.

   B. Notify me before downloading any updates and notify me again before installing them on my computer.

   C. Disable Automatic Update in the System Properties tab.

   D. Download the updates automatically and notify me when they are ready to be installed.

3. Which Windows XP version uses the performance enhancements of the Intel Itanium 2 processor?

   A. Home Edition

   B. Professional Edition

   C. Professional 64-Bit Edition

   D. Media Center Edition

4. Which version of Windows requires a minimum of 64 MB RAM and a Pentium II processor?

   A. Windows 95

   B. Windows XP Professional Edition

   C. Windows XP Professional 64-Bit Edition

   D. Windows 3.1

5. What is the minimum amount of RAM (in MB) that is needed to install Windows XP Professional?

   A. 32

   B. 64

   C. 128

   D. 256

6. Which Windows operating system cannot be upgraded to Windows XP?

   A. Windows 95

   B. Windows 98

   C. Windows 2000

   D. Windows NT 4.0

7. What is the first step in the Windows XP installation?

   A. File copy

   B. GUI mode setup

   C. Windows Welcome

   D. Text mode setup

8. What command is used to start an upgrade to Windows XP?

    A. xp.exe

    B. winnt32

    C. No command; cannot upgrade

    D. 2000up

9. Where is the My Computer icon located by default on a Windows XP computer?

    A. Desktop

    B. Start menu

    C. Taskbar

    D. Task Manager

10. Which statement best describes the Fast User Switching feature of Windows XP?

    A. Allows users to log on multiple times

    B. Allows users to switch quickly between accounts without having to log off

    C. Allows up to five users to log on simultaneously

    D. Eliminates the need to log on when the computer boots

Objectives

Upon completion of this chapter, you will be able to perform the following tasks:

- Understand the hardware requirements for multimedia
- Install or upgrade the video and sound cards
- Configure video capture and video capture boards
- Uninstall the hardware components and remove associated drivers
- Install and configure the CD-ROM and DVD drives
- Understand the differences between recordable and rewritable CDs and DVDs

Chapter 8

Multimedia Capabilities

This chapter discusses the multimedia capabilities of the PC. Multimedia presentations go beyond text and images to include video, animation, live situations, audience interaction, and sound. You learn about the basic hardware—including video cards, computer displays, and media file formats—that is used in multimedia. This chapter provides information on how to install or upgrade video and sound cards, including how to configure drivers and software. Compact disc read-only memory (CD-ROM) drives and digital versatile disc read-only memory (DVD-ROM) drives are detailed, providing you with an overview of how these drives work and the advantages of each, especially in terms of multimedia production.

Introduction to Multimedia

Most modern computer systems come equipped with the capability to display and create multimedia. The ability to use different types of media is as much a part of the modern PC as an Internet connection. This section includes the following topics:

- Basic hardware required for multimedia upgrades
- The video adapter
- Computer displays
- Sound cards and speaker systems
- Common media file formats used in multimedia applications
- MPEG hardware versus software

Basic Hardware Required for Multimedia Upgrades

The IT technician is responsible for the hardware and software that are required to run modern presentation media on the PC. The hardware can range from simple speakers to complex recording equipment.

The term *multimedia* means a combination of text, sound, and motion video. Figure 8-1 is an example of a video in the Windows Media Player.

Figure 8-1 Windows Media Player

Multimedia refers to any of the following items:

- Text and sound
- Text, sound, and still or animated graphics images
- Text, sound, and video images
- Video and sound
- Multiple display areas, images, or presentations that are presented concurrently
- Speakers or actors and props, together with sound, images, and motion video

Multimedia is distinguished from traditional motion pictures or movies in two ways. One is the scale of the production. Multimedia is usually smaller and less expensive. The second is that multimedia can add audience participation or interactive multimedia. The following are interactive elements:

- Voice commands
- Mouse manipulation

- Text entry
- Touch screen
- Video capture of the user
- Live participation during live presentations

Multimedia presentations are more complex than simple text-and-image presentations and are generally more expensive. Multimedia presentations can be included in many contexts, including the web, CDs, and so on. Basic development costs of a commercial multimedia production with video for commercial presentations can cost as much as US $1000 per minute of presentation time. Multimedia software can develop presentations at a much lower cost than commercial video productions, with the flexibility to distribute on the web or on a CD.

PC Requirements to Run Multimedia

The types of computer hardware and software that are necessary to develop multimedia on a PC vary. The minimum hardware requirements include a computer monitor, video accelerator card, and sound adapter card with attached speakers. The following components provide visual and sound output:

- A microphone can be connected to a plug on the sound adapter card to input sound.
- CD-ROM and DVD-ROM drives are common PC components that are used to input multimedia. CD-RW and DVD-RW drives can be used to both read and write to the media.
- A connection to the Internet, using a network interface card or a modem, also provides multimedia input to the system. Audio and video streaming is popular.
- Digital still pictures and video cameras are often connected through standard computer ports or special card adapters.
- A video capture card—that is, a special adapter card that samples and converts the images and sounds—can provide television and radio recordings and images.
- Motion Picture Experts Group (MPEG) hardware and web-based movie players can play movies.
- Computer games on DVDs or CDs require specialized hardware to display high-end graphics and to keep up with the fast-paced action.

The Video Adapter

A *video adapter*, also called a *display adapter* or *video board*, is an expansion card in a computer. In some computers, the video adapter is integrated into the motherboard. There are also monitors that provide digital-to-analog conversion, video RAM, and a video controller so that data can be sent to a computer display. Figures 8-2 and 8-3 show the front and side views, respectively, of a video adapter.

Figure 8-2 Front View of a Video Adapter

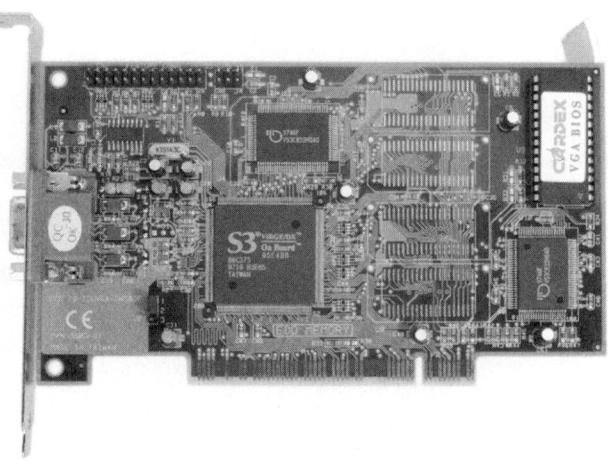

Figure 8-3 Side View of a Video Adapter

Today, most displays and video adapters adhere to the ***Video Graphics Array (VGA) standard***. VGA standards describe how data is passed between the computer and the display. This standard defines the frame refresh rates, in hertz, and the number and width of horizontal lines. The VGA standard specifies the resolution, which in turn defines the number of pixels that are on the screen. VGA supports four different resolution settings and two related image refresh rates.

In addition to VGA, most displays adhere to one or more standards set by the ***Video Electronics Standards Association (VESA)***. The VESA standards define how software determines the capability of a display. The association also identifies resolution settings beyond those of VGA. These resolutions include the following:

- 800×600 pixels
- 1024×768 pixels
- 1280×1024 pixels
- 1600×1200 pixels

What Is a Display?

A *display* or *monitor* is a computer output surface and projecting mechanism that shows text and graphics images, using one of the following technologies:

- Cathode ray tube (CRT)
- Liquid crystal display (LCD)
- Light-emitting diode (LED)
- Gas plasma
- Other image-projection technology

The display usually includes the screen or projection surface and the device that produces the information on the screen. In some computers, the display is packaged in a separate unit called a monitor. Figure 8-4 shows a typical flat-panel monitor. In other computers, the display is integrated into a unit with the processor and other parts of the computer. Some sources make the distinction that the monitor includes other signal-handling devices that feed and control the display or projection device. However, no distinction exists when all these parts become integrated into a total unit, as in the case of notebook computers. A *video display terminal (VDT)* or *video display unit (VDU)* typically refers to a terminal with a display and a keyboard.

Figure 8-4 HP 18-Inch Flat-Panel Monitor

Most computer monitors use analog signals to display an image and need to continually refresh the image that is displayed. For this reason, the computer also needs a display or video adapter. The video adapter performs the following tasks:

- Accepts the digital data that is sent by application programs
- Stores the data in video random-access memory (VRAM)
- Converts the digital data to analog data for the display-scanning mechanism using a digital-to-analog converter (DAC)

Computer Displays

Computer video displays can be characterized according to the following characteristics:

- Color capability
- Sharpness and viewability
- Screen size
- Projection technology

Color Capability

Today, most desktop displays provide color. Older notebook computers and earlier desktop computers sometimes had a less expensive monochrome display. Video displays can usually operate in one of several display modes. These modes determine how many bits describe color and how many colors can be displayed. A *Super Video Graphics Array (SVGA) monitor* can display up to 16,777,216 colors, because it can process a 24-bit-long description of a pixel. The number of bits that describe a pixel is known as its *bit-depth*. The 24-bit bit-depth is also known as *true color*. True color allows 8 bits for each of the three additive primary colors: red, green, and blue (RGB). Although humans cannot distinguish 16 million colors, the 24-bit system is necessary for graphics designers, because it allocates 1 byte for each color. The *Video Graphics Array (VGA) mode* is the lowest common denominator of display modes. Depending on the resolution setting, this mode can provide up to 256 colors. Table 8-1 shows the relationship between bit-depth and the number of colors that can be produced.

Sharpness and Viewability

The physical limitation on the potential sharpness of a screen image is the *dot pitch*. The shape of this image can be round or a vertical, slot-shaped rectangle, depending on the display technology, as illustrated in Figure 8-5. Displays typically have a dot pitch of 0.28 millimeters (mm) or smaller. This dot pitch is the diagonal distance between phosphor dots of the same color. The smaller the dot pitch, the greater the potential image sharpness.

Table 8-1 Display Bit-Depth

Bit-Depth	Number of Colors
1	2 (monochrome)
2	4 (CGA)
4	16 (EGA)
8	256 (VGA)
16	65,536 (High Color, XGA)
24	16,777,216 (True Color, SVGA)
32	16,777,216 (True Color + Alpha Channel)

Figure 8-5 Dot Pitch Illustration

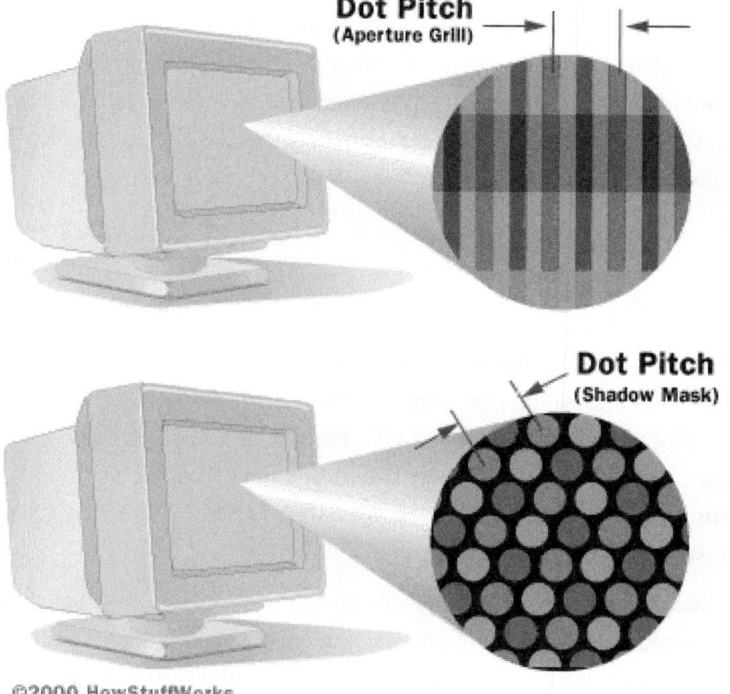

©2000 HowStuffWorks

The sharpness of a particular display image is measured in **dots per inch** (dpi). The dpi is determined by a combination of the screen resolution, which is how many pixels are projected on the screen horizontally and vertically, and the physical screen size. A low-resolution setting spread out over a larger screen reduces sharpness. On the other hand, a high-resolution setting on a smaller surface produces a sharper image, but text readability suffers.

Viewability is the ability to see the screen image from different angles. CRT displays generally provide good viewability from wide angles. Flat-panel displays, including those using LED and LCD technology, are often harder to see at angles.

Screen Size

On desktop computers, the width-to-height ratio of the display screen, known as the *aspect ratio*, is generally standardized at 4 to 3 (4:3). Screen sizes are measured diagonally, from one corner to the opposite corner, and screens can be measured in either millimeters or inches. Common desktop screen sizes are 15, 17, and 19 inches. Notebook screen sizes are somewhat smaller.

Projection Technology

Many displays use cathode ray tube (CRT) technology, which is similar to that used in most television sets. The CRT technology requires a certain distance from the beam projection device to the screen to function. Through the use of other technologies, displays can be much thinner. These thinner displays are known as flat-panel displays. Flat-panel display technologies include the following:

- LED
- LCD
- Gas plasma

Light-emitting diode (LED) and *gas plasma* technologies work by lighting up display screen positions based on the voltages at different grid intersections. *Liquid crystal displays (LCDs)* work by blocking light rather than creating it. LCDs require far less energy than LED and gas plasma technologies, which helps to maximize battery life in notebook computers. Different types of LCDs, with different characteristics, are available. LCDs are currently the primary displays that are used for notebook and other mobile computers.

Displays generally handle data input as either character maps or bitmaps. In character-mapping mode, a display has a preallocated amount of pixel space for each character. In bitmap mode, a display receives an exact representation of the screen image that is to be projected in the form of a sequence of bits. This representation describes the color values for specific X and Y coordinates, starting from a given location on the screen. Displays that handle bitmaps are also known as *all-points-addressable displays*.

Sound Cards and Speaker Systems

Most modern sound cards only have the capability of directly driving low-power headphones. If *external speakers* are used, the output of the sound card requires additional amplification. The amplification circuitry is normally included in the external speaker units. Figure 8-6 shows external speakers. The internal speaker system can also produce audio output and can be amplified through external audio amplifier systems for applications such as surround sound.

Figure 8-6 External Computer Speakers

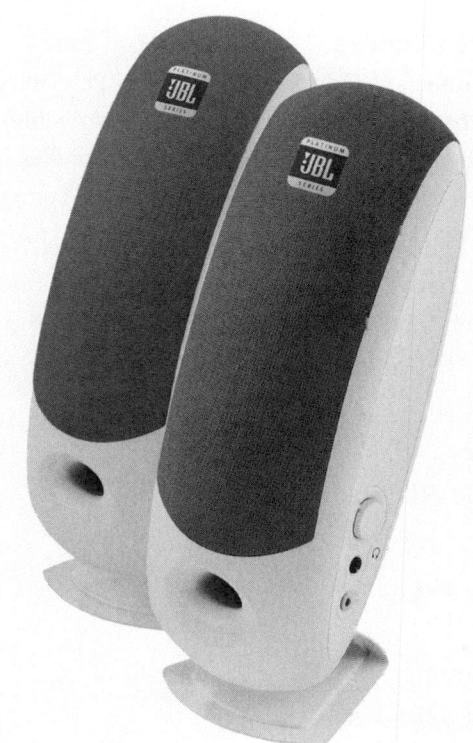

Common Media File Formats Used in Multimedia Applications

Two data-compression standards are commonly used with digitized video: the *Joint Photographic Experts Group (JPEG)* and the *Moving Picture Experts Group (MPEG)* compression standards.

JPEG is preferred for compression of full-color or grayscale images. It does not work well with cartoons, line art, or other nonrealistic images. JPEG uses an algorithm to achieve compression that allows a certain amount of loss that is not visible to the human eye. The loss in the JPEG image is only noticeable with machine analysis. The lossless mode of JPEG does not provide a compression ratio and is rarely used.

Several variations of MPEG are used today. MPEG-1 is used primarily as a cross-platform movie standard on the web. It was optimized for CD-ROM or applications at about 1.5 Mbps. MPEG-2 has become the standard for HDTV and digital satellite broadcasts. Another key feature of MPEG-2 is scalable extensions, which permit the division of a continuous video signal into two or more coded bit streams that represent the video at different resolutions, picture quality, or picture rates.

Other Compression Standards

Intel has developed another method of data compression for PCs called Indeo. *Indeo* is similar to the MPEG standard, because it was designed to be a distribution format. The Indeo standard was primarily designed to play back compressed video files from the smallest file size possible. Later versions of this standard include the MPEG compression methods.

Another compression and decompression standard that is supported by Video for Windows is *Cinepak*. This standard uses an *audio video interface (AVI)* file format to produce 40:1 compression ratios and a 30 frames-per-second capture rate, at 320×200 resolution. Microsoft Windows supports the following compression techniques:

- Cinepak
- Two versions of Indeo
- Run Length Encoding (RLE) format
- Video 1 format

Figure 8-7 shows how data compression works.

Figure 8-7 Data Compression

MPEG Hardware Versus Software

Although the JPEG format provides enough compression to allow single-frame digitized images to fit on disk drives, full-motion pictures require much greater compression to be useful with current technology. The MPEG format was created to provide compression ratios up to 200:1 with high-quality video and audio.

As with JPEG, the MPEG format removes redundant picture information from individual scenes. However, instead of simply removing redundant information from within a single frame, the MPEG compression scheme removes redundant information from consecutive scenes. In addition, the MPEG methodology compresses only key objects within a frame every 15th frame. Between these key frames, only the information that changes from frame to frame is recorded.

The MPEG standard includes specifications for audio compression and decompression in both MPEG-1 and MPEG-2. The MPEG-1 format provides CD-quality stereo output at data rates from 128 kbps to 256 kbps. The MPEG-2 specification supports CD-quality surround sound. Table 8-2 describes the different MPEG standards.

Table 8-2 MPEG Standards

	MPEG-1	**MPEG-2**	**MPEG-4**
Compression	320×280 Full-motion video	720×480 Full-motion video	Full-motion video
Application	Interactive multimedia/broadcast TV	Broadcast TV, video-on-demand	Interactive multimedia
Data rate	1.5 Mbps	4-80 Mbps	≥64 Kbps

 Worksheet 8.1.6   Multimedia Devices

In this worksheet, you match multimedia devices to the correct descriptions.

Upgrading Video with a Video Acceleration Board

You must consider several things when upgrading a video card. Before installing a card, you should understand the different types of cards, how memory is used, and the functions that are provided by the video BIOS. This section includes the following topics:

- Reviewing PCI and AGP types
- Understanding all-in-one cards

- Installing and configuring the video card driver and software
- Understanding RAMDAC and video memory
- Flashing the video board with BIOS updates

Reviewing PCI and AGP Types

Newer Pentium systems include an advanced *Accelerated Graphics Port (AGP)* interface for video graphics. The AGP interface is a variation of the PCI bus design that has been modified to handle the larger data throughput that is associated with three-dimensional graphics. Figure 8-8 shows the AGP interface on the motherboard.

Figure 8-8 Accelerated Graphics Port (AGP) Interface

The AGP specification was introduced by Intel to provide a 32-bit video channel that runs at 66 MHz in basic 1x video mode. The standard also supports two high-speed modes: a 2x (533-MBps) and a 4x (1.07-GBps) mode.

The AGP standard provides a direct channel between the AGP graphic controller and the computer system main memory. This removes the video data traffic from the PCI buses. The speed that is provided by this direct link permits video data to be stored in system RAM instead of in special video memory.

The system board typically has a single slot that is supported by a Pentium/AGP-compliant chipset. System boards that are designed for portable systems and single-board systems can incorporate the AGP function directly into the board without using a slot connector.

Understanding All-in-One Cards

Video capture software captures frames of television video and converts these frames into digital formats that can be processed by the system. Graphics packages can manipulate the contents of the video after it has been converted into digital formats. One of the popular file formats for video is the Microsoft AVI format.

Video capture cards are responsible for converting video signals from different sources into digital signals that can be manipulated by the computer. As in the audio conversion process, the video card samples the incoming video signal by feeding it through an analog-to-digital (A/D) converter. Figure 8-9 shows the audio signal going in as analog and coming out as a digital signal.

Figure 8-9 Analog-to-Digital Conversion

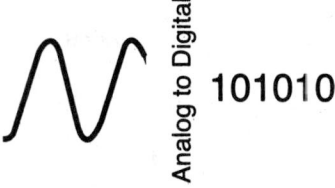

One of the jobs of the video capture card is to convert the YUV format into an RGB VGA-compatible signal. *YUV* is the color model that is used for encoding video, and it is different from RGB. Y indicates the luminosity of the black-and-white signal. U and V are color difference signals. U is red minus Y, and V is blue minus Y. YUV saves storage space and transmission bandwidth compared to RGB. To display YUV data on a computer screen, the data must be converted into the RGB format that is acceptable to the VGA card screen memory. This is done through the *color space conversion* process. An encoding circuit samples the incoming analog signal and then performs this operation. The resolution of a studio-quality TV signal is delivered in two interlaced screens at a rate of 60 fields per second. The encoder converts this signal scheme into a 640×480 image in VGA mode, delivered to the screen in a single, noninterlaced rate of 30 or more frames per second.

In addition to changing the format, the capture card also scales the image to fit the defined video window on the monitor. The capture card video signal processor adjusts the image to the correct size by adding or removing adjacent pixels as necessary. The encoder samples the analog signal at a rate of 27 MBps. This value becomes important when considering that at this rate, a 500-MB hard drive would become full in 18.5 seconds. To make the digitized video manageable and useful to the digital computer system, the signal must be compressed into smaller files.

Installing and Configuring the Video Card Driver and Software

After the video card has been installed and the monitor has been connected to the video card and plugged into the power outlet, you must install the correct drivers for the video card. At this point, the Windows 9x operating systems should do the following:

- Detect the video card
- Start the system with the basic VGA video drivers
- Ask whether you want to install the manufacturer's video drivers

Figure 8-10 shows the screen that displays when hardware installation starts.

Figure 8-10 Installing a Video Driver

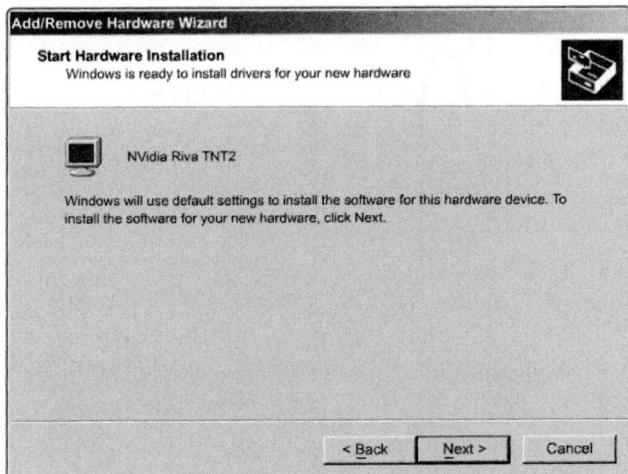

The Windows 2000 operating system is even more proactive. It does the following things:

- Detects the new video card
- Tells the user that it has found the new card
- Automatically loads the card's video drivers

The only time that the user should need to be directly involved with the system video drivers is when the Plug and Play feature fails or if the video card is not recognized by the operating system.

Lab 8.2.3 Upgrading the Video Accelerator Card

This lab provides the steps to install a video card with advanced capabilities such as three dimensions, more memory, or AGP capabilities. Removing the old video drivers and installing new ones are also covered.

Video Replacing a Video Card

This video shows the steps of replacing a video card, as discussed in this chapter.

Understanding RAMDAC and Video Memory

Image information is stored and manipulated in video memory in the standard binary format of 1s and 0s. These binary patterns control the resolution and color of each pixel on the video display screen. However, monitors are analog—not digital—devices. For the monitor to work, the digital information in the *video card memory* must be translated into analog form for export to the monitor. This is the role of the *random-access memory digital-to-analog converter (RAMDAC)* chip.

The RAMDAC chip does the following things:

- Reads the video memory content
- Converts the video memory content to analog form
- Sends the video memory content over a cable to the video monitor

The quality of this chip impacts the quality of the image, speed of the refresh rate, and maximum resolution capability. Refresh rate refers to the number of times per second that the video display screen can be redrawn.

Video Memory

The video chipset relies on video memory to render an image. The basic element of every video image is a pixel. Many pixels comprise what is displayed on the monitor. Every pixel has a location that is reserved in video memory. The maximum number of pixels that can be displayed relates to the resolution.

Resolution is commonly expressed as a pair of numbers. Each pair of numbers represents the maximum possible number of pixels on a horizontal axis and the maximum possible number pixels on a vertical axis. The basic VGA resolution of 640×480 means that 640 pixels are possible on the horizontal axis and 480 pixels are possible on the vertical axis. Enhanced VGA has a resolution of 800×600 pixels. Super VGA has a resolution of 1024×768 pixels. As the resolution increases, more memory is needed to draw the image. Higher resolution creates a sharper and clearer image. Figure 8-11 illustrates how resolution can affect the quality of an image.

When an image is displayed in color or grayscale, a certain number of bits must be assigned per dot to achieve a given color depth. If more bits are assigned per dot, more colors can be presented.

Flashing the Video Board with BIOS Updates

Although the CPU issues instructions to the video card about what to draw, the CPU does not tell the video card how to draw. The *video BIOS* is responsible for determining how an image is to be displayed. The video BIOS provides the set of video functions that can be used by the software programs to access the video hardware. The video BIOS allows software to interface with the video chipset in much the same way that the system BIOS does for the motherboard chipset. When SVGA technology became an industry standard, incompatibilities in the different video BIOS implementations led to the development of a standardized BIOS.

Figure 8-11 Quality Improves as Resolution Increases

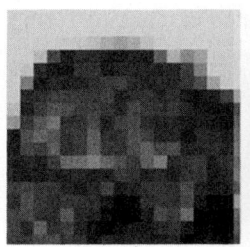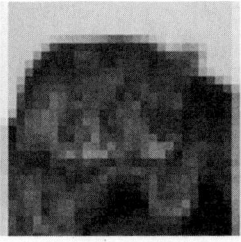

 Worksheet 8.2.5 Video Accelerators

This worksheet reviews the information that was covered on video cards and video accelerators.

Adding Audio Capabilities with a Sound Card

Audio is an integral component of the multimedia experience and is a standard feature on personal computers. Educational software and recreational software use sound effects to heighten the experience. Musicians use computer audio capabilities to create songs. Visually impaired users can have the computer "speak" information to them. The applications for computer audio are endless, but for a PC to have audio capabilities, it must have a sound card. This section includes the following topics:

- Understanding sound card operation
- Working with USB, PCI, and built-in sound
- Removing or disabling outdated sound cards
- Installing sound cards
- Connecting a CD-ROM or DVD-ROM drive to the sound card
- Installing the sound card driver and software
- Connecting MIDI and external audio sources

Understanding Sound Card Operation

A *sound card* is a device, either in the form of an expansion card or a chipset, that allows the computer to handle audio information. Figure 8-12 shows a typical sound card.

Figure 8-12 Sound Card

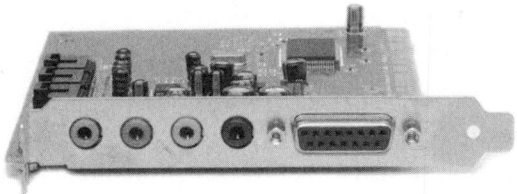

The basic responsibilities of a sound card are the input, processing, and output of audio information, as detailed in the following list:

- *Sound card input* —Sound cards can capture audio information from many different sources. These sources include microphones and CD players.

- *Sound card processing* —The processing capability of a sound card allows it to convert audio information in different formats as well as to add effects to the sound data.

- *Sound card output* —Simple sound card output devices include headphones and speakers. More complicated devices consist of surround-sound digital theater systems, digital audio tape (DAT), CD recorders, and musical devices.

Basic Components of a Sound Card

Even though many types of sound cards are available for different applications, every sound card has the following basic components:

- *Sound card processor* —The digital signal processor (DSP) is a chip, or set of chips, that is the brain of the sound card. The DSP handles the basic instructions that drive the sound card and route audio information. It can also act as the synthesizer, or music generator.

- *Sound converters* —Digital-to-analog converters (DACs) and analog-to-digital converters (ADCs) are used in the input and output process. Most audio information that is recorded from outside the computer, unless it is recorded in a digital format, must pass through the ADC. Data that is being output to speakers uses the services of the DAC.

- *Sound card memory*—More advanced sound cards use memory to store samples from musical instruments and to hold instructions for Musical Instrument Digital Interface (MIDI) devices. This memory is usually in the form of ROM, Flash, or NVRAM and can often be upgraded or expanded.

- *Sound card ports*—Sound cards can have multiple internal and external ports for connecting to input and output devices. Also known as jacks or interfaces, these ports expand the functionality of a sound card.

Sound Production and Quality

Sound cards produce audio—or synthesize—using the following methods:

- Frequency modulation (FM)
- Wavetable
- MIDI

Sound cards that use *frequency modulation (FM)* synthesis use programming to create waveforms that best match the instrument playing. These sounds are easy to produce but are unrealistic. *Wavetable sound cards* use digitized samples of real instruments to reproduce audio. These samples are stored within the card memory, which usually contains an entire orchestra of musical instruments. *Musical Instrument Digital Interface (MIDI)* is a combination of hardware and software that allows the sound card to control musical instruments and to use these instruments to output the audio. If an external instrument is not available, the sound card can use its MIDI synthesizer to play the encoded music.

The quality of a sound card is determined by its bit-depth, sample rate, and feature set. *Bit-depth for sound* refers to the sample size and bus size of the sound card. In general, the larger the sample size, the higher the quality of the sound that is reproduced. A 32-bit sample holds a much greater amount of information about an instrument than an 8-bit sample. Also, a 32-bit sound card can move data faster than an 8-bit or 16-bit card.

The *sampling rate* is the rate at which the card can record audio information. This rate is measured in kilohertz (kHz)—that is, thousands of cycles per second. Essentially, the sampling rate indicates how many samples of a sound are captured within a second. CD-quality audio uses 44-kHz sampling. Sound cards are now capable of sampling at 128 kHz and beyond. Remember, the higher the sampling rate, the more accurate the reproduction of the sound. Of course, with a higher sampling rate, the digital file that is created is larger as well. Figure 8-13 shows an audio sampling rate of 44.1 kHz.

Figure 8-13 Audio Sampling Rate

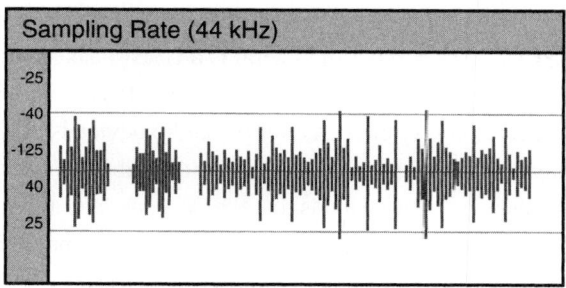

The *feature set* of a sound card is composed of specific characteristics that can be included. Higher-quality sound cards offer the following additional features:

- Three-dimensional audio coprocessors
- Device controllers
- Digital output options

Three-dimensional audio coprocessors produce spatial audio in multispeaker systems. This type of output immerses the user in a world of sound and is popular with computer games. Sound cards can also have built-in Small Computer System Interface (SCSI), Redundant Array of Independent Disks (RAID), FireWire, or other device controllers.

High-end sound cards can also offer digital output ports to allow connection to home theater systems.

 PhotoZoom   Sound Card

Use this interactive PhotoZoom to review the components of a sound card.

Working with USB, PCI, and Built-In Sound

Audio is created through USB sound, PCI sound cards, or built-in sound chipsets that are found on the motherboard. Each of these methods has advantages and disadvantages, as described in the following sections.

NOTE

SCSI is a hardware interface that allows the connection of up to 15 peripheral devices to a single board. RAID increases performance and provides fault tolerance. RAID is detailed in Chapter 9, "Advanced Hardware Fundamentals for Servers." FireWire, also known as IEEE 1394, is a high-speed serial bus, developed by Apple and Texas Instruments, that allows the connection of up to 63 devices.

USB Sound

Universal serial bus (USB) is a hot-swappable interface that connects many different types of peripherals to a PC. One such popular peripheral is a USB speaker system. These speaker systems allow the USB port to act as a sound card. Plug and Play is a major benefit of USB sound. You do not need other configurations after the audio device is plugged into the interface. The Plug and Play feature has been a standard for all Windows operating systems since Windows 95. One advantage of USB sound is that the PC generates all the information that is necessary to create sounds and music. The speakers then perform the digital-to-analog conversion. The drawback of USB sound is that it requires processing power to create audio and can hamper the performance of the computer. The effect is minimal in new PCs with more powerful processors.

To operate, USB speaker systems require only the speakers, a USB cable, and a USB port, as shown in Figure 8-14. The prices on these devices can vary from US$ 40 to US$ 400.

Figure 8-14 USB Port

PCI Sound Cards

A *PCI sound card* is an adapter card with an on-board audio processor that connects to a motherboard using a PCI slot. These cards use the PCI 32-bit or 64-bit bus to input and output audio information. An advantage of the on-board audio processor is that it creates the audio. In doing so, the audio processor bypasses the computer processor and frees precious CPU cycles. PCI sound cards usually have multiple ports for connecting to other audio peripherals. External ports include speaker outputs, microphone inputs, and digital connectors. Internal interfaces connect directly to CD-ROM and DVD-ROM drives. A disadvantage to using a PCI card is that like other adapter cards, it requires the use of an empty PCI slot and some of the computer's resources.

Built-In Sound

Many motherboard manufacturers integrate both video and audio options into their products. The *built-in sound* has an audio processor that is located on a motherboard in the form of a single chip or chipset. In this manner, built-in sound has the advantages of both USB and PCI sound options. Because the sound is built in, the setup is as simple as a USB sound card. Because built-in sound uses an audio processor like a PCI sound card, the computer CPU does not process the audio information. Motherboards with built-in sound also include the common audio ports for speakers and a microphone, as shown in Figure 8-15.

Figure 8-15 Motherboard with Built-In Sound

One benefit of built-in sound is that the price of the complete sound package is less expensive. You do not need to purchase a separate sound card. The major drawback of built-in sound is that it is difficult—and sometimes impossible—to upgrade the audio capabilities. Upgrading built-in sound usually requires disabling the audio system and installing a PCI sound card.

Removing or Disabling Outdated Sound Cards

A common upgrade for modern PCs is the addition of a newer sound card. Before adding a more capable sound card, older sound cards should be removed. Removing or disabling outdated sound cards frees resources such as IRQs and expansion slots.

Use the proper uninstall procedures to remove all the following items:

- Hardware
- Related software
- Specific drivers
- Files that could slow the system and consume resources

Uninstalling the Card in a Windows Environment

In Windows, use the Device Manager to uninstall hardware. Follow these steps to remove a sound card:

Step 1 Choose **Start**, **Settings**, **Control Panel**; select the **System Properties** icon; and click the **Device Manager** tab, as shown in Figure 8-16.

Step 2 Select the device to be removed. In this example, it is the Sound Blaster sound card.

Step 3 Click the **Remove** button.

A confirmation screen displays.

Step 4 Click **OK** to complete the process.

Figure 8-16 System Properties—Device Manager Showing the Sound Card

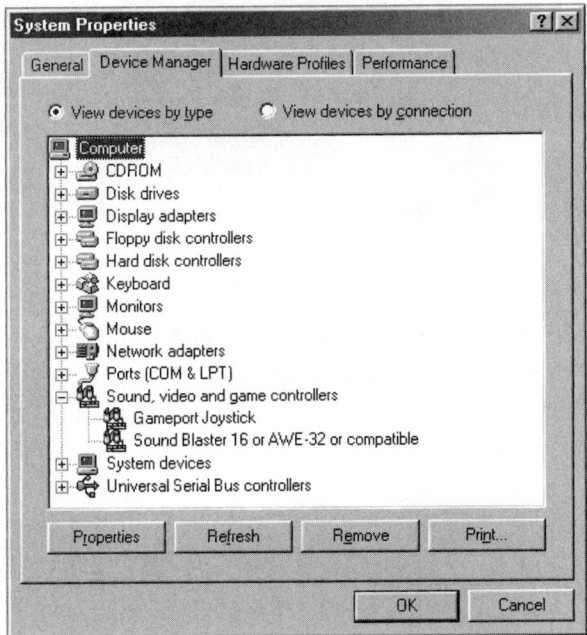

To uninstall software and drivers, select the Add/Remove Programs icon of the Control Panel. When the uninstall is complete, the computer should be shut down so that the outdated sound card can be physically removed. If the computer is restarted before the sound card is removed, the operating system might detect it and reinstall the drivers.

Disabling an outdated sound card or built-in sound is similar to the uninstall process. To disable a sound card or built-in sound, open the Device Manager, as previously described;

highlight the sound card; and click the **Properties** button. In the Properties dialog box, select the **Disable in this hardware profile** check box. This is different than removing the card, because the sound card and its drivers and files are not removed. This action can free resources while trying other sound cards to ensure compatibility. Also, a disabled sound card can easily be reenabled. Disabling built-in sound often requires you to make a change in the computer BIOS. You typically find a setting that allows you to enable or disable the on-board audio. Built-in sound must be disabled within the BIOS and the operating system.

Removing an Outdated Sound Card

To physically remove a sound card, follow the same basic steps as you would when removing other hardware from the computer. After the computer is powered off and the power cable is removed, you can open the case. An antistatic wrist strap should be worn while working inside the case. After the sound card is located, all interconnecting cables should be removed. These cables include external cables that connect to speakers or microphones and internal cables that connect to a CD-ROM drive, DVD-ROM drive, or internal speakers. After removing the screw that holds the sound card in place, use both hands to firmly grasp the card, gently rock it back and forth, and pull it from the slot. Once removed, the card should be placed in an antistatic bag for protection. Replace the adapter slot cover, case cover, and power cord, and then boot the computer to ensure that the removal process was successful.

 Worksheet 8.3.3 Sound Cards

You can find a review of the information that was provided on sound cards in this worksheet.

Installing Sound Cards

Installing a sound card is similar to installing any other adapter card. Refer to the user's guide to determine what hardware configuration settings should be made before inserting the card into the system. You should also run a diagnostic software package to check the available resources of the system before configuring the card. USB and built-in sound chipsets are part of an integrated motherboard and do not require installation. PCI sound cards must be physically installed, internal connections must be made, and the card must be configured before use. Before beginning the installation process, be sure that you have the proper tools available. A screwdriver or socket set is often needed to open the computer case and to remove the slot covers. An antistatic wrist strap must be worn at all times while handling cards and working inside the computer.

Follow these steps to install a sound card:

Step 1   Make sure that the PC is not plugged into a wall socket and that all external devices are disconnected.

Step 2   Remove the cover from the computer case.

A can of compressed air can be used to remove any dust that has built up inside the case.

Step 3   Locate an available PCI slot to accommodate the sound card, and remove the corresponding slot cover.

Be sure to save the slot cover and the screw that connects the cover to the frame.

Step 4   While wearing an antistatic wrist strap, align the tabs on the bottom side of the sound card with the open PCI slot.

Step 5   Firmly press the card into the slot, keeping even pressure along the side of the card.

Step 6   After ensuring a snug fit, replace the cover-slot screw to secure the sound card to the frame.

This stabilizes the sound card and provides the proper grounding.

Lab 8.3.4   Sound Card Installation

In this lab, the sound card is installed. The speakers and microphone are attached, and the proper drivers are installed.

Video   Installing a Sound Card

This video shows the steps for installing a sound card, as detailed in this chapter.

Connecting a CD-ROM or DVD-ROM Drive to the Sound Card

After installing the sound card, the next step is to connect any internal components and cables to the sound card. A common connection is cabling the CD-ROM or DVD-ROM drive to the sound card to produce digital audio. All CD-ROM drives have an analog audio-out connector for connecting to a sound card. This four-wire connection uses the CD-ROM digital-to-analog converter to pass two-channel analog audio to the sound card for output through connected speakers. These connectors are labeled as "Analog audio out" and are keyed on both the CD-ROM drive and sound card to ensure the correct type of connection.

Most DVD-ROM drives, as well as some newer CD-ROM drives, offer a digital audio-out connection. DVDs can include audio streams that contain multiple channels. A multispeaker sound card can separate these channels and direct the output to the correct speakers to create a surround-sound environment. The two-wire digital audio connectors are labeled and keyed on both the drive and sound card to ensure proper connection. After making one or more connections between the sound card and a drive, it is usually necessary to configure the connection using the sound card's setup application. Figure 8-17 shows the Add/Remove Hardware Wizard, which allows you to install the sound card software.

Figure 8-17 Configuring a Sound Card Connection

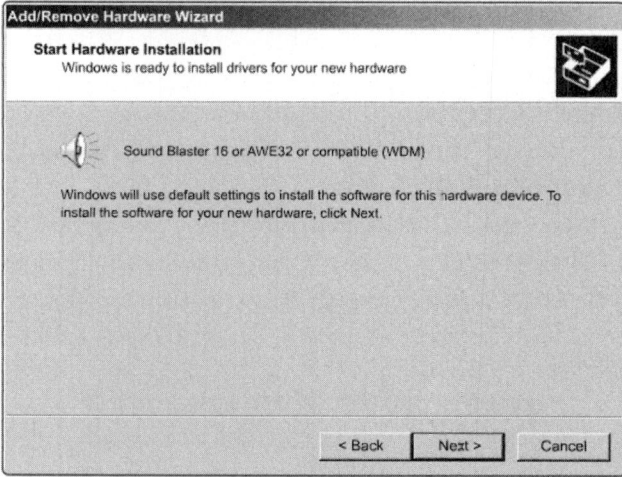

Installing the Sound Card Driver and Software

To complete the sound card installation process, the correct sound card drivers and any other audio-related applications must be installed. A sound card driver is the software that allows the computer operating system to communicate with the hardware. The driver that is being installed must match the particular sound card as well as the installed operating system. Faulty drivers can cause any of the following problems:

- Distorted audio output
- No audio output
- Reduced computer performance

After installing the sound card, start the computer. Windows begins to install a driver for the hardware. Following the notification that new hardware is detected, the operating system prompts you for a disk or CD that is supplied by the sound card manufacturer. The disk or CD typically contains various drivers for the sound card, other audio applications, and an installation program for the drivers and applications. Running the installation program allows you to choose the proper sound card driver and to install any audio applications. These audio applications can include the following:

- Music players and generators
- Audio-capture utilities
- Speech-recognition programs
- Volume/tone controls

Because the drivers that are included with the sound card can become outdated, you can download updated device drivers from the manufacturer's website.

You can also manually install a driver. After the sound card is installed physically, the driver can be installed, changed, or updated by using the Device Manager. In the Device Manager, select the sound card, click the Properties button, and click the General tab, as shown in Figure 8-18. This tab shows the general properties of the sound card. Click the Driver tab, as shown in Figure 8-19, to determine the version of the sound card driver that is currently installed. Finally, click the Driver File Details button at the bottom of the Driver tab to view the driver files that the device is using currently. These files are shown in Figure 8-20.

Figure 8-18 Device Properties—General Tab

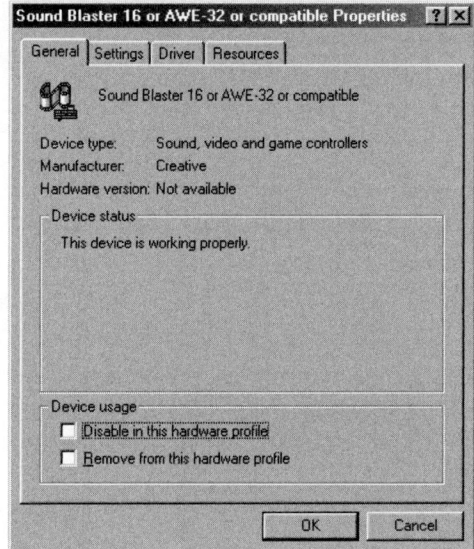

Figure 8-19 Device Properties—Driver Tab

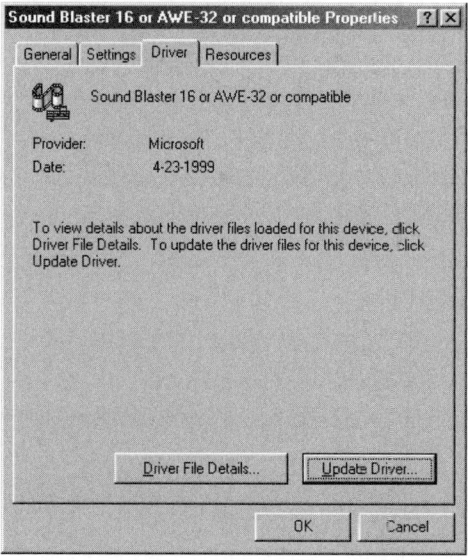

Figure 8-20 Driver File Details

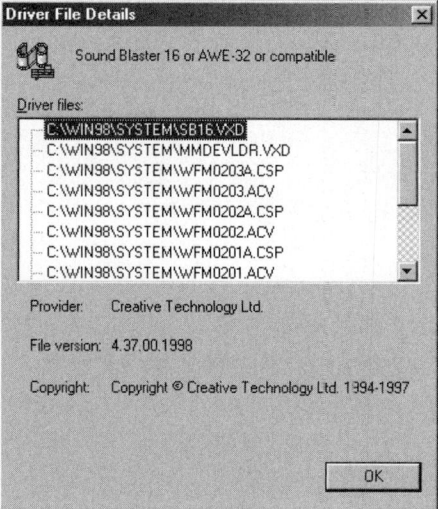

Provided that the sound card is properly configured and the software configuration matches, the sound card and speakers should work. If the speakers or sound card do not work properly, check the following items:

- Determine whether the speakers are plugged into the speaker port. It is not uncommon for the speakers to be mistakenly plugged into the card microphone (MIC) port.
- If the sound card does not record sound, make sure that the microphone is installed in the proper jack—not the speaker jack—and that it is turned on.
- Ensure that enough free disk space is available to hold the file that is being produced.

Connecting MIDI and External Audio Sources

Sound cards are not only used for audio output, but they are also used to record audio from a variety of external sources. Common external-audio source connections include the following:

- MIDI port
- Microphone-in port
- Line-in port
- Digital-in port

Although the connectivity options for sound cards vary from the professional level to the consumer grade, Figure 8-21 shows the ports on a typical sound card.

Figure 8-21 Sound Card Ports

A *MIDI port* is an industry-standard interface that connects musical devices. The basic MIDI devices are controllers and generators. Musicians often use MIDI-enabled computers to control and sequence music generators such as drum machines and synthesizers. Most sound cards have a MIDI/joystick combination port. This is commonly a female DB-15 port on the face of the sound card. A MIDI cable connects one or more devices to the sound card. Special software is required to use the MIDI functions of a sound card and is usually included as part of the device package.

Microphones can be connected to a sound card using the female 3.5-mm minijack port on the face of the sound card. Using a microphone, the user can capture his or her voice by using a recording application on the computer. Inputting audio by way of the ***microphone-in port*** requires the sound card to use its analog-to-digital converter. Some common digital audio formats include .WAV, MP3, and Ogg Vorbis files.

A sound card's ***line-in port*** has the same physical characteristics as the microphone-in port, using a female 3.5-mm minijack, but the two ports are used for two different types of sources. The microphone-in port is used with nonamplified sources. The line-in port captures audio from amplified or powered sources, such as cassette players, digital audio tape (DAT) players, external CD players, and other devices with line-out options. As with the microphone-in port, the line-in port requires the use of a sound card A/D converter.

With the popularity of digital audio sources, such as CD, Minidisk, DVD, and DAT players, sound card manufacturers are adding external digital audio source capture components. Most ***digital-in ports*** use the Sony Phillips Digital Interface (SPDIF), which is outlined in the Red Book audio standard for digital audio recording. The digital-in port on a sound card usually has one of the following configurations:

- *Toslink*—A fiber-optic port that was developed by Toshiba
- *Coaxial*—A port that uses an RCA jack
- *Minijack*—A female 3.5-mm port that is physically the same as the microphone-in and line-in ports

The major advantage of using the digital-in option is that no analog-to-digital conversion is necessary to capture the audio information. Digital audio capture produces the best possible audio reproduction.

> **NOTE**
>
> Ogg Vorbis is a new audio compression format that is free, open, and unpatented. It is roughly comparable to other formats that store and play digital music, such as MP3, VQF, and AAC.

Overview of CDs and DVDs

A major advancement in computer storage has been the CD—and more recently, the DVD. Although the floppy disk drive is still in limited use, the CD-ROM drive is currently the standard on most new computers. This section includes the following topics:

- Compact discs
- CD-R and CD-RW media
- Digital audio extraction
- DVD drives
- DVD recording
- CD recording formats
- DVD layering and formats

Compact Discs

Compact discs (CDs) are a popular type of removable media. CDs were initially intended for digital audio storage and playback but rapidly expanded into the world of personal computer data storage. The success of CDs can be attributed to their storage capacity, ruggedness, and price. Because of the widespread acceptance of this media format, CD-ROM drives are standard devices on most personal computers.

CDs are 120 mm in diameter and 1.2 mm thick, as shown in Figure 8-22. Depending on the type of reader, writer, and software that creates the CD, these discs can store up to 700 MB of data (80 minutes of audio). They are composed of a layer of polycarbonate plastic, a layer of reflective metal, and a coating of lacquer. CDs are optical media, as opposed to floppy disks, hard disks, and Zip disks, which are magnetic media.

Figure 8-22 Compact Disc

A CD-ROM drive is composed of the following items:

- Drive motor
- Laser assembly
- Tracking mechanism
- Communication circuits

The *drive motor* spins the CD up to the proper speed so that the laser assembly can read the information that is on the disc. The laser assembly consists of a laser and a lens. This *laser assembly* reads the compact disc as it spins. The *tracking mechanism* is a motor and drive system that moves the lens into the correct position to access a specific area of the disc. Finally, the *communication circuits* send the information that is read from the CD to the computer that is using the configured bus.

CD-ROM Drive Categories

CD-ROM drives are categorized as follows:

- Case type
- Bus type
- Read speed

The case type refers to an internal or external device. Bus type refers to the way that the drive communicates. The read speed is how fast the drive communicates with the CPU.

CD-ROM Case Types

CD-ROM drives can be mounted inside the computer or as an external drive. Internally mounted drives are now common. These drives draw their power from the computer's power supply and are usually connected to the computer bus through a ribbon cable.

External drives are enclosed in a case and have their own power supplies. They connect either directly to an external port on the computer—such as a USB, FireWire, or parallel port—or to a controller that is installed in one of the computer expansion slots (usually a SCSI controller).

Bus Communication

A *bus* is the communications pipeline between a computer and the installed peripherals. Common internal connections include IDE and SCSI types. Most motherboards have built-in IDE controllers and automatically recognize that a CD-ROM drive has been installed. IDE communication cables are 40-pin ribbon cables that connect to the drive and the motherboard. Although some motherboards offer built-in SCSI solutions, most applications require a SCSI adapter to be purchased and installed separately. Many different varieties of SCSI buses and assorted cabling types are available.

Speed Ratings

The **CD-ROM drive read speed** determines the rate at which information can be pulled from the CD and sent to the communications bus. In general, the higher a CD-ROM drive's read speed rating, the faster the drive. The read speed of a CD-ROM drive is measured in multiples of 150 kilobytes per second (KBps) and is denoted by a numeral followed by an x. A drive rated at 1x has a read speed of 150 KBps, or 1 times 150 KBps. A drive rated at 10x has a read speed of 1500 KBps. Data that streams from a CD, such as full-motion video, can require read speeds of 12x or more. Also, a CD-ROM drive read speed is not always uniform. A drive rated at 16x can only achieve that rate near the outer tracks of the CD while only achieving an 8x rate at the center tracks.

Installing and Configuring an IDE CD-ROM Drive

Installing and configuring an internal IDE CD-ROM drive is similar to installing an internal IDE hard drive. The CD-ROM drive needs to be connected to a 40-pin IDE cable, which is then connected to the IDE controller. The drive is usually keyed so that the cable can only be connected one way. However, it is important that pin 1 on the cable is aligned with pin 1 on the drive. An internal CD-ROM drive uses the standard Molex power connector that supplies 12 volts DC to other devices inside a PC.

The CD-ROM drive must be set to its proper operating status, which can be master, slave, or single drive. The drive should be set as a master drive only if it is the fastest drive on that particular IDE cable. Be sure to set the master/slave/single jumpers before sliding the drive into the computer case. Most CD-ROM drives have a digital audio cable that connects directly to the sound card. A CD-ROM drive that contains a DAC allows music to be played through the computer speakers without the need for overhead processing. Finally, you must install a software driver for certain CD-ROM drives to work properly.

For further information on the step-by-step installation of IDE drives, refer to Chapter 3, "Assembling a Computer."

CD-R and CD-RW Media

CD recorders, often referred to as *CD burners*, are becoming standard equipment on personal computers. CD recorders allow users to burn—or write—their own CDs containing music, data, video, or any combination thereof. Users can now do all of the following with CD recorders:

- Create compilations of audio CDs
- Make backup copies of software
- Back up critical data
- Create Video CDs (VCDs) that can be played in stand-alone DVD players

The low price of the drive and media, coupled with the generous data capacity of a CD, has made CD recorders popular. Figure 8-23 shows a CD-ROM drive on a PC. Two types of CD media are currently available: CD-R and CD-RW.

Figure 8-23 CD-ROM Drive

Compact Disc–Recordable (CD-R)

CD-R was the first of the two CD recording technologies that were conceived. Commercially produced audio and other data CDs are created using a pressing technique. This technique produces the land and pit areas of the CD that the laser assembly reads. CD-R technology uses a different strategy for writing information to a CD. CD-R media adds a layer of dye between the aluminum and plastic layers of the CD. This layer of dye is translucent and allows light to shine through to the aluminum layer, which reflects the light. When a CD-R drive writes information to the CD-R media, a laser burns areas of the dye to create opaque, nonreflective spots. When the recorded CD-R is read, the laser assembly receives reflections from only the translucent areas of the dye. This reflective/nonreflective surface easily translates into bits of data.

To accomplish the job of reading and writing CDs, CD-R drives use two lasers: a read laser and a write laser. The speed at which a CD-R can burn a CD uses the same numeric convention as CD-ROM drive read speeds. For example, a CD-R drive that can write at 3000 KBps has a 20x—or 20 times 150 kb—write speed. A drive that is listed as 24x/40x has a write speed of 24x and a read speed of 40x. One downside of CD-R media is that it cannot be rewritten to.

Compact Disc–Rewritable (CD-RW)

Like CD-R drives, *CD-RW* drives require the use of a special type of disc. The CD-RW disc is compatible with other CD reading drives, and the CD-R disc can be read by a CD-RW drive. CD-RW media include a phase-change compound layer between the aluminum and plastic layers of the CD. This compound is a special mix of chemical elements that can change physical state at certain temperatures and remain in that state indefinitely. The compound begins in a translucent, crystalline state that allows light to pass through to the reflective aluminum layer. When the CD-RW write laser burns information to the disc, certain areas of the phase-change compound are melted by superheating and are held in that phase by rapid cooling. These melted areas are opaque and nonreflective. What makes a CD-RW drive unique is that it includes a third, eraser laser. The eraser laser slowly reheats melted areas of the phase-change compound into the crystalline state. This allows the rewriting of CDs. Similar to CD-R drives, CD-RW drives are rated by the speed at which they write, rewrite, and read information. For example, a CD-RW drive listed as 24x/12x/40x has a write speed of 24x, a rewrite speed of 12x, and a read speed of 40x.

Copyright Issues

It is the responsibility of the PC technician to adhere to the copyright or licensing limitations of CDs in the workplace. Providing this information as it relates to the purchase and use of software can avoid legal conflicts.

Digital Audio Extraction

The availability and relatively low cost of CD recorders and recordable media have put custom compilation audio CDs within the reach of many users. Since the inception of audio CDs, users have wanted to create custom CDs while keeping the quality of the music that digital recording provides. *Digital Audio Extraction* (DAE) makes this possible.

DAE is the process of copying audio from a CD to another medium while keeping the audio in its original digital state. Also known as *ripping*, DAE allow users to copy tracks, or songs, from an audio CD to a computer hard drive and then to a recordable CD. Keeping the song in an all-digital format greatly reduces audio discrepancies as the song is moved from one medium to another.

When a CD player or CD-ROM drive plays a Red Book CD, which is the format used for audio CDs, the drive performs a digital-to-analog conversion in real time so that the audio can be played through speakers. Before DAE, this audio had to be re-recorded and redigitized if a user decided to copy the song to a recordable CD. This digital-to-analog-to-digital conversion was time consuming, and unwanted noise was usually introduced. Depending on the quality of the CD-ROM drive, computer hardware, and software used, DAE can quickly make nearly flawless digital copies of songs.

Copying a song from a Red Book CD is much different from copying a file from a CD. Songs are stored in tracks on the CD, and drives read these tracks as the CD spins under the laser assembly. Because the audio information is streamed to the drive, special digital audio extraction software must be used. This software reads the raw information of a track as it is streamed and collects the information into a .WAV file. This file can then be played on a computer or copied to a recordable CD, along with other songs, to create a custom audio CD.

When DAE is used to create .WAV files on a computer, those files are uncompressed and can be large. Other audio formats, such as MP3 and Ogg Vorbis, compress these raw files into much smaller files with minimal loss of song quality.

DVD Drives

The *digital versatile disc (DVD)* is a newer technology that builds on the strengths of CDs. DVDs share the same physical size as CDs, but DVDs can handle much more information. DVDs are used to store movies, audio, and data. Depending on the layering and whether the disc is single- or double-sided, a DVD can store nearly 20 times the amount of information as a CD. DVDs can store more information because they have all the following attributes:

- Provide a greater area for data storage
- Use a higher-density recording technique
- Can access multiple layers within the media

The two major markets for DVD players are the home entertainment market and the computer DVD drive market. Many consumers have a DVD player as a component in their home theater setup. This is because movies that are recorded on DVD media are digital reproductions, with vivid colors and theater-style surround sound, and these reproductions often contain other movie-related extras. Because the movie is recorded in a digital format, the quality of the movie is as close to the film's quality as possible; the quality will never deteriorate like VHS tapes can. Home DVD players also offer various audio options that feature multiple audio channels, including Dolby Surround Sound, Dolby Digital 5.1, and DTS.

Computer *DVD drives* can play movies and music as well as read data discs. Software manufacturers are beginning to offer their products on DVDs. These manufacturers can now place an entire program on a single DVD instead of using multiple, lower-capacity CDs. Another benefit of DVD drives is that they are backward compatible with CDs. A DVD drive can read DVDs and CDs, while a CD-ROM drive can only read CDs.

DVD drives are similar to CD-ROM drives in design. DVD drives are composed of a drive motor for spinning the disc, a laser assembly for reading the DVD, a tracking mechanism for moving the laser assembly into the desired area, and communication circuits for moving the data to its destination. Other optional components include decoders. All home DVD players and some computer DVD drives have an MPEG-2 decoder for decompressing the video data into a format that can be shown on a television screen or monitor. Some DVD players and drives also contain audio decoders for either Dolby Digital 5.1 or DTS audio streams. These decoders decompress the audio data and separate the information into the proper discrete channels. DVD players and drives that do not contain these decoders can use other hardware or software to accomplish the decoding.

The laser that is used in a DVD drive is different from a CD-ROM drive laser. The DVD drive laser must be able to focus on different layers of the media. While a single-layer DVD has only a single reflective layer of material, a dual-layered disc contains a semitransparent layer over the top of a completely reflective layer. The laser must be able to distinguish between the two layers by focusing on the correct layer of material that contains the desired data.

When installing a DVD drive, follow the steps for installing a CD-ROM drive, including all the safety procedures, that are detailed in Chapter 3. Follow these general steps to install a DVD drive:

1. Configure the drive jumpers.
2. Slide the drive into an open bay.
3. Connect the communication cable, usually a 40-pin IDE ribbon cable.
4. Connect the power supply.
5. Connect any necessary audio cables.

DVD drives usually have connectors for analog audio out as well as digital audio-out cables. Finally, install the device driver and check your installation by restarting the computer.

DVD Recording

Consumer demand for greater amounts of removable storage options has prompted the industry to develop methods of recording on DVDs. Figure 8-24 shows a DVD drive with record and rewrite capabilities. Currently, four different methods of DVD recording are available. Each of these technologies is vying to be the standard for DVD recording. These methods are described in the following sections.

DVD Recordable (DVD-R)

DVD-R is similar to CD-R technology in that it allows the media to be written to only one time. This method is most often used for DVD authoring and is not practical for consumers because of the price of the DVD drives. Even though price, which continues to drop, is a drawback for this technology, compatibility is not. Most DVD-ROM drives and stand-alone players can read DVD-R discs. DVD-R discs can hold 4.7 GB of data per side.

Figure 8-24 DVD Writer

DVD-RAM

Using RAM technology allows users to write and overwrite discs up to 100,000 times. *DVD-RAM* uses phase-change technology that is similar to CD-RW drives. This technology enables the user to store 4.7 GB of information on each side of the disc. Compatibility is an issue with DVD-RAM drives; most of these drives require the use of a cartridge-based disc while recording.

DVD Read/Write (DVD-RW)

The *DVD-RW* technology is designed to address compatibility and re-recording issues. Geared more toward general use than authoring, DVD-RW uses a caddyless system and allows users to rewrite information on the media approximately 1000 times. The media is compatible with most DVD-ROM drives and stand-alone players that are currently on the market. The drive uses a sequential recording technology that is used primarily for streaming media. DVD-RW is capable of writing 4.7 GB of information to each side of a disc.

DVD+RW

DVD+RW is the latest DVD recording technology, and many major corporations—including Hewlett-Packard—back it. As with DVD-RW, the technology is compatible with existing hardware, and the media is written easily to multiple times. The major advantage of DVD+RW is the ability to use a variable bit-rate when encoding certain types of media, such as streaming video. The major industry backing of this format, coupled with the affordability of the drive, should make DVD+RW the standard DVD recording format in the near future. Figure 8-25 shows a DVD+RW disc.

Figure 8-25 DVD+RW Disc

CD Recording Formats

Phillips and Sony developed the format standard for audio CDs in the early 1980s. When manufacturers realized the potential for using CDs to store information for computers, they developed even more formats to ensure compatibility when recording CDs. The two major types of CD formats are as follows:

- Logical standards
- Physical standards

Logical Standards

A *logical standard* defines the way that information is stored on the media. CDs and other computer-accessed discs use a series of tracks and sectors, also called frames on CDs, to store the data on the disc. Simply put, a CD's logical standard determines its file system structure. Currently, ISO 9660, also referred to as the High Sierra Standard, is the industry-standard format. CDs that are created using the ISO 9660 format can be accessed by most modern platforms and operating systems. Other formats—such as Rock Ridge for UNIX, HFS for Macs, and Hybrid HFS/ISO—are used today, but ISO 9660 is internationally accepted as the standard. Two formats that improve on ISO 9660 include JOLIET and UDF. JOLIET is a Microsoft version of ISO 9660 that extends the maximum number of characters in a filename from 8 to 64. Universal Disc Format (UDF) extends the maximum number of characters in a filename to 127. UDF is an emerging standard, built on ISO 9660, that is specifically designed for data storage.

Physical Standards

Physical standards define where the information is placed on a CD. Most formats fall within the Color Books. When Phillips and Sony completed the format for the audio CD, the formatting rules were published in a book with a red cover. This format quickly became known as the Red Book format, and it is the basis of the naming conventions for the other Color Book formats. Table 8-3 describes these recording formats.

Table 8-3 CD Recording Formats

Book Format	Description
Red Book	Also known as CD-DA (compact disc–digital audio), this format defines an audio CD. It specifies how songs are placed in tracks on the disc.
Yellow Book	This book was developed early on as the initial format for data. This format allows data to be written as files instead of as streaming information.
Green Book	In 1986, Phillips created this format for its new CD-I (Interactive) discs. This format was specially designed to synchronize audio and video data for multimedia applications.
Orange Book	This 1990 standard defines the physical format for recordable CDs. The standard is subdivided into three parts. Part 1 deals with magneto-optical (MO) devices; part 2 handles write-once (WO) drives; and part 3 addresses rewritable drives.
White Book	This standard addresses the method of recording MPEG-1 audio, video, and still graphics to a Video CD (VCD). These discs require a specialized player or software application to access them because the information is highly compressed.
Blue Book	This standard specifies the format of Enhanced CDs (E-CDs). E-CDs are stamped multisession discs that feature Red Book audio and Yellow Book multimedia data on a single disc.

DVD Layering and Formats

Even though DVD and CD media share the same physical size, DVDs offer a far greater storage capacity. This is made possible through the use of a higher-density data-storing technique and through the use of layering. DVD layering is the process in which the read laser of a drive is able to focus at different layers inside the disc. A dual-layered disc has an equivalent of close to twice the surface area of a regular disc. A dual-layered, double-sided disc has almost four times the surface area on which to store data. Currently, three types of DVDs and four physical formats are available.

The three DVD types are as follows:

- *DVD-ROM*—Designed for storing computer files
- *DVD-Video*—Used by stand-alone DVD players for movies and extras
- *DVD-Audio*—A newer format that includes multiple-channel audio with many options

DVD physical formats define the structure of the disc and the areas to which data is recorded, as follows:

- **DVD 5**—A single-sided, single-layer DVD with a storage capacity of up to 4.7 GB
- **DVD 9**—A single-sided, dual-layered DVD with a total storage capacity of 8.5 GB
- **DVD 10**—A double-sided, single-layer-per-side DVD with a capacity of 9.4 GB.
- **DVD 18**—A double-sided, dual-layer-per-side DVD with a total capacity of 17 GB.

Table 8-4 shows a comparison of the different DVD formats.

Table 8-4 DVD Characteristics

Physical Format	Layers Per Side	Number of Sides	Capacity (GB)	Length (Hours)
DVD 5	1	1	4.7	2.0
DVD 9	2	1	8.5	4.0
DVD 10	1	2	9.4	4.5
DVD 18	2	2	17.0	8.0

Worksheet 8.4.7   CD and DVD Terminology

This worksheet is a review of the CD and DVD terminology that was covered in this chapter.

Digitizing Video

Digital images and video are a major part of multimedia. Although images such as photos can be downloaded with software that is included with the camera, incorporating video requires the use of a video capture board. This section includes the following topics:

- Digital cameras and video cameras
- Hardware and software video capture
- Installing and configuring a video capture board

Digital Cameras and Video Cameras

Digital cameras and video cameras are essential to the creation of multimedia presentations. Understanding how these devices work and how to download the images is important for the IT technician.

Digital Cameras

A digital still camera has a series of lenses that focus light to create an image of a scene, just like a conventional film camera. Figure 8-26 shows a digital still camera. It focuses light onto a semiconductor device that records the image electronically instead of focusing this light onto a piece of film. This electronic information is broken down into digital data by the computer. This is what allows users to view, edit, and e-mail pictures and to post pictures to the Internet.

Figure 8-26 Digital Camera with Docking Station

A charge-coupled device (CCD) is the image sensor that is used by many digital cameras. CCDs capture and store image data in telescopes, scanners, digital still cameras, and digital video cameras. A good CCD can produce an image in extremely low light, and its resolution does not degrade in low light the way that film camera resolution does. Complementary Metal Oxide Semiconductor (CMOS) technology is used by some of the more inexpensive cameras. Although CMOS sensors are continually improving, CCD technology will continue to be the standard in higher-end digital cameras.

Resolution, measured in pixels, is the amount of detail that the camera can capture. Basically, more pixels mean more detail and better quality. With low resolution, pictures become grainy and look out of focus when enlarged.

Digital cameras use the following resolutions:

- **256×256 pixels**—This resolution is used in inexpensive cameras. At 65,000 total pixels, it produces a low-quality picture.
- **640×480 pixels**—This resolution is somewhat better than 256×256 resolution. It is adequate. This resolution equals 307,000 total pixels.

- **1216×912 pixels**—This resolution is in the good range. It is sufficient for printing images as well as for e-mailing pictures and posting them on a website. This is a mega-pixel image size, with 1,109,000 total pixels.
- **1600×1200 pixels**—This is high resolution. Good results are achieved when printing to larger sizes, such as 8×10. This resolution equals almost 2 million pixels.

Modern cameras are available with up to 10.2 million pixels, providing the same or even better results than film cameras.

Many digital cameras use an LCD screen, as shown in Figure 8-27. This feature makes it possible to view and delete pictures immediately. The next step is transferring the pictures to a computer. This is accomplished in several different ways.

Figure 8-27 LCD Screen on a Digital Camera

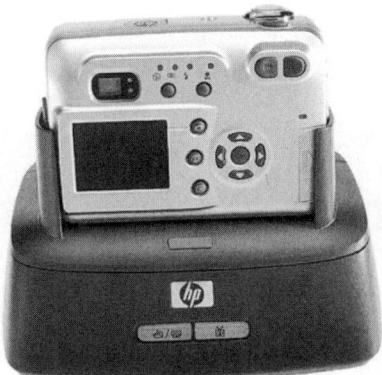

Cameras with fixed storage must be connected to the computer to download the images. This connection can be made through a serial, parallel, SCSI, or USB port. However, many newer cameras provide removable storage. This allows the images to be transferred to the computer—or even directly to a printer—without having to connect the camera.

The following list describes storage systems:

- **Built-in memory**—Built-in Flash memory that is used by many inexpensive cameras
- **SmartMedia cards**—Small Flash memory modules
- **CompactFlash**—Another form of Flash memory that is similar to but slightly larger than SmartMedia cards
- **Memory Stick**—A proprietary form of Flash memory that is used by Sony
- **Floppy disk**—An inexpensive media on which some cameras store images directly
- **Hard disk**—Built-in disk or PCMCIA card that is used for image storage
- **Writeable CD and DVD drives**—Drives that higher-end cameras use to store images

A drive or reader is required to transfer files from Flash memory to a computer. These inexpensive devices behave much like floppy drives. The devices allow images to be transferred to the computer without having to use cables.

The difference between the storage media is their capacity. A floppy disk has a fixed capacity, whereas the capacity of Flash memory devices is evolving to hold more and more data.

Digital cameras are of two primary file formats: TIFF and JPEG. JPEG is a compressed format, whereas TIFF is an uncompressed format. The JPEG file format is used most often for storing pictures. This format can provide different quality levels based on the amount of compression used.

Video Cameras

Video cameras, or camcorders, have been available for almost 20 years. They are similar to a digital camera in that they use CCD technology. The lens in a camcorder shines the light onto a CCD. The CCD measures the light with a half-inch, or 1-cm, panel of 300,000 to 500,000 tiny light-sensitive diodes called *photosites*.

The following types of video cameras are available:

- Analog
- Digital

Analog camcorders record video and audio signals as an analog track on video tape. Every time a copy of a tape is made, the image loses some image and audio quality. Analog formats lack a number of the impressive features that are found in digital camcorders. The main differences between the available analog formats are the kind of video tape that the camcorder uses and the resolution that if offers.

Analog formats include the following:

- **Standard VHS**—Uses the same type of videotapes as a regular VCR. Once recorded, these tapes can be played on a standard VCR.
- **VHS-C**—A compact VHS format. The video camera tapes are smaller than standard VHS tapes but can be played on a standard VCR with the use of an adapter.
- **Super VHS**—This format records an image with 380–400 horizontal lines, a much higher-resolution image than standard VHS formats. The video camera itself is a VCR and can be connected directly to a television or VCR to copy to standard VHS tapes.
- **Super VHS-C**—A more compact version of Super VHS that uses a smaller cassette.

- **8-mm**—Small 8-mm tapes, about the size of an audio cassette, provide about the same resolution as standard VHS. The advantage is that this format allows more compact video recorders, sometimes small enough to fit in a pocket. To view recordings, the video recorder is attached to a television.

- **Hi-8**—Similar to 8-mm camcorders, Hi-8 camcorders have a higher resolution, about 400 horizontal lines. Hi-8 tapes are more expensive than ordinary 8-mm tapes.

Digital recorders, as shown in Figure 8-28, record information in bytes rather than in frames. This allows the image to be reproduced repeatedly without losing image or audio quality. Digital video can also be downloaded to a computer, where it can be edited or posted on the Internet. Also, digital video, with typically 500 horizontal lines, has a much better resolution than analog video.

Figure 8-28 Digital Video Recorder

MiniDV Recorders

These video recorders can be small and lightweight. They record on compact cassettes, which are fairly expensive and hold 60–90 minutes of footage. The recordings are at 500 lines of resolution and can be transferred to a personal computer. MiniDV recorders can capture still pictures, just as a digital camera does. Sony has recently introduced MicroMV, a format that works in the same basic way as MiniDV but records on much smaller tapes.

Digital8 Recorders

Sony is the exclusive producer of Digital8. These units are similar to regular digital camcorders, but they use standard Hi-8 tapes, which are less expensive and can hold up to 60 minutes of footage. Digital8 recordings can be copied with no loss in quality. Digital8 recorders can be connected to a computer to download for editing or Internet use.

DVD Recorders

DVD recorders are not as common as the MiniDV models, but they are expected to gain more acceptance. DVD recorders burn video information directly onto small discs. The advantage is that each recording session is recorded as an individual track, similar to the song tracks on a CD. These tracks make it possible to jump to any section of video. DVDs can hold 30 minutes to 2 hours of video.

The newer DVD recorders support two formats: DVD-R and DVD-RAM. DVD-R camcorder discs work in most set-top DVD players. The disc can only be recorded to once. DVD-RAM makes it possible to record discs repeatedly, but the discs cannot be played in a standard DVD player. The video recorder is connected directly to the television for playback, or the movies can be copied to another format.

Memory Cards

Just like digital cameras, you can purchase digital video recorders that record directly onto solid-state memory cards, such as Flash memory cards, Memory Sticks, and SmartMedia cards.

Hardware and Software Video Capture

Video clips can be played using the Windows AVI format or through a video capture card. This is a major consideration when creating a presentation that includes a video component. Will the computer that you use have a compatible video digitizer card installed, or will the video clip be required to play through the Windows multimedia extensions?

Sources for video capture normally include VCRs and camcorders. Some capture cards include a radio frequency (RF) demodulator and a TV tuner so that video can be captured from a television broadcast signal or a cable TV input.

The output from these video-producing devices tends to be composite TV or analog S-video signals. A *video decoder circuit* converts the analog signal into a stream of digital signals. However, these are not the RGB digital signals that are useful to the VGA card. The characteristics of the decoded TV signal are defined in television industry terms as YUV, as discussed earlier in this chapter.

The digitized output from the A/D converter is applied to a video compression *Application-Specific Integrated Circuit (ASIC)*. This is a compression chip that reduces the size of the file by removing redundant information from consecutive frames. This reduction is necessary because of the large size of typical digitized video files. Video-compression schemes can reduce the size of a video file by a ratio of up to 200:1. As the sections of video are compressed, the compressed files can be applied to the system RAM or can be routed directly to the hard disk drive. The audio signal is not compressed, but it is synchronized to the video signal so that it plays in sync with the video.

When the digitized video is recalled for output purposes, the file is reapplied to the compression chip, which restores the redundant information to the frames. The output from the compression chip is applied to the digital-to-analog portion of the video-processing circuitry. The analog signals are converted back into the proper VGA format and are applied to the video-out connector at the back of the video card.

Installing and Configuring a Video Capture Board

To prepare the hardware configuration jumpers, or switches, for operation, refer to the manufacturer's documentation that is included with the video card. The factory default settings of the card usually work well, but you should examine the installed system devices for address and IRQ conflicts.

Figure 8-29 shows a video capture card. As with any other adapter card, you must remove the system's cover to install the card. Inside the unit, remove the cover of an expansion slot, making sure that the expansion slot type is compatible with the capture card edge connector. Many capture cards are full-length cards, so make sure that the slot can handle the physical dimensions of the card.

Figure 8-29 Video Capture Card

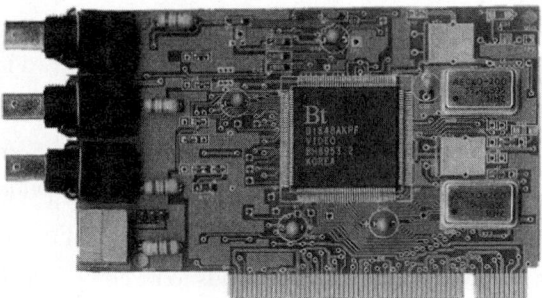

Connect the capture card to the VGA card as directed by the installation guide. Search the card manufacturer's website for details about the specific card that you are installing. Some VGA cards use an edge connector that is built into the top of the card.

Install any antennas that must be connected to the card. These could include a TV antenna, a coaxial television cable, or an FM radio antenna. Connect the video-in cables to the video source that is being used for input, and connect the audio cable to the audio source.

The audio and video connections are typically made with standard RCA cables and connectors. Connect the VGA monitor signal cable to the capture card VGA-out connector. The video signal passes through the capture card and is looped to the VGA card. This means that the screen image can be present on the monitor and the video screen simultaneously. A VGA loopback cable is connected between the capture card loopback input and the VGA card RGB-out connector.

If all the hardware and software configuration settings are correct but capture problems occur, you must troubleshoot the video capture–related hardware. In most systems, this involves a TV signal source such as a VCR or camcorder, the cabling, the capture card, and the video card.

Most capture card software provides a preview window that lets you view the video that is coming from the video source. If the source is visible in this window, the video source and the video-in cabling can be eliminated as a source of problems. However, simply being able to see the video in the window does not mean that the card can capture video.

If the video is present in the window, and the video source and cabling check okay, the hardware and software configurations should be checked closely. Check the capture software setup for the video buffer settings. Usual video buffer settings are D0000h, D800h, E000h, or E800h. Change the setting to one of the other possible values. Add a DEVICE= statement to the CONFIG.SYS file that corresponds to the new setting for the video buffer. For example, you can add the following statement:

    DEVICE=*path*\EMM386.EXE X=D000h-D700h

Finally, if problems continue, reinstall and reconfigure the capture software.

If the signal from the video source is not present in the preview window, be sure that the video source is turned on. Check the video-in cable to make sure that it is properly connected to the video-out jack of the video source and is plugged into the correct video-source input on the capture card. Check the I/O address setup of the capture card closely as well as its setting in the capture software. Check the *video capture software* to make sure that the correct video source setting is selected. While you are in the software settings window, check the video type that is selected. Make sure that the video type is set for the NTSC standard if you are in the United States, or determine that you are using the appropriate video standard in other regions.

Summary

This chapter discussed multimedia technology and the required hardware and software. Some of the important concepts to retain from this chapter include the following:

- Know the requirements and installation procedures for the specific hardware to produce multimedia using the PC. This includes the video adapter, sound card, CD-ROM drives, and DVD players.

- Understand the characteristics of the computer display or monitor, including the color capabilities, the sharpness/viewability, and the projection technology. The number of bits that describe a pixel is known as its bit-depth. The 24-bit bit-depth is known as true color.

- Familiarize yourself with the video card types and installation, and understand RAM-DAC and video memory. Video capture cards convert video signals from different sources into a digital signal that can be manipulated by the computer.

- Know the sound card types and installation, the basic components of the sound card, and the methods that sound cards use to produce audio. The basic functions of the sound card are input, processing, and output. The quality of the sound card is determined by the audio bit-depth, sampling rate, and feature set.

- Understand that CD drives are categorized by the type of case and the bus type. The CD-ROM drive read speed determines the rate at which information can be pulled from the CD and sent to the communications bus.

- Currently, CD drives can read data, record data, and rewrite data to a previously recorded CD. Although a CD drive cannot read a DVD, a DVD drive can read data from a CD. In addition, the laser that is used in a DVD drive is different from that found in a CD drive, because the DVD laser must be able to focus for single-layer DVDs and dual-layered DVDs.

The next chapter details advanced hardware fundamentals for servers. It focuses on the network server, RAID technology, memory considerations, and server upgrades.

Key Terms

Accelerated Graphics Port (AGP)   Interface that is designed to handle the intense data throughput that is associated with three-dimensional graphics.

all-points-addressable display   A display that handles bitmaps.

Application-Specific Integrated Circuit (ASIC)   A compression chip that reduces the size of a file by removing redundant information from consecutive frames.

aspect ratio   The width-to-height ratio of the display screen.

audio video interface (AVI)   A popular file format for video that produces a 40:1 compression ratio and a 30 frames-per-second capture rate, at 320×200 resolution.

bit-depth   The number of bits that describe a pixel.

bit-depth for sound   The sample size and bus size of the sound card.

built-in sound   An audio processor that is located on the motherboard.

CD burner   See *CD recorder*.

CD-R   Compact disc–recordable. CD media that can be recorded to once.

CD recorder   Allows CD media to be recorded with data, audio, or any combination of the two.

CD-ROM drive read speed   Determines the rate at which information can be pulled from the CD and sent to the communications bus.

CD-RW   Compact disc–rewritable. CD media that can be recorded to multiple times.

Cinepak   A compression/decompression standard that is supported by Video for Windows.

coaxial   Digital configuration that uses an RCA jack.

color space conversion   The process of converting the YUV signal into the RGB format that is acceptable to the VGA card screen memory.

communication circuit   Sends the information that is read from the CD to the computer using the configured bus.

compact disc (CD)   Removable media for audio and data storage.

Digital Audio Extraction (DAE)   The process of copying audio from a CD to another medium while keeping the audio in its original digital state.

digital-in port   An interface that captures digital audio.

digital versatile disc (DVD)   Removable media that is used primarily for movie and data storage.

display   A computer output surface and projecting mechanism that shows text and graphics images.

display adapter   See *video adapter*.

dot pitch   The physical limitation on the potential image sharpness of a screen image.

dots per inch (dpi)   How the actual sharpness of a display image is measured.

drive motor   Spins the CD up to the proper speed so that the laser can read the data.

DVD-Audio   New DVD format that includes multiple-channel audio.

DVD drive   Computer drive that can play/read DVDs. A DVD drive can read CDs and DVDs, whereas a CD drive can only read CDs.

DVD physical format   Defines the structure of the disc and the areas to which the data is recorded.

DVD-R   Technology that allows a DVD to be written to once.

DVD-RAM   Technology that uses random-access memory to enable users to record DVDs multiple times.

DVD-ROM   DVD format that is designed for storing computer files.

DVD-RW   Technology that allows the media to be recorded multiple times.

DVD+RW   Similar to DVD-RW, technology that uses variable bit-rate when encoding.

DVD-Video   DVD format that is used by stand-alone DVD players for movies and extras.

external speaker   Output device for the sound card.

feature set   Additional features that include three-dimensional audio coprocessors, device controllers, and digital output options.

frequency modulation (FM)   Uses programming to create waveforms that best match the instrument that is playing.

gas plasma   A type of computer display that works by lighting up display screen positions based on the voltages at different grid intersections.

hot-swappable interface   Allows peripherals to be changed while the system is running. USB is an example.

Indeo   Data compression method that was developed by Intel.

Joint Photographic Experts Group (JPEG)   A compression standard that is used with digitized video.

laser assembly   Consists of a laser and a lens that reads the CD as it spins.

light-emitting diode (LED)   A type of computer display that works by lighting up display screen positions based on the voltages at different grid intersections.

line-in port   An interface that captures audio from amplified or powered sources such as external stereos.

liquid crystal display (LCD)   A type of computer display that works by blocking light rather than creating it.

logical standard   Defines the way that information is stored on the media.

microphone-in port   An interface that connects a microphone for sound to the PC.

MIDI port   An industry-standard interface that connects musical devices.

minijack   Configuration for the digital-in port that is physically the same as the microphone-in and line-in ports.

monitor   See *display*.

Moving Picture Experts Group (MPEG)   A compression standard that is used with digitized video.

multimedia   The combination of text, sound, or motion video.

Musical Instrument Digital Interface (MIDI)   A combination of hardware and software that allows the sound card to control musical instruments and use these instruments to output the audio.

PCI sound card   An adapter card with an audio processor that connects to the motherboard through the peripheral component interconnect.

physical standard   Defines where the information is placed on the media.

random-access memory digital-to-analog converter (RAMDAC)   The firmware that translates digital information into analog form for export to the monitor.

ripping   The process of Digital Audio Extraction.

sampling rate   The rate at which the sound card can record audio information.

sound card   Device that allows the computer to handle audio information.

sound card input   Sources of sound that include microphones and CD players.

sound card memory   Usually in the form of ROM, Flash, or NVRAM and can often be upgraded or expanded. It stores samples from musical instruments and holds instructions for MIDI devices.

sound card output   Produces sound for devices such as headphones.

sound card port   Internal or external port for connecting to input and output devices.

sound card processing   The capability to convert audio information into different formats.

sound card processor   Handles the basic instructions that drive the sound card as well as the routing of audio information.

sound converter   Converts data for sound.

Super Video Graphics Array (SVGA) monitor   A monitor that can display up to 16,777,216 colors, because it can process a 24-bit-long description of a pixel.

Toslink   A fiber-optic port that was developed by Toshiba for the digital-in port.

tracking mechanism   A motor and drive system that moves the lens into the correct position to access a specific area of a CD.

true color   Also known as 24-bit bit-depth, it allows 8 bits for each of the three additive primary colors: red, green, and blue.

universal serial bus (USB)   A hot-swappable interface that connects peripherals such as the USB speaker system.

video adapter   An integrated circuit card in a computer, or in some cases a monitor, that provides digital-to-analog conversion.

video BIOS   Provides the set of video functions that can be used by the software to access the video hardware.

video board   See *video adapter*.

video card memory   Used by the video chip set. Digital information in video memory must be translated into analog form for export to the monitor.

video capture card   Converts video signals from different sources into digital signals that can be manipulated by the computer.

video capture software   Captures frames of television video and converts these frames into digital formats that can be processed by the system.

video decoder circuit   Converts the analog signal into a stream of digital signals.

video display terminal (VDT)   A terminal with a display and a keyboard.

video display unit (VDU)   See *video display terminal*.

Video Electronics Standards Association (VESA)   Association that provides standards that define how software can determine the capability of a display.

Video Graphics Array (VGA) mode   The lowest common denominator of display modes.

Video Graphics Array (VGA) standard   Standard that describes how data is passed between the computer and the display.

viewability   The ability to see the screen image from different angles.

wavetable sound card   Uses digitized samples of instruments to reproduce audio.

YUV   The color model that is used for encoding video. Y is the luminosity of the black-and-white signal. U and V are color difference signals. U is red minus Y (R–Y), and V is blue minus Y (B–Y).

Check Your Understanding

1. What is a typical VESA video resolution standard?

   A. 640×480

   B. 800×600

   C. 1040×680

   D. 1360×1280

2. What is the physical limitation on the potential sharpness of a screen image?

   A. Pixel

   B. Dot pitch

   C. Lines per inch

   D. Screen resolution

3. Which book standard is associated with audio CDs?

   A. Red Book

   B. Yellow Book

   C. White Book

   D. Orange Book

4. Which book standard is associated with data CDs?

   A. Red Book

   B. Yellow Book

   C. White Book

   D. Orange Book

5. Which book standard is associated with recordable CDs?

   A. Red Book

   B. Yellow Book

   C. White Book

   D. Orange Book

6. Which book standard is associated with video CDs?

   A. Red Book

   B. Yellow Book

   C. White Book

   D. Orange Book

7. Which video specification, introduced by Intel, provides a 32-bit video channel that runs at 66 MHz in basic 1x mode?

   A. ISA

   B. EISA

   C. PCI

   D. AGP

8. Which chip handles the basic instructions for a sound card?

   A. ADC

   B. DAC

   C. DSP

   D. DAT

9. Which of the following are common multimedia compression types?

   A. JPEG

   B. MPEG

   C. Cinepak

   D. All of the above

10. Which DVD recording technology has the ability to use a variable bit-rate when encoding certain types of media such as streaming video?

    A. DVD+RW

    B. DVD-RW

C. DVD-RAM

D. DVD-R

11. A user needs to copy audio from one CD to another without changing the original digital state of the audio. Which process can achieve this?

A. Digital Sound Conversion

B. Digital Audio Extraction

C. Digital to Analog Conversion

D. Razzing

12. Which items need to be considered when determining the quality of a sound card?

A. Bit-depth

B. Feature set

C. Sampling rate

D. All of the above

13. Which dot pitch has the greatest potential image sharpness?

A. .24 mm

B. .28 mm

C. .32 mm

D. .38 mm

14. Which of the following are CD-ROM standards that define how information is stored on CD media?

A. IEEE 1934

B. ISO 9660

C. None of the above

D. Both a. and b.

15. Which items are functions of a video capture card?

    A. Convert YUV signals to RGB signals.

    B. Sample incoming video signals using an ADC.

    C. Scale the image to fit in the window view of the monitor.

    D. All of the above.

Objectives

Upon completing this chapter, you will be able to perform the following tasks:

- Install and configure hard drives in a RAID array, external peripherals, external drive subsystems, and processors for a server
- Upgrade adapters, internal and external devices, system-monitoring agents, and service tools as they relate to a server
- Increase memory to improve network server performance
- Document the configuration for upgrading and troubleshooting purposes

Chapter 9

Advanced Hardware Fundamentals for Servers

A network server is the center of a network environment. The server allows users to access files, e-mails, programs, and printers. Fault tolerance is important for a network server, because it allows a system to continue when a hardware failure occurs. One method that provides fault tolerance is the Redundant Array of Independent Disks (RAID) technology. This chapter focuses on RAID and discusses memory upgrades, the configuration of external disk subsystems, and external compact disc read-only memory (CD-ROM) systems.

Network Server Overview

The network server is a critical component. Keeping the data that is stored on the server safe and maintaining the services that are provided to the users are extremely important tasks for the IT technician. This section includes the following topics:

- Network servers
- RAID
- RAID controllers
- Hardware RAID versus software RAID
- Hardware-based RAID configurations

Network Servers

A *network server* is a computer system in a network that is shared by multiple users. Servers are available in all sizes, from x86-based PCs to mainframes. Figure 9-1 shows examples of different network servers. A server can have a keyboard, monitor, and mouse directly attached to it. Also, one keyboard, monitor, and mouse can connect to any number of servers through a keyboard/video/mouse (KVM) switch, which is shown in Figure 9-2. Servers can also be accessed through a network connection.

Figure 9-1 Network Servers

Figure 9-2 KVM Switch

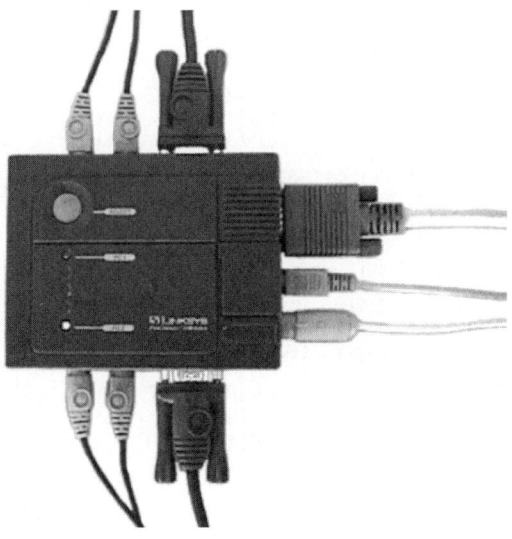

 PhotoZoom   KVM Switch

This PhotoZoom details the components of the KVM switch, with multiple servers connected.

The term *server* can refer to both the hardware and software, which is the entire computer system, or it can refer to just the software that performs the service. For example, the e-mail server can refer to the e-mail server software in a system that also runs other applications. It can also refer to a computer that is dedicated only to the e-mail server application.

 PhotoZoom   Server Component

The front and rear views of a network server are detailed in this PhotoZoom.

RAID

The *Redundant Array of Independent Disks (RAID)* technology is designed to allow some fault tolerance to prevent loss of data in the event of a disk drive failure on a network server. A disk drive is a mechanical device that can eventually fail. RAID accomplishes this fault tolerance, or redundancy, by storing the information on more than one disk drive.

RAID level 1 uses duplication of the data to provide fault tolerance. RAID levels 3, 4, and 5 use parity information that is calculated from the bit patterns of the data that is being written to the RAID array to provide fault tolerance. When a disk drive fails in a RAID 3, 4, or 5 system, the parity information can be used along with the data on the remaining disk drives in the array to calculate the data that was on the disk drive that failed. This allows the disk subsystem and the network server to keep functioning. However, the server will be slightly slower because of the calculations required to re-create the missing data. RAID level 2 is structurally different in that it does not use duplication, or parity, to provide fault tolerance. RAID 2 instead uses a special hamming code.

RAID is a term that is surrounded by a tremendous amount of misinformation. There is disagreement about how many levels of RAID are defined, whether the *A* in RAID stands for *array* or *arrays,* and whether the *I* in RAID stands for *inexpensive* or *independent.* In the past few years, many people have substituted the word independent for inexpensive.

RAID 6, 7, 10, 50, 53, and others can be found in the literature that is provided by many vendors. This chapter focuses on the types of RAID that are used most often in a network environment.

RAID was defined in 1988 in the paper "A Case for Redundant Arrays of Inexpensive Disks (RAID)," which was written by David A. Patterson, Garth A. Gibson, and Randy H. Katz at the University of California, Berkeley. The original paper defined five levels of RAID and offered the RAID solution as an alternative to the Single Large Expensive Disk (SLED) technology.

RAID 0

RAID 0 was not defined in the 1988 Berkeley paper. In fact, it is not RAID because it does not provide redundancy. RAID 0 is just an array or group of disk drives that are used as a single disk. The data is written in chunks, or stripes, to all the disk drives in the array. This improves disk input and output performance, because several chunks of data can be written or read simultaneously. If a disk drive in the RAID 0 array fails, all data in the array is lost. RAID level 0 is also often called *disk striping without parity*. Figure 9-3 shows an illustration of RAID 0.

Figure 9-3 RAID Level 0

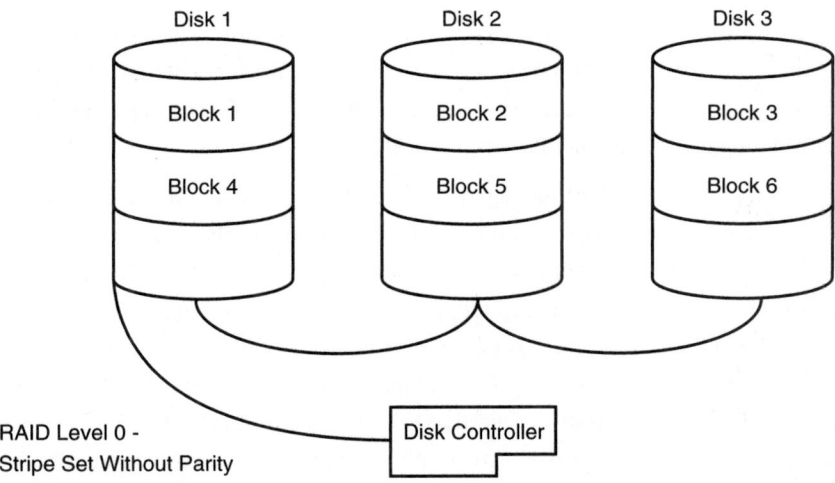

e-Lab Activity   Creating RAID 0 with Windows 2000

This e-lab goes step by step through the process of creating RAID 0. The requirements listed are necessary only when implementing RAID 0 in a network environment.

RAID 1

RAID 1 requires a minimum of two disk drives. All other RAID levels, except level 0, require at least three disk drives to implement. *RAID 1* writes all data to two separate locations. To store 20 GB of data using RAID 1, two 20-GB disk drives are required. This is a 50 percent loss of storage capacity.

RAID 1 can be implemented in the following ways:

- Disk mirroring
- Disk duplexing

In **disk mirroring**, the two disk drives are connected to the same disk controller. The only problem with disk mirroring is that if the disk controller fails, there is no access to the mirrored data. Figure 9-4 shows a diagram of disk mirroring. To eliminate this single point of failure, use disk duplexing rather than disk mirroring.

Figure 9-4 RAID Level 1 (Disk Mirroring)

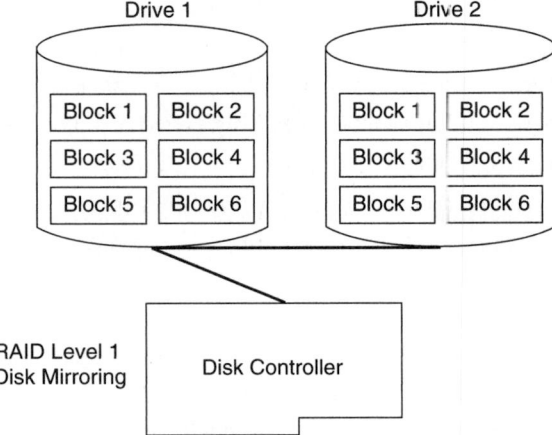

In **disk duplexing**, each disk drive in the mirrored set is connected to a different disk controller. This eliminates the single point of failure in pure disk mirroring. The only additional cost is that of the additional disk controller. Figure 9-5 shows a diagram of disk duplexing.

Figure 9-5 RAID Level 1 (Disk Duplexing)

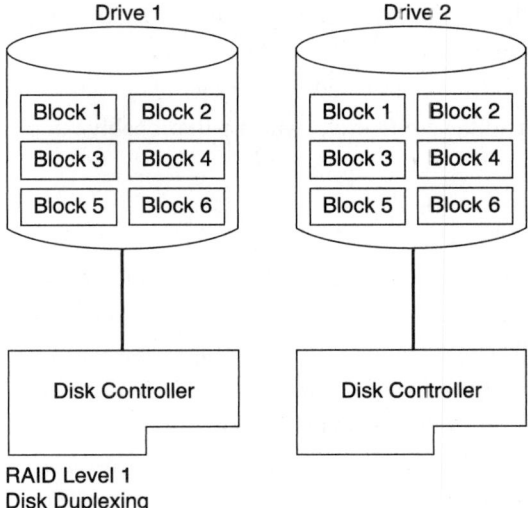

e-Lab Activity   Creating RAID 1 with Windows 2000

This e-lab goes step by step through the process of creating RAID 1. The requirements listed are necessary only when implementing RAID 1 in a network environment.

RAID 2

NOTE

A *hamming code* is an error-correction method that mixes 3 check bits at the end of each 4 data bits. When these check bits are received, they detect and correct 1-bit errors automatically.

RAID 2 uses a hamming code to create an *error-correcting code (ECC)* for all data to be stored on the RAID 2 array. The ECC can detect and correct single-bit errors and detect double-bit errors. The ECC code must be read and decoded each time data is read from the disk. RAID 2 is difficult and expensive to implement and has a high overhead. For example, RAID 2 provides 3 parity bits for each 4 data bits.

RAID 2 has no commercial implementations because of the expense and difficulty of implementation. It requires a minimum of three disk drives to implement.

RAID 3

RAID 3 uses bit-level parity with a single-parity disk to provide fault tolerance of data stored on the RAID 3 array in the event of failure of a single disk drive in the array. RAID 3 requires that all the disk drives in the array are synchronized with each other. The bits of the data and the parity information calculated from the data are written to all the disk drives in the array simultaneously. RAID 3 requires a minimum of three disk drives to create the array.

RAID 4

RAID 4 uses block-level parity with a single-parity disk to provide fault tolerance to the RAID 4 array in the event of failure of a single disk drive in the array. On a RAID 4 array, data and the parity information calculated from the data is written to the disk drives in blocks. The disk drives do not have to be synchronized, and the disk drives can be accessed independently. A minimum of three disk drives is required to create the array. The problem with RAID 4 is that the parity drive is accessed on every write operation to the RAID array. This causes heavy utilization of the parity drive, which will probably fail before the other drives in the array.

RAID 5

RAID 5 uses *disk striping with parity*. It uses block-level parity, but it spreads the parity information among all the disk drives in the disk array. This eliminates the parity drive failure that is common in RAID 4 systems. The loss of storage capacity in RAID 5 systems is equivalent to the storage capacity of one of the disk drives. If a RAID 5 array has three 10-GB disk drives, the storage capacity of the array is 20 GB, which is a loss of one-third, or 33 percent. In another example, if a RAID 5 array has seven 10-GB disk drives, the total storage capacity of the array is 60 GB, which is a loss of one-sixth, or 16.67 percent. Figure 9-6 shows a diagram of RAID 5.

Figure 9-6 RAID 5 (Disk Striping with Parity)

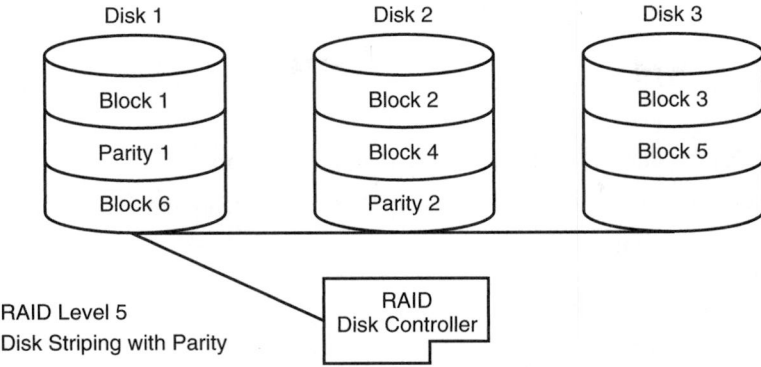

RAID 0/1

RAID 0/1 is also known as ***RAID 0+1***, and it is sometimes called ***RAID 10.*** This combination of RAIDs provides the best of both worlds. It has the performance of RAID 0 and the redundancy of RAID 1. RAID 0/1 requires at least four disk drives to implement. In RAID 0/1, two RAID 0 stripe sets, which provide high input/output performance, are mirrored. This provides the fault tolerance. Figure 9-7 shows a diagram of RAID 0/1.

Figure 9-7 RAID 0/1 (Mirrored Stripe Set Without Parity)

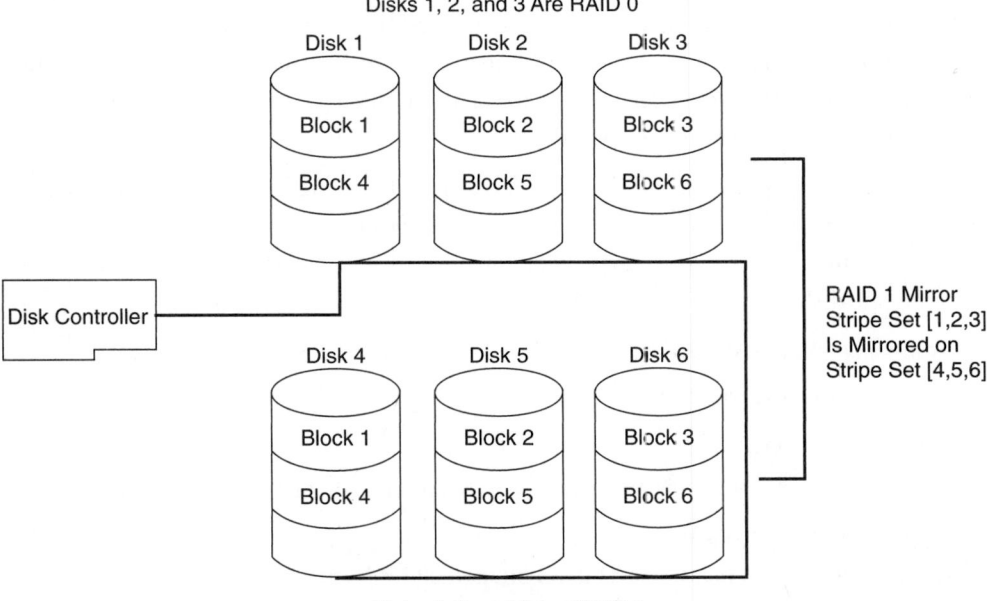

Video   Basic Disk–to–Dynamic Disk Conversion

The steps to convert a hard drive from a basic disk to a dynamic disk are shown in this video.

Lab 9.1.2   Basic Disk–to–Dynamic Disk Conversion

Upon completion of this lab, you will be able to convert a hard drive from a basic disk to a dynamic disk.

RAID Controllers

RAID controllers are specialized disk controllers that use either Advanced Technology Attachment (ATA) or Small Computer System Interface (SCSI) technologies. ATA RAID controllers are limited in the number of disks that can be attached. This is because of ATA channel limitations, which are a maximum of two channels with a maximum of two disk drives per channel, for a total of four disk drives. SCSI RAID controllers have multiple channels. Two channels are common. RAID controllers with three, four, and five channels are available. RAID controllers are generally expensive because of the sophistication that they must contain.

RAID controllers often have an on-board memory cache that ranges in size from 4 MB to 256 MB. This memory cache often has a battery backup system to prevent data loss in the event of a sudden power loss to the network server. This is important, because data written from the system memory to the RAID controller is first written to the on-board cache, and it could be several seconds before the data is written to the disk. Data on the disk drive might not be updated with the current data without the battery to supply power to the RAID controller. This could easily lead to a loss of data integrity.

The memory cache on the RAID controller can usually be configured as read cache, write cache, or a combination of both. The read cache improves the read performance. The write cache allows the processor to continue with other tasks instead of waiting for the data to be written to the disk. Figure 9-8 shows the RAID controller and the disk array.

The following features should be considered when evaluating RAID controllers:

- Number of channels
- Speed of channels
- On-board cache, which is read, write, combination, and battery backup option
- Fast host adapter (PCI)
- Bus width, which includes 16 bit, 32 bit, and 64 bit

Figure 9-8 RAID Controller and Disk Array

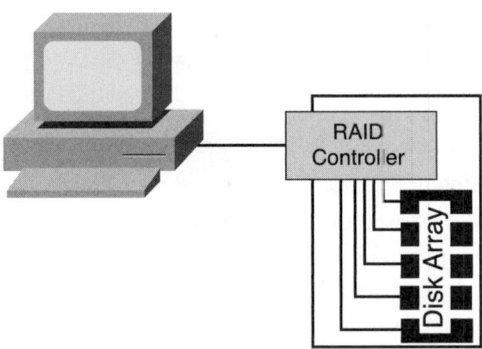

Hardware RAID Versus Software RAID

RAID is usually implemented using a RAID disk controller. However, RAID disk controllers are rather expensive. RAID can also be implemented in software by several network operating systems, including Novell NetWare, Linux, Microsoft Windows NT, and Microsoft Windows 2000. See Figure 9-9.

NOTE

When using the Windows 2000 version of RAID, the hard drive must be converted to a dynamic disk before the RAID options can be implemented.

Figure 9-9 Hardware Versus Software RAID

The network operating system determines the type of RAID that can be supported. For example, Windows NT supports levels 1 and 5, whereas Linux can support levels 0, 1, 4, and 5. Software RAID is usually implemented at the disk partition level rather than on the physical disk, as in hardware-based RAID. The disadvantage of software RAID is that it requires the network server processor to perform the work that is usually done by the RAID controller in hardware RAID. RAID 5 implemented in software requires the processor to calculate all the parity information when writing data to the RAID 5 disk array. RAID 1 implemented in software places a minimal load on the network server processor.

When RAID 5 is implemented in software, the files on the RAID array are not available until the network server operating system is running. This means that the operating system cannot be stored on, and therefore cannot boot from, a RAID 5 system implemented in software. This is not an issue when a RAID 5 system is implemented using hardware.

Software-based RAID has one advantage over hardware-based RAID. In software-based RAID, the RAID implementation can be based on disk partitions rather than entire disk drives. For example, three 10-GB partitions on three different disk drives can be used to create a software RAID 5 array. Space in different partitions on each of these disk drives could be used for some other purpose. In nearly all cases, hardware-based RAID is better than software-based RAID. However, having RAID implemented in software is much better than having no disk fault tolerance.

Worksheet 9.1.4   RAID

This worksheet is a review of the information that was covered on the different types of RAID that are used in a network environment.

Hardware-Based RAID Configurations

Network servers that contain a RAID controller must have the RAID system configured before the network operating system can be installed. Configuration of the RAID system consists of selecting physical disk drives and grouping them into one of the available RAID configurations. These configurations are usually RAID 1 or RAID 5. The network hardware vendor or the RAID hardware vendor usually supplies software to aid in the configuration of the RAID system. The disk drives of the RAID system can be internal to the network server chassis or external in a separate enclosure.

As mentioned in the previous section, RAID provides fault tolerance in case of a disk drive failure in the network server. In *hardware-based RAID*, the disk drives in the network server have RAID implemented by a special disk controller, which is the RAID controller. Some network operating systems can implement software-based RAID at the expense of an additional load on the network server processor. Most RAID controllers are designed to use SCSI disk drives. However, at least one disk controller manufacturer makes a RAID controller that uses an EIDE/ATA-2 disk drive. The RAID disk controller has its own processor to implement the RAID configuration, and this relieves the network server processor of this task.

The configuration of the RAID controller in the network server is accomplished by software that is provided by the network server or RAID controller vendor. Although it is vendor specific, all the software works basically the same way. It enables an administrator to see the disk drives that are attached to the RAID controller. First, the administrator selects the disk drives to use. Then the administrator specifies the version of RAID to implement, using the selected disk drives. The software then "prepares" the disk drives to implement the RAID solution. For example, the administrator might choose two physical disk drives and tell the RAID configuration software to use these two disk drives to implement a RAID 1 or mirroring solution. The RAID controller would tell the network server operating system that a single logical disk drive is available. In this case, the RAID controller is reading and writing to two physical disk drives.

In another example, an administrator might select five physical disk drives and tell the RAID configuration software to use these five physical drives to implement RAID 5, which is disk striping with parity. The RAID controller would tell the network server operating system that a single logical disk drive is available. In this case, the RAID controller is reading and writing data in blocks across all five disk drives in the RAID 5 disk array.

NOTE

The Server+ exam will ask questions regarding general configurations and your general understanding of RAID.

In yet another example, an administrator might select the same five physical disk drives and tell the RAID configuration software to use these disk drives to implement RAID 5, which is disk striping with parity. In addition, the single logical disk drive could be partitioned into two partitions by the RAID configuration software. The network operating system would see two logical disk drives, or one on each partition. In this case, the RAID controller is reading and writing data in blocks across all five disk drives in the RAID 5 disk array.

Figure 9-10 shows an example of how a RAID controller manages disk drives.

Figure 9-10 RAID Controller Disk Drive Presentation

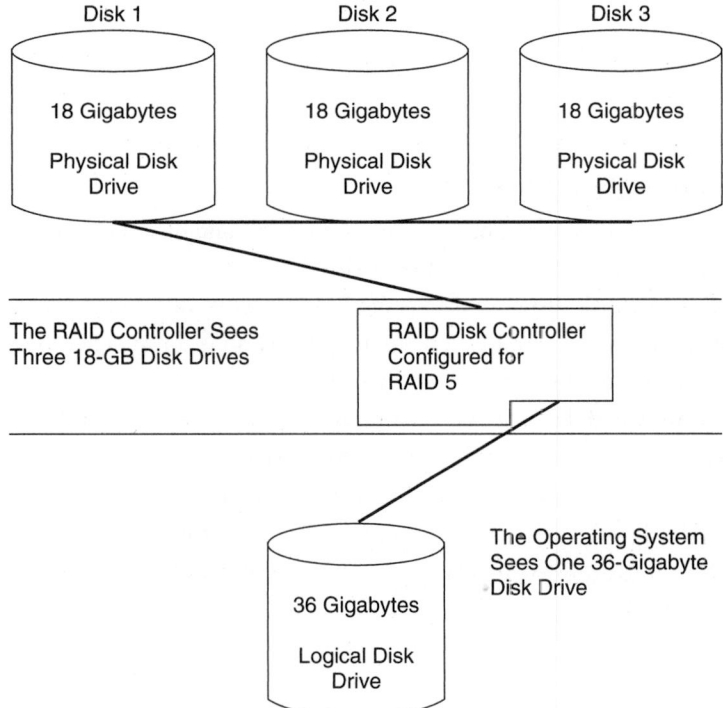

RAID 0 Configuration

RAID 0 is known as *disk striping*. Specifically, it is a stripe set without parity. RAID 0 is not fault tolerant, but it improves disk input/output performance. RAID 0 should not be used in a production-server environment. However, RAID 0 is often used in a high-powered workstation to improve disk input/output performance by reading and writing files in blocks to several disks simultaneously, as opposed to reading and writing a file sequentially to a single disk drive. To implement RAID 0, at least two disk drives are needed. Figure 9-11 shows an example of a RAID 0 implementation. For example, two 18-GB disk drives that are configured to implement RAID 0 have a storage capacity of 36 GB.

Figure 9-11 RAID 0 (Disk Striping Without Parity)

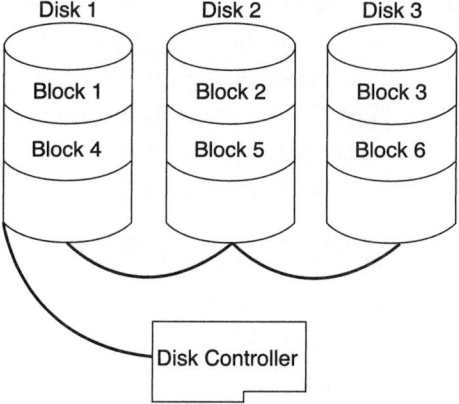

RAID 1 Configuration (Mirroring)

RAID 1 has two different implementations: disk mirroring and disk duplexing. In disk mirroring, everything that is written to one disk is also written to a second disk. Reading can be performed from either disk. Because data is duplicated on two different disk drives, the failure of one disk drive is not a serious problem, but merely an inconvenience. The network server keeps running using the single working disk drive. When time permits, the failed disk drive can be replaced, and the data on the working disk drive can be copied to the replacement. This re-creates the mirror. A minimum of two disk drives is required to implement RAID 1. In disk mirroring, both disk drives are attached to the same disk controller. The disk overhead for RAID 1 with mirroring is 50 percent. The disk controller represents a single point of failure for mirrored disk drives. Figure 9-12 shows an example of RAID 1 with the mirroring implementation.

Figure 9-12 RAID 1 (Disk Mirroring)

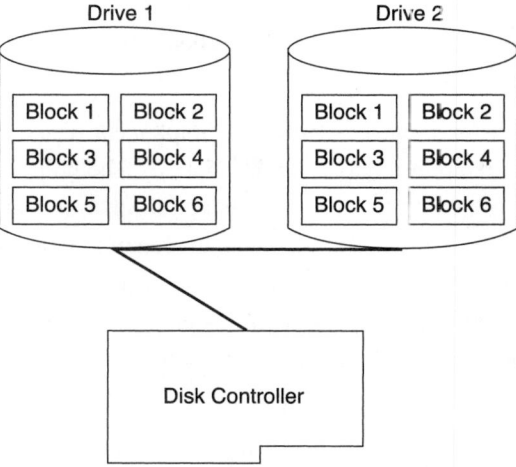

RAID 1 Configuration (Duplexing)

Disk duplexing eliminates the single point of failure that exists in disk mirroring. This is done by adding another disk controller and configuring the RAID system to duplicate data on disk drives that are attached to two different disk controllers. Generally no significant performance difference exists between disk mirroring and disk duplexing. The administrator is just adding further redundancy in the form of a second controller. The overhead of RAID 1 duplexing is 50 percent. Figure 9-13 shows an example of a RAID 1 duplexing implementation.

Figure 9-13 RAID 1 (Disk Duplexing)

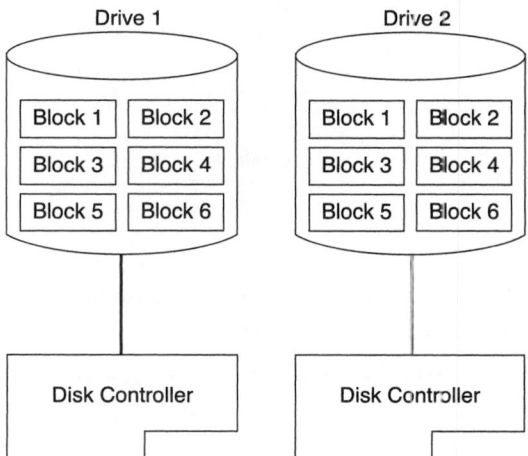

RAID 5 Configuration

RAID 5 uses a much more complicated scheme to provide fault tolerance in the case of a single disk failure. Refer to the section "RAID," earlier in this chapter, for an in-depth discussion of RAID 5.

RAID 5 requires a minimum of three disk drives to implement. The disk drives that comprise a RAID 5 solution are often referred to as a *RAID 5 array*. The failure of a single disk drive does not cause the network server to fail. The missing information that was on the failed disk can be re-created quickly using the information on the remaining disks. The failed disk drive should be replaced as quickly as possible. RAID 5 cannot survive the failure of a second disk drive after one disk drive has failed. Because of this fact, some RAID systems allow the configuration of a "hot-spare" disk drive. A hot-spare disk drive is powered up and running, but it contains no data. It is just waiting for a drive in the disk array to fail so that it can be used.

When the failure of a disk drive in the RAID array occurs, the RAID system starts rebuilding the data that was on the failed drive on the hot spare disk drive. This hot-spare methodology minimizes the amount of time it takes to get the RAID rebuilt. It also minimizes the window of time that the RAID system is vulnerable to a second drive failure that could destroy all the data stored on the RAID array. Figure 9-14 shows an example of a RAID 5 implementation.

Figure 9-14 RAID 5 (Disk Striping with Parity)

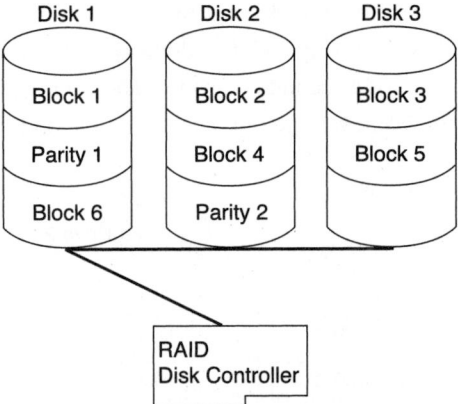

RAID 5 is more efficient than the other RAID levels because the overhead is $(1/n) * 100$, where n is the number of disk drives in the RAID 5 array. In other words, if a RAID 5 array is composed of six 18-GB disk drives, the overhead is $(1/6) * 100$, or 16.7 percent. Another way of looking at this is that the administrator loses the capacity of one of the disk drives in the RAID 5 array. This space stores the parity information. The parity information is stored across all the drives in the RAID 5 array.

The total storage capacity of the RAID 5 array is $(n-1) * c$, where n is the number of disk drives and c is the capacity of each of the disk drives. In this example, the total storage capacity of the RAID 5 array is $(6-1) * 18$, or 90 GB.

RAID 0/1 Configuration

RAID 0/1, which is sometimes called RAID 0+1 or RAID 10, involves mirroring or duplexing two RAID 0 arrays. This yields the fault tolerance of RAID 1 and the input/output speed of RAID 0. RAID 0/1 requires a minimum of four disk drives to implement. Figure 9-15 shows an example of a RAID 0/1 implementation.

Figure 9-15 RAID 0/1 (Mirrored Stripe Sets Without Parity)

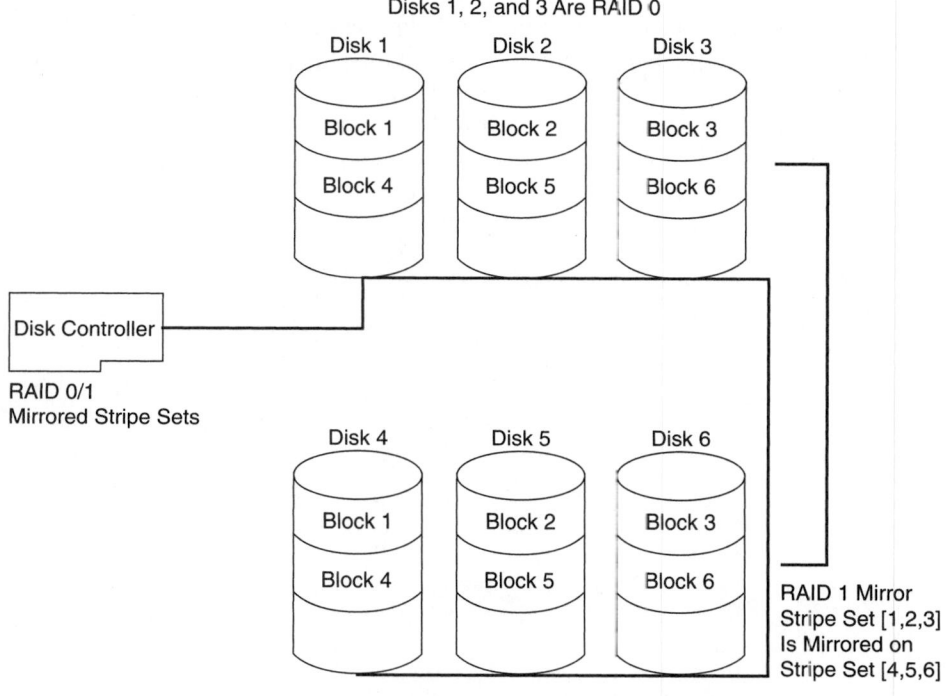

Configuring External Peripherals

Understand how to configure external peripherals such as external subsystems and CD-ROM systems, as well as how to configure external peripherals. This section includes the following topics:

- Overview of external disk subsystems
- Configuring an external disk subsystem
- Configuring an external CD-ROM system

Overview of External Disk Subsystems

External disk subsystems are necessary when the amount of disk storage cannot be accommodated by the disk drive bays that are internal to the network server chassis. These external disk subsystems can be either SCSI or Fibre Channel. Generally, Fibre Channel–based systems can support many more disk drives than a SCSI-based external system. External CD-ROM systems generally implement a *CD-ROM library*, which can accommodate a large number of CD-ROM drives and make them available to client computers on the network. See Figure 9-16. The network servers that implement CD-ROM libraries are often called *CD-ROM servers*.

Figure 9-16 CD-ROM Library

Configuring an External Disk Subsystem

Even though server-class microcomputers often have many empty bays that are designed to hold disk drives, it is often necessary to have disk drives external to the server chassis. External disk subsystems can consist of a single disk drive in its own chassis with its own power supply. On the high end, an external disk subsystem chassis can have 100 or more disk drives in it. See Figure 9-17.

Figure 9-17 Disk Subsystem

The simple external disk subsystem with only a few disk drives might just be attached to the external port on a SCSI or RAID controller. The external disk drives would then function in the same way that internal disk drives function, except that they are external to the network server chassis.

Some large external disk subsystems can have their own RAID mechanism built in. These large systems are often configured separately from the disk controller in the network server to which they are to be attached.

An administrator can often configure large external disk subsystems to be shared by more than one network server. This is one way to implement a high-availability server solution.

To connect the external disk subsystem to the network server, use a standard external SCSI cable or Fibre Channel, depending on the interface.

Generally, Fibre Channel–based external disk systems can handle a large number of disk drives. In all cases, be sure that the power switch on the external disk subsystem is turned on before turning on the network server.

Configuring an External CD-ROM System

External CD-ROM systems are often referred to as a CD-ROM library. Imagine a tower chassis with 7, 14, 21, or more CD-ROM drives. Having these CD-ROM drives attached to

NOTE

Fibre Channel can be configured point to point through a switched topology or in an arbitrated loop (FC-AL) with or without a hub, which can connect up to 127 nodes. Fibre Channel supports transmission rates of up to 2.12 Gbps in each direction, and rates of up to 4.25 Gbps are expected in the future.

a network server means that you can share all these CD-ROM drives and the CDs that they contain with all users on the network.

NOTE

To configure the external CD-ROM system, follow the manufacturer's installation and configuration instructions. Be sure that the external CD-ROM system is powered on before powering up the network server.

Attaching that many CD-ROM drives to a single network server is a simple process. It is done through a seldom-used feature called a *Logical Unit Number (LUN)*. Although LUNs are defined in the SCSI standards, they are seldom used, except on large groups of CD-ROM drives. A LUN enables an administrator to assign sub-SCSI IDs to a single SCSI ID. This means that the administrator could have seven CD-ROM drives all with the SCSI ID of 5. Each drive could have a different LUN of 1 through 7, all on the same SCSI channel. This means that on a single SCSI channel with SCSI IDs of 1 through 7, each SCSI ID could have seven LUNs. This would effectively make a total of 49 CD-ROM drives on a single SCSI channel.

Adding Hardware to a Server

Processor upgrades fall into two general categories: replacing an existing processor with a faster processor and adding an additional processor to a multiprocessor-capable network server. This section includes the following topics:

- Replacing a single processor with a faster processor
- Installing additional processors
- Upgrading the operating system for multiple processors
- Adding hard drives
- Adding memory

Replacing a Single Processor with a Faster Processor

Deciding whether a processor in a network server can be replaced with a faster processor depends on several factors. The most important factor is whether the motherboard in the network server can support a processor with a faster clock cycle. The other factors include the physical package that the existing processor uses and whether a faster processor is available that can use the same physical package, or form factor. Users can obtain this important upgrade information from the manufacturer of the network server's motherboard. Check the motherboard manufacturer's website to see whether the processor can be upgraded to a faster one. The administrator must determine whether a faster processor is available, in a form factor that is compatible with the existing processor. Upgrading to a faster processor can also require upgrading the BIOS on the system board. As a reference, Figure 9-18 shows an internal view of the server chassis. The side view is shown in Figure 9-19. A hot-swappable power supply is shown in Figure 9-20.

Figure 9-18 Internal View of the Server Chassis

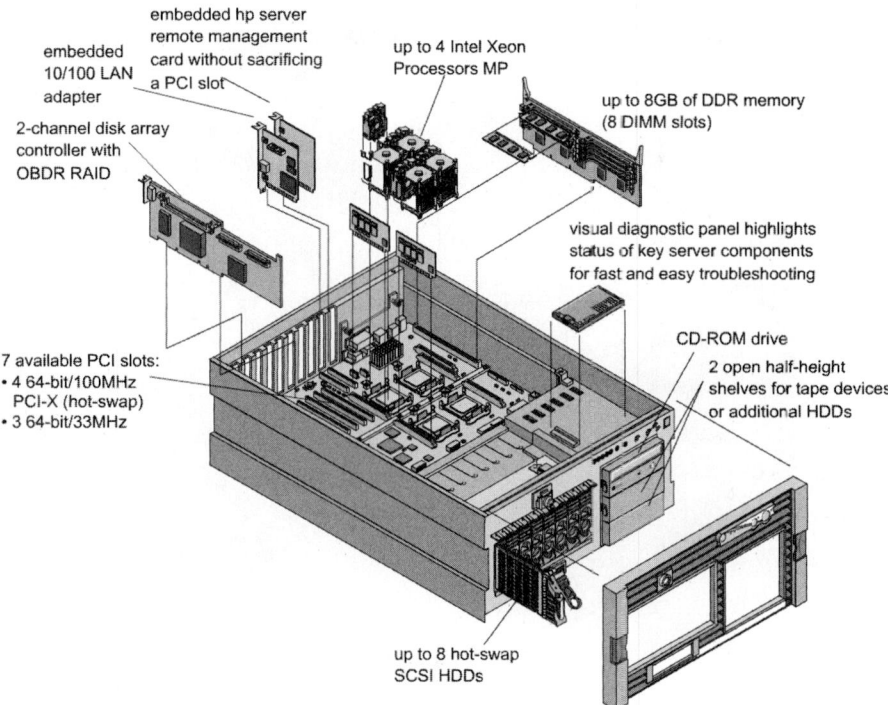

embedded hp server
remote management
card without sacrificing
a PCI slot

embedded
10/100 LAN
adapter

up to 4 Intel Xeon
Processors MP

up to 8GB of DDR memory
(8 DIMM slots)

2-channel disk array
controller with
OBDR RAID

visual diagnostic panel highlights
status of key server components
for fast and easy troubleshooting

CD-ROM drive

7 available PCI slots:
• 4 64-bit/100MHz
  PCI-X (hot-swap)
• 3 64-bit/33MHz

2 open half-height
shelves for tape devices
or additional HDDs

up to 8 hot-swap
SCSI HDDs

Figure 9-19 Side View of the Server Chassis

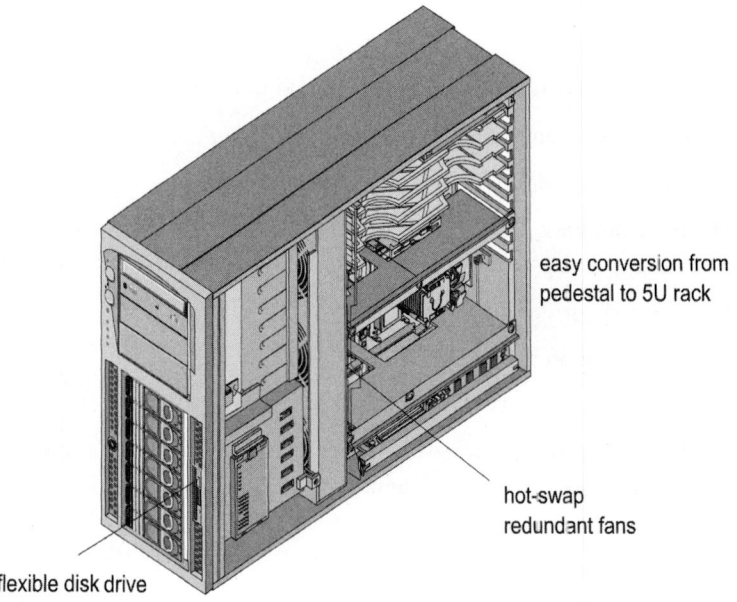

easy conversion from
pedestal to 5U rack

hot-swap
redundant fans

flexible disk drive

Figure 9-20 Hot-Swappable Power Supply

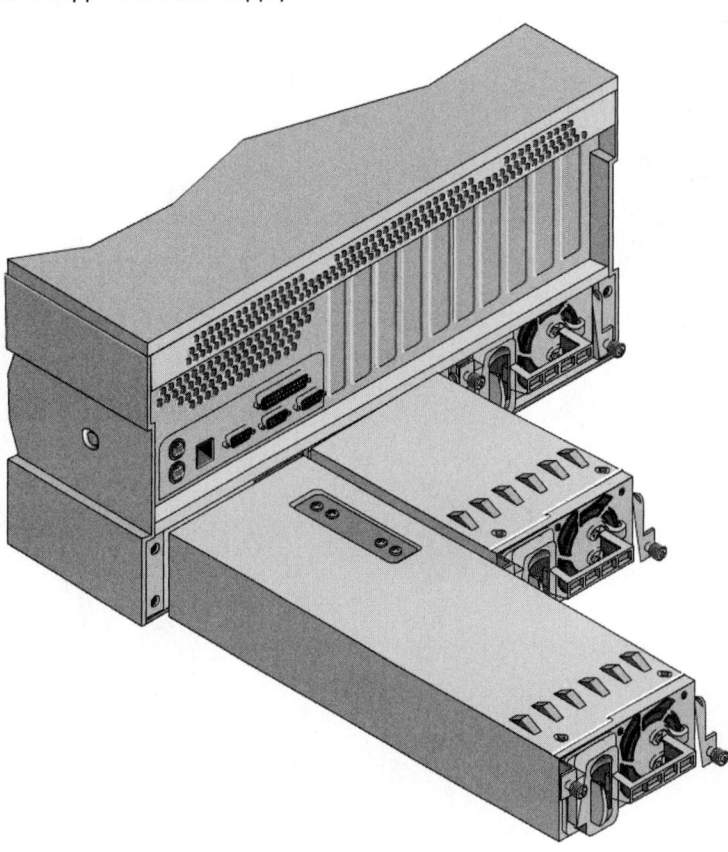

Take the following steps to perform a single-processor upgrade:

Step 1 Read the documentation that is provided by the manufacturer.

Step 2 Upgrade the system BIOS.

Step 3 Open the network server chassis (following electrostatic discharge [ESD] best practices).

Step 4 Remove the current processor.

Step 5 Insert the new processor.

Step 6 Close the network server chassis.

Step 7 Verify that the new processor is recognized by the network server hardware and the network operating system.

Installing Additional Processors

To add another processor to a multiprocessor-capable network server, the new processor must meet the following criteria:

- Be the same model of processor—such as a Pentium, Pentium Pro, Pentium II, Pentium II Xeon, Pentium III, Pentium III Xeon, Pentium 4, and so on—as the existing processor
- Have the same clock speed
- Have the same Level 2 (L2) cache size
- Match the stepping within one version (N+1)

Intel provides information on all its processors on its website so that you can tell what processor is currently in the network server so that the processor can be matched. Intel also offers a utility that detects and identifies the Intel processor that is currently in a network server.

The Intel processor identification utility is available in two versions. One operates under the Microsoft Windows operating system, and one runs from a bootable DOS floppy disk.

The Microsoft Windows version of the Intel identification utility can be downloaded from the following website:

http://support.intel.com/support/processors/tools/frequencyid/freqid.htm

Figure 9-21 shows sample output from the Windows version of the Intel identification program. The bootable floppy disk version of the Intel identification utility can be downloaded from the following website:

http://support.intel.com/support/processors/tools/frequencyid/bootable.htm

Figure 9-21 Intel Identification Program (Windows Version)

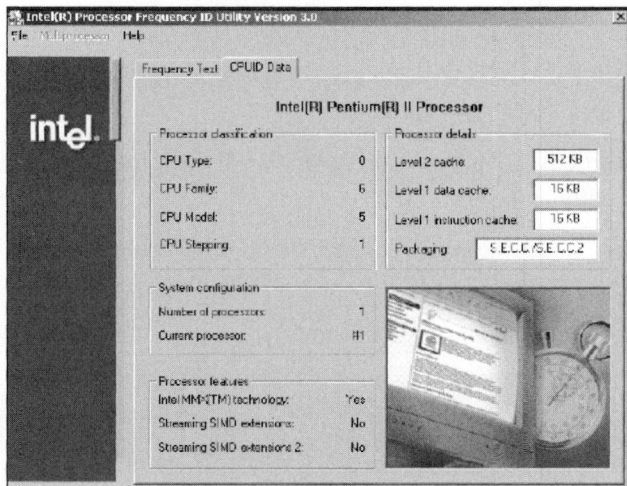

Figure 9-22 shows sample output from the bootable floppy disk version of the Intel identification program. A description of the Intel identification program, along with installation instructions, can be found at the following website:

http://support.intel.com/support/processors/tools/frequencyid/download.htm

Figure 9-22 Output from the Bootable Version of the Intel Identification Program

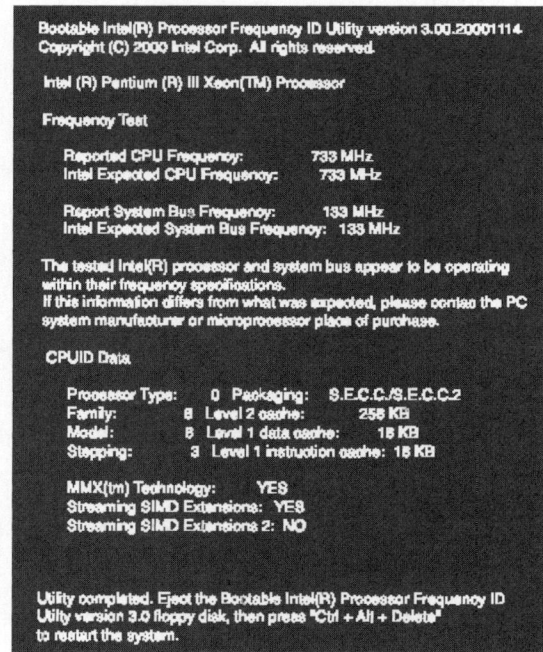

A tag on the processor can also identify the current processor. This tag contains a 5-digit spec number that starts with the letter *S*. You can use this number and the Intel website to identify the Intel processor that is in the network server.

Use the spec number from the processor label and the following Intel websites to identify the processor that is currently in the network server:

- **Pentium Pro**—http://developer.intel.com/design/pro/qit/index.htm
- **Pentium I**—http://support.intel.com/support/processors/sspec/p2p.htm
- **Pentium II Xeon**—http://support.intel.com/support/processors/sspec/p2xp.htm
- **Pentium III**—http://support.intel.com/support/processors/sspec/p3p.htm
- **Pentium III Xeon**—http://support.intel.com/support/processors/sspec/p3xp.htm
- **Pentium 4**—http://www.intel.com/support/processors/pentium4/
- **Itanium**—http://developer.intel.com/design/itanium/family

The processor to be added to the network server should come with installation instructions. The installation instructions for Intel processors are also available at the Intel website.

Intel processor installation manuals can be obtained at the following website:

http://support.intel.com/support/processors/manuals/

The following steps are used when adding a processor:

Step 1   Read any documentation that is provided by the manufacturer.

Step 2   Open the network server chassis by following ESD best practices.

Step 3   Insert the new processor.

Step 4   Close the network server chassis.

Step 5   Upgrade the system BIOS.

Step 6   Upgrade the operating system to recognize multiple processors.

Step 7   Verify that the new processor is recognized by the network server hardware and the network operating system.

Upgrading the Operating System for Multiple Processors

A network server operating system might not recognize that an additional processor has been installed on the server. The following sections detail how to correct this situation.

Windows NT Server 4.0

If the original installation of Microsoft Windows NT Server 4 was on a network server with a single processor, the Hardware Abstraction Layer (HAL) on the network server must be updated for the network server to recognize and use multiple processors. To upgrade Windows NT 4 to a multiprocessor HAL, use the UPTOMP.EXE utility that is available in the Microsoft Windows NT 4 Server Resource Kit.

For information about the processors that are recognized by the current version of Microsoft Windows NT Server 4, open a command-prompt window and type **set** in the command line.

This command prints a list of all the current environment variables. Look for the Number_of_ processors variable to see how many processors Microsoft Windows NT Server 4 recognizes. The number of processors can be determined in other ways, but this is one of the easiest.

Windows 2000 Server

If the original installation of Microsoft Windows 2000 Server was on a network server with a single processor, the HAL on the network server must be updated for the network server to recognize and use multiple processors. To install support for multiple processors on

Windows 2000, follow these steps, based on Microsoft Knowledge Base Article 234558 (previously Article Q234558):

Step 1 Choose **Start**, **Settings**, **Control Panel**, and click the **System** icon.

Step 2 Click the **Hardware** tab, and select the **Device Manager**.

Step 3 Double-click to expand the Computer branch. Note the type of support that you currently have.

Step 4 Double-click the computer type that is listed under the Computer branch. Then select the **Drivers** tab, click the **Update Driver** button, and click the **Next** button.

Step 5 Select the **Display a List of Known Drivers for This Device** radio button, and then choose the **Show All Hardware of This Device Class** radio button.

Step 6 Click the appropriate computer type (a computer type that matches your current type, except for multiple CPUs), click the **Next** button, and then click the **Finish** button.

For information about the processors that are recognized by the current version of Microsoft Windows 2000 Server, open a command-prompt window and type **set** in the command line.

This command prints a list of all the current environment variables. Look for the Number_of_ processors variable to see how many processors Microsoft Windows 2000 Server recognizes. The number of processors can be determined in other ways, but this is one of the easiest.

Novell Netware 5

If the original installation of Novell NetWare 5 was on a network server with a single processor, several changes in the configuration of the Novell NetWare 5 server must be made for it to recognize and use multiple processors. To upgrade Novell NetWare 5 so that it recognizes the additional processor, follow these steps:

Step 1 Load NWCONFIG | Multi CPU Options | Select a Platform Support Module.

Step 2 Restart the Novell NetWare 5 network server after NWCONFIG modifies the STARTUP.NCF and the AUTOEXEC.NCF files.

For information about the processors that are recognized by the current version of Novell NetWare, type **display processors** on the NetWare console.

Red Hat Linux

So that Red Hat Linux and other versions of Linux can recognize multiple processors, the Linux kernel must be rebuilt. Make sure that the main Makefile, which is usually found at

/usr/src/linux/Makefile, contains the line SMP=1. Rebuild the Linux kernel using the normal methods. For information about the processors that are recognized by the current version of Linux, type **cat /proc/cpuinfo** at the command prompt.

Worksheet 9.4.3 Adding Processors

The steps to add a new processor and to add an additional processor are reviewed in this worksheet.

Adding Hard Drives

Disk drive upgrades come in two varieties. The first type of upgrade involves adding disk drives to an existing network server, and the second type involves replacing existing disk drives with larger or faster disk drives. Upgrades to disk drives have the most potential of any upgrade to destroy data. Before attempting any disk drive upgrade, make sure that you have at least one—and preferably two—verified full backups of the data on the disk drives.

Upgrading ATA Hard Disk Drives

This section describes how to upgrade ATA hard disk drives. An example of an ATA drive is shown in Figure 9-23. To shorten the discussion, the term ATA refers to the following hard disk drives:

- Integrated Device Electronics (IDE)/ATA
- Enhanced IDE (EIDE)/ATA with Extensions (ATA-2)
- Ultra ATA

Figure 9-23 ATA Hard Drive

The process is the same for all versions of ATA disk drives.

Upgrades to ATA disks generally fall into two categories: adding disk drives and replacing existing disk drives with faster or larger disk drives.

Adding ATA disk drives to an existing ATA disk subsystem is relatively straightforward. ATA disk controllers generally have two channels to which ATA devices, such as disk drives, CD-ROM drives, and so on, can be attached. Each channel consists of a ribbon cable that can be up to 18 inches long, to which a maximum of two disk drives can be attached. One end of the channel is attached to the ATA disk controller, which can be built in to the system board. The channel, which is an 80-conductor ribbon cable, usually has two 40-pin connectors attached to it. These 40-pin connectors attach ATA disk drives to the ATA channel.

The ATA channels are usually labeled "primary" and "secondary" so that the system can distinguish between them. When only a single disk drive is attached to the ATA disk controller, a second disk drive can be attached in either of the two following ways:

- The second disk drive can be attached to the same ribbon cable as the existing disk drive using the second 80-pin connector on the ribbon cable. In this case, one disk drive must be set to the master ATA disk role and the other must be set to the slave ATA disk role. Another method would be to set Cable Select (CSEL) for both disk drives.
- The second disk drive can be attached to the secondary ATA channel using a second ribbon cable for the ATA controller. Set this single drive to either the single drive or master ATA disk role, depending on the manufacturer's instructions for configuring a single disk drive on an ATA channel.

Putting the second ATA disk drive onto the secondary channel results in having one ATA disk drive on each ATA channel. The result is that performance of the disk subsystem is enhanced.

A system Basic Input/Output System (BIOS) upgrade might be required when upgrading from small ATA disk drives to very large ATA disk drives. Older system BIOSs might not have the capability to address all the space on very large ATA disk drives. The definition of *very large* has changed over the years. Various definitions of large have been 504 MB, 1 GB, 2 GB, 4 GB, and 8.4 GB. Many of these have proven to be barriers to ATA that had to be overcome by newer, better, or improved BIOSs.

Disk drives are characterized by their rotational speed. Common rotational speeds are 5400 rpm, 7200 rpm, and 10,000 rpm. The faster the rotational speed, the faster the disk can access data. Upgrading from slow disk drives to faster disk drives involves a replacement of the disk drives.

Upgrading IDE/ATA/EIDE/ATA-2 Disk Drives to SCSI Disk Drives

You can use both IDE/ATA drives and SCSI drives together on a server. However, there is no upgrade path from IDE/ATA/EIDE/ATA-2 disk drives to SCSI disk drives. To change from IDE/ATA/EIDE/ATA-2 disk drives to SCSI disk drives, the administrator must remove all the IDE/ATA/EIDE/ATA-2 disk drives, remove or disable the built-in IDE/EIDE controller, and install a SCSI bus controller and SCSI disk drives. Remember that to boot from a SCSI disk drive, the BIOS on the SCSI bus controller must be enabled, and the SCSI ID of the boot disk must be set to 0.

Upgrading SCSI Hard Disk Drives

Upgrades to SCSI disk drives fall into two categories, as follows:

- Adding SCSI disks to an existing SCSI channel
- Replacing existing SCSI disks with disk drives that have a faster rotational speed

The SCSI disk drive in the upgrade should match the existing SCSI disk in the following ways:

- SCSI level, which is 1, 2, or 3
- Type, which is normal or wide
- Signaling system, which is SE, LVD, or differential

Adding SCSI Hard Disk Drives

Adding SCSI disk drives to an existing SCSI channel is a simple process. See Figure 9-24. To make sure that the addition works, the server administrator or hardware specialist must review the documentation of the SCSI bus. The administrator needs to know the SCSI IDs of the existing disk drives and where the SCSI bus is terminated. For internal SCSI devices, he also needs to determine whether any SCSI connectors are available on the SCSI bus ribbon cable. See Figure 9-25. If no SCSI connectors are available on the SCSI bus ribbon cable, obtain a new SCSI ribbon cable with the correct number of connectors. Then set the SCSI ID of the new disk drive to a SCSI ID that is not already in use on the SCSI bus. The SCSI terminator, shown in Figure 9-26, might also need to be removed. Remember that the SCSI bus must be terminated at both ends.

Figure 9-24 SCSI Hard Drive

Figure 9-25 SCSI Cable

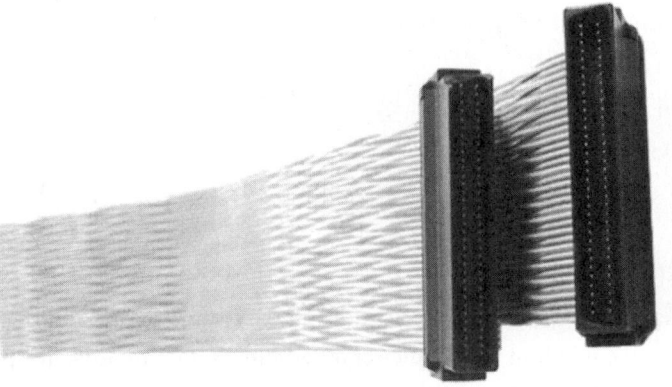

Figure 9-26 SCSI Terminator

Replacing SCSI Hard Disk Drives

Replacing an existing SCSI hard disk is just a matter of removing the old SCSI hard disk and checking the SCSI ID. Set the SCSI ID on the new SCSI hard disk to match the SCSI ID of the SCSI disk drive that was removed, and install the new SCSI hard disk. If the SCSI disk uses an SCA connector, remove the old SCSI disk drive and insert the new SCSI disk drive in its place. SCA connectors automatically set the SCSI ID of the SCSI disk drive.

Adding Drives to a RAID Array

Adding drives to a SCSI-based RAID array is no different from adding drives to a SCSI channel. The only exception is that after the disk drives are added to the array, a RAID configuration utility must be used to add the disk drives to the RAID array.

New Drives in a Separate Array

If the newly installed disk drives are configured as a separate array from the existing array, the data on the existing disk array is unaffected.

For example, if you have an existing RAID 5 array consisting of three disk drives and you have two new disk drives that need to be installed and configured as a RAID 1 array, the original RAID 5 array is not affected. No loss of data on the original array occurs. After installing the two new disk drives, use the array configuration utility to initialize the two new disk drives and configure them as a RAID 1 array. The RAID controller then has two separate RAID arrays configured. They are the original RAID 5 array, consisting of three disk drives, and the new RAID 1 array, consisting of two disk drives.

New Drives in an Existing Array

If the newly installed SCSI disk drives need to become part of an existing RAID array, the installer needs to initialize all disk drives in the array, including the existing drives. This means a loss of data on the existing disk drives.

For example, if you have an existing RAID 5 array that consists of three disk drives and you have two new disk drives that need to be installed and configured into a RAID 5 array using all five disk drives, you must initialize all five disk drives. You can then combine the five disk drives into a single RAID 5 array using all five disk drives. However, the data that was on the original RAID 5 array with the three disk drives will be destroyed in the process and must be reloaded from the backup media. The RAID controller then has a single RAID 5 array consisting of five disk drives.

Adding Memory

It has been said that you cannot have too much memory in a server. Although in many cases this is true, a few exceptions exist. One exception is that the administrator can only put as much memory in the network server as it was designed to contain. A maximum amount of memory can be supported by the processors and the control chipsets of the motherboard of the network server. The other exception is having more memory than the network server operating system can use. Keep both of these exceptions in mind when considering a memory upgrade to a network server.

Check Existing Memory

Before adding memory to a network server, the administrator should verify the current memory configuration. The documentation for the configuration of the network server should have all the details of the memory configuration. However, when this information is not readily available, the administrator needs to determine it. The most reliable way to check the existing memory configuration is to open the chassis of the network server. Try to answer the following questions:

- How many memory slots does the network server have?
- How many memory slots are empty and available for additional memory to be installed?
- What are the size, in MB, and speed of the current memory modules?
- What type of memory module is currently installed?

    Memory module types include single in-line memory modules (SIMMs), dual in-line memory modules (DIMMs), Rambus in-line memory modules (RIMMs), buffered modules, unbuffered modules, registered modules, and so on.

- What type of memory is the memory module that is used in the network server?

    Memory types include extended data out (EDO), dynamic random-access memory (DRAM), synchronous DRAM (SDRAM), and Rambus DRAM (RDRAM).

- What error-detection method is used on the memory module?

    — Methods include parity, nonparity, ECC, and non-ECC.

Answer these questions by reviewing the documentation that was shipped with the network server. This information might also be found in the log that was kept as part of the installation process.

Checking Memory Upgrade Feasibility

Before attempting a memory upgrade, first determine whether the network server hardware can support the amount of memory that is desired in the network server. Some system board control chipsets limit the amount of memory that can be used in the network server. Limitations can also apply to the maximum size of a memory module that can be placed into a single memory slot. This limits the total amount of memory as well. The best source of information about how much memory can be installed in a particular network server is the documentation that came with the network server or the network server manufacturer's website.

Verify that the network server operating system supports the amount of memory that is to be installed. Check the vendor website of the network server operating system to determine the maximum memory supported.

You might have to remove the existing memory modules and replace them with larger memory modules to achieve the total amount of memory required. An example network server could require four 128-MB modules. This network server can have only four memory slots, and two of them could be occupied by 64-MB memory modules. To achieve a total of 512 MB, the two 64-MB memory modules must first be removed.

Checking Memory Upgrade Compatibility

After answering all of these questions, check the vendor's Hardware Compatibility List for the network server to make sure that the vendor has certified the memory selected.

One other important consideration is the metal plating on the leads of the memory module. Two common metals are used on the memory module leads and the connectors in the memory slots: tin and gold. Both metals work well. However, never mix the two metals. For example, do not put gold on the memory module and tin in the connector or vice versa. This mismatching of metals causes corrosion at the contact points and results in a bad connection over time. This bad connection causes memory errors to occur.

Installing Additional Memory

After determining the feasibility of the memory upgrade and the compatibility of the memory with the network server, the last step is to install the additional memory. Be sure to install the memory according to the manufacturer's instructions. Remember that the memory modules might have a requirement to be installed in pairs or groups of four. Most network servers have SIMMs, DIMMs, or RIMMs.

Figure 9-27 shows a diagram of SIMM installation. Figure 9-28 shows a diagram of DIMM/RIMM installation.

Figure 9-27 SIMM Installation

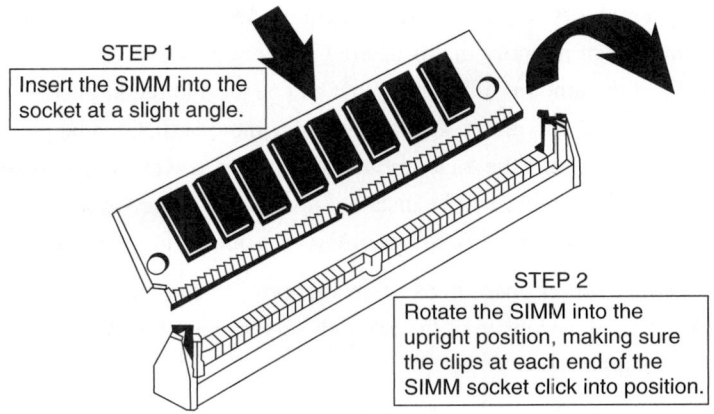

STEP 1
Insert the SIMM into the
socket at a slight angle.

STEP 2
Rotate the SIMM into the
upright position, making sure
the clips at each end of the
SIMM socket click into position.

Figure 9-28 DIMM/RIMM Installation

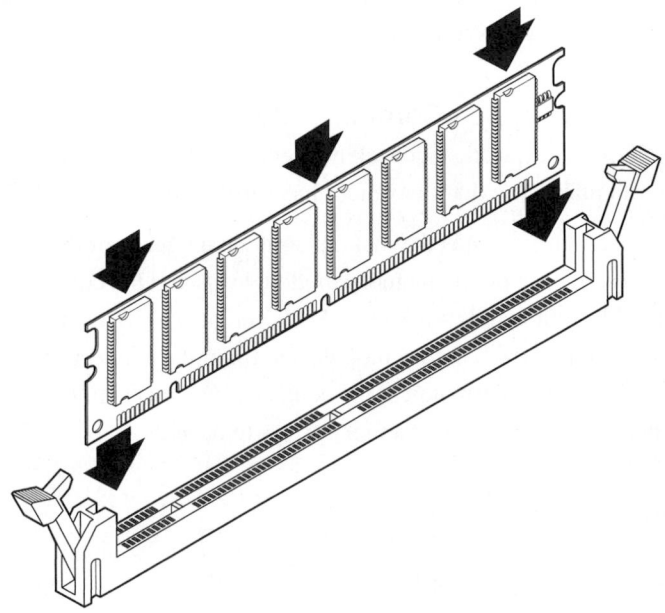

NOTE

RIMM is commonly
believed to stand for
Rambus in-line mem-
ory module. Rambus
licenses its memory
designs to semiconduc-
tor companies, which
manufacture the chips.
Kingston Technology
has trademarked the
term *RIMM* and uses
only that term.

RIMM installation differs only slightly from DIMM installation. All memory module slots
that are designed to use RIMMs must be populated. If a RIMM is not installed in a slot, a
continuity module must be installed. A continuity module contains no memory. Adding a
RIMM involves removing a continuity module and replacing it with a RIMM. Failure to have
continuity modules in the memory slots that are not occupied by RIMMs can result in a network server that does not power up.

While performing a memory upgrade, be sure to follow all safety guidelines and ESD best practices.

Upgrading Server Components

Upgrading the network server is a key function of the IT technician. Adapter upgrades fall into several categories that encompass both hardware and software. System-monitoring agents and other service tools analyze and troubleshoot system performance. This section covers the following topics:

- Upgrading adapter memory
- Upgrading adapter BIOS or firmware
- Replacing an adapter
- Upgrading peripheral devices
- Upgrading system-monitoring agents
- Upgrading service tools
- Documenting the configuration

Upgrading Adapter Memory

Network server adapters often have on-board memory that you can upgrade. Follow the adapter manufacturer's instructions to perform the memory upgrade. The following adapters use on-board memory:

- *Video adapter on-board memory* — A video adapter uses memory to store the image that is displayed on the monitor. The more memory on the video adapter, the higher the resolution and the more colors that can be supported on the video monitor.

- *SCSI adapter on-board memory* — A SCSI adapter uses on-board memory as a buffer or cache between the SCSI disk drives and the network server's memory. All read and write operations occur in the buffer rather than on the disk drive. The larger the on-board memory buffer, the faster the information can be supplied to the network server.

- *RAID controller on-board memory* — A RAID controller uses on-board memory in much the same way that a SCSI adapter uses memory — that is, as a buffer. One big difference is that the on-board memory on a RAID controller is often "backed up" by an on-board battery. This prevents the loss of data that is in the buffer if the network server loses power unexpectedly.

Upgrading Adapter BIOS or Firmware

Upgrading the BIOS or firmware on an adapter is similar to upgrading the system BIOS. The steps are vendor specific, but the steps are generally as follows:

Step 1 Locate the latest BIOS or firmware on the adapter vendor's website.

Step 2 Download the BIOS or firmware upgrade, and follow the vendor's instructions to install the upgrade.

Replacing an Adapter

Adapters are generally replaced after they fail. The replacement procedure generally follows these steps:

Step 1 Power down the network server.

Step 2 Remove the defective adapter.

Step 3 Install the new adapter.

Step 4 Power up the network server.

This process requires the network server to be taken out of operation. This results in downtime and lost productivity. However, a recent technology known as Peripheral Component Interconnect (PCI) hot plug or PCI hot swap enables the administrator to replace, upgrade, or add an adapter without powering down the network server. PCI hot plug has the following capabilities:

- *Hot replacement*—Removing a failed PCI adapter and inserting an identical adapter into the same slot while the network server is operational

- *Hot upgrade*—Replacing an existing adapter with an upgraded adapter while the network server is running

- *Hot expansion*—Installing a new adapter into a previously empty slot while the network server is running

For PCI hot plug to work, the network server hardware, the adapter drivers, and the network server operating system must be PCI hot-plug aware. The network server hardware allows power to be removed from individual PCI slots and allows adapters to be removed and inserted without the use of a screwdriver. On a PCI bus that supports hot plug, a slot release lever replaces a screw for securing the adapter in the PCI slot.

The following steps detail how to use a PCI hot plug to add an adapter:

Step 1 Open the network server chassis.

Step 2 Open the slot-release lever on an available PCI slot. This removes power from the selected PCI slot.

Step 3   Install the adapter into the selected PCI slot.

Step 4   Attach any necessary cables to the adapter.

Step 5   Close the slot-release lever to secure the adapter in the PCI slot.

Step 6   Press the PCI hot-plug button. This reapplies power to the PCI slot.

   The network server operating system locates and loads the appropriate device drivers for the adapter or prompts the installer for the location of the appropriate device drivers.

Step 7   Close the server chassis.

Upgrading Peripheral Devices

A *peripheral device* is any device that is not part of the core computer system, which includes the processor, memory, and the data bus. Peripheral devices can be either internal to the server chassis or external to the network server chassis. See Figure 9-29.

Figure 9-29 Internal and External Devices

Internal peripherals include such components as hard disk drives, CD-ROM drives, floppy disk drives, and network interface cards. Upgrading disk drives such as EIDE and SCSI drives is covered in the section "Adding Hard Drives," earlier in this chapter. Replacing, upgrading, or adding internal peripherals such as a CD-ROM drive, a DVD-ROM drive, a Zip drive, a tape drive, or a NIC requires the administrator to shut down the network server. To install the drives, follow the manufacturer's installation instructions. To install the NIC, follow the manufacturer's installation instructions after identifying an empty PCI slot into which the NIC can be installed. Be sure to download the latest drivers for the NIC from the website of the NIC vendor. Remember that some network servers have peer PCI buses; the "data load" should be balanced among the buses. This requires some knowledge of which PCI slots are on which PCI bus as well as the data load that is placed on the PCI bus by the adapters that are currently on each PCI bus.

If the adapters are not Plug and Play compatible, the administrator might have to configure them with an interrupt request (IRQ), a direct memory access (DMA) channel, and an input/output (I/O) address. The IRQ, DMA, and I/O address cannot conflict with any adapter that is already installed in the network server. As with all upgrades, be sure to follow ESD best practices.

External peripherals are devices that are external to the network server chassis, such as printers, modems, monitors, keyboards, and mice. External devices such as printers and monitors might be hot-swappable. Other external devices might require the network server to be shut down before they can be upgraded. Follow the manufacturer's installation instructions for external peripherals.

Upgrading System-Monitoring Agents

System-monitoring agents are software specific to the network server and are supplied by the network vendor. These agents are generally installed at the installer's option when using the vendor-supplied operating system installation-assistance software. As the network server vendor releases newer versions of the system-monitoring agents, the agents must be upgraded. Because the agents are extremely vendor specific, the administrator must follow the installation instructions of the vendor to upgrade the system-monitoring agents. In some cases, the network-monitoring agents can predict the impending failure of network server components such as the processor, memory, or hard disk drives.

System-monitoring agents monitor various aspects of the network server such as the configuration, mass storage, network interface card, system utilization, thermal conditions, and operating system status. The agents typically use standard protocols such as Hypertext Transfer Protocol (HTTP), Simple Network Management Protocol (SNMP), and Desktop Management Interface (DMI) to report information to a management console. The management console can be a standard web browser such as Netscape Navigator or Internet Explorer, a vendor-supplied management console such Compaq Insight Manager, or a third-party network management console such as Hewlett-Packard OpenView. Figure 9-30 shows the HP OpenView software.

As with all upgrades, follow all safety guidelines and ESD best practices.

Figure 9-30 HP OpenView Network Management Software

Upgrading Service Tools

Because of the rather unique nature of network servers compared to standard desktop micro-computers, a wide variety of service tools are sometimes necessary to configure, trouble-shoot, and maintain them. These service tools are software that is installed on the network server during the installation and configuration processes.

Network server vendors often release new versions of these tools to fix bugs, add new features, or add support for new hardware to the utilities.

Some service tools are part of the network operating system. Updates to these service tools are available from the network server operating system vendor.

These updated tools are generally available on either CDs that are supplied by the network server vendor or from the vendor's website. After receiving the updated tools, follow the vendor's installation instructions to install the updated tools on the network server. As with any upgrade, follow all safety guidelines and ESD best practices.

Upgrading the utilities on the diagnostic partition, which is only available at network server boot time, usually requires the administrator to shut down the network server. This means that the administrator needs to schedule downtime to upgrade the software utilities that are on the diagnostic partition.

Most service tools fall into the general categories that are named and described in the following sections.

Diagnostic Tools

Several sets of utilities can be categorized as *diagnostic tools*. Some diagnostic tools might be installed on the diagnostic partition and be specific to the network server. Other diagnostic tools comprise part of the network server operating system. Third-party diagnostic tools are also available.

EISA Configuration Utility

On network servers that have an EISA bus, the *Extended Industry Standard Architecture (EISA) Configuration Utility* enables the administrator to configure the components of the network server. EISA is not Plug and Play compatible, and adapters that are installed into the network server must have a configuration file loaded from a disk to allow configuration of the adapter. The EISA configuration utility is used while the network operating system is not loaded.

Diagnostic Partition Utility

The *Diagnostic Partition Utility* in the diagnostic partition enables the administrator to view and change the configuration of the hardware components in the network server without the network server operating system being loaded. This enables the administrator to troubleshoot nonfunctioning hardware components.

Server Support Utilities

Server support utilities, such as backup software and antivirus software, play a vital role in the support of the network server.

Documenting the Configuration

TIP

Documentation is a part of the upgrading and troubleshooting process. Be able to explain what the documentation process is and why it is so important.

An important part of being a good administrator is to document the problems and the procedures that are used to fix them. Good documentation allows the administrator to look up how a problem was solved at an earlier time. This, in turn, saves time fixing the problem later, and the administrator can have the server back online faster.

As the administrator installs, configures, or fixes the server, he should precisely record the success or failure of what is done. The server also generates logs. These logs are stored on the hard disk and can become rather large. Depending on the amount of hard disk space that is delegated to the log files, these files might have to be printed or archived to backup media. Older log files should be removed to make room for newer logs that are created by the server. By following this documentation process, the administrator now can quickly troubleshoot the server when a problem arises.

Document the following items during and after the server is installed and configured:

- Network operating system version.
- Update level for network operating system.
- RAID configuration.
- Server name.
- Antivirus software and version.
- Backup software and version.
- Network address for each NIC.
- Location and size of swap file(s).
- SNMP community name.
- Server-monitoring agents installed.
- System BIOS version.
- Server baseline measurements.
- Amount of memory, including the size and type of each memory module and which memory slot it occupies. Also record the number of available (empty) memory slots.
- Number of SCSI or RAID controllers.
- Channel, ID, size, and speed of each SCSI disk drive.
- SCSI ID of the tape backup system.
- SCSI ID of the CD-ROM/DVD-ROM drive.
- Size and partition structure of all IDE/ATA drives.
- Size and partition structure of SCSI drives.

Summary

This chapter discussed advanced hardware fundamentals for servers. Some of the important concepts to retain from this chapter include the following:

- Fault tolerance is the ability for a system to continue when a hardware failure occurs. Fault tolerance is important in a network server that provides users the ability to share files, programs, printers, and so on.
- Redundant Array of Independent Disks (RAID) is designed to provide fault tolerance in the event of a disk drive failure on a network server.
- RAID 1 requires two disk drives. All other RAID levels except RAID 0 require at least three disk drives. RAID 1 can be implemented in two ways: disk mirroring and disk duplexing.

- RAID is typically implemented using a RAID disk controller but can also be implemented in software. Software RAID is implemented at the disk partition level supporting RAID 0, 1, and 5. Hardware RAID is implemented on the physical disk, providing more reliable fault tolerance.

- External disk subsystems are added when the amount of disk storage cannot be accommodated by internal disk drives. Simple external disk subsystems with only a few disk drives function in the same way that internal disk drives function. Large subsystems can have their own RAID mechanism built in and are often configured separately from the network server.

- Upgrading the processor or installing an additional processor can improve the performance of the server. Before proceeding, verify that the motherboard can accommodate the upgrade or that it can support multiple processors. Check the motherboard manufacturer's manual or website for the necessary information.

- Disk drive upgrades can be accomplished by adding to the existing drives or by replacing drives with larger and faster drives.

- Increasing memory on the server can improve performance, but processors have a maximum amount of memory that they can support. Check the feasibility and compatibility of adding new memory to the existing server before proceeding.

- System-monitoring agents and service tools should be updated regularly. System-monitoring agents monitor the configuration, mass storage, NIC, system utilization, thermal conditions, and operating system status. Service tools are used to maintain the system and for troubleshooting purposes.

- Documenting the configuration of the network server is important to a network administrator. Service logs and other log files provide valuable data that is needed to troubleshoot the system if problems occur. Make sure that the information is detailed and current.

The next chapter introduces you to networking fundamentals. It discusses the types of networks, the components of a network, and connecting to the Internet.

Key Terms

CD-ROM library   Multiple CD-ROM drives in a tower that is attached to a network that can be accessed by all the users on a network.

CD-ROM server   A network server that implements a CD-ROM library.

Diagnostic Partition Utility   Enables troubleshooting of nonfunctioning hardware components.

diagnostic tools   Utilities that monitor the network server.

disk duplexing   In RAID, this refers to a mirrored set, where each disk is connected to a different disk controller.

disk mirroring   In RAID, this refers to two disk drives that are connected to the same disk controller.

disk striping with parity   RAID 5 is an example of disk striping with parity. It uses block-level parity, but it spreads the parity information among all the disk drives in the disk array.

disk striping without parity   RAID 0 is an example of disk striping without parity. It is not fault tolerant but improves disk input/output performance.

error-correcting code (ECC)   Detects and corrects single-bit errors and detects double-bit errors. It is read and decoded each time data is read from the disk.

Extended Industry Standard Architecture (EISA) Configuration Utility   Enables the configuration of the components of the network server.

external peripheral   Device that is external to the network server.

hardware-based RAID   Implements RAID using a hardware device called a RAID controller.

hot expansion   Installing a new adapter into an empty slot while the server is running.

hot replacement   Replacing an adapter while the server remains operational.

hot upgrade   Upgrading an existing adapter while the server is running.

internal peripheral   Device that is internal to the network server.

Logical Unit Number (LUN)   A seldom-used SCSI standard that enables an administrator to assign sub-SCSI IDs to a single SCSI ID, allowing one SCSI channel to support multiple CD-ROM drives.

network server   A computer that is shared by multiple users.

peripheral device   A device that is not part of the core computer system.

RAID 0   An array or group of disk drives that are used as a single disk. Data is written in chunks, or stripes, to all the drives in the array.

RAID 0/1   Provides the performance of RAID 0 and the redundancy of RAID 1. It requires at least four drives to implement.

RAID 0+1   See *RAID 0/1*.

RAID 1   Requires at least two disk drives and writes data to two separate locations.

RAID 2   Requires a minimum of three disk drives and uses a hamming code to create an ECC for all data.

RAID 3   Requires a minimum of three synchronized disk drives and uses bit-level parity with a single-parity disk for fault tolerance.

RAID 4   Requires a minimum of three disk drives that do not need to be synchronized because data is written to the drives in blocks.

RAID 5   Requires a minimum of three disk drives and uses block-level parity, but unlike RAID 4, it spreads the parity information among all the drives in the array.

RAID 10   See *RAID 0/1*.

RAID controller   A specialized device that is used in a RAID array.

RAID controller on-board memory   Used as a buffer and often backed up with an on-board battery.

Redundant Array of Independent Disks (RAID)   Provides fault tolerance to prevent loss of data in the event of a disk drive failure on a network server. Also known as Redundant Array of Inexpensive Disks.

SCSI adapter on-board memory   Uses on-board memory as a buffer or cache between the SCSI disk drives and the network server memory.

server support utilities   Used for backup and antivirus in support of the network server.

system-monitoring agent   Vendor-specific software that monitors various aspects of the network server such as the configuration, mass storage, NIC, and so on.

video adapter on-board memory   Uses memory to store the image that is displayed on the monitor.

Check Your Understanding

1. Which RAID level provides improved disk input/output but provides no redundancy?

    A. RAID 0

    B. RAID 1

    C. RAID 3

    D. RAID 5

2. Which RAID level provides redundancy at the expense of the loss of 50% of the disk storage capacity?

    A. RAID 0

    B. RAID 1

    C. RAID 3

    D. RAID 5

3. Which of the following RAID levels provides fault tolerance using parity information and a minimum of three disk drives?

    i. RAID 0

    ii. RAID 1

    iii. RAID 4

    iv. RAID 5

    A. i and ii

    B. iii and iv

    C. ii, iii, and iv

    D. i and iii

4. You have a group of six 36-GB disk drives that you want to configure as a RAID 5 array. After you have configured the RAID array with the six disk drives, what is the total storage capacity of the single logical drive that is created by the RAID array?

    A. 216 GB

    B. 180 GB

    C. 108 GB

    D. 36 GB

5. Which of the following technologies allows a network server to run more programs than can fit into its physical RAM?

   A. RAID 1

   B. RAID 5

   C. Virtual memory

   D. Backup software

6. Which of the following software packages is *not* normally installed on a network server to support its operation?

   A. Antivirus software

   B. Backup software

   C. UPS-monitoring software

   D. Spreadsheet software

7. Which RAID level does *not* provide fault tolerance?

   A. RAID 0

   B. RAID 1

   C. RAID 5

   D. RAID 10

8. After installing a second processor in a network server, the network server boots up properly and the second processor is detected by the system BIOS. However, the network server operating system does not recognize the fact that a second processor now exists in the network server. How do you correct the situation?

   A. Double the amount of memory in the network server.

   B. Configure the system BIOS to report both processors to the network operating system.

   C. Upgrade the network operating system to recognize the additional processor.

   D. Upgrade the processor software drivers to the latest version.

9. What environment variable in Microsoft Windows NT and Microsoft Windows 2000 is set to the number of processors in the network server?

   A. Number_of_processors

   B. NoProcs

   C. NumbProc

   D. Processors

10. Which of the following must be the same on the existing processor and the processor that is to be added to a multiprocessor-capable network server?

i. Level 2 cache

ii. Processor clock speed

iii. Date of manufacture

iv. Spec number

A. i and ii

B. iii and iv

C. i and iii

D. ii and iv

11. Which memory technology requires that a continuity module be inserted into all empty memory module slots in a network server?

A. SIMMs

B. SIPPs

C. RIMMs

D. DIMMs

12. A network server has a single EIDE disk drive configured as a master. You want to add a second EIDE disk drive to the same channel. How must it be configured for both disk drives to work correctly?

A. Master

B. Slave

C. CSEL

D. Secondary

13. How do you upgrade an EIDE disk subsystem to a SCSI subsystem?

A. Remove all EIDE disk drives, cables, and controllers. Add the SCSI controller, cables, and disk drives.

B. Remove the EIDE controller and replace it with a SCSI controller, using existing cables and disk drives.

C. Remove the EIDE controller, add the SCSI controller, and change the drive electronics from EIDE to SCSI.

D. Remove the EIDE disk drives, install the SCSI disk drives, and attach the SCSI disk drives to the EIDE controller.

14. Which of the following adapters usually contains on-board memory that can be upgraded?

i. Video adapter

ii. Sound card

iii. RAID controller

iv. SCSI controller

A. ii and iii

B. i, ii, and iii

C. i, iii, and iv

D. ii only

15. Your network server has dual-peer PCI buses. The RAID controller is installed in PCI bus number 1. You need to install a 100-Mbps NIC into the network server. Where do you install the NIC?

A. Into PCI bus number 1.

B. Into PCI bus number 2.

C. You cannot install a NIC and RAID controller in the same network server.

D. The NIC has its own special slot because this is a network server.

16. What problem are you most likely to encounter when adding external SCSI disk drives to a SCSI bus?

A. No available SCSI IDs

B. Exceeding the SCSI channel cable length

C. Slow performance

D. Heat

17. What are the proper combinations for installing memory modules into memory slots?

i. Gold leads on memory modules and gold contacts in memory slots

ii. Tin leads on memory modules and tin contacts in memory slots

iii. Gold leads on memory modules and tin contacts in memory slots

iv. Tin leads on memory modules and gold contacts in memory slots

A. iii and iv

B. iii only

C. iv only

D. i and ii

18. Which of the following limits the amount of memory that can be used in a network server?

    A. The control chipset on the network server motherboard

    B. The speed of the processor(s) in the network server

    C. The speed of the PCI bus

    D. The width of the data bus

19. What is the process of replacing a SCSI disk drive with an SCA connector?

    A. Remove the old SCSI disk drive and insert the new SCSI disk drive.

    B. Remove the old SCSI disk drive and note its SCSI ID. Set the SCSI ID on the new SCSI disk drive to the same SCSI ID, and insert the new SCSI disk drive.

    C. Remove the old SCSI disk drive and note its SCSI ID. Set the SCSI ID on the new SCSI disk drive to be different from the SCSI ID of the old disk drive. Insert the new SCSI disk drive.

    D. Remove the old SCSI disk drive. Set the new SCSI disk drive to CSEL. Insert the new SCSI disk drive.

Upon completion of this chapter, you will be able to complete the following tasks:

- Perform basic administrative duties that are needed to maintain a computer network
- Select a network interface card based on considerations regarding the type of network, type of media, and type of system bus
- Understand network topology and the overall structure of a computer or communication system known as the architecture
- Define protocols and the OSI model
- Compare the TCP/IP model and the OSI model
- View configuration information and troubleshoot problems
- Explain synchronous and asynchronous serial transmissions

Chapter 10

Networking Fundamentals

By definition, a computer network has two or more devices that are linked for the purpose of sharing information and resources. This chapter provides you with an overview of how networks work and how they share services. The types of networks that are detailed in this chapter include peer-to-peer, client/server, local-area network (LAN), and wide-area network (WAN). In addition, the difference between a circuit-switched and a packet-switched network is explained, as are the physical aspects and the logical topology. You learn how to add physical components to a network, including a network interface card, and how to use important utilities that aid in troubleshooting.

Introduction to PC Networking

This section includes the following topics:

- Computer networks
- File, print, and application services
- Mail services
- Directory and name services
- The Internet
- Network administration
- Simplex, half-duplex, and full-duplex transmission

Computer Networks

A *network* is a connected system of objects or people. The most common example of a network is the telephone system, which is widely known as the *Public Switched Telephone Network (PSTN)*. The PSTN allows people in virtually every corner of the world to communicate with anyone who has access to a telephone.

A *computer network* works similarly to the PSTN. It allows users to communicate with other users on the same network by transmitting data on the cables that connect them. A computer network, as illustrated in Figure 10-1, is defined as having two or more devices, such as workstations, printers, or servers. These devices are linked for the purpose of sharing information, resources, or both. Network links are made using copper cables, fiber-optic cables, or wireless connections. Wireless connections use radio signals, infrared technology, or satellite transmissions. The information and resources that are shared on a network can include data files, application programs, printers, modems, or other hardware devices. Computer networks are used in businesses, schools, government agencies, and even some homes.

Figure 10-1 Computer Network

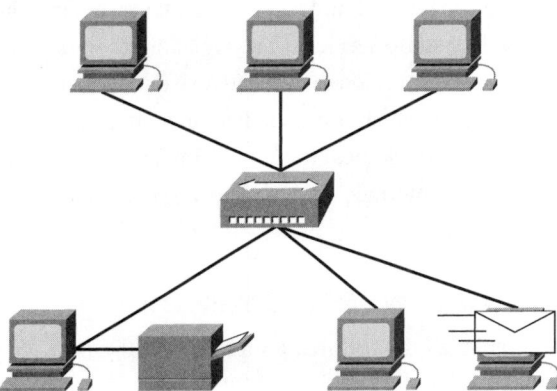

It is important to understand that networks are multilayered. A network consists of many overlapping layers, such as cabling systems, addressing schemes, and applications. The layers work together to transmit and receive data. The Open Systems Interconnection (OSI) reference model, which was created to define these multiple layers, is illustrated in Figure 10-2.

Figure 10-2 OSI Model

Application
Presentation
Session
Transport
Network
Data Link
Physical

The OSI reference model and the different ways in which computers can be networked to share resources are discussed later in this chapter.

File, Print, and Application Services

Figure 10-3 shows how computer networks offer file and print services. The need to share information is an important part of the development of computer networks. In networks, different computers take on specialized roles or functions. Once they are connected, one or more computers in the network can function as network file servers. The server is a repository for files that can be accessed and shared across the network by many users. This avoids duplication, conserves resources, and allows the management and control of key information. Network administrators can grant or restrict access to files. They also regularly copy the files to backup systems in case of problems or failures.

Figure 10-3 File, Print, and Application Services

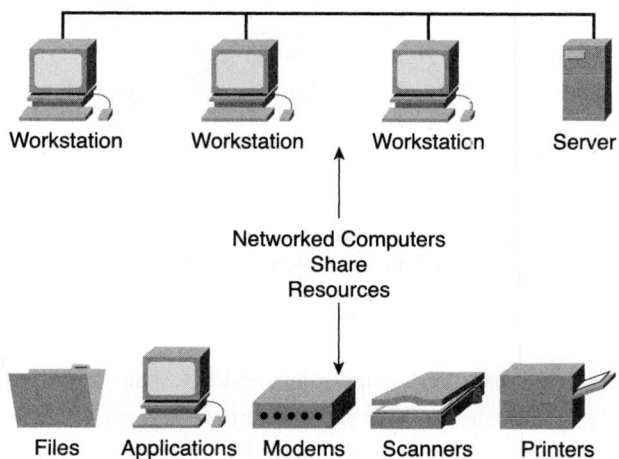

Network file services enable collaboration in the development of documents and projects. Each member of a project team can make contributions to a document or project through a shared network file service. In addition, network file services can enable the timely distribution of key files to a group of users who have an interest in that information. Finally, many people who are geographically separated can share files, games, entertainment, and other resources.

In addition to sharing computer files, networks enable users to share printing devices. *Network print services* can make a high-speed printer accessible to many users. This printer operates as if it were directly attached to individual computers. The network can send requests from many users to a central print server where these requests are processed. Multiple printer servers, each offering a different quality of output, can be implemented according to the requirements of users. Under administrative control, users can select the service that they need for a particular job. In this way, networks provide a more efficient use of expensive printing devices without duplication. Figure 10-4 illustrates one system requesting print services on a network.

Figure 10-4 Network Print Services

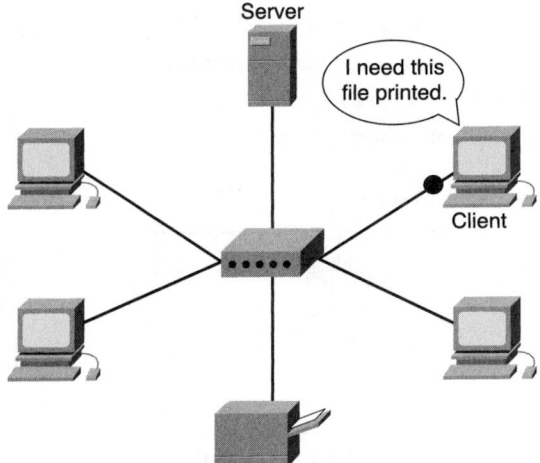

File Storage to Network Server

All network operating systems offer file and print services. Sharing information, collaborating on projects, and providing access to input and output devices are common services of computer networks. Network users can share more than information and special devices. They can also share applications, such as word processing programs, that are installed on the server. Users can run the shared applications from a server without using space on their local hard disks for the program files.

Software licensing agreements can require the purchase of additional licenses for each workstation that uses a network application. This is necessary even though only one copy is actually installed and all users are accessing that same copy. E-mail continues to be the single most widely used function of computer networks in many parts of the world.

Mail Services

From their earliest days, computer networks have enabled users to communicate by *electronic mail (e-mail)*. E-mail services work like the postal system, with one computer taking on the function of the post office. The user e-mail account operates like a post office box, where mail is held for the user until it is picked up over the network by an e-mail client program running in the user system. Figure 10-5 illustrates this concept. The e-mail is sent from the computer to the e-mail server, which acts as the post office. The server holds the e-mail until the destination client retrieves it.

Figure 10-5 Mail Services

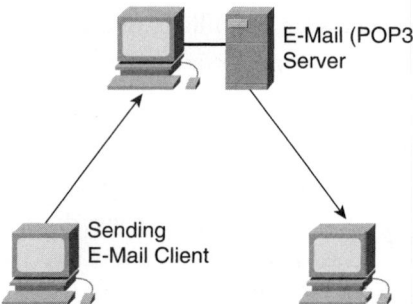

An e-mail address consists of two parts. The first part is the recipient name and the second part is the domain name. The at symbol (@) separates these two parts. An example of an e-mail address is user@cisco.com. The intended recipient is user, and the domain name is cisco.com. The domain name delivers the e-mail to the appropriate server. E-mail applications, such as Microsoft Outlook, Eudora, Netscape Mail, and Pegasus, can be different, but they can all recognize the standard e-mail format.

E-mail works as a store-and-forward application. Mail messages and the identifying information, such as sender, receiver, and time stamp, are stored on an e-mail server until the recipient retrieves his or her mail. Depending on the configuration settings and the protocol used, the messages can still be saved on the server after retrieval. Typically, e-mail messages are short communications. Current e-mail systems also allow users to attach larger files of different types to their messages. These attached files could be documents, pictures, or movies. The attachments can also be retrieved or downloaded along with the e-mail message. In this way, e-mail services are similar to file transfer services on the network.

E-mail systems have evolved together with networking technology. The rapid growth of the Internet has allowed more people to connect online. This allows immediate communication between users of the network. The store-and-forward nature of e-mail systems does not require the recipient to be connected when the e-mail is sent to him. The recipient can pick up his e-mail at a later time.

In addition to e-mail, the Internet has spawned a variety of *instant messaging services* that allow network users to chat without delay. This capability, referred to as *real time,* is when two or more users are connected to the network at the same time. Examples of common instant messaging programs include ICQ, AOL Instant Messaging (AIM), MSN Instant Messaging, Yahoo! Messenger, and Internet Relay Chat (IRC). Instant messaging requires the user to download and install software. The user then goes through the setup process to create a screen name and password. Providing additional information in a profile is optional. A multimedium instant messaging client, such as Trillian Connection Manager, provides a single interface to connect to multiple messaging services.

Directory and Name Services

Another important benefit of networks is their ability to find resources and devices wherever they are located. To enable users and systems on the network to find the services that they require, computer networks make use of *directories and name services*. Figure 10-6 illustrates the network device mappings that allow a specific file to be located. Similar to the telephone directory, the network assigns a name to users, services, and devices so that they can be identified and accessed. Knowing the name of a service on the network enables users to contact that service without having to know its physical location. In fact, a service's physical location can change and users can still find the service or device if they know its name.

Figure 10-6 Network Device Mappings

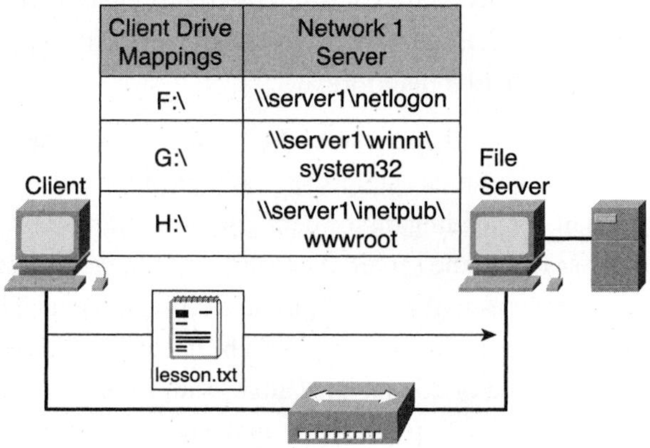

Client Drive Mappings	Network 1 Server
F:\	\\server1\netlogon
G:\	\\server1\winnt\system32
H:\	\\server1\inetpub\wwwroot

Directory and name services make a network easier to use. It is easier to work with services and other entities when they are named. Network directory and name services can translate those names into the addresses that communicate with the desired service. After the initial setup of the directory or name service, this translation takes place transparently. In addition to their ease of use, directory and name services make the network more flexible. Network designers and administrators can locate or move files, print, and perform other services with the assurance that users can still locate them by name.

The Internet

The *Internet* is a worldwide public network of networks that interconnect thousands of smaller networks to form one large "web" of communication. Many private networks, some with thousands of users, connect to the Internet by using the services of *Internet service providers (ISPs)*.

These linkages enable long-distance access to network services for information and device sharing.

The Internet functions like a highway to facilitate exchange between geographically separated users, organizations, and branches of companies. Figure 10-7 shows the highway analogy to explain bandwidth, network devices, and packets. The phrase *information superhighway* describes the benefit of the Internet to business and private communication. The Internet breaks down barriers of time and space. Figure 10-8 shows how the Internet enables the sharing of information around the globe almost instantaneously.

TIP

An ISP is a facility that enables users to connect to the Internet. For example, users sign up with an ISP and dial in. It is through the ISP that users are connected to the Internet.

Figure 10-7 Highway Analogy

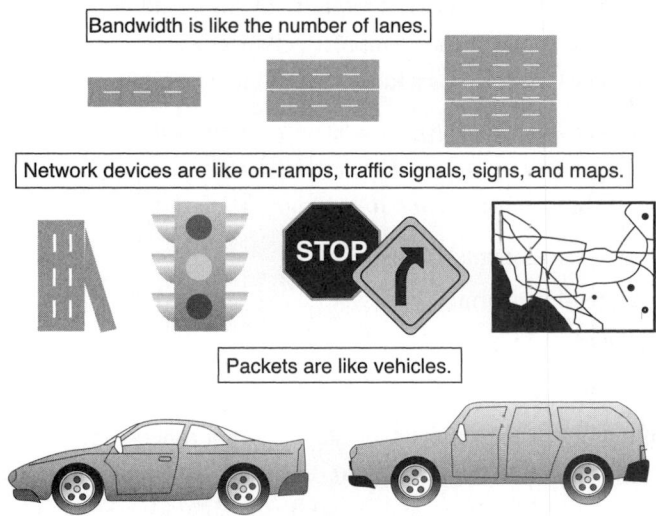

Highway Analogy for Bandwidth

Bandwidth is like the number of lanes.

Network devices are like on-ramps, traffic signals, signs, and maps.

Packets are like vehicles.

Figure 10-8 Worldwide Network

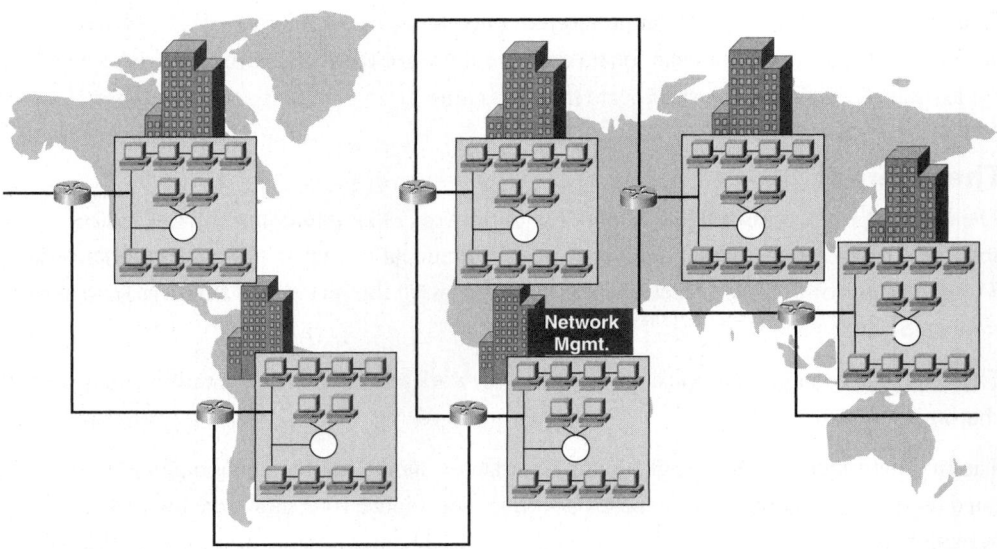

Network Administration

Businesses and individuals are becoming more dependent on computer networks for their daily activities. Because of this, it becomes vitally important that these networks function to deliver the services that users expect. Even after engineers have completed the design and installation of a new network, the network requires attention and management to deliver a consistent level of service to its users. Computer networks are dynamic. They change and grow in response to new technologies and user requirements.

The ongoing task of *network administration* is to maintain and adapt the network to changing conditions. This task belongs to network administrators and support personnel. Network administrator responsibilities include the following:

- Setting up new user accounts and services
- Monitoring network performance
- Repairing network failures
- Enforcing security

Administrators often rely on the skills of specialized support personnel to locate the sources of network problems and repair them efficiently. As networks grow, administrators must ensure that network availability is maintained while the network "migrates" to include new equipment and features. Network administrators must be skilled in using a wide range of tools on a variety of devices and systems.

Simplex, Half-Duplex, and Full-Duplex Transmission

A *data channel*, over which a signal is sent, can operate in one of three ways: simplex, half-duplex, or full-duplex. Full-duplex is often just called duplex. The distinction is in the way that the signal can travel.

Simplex Transmission

Simplex transmission is a single, one-way baseband transmission. Simplex transmission, as the name implies, is simple. It is also called unidirectional, because the signal travels in only one direction. An example of simplex transmission is the signal that is sent from the TV station to the home television. Figure 10-9 illustrates this transmission type.

Figure 10-9 Simplex Transmission

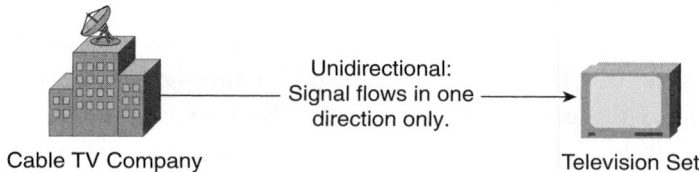

Contemporary applications for simplex circuits are rare. However, they can include remote station printers, card readers, and a few alarm or security systems, such as fire and smoke alarms. This type of transmission is not frequently used because it is not a practical mode for transmitting. The only advantage of simplex transmission is that it is inexpensive.

Half-Duplex Transmission

Half-duplex transmission is an improvement over simplex transmission because the traffic can travel in both directions. Unfortunately, the road is not wide enough to accommodate bidirectional signals simultaneously. This means that only one side can transmit at a time, as shown in Figure 10-10. Two-way radios, such as police or emergency communications mobile radios, work with half-duplex transmissions. When someone presses the button on the microphone to transmit, the person on the other end can hear what is being said. If people at both ends try to talk at the same time, neither transmission gets through.

NOTE

Modems are half-duplex devices. They can send and receive, but not at the same time. However, you can create a full-duplex modem connection with two telephone lines and two modems.

Figure 10-10 Half-Duplex Transmission

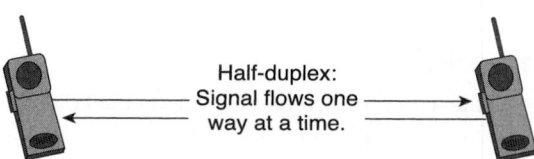

Full-Duplex Transmission

Full-duplex transmission operates like a two-way, two-lane street. Traffic can travel in both directions at the same time, as shown in Figure 10-11.

Figure 10-11 Full-Duplex Transmission

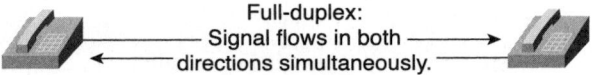

A land-based telephone conversation is an example of full-duplex communication. Both parties can talk at the same time, and both parties can hear each other—although admittedly with some difficulty.

Full-duplex networking technology increases performance because data can be sent and received at the same time. Digital subscriber line (DSL), two-way cable modem, and other broadband technologies operate in full-duplex mode. With DSL, for example, users can download data to their computer at the same time they are talking over the line.

Types of Networks

By using LAN and WAN technologies, many computers are interconnected to provide services to their users. In providing services, networked computers take on different roles or functions in relation to each other. Some types of applications require computers to function as equal partners. Other types of applications distribute work so that one computer functions to serve a number of others in an unequal relationship. In either case, two computers typically communicate with each other by using request or response protocols. One computer issues a request for a service, and a second computer receives and responds to that request. The requester takes on the role of a client, and the responder takes on the role of a server. This section includes the following topics:

- Peer-to-peer networks
- Client/server networks
- Local-area networks
- Wide-area networks

Peer-to-Peer Networks

In a *peer-to-peer network*, the networked computers act as equal partners—or peers—to each other. As peers, each computer can take on the client function or the server function alternately, as shown in Figure 10-12. For example, at one time, Workstation A can make a request for a file from Workstation B, which responds by serving the file to Workstation A. Workstation A functions as the client, whereas Workstation B functions as the server. At a later time, Workstation A and B can reverse roles. Workstation B could be the client, making a request of Workstation A, and Workstation A, as server, responds to the request of Workstation B. Workstations A and B stand in a reciprocal, or peer, relationship to each other.

Figure 10-12 Peer-to-Peer Network

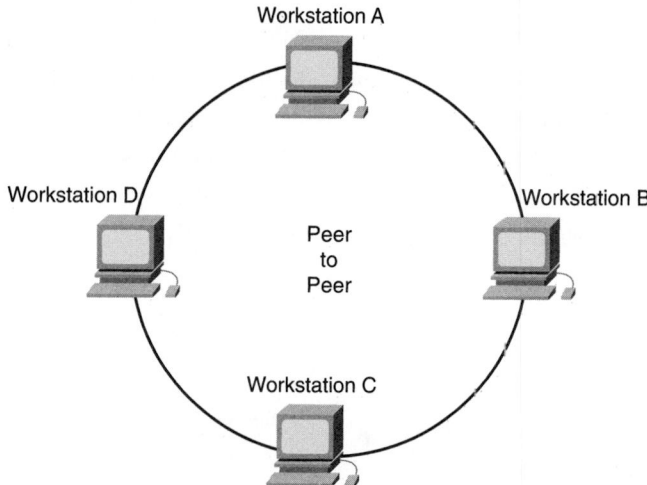

In a peer-to-peer network, individual users control their own resources. They can decide to share certain files with other users, and they can require passwords before they allow others to access their resources. Because individual users make these decisions, there is no central point of control or administration in the network. In addition, individual users must back up their own systems to be able to recover from data loss in case of failures. When a computer acts as a server, the user of that machine can experience reduced performance as the machine serves the requests from other systems.

Peer-to-peer networks are relatively easy to install and operate. No additional equipment is necessary beyond a suitable operating system in each computer. Because users control their own resources, no dedicated administrators are needed. A peer-to-peer network works well with ten or fewer computers.

As networks grow larger, peer-to-peer relationships become increasingly difficult to coordinate. They do not scale well, because their efficiency decreases rapidly as the number of computers on the network increases. Because individual users control access to the resources on their computers, security can be difficult to maintain. Client/server networks address these limitations of the peer-to-peer arrangement.

Client/Server Networks

In a *client/server network* arrangement, network services are located in a dedicated computer whose only function is to respond to the requests of clients. The *server* contains the file, print, application, security, and other services in a central computer that is continuously available to respond to client requests. Most network operating systems adopt the form of client/server relationships. Typically, desktop computers function as clients, and one or more computers with additional processing power, memory, and specialized software function as servers.

Servers are designed to handle requests from many clients simultaneously. Before a client can access the server resources, the client must identify itself and be authorized to use the resource. An account name and password are assigned to each user for this purpose. A specialized authentication server acts as an entry point, guarding access to the network, and verifies this account information. By centralizing user accounts, security, and access control, server-based networks simplify the work of network administration. Figure 10-13 illustrates a client/server network.

Figure 10-13 Client/Server Network

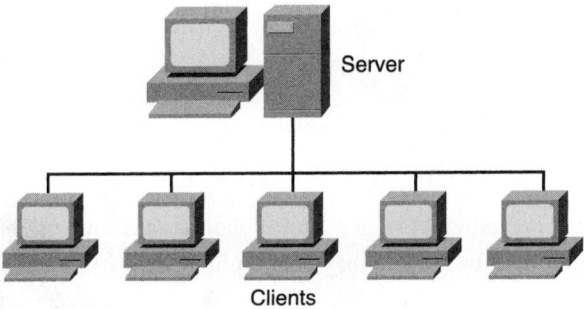

The concentration of network resources, such as files, printers, and applications, on servers also makes the data that they generate easier to back up and manage. Rather than having these resources spread around on individual machines, the resources can be located on specialized, dedicated servers for easier access. Most client/server systems also include facilities for enhancing the network by adding new services that extend the usefulness of the network.

Substantial advantages come from the distribution of functions in a client/server network. However, costs are incurred for these advantages. The aggregation of resources on server systems brings greater security, simpler access, and coordinated control. However, the server introduces a single point of failure into the network. Without an operational server, the network cannot function. In addition, servers require a trained, expert staff to administer and maintain them, which increases the expense of running the network. Server systems require additional hardware and specialized software that substantially add to the cost of the system.

Local-Area Networks

A *local-area network (LAN)* can connect many computers in a relatively small geographical area. These areas can be in a home, an office, or a campus, as shown in Figure 10-14. A LAN allows users to access high-bandwidth media, such as the Internet, and allows users to share devices such as printers.

Figure 10-14 Local-Area Network

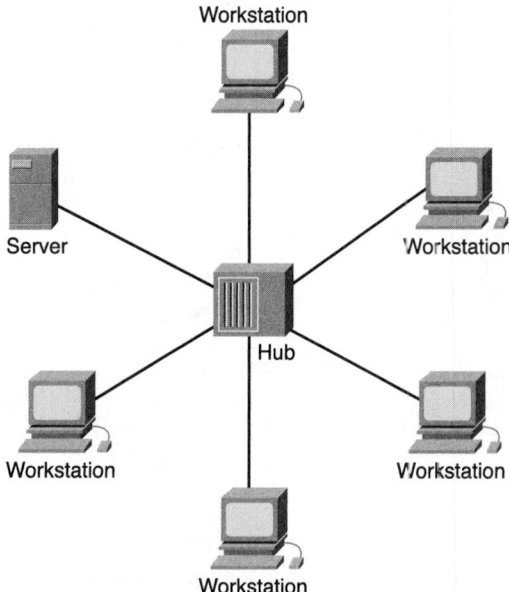

A LAN connects each computer to each of the others by using a separate communications channel. A direct connection from one computer to another is called a *point-to-point link.* If the network were designed using point-to-point links, the number of links would grow rapidly as new computers were added to the network. For each new computer, the network would need a new, separate connection to each of the other computers. This approach would be costly and difficult to manage.

In the late 1960s and early 1970s, network engineers designed a new form of network. This network enabled many computers in a small area to share a single communications channel by taking turns using it. These LANs now connect more computers than any other type of network. By allowing the computers to share a communications channel, LANs greatly reduce the cost of the network. For economic and technical reasons, point-to-point links over longer distances can then connect computers and networks in separate towns and cities, or even across continents.

The general shape or layout of a LAN is called its *topology*. Topology defines the structure of the network. This includes the physical topology, which is the actual layout of the wire or media. It also includes the logical topology, which is how the hosts access the media. Figure 10-15 illustrates some of the topologies that are discussed in detail later in this chapter.

Figure 10-15 Physical Topologies

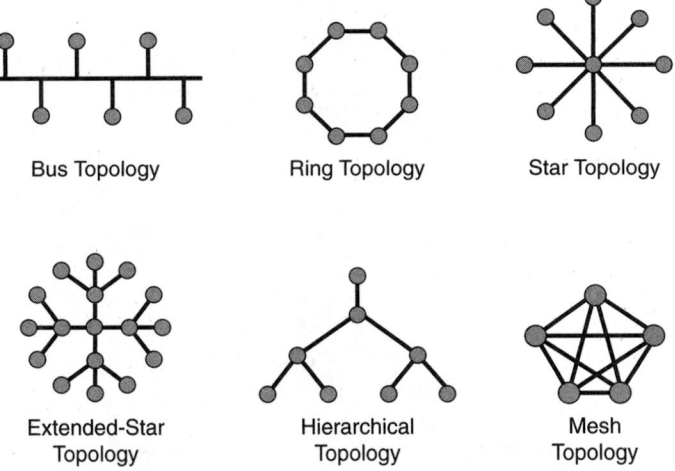

| Bus Topology | Ring Topology | Star Topology |

| Extended-Star Topology | Hierarchical Topology | Mesh Topology |

When all the computers connect to a central point, the network takes on a star topology. An alternative topology connects the computers in a closed loop. Here, the cable is run from one computer to the next and then from the second to its neighbor, until the last one is connected back to the first. This forms a ring topology. A third topology, called a bus, attaches each computer to a single, long cable. Each topology has its benefits and disadvantages. Most modern LANs are designed using some form of star topology, although ring and bus layouts are still used in some installations.

Regardless of the layout, or topology, that the network uses, all LANs require the networked computers to share the communications channel that connects them. The communications channel that they all share is called the *medium*, and it is typically a cable that carries electrical signals through copper. However, it can also be a fiber-optic cable that carries light signals through purified glass or plastic. In the case of wireless networks, the computers can use antennas to broadcast radio signals to each other. In all cases, the computers on a LAN share the medium by taking turns using the medium.

On a LAN, the rules for coordinating the use of the medium are called *Media Access Control (MAC)*. Many computers are on the network, but only one of them can use the medium at a time. Therefore, there must be some rules for deciding how each computer takes turns in sharing the network. The data link layer provides reliable transit of data across a physical link by using the MAC address. If conflicts arise when more than one computer is contending for the medium, the rules ensure that an agreed method is available to resolve the conflict. In later sections of this chapter, the major types of LANs are reviewed, including the rules for sharing the medium.

Wide-Area Networks

For economic and technical reasons, LANs are not suitable for communications over long distances. On a LAN, the computers must coordinate their use of the network, and this coordination takes time. Long distances create greater delays in communication. If a LAN were used over long distances, the computers would take more time coordinating the use of the shared medium and less time sending data messages. In addition, the costs of providing high-speed media over long distances are much greater than in the case of LANs. For these reasons, WAN technologies differ from those of the LAN.

A *wide-area network (WAN)*, as the name implies, is designed to work over a larger area than a LAN. Figure 10-16 illustrates the individual LANs that are able to communicate using a WAN.

Figure 10-16 Wide-Area Network

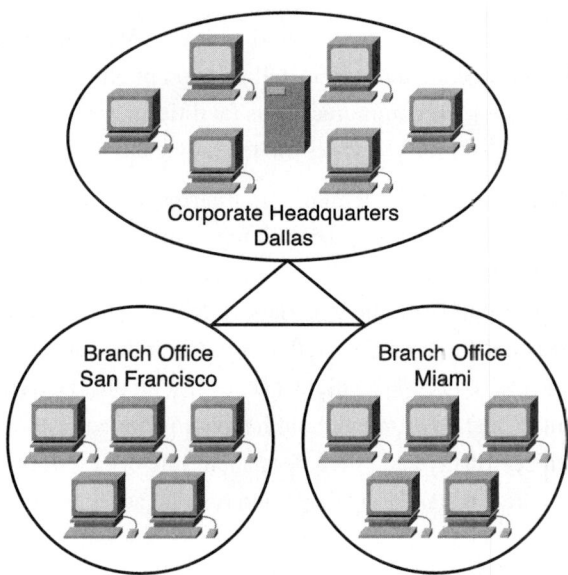

Corporate Headquarters
Dallas

Branch Office
San Francisco

Branch Office
Miami

WANs use point-to-point or point-to-multipoint serial communications lines. Point-to-point lines connect only two locations, one on each side of the line. Point-to-multipoint lines connect one location on one side of the line to multiple locations on the other side. They are called *serial lines* because the bits of information are transmitted one after another, in a series. This is illustrated in Figure 10-17 as a car traveling on a single-lane highway.

Figure 10-17 Serial Transmission

The following are some of the more common WAN technologies:

- Integrated Services Digital Network (ISDN)
- DSL
- Frame Relay
- Asynchronous Transfer Mode (ATM)
- The T (U.S.) and E (Europe) carrier series (T1, E1, T3, E3)
- Synchronous Optical Network (SONET)

Typically, individuals and companies do not build their own WAN connections. Government regulations only allow utility companies to install lines on public property. Therefore, wide-area connections make use of the communications facilities that are put in place by utility companies, called *common carriers,* such as the telephone company.

Connections across WAN lines can be temporary or permanent. Telephone or dialup lines, for example, might make a temporary connection to a remote network from a computer in a home or small office, as shown in Figure 10-18. In this case, the home or office computer makes a phone call to a computer on the boundary of the remote network. The telephone company provides the connection, or circuit, that is used for the duration of the call. After the data is transmitted, the line is disconnected, just as it is for an ordinary voice call. A company might want to transmit data at any time without having to connect and disconnect the line each time. To do so, the company can rent a permanent line or circuit from the common carrier. These leased lines are constantly available and operate at higher speeds than temporary dialup connections.

In both temporary and permanent cases, computers that connect over wide-area circuits must use either a modem or a channel service unit/data service unit (CSU/DSU) at each end of the connection.

NOTE

A channel service unit/data service unit (CSU/DSU) is a pair of communications devices that connect an in-house line to an external digital circuit. An external digital circuit could be a T1 line or direct digital signal (DDS). It is similar to a modem but connects a digital circuit rather than an analog one.

Figure 10-18 WAN Connections

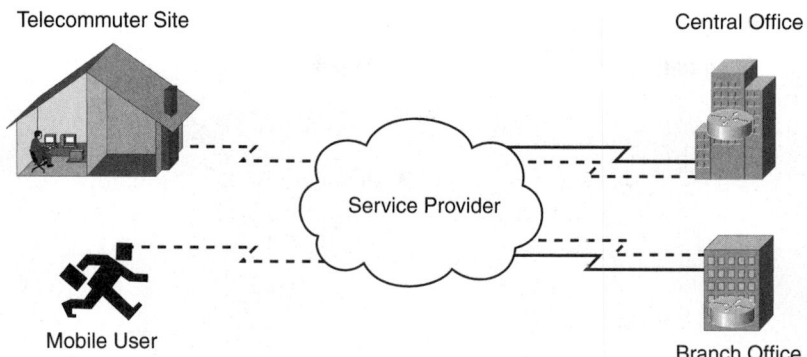

Modem devices are required because the electrical signals that carry digital computer data must be transformed, or modulated, before they can be transmitted on analog telephone lines. On the transmitting end of the connection, a modem (modulator/demodulator) transforms computer signals into phone signals. On the receiving end, the transformation is done from phone to computer signals. The modem is only one way of connecting computers or similar devices so that they can communicate over long distances. Other, much faster technologies include ISDN, Frame Relay, and ATM.

In general, WANs typically connect fewer computers than LANs and normally operate at lower speeds than LANs. WANs, however, can connect single computers and many LANs over large distances. Therefore, WANs enable networks to span entire countries—even the entire globe.

Circuit-Switched Versus Packet-Switched Networks

The public telephone system, sometimes referred to as *plain old telephone service (POTS)*, is a *circuit-switched communications network*. When a telephone call is placed on this type of network, only one physical path is used between the two telephones for the duration of that call. This pathway, called a *circuit*, is maintained for the exclusive use of the call, until the connection is ended and the telephone is hung up. Figure 10-19 illustrates this concept with one route on the map. It is the only way to get from point A to point B.

If the same number were called tomorrow from the same location as the call from today, the transmission path would probably not be the same. The circuit is created by a series of switches that use currently available network paths to set up the *end-to-end*, or *point-to-point*, call. This explains why callers can get a clear connection one day and noise and static on another. This demonstrates that a circuit-switched connection is end-to-end or point-to-point.

Figure 10-19 Circuit-Switched Networks

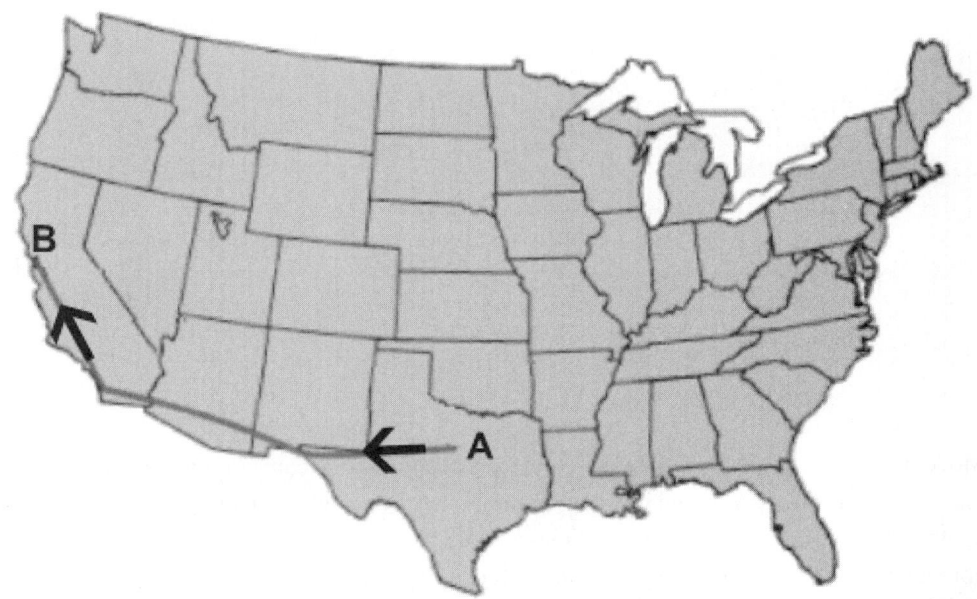

This is different from a ***packet-switched communications network***, where each packet of data can take a different route. Also, with a packet-switched network, no dedicated pathway or circuit is established. The different routes that are shown on the map in Figure 10-20 illustrate this concept. Using a packet-switched network to transfer data enables each packet to take a different route when going from point A to point B. Although all the data arrives at the same destination, it does not all travel the same path to get there. Internet traffic uses packet-switching technology.

The difference between circuit switching and packet switching can be compared to the different ways in which a large group of people travel to the same destination. For example, ***circuit switching*** is similar to loading the entire group on a bus, train, or airplane. The route is plotted out, and the entire group travels over that same route.

Packet switching is comparable to people traveling in their own automobiles. The group is broken down into individual components, just as the data communication is broken into packets. Some travelers might take interstate highways, and others might use back roads. Some might drive straight through, and others might take a more roundabout path. Eventually, all the people end up at the same destination. The group is put back together, just as packets are reassembled at the endpoint of the communication.

Figure 10-20 Packet-Switched Networks

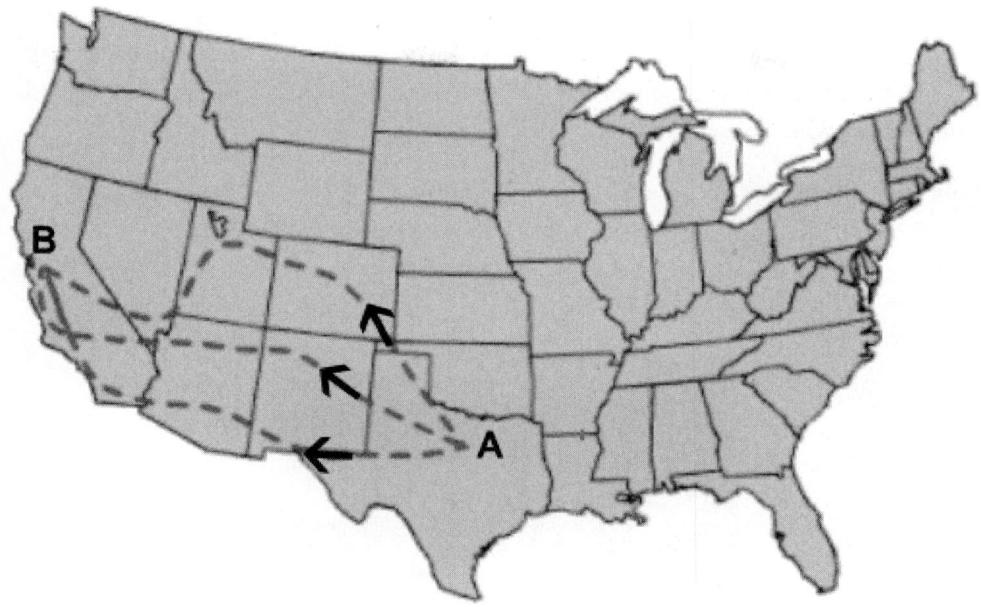

 Worksheet 10.2.5   Types of Networks

This worksheet is a review of the different types of networks that are covered in this chapter.

Adding a Network Interface Card

Before installing a network interface card, you must consider the type of network, type of media, and system bus. Once the card is installed, the IP address is set and, depending on the network, other configurations might be necessary. This section includes the following topics:

- Defining a network interface card
- Setting the IP address
- DHCP servers
- Default gateways
- Domain Name System

Defining a Network Interface Card

A *network interface card (NIC)*, shown in Figure 10-21, is a device that plugs into a motherboard and provides ports for the network cable connections. The NIC is the computer interface with the LAN. A NIC communicates with the network through serial connections and communicates with the computer through parallel connections.

Figure 10-21 Network Interface Card (NIC)

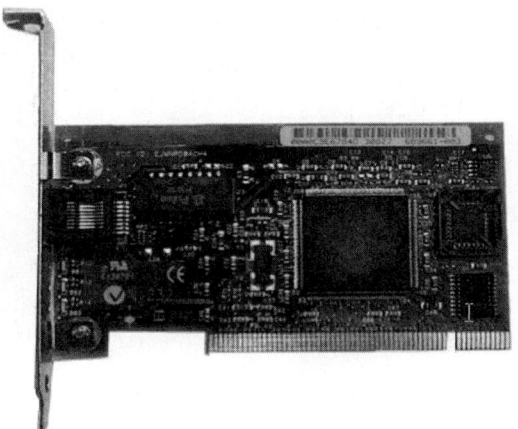

Consider the following items when selecting a NIC to use on a network:

- **The type of network**—NICs are designed for Ethernet LANs, Token Ring networks, Fiber Distributed Data Interface (FDDI) networks, and so on. An Ethernet NIC does not work with Token Ring networks and vice versa.

- **The type of media**—The type of port or connector that the NIC provides determines the specific media types to use, such as twisted-pair, coaxial, fiber-optic, or wireless.

- **The type of system bus**—The type of NIC required on the network can determine the system bus requirement in the device. A PCI slot is faster than an ISA bus. A PCI slot should be used with FDDI cards, because an ISA bus cannot handle the required speed.

A NIC is installed in the computer in an expansion slot. NICs require an interrupt request (IRQ), an I/O address, and memory space for the operating system drivers in order to perform their functions. Newer NICs are Plug and Play compatible, making the installation an easy process. The system automatically finds the new hardware after it is installed and the computer is powered on. The computer then installs the driver and sets the IRQ, I/O address, and memory space. For troubleshooting issues, refer to the manufacturer's documentation or website.

Figure 10-22 shows the components of a NIC.

Figure 10-22 NIC Components

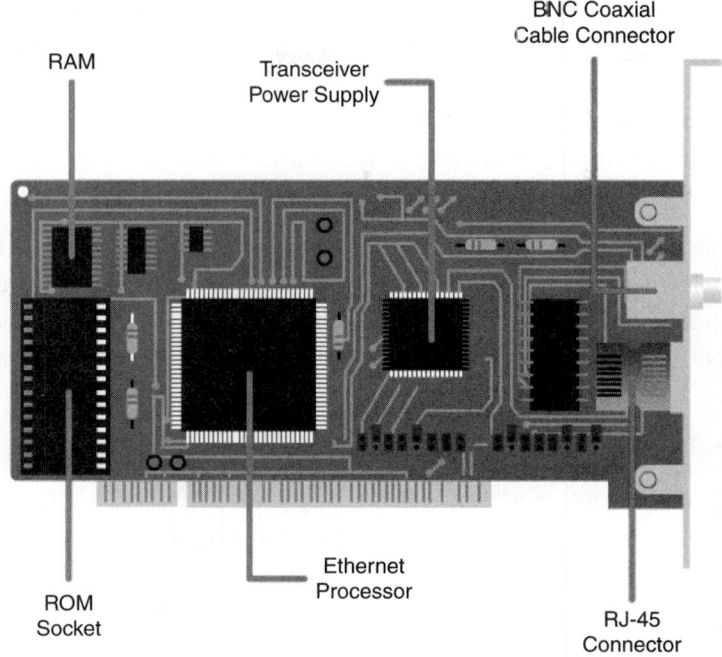

PhotoZoom   Network Interface Card

This PhotoZoom shows the different views of a NIC.

Video   Installing a NIC

The step-by-step NIC installation process is shown in this video.

Lab 10.3.1   NIC Installation

In this lab, you install and configure a network interface card. You also troubleshoot issues using the Device Manager.

Setting the IP Address

In a Transmission Control Protocol/Internet Protocol (TCP/IP) LAN, PCs use IP addresses to identify each other. These addresses allow computers that are attached to the network to locate each other. An *Internet Protocol (IP) address* is a 32-bit binary number. This binary number is divided into four groups of 8 bits known as octets. A decimal number in the range of 0 to 255 represents each *octet*. The octets are separated by decimal points. The combination 190.100.5.54 is an example of an IP address. This type of address is described as a dotted decimal representation. Each device on the network that has an IP address is known as a *node*. A node can include a host, printer, or other device. In a network, a host is the computer that is accessed by users. Because it is a node, the host has a unique IP address.

A secondary dotted decimal number, known as the *subnet mask*, always accompanies an IP address. For example, the dotted decimal number 255.255.0.0 is a subnet mask. The subnet mask is used by network devices to determine whether a particular host IP address is local or remote. A local host is on the same network segment, while a remote host is on another segment.

IP addresses for hosts on a LAN can be assigned in the following ways:

- Manually assigned by the network administrator. Figure 10-23 shows the Internet Protocol (TCP/IP) Properties dialog box in Windows that is used to manually assign IP addresses.

Figure 10-23 Manually Entering an IP Address

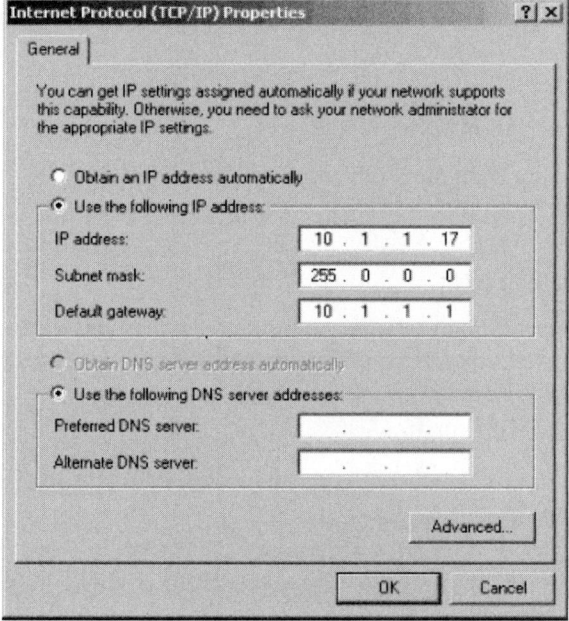

- Assigned by a Dynamic Host Configuration Protocol (DHCP) server. Figure 10-24 shows the TCP/IP Properties dialog box in Windows that is used to automatically assign IP addresses. DHCP servers are discussed in the next section.

Figure 10-24 Obtaining an IP Address Automatically

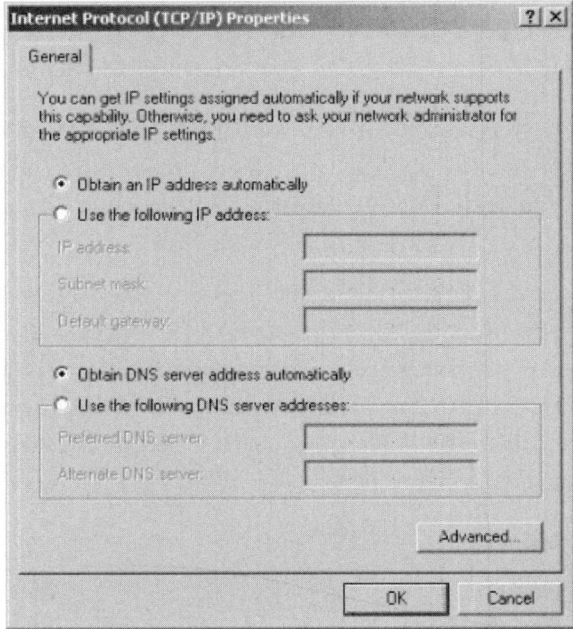

The following address settings or configurations are required to connect with the network:

- IP address
- Subnet mask
- Default gateway address

If more than a few computers are involved, manually configuring TCP/IP addresses for every host on the network can be a time-consuming process. This would also require the network administrator, who is assigning the address, to understand IP addressing. He or she would also need to know how to choose a valid address for the particular network. The IP address that is entered is unique for each host and resides in the computer driver software for the NIC. This is different from the MAC address, which resides on the NIC hardware. TCP/IP addressing is not part of the scope of this course. The default gateway address is discussed later in this chapter.

e-Lab Activity Configuring an IP Address

In this e-lab activity, you manually configure an IP address for a host.

DHCP Servers

The most common and efficient way for computers on a large network to obtain an IP address is through a *Dynamic Host Configuration Protocol (DHCP)* server. DHCP is a software utility that assigns IP addresses to PCs. The computer that is running the software is known as a DHCP server. DHCP servers hand the IP addresses and TCP/IP configuration information to computers that are configured as DHCP clients. This dynamic process eliminates the need for manual IP address assignments. However, any devices that require a static, or permanent, IP address must still have their IP address manually assigned.

The DHCP server receives a request from a host. The server then selects IP address information from a set of predefined addresses that are stored in its database. After it has selected the IP information, the server offers these values to the requesting device on the network. If the device accepts the offer, the DHCP server then leases the IP information to the device for a specific period of time. Figure 10-25 illustrates a DHCP operation, as the client makes a request of the server and the server responds.

Figure 10-25 DHCP Operation

The IP address information that a DHCP server can hand out to hosts that are starting up on the network includes the following:

- IP address
- Subnet mask
- Default gateway
- Optional values, such as a Domain Name System (DNS) server address

The use of this system simplifies the administration of a network, because the software keeps track of IP addresses. Automatically configuring TCP/IP also reduces the possibility of assigning duplicate IP addresses or invalid IP addresses. For a computer on the network to take advantage of the DHCP server services, it must be able to identify the server on the local network. This is accomplished by choosing to obtain an IP address automatically on the client software through its TCP/IP Properties dialog box. In other cases, the operating system feature *Automatic Private IP Addressing (APIPA)* enables a computer to assign itself an address if it is unable to contact a DHCP server.

Video   Configuring the NIC to Work with a DHCP Server

In this video, you learn how to configure the NIC to work with a DHCP server.

Lab 10.3.3   Configuring the NIC to Work with a DHCP Server

In this lab, you configure a NIC to use Dynamic Host Configuration Protocol (DHCP).

Default Gateways

A computer located on one network segment that is trying to communicate with another computer across the router sends its data through a default gateway. The *default gateway* is the "near-side" interface of the router. That is the interface on the router where the network segment or wire of the local computer is attached. For each computer to recognize its default gateway, the corresponding near-side router interface IP address must be entered into the host TCP/IP Properties dialog box. This information is stored on the NIC.

Domain Name System

If a LAN is large or is connected to the Internet, it is often challenging to remember the IP addresses of hosts. Most hosts are identified on the Internet by friendly computer names known as *domain names*. The Domain Name System (DNS) translates computer names, such as cisco.com, to their corresponding unique IP addresses. The DNS software runs on a computer that acts as a network server for handling the address translations. DNS software can be hosted on the network by itself or by an ISP. Address translations are used each time the Internet is accessed. The process of translating names to addresses is known as *name resolution*. Figure 10-26 illustrates how the DNS server resolves the post office name of an e-mail address.

Figure 10-26 DNS Functions

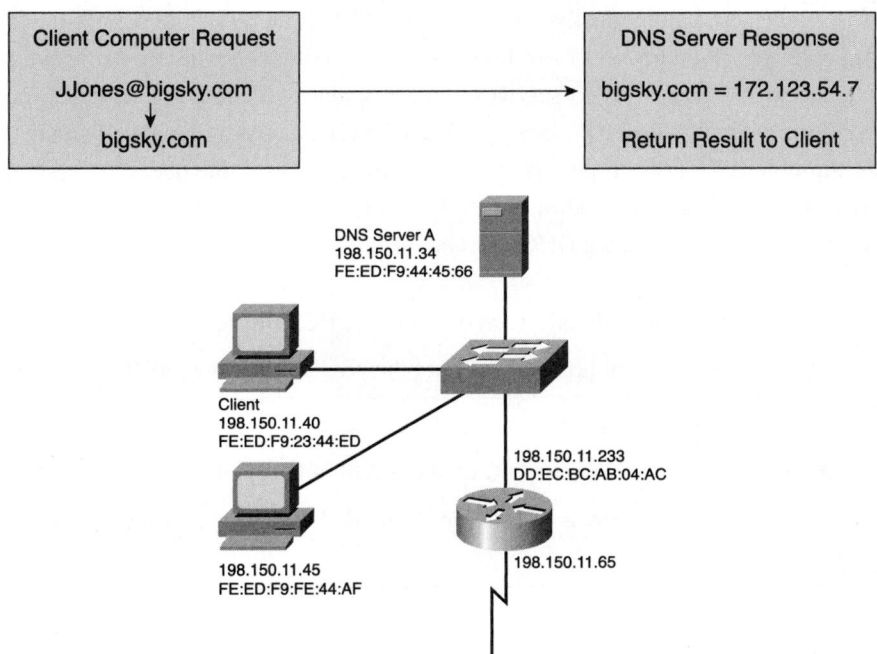

The DNS server keeps records that map the computer host names and their corresponding IP addresses. All these record types are combined in the DNS table. When a host name needs to be translated to its IP address, the client contacts the DNS server. A hierarchy of DNS servers exists on the Internet. Different servers maintain DNS information for their own areas of authority, called *zones*. A DNS server, when consulted by a computer, may not always get an IP mapping for the host name sought. If this happens, the query passes to another DNS server until the information is obtained.

DNS is not an absolute requirement to communicate on the Internet. However, without it, all communications must use IP addresses instead of host names. It is much easier for most people to remember cisco.com than 198.133.219.25.

Computers that are located on the LAN need to access and make use of the DNS services. To do so, the DNS server IP address, as well as the IP address and subnet mask, must be entered into the Internet TCP/IP Properties dialog box.

Physical Components of a Network

The physical components that are used in a network are determined by the topology. A network design includes both physical and logical considerations. This section includes the following topics:

- Network topologies
- Physical versus logical topologies
- Networking media
- Common networking devices
- Server components

Network Topologies

The *network topology* defines the way in which computers, printers, and other devices are connected. A network topology describes the layout of the wire and devices as well as the paths that are used by data transmissions. The topology greatly influences how the network functions.

The following sections discuss the different types of topologies, including bus, star, extended-star, ring, mesh, and hybrid. The physical and logical topologies of a network are also presented.

Bus Topology

Commonly referred to as a linear bus, all the devices on a *bus topology* are connected by a single cable. Figure 10-27 illustrates the bus topology. This cable proceeds from one computer to the next like a bus line going through a city. The main cable on the bus topology must be terminated at each end with a terminator. The terminator absorbs the signal when it reaches the end of the line or wire. If no terminator exists, the electrical signal that represents the data bounces back at the end of the wire, causing errors in the network. Only one packet of data can be transmitted at a time. If more than one packet is transmitted, the packets collide and must be re-sent. A bus topology that has many hosts can be slow because of these collisions. In addition, a failure at any point on the bus causes the network to stop. This topology is rarely used and would only be suitable for a home office or small business with a few hosts.

Figure 10-27 Bus Topology

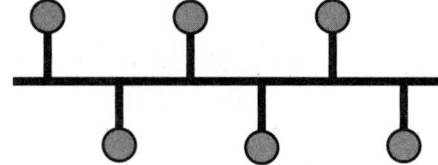

Star Topology

The *star topology* is the most commonly used architecture in Ethernet LANs. Figure 10-28 illustrates the star topology. When installed, the star topology resembles spokes in a bicycle wheel. This topology is made up of a central connection point that is a device such as a hub, switch, or router. All the cabling segments meet at this central connection point. Each host in the network is connected to the central device with its own cable.

Figure 10-28 Star Topology

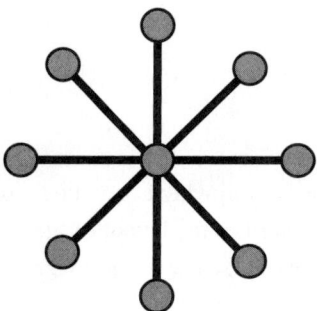

A star topology costs more to implement than a bus topology. This is because more cable is used in a star topology. Also, a central device, such as a hub, switch, or router, is needed. However, the advantages of a star topology are worth the additional costs. Because each host is connected to the central device with its own wire, if a problem exists with that cable, only that host is affected. The rest of the network is operational. This benefit is important, and it is the reason why virtually every newly designed network has this topology.

Extended-Star Topology

When a star network is expanded to include an additional networking device that is connected to the main networking device, it is called an *extended-star topology*. Figure 10-29 illustrates an extended-star topology. Larger networks, like those of corporations or schools, use the extended-star topology. This topology can be used with network devices that filter frames or packets, like bridges, switches, and routers. This topology, when used with these devices, significantly reduces the traffic on the wires by sending packets only to the wires of the destination host.

Figure 10-29 Extended-Star Topology

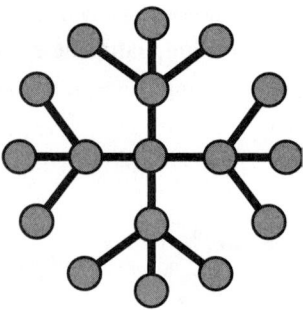

Ring Topology

The *ring topology* is another important topology in LAN connectivity. It is important to know the advantages and disadvantages of choosing a ring topology. As the name implies, hosts are connected in the form of a ring or circle. Unlike the bus topology, the ring topology has no beginning or end that needs to be terminated. Data is transmitted in a way that is unlike the bus or the star topology. A token travels around the ring, stopping at each node. A *token* is a bit setting in a specialized frame that continuously travels around a circuit. If a node wants to transmit data, it adds the data as well as the destination address to the token. This change in the bit setting is referred to as *taking the token.* The token then continues around the ring until it finds the destination node, which again changes the bit setting by taking the data out of the token. The advantage of using this method is that no collisions of data packets occur.

The two types of ring topologies are as follows:

- **Single-ring**—All the devices on the network share a single cable, and the data travels in only one direction. Each device waits its turn to send data over the network, as illustrated in Figure 10-30. An example of the single-ring topology is the Token Ring topology.

Figure 10-30 Single-Ring Topology

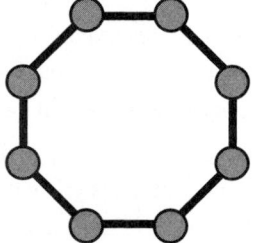

■ **Dual-ring**—The dual-ring topology is illustrated in Figure 10-31. This topology allows data to be sent in both directions, although only one ring is used at a time. This creates redundancy, or fault tolerance, meaning that in the event of the failure of one ring, data can still be transmitted on the other ring. An example of the dual-ring topology is a FDDI network.

Figure 10-31 Dual-Ring Topology

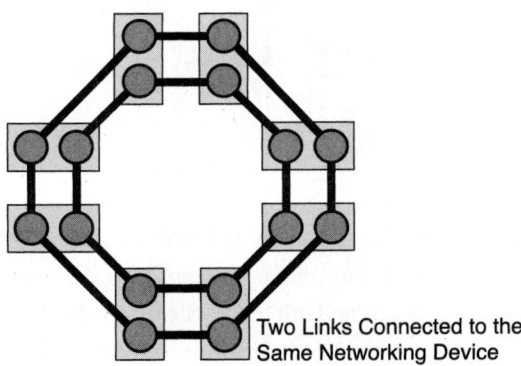

Two Links Connected to the
Same Networking Device

The most common implementation of the ring topology is in Token Ring networks. The Institute of Electrical and Electronics Engineers (IEEE) 802.5 standard uses the Token Ring access method. FDDI is a technology that is similar to Token Ring, but FDDI uses light instead of electricity to transmit data over a dual-ring topology.

Mesh Topology

The *mesh topology* connects all devices, or nodes, to each other for redundancy and fault tolerance, as shown in Figure 10-32. This topology is used in WANs to interconnect LANs and for mission-critical networks like those used by governments. Implementing the mesh topology is expensive and difficult. The two types of mesh topologies are as follows:

■ **Full-mesh**—This topology is usually reserved for backbone networks. It is expensive to implement because every node is interconnected in the network. This topology provides the greatest redundancy, because traffic can easily be redirected if one node should fail.

■ **Partial-mesh**—This topology interconnects primary nodes on the network. It is typically used to connect to full-mesh networks. It is less expensive but also provides less redundancy than a full-mesh network.

Figure 10-32 Mesh Topology

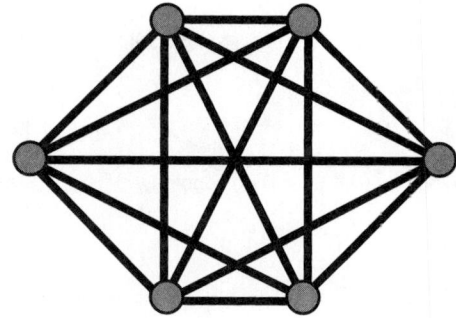

Hybrid Topology

The *hybrid topology* combines more than one type of topology. When a bus line joins two hubs of different topologies, this configuration is called a *star bus*. Businesses or schools that have several buildings, known as campuses, sometimes use this topology. The bus line transfers the data between the star topologies.

Physical Versus Logical Topologies

Network topologies are defined by the way that they are physically designed and the logical way that data is transmitted. This concept is important. Physical and logical topologies are described as follows:

- *Physical topology*—Refers to the layout of the devices and media. Physical topologies are shown in Figure 10-33.
- *Logical topology*—Refers to the paths that signal travel from one point on the network to another—that is, the way in which data accesses a medium and transmits packets across it.

These two terminologies can be confusing. This is partly because in this instance, the word *logical* has nothing to do with the way the network appears to be functioning. The physical and logical topologies of a network can be the same. For example, in a network that is physically shaped as a linear bus, the data travels in a straight line from one computer to the next. Therefore, it has both a bus physical topology and a bus logical topology.

Figure 10-33 Physical Topologies

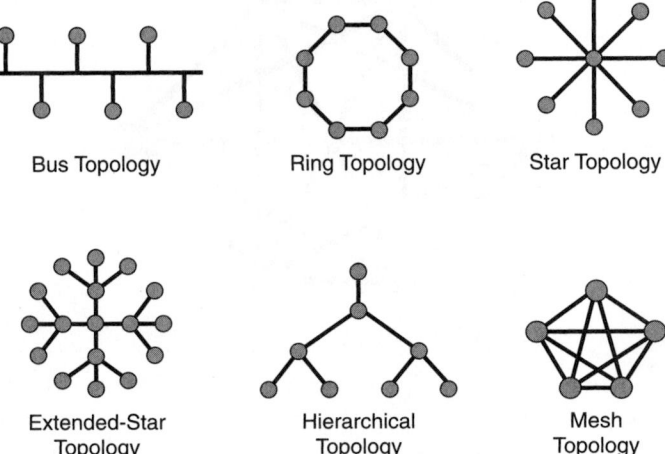

Bus Topology   Ring Topology   Star Topology

Extended-Star
Topology

Hierarchical
Topology

Mesh
Topology

A network can also have physical and logical topologies that are different. For example, a physical topology in the shape of a star can in fact have a logical ring topology. Remember that in a ring, the data travels from one computer to the next. That is because inside the hub, the wiring connections allow the signal to travel around in a circle from one port to the next, creating a logical ring. The way that data travels in a network cannot always be predicted by simply observing its physical layout.

A Token Ring network uses a logical ring topology in either a physical ring or a physical star. An Ethernet network uses a logical bus topology in either a physical bus or a physical star.

All the topologies that have been discussed can be both physical and logical, except that no logical star topology exists.

Worksheet 10.4.2   Network Topology

This worksheet is a review of the different types of topology that are covered in this chapter.

e-Lab Activity   Identifying LAN Topologies and Devices

In this e-lab, you identify the network topologies and the devices that were discussed.

Networking Media

Networking media is the means by which signals—the data—are sent from one computer to another. This can be done either by cable or by wireless means. A variety of networking media are available in the marketplace. This section discusses some of the available media types. One type uses copper for coaxial and twisted-pair cables to transmit data. Another type uses glass for fiber-optic cables to transmit data. Yet another type just uses electromagnetic waves to wirelessly transmit data.

Coaxial Cable

Coaxial cable is a copper-cored cable that is surrounded by a heavy shielding, as shown in Figure 10-34. This cable connects computers in a network. Several types of coaxial cable are available, including thicknet, thinnet, RG-59, and RG-6. RG-59 is the standard for cable TV, whereas RG-6 is used in video distribution. Thicknet is large in diameter and rigid; therefore it is difficult to install. In addition, the maximum transmission rate is 100 Mbps, significantly less than that of twisted-pair or fiber-optic cable, and thicknet's maximum run is 500 meters. A thinner version, known as thinnet or cheapernet, is occasionally used in Ethernet networks. Thinnet has the same transmission rate as thicknet.

Figure 10-34 Coaxial Cable

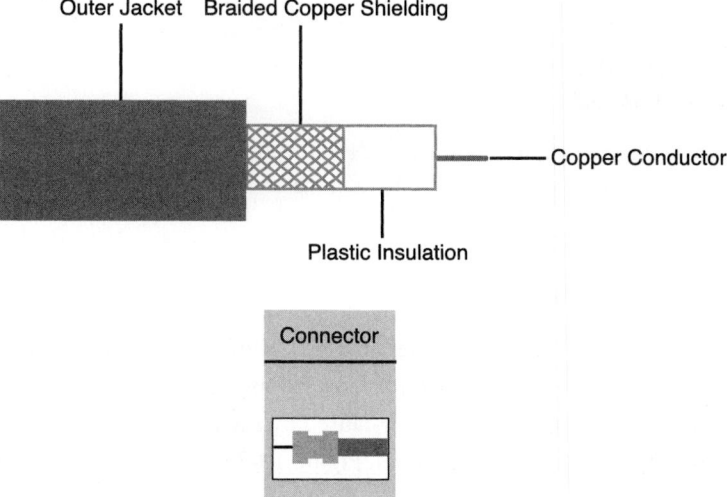

Twisted-Pair Cable

Twisted-pair is a type of cabling that is used for telephone communications and most modern Ethernet networks. A pair of wires forms a circuit that can transmit data. The pairs are twisted to provide protection against crosstalk, the noise that is generated by adjacent pairs. Pairs of copper wires that are encased in color-coded plastic insulation are twisted together. All the twisted pairs are then protected inside an outer jacket. Two basic types of twisted-pair cables are available: shielded twisted-pair (STP) and unshielded twisted-pair (UTP). Several categories of UTP wiring are also available.

STP Cable

Shielded twisted-pair (STP) cable combines the techniques of cancellation and the twisting of wires with shielding. Each pair of wires is wrapped in metallic foil to further shield the wires from noise. The four pairs of wires are then wrapped in an overall metallic braid or foil. STP reduces electrical noise, or crosstalk, from within the cable. It also reduces electrical noise, electromagnetic interference (EMI), and radio frequency interference (RFI) from outside the cable. Figure 10-35 illustrates the STP cable.

Figure 10-35 STP Cable

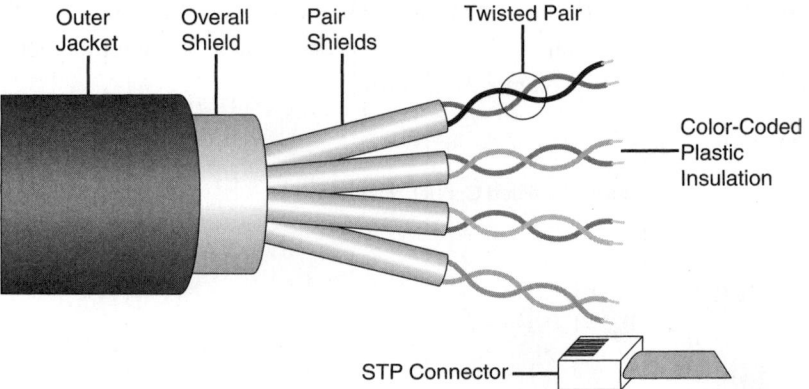

UTP Cable

Unshielded twisted-pair (UTP) cable is used in a variety of networks. It has two or four pairs of wires. This type of cable relies solely on the cancellation effect that is produced by the twisted wire pairs to limit signal degradation caused by EMI and RFI. UTP is the most commonly used cabling in Ethernet networks. Figure 10-36 illustrates the UTP cable.

Although STP prevents interference better than UTP, STP cable is more expensive and difficult to install. In addition, the metallic shielding must be grounded at both ends. If improperly grounded, the shield acts like an antenna, picking up unwanted signals. STP cable is primarily used outside North America.

Figure 10-36 UTP Cable

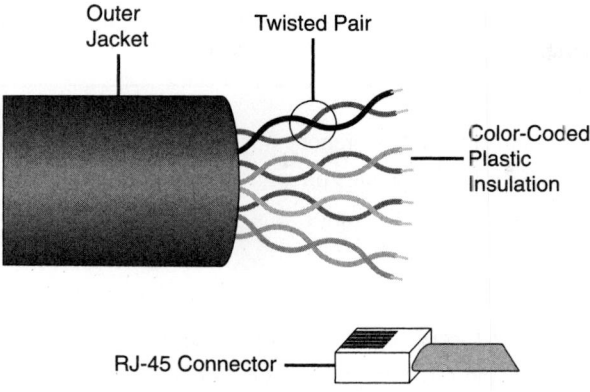

Category Rating

UTP cable is available in several categories that are based on the number of wires and number of twists in those wires. *Category 3* is the wiring used for telephone connections. It has four pairs of wires and a maximum data rate of 16 Mbps. *Category 5* and *Category 5e* are currently the most commonly used Ethernet cables. They have four pairs of wires with a maximum data rate of 1 Gbps. Category 5e cable has more twists per foot than Category 5 wiring. These extra twists further prevent interference from outside sources and the other wires within the cable. Table 10-1 summarizes the common category cables and transmission speeds.

Table 10-1 UTP Category Rating

Cable Rating Category	Number of Wire Pairs	Transmission Rate	Common Use
1	1	Voice grade (telephone only)	Not commonly used
2	4	Up to 1.544 Mbps (IEEE 802.5)	4-Mbps Token Ring
3	4 (3 twists per foot of cable length)	Up to 10 Mbps (IEEE 802.3)	Voice, 10-Mbps Ethernet, and 16-Mbps Token Ring
4	4	Up to 16 Mbps (IEEE 802.5)	10-Mbps Ethernet and 16-Mbps Token Ring
5	4	Up to 1 Gbps (1000BASE-T)	100-Mbps Ethernet and 155-Mbps ATM

PhotoZoom   Straight-Through Cable

This PhotoZoom provides a detailed view of a Cat 5 straight-through cable that is used in networking.

The latest type of cable is *Category 6*. Category 6 is similar to Category 5 and Category 5e cable except that a plastic divider separates the pairs of wires to prevent crosstalk. The pairs also have more twists than Category 5e cable.

EIA/TIA-232

EIA/TIA-232 is a standard for serial transmission between computers and other devices, such as the modem, mouse, and so on. It supports a point-to-point connection over a single copper wire, so only two devices can be connected. Virtually every computer has one EIA/TIA-232 serial port. Modems, monitors, mice, and serial printers are designed to connect to the EIA/TIA-232 port. This port also connects modems to telephones. Two types of connectors are available: a 25-pin connector (DB-25) and a 9-pin connector (DB-9). Limitations of using EIA/TIA-232 include the following:

- The signaling rate is limited to 20 Kbps.
- The signaling rate is limited because the potential for crosstalk among signal lines in the cable is high.

EIA/TIA-232 is still the most common standard for serial communication. RS-422 and RS-423 are expected to replace it in the future. Both of these standards support higher data rates and have greater immunity to EMI.

e-Lab Activity   Identifying Media Ports

In this e-lab, you identify ports that connect monitors, mice, printers, and other peripherals.

Fiber-Optic Cable

Fiber-optic cable is a networking medium that is capable of conducting modulated light transmissions. Figure 10-37 shows an example of a fiber-optic cable. To modulate light is to manipulate it so that it can transmit data. Fiber-optic refers to cabling that has a core of strands of glass or plastic, instead of copper, through which light pulses carry signals.

Figure 10-37 Fiber-Optic Cable

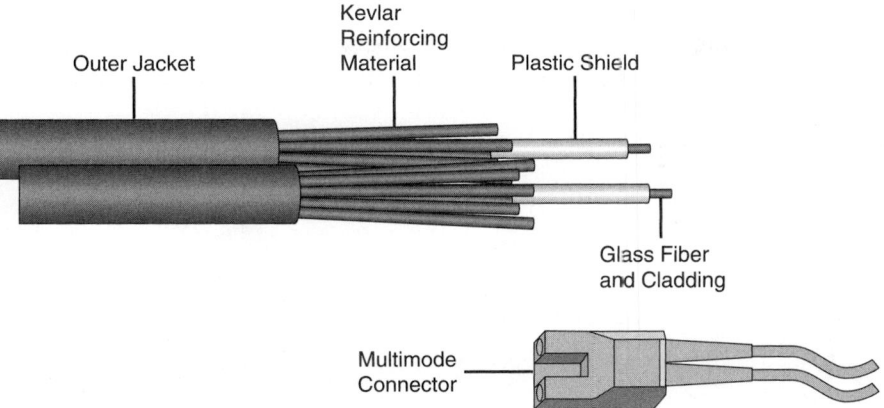

Fiber-optic cable does not carry electrical impulses as do other forms of networking media that use copper wire. Instead, signals that represent data are converted into beams of light. Figure 10-38 illustrates how data is transmitted in the form of light. Fiber has many advantages over copper in terms of transmission bandwidth and signal integrity over distance. However, fiber is more difficult to work with and more expensive than copper cabling. The connectors for fiber-optic cables are expensive, as is the labor that is necessary to terminate the ends of the cables.

Figure 10-38 Fiber Transmits Data in the Form of Light

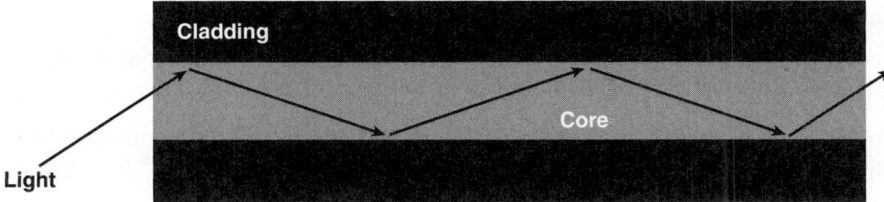

Wireless

Sometimes the cost of running cables is too high. In some cases, computers need to be movable without being tethered to cables. When this is the case, wireless is an alternative method of connecting a LAN. Wireless networks use radio frequency (RF) waves, laser waves, infrared (IR) waves, and microwaves to carry signals from one computer to another without a permanent cable connection. Wireless signals are electromagnetic waves that travel through the air, as shown in Figure 10-39. No physical medium is necessary for wireless signals, making them versatile tools with which to build a network.

Figure 10-39 Fiber-Encoding Signals as Electromagnetic Waves

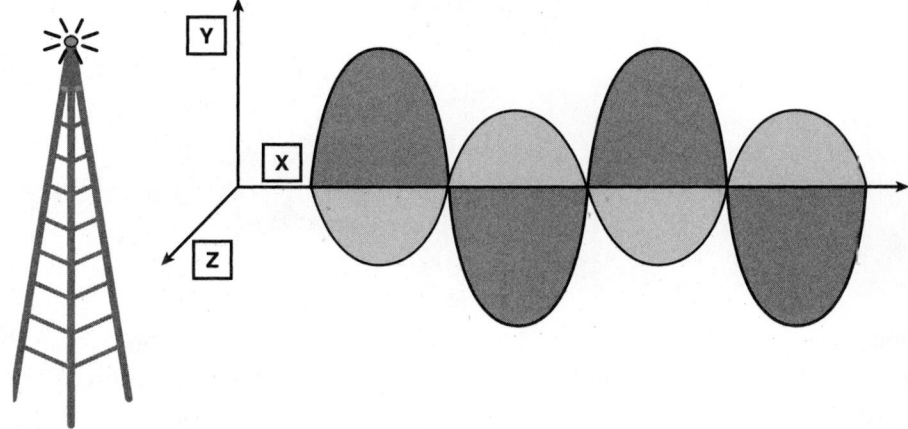

Common Networking Devices

Networking devices connect computers and peripheral devices so that they can communicate. These devices include hubs, bridges, and switches, as detailed in the following sections.

Hubs

A *hub* is a device that extends an Ethernet wire, allowing more devices to communicate with each other. When using a hub, the network topology changes from a linear bus, where each device plugs directly into the wire, to a star topology. Figure 10-40 shows an example of a Cisco hub.

Figure 10-40 Cisco Hub

Hubs share bandwidth and can be either active or passive. A passive hub transmits LAN signals as received; an active hub amplifies LAN transmission signals. Data that is arriving over the cables to a hub port is electrically repeated on all the other ports that are connected to the same Ethernet LAN. That happens except for the port on which the data was received. Hubs are sometimes called *concentrators,* because they serve as a central connection point for an Ethernet LAN. Hubs are most commonly used in Ethernet 10BASE-T or 100BASE-T networks, although other network architectures use them. Figure 10-41 illustrates how computers are connected to a hub.

Figure 10-41 Computers Attached to a Hub

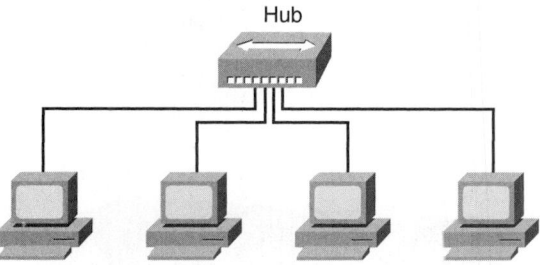

Bridges and Switches

Bridges connect network segments. The basic functionality of the bridge is its ability to make intelligent decisions about whether to pass signals on to the next segment of a network. When a bridge sees a frame on the network, it looks at the destination address. The bridge compares this address to the forwarding table to determine whether to filter, flood, or copy the frame onto another segment. Recall that a frame is the data that is being sent from one computer to another. Figure 10-42 shows a Cisco wireless bridge.

A *switch* is sometimes described as a multiport bridge. A typical bridge can have just two ports, linking two systems on the same network. The switch has several ports, as shown in Figure 10-43, depending on how many network segments are to be linked. A switch is a more sophisticated device than a bridge. The basic function of the switch is deceptively simple. It is to choose a port to forward data to its destination. Ethernet switches are becoming popular connectivity solutions because, like bridges, they increase network performance with speed and bandwidth.

Figure 10-42 Cisco Wireless Bridge

Figure 10-43 Switch

Routers

Routers are sophisticated internetworking devices. They are slower than bridges and switches, but they make "smart" decisions on how to route—or send—packets that are received on one port to a network on another port. Each port is attached to a network segment at a router interface. Routers can be computers with special network software installed on them, or they can be other devices that are built by network equipment manufacturers. Routers contain tables of network addresses, along with optimal destination routes to other networks. A Cisco router is shown in Figure 10-44.

Figure 10-44 Cisco Router

Server Components

The network server represents another physical component of a network. Server components are those components that are used exclusively with the network server. End users depend on the server to provide the services required. To keep the server running at its optimal performance, a higher level of preventive maintenance must be maintained.

Video Controller

A *video controller* does not need to support high video resolutions on the network server. A video controller that can support 1024 × 768 resolution and 64,000 colors should be sufficient for most network servers.

Video Monitor

A *video monitor* for a network server should support 800 × 600 or better video resolution. A network server should have at least a 21-inch video monitor. A liquid crystal display (LCD) monitor could also be used as a network server monitor. If the video monitor is to be installed in a server rack, the video monitor must be small enough to fit into the rack. The maximum size for a video monitor that is to be used in a server rack is about 15 inches. To save space in a server rack, newer LCD monitors that fold away when not in use are available. Figure 10-45 shows servers with a monitor installed.

Figure 10-45 Servers with a Monitor Installed

KVM Switch

A *keyboard/video/mouse (KVM) switch* is a common component in a network server rack. Multiple network servers that are installed in a single equipment rack generally have a single keyboard, video display, and mouse that can be switched among the network servers. A rack-mountable KVM switch usually fits within one rack unit. This allows sharing the keyboard, video display, and mouse among the network servers in the rack. Newer KVM switches allow the use of a hot-key sequence, such as Ctrl-Alt, to switch between the different modes of operation. The hot-key sequence can be customized if the default Ctrl-Alt combination conflicts with other applications.

CD-ROM/DVD-ROM Drive

Most server hardware includes either a CD-ROM or DVD-ROM drive. CD-ROM and DVD-ROM libraries are used in many implementations of RAID, as discussed in Chapter 9, "Advanced Hardware Fundamentals for Servers." These drives provide data storage, backup, and redundancy in the network environment. CD-ROM and DVD-ROM drives are also used for installing the operating system and other software.

Floppy Drive

A floppy disk drive is often required on a network server to load hardware drivers and to perform flash BIOS upgrades. Figure 10-46 shows a tower server with a CD-ROM drive and a floppy disk drive.

Figure 10-46 Tower Server

Universal Bus Controller

The universal serial bus (USB) is an external bus standard that supports data transfer rates of up to 12 Mbps. One USB port can have up to 127 devices connected to it. On a network server, the types of devices that might be attached to a USB port include a USB mouse, a USB modem, a USB keyboard, or a USB monitoring cable for an uninterruptible power supply (UPS). A USB bus supports Plug and Play technology and devices that can be hot-plugged. These devices can be attached to and unattached from the USB bus without powering down the network server. To use a USB port on a network server, the network operating system must be able to recognize and have drivers for the USB port. USB conforms to the IEEE Standard 1384.

The newer USB 2.0 version is 40 times faster than the previous version of USB. The raw data transfer rate of USB 2.0 is 480 Mbps. Although USB 2.0 has become the standard, you do not have to replace older USB 1.1 devices, such as generic keyboards, mice, joysticks, and some audio speakers. These devices do not require the faster speed to function properly. Devices that require more bandwidth and speed, such as web cams and high-capacity storage systems, benefit from USB 2.0 connectivity.

A new version of USB 2.0 is USB On-the-Go (OTG). This specification adds host functionality to USB mobile computing devices such as PDAs, mobile phones, digital cameras, and so on. OTG allows these peripherals to connect not only to a PC but also to other USB devices. For example, with OTG, pictures from a digital camera can be downloaded to the PC or sent directly to a printer or a PDA with video capabilities.

FireWire

The IEEE 1394 standard, known as FireWire by Apple Computer, is an external serial bus that uses the SCSI 3 standards for communications. Data transfer rates of up to 400 Mbps are achievable using the IEEE 1394 standard. A single IEEE 1394 bus can have up to 63 devices attached to it. The IEEE 1394 standard supports Plug and Play technology and hot-plugging, much like the USB standard.

Modem

Depending on the function that the modem performs on the network, you might need to install more than one modem on the server. For example, a remote-access server would need one or more modems to support dialup access to the network. To implement a fax server, one or more fax modems must be installed in the network server.

Redundant NIC

Having a *redundant NIC* in the network server allows the network server to keep communicating over the network even if a NIC fails. This is usually accomplished by having two identical NICs in the server, only one of which is communicating over the network. A special software driver for the redundant NIC constantly monitors the network communications. If the software driver determines that the currently used NIC has failed, the driver automatically switches to the other NIC.

Cooling Fan

Keeping the inside of the server chassis relatively cool is of major importance. If components inside the server chassis get too hot, they can fail. Server hardware has cooling fans to keep air circulating around the components. If only one cooling fan is installed and it fails, the inside of the server chassis will overheat and the server will fail. Many hardware manufacturers add a redundant cooling fan, which is hot swappable in the case of a cooling fan failure.

Power Supply

Server hardware can have multiple hot-swappable power supplies for redundancy. Having two—or even three—power supplies allows the power supplies to balance the electrical load. If one power supply fails, the other power supply can handle the entire electrical load. The failed power supply can be replaced with a new unit without taking the network server offline.

Server Rack

Network servers can be purchased in a chassis that can be installed in a standard 19-inch equipment rack. This conserves space in the server room.

EIA Rack Unit

The Electronic Industries Association (EIA) has specified that the standard vertical rack unit is 1.75 inches high. Server rack height is specified in rack units. For example, a 42U rack is 42×1.75 inches high. This calculates to a total of 73.5 inches—or 6 feet, 1.5 inches—high.

Rack Layout

The layout of the components in the rack is important. The rack-mounted UPSs are generally installed at the bottom of the rack because of their weight. A rack-mounted keyboard should be at the proper height to allow comfortable typing. The rack-mounted display adapter should be at eye level. Most network server rack manufacturers provide software to aid in creating a layout of the devices that are in the network rack.

Rack-Mounted Keyboard/Trackball/Monitor/LCD Panel

Rack-mounted keyboards or keyboard-and-trackball combinations that fit into a drawer that slides into the rack are available. This one keyboard can be attached to a rack-mounted KVM switch so that it can control all the network servers in the rack. The keyboard drawer is usually two rack units high.

Several options are available for the video display that is used in a rack. A standard 15-inch CRT video display can be installed on a shelf in the rack. A monitor larger than 15 inches is usually too large to fit into a rack.

Various keyboard/LCD panel combinations are also available for racks. The LCD panel can fold down and slide into the rack when not in use. The keyboard/LCD panel combination is only two rack units high.

Cable Management

Management of the various cables becomes critical when dealing with several network servers and other devices in a rack. Also, devices that are installed in a rack can usually be pulled out of the rack for service, much like a drawer is pulled out of a cabinet. The network server can be pulled out of the rack without disconnecting all the cables for the network server's devices. This is accomplished by hinged cable-management arms that are attached to the network server on one end and to the rack on the other end.

Security

The network server should have side panels to protect the internal components. The server should also have front and rear doors that are lockable to provide security for the network devices that are installed in the rack.

LAN Architectures

The architectures that are used in a LAN design determine the speed and efficiency of the network. The advantages and disadvantages of each are discussed in detail. This section includes the following topics:

- Ethernet
- Token Ring
- Fiber Distributed Data Interface

Ethernet

The Ethernet architecture is now the most popular type of LAN architecture. *Architecture* refers to the overall structure of a computer or communication system. It determines the capabilities and limitations of the system. The *Ethernet architecture* is based on the IEEE 802.3 standard. This standard specifies that a network must implement the *carrier sense multiple access collision detect (CSMA/CD)* access control method. CSMA/CD uses baseband transmission over coaxial or twisted-pair cable that is laid out in a bus topology, either a linear or star bus. Standard transfer rates are 10 Mbps or 100 Mbps, but new standards provide for Gigabit Ethernet, which is capable of attaining speeds of up to 1 Gbps over fiber-optic cable or other high-speed media.

10BASE-T

Currently, *10BASE-T* is one of the most popular Ethernet implementations; it uses a star topology. The 10 stands for the common transmission speed of 10 Mbps, the BASE stands for baseband mode, and the T stands for twisted-pair cabling. The term *Ethernet cable* describes the UTP cabling that is generally used in this architecture. STP cable can also be used. Using the 10BASE-T implementation and a later version, 100BASE-X, makes setting up and expanding networks easier. Some advantages of 10BASE-T are as follows:

- Networks that are based on the 10BASE-T specifications are relatively inexpensive. Although a hub is required to connect more than two computers, small hubs are available at a low cost. The 10BASE-T network cards are inexpensive and widely available.
- Twisted-pair cabling, especially the UTP type most commonly used, is thin, flexible, and easier to work with than coaxial cable. The twisted-pair cable uses modular RJ-45 plugs and jacks, so connecting the cable to the NIC or hub is easy.
- The 10BASE-T implementation can be upgraded. By definition, a 10BASE-T network runs at 10 Mbps. However, by using Category 5 cable or above and 10/100-Mbps dual-speed NICs, an upgrade to 100 Mbps can be achieved by simply replacing the hubs.

The 10BASE-T implementation has the following disadvantages:

- The maximum length for a 10BASE-T segment, without repeaters, is only 100 meters, or about 328 feet.
- The UTP cable that is used in such a network is more vulnerable to EMI and attenuation than other cable types.
- The extra cost of a hub might not be acceptable.

Table 10-2 summarizes the advantages and disadvantages of 10BASE-T.

Table 10-2 Advantages and Disadvantages of 10BASE-T

Advantages	Disadvantages
Relatively inexpensive.	The maximum length for a segment (without repeaters) is only 100 meters, or about 328 feet.
Twisted-pair cabling is thin, flexible, and easier to work with than coaxial cable.	More susceptible to EMI and attenuation than other cable types.
Easy to upgrade.	Additional cost of a hub might not be acceptable.

The high-bandwidth demands of many modern applications, such as live videoconferencing and streaming audio, have created a need for speed. Many networks require more throughput than is possible with 10-Mbps Ethernet. This is where 100BASE-X, also called *Fast Ethernet*, becomes important.

100BASE-X

100BASE-X is the next evolution of 10BASE-T. Available in several different varieties, it can be implemented over 4-pair Category 3, Category 4, or Category 5 UTP cable. Most implementations are over 2-pair Category 5 or 5e UTP cable or STP (100BASE-TX) cable, or as Ethernet over 2-strand, fiber-optic (100BASE-FX) cable. The following are the advantages of 100BASE-X:

- Regardless of the implementation, the big advantage of 100BASE-X is its high-speed performance. At 100 Mbps, transfer rates are ten times that of 10BASE2, 10BASE5, and 10BASE-T. The 10BASE2 and 10BASE5 implementations are outdated technologies.

- Because it uses twisted-pair cabling, 100BASE-X also shares the same advantages that are enjoyed by 10BASE-T. These include low cost, flexibility, and ease of implementation and expansion.

The disadvantages of 100BASE-X are as follows:

- 100BASE-X shares the disadvantages that are inherent to the twisted-pair cabling of 10BASE-T, such as susceptibility to EMI and attenuation.

- 100-Mbps NICs and hubs are generally somewhat more expensive than those designed for 10-Mbps networks, but prices have dropped as 100BASE-X has gained in popularity.

- Fiber-optic cable remains an expensive cabling option, not so much because of the cost of the cable itself but because of the training and expertise that are required to install it.

Table 10-2 summarizes the advantages and disadvantages of 100BASE-X.

Table 10-3 Advantages and Disadvantages of 100BASE-X

Advantages	Disadvantages
High-speed performance.	Susceptible to EMI and attenuation.
Low cost.	100-Mbps NICs and hubs are generally more expensive.
Flexibility.	Requires better-trained installers and technicians.
Ease of implementation and expansion.	

1000BASE-T

1000BASE-T is commonly known as *Gigabit Ethernet*. The *1000BASE-T* architecture supports data transfer rates of 1 Gbps, which is remarkably fast. For the most part, Gigabit Ethernet is a LAN architecture. However, its implementation over fiber-optic cable makes it suitable for metropolitan-area networks (MANs). The greatest advantage of 1000BASE-T is its performance. At 1 Gbps, it is ten times as fast as Fast Ethernet and 100 times as fast as standard Ethernet. This allows bandwidth-intensive applications, such as live video, to be implemented throughout an intranet. The main disadvantages that are associated with 1000BASE-T are those common to all UTP networks, as detailed in the previous sections on 10BASE-T and 100BASE-T architectures. Table 10-4 summarizes the advantages and disadvantages of 1000BASE-T.

Table 10-4 Advantages and Disadvantages of 1000BASE-T

Advantages	Disadvantages
At 1 Gbps, it is ten times as fast as Fast Ethernet and 100 times as fast as standard Ethernet.	The main disadvantages that are associated with 1000BASE-T are those common to all UTP networks.
Can be used to implement bandwidth-intensive audio and video applications.	

Token Ring

IBM originally developed *Token Ring* as a reliable network architecture based on the token-passing access control method. It is often integrated with IBM mainframe systems such as the AS400. Token Ring was intended to be used with PCs, minicomputers, and mainframes. It works well with Systems Network Architecture (SNA), which is the IBM architecture that is used for connecting to mainframe networks.

The Token Ring standards are defined in IEEE 802.5. It is a prime example of an architecture whose physical topology is different from its logical topology. The Token Ring topology is referred to as a star-wired ring, because the outer appearance of the network design is a star. The computers connect to a central hub, called a multistation access unit (MSAU). However, inside the device, the wiring forms a circular data path, creating a logical ring. Figure 10-47 shows the Token Ring topology implemented on a network.

Figure 10-47 Token Ring Implementation

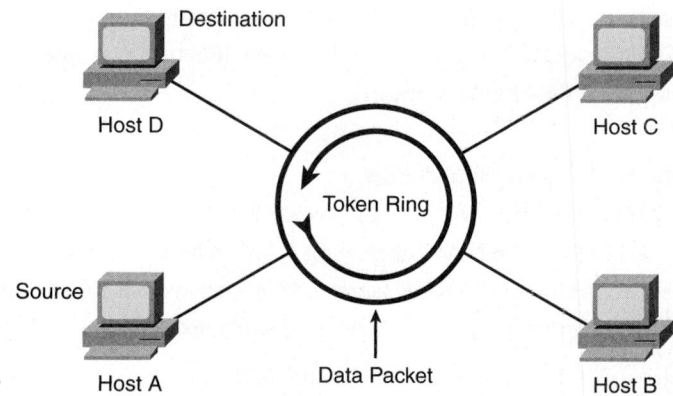

Token Ring is so named because of its logical topology and its MAC method of token passing. The transfer rate for Token Ring can be either 4 Mbps or 16 Mbps.

Token Ring is a baseband architecture that uses digital signaling. In that way, it resembles Ethernet, but the communication process is different in many respects. Token Ring is an active topology. As the signal travels around the circle to each network card, it is regenerated before being sent on its way.

In an Ethernet network, all computers are created physically equal. At the software level, some computers can act as servers and control network accounts and access. However, the servers communicate physically on the network in the same way as the clients.

The Monitor of the Ring

In a Token Ring network, the first computer that comes online becomes the "monitor" and must keep track of how many times each frame circles the ring. This computer has the responsibility of ensuring that only one token is out on the network at a time.

The monitor computer periodically sends a signal called a *beacon,* which circulates around the ring. Each computer on the network looks for the beacon. If a computer does not receive the beacon from its nearest active upstream neighbor (NAUN) when expected, it puts a message on the network. This message notifies the monitoring computer that the beacon was not received, along with its own address and that of the NAUN that failed to send when expected. In most cases, this causes an automatic reconfiguration that restores communications.

Data Transfer

A Token Ring network uses a token to control access to the cable. A token is initially generated when the first computer on the network comes online. When a computer wants to transmit, it waits for and then takes control of the token when it comes its way. The token can travel in either direction around the ring, but only in one direction at a time. The hardware configuration determines the direction of travel.

Fiber Distributed Data Interface

Fiber Distributed Data Interface (FDDI) is a type of Token Ring network. Its implementation and topology differ from the IBM Token Ring LAN architecture, which IEEE 802.5 governs. FDDI is often used for MANs or larger LANs, such as those that connect several buildings in an office complex or campus. MANs typically span a metropolitan area.

As its name implies, FDDI runs on fiber-optic cable. FDDI combines high-speed performance with the advantages of the token-passing ring topology. FDDI runs at 100 Mbps, and its topology is a dual ring. The outer ring is called the primary ring, and the inner ring is called the secondary ring.

Normally, traffic flows only on the primary ring. If the primary ring fails, the data automatically flows onto the secondary ring in the opposite direction. When this occurs, the network is said to be in a wrapped state. This provides fault tolerance for the link. Figures 10-48 and 10-49 illustrate how FDDI works.

Computers on an FDDI network are divided into two classes, as follows:

- *FDDI Class A*—Computers are connected to the cables of both rings.
- *FDDI Class B*—Computers are connected to only one ring.

A FDDI dual ring supports a maximum of 500 nodes per ring. The total distance of each length of the cable ring is 62 miles, or 100 kilometers. A repeater, a device that regenerates signals, is needed every 1.24 miles, or 2 kilometers. For this reason, FDDI is not considered to be a WAN link.

Figure 10-48 FDDI

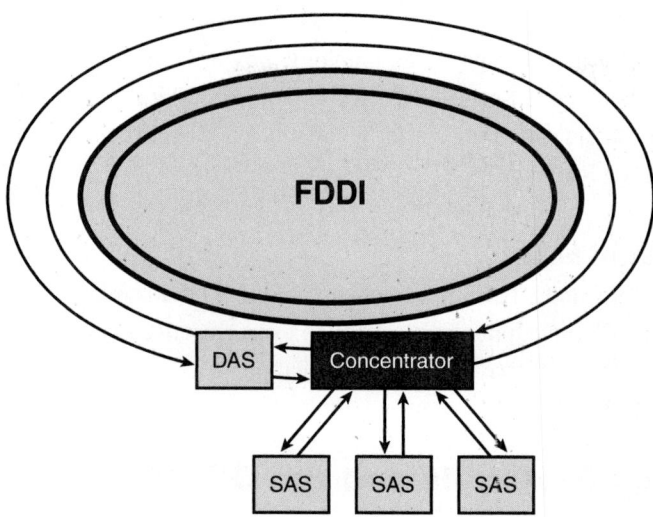

Figure 10-49 FDDI with a Break in the Cable

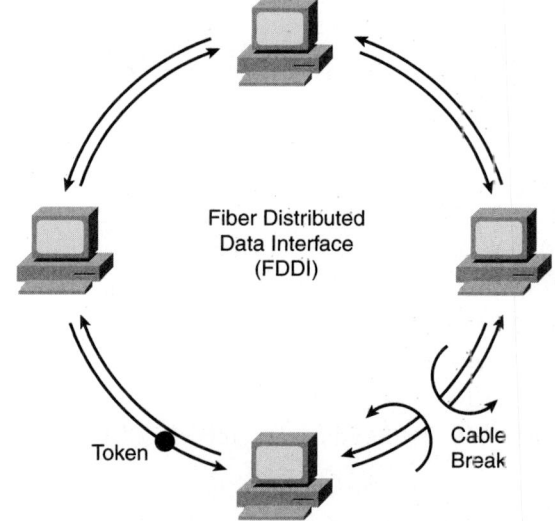

The specifications that have been described so far refer to a FDDI that is implemented over fiber-optic cable. It is also possible to use the FDDI technology with copper cabling. This is called *Copper Distributed Data Interface (CDDI)*. The maximum distances for CDDI are considerably lower than those for FDDI.

Advantages of FDDI

FDDI combines the advantages of token passing on the ring topology with the high speed of fiber-optic transmission. The dual-ring topology provides redundancy and fault tolerance. The fiber-optic cable is not susceptible to EMI and noise, and it is more secure than copper wiring. Fiber-optic cable can send data for greater distances between repeaters than Ethernet and traditional Token Ring.

Disadvantages of FDDI

As always, high speed and reliability come with a price. FDDI is relatively expensive to implement, and the distance limitations, although less restrictive than those of other LAN links, make it unsuitable for true WAN communications.

Networking Protocols and the OSI Model

TCP/IP is based on the layers of the OSI model. These guidelines define how data is transferred over a network. The protocols perform specific functions as data moves through each layer. This section includes the following topics:

- OSI model overview
- Defining a protocol
- Transmission Control Protocol/Internet Protocol (TCP/IP)
- Internetwork Packet Exchange/Sequenced Packet Exchange
- NetBEUI
- AppleTalk

OSI Model Overview

The *Open Systems Interconnection (OSI)* reference model is an industry-standard framework that divides the functions of networking into seven distinct layers. It is one of the most commonly used tools for teaching and reference in networking. The *International Organization for Standardization (ISO)* developed the OSI model in the 1980s.

The OSI reference model contains seven layers, as shown in Figure 10-50. Each layer provides specific services to the layers that are above and below it for the network to work effectively. At the top of the model is the application interface. This layer enables the smooth usage of such applications as word processors and web browsers. At the bottom is the physical side of the network. The physical side includes the cabling, hubs, and other hardware, but it does not include bridges/switches or routers. Recall that cabling was discussed earlier in this chapter.

Figure 10-50 OSI Reference Model

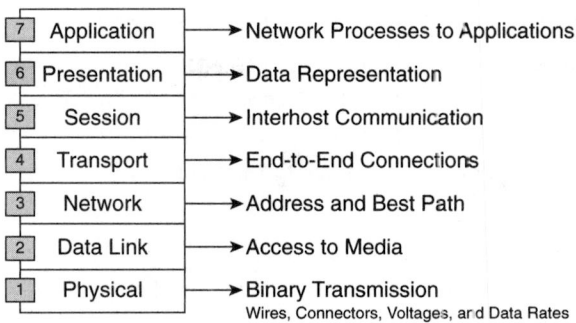

How Does the OSI Model Work?

A message begins at the top application layer and moves down the OSI layers to the bottom physical layer. One example is the sending of an e-mail message. Figure 10-51 shows the progression of the e-mail as it descends the layers and information or headers are added. A header is layer-specific information that explains what functions the layer carried out.

Figure 10-51 E-Mail Message

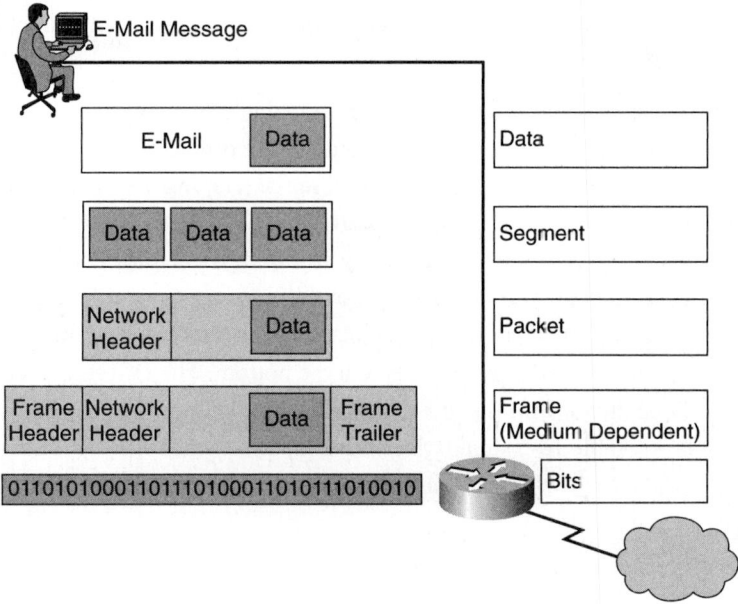

Figure 10-52 illustrates the layers of the OSI model that the e-mail goes through.

TIP

Use the following mne-
monics to help you
remember the seven
layers of the OSI
model: "**A**ll **P**eople
Seem **T**o **N**eed **D**ata
Processing" or "**P**lease
Do **N**ot **T**hrow **S**ausage
Pizza **A**way."

Figure 10-52 OSI Layers of an E-Mail

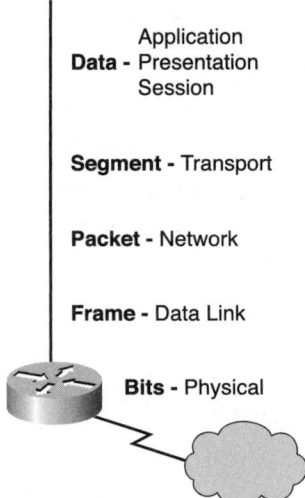

TIP

Know the layers of the
OSI reference model
and the purpose of each
layer from top to bot-
tom and bottom to top.

Conversely, at the receiving end, headers are stripped from the message as it travels up the corresponding layers and arrives at its destination. The process of data being encapsulated on the sending end and data being de-encapsulated on the receiving end is the function of the OSI model.

Communication across the layers of the reference model is achieved because of special net-working software programs called *protocols*. Protocols are discussed in the sections that follow. The OSI model was intended to be a model for developing networking protocols. However, most of the protocols that are now used on LANs do not necessarily respond exactly to these layers. Some protocols fall neatly within the boundaries between these lay-ers, while others overlap or provide services that overlap or span several layers. This explains the meaning of "reference" as it is used in conjunction with the OSI reference model. Tradi-tionally, layer diagrams are drawn with Layer 1 at the bottom. The OSI reference model could just as easily be drawn with Layer 1 at the top. What is important to understand is the function of each layer. Table 10-5 summarizes these functions, the type of data that each layer handles, and the type of hardware that can work at that layer.

Table 10-5 OSI Model Layers and Their Functions

Layer Number	Layer Name	Protocol Data Unit	Mnemonic	Purpose
7	Application	Data	All	Provides network services to application processes (such as e-mail, FTP, and Telnet).
6	Presentation	Data	People	Ensures that data is readable by the receiving system. Deals with data representation.
5	Session	Data	Seem	Establishes, manages, and terminates sessions between applications.
4	Transport	Segment	To	Handles information flow control, fault detection and recovery, and data transport reliability.
3	Network	Packet	Need	Provides addressing and best-path selection between two end systems.
2	Data Link	Frame	Data	Provides reliable transfer of data across media using physical addressing and the network topology.
1	Physical	Bits	Processing	Consists of voltages, wires, and connectors.

e-Lab Activity   OSI Model

This e-lab activity is a review of the seven layers of the OSI model.

The following sections discuss examples of the networking protocols that are mentioned in this section.

Defining a Protocol

A *protocol* is a controlled sequence of messages that are exchanged between two or more systems to accomplish a given task. Protocol specifications define this sequence, together with the format or layout of the messages that are exchanged. Protocols use control structures in each system to coordinate the exchange of information between the systems. Protocols operate like a set of interlocking gears. Computers can precisely track protocol connection points as they move through the sequence of exchanges. Timing is crucial to network operation. Protocols require messages to arrive within certain time intervals, so systems maintain one or more timers during protocol execution. Protocols also take alternative actions if the network does not meet the timing rules. To do their work, many protocols depend on the operation of other protocols in the group or suite of protocols. Protocol functions include the following:

- Identifying errors
- Applying compression techniques
- Deciding how data is to be sent
- Addressing data
- Deciding how to announce sent and received data

Transmission Control Protocol/Internet Protocol (TCP/IP)

The *Transmission Control Protocol/Internet Protocol (TCP/IP)* suite of protocols has become the dominant standard for internetworking. TCP/IP was originally defined by researchers in the United States Department of Defense (DoD). TCP/IP represents a set of public standards that specify how packets of information are exchanged between computers over one or more networks.

The TCP/IP protocol suite includes a number of major protocols, and each performs a specific function. Figure 10-53 illustrates the relationship between the OSI model and the TCP/IP model.

Figure 10-53 OSI Model Versus the TCP/IP Model

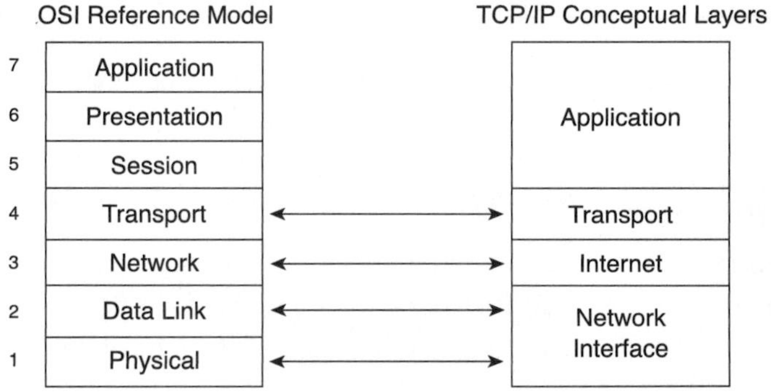

Application Protocols

The *application layer* is the fourth layer in the TCP/IP model. It provides the starting point for any communication session. An overview of the TCP/IP application layer is shown in Figure 10-54.

Figure 10-54 TCP/IP Application Layer

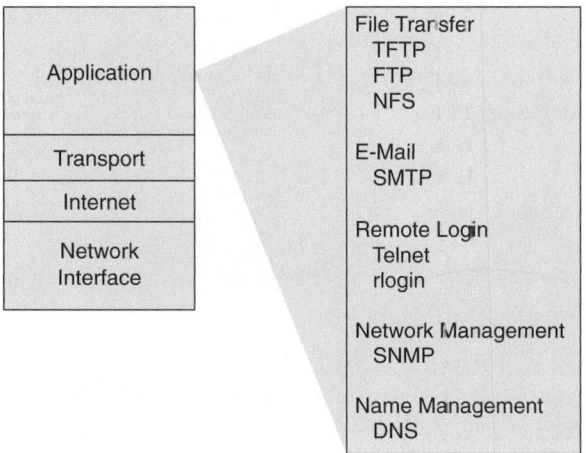

The following protocols and services are used at the application layer:

- *Hypertext Transfer Protocol (HTTP)*—Governs how files—such as text, graphics, sounds, and video—are exchanged on the Internet. The Internet Engineering Task Force (IETF) developed the standards for HTTP. HTTP 1.1 is the current version. As its name implies, HTTP is used to exchange hypertext files, and these files can include links to other files. A web server runs an HTTP service or daemon. A *daemon* is a program that services HTTP requests. These requests are transmitted by HTTP client software, which is another name for a web browser.

- *Hypertext Markup Language (HTML)*—A page-description language. Web designers use HTML to indicate to web browser software how the page should look. HTML includes tags to indicate boldface type, italics, line breaks, paragraph breaks, hyperlinks, insertion of tables, and so on.

- *Telnet*—Enables terminal access to local or remote systems. The Telnet application accesses remote devices for configuration, control, and troubleshooting.

- *File Transfer Protocol (FTP)*—An application that provides services for file transfer and manipulation. FTP uses the session layer to allow multiple simultaneous connections to remote file systems.

- *Simple Mail Transport Protocol (SMTP)*—Provides messaging services over TCP/IP and supports most Internet e-mail programs.
- *Domain Name System (DNS)*—Provides access to name servers, where network names are translated to the addresses used by Layer 3 network protocols. DNS greatly simplifies network usage by end users.

Transport Protocols

The *transport layer* is the third layer in the TCP/IP model. It provides an end-to-end management of the communications session. An overview of the TCP/IP transport layer is shown in Figure 10-55.

Figure 10-55 TCP/IP Transport Layer

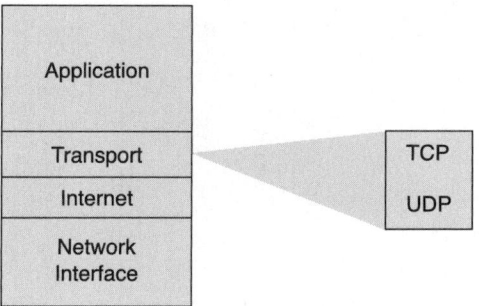

The following protocols are used in the transport layer:

- *Transmission Control Protocol (TCP)*—The primary Internet protocol for the reliable delivery of data. TCP includes facilities for end-to-end connection establishment, error detection and recovery, and metering the rate of data flow into the network. Many standard applications—such as e-mail, web browsers, file transfer, and Telnet—depend on the services of TCP. TCP identifies the application that is using it by a port number.
- *User Datagram Protocol (UDP)*—Offers a connectionless service to applications. UDP uses lower overhead than TCP and can tolerate a level of data loss. Network management applications, network file systems, and simple file transport use UDP. Like TCP, UDP identifies applications by port number.

Network Protocols

Network protocols make up the Internet layer, the second layer in the TCP/IP model. This layer provides internetworking for the communications session. An overview of the TCP/IP Internet layer is shown in Figure 10-56.

Figure 10-56 TCP/IP Internet Layer

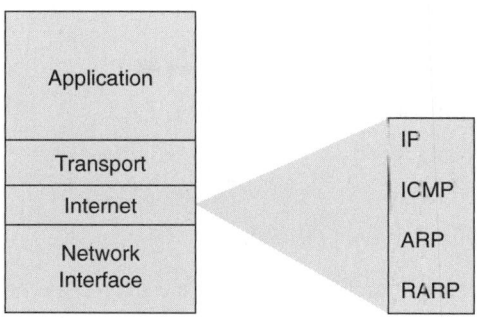

The following protocols are used in the Internet layer:

- *Internet Protocol (IP) address*—Provides source and destination addressing. In conjunction with routing protocols, the IP address provides packet forwarding from one network to another toward a destination.

- *Internet Control Message Protocol (ICMP)*—Used for network testing and troubleshooting, it enables diagnostic and error messages. ICMP echo messages are used by the ping application to test whether a remote device is reachable.

- *Routing Information Protocol (RIP)*—Operates between router devices to discover paths between networks. In an intranet, routers depend on a routing protocol to build and maintain information about how to forward packets toward the destination. RIP chooses routes based on the distance or hop count.

- *Address Resolution Protocol (ARP)*— Maps an IP address to a physical machine address. End stations as well as routers use ARP to discover local addresses.

Internetwork Packet Exchange/Sequenced Packet Exchange

Internetwork Packet Exchange/Sequenced Packet Exchange (IPX/SPX) is the protocol suite that was originally used by Novell Corporation's network operating system, NetWare. IPX/SPX delivers functions similar to those that are included in TCP/IP. To enable desktop client systems to access NetWare services, Novell deployed a set of application, transport, and network protocols. NetWare client/server systems are not tied to particular hardware platforms. However, the native—or original—NetWare protocols remained proprietary. Unlike TCP/IP, the Novell IPX/SPX protocol suite remained the property of one company. Pressure to standardize the way that networks are built has caused IPX/SPX exposure to weaken. In its current releases, Novell supports the TCP/IP suite. However, there remains a large installed base of NetWare networks that continue to use IPX/SPX.

Common examples of the protocol elements that are included in the Novell IPX/SPX protocol suite are as follows:

- Service Advertising Protocol (SAP)
- Novell Routing Information Protocol (Novell RIP)
- Netware Core Protocol (NCP)
- Get Nearest Server (GNS)
- Netware Link Services Protocol (NLSP)

A detailed discussion of the role and functions that are played by these protocol elements in networking and internetworking is not within the scope of this book.

NetBEUI

NetBIOS Extended User Interface (NetBEUI) is a protocol that is used primarily on small Windows NT networks. It was used earlier as the default networking protocol in Windows 3.11, Windows for Workgroups, and LAN Manager. NetBEUI has a small overhead, but it cannot be routed or used by routers to talk to each other on a large network. NetBEUI is a simple protocol that lacks many of the features that enable protocol suites such as TCP/IP to be used on networks of almost any size.

NetBEUI cannot be used to build large networks or to connect several networks. However, it is suitable for small peer-to-peer networks, involving a few computers that are directly connected to each other. NetBEUI can be used in conjunction with another routable protocol such as TCP/IP. This gives the network administrator the advantage of the high performance of NetBEUI within the local network and the capability to communicate beyond the LAN over TCP/IP.

 Worksheet 10.6.5   The OSI Model, TCP/IP, and Protocols

This worksheet is a review of the OSI model, TCP/IP, and the protocols that are covered in this chapter.

AppleTalk

AppleTalk is a protocol suite that is used to network Macintosh computers. It is composed of a comprehensive set of protocols that span the seven layers of the OSI reference model. AppleTalk protocols were designed to run over LocalTalk, which is the Apple LAN physical topology. These protocols are also designed to run over major LAN types, notably Ethernet and Token Ring.

Examples of AppleTalk protocols are as follows:

- AppleTalk Filing Protocol (AFP)
- AppleTalk Data Stream Protocol (ADSP)
- Zone Information Protocol (ZIP)
- AppleTalk Session Protocol (ASP)
- Printer Access Protocol (PAP)

A detailed discussion of these protocol elements is not within the scope of this book.

Like Novell, Apple Computer also developed its own proprietary protocol suite to network Macintosh computers. Also like Novell, a sizeable number of customers still use AppleTalk to interconnect their systems. But just as other companies have transitioned to the use of TCP/IP, Apple now fully supports the public networking protocol standards.

TCP/IP Utilities

TCP/IP utilities are a complex collection of protocols. Most vendors implement the suite to include a variety of utilities for viewing configuration information and troubleshooting problems. In the sections that follow, some common TCP/IP utilities are explored.

This section includes the following topics:

- Packet Internet Groper
- ARP
- RARP
- NSLOOKUP
- Netstat
- Nbtstat
- ipconfig, winipcfg, config, and ifconfig
- tracert, iptrace, and traceroute

Utilities that perform the same function or functions can be given different names by different vendors. How these utilities are used in software troubleshooting is discussed in a later chapter.

Packet Internet Groper

Packet Internet Groper (ping) is a simple but highly useful command-line utility that is included in most implementations of TCP/IP. Ping can be used with either the host name or the IP address to test IP connectivity. Ping works by sending an ICMP echo request to the destination computer. The receiving computer then sends back an ICMP echo reply message.

You can also use ping to find the IP address of a host when the name is known. If **ping apple.com** is typed at the command line, as shown in Figure 10-57, the IP address from which the reply is returned displays.

Figure 10-57 Ping Utility

```
c:\>ping apple.com
Pinging apple.com [17.254.3.183] with 32 bytes of data:
Reply from 17.254.3.183: bytes=32 time=430ms TTL=90
Reply from 17.254.3.183: bytes=32 time=371ms TTL=90
Reply from 17.254.3.183: bytes=32 time=370ms TTL=90
Reply from 17.254.3.183: bytes=32 time=371ms TTL=90

Ping statistics for 17.254.3.183:
    Packets: Sent = 4, Received = 4, Lost = 0 <0% loss.,
Approximate round trip times in milli-seconds:
    Minimum = 370ms, Maximum = 430ms, Average = 385ms
```

Video   Troubleshooting a NIC Using the ping Command

This video demonstrates how to troubleshoot a network connection using the **ping** command.

Lab 10.7.2   Troubleshooting a NIC Using the ping Command

In this lab, you use the **ping** command to test connectivity and problems based on **ping** command results.

ARP

The Address Resolution Protocol (ARP) is the way that networked computers map IP addresses to physical hardware (MAC) addresses that are recognized in a local network. ARP builds and maintains a table called the *ARP cache*, which contains these mappings for the IP address to the MAC address. The ARP cache is the means by which a correlation is maintained between each MAC address and its corresponding IP address. ARP provides the protocol rules for making this correlation and provides address conversion in both directions.

The following switches can be used with the ARP command:

- *-a* – Displays the cache
- *-s* – Adds a permanent IP-to-MAC address mapping
- *-d* – Deletes an entry from the ARP cache

Other switches are included with specific vendor implementations of ARP.

RARP

Machines that do not know their IP addresses use *Reverse Address Resolution Protocol (RARP)*. This protocol obtains IP address information based on the physical or MAC address. A physical machine in a LAN can make a request to learn its IP address. RARP provides the rules to make this request from the gateway server ARP table or cache. A gateway server is a computer or router that is configured to receive information from computers in the local network. Then information is sent to computers in a remote location, such as the Internet, or to other areas in a large internetwork.

NSLOOKUP

Another utility, *NSLOOKUP*, returns the IP address for a given host name. This utility can also do the reverse and find the host name for a specified IP address. For example, entering **cisco.com** at the command prompt would deliver 198.133.219.25, which is the Cisco IP address.

Netstat

It is often useful to view network statistics. The *netstat* command is used in Windows and UNIX/Linux to display TCP/IP connection and protocol information. Novell uses the tcpcon Netware Loadable Module (NLM) to accomplish this.

The **netstat** command provides a list of connections that are currently active, as shown in Figure 10-58. **Netstat** statistics can be useful in troubleshooting TCP/IP connectivity problems. Adding the -s switch to this command shows the information in summary mode. These error reports are especially helpful in diagnosing hardware and routing problems.

Figure 10-58 Netstat Command

```
c:>netstat
Active Connections
   Proto   Local Address      Foreign Address               State
   TCP     DS2000:3301        msgr-ns18.hotmail.com:1863    ESTABLISHED
   TCP     DS2000:3450        constellation.tacteam.net:3389 ESTABLISHED
   TCP     DS2000:3860        ultra1.dallas.net:pop3        TIME_WAIT
   TCP     DS2000:3861        aux153.plano.net:pop3         TIME_WAIT
```

Nbtstat

The Microsoft TCP/IP stacks that are included in Windows operating systems provide the *nbtstat* utility, which displays NetBIOS information. Figure 10-59 shows the syntax and switches that are available with the **nbtstat** command.

> **NOTE**
>
> ARP maps IP addresses to MAC addresses. RARP, the reverse of ARP, maps MAC addresses to IP addresses.

Figure 10-59 Nbtstat Command: Syntax and Switches

```
c:\>nbtstat

Displays protocol statistics and current TCP/IP connections using NBT
(NetBIOS over TCP/IP).
NBTSTAT [ [-a RemoteName] [-A IP address] [-c] [-n]
        [-r] [-R] [-RR] [-s] [-S] [interval] ]
  -a   (adapter status) Lists the remote machine's name table given
its name
  -A   (Adapter status) Lists the remote machine's name table given
its
                        IP address.
  -c   (cache)          Lists NBT's cache of remote [machine] names
and their IP
  addresses
  -n   (names)          Lists local NetBIOS names.
  -r   (resolved)       Lists names resolved by broadcast and via WINS
  -R   (Reload)         Purges and reloads the remote cache name table
  -S   (Sessions)       Lists sessions table with the destination IP
addresses
  -s   (sessions)       Lists sessions table converting destination IP
                        addresses to computer NETBIOS names.
  -RR  (ReleaseRefresh) Sends Name Release packets to WINs and then,
starts Refresh

  RemoteName   Remote host machine name.
  IP address   Dotted decimal representation of the IP address.
  interval     Redisplays selected statistics, pausing interval
               seconds between each display. Press Ctrl+C to stop
               redisplaying statistics.
```

Ipconfig, Winipcfg, Config, and Ifconfig

TCP/IP configuration information can be displayed using different utilities. Depending on the operating system employed, the following utilities are used:

- **ipconfig**—Windows NT and Windows 2000 (command line), as shown in Figure 10-60

Figure 10-60 Ipconfig Utility

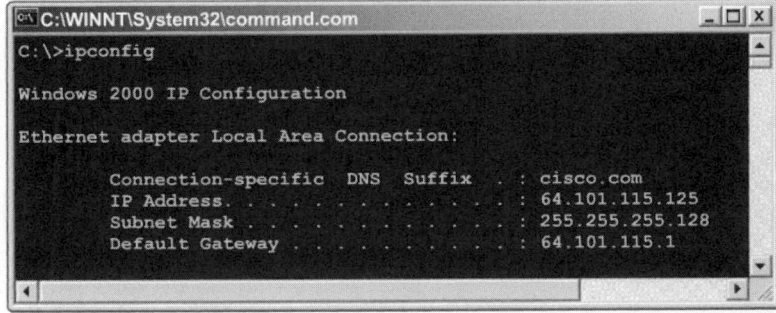

```
C:\WINNT\System32\command.com                                    _ □ ×
C:\>ipconfig

Windows 2000 IP Configuration

Ethernet adapter Local Area Connection:

        Connection-specific  DNS  Suffix  . : cisco.com
        IP Address. . . . . . . . . . . . : 64.101.115.125
        Subnet Mask . . . . . . . . . . . : 255.255.255.128
        Default Gateway . . . . . . . . . : 64.101.115.1
```

- **winipcfg**—Windows 95, 98, and Me (graphical interface), as shown in Figure 10-61

Figure 10-61 Winipcfg Utility

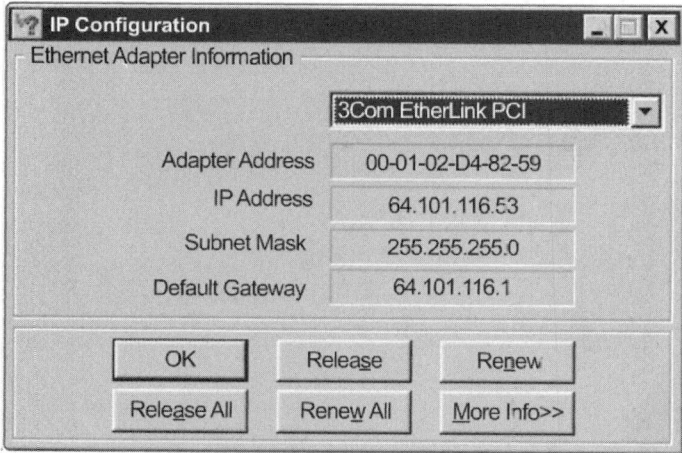

- **config**—NetWare (server console)

Figure 10-62 Novell Config Output

```
File server name: CD7C3103
IPX internal network number: CD7C3103
Server Up Time:   60 Days 1 Hour 1 Minute 17 Seconds

Intel(R) 8255x-based Network Connection
       Version 2.28   November 13, 2000
       Hardware setting: Slot 201, I/O ports 2000h to 201Fh,
                         Memory FD000000h to FD000FFFh,
                         Interrupt 9h
       Node address: 00034742479B
       Frame type: ETHERNET_II
       Board name: CE100B_1_EII
       LAN protocol: IANS Intel Teaming
       LAN protocol: IPX network CD7C3180

Intel(R) 8255x-based Network Connection
       Version 2.28   November 13, 2000
       Hardware setting: Slot 202, I/O ports 2020h to 203Fh,
                         Memory FD001000h to FD001FFFh,
                         Interrupt 9h
       Node address: 00034742479C
       Frame type: ETHERNET_II
       Board name: CE100B_2_EII
       LAN protocol: IANS Intel Teaming

Intel Advanced Network Services
       Version 2.17   June 13, 2000
       Hardware setting:
       Node address: 00034742479B
       Frame type: ETHERNET_II
       Board name: FEC_TEAM_EII
       LAN protocol: ARP
       LAN protocol: IP Addr:205.124.49.3 Mask:255.255.255.0

       LAN protocol: IPX network CD7C3180

Tree Name: GRANITE-SCHOOL-DISTRICT-5
```

- **ifconfig**—UNIX and Linux (command line), as shown in Figure 10-63

Figure 10-63 Linux Ifconfig Output

```
[root@jesselinux root]# ifconfig
eth0      Link encap:Ethernet  HWaddr 00:00:86:48:3E:85
          inet addr:64.101.115.124  Bcast:255.255.255.255
Mask:255.255.255.128
          UP BROADCAST NOTRAILERS RUNNING  MTU:1500  Metric:1
          RX packets:50156 errors:0 dropped:0 overruns:0 frame:0
          TX packets:4687 errors:0 dropped:0 overruns:0 carrier:0
collisions:0
          RX bytes:9440811 (9.0 Mb)  TX bytes:465497 (454.5 Kb)

lo        Link encap:Local Loopback
          inet addr:127.0.0.1  Mask:255.0.0.0
          UP LOOPBACK RUNNING  MTU:16436  Metric:1
          RX packets:62 errors:0 dropped:0 overruns:0 frame:0
          TX packets:62 errors:0 dropped:0 overruns:0 carrier:0
collisions:0
          RX bytes:3604 (3.5 Kb)  TX bytes:3604 (3.5 Kb)

[root@jesselinux root]#
```

The configuration utilities can provide a wealth of information, including the currently used IP address, MAC address, subnet mask, and default gateway. The utilities can show the addresses of DNS and WINS servers, DHCP information, and services enabled. A variety of switches are available, depending on the vendor and specific utility.

Tracert, Iptrace, and Traceroute

Tracing the route that a packet takes on its journey from source computer to destination host is often useful. TCP/IP stacks include a route-tracing utility that enables users to identify the routers through which the message passes. The following options depend on the operating system that is used:

- *tracert*—Windows, as shown in Figure 10-64
- *iptrace*—NetWare NLM
- *traceroute*—UNIX/Linux, as shown in Figure 10-65

Figure 10-64 Tracert Option

```
C:\WINNT\System32\cmd.exe                                          _ □ X

C:\>tracert www.hp.com
Tracing route to www.hp.com [192.6.234.8] over a maximum of 30 hops:
1    <10 ms    <10 ms    <10 ms  phx2-00-gw1.cisco.com [187.101.115.2]
2    31 ms    31 ms     32 ms  sjce-dirty-gw1.cisco.com
[115.107.240.197]
3    31 ms    16 ms     31 ms  barrnet-gw.cisco.com [90.107.239.54]
4    31 ms    31 ms     32 ms  12.127.200.81
5    31 ms    31 ms     31 ms  gbr3-p80.la2ca.ip.att.net
[12.122.2.250]
6    31 ms    47 ms     47 ms  ggr1-p360.la2ca.ip.att.net
[12.123.28.129]
7    31 ms    47 ms     31 ms  lax-brdr-01.inet.qwest.net
[205.171.1.129]
8    31 ms    47 ms     32 ms  lax-core-01.inet.qwest.net
[205.171.19.37]
9    78 ms    109 ms    94 ms  iah-core-01.inet.qwest.net
[205.171.5.161]
10   94 ms    93 ms     94 ms  tpa-core-02.inet.qwest.net
[205.171.5.105]
```

Figure 10-65 Linux Traceroute Output

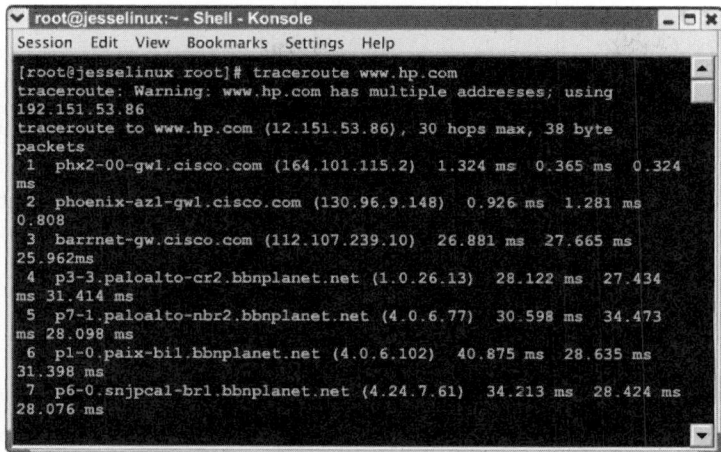

Each of these utilities can trace a packet. The determining factor is the operating system or software environment.

Connecting to the Internet

Different ways are available to connect to the Internet, including dialup, DSL, and cable; each has its advantages and disadvantages. Understanding the different ways of connecting and knowing how signals are transmitted are helpful for the IT technician when troubleshooting. This section includes the following topics:

- Synchronous and asynchronous serial lines
- Modems
- Dial-Up Networking, modem standards, and AT commands
- ISPs and Internet backbone providers
- Digital subscriber lines
- Cable modems
- Cable modems versus DSL Internet technologies
- ISDN connections
- Satellite dishes

Synchronous and Asynchronous Serial Lines

Serial lines that are established over serial cabling connect the standard EIA/TIA-232 communication (COM) ports of the computer. Serial transmission sends data one bit at a time. This was previously illustrated with a car on a one-lane highway. Analog or digital signals depend on changes in the state—that is, modulations—to represent the binary data. To correctly interpret the signals, the receiving network device must know precisely when to measure the signal. Therefore, timing becomes important in networking. In fact, the biggest problem with sending data over serial lines is keeping the transmitted data bit timing coordinated. The following two techniques provide proper timing for serial transfers: synchronous serial transmission and asynchronous serial transmission.

Synchronous Serial Transmission

Synchronous serial transmission data bits are sent together with a synchronizing clock pulse, as shown in Figure 10-66. In this transmission method, a built-in timing mechanism coordinates the clocks of the sending and receiving devices. This is known as *guaranteed state change synchronization.* Guaranteed state change synchronization is the most commonly used type of synchronous transmission method.

Figure 10-66 Synchronous Serial Transmission

Synchronous Transmission

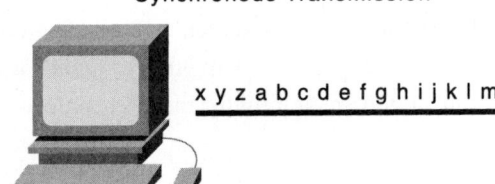

x y z a b c d e f g h i j k l m

Asynchronous Serial Transmission

Asynchronous serial transmission data bits are sent without a synchronizing clock pulse. This transmission method uses a start bit at the beginning of each message. Asynchronous serial transmission is illustrated in Figure 10-67. The spaces between the data indicate the start and stop bits. When the receiving device gets the start bit, it can synchronize its internal clock with the sender clock.

PC serial ports and most analog modems use the asynchronous communication method. Digital modems, also called terminal adapters, and LAN adapters use the synchronous method. The industry standard for the serial line interface is the Electronic Industries Association (EIA) *RS-232C* standard.

Figure 10-67 Asynchronous Serial Transmission

Asynchronous Transmission

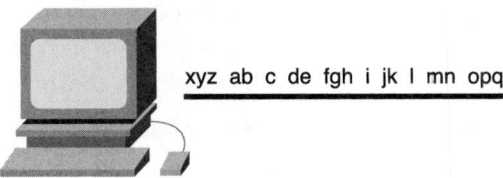

xyz ab c de fgh i jk l mn opq

Asynchronous and Synchronous Devices

PC and modem makers have developed single-chip devices that perform all the functions that are necessary for serial transfers to occur. These devices are called *Universal Asynchronous Receiver/Transmitters (UARTs)*. The synchronous devices are known as *Universal Synchronous/ Asynchronous Receiver/Transmitters (USARTs)* and can handle both synchronous and asynchronous transmissions.

Modems

The *modem* is an electronic device that is used for computer communications through telephone lines. It allows data transfer between one computer and another. The UARTs convert byte-oriented data to serial bit streams. Blocks of data are handled by software. *Internal modems* combine a UART and a modem on-board.

Modems convert digital data to analog signals and analog signals back to digital data. The term *modem* derives from the function of the device. The process of converting analog signals to digital and back again is called modulation/demodulation—modem, for short. Modem-based transmission is remarkably accurate, despite the fact that telephone lines can be noisy because of clicks, static, and other problems.

The following list details the four main types of modems:

- *Expansion card modems*—These modems, as shown in Figure 10-68, are the most common type. They plug into the motherboard expansion slots, either the ISA or PCI slots, and are called *internal modems.*

- *Personal Computer Memory Card International Association (PCMCIA) modems*— These modems, as shown in Figure 10-69, are a variation of modems that are designed for easy installation in notebook computers. Also known as PC card modems, they look like credit cards and are small and portable.

- *External modems*—These modems can be used with any computer. The connection type depends on the type of modem that is used. External dialup modems plug into a serial port, either COM1 or COM2, as shown in Figure 10-70. External modems, such as the Linksys cable modem, shown in Figure 10-71, or DSL modems, are generally connected through a USB port or through the network card on the back of the computer.

- *Built-in modems*—These internal modems are used in some notebook or laptop computers.

Figure 10-68 Typical Expansion Card Modem

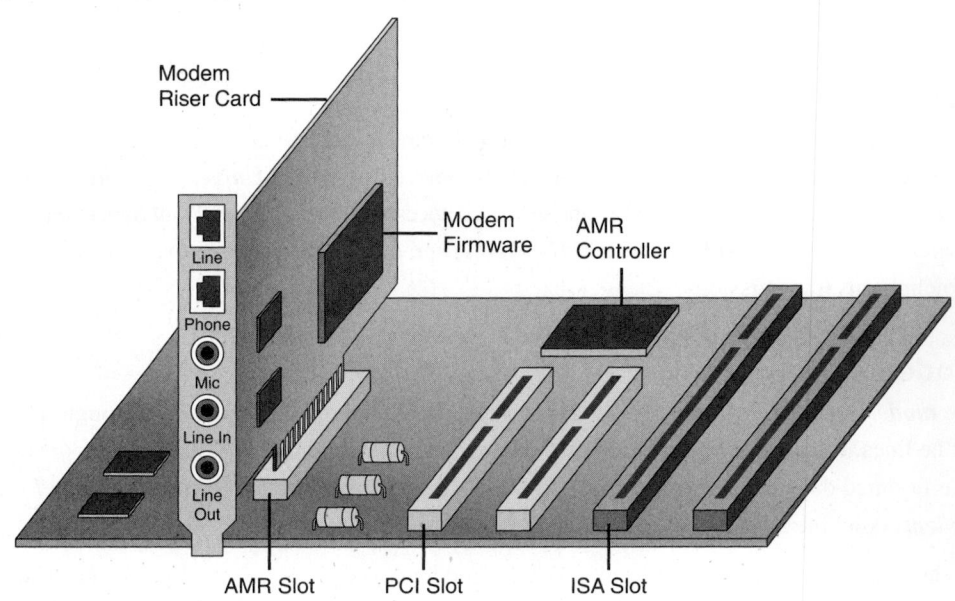

Figure 10-69 PC Card Modem

Figure 10-70 External Dialup Modem

Figure 10-71 Linksys Cable Modem

Internal modems simply plug into one of the expansion slots that are on the motherboard. These internal modem varieties do not take up extra space on the desktop. They usually cost slightly less than the modems that are externally plugged into the computer. To configure internal modems, the IRQ and I/O addresses are selected by setting jumpers. No configuration is needed for a Plug and Play (PnP) modem, which is installed on a motherboard that supports PnP. A modem that uses an available serial (COM) port must be configured. In addition, the software drivers that come with the modem must be installed for the modem to work properly.

External modems are typically a bit more expensive than the internal varieties. Plugging the external units into one of the serial ports connects them to the computer. The computer case does not have to be opened. Newer USB modems are plugged into a USB port or hub. An external modem uses the IRQ and I/O address that is assigned to the serial port. A status light on the modem indicates whether the modem is online. Software must be installed for the external modem to work properly.

In most current modem types, a phone line is plugged into a standard RJ-11 telephone jack. Other modem types and devices, such as cable modems and DSL modems, are discussed later in this chapter.

Dial-Up Networking, Modem Standards, and AT Commands

When computers use the public telephone system or network to communicate, it is called *Dial-Up Networking (DUN)*. Computers connect to the phone network using modems. Modems communicate with each other using audio tone signals. This means that modems can duplicate the dialing characteristics of a telephone. When a computer is running Windows 95 or a later version, DUN establishes the connection with a modem that connects to a LAN or a WAN. DUN creates a Point-to-Point Protocol (PPP) connection between the two computers over a phone line. In this process, PPP causes the modem to act like a network interface card. PPP is the WAN protocol that transports the networking protocol of TCP/IP, IPX/SPX, or Net-BEUI over the telephone line. This allows network activity between the connected PCs.

To enable DUN, the modem must operate in one of the following states:

- *Local command state*—The modem is offline. It receives commands and provides status information to the host computer to which the modem is installed.
- *Online state*—The modem is transferring data between the host machine and a remote computer through the telephone system.

Three activities occur during the local command and online states: dialing, data exchange, and answering. The modem normally shifts between the two states. This happens, for example, when the computer tells the modem to go online and dial out to another unit, or if the modem receives an incoming call.

After the line connection has been established, a "handshaking sequence" takes place between the two modems and the computers. This is a flurry of short events that take place between the two systems. The handshake establishes the readiness of the two modems and their computers to exchange data. Dialup modems send data over the serial telephone line in the form of an analog signal. Analog signals can be drawn as waves because they change gradually and continuously. Recall that digital communications are based on the binary format. In the binary system, the digital signals represent 1s and 0s. These signals must be converted to an analog waveform to travel across telephone lines. The signals are converted back to the digital form—1s and 0s—by the receiving modem so that the receiving computer can understand the data.

The outcome of the handshake and the negotiation between the sending and receiving devices is the establishment of a common modulation that is supported by both computers. This completes the process of a session negotiation so that effective data exchange can occur.

Other devices can determine the speed of data transfer. As previously mentioned, small, single-chip devices can run the COM port to which an external modem is attached. These are the UART chips. The type of UART chip that is used determines the top speed at which the devices can communicate using the port. Current UART 16450 and 16550 chips enable speeds of up to 115,200 bps, and the 16650 chip supports a transmission rate of up to 230,400 bps.

AT Commands

All modems require software to control the communication session. The ***Hayes-compatible command set*** is the set of commands that most modem software uses. These commands are named after the Hayes Microcomputer Products Company, which first defined them. The Hayes command set is based on a group of instructions that always begins with a set of attention characters (AT), followed by the command characters. Because these attention characters are an important part of a Hayes command, the command set is usually referred to as the ***AT command set***.

Simply put, the AT commands are modem control commands. The AT command set issues dial, hangup, reset, and other instructions to the modem. Most modem user's manuals contain a complete listing of the AT command set, as shown in Table 10-6. This table is a summary of the most commonly used AT commands. Note that the standard Hayes-compatible code to dial is ATD*xxxxxxx*.The AT string usually contains no spaces. If a space is inserted, most modems ignore it. The *x*s signify the number dialed. Ten digits are used for a local call (that is, area code + phone number, and 11 digits are used for a long-distance call (that is, 1 + the area code + phone number). A *W* indicates that the modem will wait, for example, when dialing a 9 for an outside line so that a dial tone is established before proceeding. A *T* is sometimes added to signify tone dialing, or a *P* is added to signify pulse dialing.

Table 10-6 Commonly Used Modem (AT) Control Commands

AT Command	Function
AT	Attention code that precedes all modem action commands
ATDP*xxxxxxx*	Dial the phone number, *xxxxxxx*,using pulse dialing
ATDT*xxxxxxx*	Dial the phone number, *xxxxxxx*,using tone dialing
ATA	Answer the phone immediately
ATHO	Hang up the phone immediately
ATZ	Reset the modem to its power-up settings
ATF	Reset modem parameters and settings to the factory defaults
AT+++	Break the signal, change from data mode to command mode
P	Signifies pulse dialing
T	Signifies tone dialing
W	Indicates that the modem will wait

ISPs and Internet Backbone Providers

Services of an Internet service provider (ISP) are required to surf the Internet.

The connection to the Internet is tiered. This means that the ISP can link to a larger regional ISP. This ISP, in turn, might connect to one of a number of nationwide computer centers. Therefore, by just sitting in front of a computer and browsing the Internet, you can benefit from hundreds or even thousands of computers that are networked. This enables access to all kinds of documents, music downloads, and videos from around the world.

When connecting to an ISP, the computer becomes a remote client on the ISP local network. It is amazing how far the Internet has gone toward turning the world into one "global village." At the onset of the Internet era, a local computer or LAN had to have a direct connection to the Internet backbone. This was not affordable for individuals and smaller companies. Now, new technologies have led to easier and cheaper ways of building networks. ISPs now play a critical role in providing Internet access to most homes and businesses. ISPs use the more expensive and complex equipment to establish a point of presence (POP), or access point, on the Internet. These ISPs either lease the dedicated high-speed lines from a telephone company or, in the case of large ISPs, install their own lines. Note that a very small, local ISP might not link directly to the Internet backbone. Instead, the ISP might go through a larger regional ISP that is directly connected. Not all ISPs are created equal.

Internet Infrastructure Example

The current United States Internet infrastructure consists of a commercial backbone and a high-speed service known as the ***Very High-Speed Backbone Network Service (vBNS)***. The vBNS connects five supercomputer networks across the country and is used for scientific research purposes, as described in Table 10-7. The commercial backbone is basically an internetwork of commercially operated networks. In the United States, for example, the following companies provide the commercial backbone:

- Cable and Wireless USA
- Sprint
- AT&T
- BBN Planet

ISPs connect to the commercial networks. Usually the backbone providers and ISPs enter into agreements, called *peering agreements.* These agreements allow the backbone providers and ISPs to carry the network traffic of each other. In the United States, much of the physical cabling is still owned by the Regional Bell Operating Companies (RBOCs). These companies then lease the cabling to the providers. The provider networks connect with T1, T3, OC-3, or E1 lines. T1, T3, and OC-3 lines are used in North America. E1 lines are used in Europe and most other parts of the world.

Table 10-7 vBNS Details

Supercomputer Center	Location
National Partnership for an Advanced Computational Infrastructure (NPACI)	San Diego, California
National Center for Atmospheric Research	Boulder, Colorado
National Center for Supercomputing Applications (NCSA)	Urbana, Illinois
Pittsburgh Supercomputing Center	Pittsburgh, Pennsylvania
Cornell Theory Center	Ithaca, New York

In the United States, an ISP that cannot connect directly to the national backbone is charged a fee to connect to a regional provider. Regional providers are listed in Table 10-8. Regional providers link to the national backbone through a *Network Access Point (NAP)*. A NAP, which provides data switching, is the point at which access providers are interconnected, as shown in Table 10-9. However, not all Internet traffic goes through NAPs. Some ISPs that are in the same geographic area make their own interconnections and peering agreements. A *Metropolitan Area Exchange (MAE)* is the point where ISPs connect to each other and traffic is switched among them. MAE EAST, which is located in the Washington, D.C., area and MAE WEST, located in Silicon Valley, California, are the first-tier MAEs in the United States.

Regional providers are instrumental in allowing small ISPs to connect to the National Internet Backbone.

In other countries or regions of the world where the Internet infrastructure has fully developed, the structural organization is similar to that in the United States. However, for smaller regions or countries that have a smaller or developing infrastructure, there are fewer access layers than in the United States.

Table 10-8 Regional Providers

Provider	Region Covered
NEARNET and NYSERNet	Northeastern part of the United States
BARRNet	North-central California
MIDnet	Central part of the United States
CICnet	Midwestern part of the United States
SURAnet	Southeastern part of the United States
Westnet	Western part of United States

Table 10-9 NAP Details

Location	Operating Company
Washington, D.C.	WorldCom
New York, New York	Sprint
San Francisco, California	Pacific Bell
Chicago, Illinois	Ameritech

Digital Subscriber Lines

Digital subscriber line (DSL) is an always-on technology. This means that the user does not need to dial in each time that she wants to connect to the Internet. DSL is a relatively new technology that is currently being offered by phone companies as an add-on service over existing copper wire or phone lines.

DSL is available in the following varieties:

- *Asymmetric DSL (ADSL)*—Currently the most common implementation. It has speeds that vary from 384 kbps to more than 6 Mbps downstream. The upstream speed is typically lower.

- *High Data Rate DSL (HDSL)*—This type is symmetrical—that is, an equal amount of bandwidth is available in both directions. It carries the same bandwidth as a T1 line in North America or an E1 line in Europe (2,320 kbps).

- *Symmetric DSL (SDSL)*—Provides the same speed with a single pair of copper wires as HDSL, about 2.3 Mbps, for uploads and downloads.

- *Very High Data Rate DSL (VDSL)*—Is capable of bandwidths from 13 Mbps to 52 Mbps.

- *Integrated Services Digital Network (ISDN)*—Sometimes called IDSL, this is DSL service over ISDN lines. It is a set of CCITT/ITU standards for digital transmission over ordinary telephone copper wire as well as over other media, with a top speed of 144 kbps. ISDN is available in areas that do not qualify for other DSL implementations. An ISDN adapter at both ends, user side in place of the modem and service provider, is required. ISDN is generally available in urban areas in the United States and in Europe from the local phone company.

Table 10-10 summarizes the different varieties of DSL. The generic term for DSL, including all its implementations, is *x*DSL.

Table 10-10 DSL Types

DSL Variety	Average Speed	Pros	Cons
ADSL	Downstream speeds of 384 kbps to 6 Mbps; upstream speeds lower.	Most widely implemented DSL variety; relatively inexpensive.	Much lower upstream speed. Installed only within 17,500 feet of a telco central office.
SDSL	Up to 3 Mbps for both upstream and downstream.	Same upstream and downstream data speeds.	Generally more expensive and less widely available than ADSL.
IDSL	144 kbps for both upstream and downstream.	Can be installed in many locations where other DSL varieties are not available because of distance.	Considerably lower speed and more expensive than ADSL.
HDSL	768 Kbps for both upstream and downstream.	Generally faster than IDSL and some implementations of ADSL.	Not widely available.
VDSL	13 Mbps to 52 Mbps for both upstream and downstream.	Extremely high speed for multimedia, such as live audio and video.	Most expensive DSL type; not widely available.

Transfer rates are often broken down into upstream and downstream rates. *Upstream* is the process of transferring data from the end user to the server. *Downstream* is the process of transferring data from the server to the end user. For example, when a user submits his username and password to gain access to e-mail, he is uploading that data, or transferring that data upstream, to the e-mail server. When the contents of the mailbox are displayed on the web browser, that data is downloaded, or transferred downstream, to the computer.

ADSL is currently the most common DSL technology. Its high downstream speed, typically 1.5 Mbps, is a significant benefit. This is because most Internet users spend the majority of their time doing tasks that require a lot of downloading, such as checking e-mail and surfing the web. The lower upload speed is insufficient when hosting a web server or FTP server, both of which involve upload-intensive Internet activities.

ADSL uses a technology called frequency-division multiplexing (FDM) to split bandwidth to create multiple channels. Other DSL implementations use another technique known as echo cancellation, which is more efficient but also more expensive. Either way, this ability to create multiple channels allows a DSL user to surf the Internet while concurrently having a voice conversation over the same phone line. The advantages and disadvantages of cable modems are discussed in the next section.

Cable Modems

A *cable modem* acts like a LAN interface by connecting a computer to the Internet. The cable modem connects a computer to the cable company's network through the same coaxial cabling that feeds cable TV (CATV) signals to a television set. Cable modems are generally designed to provide Internet access only. Analog modems or ISDN adapters allow dialing in to a service provider or a remote-access server. With a cable modem, the cable company must be used.

The cable modem service is also an always-on technology, similar to DSL. A standard cable modem has two connections. One port is connected to the TV wall outlet, and the other is connected to the subscriber's PC. The cable modem can then communicate over the cable network to a device called a Cable Modem Termination System (CMTS). The speed of the cable modem depends on traffic levels and how the overall network is set up. Although the server being contacted is at a remote location, cable modem access is more like a direct LAN connection than remote access. A dialup connection might be required for data upload using the local phone line. This is because the cable company infrastructure is still one-way. In such a case, a phone jack is built into the cable modem.

Cable modems are capable of receiving and processing multimedia content at 30 Mbps. This is hundreds of times faster than a normal telephone connection to the Internet. In reality, subscribers can expect to download information at speeds of 0.5 to 1.5 Mbps, because the bandwidth is shared by a number of other users in the neighborhood. The modem receives digitally altered signals. A demodulator is built into the modem and, if it is a two-way modem, a burst modulator is used to transmit data upstream.

Internal and External Units

Cable modems are available as internal and external units. Most internal cable modems are in the form of PCI cards. An external cable modem is a small box with a coaxial CATV cable connection. A splitter is typically used to divide the signal between the TV and the cable modem. The splitter box is connected to an Ethernet card in the computer through UTP Ethernet cable. External USB devices can also be available to connect the modem to the computer's USB port without requiring an Ethernet card.

No standard currently exists for cable modems in the cable access industry. As a result, many competing proprietary products are found. Cable service, speed, reliability, setup, and configurations can vary significantly from one cable company to another. The most common cable modems are currently made by Cisco Systems, Linksys, 3Com, Com21, Bay Networks, Motorola, RCA, Toshiba, and Terayon. Figure 10-72 shown a Cisco uB900 Series cable modem.

Figure 10-72 Cisco Cable Modem

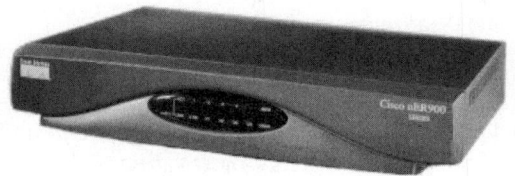

The *Data Over Cable Service Interface Specification (DOCSIS)*, developed by CableLabs, defines the interface standards that regulate cable modems and the supporting equipment. Companies that receive this certification can produce cable modems for retail customers. This allows users to buy a cable modem instead of having to lease one from the cable company. HDTV and web-enabled set-top boxes for regular television are also supported by the standard.

Cable Modems Versus DSL Internet Technologies

When comparing cable modems and DSL Internet technologies, both have their pros and cons. DSL service can be added incrementally in an area. This means that the service provider can start up with a handful of clients and upgrade the bandwidth to coincide with the growth in subscriber numbers. DSL is also backward compatible with analog voice signals and makes good use of the existing local loop. This means that little needs to be done to use the cable service simultaneously with normal phone service. However, DSL suffers from distance limitations. Most DSL service offerings currently require the customer to be within 18,000 feet of the provider's central office (CO) location. In addition, the longer and older loops present problems, and the best form of voice support is still being debated. Also, the upstream, or upload, speed is usually considerably lower than the downstream, or download, speed.

In contrast, cable modem technology presents plenty of relatively inexpensive bandwidth. In fact, the downstream and upstream Internet channels are seen as just another premium TV channel by the system. This is a major advantage, especially when hosting a web server or FTP server, which involve upload-intensive Internet tasks. The use of fiber, specifically hybrid fiber coax (HFC), greatly addresses some of the service shortcomings that are initially encountered with this technology. Unfortunately, the cabling infrastructure that is needed to support cable modem technology has been upgraded slowly. As a result, most homes in the United States cannot use this technology. Upgrading is a big investment, particularly for small providers.

The advantages and disadvantages of these two Internet technologies are summarized in Tables 10-11 and 10-12.

Table 10-11 Advantages and Disadvantages of DSL

Advantages	Disadvantages
Offers speeds up to and exceeding those of T-1 lines, at a fraction of the cost.	Availability is still limited, with service for most varieties only possible for users who live within a specified number of feet from the central office (CO) of the service provider.
Service can be added incrementally as more users subscribe.	The telephone company central office (CO) that is servicing the location must have DSL equipment installed.
Both voice and data can be transmitted over the same line at the same time.	The best form of voice support is still being debated.
Is an always-on technology. This means that users do not need to dial in each time they want to connect to the Internet.	
Is backward compatible with conventional analog phones.	

Table 10-12 Advantages and Disadvantages of Cable Modems

Advantages	Disadvantages
Existing cable TV systems offer plenty of available bandwidth for both upstream and downstream traffic.	Almost always requires an overhaul of the existing cable infrastructure and is expensive for smaller providers.
Cable TV infrastructure upgrade with HFC has addressed many of the existing service bottlenecks.	Being a shared media structure, the more users that are on the network, the less bandwidth that is available for each user.

Worksheet 10.8.7 Connecting to the Internet

This worksheet reviews the information that is provided on Internet connectivity.

ISDN Connections

Connecting to the Internet presents the IT technician with new challenges. Users always want the fastest connection, so the technician must understand how the Internet works and what connection options are available.

ISDN is an alternative to using analog telephones lines to establish a connection. Figure 10-72 illustrates a logical representation of an ISDN connection. Using an ISDN connection has many advantages over using telephones lines. One of these advantages is speed. ISDN uses a pair of 64-kbps digital lines to connect, which provides a total of 128 kbps throughput. This is much better than using a telephone line, which provides a maximum speed of 56 kbps. (Telephone lines rarely exceed 53 kbps because of analog transmission limitations.) Although using ISDN is better than using telephones lines, an even better alternative to ISDN is DSL or cable modem services. Figure 10-73 is an illustration of an ISDN connection.

Figure 10-73 ISDN Connection

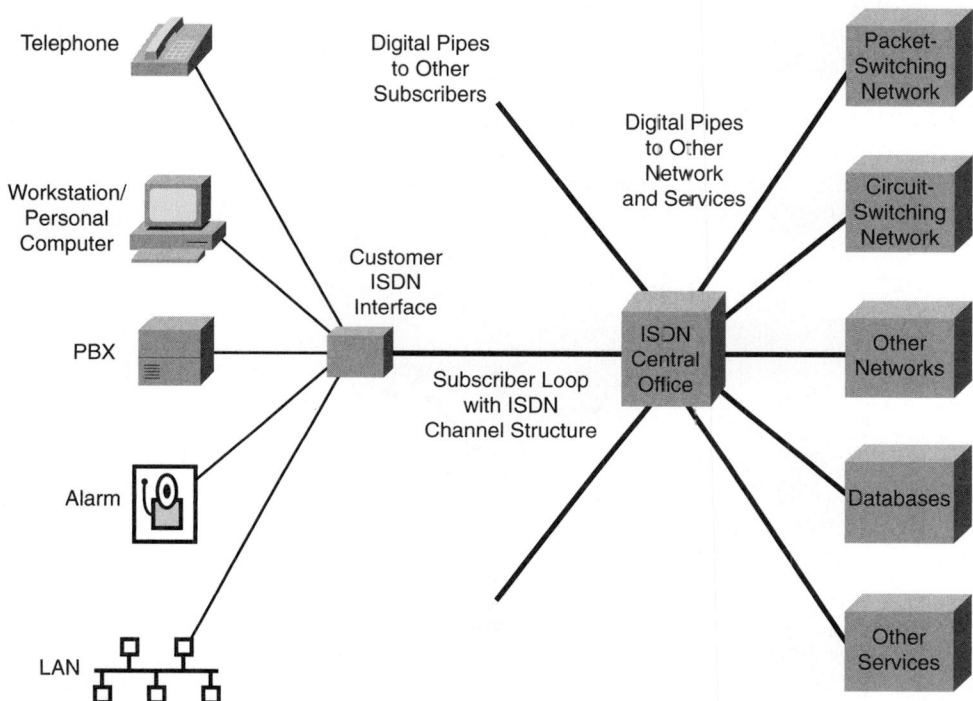

Instead of using a modem to connect to a remote computer, ISDN uses a terminal adapter. A terminal adapter is an external device that acts much like an external modem does. However, you can use an internal device that plugs into one of the PCI slots in the computer. These internal ISDN devices are called *ISDN modems.*

The terminal adapter essentially performs the same role that a modem plays in a PPP connection. Establishing a connection with the terminal adapter is done the same way as with a modem and a PPP connection.

Satellite Dishes

Users in rural areas or those who have no other access to high-speed Internet service might want to consider a satellite dish connection. Figure 10-74 shows a satellite dish. Satellite Internet does not require a phone line or cable. Two-way communication—that is, for upload and download—is achieved with a satellite dish. The download speed is up to 500 kbps, whereas the upload speed is one-tenth of that. A two-way satellite Internet connection consists of the following:

- A round dish
- Two modems—one for uplink and one for downlink
- Coaxial cables between the dish and modems

Figure 10-74 Satellite Dish

Satellite dishes in North America require a clear view to the south, because orbiting satellites are located over the equator. Just like with satellite TV, heavy rains and high winds can affect the Internet signals.

Two-way satellite Internet uses IP multicasting technology. Up to 5,000 channels of communication can be simultaneously served by a single satellite. By sending data in compressed format, IP multicasting can send data from one point to many points, all at the same time. The size of the data and the bandwidth are reduced with compression. The usual dialup, land-based earthbound systems have bandwidth limitations that prevent multicasting of this magnitude.

Summary

This chapter discussed network fundamentals. Some of the important concepts to retain from this chapter include the following:

- A network is a connected system of objects or people. The most common example of a network is the telephone system. A computer network is defined as having two or more devices, such as workstations, printers, or servers. These devices are linked for the purpose of sharing information, resources, or both.

- The three transmission methods that send signals over data channels are simplex, half-duplex, and full-duplex. Full-duplex networking technology increases performance, because data can be sent and received at the same time. DSL, two-way cable modem, and other broadband technologies operate in full-duplex mode.

- A peer-to-peer network is easy to install, and no additional equipment or dedicated administrator is required. Users control their own resources, and this type of network works best with a small number of computers. A client/server network uses a dedicated system that functions as the server. The server responds to requests made by users or clients that are connected to the network.

- A LAN uses a direct connection from one computer to another called a point-to-point link. A LAN is suitable for a small area, such as a home, building, or school. A WAN uses point-to-point or point-to-multipoint serial communications lines to communicate over greater distances.

- A NIC is a device that plugs into a motherboard and provides ports for the network cable connections. The NIC is the computer interface with the LAN. When choosing a NIC, consider the type of network, type of media, and type of system bus. PCI slots should be used with FDDI cards, because an ISA bus cannot handle the required speed.

- The network topology defines the way in which computers, printers, and other devices are connected. Physical topology describes the layout of the wire and devices as well as the paths that are used by data transmissions. Logical topology is the path that signals travel from one point to another. Topologies include bus, star, ring, and mesh.

- Networking media is the means by which signals—or data—are sent from one computer to another. This data sending can be accomplished by using either a cable or a wireless connection. Cable methods include copper, coaxial, twisted-pair, glass, and fiber-optic. Wireless media use electromagnetic waves to transmit data.

- Networking devices connect computers and peripheral devices so that they can communicate. These devices include hubs, bridges, and switches. The type of device that is implemented depends on the type of network.

- Server components are specific to the network server. The peripheral devices, such as the monitor, CD-ROM drive, and floppy drive, are no different from a PC, except a higher level of preventive maintenance is required to keep the server running at peak performance.

- Ethernet architecture is now the most popular type of LAN architecture. Architecture refers to the overall structure of a computer or communication system. It determines the capabilities and limitations of the system. The Ethernet architecture is based on the IEEE 802.3 standard. This standard specifies that a network must implement the CSMA/CD access control method.

- The OSI reference model is an industry-standard framework that divides the functions of networking into seven distinct layers. These layers include application, presentation, session, transport, network, data link, and physical. You should understand the purpose of each layer.

- The TCP/IP suite of protocols has become the dominant standard for internetworking. TCP/IP represents a set of public standards that specify how packets of information are exchanged between computers over one or more networks. The TCP/IP model is made up of four layers that carry out all the functions of the OSI model.

- Synchronous serial transmission occurs when data bits are sent together with a synchronizing clock pulse. In this transmission method, a built-in timing mechanism coordinates the clocks of the sending and receiving devices. This is known as guaranteed state change synchronization. Guaranteed state change synchronization is the most common type of synchronous transmission method.

- Asynchronous serial transmission occurs when data bits are sent without a synchronizing clock pulse. This transmission method uses a start bit at the beginning of each message. When the receiving device gets the start bit, it can synchronize its internal clock with the sender's clock.

- A modem is an electronic device that is used for computer communications through telephone lines. The modem allows data transfer between one computer and another. UARTs convert byte-oriented data to serial bit streams. All modems require software to control the communication session. The set of commands that most modem software uses is known as the Hayes-compatible command set.

In the next chapter, you learn about printers and printing. That chapter discusses buying a printer, connecting and sharing printers, managing print jobs, and dealing with paper problems.

Key Terms

10BASE-T   Transmission speed of 10 Mbps, baseband mode with twisted-pair cabling. It is one of the most popular Ethernet implementations and uses a star topology.

*100BASE-*X   High-speed performance, typically implemented over 2-pair Category 5 or 5e UTP or STP (100BASE-TX) cable, or as Ethernet over 2-strand fiber-optic (100BASE-FX) cable.

1000BASE-T   Primarily a LAN architecture, but it can be used for metropolitan-area networks (MANs) over fiber-optic cable. It supports data transfer rates of 1 Gbps.

Address Resolution Protocol (ARP)   Discovers the local address (MAC address) of a station on the network when the station's IP address is known. End stations as well as routers use ARP to discover local addresses.

> *-a*   Switch used with the ARP command that displays the cache.
>
> *-d*   Switch used with the ARP command that deletes an entry from the ARP cache.
>
> *-s*   Switch used with the ARP command that adds a permanent IP-to-MAC address mapping.

AppleTalk   A protocol suite that networks Macintosh computers. It is composed of a comprehensive set of protocols that span the seven layers of the OSI reference model. AppleTalk protocols were designed to run over the major LAN types, notably Ethernet and Token Ring, as well as Apple's own LAN physical topology, LocalTalk.

application layer   The fourth layer in the TCP/IP model. It is the starting point for communication sessions.

architecture   The overall structure of a computer or communication system.

ARP cache   The means by which a correlation is maintained between each MAC address and its corresponding IP address.

Asymmetric DSL (ADSL)   Currently the most common DSL implementation. Its speeds vary from 384 kbps to more than 6 Mbps downstream. The upstream speed is typically lower.

asynchronous serial transmission   Transmission in which data bits are sent without a synchronizing clock pulse. This transmission method uses a start bit at the beginning of each message. When the receiving device gets the start bit, it can synchronize its internal clock with the sender's clock.

AT command set   Issues dial, hangup, reset, and other instructions to the modem. It is based on the Hayes command set; the AT stands for attention.

Automatic Private IP Addressing (APIPA)   An operating system feature that enables a computer to assign itself an address if it is unable to contact a DHCP server.

bridge   Connects network segments based on intelligent decisions. The bridge compares the destination address to the forwarding table to determine whether to filter, flood, or copy the frame onto another segment.

built-in modem   Used internally in some notebook or laptop computers.

bus topology   Connects all devices on a single cable.

cable modem   Acts like a LAN interface by connecting a computer to the Internet. The cable modem connects a computer to the cable company's network through the same coaxial cabling that feeds cable TV (CATV) signals to a television set.

carrier sense multiple access collision detect (CSMA/CD)   The LAN access method that is used in an Ethernet network. A device checks to see whether the network is quiet (senses the carrier). If it is not, the device waits a random amount of time before retrying. If the network is quiet and two devices access the line at the same time, their signals collide. When the collision is detected, the two devices back off and each waits a random amount of time before retrying.

Category 3   Cable that is primarily used in telephone connections.

Category 5   Cable that contains four pairs of wires, with a maximum data rate of 1 Gbps.

Category 5e   Cable that provides more twists per foot than Category 5 at the same data rate of 1 Gbps.

Category 6   Cable that is enhanced with more twists than Category 5e cable. It contains a plastic divider that separates the pairs of wires to prevent crosstalk.

circuit   The pathway that a data transmission takes.

circuit-switched communications network   Developed for use primarily by the telephone, it provides one physical path that is used for the duration of the transmission.

circuit switching   Basic switching process whereby a circuit between two users is opened on demand and maintained for their exclusive use for the duration of the transmission.

client/server network   A network in which services are located in a dedicated computer that responds to client (or user) requests.

coaxial cable   Copper-cored cable that is surrounded by a heavy shielding.

computer network   Two or more devices—such as workstations, printers, or servers—that are linked for the purpose of sharing information, resources, or both.

Copper Distributed Data Interface (CDDI)   The FDDI technology with copper cabling.

data channel   The "road" over which a signal is sent.

Data Over Cable Service Interface Specification (DOCSIS)   Developed by CableLabs, this specification defines the interface standards that regulate cable modems and the supporting equipment.

default gateway   The route taken so that a computer on one segment can communicate with a computer on another segment.

Dial-Up Networking (DUN)   When computers use the public telephone system or network to communicate.

digital subscriber line (DSL)   An always-on technology that allows users to connect to the Internet.

directories and name services   Allow users to find people and services on a computer network.

Domain Name System (DNS)   Translates computer names into IP addresses.

downstream   The process of transferring data from the server to the end user.

Dynamic Host Configuration Protocol (DHCP)   A software utility that automatically assigns IP addresses in a large network.

electronic mail (e-mail)   The ability for users to communicate over a computer network.

end-to-end   Refers to the temporary pathway that is currently available for a telephone.

Ethernet architecture   Based on the IEEE 802.3 standard, which specifies that a network must implement CSMA/CD.

expansion card modem   The most common type of modem. These modems plug into the motherboard expansion slots (ISA or PCI) and are called internal modems.

extended-star topology   A star topology that is expanded to include additional networking devices.

external modem   A modem that can be used with any computer. These modems plug into a serial port (COM1 or COM2) on the back of the computer. External modems, such as cable modems, are typically used for high-speed connections.

Fast Ethernet   See *100BASE-X*.

FDDI Class A   Computers that are connected to the cables of both rings.

FDDI Class B   Computers that are connected to only one ring.

Fiber Distributed Data Interface (FDDI)   A type of Token Ring network that is used in larger LANs or MANs (metropolitan-area networks).

fiber-optic cable   Conducts modulated light to transmit data.

File Transfer Protocol (FTP)   An application that provides services for file transfer and manipulation.

full-duplex transmission   Data transmission that can go two ways at the same time. An Internet connection using DSL service is an example.

Gigabit Ethernet   See *1000BASE-T*.

half-duplex transmission   Data transmission that can go two ways, but not at the same time. A telephone and two-way radio are examples.

Hayes-compatible command set   Set of AT commands that most modem software uses. This command set is named after the Hayes Microcomputer Products Company, which first defined them.

High Data Rate DSL (HDSL)   Provides a bandwidth of 768 kbps in both directions.

hub   A device that extends an Ethernet wire to allow more devices to communicate with each other.

hybrid topology   Combines more than one type of topology.

Hypertext Markup Language (HTML)   A page-description language.

Hypertext Transfer Protocol (HTTP)   Governs how files are exchanged on the Internet.

information superhighway   The benefit of the Internet to business and private communications.

instant messaging (IM) services   The ability for users to communicate in real time, or without delay, over a computer network.

Integrated Services Digital Network (ISDN)   A set of CCITT/ITU standards for digital transmission over ordinary telephone copper wire as well as over other media, with a top speed of 144 kbps. ISDN is available in areas that do not qualify for other DSL implementations.

internal modem   Plugs into one of the expansion slots on the motherboard. No configuration is needed for a Plug and Play (PnP) modem, which is installed on a motherboard that supports PnP.

International Organization for Standardization (ISO)   Organization that developed the OSI model in the 1980s.

Internet   A worldwide public network of networks that interconnect thousands of smaller networks to form one large "web" of communication.

Internet Control Message Protocol (ICMP)   Used for network testing and troubleshooting, it enables diagnostic and error messages. ICMP echo messages are used by the ping application to determine whether a remote device is reachable.

Internet Protocol (IP)   Provides source and destination addressing and, in conjunction with routing protocols, packet forwarding from one network to another toward a destination.

Internet Protocol (IP) address   A 32-bit binary number that is divided into 4 groups of 8 bits, known as octets.

Internet service provider (ISP)   A private network that enables users to connect to the Internet.

iptrace   NetWare NLM utility that traces the route that a packet takes from the source computer to the destination host.

Internetwork Packet Exchange/Sequenced Packet Exchange (IPX/SPX)   The protocol suite that was originally used by Novell Corporation's Network Operating System, NetWare. It delivers functions similar to those that are included in TCP/IP.

keyboard/video/monitor (KVM) switch   A switch that allows a single keyboard, video display, and mouse to be used with all network servers.

local-area network (LAN)   A communication network that covers a small geographical area and is under the control of a single administrator.

local command state   The modem is offline. It receives commands and provides status information to the host computer to which the modem is installed.

logical topology   The paths that signals travel from one point on a network to another.

Media Access Control (MAC)   The rules for coordinating the use of the medium on a LAN.

medium   The communication channel or cable that enables computers to communicate over a network.

mesh topology   Interconnects devices to provide redundancy and fault tolerance.

Metropolitan Area Exchange (MAE)   The point where ISPs connect to each other and where traffic is switched between them. MAE EAST, located in the Washington, D.C., area and MAE WEST, located in Silicon Valley, California, are the first-tier MAEs in the United States.

modem   An electronic device that is used for computer communications through telephone lines.

name resolution   The process of translating an IP name into an IP address.

nbtstat   Used by Windows to display NetBIOS information.

NetBIOS Extended User Interface (NetBEUI)   A protocol that is used primarily on small Windows NT networks. NetBEUI is a simple protocol that lacks many of the features that enable protocol suites such as TCP/IP to be used on networks of almost any size.

netstat   A command that is used in Windows and UNIX/Linux to display TCP/IP connection and protocol information.

network   A connected system of objects or people.

Network Access Point (NAP)   The point at which access providers are interconnected.

network administration   The task of maintaining and upgrading a private network that is done by network administrators.

network file services   Allow documents to be shared over a network to facilitate the development of a project.

network interface card (NIC)   The computer's interface with the LAN.

network print services   Make printers available to many users.

network protocols   Make up the Internet layer, the second layer in the TCP/IP model.

network topology   The way that computers, printers, and other devices are connected.

networking media   The means (either cable or wireless) by which signals are sent from one computer to another.

NSLOOKUP   Returns the IP address for a given host name. This command can also do the reverse and find the host name for a specified IP address.

octet   A decimal number in the range of 0 to 255 that represents 8 bits.

online state   The state in which the modem is transferring data between the host machine and a remote computer through the telephone system.

Open Systems Interconnection (OSI)   Industry-standard reference model that divides the functions of networking into seven distinct layers.

Packet Internet Groper (ping)   A simple but highly useful command-line utility that is included in most implementations of TCP/IP. Ping can be used with either the host name or the IP address to test IP connectivity.

packet switching   Each packet is then transmitted individually and can even follow different routes to its destination. After all the packets forming a message arrive at the destination, they are recompiled into the original message.

packet-switched communications network   Network in which individual packets of data can take any available route. The route does not have to be dedicated, as in a circuit-switched network.

peer-to-peer network   A network in which computers act as equal partners.

Personal Computer Memory Card International Association-(PCMCIA) modem   A type of modem that is designed for easy installation in notebook computers. Also known as PC cards, these modems look like credit cards and are small and portable.

physical topology   The layout of the devices and media.

ping   See *Packet Internet Gopher.*

plain old telephone service (POTS)   The public telephone system.

point-to-point   A direct connection from one computer to another.

protocol   A controlled sequence of messages that are exchanged between two or more systems to accomplish a given task.

Public Switched Telephone Network (PSTN)   The telephone system that allows people in every corner of the world to communicate with anyone who has access to a telephone. It is the most common example of a network.

redundant NIC   In a network server, it serves as a backup NIC.

Reverse Address Resolution Protocol (RARP)   A protocol that obtains IP address information based on the physical or MAC address.

ring topology   A common topology in Ethernet LANs. This topology connects devices in the shape of a ring. Ring topology can be single, where data travels in one direction, or dual, where data is sent bidirectionally.

router   A networking device that makes smart decisions on how to send data packets.

Routing Information Protocol (RIP)   Operates between router devices to discover paths between networks. In an intranet, routers depend on a routing protocol to build and maintain information about how to forward packets toward the destination. RIP chooses routes based on the distance, or hop count.

RS-232C   The industry standard for serial transmissions between computers and other devices.

server   A repository for files that can be accessed and shared across a network by many users.

shielded twisted-pair (STP)   A pair of wires that form a circuit to transmit data. The wires are wrapped in metallic foil to shield them from noise.

Simple Mail Transport Protocol (SMTP)   Provides messaging services over TCP/IP and supports most Internet e-mail programs.

simplex transmission   A single, one-way data transmission.

star topology   Common in Ethernet LANs, it is made up of a central connection point (for example, a hub) where all cabling segments meet.

subnet mask   The second group of numbers in an IP address.

switch   Also known as a multiport bridge.

Symmetric DSL (SDSL)   Provides the same speed, up to 3 Mbps, for uploads and downloads.

synchronous serial transmission   Transmission in which data bits are sent together with a synchronizing clock pulse. In this transmission method, a built-in timing mechanism coordinates the clocks of the sending and receiving devices.

TCP/IP utilities   Most vendors implement this suite to include a variety of utilities for viewing configuration information and troubleshooting problems.

Telnet   Enables terminal access to local or remote systems.

token   A bit setting in a specialized frame that continuously travels around a circuit.

Token Ring   Based on the token-passing access control method.

topology   Defines the structure of the network. This includes the physical topology, which is the actual layout of the wire or media. It also includes the logical topology, which is how the hosts access the media.

traceroute   UNIX/Linux utility that traces the route that a packet takes from the source computer to the destination host.

tracert   Windows utility that traces the route that a packet takes from the source computer to the destination host.

Transmission Control Protocol (TCP)   The primary Internet protocol for the reliable delivery of data. TCP includes facilities for end-to-end connection establishment and error detection and recovery, and for metering the rate of data flow into the network.

Transmission Control Protocol/Internet Protocol (TCP/IP)   A suite of protocols that has become the dominant standard for internetworking.

transport layer   The third layer in the TCP/IP model. It provides end-to-end management of the communication session.

twisted-pair   A pair of wires that form a circuit to transmit data.

Universal Asynchronous Receiver/Transmitter (UART)   This type of chip determines the top speed at which devices can communicate using a port.

Universal Synchronous/Asynchronous Receiver/Transmitter (USART)   Handles both synchronous and asynchronous transmissions.

unshielded twisted-pair (UTP)   A twisted pair of wires that relies on the cancellation effect to limit signal degradation.

upstream   The process of transferring data from the end user to the server.

User Datagram Protocol (UDP)   Offers a connectionless service to applications. UDP uses lower overhead than TCP and can tolerate a level of data loss.

Very High Data Rate DSL (VDSL)   DSL that is capable of bandwidths from 13 Mbps to 52 Mbps.

Very High-Speed Backbone Network Service (vBNS)   The current U.S. Internet infrastructure that consists of a commercial backbone and a high-speed service.

video controller   Does not need to support high video resolutions on a network server. A video controller that can support 1024×768 resolution and 64,000 colors should be sufficient for most network servers.

video monitor   A monitor that should support 800×600 or better video resolution for a network server.

wide-area network   A communication network that covers a large geographical area.

Check Your Understanding

1. What is the largest network of computers in the world called?

   A. DoD

   B. The World Wide Web

   C. The Internet

   D. Microsoft

2. What is the general shape or layout of a LAN called?

   A. Configuration

   B. Topology

   C. Ethernet

   D. Medium

3. What is the term for three or more computers that share communications?

   A. Operating system

   B. Network

   C. Remote connection

   D. Sharing violation

4. Which of the following is not networking media?

   A. Coaxial cable

   B. Twisted-pair cable

   C. Fiber-optic cable

   D. KVM switch

5. What is used to translate computer names, such as cisco.com, into their corresponding unique IP addresses?

   A. DNS

   B. MAC

   C. DHCP

   D. NAT

6. Which of the following defines the rules for coordinating the use of the medium on a LAN?

   A. DNS

   B. MAC

   C. DHCP

   D. NAT

7. What is the most common and efficient way for computers on a large network to obtain an IP address?

   A. A DHCP server

   B. Through DNS

   C. Manually

   D. Remotely

8. Which of the following is not a basic network architecture?

 A. Extended-star

 B. Ring

 C. Extended-ring

 D. Star

9. What does NIC stand for?

 A. No information current

 B. Network interface card

 C. Network Internet Community

 D. Network Isolation Committee

10. What is an IP address?

 A. A 16-bit binary number

 B. A 32-bit binary number

 C. A 32-bit hexadecimal number

 D. A 16-bit decimal number

11. When using a hub, the network topology changes from a linear bus to what?

 A. It does not change.

 B. Star topology.

 C. Extended-star.

 D. Extended-bus.

12. What is the standard Internet addressing scheme that creates the link between international subnetworks?

 A. Internet address

 B. IP address

 C. Web address

 D. MAC address

13. If you are using a Token Ring network, when does each station transmit?

   A. When no other stations are using the network

   B. Only when that station has been given transmission time

   C. Only when the station processes the token

   D. Only when another station on the network permits

14. What does KVM stand for?

   A. Keyboard/virtual/mouse

   B. Keyboard/video/mouse

   C. Keyboard/video/microprocessor

   D. Keylock/video/mouse

15. Which of the following is a cable with a braided copper shield around it and only a single conductor?

   A. UTP

   B. STP

   C. FDDI

   D. Coax

16. What is a popular Ethernet implementation that uses a star topology, twisted-pair cabling, and a common transmission speed of 10 Mbps?

   A. 100BASE2

   B. 10BASE-X

   C. 10BASE-T

   D. 10BASE-S

17. What do you do if you ping an IP address and cannot get a response?

   A. Use the **tracert** command.

   B. Use the **MSD** command.

   C. Try a different IP address.

   D. Ask the site when it will be running.

18. How many layers make up the OSI reference model?

  A. Six

  B. Seven

  C. Eight

  D. Nine

19. Which layer of the OSI model describes the cable and how it is attached?

  A. Network

  B. Transport

  C. Data link

  D. Physical

20. Which layer of the OSI model is responsible for establishing a unique logical address?

  A. Network

  B. Transport

  C. Data link

  D. Physical

21. Which layer of the OSI model is responsible for the reliable delivery of data?

  A. Presentation

  B. Data link

  C. Session

  D. Transport

22. Which layer of the OSI model translates data into an appropriate transmission format?

  A. Application

  B. Network

  C. Presentation

  D. Data link

23. To access the Internet, which network protocol is required?

  A. TCP/IP*

  B. ISP

  C. IPX/SPX

  D. DNS

24. Which of the following dialup protocols offers the fastest connections?

   A. ISP

   B. PPP

   C. TCP

   D. IP

25. What is required to receive a direct connection to the Internet?

   A. At least two routers between the local network and the Internet

   B. Only a bridge between the local network and the Internet

   C. Only a hub between the local network and the Internet

   D. Only one router between the local network and the Internet

Upon completion of this chapter, you will be able to complete the following tasks:

- Understand the basic types of printers that are used with the PC
- Understand the major components of popular printer types and know how they work
- Understand how different types of printers operate and know the processes that they use to place images on paper
- Understand considerations when buying a printer
- Troubleshoot printer problems and replace defective components
- Install various types of printers on a PC
- Explain the different types of printer connections and their configurations
- Understand appropriate safety measures when servicing printers

Chapter 11

Printers and Sharing

This chapter provides detailed information about printers and sharing printers. You learn how different printers operate, what to consider when purchasing a printer, and how to connect printers to a PC or to a network. Print management, including using the queue and configuring printer options, is covered. In addition, you learn how to troubleshoot basic printer problems such as paper jams.

Understanding Printers and Printing

Most homes and businesses have an ink jet printer, a laser printer, or both. In some situations, a dot matrix printer is used because it can handle continuous forms. Understanding how these printers work can help the IT technician troubleshoot and repair common problems. This section includes the following topics:

- Printer overview
- Understanding dot matrix printer operation
- Understanding ink jet printer operation
- Understanding laser printer operation

Printer Overview

Printers are an important part of modern PC systems. Hard copies of computer and online documents are as important today as they were when the paperless revolution began several years ago. Modern computer technicians must be able to understand the operation of various types of printers to install, maintain, and troubleshoot printer problems.

The most common printers today are electrophotographic-type laser printers and sprayed ink jet printers, as shown in Figure 11-1. Older impact-type dot matrix printers are still used in many offices and homes, but finding replacement parts for these units is becoming difficult.

Figure 11-1 Ink Jet (left) and Laser Printer (right)

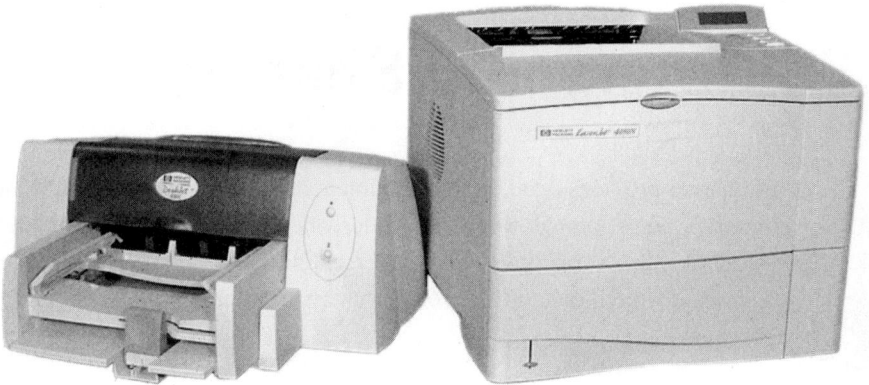

Some industries use thermal printers. This is a nonimpact type of printer that uses heat to transfer images to paper. The printhead contains small resistive heating pins that melt a wax-based ink onto plain paper or burn dots onto paper that is specially coated for the process. The two types of thermal transfer printers are direct thermal and thermal wax transfer.

Direct Thermal Printers

Direct thermal printers do not use ribbons. This printer creates the image by burning dots onto a specially coated paper as the paper passes over the heated printhead. Older fax machines used direct thermal printing.

Thermal Wax Transfer Printers

Thermal wax transfer printers use a thermal transfer ribbon that contains a wax-based ink. Heat is applied to the ribbon by the thermal printhead, which melts the ink onto the paper. A thermal transfer ribbon generally has the following layers:

- The base material
- The heat-melting ink
- The coating on the print side of the base material

The coating and base material help keep ink from adhering to the printhead. Otherwise, poor print quality results. Two types of thermal transfer ribbons are available: monochrome and color.

Dye-Sublimation Printers

Another type of printer used today is the dye-sublimation printer. Instead of using ink, dye-sublimation printers use a transparent film roll with embedded solid dyes. These solid dyes correspond to the following four basic colors that are used in printing:

- Cyan
- Magenta
- Yellow
- Black

As the printhead warms, it passes over the film, causing the dyes to vaporize and permeate the paper. The dyes then turn back to a solid, which leaves the color infused in the paper. Because a special glossy paper is used, the prints look like those from a photo lab. The dye-sublimation process also is used for various heat presses. For example, a reversed image is printed on a dye-sublimation printer and then transferred to a mug or T-shirt using a mug press or flat press.

Printer Connections and Drivers

Printers are connected to PCs with USB ports, FireWire ports, serial ports, parallel ports, network cable connections, or wireless connections. Wireless types of connections include infrared (IR) and radio frequency (RF) technologies.

Printer drivers are software that must be installed on the PC so that the computer can communicate with the printer and coordinate the printing process. Printer drivers vary according to printer type, manufacturer, and model and PC operating system.

The next section discusses how the most popular printers work.

Understanding Dot Matrix Printer Operation

The *dot matrix printer*, shown in Figure 11-2, belongs to a printer class called *impact printers*. In this type, the printhead impacts a printer tape or inked ribbon to form characters on the paper.

In the dot matrix printer, this impact happens as the printhead fires pins or print wires at an ink ribbon, which contacts the paper and leaves a mark. The printhead—the assembly that contains the pins—moves from left to right across the paper, one line at a time. This creates letters out of the circular dots of ink that impact the paper. Many dot matrix printers also print bidirectionally—that is, left to right and right to left; this increases the printer's speed. Coils of wires form electromagnets that are called *solenoids*. The solenoid fires, and the pin impacts the ribbon.

WARNING

The printhead on a dot matrix printer can become hot. Allow it to cool completely before attempting to touch it.

Figure 11-2 Dot Matrix Printer

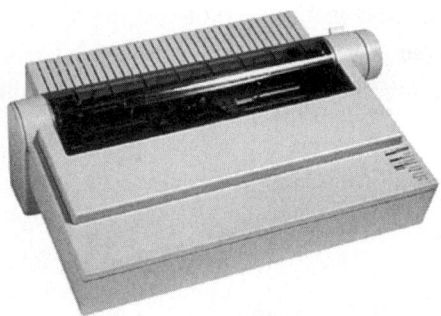

The number of pins in a dot matrix printer indicates the quality of the printer. For example, 9-pin, 24-pin, and 48-pin printers are available. This number indicates how many pins are vertically aligned in the printhead. The highest quality of print that is produced by the dot matrix printer is referred to as *near letter quality (NLQ)*. The speed of the dot matrix printer is measured in characters per second (cps).

Most dot matrix printers use continuous-feed paper. This paper has perforations between each sheet and a perforated strip on each side. These perforations allow the paper feeder to feed the paper and prevent skewing or shifting. Sheet feeders, which print one page at a time, have been added to some higher-quality office printers. A large roller, called the *platen*, applies pressure to keep the paper from slipping. If a multiple-copy paper is used, the platen gap can be adjusted to the thickness of the paper.

Dot matrix printers are currently used in limited situations. These situations include harsh environments, such as manufacturing plants, where other printers would fail, and environments that require the use of multipart forms, such as shipping offices.

Understanding Ink Jet Printer Operation

Color ink jet printers are the most common type of printers in home use today. This is because of their low cost and moderate print quality. Ink jet printers usually print one row of dots in a line at a time. They are typically faster and quieter than dot matrix printers.

The color ink jet printer, as shown in Figure 11-3, uses liquid ink-filled cartridges that force out and spray ink particles at the page through tiny holes called *nozzles*. The ink particles are forced out by applying pressure and heat that is generated by electricity or an electrical charge. Pressure inside the ink cartridge reservoir is less than the ambient pressure. When the electricity is applied, the internal pressure rises. This pressure causes small dots of ink to be forced out through the nozzles. Figure 11-4 shows the components of a typical ink jet printer.

Figure 11-3 HP DeskJet Color Ink Jet Printer

Figure 11-4 Components of an Ink Jet Printer

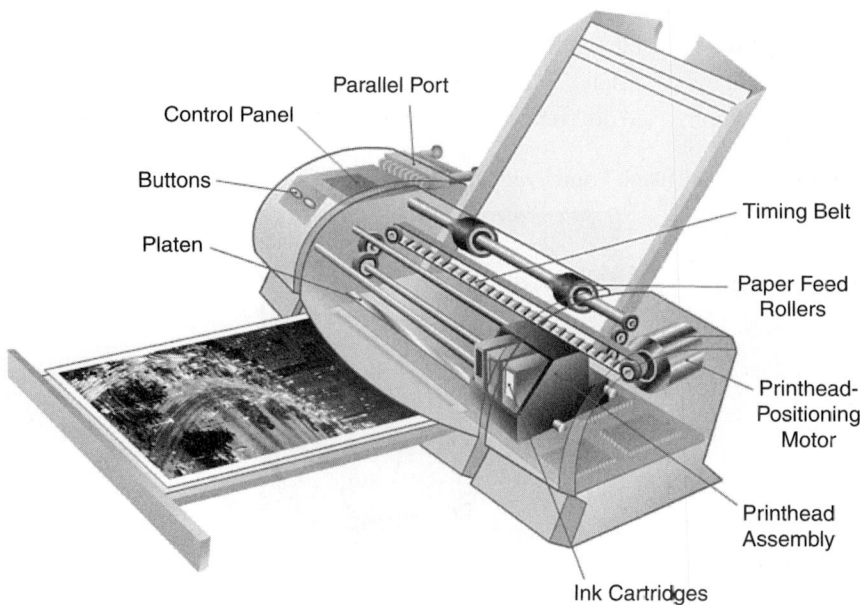

Ink jet printers have two kinds of printheads. One common brand of ink jet printer, called a thermal bubble printer, uses a thermal-shock printhead. This printhead has a heating element that surrounds each nozzle. When an electrical current heats the nozzle, the ink expands. When the ink expands, it is forced out through the nozzle. This is the method that is used by HP ink jet printers.

Another common brand of ink jet printer operates based on electrostatic charges. When the deflection plates are electrically charged, the size and shape of the nozzle changes. This causes the nozzle to act like a pump. This pumping action forces ink through the nozzle to the paper. These printheads are called *piezoelectric* printheads.

Ink jet printers generally use plain paper, but they can also use specific ink jet paper, when high-quality prints or photographs are required.

When the ink jet print operation is complete and the paper leaves the printer, the ink often remains wet. Touching the paper immediately can smear the ink and smudge the printout. Most inks dry in 10–15 seconds.

The quality of print for an ink jet printer is measured in ***dots per inch (dpi)***, and the print speed is measured in ***pages per minute (ppm)***.

Understanding Laser Printer Operation

Today, the ***laser printer*** is the printer most commonly used in business environments for monochrome printing such as text. It provides high resolution, superior operation, and speed. The laser printer uses static electricity and a laser to form images on the paper. However, its internal operation is more complex than other types of printers. Figure 11-5 shows a laser printer that can accommodate different paper sizes and collates for large projects.

Figure 11-5 HP LaserJet 8150dn Printer with Accessories

As with photocopiers, static electricity is used in the operation of a laser printer. This is the same static electricity that causes lightning or causes oppositely charged particles to attract each other. This attraction temporarily attaches small dry-ink particles called *toner* to a statically charged image on an electrophotographic drum. A laser beam draws this image.

Figure 11-6 illustrates the components of a laser printer. The central part of the laser printer is its ***electrophotographic drum***. The drum is a metal cylinder that is coated with a light-sensitive insulating material. When a beam of laser light strikes the drum, the drum becomes a conductor at the point where the light hits it. As the drum rotates, the laser beam draws an electrostatic image on the drum called the *image*. The undeveloped image, or **latent image**, is passed by a supply of dry ink or toner that is attracted to it. The drum turns and brings this image in contact with the paper, which attracts the toner from the drum. The paper is passed through a fuser that is made up of hot rollers, which melt the toner onto the paper.

Figure 11-6 Components of a Laser Printer

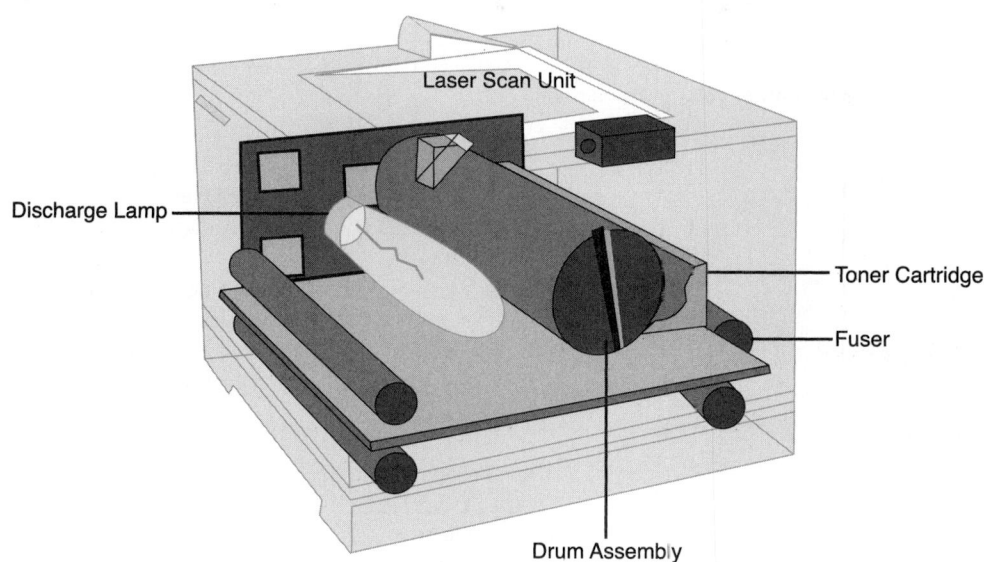

This laser-printing process is completed in six steps. Each of the steps is detailed as follows:

Step 1   *Cleaning* —When an image has been deposited on the paper and the drum has separated from the paper, any remaining toner must be removed from the drum. One method of cleaning uses a blade to scrape all excess toner from the drum. Other printers use an AC voltage on a wire that removes the charge from the drum surface and allows the excess toner to fall away from the drum. The excess toner is stored in a used toner container that can be emptied or discarded.

Step 2   *Conditioning* —This step involves removing the old latent image from the drum and clearing or conditioning the drum for a new latent image. Placing a special wire, grid, or roller that is charged to about –6000 volts DC uniformly across the surface of the drum accomplishes this. This charged wire or grid is referred to as the *primary corona wire.* Some printers provide this charge by using a conditioning roller. The charge that is impressed on the surface of the drum is –600 to –1000 volts DC.

CAUTION

The photosensitive drum is light sensitive and should never be exposed to light for long periods of time.

WARNING

The voltage device that erases the drum is dangerous. It is called the *primary corona wire* or grid, or the conditioning roller. This voltage can be as high as –6000 volts. Only certified technicians should work on the drum to make sure that it is properly discharged.

Step 3   *Writing*—This process involves scanning the photosensitive drum with the laser beam. Every portion of the drum that is exposed to the light has the surface charge reduced to about –100 volts DC. This electrical charge is numerically lower than that on the remainder of the drum. As the drum turns, an invisible latent image is created on the drum. Figure 11-7 illustrates the various voltage transitions that are involved in creating a printed page in the laser printing process.

Figure 11-7 Laser Printing Voltage Transitions

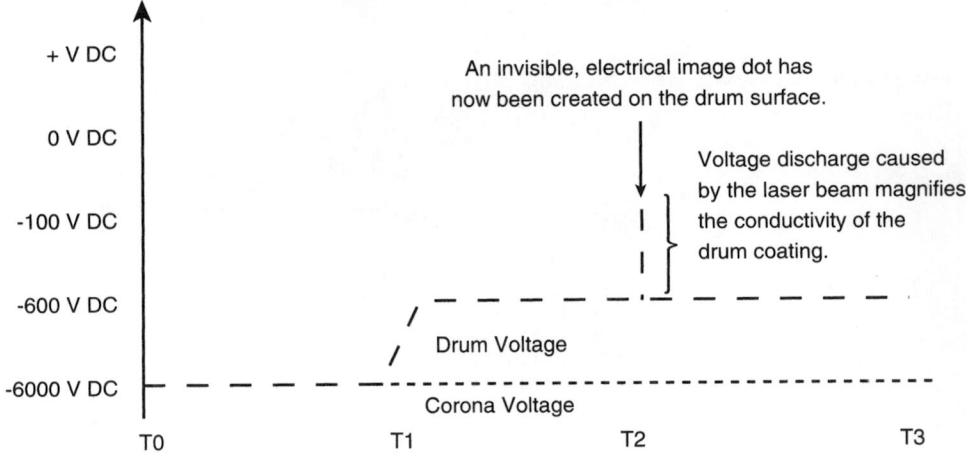

Step 4   *Developing*—This is the step where the toner is applied to the latent image. Inside the toner unit are developer particles made up of magnetic materials. These magnetic particles are coated with a plastic-like material. A triboelectric charge on the developer particles causes it to attract toner. The toner, as a result, is charged to about –200 volts DC. This causes the toner to be attracted to the more positive, or –100 volts DC, areas of the photosensitive drum. However, the toner is repelled by the more negative, or –600 volts DC, areas. Typically, a cylinder within the toner unit releases toner so it can fall against a control blade or developer blade as the developer rollers travel. Also known as the *restricting blade,* the control blade keeps toner from pouring onto the drum. Instead, the blade holds the toner at a microscopic distance away from the drum. The toner then leaps from the control blade to the drum where it is attracted by the more positively charged latent image.

Step 5   *Transferring*—In this step, the toner that is attached to the latent image is transferred to the paper. The transfer or secondary corona places a positive charge on the paper. Because the drum was charged negatively, it attracts the negative toner image from the drum to the paper. The image is now on the paper and is held in place by the positive charge.

Step 6   *Fusing* —The toner particles on the paper are only there because of the charge that is present. The particles are kept permanently in place by the fusing process. In this process, the printing paper is rolled between a heated roller and a pressure roller. As the paper rolls, the top fuser roller is heated to about 350°F, which melts the loose toner powder that is fusing with the fibers in the paper. This operation is called *fixing* by some manufacturers. After the fusing operation is complete, the paper is moved to the output tray as a printed page.

A good way to memorize the order of the laser-printing steps for certification is to use the first letter from each step to create a mnemonic, which is **C**ontinuous **C**are **W**ill **D**elay **T**rouble **F**orever. The steps are shown graphically in Figure 11-8.

Figure 11-8 Six Steps of the Laser-Printing Process

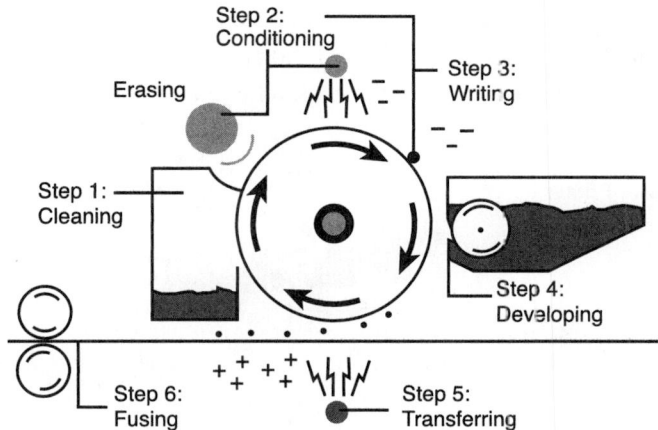

Buying a Printer

When buying a printer, you should consider several important factors. How much printing is to be done and what type of quality is required are a couple of these considerations. Weighing the advantages and disadvantages of both laser printers and ink jet printers can help when deciding which type to buy. This section includes the following topics:

- Print capacity and speed
- Print quality and resolution
- Printer reliability
- Cost of ownership
- Laser versus ink jet printers

Print Capacity and Speed

Printer capacity and speed are important factors in the overall decision of buying a printer. If speed is an important consideration, lower-end ink jet printers are not a good choice. Speed is less important when printers are for home use or small-office environments. Ink jet printers can generally print text at 2 to 6 pages per minute (ppm). Printing a page of graphics can take several minutes. Compare this with color laser printers, which can print at 16 ppm and send out the first page in about 10 seconds. Which printer to buy is usually based on how much speed is needed and how much you can spend on the printer. Having an understanding of the capacity and speed of printers is important in making the right printer selection.

Laser printers can cost from US $150 to US $100,000. Several types of laser printers are used today. A personal laser printer, as shown in Figure 11-9, can print about 8 ppm and is sufficient for home and small-business use. A workgroup printer is typically used in an office environment as part of a network. Here, multiple users send print jobs to a centralized workgroup printer with a print speed of about 24 ppm. A production printer is used when a higher capacity is required. These are the most expensive printers that are used in a commercial copy or publishing environment. They can print up to 700 ppm and operate 24 hours a day, 7 days a week. Production printers require an increased level of maintenance to keep them running efficiently.

Figure 11-9 HP Laser Printer

Print Quality and Resolution

Both ink jet and color laser printers can produce professional-quality photos. However, if you are considering an ink jet printer, it is important to know that all ink jets are not equal. Figure 11-10 shows a color ink jet printer. All ink jet printers are not capable of professional-quality printing. The higher-end ink jet printers generally have better quality, especially when used with high-quality paper. Some ink jet printers are specially designed to produce top-quality photos, but these units tend to print text poorly. The print quality is a factor of the resolution capabilities of the printer; resolution is discussed in the next section.

Figure 11-10 Color Ink Jet Printer

Resolution

Print resolution refers to the number of tiny dots that the printhead is capable of placing per inch when forming an image. For most laser printers on the market today, the standard resolution is 600 dots per inch (dpi). This resolution is sufficient for normal printing, including small desktop publishing jobs. However, the high-end production printer, mentioned in the previous section, can have a resolution of 2400 dpi. Some laser printers still feature a 300-dpi resolution. Note that this resolution can cause jagged lines to appear on the outer edges of an image. Some manufacturers have created a solution for this. For example, the Hewlett-Packard Resolution Enhancement Technology (RET) is designed to correct this problem. RET works by inserting smaller dots at the edges of lines to smooth the rough edges. Although RET does not improve the resolution, the printed document looks better.

Printer resolution is an important factor to consider when buying a printer or when recommending the purchase of a printer. The higher the resolution is, the higher the image quality. Unless photo-quality printing is required, the standard resolution of 600×600 dpi is more than adequate for most printing. Also, check to see whether the printer offers a range of resolutions. If so, the user can choose different resolutions, such as draft mode, for different printing jobs.

Printer Reliability

Some printers are practically designed to have a short life span. Some brands of printers are more reliable than others. In general, it makes better economical sense to spend a bit more originally and have a durable printer. For example, it is more economical to spend US $900 on a printer that can last for 5 years than it is to spend US $250 each year to replace a printer that is worn out or broken. When considering a printer brand, examine the printer's construction. See whether the cartridge is attached to the printhead. Replacing a printhead is much more expensive than just replacing a print cartridge. Try to determine the ease of replacing parts as well as part availability.

Testing the Printer

Never buy a printer without testing it first in the store. Read the printer specifications, and see how the printer measures up to those specifications when it runs. Observe how the printer produces both a page of text and a page of graphics or a photo. Many printers cannot do both well. In addition, observe the print quality with different types of paper. If you are considering a color ink jet printer, pay particular attention to the sharpness of the text and images, as shown in Figure 11-11. Some ink jet printers do a poor job when printing sharp lines.

Figure 11-11 Printer Sharpness Is Important

Cost of Ownership

It is important to check the related costs, such as cartridges, toner, replacement parts, printing paper, and so on. Consider the frequency of replacement and the amount of consumables that are required to run the printer yearly or per business cycle. These issues account for the cost of operating the printer and the Total Cost of Ownership (TCO).

To print true black, most ink jet printers need to have a separate black cartridge. Look for ink jet printers that have separate cartridges for each color. It is cheaper to replace just the color that is needed than to replace an entire cartridge that contains several colors. Note that replacing a color laser toner cartridge is more expensive than replacing an ink jet cartridge, but printing with a color laser typically costs less per page.

Supplies for the ink jet and laser printers are shown in Figure 11-12.

Figure 11-12 Printer Supplies for the Ink Jet Printer and Laser Printer

Laser Versus Ink Jet Printers

A laser printer is different from an ink jet in several ways. Figures 11-13 and 11-14 show a typical laser printer and ink jet printer. In addition to the cost difference when purchasing these printers, the following list details additional considerations:

- The toner or ink in a laser printer is dry. In an ink jet, the ink is wet.
- An ink jet printer is about ten times more expensive to operate, over time, than a laser printer, because ink needs to be replenished more frequently than toner.
- The printed document from an ink jet printer can smear if it is still wet. A laser printed document will not smear.

- An ink jet printer is sufficient if the printing needs are minimal. However, for high-volume printing, a laser printer would be a better choice.
- Consider a monochrome laser printer for large-volume work and an ink jet for small and color jobs to accommodate printing requirements.

Figure 11-13 Laser Printer

Figure 11-14 Ink Jet Printer

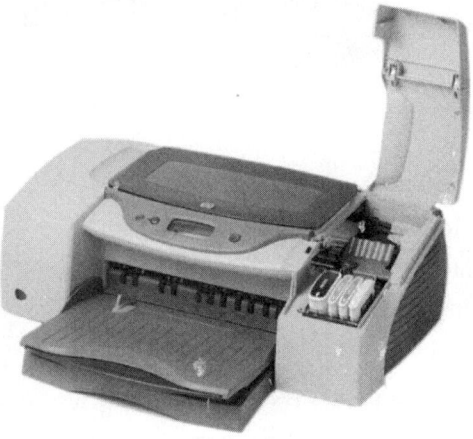

In terms of similarities, both ink jet and laser printers operate quietly and allow fonts to be added by using font cartridges or by installing soft fonts.

Connecting a Printer

Another consideration when purchasing a printer is the communication type. This determines how the printer will be connected to a computer or to the network. You should understand how printers are maintained and upgraded. Once you have installed a printer, you should print a test page. This section includes the following topics:

- Using serial, parallel, SCSI, USB, FireWire, network, and infrared communication types
- Understanding page description languages
- Installing and updating printer drivers
- Installing and replacing ink and toner
- Installing and adjusting print media
- Installing additional printer memory
- Adding a local printer
- Printing a test page

Using Serial, Parallel, SCSI, USB, FireWire, Network, and Infrared Communication Types

Printers require a method of communicating with the computers that they serve. Communication is accomplished through the ports on both the printer and the computer. Communication can also be accomplished by using wireless technologies such as infrared signals. Most printers use serial, parallel, SCSI, and USB ports, with the appropriate network cables, to receive information from computers. Each of these types is described in the sections that follow. A discussion of FireWire, network, and infrared communications is also included.

Serial Ports

Serial ports are usually found on dot matrix printers that do not require high-speed transfers of data. Serial data transfer moves single bits of information in a single cycle. Serial ports are D-shell ports that are categorized as being either male or female and are defined by the number of pins that are available for each port. Common serial cables include those with 9-pin connectors on both ends, 25-pin connectors on both ends, and a combination of the two. The ends of the printer cables are usually secured to the ports on the printer and PC with thumbscrews. The maximum length of serial cable is 50 feet (18 meters). Figure 11-15 shows an RS-232C serial interface cable.

Figure 11-15 RS-232C Serial Interface Cable

Parallel Ports

Printers' ***parallel ports*** use parallel communication. This provides faster data transfer rates than serial printers, because parallel data transfer moves multiple bits of information in a single cycle. Therefore, a wider path is provided for information that is moving to or from the printer. Figure 11-16 compares the data transfer between parallel and serial connections. IEEE 1284 is the current standard for parallel printer cables; this standard specifies a maximum cable length of about 32 feet (10 meters). Other standards, such as Enhanced Parallel Port (EPP) and Enhanced Capabilities Port (ECP), allow bidirectional communication across the parallel cable. A parallel printer cable has two unique ends. Figure 11-17 shows a Type A 25-pin DB-25 connector. The Type A connector is attached to the PC or daisy-chained peripheral and has two screws that are hand-tightened. Figure 11-18 shows a 36-pin Centronics connector. The Centronics connector attaches to the printer and is secured in place with the port clips.

SCSI

Small Computer System Interface (SCSI) is a type of interface that uses parallel communication technology to achieve high data transfer rates. Many types of SCSI interfaces exist. The most common are as follows:

- SCSI 1, or plain SCSI
- SCSI 2, or wide SCSI
- SCSI 3, or fast SCSI

SCSI printers and computers require the proper cabling for the ports. These ports can be DB-50, mini-DB-50, and DB-68. All of these connectors can be either male or female. Figure 11-19 shows the SCSI cable types and connectors.

Figure 11-16 Serial and Parallel Data Transfer Compared

Parallel Connector (25 Pin Male)

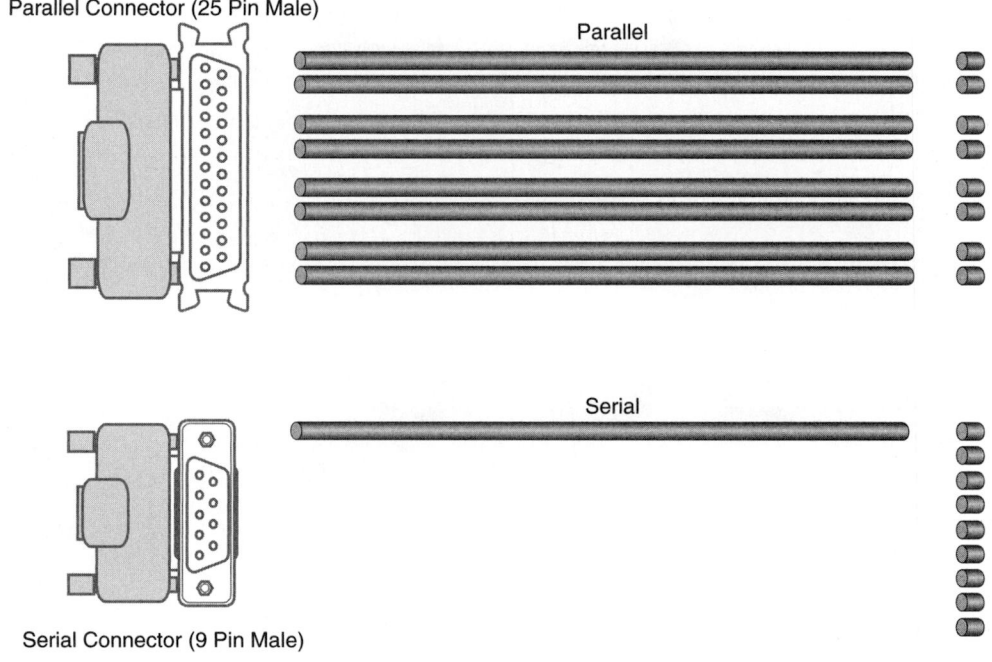

Serial Connector (9 Pin Male)

Figure 11-17 DB-25 Parallel Cable Connector

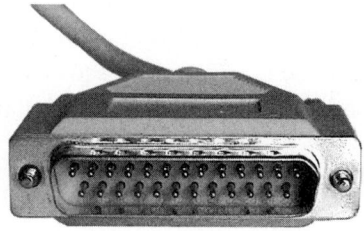

Figure 11-18 Centronics Parallel Cable Connector

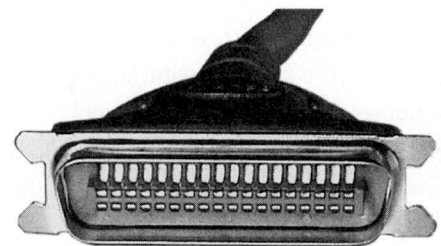

Figure 11-19 SCSI Cable Types and Connectors

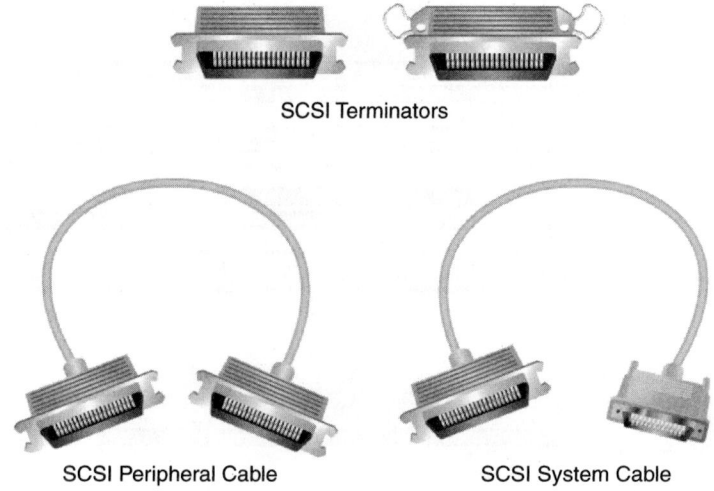

SCSI Terminators

SCSI Peripheral Cable   SCSI System Cable

USB

Universal serial bus (USB) is a common communication type, not only for printers but also for other devices because of its speed and ease of setup. Newer operating systems offer Plug and Play USB support. When a device is added to a computer system through a USB port, it is automatically detected, and the driver installation process begins. A USB cable is a four-wire cable that has two unique ends, as shown in Figure 11-20. The slimmer end is the USB Type A connector that connects to the PC. The wider, square end is the USB Type B connector, which connects to the printer. These ends are keyed so that they can only fit one way into each port.

FireWire

FireWire, also known as i.LINK or IEEE 1394, is a high-speed, platform-independent communication bus that interconnects digital devices such as printers, scanners, cameras, hard drives, and so on. Figure 11-21 shows an example of FireWire. Developed by Apple, FireWire was designed to allow peripherals to seamlessly plug into a computer. It also allows a device, such as printer, to be hot-plugged. FireWire provides a single plug-and-socket connection on which up to 63 devices can be attached, with data transfer speeds of up to 400 Mbps. In the future, IEEE 1394 implementations are planned to replace and consolidate serial and parallel interfaces, such as Centronics parallel, RS-232C, and SCSI interfaces. The first printers to feature FireWire are just reaching the market.

Figure 11-20 USB Cable and Connectors

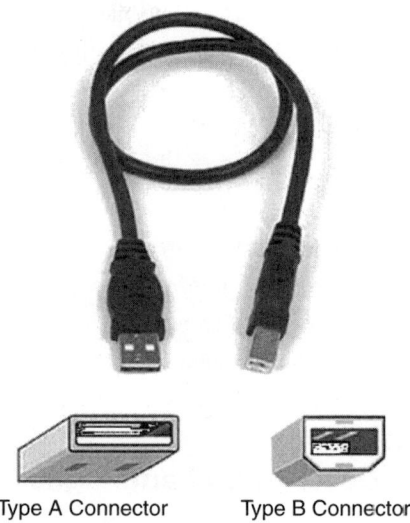

Type A Connector   Type B Connector

Figure 11-21 FireWire Cable and Connectors

Network

Network printers are commonly used in the workplace, because they act as shared resources for all users on the network. Users are not required to have their own printers. These printers have high-speed outputs and offer many options, such as LAN fax, duplex, and finishers.

Connecting a printer to the network requires cabling that is compatible with the existing network. Most network printers ship with an RJ-45 interface for connection into an Ethernet network. Other connection options include Bayonet Neill-Concelman or British Naval Connectors (BNC) and Token Ring ports. The maximum length of a Category 5 cable, used to connect a printer to the network, is 328 feet (100 meters).

Infrared

Current wireless printing technology is built on *infrared* technology, which uses a spectrum of light that is invisible to the human eye. For infrared communication to take place between a printer and a computer, a transmitter and a receiver are required on both devices. When setting up an infrared printer, a clear line of sight must exist between the transmitter and receiver, with a maximum distance of about 3 feet (1 meter) between the devices.

Understanding Page Description Languages

Page Description Language (PDL) is a code that describes the contents of a document in a language that a printer can understand. These contents include text, graphics, and the overall formatting of the document. PDLs are used by software applications to send *What You See Is What You Get (WYSIWYG)* images to the printer so that the printer output mirrors the document as laid out on the screen. PDLs also speed the printing process by sending larger amounts of data to the printer at a time. Finally, PDLs handle fonts that are used by the printer. *Fonts* are sets of formatted text types that can be scaled to various sizes and weights without lowering the quality of the text. Fonts are either raster based, consisting of multiple dots, or vector based, consisting of complicated, outline-oriented fonts. Today, the commonly used PDLs are as follows:

- *Printer Control Language (PCL)* —PCL was developed by Hewlett-Packard (HP) to allow software applications to communicate with HP and HP-compatible laser printers, ink jet printers, and plotters. It is the standard PDL on which many others are based.
- *PostScript (PS)* —PS was developed by Adobe Systems to allow fonts or text types to share the same characteristics on-screen as well as on paper.
- *Interpress* —Interpress was developed by Xerox to handle its line of high-speed laser printers.

Most current printers can understand multiple PDLs, such as PCL and PS, and can use any of the available languages if the proper printer driver is installed.

Installing and Updating Printer Drivers

Printer drivers are software programs that allow the computer and printer to communicate. These programs also provide the user with an interface with which to configure the printer options. Every printer model has a unique driver program. Printer manufacturers frequently update drivers to increase the performance of the printer, add new and improved printer options, and address general compatibility issues. These drivers can be downloaded from the printer manufacturer's website. The process of installing and updating a printer driver is described in the following steps:

Step 1 **Determine the version of the installed printer driver**—All printer manufacturers use version numbers to uniquely identify printer driver software. In general, the higher the version number, the newer the printer driver software. You should know the version of the currently installed printer driver to ensure that you don't replace it with an earlier version.

Step 2 **Determine whether a newer, compatible driver is available**—Visit the printer manufacturer's website. The URL for the site is usually http:// www.*manufacturer_name* .com. If this is not the case, use a search engine to find the manufacturer's site. Because driver updates occur frequently, most websites have a link from the main page directly to the drivers or support page. After you have found the driver page and located a newer version of the printer driver, research the printer driver to ensure that it is compatible with the system. Compatibility issues include the following:

- Required operating system
- System hardware specifications, such as RAM, hard drive space, and so on
- Application
- Communication cabling

Step 3 **Download the driver**—Once you have determined that the driver is compatible with the system, download the printer driver file(s) to your local machine. Be sure to download all necessary files as well as any documentation for installing the newer software. These items should be downloaded and saved in a separate folder on the computer.

Step 4 **Install the downloaded driver**—You can install the downloaded driver either automatically or manually. Most printer drivers are packaged with extra software that, when executed, automatically searches the system for an older driver and replaces that driver with the new one. Manual printer driver installation is accomplished by moving or copying files to certain locations on the computer and letting the operating system know about the changes.

Step 5 **Test the newly installed printer driver**—The final step in updating a printer driver is to test the driver to ensure that it is working correctly. You should run multiple tests to ensure compatibility. These tests should include using applications to print different types of documents, changing and trying out each printer option, and noting any problems that occur. If problems occur once the new driver software is installed, restart the computer and printer and run the tests again. If the problems are still present, contact the printer manufacturer or visit the manufacturer's website to report any bugs.

Installing and Replacing Ink and Toner

Follow the manufacturer's specifications to install the printer ink cartridges, toner units, and ribbons. Some ink jet printers must be powered on before installing ink cartridges. An example of a replacement cartridge for a laser printer is shown in Figure 11-22, and a replacement cartridge for an ink jet printer is shown in Figure 11-23.

Figure 11-22 Laser Printer Cartridge

Figure 11-23 Ink Jet Printer Cartridge

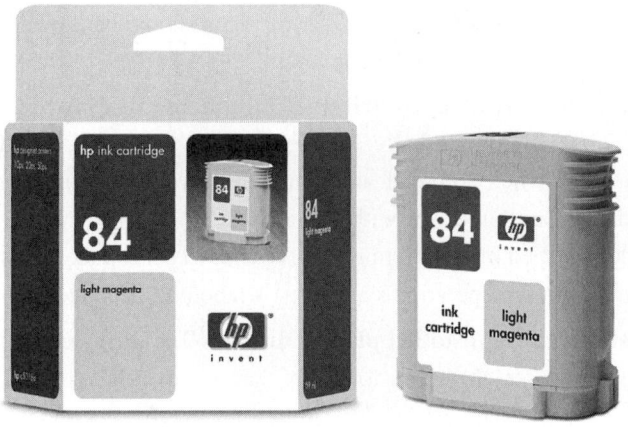

In general, laser and dot matrix printers should not be powered on when installing the toner unit or print ribbon. Always take the following precautions when installing toner units, ink cartridges, or ribbons:

- Laser printer toner units should be shaken vigorously in a side-to-side manner to evenly distribute the toner inside the hopper. If toner spills out of the cartridge, it can be wiped up with a damp cloth.

- Ink jet printer cartridges can be fragile. Be sure to handle them with care, and do not touch the printhead or foil contacts. This could clog the nozzles and cause erratic output. Also, be sure to install the correct color cartridge in the correct slot in the printer.

- Printer ribbons should be handled on the plastic ends only. Never touch the ribbon.

- Check the expiration date. Many manufacturers include an expiration date on their cartridges. After this date, the ink cartridge might work erratically or might not work, even with the remaining ink. Any guarantee is void after this date.

- Ink cartridges, toner units, and ribbons should be recycled according to the environmental recommendations. Manufacturers typically include the packing material in which to return toner units.

Installing and Adjusting Print Media

Print media is the material on which the final output is placed. Traditionally, this media has been paper. However, recent advances in printer technology allow other materials to be printed upon, such as transparency media, slides, card stock, and so on. Before installing any print media, be sure that it meets the specification of the printer. Physical size, weight, texture, and absorbency should all be taken into consideration.

Use the following steps when installing print media:

Step 1   **Adjust the appropriate media tray**—Most printers can handle multiple media types and provide different media trays and feed options. Identify the proper media-handling input tray first. For example, HP ink jet printers require users to place regular, 20-lb bond paper in the lower media tray, whereas heavier stock is single-sheet fed at a different location. Once the tray has been identified, adjust the tray so that the media fit is correct. Most media trays have adjustable guides, as shown in Figure 11-24, that keep the media lined up as it enters the printer. Adjust these guides carefully, because too much slack can cause a misfeed and too much pressure can cause a jam. Also, determine whether the printer has a media-selection lever near the input tray(s). This lever or button sets the height of the rollers that pull the media from the tray.

Figure 11-24 Ink Jet Printer Media Tray and Guide

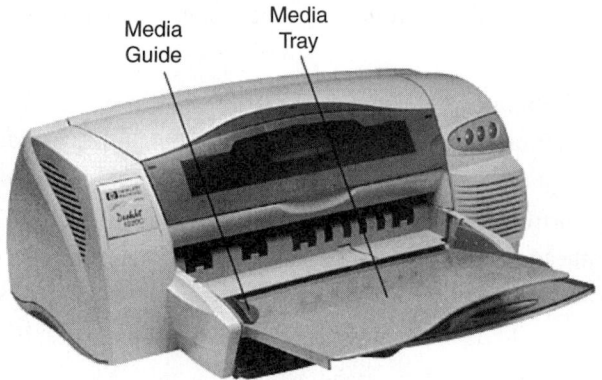

Media
Guide

Media
Tray

Step 2   **Prepare the media**—When using a stack of media, be sure to fan the media to reduce the effect of static electricity. Static electricity can cause multiple sheets to cling to one another, which can cause a printer jam. The print surface of the media must also be properly placed. Most transparencies and many paper types have a special printing surface that is indicated on the media packaging. Failure to print on the correct surface can cause poor output and can harm the printer.

Step 3   **Make other physical adjustments to the printer**—Many printers now have multiple media-output options. For example, printed plain paper can fall into a catch tray, while printed envelopes are held at the end of the output path for the user to retrieve one at a time. If a printer has these capabilities, it usually has a switch with which to select output paths; this can be the same as an input switch. If the printer output is to be placed into an output tray, be sure to adjust the guides on that tray for the intended media.

Step 4   **Configure the printer driver for the proper media**—This is accomplished on the computer using the printer setup option. In print setup, the user can inform the printer of the following specifics of the media:

- Size
- Weight
- Texture
- Absorbency
- Media input tray
- Output path

Bypassing this final step can lead to many printer errors.

Installing Additional Printer Memory

The main method of speeding up a printer and allowing it to handle more complex print jobs is to increase the printer's memory. All printers now have at least a small amount of RAM. Generally, the more memory a printer has, the more efficiently it works, and the requirements for the computer resources, such as CPU cycles and RAM, become smaller. This memory is used for tasks such as job buffering and page creation or drawing.

Print-job buffering is the ability of the printer to capture as much of the print job into its internal memory as possible. This allows the computer to focus on other tasks instead of waiting to send the remaining data in the print job to the printer. Buffering is common on laser printers and plotters as well as on higher-end ink jet and dot matrix printers. *Page creation* is the process of the printer re-creating the entire page of a document before outputting it. This allows the printer to output an entire page at a time while creating the next page to be printed. This is a key component of laser printers, because these pages are drawn onto the drum and then transferred to paper.

The first step in installing additional printer memory is to consult the printer documentation to determine the following:

- **Memory type**—Memory specifications include the physical type of memory, speed, and capacity. Some printer manufacturers use standard types of memory in their printers, as shown in Figure 11-25, whereas others require the use of special or proprietary memory.

Figure 11-25 Dual In-Line Memory Module (DIMM)

- **Memory population and availability**—If a printer has multiple memory upgrade options or slots, you should know how many slots are used and how many are available. This can require opening a compartment on the printer to check the RAM population.

■ **Proper procedures**—Each printer manufacturer has its own set of procedures for memory upgrades. The procedure list can include the steps for physically accessing the memory area of the printer, removing or installing the memory, and initializing the printer, as well as any other software or driver changes that must be made before using the printer.

Adding a Local Printer

Adding a local printer is a relatively easy process. In Windows 2000, choose **Start, Settings, Printers**. Figure 11-26 shows the Printers window. Double-click the **Add Printer** icon. The Add Printer Wizard then launches, as shown in Figure 11-27. The wizard asks whether the printer to be added is local or part of the network. If the printer is directly connected to the computer other than through a network port, choose **Local printer**, as shown in Figure 11-28. Connecting to a network printer is discussed in the next section.

Choose the port to be assigned. Figure 11-29 shows the most common port for local printers, which is LPT1. The printer manufacturer and model type must be provided. Choose the correct model from the list. If the model is not displayed, check the printer's user's guide for help in choosing a model from the same manufacturer with a similar name. For example, if the printer is an HP DeskJet 550 and that model is not listed in the Add Printer Wizard, the closest model would be the HP DeskJet 500.

Figure 11-26 Printers Window

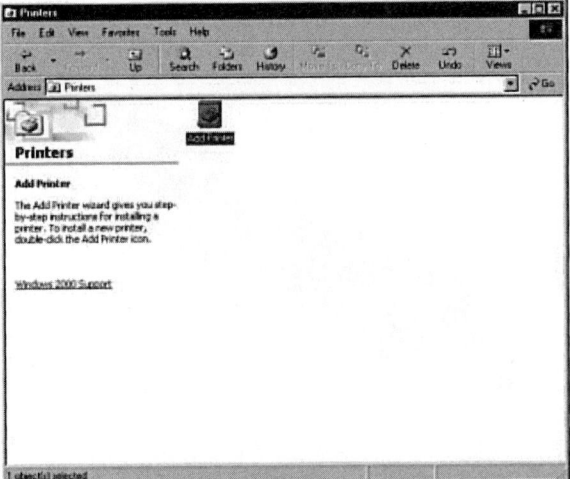

Figure 11-27 Add Printer Wizard

Figure 11-28 Adding a Local Printer

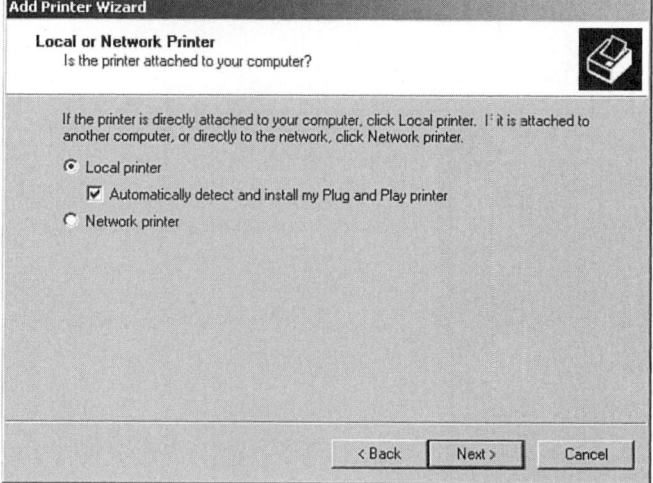

Figure 11-29 Selecting a Printer Port

After a printer is chosen, the wizard notifies you that the printer is now ready to use, as shown in Figure 11-30. This does not mean, however, that the printer and the computer are communicating properly. To verify this, you should print a test page.

Figure 11-30 Completing the Add Printer Wizard

Video   Adding a Printer

The steps to add a network printer to a workstation PC are demonstrated in this video.

Lab 11.3.7   Adding an Ink Jet Printer to a Computer

In this lab, you connect a printer to a PC, install the correct printer driver, and verify the communication by printing a test page.

Printing a Test Page

Printing a test page is the final step when connecting a printer. This ensures that the printer is functioning properly, the driver software is installed and working correctly, and the printer and computer are communicating.

You can print a test page in any of the following ways:

- **Use the Print Test Page option in the Add Printer Wizard**—After adding a new printer to a computer, you are given the option of printing a test page. See Figure 11-31. If you skip this step or make a change and would like to print another test page, you can access this option through the next method.

Figure 11-31 Printing a Test Page

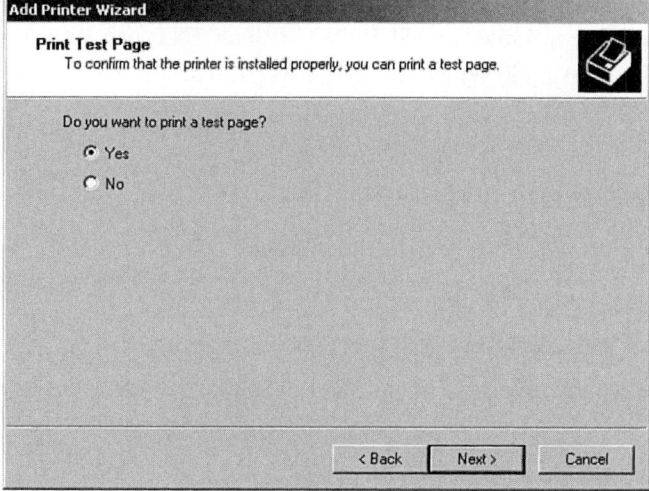

- **Access the Print Test Page option**—In Windows, choose **Start**, **Settings**, and choose the **Printers** folder. Alternatively, double-click to open **My Computer** and then open the **Printers** folder. Right-click the **Printers** icon, and choose **Properties** from the drop-down menu that appears. This opens a dialog box that contains most of the customizable features of that printer. Near the bottom of the General tab, you should find the **Print Test Page** button. Click this button to initiate the printing of a test page. This is followed by another dialog box, which asks you whether the page printed correctly. If it did not, the built-in help files can walk you through the troubleshooting steps.

- **Use an application to print a test page**—All computers have a basic text application installed. In Windows, a good application to use is a text editor such as Notepad or WordPad. Start the text editor by choosing **Start**, **Programs**, **Accessories**, and then select either **Notepad** or **WordPad**. After typing in a few lines of text in the application, choose **File**, **Print**. If the printer is installed and configured correctly, it should print the text that is on the screen. To test the graphics or color capabilities of the printer, start a drawing application, such as Paint, and print a test page. If a file has already been created and saved, in Windows Explorer, right-click the file and select **Print** from the drop-down menu that appears. This causes Windows to open the file in the associated application and print it automatically.

- **Send a file directly to a parallel port printer using the command line**—You can also use command-line statements to send a file directly to the printer. When command-line–oriented operating systems were the only operating systems on computers, this was a common way to test the printer as well as to print documents. Printing from the command line is limited to ASCII files, such as .TXT and .BAT files. To begin a command-line session in Windows, choose **Start**, **Run**. At the command line, type **COMMAND.COM** and click the **OK** button. This opens a shell session. At the command-line prompt, type the following command:

  TYPE THEFILE.TXT > PRN

In this command, each element is described as follows:

- **TYPE:** This command sends the file to an output device.
- **THEFILE.TXT:** This is the ASCII file that is to be printed.
- **>:** This character redirects the file to a specific output device.
- **PRN:** This command sets the printer to be the output device.

If an ASCII file is not available, the current directory can be printed using the following command:

  DIR > PRN

NOTE

The **DIR>PRN** command should be used with caution. The directory might be large, and printing it can use a lot of paper.

Sharing a Printer

You can share a printer in several ways in a network environment. On smaller networks, the printer can be installed on a PC and accessed by other users. In larger networks, a print server handles large volumes of print requests most efficiently. This section includes the following topics:

- Host-based printing technology
- Printer switches
- Built-in printer fonts and font cards
- Configuring printer sharing
- Adding a network printer
- Installing print services
- The network print server
- Printer network interface cards

Host-Based Printing Technology

When a computer sends a document to a printer for output, the information must be translated from the operating system format to the Page Description Language (PDL) of the printer. The PDL then creates a raster or bitmap image of the document, and the printer outputs the image. These language translations and the drawing of the raster image can be time consuming. A method of speeding up print jobs is through the use of host-based printing.

Host-based printing, also known as ***Graphical Device Interface (GDI)*** printing, is Windows technology in which the operating system communicates directly with the printer and sends the printer an image that is ready to print. Because no translations need to be made and because the computer sends the data to the printer at the rate that it is actually printed, the speed of the printing process is significantly improved. Printers that take advantage of host-based printing technology are usually less expensive than traditional PDL-based printers. Because the computer CPU and memory are doing all the work, manufacturers no longer have to place complicated processors or memory buffers in their printers. Therefore, host-based printing technology takes advantage of the power of the computer and the efficiency of the operating system. To increase the performance of the printer, users can upgrade the PC and update the printer driver.

Host-based printing technology has the following drawbacks:

- A printer-specific driver must be installed. Many PDL-based printers can use generic drivers, but GDI printer drivers are printer-specific so that the operating system knows how to communicate with the printer.

■ Host-based printers that are placed on a network require a direct connection to a host and require printer sharing to be configured. This host then becomes a print server, which can limit the role that the computer can perform.

Printer Switches

You often need to have multiple printers available to handle different types of print jobs. Standard monochrome laser printers are fast and can produce clear text output, whereas ink jet printers turn out photo-realistic prints on various media. For the most part, if multiple printers are to be connected to a single host PC and the user needs to connect or disconnect the desired printer on demand, the printers must connect to different ports, such as parallel and USB, multiple USBs, and so on. The alternative is to use a printer switch.

A *printer switch* is a piece of hardware that takes data input from one or more devices and routes it to one or more output devices. Figure 11-32 shows the front and rear views of a printer switch. Also known as A/B switches or data switches, these devices allow a host to access two or more output devices with the flick of a switch. Used primarily in home offices, both manual and automatic versions are available. In addition to printers, output devices can be Zip drives or CD-R drives.

Figure 11-32 Views of a Printer Switch

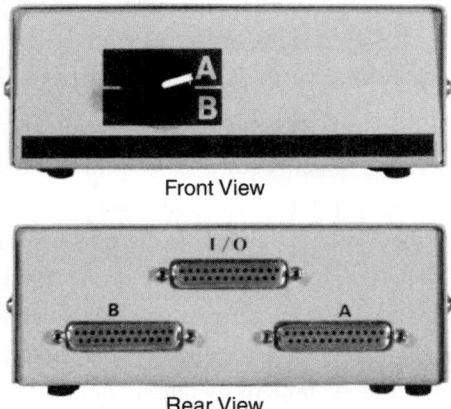

Front View

Rear View

The parallel port is still the standard printer interface port on the PC. Most PCs are assembled with only a single parallel port. Even though you can install and configure a second parallel port, the easiest method of having access to multiple printers on a single host is through the use of a parallel printer switch. The switching device connects to a host parallel port and gives the host access to two user-selectable parallel ports. Some models can have more ports, depending on the model of the switch. The port that the host connects to is labeled "Input" or "Host," and the output ports are usually labeled "A" and "B." Inside the printer switch is mechanical or digital circuitry that performs the switching when the user selects the port that is connected to the desired output device. The user selects the device by turning a knob, flipping a switch, or pressing a button.

A printer switch is simple to set up and use, but follow these rules before installing one:

- A printer switch can only direct output to one device at a time.
- Each printer or other device that is connected to the switch must be installed and configured properly on the host. The correct printer and device drivers are still needed for printer operation.
- The correct printer must be chosen for each print job. Checking to see that the printer switch is set to that printer does this.
- Check the printer manual to ensure that the printer and switch are compatible. Many printers require precise bidirectional signaling from the host, so the printer switch must be able to handle this.
- Electronic, rather than mechanical, switch boxes can be used for laser printers. Because of the way that laser printers work, they do not operate well with mechanical switches.

Built-In Printer Fonts and Font Cards

A *font* is a complete set of characters of a particular typeface that are used for display and printing purposes. These characters include letters, numbers, and other symbols that share a common theme or look. Fonts can be modified by size, weight, and style. Groups of fonts with differing styles are called *font families*. Display fonts are used for screen output, and print fonts are used for hard copy output. Display fonts and print fonts try to match one another as closely as possible to ensure that the user has true WYSIWYG output. When you are using host-based printing technology, virtually any font that can be displayed on the screen can be outputted to the printer. However, using true print fonts can speed the printing process.

Print fonts come in two different varieties: built-in printer fonts and font cards. Both of these are described in the following sections.

Built-In Printer Fonts

With *built-in printer fonts*, also known as *resident fonts*, the character sets are part of the firmware or ROM that includes software that is built into the printer. These are usually common fonts of serif and sans serif types. Upgrading a built-in printer font is limited by the specifications of the printer. Many printers require a firmware change for an upgrade, which can be a costly and difficult task. Other printers allow users to download fonts, also called *soft fonts,* directly to the printer, where the firmware can be flash-upgraded or the fonts can be saved to another part of the printer's memory.

Font Cards

Many printers, especially laser printers, have expansion slots that are similar to those found in personal computers. These slots allow memory upgrades, different printer interfaces, and font upgrades. Font upgrades are accomplished through the use of *font cards*. These are hardware cards that contain firmware that hold other print fonts. Font cards can be purchased with single or multiple font families and are easy to install and configure. Users can also swap font cards for use in particular print jobs. These cards must be purchased for specific printers, because printer expansion slots vary by manufacturer.

Configuring Printer Sharing

Printer sharing allows multiple users or clients to access a printer that is directly connected to a single computer, which is the print server. Sharing resources, like printers, was one of the reasons that networks were developed. Having a group of users share a single printer is far more economical than buying each user a printer.

NOTE

In a mixed operating system environment, compatible printers for each operating system are needed on the print server. In addition, if you have different printers, the drivers for each printer must be placed on the server.

For print sharing to work, special software must be installed and configured on the print server. Then the clients must be configured to access the printer that is located on the print server. Although third-party software applications are available, most personal computer operating systems have built-in printer-sharing capability.

In Windows, this option is called File and Print Sharing. Although Windows 2000 installs this component automatically, you can easily add it to the other Windows operating systems. To install File and Print Sharing or to verify that it is installed on a Windows 9*x* computer, right-click **My Network Places** in Windows Me or **Network Neighborhood** in Windows 95/98, and choose **Properties** from the drop-down menu that appears. The window that is shown in Figure 11-33 is displayed. You can determine whether File and printer sharing for Microsoft Networks is installed. If it is not installed, click the File and Print Sharing button and select the **I want to be able to give others access to my files** option, the **I want to be able to allow others to print my from printer(s)** option, or both. Remember: The printer must be installed and configured on the print server before printer sharing can work.

After verifying that the printer-sharing software is installed, the server must know which printers it is going to share. In the Printers folder, right-click the printer to share, choose **Properties** from the drop-down menu that appears, and select the **Sharing** tab. Choose the option to share the printer, and assign it a unique name.

Figure 11-33 Network Window Showing the Configuration Tab Selected

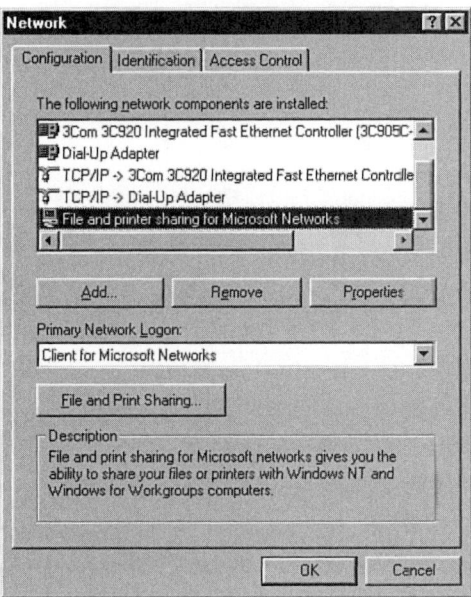

Finally, each client computer that is to access the printer must have the correct printer drivers installed. Use the Add Printer Wizard to find and install the shared printer. If configured properly, the client will automatically download the driver information from the server.

Video   Setting Up Print Sharing Capabilities

This video demonstrates the steps that are required to enable printer sharing over a network.

Lab 11.4.4   Setting Up Printer-Sharing Capabilities

Upon completion of this lab, you will be able to verify communication between the server and the client, set up the print server, configure the client, and test the client's print capability.

Adding a Network Printer

Two basic types of computer networks exist: peer-to-peer and client/server. Peer-to-peer networks are small computer networks in which each computer has an equal responsibility.

Client/server networks can be of various sizes and are made up of client computers and servers. Clients are workstations that request the services of servers, such as application information, e-mail, web pages, and printer services. A client/server network with a printer is illustrated in Figure 11-34.

Figure 11-34 Client/Server Network Printer

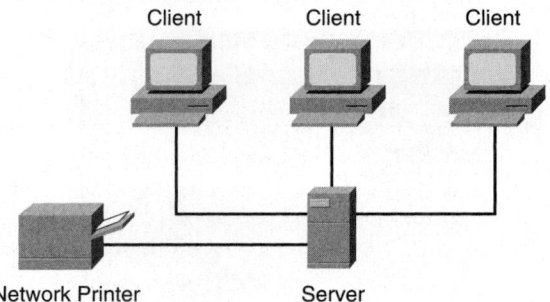

A *network printer* is attached directly to the network, as are the client workstations. The network server manages all requests by the workstations to use the printer.

Configuring a printer to print over a network involves a method that is similar to accessing a server resource or drive on the network. You cannot simply connect a printer to a print server to allow printing over the network. The network operating system has utilities that allow network printing to be set up and managed.

The following steps are involved in network printing:

Step 1 The application formats the document to be printed into data that the printer can understand and sends out the data.

Step 2 The redirector in the computer sends the data out on the network, and the data then travels to the print server.

Step 3 The print spooler in the software on the print server places the data in a print queue, which are print jobs waiting to be processed. A print spooler is a collection of dynamic link libraries (DLLs) that acquire, process, catalog, and dispense print jobs to the printer.

Step 4 The print data is held in the print queue until the printer is ready to print it.

Installing Print Services

Depending on the network operating system used, the procedure for installing print services can vary. However, some basic procedures that are common to most networks are as follows:

- Printer drivers must be installed to allow the printer to communicate with the print server.

- A printer name must be assigned so that users on the network can find and share the printer.

- The output destination information must be supplied so that the print director knows where to send the print job.

- Setting information and output format details must be identified so that the network can know how to process the print job.

Most network operating systems have their own utilities to set up printers with the previously listed information. This is called the Print Manager in most Windows operating systems.

The Network Print Server

A network print server is a computer that is dedicated to handling client print jobs in the most efficient manner. Because it handles requests from multiple clients, a print server is usually one of the most powerful computers on the network. A print server should have the following components:

- **A powerful processor**—Because the print server uses its processor to manage and route printing information, it needs to be fast enough to handle all incoming requests.

- **Adequate hard disk space**—A print server captures print jobs from clients, places them in a print queue, and feeds them to the printer in a timely way. This requires the computer to have enough storage space to hold these jobs until they are completed.

- **Adequate memory**—The server processor and RAM handle feeding print jobs to a printer. If a server's memory is not large enough to handle an entire print job, the job must be fed from the hard drive, which is much slower.

The server needs to be reliable. It must be available at all times to all users, and this requires a reliable connection to the network.

The print server has two purposes. The first is to provide client access to print resources. The second is to provide feedback to the users. When using printers that connect directly to the network, the print server routes print jobs to the proper printer, as shown in Figure 11-35. With host-based printing technology, the print server acts as the interpreter between the client and the printer to which it is directly connected. This is illustrated in Figure 11-36. If configured properly, the print server can also send clients the printer driver software that is needed to access the printer.

Figure 11-35 Printers That Connect Directly to the Network

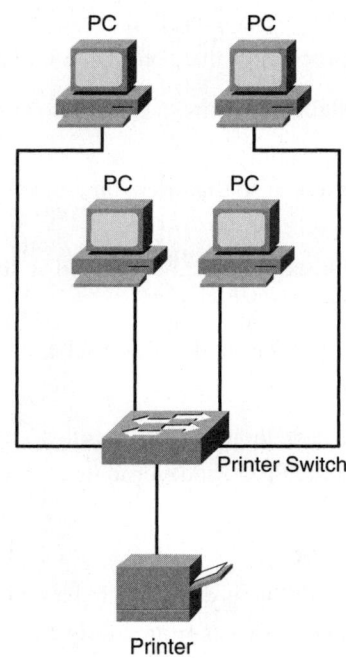

Figure 11-36 Print Server

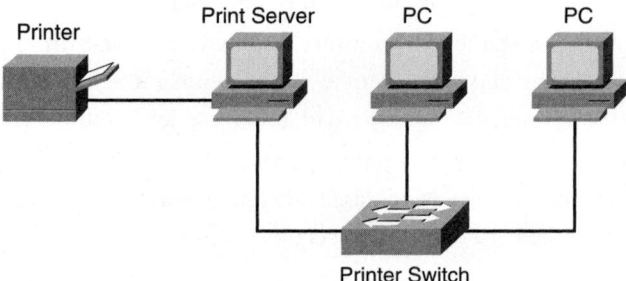

Because print servers manage print jobs through a print queue, they can also provide feedback about the printers to the users on the network. This feedback can include a confirmation message that a print job has been completed, an estimated time of print-job completion, and any errors that might have been encountered in the printing process. These errors can include printer out of paper, out of toner or ink, wrong paper type, paper jam, and so on. Figure 11-37 shows a confirmation message from a print server, indicating that a print job has been completed.

Figure 11-37 Printing Completion Message

Printer Network Interface Cards

For a printer to connect directly to a computer network, it must have the proper type of port for network connection. A *printer network interface card (NIC)* is an adapter that the printer uses to access the network media. This NIC can be built into the printer or can be in the form of an expansion card. Currently, the most commonly used printer NICs have RJ-45 ports to connect to copper-cable–based Ethernet networks, as shown in Figure 11-38. Category 5 cable is typically used to connect the printer NIC to a network hub or switch. Other printer NIC types include the following:

- BNC
- RJ-11, which is 4-wire telephone cable
- Wireless, which uses infrared or radio frequency waves

Figure 11-38 Printer NIC

Managing a Printer

The network administrator is typically responsible for managing the printers in a network environment. This includes accessing the printer queue and configuring options. This section includes the following topics:

- Using the printer queue to manage print jobs
- Setting print times for large or less important documents
- Selecting a default printer
- Configuring individual printer options
- Using printer accessories

Using the Printer Queue to Manage Print Jobs

The purpose of sharing a printer or using a network printer is to make the printer available for multiple users. However, printers can only process a single print job at a time. When a print job is sent to a printer while it is busy, that print job is held in the printer queue, as shown in Figure 11-39.

Figure 11-39 Windows Printer Queue

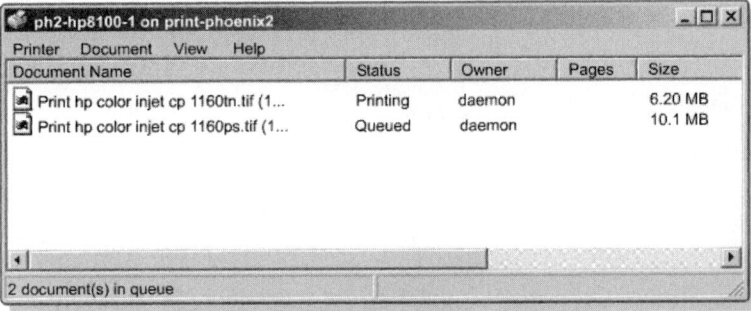

A *printer queue* is a temporary holding area for print jobs. The jobs in the queue are fed to the printer when it is ready for the next job. This queue is an area of memory that is set aside on the print server for managing print jobs. When a user decides to print a document, it is immediately sent to the printer queue. If no other jobs are in the queue, the job is processed at once. Printer queues, by default, use the first in, first out (FIFO) rule. This rule means that the print job that reaches the queue first receives the highest priority and is output before all other jobs.

The printer queue is also a management tool that can be used to view and manipulate print jobs. The queue can show information about each print job and the progress of the job as it is being fed to the printer. This information includes the user identification, job start time, and current status of the print job. Some print job manipulation tasks that can be performed in the printer queue are as follows:

- **Deleting print jobs**—The printer queue can be used to delete single, multiple, or all the print jobs that are currently being held in the queue. This is useful if an error occurs or if multiple copies of a document are accidentally sent to the printer.

- **Rearranging print jobs**—Even though the printer queue uses FIFO, the order in which jobs are processed can be changed. Higher-priority print jobs can be placed closer to the top of the queue, whereas low-priority jobs can be taken to the bottom of the list.

- **Pausing the printer**—Sometimes it is beneficial to temporarily pause the printing process. Choosing to pause printing puts the queue in a "wait state." During this pause time, changes such as deletions or rearrangements can be made within the queue. Then, operations can be made on the printer, such as changing media type, ink, or toner. The printer queue is taken out of pause mode to resume processing the print jobs.

The task of managing the printer queue must be restricted to a few individuals, such as the network administrator and print server administrator. The network administrator can then determine the priority of users and print jobs. For example, the network administrator can prioritize all print jobs from the president and vice presidents of the company or from the accounting department. If every user were given access to the printer queue, each user might attempt to have his job printed first.

Setting Print Times for Large or Less Important Documents

In busy, high-print-volume environments, where multiple users share access to printers, a large print job can tie up a printer for a significant amount of time. This can, in effect, reduce the efficiency of those requiring the services of the printer. In these situations, it is beneficial to set print times for large or less important documents. If a document is not needed immediately, it can be set to print after business hours or during a lunch break.

Selecting a Default Printer

The *default printer* is the printer to which all print jobs are sent if another printer is not selected. With simple applications like Notepad, selecting the option to print sends the document to the default printer. Other applications allow the user to choose any of the installed printers, but these applications list the default printer as the first option. Any computer with a printer installed has a default printer. If a single printer is installed, it becomes the default printer. As other printers are installed, the user must decide which printer to assign as the default printer.

Choosing or changing a computer's default printer can be done in the following ways:

■ **Designating during printer installation**—Each time a printer is installed on a computer, the user is given the opportunity to designate that printer as the default printer.

■ **Selecting manually**—Opening the Printers folder in Windows allows the user to see icons that represent all installed printers. A list of installed printer icons can be viewed by choosing **Start**, **Settings**, **Printers** or by opening the Control Panel from the Windows 9*x* Desktop. The current default printer has a small check mark in a dark circle on its icon, as shown in Figure 11-40. Designating a new default printer can be done by right-clicking that printer's icon and choosing **Set as Default** from the drop-down menu that appears. Figure 11-41 shows setting the default printer option.

■ **Using the printer queue**—When viewing the queue of a particular printer, that printer can be designated as the default printer by choosing **Printer**, **Set as Default**.

Figure 11-40 Windows Default Printer

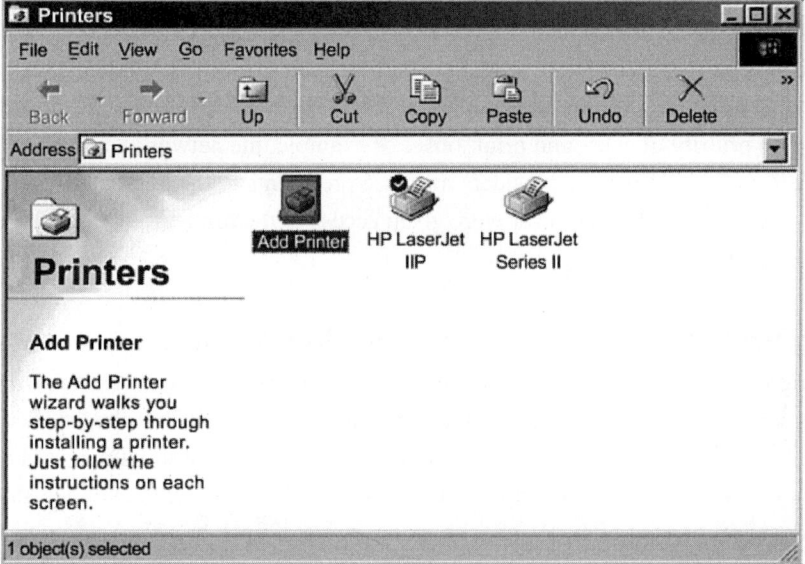

Configuring Individual Printer Options

Each model of printer can have its own set of user-selectable options. The two main categories of printer options are media handling and printer output.

Figure 11-41 Setting the Default Printer

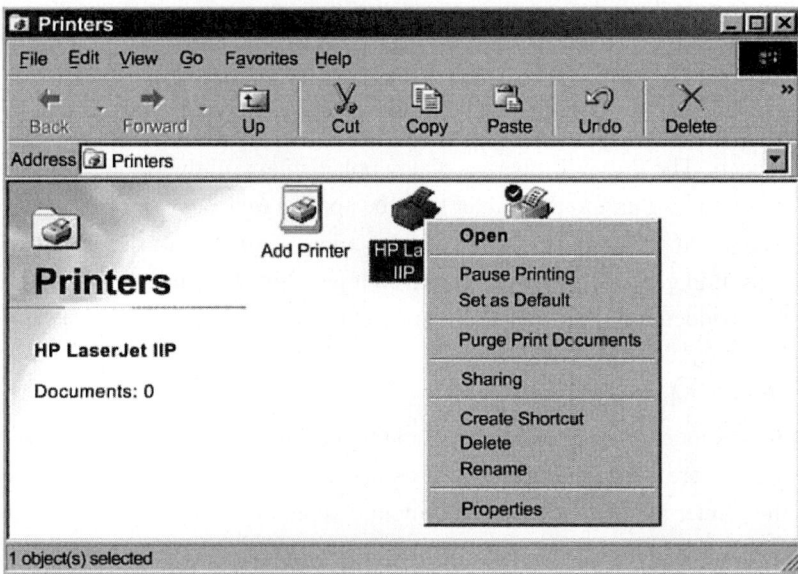

In general, ***media-handling options*** set the way that a printer handles the media and can include the following:

- Input paper tray selection
- Output path selection
- Media size and orientation
- Paper weight selection

Printer-output options deal with how the ink or toner is placed on the media and include these common options:

- Color management
- Print quality
- Print speed

Although some printer options can be selected through physical switches that are located on the printer, most printer options are now configured through the printer driver. Two methods of selecting individual printer options are global and per-document. They are described in the following sections.

Global Method

The global method refers to printer options that are set for all documents. Each time a document is printed, the *global print options* are used, unless they are overridden by per-document selections. Global printer configuration changes are made by choosing **Start**, **Settings**, **Printers**. Right-click the individual printer, and choose **Properties** from the drop-down menu that appears. The Printer Properties dialog box displays all the printer options. At this point, configuration changes to the printer must be applied to become the default printer settings. For example, if a user prefers not to use the color capabilities of the ink jet printer, she can select to print in grayscale (black) only. Even though these settings become the defaults, they can be overridden using the per-document method of configuring printer options.

Per-Document Method

Most modern computer users print many different types of documents. Letters, spreadsheets, and digital images are common document types that can require different settings to be configured on the printer before output. Most computer applications allow the user to override any globally selected printer options through the use of *per-document printer settings*. Within the application that creates the document, a user can select **File**, **Print** to access printer options. The default settings appear but can be changed for the specific document to be printed. A user who has been writing letters using a word processor might want to change the color and print-quality options of a particular printer before printing a full-color photograph.

 Lab 11.5.4 Managing Files in a Printer Queue

Upon completion of this lab, you will be able to open the printer queue, add jobs to the printer queue, delete a job from the printer queue, rearrange jobs in the printer queue, and purge all jobs that are held in the printer queue.

Using Printer Accessories

Additional printer components can be used to speed the printing process for larger jobs. Most printers have a paper tray that holds a supply of paper as well as a sheet feeder that is used for specialty printing. Extra paper trays can be added to accommodate different sizes of paper—such as legal, executive, and envelopes—or for different types of paper such as a company letterhead. High-end printers often include a finisher that can collate and staple the paper. Options can include how the paper is sorted and where the staple is placed.

Combination printers that also fax, scan, and copy (as shown in Figure 11-42) allow users to manage these functions using software that typically comes with the printer. The obvious advantage is that these printers use only one connection to the computer instead of requiring multiple ports.

Figure 11-42 Combination Printer

Dealing with Paper Problems

Issues with paper make up the majority of problems that occur with printers. The IT technician must know how to clear paper jams and troubleshoot mechanical failures. This section
includes the following topics:

- Obstructions in the paper path
- Stripped and broken drive gears
- Stepper motor problems
- Defective registration roller and other feed rollers
- Wrong type of paper
- High humidity
- Paper dusting

Obstructions in the Paper Path

The majority of printer problems are paper jams. In fact, many of the problems are related
to the paper itself. Fragments of paper that are torn in the printing process must often be
removed from the paper path. This usually involves understanding the path that the paper
travels, from the registration roller to the output roller. A closer visual check of this path usually discloses the location of the fragment. Take care not to damage the printer while removing the obstruction.

Parts that drive paper movement can fail and cause paper to crumple or fold while moving through the path. This disables the printer and requires the removal of any trapped paper. Again, care in removal must be emphasized. Never remove a paper jam by pulling the paper in the opposite direction; the printer gears could be damaged. Such jams should be cleared by pulling the paper out in the same direction that it goes through the printer.

A paper jam can occur when the wrong type of paper is used. This can cause more than one page to enter the registration rollers, a problem that is called *paper clumping*. A bad separator pad can also cause clumping and should be replaced.

Most of the problems that require service in laser printers are rooted in the paper dust that is accumulated in the paper path. This paper dust requires regular cleaning to prevent costly service at a later date. However, it is difficult to clean something that is not easily seen. The technician must open or take apart the printer and clean all the places where the dust accumulates. He must know where to clean and how to clean. Consult the printer's service documentation for cleaning instructions. Because static charges are present in the laser-printing process, dust also accumulates outside the paper path. At some point, this dust will fall back into the paper path, causing jams.

Replacing toner units and removing paper jams can release toner that has not been fused to the paper. Use compressed air or a toner vacuum to remove excess toner. If toner leaves a smear on the printer, use an approved solvent to clean the affected area.

 Worksheet 11.6.1   Paper Jams

This is a true/false worksheet that tests your knowledge of clearing paper jams.

Stripped and Broken Drive Gears

When clumping or other jam failures occur, the drive system can overload. This can result in a broken gear or teeth being stripped from a gear. The only solution is to replace the gear. Be sure to understand the timing of the paper movement. Service instructions are necessary, even for skilled technicians, to perform this repair properly.

Stepper Motor Problems

NOTE

Technicians without proper training should not fix issues such as stepper motor problems. Only a manufacturer's technician or a certified service technician should repair these more severe problems.

Stepper motors are used in printers to position the printhead as well as to move paper through the printer, as shown in Figure 11-43. Stepper motors are usually trouble-free. Overloading, however, can damage the motor. In this situation, replacement of the motor is required. Timing of the print process must be observed. Follow the manufacturer's procedure for motor replacement. Improper solder connections on stepper motors can cause intermittent problems. Properly resoldering these connections can correct this condition.

Figure 11-43 Stepper Motor

Defective Registration Roller and Other Feed Rollers

The rubber that is used on feed rollers can become hardened over time. Paper slippage on these rollers can cause jams. Solutions that clean and soften rubber are available as a remedy for this problem. If these solutions do not correct the problem, the rollers should be replaced.

Wrong Type of Paper

Most printers are designed for a specific type and weight of paper. When problems occur, such as clumping or folding, check the type of paper being used to determine whether it is in compliance with the printer manufacturer's recommendations. Figure 11-44 shows different types of paper.

Figure 11-44 Different Types of Printing Paper

High Humidity

A majority of the printers that are used today print on cut sheets of paper. Paper-handling problems are more likely to occur in single-sheet printers than in older printers that required tractor-feed sheets of paper. These problems include jams and paper clumping. One of the primary causes of these problems is damp paper. Paper has a tendency to absorb moisture when it is stored. A cool, dry place is the best place to store paper. High-humidity areas should not be used for paper storage. The paper package should not be opened until it is ready to be used, as shown in Figure 11-45. It is good to riffle, or fan, the edges of the paper sheets before placing them in the printer.

Figure 11-45 Keep Paper in Its Package Until Ready for Use

Paper Dusting

Paper should be kept in its original wrapper until needed. This keeps the paper clean and dry. In extreme cases, compressed air can be used to dust the paper before putting it in the printer. This is especially useful if the printer is in a dusty environment or has experienced problems related to dust.

Summary

This chapter discussed the basics of printers and printer sharing. Some of the important concepts to retain from this chapter include the following:

- Printer types used today include laser, ink jet, and dot matrix. Of the three, the laser printer has the most complicated operation process and the highest price. High resolution, superior operation, and high speed make the laser unit the preferred printer today.

- The laser printer process is composed of the following six steps:

Step 1   Cleaning removes toner from the drum.

Step 2   Conditioning removes the old image and prepares the drum for a new image.

Step 3   Writing scans the photosensitive drum with the laser beam. At this step, the latent image is created.

Step 4   Developing is where the toner is applied to the latent image.

Step 5   Transferring is where the toner that is attached to the latent image is transferred to the paper.

Step 6   Fusing is where the printed paper is rolled between a heated roller and a pressure roller.

- Considerations when purchasing a printer include the following:
  - The print capacity, or the amount of printing a printer can handle
  - The speed of the printer, expressed in pages per minute (ppm)
  - The quality of the print produced
  - The resolution, or dots per inch (dpi), that the printer is capable of producing
  - The actual cost of ownership, which includes the type of paper the printer uses, the cost of ink replacement cartridges or toner units, and the warranty
- A printer communicates by using cables that connect to ports on the computer and the printer or by using wireless technologies such as infrared signals. The type of printer that is used determines whether a serial, parallel, SCSI, USB, or FireWire port is used. The parallel port is the standard printer interface port on the PC.
- Networked printers save resources. For an Ethernet connection, the RJ-45 connector is used. Other connection options include BNC and Token Ring ports. The maximum length of a Category 5 cable that connects a printer to the network is 100 meters (328 feet).
- A document must be translated from the operating system format to the Page Description Language (PDL) of the printer. A raster or bitmap image of the document is then created, and the printer outputs the image. This method is sped up with the use of host-based printing, which allows the operating system to communicate directly with the printer.
- A hardware device that allows a computer to route data to two printers or devices is called a printer switch, an A/B switch, or a data switch.
- A network print server is a computer that is dedicated to handling multiple print requests from multiple clients. The print server should provide access to print services and provide feedback to the users. A network print server should have a powerful processor, adequate hard disk space, and sufficient memory.

- The print queue in Windows is a temporary holding area for print jobs that are sent to the printer. In the queue, the network administrator can manage print jobs by pausing, deleting, or rearranging the jobs that are waiting to be processed.

- Preventive maintenance for printers includes keeping the printer clear of obstructions that can cause a paper jam, using the proper paper, keeping dust to a minimum, and keeping humidity levels low.

The next chapter provides information about proper preventive maintenance. It discusses hardware and software preventive maintenance, electrostatic discharge (ESD), and power issues.

Key Terms

built-in printer font   Resident font that is part of ROM and is built into the printer.

cleaning   The first step in the laser printer process that removes toner from the drum.

color ink jet printer   Type of printer that uses liquid-ink–filled cartridges that spray ink to form an image on the paper.

conditioning   The second step in the laser printer process that prepares the drum for a new image.

default printer   The first option that an application uses when the user clicks the printer icon. The default printer can be changed by the user.

developing   The fourth step in the laser printer process that applies toner to the latent image.

dot matrix printer   A printer that works by impacting the ribbon to place an image on the paper.

dots per inch (dpi)   How the quality of print is measured on a dot matrix printer.

electrophotographic drum   The central part of the laser printer.

FireWire   High-speed, platform-independent communication bus that interconnects digital printers and other devices.

font   A complete set of characters of a particular typeface that are used for display and printing purposes.

font card   Expansion card that allows memory upgrades, different printer interfaces, and font upgrades.

fusing   The sixth step in the laser printer process that rolls the paper between a heated roller and a pressure roller.

global print options   Allow a printer to be selected and used for all applications.

Graphical Device Interface (GDI) printing   See *host-based printing*.

host-based printing   Technology in which the operating system communicates directly with the printer and sends the printer an image that is ready to print.

impact printer   Class of printer that includes dot matrix and daisy wheel.

infrared   Type of communication that uses a spectrum of light to transmit and receive.

Interpress   PDL that was developed by Xerox to handle its line of high-speed printers.

laser printer   Type of printer that uses static electricity and a laser to form the image on the paper.

latent image   In laser printers, the undeveloped image.

media-handling options   Options by which a printer handles media, including the orientation, size, and weight of the paper.

near letter quality (NLQ)   The highest quality of print that is produced by a dot matrix printer.

network printer   Printer connected to the computer network that is set up to be shared by multiple users.

Page Description Language (PDL)   Code that describes the contents of a document in a language that the printer can understand.

pages per minute (ppm)   Designation for measuring the speed of a printer.

parallel port   Transfers multiple bits of information in a single cycle.

per-document printer settings   Allow global settings to be overridden for an individual document.

platen   The large roller in a dot matrix printer.

PostScript (PS)   Developed by Adobe Systems to allow fonts to share the same characteristics on-screen and on paper.

primary corona wire   Also called the grid or conditioning roller, it is the voltage device that erases the drum.

print resolution   The number of tiny dots that the printhead is capable of placing per inch on the paper when forming an image.

Printer Control Language (PCL)   Developed by Hewlett-Packard to allow software applications to communicate with HP and HP-compatible laser printers.

printer driver   Software that must be installed on a PC so that the printer can communicate and coordinate the printing process.

printer network interface card (NIC)   An adapter that the printer uses to access the network media.

printer-output options   Determine how the ink or toner is transferred to the paper and include color management, print quality, and speed.

printer queue   A temporary holding area for print jobs. The jobs in the queue are fed to the printer when it is ready for the next job.

printer switch   Hardware that routes data input from one device to another. Also known as an A/B switch.

resident font   See *built-in printer font*.

serial port   Transmits data to the printer one character at a time.

Small Computer System Interface (SCSI)   Type of interface that uses parallel communication technology to achieve high data transfer rates.

solenoid   Coil of wires that form electromagnets that fire the pins in a dot matrix printer.

transferring   The fifth step in the laser printer process where toner is detached from the latent image and transferred to the paper.

universal serial bus (USB)   Type of interface for printers and other devices that are Plug and Play–compatible.

What You See Is What You Get (WYSIWYG)   Printer output that matches what the user sees on-screen.

writing   The third step in the laser printer process where the photosensitive drum is scanned with a laser beam.

Check Your Understanding

1. What are the coils of wire that form electromagnets in a dot matrix printer called?

    A. Rollers

    B. Solenoids

    C. Platens

    D. Energizers

2. Which part of a dot matrix printer can produce a burn if touched?

    A. Platen

    B. Rollers

    C. Printhead cable

    D. Printhead

3. Which of the following is a nonimpact type of printer?

    A. Dot matrix

    B. Ink jet

    C. Daisy wheel

    D. Feed

4. What type of printer forces ink through a nozzle when heated by an electrical current?

   A. Laser

   B. Dot matrix

   C. Ink jet

   D. A plotter

5. When an ink jet printer has completed a print job, which of the following describes the ink?

   A. Often still wet

   B. Very hot

   C. Charged with electrostatic particles

   D. Has a uniform positive charge

6. The quality of print for an ink jet printer is measured in which of the following terms?

   A. rpm

   B. dpi

   C. kps

   D. lpi

7. The photosensitive drum of a laser printer should never be exposed to which of the following for long periods of time?

   A. Light

   B. Toner

   C. Rollers

   D. Energizers

8. To fix the toner to the paper, the top fuser roller in a laser printer is heated to what temperature?

   A. 250°F

   B. 350°F

   C. 150°F

   D. 450°F

9. What is the primary corona wire of a laser printer?

  A. A device that applies the toner

  B. The voltage device that erases the drum

  C. A negative voltage device that scans the drum

  D. A positive voltage device that scans the drum

10. What is the name of the step in which the toner is applied to the latent image?

  A. Developing

  B. Conditioning

  C. Redeveloping

  D. Transferring

11. What phase occurs between the conditioning phase and the developing phase in the laser printer process?

  A. Charging

  B. Writing

  C. Fusing

  D. Cleaning

12. Which command and control languages are most commonly associated with printers?

  A. PCL and PostScript

  B. PPP and PC Script

  C. Electrophotographic and PCL

  D. PCL and PPP

13. What type of data transfer moves single bits of information in a single cycle?

  A. Ethernet

  B. Serial

  C. Parallel

  D. Infrared

14. What is a printer driver?

    A. A hardware device that enables color printing

    B. A software program that allows the computer and the printer to communicate

    C. Software that installs fonts for the printer

    D. A part of the solenoid

15. How do you open the print queue in Windows 2000?

    A. Click the printer PostScript icon.

    B. Choose **Start**, **Settings**, **Printers** and double-click the appropriate printer.

    C. Choose **File** where the document was created.

    D. Click the desired printer in the My Documents folder.

16. How do you reorder a print job in a print queue in Windows 2000?

    A. Drag and drop it to the **Start**, **Print**, **Top Queue** icon.

    B. It is not possible.

    C. Drag and drop it to the desired position in the queue.

    D. Choose **Print Order** in My Computer.

17. What is the first thing you should do when troubleshooting a printer problem?

    A. Check the power and paper.

    B. Check for IRQ conflicts.

    C. Reinstall the print driver.

    D. Remove the ink cartridge or toner cartridge and reinstall it.

18. What does Windows 2000 use to make printer setup easier?

    A. Queue support

    B. Plug and Play support

    C. Updated printer support

    D. Port support

19. What causes the majority of printer problems?

    A. Paper jams

    B. Toner units

    C. Stripped gears

    D. Defective rollers

Upon completion of this chapter, you will be able to complete the following tasks:

- Document the procedures for preventive maintenance and for keeping the maintenance log
- Follow the appropriate environmental guidelines for the proper disposal of computer components
- Protect against electrostatic discharge
- Perform preventive maintenance on computer components
- Run software utilities and antivirus software to maintain system integrity
- Understand the power issues that affect computer systems

Chapter 12

Preventive Maintenance

The goal of a preventive maintenance program is to avoid costly computer repairs. This chapter stresses the importance of preventive maintenance and describes the tools that are necessary to achieve it. Proper maintenance can help prolong the life of hardware. Software utilities can make a computer system faster and more efficient. This chapter also discusses important safety guidelines for working on a computer and disposing of components.

Preventive Maintenance and the Technician

The IT technician is usually the first one called for computer problems. Knowing the right questions to ask is just as important as having the right tools. Environmental guidelines and Material Safety Data Sheets (MSDSs) can provide the information that is needed when computer components reach the end of their life. This section includes the following topics:

- Elements of a preventive maintenance program
- Tools and equipment
- Environmental guidelines
- Environmental guidelines for a server room
- Proper disposal of hazardous materials
- Using Material Safety Data Sheets

Elements of a Preventive Maintenance Program

The main goal of any preventive maintenance program is to protect a system from future problems. The following three questions need to be answered when developing a *preventive maintenance policy*:

- **When should preventive maintenance be scheduled?**

  Exact times depend on specific requirements. What is important is that you have a schedule. When developing a preventive maintenance policy, determine whether automated tasks can be done overnight and what upgrades must be done at night or on weekends. A schedule should be created for specific tasks to be completed at certain times of the day, week, and month.

- **What type of maintenance is necessary?**

  The type of maintenance that is performed depends on individual circumstances. Systems that are constantly updating, for example, must be backed up more frequently. Systems that access the Internet need constant virus scanning. Make these determinations as part of the preventive maintenance policy, because it is easier to address minor problems rather than to wait for major problems to develop. Every time a maintenance task is performed on a computer system, it should be noted in a preventive maintenance log. Each entry should list the date, time, name of the technician, and the computer system on which the maintenance was done.

- **How will the system be maintained?**

  The easy answer is "according to a preventive maintenance policy." Once a preventive maintenance policy is developed, it must be followed. Maintain current information on system components, including any updates. Keep the work area clean and dust-free. Keep logs of periodic changes and other types of documentation that can be helpful in future diagnostics and troubleshooting.

The following sections describe how to maintain specific components of a computer system.

Tools and Equipment

A technician should have a toolbox that contains the basic tools, as shown in Figure 12-1.

Figure 12-1 Typical Technician's Tool Set

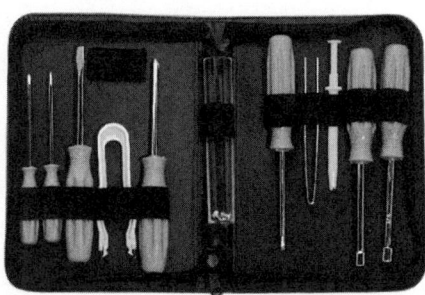

In addition, a toolkit should include the following items:

- Antistatic wrist strap or other antistatic device
- Flat-head screwdriver
- Phillips-head screwdriver
- Nut drivers
- Needle-nose pliers
- Diagonals or crosscut pliers
- Mirror to help see in tight places
- Digital multimeter
- Flashlight

A technician's toolset should contain a variety of flat-head and Phillips-head screwdrivers. Technicians encounter many different types of screws and nuts. Certain screws might require different lengths of screwdrivers so that the technician can access them. Magnetic tools, although handy, should not be used inside the computer because they can be hazardous to internal components. A sufficiently strong magnet can generate enough current to damage the hard drive, motherboard, or other internal component.

Technicians spend a lot of time working with wiring and cabling. Sometimes, a wire or cable must be cut. Diagonals or crosscut pliers allow technicians to cut wires and cabling to their exact specifications.

A tool set should also include a socket set. Most computer screws fit hex-style sockets, and the technician can use a nut driver to loosen or tighten hex-style screws. A mirror can be used to see into tight spots or around corners.

An antistatic vacuum cleaner, canned air, various solvents, and lint-free cloths should also be available. Antistatic vacuum cleaners should be used for computer components, because normal vacuum cleaners generate static. The vacuum cleaner should be specially certified for use with a computer. A typical vacuum cleaner should not be used to clean toner from a laser cartridge. The fine consistency of toner particles requires a vacuum cleaner with a higher level of filtration.

Canned air is one of the most useful tools for cleaning computer components. A can of air can remove dust from the inside of a computer without creating static. Do not let dust get blown into inaccessible areas. A lint-free cloth can be used with some water and mild soap to clean the outside of a computer case or component.

Digital Multimeter

NOTE

Before using a DMM for testing, verify that it is set to the proper function. For example, to test DC readings for the motherboard, verify that the DMM is set to the DC voltage function.

The tool set should also include a *digital multimeter (DMM)*, as shown in Figure 12-2. A DMM combines the functionality of a voltmeter, ohmmeter, and ammeter into one easy measuring device. Table 12-1 is a list of important DMM terms.

Figure 12-2 Digital Multimeter

Table 12-1 Digital Multimeter Terms

Term	Definition
Voltage (V)	The electrical potential difference between two points in a wire. Voltage is measured in volts (abbreviated V). In North America, wall outlets supply 120V, whereas in Europe, wall outlets supply 240V.
Current (Amps or A)	The flow of electrons through the wire. Current is measured in amperes (or amps, abbreviated A).
Power	Voltage multiplied by current—that is, V * A.
Resistance (Ohms or R)	The opposition to the flow of electricity through a substance.
Capacitance	The number of electrons that a capacitor can hold under a given electrical pressure (voltage). Capacitors store electrons (electricity) for a short period of time.

A DMM can perform electrical tests and measure voltage, amps, and ohms in both alternating and direct current. A DMM can be used to test power supplies, DC/AC voltage and polarity, resistance, diodes, continuity, coaxial cable, fuses, and batteries.

You should know the range of expected results before performing a test. For example, before performing a motherboard test for DC voltage, you should know that expected results could be ±12 V or ±5 V. Technicians can expect these voltage readings on the motherboard to vary by about 5 percent.

When you are using a DMM to measure a device with unknown voltage settings, the DMM should be set to the highest voltage setting or range.

The *DC voltage test* checks for live DC circuits. This test is usually performed on motherboard circuits. A parallel test should be conducted on the circuits. A parallel test is performed by connecting a circuit to the red measuring lead and connecting the black reference lead to a ground.

A DMM resistance or continuity test can be performed to verify that a device or a conductor has zero resistance. For example, resistance tests can be performed to test fuses. First, the technician must disconnect one end of the fuse from the system. If the DMM is set at 1 ohm, a good fuse should read close to 0 ohms. If the fuse is bad, the reading will be close to infinite.

Make sure that the power is turned off before performing a resistance test. The technician and the meter can be seriously damaged if the power is turned on. Also, a circuit must be removed from the system before resistance testing can take place. A component can be isolated from the system board by unsoldering one or both ends of the circuit.

The DMM can be set to produce a sound when no resistance is detected and continuity exists. This typically tests continuity in RAM modules. First, the module is unplugged from the motherboard. Then the red and black probes are touched to both end pins of the module simultaneously. A sound indicates continuity. If no sound is heard, the chip is most likely defective.

The *AC voltage test* is also used for checking system components. This test mainly checks power supplies and requires extreme caution. The electrical current that is supplied by a power supply unit can be harmful. Voltage from the DC output can also be tested with the AC voltage function.

Loopback Plugs

Loopback plugs, also called *loopback adapters,* are used for loopback tests that provide important diagnostic information. Different types of loopback plugs are available for troubleshooting. For example, loopback plugs are available to test serial and parallel ports, USB

NOTE

The PC power supply must have a load on it before making any output tests on the leads. A component such as the hard drive must be running and drawing power before the power supply can produce any DC output. This is called a *switched power supply.*

ports, and RJ-45 connectors for network connectivity. Loopback testing works by sending out signals and verifying that the returned signal is valid. Diagnostic information can be gained from individual pins, ports, controllers, and printer output. Figure 12-3 illustrates the connections that enable the loopback test on a parallel loopback plug.

Figure 12-3 Loopback Plug

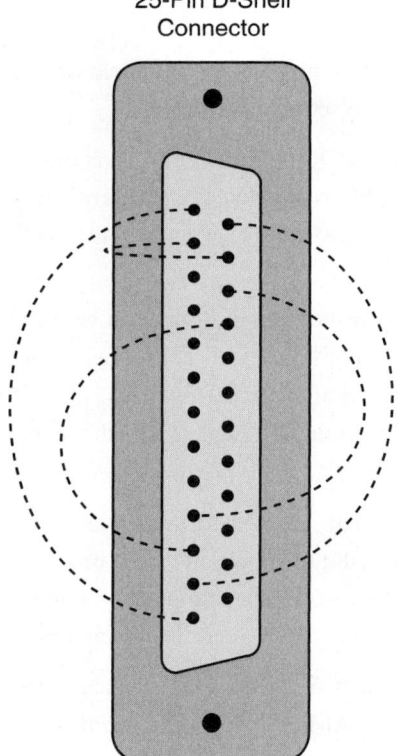

25-Pin D-Shell
Connector

Other loopback plugs are wrapped—that is, the wires are wrapped around and do not go from end to end. These wrap plugs do not work as adapters.

Lab 12.1.2   Using a Digital Multimeter

In this lab, you identify and record power supply specifications and connecter types. This lab also focuses on the use of a multimeter to safely test and record voltage readings.

Environmental Guidelines

Computers and other computing devices eventually become unusable. This can be caused by one of the following reasons:

- Parts or components begin to fail more frequently because the machine is old and uneconomical.
- The computer becomes obsolete for the application for which it was originally intended.
- Newer machines with improved features replace earlier models.

Eventually, the question of how to dispose of old computers or parts arises. Can they be placed in a garbage bin and buried in a landfill?

Computers and peripherals contain some environmentally unfriendly materials. Most computer components are either hazardous or contain some level of hazardous substances. Waste materials are listed as hazardous because they are known to be harmful to human health and the environment when not managed properly. Also known as *toxic waste,* hazardous materials typically contain high concentrations of heavy metals such as cadmium, lead, or mercury. Computer printed circuit boards consist of plastics, precious metals, fiberglass, arsenic, silicon, gallium, and lead. Cathode ray tube (CRT) monitors contain glass, metal, plastics, lead, barium, and rare-earth metals. Batteries from portable systems can contain lead, cadmium, lithium, alkaline manganese, and mercury.

Many of the cleaning substances that are used on computer equipment can also be classified as hazardous materials. However, no widespread U.S. regulations exist regarding placing these cleaning substances in landfills. The situation is similar in most other parts of the world. The rest of this section focuses on items that require special disposal procedures to comply with environmental guidelines. This includes batteries, CRTs or monitors, chemical solvents or cans, and toner kits or printer cartridges. Finally, the Material Safety Data Sheet (MSDS) is discussed.

Environmental Guidelines for a Server Room

In the server room, temperature is important. The server should never be located near ductwork or next to the air conditioner. Items such as motors and microwaves can cause interference. Electromagnetic interference (EMI) should also be avoided. Only isolated grounding circuits should be used.

The area around the server should be kept free of debris and clutter. Ideally, the server should be locked in a closet with limited access and with no likelihood of being bumped, jostled, accessed directly, or otherwise disturbed by nonadministrators. For the safety of the technicians and the equipment, all cables and wires should be secured.

The space above a dropped ceiling, which is between the ceiling and the floor of the next level of a building, is extremely important for network administrators and fire marshals. This space, called the *plenum,* is a convenient place to run network cables around a building. The plenum is typically an open space in which air circulates freely. Therefore, fire marshals pay special attention to it.

The most common outer covering for copper-based cabling is polyvinyl chloride (PVC). PVC cabling gives off poisonous fumes when it burns. Fire codes prohibit PVC cabling in the plenum to prevent poisonous fumes from circulating freely throughout the building.

Plenum-grade copper-based cabling is designed for use without conduit in plenums, walls, and other areas where fire codes prohibit PVC cabling. Plenum-grade cabling is less flexible and more expensive than PVC cabling, so it is used primarily where PVC cabling cannot be used.

Temperature

The following items control the temperature of the computing environment:

- During cold weather, the heating system maintains the temperature at a comfortable level. This is applicable to open-office and server room environments.
- During hot weather, the air conditioning ensures that the server remains below the maximum operating temperature. Most enterprise data centers are air conditioned year-round because of the heat that is generated by the equipment.

When a new server is being implemented, it is important to check the number of British Thermal Units (BTUs) that the server puts out. This is sometimes difficult to determine, because the BTUs are frequently omitted from the server specifications. The technician must also make sure that the air conditioning unit can cool the aggregate number of BTUs. If the server is to be rack mounted, the technician should also make sure that the rack is well ventilated. If possible, the rack should contain some sort of airflow management, such as a fan, to ensure that the server stays cool in a closed rack enclosure.

Air conditioning systems that are used in critical environments such as data centers measure their cooling capacity based on the volume of air in the data center. One of the easiest environmental issues to identify is the temperature. A hot computer room indicates a problem. Network technicians should be aware of the operating temperatures for computer equipment. A typical server would operate in the following ranges:

- Operating temperature: 50°F to 95°F
- Storage temperature: 40°F to 95°F
- Maximum heat dissipation: 10,000 BTU/hour

In this example, if the server storage area exceeds 95°F, a serious problem is likely to occur.

Humidity

Humidity is another important environmental factor for a server room. Moisture that results from too much humidity in the air can damage the server's electronic components. If the environment is too dry, electrostatic discharge (ESD) can occur. ESD is discussed later in this chapter.

If the server is in a controlled environment, such as an air conditioned office, server room, or data center, the air conditioning and heating units usually control the humidity. A dehumidifier or humidifier should not be used to control humidity because these devices are unreliable. A humidifier or a dehumidifier would also introduce a water source that could potentially damage a server. A network server should be kept in a climate-controlled room that maintains relative humidity in the range of 20 to 50 percent.

Air Quality

No discussion of a server operating environment would be complete without a discussion of the air quality. This is generally not an issue in a data center environment, but it can be an issue when servers are placed in areas with a lot of dust and debris in the air. The fans on a server can pull all the dust in the air through the system and deposit it on the components. If the components become covered with dust, they can overheat and fail. If the equipment is in an area where the air quality is questionable, the network technician should schedule weekly or monthly maintenance to clean out the system using a computer vacuum cleaner or canned air.

Fire Suppression

Servers can be installed in several different environments. Network technicians must be aware of fire-suppression considerations in these areas.

In most data center environments, an inert gas-based fire-suppression system is in place that works by eliminating all the oxygen in the air. Halon was a favorite for many years but has been outlawed in many countries. It has been replaced by more environmentally friendly gases such as carbon dioxide. Table 12-2 lists some commonly used replacement chemicals for Halon.

Carbon dioxide extinguishes a fire by reducing the oxygen content of the protected area below the point where the area can support combustion. DuPont originally developed FE13 as a chemical refrigerant; it suppresses fire by absorbing heat from a fire until the atmosphere can no longer support the fire.

Table 12-2 Halon Replacement Chemicals

Chemical Name	Trade Name	Manufacturer
PFC-3-1-10	CEA-410	3M Specialty Chemicals
HFC-23	FE 13	DuPont
HFC-227ea	FM-200	Great Lakes Chemical
IG-541	Inergen	Ansul Fire Protection
CO_2	—	Various, including Kidde, Fire Protection Systems, and Ansul Fire Protection

Another type of fire suppression is the use of foam to extinguish the fire. Foam fire-suppression systems work by separating the fire from the oxygen in the air. Depending on the type of foam system, this can be done by using the foam to blanket the fuel surface, smothering the fire by cooling the fuel with the water content of the foam, or suppressing the release of flammable vapors that can mix with the air and burn.

Many server rooms include the same sprinkler system that is used in the office space. This is generally a bad idea. Water is one of the worst things that can be poured on an electrical fire. A fire in a wastebasket on one end of the floor could trigger a sprinkler system that would result in extensive damage to servers and other electrical components. Therefore, sprinkler systems should be disabled in a server room.

An ABC or BC fire extinguisher is recommended for a server room. Table 12-3 explains the meaning of the letters on a fire extinguisher.

Table 12-3 Fire Extinguisher Ratings

Letter Rating	Type of Fire to Extinguish
A	Fires where ordinary combustibles—such as wood, cloth, and paper—are burning
B	Fires where flammable liquids, oils, and grease are burning
C	Fires with live electrical equipment
D	Fires that contain combustible metals such as magnesium, potassium, and sodium

The fire extinguisher should be mounted in a prominent location, either directly inside the entrance to the server room or on the wall outside the door. If the server room experiences a fire, the network technician should be able to access a fire extinguisher that is rated for electrical fires.

In a shared office environment, it is generally not practical to disable the sprinklers. In this situation, it is best to shield the server from any possible water from the sprinklers. For example, the server can be placed under a desk or enclosed in a sealed rack. This environment should also include an ABC or BC fire extinguisher.

Flooding

Flooding is a critical problem for computers and servers. If equipment is not saved before the flood, it usually becomes damaged or unrecoverable. The following actions can save equipment from an impending flood:

- Remove all removable media and backup tapes from the premises prior to the flooding. Store these media in waterproof containers so that the data can be recovered as part of a disaster-recovery program.
- Power off all servers and move them to the highest location in the building. If possible, remove them from the building and store them on high ground. The power is usually shut off before the flooding has time to damage the servers.

If a network administrator must recover the data from drives in a flooded area, the exposure to moisture should be minimized.

If the servers have been flooded, they are probably not going to be dependable. If the network administrator wants to try to recover them, all components should be removed and dried as quickly as possible. Allow the components to air dry for at least 48 hours before cleaning and testing them. Corrosion and moisture on the components are two areas of concern. If an electric current is applied to a motherboard with droplets of water on it, this could cause extensive damage to the electrical components.

A disaster-recovery plan is important for situations such as flooding. If data is backed up and stored in a separate location, a system can be restored after damages from flooding and other disasters.

Monitoring the Server State

The server state should be monitored in relation to its environment. To prevent environmental factors from affecting the server, the temperature, line voltage, and other environmental operating statistics should be monitored. The server temperature can be measured with a thermometer. A new generation of add-on server cards also provides detailed information about the environmental state of the server.

The best way to monitor the network servers is to add a hardware remote management card. This card provides detailed information about the internal environment of the server. The information is usually available for hardware components such as active hard drives and processor utilization, and can include operating system statistics. From an environmental perspective, you should have access to information such as system temperature and line voltage. Many remote management cards allow administrators to set temperature thresholds to alert the technician if the server temperature exceeds the operating range.

Proper Disposal of Hazardous Materials

The list of substances that have been identified as being hazardous in the workplace is constantly growing. Some substances, like adhesives, solvents, and abrasives, present fairly obvious hazards to humans and the environment. Others, like the toner in office copiers and printers or some cleaning and disinfectant products, might not be as obvious. Proper disposal is therefore a matter of safety as well as law. Check regulations concerning disposal of hazardous materials to ensure that you are in compliance.

Proper Disposal of Batteries

Batteries often contain rare-earth metals that can be harmful to the environment. Batteries from portable computer systems can contain lead, cadmium, lithium, alkaline manganese, and mercury. These metals do not decay and can remain in the environment for many years if not carefully disposed of. Mercury, which is commonly used in the manufacturing of batteries, is extremely toxic and harmful to humans. Lead and the other metals are not as harmful as mercury. However, they can still harm the environment.

Because of these metals, depleted batteries are classified as hazardous materials. The disposal of batteries is tightly controlled at the national, state, and local levels. In addition to the U.S. federal guidelines, most states and local communities in the United States have laws about the proper disposal of batteries.

The desired method for the disposal of batteries is recycling. All batteries, including lithium-ion, nickel-cadmium, nickel metal hydride, and lead-acid, are subject to the special disposal procedures to comply with existing environmental guidelines. However, because regulations vary among different states and countries, the trash removal services for a company or a local community should be contacted for more information. These services can either arrange for special disposal facilities or provide a supplier that can safely remove batteries.

Proper Disposal of Monitors or CRTs

CRTs must always be handled with care because of the potentially lethal voltage that is maintained, even after they are disconnected from a power source. CRTs also contain glass, metal, plastics, lead, barium, and rare-earth metals. According to the U.S. Environmental Protection Agency (EPA), CRT monitors contain approximately 4 pounds of lead. The exact amount depends on the size and make of the monitor. Most of the components of end-of-life CRT monitors can be salvaged or recycled. Monitors must be disposed of in compliance with environmental regulations. Consult your local waste collection agent or recycling company for information on how to dispose of end-of-life CRTs.

Proper Disposal of Toner Kits, Cartridges, and Developers

Used printer toner kits, cartridges, and developers can be destructive to the environment. Their sheer volume necessitates caution in the way that they are handled and disposed of.

Laser printer toner cartridges can be recycled. When a new toner cartridge is purchased, some suppliers take the old cartridge for a small credit. Most often, the new cartridge provides a mailer for returning the old cartridge to the manufacturer. The cartridge is recycled, reloaded with toner and developer, and then resold. This is the preferred method for disposing of toner cartridges. Although ink jet printer cartridges can be refilled and reused with "do it yourself" kits, this is not recommended. Ink from these kits has been known to leak into the printer, causing irreversible damage. Also, using refilled ink jet cartridges can void the ink jet printer's warranty.

Proper Disposal of Chemical Solvents and Aerosol Cans

The chemicals and solvents that clean computers are another source of environmental problems. When drained or evaporated into the environment, these chemicals can cause significant damage. Therefore, it is usually necessary to clear these items with the local waste management agencies before disposing of them. Contact the sanitation provider to learn how and where to dispose of these chemicals. Never pour them down the sink or dispose of them in a drain that connects to the public sewers.

Free liquids are substances that can pass through a standard paint filter. Many dump sites cannot handle free liquids, and these liquids cannot be disposed of in a landfill. Therefore, solvents and other liquid cleaning materials must be properly categorized and disposed of at an appropriate disposal center.

Any cans or bottles that the solvents and other cleaning supplies were supplied in must also be specially treated. Make sure that they are identified and treated as special hazardous waste. If the contents are not completely used, some aerosol cans can explode when exposed to heat.

 Worksheet 12.1.4 Environmental Considerations

This worksheet reviews the important considerations regarding hazardous materials and the environment.

Using Material Safety Data Sheets

A *Material Safety Data Sheet (MSDS)* is a fact sheet that summarizes information about material identification. This information includes hazardous ingredients that can affect personal health, cause fire hazards, and require first aid. The chemical reactivity and incompatibilities include spill, leak, and disposal procedures and protective measures for the safe handling and storage of materials. To determine whether a material that is used in PC repairs or preventive maintenance is classified as hazardous, consult the manufacturer's MSDS. The Occupational Safety and Health Administration (OSHA), shown in Figure 12-4, developed these data sheets on the proper handling of hazardous materials. All hazardous materials must be accompanied by an MSDS when they change hands. Some of the products that are purchased for computer repairs or maintenance include relevant MSDS information in the manual. If the MSDS is not available, visit http://www.msdssearch.com for current information.

Figure 12-4 OSHA Logo

OSHA requires organizations that work directly with these materials to post MSDSs in a prominent location. An MSDS is a valuable source of information that can include the following:

- The name of the material
- The physical properties of the material
- Any hazardous ingredients the material contains
- Reactivity data, such as fire and explosion data
- Spill or leak procedures
- Special precautions
- Health hazards
- Special protection requirements

An MSDS is valuable in determining how best to dispose of potentially hazardous materials. Local regulations concerning acceptable disposal methods should always be checked before disposing of any electronic equipment.

Preventive Maintenance and Electrostatic Discharge

Electrostatic discharge (ESD) is everywhere. When ESD builds and discharges, it can affect sensitive electronic components. Taking the proper precautions and using the appropriate equipment can control the potential damage. This section includes the following topics:

- Electrostatic discharge overview
- Antistatic bags
- Grounding wrist straps
- Compressed air
- Grounded workbench

Electrostatic Discharge Overview

Static electricity is the buildup of an electric charge on a surface. This buildup can end up zapping something that it can damage. A zap is known as an *electrostatic discharge (ESD)*. ESD is the worst enemy of the fine electronics that are found in computer systems. This is why it has been discussed in almost every chapter of this book.

At least 3000 volts must be built up before a person can feel an ESD. If the discharge causes pain or makes a noise, the charge was probably above 10,000 volts. Most computer chips run on less than 5 volts of electricity. A computer component could be damaged by less than 3000 volts of static buildup. Table 12-2 summarizes some important guidelines for working with static electricity.

Table 12-4 Dos and Don'ts of Static Electricity

Do	Don't
Work at an antistatic workstation that is equipped with tiled floors, a grounding strap, and a grounding mat.	Walk across the room and then handle an electronic component without grounding yourself.
If possible, make sure that the relative humidity is greater than 50%.	Touch pins or leads on a circuit board.

Worksheet 12.2.1   Electrostatic Discharge (ESD)

This worksheet is a review of ESD information, including the damage that it can cause and the necessary precautions that you should take.

Avoiding ESD

To avoid ESD, it helps to know when it is most likely to occur. The potential for ESD increases significantly when the humidity is low. The potential for static electricity is also higher if the temperature is low or if carpeting is on the floor. Table 12-5 lists the different conditions that can cause static buildup.

Table 12-5 Conditions That Can Cause Static Buildup

Type of Generation	Volts Generated at 10%–25% Relative Humidity	Volts Generated at 65%–90% Relative Humidity
Walking on carpet	35,000	1500
Walking on vinyl tile	12,000	250
Working at a bench	6,000	100
Picking up a poly bag from a bench	20,000	1200
Moving a chair with urethane foam	18,000	1500

A good working area should include antistatic tile on the floors, grounded workbenches with antistatic mats, and wrist straps. All grounding devices must share a common ground. The area should be clean and well lit, and the humidity level should be maintained between 20 percent and 50 percent. All of these elements can significantly reduce the risk of ESD.

After the computer case has been opened, the technician should be grounded to the case by touching an exposed metal part of it. Touch a bare metal portion, because if a painted part of the case is touched, it might not release static buildup. After any static buildup has been discharged into the exposed case, attach the grounding wrist strap to the case to help prevent additional buildup. An ESD-free environment is crucial to preventive maintenance when opening the computer case.

Many things can cause a computer system to fail. The most common items are dust buildup, extreme temperatures, and rough handling. The amount of dust and the potential for static electricity in the computer area determine how often the PC must be cleaned.

If a computer is not cleaned regularly, dust can build up on the internal components, such as the fan bearings and printed circuit boards. A fan with a large amount of dust buildup could stop working and cause the system to overheat. This is especially true with newer CPUs. If the processor fan stops working, the computer can either malfunction or shut down, and the processor can be damaged.

Keep the inside of the computer clean. To properly clean inside the computer case, unplug the unit and move it away from other equipment. Use a can of compressed air to blow out all the dust within the case. Be sure to follow the directions carefully. This process should be done at least once a year, if an area is not dusty, and two or three times a year in dusty areas. This process can serve two purposes. After the dust has been removed, the motorized components will work more efficiently for a longer period of time. Also, preventing the buildup of dust reduces the chances of ESD.

Extreme temperatures are hazardous to computers and should be avoided. If a computer system overheats, several problems can occur, such as system malfunctions and data loss. To prevent this, make sure that the ventilation mechanisms of the case are properly functioning and that the room is at a reasonable temperature.

Rough handling can also cause damage to a computer. Be careful when moving a system to avoid loosening internal components. If a component becomes loose while the machine is turned off, it could be damaged when the unit is turned back on.

Antistatic Bags

Special packing materials are used with microchips and printed circuit boards. These packing materials range from special molded plastics and foams for microchips to antistatic bags for circuit boards. Do not remove a component from special packaging until it is ready to be installed. Figure 12-5 shows an *antistatic bag* that can temporarily store parts and components when disassembling a computer for cleaning or other types of preventive maintenance.

Figure 12-5 Antistatic Bag

Grounding Wrist Straps

When working on a computer or its components, certain tools should be used to reduce the risk of ESD. A *grounding wrist strap*, which is shown in Figure 12-6, provides a place for the static to go before discharging through sensitive computer components.

Figure 12-6 Grounding Wrist Strap

Compressed Air

Two other items that can be used when working on computers are *antistatic spray* and *compressed air*. The latter is shown in Figure 12-7. These products can be used on floors, desks, and some types of equipment. Follow the label's safety instructions when using these items.

Figure 12-7 Compressed Air

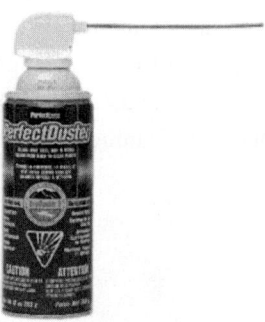

Grounded Workbench

Grounding the workbench is a common practice in many lab and work environments. Figure 12-8 illustrates a typical workbench. When the surface is grounded, computers and other electronic devices do not require a grounding mat during repairs.

Figure 12-8 Grounded Workbench

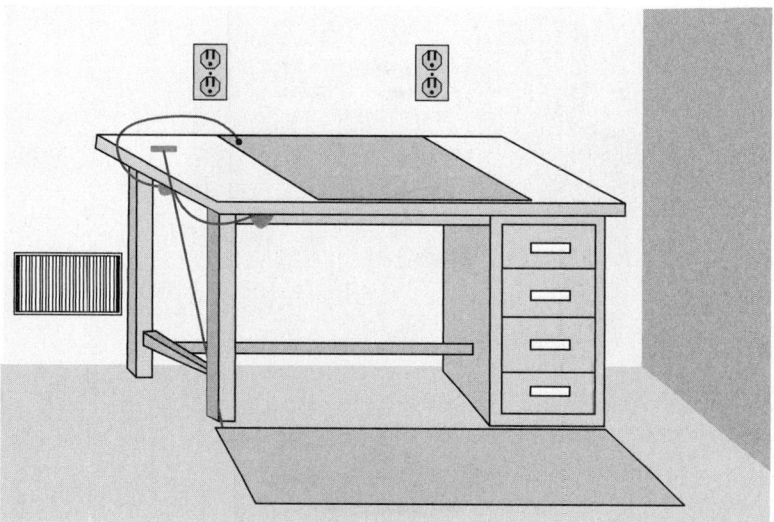

Preventive Maintenance for Computer Peripherals

The goal of preventive maintenance for computer peripherals is to help reduce downtime. In addition, it is far less expensive to maintain these types of components than to replace them. This section include the following topics:

- Monitors
- Mice
- Keyboards
- Printers
- Scanners

Monitors

A display unit is shown in Figure 12-9. Because the display unit is the most visible piece of computer equipment, it should be kept clean for both appearance and functionality. The information in this section applies to both CRT and LCD screen types.

When cleaning a display, make sure that the device is unplugged from the wall. Use a damp cloth with a mild detergent to wipe down the entire display unit and remove dust buildup. Dampen another cloth with water to remove cleaner residue on the surface of the monitor. Avoid using too much water to prevent drips. After cleaning the display, use a dry cloth to complete the job. Be careful when cleaning to avoid scratching the screen portion of the monitor.

Figure 12-9 CRT Monitor

HP p930 Monitor

After cleaning the monitor, make sure that the power cord is plugged in securely.

Mice

Mice can be either mechanical or optical. Both types of mice are shown in Figure 12-10.

Figure 12-10 Mechanical Mouse (left) and Optical Mouse (right)

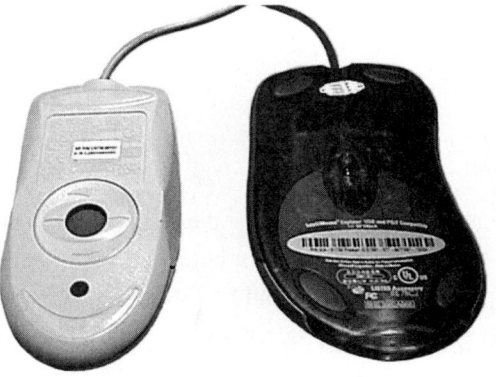

A mechanical mouse might not function properly if it becomes dirty. When dust settles on the mouse pad, it gets swept up into the moving parts of the mouse. This causes a buildup on the rollers inside the mouse. The fastest way to clean a mechanical mouse is to remove the plate on the bottom of the unit, remove the ball, and then gently scrape the dust buildup from the rollers. The buildup can be removed with a fingernail or other gentle scraping tool. Another cleaning method is to use isopropyl alcohol or methanol with a cotton swab.

An optical mouse might need to be cleaned with a damp cloth on its sensor surface. However, this could damage the mouse and should only be done if the mouse functions erratically. Be sure to unplug an optical mouse before cleaning it. Do not expose your eyes to the mouse's laser.

Keyboards

A keyboard receives more physical abuse than any other component of a computer system. Keyboards are also exposed to the environment, which allows dust to build up on the keyboard over time. Periodic cleaning of the keyboard can prolong the life span and prevent malfunction. The keys on a keyboard can be removed, as shown in Figure 12-11. This allows easy access to the areas where dust collects. A soft brush or cotton swab can remove dirt from under the keys. Compressed air can blow out dust from below the keys. The keyboard should be held vertically or in an inclined position while using the air to blow out the dirt and dust. This prevents large dirt and dust particles from remaining stuck in the interior corners, springs, and foam material beneath the keys.

Figure 12-11 Keyboard with Keys Removed

Printers

Printers have many moving parts within them. Therefore, they require a higher level of maintenance. Printers produce impurities that collect on the components within the device. Over time, these impurities need to be removed. Otherwise, they can cause the printer to malfunction.

When working with dot matrix printers, the roller surfaces should be cleaned with a damp cloth. The power cord should be unplugged before applying the cloth.

On an ink jet printer, the paper-handling mechanism can collect particles of paper over time. These particles can be removed with a damp cloth when the unit is unplugged. Figure 12-12 shows an ink jet printer.

Figure 12-12 Ink Jet Printer

WARNING

It is important to unplug the laser printer before cleaning because of the high amounts of voltage that it can discharge.

Laser printers usually require little maintenance unless they are in a dusty area. Certain older units also require more maintenance than newer ones. When cleaning a laser printer, a special vacuum cleaner must be used for toner removal. If a household vacuum cleaner is used, the toner particles can pass through the filtration system and get into the air.

The type of paper and ink that are used in a printer are important for the following reasons:

- **Paper selection**—The right type of paper can help the printer last longer and print more efficiently. In most computer-supply stores, several types of paper are available. Each type of paper is clearly labeled with the type of printer for which it is intended. Paper types include ink jet and laser printer paper. The printer manufacturer usually recommends the use of a certain type of paper in its user's manual.

- **Ink selection**—The printer manual also lists the brand and type of ink that are recommended by the printer manufacturer. If the wrong type of ink is installed, the printer might not work and the print quality can be reduced. Avoid trying to refill ink cartridges because the ink can leak out.

Scanners

Figure 12-13 shows a scanner. Keep the scanner surface clean. If the glass becomes dirty, consult the manufacturer's manual for cleaning recommendations. If the manual does not list recommendations, use a glass cleaner and a soft cloth to protect the glass from getting scratched.

Figure 12-13 Scanner

If the inside of the glass becomes dirty, check the manual for instructions on how to open the unit or remove the glass from the scanner. If possible, thoroughly clean both sides, and replace the glass as it was originally set in the scanner.

Lab 12.3.5   Cleaning Computer Components

In this lab, you learn the proper procedure to clean computer components.

Worksheet 12.3.5   Preventive Maintenance for Components

This worksheet tests your knowledge of computer components and the proper maintenance of each component.

Computer Software for Preventive Maintenance

Software utilities are the primary tool of the IT technician. The most common utilities are antivirus programs and firewalls. Many professional programs are available to help diagnose and fix system problems, but a number of programs are available as part of a successful preventive maintenance policy. This section includes the following topics:

- Software utilities
- User responsibilities
- Antivirus applications
- Firewalls

Software Utilities

Several utilities are included with DOS and Windows that can help maintain system integrity. If used on a regular basis, the following utilities can increase system speed and efficiency:

- *ScanDisk* — This utility checks the integrity of files and folders or thoroughly checks the system by scanning the disk for physical errors. It can be used on any formatted disk that the operating system can read. This program should be used whenever the system is not shut down properly, or at least once a month. Figure 12-14 shows ScanDisk in progress on drive C.

Figure 12-14 ScanDisk

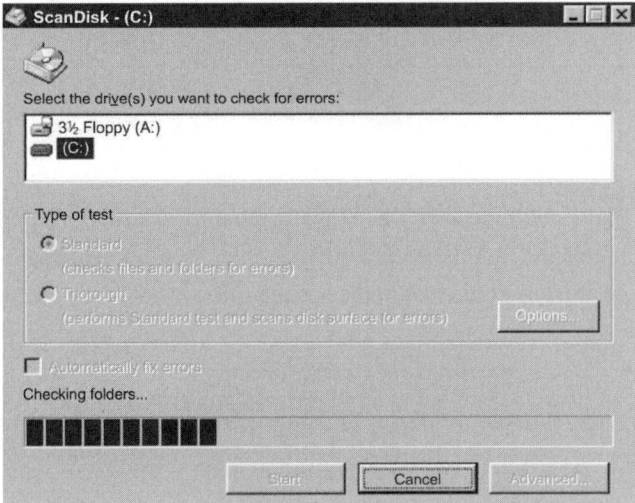

- *Defragmenter* — When a program or data is written to the hard drive, it can be distributed over various portions of the hard drive. This is known as *fragmentation.* Fragmentation lowers the performance of a drive. The Defragmenter utility optimizes space on the hard drive by moving the fragments back together where space is available; this allows programs to be read more quickly. Technicians generally start the Defragmenter after using the ScanDisk utility. The Defragmenter can also be set up to run automatically at regular intervals for systems where files are created and deleted frequently. Figure 12-15 shows the Defragmenter utility being used on drive C.

Figure 12-15 Defragmenter

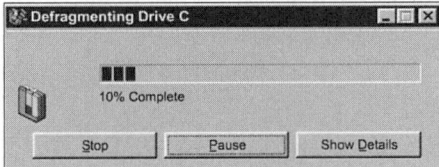

- *CHKDSK /f*—This DOS command checks the file system for errors and can be compared to the ScanDisk utility for Windows 2000 and XP. As shown in Figure 12-16, CHKDSK runs on the command line.

Figure 12-16 CHKDSK /f

```
C:\WINNT\system32\cmd.exe                                          _|□|×|
Microsoft Windows 2000 [Version 5.00.2195]
(C) Copyright 1985-2000 Microsoft Corp.

C:\Documents and Settings\glambeth>I:

I:\>chkdsk /f

CHKDSK is verifying files (stage 1 of 3)...
File verification completed.
CHKDSK is verifying indexes (stage 2 of 3)...
Index verification completed.
CHKDSK is verifying security descriptors (stage 3 of 3)...
Security descriptor verification completed.

 18824368 KB total disk space.
  1671012 KB in 271 files.
      136 KB in 20 indexes.
        0 KB in bad sectors.
    66840 KB in use by the system.
    65536 KB occupied by the log file.
 17086380 KB available on disk.

     4096 bytes in each allocation unit.
  4706092 total allocation units on disk.
  4271595 allocation units available on disk.

I:\>
```

- *REGEDIT*—The registry is a database that holds configuration data about the hardware and environment of the PC. REGEDIT is a command that is used by advanced technicians. The Registry Editor, shown in Figure 12-17, provides access to the registry in a view that is similar to that of Windows Explorer. If anything is changed in the registry, system errors or malfunctions could occur. Changes cannot be undone, so extreme caution is advised when using this program.

Figure 12-17 Registry Editor

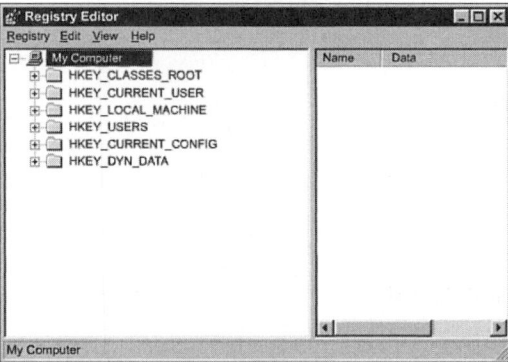

Lab 12.4.1 Using the ScanDisk and Defragmenter Utilities

In this lab, you use the ScanDisk and Defragmenter utilities to scan a hard drive, defragment the drive to check for errors, and defragment files.

 Video Using the ScanDisk and Defragmenter Utilities

The ScanDisk and Defragmenter utilities are used for preventive maintenance and troubleshooting. This video demonstrates how to access and start each utility.

User Responsibilities

A computer user can do several things to make the system work properly. System utilities can enhance performance in the following ways:

- Managing applications
- Managing files and folders
- Backing up your work

Managing Applications

When installing applications, use the Add/Remove Programs utility. Certain applications do not use an install shield, and if the setup program crashes in the middle of the installation, it could cause the system to fail. The Add/Remove Programs utility can also be used to remove an application from the system.

Managing Files and Folders

The file-management system of an operating system is designed to keep data in a hierarchical tree. The hard drives should be organized with work files and programs in different locations. This makes it easier to find and back up files.

Backing Up Your Work

Because a system could fail at any time, personal files should be backed up regularly. The best way to back up data is to copy it onto a form of removable media such as a floppy disk, CD, or Zip disk. The media should be stored far away from the computer, preferably in a different building, to prevent all data from being lost in a fire. Do not use the same disk repeatedly. Use multiple disks, and create multiple copies of the same data.

Antivirus Applications

A *computer virus* is a program that has been written by someone with malicious intent. After a computer has been infected, the virus can be spread to other machines through a network connection or by removable media.

An *antivirus application* can prevent a virus from infecting the system. Antivirus programs can also be run on command and can scan the entire computer or a specific file for viruses. If a virus is found, the antivirus software can either clean or isolate the infected file. If a file becomes isolated, the user typically cannot open it. The virus definitions that are used by the antivirus program must be updated often. An automatic virus definition update is the preferred method.

Viruses are typically sent as e-mail attachments. After being opened, the attachment allows the virus to infect the computer. The virus can resend itself to other computers using e-mail addresses that are found in programs such as Microsoft Outlook. Other users often assume that the e-mail is legitimate, which can allow the virus to spread.

CAUTION

Be suspicious of e-mail attachments with executable extensions such as .exe, .bat, .com, and .vbs. Make sure that your antivirus software scans e-mail attachments. When in doubt, contact the sender before opening an attachment.

Types of Viruses

You should recognize the different types of viruses and what they do. The following is a list of typical viruses:

- *File virus*—This common virus modifies an existing program so that the use of a seemingly safe program activates the virus.
- *Boot-sector virus*—This kind of virus targets the boot sector of every floppy or hard disk. If the boot sector of the primary hard drive is infected, the virus can be activated every time the computer is started.
- *Macro virus*—This type of virus uses the built-in macro programming languages in word processors. Macros are used for the automatic formatting of documents. However, macros can also be written to do mischievous or damaging things.

If a computer system is behaving strangely and no hardware problems are found, a virus can still exist. The virus can act like a hardware failure. If antivirus software is installed, run it to make sure that the system is clean and then schedule it to run on a regular basis.

Firewalls

Many people are beginning to take advantage of the always-on feature of broadband technologies. Broadband users must be aware of the security risks that are associated with connecting a computer to the outside world. Security breaches on a home computer can allow a hacker to steal stored data or to use the computer to hack into other computers.

Many steps can be taken to minimize the security risk of connecting a computer to the Internet. A home firewall can prevent hacker attacks on a home computer. Firewalls are the most popular method of protecting corporate LANs from outside intruders. A firewall is a hardware or software system that prevents unauthorized people from accessing sensitive data. A home firewall is normally located at the interface between the local devices and the high-speed broadband connection. All data, video, and voice traffic between these two networks is examined by the firewall. A typical home firewall system also does the following things:

- Closes the broadband connection after detecting an attempt to hack into a digital appliance
- Allows different family members to set their own levels of security
- Records all broadband Internet access events

After you install a firewall, certain ports must be opened to use e-mail services and the Internet. SMTP uses port 25 and POP3 uses port 110 to transmit and receive e-mails. Port 80 must also be opened for HTTP, the standard protocol that supports the exchange of information on the World Wide Web.

Windows XP has a built-in firewall called the Internet Connection Firewall (ICF). Figure 12-18 shows this setting in the Local Area Connection Properties dialog box. ICF is a software component that blocks unsolicited traffic from the Internet. ICF monitors all the outbound and inbound communications of a computer. If ICF does not recognize a packet that is being sent or received, the packet is dropped. Windows XP can create a plain-text log of all events, such as packets being dropped. ICF can block all unsolicited incoming packets by default. If a computer is using an FTP Server, click the Services tab in the Advanced Settings dialog box, as shown in Figure 12-19. Select the **FTP Server** check box to allow this service through the ICF.

Video   Internet Connection Firewall

This video demonstrates how to enable the ICF in Windows XP.

Figure 12-18 ICF Screen

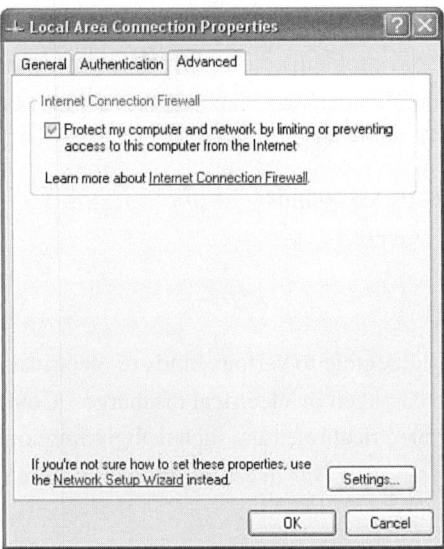

Figure 12-19 Advanced Settings Dialog Box

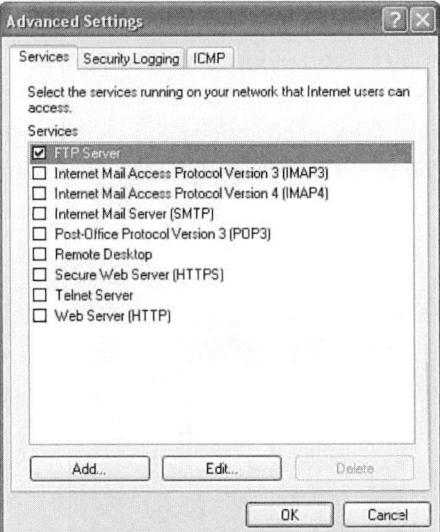

Preventive Maintenance and Power Issues

Although electricity is a necessity to run computer systems and all the required peripherals, it can also be the cause of serious problems. Some power issues cannot be prevented, but precautions can be taken to minimize damage. This section includes the following topics:

- Power issues
- Surge suppressors and power supplies
- UPS in a server environment

Power Issues

Computer components are vulnerable to various kinds of electrical fluctuations. The delicate internal components can be damaged by electrical discharges. Computers can be damaged or destroyed by high levels of electrical releases, such as lightning, or low levels, such as static electricity. The following types of power interruptions can cause a system to malfunction or fail:

- *Blackout*—A blackout is the complete loss of power for any amount of time because of a natural event (such as bad weather) or a human-error type of accident (such as during construction).

- *Brownout/sag*—A brownout is a drop in power, as illustrated in Figure 12-20. A sag is a brownout that lasts for less than a second. These incidents occur when voltage on the power line falls below 80 percent of the normal voltage. Overloaded circuits can cause this. Utility companies can intentionally cause brownouts to reduce the power that is drawn by users during peak-demand periods. Sags and brownouts account for a large portion of the power problems that affect networks and computing devices.

Figure 12-20 Brownout or Sag

■ *Noise*—Noise is caused by interference from radio broadcasts, generators, and lightning, as illustrated in Figure 12-21. Noise results in unclean power, which can cause errors in a computer system.

Figure 12-21 Noise

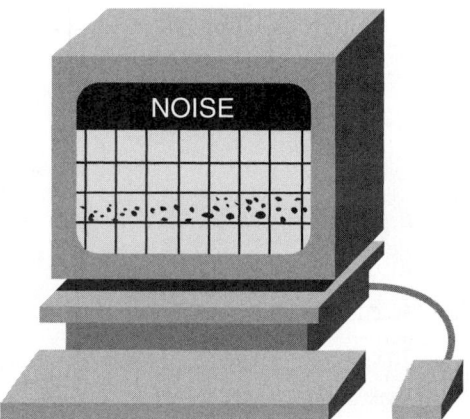

■ *Spike*—Spikes are sudden increases in voltage that are much higher than normal levels, as illustrated in Figure 12-22. A spike typically lasts for 1–2 seconds. Spikes are usually caused by lightning strikes, but they can also occur when the utility system comes back online after a blackout.

Figure 12-22 Spike

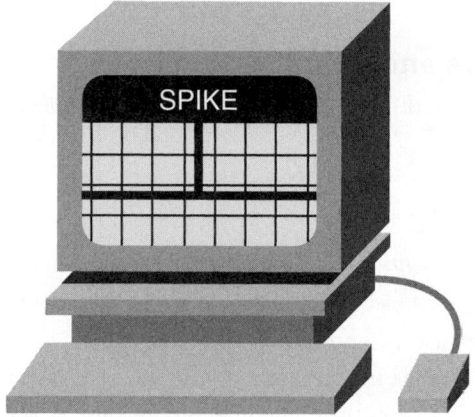

■ *Power surge*—A power surge is a dramatic increase in voltage above the normal flow of electrical current, as illustrated in Figure 12-23. Power surges are also referred to as *transient voltage.* For example, if a standard wall outlet in the United States increases from 120V to 250V, this is known as a power surge. A power surge lasts more than 3 nanoseconds. A nanosecond is one-billionth of a second. Surge suppressors can help protect delicate computer components from power surges.

Figure 12-23 Power Surge

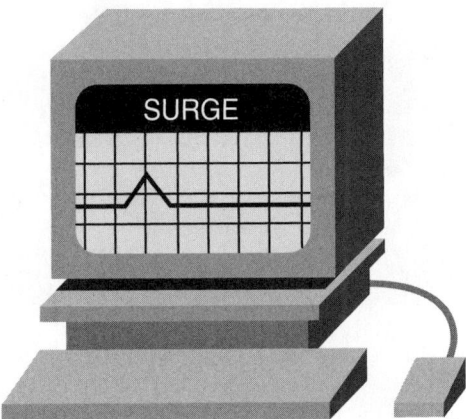

Having an understanding of the different power issues that can affect computer systems can simplify the prevention of problems. The next section discusses the devices that protect computer equipment from power issues.

Surge Suppressors and Power Supplies

This section introduces three different devices that protect sensitive computer equipment from power issues.

Surge Suppressors and Power Supplies

Figure 12-24 shows a *surge suppressor.* Surge suppressors, which are also called surge protectors, can help guard against electrical surges and spikes by diverting extra voltage to the ground. Surge suppressors use a component called a metal oxide varistor (MOV) to divert the overvoltage. A clamping voltage triggers the MOV. If the voltage is above the maximum, it is diverted to the MOV and bypasses the computer components. This ensures that the voltage that is supplied to a device stays below a certain level. Protectors mainly stop spikes from damaging the hardware. They also prevent high-voltage power surges from damaging computer equipment. Surge suppressors usually have a built-in fuse that prevents excess amounts of power from flowing through the unit. However, a surge suppressor is useless during brownouts or blackouts.

Figure 12-24 Surge Suppressor

Standby Power Supplies

A *standby power supply (SPS)* has a battery to supply power when the incoming voltage drops below the normal level. This backup battery, illustrated in Figure 12-25, is on standby during the normal operation of the unit. When the voltage drops, the battery provides DC power to a power inverter, which converts it to AC power for the computer. The problem with this device is the time that it takes to switch over to the battery. If the switching device fails, the battery cannot supply power to the computer.

Figure 12-25 Standby Power Supply (SPS)

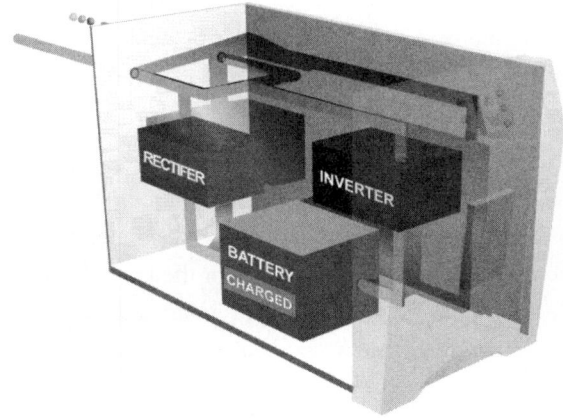

Uninterruptible Power Supplies

An ***uninterruptible power supply (UPS)*** is comparable to an SPS. However, a UPS requires battery power to operate. As illustrated in Figure 12-26, the power that is entering the unit recharges the batteries when they are not in use. The power from the battery is sent to an inverter, which sends AC power to the computer. This device protects against AC power issues. A UPS provides a limited supply of power during a power failure. The UPS usually provides enough power to allow you to save and exit your work and power off the computer. A UPS can also help guard against power sags or brownouts. Most people prefer to use a UPS over an SPS because of the switching time that is involved with an SPS. A UPS provides a steady stream of power with no delay.

Figure 12-26 Uninterruptible Power Supply (UPS)

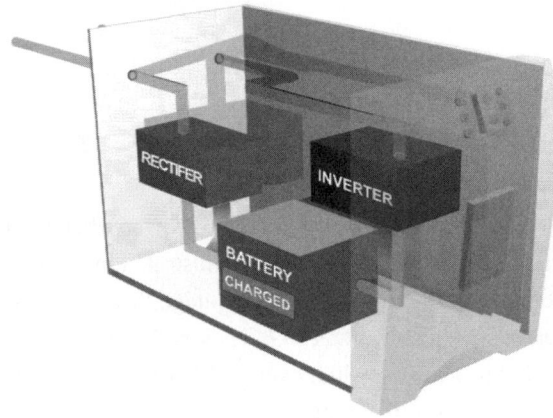

Overall, the best protection against power issues is a properly grounded building with enough battery power to run all equipment in case of a power outage.

UPS in a Server Environment

A UPS can be freestanding, as shown in Figure 12-27, or rack mounted, as shown in Figure 12-28. The UPS is plugged directly into the power source. The server and its components are then plugged into the UPS. A serial or USB cable that connects the UPS to a port on the server allows the network operating system to monitor the UPS. Therefore, the system can know when the power has failed and the UPS is providing battery power. A rack-mounted UPS is generally installed as the lowest device in a server rack because of the weight of the batteries.

Figure 12-27 Freestanding UPS

Figure 12-28 Rack-Mounted UPS

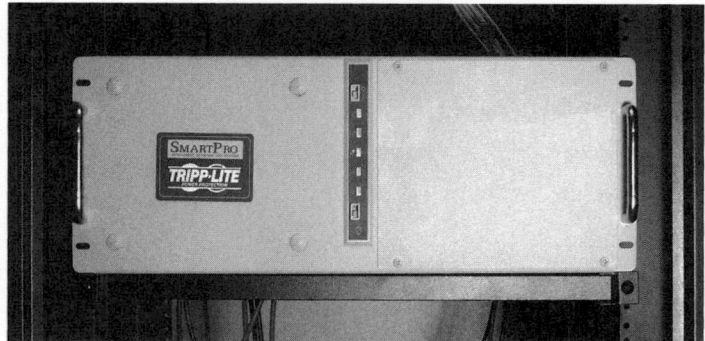

Configuring the UPS

After installing UPS-monitoring software, network administrators must configure the following parameters:

- Time to wait before sending a warning to clients that the server is running on battery power. This is generally a few seconds to allow time for the power to be restored and to prevent warning messages from being sent during momentary power losses.

- Time to wait before beginning a shutdown of the network server. This is generally a few minutes.
- Name of a program or group of commands to run as part of the shutdown process. This can be the name of the server shutdown command, or it could include programs that perform tasks, such as sending a message to the pager of the network administrator.

The UPS-monitoring software checks the status of the UPS. Status items include the voltage level that is entering the UPS and the voltage level that is leaving the UPS. Some UPS manufactures provide sophisticated software that allows the administrator to remotely manage the UPS over the Internet.

Upgrading the UPS

Upgrading a UPS can require replacing the UPS battery or upgrading to a UPS with a larger VA (volt/amp) rating. A UPS upgrade might be required for any of the following reasons:

- The current UPS does not provide power for a long enough time period for the network server to shut down properly.
- The network server power requirements have increased because power-consuming hardware, such as an internal hard disk drive, has been added to the network server.
- The amount of equipment that must be supported by the UPS during a power failure has increased.

Replacing a UPS

To replace a UPS, the network administrator must schedule downtime and then shut down the network server. Perform the following steps when recharging or replacing the UPS:

Step 1   Shut down the network server.

Step 2   Turn off all devices that are connected to the UPS.

Step 3   Turn off the UPS.

Step 4   Disconnect all power cords from the UPS.

Step 5   Disconnect the UPS power cord from the power source.

Step 6   Disconnect the UPS-monitoring cable.

Step 7   Remove the UPS from the server rack, if necessary.

Step 8   Install the new or fully charged UPS.

Step 9   Plug the UPS into the power source.

Step 10   Plug the power cords of the devices to be supported by the UPS into the UPS.

Step 11   Connect the UPS-monitoring cable.

Step 12   Turn on the UPS.

Step 13 Power up the network server and other devices that are plugged into the UPS.

Step 14 Upgrade and reconfigure the UPS-monitoring software on the network server.

Before installing a UPS, plug it into a power source to charge its batteries. The initial charge time is usually 12 hours or more. Follow the manufacturer's instructions for unpacking the UPS and preparing it for use.

Check the power requirements of the new UPS to determine whether the existing power source is adequate and the amperage is correct. The new UPS might require a different power plug or monitoring cable than the old UPS. The UPS-monitoring software might need to be updated or replaced. Check to see that the new UPS can fit into the same space as the old UPS.

The batteries in a UPS are rechargeable, but they do not last forever. At some point, the UPS battery must be replaced. To replace the battery in a UPS, consult the UPS manufacturer's instructions. Some UPS battery-replacement operations can be performed while the network server is operating and the UPS is supplying power to the server. This is called a *battery hot swap*. Many battery replacements require the UPS to be turned off. If the UPS must be turned off, shut down the network server before replacing the battery.

Summary

This chapter discussed preventive maintenance and the importance of keeping computer hardware in good working condition to avoid costly repairs. Some important concepts from this chapter include the following:

- Three important questions for developing a preventive maintenance policy are when, what, and how. Preventive maintenance should be done on a regular basis, and each task should be recorded in a maintenance log. Documentation should explain how the maintenance is carried out so that it is consistent and thorough.

- The tools and equipment that are required to maintain computer components include a basic toolkit, an antistatic vacuum, canned air, and lint-free cloths.

- Adhere to environmental guidelines for the proper disposal of CRTs, batteries, printing supplies, and other components. A Material Safety Data Sheet lists specific hazards and special handling procedures.

- Electrostatic discharge protection devices and ESD-free environments can prevent many problems. ESD can be prevented by using a wrist strap with an antistatic mat or by using a grounded workbench when working on a system.

- Individual computer components must be cleaned on a regular basis. These components must be unplugged during cleaning.

- Software utilities such as ScanDisk and Defragmenter manage applications and files to optimize system performance.

- A firewall is a hardware or software system that prevents unauthorized people from accessing sensitive data. Windows XP includes a personal firewall that can be set up to protect a home or office network.

- Special devices are used to protect computer equipment from different types of power interruptions that can cause system malfunctions.

The next chapter covers troubleshooting basics for computer hardware. The chapter explains how to determine the cause of hardware problems and how to resolve them.

Key Terms

AC voltage test   Used to check system components, including power supplies.

antistatic bag   Special packaging material that protects components from ESD.

antistatic spray   Reduces ESD and cleans and repels dust from electronic equipment.

antivirus application   A program that is installed on the system to prevent computer viruses from infecting the computer.

blackout   A complete loss of power.

boot-sector virus   Targets the boot sector of the system so that the virus is run when the computer starts.

brownout   A temporary drop in power.

CHKDSK /f   DOS utility that checks the system for errors.

compressed air   Also called canned air, it is air under pressure in a can that blows dust off of computer components without creating static.

computer virus   A program with malicious intent.

DC voltage test   Checks for live DC circuits.

Defragmenter   Utility that optimizes space on the hard drive.

digital multimeter (DMM)   Combines the functionality of a voltmeter, ohmmeter, and ammeter into one easy measuring device.

electrostatic discharge (ESD)   The buildup of an electric charge on a surface.

file virus   Modifies an existing program so that upon execution, the virus carries out the malicious intent.

free liquid   A substance that can pass through a standard paint filter. Many dump sites cannot handle free liquids.

grounding wrist strap   Provides a place for the static before being discharged through sensitive computer components.

loopback plug   Tests serial and parallel ports, USB ports, and RJ-45 connectors for network connectivity. Loopback testing works by sending out signals and verifying that the returned signal is valid. Also called loopback adapters.

macro virus   Takes advantage of programming languages to attack a system.

Material Safety Data Sheet (MSDS)   A fact sheet that identifies hazardous materials.

noise   Interference that causes unclean power.

power surge   A brief increase in voltage that is usually caused by high demands on the power grid in a local area.

preventive maintenance policy   The detailed program that determines maintenance timing, the type of maintenance performed, and the specifics of how the maintenance plan is carried out.

REGEDIT   A utility that is used to edit the registry.

sag   A brownout that lasts for less than a second.

ScanDisk   Utility that checks the integrity of files and folders on the hard drive.

spike   A sudden increase in voltage that is usually caused by lightning strikes.

standby power supply (SPS)   Battery backup that is enabled when voltage levels fall below normal.

surge suppressor   Device that makes sure that the voltage going to another device stays below a certain level.

uninterruptible power supply (UPS)   Power supplied by a battery that is constantly recharged by a regular power source.

Check Your Understanding

1. Which of the following is not used to clean computer components?

   A. Canned air

   B. Lint-free cloths

   C. Soap and water

   D. Regular vacuum

2. What is the proper way to dispose of batteries that are used in portable computers?

   A. Recycling.

   B. Recharging.

   C. Designated landfill.

   D. Special disposal is not required.

3. What does the acronym MSDS stand for?

   A. Maintenance Standard Data Specifications

   B. Material Safety Data Sheet

   C. Material Standard Distribution Sheet

   D. Maintenance Safety Data Specifications

4. What is the name for substances that can pass through a standard paint filter?

   A. Free liquids

   B. Micro liquids

   C. Municipal liquids

   D. Macro liquids

5. What does the acronym ESD stand for?

   A. Electrostandard discharge

   B. Electric Static Disarray

   C. Electrostatic discharge

   D. Electro Standard Direct

6. How many volts must be built up for a person to feel an ESD?

   A. 3000

   B. 300

   C. 10,000

   D. 1,000

7. Once a computer case has been opened, a technician should do which of the following?

   A. Work quickly.

   B. Wear a grounding wrist strap.

   C. Raise the humidity.

   D. Work on carpet.

8. Which of the following temporarily stores parts and components when disassembling a computer for cleaning or other types of preventive maintenance?

   A. Metal box

   B. Cloth bag

   C. Magnetic board

   D. Antistatic bag

9. What component of a computer system receives more physical abuse than any other?

   A. Mouse

   B. Keyboard

   C. Monitor

   D. Printer

10. An erratic mouse is most likely due to which of the following?

    A. One of the potentiometers has failed.

    B. The mouse driver is corrupt.

    C. The mouse is plugged into the wrong port.

    D. The mouse needs cleaning.

11. Which utility checks the integrity of files and folders?

    A. ScanDisk

    B. Defragmenter

    C. CHKDSK

    D. REGEDIT

12. Which utility reorganizes files on a hard drive?

    A. ScanDisk

    B. Defragmenter

    C. CHKDSK

    D. REGEDIT

13. What term describes a complete loss of power?

    A. Blackout

    B. Brownout

    C. Spike

    D. Sag

14. What term describes a drop in power?

    A. Blackout

    B. Brownout

    C. Spike

    D. Surge

15. What term describes a sudden increase in voltage that is higher than normal levels?

 A. Blackout

 B. Brownout

 C. Spike

 D. Sag

16. What term describes a brief increase in voltage?

 A. Blackout

 B. Surge

 C. Spike

 D. Sag

17. When should you run antivirus software?

 A. When notified of a potential virus

 B. On a regular basis

 C. When the system is acting strangely

 D. All of the above

18. What term describes a system that runs off of a battery that is constantly charged?

 A. Uninterruptible power supply (UPS)

 B. Standby power supply (SPS)

 C. Uninterruptible power plug (UPP)

 D. Uninterruptible power unit (UPU)

19. What does a surge suppressor do?

 A. Keeps voltage high for better transmission

 B. Keeps voltage below a certain level

 C. Is used in the plenum of a building

 D. Works with software to even out voltage levels

20. What term describes a system that has a battery take over when needed?

 A. Uninterruptible power supply (UPS)

 B. Standby power supply (SPS)

 C. Uninterruptible power plug (UPP)

 D. Uninterruptible power unit (UPU)

Upon completing this chapter, you will be able to perform the following tasks:

- Use the steps in the troubleshooting cycle
- Gather correct data from the user to properly troubleshoot the computer problem
- Isolate hardware problems from software problems
- Troubleshoot hardware components
- Identify the most common failure points of computer components
- Identify common field-replaceable units

Chapter 13

Troubleshooting PC Hardware

This chapter discusses the troubleshooting process for computer hardware components. The troubleshooting cycle details the techniques that can diagnose computer problems and implement the solutions. When the diagnosis has been made, you learn the steps that are necessary to correct problems with hardware, peripherals, Internet connections, and network-access devices.

Troubleshooting Basics

Following the steps in the troubleshooting process allows the technician to effectively determine the cause of a problem and offer potential solutions. In addition, the technician must know which tools to use and how to dispose of components in an environmentally safe manner. This section includes the following topics:

- Troubleshooting overview
- Troubleshooting steps
- Troubleshooting tools
- Diagnostic software
- Disposal actions

Troubleshooting Overview

Effective *troubleshooting* uses proven techniques to diagnose and fix computer problems. A series of logical steps make the troubleshooting process the most efficient way to solve a computer problem.

Figure 13-1 displays the troubleshooting process. The cycle starts with identifying the problem. Then, information must be gathered to define the causes. Next, a solution is developed and implemented. Finally, the solution is verified. If the problem is resolved, the troubleshooting cycle ends by documenting the solution. If the problem is not resolved, the cycle starts over, and the process repeats until a solution is found. Each of these steps is detailed in the following sections.

Figure 13-1 Troubleshooting Cycle Flow Chart

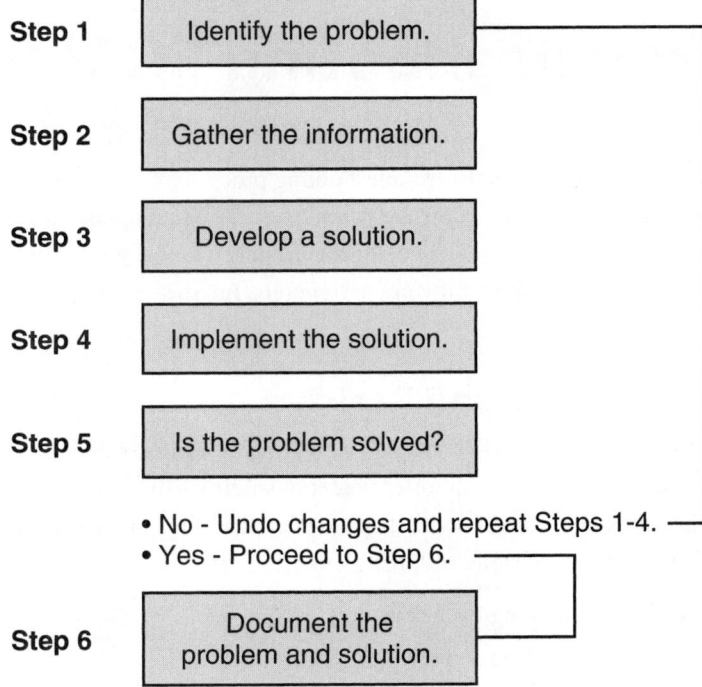

Troubleshooting Steps

As depicted in Figure 13-1, the steps for troubleshooting are as follows:

Step 1   Identify the problem.

Step 2   Gather the information.

Step 3   Develop a solution.

Step 4   Implement the solution.

Step 5   Verify that the problem is solved.

Step 6   Document the problem and solution.

Each of these steps is detailed in the following sections.

Step 1: Identify the Problem

In this step, the problem is identified. This includes defining the general symptoms so that the possible causes can be determined. The outcome is a detailed statement that clearly describes the problem. Without a clear understanding of the problem, the technician cannot gather the necessary information to develop an appropriate solution.

To identify the problem, perform the following tasks:

- Identify symptoms and associated causes
- List ideas and possibilities (brainstorm)
- Create a clear and concise problem statement

Worksheet 13.1.2   Troubleshooting Basics

Test your basic knowledge of troubleshooting techniques.

Step 2: Gather the Information

When the problem has been identified, the next step is to gather information so that a solution can be developed. Fast and efficient troubleshooting involves gathering the correct information to develop an accurate solution. Computer problems can range from simple to extremely complex. However, computer problems can become increasingly complicated if the technician does not have the correct information.

Technicians have many resources available to help them to diagnose the problem. Technicians can use digital multimeters (DMMs), software-based diagnostic tools, and the user to gain information. Technicians can visually inspect the systems, look for broken components, and listen for evidence of a problem.

The user can provide insights into how the computer was operating before the system had problems. The technician can document any changes that were made by the user that might have adverse effects on the system. The user can also describe any changes to the system, errors that were received, and the system performance leading up to the problem.

It is the technician's responsibility to develop a rapport with the user. Part of this involves knowing how to properly question the user. A professional approach establishes the required trust that enables the user to discuss any changes. For example, it would not be easy for a user to contact tech support and report that he had opened an e-mail attachment, and that his machine is now infected with a virus. But that is what must happen, or the entire network can become infected.

NOTE

By keeping current and accurate system information on each computer in a network, the IT technician can determine whether the user has accidentally made changes or has forgotten about changes that can affect the system performance and cause system errors. The IT technician is in an excellent position to educate users about the policies regarding acceptable use.

CAUTION

Do not reproduce the error if it can adversely affect the computer components. For example, do not reproduce a problem such as an arcing power supply.

The following is a list of typical questions that the technician should ask:

- Can the error be described? Document the description of the problem.

- Was an error message received? Computers are manufactured with self-diagnostic tools. If the computer fails one of the self-diagnostics tests, the unit typically generates an error message.

- Ask the user to recall the error message or re-create it. In the case of a power-on self-test (POST) error, ask the user for the type (number and pattern) of beeps heard.

- Has the problem or error occurred before? Try to establish a timeline for the event. A timeline can help identify potential causes of the event. If the problem has happened before, document the changes that were made to the system.

- Has the system been changed in any way? Identify recent changes to the hardware or software. Changes that were made in an attempt to correct previous problems can be the source of the current problem. Also, adding or removing hardware and software can create unforeseen problems with system resources. Many updates are automatic, and the user might not be aware that a change has taken place.

Reproducing the problem can allow the user to precisely describe the error. An on-site technician can then see and experience the problem firsthand.

After asking all the necessary questions, obtaining answers, and assessing the answers, the problem should be isolated as being hardware or software related. The problem can then be isolated to a specific component or part of the system. Then, the technician can proceed with developing a potential solution to the problem, as outlined in the next section.

Network Server Problem Solving

The following list presents a few typical questions to ask when a problem exists with a network server:

- When was the last time that the network server was operational?

- What has changed since the last time the network server was operational?

- What hardware has been recently added to or removed from the network server?

- What software has been recently added to or removed from the network server?

- Who first reported the problem with the network server?

- Where is the network server logbook?

- How does the failure of the network server affect the operation of the corporation?

Use your senses to answer the following questions:

- Is the server room too hot or too cold?

- Is the server room above the maximum operating humidity for the equipment?

- Can you smell anything burning in the server room?
- Is smoke visible in the server room?
- Are server alarms sounding?
- Are UPS alarms sounding?
- Are error lights flashing on disk drives?
- Are any of the network server components hot to the touch?
- Are power cords disconnected from any of the components?
- Are network cables disconnected from any of the network devices, including the servers?
- Are all external SCSI cables properly connected?

Using your senses to answer these basic questions is an integral part of troubleshooting. Also important are hardware/software tools and utilities.

Step 3: Develop a Solution

Creating a potential solution is the third step in the troubleshooting process. The technician assesses the gathered data. He or she uses experience, logic, reasoning, and common sense to develop a solution. Sometimes, the initial diagnosis proves unsuccessful and the strategy must be revised. Troubleshooting is an acquired skill that improves with time and experience.

To develop a solution, perform the following tasks:

- Compile gathered information.
- Assess the information.
- Consider the most likely cause.
- Develop a solution based on your experience and the information that you gathered.

Step 4: Implement the Solution

The fourth step in the troubleshooting cycle is implementing the solution. Essentially, this step involves the technician working on the computer. The technician attempts the solution through hands-on manipulation of the computer components, which can be hardware or software. Remember the following things when implementing a solution to a problem:

- Back up critical data before making any changes that have the potential to corrupt data that is stored on the computer.
- Start with the simple things first.
- Change only one thing at a time, and double-check the effect of the change on the computer.
- Reverse any changes that make the problem worse or cause further harm to the system.

Step 5: Verify That the Problem Is Solved

Verifying that the problem is solved is the next step in the troubleshooting cycle. After the solution has been implemented, the technician can run diagnostic tests, visually inspect, and listen to the system to verify that the problem is solved. Then, the technician must verify that the user is satisfied with the results. If the system is operating properly, the technician moves on to Step 6: documenting the details of the problem and the ultimate solution.

If the system is not operating correctly, the technician must undo any changes that were made to the system and return to the beginning of the troubleshooting cycle. If more information is needed, the technician should return to problem identification in Step 1.

Step 6: Document the Problem and Solution

Documenting is the final step of the troubleshooting process. It is important to document all the changes that were introduced to the system as a result of solving the problem. This record can be the starting point for troubleshooting future problems. The documentation can also eliminate an entire set of suspect problems.

Documentation over time tracks all the changes or modifications that were made to a system. Future problems with the system can then be diagnosed more easily by a different technician. Records of previous repairs are invaluable troubleshooting tools that can educate the technician on the previous state of the machine.

The following items are involved in documenting the problem and solution:

- Document all changes that were made to system.
- Document the initial problem and the subsequent resolution.
- Document when the problem was resolved.
- Document who resolved the problem.

 Lab 13.1.7   The Steps of the Troubleshooting Cycle

Upon completion of this lab, you will be able to describe the importance of and identify the steps in the troubleshooting cycle.

Troubleshooting Tools

To correctly troubleshoot hardware problems, technicians need to be equipped with the right tools, as shown in Figure 13-2. Technicians should be prepared for a wide range of circumstances and should take tools with them to remote locations. The tools in a tool set should include both mechanical and digital tools.

Figure 13-2 Typical Tool Set

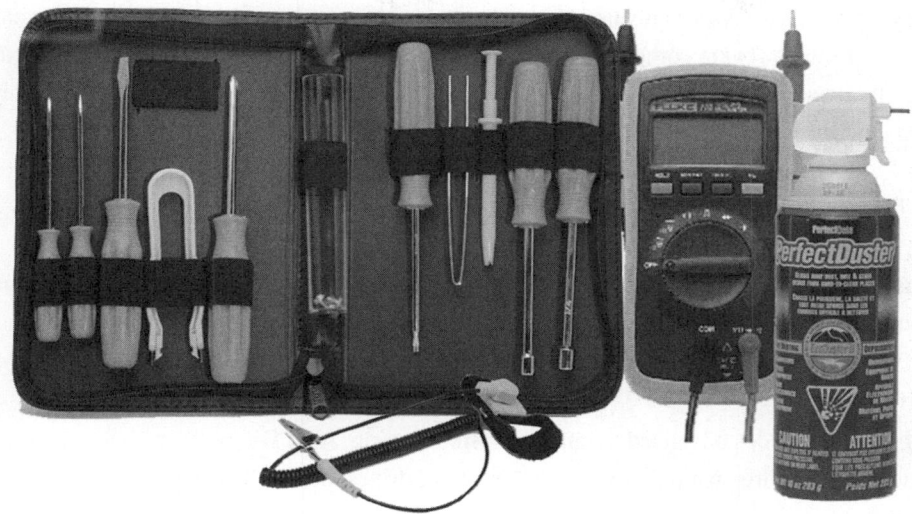

Diagnostic Software

Many commercial software products are available to assist in troubleshooting computer problems. These products, referred to as *diagnostic software*, are also helpful in preventing potential system failures. Some of the more popular programs are included in the following list:

- **SpinRite**—http://grc.com/default.htm
- **Checkit**—http://www.smithmicro.com/
  default.tpl?cart=1077398154141037&group=product_full&sku=CKDWINEE
- **PC Technician**—http://www.windsortech.com/
- **AMI Diags**—http://www.amidiag.com
- **SiSoft Sandra**—http://www.3bsoftware.com/

A number of other products are also available. Many are freeware or shareware and can help solve both hardware and software problems.

SpinRite

SpinRite is a program for recovering data from a crashed hard drive. SpinRite is a stand-alone application that is capable of booting independent of DOS. It has gained market recognition and has been successful in difficult cases. SpinRite can also help prevent hard drive failures. If loaded before a failure, it can warn users of a potential problem and can prevent a crash by isolating problem areas of the hard drive. The problem areas are designated as corrupt. If an area has been corrupted, it cannot be used to read or write data.

Checkit

Checkit performs system analysis and testing. It can provide the technician with performance reports for the hardware components. Checkit can perform loopback testing using loopback plugs. It can also verify proper operation of the CPU, PCI slots, DMA, CMOS, cache, keyboard, and the first 64 MB of video RAM.

PC Technician

PC Technician is a stand-alone diagnostic tool that operates independently of DOS. PC Technician can perform diagnostic tests on parallel ports, serial ports, hard drives, keyboards, video adapters, and RAM.

AMI Diags

AMI Diags provides advanced diagnostic system testing. AMI Diags can provide reports on memory, serial ports, parallel ports, modems, hard drives, the keyboard, the BIOS, and video adapters.

SiSoft Sandra

SiSoft System Analyzer, Diagnostic, and Reporting Assistant (Sandra) is a program that provides a set of diagnostic tools that can aid in troubleshooting and benchmarking computer components. Sandra can test the performance of the CPUs, modem, video card, memory, BIOS, and hard drives.

Disposal Actions

Proper disposal practices should be followed when disposing of hazardous materials such as chemicals, batteries, CRTs, and printer cartridges. Technicians should be informed of the local regulations for disposing of computer components. Information for disposing of computer components is covered in Chapter 12, "Preventive Maintenance."

Troubleshooting the Hardware Box

The steps of the troubleshooting process can help determine that a problem is hardware related. The technician must then determine which component is causing the problem and whether it can be fixed or must be replaced. The field-replaceable unit (FRU) is usually a quick fix for hardware problems. It allows the technician to remove the component for further evaluation and gets the user back to work. This section includes the following topics:

- Overview of field-replaceable units
- POST errors
- CMOS/BIOS errors

- Motherboard-related errors
- CPUs
- RAM
- Cable issues
- Ports
- The video system
- Secondary storage devices
- Sound cards
- Power supply issues
- Box cooling issues

Overview of Field-Replaceable Units

Devices that can be replaced or added in the field are called *field-replaceable units (FRUs)*. Some of the common FRUs are illustrated in Figure 13-3.

Figure 13-3 Field-Replaceable Units

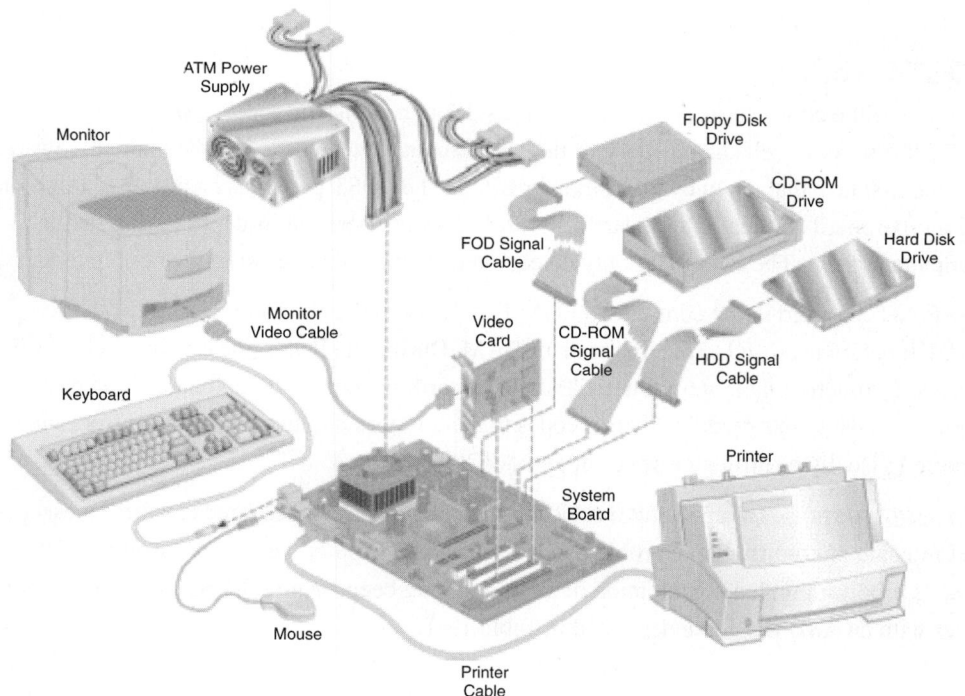

FRUs do not require soldering and are easy to remove and install. For example, a PCI sound card is considered an FRU. A sound card can be removed with no special tools required. The following is a list of common FRUs:

- Monitors
- Keyboards/mice
- Modular expansion cards
- Most microprocessors
- Power supplies
- RAM: DIMMs, SIMMs, RIMMs, and so on
- Floppy and fixed disk drives
- Motherboards

When a component is replaced as an FRU, make sure to document the symptoms that are described and record the replacement unit's serial number. This documentation could help if a pattern of problems develops. A manufacturer's defect, power issues, or ESD could be the cause of component failure, and detailed documentation can help pinpoint whether certain components are failing more often than others.

POST Errors

Every time the computer is powered on, it runs through a *power-on self-test (POST)*. The POST is a series of self-diagnostic tests that the computer executes to test the major hardware. It is the first task that is run by the computer BIOS. The POST performs basic test routines on the motherboard and major hardware devices. It does not perform in-depth testing on the computer system. The POST can only detect major failures that can stop the bootup process.

The POST is stored in the computer's ROM BIOS. When the computer is turned on, the POST function is passed to the first bank of RAM. During the POST, the computer checks for a properly functioning system timer, CPU, video card, memory, and keyboard. If an error occurs, the BIOS has predefined error codes that are reported to the user. These errors can be reported visually or through a series of audio POST codes.

The *audio POST codes* are useful troubleshooting aids. These codes represent error messages that indicate or confirm that a problem exists with the computer hardware. An audio POST code is produced with a combination of short and long beeps. Audio POST codes for a computer with an AMI BIOS are described in Table 13-1.

Table 13-1 AMI BIOS POST Errors (Audible Error Codes)

Audible Code	Error Message	Description
(No sound)	Not plugged in or bad power supply	The power supply is either bad or is not plugged in.
1 short beep	DRAM refresh failure	The programmable interrupt timer or controller might be bad.
2 short beeps	Memory parity error	A memory parity failure has occurred in the first 64 KB of RAM.
3 short beeps	Base 64-KB RAM error	A memory failure has occurred in the first 64 KB of RAM.
4 short beeps	System timer error	A failure has occurred with the system timer or with the first bank of memory.
5 short beeps	Microprocessor error	A failure has occurred with the CPU.
6 short beeps	Keyboard/Gate A20 failure	A failure has occurred with the keyboard.
7 short beeps	Virtual mode exception error	A failure has occurred with the motherboard or CPU.
8 short beeps	Video display memory error	A failure has occurred with the video adapter.
9 short beeps	ROM BIOS checksum failure	A failure has occurred with the BIOS chip.
10 short beeps	CMOS shutdown register read/write error	The CMOS shutdown has failed.
11 short beeps	Cache error	The L2 cache is faulty.
1 long beep and 2 short beeps	Video system failure	A failure has occurred with the video display, or the cable is not attached.
1 long beep	Normal operation	The computer has passed the POST and is performing normally.

The error reports that are generated by the POST can vary slightly depending on the BIOS that is installed on the computer. For specific information about POST errors, refer to your BIOS documentation or the BIOS manufacturer's website. Error messages, such as those shown in Table 13-2, apply only to the referenced BIOS. Visit the following website for BIOS code information:

http://bioscentral.com

Table 13-2 Display Errors

Error Message	Description
Visual Display Error Messages	
CMOS BATTERY LOW	A failure has occurred with the CMOS battery or the checksum test.
CMOS SYSTEM OPTION NOT SET	A failure has occurred with the CMOS battery or the checksum test.
CMOS CHECKSUM FAILURE	The checksum test failed, or the CMOS battery is low.
CMOS DISPLAY MISMATCH	A failure has occurred in the display type verification.
CMOS MEMORY SIZE MISMATCH	A setup and system configuration failure has occurred.
CMOS TIMER AND DATE NOT SET	A setup and system configuration failure has occurred with the timer circuitry.
Nonfatal Errors Without Setup Option	
KEYBOARD ERROR	A keyboard failure has occurred.
KEYBOARD LOCKED	A keyboard failure has occurred.
CH-X TIMER ERROR	A channel X (0, 1, or 2) timer failure has occurred.
DISPLAY SWITCH SETTING NOT PROPER	A display type error has occurred.

Table 13-2 Display Errors (Continued)

Error Message	Description
Nonfatal Errors Without Setup Option (Continued)	
FDD CONTROLLER ERROR	A floppy drive setup failure has occurred.
HDD CONTROLLER ERROR	A hard drive setup failure has occurred.
C: DRIVE ERROR	A hard drive setup failure has occurred.
D: DRIVE ERROR	A hard drive setup failure has occurred.
System-Halted Errors	
INVALID SWITCH MEMORY FAILURE	An error with real-/protected-mode changeover has occurred.
8042 GATE A20 ERROR	The GATE A20 portion of the keyboard controller has failed.
CMOS INOPERATIONAL	The CMOS shutdown register test has failed.
DMA ERROR	The DMA on the motherboard has failed.
DMA #1 ERROR	The first DMA on the motherboard has failed.
DMA #2 ERROR	The second DMA on the motherboard has failed.

POST Card Error Indicators

A *POST card* is a device that helps troubleshoot computer problems that occur before the BIOS can report an error. Sometimes a computer fails before a BIOS error can be reported. When this happens, a POST card is useful, because it provides the technician with a digital readout of POST errors. POST cards are useful for troubleshooting power supply voltages, IRQ/DMA conflicts, and motherboard timers. Also, POST cards are compatible with either ISA or PCI slots.

POST card error messages are displayed on the card itself, in either binary or hex format. No video display is necessary to read the error message. Figure 13-4 shows a picture of a POST card. Notice the LCD and hexadecimal BIOS code.

Figure 13-4 POST Card

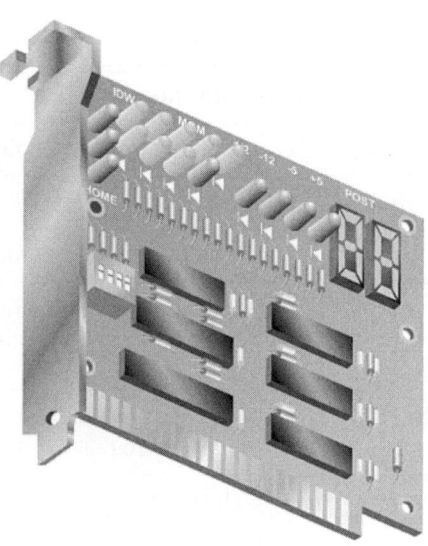

Lab 13.2.2 Identifying POST Errors

Upon completion of this lab, you will be able to identify common POST errors. The ability to identify POST errors is essential when troubleshooting computers.

CMOS/BIOS Errors

The *Complementary Metal Oxide Semiconductor (CMOS)* or *nonvolatile random-access memory (NVRAM)* stores the system startup configuration and parameters. Common errors that are associated with the BIOS include CMOS checksum errors, IRQ/DMA conflicts, hard drive errors, memory errors, and CPU problems. Table 13-3 provides common errors that can be received by the computer operator.

Checking the System BIOS

When a computer or network server is powered up, the version number of the system BIOS usually displays. Check the vendor's website to determine whether the version of the system BIOS that is installed is the latest available. If a newer version of the system BIOS is available, download the upgrade and follow the vendor's instructions to update the system BIOS on the computer or network server. Most network servers and computers have a BIOS that is flashable, meaning that it can be easily erased and updated using software.

Table 13-3 CMOS/BIOS-Related Errors

Symptom/Error	Problem	Solution
CMOS battery is low	Low CMOS battery, either internal or external.	For internal batteries, leave the computer on to recharge the batteries. For external batteries, buy replacements. If the problem still exists, you might have to replace the CMOS chip. The CMOS chip is usually soldered onto most motherboards. Decide whether to replace the entire board or to resolder the new CMOS chip.
CMOS checksum error	CMOS battery failure.	Replace the CMOS battery.
Incorrect CPU speed shown	CPU speed mismatch.	Reset or update the BIOS. Also, verify the jumper settings on the motherboard.
Inaccessible boot device	Hard drive is not valid.	Verify the boot order in the BIOS, and verify the jumper settings.
Incorrect memory size	Memory mismatch.	Verify the compatibility of memory; switch out memory with known good memory.

Accessing the CMOS

To access the CMOS setup utility, press the setup key during the boot process. The setup key must be pressed early in the boot process or the system will load the installed OS. If the video display is functional, a prompt to enter setup by pressing a certain key is usually displayed. The CMOS setup key is usually F1, F2, or Delete. However, no standard exists, so verify the setup key with the proper documentation. Figure 13-5 shows a typical CMOS setup utility screen.

Identifying a Faulty/Incorrect CMOS Setting

One way to help resolve CMOS-related errors is to reset the CMOS settings to default. Resetting the CMOS clears the memory and all potentially corrupted data. Clearing the CMOS memory is useful when the computer does not boot. You can clear the CMOS memory in two ways. One way is to move the motherboard jumpers manually to the "Clear CMOS" position for a few seconds. To locate these jumpers, consult the motherboard manufacturer's documentation.

Figure 13-5 CMOS Setup Utility Screen

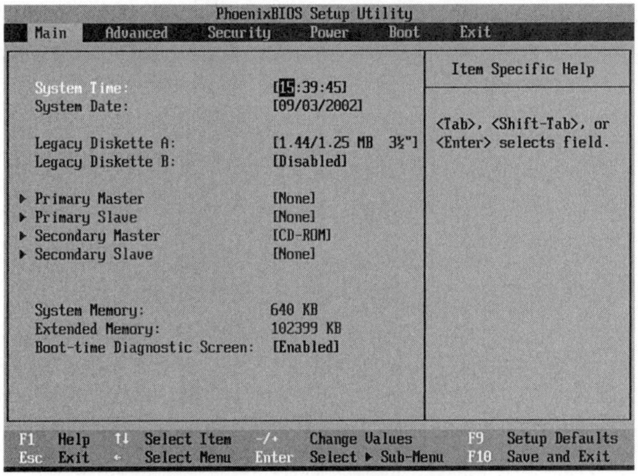

```
                        PhoenixBIOS Setup Utility
   Main    Advanced    Security    Power    Boot    Exit

                                                      Item Specific Help
   System Time:                [15:39:45]
   System Date:                [09/03/2002]
                                                   <Tab>, <Shift-Tab>, or
   Legacy Diskette A:          [1.44/1.25 MB  3½"]  <Enter> selects field.
   Legacy Diskette B:          [Disabled]

 ▶ Primary Master             [None]
 ▶ Primary Slave              [None]
 ▶ Secondary Master           [CD-ROM]
 ▶ Secondary Slave            [None]


   System Memory:              640 KB
   Extended Memory:            102399 KB
   Boot-time Diagnostic Screen: [Enabled]



 F1   Help   ↑↓  Select Item   -/+   Change Values    F9   Setup Defaults
 Esc  Exit    ←  Select Menu   Enter Select ▶ Sub-Menu F10  Save and Exit
```

If the preceding procedure fails to clear the CMOS, you can remove the CMOS battery, which is the small round battery on the motherboard, as shown in Figure 13-6.

Figure 13-6 CMOS Battery

Follow these steps to remove the CMOS battery:

Step 1   Turn off the computer and unplug it.

Step 2   Remove the CMOS battery from the motherboard.

Step 3   Short (connect) the negative and positive battery connections that are located on the motherboard using a conducting material such as a wire or a screwdriver head.

Step 4   Replace the CMOS battery in its original position on the motherboard.

Step 5   Plug in the computer and power it on to reboot the system.

Upgrading the BIOS

A BIOS upgrade can include patches, fixes, additional features, and support for the latest devices to resolve any problems. If the system is operating properly, a BIOS upgrade is not recommended. If the BIOS is updated incorrectly, it could damage the motherboard and peripheral devices. It could also void the manufacturer's warranty.

Special consideration must be taken before upgrading the BIOS. The motherboard must have a flash BIOS and support the upgraded version. The BIOS chip also must support the upgrade version number. Only when these criteria are met can the BIOS be successfully updated.

Always obtain this information before attempting a flash BIOS upgrade. Generally, if the motherboard has PCI slots, it has a flash BIOS. The BIOS revision number should display during startup. It should be in the following format: #401A0-1234. In this example, the revision number is 1234. The motherboard revision number is printed on the board. On newer motherboards, the revision number is located near the CPU or the center of the motherboard.

To upgrade a flash BIOS, follow these general steps:

Step 1   Obtain the latest BIOS program from the vendor, generally from the vendor's website.

Step 2   Follow the vendor's instructions when loading the BIOS upgrade program onto a floppy disk.

Step 3   Shut down and reboot the computer or server from the floppy disk that contains the BIOS upgrade program and the latest BIOS code.

Step 4   Follow the on-screen instructions when performing the BIOS upgrade.

Step 5   Never interrupt the flash BIOS upgrade process. This could result in a computer or network server that cannot be booted. When this happens, the system must usually be returned to the manufacturer for repair/replacement, resulting in downtime and lost productivity.

Upgrading Adapters

To upgrade the BIOS or firmware on adapters, such as a SCSI adapter or a RAID controller, follow these general steps:

Step 1   Locate the latest BIOS or firmware on the adapter vendor's website.

Step 2   Download the BIOS or firmware upgrade, and follow the vendor's instructions to install the upgrade.

Motherboard-Related Errors

The motherboard coordinates the proper functioning of the system components. It allows devices to communicate and work with each other. If the motherboard is malfunctioning, it must be replaced. The following scenarios illustrate possible problem situations and describe the procedures to resolve them. Figure 13-7 shows a typical motherboard.

Figure 13-7 Motherboard

Scenario 1: Computer Does Not Boot and Appears Inoperative

If the computer does not boot and appears to be inoperative, follow these steps:

Step 1   Check the external power supply. Verify that the wall outlet is working and that the cable is properly connected to the computer. Check the voltage setting on the power supply. A power-supply switch that is set incorrectly can keep the PC from booting.

Step 2   Inspect the cabling inside the computer case. Make sure that the motherboard and the drives are connected to the internal power supply.

Step 3   Inspect the mounting of the motherboard. The motherboard is separated from the case by rubber buffers on each mount point and should not be touching the metal base. If these buffers (made of either rubber or plastic) are not properly installed, the motherboard could short.

Step 4   Remove each expansion card, and try to reboot the system. If the computer boots, the expansion card that was removed was faulty.

Step 5   Check the drive controllers. Remove them and try to boot the computer. If it boots, the problem can be isolated to one of the drives.

Step 6   Remove any modular video cards. If the computer boots, replace the defective video card with a valid video card and try to reboot.

Step 7   Replace the first bank of RAM with a known-good bank of RAM.

If the computer is still not operational, the motherboard probably needs to be replaced.

Scenario 2: Motherboard Jumper Settings Are Reconfigured

DIP switches and jumpers are on the surface of most motherboards. The switch settings or jumper settings can be reconfigured during troubleshooting. For example, on some motherboards, the CMOS startup utility can be entered by a particular placement of the jumpers. If these jumpers are not returned to their original configuration, the computer will not operate correctly. To verify motherboard jumper settings, consult the motherboard's documentation or the manufacturer's website.

Scenario 3: ROM Chip and Motherboard Are Incompatible

During the POST routines, the POST compares the compatibility of the ROM chip and the motherboard. If the POST fails, the user receives a "BIOS ROM checksum error" message. This error signifies that the ROM chip and motherboard are not compatible. The ROM chip must be replaced with a chip that is compatible with the motherboard.

CPUs

The symptoms of a processor error include slow performance, POST beep errors, or a system that is not operating properly. These errors usually indicate that an internal error has occurred. Internal errors can also cause intermittent failures. If the system continuously counts RAM or freezes while counting the RAM, the CPU might be creating the errors and might need to be replaced.

Cooling Issues

Figure 13-8 shows a fan, and Figure 13-9 shows the fan attached to the heat sink. Most CPUs have an on-board fan to provide cooling to the CPU. If the system freezes—or is overheating—the CPU fan might be malfunctioning.

Figure 13-8 CPU Fan

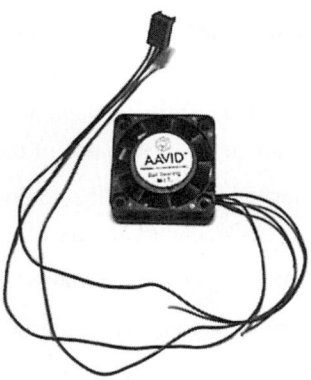

Figure 13-9 Heat Sink with the CPU Fan

Proper maintenance of internal components can help prevent costly repairs to the CPU. Keep the computer in a well-ventilated area, clean the vents regularly, routinely replace case slots, and clean the inside of the computer. A proper cooling fan for the specific CPU is also required.

CPUs can also become loose because of the expansion of metals when heated and the contraction of metals when cooled. Metal fluctuation can eventually cause the CPU to become unstable and can affect performance. Visually inspect the CPU, and push it back into place if it appears to be loose. With a ZIF socket, a loose CPU should be reseated by "unlocking" the socket, reinserting the CPU, and relocking the socket (lowering the lever).

Voltage Supply Issues

To run properly, CPUs must be set to receive the correct voltages. Motherboards that use Socket 5, Socket 7, or Super Socket 7 chips need to use voltage regulators. Those that use Socket 370, Slot 1, Slot A, or Socket A have an automatic voltage-regulation feature. This capability allows the CPU to determine the voltage setting automatically. Typically, the voltage regulators are built into the board. They must be set at the proper voltage, or the CPU can be damaged. Properly inspect and examine the motherboard, CPU chip, and motherboard documentation to find the correct CPU voltage. Figure 13-10 shows the different types of CPU socket designs.

Figure 13-10 CPU Socket Designs

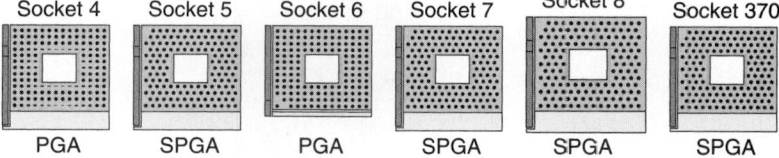

RAM

Today, most RAM implementations are synchronous dynamic RAM (SDRAM) and Rambus dynamic RAM (RDRAM). SDRAM chips with 168-pin DIMMs are the most common types of modules. Before SDRAM and RDRAM, dynamic RAM (DRAM) was prevalent. Older Pentiums used fast page mode (FPM) and extended data-out (EDO) RAM. FPM and EDO RAM are 72-pin memory modules. A description of these RAM types is as follows:

- *Dynamic RAM (DRAM)*—DRAM is a classic form of RAM and has since been replaced by the faster and less expensive SDRAM. DRAM stores data electrically in a storage cell and refreshes the storage cell every few milliseconds.

- *Extended data-out RAM (EDO RAM)*—EDO RAM is faster than DRAM. EDO RAM has also been replaced by SDRAM. EDO RAM is an improvement on DRAM because it has advanced timing features. EDO RAM extends the amount of time that data is stored and has a reduced refresh rate. This alleviates the CPU and RAM from timing constraints and improves performance.

- *Fast page mode (FPM) RAM*—FPM RAM is a type of DRAM that allows faster access to data in the same row or page. It eliminates the need for an address row if data in the previous row was accessed.
- *Synchronous DRAM (SDRAM)*—SDRAM replaced DRAM, FPM RAM, and EDO RAM. SDRAM is an improvement because it synchronizes data transfer between the CPU and memory. SDRAM allows the CPU to process data while another process is being queued. Figure 13-11 shows an SDRAM module.

Figure 13-11 SDRAM Module

- *Double data rate SDRAM (DDR SDRAM)*—DDR SDRAM is a newer form of SDRAM that can theoretically improve memory clock speed to 200 MHz or more.
- *Single in-line memory module (SIMM)*—A SIMM is a memory module with 30 or 72 pins, as shown in Figures 13-12 and 13-13. SIMMs are considered legacy components and can be found in older machines. SIMMs with 72 pins can support 32-bit transfer rates, and 32-pin SIMMs can support 16-bit transfer rates.

Figure 13-12 30-Pin SIMM

30-Pin SIMM

Figure 13-13 72-Pin SIMM

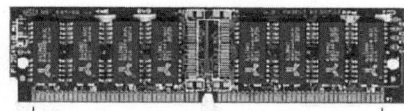

72-Pin SIMM

- *Dual in-line memory module (DIMM)* — A DIMM is a memory module with 168 pins, as shown in Figure 13-14. DIMMs are commonly used today and support 64-bit transfer. SO-DIMMs (small outline DIMMs) have 72 pins and are primarily used for portable computers.

Figure 13-14 168-Pin DIMM

168-Pin DIMM

- *Rambus in-line memory module (RIMM)* — A RIMM is a 184-pin memory module that uses only RDRAM, as illustrated in Figure 13-15. Smaller modules, called SO-RIMMs (small outline RIMMs), have a 160-pin connector. Some systems require that RIMMs be added in identical pairs, whereas others allow single RIMMs to be installed.

Figure 13-15 Direct Rambus DRAM

More information about specific memory types can be obtained from the manufacturer's website.

Troubleshooting RAM Issues

RAM failures are either sudden or intermittent. Overused or defective memory can cause the system to fail at any time. System performance is a good indication of the state of the memory. If the system is running smoothly and applications rarely stall, the RAM workload is well within the RAM specifications. If the computer is multitasking and freezes frequently, the RAM is probably insufficient for the workload or is defective.

Troubleshooting the RAM modules is straightforward. RAM is inexpensive and easy to replace. Technicians can easily remove the suspected memory and add a valid module. If the problem is resolved, the RAM module is probably no longer operative. If the memory problem still exists, consult the motherboard manufacturer's documentation. Some motherboards require memory modules to be installed in a particular slot order or require jumpers to be set. Figures 13-16, 13-17, and 13-18 show the correct way to install SIMMs, DIMMs, and RIMMs.

Figure 13-16 Installing a SIMM

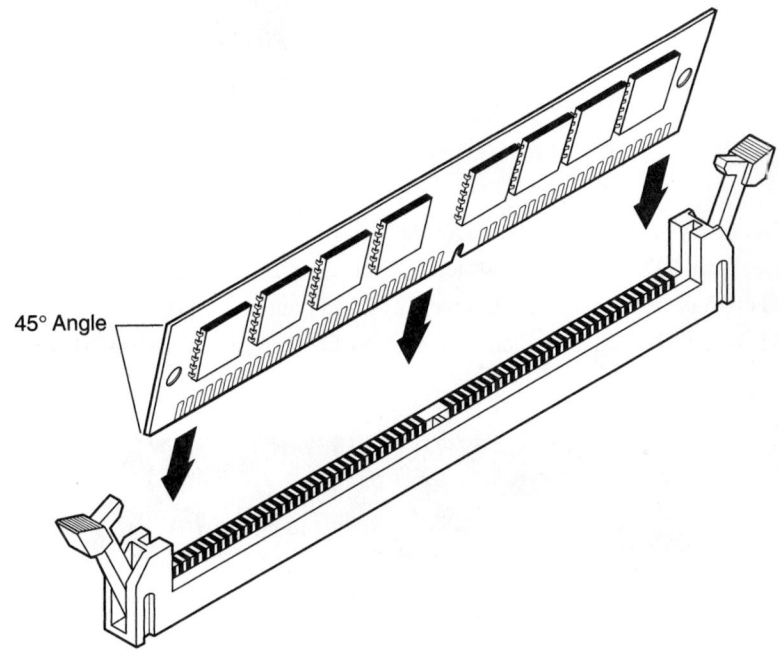

45° Angle

Figure 13-17 Installing a DIMM

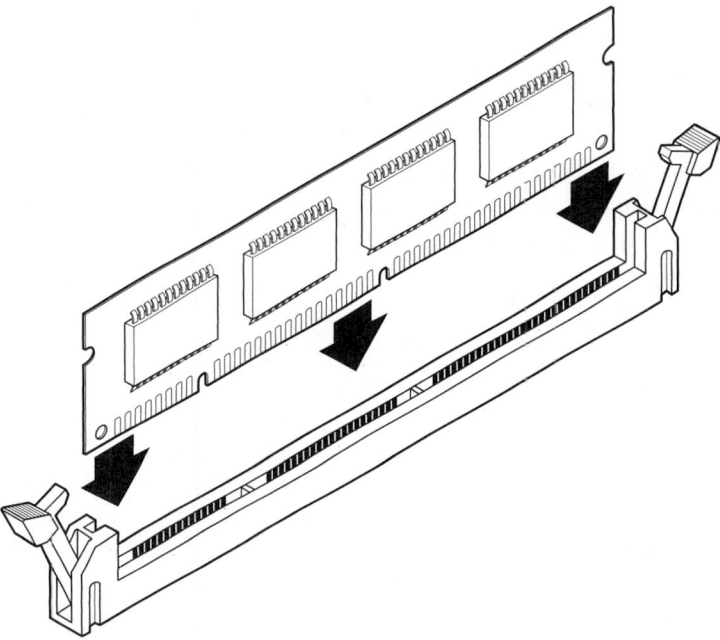

Figure 13-18 Installing a RIMM

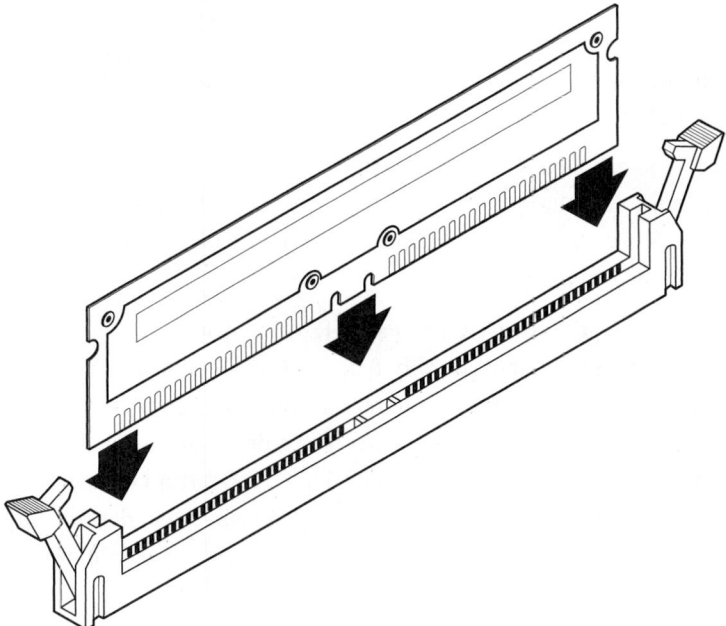

Also, verify that the module has been correctly installed. Memory modules are notched and can only be inserted in one direction. If you suspect an improper installation, remove the module and visually inspect the module socket. Clean the contacts and check for corrosion. Remove any debris, dust, or dirt, and reset the memory module. Verify that the latches have not been damaged and that they securely hold the module in place.

Modern computers run software applications that are memory intensive. These programs continually put stress on the memory modules, potentially causing them to fail. The symptoms for failed memory include the following:

- HIMEM.SYS has trouble loading.
- The computer appears inoperative and does not boot.
- Windows is unstable, or programs are freezing.
- POST errors exist.

RAM Compatibility Issues

SDRAM modules come in various speeds. The most common SDRAM speeds are PC-66, PC-100, and PC-133. The speed of SDRAM is measured in megahertz (MHz). SDRAM with a higher MHz rating indicates a higher-performing memory module. SDRAM can have compatibility issues with the bus on the motherboard. The speed of the SDRAM module must match the speed of the bus. Common bus speeds are PC-100 or PC-133. When purchasing RAM modules, verify the bus speed and buy a compatible RAM module.

The speed of EDO and FPM memory modules are measured in nanoseconds (ns). The memory module with the lowest ns rating is the fastest. EDO and FPM RAM can also have compatibility issues with the system bus.

Faster DRAM can be installed on a slower system bus, and performance will not be affected. The system operates at the bus speed, even if faster memory is installed. However, a slower or mixed DRAM module cannot be installed on a system with faster DRAM requirements or DRAM that is clocked differently.

Legacy machines can require parity RAM. Parity RAM performs an error-checking calculation that adds an extra bit (a 9th bit) to every 8 bits to provide a mechanism that detects whether a bit has changed. Today, RAM is nonparity and does not perform parity calculations on data. Never mix parity and nonparity SIMMs. For older systems, the setup utility has an option for enabling or disabling RAM parity checking. Also, error correction code (ECC) RAM and non-ECC RAM cannot be mixed. ECC RAM can correct data errors and is typically found in file servers. The following scenario helps to illustrate an issue with RAM.

Scenario

After a recent memory update, the computer does not boot and the memory is not being correctly recognized. These errors usually occur when a clocking issue exists with SDRAM. Computers require SDRAM to be either 2-clock or 4-clock. Legacy equipment usually requires 2-clock SDRAM. Newer computers usually require 4-clock SDRAM. Different clock rates are not compatible and cannot be mixed. In this scenario, the clock rating is probably not compatible with the motherboard specifications, and the SDRAM cannot be used. Consult the motherboard documentation to find the compatible clock rating for SDRAM modules.

Cable Issues

Many cabling issues can be easily determined because they are due to faulty physical connections. Reconnecting cables resolves many problems.

Another common cable issue is mismatched interfaces. Different cables look very similar. Always verify that the proper cable is being used with the proper interface.

Placing cable near an electrical source can cause signaling problems. Electromagnetic energy can pass through the cable and interfere with the data being transmitted by that cable. The concept of signal distortion is illustrated in Figure 13-19.

Figure 13-19 Signal Distortion

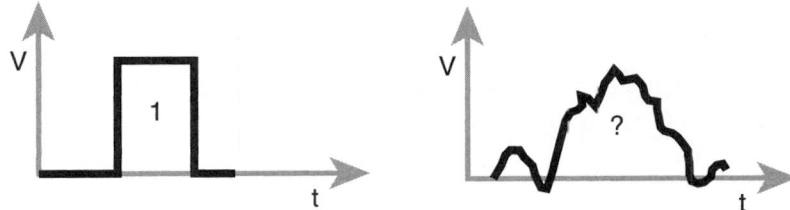

Ports

A slow or inoperative peripheral device is indicative of a port problem. Common symptoms include the following:

- Inoperative port.
- "Device not found" error message.
- Peripheral device is slow or has unacceptable performance.

Port problems can generally be attributed to the following:

- A bad cable connection
- An inoperable peripheral device
- Software problems
- Outdated or missing drivers
- A defective port

Common port/connection problems are usually found on the following ports:

- Parallel
- Serial
- USB
- FireWire
- i.Link
- AGP Video

Figure 13-20 shows common ports on a motherboard. These ports are discussed in Chapter 2, "How Computers Work," and Chapter 3, "Assembling a Computer."

Figure 13-20 Ports

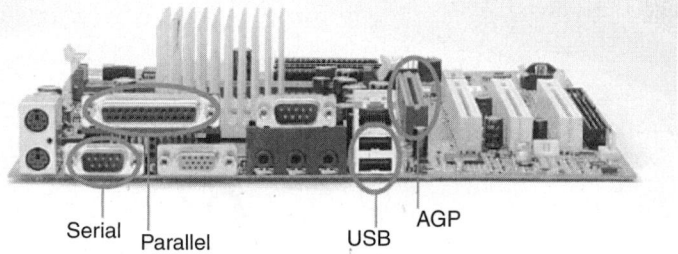

The Video System

When a computer is having video display errors, the system might boot normally but no video displays on the monitor. Troubleshooting the video display starts outside the computer case. The technician should begin by verifying that the monitor is turned on and plugged into a functional wall outlet or socket. Test the wall socket by plugging in an operational device such as a radio. After the connection has been verified, check the connections to the computer case. The IBM standard female DB-15 HD (high-density) connector consists of three rows of five pins each. It is located on the back of computer case and is the most common monitor

> **NOTE**
>
> Some computers have two video cards. If this is the case, try connecting the video cable to each video card. If the video problem still exists, one of the cards must be disabled and the other card enabled. This is usually required when the video card is integrated into the motherboard. The on-board video card can be autodetected and reinstalled as new hardware at each startup. In this case, the on-board video card is the operational card. Plugging the monitor into the on-board video card can provide access to the CMOS setup. Change the video settings, exit and save the changes, plug the monitor into the modular video card, and start the system.

connection. Figure 13-21 shows the IBM standard female DB-15 connector circled on a motherboard with integrated video. For Mac systems, the DB-15 connector has one row of eight pins and another row of seven pins.

Figure 13-21 IBM Standard Female DB-15 HD Connector

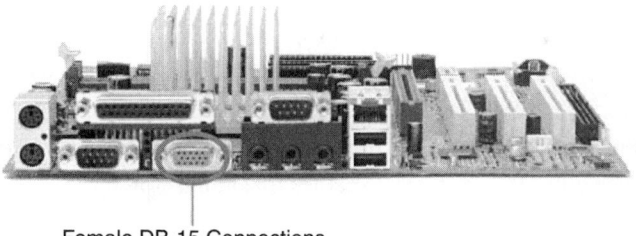

Female DB-15 Connections

After all the connections have been correctly made, open the case and verify that the video card is properly inserted. The video card might have to be removed and reseated to double-check the installation. If the video card is in a PCI slot, install the video card in another PCI slot. Some video cards need to be inserted into a particular PCI slot to work properly.

Video cards can also have problems that are related to software. Always verify that the latest driver is installed for the video card. Use the disks that came with the card or visit the manufacturer's website.

Video Monitor

The problems that are associated with the video monitor are usually caused by the configurations of the video card. High-performing video cards can overload a lower-performing monitor. Overloading the monitor can cause damage to the circuitry. If the monitor is being overloaded by the output of the video card, set the video card output to standard VGA settings of 640×480 pixels. Troubleshoot the monitor settings if the problem still occurs by checking the contrast and brightness settings if the screen appears blank. If advanced monitor settings are incorrect, they can adversely affect the video display.

Secondary Storage Devices

Some computers are configured with two different hard drives. Configuring a computer with two hard drives increases space for backup data and data storage. If two IDE hard drives are configured on the same ribbon cable, they must have a master-slave relationship. During normal operation, the computer boots from the OS that is loaded on the hard drive that is set to master. Once the computer boots up, the master drive can manage the slave drive, which is the drive with the jumper set to slave. The hard drive that is set to slave provides extra storage capabilities.

WARNING

Troubleshooting the internal components of a monitor can be fatal. The cathode ray tube (CRT) contains a capacitor and can potentially store 25,000 volts. This voltage can be stored long after the monitor has been disconnected. Never assume that this voltage is not present. Troubleshooting the internal components of a monitor is only recommended for experienced, certified technicians.

When two drives are installed, the majority of problems result from improperly set jumpers or incorrect BIOS settings. Hard drive manufacturers decide the jumper settings, so the technician must consult the hard drive manual or the manufacturer's website for specific details. However, each drive must be set to Master, Slave, or Cable Select. The hard drive that contains the OS becomes the master, and the secondary drive is the slave.

Cable Select (CSEL) is an option that decides master/slave hard drive relationships based on the position of the drive on the IDE cable. For CSEL to work properly, each device must have its jumpers set to CSEL, CSEL cabling must be used, and the host interface connector must support CSEL. Figure 13-22 shows a typical hard drive with the available configuration jumper settings as well as the appropriate cables that connect it.

Figure 13-22 Hard Drive with Cables

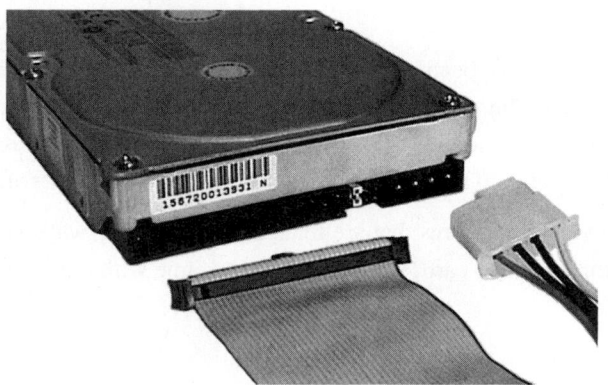

Sound Cards

Legacy sound cards had well-documented interrupt conflicts with other devices, typically peripheral devices. Hardware errors can be caused by a physically damaged sound card and improperly set jumpers. Most modern sound cards are Plug and Play (PnP) compatible. Installation involves inserting the sound card into the appropriate expansion slot, booting the computer, and loading the driver. Check the manufacturer's website for recent driver updates.

If a user is experiencing sound card problems, start outside the computer case and then look inside the case. Verify that the speakers are turned on and attached to the correct speaker port. A common error is plugging the speaker jack into the microphone port. The microphone jack is used for recording sound. If the problem is related to balancing the sound output, this can easily be corrected. From Windows, access the volume controls by double-clicking the speaker icon on the toolbar or by choosing **Start**, **Programs**, **Accessories**, **Entertainment**,

Volume Control. Verify that the balance is correct and that settings are not muted. Figure 13-23 shows the sound card volume controls.

Figure 13-23 Sound Card Volume Controls

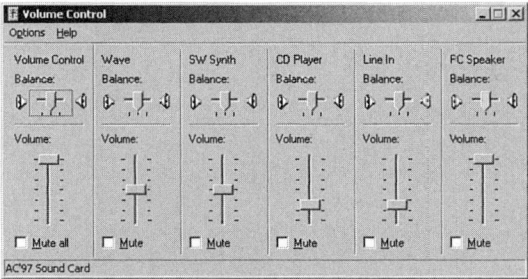

Intermittent problems or a sound card that does not function usually indicate symptoms of resource conflicts. If the sound card is in conflict with another device, it can operate sporadically. For example, if the sound card does not work when a document is printed, this can indicate that resources are conflicting. The resources might have been configured to use the same IRQ channel.

To troubleshoot these conflicts, the first step is to verify hardware and software configurations. The majority of these problems include uninstalled or outdated drivers, and resource conflicts. Software diagnostic tools can help reveal interrupt conflicts. Most diagnostic tools include diagnostic testing for the sound card. Running these tests can provide information on the computer's multimedia performance.

The Windows OS has management features to diagnose the problem. In Windows 98/2000, right-click the My Computer Desktop icon and select **Properties** from the menu that appears. The System Properties dialog box opens. Click the **Hardware** tab, and click the **Device Manager** button. The Device Manager opens. Click the plus sign next to **Sound, video, and game controllers**. If the system detects a conflict, it places a yellow question mark next to the device, as shown in Figure 13-24. If the system has a disabled device, it places a red X next to the device.

Right-click the device to view the resources that the device is using and the conflicting device. To access the Resource Manager, right-click the device, select **Properties** from the menu that appears, and click the **Resources** tab. Figure 12-25 shows the screen that displays the information concerning any conflicting devices.

Figure 13-24 Device Manager

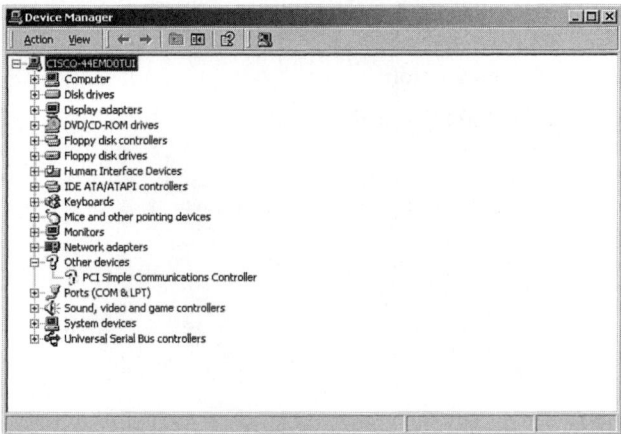

Figure 13-25 Resources Tab

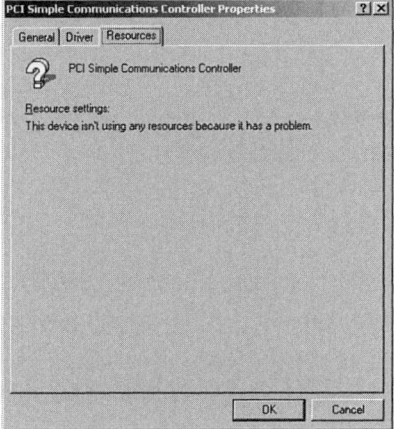

The Device Manager also lets you determine whether the correct audio driver is installed and whether the settings match those that are recommended by the sound card manufacturer. If the drivers are missing or wrong, they must be added to the system by using the Found New Hardware Wizard in the Control Panel. Figure 13-26 shows the screen that displays when new hardware is found.

Figure 13-26 Found New Hardware Wizard

Power Supply Issues

The power supply plays a vital role in the operation of a computer system. If the power supply is not working properly, the computer components can receive the wrong voltages and might not operate correctly.

The power supply converts the current coming from the wall outlet from alternating current (AC) to direct current (DC). As shown in Figure 13-27, the AC comes from the wall outlet and is 120V or 240V, depending on the country or region.

Figure 13-27 Alternating Current Entering the Power Supply

The alternating current is converted into +3.3V, ±5V, and ±12V DC. After the current is converted from AC to DC, the power supply provides the following important functions to the computer:

TIP

When a PC randomly reboots or locks up after running for a time, it might have a faulty power supply.

- **Supplies power**—The power supply is responsible for delivering the correct amount of DC power to the system components. All the system components are powered by the power supply. For example, the microprocessor, modular cards, RAM, and drives all receive DC power from the power supply.

- **Acts as a cooling mechanism**—This is the less obvious function of the power supply. However, this function should not be overlooked because it is an important role in system performance. Computer systems perform better if they are properly ventilated and cooled. An on-board fan, attached to most power supplies, cools the power supply and internal components, as shown in Figure 13-28.

Figure 13-28 Power Supply Airflow Supply

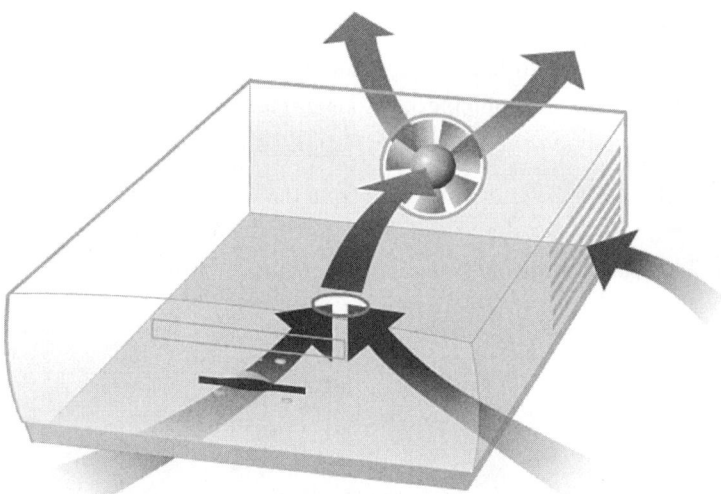

Box Cooling Issues

Computer components are susceptible to heat. The components operate at high speeds and in tight spaces. For example, hard drives operate at 7200 rpm and can be located only centimeters from one another. This environment is conducive to heat buildup, which can be harmful to the components. Every computer case needs proper airflow for the components to perform at their optimal levels.

The power supply usually generates the majority of the airflow. The fan on a power supply cools the power-supply unit and other internal components of the system. The fan pulls the air in over the internal components, motherboard, chip, and modular cards and pushes hot air out the back of the computer case. This is typically the case with the newer ATX form factors. With the older AT systems, the fan pulls air from the outside and blows it directly over the motherboard components. Most modern processors also have a fan that is attached directly to the CPU to cool the unit. Verify that the fans are working by listening for them. The fans should quietly run in the background and should not make loud or excessive noises.

The computer case plays an important role in cooling the internal components and is designed with cooling features. Computer cases have air-intake vents that are usually cut into the sides or front of the case. In the back of the case, an air-output vent provides the exit point for the airflow. Air enters the front of the case, pulled by the system fan located at the front. The air flows across the components and exits the back of the case as hot air. The power-supply fan helps the air circulation. The diagrams in Figures 13-29 and 13-30 show the airflow through a typical computer.

Figure 13-29 Proper Airflow

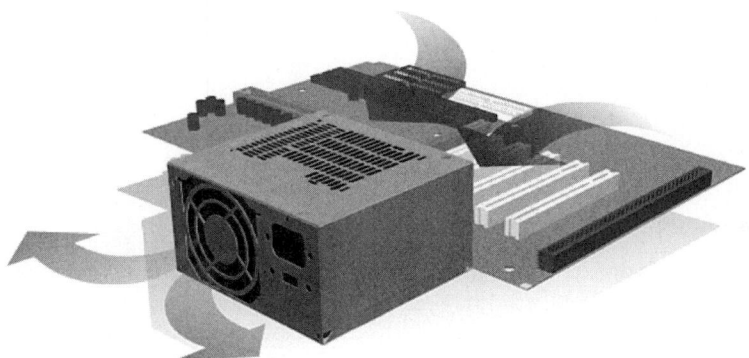

It is important to keep the air vents clean of any debris. These vents attract dirt and dust, which can prohibit airflow. The air vents should be cleaned frequently with a vacuum or a damp cloth. Use only a vacuum that is specially certified for computer cleaning.

Additional cooling fans can be added for computers that are used for long periods of time or are located in warmer environments. Computer systems that run cooler last longer and perform better.

Adding cooling fans is an example of proactive management. Proactive management occurs when a technician looks for potential problems before they become serious issues. It is a method of minimizing computer problems.

Figure 13-30 Airflow Through the Computer Case

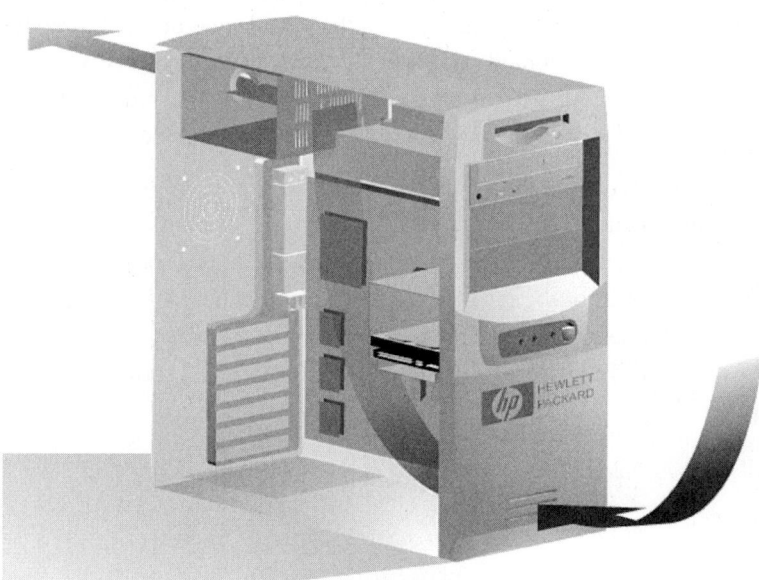

 e-Lab Activity   Power-Supply Issues

This e-lab covers the issues that relate to the power that is supplied to the computer system.

Troubleshooting Peripheral Devices

The steps of the troubleshooting process can help determine whether a computer problem is related to an input/output device. If the problem is server related, the SCSI interface can be the cause. If the problem is related to accessing the Internet or the network, use the troubleshooting steps to diagnose a solution. This section includes the following topics:

- Input devices
- Output devices
- SCSI interface issues
- Internet/network-access devices

Input Devices

An *input device*, such as a keyboard, mouse, scanner, and digital camera, transfers data into the computer. Most input devices are detected at startup.

When troubleshooting input devices, make sure that the device is properly connected. Verify that the cable is in good working condition and is not frayed. As with any hardware problem, start from the outside of the case.

After checking the physical connections of the input device, try rebooting the computer. Sometimes, an input device gets disconnected while in operation and a reboot is required. Pay attention to errors that display during startup. The errors are indicated as either a text message on the video display or a POST beep code. For example, if a keyboard is not properly connected, the user might get a beep code or a 301 error message.

Two common errors with input devices are incorrect character input and unrecognized devices. Both of these errors can result from a bad or outdated driver. Always check the manufacturer's website for updated device drivers. Input devices need the right driver to work correctly.

Keyboards

Keyboards are heavily used input devices. Because of the heavy workload and numerous movable components, keyboard failures are frequent. The best protection against keyboard errors is proactive maintenance. Table 13-4 lists some of the most common errors that are associated with the keyboard.

Table 13-4 Common Keyboard Errors

Problem/Error	Solution
Keyboard is running on legacy equipment and isn't supported.	Keyboards are either AT or XT compliant. However, an AT keyboard does not work with an XT-compliant computer, and vice versa. An AT-compliant keyboard is used in a 286 or higher system for this discussion. However, some AT keyboards can work with both types using a configuration DIP switch or a normal slider switch that is located on the bottom of the keyboard. Check to see whether these switches are set properly when troubleshooting keyboards.
Gate A20 failure.	Indicates that a 286 or higher system must switch to protected mode to use more than 1 MB RAM. The solution is to verify XT or AT configuration. Replace the keyboard with a known-good keyboard. Finally, replace the motherboard.

continues

Table 13-4 Common Keyboard Errors (Continued)

Problem/Error	Solution
Voltage issue.	Troubleshoot the keyboard connections to the motherboard, checking the voltage. Clock pins should measure between +2.0V and +5.5V. Power pins should measure between +2.0V and +5.5V. Data pins should measure between +4.8V and +5.5V.
Keyboard is not properly connected (301 error message or keyboard error).	Verify the connection, and reboot the computer. Remove and clean stuck keys. Clean the keyboard (using distilled water). If the problem still exists, replace the keyboard.

Mouse

The mouse is also a heavily used input device. Mice are prone to bad performance, mainly because dust and dirt can get into the components. Maintain a clean environment, and clean the mouse frequently for optimal performance. Table 13-5 lists some of the most common mouse errors.

Table 13-5 Common Mouse Problems

Problem/Error	Solution
Unrecognized or malfunctioning mouse	Remove outdated mouse drivers, and install a current driver. Also, make sure that the mouse is properly connected.
Erratic movement of the cursor	Clean the ball and the rollers that are located on the bottom of the mouse. Also, you might need to reconfigure the mouse settings. In a Windows environment, this is done through the Control Panel. If the problem still exists, replace the mouse.

Scanners

Most scanner errors are either a direct result of a bad software installation or an improperly connected device. Table 13-6 lists the most common errors that are associated with scanners.

Table 13-6 Common Scanner Problems

Problem/Error	Solution
Bad software installation; device is not recognized.	Incomplete software installation. Reinstall software and necessary drivers.

Table 13-6 Common Scanner Problems (Continued)

Problem/Error	Solution
Low-quality image on monitor.	Scanners use 24-bit color (with 16 million color variations), and the monitor resolution might be set too low. Change the monitor settings to display true color (24-bit color).
Slow or erratic performance.	Two devices might be daisy-chained (that is, chaining several devices on one cable). To access more than one peripheral on a parallel port, use a switch box. This is a device that switches between the two peripherals, using each device independent of the other.
Vertical streaks on the image.	Scanners can pick up dust or smudges on the glass. Use a damp cloth to clean the glass. Make sure that the glass is free of dust, dirt, and other particles.

Parallel Ports

Parallel ports rarely fail. However, a more common problem is slow performance from a parallel device. The most common errors that are associated with parallel ports are listed in Table 13-7.

Table 13-7 Common Parallel Port Errors

Problem/Error	Solution
Cable cannot supply the necessary data transfer rates.	Troubleshoot with a cable that has been verified to work.
Legacy equipment does not support new product requirements, or a hardware defect exists.	Upgrade the ports.
Outdated or bad drivers.	Update or reload the drivers.
IRQ conflict (two devices sharing same device).	Remove a conflicting device. (ISA cards are often the problem: IRQ5 conflicts with LPT2, or IRQ7 conflicts with LPT1.)
Wrong mode is selected. (Modes include EPP, ECP, and EPP/ECP.)	Use an IEEE 1284–compatible cable, which supports all parallel port modes.

USB Ports

Most new computers are equipped with a ***universal serial bus (USB) port.*** Today, USB ports are replacing the older serial ports that were found on most computers. USB devices are based on Plug and Play (PnP) technology. This means that USB devices should install and operate with minimal configuration. However, this does not mean that USB devices are free from errors. The following common failures are associated with USB devices:

- Missing or outdated driver
- Wrong cabling
- Defective hardware
- Resource conflicts

USB devices should load automatically in most versions of Windows. Windows 95 OSR2, 98, Me, 2000, and XP support USB. However, Windows NT does not support the USB standard. While the user is installing a USB device, Windows sometimes prompts the user for the location of a USB device driver. USB devices are usually packaged with a disk that contains the device driver, or users can visit the manufacturer's website to obtain the latest driver.

USB devices connect through ***USB cables.*** The USB device and cable must be the same speed to function properly. USB cables come in two speeds: low and high. If a faster device is connected to a slower cable, the signal can become corrupted over long distances. If a cable problem is suspected, replace the cable with a faster cable.

USB devices require an IRQ channel to work properly. The easiest way to check for a resource conflict is to use the Device Manager. To access the Device Manager in Windows, right-click **My Computer**, select **Properties** from the menu that appears, and click the **Hardware** tab. Click the **Device Manager** button. The Device Manager opens, displaying the computer hardware devices. The Device Manager indicates any device conflicts with an exclamation mark highlighted in a yellow circle. If this occurs, verify that the device is properly installed and that the system resources have been allocated correctly.

Output Devices

An ***output device*** displays or prints data that is processed by the computer. The computer communicates with an output device when the user sends the request. Printers are output devices that are frequently used. Because of this constant usage, problems can occur. Proper cleaning of the printer can reduce downtime, loss of productivity, and repair costs.

The length of time between cleaning depends on the usage of the printer. Printer maintenance involves visually inspecting the printer for dirt, dust, paper jams, and other debris that can affect printer performance; error messages can also be shown on some printers. Preventive maintenance cannot prevent all printer errors. Printers are intricate, delicate devices that can fail in many areas.

Printing a self-test page can help the technician isolate a printer error. The self-test capability is a convenient troubleshooting and diagnostic tool. If nothing prints, check all connections. Make sure that the printer is turned on, the paper has been properly loaded, and the printer is online. Verify that the printer is the default printer in the Control Panel. To make a printer the default printer, select the Printers icon in the Control Panel.

Common Printer Errors

Printer errors can range from minor paper jam problems to major issues with internal components. The degree of troubleshooting required depends on the age and type of printer. At some point, an older printer that has continuous problems needs to be replaced. Consider this option if the older printer constantly jams or overheats, or if the output quality is unacceptable. Analysis should include repair costs versus the cost of a replacement. Note that repair is usually a better option when dealing with expensive, high-end printers.

Troubleshooting a paper jam is a common task for most technicians. The usual symptom is an error message or failure of the paper to advance. Check the paper loader for jammed paper or an overloaded paper tray. Clean any jammed paper, and visually inspect the paper path for any obstructions. Ensure that the printer is configured for the correct paper tray. Check the paper-feed motor, and replace it if necessary.

If the printer shuts down intermittently, the thermistor could be causing the problem. A thermistor keeps the printer from overheating. To check a thermistor, shut off the printer until it cools completely and then turn it back on. Observe how it works for a period of time. If, after operating for some time, the printer shuts down, the thermistor might be the problem. A thermistor is generally replaced and not repaired. Check the printer's manual for more information, or visit the manufacturer's website.

Troubleshooting Ink Jet Printers

If an ink jet printer is not printing clearly or correctly, clogged nozzles on the printhead can be causing the problem. Visually inspect the printhead for debris that restricts the flow of ink. Printheads can be cleaned by the printer software, if available, or manually by the technician. Select the Printers icon in the Control Panel to determine whether the printer is capable of performing a self-cleaning operation. Manual cleaning varies among manufacturers. Check the printer's manual for instructions on how to clean an ink jet printer.

If the ink jet printer indicates that it is offline but is connected, verify that the cables are properly connected. The cable between the computer and printer has probably been disconnected.

Troubleshooting Dot Matrix Printers

Dot matrix printers use a series of pins, which are located on the printhead, to transfer ink to paper. These pins repeatedly strike the ribbon and then the paper. Over time, these pins can become clogged with dust and ink. To resolve this problem, first unplug the dot matrix printer. Paying close attention to how the printhead is installed, carefully remove it from the ribbon cable. Next, soak the printhead in denatured alcohol. Place the pins in the denatured alcohol for 2–3 minutes. Let the printhead dry, and then reinstall it properly. Run the printer self-test without the ribbon attached to the printhead. This allows excess or residual ink to be removed from the pins. Replace the ribbon after the pins are free of any excess ink.

If the characters are not properly aligned on the page, the ribbon cable might be misaligned with the printhead. Verify that the ribbon cable and printhead are properly spaced. Also, verify that the ribbon is advancing properly. Consult the printer's manual to verify the proper printer-control settings.

Troubleshooting Laser Printers

To efficiently troubleshoot laser printers, technicians must be familiar with the components of a laser printer. Table 13-8 lists the most common laser printer problems.

Table 13-8 Common Laser Printer Problems

Problem/Error	Solution
Printer is online and properly connected but does not print.	Toner cartridge might be empty. If so, replace it.
Vertical lines are printed.	Toner cartridge is most likely broken and needs to be replaced.
Pages are dirty.	Toner cartridge is most likely broken and needs to be replaced.
Paper is not feeding correctly.	Could be caused by a paper jam. Manually feed the paper or change the software configuration.

Students can read more about troubleshooting printers and issues that are related to paper jams in Chapter 11, "Printers and Sharing."

Worksheet 13.3.2   Troubleshooting Printers

Test your knowledge of dot matrix, ink jet, and laser printers by completing this true/false worksheet.

SCSI Interface Issues

SCSI drives require a controller that is separate from the IDE controller. This controller operates with ROM BIOS under DOS and Windows. The ROM BIOS contains management, surface verification, and low-level format applications. The SCSI BIOS is accessed during the bootup process by pressing the setup key or key combination.

The SCSI bus operation and the transfer rate are controlled by adapter settings. If a transfer speed mismatch occurs among the SCSI controllers, the drive might have input/output (I/O) errors. I/O errors, although not fatal to a computer, can cause the system to lock up.

Also, to ensure optimal performance, enable parity checking and host adapter termination.

SCSI devices must have unique SCSI IDs. SCSI devices cannot share ID numbers. The location of the SCSI ID on the bus is not important. The SCSI IDs do not need to be placed sequentially on the bus. Be sure that devices do not share the same ID numbers. If SCSI devices share the same ID, errors can occur.

The actual ID priority sequence (from highest to lowest) is 7, 6, 5, 4, 3, 2, 1, 0, 15, 14, 13, 12, 11, 10, 9, 8. The SCSI host controller should be set to SCSI ID 7. This gives the SCSI host controller the highest priority. Hard drives should be set with lower IDs. Hard drives have the potential to consume a large amount of the bus speed. Setting the hard drives to a lower priority allows time-sensitive information to have a higher priority. Use IDs 6, 5, and 4 for CD-RW drives and other streaming-media drives. SCSI controllers are configured with the following parameters:

- Sync negotiation
- Transfer rate
- BIOS scan
- Send start unit command

SCSI fixed disk I/O errors can occur if the SCSI parameters are configured incorrectly. SCSI controllers allow drive configuration for larger SCSI drives. If these parameters are not set correctly, the drive might be inaccessible. This error can be fixed if the configuration parameters are correctly set for the SCSI controllers.

A SCSI drive can have built-in or external termination that can be enabled or disabled. The SCSI bus must be terminated at both ends of the controller and must have two termination points: one at the beginning and one at the end of the SCSI bus. The ending termination point must be within 4 inches of the ending points of the bus. The drives on the SCSI bus must run sequentially—drive A to B, B to C, C to D, and so on. The SCSI bus must not contain a Y-shaped drive configuration.

NOTE

Attach the SCSI controller set to the last SCSI ID, which is SCSI ID 7. I/O errors can result if the SCSI ID is not set to 7.

SCSI Interface Levels

Many network servers (and some PCs) have SCSI ports built into them. SCSI ports are supported by all major operating systems. Several levels of SCSI exist, including SCSI-1, which evolved into SCSI-2 and SCSI-3. These three SCSI levels are mostly outdated. Other SCSI levels are Ultra-SCSI, which is a widely implemented SCSI standard, and Ultra-3, which is the latest SCSI standard. Although not all devices support all levels of SCSI, the evolving SCSI standards are generally backward compatible. All the SCSI standards have different speeds. When installing SCSI drives and other devices, you must consider the cabling. The cable length specifications for the various SCSI types are summarized in Table 13-9. SCSI devices can malfunction when these specifications are ignored during installation and configuration.

Table 13-9 SCSI Interfaces

SCSI Type	Maximum Cable Length (Meters)	Maximum Speed (MBps)	Maximum Number of Devices
SCSI-1	6	5	8
SCSI-2	6	5–10	8 or 16
Ultra SCSI-3, 8-/16-bit	1.5	20/40	8/16
Ultra-2 SCSI	12	40	8
Wide Ultra-2 SCSI	12	80	16
Ultra-3 (Ultra-160/m) SCSI	12	160	16

e-Lab Activity   SCSI Termination

In this e-Lab, you determine the correct location for SCSI termination.

Internet/Network-Access Devices

Network problems range from an unattached Category 5 cable to advanced protocol issues. Discussing advanced network problems is beyond the scope of this chapter. However, basic techniques for troubleshooting common network problems are presented.

Begin network troubleshooting by determining whether the system has undergone recent changes. Reverse the changes, and see whether the problem is resolved. If so, the problem was with the recent change.

The next area to troubleshoot is the physical layer. Start outside the computer case with the cabling. The cabling should run from the wall jack to the back of the computer or external modem. Verify that the cable is attached to the correct wall jack or port and that the cable is functional.

The LED indicator lights can tell the installer the following things:

- Whether the network adapter is properly connected to the computer
- Whether the network adapter can link to other adapters on the network
- Whether network activity exists

Most desktop computers have a NIC with one, two, or three diagnostic LED indicators. A single light on the card can serve the dual purpose of both link integrity and link activity. The single light blinks on and off as messages are sent across the network. It remains on steadily when no message traffic exists.

A NIC with two lights uses one as a link-integrity indicator and the other as a link-activity indicator. If the link-integrity indicator is lit, it signifies a physical connection between the network card and some other piece of hardware. When the second light blinks on and off as messages are sent across the network, the correct cable is selected.

A NIC with three lights, as shown in Figure 13-31, uses one as a link-integrity indicator, another as a link-activity indicator, and a third to show full-/half-duplex transfer rates.

Figure 13-31 NIC Lights

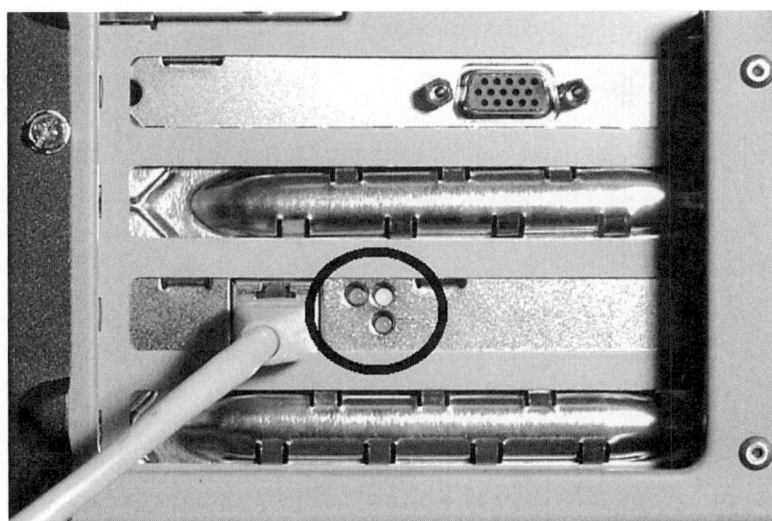

Modems usually have indicator lights that can diagnose a problem. An external modem has indicator lights on the front of the unit, whereas an internal modem has indicator lights that are similar to a NIC. Each modem manufacturer has a different set of lights, but each generally features a power, status, and activity light. These lights can help isolate any problem. For example, the status light can indicate that the modem is not online. Verify the connections. Unplug and then plug the cables back in and retest.

If the problem still exists after all the connections have been verified, look inside the computer box. Make sure that the NIC or modem is properly inserted into the expansion slot. Remove and reinstall the card to ensure that it is properly seated.

Most network adapter problems involve conflicting resource and configuration settings. Common resource problems are conflicting IRQs, I/O addresses, and memory. Common configuration errors include adapter card speed mismatch and defective drivers.

 Worksheet 13.3.4 Troubleshooting Hardware

Use this worksheet to test your knowledge of the basic terms and the procedures that are used when troubleshooting hardware.

Summary

This chapter discussed troubleshooting methods, including tips and tricks to solve computer problems. The following topics were discussed:

- The six steps in the troubleshooting process are identifying the problem, gathering the information, developing the solution, implementing the potential solution, verifying that the problem is resolved, and documenting the solution.

- Diagnostic software—such as SpinRite for recovering data from a crashed hard drive, and Checkit, PC Technician, AMI Diags, and SiSoft Sandra, which perform system analysis and testing—are valuable tools for the IT technician.

- Field-replaceable units are monitors, keyboards, expansion cards, and memory upgrades that can be easily replaced. Some FRUs can be changed out easily, whereas others can require accessing the computer case.

- The POST is a series of self-diagnostic tests that a computer runs through to test major hardware. Any errors are reported visually or as a series of audio POST codes to indicate specific problems. Audio POST codes are BIOS specific and are helpful in the troubleshooting process.

- Accessing the BIOS is done to obtain low-level hardware and software configuration information. In addition, the BIOS can be accessed for upgrades for support devices.

- Overused or defective memory can cause the system to fail at any time. System performance is a good indication of the state of the memory. Test RAM for any sudden or intermittent failures.

- Two functions are provided by the power supply in a computer system: delivering the appropriate amount of DC power to the components and cooling the system with an on-board fan.

- Problems with peripheral devices can usually be resolved by checking cables and ports. The Device Manager can determine whether IRQ conflicts exist.

- Check recent changes to the system to troubleshoot network-access problems. Reverse the changes, and see whether the problem is resolved. Indicator LEDs on NICs can verify connectivity.

The next chapter details troubleshooting basics for computer software. The steps that are used to determine the cause of specific problems and the steps that are followed to resolve software problems are detailed.

Key Terms

AMI Diags Program that provides advanced system testing and reports on memory, serial ports, parallel ports, modems, hard drives, keyboards, BIOSs, and video adapters.

audio POST codes A reporting system for errors that are found by the BIOS during the POST, represented by a series of beeps.

Cable Select (CSEL) An option that decides master/slave hard drive relationships based on the position of the drive on the IDE cable.

Checkit Program that performs system analysis and testing.

Complementary Metal Oxide Semiconductor (CMOS) Stores the system startup configurations and parameters.

diagnostic software Programs that assist in the troubleshooting process.

double data rate SDRAM New synchronous dynamic RAM that increases memory clock speed to at least 200 MHz.

dual in-line memory module (DIMM) Memory module with 168 pins. Supports 64-bit data transfers.

dynamic RAM (DRAM) Works by storing data electrically in a storage cell and refreshing the storage cell every few milliseconds.

extended data-out RAM (EDO RAM) Extends the amount of time that data is stored and has a reduced refresh rate.

fast page mode (FPM) RAM A type of DRAM that eliminates the need for an address row if data in the previous row was accessed. It allows faster access to data in the same row or page.

field-replaceable unit (FRU) Computer component that can be easily replaced.

input device Device that transfers data into the computer. This includes the keyboard, mouse, scanner, and so on.

nonvolatile random-access memory (NVRAM) Stores the system startup configurations and parameters.

output device Device that displays or prints data that is processed by the computer.

PC Technician Program that operates independently of DOS to perform diagnostic tests on parallel ports, serial ports, hard drives, keyboards, video adapters, and RAM.

POST card Device that can digitally report errors if the computer fails before a BIOS error can be generated.

power-on self-test (POST)   A series of self-diagnostic tests that the computer performs to test the major hardware.

Rambus in-line memory module (RIMM)   Memory module with 184 pins. Uses only RDRAM.

single in-line memory module (SIMM)   Memory module with 30 or 72 pins. It supports both 16-bit and 32-bit data transfers.

SiSoft System Analyzer, Diagnostic, and Reporting Assistant (Sandra)   Program that aids in troubleshooting and benchmarking computer components.

SpinRite   Program that is used for recovering data from a crashed hard drive.

synchronous DRAM (SDRAM)   Allows the CPU to process data while another process is being queued.

troubleshooting   A series of logical steps that diagnose a computer problem.

universal serial bus (USB) port   USB ports are replacing the older serial ports that were found on most computers. USB devices are based on Plug and Play (PnP) technology, and they install with minimal configuration.

USB cable   Connects a USB device to the computer. The device and cable must be the same speed.

Check Your Understanding

The following are review questions for the A+ exam. Answers are found in Appendix B.

1. What is the first step in troubleshooting a PC problem?

   A. Remove the cover.

   B. Unplug all the cords from the computer.

   C. Remove all optional equipment from the system.

   D. Eliminate the user as the source.

2. What setting should you use on a multimeter when checking a power-supply unit?

   A. AC voltage

   B. DC voltage

   C. Ohms

   D. Amps

3. How many changes should you make at a time when troubleshooting a PC?

   A. One.

   B. Two.

   C. Three.

   D. It doesn't matter.

4. What is the most likely cause for a shaky video display?

   A. Faulty monitor

   B. Faulty cables

   C. Faulty video adapter

   D. Incorrect settings

5. What is the first thing to do if a new monitor is not working?

   A. Adjust the brightness and contrast.

   B. Check the monitor for broken parts.

   C. Measure the voltage inside the monitor.

   D. Make sure that the power cord is firmly plugged in.

6. A high-performing video card can overload which of the following lower-performing units?

   A. Keyboard

   B. Monitor

   C. Mouse

   D. Printer

7. An audio POST code with one long beep and two short beeps during the bootup process indicates a problem with which of the following?

   A. Video controller

   B. Floppy drive

   C. Hard drive

   D. Mouse

8. When a PC randomly reboots or locks up after running for a time, what might the problem be?

   A. Monitor problem

   B. Faulty expansion card

   C. Bad hard drive

   D. Faulty power supply

9. What does USB stand for?

   A. Ultimate serial bus.

   B. Universal steering bus.

   C. Unified serial bus.

   D. Universal serial bus.

10. What is the problem if the PC clock resets when you turn the computer off?

   A. Defective CMOS battery

   B. Defective BIOS chip

   C. Faulty power cord

   D. Faulty motherboard

11. A new mouse has been installed but does not work. Which of the following is *not* the cause?

   A. It is plugged in to the wrong port.

   B. The operating system needs to be reinstalled.

   C. It requires a new driver.

   D. It is a faulty mouse.

12. An erratic mouse is most likely a result of which of the following?

   A. One of the potentiometers has failed.

   B. The unit has a corrupt mouse driver.

   C. The mouse is plugged in to the wrong port.

   D. The mouse needs cleaning.

13. What can create a memory problem?

    A. Installing different-speed memory modules

    B. Skipping over an empty memory socket

    C. Not installing memory in pairs

    D. Using memory from different manufacturers

14. One of your memory modules is unusually hot. What does this indicate?

    A. It is normal.

    B. It needs a new cooling fan.

    C. The voltage to the memory is insufficient.

    D. It is defective or becoming defective.

15. What symbol is typically used in Windows to indicate a disabled hardware device?

    A. A yellow question mark on the hardware icon

    B. A circled exclamation point on the hardware icon

    C. An upside-down question mark

    D. A red X

16. What symbol is typically used in the Windows Device Manager to indicate that a device has a problem?

    A. A question mark on the hardware icon

    B. A yellow exclamation point

    C. An upside-down question mark

    D. A blinking, red X

17. Which of the following is a good way to test a problem with RAM?

    A. Run a diagnostic program.

    B. Remove the module.

    C. Use a digital multimeter.

    D. Replace the module with a new one to see if the problem reoccurs.

18. The computer fails to start after you install a new sound card. What is the most likely cause of this problem?

    A. The sound card is not compatible.

    B. Not enough memory is present in the system.

    C. An interrupt conflict between the sound card and another device has occurred.

    D. The sound card needs a different DMA setting.

19. A computer powers up but does not attach to the network. After rebooting, the problem persists. Which of the following is a possible solution?

    A. Reinstall the NIC.

    B. Check the Device Manager for network adapter conflicts.

    C. Perform diagnostic tests on the Internet.

    D. Perform diagnostic tests on the server.

20. What is the best source for troubleshooting information?

    A. The user

    B. The manufacturer's website

    C. Other technicians

    D. All of the above

Upon completion of this chapter, you will be able to perform the following tasks:

- Communicate with the user to determine the cause of system problems
- Create a bootable disk that enables the technician to access the system when it does not boot
- Recognize DOS error messages, know what causes them, and know how to address them
- Understand startup modes, including normal and the different safe modes that are used for troubleshooting
- Troubleshoot Windows installation problems, memory usage problems, and system lockup errors
- Use Windows system tools, the Device Manager, and system editors to diagnose and fix computer errors
- Understand the registry structure and the key for every process that is running on the system
- Know the different types of backup procedures to make sure that the system can be restored

Chapter 14

Troubleshooting Software

This chapter discusses general troubleshooting procedures for software and operating systems. It also provides helpful tips for gathering the information that is needed to diagnose and repair common computer problems.

Troubleshooting Process

The process that is used to troubleshoot issues allows the IT technician to identify and resolve problems systematically. Using the available resources, the problem is first identified as being hardware or software related. This section includes the following topics:

- Overview of the troubleshooting process
- Gathering user information
- Reproducing error symptoms
- Identifying recent software changes
- Determining whether a problem is hardware or software related
- Fixing the software

Overview of the Troubleshooting Process

The troubleshooting process usually begins with the users because they have the most valuable information. User input can help narrow the search for the problem that is affecting the computer. The main goal of troubleshooting is to allow users to work with their systems. The process starts when the user calls for support, as illustrated in Figure 14-1.

Figure 14-1 User Calling for Support

Gathering User Information

Before troubleshooting a computer, talk to users to gather information regarding their problems. Sometimes users can explain what they might have done to cause the problem. Determine what they were doing when they began to experience issues. For example, find out what applications they were using or whether they were attempting to install or uninstall hardware or software. This information provides a good starting point for troubleshooting the computer.

Eliciting information from users can be a tricky process. Some users are easy to deal with and answer all questions honestly. However, this is not the case with others. In a working environment, many users are limited in what they can do with their computers. The administrator determines the level of access for each user. Unfortunately, many computer problems result from users who are trying to do something that they are not supposed to be doing, such as installing software or downloading files from the Internet. If a user's system is not working because of these actions, he or she is less likely to say what is wrong.

Administrators or service technicians usually know more about computers than users. Be patient with users, and do not get frustrated or say something that makes them feel inferior. A trivial problem that is obvious to the administrator can be something that the user does not understand. Be polite when eliciting information from users.

Reproducing Error Symptoms

After talking to the user, administrators should try to reproduce the error symptoms. Reproducing the error symptoms is helpful, because determining when the error occurs in the process can help identify where the search for the problem should begin. For example, if a user states that an error message appears during the bootup process, rebooting the computer can reproduce the error symptoms. This can determine at what point in the boot process the computer stops or the error is generated.

Identifying Recent Software Changes

Identifying any changes that the user has made to the software environment can simplify the troubleshooting process. Many computer problems result from users installing or uninstalling software. Sometimes users delete important folders or files by accident. Users can provide valuable information about recent changes that have been made.

Recently installed software can be incompatible with the operating system, or it could have overwritten or deleted important files. Sometimes a user uninstalls software and accidentally deletes files that are necessary for the operating system to function properly.

Determining Whether a Problem Is Hardware or Software Related

Computer hardware refers to the physical components of the computer, and *software* refers to the operating system and programs. Hardware and software are closely related and work with each other, which can make problem solving difficult. It is important to determine whether computer problems are related to hardware failures or software issues.

Hardware Issues

Look at the bootup sequence to begin isolating the problem. When the computer boots up, the user should hear a single beep after the power-on self-test (POST) and before the boot process begins. Basic system hardware problems are displayed before this beep. The operating system and software do not start until after this beep. Only the BIOS and basic system hardware are active before the beep.

Hardware-related issues are either configuration errors or **hardware failures**. Basic system hardware failures can prevent the operating system from loading. After the BIOS and basic system hardware have been checked and passed, the operating system starts to load, as shown in Figure 14-2.

If the hardware is unable to load, this can indicate that a component has failed. After determining which hardware component has failed, replace the component and retry the boot process.

Configuration errors result from a mismatch between the programmed configuration of the system and the equipment that is installed in the system. After installing software, users can enter some parameters into programs to match their capabilities to the computer configuration. If these parameters are set incorrectly, the software cannot detect the system hardware and an error occurs. Hardware-specific troubleshooting issues are covered in Chapter 13, "Troubleshooting PC Hardware."

Figure 14-2 Boot Process

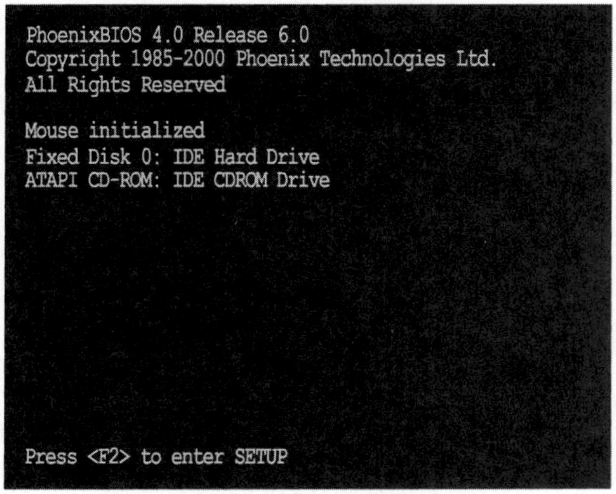

```
PhoenixBIOS 4.0 Release 6.0
Copyright 1985-2000 Phoenix Technologies Ltd.
All Rights Reserved

Mouse initialized
Fixed Disk 0: IDE Hard Drive
ATAPI CD-ROM: IDE CDROM Drive




Press <F2> to enter SETUP
```

Fixing the Software

After identifying and locating the problem, it is time to fix the software. The method that is used to fix the software depends on the problem. It might be necessary to copy some files from the installation CD of the operating system or an installed application to the hard drive. The paths for shortcuts to the executable files of an installed application might need to be changed. Reinstalling the software can eliminate errors sometimes. This chapter discusses many techniques and troubleshooting aids for resolving software-related problems.

DOS Troubleshooting Issues

Troubleshooting DOS requires an understanding of the bootup process and the error messages that display when problems occur. The IT technician must be able to use the tools that detect and resolve these issues. This section includes the following topics:

- System boot problems
- DOS error messages
- Invalid directory errors

System Boot Problems

The bootup procedure reveals a great deal of information about the status of a system. Some errors can be identified and eliminated during the bootup process. A problem that is related to the bootup process can prevent the operating system from loading. An understanding of the boot process can help determine which section failed if the system does not boot past a particular point. For example, if the system boots to the point where it is checking the floppy drive, and the floppy drive light does not come on, the problem exists in the floppy drive.

The Bootable Disk

Every system administrator should have a bootable disk for each OS that is used in the network. Many systems can have issues that cannot be resolved or a corrupt operating system that can prevent the system from booting up. A **bootable disk** allows administrators to boot from a floppy disk instead of the hard drive. Simply insert the disk into the floppy drive and restart the computer. Make sure that the BIOS is set to boot from the floppy drive. Figure 14-3 shows the BIOS settings for booting from the floppy drive. The bootable disk contains the necessary files to boot the system while bypassing the corrupted files on the hard drive. Booting from a bootable disk brings up a DOS prompt. This allows the administrator to recopy files, inspect the hard drive partition, or reformat the drive.

Figure 14-3 BIOS Settings: Booting to a Floppy Disk

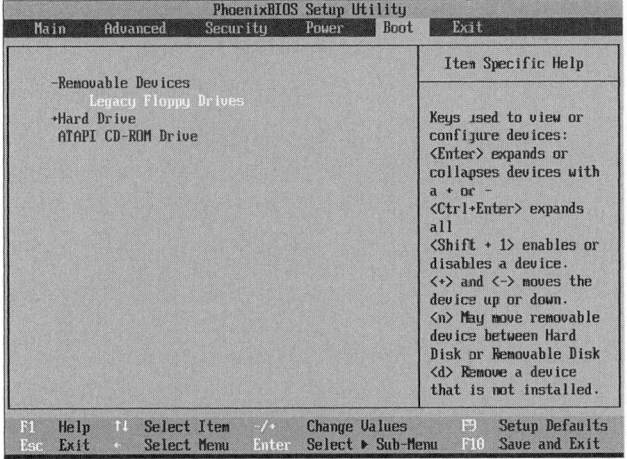

Hidden Files

A **hidden file** has a special attribute turned on and is not normally visible to users. For example, hidden files are not listed when the DOS **DIR** command is executed. However, most file-management utilities allow hidden files to be viewed.

DOS hides some files, such as MSDOS.SYS and IO.SYS, so that users do not accidentally corrupt or delete them. These two files are special files that are located in the operating system's root directory. Without them, the system cannot boot. The hidden attribute for a normal file can also be turned on to prevent users from viewing or corrupting the file. The **ATTRIB** command is used to view and change file attributes.

The Command Interpreter

COMMAND.COM is the *command interpreter*. It is the most important system file; the computer cannot boot without it. COMMAND.COM contains the most commonly used commands of the operating system. COMMAND.COM is loaded into RAM during bootup. It contains internal commands that can be run quickly. External commands are located in multiple locations on the physical storage medium. These commands are loaded into RAM before being executed, which makes them much slower.

When a DOS command is entered at the DOS prompt, the COMMAND.COM program examines it to determine whether it is internal or external. Internal commands are recognized and executed immediately. External commands are stored in the \DOS directory, and the COMMAND.COM file must browse through the directory to find the command program.

When DOS runs an application, COMMAND.COM finds the program, loads it, and gives it control of the system. When the program is shut down, control is passed back to the command interpreter.

DOS Switches

Many common DOS switches are discussed in Chapter 4, "Operating System Fundamentals." This chapter introduces a few more switches that are useful in troubleshooting software problems. As a review, DOS switches configure DOS commands to perform specific functions. For example, DOS switches are used in the CONFIG.SYS file to configure DOS to emulate different hardware configurations. The **SWITCHES** command is useful when using older applications with a new enhanced keyboard that is incompatible with the operating system. Entering the **SWITCHES=/K** command in the CONFIG.SYS file configures the keyboard to act like a standard keyboard.

These switches can be helpful when troubleshooting computer systems. They can also be used to manipulate the DOS commands.

The following is a list of common switches:

- **/K**—Causes an enhanced keyboard to act like an older, standard keyboard
- **/F**—Removes the 2-second delay that occurs when the "Starting MS-DOS" message is displayed on the screen in DOS version 6
- **/N**—Disables the F5 and F8 keys during system startup for DOS version 6
- **/W**—Tells DOS that the WINA20.386 file has been moved to a directory other than the root directory

Bootable Disk Utility Files

A DOS boot disk can be used to boot the system to the DOS prompt. This allows a system to start so that troubleshooting can begin. FORMAT.EXE and FDISK.EXE are two useful utilities that can be added to the boot disk.

FORMAT.EXE

If an operating system is corrupted beyond repair, the ***FORMAT.EXE*** command can be used to erase the disk and reformat it if necessary. The command prepares a new disk for use with an operating system. As a result, when using FORMAT.EXE, all the current information on the hard drive is erased.

FDISK.EXE/MBR

FDISK is one of the most commonly used MS-DOS commands, even with newer operating systems such as Windows 2000 and XP. FDISK allows the technician to delete and create partitions on the hard drive. After using the boot disk to boot to a DOS prompt, type **FDISK** to enter the FDISK Options screen. Figure 14-4 shows the FDISK options that allow changes to be made to the hard disk partitions.

Figure 14-4 FDISK Options

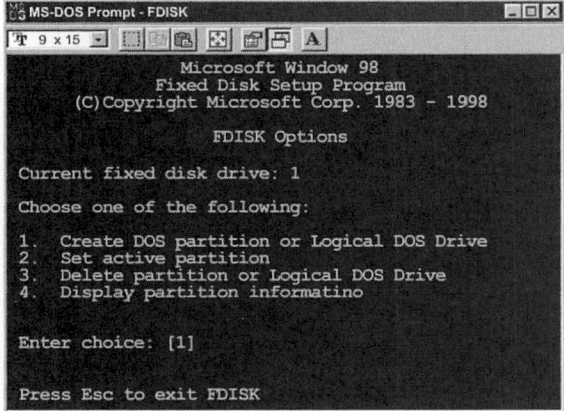

If a computer is unable to boot, this usually indicates that the ***Master Boot Record (MBR)*** has been damaged or corrupted. This can be caused by a virus or by files that have been deleted. The MBR is a program that is executed when a computer boots up. The MBR usually resides on the first sector of the hard drive. The program begins the boot process by referencing the partition table to determine which partition to use for booting. The MBR then transfers program control to the boot sector of that partition to continue the boot process. In DOS and Windows systems, the MBR is created with the ***FDISK /MBR*** command. This command rewrites the MBR to allow the system to boot up again.

Bootable Configuration Files

The two main configuration files that a computer uses to boot are CONFIG.SYS, which is shown in Figure 14-5, and AUTOEXEC.BAT, which is shown in Figure 14-6.

Figure 14-5 CONFIG.SYS File

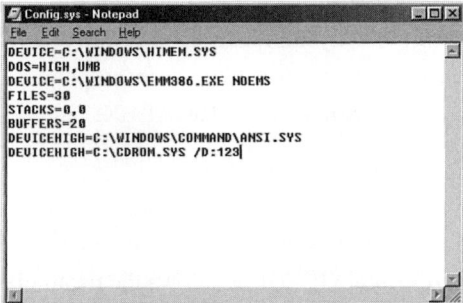

CONFIG.SYS is a special file that contains setup or configuration instructions for the computer system. The commands in this file configure the DOS program for use with devices and applications in the system. The commands also set up the memory managers in the system. After the commands in CONFIG.SYS have been completed, DOS begins searching for the *AUTOEXEC.BAT* file. This file contains a list of DOS commands that are automatically executed when DOS is loaded into the system.

Figure 14-6 AUTOEXEC.BAT File

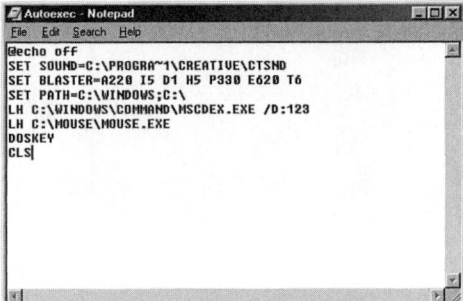

The system can still boot if these files are missing or corrupted. However, these two files are essential for the complete bootup process to occur with the DOS operating system. They contain information that is used to change the operating system for personal use. They also contain the requirements of different software application packages. A system would require troubleshooting if either of these files became damaged or corrupted.

DOS Error Messages

Error messages are commonly displayed when operating systems require troubleshooting. Many factors can cause error messages to display. As technicians gain troubleshooting experience, these messages become easier to recognize and address. Error messages usually appear when the operating system identifies a problem or when users try to open an application that the operating system cannot recognize.

Bad or Missing COMMAND.COM

In the DOS environment, the "Bad or Missing COMMAND.COM" error message is common. This error message can appear for the following reasons:

- The COMMAND.COM file cannot be found on the hard drive.
- The COMMAND.COM file is not located in the hard drive root directory. This usually occurs when a new hard drive or operating system is installed.
- The user accidentally erased the COMMAND.COM file from the root directory.

This error message does not mean that the operating system has been corrupted and must be reinstalled. If this message appears, use the bootable disk and type **SYS C:** at the DOS prompt. The **SYS** command copies the IO.SYS, MSDOS.SYS, and COMMAND.COM system files from the boot disk to the hard drive. Remove the bootable disk, and reboot the system.

Configuration File Errors

Two other common error messages that are associated with the CONFIG.SYS and the AUTOEXEC.BAT files are the "Error in CONFIG.SYS Line XX" and "Error in AUTOEXEC.BAT Line XX" messages. The line specified by the XX in the error message contains a syntax error that prevents these files from operating. This means that the files contain a spelling, punctuation, or usage error. This can also produce an unrecognized command error. Sometimes missing or corrupted files are detected by the CONFIG.SYS and AUTOEXEC.BAT files. To correct these files, enter them at the DOS prompt and edit them with a text editor by correcting the appropriate line in the specified file. Reload the indicated file, and restart the computer.

REM Statements

Administrators must be familiar with the REM statements in the CONFIG.SYS and AUTOEXEC.BAT files to edit these files. REM stands for REMark. The REM statements prevent a line from being read or executed when the CONFIG.SYS and AUTOEXEC.BAT files are being used, for example, when the computer boots up. If Windows 98 is being used and you have problems booting because DOS-based applications are causing the system to stall, reboot the computer and press **F8** when the "Starting Windows 98" message is displayed. Restart in MS-DOS mode, and edit the AUTOEXEC.BAT file from this point. Press **F5** to skip AUTOEXEC.BAT and CONFIG.SYS when the message "Starting MS-DOS" displays. Place a REM statement at the beginning of any application statements that were preventing the system from booting. When the system is restarted, the lines that begin with "REM" are not executed in the bootup process, and the system should start up. Figure 14-7 shows the AUTOEXEC.BAT file with REM statements added.

Figure 14-7 REM Statements

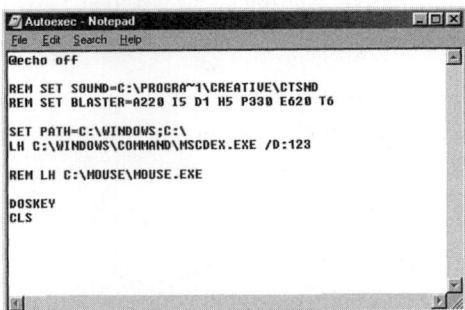

REM statements can be used in the CONFIG.SYS file, which contains configuration information about the system hardware and devices. For example, a device driver might be preventing the system from booting up properly. Edit the CONFIG.SYS file by placing a REM statement at the beginning of the line for the device driver. This temporarily prevents the driver from loading when the CONFIG.SYS file is loaded.

The first thing to do when troubleshooting a HIMEM.SYS error is to use the System Editor to check the entry in the CONFIG.SYS file for accuracy. In Windows 98, the HIMEM.SYS statement must be present—and correct—for the operating system to load. Also, make sure that the version and location of the HIMEM.SYS file are correct.

Extended Memory Access (HIMEM.SYS)

DOS 4.0 and higher versions have a memory-management program called *HIMEM.SYS* that manages the extended memory above the 1024-KB level. When this utility is loaded, it shifts most of the operating system functions into the high memory area of extended memory. Add the following line to the CONFIG.SYS file to activate this function:

    DEVICE=C:\DOS\HIMEM.SYS

This command loads the DOS Extended Memory Specification (XMS) driver. This causes HIMEM.SYS to be executed automatically when the computer is started.

Expanded Memory Access (EMM386.EXE)

The *EMM386.EXE* utility is another memory-management program that provides system access to the upper memory area of RAM. This program works with the HIMEM.SYS utility to enable the system to conserve conventional memory by moving device drivers and memory-resident programs into the upper memory area.

Troubleshooting issues commonly occur with this program because of conflicts in the allocation of the upper memory blocks. This can be caused by a missing or incorrect HIMEM.SYS file or conflicting drivers. To detect this type of memory conflict, start Windows by typing **WIN /D:X** at the DOS prompt. This command bypasses the upper memory portion in the bootup process. If Windows starts up after using this switch, the system has identified that an upper memory block conflict exists and needs to be resolved. To resolve the conflicting driver issue, run the MSD.EXE diagnostic tool to examine the drivers that use the upper memory block. After locating a conflicting driver, add an EMMEXCLUDE= line to the [386Enh] section of the SYSTEM.INI file. This statement in the SYSTEM.INI file prevents Windows from trying to use the space to establish buffers.

The MS-DOS–based automated memory optimizer is called the MEMMAKER utility. This utility automatically configures memory allocation when run with the /BATCH switch.

Figure 14-8 summarizes information about the MS-DOS memory layout.

Figure 14-8 MS-DOS Memory Layout

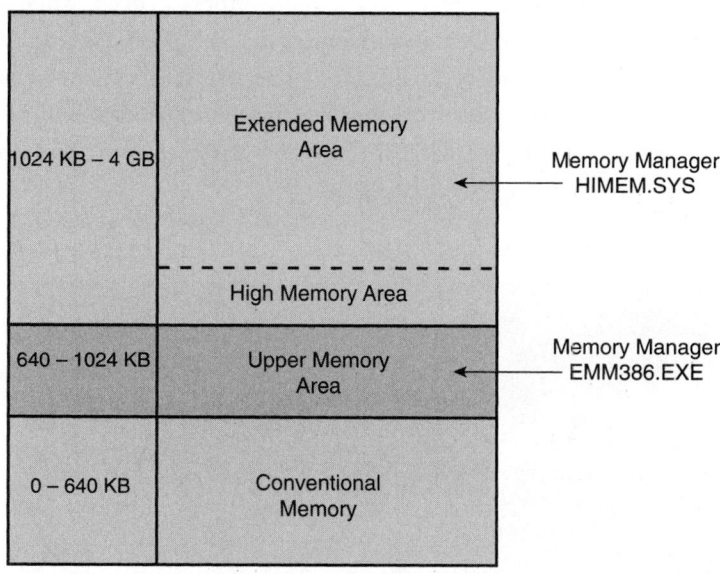

LASTDRIVE= Errors

The *LASTDRIVE=* command is contained in the CONFIG.SYS file and specifies the maximum number of drives that the system can access. Common troubleshooting issues with this command can be fixed by editing the CONFIG.SYS file. The parameter that contains the actual number of drives might be incorrect; this value might have to be manually edited. After correcting this value, restart the system and see whether it boots properly. If the available disk drives are set to a letter value that is lower than what is required of the existing system, DOS automatically overrides the letter value to accommodate the drives that are installed in the system. The number of drives should only be increased if additional drives are going to be used, because each drive letter above E decreases the amount of RAM that is available for other purposes.

DEVICEHIGH= Errors

The *DEVICEHIGH=* command loads drivers into the upper memory area instead of loading them into conventional memory. Errors commonly occur when this command attempts to load a device-driver file that is too large to fit in the buffer space that is available in a block of the upper memory area. This can cause the system to lock up. Use the MEM /D command to determine details on the current memory utilization and what is loaded.

Invalid Directory Errors

An invalid directory error is shown in Figure 14-9. These errors can occur while attempting to navigate through the file system in DOS. For example, if a hard drive contains two partitions and only the first partition has been formatted, attempting to access the second partition drive letter results in an invalid directory error. This error also appears when a user tries to access a directory that has been deleted or damaged. If the system has been backed up, recopy the directory to the hard drive and try to access it again.

Figure 14-9 Invalid Directory Error Message

Common Windows Operating System Problems

Typically, operating system installations proceed without incident, but occasionally, errors can occur. It is important for the IT technician to understand all the steps of the installation process and to know how to recognize problems. This section includes the following topics:

- Troubleshooting setup (installation) problems: Review
- Troubleshooting startup (booting) problems
- Understanding Windows memory usage problems
- Troubleshooting Windows missing/corrupt .DLL or .VxD files
- Troubleshooting system lockup errors
- Troubleshooting shutdown problems

Troubleshooting Setup (Installation) Problems: Review

Common installation hardware-related issues are identified by insufficient memory and incompatible device driver errors. Before attempting to resolve hardware problems, consult the Microsoft website to see whether the hardware is compatible with the operating system that is being installed. If the hardware is not supported, it should be replaced. Figure 14-10 shows the insufficient disk space error message.

Figure 14-10 Insufficient Disk Space Message

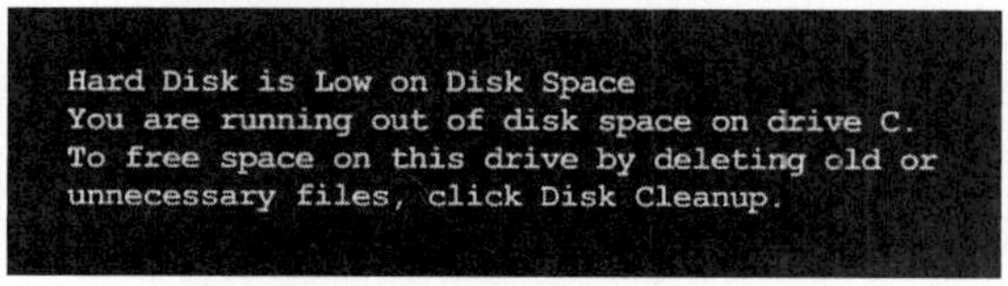

```
Hard Disk is Low on Disk Space
You are running out of disk space on drive C.
To free space on this drive by deleting old or
unnecessary files, click Disk Cleanup.
```

Troubleshooting Startup (Booting) Problems

Startup issues typically involve problems with hardware, configuration, and boot or operating systems. Some of these problems can simply prevent system activities from occurring, whereas others can produce error messages that make it easy to find the cause.

The problem is most likely hardware related if the system produces an error message or a beep-coded error signal before the normal POST beep. The normal POST beep signals that the BIOS has passed the POST and that the operating system is about to load. If the error message or beep-coded error signal occurs after the normal POST beep, the problem is most likely software related.

Creating a Windows 9x Startup Disk

A startup or boot disk allows diagnostic programs to identify the cause of computer problems. A blank floppy disk should be used to create a boot disk. Any files that are on the disk will be erased by creating this boot disk.

Use the following steps to create a Windows 98 startup disk:

Step 1   Label a blank disk as the Windows 98 startup disk.

Step 2   Choose **Start**, **Settings**, **Control Panel**.

Step 3   Double-click the **Add/Remove Programs** icon.

Step 4   Click the **Startup Disk** tab, and then click the **Create Disk** button, as shown in Figure 14-11.

Step 5   Insert the blank floppy disk into the disk drive, and click the **OK** button.

Figure 14-11 Creating a Startup Disk

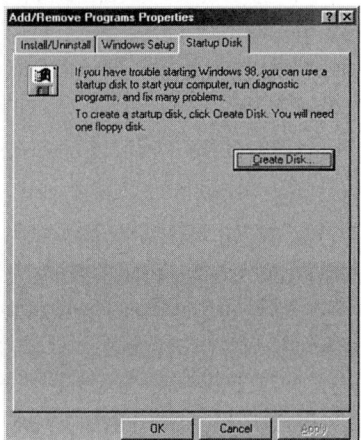

Using the Windows 9x Startup Disk

The Windows 9x startup disk gives technicians access to the system when the OS becomes corrupted. To use the disk, insert it into the floppy drive and restart the system. Use the Windows 9x startup disk to access the operating system files, and use the troubleshooting tools on the disk to identify the cause of the problem.

In addition to the files that are needed to start the system in a minimal or DOS mode, the Windows 9x startup disk provides many diagnostic programs and CD-ROM drivers. The startup disk also contains a RAM drive and an **EXTRACT.EXE** command. This command copies .CAB files from the Windows 98 CD.

Using Windows System Tools to Troubleshoot Startup Problems

The Windows operating system provides many system troubleshooting tools. These tools can isolate and correct many computer issues. Load the system tools configuration utility from the command line by typing **MSCONFIG.EXE**. Figure 14-12 shows the screen that displays. This troubleshooting tool can load device drivers and software options. This utility can also systematically view the CONFIG.SYS and the AUTOEXEC.BAT files. It can enable or disable items until all the problems are identified.

Figure 14-12 MSCONFIG Display

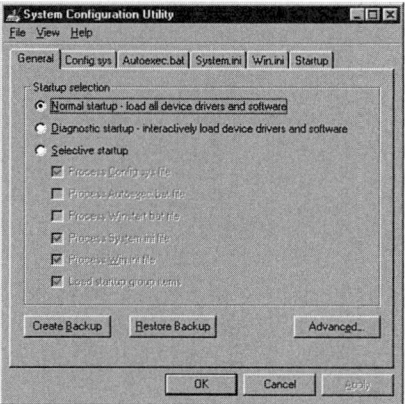

If your inspection of the CONFIG.SYS and AUTOEXEC.BAT files does not solve the problem, the system tools utility provides other options. Lower-level configuration settings, such as real-mode disk access and VGA standard video settings, can be inspected. The Device Manager can also be started from the MSCONFIG view option, allowing you to troubleshoot protected-mode device drivers. You can also check to verify that system files are not missing or corrupt. Other items that can be inspected are corrupt registry entries, viruses, and possible hardware conflicts.

Understanding Windows Memory Usage Problems

Memory usage errors occur when the operating system or an application attempts to access a memory location that is unallocated. When this type of conflict occurs, the unallocated memory location becomes corrupted and usually causes the operating system to crash. This could occur if multiple applications are being used and one application attempts to use the memory space of another. When this happens, the operating system generates an error message or stops processing and locks up. The typical error message is "This operation has performed an illegal operation and is about to be shut down."

Some memory usage errors are nonfatal, which means that they do not cause the application or the system to lock up. These errors give users the option to continue working or to shut down the application. Users should shut down the application. Otherwise, it could become unstable and lock up, causing a loss of unsaved data.

If a Windows memory error affects the Windows core files KRNLXXX.EXE, GDI.EXE, or USER.EXE, restart the Windows operating system.

Windows Resources Low Issues

When the Windows resource level gets too low, applications or the operating system can lock up. This type of error indicates that the operating system is running out of real and virtual memory. The system performance begins to degrade and slow down. This usually occurs when many applications are being used at the same time or when the system has not been restarted in a long time. The System Tray, located in the lower-right corner of the screen, contains programs that are constantly operating in the background, even though they are not being used. These programs are using system resources. Any unnecessary icons in the System Tray should be disabled or removed to free more resources for other applications.

General Protection Fault Problems

A *general protection fault (GPF)* occurs when an application attempts to access an unallocated memory location. Figure 14-13 shows the screen that is displayed. GPFs are usually caused when programs use illegal instructions to access protected areas of memory. In earlier versions of Windows, a GPF would crash the system and require it to be rebooted. Any unsaved data would be lost in the process. The latest versions of Windows remain stable after a GPF so that users can close the error message and save their data before closing the application or restarting the system.

Figure 14-13 General Protection Fault (GPF) Message

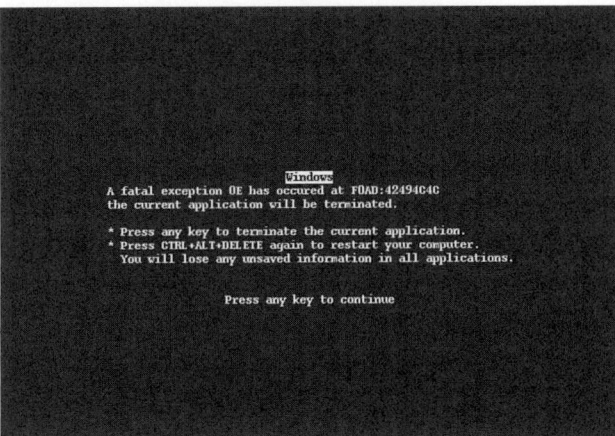

GPFs can be caused by trying to use applications that are not written for the Windows operating system, selecting the wrong machine or network during installation, or using incorrect versions of DOS in the system. A CONFIG.SYS or AUTOEXEC.BAT file that contains unsupported programs or drivers could also be a cause.

Troubleshooting Windows Missing/Corrupt .DLL or .VxD Files

Two important types of files are associated with the Windows operating system: .VxD and .DLL files. It is important to learn what these files do and to understand how to repair them because they are critical to the health of the system. If these files are deleted or become corrupted, the system will no longer run properly. A *.VxD file* is a virtual device driver and is only found in the Windows 9*x* operating systems. These .VxD files take the place of the **DEVICE=** and **LOADHIGH=** commands for devices that are in versions of DOS. The .VxD files are protected-mode drivers that allow multiple applications to access a system hardware or software resource. The *x* in .VxD represents a particular type of driver. For example, a .VDD file is a display adapter driver and a .VPD file is a printer driver. If these .VxD files are missing or corrupted, many devices can fail. As a result, the system might not start up or might not start up properly. If this happens, try reloading the driver that came with the hardware or try to update the driver by downloading it from the manufacturer's website.

Another file, called a *dynamic link library (.DLL) file*, can communicate with the Windows core directly. These small files store subroutines that either come with an application or are created by the programmer. Loss or corruption of .DLL files can cause an application to lock up or can prevent it from loading. Windows 95, 98, and 2000 applications use the operating system as a pool of resources (such as memory, modem, video, and printer). Programs or .DLL files make "calls" to these three modules when they need to place something on the screen, to check the status of the mouse, to use memory, or to gain access to other items. Problems arise when a new application is installed and updates one of the shared .DLL files, thereby creating a .DLL conflict. As a result of this conflict, older applications might not be able to handle the updated file and fail to work.

SFC Utility

The Windows operating system includes many tools, such as the *System File Checker (SFC)*, to make it more stable and dependable. The SFC is a command-line utility that scans the operating system files to ensure that they are the correct Microsoft versions. Although it is no longer a widespread problem, some applications can replace system files, such as .VxD or .DLL files, with different files of the same name. This eventually prevents a computer system from working. The operating system is no longer stable and can have difficulty booting after installing or uninstalling some applications or utilities.

The SFC is a tool that allows users to scan their system and verify that the versions of protected system files are up to date. If a protected system file has moved or has been deleted, the SFC automatically replaces the file with the correct version from the .DLL cache folder. Figure 14-14 shows the SFC.

Figure 14-14  Windows Missing/Corrupt .DLL or .VxD Files

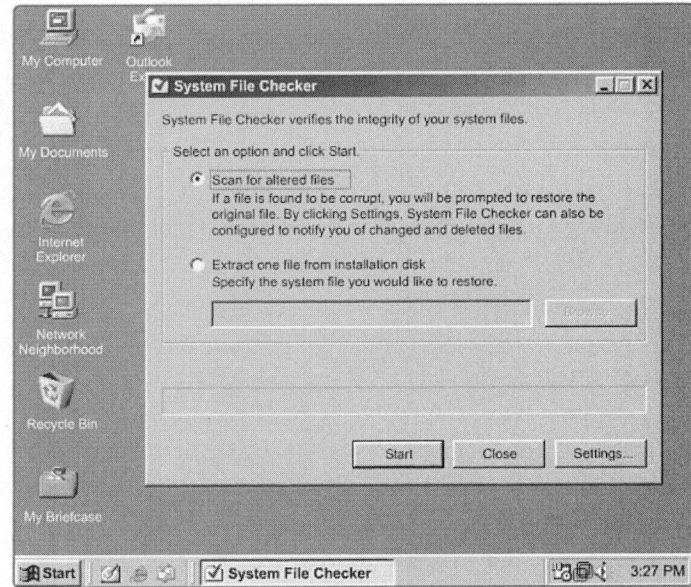

Locating/Replacing Missing or Corrupt .DLL or .VxD Files

The SFC utility scans the hard drive for damaged and missing Windows files and corrects problems. An operating system CD must be available for restoring missing files to the proper location on the system. This utility works in Windows 98 and Windows 2000. In Windows 2000, type **SFC /SCANNOW** at a command prompt. To return to the default Windows file protection operation, type **SFC /ENABLE**. In this mode, the **SFC** automatically prompts the user to restore the correct system file version when it detects that an application has overwritten a file. Do not forget to enable this option before exiting the command-prompt window.

Although running the SFC utility can solve a problem most of the time, many programs load a restore file in their own folder. This can be fixed in several ways.

One example is an error with the MFC42.DLL files. First, rename any MFC42.DLL files that can be found, other than those in the **\SYSTEM** and **\CABS** folders, from MFC42.DLL to MFC42.OLD, and reboot the computer. This can only be done from a DOS prompt. If the problem is resolved, the filename can be changed back to the original. Do this one file at a time. If three MFC42.DLL files are found, rename the first one. Reboot, and if the problem remains, rename the next one and continue the process. Eventually only one copy of this file should exist in the **\SYSTEM** folder and in the **\CABS** folder.

If this does not fix the problem, rename the MFC42.DLL file in the system folder to MFC42.OLD. Then copy one of the other MFC42.DLL files that were found in the other folders to the **C:\WINDOWS\SYSTEM** folder and rename it MFC42.DLL. The object is to use the other copies of the files and see whether they work. This approach usually solves the problem of missing or corrupted .DLL files.

Troubleshooting System Lockup Errors

The majority of system lockup errors occur when a memory allocation error exists or when system resources are too low. Memory allocation errors were discussed earlier in this chapter. Use only one or two applications at a time to help prevent system lockup problems. The screen shown in Figure 14-15 is displayed when the user presses Ctrl-Alt-Delete. A more permanent solution is to add system resources. For example, the processor could be upgraded or memory could be added.

Figure 14-15 System Lockup Errors

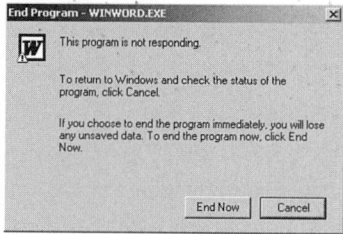

Troubleshooting Shutdown Problems

Sometimes technicians receive troubleshooting calls from users whose systems do not shut down. This is usually caused by an application that is still operating in the background. This application might have encountered an error and the application processes might be hanging up the system and preventing it from shutting down. If this occurs, one solution is to press Ctrl-Alt-Delete. The screen shown in Figure 14-16 appears. The application can be shut down manually, and then the system can be shut down. Further troubleshooting steps should be taken to determine what caused the application to hang up.

Figure 14-16 Troubleshooting Shutdown Problems

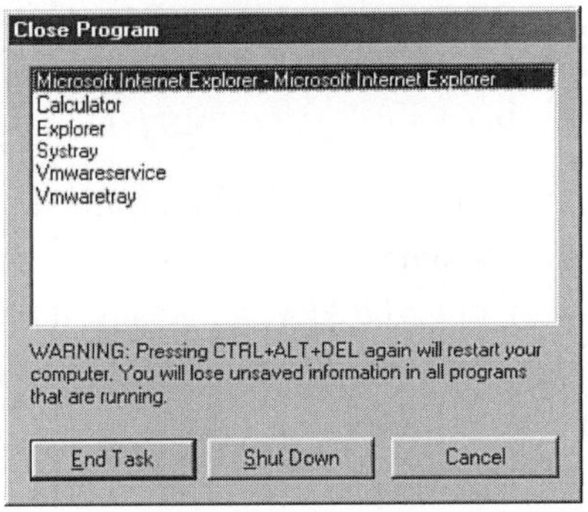

Troubleshooting Windows 9*x*

Most of the time, an upgrade to Windows 9*x* is completed successfully. Understanding the upgrade process can benefit the IT technician for times when errors occur. This section includes the following topics:

- Upgrade issues
- Error codes and startup messages
- Windows 9*x* startup modes
- Windows 9*x* error log files
- Windows virtual memory errors

Upgrade Issues

Problems that are encountered during upgrades to Windows 9*x* are related to hardware, software, or both. Before starting an upgrade, consult the Microsoft website to see whether the hardware is compatible. Make sure that the hardware meets the minimum system recommendations. Check with the hardware component manufacturers and the software publishers to determine whether updated drivers are needed for the upgrade.

The minimum system requirements for a Windows 98 upgrade are as follows:

- 486DX (66-MHz) or faster processor
- 16 MB of memory
- 225 MB of free hard disk space for a full installation on a FAT16 drive
- 175 MB of free hard disk space for a full installation on a FAT32 drive
- VGA or higher resolution monitor
- Keyboard

- CD-ROM drive (optional but recommended)
- High-density 3-1/2-inch floppy disk drive if no bootable CD-ROM drive is available

The Microsoft website includes a list of recommendations that identify the type of processor and amount of RAM that are required to use the selected operating system.

Error Codes and Startup Messages

Error codes that are generated at system startup usually indicate hardware problems, configuration problems, or bootup problems that are associated with the operating system. These types of errors can result in a startup failure. These problems must be fixed before the system can boot up properly. If one of these errors appears, use a bootable floppy disk, discussed earlier in this chapter, to boot the system and begin the troubleshooting process.

No Operating System Found

The "Missing operating system" error message is shown in Figure 14-17. If this message appears during startup, it probably indicates a failed hard drive or a damaged or corrupted MBR. The error message "No operating system found" might also appear if the command interpreter, or COMMAND.COM, file is missing. To troubleshoot the problem, first check to make sure that the hard drive and all cables are properly installed. If the problem continues, start the system with a boot disk that contains the **FDISK.EXE** file and use the **FDISK / MBR** command to fix the Master Boot Record on the hard drive. It might be necessary to run diagnostics on the hard drive to determine whether a hard drive failure has occurred.

NOTE

The error message that you see depends on the type of the BIOS and the version of the BIOS that is on the machine.

Figure 14-17 Error Message: Missing Operating System

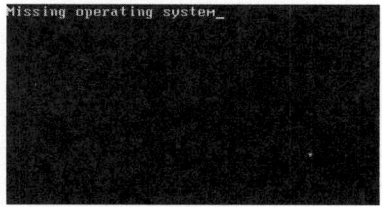

Windows Protection Error

The error message "Windows protection error" can occur when a computer loads or unloads a virtual device driver (VxD). The VxD that did not load or unload is usually mentioned in the error message. Sometimes it is impossible to identify the VxD that caused the error. Windows protection error messages can occur for the following reasons:

- A real-mode driver and a protected-mode driver are in conflict.
- The registry is damaged.
- The WIN.COM file or the COMMAND.COM file is infected with a virus or is damaged.

- A protected-mode driver is loaded from the SYSTEM.INI file, and the driver is already initialized.
- There is a physical input/output (I/O) address conflict or a random-access memory (RAM) address conflict.
- The Complementary Metal Oxide Semiconductor (CMOS) settings are incorrect for built-in peripheral devices such as cache settings, CPU timing, and hard disks.
- The Plug and Play feature of the computer Basic Input/Output System (BIOS) is not working correctly.
- The computer contains a malfunctioning cache or malfunctioning memory.
- The computer motherboard is not working properly.

Illegal Operation

The error message "Illegal operation" indicates that a specific program is having a problem. The *illegal operation* designation covers a wide range of errors. It can take some time to identify the cause. The most common causes of an "Illegal operation" error message are as follows:

- Problems between the program and a software driver in the operating system
- Memory-management problems between the program and an open program in the background
- Problems and conflicts with different .DLL files, which are added to the system when software programs are installed
- Hardware conflicts
- Defective RAM chips
- Program bugs

To pinpoint the cause, ask the following questions:

- Is a program that has always worked now crashing unexpectedly?
- Have new hardware devices or software been added or removed recently?

Tracing the origins of a problem to a specific event can help isolate the likely causes. An incompatible printer driver can also cause the "Illegal operation" error, even if the error is not generated when printing.

Error Message: Device Is Not Found

The WIN.INI file contains parameters that can be altered to change the Windows environment and software settings to user preferences. WIN.INI is a software initialization file for

Windows. It contains information about some Windows defaults, the placement of windows, color settings for the screen, available ports, printers, fonts, and software applications. The SYSTEM.INI file contains hardware-setting information for the drivers that Windows uses for configuration. When the error message "A device referenced in SYSTEM.INI, WIN.INI, or registry is not found" displays, it usually means that these files contain an entry that is no longer installed in the system. To fix this error, open the files and edit them to remove the lines that are referencing the hardware or software. Alternatively, the technician could reinstall the missing files or application.

Failure to Start GUI

The operating system files that control the graphical user interface (GUI) can become corrupted and generate the "Failure to start GUI" error message. If this occurs, start the operating system from the DOS prompt—that is, the command line. From the DOS prompt, troubleshoot the operating system to repair the files that start the GUI.

Windows 9*x* Startup Modes

Access the Windows 9*x* Startup menu by pressing **F8** when the "Microsoft Windows 9*x* Startup Menu" screen is displayed. The menu offers several startup options, including normal, logged, safe mode, step-by-step confirmation, and DOS modes, as shown in Figure 14-18. These startup modes are helpful for troubleshooting startup issues. In normal mode, the system boots as it normally would with all the proper drivers and registry files. The logged mode boots just like the normal mode, but the OS creates an error log that contains the performed steps and their outcomes.

Figure 14-18 Windows 9*x* Startup Modes

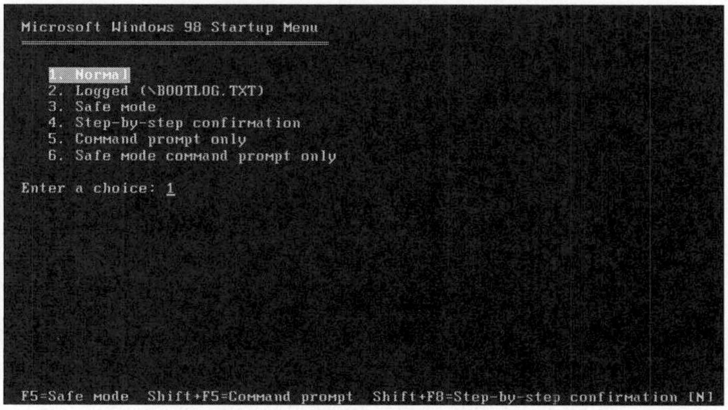

Safe Mode

Safe mode is a troubleshooting tool for Windows. It is similar to the command-line switches for Windows 3.x. Safe mode allows access to Windows using only the most basic drivers. The properties of safe mode are as follows:

- The AUTOEXEC.BAT and CONFIG.SYS files are not loaded.
- The main portion of the registry is not loaded.
- In the WIN.INI file, the load= and run= lines are not loaded.
- In the SYSTEM.INI file, the [Boot] and [386Enh] sections are not loaded.

Starting Windows 9x in safe mode bypasses the real-mode configuration and loads a protected-mode configuration. This disables Windows 95 device drivers and uses the standard VGA display adapter. If the problem that you are trying to solve does not occur in safe mode, you might have a conflict with hardware settings, real-mode configuration issues, incompatible legacy Windows programs or drivers, or registry damage.

While Windows is in safe mode, the Device Manager should be checked for any hardware device conflicts. If conflicts exist, it might be necessary to change interrupt request (IRQ) or direct memory access (DMA) settings. If no conflicts exist, the problem is probably software related.

Safe mode is the best troubleshooting tool in Windows, but safe mode does not state exactly where the problem is. You can perform the following troubleshooting steps in safe mode:

- Choose **Start**, **Settings**, **Control Panel**, double-click the **System** icon, click the **Performance** tab, click the **Graphics** button, and set the hardware acceleration to **None**.
- Choose **Control Panel**, **System**, **Performance**, **File System** to set read-ahead to **None**.
- Choose **Control Panel**, **Display**, **Settings**, **Change Display Type** to change the video driver to a standard VGA.
- Restart the computer in normal mode each time something is changed.

If the problem is software related, consider editing the WIN.INI file. Only two lines in the WIN.INI file do not load in safe mode. These are the RUN= and the LOAD= lines. Mark out these lines by placing a semicolon in front of them, and then try to start the computer normally. If this solves the problem, something that is loading on these lines is causing the problem.

If the problem is hardware related, consider editing the SYSTEM.INI file. The [Boot] and [386Enh] sections in the SYSTEM.INI file should be examined. These are the only two sections that are not loaded when booting into safe mode. A line with an .EXE extension generally indicates a program that is loading. Mark these lines out by placing a semicolon in front of them. Also, look for lines that access .386 files. These are legacy drivers. These drivers might be necessary for operating sound cards, modems, and other devices, but most manufacturers offer updated drivers.

Command Prompt Only Mode

Some systems can also be started in DOS mode to troubleshoot problems. Enter DOS mode by selecting the command prompt only mode. This mode provides the ability to troubleshoot the operating system from the command-line interface using command-line tools and DOS editors. Loading the HIMEM.SYS, the IFSHLP.SYS, or any of the Windows 9x files can also be avoided. Choose this startup option if the system does not boot into safe mode.

WIN Switches

The *WIN switches* provide the ability to start up Windows from the command line. The **WIN /D** command troubleshoots and isolates problems with the operating system. Modify the /D switch to start Windows in a number of different configurations. Use these different configurations to start Windows with different options to troubleshoot specific areas of the operating system, as follows:

- **WIN /D:F**—Disables 32-bit disk access.
- **WIN /D:M**—Starts Windows in safe mode or safe mode with networking.
- **WIN /D:S**—Prohibits Windows from using the address space between F000h and FFFFFh.
- **WIN /D:V**—Prevents Windows from controlling disk transfers. The hard drive transfers are instead handled by the BIOS.

The various switches allow users to manipulate Windows to troubleshoot specific areas of the operating system.

Windows 9x Error Log Files

When troubleshooting a computer system, it can be difficult to determine exactly what the error is or why it occurred. It might be easy to recognize and solve the problem, but it is important to identify the cause of the error. Fixing the problem without fixing the cause does not prevent the problem from reoccurring. Windows 9x maintains error log files of system operations; these files list the events that led to the error. The filenames of these log files are indicative of the type of information that they track. Table 14-1 shows the function and location of each log file and indicates when each log file is created.

Table 14-1 Summary of Log Files

Filename	When Created	Function	Location
SETUPLOG.TXT	When the Setup program fails before hardware detection	Windows 98 can recover by reading this file. This file can also be used for troubleshooting errors that occur during installation.	Located in the root directory. The file determines where the system stalled, what to redo, and what to skip.
DETCRASH.LOG	When the Setup program fails during hardware detection	This file records information about the detection module that was running and the memory resources or I/O port that was being accessed when the program failed.	Only the Setup program can read this file. If the detection process is completed successfully, this file is deleted. The file can be found in the C:\ directory.
DETLOG.TXT	Every time that the detection process runs	This file contains a record of a specific hardware device that was detected and identifies the parameters for the detected device.	Located in the root directory after Windows 98 is installed. This file indicates the start of a detection test and whether the test was completed.

The *BOOTLOG.TXT* file contains the information that is collected while the system is booting up. This file is created during the Windows installation process. It is not automatically updated each time the system boots. The file can be updated by pressing **F8** during startup and choosing the logged option or by starting Windows with the **WIN /B** command.

The log information is recorded in five steps, as follows:

Step 1   **Loading real-mode drivers**—The system loads the real-mode drivers and reports an error in the log if it is unsuccessful in loading these drivers.

Step 2   **Loading virtual device drivers (VxDs)**—The system loads the virtual device drivers and reports an error in the log if it is unsuccessful in loading these drivers.

Step 3   **Initialization of critical VxDs**—The system initializes critical VxDs and reports an error in the log if it is unsuccessful in initializing these VxDs.

Step 4   **Device initialization of VxDs**—This log shows all the VxDs that have been successfully initialized. In this section, each device is initialized and a success or failure report of the initialization is generated.

Step 5   **Successful initialization of VxDs**—This section verifies the successful completion of the initialization of the system VxDs.

SETUPLOG.TXT

The *SETUPLOG.TXT* file is created during the installation process and contains the system setup information. It can be used for safe-recovery situations and is stored in the system root directory. The entries in this file are listed in the order that they occurred during the startup process. This can be helpful when troubleshooting because it shows exactly where an error occurred.

DETCRASH.LOG

If the system crashes during the hardware-detection phase of the startup process, the *DETCRASH.LOG* file is created. This file contains information about the processes that were operating when the crash occurred. This file cannot be read directly because it is in binary form.

DETLOG.TXT

Use the *DETLOG.TXT* file to read the information that is generated when the DETCRASH.LOG file is created. The DETLOG.TXT file indicates which components have been detected by the system and which ones have not. This file is essentially a detailed report of the hardware-detection phase of the system's Plug and Play operation.

Windows Virtual Memory Errors

Many operating systems, such as Windows, have huge memory requirements that exceed the amount of physical memory, or RAM, in the system. Even if enough physical memory exists to operate Windows, other applications on the system can require more memory. Without virtual memory, it would be impossible to run these applications.

Virtual memory is the part of the hard drive that is reserved for the operating system to do paging. Data is stored in pages, and only a certain number of pages can fit in the physical memory, or RAM, at the same time. The operating system moves some of the pages to the virtual memory so that the current pages can be kept in physical memory, which is faster. This process is called *swapping*. A swap file is essentially a large file that can contain thousands of these pages on a reserved portion of the hard drive.

Virtual Memory Settings

The default paging file size is 2 MB. The recommended paging file size for Windows 2000 is equal to 1.5 times the total amount of RAM. Windows sets a default paging file size during installation. Figure 14-19 shows the Virtual Memory dialog box. If many applications are operating simultaneously, it can be beneficial to use a larger paging file or multiple paging files. Unused space in the paging file remains available to the internal Windows Virtual Memory Manager.

Figure 14-19 Virtual Memory Settings

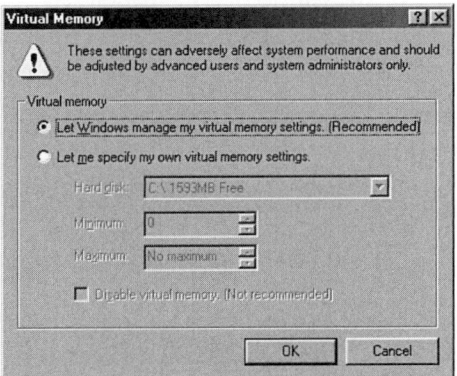

If Windows detects that the Windows paging file is set too low, a "Virtual memory minimum is too low" error message appears after the user logs on. The message indicates that Windows is increasing the size of the paging file. During this process, programs can operate more slowly or pause because memory requests by the applications have been denied.

SWAP File Errors

Swap file errors or "Swap file corrupt" messages indicate that the permanent swap file that was created for Windows has become corrupt. Swap file errors commonly indicate that little free space remains on the hard drive. This error can also appear when disk-management functions like FORMAT and FDISK are operating. Sometimes the swap file can be overwritten or become corrupted. If the swap file becomes corrupted or disabled, it can be re-created. Another fix is to reinstall the operating system.

Worksheet 14.4.5   Troubleshooting Software

This worksheet tests your knowledge of troubleshooting software by matching the terms with the correct descriptions.

Using System Tools and System Editors to Troubleshoot Windows 9x/2000

The IT technician can use system tools and system editors extensively when troubleshooting issues with Windows 9x and 2000. In addition, the Device Manager provides system status for components. This section includes the following topics:

- Using system tools
- Using the Device Manager to troubleshoot
- Using system editors

Using System Tools

Windows 9x and 2000 have many system tools that are helpful when troubleshooting. These include administrative and diagnostic tools that can help fix problems with the computer system.

TIP

Know what the different system tools are, how to access them, and how to use them in Windows.

Event Viewer: "Event Log Is Full"

Figure 14-20 shows the *Event Viewer*, which monitors system, application, and security events in Windows 9x. System events include successful and failed Windows component startups. Application events store information about system applications and their performance. Security events store information that is related to system security, such as logons and logoffs, file and folder access, and the creation of a new Active Directory.

Figure 14-20 Event Viewer

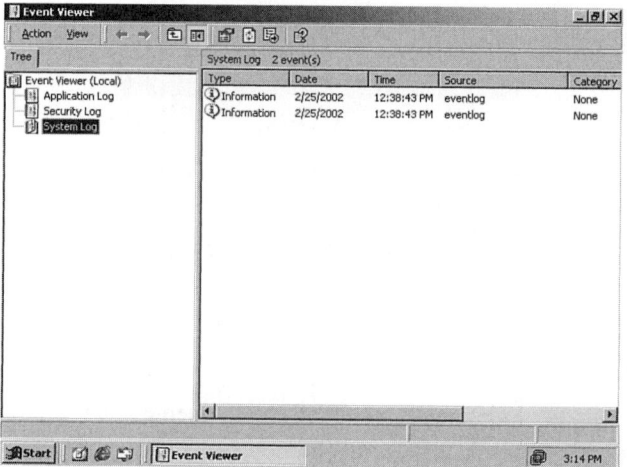

The Event Viewer also creates categories of system and application events. Information events indicate that an application, service, or driver has loaded successfully. Warning events identify things that can be harmful in the future. Error events indicate that an application, service, or driver has failed to load. Because the security log is limited in size and a large number of routine audit records can make it difficult to find records that suggest a security problem, carefully consider how to audit object access. Too many audit records can require a frequent review and clearing of the security log. This can generate an "Event log is full" error message. When this occurs, open the event log and delete some of the entries.

Dr. Watson Utility

The *Dr. Watson utility* isolates and corrects general protection faults (GPFs). When a GPF cannot be traced to the operating system, it is usually caused by an application. The Dr. Watson utility can operate in the background while an application is being used. The utility monitors application operations and logs important events in the DRWATSON.LOG file. This log provides details about events that cause GPFs and can be used to diagnose technical problems. If an error occurs more than once in the same application, the software might need to be updated with a patch.

SCANREG.EXE

The *SCANREG.EXE* file scans the registry for corruption. This file should be used if system troubleshooting indicates that an error is caused by a corrupted registry entry. Figure 14-21 shows the Windows registry being scanned. If the scan produces corrupted files, try to repair them by inserting the installation CD and choosing the repair installation option.

Figure 14-21 Running SCANREG.EXE

DEFRAG.EXE

System performance can be degraded when files are fragmented on the hard drive. As files are added and deleted, pieces of files are scattered through the hard drive. This degrades performance and can also cause the system or applications to lock up. Use the *DEFRAG.EXE* file to start the Defragmenter utility. Figure 14-22 shows the DEFRAG.EXE utility operating.

This utility reorganizes and rewrites all the files on the hard drive to the beginning of the drive, which simplifies information retrieval.

Figure 14-22 Running DEFRAG.EXE

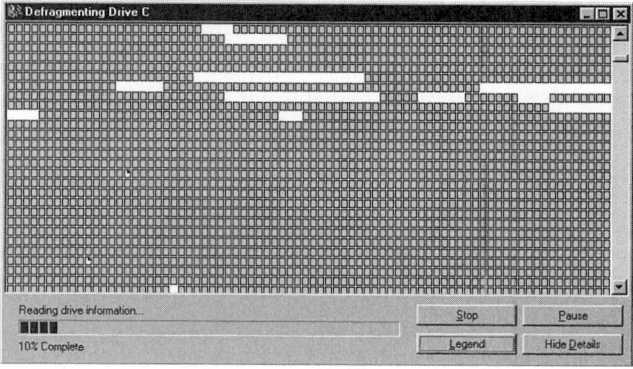

CHKDSK.EXE

The ***CHKDSK.EXE*** file is a command-line tool that recovers lost allocation units from the hard drive. The lost allocation units occur when an application terminates unexpectedly. Over time, lost allocation units can accumulate and occupy large amounts of disk space. By adding the /F switch to the CHKDSK.EXE command, the lost allocation units can be converted into files so that they can be viewed and deleted if necessary. This utility optimizes disk storage space by locating and removing files that have been corrupted.

SCANDSKW.EXE

ScanDisk for Windows, or ***SCANDSKW.EXE***, is a disk-checking and repair tool that checks the integrity of the media and repairs any problems. The media includes hard disks and floppy disks.

MSCONFIG.EXE

Load the system tools configuration utility from the command line by typing ***MSCONFIG.EXE***. This troubleshooting tool interactively loads device drivers and software options. This utility allows you to systematically view the lines of the CONFIG.SYS and AUTOEXEC.BAT files and to decide whether to load each line. Items can be enabled or disabled until all the problems are identified.

EDIT.COM

EDIT.COM is a windows troubleshooting tool that can be used to view and edit configuration files such as AUTOEXEC.BAT, CONFIG.SYS, and .INI files.

Using the Device Manager to Troubleshoot

The Windows Device Manager allows the hardware on a system to be viewed in a graphical interface and is helpful for managing and troubleshooting the system. The Device Manager, which is shown in Figure 14-23, can be used to disable, uninstall, and update device drivers. The Device Manager can also determine whether the system hardware is working properly and whether the correct drivers are installed for the hardware. Each device that is having a problem can be labeled so that the hardware that is not installed properly can be easily identified. When device configurations are being changed manually, the Device Manager can help avoid problems. The Device Manager identifies free resources and assigns devices to those resources, disables devices to make resources available, and reallocates resources if necessary. In Windows 2000, users must be logged on as members of the administrators group to change resource settings. Even if a user is logged on as an administrator, policy settings on a network might prevent him or her from changing resources.

Figure 14-23 Device Manager

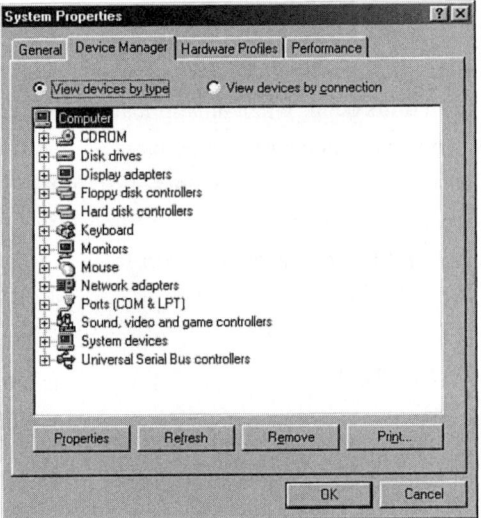

Using the System Editors

The Windows operating systems contain important editors. These editors allow Windows settings to be changed and customized to any policy that the system administrator desires. A system administrator can use the SYSEDIT.EXE and POLEDIT.EXE files to edit configuration settings to the user interface. In Windows 2000, the Group Policy Editor (GPE) allows the administrator to edit a policy for an entire group of users at one time.

SYSEDIT.EXE

Choose **Start, Run**, and type **SYSEDIT** in the command line. This opens the *SYSEDIT.EXE* file, which is the system editor tool. The SYSEDIT utility modifies text files such as .INI files and the CONFIG.SYS and AUTOEXEC.BAT files. The SYSEDIT commands are similar to those in other Windows-based text-editing programs. Figure 14-24 shows the System Configuration Editor.

Figure 14-24 System Configuration Editor

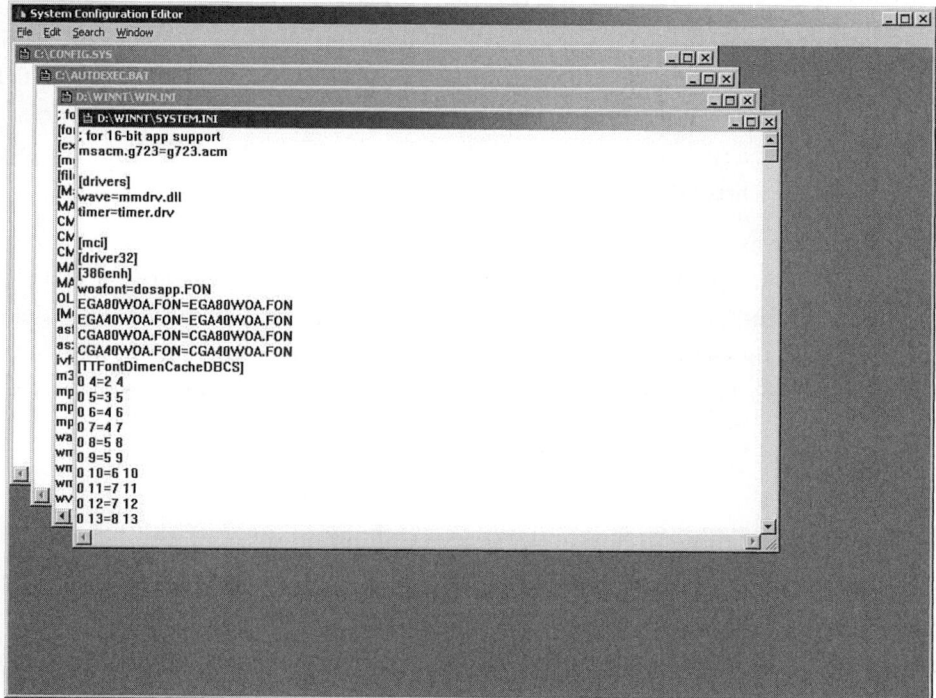

POLEDIT.EXE

Use the System Policy Editor, or *POLEDIT.EXE*, to set up different security restrictions for different users. Use it to set one policy for a entire group, to configure Desktops for roving users so that any computer they use can have the same look, or to protect a computer if it is unplugged from the network.

The Windows System Policy Editor is a powerful tool that creates and edits local registry values to standardize Desktop settings, prevent users from modifying hardware and environment settings, and control or restrict user actions.

The Windows System Policy Editor also prevents security problems such as file tampering, data losses as a result of accidental system software changes, or users being locked out of their computers.

Group Policy Editor

Group policies can refine and centralize the management of a user's Desktop environment. Group policies can control the programs that are available to users, the programs that appear on a user's Desktop, and the Start menu options.

The *Group Policy Editor (GPE)* is a group of configuration settings that a system administrator can apply to objects in the Active Directory database. A group policy editor controls the work environment of users in a domain. Group policies can also control the work environment for accounts in a specific organizational unit. Group policies can be set at the site level by using the Active Directory Sites and Services snap-in.

A group policy consists of the settings that control how an object and subobjects behave. Group policies allow a group policy administrator to provide users with a fully populated Desktop environment. This environment can include a customized Start menu, applications that are automatically set up, and restricted access to files, folders, and Microsoft Windows 2000 system settings. Group policies can also determine the rights of user accounts and groups.

Windows 9*x*/2000 Registry Problems

The registry structure of the Windows 2000 operating system is different from that of Windows 98. Both operating systems can be installed on a single machine, but they must be configured to dual-boot. This section focuses on the Windows 2000 registry and includes the following topics:

- Understanding the registry files
- Understanding the registry structure
- Editing the registry
- Cleaning the registry

Understanding the Registry Files

The registry files contain all the system configuration information. This includes the local hardware configuration, the network environment, file associations, and user configurations.

USER.DAT and SYSTEM.DAT are the registry files that contain all the contents of the registry. The following system files are related to the registry:

- *USER.DAT*—This file contains all the information that is specific to the user. This file maintains user profiles, such as mouse speed, wallpaper, and color scheme.

- *USER.DA0*—When Windows successfully boots up, the USER.DA0 file is created. This file is a backup of the USER.DAT file. If the USER.DAT file becomes corrupted or is deleted, rename the USER.DA0 file USER.DAT, and the registry can be restored.

- *SYSTEM.DAT*—This file holds hardware profiles, computer-specific profiles, and settings information. When a new piece of hardware, such as a video card, is installed, the SYSTEM.DAT file is updated.

- *SYSTEM.DA0*—Like the USER.DA0 file, the SYSTEM.DA0 file is also created when Windows successfully boots. This file is a backup of the SYSTEM.DAT file. If the SYSTEM.DAT file becomes corrupted or is deleted, rename the SYSTEM.DA0 file SYSTEM.DAT, and the registry can be restored.

- *SYSTEM.INI*—This file contains hardware information for the drivers that Windows uses for configuration. When the operating system needs to reference hardware information, it uses the SYSTEM.INI file.

- *WIN.INI*—This file contains parameters that can be altered to change the Windows environment or software settings based on user preferences. The WIN.INI file is a software initialization file for Windows. It contains information about some Windows defaults, the placement of windows, color settings for the screen, and available ports, printers, fonts, and software applications.

NOTE

WIN.COM is another registry file that controls the initial environment. It checks and loads Windows 95 core components when Windows 95 is loading.

TIP

Know how to access the Registry Editor and the files that are associated with the registry.

Understanding the Registry Structure

Understanding the purpose of the registry structure subtrees can help you troubleshoot and maintain the computer. A key exists for every system process in the Registry Editor, as shown in Figure 14-25. The following five subtrees, or subtree keys, are displayed in the Registry Editor window:

- *HKEY_USERS*—Contains the system default settings data that controls individual user profiles and environments, such as desktop settings, Windows environment, and custom software settings.

- *HKEY_CURRENT_CONFIG*—Contains data on the active hardware profile that is selected during the boot process. This information is used to configure settings for the device drivers to load and for the display resolution to use.

- *HKEY_CLASSES_ROOT*—Contains software configuration data for all software that is installed on the computer.

TIP

Know each subtree key, and describe what it does in the registry.

■ *HKEY_CURRENT_USER*—Contains data about the user who is currently logged on to the computer. Retrieves a copy of each user account that is used to log on to the computer and stores it in the registry.

■ *HKEY_LOCAL_MACHINE*—Contains all configuration data for the computer, including hardware and operating system data such as bus type, system memory, device drivers, and startup control data. Applications, device drivers, and the operating system use this data to set the computer configuration. The data in this subtree remains constant, regardless of the user.

Figure 14-25 Registry Keys

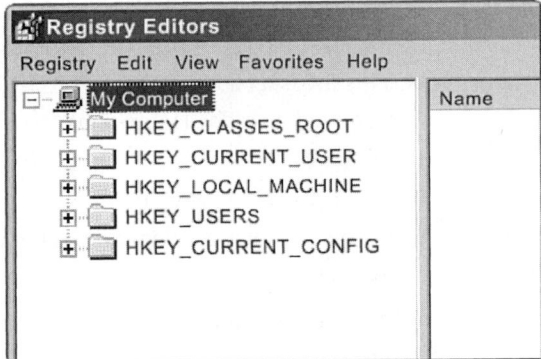

Editing the Registry

Most users do not have to edit the registry, but the troubleshooting responsibilities of a computer technician can include viewing, editing, backing up, and restoring the registry. The contents of the registry can be edited and viewed through the registry editors. Access the registry editors by choosing **Start**, **Run**, and typing **REGEDIT** or **REGEDT32** in the command window. When this command is entered, you see an interface with the registry subtrees window, allowing you to search all registry values. This allows you to manually change any registry value.

REGEDIT.EXE and REGEDT32.EXE

REGEDIT.EXE, which is shown in Figure 14-26, was designed to work with Windows 9*x,* but it also works with Windows 2000. Figure 14-27 shows REGEDT32.EXE. REGEDT32.EXE is recommended for use with Windows 2000, and REGEDIT.EXE is recommended for Windows 9*x.* REGEDT32 is automatically installed in the SYSTEMROOT\SYSTEM32 folder. REGEDIT.EXE is automatically installed in the SYSTEMROOT folder. Use these commands to navigate and edit the registry manually.

Figure 14-26 REGEDIT.EXE

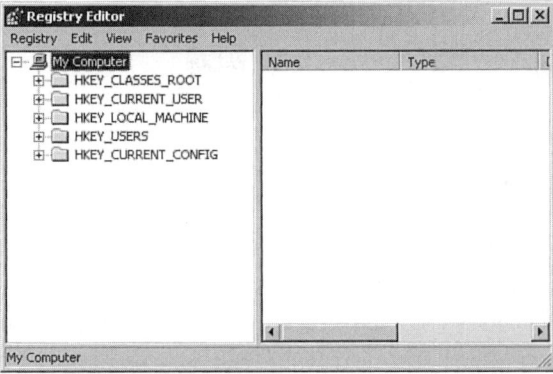

Figure 14-27 REGEDT32.EXE

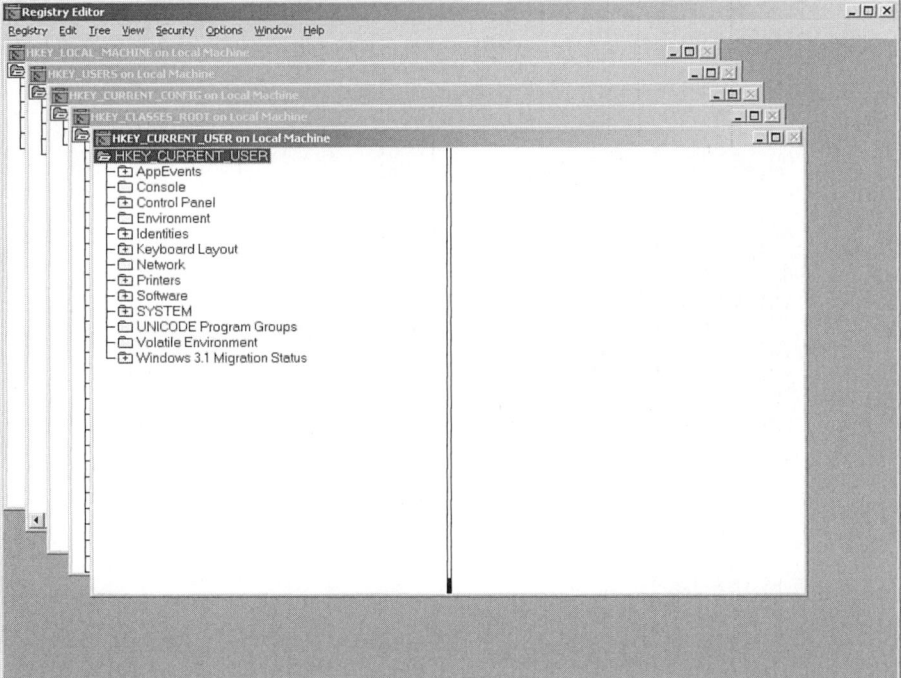

Third-Party Registry-Editing Tools

Navigating and editing the Windows registry can be a difficult and confusing task, even for the most experienced technician. The operating system can be damaged beyond repair if the wrong value is inserted or deleted. To make editing the registry an easier and safer task, use third-party registry-editing tools. Some popular tools are Norton WINDOCTOR, McAffee Registry Wizard, and PC Doctor OnCall. These tools provide an interface that is easier to use and navigate than the standard Windows registry editors.

Cleaning the Registry

An important part of maintaining a healthy computer is cleaning the registry. As the system is used and applications are installed and uninstalled, values are left behind in the registry. These values remain, even if the Add/Remove Programs Wizard is used, as shown in Figure 14-28. If the registry becomes cluttered with old files and old application registry entries, system performance can suffer.

Figure 14-28 Add/Remove Programs Wizard

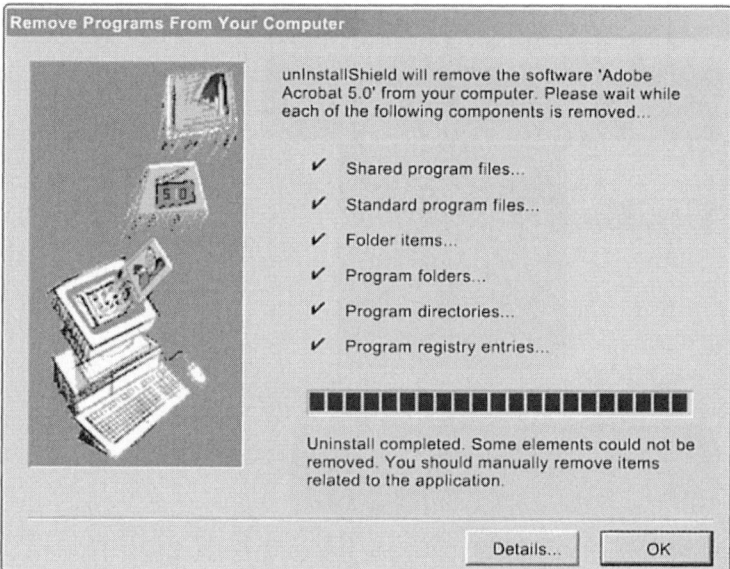

Third-Party Registry-Cleaning Tools

Third-party registry-cleaning tools are recommended for cleaning the registry. Popular cleaning tools are Norton WINDOCTOR and Microsoft RegCleaner.

Troubleshooting Windows NT 4/2000

Troubleshooting the common problems with Windows NT and Windows 2000 requires an understanding of the different startup modes and the Recovery Console. Knowledge of the installation process can benefit the technician when installing or upgrading a system. This section includes the following topics:

- Windows NT/2000 installation problems: Review
- Windows NT/2000 upgrade issues
- Windows NT startup modes
- Windows 2000 startup modes
- Windows 2000 Recovery Console

Windows NT/2000 Installation Problems: Review

The most common types of problems that occur when installing Windows NT or 2000 are hardware and software compatibility issues. Before installing Windows 2000, make sure that the hardware is capable of running it. The processor must be at least in the Pentium class. The system is also required to have at least 64 MB RAM. The hard drive or partition that the operating system files are installed on must be at least 2 GB in size. A VGA monitor and a CD-ROM drive that is capable of reading at least at 12X speed are also required. Windows 2000 is a network operating system, and to enable networking, a network card is required.

A Microsoft tool called the Hardware Compatibility List (HCL) can be used before installing Windows 2000 to verify that the hardware is compatible with Windows 2000. Microsoft provides tested drivers only for devices that are included on this list. Using hardware that is not listed on the HCL can cause problems during and after installation. View this HCL by opening the HCL.TXT file in the Support folder on the Windows 2000 Professional CD.

Windows NT/2000 Upgrade Issues

The issues that occur when upgrading to Windows NT and 2000 are similar to the issues that occur when performing Windows 9x upgrades. As with Windows 9x, problems that occur during upgrades to Windows 2000 can be hardware or software related, or they can be related to both. Before starting an upgrade, consult the Microsoft website to make sure that the hardware is compatible. Check with the manufacturers of the hardware components and software to see whether they have updated drivers that are necessary for the upgrade. The system requirements for Windows 2000 Pro are as follows:

TIP

Make sure that you know the minimum requirements for Windows 2000 Pro.

- 133-MHz Pentium or higher microprocessor
- 64 MB RAM
- 2-GB hard disk with at least 650 MB of free space
- VGA or higher resolution monitor
- Keyboard
- Mouse
- CD-ROM drive
- High-density 3-1/2-inch floppy disk drive if no bootable CD-ROM drive is available

Windows NT Startup Modes

Startup mode options are also available in Windows NT. However, the startup process for Windows NT is different from that for Windows 9x. The Windows NT startup depends on the boot loader file, or BOOT.INI. The NTLDR program uses this file to generate a boot loader menu that is displayed on-screen; you select an operating system from this menu. Also from this menu, choose to start the system in VGA mode or last known good hardware configuration mode. These modes are explained shortly, because they are also included with Windows 2000.

Windows 2000 Startup Modes

Windows 2000 also provides a choice of startup modes. In addition to the safe mode options that are available in Windows 9x, Windows 2000 provides an advanced options menu with additional features. Figure 14-29 shows the options that are available to enable boot logging, VGA mode, last known good configuration mode, and debugging mode.

Normal and Safe Mode Boot Modes

Windows 2000 allows users to boot normally, boot to safe mode, boot to safe mode with networking, or boot to safe mode with a command prompt. As with Windows 9x, Windows NT and 2000 provide a way to boot the system into safe mode with minimal drivers to allow troubleshooting.

Enable Boot Logging

If the enable boot logging startup mode is chosen, a NTBTLOG.TXT file is created. This is similar to the BOOTLOG.TXT file in Windows 9x and contains a listing of all the drivers and services that the system attempts to load during the bootup process. Use this startup mode to determine what device or service is causing the system to fail.

Figure 14-29 Windows 2000 Advanced Options Menu

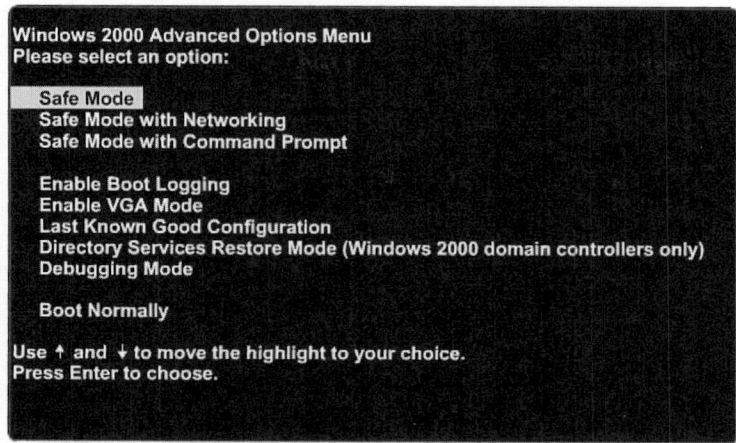

Enable VGA Mode

Use the enable VGA startup mode if you experience display problems while booting up. This mode loads the standard VGA driver instead of the driver for your video card. Boot into VGA mode, and reconfigure the display setting.

Last Known Good Configuration

If the system begins to fail after a new device driver is loaded, use the last known good configuration startup mode option. This option enables the system to start from the point of the last successful user logon, before the new device driver was installed.

Debugging Mode

The debugging mode startup feature enables the use of special debugger utilities. These utilities access the kernel for troubleshooting and analysis by starting the operating system in a kernel debug mode.

Lab 14.7.4   Booting into Safe Mode

Upon completion of this lab, you will be able to boot the PC using the advanced troubleshooting options of Windows 2000.

Windows 2000 Recovery Console

The Windows 2000 ***Recovery Console*** is a command-line interface that performs a variety of troubleshooting and recovery tasks. These tasks include starting and stopping services,

TIP

Know how to use the Windows 2000 Recovery Console.

reading and writing data on local drives such as drives that are formatted with the NT file system, and formatting hard disks. Figure 14-30 shows the startup screen with the Recovery Console option. After starting the Recovery Console, use the commands from the command line to remove, replace, or copy corrupted files.

Figure 14-30 Windows 2000 Recovery Console

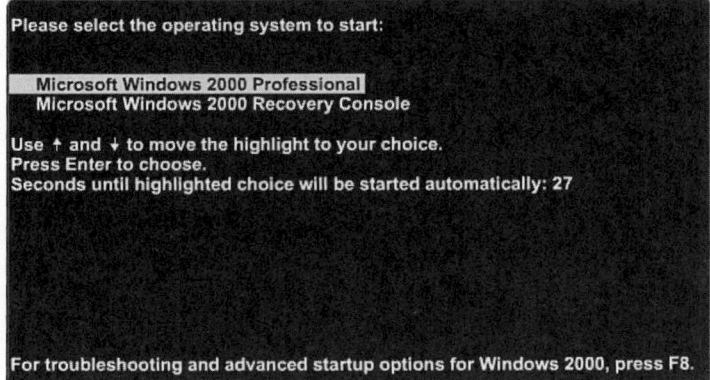

You can start the Recovery Console in several ways. First, try inserting the Windows 2000 CD into the CD-ROM drive and wait for the Microsoft Windows 2000 CD dialog box to open. If the dialog box does not open, choose **Start**, **Run** and type **CMD**. This displays the command-prompt window. Change to the drive letter of the CD-ROM drive, navigate to the I386 folder, and type **WINNT32 /CMDCONS**. After the Recovery Console is installed, it can be accessed from the Please Select Operating System to Start menu. The Recovery Console can also be started by using the Windows 2000 setup disks or CD to start the system and selecting the Recovery Console option when prompted.

FIXMBR and FIXBOOT

The *FIXMBR* command can be used with the Recovery Console to fix hard drive problems. The **FIXMBR** command repairs the Master Boot Record (MBR). The syntax for this command is **FIXMBR [*device name*]**. If the device name parameter is omitted, **FIXMBR** rewrites the MBR on the boot device. A device name can be specified to write an MBR to a different drive such as a floppy disk or a secondary hard disk. Use the **MAP** command to retrieve a list of device names. An example of a valid device name is MAP\Device\HardDisk0.

The *FIXBOOT* command writes a new boot sector onto the system partition. The syntax for the command is **FIXBOOT [*drive:*]**. If the drive is not specified, **FIXBOOT** writes the boot sector to the default boot partition. Specify a drive if the boot sector is to be written to a volume other than the default boot partition.

Lab 14.7.5   Using the Windows 2000 Recovery Console

In this lab, you learn how to use and implement the Windows 2000 Recovery Console.

Troubleshooting Windows XP

Troubleshooting the Windows XP installation is similar to that of Windows 2000, but the technician must understand certain specific issues. It is preferable to perform a clean installation of Windows XP as opposed to an upgrade. In addition, you should verify hardware compatibility. This section includes the following topics:

- Windows XP installation problems
- Windows XP upgrade issues
- Windows XP startup modes
- Windows XP Recovery Console

Windows XP Installation Problems

Some of the peripherals might not work correctly during the setup process. Begin troubleshooting by checking the system BIOS. An outdated BIOS can cause problems with disk partitioning, power management, peripheral configuration, and other important low-level functions. Identify the BIOS manufacturer, and determine whether an update is available. When the computer is using the most current version of the BIOS, enter the BIOS setup and select the **Non-Plug and Play** operating system option. Even though Windows XP is a Plug and Play operating system, the BIOS option can prevent Windows XP boot loader from accessing devices at startup. The BIOS option was intended for previous versions of Windows.

To boot the bootable CD during the installation process, enter the BIOS setup and change the boot sequence. The setting can be configured multiple ways, and each BIOS is different.

The system can crash after the text-mode setup is complete. This indicates that the setup is not compatible or that the driver for the disk subsystem is missing. If the computer comes with a high-performance IDE controller or SCSI device, Windows XP might not include a compatible driver. Downloading a driver that is compatible with Windows XP, copying the driver to a floppy disk, and rebooting the system can solve this problem. When the text-mode setup starts, you are prompted to press F6 to install third-party drivers. After the files are loaded, setup prompts you to insert the floppy disk that contains the driver. After the driver is installed, Windows XP setup continues with the installation.

Windows XP Upgrade Issues

The issues that can occur when upgrading to Windows XP are similar to those that occur when performing Windows 9x, NT, and 2000 upgrades. As with Windows 9x, NT, and 2000, problems that occur during upgrades to Windows XP can be hardware or software related, and sometimes both. Before an upgrade is started, consult the Microsoft website to see whether the hardware is compatible. Check with the manufacturers of the hardware components and software to see whether they have updated drivers that are necessary for the upgrade. The minimum system requirements for the Windows XP Home Edition and Professional Edition are as follows:

TIP

Know the minimum system requirements for Windows XP Home and Professional Editions.

- Pentium 233-MHz processor or faster, with 300-MHz recommended
- 64 MB RAM, with 128 MB recommended
- 1.5 GB of available hard disk space
- CD-ROM or DVD-ROM drive
- Keyboard and Microsoft Mouse, or a compatible pointing device
- Video adapter and monitor, with Super VGA resolution of 800×600 or higher
- Sound card
- Speakers or headphones
- Network interface card if using Windows XP Professional in the corporate environment

Windows XP Startup Modes

The Windows XP operating systems provide a choice of startup modes that are similar to those for the Windows 9x operating systems. However, Windows XP provides an advanced options menu that provides features in addition to the safe mode options, as shown in Figure 14-31.

Part of being able to successfully troubleshoot the Windows operating system is being able to troubleshoot the applications that are installed on the operating system. At least half of all troubleshooting calls are concerned with troubleshooting applications.

Normal and Safe Boot Modes

Windows XP allows users to boot to normal mode, safe mode, safe mode with networking, or safe mode with command prompt. As with Windows 9x, Windows NT/2000 provides a means of booting the system into safe mode with minimal drivers to allow troubleshooting.

Figure 14-31 Windows XP Startup Modes

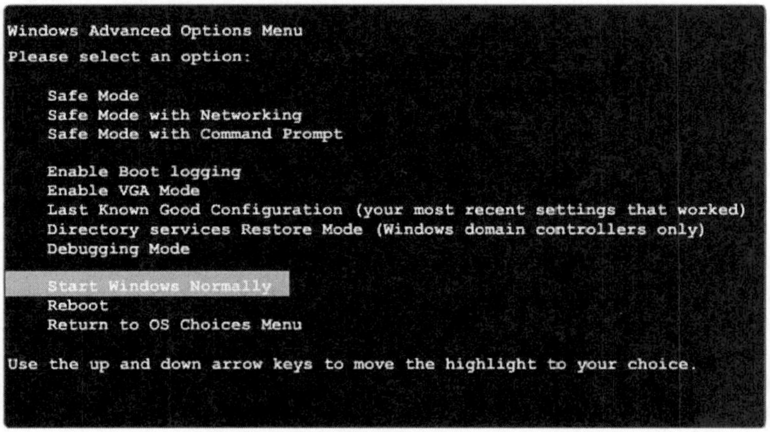

```
Windows Advanced Options Menu
Please select an option:

    Safe Mode
    Safe Mode with Networking
    Safe Mode with Command Prompt

    Enable Boot logging
    Enable VGA Mode
    Last Known Good Configuration (your most recent settings that worked)
    Directory services Restore Mode (Windows domain controllers only)
    Debugging Mode

    Start Windows Normally
    Reboot
    Return to OS Choices Menu

Use the up and down arrow keys to move the highlight to your choice.
```

Enable Boot Logging

If the enable boot logging startup mode is chosen, a NTBTLOG.TXT file is created. This file works similar to the Windows 9x BOOTLOG.TXT file. The NTBTLOG.TXT file contains a listing of all the drivers and services that the system attempts to load during the boot process. Use this startup mode to determine what device or service is causing the system to fail.

Enable VGA Mode

Use the enable VGA startup mode if you experience display problems while booting up. This mode loads the standard VGA driver instead of the driver for your video card. Boot into VGA mode, and reconfigure the display setting with the "Enable VGA mode" startup mode.

Last Known Good Configuration

If a new device driver is loaded into the system and then the system begins to fail, use the last known good configuration startup mode option. This option enables the system to start from the point of the last successful user logon, before the new device driver was installed.

Windows XP Recovery Console

The Windows XP Recovery Console is a command-line interface that performs a variety of troubleshooting and recovery tasks. These tasks include starting and stopping services, reading and writing data on a local drive (including drives that are formatted with the NT file system), and formatting hard disks. After the Recovery Console has been started, enter commands at the command prompt to remove, replace, or copy corrupted files.

TIP

Know how to use the Windows XP Recovery Console.

You can start the Recovery Console in several ways. One way is to insert the Windows XP CD into the CD-ROM drive and wait for the Microsoft Windows XP CD dialog box to open. The option to open the Recovery Console displays. Press **R** to run the Recovery Console.

Another way to start the Recovery Console is to choose **Start**, **Run** and type **CMD** in the command window. This displays the command-prompt window. Change to the drive letter of the CD-ROM drive, navigate to the I386 folder, and type **WINNT32 /CMDCONS** at the command prompt.

After the Recovery Console is installed, it can be accessed from the Please Select Operating System to Start menu.

FIXMBR and FIXBOOT

The **FIXMBR** command can be used with the Recovery Console to fix hard drive problems. The **FIXMBR** command repairs a Master Boot Record (MBR). The syntax for this command is **FIXMBR** [*device name*], as shown in Figure 14-32. If the [*device name*] parameter is omitted, **FIXMBR** rewrites the MBR on the boot device. A device name can be specified to write an MBR to a different drive such as a floppy disk or secondary hard disk. Use the **MAP** command to retrieve a list of device names. An example of a valid device name is MAP\Device\HardDisk0.

Figure 14-32 FIXMBR

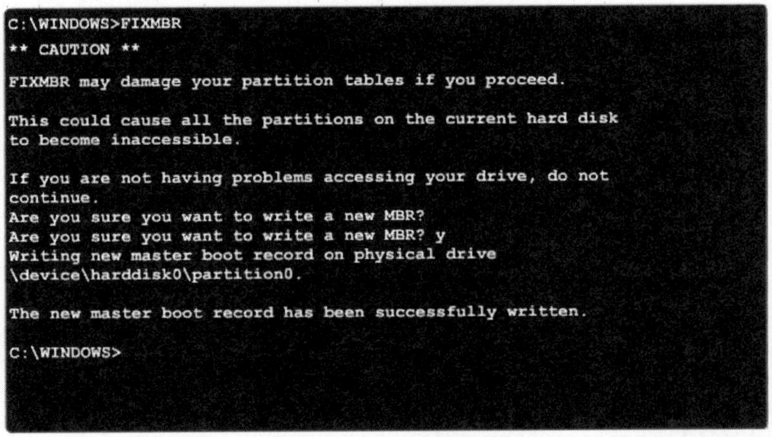

```
C:\WINDOWS>FIXMBR
** CAUTION **

FIXMBR may damage your partition tables if you proceed.

This could cause all the partitions on the current hard disk
to become inaccessible.

If you are not having problems accessing your drive, do not
continue.
Are you sure you want to write a new MBR?
Are you sure you want to write a new MBR? y
Writing new master boot record on physical drive
\device\harddisk0\partition0.

The new master boot record has been successfully written.

C:\WINDOWS>
```

The **FIXBOOT** command writes a new boot sector onto the system partition. The syntax for the command is **FIXBOOT** [*drive:*], as shown in Figure 14-33. If you do not specify the [*drive* :] option, **FIXBOOT** writes the boot sector to the default boot partition. Specify a different drive if a boot sector is to be written to a volume other than the default boot partition.

Figure 14-33 FIXBOOT

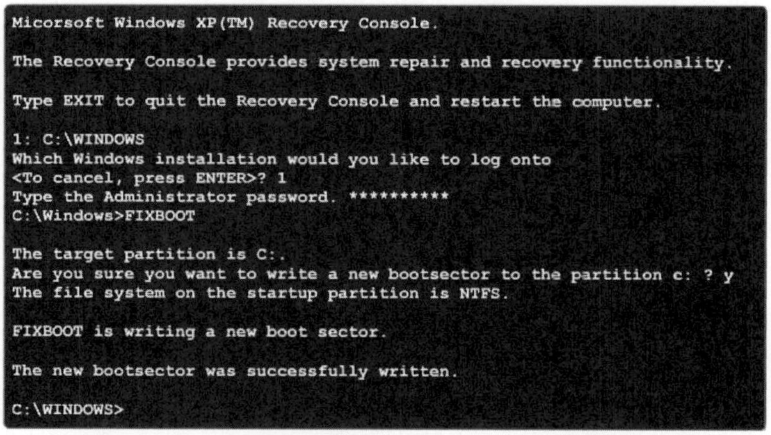

```
Micorsoft Windows XP(TM) Recovery Console.

The Recovery Console provides system repair and recovery functionality.

Type EXIT to quit the Recovery Console and restart the computer.

1: C:\WINDOWS
Which Windows installation would you like to log onto
<To cancel, press ENTER>? 1
Type the Administrator password. **********
C:\Windows>FIXBOOT

The target partition is C:.
Are you sure you want to write a new bootsector to the partition c: ? y
The file system on the startup partition is NTFS.

FIXBOOT is writing a new boot sector.

The new bootsector was successfully written.

C:\WINDOWS>
```

Troubleshooting Applications

As an IT technician, you will be called on to troubleshoot both DOS and Windows applications. You should understand each operating system and the diagnostic tools that are used with each OS. This section includes the following topics:

- Troubleshooting DOS applications
- Troubleshooting NT/2000 applications

Troubleshooting DOS Applications

To successfully troubleshoot the Windows operating system, it might be necessary to troubleshoot the applications that are installed on the operating system. Figure 14-34 shows the system File Checker command.

Missing or Corrupted .DLL or .VXD Files

Dynamic link library (.DLL) files are small files that store subroutines that either come with an application or are written by the programmer. The loss or corruption of .DLL files can cause an application to lock up or can prevent it from loading. Problems occur when a new application is installed and then updates the shared .DLL files. This creates a .DLL conflict. As a result of this conflict, older applications might not be able to use the updated file and might not work properly.

Figure 14-34 System File Checker

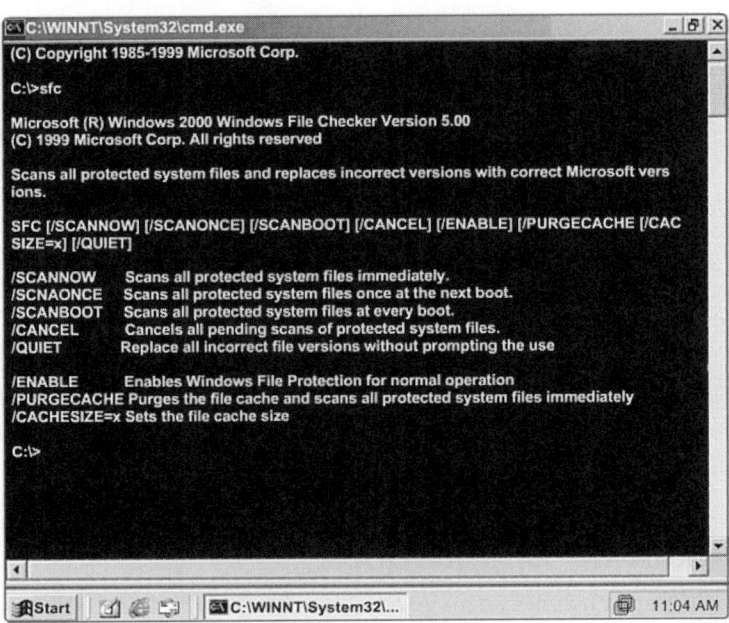

Troubleshooting NT/2000 Applications

Windows NT and 2000 often experience the same application errors as Windows 9x. For example, the application properties can be incorrect, the registry entries can be missing or corrupted, or the .DLL files can be corrupted. The Windows NT and 2000 operating systems are usually part of an integrated network, which introduces many potential problems. For example, the permissions that are set on files or folders might be too restrictive for users, or they might not be restrictive enough.

Windows 2000 Task Manager

The Windows 2000 Task Manager is used to troubleshoot applications. Access the *Task Manager* by pressing Ctrl-Alt-Delete and clicking the Task Manager tab. As shown in Figure 14-35, the Task Manager displays a list of active applications to help identify the applications that are not responding. The Task Manager can be used to switch to a particular application for troubleshooting, if necessary. It can also end the application if it has crashed and is not responding.

Figure 14-35 Windows 2000 Task Manager

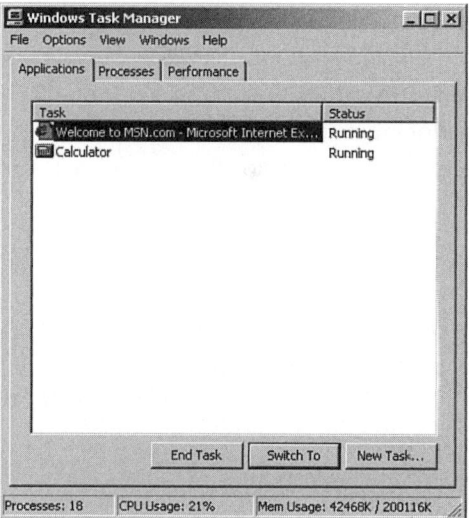

The Processes tab provides information to help identify applications that are slowing system operations. Sometimes when an application crashes, it affects the system's processor and causes the rest of the system to lock up or slow to a point where it becomes unusable. The Processes tab shows the percentage of the CPU that an application is using. If an application is not responding and it is using a large percentage of the CPU, close the application and see whether the system returns to normal.

The Performance tab allows users to view a graphical interface that shows the processor performance and memory usage. Past and current usage can be viewed to obtain information about the applications that were running and when they caused the system to lock up.

Windows Data Backup and Recovery

The importance of a backup strategy cannot be emphasized enough. The type of data determines how often a backup must be scheduled. System files do not need to be backed up as often as work that is done on a daily basis. Understanding the tools that are used to back up and recover files can benefit the technician when serious problems cause data to be lost. This section includes the following topics:

- Windows registry backup and recovery tools
- Windows data and application backup and recovery tools
- Types of data backup procedures

Windows Registry Backup and Recovery Tools

Technicians can encounter blue screens that are sometimes called the "blue screen of death," pop-up boxes that report errors, and other messages that indicate that the registry is corrupted or cannot load a device. When the database or registry is corrupt, the only solution is to reinstall Windows. These types of errors are common. However, data loss can be prevented with proper backup and recovery tools. The method for backing up the registry depends on the operating system in use.

Windows 95

Previous sections of this chapter discussed the SYSTEM.DAT and USER.DAT files. Windows 95 usually creates a backup copy of the registry each time the operating system is started. It copies SYSTEM.DAT to SYSTEM.DA0 and USER.DAT to USER.DA0. If Windows 95 has not replaced either backup file with a corrupted registry, the .DAT files can be restored. This would be the case if Windows 95 has not been restarted since the registry became corrupted. Copy SYSTEM.DA0 to SYSTEM.DAT and USER.DA0 to USER.DAT to recover the last copy of the uncorrupted registry files.

Windows 98/Me

Windows 98 does not copy the registry to .DA0 files when the operating system starts. Instead, it provides a program called the Registry Checker. The Registry Checker, or SCANREGW.EXE, backs up the registry to a .CAB file once a day. The .CAB file puts the registry in the C:\WINDOWS\SYSBCKUP folder, which is a hidden folder. The first backup is named RB000.CAB, the second backup is RB001.CAB, and so on. The file with the most recent date is the latest backup. The Registry Checker can also make additional backup copies of the registry. To make an additional copy of the registry, choose **Start**, **Run**, type **SCANREGW** in the command window, and click the **OK** button. After scanning the registry for errors, you are asked whether you want to make another backup of the registry. Click the **Yes** button, and the Windows Registry Checker backs up the registry to another .CAB file and displays a dialog box stating that it is finished. Click the **OK** button to close the Windows Registry Checker.

Windows NT

Windows NT 4.0 offers several ways to back up and recover the registry or the individual hives in the registry. A *hive* is a collection of registry keys, subkeys, and values that are stored in a file. The easiest way to back up the registry is by using the Emergency Repair Disk (ERD). The ERD copies local hive files that are found in the SYSTEMROOT\SYSTEM32\CONFIG folder to the SYSTEMROOT\REPAIR folder.

The files can also be copied to a floppy disk. Use the Windows NT Resource Kit backup utilities or a third-party backup program to copy the hive files to tape.

When the ERD process is run from the NT Backup utility, the current registry hives can be backed up to the repair directory on the system hard drive before the ERD floppy is created. If this option is chosen, all registry hives are copied to the SYSTEMROOT\REPAIR\ REGBACK folder. This option also copies the current user NTUSER.DAT file to the REGBACK folder. The user-specific COM Classes portion of the user profile is copied to a file called USRCLASS.DAT. This is the equivalent of NT 4.0 running RDISK.EXE, which is a recovery disk program, with the option to create the files on the hard drive instead of a floppy disk. If necessary, these saved registry hives can be used during a system repair process.

Windows 2000

The registry backup is part of the system state backup, which also includes critical boot files, on-domain controllers, and the Active Directory database. Start the Windows 2000 backup utility by using one of the following methods:

- Choose **Start**, **Programs**, **Accessories**, **System Tools**, **Backup**.
- Choose **Start**, **Run**, and type **NTBACKUP** in the run window.

Figure 14-36 shows the screen that is displayed. When the system backup begins, a welcome page appears, with wizards for automating the backup and restoration processes.

Figure 14-36 Windows 2000 Backup and Recovery

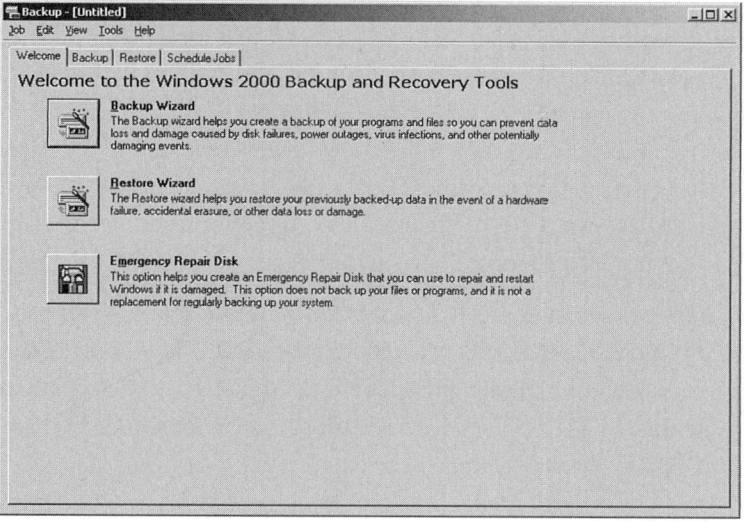

To back up the registry with the Windows 2000 Backup utility, choose the Backup Wizard or select the Backup tab. If the wizard is used, you are asked what you want to back up. If the backup is running on a Windows 2000 Domain Controller, back up the Active Directory, the registry, and the data by selecting the option to back up System State data, as shown in Figure 14-37.

Figure 14-37 Windows 2000 Backup: System State

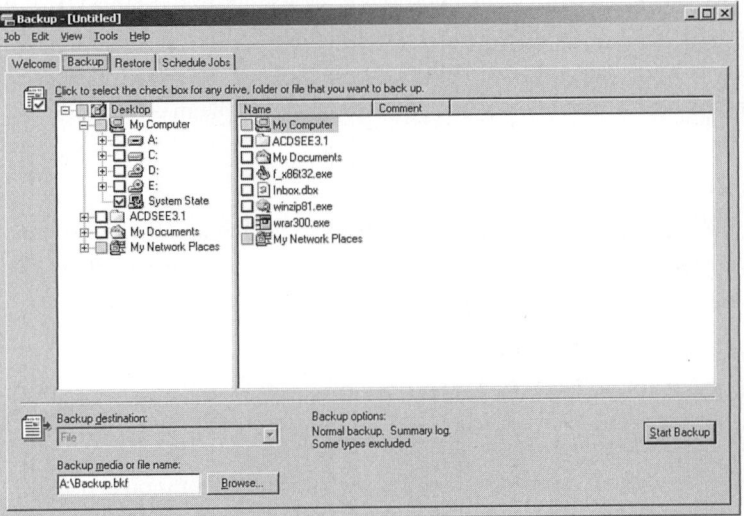

After choosing to back up the System State, select disks, files, or tapes as the media. The Backup utility backs up all necessary hives in the SYSTEMROOT\SYSTEM32\CONFIG directory, including Default, Software, System, SAM, and Security. The utility also backs up system files, user profiles, and any part of the system that is required for a complete system restoration. This can potentially mean a lot of data, depending on the size of the user profiles and registry hive files that are stored on the machine. To perform selected backup of registry hive files, use a tool from the Resource Kit, such as REGBACK.

The Windows 2000 Backup utility gives you the option to create an ERD. It backs up only three files: AUTOEXEC.NT, CONFIG.NT, and SETUP.LOG. The SETUP.LOG file is a list of the system files on the machine and includes a checksum value that indicates the correct version of the file. Use SETUP.LOG to restore corrupt system files when booting from a Windows 2000 CD, and choose the Repair option.

Windows XP

Backup in Windows XP is similar to the backup function in Windows 2000. It is started by choosing **Start**, **Programs**, **Accessories**, **System Tools**, **Backup**. Select the check box to open the Backup Utility Advanced Mode, as shown in Figure 14-38. New in Windows XP is the Restore and Manage Media tab. This tab expands on the previous option to enable users not only to restore data but also to manage the type of media that it is being restored from.

Figure 14-38 Windows XP Backup System State

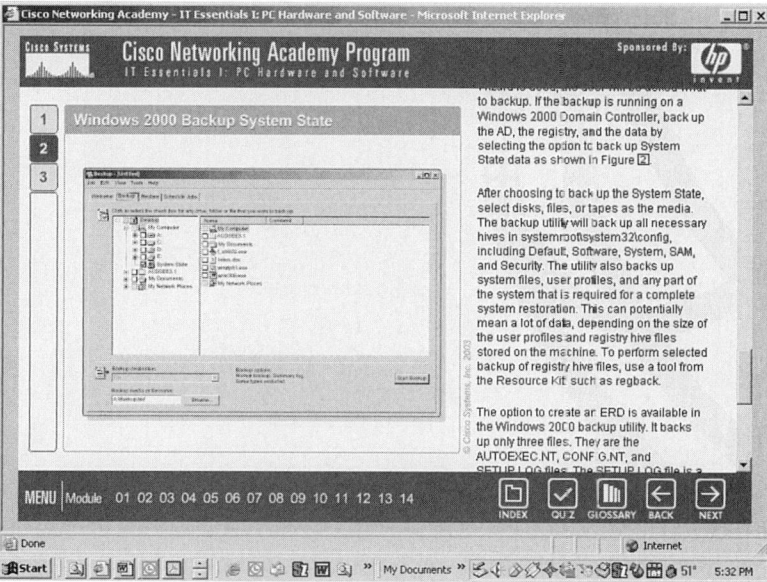

Windows Data and Application Backup and Recovery Tools

You can back up data and applications in several ways. Windows comes with backup utilities that are installed with the operating system, or third-party utilities can be purchased to back up data and applications. The chosen backup method depends on the type and amount of data that is being backed up. In Windows 2000, the Backup Wizard can be used by executing the **NTBACKUP** command from the Run window. As shown in Figure 14-39, specify what to back up by choosing one of the following options:

- **Back Up Everything on My Computer**—Backs up all files on the computer, except the files that the Backup Wizard excludes by default, such as certain power-management files.

- **Back Up Selected Files, Drives, or Network Data**—Backs up selected files and folders. When this option is selected, the Backup Wizard provides a hierarchical view of the computer and the network through My Network Places.
- **Only Back Up the System State Data**—Backs up important system components, such as the registry and the boot files.

Figure 14-39 Using the Backup UtilityWizard

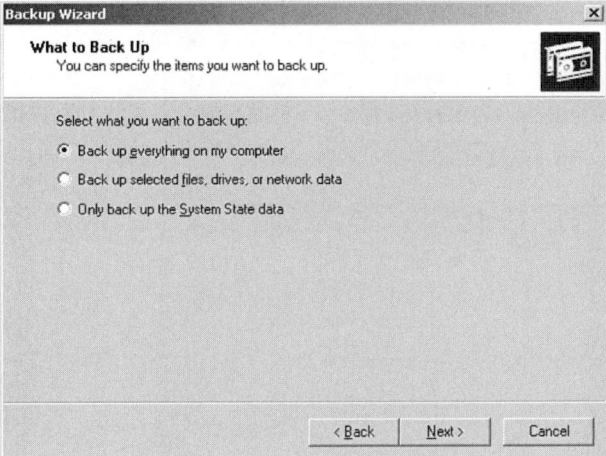

For Windows 9*x*, use the **BACKUP** and **RESTORE** commands to back up data. The backup command *BACKUP.EXE* can be used to begin the backup process. This does not install automatically when Windows 9*x* is installed. Install it by adding it from the Windows Setup tab in the Add/Remove Programs icon in the Control Panel. When this backup program is used, you are prompted to create a new backup job, open an existing backup job, or restore backed up files.

Types of Data Backup Procedures

In this section, some common backup procedures, such as normal, incremental, differential, and daily, are discussed. The first three backup procedures are the most common. Figure 14-40 shows the backup types that are available.

Normal Backup

A *normal backup* is also called a *full backup*. During a normal backup, all files on the disk are stored to tape or other backup media, and the archive bit for all files is set to off or cleared.

Figure 14-40 Windows 2000 Backup Types

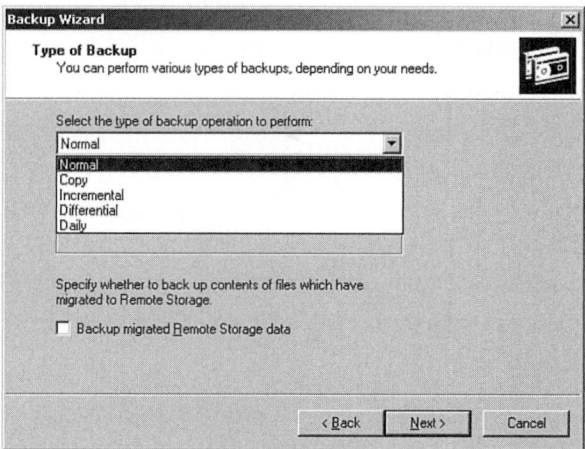

A daily backup generally requires only one tape to restore the data. It is impractical to run a full backup each day because of the amount of time it requires. Copy backups and daily backups do not reset the archive bit, and both are used to back up selected files.

Incremental Backup

An *incremental backup* procedure backs up all the files that have been created or modified since the last full backup. Incremental backups have two important characteristics. First, they must be used in conjunction with a full backup. Second, any file that is created or modified has its archive bit reset to off, or cleared, so that the file will not be saved during the next incremental backup.

For example, if a full backup were performed on a Monday, this would reset all the archive bits on the files. On Tuesday, an incremental backup would be performed to a separate tape. This would store all the files that were modified on Tuesday and reset their archive bits to off. This process is repeated for every business day of the week, each with a separate tape. This provides a complete backup of all files that were modified during the week. On the following Monday, the entire process would begin again.

The advantages and disadvantages of an incremental backup are as follows:

- **Advantage**—This type of backup scheme requires the least amount of time each day. Therefore, it has the smallest impact on the network resources in a networked environment.

- **Disadvantage**—If users need to restore the complete system backup, they must first restore the full backup tape and then restore all the incremental backup tapes in order. This takes a great deal of time, and if one of the tapes is bad, some information will be lost.

Differential Backup

A *differential backup* procedure backs up all the files that have been created or modified since the last full backup. The difference between a differential backup and an incremental backup is that after a file is saved in a differential backup, the archive bit is not reset to off. Each time a differential backup is performed, all the files that were modified or created since the last full backup will be saved again.

If a full backup were performed on a Monday, it would reset all the archive bits on the files. On Tuesday, a differential backup would be performed on a different tape. This would store all the files that were modified on Tuesday, but it would not reset their archive bits to off. This process is repeated for every business day of the week, using the same tape. A differential backup also provides a complete backup of network data in a networked environment.

The advantages and disadvantages of a differential backup are as follows:

- **Advantages**—Differential backups only require two tapes to create and restore a complete system backup.
- **Disadvantages**—The files that were backed up on previous days are stored again, which requires extra network resources. If the differential backup tape is damaged and the restore is performed on a Friday, for example, the data from four days will be lost and must be reentered.

Copy Backup

A *copy backup* backs up files that are selected by a user. A copy backup does not reset the archive bit after saving a file.

Daily Backup

A *daily backup* only backs up the files that are modified on the day of the backup. Daily backups do not reset the archive bit.

 Lab 14.10.3   Windows Registry Backup and Recovery

In this lab, you learn how to back up the registry and perform a recovery of the registry.

TIP

Know the different types of backup options, and understand how they are used.

Windows-Specific Printer Software Problem Troubleshooting

Printer drivers can be a problem when a new printer is added or when the operating system is upgraded. Most problems can be corrected by accessing the printer queue. This section includes the following topics:

- Print spoolers
- Print queues
- Incorrect/incompatible printer drivers

Print Spoolers

The word *spool* represents Simultaneous Peripheral Operations On-Line. *Spooling* refers to the process of loading documents into a buffer, which is usually an area on a hard drive, until the printer is ready. This allows users to place multiple print jobs into a queue and print them in the background instead of waiting for each print job to be completed. The print spooler is the printer-managing function, and its support components are integrated into a single print-processing architecture.

Setup

The print spooler is installed in Windows when the printing services and the printer are installed. The print spooler sends print data to the printer when the data is ready. The settings can be changed through the My Computer icon on the Desktop or by choosing **Start**, **Settings**, **Printers**, as shown in Figure 14-41.

Figure 14-41 Printer Settings

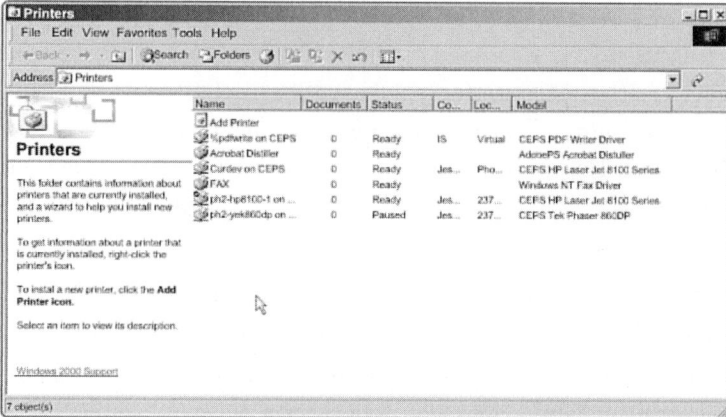

Printer Queues

Even the most advanced network printers can process only one print job at a time. When a print job is sent to a printer while it is busy, that print job is held in the printer queue, as shown in Figure 14-42.

Figure 14-42 Printer Queue

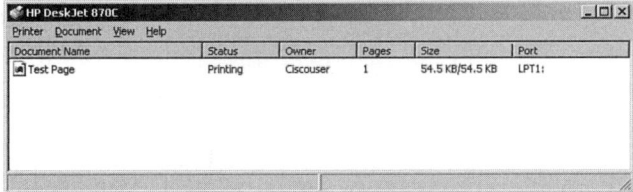

A *printer queue* is a temporary holding area for print jobs. The printer queue sends the next job to the printer when the printer becomes available. The queue is an area of memory that is set aside on the print server for managing print jobs. When a user prints a document, it is sent to the printer queue. If no other jobs are in the queue, the print job is processed immediately. Printer queues, by default, use the first in, first out (FIFO) rule. The print job that reaches the queue first receives the highest priority and is output before other jobs.

Setup

The printer queue is automatically set up and configured when the printer is installed. The printer queue can be configured in the Properties menu of the printer. The size of the queue can be specified. Printing priorities can also be set so that user files with higher priority are printed before other files.

Clearing Print Jobs

The printer queue is also a management tool that can be used to view and manipulate print jobs. The queue shows information about each print job and the progress of the job as it is being fed to the printer. This information includes user identification, the job start time, and the current status of the print job. The following print-job manipulation tasks can be performed in the printer queue:

- **Deleting print jobs**—The printer queue can be used to delete specific print jobs or delete all the jobs that are currently held in the queue. This is useful if an error occurs or if multiple copies of a document are accidentally sent to the printer.
- **Rearranging print jobs**—Even though the printer queue uses FIFO by default, the processing order of print jobs can be changed. Higher-priority print jobs can be moved to the top of the queue while lower-priority jobs can be moved to the bottom of the list.

■ **Pause the printer**—Pausing the printing process puts the queue in a wait state. During this time, changes such as deletions or rearrangements can be made within the printer queue. Changes can also be made to the printer, such as changing the media type, ink, or toner. The printer queue can then resume processing the print jobs.

Redirecting

Print documents can be redirected to a different printer. For example, if a printer is connected to a faulty device, the documents can be redirected to prevent users from having to resubmit the documents. All print jobs for a printer can be redirected collectively, but individual documents cannot be redirected. The new printer must use the same printer driver as the current printer.

To redirect documents to a different printer, choose **Start**, **Settings**, **Printers**. Right-click a printer icon, and choose **Properties** from the menu that appears. Click the **Details** tab, and click the **Add Port** button. In the Add Port dialog box, select the **Other** radio button and choose **Local Port**. In the Port Name dialog box, type the name of the printer to redirect the documents to, for example, \\PRNTSRV9\HPLASER4XL, and then click the **OK** button.

TIP

Understand the most common printers problems, and know how to fix them.

Incorrect/Incompatible Printer Drivers

The printer driver is important for a printer to work correctly. Drivers are necessary for the operating system to communicate with the system hardware. If the proper drivers are not installed, the system cannot print. Error messages will probably appear, stating that the incorrect driver has been installed and that the operating system is unable to find the printer.

Incorrect Printer Drivers

Drivers are usually included with a printer. However, they are not always the correct printer drivers for the operating system being used. Most manufacturers maintain a website that contains downloadable printer drivers.

Sometimes the correct printer drivers are installed and the printer still does not work. This usually means that the printer hardware is not compatible with the system hardware or operating system.

Incorrect Printer Software Parameter Settings/Switches

Some printers and printer drivers have numerous software and parameter settings or switches. After installing the drivers, the specific settings or switches might need to be configured before the printer can work properly. For example, you could have a nonstandard paper size in the printer. The current settings might not recognize the paper size, and the printer settings must be changed for the printer to operate.

Windows-Specific Networking Software Connection Troubleshooting

Many Windows-specific connection issues are due to improper configuration. Making sure that the client can communicate with the server, along with diagnosing error messages, is an important function for the IT technician. This section includes the following topics:

- Error messages
- Incorrect parameter settings/switches
- Incorrect protocols or protocol properties
- Incorrect client or client properties
- Missing or incorrect bindings
- Incorrect service selection
- Incorrect primary network logon settings
- Incorrect computer name or workgroup name
- Network troubleshooting software utilities

Error Messages

This chapter has discussed troubleshooting the various error messages that display because of operating system issues, application issues, and driver issues. Technicians also need to troubleshoot software issues that are related to networking.

Error Message: Cannot Log On to Network—NIC Not Functioning

One error message that is typically related to networking issues is "Cannot log on to network—NIC not functioning." This message can appear for several reasons. For example, the network interface card (NIC) might need to be replaced. This can be done by opening the system case and replacing the old NIC with a new one. First, check the NIC on the back of the system and verify whether the NIC LED light is on. A green light usually means that the card is good and does not need to be replaced. Ping the card with its local loopback address, which is 127.0.0.1, or use the **PING LOCALHOST** command, as shown in Figure 14-43. This command sends a packet out and back to the NIC to see whether it is functioning properly. If a message appears stating that the packet was not received, the NIC is defective and must be replaced. If the **PING** command receives a response, the NIC is working properly.

Figure 14-43 Testing NIC Functionality

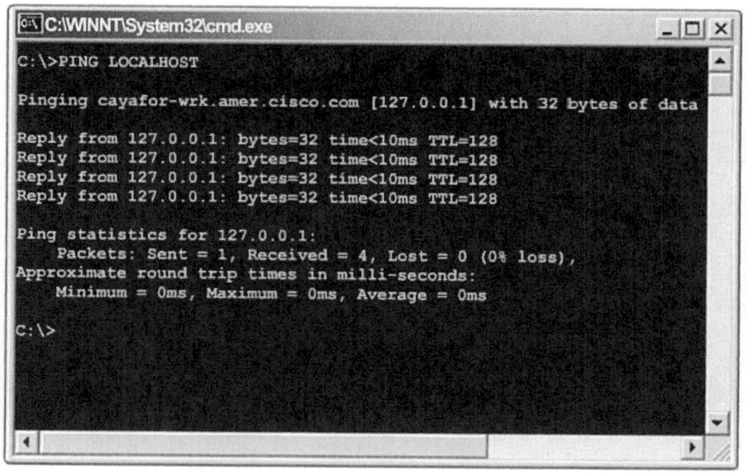

```
C:\WINNT\System32\cmd.exe                                    _ □ ×

C:\>PING LOCALHOST

Pinging cayafor-wrk.amer.cisco.com [127.0.0.1] with 32 bytes of data

Reply from 127.0.0.1: bytes=32 time<10ms TTL=128
Reply from 127.0.0.1: bytes=32 time<10ms TTL=128
Reply from 127.0.0.1: bytes=32 time<10ms TTL=128
Reply from 127.0.0.1: bytes=32 time<10ms TTL=128

Ping statistics for 127.0.0.1:
    Packets: Sent = 1, Received = 4, Lost = 0 (0% loss),
Approximate round trip times in milli-seconds:
    Minimum = 0ms, Maximum = 0ms, Average = 0ms

C:\>
```

NIC Driver Software Issues

The NIC driver software issues can include incorrect versions of the driver, corrupt drivers, or incompatible drivers. If a driver is an incorrect version, contact the manufacturer to obtain the correct one. The correct driver can usually be downloaded from the manufacturer's website. Figure 14-44 shows the HP download site, with the drivers that are available. If the driver is corrupted, a version that is not corrupted can be obtained from the website. If other conflicts with the operating system produce an error, the driver might work if the cause of the conflict is fixed. If an incompatible driver error message appears, check to see which version of the driver is installed and update the driver to match the version that is required by the operating system, as shown in Figure 14-45.

TIP

Know how to trouble-shoot a NIC.

Incorrect Parameter Settings/Switches

Incorrect parameter settings and switches can also apply to the NIC drivers. Some NICs and NIC drivers have many software and parameter settings or switches. The NIC might not be functioning even if the correct driver has been installed. The software settings or switches might need to be configured before the NIC can work properly. Figure 14-46 shows the advanced settings for a NIC.

Figure 14-44 HP Driver Download Site

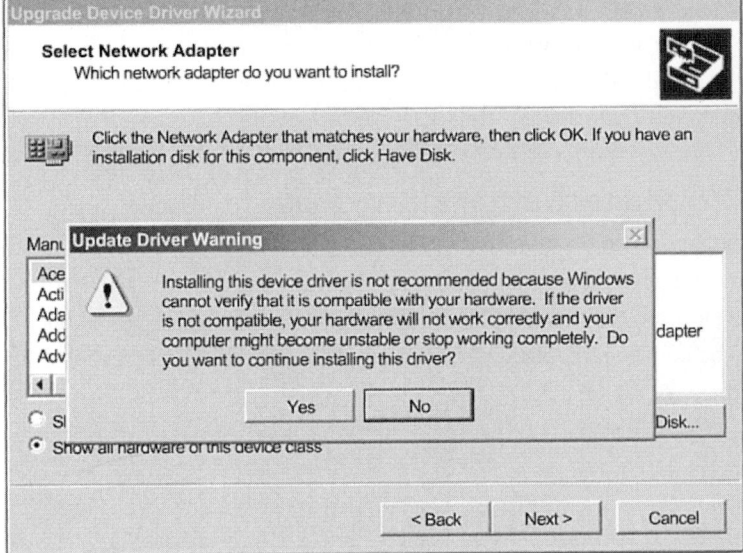

Figure 14-45 Incorrect Drivers

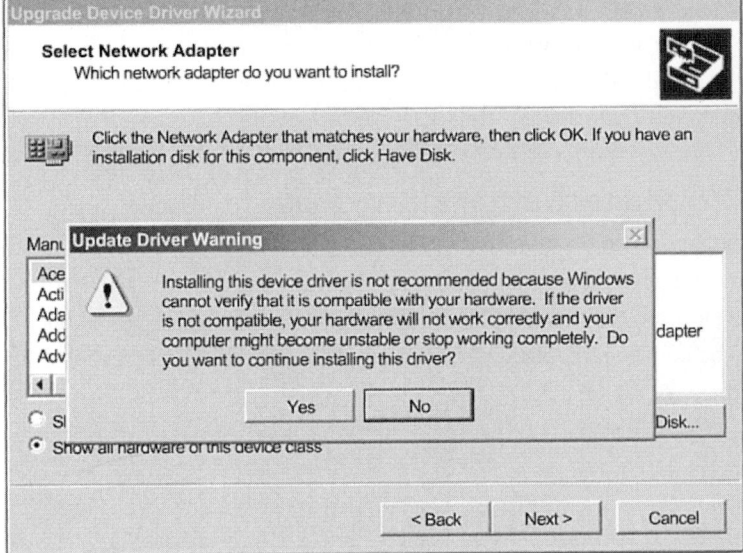

Figure 14-46 Advanced NIC Settings

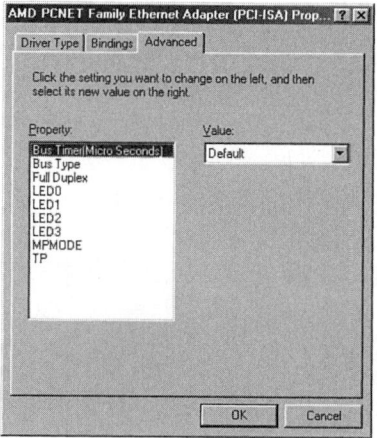

Incorrect Protocols or Protocol Properties

Before a system can successfully log on to the network, the protocols must be set correctly. If they are not, the user cannot see any of the computers on the network or access any of the network resources. After determining whether the network is using TCP/IP, IPX/SPX, or another protocol, access the Network Properties screen, as shown in Figure 14-47. Check the protocol properties to see whether they are set properly. For example, the correct protocol might be installed but the IP address settings might be incorrect. Both items must be correct to access the network.

Figure 14-47 Network Properties

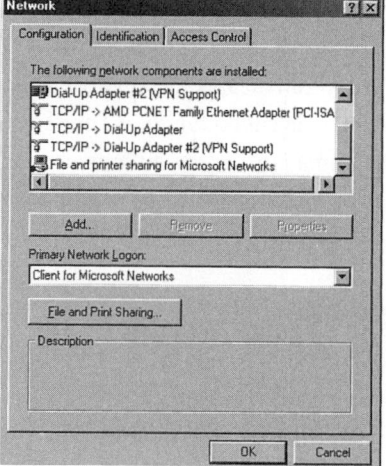

Incorrect Client or Client Properties

The proper client and client properties must also be installed. For example, if Novell NetWare is running and the system needs to connect to resources on the Novell servers, the client for Novell NetWare must be installed on the Windows operating system. If the proper clients are not installed, users cannot access the resources on the servers. Figure 14-48 shows the Microsoft Client Settings screen.

Figure 14-48 Client Properties

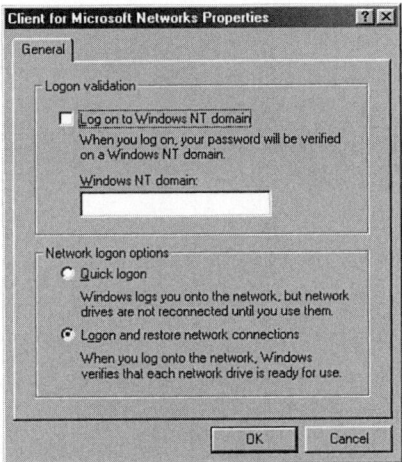

Missing or Incorrect Bindings

Technicians must understand how network bindings affect networked computers. For example, network bindings must be manipulated to run two different protocols on two different network adapters in a server. Changing the order of bindings can optimize network performance.

Transport protocols are assigned to run on specific network adapters. Creating this association between protocols and adapters is called *binding*. The most frequently used protocol is usually listed first in the binding on a NIC. If the bindings are missing or incorrect, the NIC cannot function and the user cannot access the network. Figure 14-49 shows the Bindings tab of the NIC properties screen.

Incorrect Service Selection

Network services provide added features to clients on the network. For example, File and Print Sharing is a popular service on nearly every network. If this feature is not installed, files or printers cannot be shared over the network. Figure 14-50 shows the screen that enables file and print sharing.

Figure 14-49 Bindings Tab

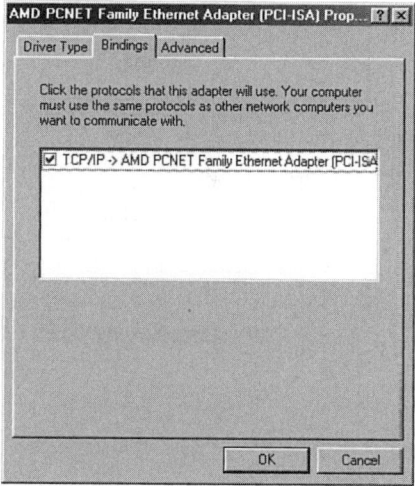

Figure 14-50 File and Print Sharing Services

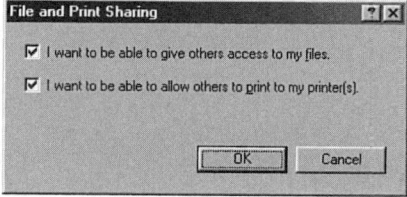

Incorrect Primary Network Logon Settings

Network access begins with the logon feature, as shown in Figure 14-51. If a user cannot log on, he or she cannot access the Desktop or any of the network resources. If this happens, log on with the administrator account and make sure that the account settings are correct. Check the password setting, and make sure that it has not expired or been locked out.

Incorrect Computer Name or Workgroup Name

Figure 14-52 shows the Identification tab in the Network window. If the computer name or workgroup name is incorrect, the system cannot access the network. This can result in the following error messages:

- User cannot see any other computers on the local network.
- User cannot see any other computers on different networks.
- Clients cannot see the DHCP server, but do have an IP address.

Figure 14-51 Primary Network Logon

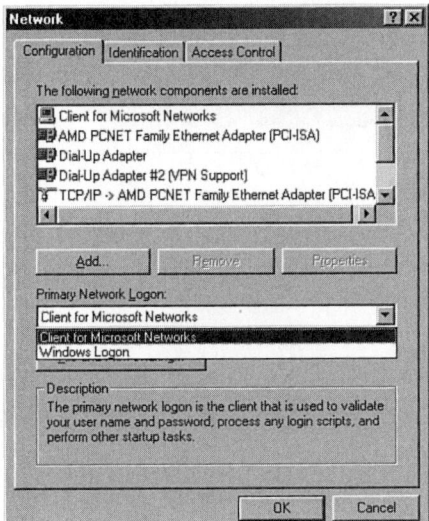

Figure 14-52 Computer Identification on the Network

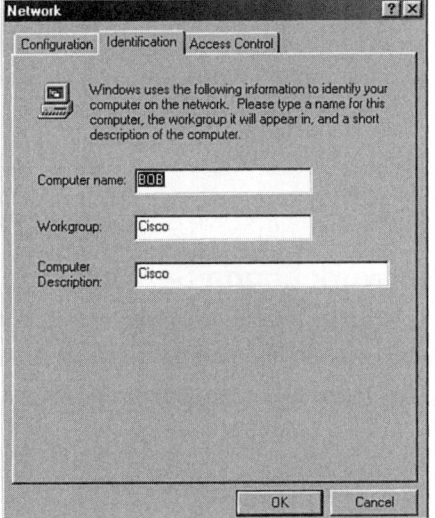

When a computer is added to a network domain, an account is created that allows the computer to access resources in that domain. The computer name is registered, and if the name changes, the domain controller does not recognize the computer and access is denied. The same rule applies to the workgroup name. If a computer has an incorrect workgroup name, network access is denied. Administrators can change the computer name and then re-create an account in the domain for the new name if they forget the name of the computer.

Network Troubleshooting Software Utilities

Windows provides some useful network troubleshooting tools to help determine why a user is unable to access a network. These tools allow technicians to test connections, check settings, and trace the route of packets on a network to identify the problem.

PING.EXE

The *Packet Internet Groper (PING)* determines whether a specific IP address is accessible. It works by sending a packet to the specified address and waiting for a reply. PING is used primarily to troubleshoot Internet and network connections. Figure 14-53 shows the PING command.

Figure 14-53 PING Command (PING.EXE)

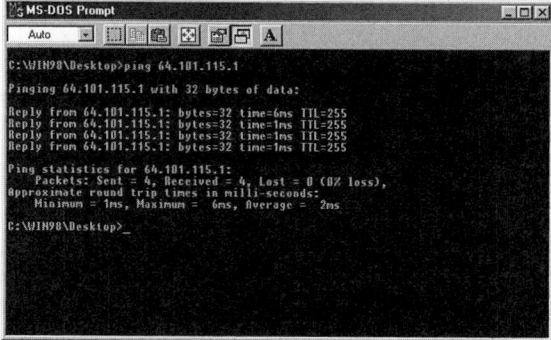

TRACERT.EXE

The *TRACERT.EXE* utility traces a packet from the computer to an Internet host. It shows how many hops the packet requires to reach the host and how long each hop takes. If website pages are appearing slowly, use TRACERT.EXE to identify where the longest delays are occurring. Figure 14-54 shows the TRACERT command.

The TRACERT.EXE utility sends packets with Time-to-Live (TTL) fields. The TTL value specifies how many hops the packet is allowed before it is returned. When a packet cannot reach its destination because the TTL value is too low, the last host returns the packet and identifies itself. By sending a series of packets and increasing the TTL value with each successive packet, TRACERT.EXE identifies all the intermediary hosts.

Figure 14-54 TRACERT Command (TRACERT.EXE)

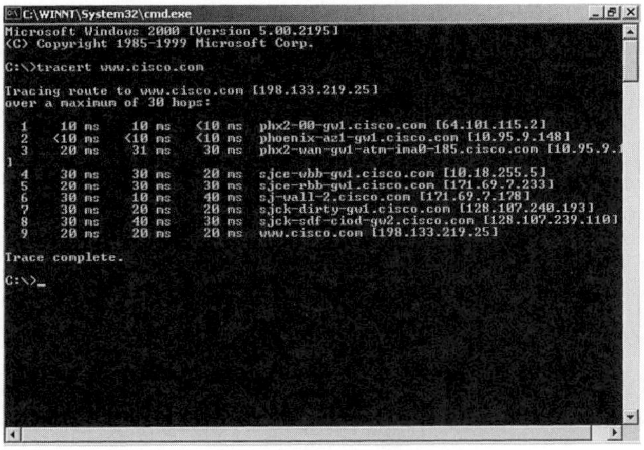

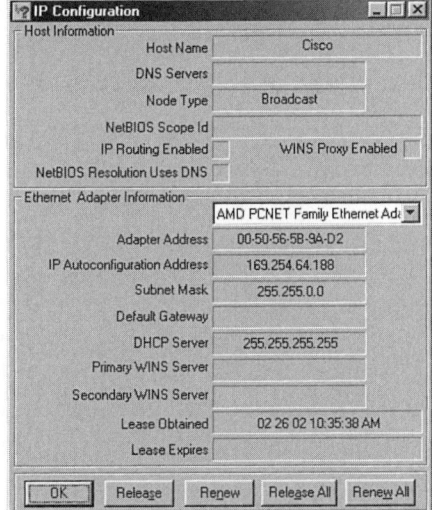

WINIPCFG.EXE

Windows IP Configuration, or the *WINIPCFG.EXE* utility, allows technicians to view the basic IP networking settings of a Windows 95, 98, or Me computer.

IP addresses, which allow computers to interact with the Internet, are allocated and assigned by the Dynamic Host Configuration Protocol (DHCP). When the system boots up, it sends a request to the DHCP server for an IP address. The DHCP server finds an available IP address and assigns it to the computer. Figure 14-55 shows the IP configuration from the WINIPCFG utility.

Figure 14-55 WINIPCFG Utility (WINIPCFG.EXE)

The WINIPCFG utility allows technicians to receive new IP information, such as addresses, masks, or gateways, without rebooting. The IP information can be released by clicking the Release button. Clicking the Renew button assigns a new IP address to the computer from the DHCP server. Obtaining new information can help with IP-related problems.

To use WINIPCFG, choose **Start**, **Run** and type **WINIPCFG** in the command window. Then click the **OK** button. This command can also be run from a DOS prompt.

IPCONFIG.EXE

The *IPCONFIG.EXE* utility is the Windows NT and 2000 equivalent of the WINIPCFG.EXE utility. The IPCONFIG utility allows users to view the IP address information, the WINS server addresses, the DNS server addresses, and the DHCP server addresses. New IP addresses can be obtained by using the /RELEASE or /RENEW switches. Unlike the **WINIPCFG** command, the **IPCONFIG** command must be run from the DOS prompt. It cannot be typed in the command window by choosing **Start**, **Run**. Figure 14-56 shows the **IPCONFIG** command being run from the DOS prompt.

Figure 14-56 IPCONFIG Utility (IPCONFIG.EXE)

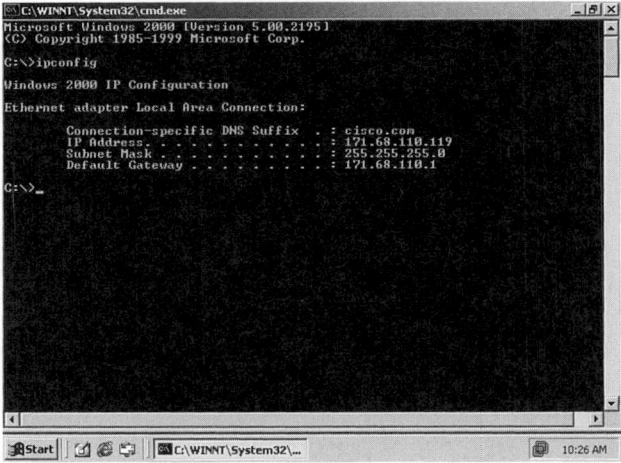

NET VIEW Command

The *NET VIEW* command displays a list of domains, a list of computers, and a list of resources for a computer. The **NET VIEW** command is a command-line interface that performs most of the browsing functions that are available in Network Neighborhood or My Computer. However, users cannot view a list of workgroups.

The syntax for the **NET VIEW** command is as follows:

NET VIEW [*computername* | /DOMAIN[:*domainname*]]

If the **NET VIEW** command is entered with no parameters, it displays a list of computers in the domain. The *computername* parameter should identify the computer with the resources that are to be displayed. The *domainname* parameter should identify the domain whose computer names are to be viewed. Using the /DOMAIN switch displays all domain names on the network. Type these commands from the DOS prompt.

NETSTAT

The Network Statistics, or *NETSTAT.EXE* utility, displays the current TCP/IP network connection and protocol information for the computer. The **NETSTAT** command displays the contents of various network-related data structures. Many different output formats are available, depending on the information that is being presented. For example, this command can display a list of active sockets for each protocol that is being used. It can present the contents of other network data structures according to the option selected. The NETSTAT utility can also display information about packet traffic on the configured network interfaces. Figure 14-57 shows the **NETSTAT** command being run from the command prompt.

Figure 14-57 NETSTAT Command (NETSTAT.EXE)

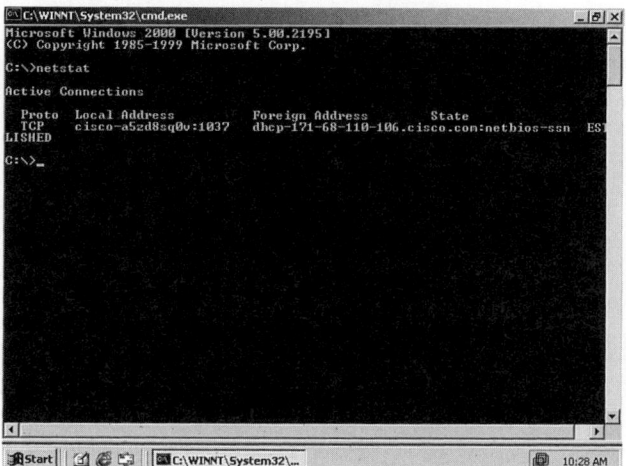

Figure 14-58 illustrates how the TRACEROUTE command works with multiple hops, providing more detailed information about the connection. Compare this to the illustration of a typical **PING** command that determines basic connectivity between two PCs, as shown in Figure 14-59.

Figure 14-58 TRACEROUTE Operation

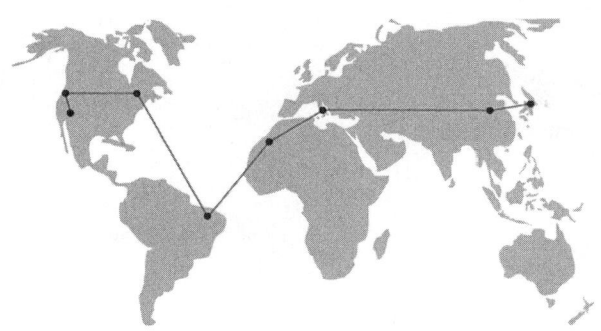

Figure 14-59 PING Operation

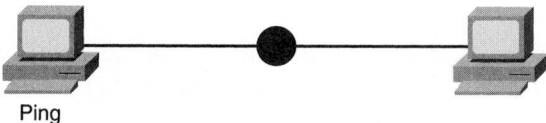

Ping

Windows 9*x*, NT, 2000, and XP Help

The Help files that are provided with the Windows operating system are a valuable tool. They not only provide information on specific topics but also list resources for additional information. This section includes the following topics:

- Help and troubleshooting files
- Troubleshooting and information resources

Help and Troubleshooting Files

The Windows 9*x*, NT, 2000, and XP operating systems all include a built-in help center, with numerous troubleshooting files for basic system troubleshooting tasks. The Windows 9*x*, 2000, and XP Help files are more comprehensive than the Windows NT Help files. The Help files utility can be accessed from the Start menu or from the Help icon on the standard toolbar.

Windows 98 and more recent Windows operating systems have increased the Help file database, added troubleshooting tools, and incorporated a web browser to access online help. The online access provides many helpful resources from Microsoft and other sources. Figure 14-60 shows the Windows Help screen.

Figure 14-60 Windows Help Screen

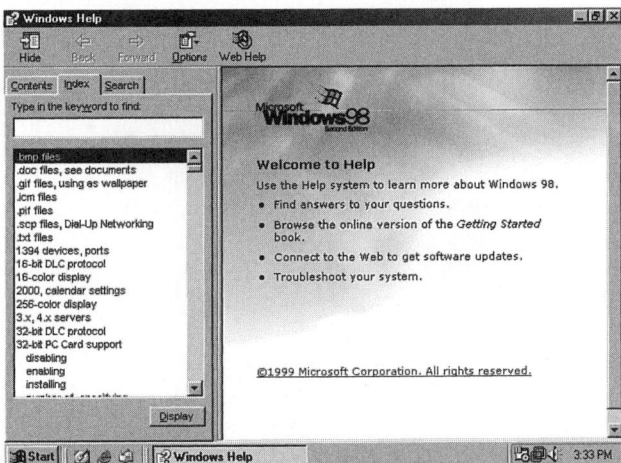

Window XP includes a new Help feature called the Help and Support Center, which is shown in Figure 14-61. The Help and Support Center home page includes links to basic tools and utilities such as Disk Defragmenter, System Configuration Utility, Network Diagnostics, and Windows Update. All of these utilities can be run from the Help and Support Center window. Additional links provide up-to-date system information about current configurations and installed services, software, and hardware. Other links include the Microsoft Knowledge Base and a variety of Windows-specific newsgroups. Remote Assistance allows experienced users to connect directly to a computer that is experiencing problems and make configuration changes or repairs.

Troubleshooting and Information Resources

If answers are not found in the Help and Troubleshooting Files database, other resources are available, such as the Windows 9x, NT, and 2000 resource kits and various websites.

Windows 9x/NT/2000 Resource Kits

The Windows 9x, NT, and 2000 resource kits contain solutions for almost every troubleshooting issue. Figure 14-62 shows a Windows 2000 Professional Resource Kit. These resource kits provide CDs and textbooks with thousands of pages of in-depth technical information and reference materials. The kits also include many features and troubleshooting tools that can be installed on a computer system. For example, they provide hundreds of utilities for troubleshooting and maintaining a network. These resource kits are not included with the operating system installation CD.

Figure 14-61 Windows XP Help and Support Center

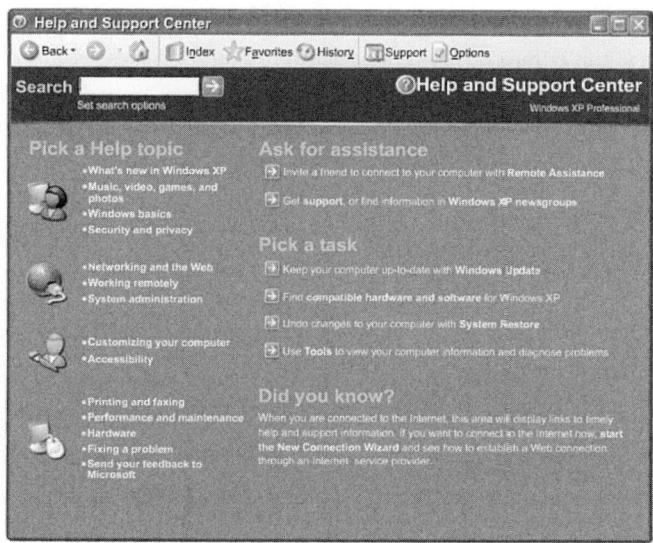

Figure 14-62 Windows 2000 Professional Resource Kit

Internet Help

Another good source of help and troubleshooting aids is the Internet. Many websites provide useful information about common Windows operating system issues. For example, the Microsoft website has a huge database of troubleshooting pages called the *Microsoft Tech-Net*. Other websites for troubleshooting operating system issues can be found by using the Search feature built in to Windows.

Summary

This chapter discussed troubleshooting software. Some of the important concepts to retain from this chapter include the following:

- The steps to take to identify an error are defining whether the issue is hardware or software related, questioning the user, reproducing the error, and identifying changes to the system.

- When dealing with system boot problems, an important tool to use is the bootable disk. Booting with a floppy disk allows technicians to recopy files, inspect the hard drive partition, or reformat the hard drive. It also provides the ability to navigate through the files on the disk.

- The MBR resides on the first sector of the hard drive, and if it has been damaged, the computer will not boot. The **FDISK /MBR** command rewrites the MBR so that the system can boot.

- DOS error messages typically occur when the operating system identifies a problem or when a user attempts to run an application that the operating system cannot recognize. Error messages include bad or missing commands, configuration file errors, and memory errors.

- A startup disk is created to start the computer when the operating system becomes corrupted. Shutdown problems are usually caused by an application that is still running in the background. Pressing Ctrl-Alt-Delete opens the Task Manager, which allows users to end an application that has stopped or to restart the computer.

- A GPF occurs when an operating system application attempts to access an unallocated memory location. Running applications that are not written for the Windows operating system, selecting the wrong machine or network during installation, or using incorrect versions of DOS in the system can cause a GPF.

- Safe mode is a troubleshooting tool in Windows. Safe mode involves the following actions:
  - The AUTOEXEC.BAT and CONFIG.SYS files are not loaded.
  - The registry is not loaded.
  - The load= and run= lines are not loaded in WIN.INI.
  - The [Boot] and [386Enh] sections are not loaded in SYSTEM.INI.

  Safe mode allows the technician to access the Device Manager and to run system utilities.

- The Registry Editor is accessed by typing **REGEDIT** or **REGEDT32** in the Run dialog box. Six registry files contain all the system configuration information. Understanding the registry subtree keys is helpful for troubleshooting and maintaining the computer. Registry-editing tools can be used to remove unused files from the registry. These files can cause problems and degrade system performance.

- One of the most important tasks to perform is a regular backup. The only way that data can be recovered is if it has been backed up. Normal or full backups store all files. Incremental backups save the files that have been created or modified since the last full backup. Differential backups are similar to incremental backups, except that the archive bit is not reset. Copy backups back up user-selected files but do not reset the archive bit.

- Device drivers are important for computer components such as NICs and printers. The most reliable place to find and download a current driver for a device is the manufacturer's website.

- Help is available in the Windows operating system and can be accessed from the Start menu. Additional information is also available on the Microsoft website.

Key Terms

AUTOEXEC.BAT   Contains a list of DOS commands that can automatically execute when DOS is loaded into the system.

BACKUP.EXE   Starts the backup process.

bootable disk   A troubleshooting tool that allows the computer to boot from a disk when the hard drive will not boot.

BOOTLOG.TXT   A file that contains the system information that is collected as the system is booting up.

CHKDSK.EXE   A command-line tool that recovers lost allocation units from the hard drive.

command interpreter   Also known as COMMAND.COM in Windows 95/98 and CMD.EXE in Windows NT/2000, it displays the DOS prompt and executes the commands that are typed at the prompt.

CONFIG.SYS   A file that contains setup or configuration instructions for the computer system.

copy backup   Backs up user-selected files to tape. This backup does not reset the archive bit to off.

daily backup   Backs up only the files that are modified on the day of the backup. This backup does not reset the archive bit to off.

DEFRAG.EXE   Rearranges the data and rewrites all the files on the hard drive to the beginning of the drive, making it easier and faster for the hard drive to retrieve data.

DETCRASH.LOG   File that is created if the system crashes during the hardware-detection phase of the startup process.

DETLOG.TXT   Used to read the information that is generated when the DETCRASH.LOG file is created.

DEVICEHIGH =   Command that loads drivers into the upper memory area instead of loading them into conventional memory.

differential backup   Backs up all the files that have been created or modified since the last full backup. It does not reset the archive bit.

Dr. Watson utility   Isolates and corrects GPFs.

dynamic link library (.DLL) file   Stores subroutines for a program.

EDIT.COM   A Windows troubleshooting tool that can view and edit configuration files such as AUTOEXEC.BAT and CONFIG.SYS as well as .INI files.

EMM386.EXE   Memory-management program that provides the system with access to the upper memory area of RAM.

Event Viewer   Monitors system events, application events, and security events in Windows 9*x*.

FDISK   Deletes and creates partitions on the hard drive.

FDISK /MBR   Command that creates or rewrites the MBR so that the system can boot up.

FIXBOOT   Command that writes a new boot sector onto the system partition.

FIXMBR   Command that is used with the Recovery Console to fix hard drive problems.

FORMAT.EXE   Erases a hard drive and prepares the disk for data.

full backup   Also called a *normal backup*, it backs up all files on a disk.

general protection fault (GPF)   An error that occurs when one of the operating system applications attempts to access an unallocated memory location.

Group Policy Editor (GPE)   Edits the configuration settings in a network environment.

hardware failures   A malfunction of a computer component that can prevent the OS from loading.

hidden file   A file that users typically cannot see.

HIMEM.SYS   Memory-management program that manages the extended memory above 1024 KB.

HKEY_CLASSES_ROOT   Subtree that contains software configuration data for all the software that is installed on the computer.

HKEY_CURRENT_CONFIG   Subtree that contains data on the active hardware profile that is selected during the boot process. This information is used to configure settings for the device drivers to load and for the display resolution to use.

HKEY_CURRENT_USER   Subtree that contains data about the user who is currently logged on to the computer. This subtree retrieves a copy of each user account that is used to log on to the computer and stores it in the registry.

HKEY_LOCAL_MACHINE   Subtree that contains all configuration data for the local computer, including hardware and operating system data such as bus type, system memory, device drivers, and startup control data. Applications, device drivers, and the operating system use this data to set the computer configuration. The data in this subtree remains constant, regardless of the user.

HKEY_USERS   Subtree that contains the system default settings data that controls individual user profiles and environments such as Desktop settings, windows environment, and custom software settings.

illegal operation   Error message in Windows that indicates that the system has encountered a problem.

incremental backup   Backs up all the files that have been created or modified since the last full backup and resets the archive bit.

IPCONFIG.EXE   Utility that is the Windows NT/2000 equivalent of the **WINIPCFG.EXE** command in Windows 95, 98, and Me. It performs the same functions as the **WINIPCFG.EXE** command in that it allows users to view all the IP address information as well as the WINS server addresses, DNS server addresses, and the DHCP server addresses.

LASTDRIVE =   Command that is contained in the CONFIG.SYS file. It specifies the maximum number of drives that the system can access.

Master Boot Record (MBR)   The program that is responsible for starting the boot process. It determines which partition is used for booting the system and transfers control to the boot sector of that partition, which continues the boot process.

Microsoft TechNet   A Microsoft website that has a huge database of troubleshooting pages.

MSCONFIG.EXE   A command-line tool that interactively loads device drivers and software options.

NET VIEW   Command that displays a list of domains, a list of computers, and a list of resources for a computer.

NETSTAT.EXE   Utility that displays the current TCP/IP network connections and protocol information for the computer.

normal backup   Also called a *full backup*. All files on the disk are stored to tape or other backup media, and the archive bit for all files is set to off, or cleared.

Packet Internet Groper (PING)   Utility that determines whether a specific IP address is accessible.

POLEDIT.EXE   Sets up different security restrictions for different users.

printer queue   A temporary holding area for print jobs that are fed to the printer when it is ready for the next job.

Recovery Console   A command-line interface that performs a variety of troubleshooting and recovery tasks in Windows 2000 and XP.

SCANDSKW.EXE   Also known as ScanDisk for Windows, this utility checks the integrity of the media to repair problems that occur.

SCANREG.EXE   Scans the registry for corruption.

SETUPLOG.TXT   File that is created during the installation process and contains the system setup information.

spooling   The process of loading documents into a buffer (usually an area on a hard drive) until the printer is ready for the documents.

SYSEDIT.EXE   Modifies text files such as the .INI files as well as the CONFIG.SYS and AUTOEXEC.BAT files.

SYSTEM.DA0   Like the USER.DA0 file, the SYSTEM.DA0 file is created when Windows successfully boots. This file is a backup of the SYSTEM.DAT file. If the SYSTEM.DAT file gets corrupted or is deleted, rename the SYSTEM.DA0 file SYSTEM.DAT to restore the registry.

SYSTEM.DAT   A file that holds hardware, computer-specific profile, and setting information.

SYSTEM.INI   A file that contains hardware-setting information for the drivers that Windows uses for configuration. When the operating system needs to reference information about the hardware, it uses the SYSTEM.INI file.

System File Checker (SFC)   A command-line utility that scans the operating system files to ensure that they are the correct ones.

Task Manager   Displays active applications and identifies those applications that are not responding so that they can be shut down.

TRACERT.EXE   A utility that traces a packet from the computer to an Internet host.

USER.DA0   Created when Windows successfully boots up. This file is a backup of the USER.DAT file. If the USER.DAT file gets corrupted or is deleted, rename the USER.DA0 file USER.DAT to restore the registry.

USER.DAT   File that contains all the information that is specific to the user.

.VxD file   A virtual device driver that takes the place of the *DEVICE=* and *LOADHIGH=* commands.

WIN.COM   A registry file that controls the initial environment checks and loads Windows 95 core components during bootup.

WIN.INI   A file that contains parameters that can be altered to change the Windows environment or software settings to suit the user's preferences. The WIN.INI file is a software initialization file for Windows. It contains information about some Windows defaults, the placement of windows, the color settings for the screen, and available ports, printers, fonts, and software applications.

WINIPCFG.EXE   Also known as Windows IP Configuration, it is a tool that allows the technician to view the basic IP networking settings of a Windows 95, Windows 98, or Windows Me computer.

WIN switch   Allows the technician to start Windows from the command line.

Check Your Understanding

The following are review questions for the A+ exam. Answers are found in Appendix B.

1. What are the three things that make a successful technician?

    A. Communication, local employees, smart dresser

    B. Communication skills, technical skills, troubleshooting skills

    C. Sense of humor, large inventory of parts, resource kits

    D. Location, location, location

2. Hardware-related issues are either configuration errors or which of the following?

    A. Communication failures

    B. Peripheral errors

    C. Software failures

    D. Hardware failures

3. To isolate the computer's problem during the troubleshooting process, you would do all *except* which of the following tasks?

    A. Reproduce the problem.

    B. Classify the problem.

    C. Reconfirm the problem.

    D. Remove all the internal components before doing anything else.

4. What is the MS-DOS–based automated memory optimizer called?

    A. MEM

    B. MEMMAKER

    C. REM

    D. MSD

5. Which key is pressed to skip the AUTOEXEC.BAT and CONFIG.SYS files when the message "Starting MS-DOS" displays?

    A. F5

    B. F6

    C. F7

    D. F8

6. Which of the following can recover files from damaged disks?

    A. RECOVER and FDISK

    B. RECOVER and UNFORMAT

    C. SCANDISK and UNFORMAT

    D. SCANDISK and UNFORMAT

    E. SCANDISK and CHKDSK

7. If you have ScanDisk, you do not need to run which of the following?

    A. FORMAT

    B. CHKDSK

    C. FDISK

    D. Volume

8. Which utility can be used to increase access speed by rearranging files and directories on the hard drive?

    A. SORT

    B. SCANDISK

    C. DEFRAG

    D. FORMAT

9. An "Insufficient memory to run this application" error displays. What should you do?

   A. Install a hard drive with more free space.

   B. Increase the size of your swap file.

   C. Buy more ROM chips.

   D. Buy a new computer.

10. Which of the following software problems can corrupt files?

    A. Faulty hard drive

    B. Downloading problems

    C. Getting bad writes during a copy

    D. All of the above

11. What is the most common symptom of a corrupted file?

    A. Overheating

    B. Inconsistent lockups

    C. Consistent lockups

    D. Unable to start computer

12. You choose **Start**, **Run**. What command allows you to access the registry from the command window?

    A. REGISTRY

    B. REGEDIT

    C. SYSEDIT

    D. SYSTEM

13. What is the first utility you should run if a computer locks up?

    A. REGISTRY

    B. SCANDISK

    C. FORMAT

    D. UNLOCK

14. Why does a GPF occur?

    A. The hard disk cannot store any more data.

    B. An application is using too many system resources.

    C. An application is trying to write to a memory space that is occupied by another application.

    D. A memory module in the computer is defective.

15. What causes a page fault in Windows 98?

    A. Device drivers that are corrupt

    B. Applications that are poorly written

    C. Hard drives that are faulty

    D. All of the above

16. A NIC was working fine, but now it is causing connectivity problems. What do you do first?

    A. Just install a new NIC.

    B. Upgrade the NIC driver.

    C. Contact the vendor for any updates and patches.

    D. Check the LEDs on the back of the NIC.

17. Which two files do not load in safe mode?

    A. AUTOEXEC.BAT and CONFIG.SYS

    B. SYSTEM.INI and AUTOEXEC.BAT

    C. CONFIG.SYS and MEMMAKER

    D. AUTOEXEC.INI and MEMMAKER

18. The resource window for a device in the Device Manager *does not* display which of the following?

    A. IRQ

    B. I/O address

    C. Settings button

    D. Delete settings button

19. Which utility determines whether a specific IP address is accessible?

   A. TRACERT.EXE

   B. WINIPCFG.EXE

   C. PING.EXE

   D. NETSTAT.COM

20. Which utility traces a packet from the computer to an Internet host?

   A. TRACERT.EXE

   B. WINIPCFG.EXE

   C. PING.EXE

   D. NETSTAT.COM

The Information Technology Professional

The Cisco Networking Academy Program has driven great change in the information technology (IT) workforce in the last five years. To a significant extent, the Networking Academy Program enables students to enter the IT workforce with a good salary by pursuing a series of certifications within certain IT career tracks. IT careers can be classified as software, hardware, and nontechnical. There can be overlaps, but the categories in the matrix below are fairly representative—most IT jobs fit into one of these categories. Some careers are inherently hybrid, such as that of the network engineer and the network administrator.

What Is IT

IT touches almost every aspect of the modern-day work world. Computers are now used in almost every occupation imaginable. If IT is defined as any job that uses computers or electronic devices, this would mean that IT encompasses almost all jobs! A more accurate interpretation of IT includes only those jobs where the primary focus of the job is the computer itself, the computer software, or the electronic devices. A career in IT is one where the product of the work is an electronic device, a software program, or information. An IT career might also be a parallel effort, such as sales or marketing of the computer-related product.

For the purposes of this book, the term *information technology* means "that which concerns the advance of computer science and technology, and the design, development, installation, and implementation of information systems and applications."

Careers in IT and Setting Career Goals

The range of careers in IT is very broad. Something can be found for every personality in a wide salary range. Do you want to be a computer programmer? A system administrator? A hardware designer? A network engineer? A project manager? These are just a sample of the careers in the IT industry.

All IT careers have a technical component in common. But keep in mind that companies employing IT workers also offer a wide range of jobs that are not directly technical in nature, for example, sales and marketing professionals, accountants, financial analysts, attorneys, managers, and executives.

IT professionals usually have a strong technical ability, but this doesn't necessarily imply a college or university education. Various career tracks, such as MCSE and CCNA/CCNP/ CCIE certifications, are options that you can pursue as a means of entering the IT industry. However, it is often helpful to have a college degree when entering this field, especially in software development, engineering, and management positions.

Some IT job titles can be misleading. For example, a person can become a network engineer or system engineer for some companies without having a college degree if he or she has the appropriate certifications and experience. Other types of engineering careers, such as computer, electrical, mechanical, and civil engineering, require bachelor's, master's, or doctor's degrees. Knowing your personal strengths and interests makes it easier to plan a career in the IT world. It's easiest to enter the IT industry as a young person with a college education or a set of appropriate certifications, but many people have successfully entered the field later in life. Those who choose to make the transition from careers unrelated to IT often take specialized training in colleges or technical schools. If you're still in school, prepare for a career in the IT industry by focusing on math and the sciences as much as possible. The analytical thinking that is required in math and science is exactly the type of thinking that is required for the troubleshooting and problem-solving that are common in IT jobs.

Communication skills are also very important in the IT world, just as they are in most professions. These skills include one-on-one communication, interviewing skills, and public speaking. They are learned by practice and in courses in English and communications.

Career Paths in IT

The job market in the IT sector continues to grow rapidly (see *www.itprc.com/jobs.htm*). The U.S. government's projections show that the fastest-growing occupations in the IT sector are as follows (see *http://stats.bls.gov/news.release/ecopro.t06.htm*):

- Computer software engineers, applications
- Computer support specialists

- Computer software engineers, systems software
- Network and computer systems administrators
- Network systems and data communications analysts
- Desktop publishers
- Database administrators
- Computer systems analysts

The following list, taken from the University of Washington's IT career page, is a sample of careers in information technology (see *www.washington.edu/students/it/careers.htm*):

- Computer engineer
- Computer programmer
- Computer scientist
- Computer user
- Database administrator
- Database specialist
- Interface designer
- Network specialist
- Software engineer
- Statistician
- Systems analyst
- Technical communicator
- Web designer

Nontechnical IT careers include accounting, sales, marketing, law, and project management; however, the focus in this book is on technically oriented IT careers.

The most popular software jobs include networking, Internet/intranet and e-commerce development, network security, and database administration.

The sections that follow provide brief descriptions of some key IT careers in software.

Programmers

Computer programmers write computer code that makes the computer perform various functions. This requires much attention to detail and a strong technical aptitude. Programmers write software according to the specifications determined by systems analysts.

Systems Analysts and Software Engineers

Systems analysts produce specifications for adapting existing systems or creating new ones. The design process is generally lengthy and complex. Note that a system analyst can be involved with overseeing the development of hardware devices, if this is part of the overall system.

Technical Writers

Technical writers produce a variety of technical publications, including instructional materials, technical manuals, product documentation, and so on. They might produce materials to assist end users with hardware devices and software applications, such as online help, user's manuals, installation manuals, guided tours, and tutorials.

Multimedia Developers

Multimedia developers have the skills of the computer programmer and the artist. They produce multimedia documents that can contain graphics, text, and digital audio and video with interactivity.

Multimedia development is a rapidly changing field. New advances in hardware and software continue to improve the functionality of multimedia development tools.

Multimedia is still in its infancy. The people who are making multimedia work are taking newly created tools and inventing the ways in which the tools are used.

Those who work as multimedia developers probably started in other careers. They could have been graphic designers, software engineers, writers, publishers, or educators, or might have worked in one of the many other fields that contribute to what we think of as multimedia.

Interface Designers

Human–computer interaction is a relatively new field of research in computer science that addresses ergonomic and interaction issues in computing. Interface designers use human factor analysis, graphic design theory, and other methodologies to design the user interface of a computer system. The user interface—the communication system between the user and the computer—determines how a user is led through a program or process, providing a likely path or paths for the user to navigate. The interface also provides a conceptual structure for organizing large amounts of information. Furthermore, the user interface offers tools for filtering information and then retrieving it at a later point, according to a predetermined set of criteria.

Web Developers

Web developers design, produce, build, and support websites and e-commerce sites. Web development isn't a single function but rather a series of functions. Some functions overlap, for example, programming and database administration. Other functions, such as web design and content management, generally don't overlap, but those responsible for either function need to work closely together.

Because of the variety of skills brought to bear on building and maintaining a website, web development is a difficult job to define. The functions performed by a web developer vary widely. They include website design, database administration, software programming, content management, e-marketing, information architecture, and production management.

Web developers are charged with designing, building, programming, populating with content, marketing, supporting, and managing a website. Developers manage server migrations, download times, and site crashes, in a virtual space driven by databases where user experience (measured in page views, site traffic, time spent surfing, and conversion to membership or paying customer) is the key to a website's success.

Database Developers

Database developers follow a product development cycle that is similar to that of software engineers. In general the development cycle of a database is as follows:

1. **Gather user requirements**—At the beginning of the cycle, a database developer interviews the people who will be using the database to find out what kinds of queries and reports the users need.

2. **Design the database**—A web designer or graphics designer might work with the database developer to create a storyboard, that is, a series of pictures showing how users will access the computer database and what kinds of answers they expect from a query. This storyboard is shown to users for feedback.

3. **Build the database**—The database developer builds the database, and a data entry person puts all the information into the database.

4. **Gather feedback**—Once the database is ready to use, the database developer requests feedback on how it works.

5. **Modify the database**—Depending on the feedback received, the database developer can make modifications to the database.

6. **Maintain the database**—Eventually, when the database is in production, a database administrator takes over. This person is responsible for making sure that the database runs smoothly, is backed up regularly, and is kept up to date.

Related IT Careers

The software careers described typically require a college education, with the possible exception of multimedia and web development. Courses or degrees in math or computer science are recommended for these careers.

Many IT careers are related to electrical and computer engineering. Computer engineers and electrical engineers design, build, test, and evaluate new computer chips, circuit boards, computer systems, and peripheral devices. The goal of computer engineering is to produce computing devices that run reliably, efficiently, and economically.

Different kinds of engineers handle different aspects of the production process. Development engineers often work in research and development departments of computer firms, and conceive of new product ideas. Design engineers work with development engineers to design the product. Production engineers supervise the production process (and associated staff) in manufacturing the product once it has been designed. Quality assurance engineers control the production process, making sure that the product is manufactured properly and that no flaws occur in production.

Device development engineers develop electronic components, such as transistors, integrated circuits, Application-Specific Integrated Circuits (ASIC), etc. Most circuits are built on silicon chips, making the circuitry microscopic. Chip designers, integrated circuit designers, and logic designers are all involved in circuit design. Computer hardware is designed by combining circuitry so that the various functions of the component circuits work together to perform larger functions. Much of computer engineering takes place on the level of microprocessors and other specialized boards (for example, graphics, audio, and networking boards) that add functionality to a computer. The first task of a design engineer is to determine the precise function of the planned device. Having established the project specifications, the engineer (or more likely, the team of engineers and other personnel) designs the components, assembles them, tests the new device, and evaluates the design for its overall effectiveness, cost, reliability, and safety. This process applies regardless of the end product.

Engineers often use computer-aided design (CAD) software to produce and analyze designs. CAD software is powerful design software that automates the drafting and design process for mechanical and electronic applications. With CAD software, engineers can create three-dimensional models of objects that can then be manipulated by computer. This allows the engineer to experiment with different designs that would be too costly to produce as prototypes.

Computer and electrical engineers design computers of all descriptions, but they also design industrial robots, industrial automated systems, and artificial intelligence–based hardware systems. These engineering jobs require bachelor's degrees or graduate (master's or doctor's) degrees.

With the rapid change in technology, job titles come and go. Some careers in the IT industry don't lend themselves to categorization. Many of these jobs are hybrid jobs; they are not only difficult to classify, but they also have no prescribed mechanism for entry into the field. Many of these careers do not require a college education and can be entered through the training and certification process. However, a college education is always an advantage in getting a job and usually commands a higher salary.

One hybrid career is that of the network engineer. A network engineer is responsible, either as a consultant or as a corporate employee, for troubleshooting and maintaining computer networks. This involves configuring networking equipment such as routers and switches. A network engineer or system engineer can also play a critical role in the design process of a computer network for a company that is upgrading or expanding its network. Most of the work of a network engineer is software based, but the software is integrated into various types of network hardware with which the network engineer must also be familiar.

Whereas a network administrator usually works at a single location with the responsibility for a single network or internetwork, the network engineer has wider responsibilities and can work across several sites with more than one company.

Another hybrid career is that of system administrator. A system administrator is responsible for maintaining a multiuser computer system, including a local-area network (LAN). Typical duties are as follows:

- Adding and configuring new workstations
- Setting up user accounts
- Installing system-wide software
- Performing procedures to prevent the spread of viruses
- Allocating mass storage space

The system administrator is sometimes called the *sys **admin***. Small organizations might have just one sys admin, while larger enterprises usually have a team of system administrators. The sys admin might work on several operating systems or platforms, such as Windows 2000 Server and Solaris.

Another category of IT careers involves the support of products that have already been released. Desktop support, technical support, and help desk positions are closely related and sometimes interchangeable. When an end user has problems, it is the job of the technical support personnel to help that person. Technical support and help desk positions are often a "foot in the door" to an IT company, and they can lead to more challenging, higher-paying positions.

Software testing, another key IT job, is critical for the success of a software program. In this area, software bugs are discovered and eliminated before the product is released to the end user. Many careers are available in software testing.

Working as a technical assistant to an engineer or project manager is an excellent means of entry into the IT industry. This type of position often leads to better opportunities, so it is wise to take such a position when entering the IT field.

A technical trainer is highly valued, because someone has to teach all these IT experts and keep them up to date with the latest technologies! Becoming a trainer in the IT field usually involves some college education, a set of required certifications, and verification of one's teaching ability.

This list of IT careers is far from complete, but the major categories have been covered. You should have a good idea of the types of jobs that are available, and perhaps have enough information to decide which IT career is best for you.

In many cases, there is a strong association between careers and personality types. (See *www.haleonline.com/psych/* or *www.ibiblio.org/pub/academic/psychology/ alt.psychology.personality/profiles/*.) Understanding your personality type can help you choose a career, but don't take this too seriously—there's always room for change.

Try to avoid locking yourself into a particular career just because you think that's what you're supposed to do. It helps to remain open to the idea of changing careers as you move through your work life. Changing careers has become common. The U.S. Department of Labor (DOL) has determined that workers will have 8 to 10 jobs on average prior to their retirement. The DOL also notes that job changing declines with age and work experience. (See "Report on the American Workforce" at *http://stats.bls.gov/opub/rtaw/rtawhome.htm*.)

Degree Programs in IT

Traditionally, colleges or universities were the only avenues to a professional career. For some careers, such as medicine, law, or academia, this is still true. However, the IT explosion over the last few decades has changed many traditions. For example, it is now fairly common for colleges and universities to accept work experience for college credit.

It is now possible for an individual to become an IT professional and command a relatively high salary without having a formal postsecondary education. (Remember that a college education always improves your opportunities in the IT world and in other careers.)

If you pursue a career in engineering (for example, as an electrical or computer engineer), you must complete a four-year degree in the appropriate field. To become a software developer, programmer, or systems analyst, you are almost always required to have at least a four-year degree in computer science or information systems. To become an IT project manager, you often need a four-year degree in business administration. However, project managers come from a broad range of backgrounds, so the degree requirements are somewhat flexible.

Just as it improves your opportunities in general to get a college degree, the more advanced your degree, the better your chances of getting a job in the field of your choice with the salary range you desire. Unfortunately, nothing is certain. However, you improve your chances of doing what you want to do and getting paid what you want to earn by obtaining an advanced degree.

Many two-year college programs are available for entry into the IT workforce. Community colleges and junior colleges have IT programs that are designed solely to teach you to work in the IT world. These schools often have placement services to help you find a job after graduation. These colleges also have internships with local companies that are part of earning your degree. These internships can open the door to a new career.

Certification Tracks in IT

Certification programs, such as MCSE and CCNA/CCNP/CCIE, have driven the greatest change in the IT workforce in the last 20 years. To a significant extent, these certification options have replaced college education and have forced colleges to rethink the way they deliver education.

It is now possible to enter the IT workforce with a good salary by pursuing a series of certifications. Companies such as Cisco Systems, Microsoft, Novell, and Sun Microsystems create these certifications. These corporations create training programs and exams that map to specific courses. The exams test the mastery of subject matter related to specific software or hardware.

The courses associated with the certifications are not inexpensive, and the high cost is often a hurdle to obtaining the required training. Many corporate and government programs subsidize a portion of the cost of these courses, so it's important to do some research to see what options are available to you. It might cost you US$ 10,000 to US$ 15,000 to receive the required training and practice for the MCSE 2000 certification. For the prestigious CCIE certification, it is common for an individual to invest US$ 20,000 to US$ 40,000 over several years.

Programs such as the Cisco Networking Academy Program, begun in 1997, are integrated into high school, two-year college, and four-year college programs. These are relatively new options for students that allow exposure to the same material and training as in the costly certification programs, but for a much lower financial investment. However, you must be enrolled in one of these educational institutions to receive the training; this often means going to college. With the notable exception of the CCIE, all the major certifications can be obtained strictly by reading books, memorizing facts, and practicing exam questions found on the Internet. However, if you don't perform hands-on labs to internalize the concepts laid out in the certification books, you aren't particularly useful to a company. Employers are aware that these certifications can be obtained without mastery of the hands-on skills required to work in industry. However, employers are interested in your ability to create software, configure servers, or configure networking hardware for their enterprise, not in the paper certifications that you might have.

The hundreds of hours of hands-on practice that are needed to reinforce a theoretical knowledge base are difficult to complete and might require some investment in equipment. Most veterans of the IT industry say that it is a worthwhile investment. There is no sure path to success in the IT world. You must have the desire to pursue an IT career. It's important to enjoy what you're doing; if not, you're probably pursuing the wrong career goal. A successful pursuit of your goals requires much hard work. But if you enjoy what you're doing, the hard work can add to the enjoyment and sense of satisfaction.

Summary

This appendix described the various careers that are available in information technology and the educational paths that lead to these careers. You need to have fairly strong technical skills to succeed in the world of information technology. This means taking math and science courses to build these skills. If information technology courses are available at the school you are attending, take advantage by enrolling in these courses. Courses in system administration, computer programming, database administration, electronics, and operating systems can all aid your success in IT.

The world of IT is diverse, and there's no end to the opportunities. If you choose to pursue a career in IT, you've chosen a field that has a great range of possibilities and potential for growth. The most common ingredient to success in IT is the desire to learn more and keep current about the latest information in the field. If you don't like change, this is not the field for you, because your IT career is guaranteed to involve constant change.

Information Technology Industry's Certifications Outline

I. 3Com

    1. 3Com Certified Solutions Associate—Designed to provide networking professionals with introductory technology, product, and solutions knowledge. Primarily aimed at employees working in nontechnical capacities such as sales, marketing, and management who require fundamental knowledge of network technologies, product options, and recommended business solutions.

2. 3Com Certified Solutions Expert—Designed for systems engineers and other technical professionals with a need to identify customers' needs and to recommend, design, and install 3Com solutions. Developed for IT/MIS staff with focus on determining customer needs, designing and installing custom solutions, and maintaining client systems after installations.

3. Focused specializations such as network telephony can be obtained to recognize expertise above and beyond Solutions Expert.

II. Adobe

1. ACE: Adobe Certified Expert—For graphic designers, web designers, developers, and business professionals who wish to be recognized experts using Adobe products. Adobe product proficiency exam must be passed for a specific Adobe software product to be shown as a highly skilled, expert-level user.

III. Adaptec

1. ACSP: Adaptec Certified Storage Professional—Program for IT professionals and resellers teaching complex storage technologies and the implementation and support for storage solutions based on these technologies. Provides a training platform to allow IT professionals to build technical expertise using basic to advanced storage solutions. ACSP for RAID provides in-depth knowledge of Adaptec RAID products, server technologies, implementation, and troubleshooting techniques for increased array performance.

IV. Allaire

1. Certified ColdFusion Developer—Designed for any IT professional that desires recognition of expert-level knowledge of CFML, with exceptional handling skills, and the ability to manage user sessions. Scoring 80 percent or better on the exam gains Advanced ColdFusion Developer status. This entitles a person to use logos and letterheads, as well as to have a listing in the Macromedia directory.

2. Certified Website Developer—Proof to employers and potential clients of expertise in web page design and authoring skills. This certification represents a thorough understanding of web page design, web page authoring, and supporting technologies at a professional level.

V. Check Point

1. CCSA: Check Point Certified Security Administrator—This is the foundation-level certification for individuals who wish to manage basic installations of Check Point's VPN-1/FireWall-1. The designation indicates the ability to

install, configure, and use the VPN-1 and FireWall-1, apply NAT (Network Address Translation) rules in firewall configurations, and authenticate users in the environment.

2. CCSE: Check Point Certified Security Expert—Demonstrates in-depth knowledge for establishing, managing, and implementing complex installations of VPN-1/FireWall-1. This advanced certification also teaches content security, encryption schemes, remote access using a VPN, server load balancing, modifying attack detection parameters, and setting up tracking within VPN-1/FireWall-1.

3. CCAE: Check Point Certified Addressing Engineer—Focused certification for managing Check Point's Meta IP. Program teaches security specialists how to configure policy-based network management for user-centric networks, installing Meta IP or upgrading to Meta IP, configuring Meta IP, and structuring automated IP address allocation as well as load balancing and troubleshooting.

4. CCQE: Check Point Certified Quality of Service Engineer—Provides the skills and knowledge required to implement and manage Check Point's FloodGate-1. This certification proves knowledge of installation and navigation of FloodGate-1, integration of FloodGate-1 with VPN-1/FireWall-1, creation and configuration of standard and bandwidth policies, use of network objects, services, and resources managers.

VI. Cisco Systems

A. *Network Installation and Support*

1. CCNA: Cisco Certified Network Associate—Certification in the fundamentals of networking for the small office/home office market. Provides the knowledge to install, configure, operate LAN, WAN, and dialup services for small networks of 100 nodes or fewer using numerous protocols.

2. CCNA WAN Switching—CCNA concentrating on the apprentice knowledge of WAN switched networks and the installation of WAN switches: IPX, IGX, BPX, AXIS, Shelf, and modems.

3. CCNP: Cisco Certified Network Professional—Provides advanced knowledge concerning the installation, configuration, operation of LAN and WAN, and dial access services for organizations with networks with 100 to more than 500 nodes using many different protocols.

4. CCNP WAN Switching—Advanced certification indicating journeyman knowledge of WAN switched networks. Provides the knowledge to configure, operate, troubleshoot, and manage WAN switched networks.

5. CCIE Routing and Switching: Cisco Certified Internetwork Expert—Certification for the high-level network professional concentrating on IP and IP routing, non-IP desktop protocols such as IPX, and bridge and switch related technologies.

B. *Network Engineering and Design*

   1. CCDA: Cisco Certified Design Associate—Fundamental certification indicating apprentice knowledge of network design for the small office/home office market. Shows ability to design routed and switched networks involving LAN, WAN, and dial access services for organizations with 100 or fewer nodes.

   2. CCDP: Cisco Certified Design Professional—Indicates advanced knowledge of designing routed and switched networks involving LAN, WAN, and dial access services for organizations with 100 to over 500 nodes.

   3. CCDP WAN Switching—Advanced certification concentrating on designing and implementing an ATM network (with CBR, ABR, and VBR traffic) and a Frame Relay network (with CIR and MIR traffic parameters); troubleshooting a WAN switched network; and managing traffic and voice technologies.

C. *Communications and Services*

   1. CCIP: Cisco Certified Internetwork Professional—Shows competency in infrastructure or access solutions in a Cisco end-to-end environment. Indicates detailed understanding of diverse telecommunications technologies including IP routing, IP multicast, cable, DSL, content networking, or IP telephony.

   2. CCIE Communications and Services: Cisco Certified Internetwork Expert—Shows mastery of IP and IP routing, optical, DSL, dial, cable, wireless, WAN switching, content networking, and voice.

D. *Cisco Qualified Specialist*

   1. Cable—Provides the knowledge and skills required to support and deploy Cisco cable two-way data services including proficiency in DOCSIS, DVB, RF, and Cisco IOS.

   2. Security—Designation focusing on the design, installation, and support of Cisco security solutions in the network security market.

   3. Internet Solutions—Targets individuals involved in e-business solutions, and designing and delivering the underlying network architectures. Emphasizes the skills and knowledge in the areas of applications, tools, operating systems, and networks pertaining to systems planning to bring together Cisco services with Internet business solutions.

   4. SNA/IP Design or Support Specialist—Designation to show knowledge and proficiency in the design, installation, and support of Cisco SNA/IP integration solutions.

VII.   Citrix

1. CCA: Citrix Certified Administrator—For system administrators and resellers who wish to show a thorough knowledge of Citrix products for Windows and UNIX.

2. CCEA: Citrix Certified Enterprise Administrator—An advanced technical certification building on the CCA program. This certification shows expanded knowledge of Citrix products and provides more extensive education of the installation and administration of Citrix Management Services, Load Balancing Services, Program Neighborhood, and NFuse.

3. CCSP: Citrix Certified Sales Professional—A continued certification designed for individuals who wish to expand their customer base by acquiring advanced knowledge of Citrix technology, products, services and know how to sell and market them.

4. CCI: Citrix Certified Instructor—Demonstrates exceptional knowledge of the MetaFrame and WinFrame product lines and their underlying operating systems. Ensures the highest level of instruction on Citrix products.

VIII.   Cognos, Inc.

1. CCPP—Cognos Certified Professional Program.

2. BI Author—Foundation knowledge and skills concerning understanding of client tools from the user and administrator perspective.

3. BI Administrator—Addresses advanced techniques and troubleshooting skills.

4. BI Architect—Focusing on data modeling, data mart creation, and metadata delivery.

5. BI Engagement Manager—Ensures the ability to define and promote successful enterprise BI application deployment.

IX.   Compaq

1. APS: Accredited Platform Specialist—Certifies warranty-level support skills and remedial maintenance for warranty-trained technicians. Predominantly hardware focused, the certification provides knowledge of diagnostic tools, troubleshooting methodologies, FRU call out and replacement, hardware and driver configuration, installation, and upgrade.

2. API: Accredited Platform Integrator—Designed to provide certification of basic networking, system integration and support skills for Compaq customers, resellers, and service support staff. Accreditation focuses on system architecture, product specification, implementation, optimization, and hardware-OS management and administration.

3. ASE: Accredited Systems Engineer—Certifies advanced networking, systems integration and support skills for systems engineering specialists and advanced integration of hardware and operating system. Courseware includes advanced systems architecture, challenging implementations, and advanced troubleshooting.

4. Master ASE: Master Accredited Systems Engineer—Building on the ASE certification, the Master ASE demonstrates design and integration of solutions based upon customer business needs. Courseware includes advanced management, solutions planning, and system, network and application architectures.

X. CompTIA

1. A+ Service Technician Certification—Covering a broad range of hardware and software technologies, the certification acknowledges competency of entry-level (6 months experience) computer service technicians. CompTIA A+ program is backed by major computer hardware and software vendors and defines basic computer technical and safety standards.

2. CDIA: Certified Document Imaging Architect—Acknowledges competency and professionalism in the document imaging industry. The CDIA shows critical knowledge of planning, designing, and specifying all major areas of an imaging system.

3. EBiz+—Shows the knowledge surrounding basic concepts, key issues, and critical technologies of e-business. This certification is designed for anyone working in an e-business environment.

4. INet+—Targets IT professionals who wish to demonstrate a baseline of technical knowledge in a variety of Internet-related careers. Covering Internet basics, Internet development, networking, security, Internet, intranet, and extranet technologies. This certification helps managers determine a prospective employee's knowledge and skill level.

5. IT Project+—An industry-recognized certification that shows competency and professionalism in IT project management. Courseware includes basic business knowledge, interpersonal skills, and project management processes needed to manage IT projects.

6. Linux+—Credential measuring Linux knowledge and skills. This certification is a fundamental building block for any individual interested in an entry-level job using Linux such as help desk, sales/marketing, or application developers.

7. Network+—Shows knowledge of networking professionals with 18–24 months of experience in the IT industry. Courseware covers a wide range of networking technologies to prepare candidates for a variety of networking roles.

8. Server+—Shows competency dealing with advanced PC hardware issues such as RAID, SCSI, multiple-CPU PCs, and SANs, to name a few.

9. CTT+: Certified Technical Trainer—A cross-industry credential certifying an instructor who has achieved a standard of excellence in the technical training industry. Although this certification is endorsed by the computer industry, it can be applied to any industry that provides technical training and education.

XI. Computer Associates

A. *CACP—Computer Associates Certified Professional Program*

1. Project Engineer Certification—For individuals who have successfully demonstrated the effective utilization of Project Engineer for planning and monitoring projects. Signifies a deep understanding of Project Engineer's functionality and ability to assist others with the utilization of Project Engineer.

2. Process Continuum/Process Engineer Specialist—Demonstrates skills to manage the Process Continuum libraries and development of custom processes to fulfill the business mission of an organization.

3. ERwin Logical Modeling Specialist—Teaches a solid understanding of logical data modeling in ERwin, ability to explain data modeling theory for IDEF1x and IE methodologies, and development of logical data models using ERwin.

4. ERwin Physical Modeling Specialist—Demonstrates understanding of physical model creation from a script file, ability to modify the resulting physical model to implement additional requirements, and understanding the implementation of ERwin for model-based maintenance of the DBMS.

5. BPwin Business Modeling Specialist—Certification demonstrating ability to successfully collect information necessary for construction business models and translating them into valid diagrams, linking BPwin business models with ERwin data models, and understanding and developing business process models using BPwin.

6. CACP Network Specialist—Qualifies an individual to safeguard service levels by monitoring network performance and utilization, increase productivity by maximizing response times, solve problems with virtual LANs, troubleshoot problems with network devices, and plan effectively for the future of the network.

7. CACP Help Desk Specialist—Provides the ability to respond more quickly by integrating the help desk with Unicenter TNG event monitoring, reduce user downtime by reusing proven solutions, and improve users' access to solutions by creating self-service help environments.

8. CACP Storage Specialist—Teaches the skills to optimize backup performance by diagnosing system components to isolate bottlenecks, streamline administrative by automating a series of tasks, restoring a single file or multiple files or server, protecting data on local and remote servers from one central location, and preparing an airtight strategy for critical data recovery.

9. CACP Desktop Specialist—Qualifies an IT professional to be able to reduce total cost of ownership for desktop environments by automating software delivery, streamline day-to-day operations by monitoring and troubleshooting desktop hardware and software configurations, control software cost by metering usage, and improve productivity by delivering software according to predefined policies.

10. CACP Security Specialist—Provides the knowledge to verify security measures by centrally auditing data integrity, design and implement an architecture to utilize and optimize Unicenter TNG security, streamline administration by establishing one security architecture for multiple platforms, and control access to data by user, user group, and asset group.

11. CUE: Certified Unicenter Engineer—The standard for enterprise management software; CUE certification is a multifaceted education program providing training for engineers deploying CA's Unicenter TNG enterprise management solution. CUEs demonstrate in-depth knowledge of Unicenter TNG architecture and enterprise management tools, and can effectively plan and execute the deployment of Unicenter TNG.

12. CUA: Certified Unicenter Administrator—This certifies technical professionals with the ability to monitor the performance of a company's IT resources, maintain policies for Unicenter TNG throughout the network, leverage Unicenter TNG's security features to enhance existing operating system security, and analyze problems within the enterprise and resolve them with Agent technology utilities.

XII. Corel Corporation

1. Corel Certified Proficient User—Indicates a proficiency in the use of CorelDRAW9, Corel PHOTO-PAINT9, WordPerfect8 and 9, QuattroPro9, and Corel Presentations9. This certification covers the basic features and functions of the applications.

2. Corel Certified Expert User—Building on the Proficient User certification, the Expert User designation indicates an expert understanding in the use of CorelDRAW9 and WordPerfect8 and 9. This certification covers the more advanced capabilities of the software.

3. CCI: Corel Certified Instructor—Qualified instructors must be able to teach users whose skills range from beginner to expert and be able to perform all tasks associated with the proficient and expert level exams. Instructors have expert-level competency with each of Corel's applications.

XIII. DRI—Disaster Recovery Institute International

1. ABCP: Associate Business Continuity Planner—Supports entry-level proficiency in business continuity planning and provides the basis for moving up to a CBCP.

2. CBCP: Certified Business Continuity Professional—For IT professionals skilled in the business continuity/disaster recovery industry. Designed for individuals with two or more years experience in the field.

3. MBCP: Master Business Continuity Professional—The highest certification designed for individuals with at least five years in the business continuity/ disaster recovery industry. MBCPs must have significant demonstrated knowledge of business continuity/disaster recovery.

XIV. ETA—Electronics Technicians Association

1. CET: Certified Electronics Technician—Denotes proficiency in electronics for individuals who excel in areas of electronics equipment, service, and support. The CET consists of a four-level program from associate to journeyman to senior, and on to master level. The different levels depend on test scores and work experience and/or training in the electronics industry.

2. CSS: Customer Service Specialist—Certification specializing in the knowledge of customer and fellow worker basic human relations concepts. A CSS must have great knowledge in several human relations areas and must have at least a minimal knowledge of their company's products or services in order to express themselves.

3. FOIC: Fiber Optics Installer Certification—Provides assurance that an individual has the knowledge of the basic concepts of fiber optics safety, installation, and service.

4. CNST: Certified Network Systems Technician—Credential of knowledge of computer basic concepts which are applicable to all the various specialty areas of the computer industry. Two levels of CNST can be achieved: Journeyman CNST and Senior CNST.

5. CST: Computer Service Technician—Certifies knowledge of computer electronics basic concepts which are applicable to all the various specialty areas of the computer industry.

6. CWS: Certified Web Specialist—CWSs focus on the ability to solve problems related to the operation, maintenance, and upgrading of World Wide Web home pages. This certification is designed to provide customer service skills that allow working relationships with users that efficiently convey descriptions of difficulties, problems initiated by the user, or needs of the company.

7. CNCT: Certified Network Computer Technician—Certification focusing on computer operating systems' functions, structure, operation, hardware installation, configuration, and upgrading.

8. CECT: Certified Electronic Commerce Technician—Assures the ability of an individual to administer Windows NT Server, perform basic HTML and web design, perform basic web programming and JavaScript, plan and implement SQL and SQL server 7, provide connectivity with active server pages and databases, and implement basic Internet security and disaster planning.

XV. Help Desk Institute

1. HDA: Help Desk Analyst—Designed for entry-level help desk analysts with 9 to 18 months' experience. This certification shows possession of all the necessary skills to handle inbound service requests, problem-solving skills, understanding of incident and call-process flows, superior customer service, and professional problem escalation and notification procedures.

2. HDSE: Help Desk Support Engineer—Designed for experienced help desk and external support-center consultants showing an understanding of technologies, processes, and key factors that optimize help desk performance.

3. HDM: Help Desk Manager—Certification for experienced help desk managers responsible for day-to-day operations of the help desk. Courseware includes management of service levels with customers and secondary-support personnel, conducting team-building techniques, measurement of customer satisfaction, and determining appropriate use of technology.

XVI. Hewlett-Packard

A. *HP STAR*

1. CSE: Certified Systems Engineer—For anyone who can properly recommend, install, configure, and manage HP NetServers. This is a professional-level certification targeted primarily at systems engineers employed by HP authorized resellers.

2. CSC: Certified Systems Consultant—Focusing on the HP Solutions area of expertise with emphasis in either the NetServer Assured Availability or Microsoft Server Cluster Solutions. This certification builds on the CSE award.

XVII. IBM Corporation

A. *Certified e-Business Professional—Designed to increase and validate the IT professional's e-business proficiency.*

   1. Solution Advisor—Designed for sales representatives who demonstrate expertise in solution selling. This certification validates the ability to engage customers, develop
   e-business strategic visions, manage the customer relationship, and translate customer requirements into e-business opportunities.

   2. Solution Designer—Proves the ability to translate customer business requirements into an e-business solution. This certification teaches how to design a secure, scalable solution utilizing the IBM framework for e-business and best practices using existing customer environments.

   3. Solution Technologist—Focuses on a well-rounded perspective of e-business, and deep technical skills required to implement key IBM or qualifying e-business products. A great understanding of how to articulate e-business, issues, strategy, and methodologies is needed to receive this certification.

   4. Certified Specialist—A great number of Certified Specialist certifications can be obtained for each of IBM's products including application development, DB2 Universal Database, the IBM @.server series of computers, networking software, retail store solutions, storage and storage management, among others.

B. *Certified Developer*

   1. MQSeries—Certifies ability to design, code, and implement software using MQSeries.

   2. XML and related technologies—Designed for developers of applications that make use of XML, this certification demonstrates a broad knowledge of XML concepts and related technology, information modeling, XML processing, rendering, and query. This certification is part of the e-Business—Solution Technologist program.

C. *Certified Solution Developer*

   1. IBM VisualAge for Java—Certifies sound object-oriented analysis and design techniques based on UML, design, implementation, deployment of Java-based solutions including applications, applets, and servlets.

   2. IBM Websphere Application Server—Certifies knowledge of designing and building the components needed for an Internet/intranet site and the ability to provide technical assistance for IBM Websphere Application Server components.

3. Certified Enterprise Developer—Shows the ability to design, create, and maintain Java 2 Enterprise Edition components including Enterprise JavaBeans and JavaServer Pages, deployment and configuration of these components, and support for the clients that access them. This developer has the administration skills required to tune the application to meet performance needs.

4. Certified Solutions Expert—Indicates solution development needs for numerous IBM products including CICS web enablement, DB2 Universal Database, IBM WebSphere, MQSeries, and ViaVoice, among others.

5. Certified Systems Expert—Many IBM products offer the Systems Expert certification including application development with IBM WebSphere, IBM @.server series, networking software, and OS/2 Warp, among others.

6. Certified Advanced Technical Expert—Offered to IT professionals with expert level training with AIX and IBM @.server PSeries and DB2 Universal Database for Clusters, DRDA, and DB2 Data Replication.

XVIII. Information Systems Audit and Control Association

1. CISA: Certified Information Systems Auditor—Designed for the IS audit, control, and security professional. This certification assures an individual qualification in the skills surrounding IS audit, control, and security.

XIX. Inprise Corp (Formerly Borland)

1. Inprise Product Certification—Demonstrates knowledge of Borland products' advanced features. This certification indicates a thorough understanding of the use of these features to create, debug, and deploy software applications.

2. Inprise Trainer Certification—Designed to ensure consistent, high-quality teaching for customers. Individuals must demonstrate thorough product knowledge and excellent teaching skills.

XX. ISC2—International Information Systems Security Certification Consortium

1. CISSP: Certified Information Systems Security Professional—Designed for the security professional and demonstrates knowledge in access control, computer operations security, cryptography, application program security, risk management, communications security, computer architecture, systems security, physical security, policy and standards, and ethics.

XXI. IPG—International Programmers Guild

1. Certified Programmer—The IPG's Professional Certification Program has four components: technical proficiency, analytical skill development, conformity to the Code of Ethics, and final certification by the IPG's Master Programmer. Upon fulfillment of a minimum of mandatory standards, members receive their designation as Professional Programmer.

A. *ISCET—International Society of Certified Electronics Technicians*

1. CET: Certified Electronics Technician—Signifies the degree of theoretical knowledge and technical proficiency of practicing technicians. In the absence of governmental licensing, this certification program can help assure consumers that the person entrusted to service their electronic products possesses the knowledge, training, and experience necessary to do a good job.

XXII. IWA—International Webmasters Association

A. *CWP: Certified Web Professional*

1. CWP Site Designer—Implements and maintains websites using authoring and scripting languages, content creation and management tools, and digital media.

2. CWP Internetworking Specialist—Defines network architecture, identifies infrastructure components, and monitors and analyzes network performance. This individual also designs and manages TCP/IP networks.

3. CWP Enterprise Developer—Builds n-tier database and legacy connectivity solutions for web applications, using Java, Java application programming interfaces, Java Database Connectivity solutions, middleware tools, and distributed object models.

4. CWP e-Commerce Specialist—Understands the uses of secure electronic transactions, cryptography standards, certificate authorities, and electronic services. This certification shows expertise in the standards, technologies, and practices in electronic commerce.

5. CWP Security Specialist—Implements security policies, identifies security threats and develops countermeasures using firewalls and attack-recognition technologies. This individual is an expert in transaction and payment security solutions.

6. CWP Server Administrator—Manages and tunes e-Commerce infrastructure including web servers, FTP, news, and mail servers for midsize to large businesses. Server administrators configure, manage, and deploy e-Business solutions servers.

7. CWP Application Developer—Builds client and server-side web applications using rapid application development tools and component technologies to implement two-tier database connectivity solutions.

8. Master CWP—Offered to experts of Administrator, Designer, and Enterprise Developer, this certification demonstrates a much more in-depth knowledge of each designated certification and a mastery of the skill sets involved.

XXIII. Institute for Certification of Computing Professionals

A. *ACP: Associate Computing Professional—Designed for new entrants into the IT field and new graduates of college or degree programs. This certification validates an individual's knowledge of the general computing industry and specific programming skills. The testing also identifies strengths within a person's area of expertise.*

B. *CCP: Certified Computing Professional*

1. CDP: Certificate in Data Processing—Sought after by individuals requiring proof of mastery in the area of data processing.

2. CCP: Certified Computer Programmer—Designed for programmers who want to validate their programming skills.

3. CSP: Certified Systems Professional—This program was developed to show expertise in the areas of system development, systems programming, core IT skills, systems security, and business information systems.

XXIV. LPI—Linux Professional Institute

A. *LPIC: Linux Professional Institute Certified—There are three levels to this certification:*

1. Level 1—Shows the ability of an individual to work at the UNIX command line, perform easy maintenance tasks, and install and configure a workstation and connect it to a network.

2. Level 2—Moves beyond basic knowledge and proves ability to plan, implement, maintain, secure, and troubleshoot a small mixed network. The individual can also supervise assistants and advise management on automation and purchases.

3. Level 3—This is the master level of the LPIC. Candidates should be able to design and implement complex automation solutions, initiate projects and implement them, and act as a consultant to higher management.

XXV. Lotus

1. CLP: Certified Lotus Professional—Demonstrates expertise of a job function and represents a high level of technical knowledge of Lotus software. The CLP indicates a highly competent and experienced individual.

2. CLS: Certified Lotus Specialist—Recognizes a basic level of technical expertise with Lotus Software such as Domino, Notes, cc:Mail, and SmartSuite.

3. CLI: Certified Lotus Instructor—Directed toward technical training professionals whose expertise and experience demonstrate their ability to present Lotus's courseware in a professional and understandable format.

4. CLEI: Certified Lotus End-User Instructor—Much like the CLI, this certification is geared toward training professionals who have experience presenting Lotus's end-user courseware.

XXVI. Lucent

1. LCTE: Lucent Certified Technical Expert—Designed to show a high level of knowledge and skill in networking and Lucent Technologies products, this certification is for network administrators, consultants, engineers, and any other individual interested in showing advanced technical knowledge of Lucent Technologies products.

XXVII. Marconi

1. PNE: Marconi Public Network Engineer—Verifies basic technical competency skills on Marconi's Service Provider products including ASX/TNX switches, SE-420/440, and CellPath 90 voice/data Internet Access Devices. This certification shows the ability to install, configure, and maintain Marconi Service Provider Products.

2. ENE: Marconi Enterprise Network Engineer—For systems engineers, and technical operations personnel. This certification demonstrates basic competency skills on Marconi's Enterprise products such as ASX switches, ESX/NSX switches/routers, and other ES switches.

3. PIP: Marconi Product Installation Professional—Verifies the basic installation competency skills on Marconi's entire product line. Candidates should be able to install a suite of Marconi BBSR products to satisfy a given networking scenario.

XXVIII. Microsoft

A. *Technical Certifications*

1. MCP: Microsoft Certified Professional—Numerous MCP certifications are available for individuals who have the skills to successfully implement a Microsoft product or technology as part of a business solution in an organization.

2. MCP + Internet—A credential for professionals who install and configure server products, manage server resources, plan security, and troubleshoot problems. This certification is designed for network administrators and website server managers.

3. MCP + Site Building—For IT professionals who plan, build, maintain, and manage websites using Microsoft technologies and products. This credential is for individuals who manage sophisticated, interactive websites with database connectivity, multimedia, and searchable content.

4. MCSD: Microsoft Certified Solution Developer—The premier certification for individuals who design and develop business solutions with Microsoft technologies. MCSDs are able to develop desktop applications and multiuser, web-based, and transaction-based applications. These professionals analyze business requirements and maintain solutions.

5. MCSE: Microsoft Certified Systems Engineer—For professionals who analyze the business requirements and design and implement the infrastructure for business solutions based on the Windows 2000 platform and Microsoft server software. MCSEs are able to install, configure, and troubleshoot network systems.

6. MCSE + Internet—For individuals who enhance, deploy, and manage sophisticated intranet and Internet solutions with Microsoft operating systems and server software. These professionals are also able to analyze and manage websites.

7. MCDBA: Microsoft Certified Database Administrator—Shows an individual's ability to install, configure, implement, and administer Microsoft SQL Server databases, derive physical database designs, develop logical data models, and manage and maintain databases.

8. MCT: Microsoft Certified Trainer—The exclusive product educators for Microsoft's official curriculum. These professionals are instructionally qualified and technically certified by Microsoft to deliver Microsoft courseware to IT professionals and developers.

XXIX. Desktop Certifications

1. MOUS: Microsoft Office User Specialist—Demonstrates desktop skills with Microsoft Office products, both Microsoft business productivity applications and Microsoft Project applications. MOUSs must prove exceptional ability to utilize the advanced functionality of these applications.

2. MOUS Master Instructor Certificate—An award given to those instructors who verify their technical expertise at the MOUS Master level in either the Microsoft Office 97 applications or Microsoft Office 2000 applications.

3. MOUS Project 2000—Offered to demonstrate an individual's advanced knowledge and skills using Microsoft Project 2000 and Microsoft Project Central. MOUS certifications are not substitutes for methodological certifications; they are a measurement of an individual's ability to productively use these tools.

XXX. Motorola

1. Colleagues Certification—This program provides a benchmark of achievement for those who sell, design, and operate Vanguard networking equipment. Four certifications are offered reflecting expertise in each area respectively: Sales Specialist, Design Specialist, and Operations Specialist. The final certification, MCNE: Motorola Certified Networking Engineer, is awarded to those who have passed each of the three specialist exams.

XXXI. Nortel

1. NNCFC: Nortel Networks Certified Field Specialist—For entry- to mid-level individuals, this certification shows a basic level of technical proficiency to install, commission, and provision equipment at a customer site.

2. NNCSS: Nortel Networks Certified Support Specialist—Demonstrates a basic level of technical proficiency to maintain a live system such as problem identification, provisioning, upgrading, operations, administration, maintenance, and troubleshooting.

3. NNCAS: Nortel Networks Certified Account Specialist—Provides a basic level of technical proficiency to support Nortel Networks solutions including the ability to analyze customer business needs in the areas of products, solutions, interoperability, and value proposition. This certification is designed for the entry-level sales representative.

4. NNCDS: Nortel Networks Certified Design Specialist—Designed for the entry- to mid-level technical sales and systems engineers. This certification shows basic levels of proficiency to support Nortel Networks solutions. Skill sets necessary include network management, functionality, interoperability, architecture, and topology.

5. NNCSE: Nortel Networks Certified Support Expert—Available to the mid- to senior-level professional; an NNCSE must demonstrate expertise with problem identification, provisioning, upgrades, configuration, operations, administration, maintenance, and troubleshooting within Nortel networks.

6. NNCDE: Nortel Networks Certified Design Expert—An NNCDE must be able to optimize customer networks using Nortel Networks solutions. Targeted to the mid- to senior-level professional, this certification incorporates an increased level and range of network components to plan and optimize network management, functionality, interoperability, service, architecture, and topology.

7. NNCA: Nortel Networks Certified Architect—Shows the ability to analyze and resolve challenging internetworking environments. NNCAs must be able to illustrate and document significant dimensions of their professional accomplishments.

XXXII. Novell

1. CNA: Certified Novell Administrator—CNA certification gives an individual the ability to support software users in various work environments by specializing in one or more of the various Novell applications. CNAs are able to set up user workstations, manage users and resources on a network, execute network applications and shares, set up printing, and handle routine software maintenance.

2. CNE: Certified Novell Engineer—The CNE specializes in one or more of Novell's applications to support customers who have various technologies and networks. CNEs are able to integrate diverse network clients, use TCP/IP to design an internetwork, change a LAN to an intranet, centrally distribute software, configure and troubleshoot complex printing problems, design, analyze, and integrate a Novell Directory Services implementation.

3. CNI: Certified Novell Instructor—Designed for the IT educator interested in teaching individuals the technology and courseware of any of Novell's applications. The CNI is recognized worldwide.

4. CNS: Certified Novell Salesperson—This accreditation certifies the ability to position and sell business solutions from Novell.

5. MCNE: Master Certified Novell Engineer—Shows expertise in the ability to manage and troubleshoot cross-platform networks, integrate multivendor application servers with NDS, manage network databases, route and bridge applications over the LAN, manage advanced e-mail and post office services, secure WAN and LAN, and internetwork configurations.

XXXIII. Oracle

1. OCP: Oracle Certified Professional—Consists of five areas of certification showing expertise with Oracle's applications, development, and operation. They are: Oracle Database Administrator, Oracle Application Developer, Oracle Database Operator, Oracle Financial Applications Consultant, and Oracle Java Developer.

XXXIV. Paradyne

1. WAN A.C.E. Certification—Designed for system engineers, resellers, and distributors. This certification shows competency with the applications, functions, controls, configuration, and options of the Paradyne Analog, DDS, T1, FrameSaver, and Hotwire products.

2. FrameSaver Certification—Qualifies an IT professional to install, operate, and maintain Paradyne's 9624 and 9124 Service Level Verifier Solutions. Courseware includes how to install and configure SLVS products, how to use statistics and diagnostic tests, and how to use the performance wizard to collect data.

3. Hotwire Certification—This credential shows knowledge required to install, operate, and maintain ReachDSL, MVL, RADSL, and IDSL, and how to use Paradyne's OpenLane NMS application.

XXXV. QAI—Quality Assurance Institute

1. CQA: Certified Quality Analyst—Indicates a professional level of competence in the principles and practices of quality assurance in the IT profession. Required knowledge includes auditing and control, human resource principles, training and development, quality management, management techniques, and disaster recovery, among others.

2. CSTE: Certified Software Test Engineer—Establishes standards for initial qualification and provides direction for the testing process. Required knowledge includes test tactics, professional development, quality principles, test design, test principles and concepts, quantitative measurement, and test reporting, among others.

3. CSA: Certified SPICE Assessor—Recognizes individuals that have acquired the knowledge, skills and experience required to conduct ISO/IEC TR 15504-conformant assessment. Candidates must demonstrate knowledge and skills in ISO/IEC TR 15504, assessments experience, software engineering, communications, and human resources.

XXXVI. Red Hat

1. RHCE: Red Hat Certified Engineer—Certifies an individual at server system administration, setup of network services, and basic server security. An RHCE must show competency in the ability to install and configure Red Hat Linux, understand limitations of hardware, configure basic networking and file systems, configure the X Window System, carry out basic diagnostics and troubleshooting, and set up common IP services.

XXXVII. RSA Security

1. RSA/CA: RSA Certified Administrator—Designed for security professionals who demonstrate knowledge and skill in maintaining enterprise security systems that use RSA Security's products.

2. RSA/CSE: RSA Certified Engineer—For security professionals with comprehensive knowledge and skill in installing and configuring enterprise security systems that use RSA Security's products. This security professional will also have a basic understanding of security administration tasks.

3. RSA/CI: RSA Certified Instructors—Designed for professionals skilled in teaching individuals how to deploy and maintain security systems that use RSA Security's products.

XXXVIII. Sair Linux and GNU

1. LCA: Linux Certified Administrator—Evidence of the ability to perform as a power user with the Linux OS. LCAs are able to install, configure, administer, network, and secure the operating system at a basic knowledge level.

2. LCE: Linux Certified Engineer—Requires mastery of the LCA knowledge base. The LCE has the ability to perform as a Linux System Manager.

3. MLCE: Master Linux Certified Engineer—For Senior System Managers, this achievement incorporates the LCA and LCE knowledge base to acquire in-depth knowledge of the inner workings of Linux and its associated tools.

XXXIX. SCO

1. CUSA: SCO Certified UNIX Systems Administrator—There are two tracks to becoming CUSA certified: UnixWare7 Administration and OpenServer Release 5 Administration. CUSA is the foundation level for certification with UNIX systems.

2. ACE: SCO Advanced Certified Engineer—The ACE provides a more in-depth knowledge and understanding of UnixWare7 and OpenServer Release 5 administration.

3. Master ACE: SCO Master Advanced Certified Engineer—The top tier to the UNIX certification program. The Master ACE signifies mastery of the skills and abilities to administer UNIX operating systems.

XL. Sniffer Technologies

1. SCP: Sniffer Certified Professional—The beginning level of the Sniffer certification model. The SCP program is designed to recognize network professionals who can demonstrate an in-depth understanding of Sniffer Technologies software.

2. SCE: Sniffer Certified Expert—The SCE designation shows expert-level knowledge of Sniffer Technologies software. An SCE must be able to implement distributed Sniffer System/RMON Pro, and understand Ethernet, WAN, ATM, Windows NT/2000, TCP/IP, and wireless LAN analysis and troubleshooting.

3. SCM: Sniffer Certified Master—The SCM must complete all SCE and SCP requirements and understand networking technologies at a master's level.

XLI. Sun Microsystems

A. *Java*

1. Sun Certified Programmer—Designed for the experienced programmer to demonstrate the use of basic syntax and structure of the Java programming language.

2. Sun Certified Developer—Designed for the Sun Certified Java Programmer who has a need to further apply this knowledge to develop complex, production-level applications.

3. Sun Certified Web Component Developer—For Sun Certified Java Programmers who use Java technology servlet and JavaServer Pages APIs to develop web applications.

4. Sun Certified Enterprise Architect—Developed for enterprise architects responsible for designing Enterprise Edition Java-compliant applications that are scalable, flexible, and highly secure.

B. *Solaris*

1. Sun Certified System Administrator—Designed for system administrators who perform essential system administration procedures using Solaris. This certification shows the ability to administer a networked server running on the Solaris Operating Environment.

2. Sun Certified Network Administrator—Given to experienced system administrators capable of administering Sun systems in a networked environment including LANs and the Solaris Operating Environment.

XLII. Sybase

1. SCP: Sybase Certified Professional—The SCP is capable of designing and implementing real-world solutions using the Sybase database software including EAServer, Enterprise Portal, PowerBuilder, Adaptive Server Enterprise, Adaptive Server Anywhere, and SQL Server 11 and Adaptive Server Enterprise 11.5.

XLIII. Sysoft

1. CEP: Certified e-Business Professional—Certification offered to economy professionals, building and managing integrated e-Business architecture and process technologies. Courseware includes Internet, broadband, wireless, e-Business process improvement, customer relationship and more.

XLIV. Symantec Corp.

1. SPS: Symantec Product Specialist—Focuses on a single security product and its functionality in an overall security system.

2. SCSE: Symantec Certified Security Engineer—An SCSE is involved in the design, integration, and deployment of comprehensive enterprise security solutions. This IT security professional has product-specific training, a high-level understanding of a broad range of security solutions, and in-depth knowledge within a specific security area such as vulnerability management and intrusion detection.

3. SCSP: Symantec Certified Security Practitioner—This certifies a senior security consultant who demonstrates in-depth knowledge and expertise across the complete range of security disciplines. The SCSP has attained certification in all the security solutions categories.

XLV. TIBCO

1. TIBCO Certified Administrator—Demonstrates knowledge in the fundamentals of TIBCO's distributed system technologies and the ability to administer and configure TIB/Rendezvous, TIBCO's messaging system.

2. TIBCO Certified Developer—Qualifies an IT professional to solve the increasing complexities of enterprise application integration. Courseware includes developing applications with TIB/Rendezvous, TIB/Hawk, and TIB/Adapter SDK.

3. TIBCO Certified Solutions Administrator—Builds on the Certified Administrator certification, providing a more in-depth knowledge and mastery of the skills necessary for administrating TIBCO's distributed system technologies.

4. TIBCO Certified Solutions Developer—The second tier in the Certified Developer certification, providing a more in-depth knowledge and understanding of solution development in application integration.

5. TIBCO Certified Education Consultant—To become a Certified Education Consultant, an individual must become accredited in the Certified Solutions Administrator and Certified Solutions Developer areas at the Education Consultant level.

XLVI. **TruSecure—These certifications will be available soon to enhance and improve skills specifically focused on network and computer security.**

1. ICSA: ICSA Certified Security Associate

2. ICSE: ICSA Certified Security Expert

3. ICSP: ICSA Certified Security Professional

Answers to the Check Your Understanding Questions

Chapter 1

1. ARPANET was a precursor to the modern Internet. In the 1960s, which U.S. government agency was instrumental in developing ARPANET?

   A. Department of Defense

2. Which software application allows the user to collect and organize information so that its contents can be easily accessed, managed, and updated?

   C. Database software

3. What is the hexadecimal equivalent to the binary number 11100110?

   B. E6

4. While working on computer equipment, it is essential to have a safe, efficient work environment. Which of the following is a basic lab safety principle?

   C. Workbench power outlets should be properly grounded and sufficient in number to accommodate the system power and other electrical needs.

5. What is the binary conversion of the decimal number 204?

   D. 11001100

6. It is important to wear an ESD wrist strap while working on all computer components except which of the following?

   A. Video monitor

7. Which of the following would be a primary attribute of a mainframe environment?

   C. Dumb terminal use

8. What is the most accepted safe method to shut down a computer while in the Windows 9x environment?

   B. Select the Shut Down option from the Start menu.

9. Which numbering system is based on powers of 2?

   C. Binary

10. The CRT in a monitor can be charged to as much how many volts?

    D. 20,000

Chapter 2

1. Which basic operating system function receives data from the keyboard?

   A. Input

2. Which I/O port address does the LPT1 printer port commonly use?

   D. 378

3. In MS-DOS, which of the following actions results in a warm boot?

   B. Pressing Ctrl-Alt-Delete twice

4. Which type of motherboard supports 3.3 volts?

   D. ATX

5. Which computer resource allows hardware devices to communicate with the processor?

   C. IRQ number

6. Which process uses special software to upgrade the BIOS (Basic Input/Output System)?

   D. Flashing

7. What type of RAM (random-access memory) is used for cache memory?

   C. SRAM (static random-access memory)

8. How many universal serial bus (USB) devices can be connected to a USB port?

   B. 127

9. Which type of storage device uses a laser to record information?

   C. CD-RW drive

10. Which of the following performs a quick self-diagnostic check of the system hardware early in the boot sequence?

    B. The POST, which is located in ROM

Chapter 3

1. Which computer component can contain a dangerous amount of voltage?

   B. Monitor

2. What is the purpose of the computer's power supply?

   B. Convert AC (alternating current) to DC (direct current)

3. What is the result of incorrectly attaching the LED connectors to the motherboard?

   C. The LED status light will not work.

4. How are hard drives and CD-ROM drives configured to be master and slave drives?

   C. By setting jumpers

5. How many volts do disk drive motors require?

   C. 12

6. What color is the ground wire for a computer power supply?

   B. Black

7. What is the purpose of a heat sink?

   A. To cool the computer processor

8. Which of the following is a valid statement about the P8 and P9 connectors on a power supply?

   B. They connect to the motherboard with black wires in the middle.

9. When booting the system, keys/key combinations allow the user to access the CMOS setup screen. They include Delete, Ctrl-Alt-Esc, and F2 depending on the version of BIOS used?

   A. True

10. How do you best prevent damaging a computer with static electricity?

    D. Always wear an ESD strap when working inside a computer.

11. What type of current can kill you?

    D. AC and DC.

12. The power supply voltage can be checked by measuring the P8 and P9 connections with which of the following devices?

    C. Multimeter

13. What is a memory bank?

    B. The actual slot that memory is inserted into

14. To install a DIMM, you need to do which of the following items?

    A. Line up straight over the socket and press in

Chapter 4

1. What is the definition of an operating system?

    C. A software program that controls thousands of operations, provides an interface between the user and the computer, and runs applications

2. Which of the following is not a valid operating system?

    C. LAN

3. What does DOS stand for?

    B. Disk Operating System

4. What is the maximum length of a DOS filename?

    A. 8 characters with an extension of 3 characters

5. What three files are necessary on a DOS boot disk?

    C. IO.SYS, MSDOS.SYS, COMMAND.COM

6. Where is the statement LOADHIGH used?

    B. AUTOEXEC.BAT

7. When typing in DOS, which program is a good shortcut tool?

    D. DOSKEY

8. Which of the following is an external DOS command?

    C. FDISK

9. Which of the following is an internal DOS command?

    D. DIR

10. Which of the following commands shows all the system files within a directory?

    A. DIR *.SYS

11. The .INI file type usually contains what type of information?

    D. Parameter information about a program

12. When inserted in the CONFIG.SYS file, what does the DEVICE= statement mean?

    D. It loads a device driver.

13. What is another name for conventional memory?

    B. Base memory

14. What are the memory addresses from 0 to 640 KB called?

    D. Conventional memory

15. What is extended memory?

    D. All memory above 1024 KB

16. What is the first 64 KB of extended memory called?

    C. HMA

17. What is virtual memory?

    D. The process of manipulating disk space to create more memory

18. What program is used to find and repair lost clusters?

    A. SCANDISK

19. Which program is used to set up a partition on a hard drive?

    B. FDISK

20. What does TSR stand for?

    A. Terminate-and-stay-resident

21. Why would a read-only attribute be applied to a file?

    A. So it cannot be changed

22. What key/key sequence do you press to step through the startup files when DOS starts?

    C. F8

Chapter 5

1. What does Windows Explorer display?

   C. Hierarchical structure of files, folders, and drives

2. What is the first thing that needs to be done with a new hard drive?

   A. Partitioning

3. What is the second thing that needs to be done with a new hard drive?

   B. Formatting

4. In Windows 98, what utilities are used to set up the hard drive?

   C. FDISK and FORMAT

5. What is another name for the active partition?

   A. Bootable partition

6. The extended partition can be subdivided into a maximum how many logical drives?

   D. 23

7. What section of the hard drive stores the location of the operating system?

   A. Boot sector

8. When upgrading Window 98, what is the earliest DOS version that will allow it?

   C. It is not possible to upgrade from DOS; a previous version of Windows must exist in order to upgrade.

9. What is the first thing you should try if the computer does not boot after installing the operating system?

   A. Restart the computer

10. Is it possible to upgrade a Windows 98 computer to Windows 2000?

    A. Yes

11. What does ScanDisk do?

    D. Marks bad clusters

12. What program is used to edit the registry?

    D. REGEDIT

13. What should you do if the Windows 98 installation procedure fails?

B. Restart the computer using safe mode.

14. What does the IO.SYS file do in Windows 98?

A. Loads the basic device drivers and sets the basic system headings

15. In Windows 98, how do you remove or view devices and their properties?

B. Choose Start, Settings, Control Panel, System, Device Manager

16. In Windows 98, how do you make a startup disk?

B. Choose Start, Settings, Control Panel, Add/Remove Programs, Startup Disk tab, Create Disk

17. How do you restore a file if you delete it from the Windows 98 Desktop?

C. From the Recycle Bin

18. By default, how much space on the hard drive is set aside for the Recycle Bin in Windows 98?

A. 10%

19. How can you view the version of Windows that is currently installed?

B. Right-click My Computer and choose Properties from the menu that appears

20. How do you view the file or folder properties in Windows 98?

B. Right-click the icon and select Properties from the menu that appears

21. How do you locate an object in Windows 98?

D. Choose Start, Find

22. Which of the following characters cannot be used when naming a DOS file?

B. > (greater-than sign)

23. If a printer is changed in DOS, what must be done?

B. Change each application's printer driver

24. Creating a shortcut in Windows 98 allows the user to do which of the following?

B. Execute applications more easily

25. Windows 98 does not support which of the following types of applications?

B. UNIX programs

Chapter 6

1. Why is a system attribute applied to a file?

   D. So that the OS knows it is a system file

2. What file system limits filenames to eight characters in length?

   B. FAT16

3. The FAT32 file system is designed to support hard drives up to what size?

   A. 2048 GB

4. Which of the following file systems is capable of managing global and enterprise-level operating systems?

   C. NTFS

5. What file system is used by OS/2?

   D. HPFS

6. Which of the following is an advanced startup feature that is available for troubleshooting?

   B. Safe mode

7. What is the term for the ability to restore a disk to a consistent state with minimal data loss?

   A. Fault tolerance

8. What is the Windows registry?

   C. A database of configuration settings

9. What does POST stand for?

   D. Power-on self-test

10. Which of the following describes the Plug and Play feature?

    A. Eliminates the need to manually configure jumpers on the hardware

11. Which of the following is a tool that provides a list of files that a user has access to?

    C. Access Control List

12. Users can gain access to an encrypted file if they are assigned which of the following?

    A. Public key

13. The NTLDR uses which of the following files?

    D. NTDETECT.COM, BOOT.INI, BOOTSECT.DOS

14. Which of the following is a portion of a disk that functions as a physically separate unit of storage?

    A. Partition

15. Which of the following provides a secure set of records about the components that control the OS?

    B. Registry

16. Which of the following is a library of hardware drivers that operate between the OS and hardware that is installed on the system?

    A. Hardware Abstraction Layer

17. Which of the following is a tool, used before installing Windows 2000, that verifies that the hardware will work?

    C. Hardware Compatibility List

18. The Windows Compact installation option is used for which of the following?

    A. Computer with a limited amount of hard drive space

19. In Windows NT/2000/XP, which of the following allows the administrator to control just about everything that is related to the local computer?

    B. Administrative Tools

20. What is the term for setting up Windows to boot to Windows 2000 or Windows 98?

    C. Dual-booting

Chapter 7

1. Which of the following is not included in the Windows XP Home Edition?

    A. Roaming profiles

2. Which setting prompts the user after updates have been downloaded and are available to install?

    D. Download the updates automatically and notify me when they are ready to be installed.

3. Which Windows XP version uses the performance enhancements of the Intel Itanium 2 processor?

    C. Professional 64-Bit Edition

4. Which version of Windows requires a minimum of 64 MB RAM and a Pentium II processor?

   B. Windows XP Professional Edition

5. What is the minimum amount of RAM (in MB) that is needed to install Windows XP Professional?

   B. 64

6. Which Windows operating system cannot be upgraded to Windows XP?

   A. 95

7. What is the first step in the Windows XP installation?

   A. File copy

8. What command is used to start an upgrade to Windows XP?

   B. winnt32

9. Where is the My Computer icon located by default on a Windows XP computer?

   B. Start menu

10. Which statement best describes the Fast User Switching feature of Windows XP?

    B. Allows users to switch quickly between accounts without having to log off

Chapter 8

1. What is a typical VESA video resolution standard?

   B. 800×600

2. What is the physical limitation on the potential sharpness of a screen image?

   B. Dot pitch

3. Which book standard is associated with audio CDs?

   A. Red Book

4. Which book standard is associated with data CDs?

   B. Yellow Book

5. Which book standard is associated with recordable CDs?

   D. Orange Book

6. Which book standard is associated with video CDs?

   C. White Book

7. Which video specification, introduced by Intel, provides a 32-bit video channel that runs at 66 MHz in basic 1X mode?

   D. AGP

8. Which chip handles the basic instructions for a sound card?

   C. DSP

9. Which of the following are common multimedia compression types?

   D. All of the above

10. Which DVD recording technology has the ability to use a variable bit-rate when encoding certain types of media such as streaming video?

    A. DVD+RW

11. A user needs to copy audio from one CD to another without changing the original digital state of the audio. Which process can achieve this?

    B. Digital Audio Extraction

12. Which items need to be considered when determining the quality of a sound card?

    D. All of the above

13. Which dot pitch has the greatest potential image sharpness?

    A. .24 mm

14. Which of the following are CD-ROM standards that define how information is stored on CD media?

    B. ISO 9660

15. Which items are functions of a video capture card?

    D. All of the above

Chapter 9

1. Which RAID level provides improved disk input/output but provides no redundancy?

   A. RAID 0

2. Which RAID level provides redundancy at the expense of the loss of 50% of the disk storage capacity?

   B. RAID 1

3. Which of the following RAID levels provide fault tolerance using parity information and a minimum of three disk drives?

   i. RAID 0

   ii. RAID 1

   iii. RAID 4

   iv. RAID 5

   B. iii and iv

4. You have a group of six 36-GB disk drives that you want to configure as a RAID 5 array. After you have configured the RAID array with the six disk drives, what is the total storage capacity of the single logical drive that is created by the RAID array?

   B. 180 GB

5. Which of the following technologies allows a network server to run more programs than can fit into its physical RAM?

   C. Virtual memory

6. Which of the following software packages are *not* normally installed on a network server to support its operation?

   D. Spreadsheet software

7. Which RAID level does *not* provide fault tolerance?

   A. RAID 0

8. After installing a second processor in a network server, the network server boots up properly and the second processor is detected by the system BIOS. However, the network server operating system does not recognize the fact that a second processor now exists in the network server. How do you correct the situation?

   C. Upgrade the network operating system to recognize the additional processor.

9. What environment variable in Microsoft Windows NT and Microsoft Windows 2000 is set to the number of processors in the network server?

   A. Number_of_processors

10. Which of the following must be the same on the existing processor and the processor that is to be added to a multiprocessor-capable network server?

    i. Level 2 cache

    ii. Processor clock speed

    iii. Date of manufacture

iv. Spec number

A. i and ii

11. Which memory technology requires that a continuity module be inserted into all empty memory module slots in a network server?

    C. RIMMs

12. A network server has a single EIDE disk drive configured as a master. You want to add a second EIDE disk drive to the same channel. How must it be configured for both disk drives to work correctly?

    B. Slave

13. How do you upgrade an EIDE disk subsystem to a SCSI subsystem?

    A. Remove all EIDE disk drives, cables, and controllers. Add the SCSI controller, cables, and disk drives.

14. Which of the following adapters usually contain on-board memory that can be upgraded?

    i. Video adapter

    ii. Sound card

    iii. RAID controller

    iv. SCSI controller

    C. i, iii, and iv

15. Your network server has dual-peer PCI buses. The RAID controller is installed in PCI bus number 1. You need to install a 100-Mbps NIC into the network server. Where do you install the NIC?

    B. Into PCI bus number 2.

16. What problem are you most likely to encounter when adding external SCSI disk drives to a SCSI bus?

    B. Exceeding the SCSI channel cable length

17. What are the proper combinations for installing memory modules into memory slots?

    i. Gold leads on memory modules and gold contacts in memory slots

    ii. Tin leads on memory modules and tin contacts in memory slots

    iii. Gold leads on memory modules and tin contacts in memory slots

    iv. Tin leads on memory modules and gold contacts in memory slots

    D. i and ii

18. Which of the following limits the amount of memory that can be used in a network server?

    A. The control chipset on the network server motherboard

19. What is the process of replacing a SCSI disk drive with an SCA connector?

    A. Remove the old SCSI disk drive and insert the new SCSI disk drive.

Chapter 10

1. What is the largest network of computers in the world called?

    C. The Internet

2. What is the general shape or layout of a LAN is called?

    B. Topology

3. What is the term for three or more computers that share communications?

    B. Network

4. Which of the following is not networking media?

    D. KVM switch

5. What is used to translate computer names, such as cisco.com, into their corresponding unique IP addresses?

    A. DNS

6. Which of the following define the rules for coordinating the use of the medium on a LAN?

    B. MAC

7. What is the most common and efficient way for computers on a large network to obtain an IP address?

    A. A DHCP server

8. Which of the following is not a basic network architecture?

    C. Extended-ring

9. What does NIC stand for?

    B. Network interface card

10. What is an IP address?

    B. A 32-bit binary number

11. When using a hub, the network topology changes from a linear bus to what?

   B. Star topology.

12. What is the standard Internet addressing scheme that creates the link between international subnetworks?

   B. IP address

13. If you are using a Token Ring network, when does each station transmit?

   C. Only when the station processes the token

14. What does KVM stand for?

   B. Keyboard/video/mouse

15. Which of the following is a cable with a braided copper shield around it and only a single conductor?

   D. Coax

16. What is a popular Ethernet implementation that uses a star topology, twisted-pair cabling, and a common transmission speed of 10 Mbps?

   C. 10BASE-T

17. What do you do if you ping an IP address and cannot get a response?

   A. Use the tracert command.

18. How many layers make up the OSI reference model?

   B. Seven

19. Which layer of the OSI model describes the cable and how it is attached?

   D. Physical

20. Which layer of the OSI model is responsible for establishing a unique logical address?

   A. Network

21. Which layer of the OSI model is responsible for the reliable delivery of data?

   D. Transport

22. Which layer of the OSI model translates data into an appropriate transmission format?

   C. Presentation

23. To access the Internet, which network protocol is required?

   A. TCP/IP*

24. Which of the following dialup protocols offers the fastest connections?

B. PPP

25. What is required to receive a direct connection to the Internet?

D. Only one router between the local network and the Internet

Chapter 11

1. What are the coils of wire that form electromagnets in a dot matrix printer called?

B. Solenoids

2. Which part of a dot matrix printer can produce a burn if touched?

D. Printhead

3. Which of the following is a nonimpact type of printer?

B. Ink jet

4. What type of printer forces ink through a nozzle when heated by an electrical current?

C. Ink jet

5. When an ink jet printer has completed a print job, which of the following describes the ink?

A. Often still wet

6. The quality of print for an ink jet printer is measured in which of the following terms?

B. dpi

7. The photosensitive drum of a laser printer should never be exposed to which of the following for long periods of time?

A. Light

8. To fix the toner to the paper, the top fuser roller in a laser printer is heated to what temperature?

B. 350 ÷F

9. What is the primary corona wire of a laser printer?

B. The voltage device that erases the drum

10. What is the name of the step in which the toner is applied to the latent image?

A. Developing

11. What phase occurs between the conditioning phase and the developing phase in the laser printer process?

    B. Writing

12. Which command and control languages are most commonly associated with printers?

    A. PCL and PostScript

13. What type of data transfer moves single bits of information in a single cycle.

    B. Serial

14. What is a printer driver?

    B. A software program that allows the computer and the printer to communicate

15. How do you open the print queue in Windows 2000?

    B. Choose Start, Settings, Printers and double-click the appropriate printer.

16. How do you reorder a print job in a print queue in Windows 2000?

    C. Drag and drop it to the desired position in the queue.

17. What is the first thing you should do when troubleshooting a printer problem?

    A. Check the power and paper.

18. What does Windows 2000 use to make printer setup easier?

    B. Plug and Play support

19. What causes the majority of printer problems?

    A. Paper jams

Chapter 12

1. Which of the following is not used to clean computer components?

   D. Regular vacuum

2. What is the proper way to dispose of batteries that are used in portable computers?

   A. Recycling.

3. What does the acronym MSDS stand for?

   B. Material Safety Data Sheet

4. What is the name for substances that can pass through a standard paint filter?

   A. Free liquids

5. What does the acronym ESD stand for?

   C. Electrostatic discharge

6. How many volts must be built up for a person to feel an ESD?

   A. 3000

7. Once a computer case has been opened, a technician should do which of the following?

   B. Wear a grounding wrist strap.

8. Which of the following temporarily stores parts and components when disassembling a computer for cleaning or other types of preventive maintenance?

   D. Antistatic bag

9. What component of a computer system receives more physical abuse than any other?

   B. Keyboard

10. An erratic mouse is most likely due to which of the following?

    D. The mouse needs cleaning.

11. Which utility checks the integrity of files and folders?

    A. ScanDisk

12. Which utility reorganizes files on a hard drive?

    B. Defragmenter

13. What term describes a complete loss of power?

    A. Blackout

14. What term describes a drop in power?

    B. Brownout

15. What term describes a sudden increase in voltage that is higher than normal levels?

    C. Spike

16. What term describes a brief increase in voltage?

    B. Surge

17. When should you run antivirus software?

    D. All of the above

18. What term describes a system that runs off of a battery that is constantly charged?

    A. Uninterruptible power supply (UPS)

19. What does a surge suppressor do?

B. Keeps voltage below a certain level

20. What term describes a system that has a battery take over when needed?

B. Standby power supply (SPS)

Chapter 13

1. What is the first step in troubleshooting a PC problem?

D. Eliminate the user as the source.

2. What setting should you use on a multimeter when checking a power-supply unit?

B. DC voltage

3. How many changes should you make at a time when troubleshooting a PC?

A. One.

4. What is the most likely cause for a shaky video display?

C. Faulty video adapter

5. What is the first thing to do if a new monitor is not working?

D. Make sure that the power cord is firmly plugged in.

6. A high-performing video card can overload which of the following lower-performing units?

B. Monitor

7. An audio POST code with one long beep and two short beeps during the bootup process indicates a problem with which of the following?

A. Video controller

8. When a PC randomly reboots or locks up after running for a time, what might the problem be?

D. Faulty power supply

9. What does USB stand for?

D. Universal serial bus.

10. What is the problem if the PC clock resets when you turn the computer off?

A. Defective CMOS battery

11. A new mouse has been installed but does not work. Which of the following is *not* the cause?

B. The operating system needs to be reinstalled.

12. An erratic mouse is most likely a result of which of the following?

D. The mouse needs cleaning.

13. What can create a memory problem?

A. Installing different-speed memory modules

14. One of your memory modules is unusually hot. What does this indicate?

D. It is defective or becoming defective.

15. What symbol is typically used in Windows to indicate a disabled hardware device?

D. A red X

16. What symbol is typically used in the Windows Device Manager to indicate that a device has a problem?

B. A yellow exclamation point

17. Which of the following is a good way to test a problem with RAM?

D. Replace the module with a new one to see if the problem reoccurs.

18. The computer fails to start after you install a new sound card. What is the most likely cause of this problem?

C. An interrupt conflict between the sound card and another device has occurred.

19. A computer powers up but does not attach to the network. After rebooting, the problem persists. Which of the following is a possible solution?

B. Check the Device Manager for network adapter conflicts.

20. What is the best source for troubleshooting information?

D. All of the above

Chapter 14

1. What are the three things that make a successful technician?

B. Communication skills, technical skills, troubleshooting skills

2. Hardware-related issues are either configuration errors or which of the following?

D. Hardware failures

3. To isolate the computer's problem during the troubleshooting process, you would do all *except* which of the following tasks?

   D. Remove all the internal components before doing anything else.

4. What is the MS-DOS–based automated memory optimizer called?

   B. MEMMAKER

5. Which key is pressed to skip the AUTOEXEC.BAT and CONFIG.SYS files when the message "Starting MS-DOS" displays?

   A. F5

6. Which of the following can recover files from damaged disks?

   E. SCANDISK and CHKDSK

7. If you have ScanDisk, you do not need to run which of the following?

   B. CHKDSK

8. Which utility can be used to increase access speed by rearranging files and directories on the hard drive?

   C. DEFRAG

9. An "Insufficient memory to run this application" error displays. What should you do?

   B. Increase the size of your swap file.

10. Which of the following software problems can corrupt files?

    D. All of the above

11. What is the most common symptom of a corrupted file?

    C. Consistent lockups

12. You choose **Start**, **Run**. What command allows you to access the registry from the command window?

    B. REGEDIT

13. What is the first utility you should run if a computer locks up?

    B. SCANDISK

14. Why does a GPF occur?

    C. An application is trying to write to a memory space that is occupied by another application.

15. What causes a page fault in Windows 98?

    D. All of the above

16. A NIC was working fine, but now it is causing connectivity problems. What do you do first?

    D. Check the LEDs on the back of the NIC.

17. Which two files do not load in safe mode?

    A. AUTOEXEC.BAT and CONFIG.SYS

18. The resource window for a device in the Device Manager *does not* display which of the following?

    D. Delete settings button

19. Which utility determines whether a specific IP address is accessible?

    C. PING.EXE

20. Which utility traces a packet from the computer to an Internet host?

    A. TRACERT.EXE

.VxD file   A virtual device driver that takes the place of the ***DEVICE=*** and ***LOADHIGH=*** commands.

10BASE-T   Transmission speed of 10 Mbps, baseband mode with twisted-pair cabling. It is one of the most popular Ethernet implementations and uses a star topology.

*100BASE-*X   High-speed performance, typically implemented over 2-pair Category 5 or 5e UTP or STP (100BASE-TX) cable, or as Ethernet over 2-strand fiber-optic (100BASE-FX) cable.

1000BASE-T   Primarily a LAN architecture but it can be used for metropolitan-area networks (MANs) over fiber-optic cable. It supports data transfer rates of 1 Gbps.

AC voltage test   Used to check system components, including power supplies.

Accelerated Graphics Port (AGP)   Dedicated high-speed bus that supports the high demands of graphical software. This slot is reserved for video adapters only.

Access Control Entry (ACE)   An entry to the ACL.

Access Control List (ACL)   A list managed by the administrator that displays files that a user has access to and the type of access that has been granted.

Add New Hardware Wizard   Installs new hardware on the computer.

Add Printer Wizard   Installs a new printer on the system.

Add/Remove Programs   Installs programs on and removes programs from the computer.

address bus   A unidirectional pathway that carries addresses that are generated by the CPU to the memory and I/O elements of the computer.

Address Resolution Protocol (ARP)   Discovers the local address (MAC address) of a station on the network when the station's IP address is known. End stations as well as routers use ARP to discover local addresses:

-a   Switch used with the ARP command that displays the cache.

-d   Switch used with the ARP command that deletes an entry from the ARP cache.

-s   Switch used with the ARP command that adds a permanent IP-to-MAC address mapping.

Administrative Tools   Utility that enables the administrator to control the computer system.

algorithm   A systematic description or method of how to carry out a series of steps to complete a certain task.

all-points-addressable display   A display that handles bitmaps.

AMI Diags   Program that provides advanced system testing and reports on memory, serial ports, parallel ports, modems, hard drives, keyboards, BIOSs, and video adapters.

antistatic bag   Special packaging material that protects components from ESD.

antistatic spray   Reduces ESD and cleans and repels dust from electronic equipment.

antivirus application   A program that is installed on the system to prevent computer viruses from infecting the computer.

AppleTalk   A protocol suite that networks Macintosh computers, it is comprised of a comprehensive set of protocols that span the seven layers of the OSI reference model. AppleTalk protocols were designed to run over the major LAN types, notably Ethernet and Token Ring, as well as Apple's own LAN physical topology, LocalTalk.

application layer   The fourth layer in the TCP/IP model. It is the starting point for communication sessions.

application software   Accepts input from the user and then manipulates it to achieve a result. This result is known as the output.

Application-Specific Integrated Circuit (ASIC)   A compression chip that reduces the size of a file by removing redundant information from consecutive frames.

architecture   The overall structure of a computer or communication system.

archive file   A backup copy of files.

Arithmetic/Logic Unit (ALU)   Performs fundamental math operations and logical operations in order to make comparisons and decisions. How a program is executed is determined by logical operations.

ARP cache   The means by which a correlation is maintained between each MAC address and its corresponding IP address.

ASD.EXE   Skips a driver when the operating system fails during bootup.

aspect ratio   The width-to-height ratio of the display screen.

Asymmetric DSL (ADSL)   Currently the most common DSL implementation. Its speeds vary from 384 kbps to more than 6 Mbps downstream. The upstream speed is typically lower.

asynchronous   Without respect to time. In terms of data transmission, asynchronous means that no clock or timing source is needed to keep both the sender and the receiver synchronized.

asynchronous serial transmission   Transmission in which data bits are sent without a synchronizing clock pulse. This transmission method uses a start bit at the beginning of each message. When the receiving device gets the start bit, it can synchronize its internal clock with the sender's clock.

AT command set   Issues dial, hangup, reset, and other instructions to the modem. It is based on the Hayes command set; the AT stands for attention.

AT power supply   Uses two 6-pin motherboard power connectors, usually labeled P8/P9.

ATTRIB   Command that displays, sets, or removes one or more attributes.

attribute   A set of parameters that describe a file.

ATX power supply   Uses a single 20-pin power connector, P1.

audio POST codes   A reporting system for errors that are found by the BIOS during the POST, represented by a series of beeps.

audio visual interface (AVI)   A popular file format for video that produces a 40:1 compression ratio and a 30 frames-per-second capture rate, at 320×200 resolution.

Audio/Modem Riser (AMR)   A plug-in card for an Intel motherboard that contains all the analog functions, or codecs, that are required for audio and modem operation.

AUTOEXEC.BAT   Configuration file that is used by the operating system. The file contains a batch of DOS commands that are automatically carried out when DOS is loaded into the system.

Automatic Private IP Addressing (APIPA)   An operating system feature that enables a computer to assign itself an address if it is unable to contact a DHCP server.

Automatic Update   Allows the user to configure when and how the Windows Update feature checks for critical updates.

BACKUP.EXE   Starts the backup process.

backward compatible   Hardware or software systems that can use interfaces and data from earlier versions of the system or with other systems. Also known as backward-compatible or backwards compatible.

base memory   See *conventional memory*.

basic disk   A physical disk that contains the primary partition, extended partition, or logical drive.

basic disk storage   Industry standard for all versions of Windows.

Basic Input/Output System (BIOS)   The program stored in a ROM chip in the computer that provides the computer with basic code to control the computer's hardware and to perform diagnostics on it. The BIOS prepares the computer to load the operating system.

BIOS exit options   The two options are Exit Without Saving Setup and Save and Exit Setup.

BIOS Features setup screen   Provides advanced features that control the behavior of the system.

BIOS function   Runs basic device test programs and then seeks to configure the appropriate devices.

BIOS setup   Allows you to customize a computer to function optimally based on its hardware and software profiles.

bit   The smallest unit of data in a computer. A bit can take the value of either 1 or 0. A bit is the binary format in which data is processed by computers.

bit-depth   The number of bits that describe a pixel.

bit-depth for sound   The sample size and bus size of the sound card.

blackout   A complete loss of power.

block   See *cluster*.

boot file   A file that starts the system.

boot sector   Contains information about how the disk is organized. The first area on each logical drive.

bootable disk   A troubleshooting tool that allows the computer to boot from a disk when the hard drive will not boot.

BOOTLOG.TXT   A file that contains the system information that is collected as the system is booting up.

boot-sector virus   Targets the boot sector of the system so that the virus is run when the computer starts.

bootstrap program   A small program located in the BIOS chip that locates and loads the operating system into RAM.

bridge   Connects network segments based on intelligent decisions. The bridge compares the destination address to the forwarding table to determine whether to filter, flood, or copy the frame onto another segment.

brownout   A temporary drop in power.

built-in modem   Used internally in some notebook or laptop computers.

built-in printer font   Resident font that is part of ROM and is built into the printer.

built-in sound   An audio processor that is located on the motherboard.

bus   The media through which data is transferred from one part of a computer to another. The bus can be compared to a highway on which data travels within a computer. See also address bus, control bus, and data bus.

bus topology   Connects all devices on a single cable.

byte   A unit of measure that describes the size of a data file, the amount of space on a disk or other storage medium, or the amount of data being sent over a network. One byte consists of 8 bits of data.

C drive   Generally the label for the first hard drive in a computer system.

cable modem   Acts like a LAN interface by connecting a computer to the Internet. The cable modem connects a computer to the cable company's network through the same coaxial cabling that feeds cable TV (CATV) signals to a television set.

Cable Select (CSEL)   A setting that allows the IDE adapter to select which IDE or EIDE disk drive will function as master and which IDE or EIDE disk drive will function as slave.

cache   A data storage area that provides high-speed access for the system.

carrier sense multiple access collision detect (CSMA/CD)   The LAN access method that is used in an Ethernet network. A device checks to see whether the network is quiet (senses the carrier). If it is not, the device waits a random amount of time before retrying. If the network is quiet and two devices access the line at the same time, their signals collide. When the collision is detected, the two devices back off and each waits a random amount of time before retrying.

Category 3   Cable that is primarily used in telephone connections.

Category 5   Cable that contains four pairs of wires, with a maximum data rate of 1 Gbps.

Category 5e   Cable that provides more twists per foot than Category 5 at the same data rate of 1 Gbps.

Category 6   Cable that is enhanced with more twists than Category 5e cable. It contains a plastic divider that separates the pairs of wires to prevent crosstalk.

CD   Command that changes or displays the current directory *CD burner*. See *CD recorder*.

CD recorder   Allows CD media to be recorded with data, audio, or any combination of the two.

CD   Command in the AUTOEXEC.BAT file that causes the DOS default directory to change to the root directory.

CD-R   Compact disc–recordable. CD media that can be recorded to once.

CD-ROM drive read speed   Determines the rate at which information can be pulled from the CD and sent to the communications bus.

CD-ROM library   Multiple CD-ROM drives in a tower that is attached to a network that can be accessed by all the users on a network.

CD-ROM server   A network server that implements a CD-ROM library.

CD-RW   Compact disc–rewritable. CD media that can be recorded to multiple times.

central processing unit (CPU)   On the motherboard, it is a chip contained on a single integrated circuit called the microprocessor. The CPU contains two basic components, a control unit and an Arithmetic/Logic Unit (ALU).

Checkit   Program that performs system analysis and testing.

CHKDSK /f   DOS utility that checks the system for errors.

CHKDSK.EXE   A command-line tool that recovers lost allocation units from the hard drive.

Cinepak   A compression/decompression standard that is supported by Video for Windows.

circuit switching   Basic switching process whereby a circuit between two users is opened on demand and maintained for their exclusive use for the duration of the transmission.

client/server network   A network in which services are located in a dedicated computer that responds to client (or user) requests.

circuit   The pathway that a data transmission takes.

circuit-switched communications network   Developed for use primarily by the telephone, it provides one physical path that is used for the duration of the transmission.

cleaning   The first step in the laser printer process that removes toner from the drum.

Clipboard   Temporary storage area that is used with the Cut, Copy, and Paste commands.

cluster   A combination of two or more sectors.

CMOS Configuration setup utility   Used to determine and change if necessary the options that are used in BIOS.

COASt   An acronym for "cache on a stick," COASt provides cache memory on many Pentium-based systems.

coaxial   Digital configuration that uses an RCA jack.

coaxial cable   Copper-cored cable that is surrounded by a heavy shielding.

cold boot   Powering up a computer from the off position.

color ink jet printer   Type of printer that uses liquid-ink–filled cartridges that spray ink to form an image on the paper.

color space conversion   The process of converting the YUV signal into the RGB format that is acceptable to the VGA card screen memory.

command interpreter   Also known as COMMAND.COM in Windows 95/98 and CMD.EXE in Windows NT/2000, it displays the DOS prompt and executes the commands that are typed at the prompt.

command line   The primary user interface in DOS.

communication circuit   Sends the information that is read from the CD to the computer using the configured bus.

Communications and Networking Riser (CNR)   A 30-pin interface with LAN and home networking functions. CNR accommodates two formats, making various audio/modem and audio/network combinations possible.

compact disc (CD)   An optical storage medium that can store up to 680 MB of data. CDs can be played and written to using CD-ROM, CD-RW, and other types of CD drives. Removable media for audio and data storage.

compact disc read-only memory (CD-ROM) drive   A storage device that reads information that is stored on a compact disc (CD).

Complementary Metal Oxide Semiconductor (CMOS)   The chip that stores the settings that you make with the BIOS configuration program.

compressed air   Also called canned air, it is air under pressure in a can that blows dust off of computer components without creating static.

compression state   Describes whether a file is compressed or uncompressed.

compression tool   An option to compress a file or folder to make it smaller.

computer network Two or more devices, such as workstations printers, or servers, that are linked for the purpose of sharing information, resources, or both.

computer system Consists of hardware and software components. Hardware is the physical equipment such as the case, floppy disk drives, keyboards, monitors, cables, speakers, and printers. The term *software* describes the programs that operate the computer system.

computer virus A program with malicious intent.

computer-aided design (CAD) Used for generic design or specialized uses such as architectural, electrical, and mechanical. More complex forms of CAD are solid modeling and parametric modeling, which allow objects to be created with real-world characteristics.

conditioning The second step in the laser printer process that prepares the drum for a new image.

CONFIG.SYS A file that contains setup or configuration instructions for the computer system. Configuration file that is used by the operating system. This file loads drivers and changes settings at startup.

control bus Carries the control and timing signals that are needed to coordinate the activities of the entire computer. Control bus signals are not necessarily related to each other. Some are output signals from the CPU, and others are input signals to the CPU from I/O elements of the system.

control unit Instructs the computer system on how to follow the program instructions, directs the movement of data to and from processor memory, and temporarily holds data, instructions, and processed information in its ALU.

conventional memory Includes all memory addresses from 0 to 640 KB.

cookie A small text file that is stored on the PC's hard disk that allows a website to track the user's personal association to that site.

Copper Distributed Data Interface (CDDI) The FDDI technology with copper cabling.

COPY Command that copies one or more files from one location to another.

/A Switch that is added to the COPY command to copy ASCII files.

/B Switch that is added to the COPY command to copy binary files.

/V Switch that is added to the COPY command to verify an action.

/–Y Switch that is added to the COPY command to display a confirmation prompt before overwriting an existing file.

/Y Switch that is added to the COPY command to replace an existing file without a confirmation prompt.

copy backup   Backs up user-selected files to tape. This backup does not reset the archive bit to off.

Create Shortcut   Creates a link to a file or application.

cut   Removes a file and saves it to the Clipboard.

cylinder   All the tracks on a hard disk with the same number.

daily backup   Backs up only the files that are modified on the day of the backup. This backup does not reset the archive bit to off.

data bus   A bidirectional pathway for data flow. Data can flow along this bus from the CPU to memory during a write operation, and data can move from the computer memory to the CPU during a read operation.

data channel   The "road" over which a signal is sent.

Data Over Cable Service Interface Specification (DOCSIS)   Developed by CableLabs, this specification defines the interface standards that regulate cable modems and the supporting equipment.

data transfer rate   Refers to how fast the computer can transfer information into memory.

database   An organized collection of data that can be easily accessed, managed, indexed, searched, and updated.

DATE   Command in the AUTOEXEC.BAT file that causes DOS to prompt the user for the date.

DC voltage test   Checks for live DC circuits.

default gateway   The route taken so that a computer on one segment can communicate with a computer on another segment.

default printer   The first option that an application uses when the user clicks the printer icon. The default printer can be changed by the user.

DEFRAG.EXE   Rearranges the data and rewrites all the files on the hard drive to the beginning of the drive, making it easier and faster for the hard drive to retrieve data.

defragmenter   Rearranges clusters for more efficient hard drive access.

DEL   Command that removes named files.

DELTREE   Command that removes the directory, including all files and subdirectories.

Desktop   The area of the screen that Windows boots to. The main display screen in Windows.

Details mode   The view option that provides the most details of a file.

DETCRASH.LOG   File that is created if the system crashes during the hardware-detection phase of the startup process.

DETLOG.TXT   Used to read the information that is generated when the DETCRASH.LOG file is created.

developing   The fourth step in the laser printer process that applies toner to the latent image.

device driver   Program that tells the operating system how to control specific devices.

Device Manager   Displays a list of all the hardware that is installed on the system.

DEVICEHIGH   Option that puts upper memory blocks into use, when HIMEM.SYS and EMM386.EXE have been loaded.

DEVICEHIGH =   Command that loads drivers into the upper memory area instead of loading them into conventional memory.

Diagnostic Partition Utility   Enables troubleshooting of nonfunctioning hardware components.

diagnostic software   Programs that assist in the troubleshooting process.

diagnostic tools   Utilities that monitor the network server.

Dial-Up Networking (DUN)   When computers use the public telephone system or network to communicate.

differential backup   Backs up all the files that have been created or modified since the last full backup. It does not reset the archive bit.

Digital Audio Extraction (DAE)   The process of copying audio from a CD to another medium while keeping the audio in its original digital state.

digital multimeter (DMM)   Combines the functionality of a voltmeter, ohmmeter, and ammeter into one easy measuring device.

digital subscriber line (DSL)   An always-on technology that allows users to connect to the Internet.

digital versatile disc (DVD)   Removable media that is used primarily for movie and data storage.

digital-in port   An interface that captures digital audio.

DIR   Command in the AUTOEXEC.BAT file that causes a DOS DIR command to be performed automatically.

direct memory access (DMA)   A method for transferring data from the computer's main memory directly to the device that needs it without requiring the data to pass to and from the CPU. This makes the data transfer faster.

directories and name services   Allow users to find people and services on a computer network.

directory tree   A graphical representation of a disk drive's directory organization.

directory   Related program and data files organized and grouped together in the DOS file system.

directory   A place to store data in the Windows file-management system.

disk duplexing   In RAID, this refers to a mirrored set, where each disk is connected to a different disk controller.

disk management   The process of optimizing disk space.

disk mirroring   In RAID, this refers to two disk drives that are connected to the same disk controller.

Disk Operating System (DOS)   A collection of programs and commands that control over-all computer operations in a disk-based system. DOS, which is sometimes called MS-DOS, was designed for the IBM PC.

disk quotas   Provide the ability to assign limits to the amount of hard disk space that users are allocated.

disk striping with parity   RAID 5 is an example of disk striping with parity. It uses block-level parity, but it spreads the parity information among all the disk drives in the disk array.

disk striping without parity   RAID 0 is an example of disk striping without parity. It is not fault tolerant but improves disk input/output performance.

display   A computer output surface and projecting mechanism that shows text and graphic images.

display adapter   See *video adapter*.

Display utility   Allows the user to adjust the look of the computer screen.

Domain Name System (DNS)   A system that provides a way to map friendly host names to IP addresses. Translates computer names into IP addresses.

DOS boot disk   Disk that boots a computer to the DOS prompt.

DOS command   An instruction that is executed from a DOS command line.

DOS=HIGH   Option that is added to the CONFIG.SYS file to tell the operating system to move a portion of the OS into the high memory area.

DOSKEY   Command in the AUTOEXEC.BAT file that loads the DOSKEY program into memory.

dot matrix printer   A printer that works by impacting the ribbon to place an image on the paper.

dot pitch   The size of an individual beam that lights up a point of a phosphor on the screen.

dots per inch (dpi)   How the quality of print is measured on a dot matrix printer.

double data rate SDRAM   New synchronous dynamic RAM that increases memory clock speed to at least 200 MHz.

downstream   The process of transferring data from the server to the end user.

Dr. Watson utility   Isolates and corrects GPFs.

drive label   A name that is assigned to a newly created drive. It can be up to 11 characters in length.

drive letter   Distinguishes the logical drives in Windows.

drive motor   Spins the CD up to the proper speed so that the laser can read the data.

dual in-line memory module (DIMM)   A circuit board with a 64-bit data bus that holds memory chips. Memory module with 168 pins. Supports 64-bit data transfers.

dual-boot   An option that provides the choice to boot the system to either Windows 2000 or Windows 98, if both are installed.

DVD drive   Computer drive that can play/read DVDs. A DVD drive can read CDs and DVDs, while a CD drive can only read CDs.

DVD physical format   Defines the structure of the disc and the areas to which the data is recorded.

DVD+RW   Similar to DVD-RW, technology that uses variable bit-rate when encoding.

DVD-Audio   New DVD format that includes multiple-channel audio.

DVD-R   Technology that allows a DVD to be written to once.

DVD-RAM   Technology that uses random-access memory to enable users to record DVDs multiple times.

DVD-ROM   DVD format that is designed for storing computer files.

DVD-RW   Technology that allows the media to be recorded multiple times.

DVD-Video   DVD format that is used by standalone DVD players for movies and extras.

dynamic disk storage   A method of data storage that uses the hard drives to create multidisk volumes.

Dynamic Host Configuration Protocol (DHCP)   A software utility that automatically assigns IP addresses in a large network.

dynamic link library (.DLL) file   Stores subroutines for a program.

dynamic RAM (DRAM)   Works by storing data electrically in a storage cell and refreshing the storage cell every few milliseconds.

dynamic random-access memory (DRAM)   A type of RAM that holds only its data if it is continuously accessed by special logic called a refresh circuit.

EDIT.COM   A Windows troubleshooting tool that can view and edit configuration files such as AUTOEXEC.BAT and CONFIG.SYS as well as .INI files.

EDIT   Command that views, modifies, or creates files:

- *ance   /B*   Commonly used with the EDIT command, this switch displays monochrome mode.

- */H*   Commonly used with the EDIT command, this switch displays the maximum number of lines possible for the hardware.

- */R*   Commonly used with the EDIT command, this switch loads files in read-only mode.

electrically erasable programmable read-only memory (EEPROM)   A special type of PROM that can be erased by exposure to an electrical charge.

electronic mail (e-mail)   The ability for users to communicate over a computer network. The exchange of computer-stored messages by network communication.

electrophotographic drum   The central part of the laser printer.

electrostatic discharge (ESD)   The discharge of static electricity from one conductor to another conductor of a different potential.

Emergency Repair Disk (ERD)   Disk that restores the operating system.

EMM386.EXE   Memory manager that emulates expanded memory and makes upper memory available for use by the operating system.

encryption   A security feature that applies a coding to a file so that only authorized users can view the file.

Encryption File System (EFS)   A Microsoft specific file system for encryption.

end-to-end   Refers to the temporary pathway that is currently available for a telephone.

Enhanced Integrated Drive Electronics (EIDE)   An enhanced version of the standard IDE interface that connects hard disks, CD-ROM drives, and tape drives to a PC.

erasable programmable read-only memory (EPROM)   A special type of memory that can be erased by exposure to ultraviolet light.

error-correcting code (ECC)   Detects and corrects single-bit errors and detects double-bit errors. It is read and decoded each time data is read from the disk.

Ethernet architecture   Based on the IEEE 802.3 standard, which specifies that a network must implement CSMA/CD.

Event Viewer   Monitors system events, application events, and security events in Windows 9x.

Expanded Memory Specification (EMS)   Memory that is accessed in 16-KB pages from a 64-KB page frame, established in unused UMBs.

expanded memory   Memory that is closely related to upper memory. It is also called the *Expanded Memory Specification (EMS)*. This memory can be accessed in 16-KB pages from a 64-KB page frame.

expansion card modem   The most common type of modem. These modems plug into the motherboard expansion slots (ISA or PCI) and are called internal modems.

expansion slot   An opening in a computer where a PC card can be inserted to add capabilities to the computer.

extended data-out RAM (EDO RAM)   Extends the amount of time that data is stored and has a reduced refresh rate.

Extended Industry Standard Architecture (EISA) Configuration Utility   Enables the configuration of the components of the network server.

Extended Memory Specification (XMS)   Primary memory area used by Windows 9x.

extended memory   Memory above 1 MB.

extended partition   Second partition on the hard drive.

extended-star topology   A star topology that is expanded to include additional networking devices.

external command   Command that is not part of COMMAND.COM and that must be loaded from secondary storage before being executed.

external modem   A modem that can be used with any computer. These modems plug into a serial port (COM1 or COM2) on the back of the computer. External modems, such as cable modems, are typically used for high-speed connections.

external peripheral   Device that is external to the network server.

external speaker   Output device for the sound card.

F5   Pressed during the boot process, this key causes the system to skip the CONFIG.SYS file, including the AUTOEXEC.BAT file.

F8   Pressed during the boot process, this key allows the system to proceed through the CONFIG.SYS file (and the AUTOEXEC.BAT file if needed), waiting for confirmation from the user.

Fast Ethernet   See *100BASE-X*.

fast page mode (FPM) RAM   A type of DRAM that eliminated the need for an address row if data in the previous row was accessed. It allows faster access to data in the same row or page.

FAT32   Offered first in Windows 98, this is an improved version of the original FAT (FAT16).

fault tolerance   The ability to restore a disk to a consistent state with minimal data loss.

FDDI Class A   Computers that are connected to the cables of both rings.

FDDI Class B   Computers that are connected to only one ring.

FDISK /MBR   DOS command that helps to rebuild the operating system boot record on the hard drive.

FDISK   Command that deletes and creates partitions on the hard drive:

> *\STATUS*   Switch that displays partition information when used with the FDISK command.

feature set   Additional features that include three-dimensional audio coprocessors, device controllers, and digital output options.

Fiber Distributed Data Interface (FDDI)   A type of Token Ring network that is used in larger LANs or MANs (metropolitan-area networks).

fiber-optic cable   Conducts modulated light to transmit data.

field-replaceable unit (FRU)   Computer component that can be easily replaced.

file   A block of logically related data that is given a single name and is treated as a single unit.

File Allocation Table (FAT)   A table of records that includes the location of every directory, subdirectory, and file on the hard drive.

file details   Attributes for an individual file that include the size, type, and date modified.

file extension   Describes the file format or the type of application that created a file.

file management   The hierarchical structure of files, folders, and drives in Windows.

File Transfer Protocol (FTP)   An application that provides services for file transfer and manipulation.

file virus   Modifies an existing program so that upon execution, the virus carries out the malicious intent.

file-management file   Enables the system to manage data.

file-management system   Used by the operating system to organize and manage files.

filename   The logical name that is given to a collection of data.

FireWire   A high-speed, platform-independent communication bus. The FireWire interconnects digital devices such as digital video cameras, printers, scanners, digital cameras, and hard drives.

firmware   A program that is embedded in a silicon chip rather than stored on a floppy disk.

FIXBOOT   Command that writes a new boot sector onto the system partition.

FIXMBR   Command that is used with the Recovery Console to fix hard drive problems.

flash BIOS   Allows an upgrade of the software in the BIOS chip from a floppy disk that is provided by the manufacturer, without replacing the chip. The upgrade can also be accomplished by downloading an update from the website for the manufacturer.

Flash ROM   A special type of memory that can be reprogrammed in blocks of data instead of 1 byte at a time.

flat-file database   Stores information in a single table.

floppy disk drive (FDD)   A device that spins a magnetic floppy disk to read data from and write data to it.

folder   A place to store data in the Windows file-management system.

font   A complete set of characters of a particular typeface that are used for display and printing purposes.

font card   Expansion card that allows memory upgrades, different printer interfaces, and font upgrades.

FORMAT   Command that erases all information from a computer disk or hard drive.

> ***/Q***   This switch, added to the FORMAT command, performs a quick format but does not clear the FAT.

> ***/S***   This switch, added to the FORMAT command, copies system files.

> ***/U***   This switch, added to the FORMAT command, performs an unconditional format.

FORMAT.EXE   Erases a hard drive and prepares the disk for data.

formatting   Preparing a hard drive to store data.

free liquid   A substance that can pass through a standard paint filter. Many dump sites cannot handle free liquids.

frequency modulation (FM)   Uses programming to create waveforms that best match the instrument that is playing.

full backup   Also called a ***normal backup***, it backs up all files on a disk.

full-duplex transmission   Data transmission that can go two ways at the same time. An Internet connection using DSL service is an example.

fusing   The sixth step in the laser printer process that rolls the paper between a heated roller and a pressure roller.

gas plasma   A type of computer display that works by lighting up display screen positions based on the voltages at different grid intersections.

general protection fault (GPF)   An error that occurs when one of the operating system applications attempts to access an unallocated memory location.

Gigabit Ethernet   See ***1000BASE-T***.

gigahertz (GHz)   One billion cycles per second. This is a common measurement of the speed of a processing chip.

global print options   Allow a printer to be selected and used for all applications.

Graphical Device Interface (GDI) printing   See ***host-based printing***.

graphical user interface (GUI)   A graphical display that represents the procedures and programs that can be executed by the computer.

graphics application   Creates or modifies graphical images. The two types of graphical images include object- or vector-based images, and bitmaps or raster images.

grounding wrist strap   Provides a place for the static before being discharged through sensitive computer components.

Group Policy Editor (GPE)   Edits the configuration settings in a network environment.

half-duplex transmission   Data transmission that can go two ways, but not at the same time. A telephone and two-way radio are examples.

hard disk drive (HDD)   The device that stores and retrieves data from hard disks.

Hardware Abstraction Layer (HAL)   A library of hardware drivers that communicate between the operating system and the hardware that is installed.

Hardware Compatibility List (HCL)   A tool that verifies that hardware is compatible with the operating system.

hardware failures   A malfunction of a computer component that can prevent the OS from loading.

hardware profile   Windows NT, Windows 2000, and XP can save two or more profiles in which an administrator can control whether a piece of hardware loads. The registry stores these hardware profile configurations.

Hardware Profiles   Tab that allows the user to set up different hardware configurations for the same operating system.

hardware-based RAID   Implements RAID using a hardware device called a RAID controller.

Hayes-compatible command set   Set of AT commands that most modem software uses. This command set is named after the Hayes Microcomputer Products Company, which first defined them.

heat sink   A device that dissipates heat from electronic components into the surrounding air.

Help   Tips and instructions on how to use Windows.

hertz (Hz)   A unit of frequency measurement. It is the rate of change in the state, or cycle, in a sound wave, alternating current, or other cyclical waveform. Hertz is synonymous with cycles per second, and it describes the speed of a computer microprocessor.

hidden file   A file that is not listed in a standard DOS directory listing; the file can be seen only with a specific command.

High Data Rate DSL (HDSL)   Provides a bandwidth of 768 kbps in both directions.

High Performance File System (HPFS)   Older file system that was used with Windows NT 3.51.

high-level formatting   Creates the logical structure on the drive that tells the system what files are on the disk and where they can be found.

HIMEM.SYS   Device driver that converts memory, starting at 1 MB, to be available as XMS or extended memory. Memory-management program that manages the extended memory above 1024 KB.

HKEY_CLASSES_ROOT   Subtree that contains software configuration data for all the software that is installed on the computer.

HKEY_CURRENT_CONFIG   Subtree that contains data on the active hardware profile that is selected during the boot process. This information is used to configure settings for the device drivers to load and for the display resolution to use.

HKEY_LOCAL_MACHINE   Subtree that contains all configuration data for the local computer, including hardware and operating system data such as bus type, system memory, device drivers, and startup control data. Applications, device drivers, and the operating system use this data to set the computer configuration. The data in this subtree remains constant, regardless of the user.

HKEY_USERS   Subtree that contains the system default settings data that controls individual user profiles and environments such as Desktop settings, windows environment, and custom software settings.

host-based printing   Technology in which the operating system communicates directly with the printer and sends the printer an image that is ready to print.

hot expansion   Installing a new adapter into an empty slot while the server is running.

hot replacement   Replacing an adapter while the server remains operational.

hot upgrade   Upgrading an existing adapter while the server is running.

hot-swappable interface   Allows peripherals to be changed while the system is running. USB is an example.

hub   A device that extends an Ethernet wire to allow more devices to communicate with each other.

HWINFO.EXE   A utility that provides a detailed collection of information about the computer.

hybrid topology   A combination of one or more topologies.

Hypertext Markup Language (HTML)   A page-description language.

Hypertext Transfer Protocol (HTTP)   Governs how files are exchanged on the Internet.

icon   An image that represents an application or a capability.

illegal operation   Error message in Windows that indicates that the system has encountered a problem.

impact printer   Class of printer that includes dot matrix and daisy wheel.

incremental backup   Backs up all the files that have been created or modified since the last full backup and resets the archive bit.

Indeo   Data compression method that was developed by Intel.

Industry Standard Architecture (ISA)   A 16-bit expansion slot that transfers data with the motherboard at 8 MHz.

information superhighway   The benefit of the Internet to business and private communications.

infrared   Type of communication that uses a spectrum of light to transmit and receive.

input   Supplying information to the computer using the keyboard or mouse.

input device   Device that transfers data into the computer. This includes the keyboard, mouse, scanner, and so on.

input/output (I/O)   An operation, program, or device that transfers data to or from a computer. Typical I/O devices are printers, hard disks, keyboards, and mice.

instant messaging (IM) services   The ability for users to communicate in real time, or without delay, over a computer network.

Integrated Drive Electronics (IDE)   A type of hardware interface that connects hard disks, CD-ROM drives, and tape drives to a PC.

Integrated Services Digital Network (ISDN)   A set of CCITT/ITU standards for digital transmission over ordinary telephone copper wire as well as over other media, with a top speed of 144 kbps. ISDN is available in areas that do not qualify for other DSL implementations.

internal command   A command that is built into the operating system. These commands are part of the command interpreter and are loaded into RAM when the system first boots.

internal modem   Plugs into one of the expansion slots on the motherboard. No configuration is needed for a Plug and Play (PnP) modem, which is installed on a motherboard that supports PnP.

internal peripheral   Device that is internal to the network server.

International Organization for Standardization (ISO)   Organization that developed the OSI model in the 1980s.

Internet   A worldwide public network of networks that interconnect thousands of smaller networks to form one large "web" of communication.

Internet Control Message Protocol (ICMP) Used for network testing and troubleshooting, it enables diagnostic and error messages. ICMP echo messages are used by the ping application to determine whether a remote device is reachable.

Internet Protocol (IP) address A 32-bit binary number that is divided into 4 groups of 8 bits, known as octets. Provides source and destination addressing and, in conjunction with routing protocols, packet forwarding from one network to another toward a destination.

Internet service provider (ISP) A private network that enables users to connect to the Internet.

Internetwork Packet Exchange/Sequenced Packet Exchange (IPX/SPX) The protocol suite that was originally used by Novell Corporation's Network Operating System, NetWare. It delivers functions similar to those that are included in TCP/IP.

Interpress PDL that was developed by Xerox to handle its line of high-speed printers.

interrupt request (IRQ) A request from a device for communication with the CPU.

IPCONFIG.EXE Utility that is the Windows NT/2000 equivalent of the WINIPCFG.EXE command in Windows 95, 98, and Me. It performs the same functions as the WINIPCFG.EXE command in that it allows users to view all the IP address information as well as the WINS server addresses, DNS server addresses, and the DHCP server addresses.

iptrace NetWare NLM utility that traces the route that a packet takes from source computer to destination host.

Joint Photographic Experts Group (JPEG) A compression standard that is used with digitized video.

jumper A pair of prongs that are electrical contact points set into the computer motherboard or an adapter card.

kernel The main module of the operating system that provides all the essential services that are needed by applications.

kernel load Boot phase that begins with NTOSKRNL.EXE loading with the HAL.DLL file.

keyboard/video/monitor (KVM) switch A switch that allows a single keyboard, video display, and mouse to be used with all network servers.

kilobit (kb) 1024, or approximately 1000, bits.

kilobits per second (kbps) A measurement of the amount of data that is transferred over a connection such as a network connection. A data transfer rate of 1 kbps is a rate of approximately 1000 bits per second.

kilobyte (KB) 1024, or approximately 1000, bytes.

kilobytes per second (KBps)   A measurement of the amount of data that is transferred over a connection such as a network connection. A data transfer rate of 1 KBps is a rate of approximately 1000 bytes per second.

laser assembly   Consists of a laser and a lens that reads the CD as it spins.

laser printer   Type of printer that uses static electricity and a laser to form the image on the paper.

LASTDRIVE =   Command that is contained in the CONFIG.SYS file. It specifies the maximum number of drives that the system can access.

latent image   In laser printers, the undeveloped image.

light-emitting diode (LED)   A type of computer display that works by lighting up display screen positions based on the voltages at different grid intersections. Also called a status light, the LED indicates whether components inside the computer are on or working.

line-in port   An interface that captures audio from amplified or powered sources such as external stereos.

liquid crystal display (LCD)   A type of computer display that works by blocking light rather than creating it.

LOADHIGH   See *DEVICEHIGH* .

local command state   The modem is offline. It receives commands and provides status information to the host computer to which the modem is installed.

Local Security Policy   The options that are selected to ensure a secure computer network.

local user   An account created that gives a user access to the network.

local-area network (LAN)   A communication network that covers a small geographical area and is under the control of a single administrator.

logic gates   Electronic circuits that responds to AND, OR, NOT, and NOR signals.

logical drive   Section that the partition can be divided into.

logical standard   Defines the way that information is stored on the media.

logical topology   The paths that signals travel from one point on a network to another.

Logical Unit Number (LUN)   A seldom-used SCSI standard that enables a user to assign sub-SCSI IDs to a single SCSI ID, allowing one SCSI channel to support multiple CD-ROM drives.

logon   The final step in the bootup process.

loopback plug   Tests serial and parallel ports, USB ports, and RJ-45 connectors for network connectivity. Loopback testing works by sending out signals and verifying that the returned signal is valid. Also called loopback adapters.

low-level formatting   Marks the disk into sectors and cylinders, and defines the placement of the sectors and cylinders on the disk.

Macintosh   An operating system, based on the UNIX core technology, that is designed to be user-friendly.

macro virus   Takes advantage of programming languages to attack a system.

mainframe   A powerful machine that consists of centralized computers that are usually housed in secure, climate-controlled rooms. End users interface with the computers through dumb terminals.

Master Boot Record (MBR)   The program that is responsible for starting the boot process. It determines which partition is used for booting the system and transfers control to the boot sector of that partition, which continues the boot process. Allows programs such as DOS to load into RAM. The required boot record on any disk that is created as a boot or system disk.

master jumper setting   Designation of primary for an IDE device or hard drive.

Material Safety Data Sheet (MSDS)   A fact sheet that identifies hazardous materials.

MD   See *MKDIR*.

Media Access Control (MAC)   The rules for coordinating the use of the medium on a LAN.

media-handling options   Options by which a printer handles media, including the orientation, size, and weight of the paper.

medium   The communication channel or cable that enables computers to communicate over a network.

megabit   1,048,576 bits (approximately 1 million bits).

megabits per second (Mbps)   A common measurement of the amount of data that is transferred over a connection such as a network connection. A data transfer rate of 1 Mbps is a rate of approximately 1 million bits or 100 kilobits per second.

megabyte (MB)   1,048,576 bytes (or approximately 1 million bytes).

megahertz (MHz)   One million cycles per second. This is a common measurement of the speed of a processing chip.

MEM   Command that displays a table showing how memory RAM is currently allocated:

/C   This switch, when added to the MEM command, lists programs that are currently loaded into memory and shows how much conventional and upper memory each program is using.

/D   This switch, when added to the MEM command, lists the programs and internal drivers that are currently loaded into memory.

/F   This switch, when added to the MEM command, lists the free areas of conventional and upper memory.

/P   This switch, when added to the MEM command, pauses the display at each screen of information.

MemMaker   System memory tool that simplifies the task of placing TSRs into upper memory.

mesh topology   Interconnects devices to provide redundancy and fault tolerance.

Metropolitan Area Exchange (MAE)   The point where ISPs connect to each other and where traffic is switched between them. MAE EAST, located in the Washington, D.C., area and MAE WEST, located in Silicon Valley, California, are the first-tier MAEs in the United States.

microphone-in port   An interface that connects a microphone for sound to the PC.

microprocessor   A chip that contains a CPU.

Microsoft TechNet   A Microsoft website that has a huge database of troubleshooting pages.

MIDI port   An industry-standard interface that connects musical devices.

minijack   Configuration for the digital-in port that is physically the same as the microphone-in and line-in ports.

mirrored volume   Contains two identical copies of a simple volume that stores the same data on two separate hard drives.

MKDIR   Command that creates a new directory.

Mobile Daughter Card (MDC)   Contains audio and modem circuits for a laptop computer. It is the equivalent of the AMR for laptop computers.

modem   Short for modulator/demodulator. An electronic device that is used for computer communications through telephone lines. A device that converts digital and analog signals. At the source, a modem converts digital signals to a form that is suitable for transmission over analog communication facilities. At the destination, the analog signals are returned to their digital form. Modems allow data to be transmitted over voice-grade telephone lines.

monitor   A display device that works with the installed video card to present output from a computer. The clarity of a CRT monitor is based on video bandwidth, dot pitch, refresh rate, and convergence. See *display*.

MORE   Command that displays output one screen at a time.

motherboard   The main circuit board in a computer. This board connects all the hardware in the computer.

motherboard location map   Shows where the major components and hardware are located on the motherboard.

Moving Picture Experts Group (MPEG)   A compression standard that is used with digitized video.

MSCONFIG.EXE   A command-line tool that interactively loads device drivers and software options. Allows the user to control how the system is started.

multimedia   The combination of text, sound, and motion video.

multimeter   A device that tests high-voltage devices.

multiprocessing   Allows a computer to have two or more CPUs that programs share.

multitasking   The computer's ability to run multiple applications at the same time.

multithreading   The capability of a program to be broken into smaller parts that can be loaded as needed by the operating system.

multiuser   The ability for two or more users to run programs and share resources.

Musical Instrument Digital Interface (MIDI)   A combination of hardware and software that allows the sound card to control musical instruments and use these instruments to output the audio.

My Computer icon   Provides access to all the installed drives, which are computer storage components.

My Documents icon   A shortcut to personal or frequently accessed files.

name resolution   The process of translating an IP name into an IP address.

nbtstat   Used by Windows to display NetBIOS information.

near letter quality (NLQ)   The highest quality of print that is produced by a dot matrix printer.

NET VIEW   Command that displays a list of domains, a list of computers, and a list of resources for a computer.

NetBIOS Extended User Interface (NetBEUI)   A protocol that is used primarily on small Windows NT networks. NetBEUI is a simple protocol that lacks many of the features that enable protocol suites such as TCP/IP to be used on networks of almost any size.

NETSTAT.EXE   Utility that displays the current TCP/IP network connections and protocols information for the computer.

netstat   A command that is used in Windows and UNIX/Linux to display TCP/IP connection and protocol information.

network   A group of computers that are connected to share resources.

Network Access Point (NAP)   The point at which access providers are interconnected.

network administration   The task of maintaining and upgrading a private network that is done by network administrators.

network file services   Allow documents to be shared over a network to facilitate the development of a project.

network interface card (NIC)   The computer's interface with the LAN. This card typically is inserted into a PCI or PCMCIA (PC card) slot in a computer and connects to the network medium, which in turn is connected to other computers on the network.

network operating system (NOS)   An operating system that enables the server to track multiple users and programs.

network print services   Make printers available to many users.

network printer   Printer connected to the computer network that is set up to be shared by multiple users.

network protocols   Make up the Internet layer, the second layer in the TCP/IP model.

network server   A computer that is capable of handling multiple users and multiple jobs.

network topology   The way that computers, printers, and other devices are connected.

networking media   The means (either cable or wireless) by which signals are sent from one computer to another.

nibble   Half a byte, or four bits.

noise   Interference that causes unclean power.

nonvolatile random-access memory (NVRAM)   Stores the system startup configurations and parameters.

normal backup   Also called a *full backup*. All files on the disk are stored to tape or other backup media, and the archive bit for all files is set to off, or cleared.

NSLOOKUP   Returns the IP address for a given host name. This command can also do the reverse and find the host name for a specified IP address.

NT File System (NTFS)   Designed to manage global and enterprise-level operating systems.

NTDETECT.COM   Used by Intel-based systems to detect hardware that is installed in a system.

octet   A decimal number in the range of 0 to 255 that represents 8 bits.

online state   The state in which the modem is transferring data between the host machine and a remote computer through the telephone system.

Open Systems Interconnection (OSI)   Industry-standard reference model that divides the functions of networking into seven distinct layers.

operating system (OS)   A program that controls the hardware and manages all the other programs in a computer.

output   Data that is sent to the video screen or printer.

output device   Device that displays or prints data that is processed by the computer.

Packet Internet Gopher (ping)   A simple but highly useful command-line utility that is included in most implementations of TCP/IP. Ping can be used with either the host name or the IP address to test IP connectivity.

packet-switched communications network   Network in which individual packets of data can take any available route. The route does not have to be dedicated, as in a circuit-switched network.

Page Description Language (PDL)   Code that describes the contents of a document in a language that the printer can understand.

pages per minute (ppm)   Designation for measuring the speed of a printer.

parallel port   A type of bus that transfers multiple streams of data simultaneously.

partition table   Partition information created by FDISK.

partitioning and formatting   Prepare the hard drive for the installation of an operating system.

paste   Places a copy of what is on the clipboard to the indicated location.

PATH=C:\;C:\DOS;C:\MOUSE   Sample command in the AUTOEXEC.BAT file that creates a specific set of paths that DOS uses to search for executable files.

PC Technician   Program that operates independently of DOS to perform diagnostic tests on parallel ports, serial ports, hard drives, keyboards, video adapters, and RAM.

PCI sound card   An adapter card with an audio processor that connects to the motherboard through the peripheral component interconnect.

peer-to-peer network   A network in which computers act as equal partners.

per-document printer settings   Allow global settings to be overridden for an individual document.

Performance   Tab that displays information about the system.

Peripheral Component Interconnect (PCI) configuration screen   Contains the feature settings that control the system I/O bus and IRQ and DMA allocation for ISA and PCI PnP devices.

Peripheral Component Interconnect (PCI)   A 32-bit local bus slot that allows the bus direct access to the CPU for devices such as memory and expansion boards and allows the CPU to automatically configure the device using information that is contained on the device.

peripheral device   A device that is not part of the core computer system.

permissions   File and directory permissions that specify which users and groups can gain access to files and folders.

personal computer (PC)   A standalone device that is independent of all other computers.

Personal Computer Memory Card International Association (PCMCIA)   An organization that developed the standards for small, credit card-sized devices called PC cards. PC cards are designed to add memory and peripheral devices to portable computers.

Personal Computer Memory Card International Association (PCMCIA) modem   A type of modem that is designed for easy installation in notebook computers. Also known as PC cards, these modems look like credit cards and are small and portable.

physical memory   Memory that is divided into four categories: conventional, upper/expanded, high, and extended.

physical standard   Defines where the information is placed on the media.

physical topology   The layout of the devices and media.

ping   See *Packet Internet Gopher*.

pixel   An element that is the smallest part of a graphic image. Many pixels placed close together make up the image on the computer monitor.

plain old telephone service (POTS)   The public telephone system.

platen   The large roller in a dot matrix printer.

Plug and Play (PnP) configuration screen   Contains the feature settings that control the system I/O bus and IRQ and DMA allocation for ISA and PCI PnP devices.

point-to-point   A direct connection from one computer to another.

POLEDIT.EXE   Sets up different security restrictions for different users.

POST card   Device that can digitally report errors if the computer fails before a BIOS error can be generated.

PostScript (PS)   Developed by Adobe Systems to allow fonts to share the same characteristics on-screen and on paper.

Power Management setup screen   Controls the optional power management for devices on the computer.

power supply   Provides electrical power for every component inside the system unit.

power surge   A brief increase in voltage that is usually caused by high demands on the power grid in a local area.

power-on self-test (POST)   A diagnostic test of memory and hardware when the system is powered up.

presentation application   Permits the organization, design, and delivery of presentations in the form of slide shows and reports. Also known as business graphics.

preventive maintenance policy   The detailed program that determines maintenance timing, the type of maintenance performed, and the specifics of how the maintenance plan is carried out.

primary corona wire   Also called the grid or conditioning roller, it is the voltage device that erases the drum.

primary partition   First partition on the hard drive.

print resolution   The number of tiny dots that the printhead is capable of placing per inch on the paper when forming an image.

Printer Control Language (PCL)   Developed by Hewlett-Packard to allow software applications to communicate with HP and HP-compatible laser printers.

printer driver   Software that must be installed on a PC so that the printer can communicate and coordinate the printing process.

printer network interface card (NIC)   An adapter that the printer uses to access the network media.

printer queue   A temporary holding area for print jobs. The jobs in the queue are fed to the printer when it is ready for the next job.

printer switch   Hardware that routes data input from one device to another. Also known as an A/B switch.

printer-output options   Determine how the ink or toner is transferred to the paper and include color management, print quality, and speed.

processing   Manipulating data according to the user's instructions.

program   Instructs the computer on how to operate. Also known as computer software.

PROMPT-PG   Command in the AUTOEXEC.BAT file that causes the active drive and directory path to be displayed on the command line.

protected mode   An area of memory that has no effect on other programs.

protected-mode memory addressing   Allows one program to fail without bringing down the rest of the system.

protocol   A controlled sequence of messages that are exchanged between two or more systems to accomplish a given task.

public key   Provides access to encrypted files.

Public Switched Telephone Network (PSTN)   The telephone system that allows people in every corner of the world to communicate with anyone who has access to a telephone. It is the most common example of a network.

RAID 0   An array or group of disk drives that are used as a single disk. Data is written in chunks, or stripes, to all the drives in the array.

RAID 0/1   Provides the performance of RAID 0 and the redundancy of RAID 1. It requires at least four drives to implement.

RAID 0+1   See *RAID 0/1*.

RAID 1   Requires at least two disk drives and writes data to two separate locations.

RAID 10   See *RAID 0/1*.

RAID 2   Requires a minimum of three disk drives and uses a hamming code to create an ECC for all data.

RAID 3   Requires a minimum of three synchronized disk drives and uses bit-level parity with a single-parity disk for fault tolerance.

RAID 4   Requires a minimum of three disk drives that do not need to be synchronized because data is written to the drives in blocks.

RAID 5   Requires a minimum of three disk drives and uses block-level parity, but unlike RAID 4, it spreads the parity information among all the drives in the array.

RAID controller on-board memory   Used as a buffer and often backed up with an on-board battery.

RAID controller   A specialized device that is used in a RAID array.

RAID-5 volume   Consists of three or more parts of one or more drives or three or more entire drives.

RAM drive   A drive that is created by setting aside a portion of RAM to emulate the drive.

RAM   See *physical memory.*

Rambus in-line memory module (RIMM)   Memory module with 184 pins. Uses only RDRAM.

random-access memory (RAM)   Computer memory that can be accessed randomly, that is, any byte of memory that can be accessed without touching the preceding bytes.

random-access memory digital-to-analog converter (RAMDAC)   A specialized form of memory that is designed to convert digitally encoded images into analog signals for display. This memory is composed of an SRAM component (for storing the color map) and three digital-to-analog converters (DACs), one for each electron gun.

RD   See *RMDIR.*

read-only file   A file that can be opened and read, but not changed.

read-only memory (ROM)   A type of memory, prerecorded on a chip, that can only be read. This type of memory retains its contents when power is not being supplied to the chip.

real mode memory addressing   Assigns real addresses to real locations in the first 1024 KB (1 MB) of RAM for DOS applications.

Recovery Console   A command-line interface that performs a variety of troubleshooting and recovery tasks in Windows 2000 and XP.

Recycle Bin   Stores files, folders, graphics, and web pages that have been deleted from the hard disk.

Redundant Array of Independent Disks (RAID)   Provides fault tolerance to prevent loss of data in the event of a disk drive failure on a network server. Also known as Redundant Array of Inexpensive Disks.

redundant NIC   In a network server, it serves as a backup NIC.

REGEDIT   A utility that is used to edit the registry.

REGEDIT.EXE   Displays the registry in a hierarchical format.

registry   A hierarchical database for the information that is used by the Windows operating system.

registry subtree   Part of the hierarchical structure of the registry.

relational database   A collection of flat-file databases, or tables, that are linked through some relationship.

Remote Assistance   A troubleshooting tool that allows administrators to connect to a client machine across any distance over the Internet.

Remote Desktop Connection   Allows the user to work on a Windows XP Professional computer from any other computer.

reserved memory   See *upper memory*.

resident font   See *built-in printer font*.

Resultant Set of Policy (RSoP)   A Windows XP tool that plans, monitors, and troubleshoots group policy.

Reverse Address Resolution Protocol (RARP)   A protocol that obtains IP address information based on the physical or MAC address.

ring topology   A common topology in Ethernet LANs. This topology connects devices in the shape of a ring. Ring topology can be single, where data travels in one direction, or dual, where data is sent bidirectionally.

ripping   The process of Digital Audio Extraction.

riser card   Physically extends a slot so that a chip or card can be plugged into it.

RMDIR   Command that removes a directory or subdirectory.

ROM BIOS   The chip where the BIOS is stored allowing accessibility for the system.

root   The top level of a directory.

root directory   The file system's main directory.

router   A networking device that makes smart decisions on how to send data packets.

Routing Information Protocol (RIP)   Operates between router devices to discover paths between networks. In an intranet, routers depend on a routing protocol to build and maintain information about how to forward packets toward the destination. RIP chooses routes based on the distance, or hop count.

RS-232C   The industry standard for serial transmissions between computers and other devices.

safe mode   An option when booting the system that loads only the basic devices that Windows needs to run. It is used for troubleshooting.

sag   A brownout that lasts for less than a second.

sampling rate   The rate at which the sound card can record audio information.

ScanDisk utility   Prior to installation, this tool looks at all the files on the drive.

SCANDISK   DOS program designed to detect and repair errors on the hard drive or floppy drive.

> *\/ALL*   This switch, added to the SCANDISK command, checks and repairs all local drives at the same time.
>
> *\/AUTOFIX*   This switch, added to the SCANDISK command, fixes errors without further input.
>
> *\/CHECKONLY*   This switch, added to the SCANDISK command, checks for errors but makes no repairs.

SCANDSKW.EXE   Also known as ScanDisk for Windows, this utility checks the integrity of the media to repair problems that occur.

SCANREG.EXE   Backs up or repairs the system's registry.

SCSI adapter on-board memory   Uses on-board memory as a buffer or cache between the SCSI disk drives and the network server memory.

sector   Unit of storage (512 bytes) within a track.

serial port   A type of bus that transmits data 1 bit at a time.

server support utilities   Used for backup and antivirus in support of the network server.

server   A repository for files that can be accessed and shared across a network by many users. See *network server*.

SET TEMP C:\TEMP   Command in the AUTOEXEC.BAT file that sets up an area for temporarily holding data in a directory called TEMP.

setup program   Adds new configuration data to the registry when new hardware and applications are installed.

SETUPLOG.TXT   File that is created during the installation process and contains the system setup information.

shielded twisted-pair (STP)   A pair of wires that form a circuit to transmit data. The wires are wrapped in metallic foil to shield them from noise.

Simple Mail Transport Protocol (SMTP)   Provides messaging services over TCP/IP and supports most Internet e-mail programs.

simple volume   A basic disk that contains disk space from a complete single disk and is not fault tolerant.

simplex transmission   A single, one-way data transmission.

single in-line memory module (SIMM)   Memory module with 30 or 72 pins. It supports both 16-bit and 32-bit data transfers.

SiSoft System Analyzer, Diagnostic, and Reporting Assistant (Sandra)   Program that aids in troubleshooting and benchmarking computer components.

slave jumper setting   Designation as secondary for a hard drive or CD-ROM drive.

Small Computer System Interface (SCSI)   A parallel interface standard that supports multiple devices on the same cable and achieves faster data transmission rates than standard buses.

SMARTDRV.EXE 1024 2048   Command in the AUTOEXEC.BAT file that configures the system for a 1-MB disk cache in DOS and a 2-MB cache in Windows.

solenoid   Coil of wires that form electromagnets that fire the pins in the dot matrix printer.

sound card input   Sources of sound that include microphones and CD players.

sound card memory   Usually in the form of ROM, Flash, or NVRAM and can often be upgraded or expanded. It stores samples from musical instruments and holds instructions for MIDI devices.

sound card output   Produces sound for devices such as headphones.

sound card port   Internal or external port for connecting to input and output devices.

sound card processing   The capability to convert audio information into different formats.

sound card processor   Handles the basic instructions that drive the sound card as well as the routing of audio information.

sound card   Device that allows the computer to handle audio information.

sound converter   Converts data for sound.

Sounds utility   Allows the user to adjust the system sounds.

spanned volume   Includes disk space from multiple hard disks (up to 32 disks). It is not fault tolerant.

spike   A sudden increase in voltage that is usually caused by lightning strikes.

SpinRite   Program that is used for recovering data from a crashed hard drive.

spooling   The process of loading documents into a buffer (usually an area on a hard drive) until the printer is ready for the documents.

spreadsheet   Calculates a range of numerical values and carries out large and complex calculations.

standby power supply (SPS)   Battery backup that is enabled when voltage levels fall below normal.

star topology   Common in Ethernet LANs, it consists of a central connection point (for example, a hub) where all cabling segments meet.

Startup menu   Unique security feature in the Windows 2000/NT operating systems. A multistep process is used to get to the Startup menu.

static RAM (SRAM)   A type of RAM that holds its data without being refreshed, for as long as power is supplied to the circuit.

storage   Keeping track of files for later use. Examples of storage devices include floppy disks and hard drives.

stripped volume   Also known as RAID-0. Combines areas of free space from multiple hard disks, up to 32, into one logical volume. It is not fault tolerant.

subdirectory   A directory within a directory in DOS.

subfolder   Folder within a folder in the Windows file system.

subnet mask   The second group of numbers in an IP address.

Super Video Graphics Array (SVGA) monitor   A monitor that can display up to 16,777,216 colors, because it can process a 24-bit-long description of a pixel.

surge suppressor   Device that makes sure that the voltage going to another device stays below a certain level.

swap file   Implements virtual memory by swapping files between RAM and the hard disk drive.

switch mode power supplies (SMPS)   Uses a high-frequency switch or transistor to maintain the output voltage.

switch   An operation that is added to a DOS command to modify the output of that command. Also known as a multiport bridge.

Symmetric DSL (SDSL)   Provides the same speed, up to 3 Mbps, for uploads and downloads.

synchronous DRAM (SDRAM)   Allows the CPU to process data while another process is being queued.

synchronous serial transmission   Transmission in which data bits are sent together with a synchronizing clock pulse. In this transmission method, a built-in timing mechanism coordinates the clocks of the sending and receiving devices.

SYSEDIT   Standard text editor that edits system configuration files.

SYSEDIT.EXE   Modifies text files such as the .INI files as well as the CONFIG.SYS and AUTOEXEC.BAT files.

system board   See *motherboard*.

system bus   A parallel collection of conductors (the metallic traces on the circuit board) that carry data and control signals from one component to the other.

system disk   A disk that is created to boot the computer to the operating system for troubleshooting purposes. It contains the three required system files. Also known as a DOS boot disk.

System File Checker (SFC)   A command-line utility that scans the operating system files to ensure that they are the correct ones.

system file   A file that is required by DOS to boot the system.

system memory   See *physical memory*.

System Properties   A tool in the Windows Control Panel that displays information relating to the system.

System Restore   A Windows XP service that runs in the background and allows the user to restore the OS to a predefined point in time.

system unit   Typically a metal-and-plastic case that contains the basic parts of the computer system.

SYSTEM.DA0   Like the USER.DA0 file, the SYSTEM.DA0 file is created when Windows successfully boots. This file is a backup of the SYSTEM.DAT file. If the SYSTEM.DAT file gets corrupted or is deleted, rename the SYSTEM.DA0 file SYSTEM.DAT to restore the registry.

SYSTEM.DAT   A file that holds hardware, computer-specific profile, and setting information.

SYSTEM.INI   A file that contains hardware-setting information for the drivers that Windows uses for configuration. When the operating system needs to reference information about the hardware, it uses the SYSTEM.INI file.

system-monitoring agent   Vendor-specific software that monitors various aspects of the network server such as the configuration, mass storage, NIC, and so on.

Task Manager   Displays active applications and identifies those applications that are not responding so that they can be shut down.

TCP/IP utilities   Most vendors implement this suite to include a variety of utilities for viewing configuration information and troubleshooting problems.

Telnet   Enables terminal access to local or remote systems.

TIME   Command in the AUTOEXEC.BAT file that causes DOS to prompt for the date and the time.

Token Ring   Based on the token-passing access control method.

token   A bit setting in a specialized frame that continuously travels around a circuit.

topology   Defines the structure of the network. This includes the physical topology, which is the actual layout of the wire or media. It also includes the logical topology, which is how the hosts access the media.

Toslink   A fiber-optic port that was developed by Toshiba for the digital-in port.

traceroute   UNIX/Linux utility that traces the route that a packet takes from source computer to destination host.

tracert   Windows utility that traces the route that a packet takes from source computer to destination host.

TRACERT.EXE   A utility that traces a packet from the computer to an Internet host.

track   Magnetic area that is created by formatting the hard drive.

tracking mechanism   A motor and drive system that moves the lens into the correct position to access a specific area of a CD.

transferring   The fifth step in the laser printer process where toner is detached from the latent image and transferred to the paper.

Transmission Control Protocol (TCP)   The primary Internet protocol for the reliable delivery of data. TCP includes facilities for end-to-end connection establishment and error detection and recovery, and for metering the rate of data flow into the network.

Transmission Control Protocol/Internet Protocol (TCP/IP)   A suite of protocols that has become the dominant standard for internetworking.

transport layer   The third layer in the TCP/IP model, it provides end-to-end management of the communication session.

troubleshooting   A series of logical steps that diagnose a computer problem.

true color   Also known as 24-bit bit-depth, it allows 8 bits for each of the three additive primary colors: red, green, and blue.

tweening   A process used primarily in graphics design that defines two key points in a frame and then uses the computer to calculate the "in between" frames

twisted-pair   A pair of wires that form a circuit to transmit data.

Uninterruptible power supply (UPS)   Power supplied by a battery that is constantly recharged by a regular power source.

Universal Asynchronous Receiver/Transmitter (UART)   An integrated circuit, attached to the parallel bus of a computer that is used for serial communications. The UART translates between serial and parallel signals, provides transmission clocking, and buffers data that is sent to or from the computer.

universal serial bus (USB) port   USB ports are replacing the older serial ports that were found on most computers. USB devices are based on Plug and Play (PnP) technology, and they install with minimal configuration.

Universal Synchronous/Asynchronous Receiver/Transmitter (USART)   Handles both synchronous and asynchronous transmissions.

UNIX   An operating system that is used primarily to run and maintain computer networks.

unshielded twisted-pair (UTP)   A twisted pair of wires that relies on the cancellation effect to limit signal degradation.

upper memory   Includes memory addresses that fall between 640 KB and 1024 KB.

upper memory block (UMB)   Allocated memory in upper memory.

upstream   The process of transferring data from the end user to the server.

USB cable   Connects a USB device to the computer. The device and cable must be the same speed.

User Datagram Protocol (UDP)   Offers a connectionless service to applications. UDP uses lower overhead than TCP and can tolerate a level of data loss.

user interface   The part of the operating system that allows the user to communicate with the computer. User interfaces can be command-line text oriented or the simplified GUI.

user profile   A specific setting for the user who is logged on to the computer.

User State Migration Tool (USMT)   Used by IT administrators for migrating multiple users in large deployments of Windows XP Professional in a corporate environment.

USER.DA0   Created when Windows successfully boots up. This file is a backup of the USER.DAT file. If the USER.DAT file gets corrupted or is deleted, rename the USER.DA0 file USER.DAT to restore the registry.

USER.DAT   File that contains all the information that is specific to the user.

utility file   Enables the user to manage system resources, troubleshoot the system, and configure the system settings.

utility program   Program that maintains and repairs the operating system.

Very High Data Rate DSL (VDSL)   DSL that is capable of bandwidths from 13 Mbps to 52 Mbps.

Very High-Speed Backbone Network Service (vBNS)   The current U.S. Internet infrastructure that consists of a commercial backbone and a high-speed service.

video adapter on-board memory   Uses memory to store the image that is displayed on the monitor.

video adapter   An integrated circuit card in a computer, or in some cases a monitor, that provides digital-to-analog conversion.

video BIOS   Provides the set of video functions that can be used by the software to access the video hardware.

video board   See *video adapter*.

video capture card   Converts video signals from different sources into digital signals that can be manipulated by the computer.

video capture software   Captures frames of television video and converts these frames into digital formats that can be processed by the system.

video card memory   Used by the video chip set. Digital information in video memory must be translated into analog form for export to the monitor.

video controller   Does not need to support high video resolutions on a network server. A video controller that can support 1024×768 resolution and 64,000 colors should be sufficient for most network servers.

video decoder circuit   Converts the analog signal into a stream of digital signals.

video display terminal (VDT)   A terminal with a display and a keyboard.

video display unit (VDU)   See *video display terminal*.

Video Electronics Standards Association (VESA)   Association that provides standards that define how software can determine the capability of a display.

Video Graphics Array (VGA) mode   The lowest common denominator of display modes.

Video Graphics Array (VGA) standard   Standard that describes how data is passed between the computer and the display.

video monitor   A monitor that should support 800×600 or better video resolution for a network server.

video RAM (VRAM)   This type of memory is used by video adapters and can be accessed by two different devices at the same time.

viewability   The ability to see the screen image from different angles.

virtual memory   Created by manipulating hard disk space to provide more memory than is actually installed.

Virus Scan   Utility that checks all hard drives for viruses.

warm boot   Restarting a computer that is already turned on by pressing Ctrl-Alt-Delete twice or by pressing the Reset button.

wavetable sound card   Uses digitized samples of instruments to reproduce audio.

web browser   An application that locates and displays pages from the World Wide Web (WWW).

What You See Is What You Get (WYSIWYG)   Printer output that matches what the user sees on-screen.

wide-area network (WAN)   A communication network that covers a large geographical area.

WIN switch   Allows the technician to start Windows from the command line.

WIN.COM   A registry file that controls the initial environment checks and loads Windows 95 core components during bootup.

WIN.INI   A file that contains parameters that can be altered to change the Windows environment or software settings to suit the user's preferences. The WIN.INI file is a software initialization file for Windows. It contains information about some Windows defaults, the placement of windows, the color settings for the screen, and available ports, printers, fonts, and software applications.

Windows 98 Setup wizard   Guides the user through the installation process.

Windows Explorer   A Windows utility that represents the file-management structure.

Windows NT kernel   Loads the correct device drivers in the proper order.

Windows RAM (WRAM)   This special type of VRAM provides even better performance than standard VRAM by supporting two ports for memory exchange.

WINIPCFG.EXE   Also known as Windows IP Configuration, it is a tool that allows the technician to view the basic IP networking settings of a Windows 95, Windows 98, or Windows Me computer.

word processor   An application that creates, edits, stores, and prints documents.

wrist strap   A device that is attached to the technician's wrist and then clipped to the metal system chassis to prevent ESD damage by channeling static electricity from the person to the ground.

writing   The third step in the laser printer process where the photosensitive drum is scanned with a laser beam.

WSCRIPT.EXE   Allows configuration of the properties that relate to the Windows scripting host.

YUV   The color model that is used for encoding video. Y is the luminosity of the black and white signal. U and V are color difference signals. U is red minus Y (R–Y), and V is blue minus Y (B–Y).

zero-insertion-force (ZIF) socket   A special type of chip socket that permits the insertion and removal of the chip without any tools by using virtually no force.

Index

D